Renault Laguna

Owners Workshop Manual

Peter T. Gill

Models covered

(4283 - 368 - 9AM1)

Hatchback & Sport Tourer (Estate), including special/limited editions
Petrol engines: 1.6 litre (1598 cc), 1.8 litre (1783 cc) & 2.0 litre (1998 cc)
Turbo-Diesel engines: 1.9 litre (1870 cc) & 2.2 litre (2188 cc)

Does NOT cover models with 2.0 litre iDE, 2.0 litre turbo or 3.0 litre V6 petrol engines
Does NOT cover 'Phase 2' model range introduced February 2005

ABCDE
FGHIJ
KLMNO
PQRS

A book in the **Haynes Service and Repair Manual Series**

ISBN **978 1 84425 283 1**

British Library Cataloguing in Publication Data
A catalogue record for this book is available from the British Library.

Printed in the USA

Haynes Publishing
Sparkford, Yeovil, Somerset BA22 7JJ, England

Haynes North America, Inc
861 Lawrence Drive, Newbury Park, California 91320, USA

Haynes Publishing Nordiska AB
Box 1504, 751 45 UPPSALA, Sverige

Contents

Contents

REPAIRS AND OVERHAUL

Advanced driving

Many people see the words 'advanced driving' and believe that it won't interest them or that it is a style of driving beyond their own abilities. Nothing could be further from the truth. Advanced driving is straightforward safe, sensible driving - the sort of driving we should all do every time we get behind the wheel.

An average of 10 people are killed every day on UK roads and 870 more are injured, some seriously. Lives are ruined daily, usually because somebody did something stupid. Something like 95% of all accidents are due to human error, mostly driver failure. Sometimes we make genuine mistakes - everyone does. Sometimes we have lapses of concentration. Sometimes we deliberately take risks.

For many people, the process of 'learning to drive' doesn't go much further than learning how to pass the driving test because of a common belief that good drivers are made by 'experience'.

Learning to drive by 'experience' teaches three driving skills:

- ☐ Quick reactions. (Whoops, that was close!)
- ☐ Good handling skills. (Horn, swerve, brake, horn).
- ☐ Reliance on vehicle technology. (Great stuff this ABS, stop in no distance even in the wet...)

Drivers whose skills are 'experience based' generally have a lot of near misses and the odd accident. The results can be seen every day in our courts and our hospital casualty departments.

Advanced drivers have learnt to control the risks by controlling the position and speed of their vehicle. They avoid accidents and near misses, even if the drivers around them make mistakes.

The key skills of advanced driving are **concentration,** effective all-round **observation, anticipation** and **planning.** When **good vehicle handling** is added to these skills, all driving situations can be approached and negotiated in a safe, methodical way, leaving nothing to chance.

Concentration means applying your mind to safe driving, completely excluding anything that's not relevant. Driving is usually the most dangerous activity that most of us undertake in our daily routines. It deserves our full attention.

Observation means not just looking, but seeing and seeking out the information found in the driving environment.

Anticipation means asking yourself what is happening, what you can reasonably expect to happen and what could happen unexpectedly. (One of the commonest words used in compiling accident reports is 'suddenly'.)

Planning is the link between seeing something and taking the appropriate action. For many drivers, planning is the missing link.

If you want to become a safer and more skilful driver and you want to enjoy your driving more, contact the Institute of Advanced Motorists at www.iam.org.uk, phone 0208 996 9600, or write to IAM House, 510 Chiswick High Road, London W4 5RG for an information pack.

Working on your car can be dangerous. This page shows just some of the potential risks and hazards, with the aim of creating a safety-conscious attitude.

General hazards

Scalding

- Don't remove the radiator or expansion tank cap while the engine is hot.
- Engine oil, automatic transmission fluid or power steering fluid may also be dangerously hot if the engine has recently been running.

Burning

- Beware of burns from the exhaust system and from any part of the engine. Brake discs and drums can also be extremely hot immediately after use.

Crushing

- When working under or near a raised vehicle, always supplement the jack with axle stands, or use drive-on ramps. ***Never venture under a car which is only supported by a jack.***
- Take care if loosening or tightening high-torque nuts when the vehicle is on stands. Initial loosening and final tightening should be done with the wheels on the ground.

Fire

- Fuel is highly flammable; fuel vapour is explosive.
- Don't let fuel spill onto a hot engine.
- Do not smoke or allow naked lights (including pilot lights) anywhere near a vehicle being worked on. Also beware of creating sparks (electrically or by use of tools).
- Fuel vapour is heavier than air, so don't work on the fuel system with the vehicle over an inspection pit.
- Another cause of fire is an electrical overload or short-circuit. Take care when repairing or modifying the vehicle wiring.
- Keep a fire extinguisher handy, of a type suitable for use on fuel and electrical fires.

Electric shock

- Ignition HT voltage can be dangerous, especially to people with heart problems or a pacemaker. Don't work on or near the ignition system with the engine running or the ignition switched on.
- Mains voltage is also dangerous. Make sure that any mains-operated equipment is correctly earthed. Mains power points should be protected by a residual current device (RCD) circuit breaker.

Fume or gas intoxication

- Exhaust fumes are poisonous; they often contain carbon monoxide, which is rapidly fatal if inhaled. Never run the engine in a confined space such as a garage with the doors shut.

- Fuel vapour is also poisonous, as are the vapours from some cleaning solvents and paint thinners.

Poisonous or irritant substances

- Avoid skin contact with battery acid and with any fuel, fluid or lubricant, especially antifreeze, brake hydraulic fluid and Diesel fuel. Don't syphon them by mouth. If such a substance is swallowed or gets into the eyes, seek medical advice.
- Prolonged contact with used engine oil can cause skin cancer. Wear gloves or use a barrier cream if necessary. Change out of oil-soaked clothes and do not keep oily rags in your pocket.
- Air conditioning refrigerant forms a poisonous gas if exposed to a naked flame (including a cigarette). It can also cause skin burns on contact.

Asbestos

- Asbestos dust can cause cancer if inhaled or swallowed. Asbestos may be found in gaskets and in brake and clutch linings. When dealing with such components it is safest to assume that they contain asbestos.

Special hazards

Hydrofluoric acid

- This extremely corrosive acid is formed when certain types of synthetic rubber, found in some O-rings, oil seals, fuel hoses etc, are exposed to temperatures above 400°C. The rubber changes into a charred or sticky substance containing the acid. *Once formed, the acid remains dangerous for years. If it gets onto the skin, it may be necessary to amputate the limb concerned.*
- When dealing with a vehicle which has suffered a fire, or with components salvaged from such a vehicle, wear protective gloves and discard them after use.

The battery

- Batteries contain sulphuric acid, which attacks clothing, eyes and skin. Take care when topping-up or carrying the battery.
- The hydrogen gas given off by the battery is highly explosive. Never cause a spark or allow a naked light nearby. Be careful when connecting and disconnecting battery chargers or jump leads.

Air bags

- Air bags can cause injury if they go off accidentally. Take care when removing the steering wheel and/or facia. Special storage instructions may apply.

Diesel injection equipment

- Diesel injection pumps supply fuel at very high pressure. Take care when working on the fuel injectors and fuel pipes.

Warning: Never expose the hands, face or any other part of the body to injector spray; the fuel can penetrate the skin with potentially fatal results.

Remember...

DO

- Do use eye protection when using power tools, and when working under the vehicle.
- Do wear gloves or use barrier cream to protect your hands when necessary.
- Do get someone to check periodically that all is well when working alone on the vehicle.
- Do keep loose clothing and long hair well out of the way of moving mechanical parts.
- Do remove rings, wristwatch etc, before working on the vehicle – especially the electrical system.
- Do ensure that any lifting or jacking equipment has a safe working load rating adequate for the job.

DON'T

- Don't attempt to lift a heavy component which may be beyond your capability – get assistance.
- Don't rush to finish a job, or take unverified short cuts.
- Don't use ill-fitting tools which may slip and cause injury.
- Don't leave tools or parts lying around where someone can trip over them. Mop up oil and fuel spills at once.
- Don't allow children or pets to play in or near a vehicle being worked on.

Renault Laguna GT Hatchback

The Renault Laguna II was introduced into the UK in February 2001, replacing the previous Laguna range. The model range was originally introduced into the UK in 1994 to supersede the ageing Renault 21. All Renault Laguna II models are of five-door Hatchback or Estate (Sport Tourer) design. Some of the new design innovations inside the car offered are: keyless card entry system, tyre pressure monitor, engine immobiliser and an assortment of handy storage compartments.

A range of four-cylinder petrol engines and diesel engines are available (a V6 petrol engine is available, but is not covered by this manual). All engines are mounted transversely at the front of the vehicle with front-wheel-drive and fully independent front and semi-independent rear suspension. Models may be fitted with five or six-speed manual, or four or five-speed automatic transmissions, mounted at the left-hand side of the engine.

With all-wheel disc brakes, ABS and Brake Assist on every model, it's clear that Renault have made a big commitment to active as well as passive safety with the new car

All models have a high trim level, which is very comprehensive in the upper model range. Central locking, electric windows, an electric sunroof, a trip computer, anti-lock brakes, air conditioning and cruise control are all available. A high level of passenger safety is included, consisting of airbag(s) and seat belt pretensioners, which are standard on all models.

Renault Laguna 2.2 litre dCi Sport Tourer

The car has a high equipment level, even at the lower end of the model range. Besides the valuable safety equipment already mentioned, all feature air conditioning, trip computer, engine immobiliser, rear seat headrests, CD player, remote central locking, and electric windows. Rain sensitive wipers and opening tailgate window (Sport Tourer) are among the equipment fitted higher up the range.

Your Renault Laguna Manual

The aim of this manual is to help you get the best value from your vehicle. It can do so in several ways. It can help you decide what work must be done (even should you choose to get it done by a garage), provide information on routine maintenance and servicing, and give a logical course of action and diagnosis when random faults occur. However, it is hoped that you will use the manual by tackling the work yourself. On simpler jobs, it may even be quicker than booking the car into a garage and going there twice, to leave and collect it. Perhaps most important, a lot of money can be saved by avoiding the costs a garage must charge to cover its labour and overheads.

The manual has drawings and descriptions to show the function of the various components, so that their layout can be understood. Then the tasks are described and photographed in a clear step-by-step sequence.

References to the 'left' or 'right' of the vehicle are in the sense of a person in the driver's seat, facing forwards.

Acknowledgements

Certain illustrations are the copyright of Renault UK Limited, and are used with their permission. Thanks are due to Draper Tools Limited, who provided some of the workshop tools, and to all those people at Sparkford who helped in the production of this manual.

We take great pride in the accuracy of information given in this manual, but vehicle manufacturers make alterations and design changes during the production run of a particular vehicle of which they do not inform us. No liability can be accepted by the authors or publishers for loss, damage or injury caused by any errors in, or omissions from, the information given.

Project vehicles

The main vehicle used in the preparation of this manual, and which appears in many of the photographic sequences, was a Renault Laguna 2.2 litre, dCi, Sport Tourer. Also used was the Renault Laguna 1.8 litre, 16V, Hatchback.

The following pages are intended to help in dealing with common roadside emergencies and breakdowns. You will find more detailed fault finding information at the back of the manual, and repair information in the main chapters.

If your car won't start and the starter motor doesn't turn

- ☐ If it's a model with automatic transmission, make sure the selector is in P or N.
- ☐ Open the bonnet and make sure that the battery terminals are clean and tight.
- ☐ Switch on the headlights and try to start the engine. If the headlights go very dim when you're trying to start, the battery is probably flat. Get out of trouble by jump starting (see next page) using a friend's car.

If your car won't start even though the starter motor turns as normal

- ☐ Is there fuel in the tank?
- ☐ Has the engine immobiliser been deactivated? This should happen automatically, or when the keycard is inserted into the facia slot. However, if a faulty card causes the card reader slot to flash rapidly, consult a Renault dealer for advice.
- ☐ If it's a model with automatic transmission, the footbrake must be applied, and the selector must be in N or P.
- ☐ Is there moisture on electrical components under the bonnet? Switch off the ignition, then wipe off any obvious dampness with a dry cloth. Spray a water-repellent aerosol product (WD-40 or equivalent) on ignition and fuel system electrical connectors like those shown in the photos. Pay special attention to the ignition coil wiring connectors. (Note that diesel engines don't usually suffer from damp).

A Check the condition and security of the battery connections.

B With the ignition off, check that the wiring connectors are securely connected to the four ignition coils (petrol models).

C Check that the camshaft position sensor wiring plug is securely connected.

Check that electrical connections are secure (with the ignition switched off) and spray them with a water-dispersant spray like WD-40 if you suspect a problem due to damp

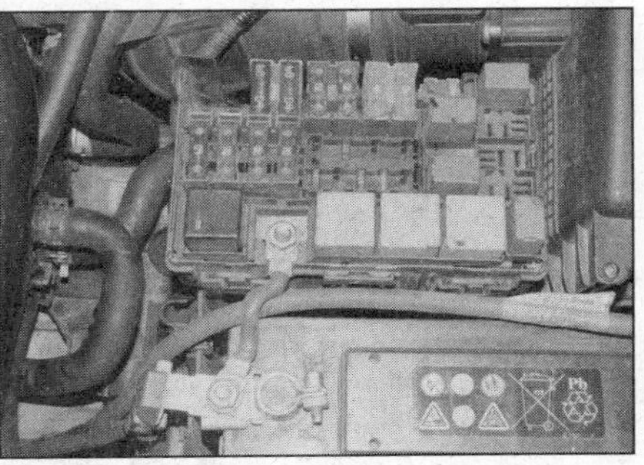

D Check all fuses and relays in the engine compartment fusebox (with the ignition switched off).

Jump starting

When jump-starting a car using a booster battery, observe the following precautions:

- ✔ Before connecting the booster battery, remove the keycard from the facia slot.
- ✔ Ensure that all electrical equipment (lights, heater, wipers, etc) is switched off.
- ✔ Take note of any special precautions printed on the battery case.
- ✔ Make sure that the booster battery is the same voltage as the discharged one in the vehicle.
- ✔ If the battery is being jump-started from the battery in another vehicle, the two vehicles MUST NOT TOUCH each other.
- ✔ Make sure that the transmission is in neutral (or PARK, in the case of automatic transmission).
- ✔ Once the booster battery has been connected, insert the keycard into the facia slot.

Jump starting will get you out of trouble, but you must correct whatever made the battery go flat in the first place. There are three possibilities:

1 The battery has been drained by repeated attempts to start, or by leaving the lights on.

2 The charging system is not working properly (alternator drivebelt slack or broken, alternator wiring fault or alternator itself faulty).

3 The battery itself is at fault (electrolyte low, or battery worn out).

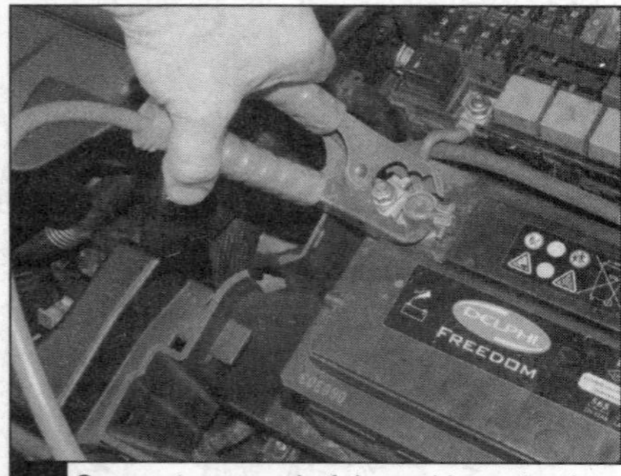

1 Connect one end of the red jump lead to the positive (+) terminal of the flat battery

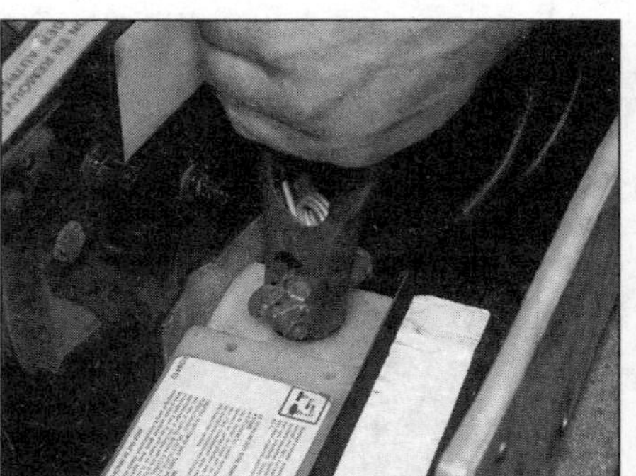

2 Connect the other end of the red lead to the positive (+) terminal of the booster battery.

3 Connect one end of the black jump lead to the negative (-) terminal of the booster battery

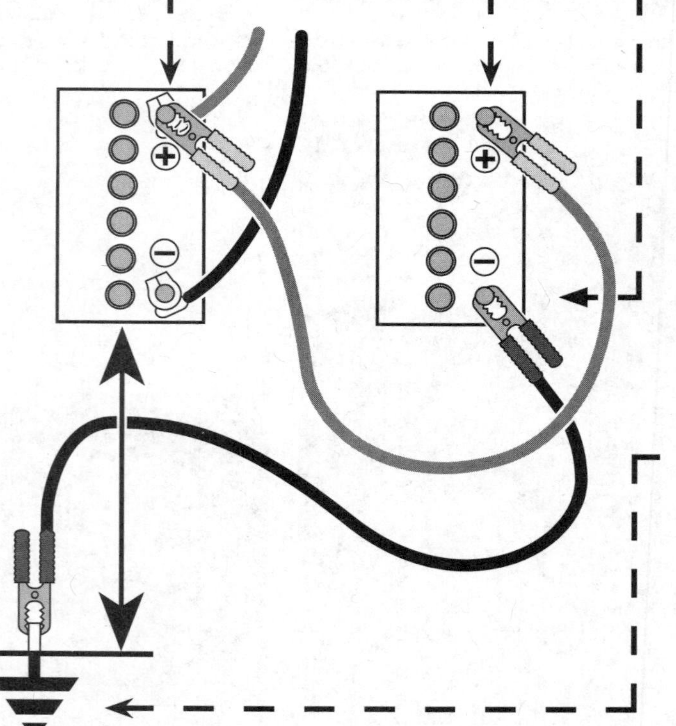

4 Connect the other end of the black jump lead to a bolt or bracket on the engine block, well away from the battery, on the vehicle to be started.

5 Make sure that the jump leads will not come into contact with the fan, drive-belts or other moving parts of the engine.

6 Start the engine using the booster battery and run it at idle speed. Switch on the lights, rear window demister and heater blower motor, then disconnect the jump leads in the reverse order of connection. Turn off the lights etc.

Wheel changing

Warning: Do not change a wheel in a situation where you risk being hit by other traffic. On busy roads, try to stop in a lay-by or a gateway. Be wary of passing traffic while changing the wheel – it is easy to become distracted by the job in hand.

Preparation

- ☐ When a puncture occurs, stop as soon as it is safe to do so.
- ☐ Park on firm level ground, if possible, and well out of the way of other traffic.
- ☐ Use hazard warning lights if necessary.
- ☐ If you have one, use a warning triangle to alert other drivers of your presence.
- ☐ Apply the handbrake and engage first or reverse gear (or Park on models with automatic transmission).
- ☐ Chock the wheel diagonally opposite the one being removed – a couple of large stones will do for this.
- ☐ If the ground is soft, use a flat piece of wood to spread the load under the jack.

Changing the wheel

1 The spare wheel and tools are located in the luggage compartment, under the boot carpet/floor panel. Lift the panel and engage the handle with the hook on the rear seat back to hold the floor panel open.

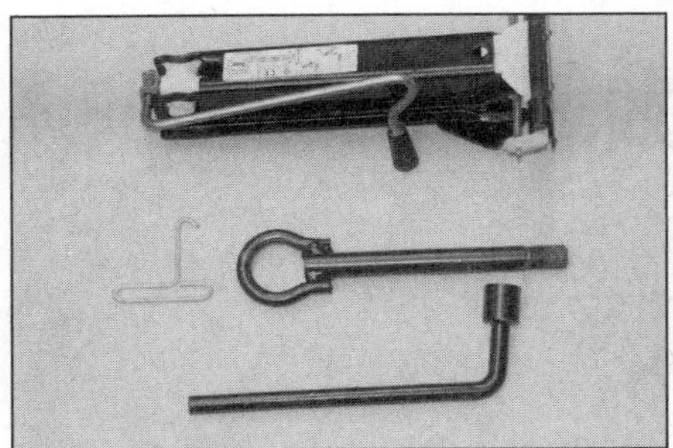

2 The vehicle jack is stored in the tool tray inside the spare wheel; this also contains the wheelbrace, towing eye, and hubcap removal tool.

3 Lift out the tool tray, unscrew the spare wheel retaining plate from the centre of the wheel, and lift out the spare wheel.

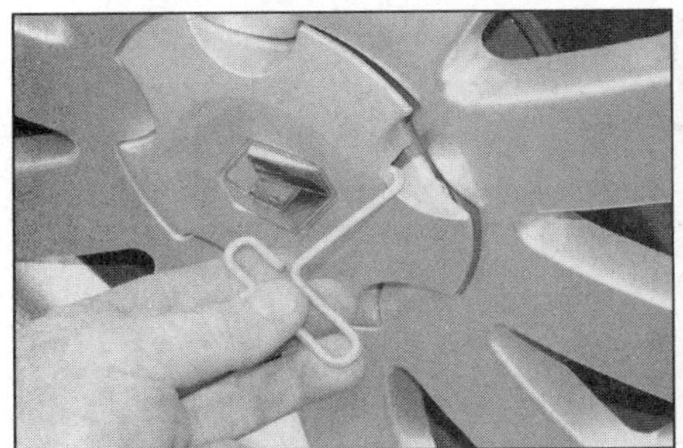

4 Remove the wheel trim or centre cap from the punctured wheel, using the tool provided.

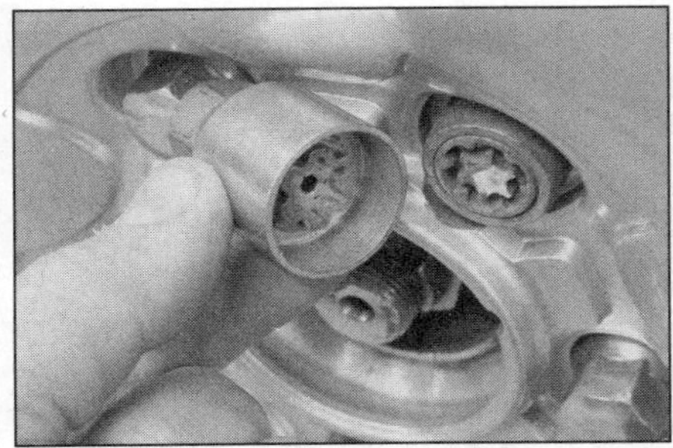

5 Use the wheelbrace to loosen each wheel bolt by half a turn, a key will be required to remove any locking wheel nuts.

6 Locate the jack head into the jacking point nearest the wheel to be changed. The jacking points are small 'plates' on the base of the sill (don't jack the car at any other point on the sill).

7 Turn the jack's handle clockwise until the wheel is raised clear of the ground. Remove the bolts and lift the punctured wheel clear. Fit the spare wheel, refit the wheel bolts, and tighten moderately with the wheelbrace.

8 Lower the car to the ground, and then finally tighten the wheel bolts in a diagonal sequence. Refit the wheel trim or centre cap, where possible. Ideally, the wheel bolts should be slackened and retightened to the specified torque at the earliest opportunity.

Finally . . .

- ☐ Remove the wheel chocks.
- ☐ Stow the jack and tools in the spare wheel.
- ☐ Some spare wheels are for temporary use only, if so, drive with extra care, especially when cornering – limit yourself to a maximum of 70 mph, and to the shortest possible journeys, while it is fitted.
- ☐ Check the tyre pressure on the wheel just fitted. If it is low, or if you don't have a pressure gauge with you, drive slowly to the nearest garage and inflate the tyre to the correct pressure. Note: *The tyre pressure monitoring system will register a fault until the punctured wheel is repaired and refitted – see Chapter 10.*
- ☐ Have the damaged tyre or wheel repaired as soon as possible.

Identifying leaks

Puddles on the garage floor or drive, or obvious wetness under the bonnet or underneath the car, suggest a leak that needs investigating. It can sometimes be difficult to decide where the leak is coming from, especially if the engine bay is very dirty already. Leaking oil or fluid can also be blown rearwards by the passage of air under the car, giving a false impression of where the problem lies.

Warning: Most automotive oils and fluids are poisonous. Wash them off skin, and change out of contaminated clothing, without delay.

The smell of a fluid leaking from the car may provide a clue to what's leaking. Some fluids are distinctively coloured. It may help to clean the car carefully and to park it over some clean paper overnight as an aid to locating the source of the leak.
Remember that some leaks may only occur while the engine is running.

Sump oil

Engine oil may leak from the drain plug...

Oil from filter

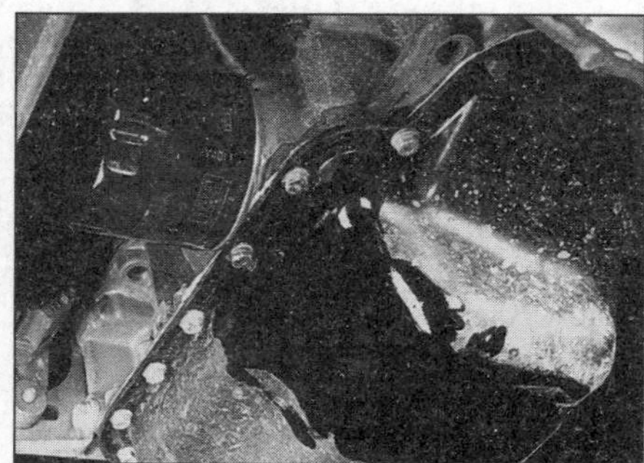

...or from the base of the oil filter.

Gearbox oil

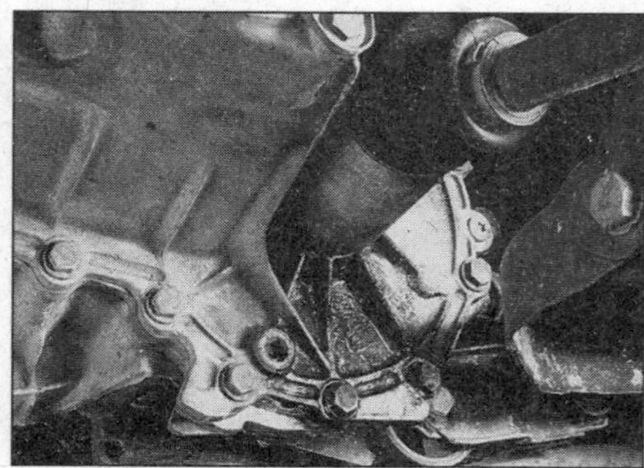

Gearbox oil can leak from the seals at the inboard ends of the driveshafts.

Antifreeze

Leaking antifreeze often leaves a crystalline deposit like this.

Brake fluid

A leak occurring at a wheel is almost certainly brake fluid.

Power steering fluid

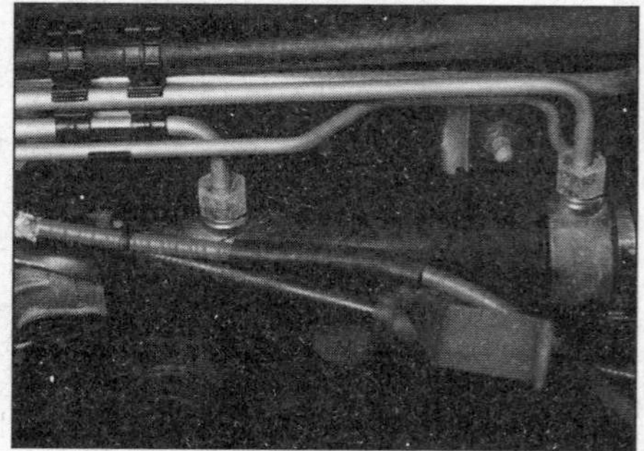

Power steering fluid may leak from the pipe connectors on the steering rack.

Towing

When all else fails, you may find yourself having to get a tow home – or of course you may be helping somebody else. Long-distance recovery should only be done by a garage or breakdown service. For shorter distances, DIY towing using another car is easy enough, but observe the following points:

☐ Use a proper tow-rope – they are not expensive. The vehicle being towed must display an ON TOW sign in its rear window.

☐ Always turn the ignition key to the 'On' position when the vehicle is being towed, so that the steering lock is released, and the direction indicator and brake lights work.

☐ A towing eye is supplied as part of the vehicle tool kit. The towing eye is clipped into the tool storage tray in the spare wheel (see *Wheel changing* in this Section).

☐ Before being towed, release the handbrake and select neutral on the transmission.

☐ On models with automatic transmission, special precautions apply, with it being preferable to tow the vehicle with the front wheels off the ground. In exceptional cases, the vehicle can be towed with all wheels on the ground for a maximum distance of 20 miles at no more than 15 mph. If in doubt, do not tow, as transmission damage may result.

☐ Note that greater-than-usual pedal pressure will be required to operate the brakes, since the vacuum servo unit is only operational with the engine running.

☐ Because the power steering will not be operational, greater-than-usual steering effort will also be required.

☐ The driver of the car being towed must keep the tow-rope taut at all times to avoid snatching.

☐ Make sure that both drivers know the route before setting off.

☐ Only drive at moderate speeds and keep the distance towed to a minimum. Drive smoothly and allow plenty of time for slowing down at junctions.

Caution: To prevent damage to the catalytic converter, a vehicle must not be push-started, or started by towing, when the engine is at operating temperature. Use jump leads (see 'Jump starting').

Introduction

There are some very simple checks which need only take a few minutes to carry out, but which could save you a lot of inconvenience and expense.

These *Weekly checks* require no great skill or special tools, and the small amount of time they take to perform could prove to be very well spent, for example:

☐ Keeping an eye on tyre condition and pressures, will not only help to stop them wearing out prematurely, but could also save your life.

☐ Many breakdowns are caused by electrical problems. Battery-related faults are particularly common, and a quick check on a regular basis will often prevent the majority of these.

☐ If your car develops a brake fluid leak, the first time you might know about it is when your brakes don't work properly. Checking the level regularly will give advance warning of this kind of problem.

☐ If the oil or coolant levels run low, the cost of repairing any engine damage will be far greater than fixing the leak, for example.

Underbonnet check points

◀ **1.8 litre (F4P) petrol engine (1.6 and 2.0 litre similar)**

A *Engine oil level dipstick*
B *Engine oil filler cap*
C *Coolant expansion tank*
D *Brake fluid reservoir*
E *Screen washer fluid reservoir*
F *Power steering fluid reservoir*
G *Battery*

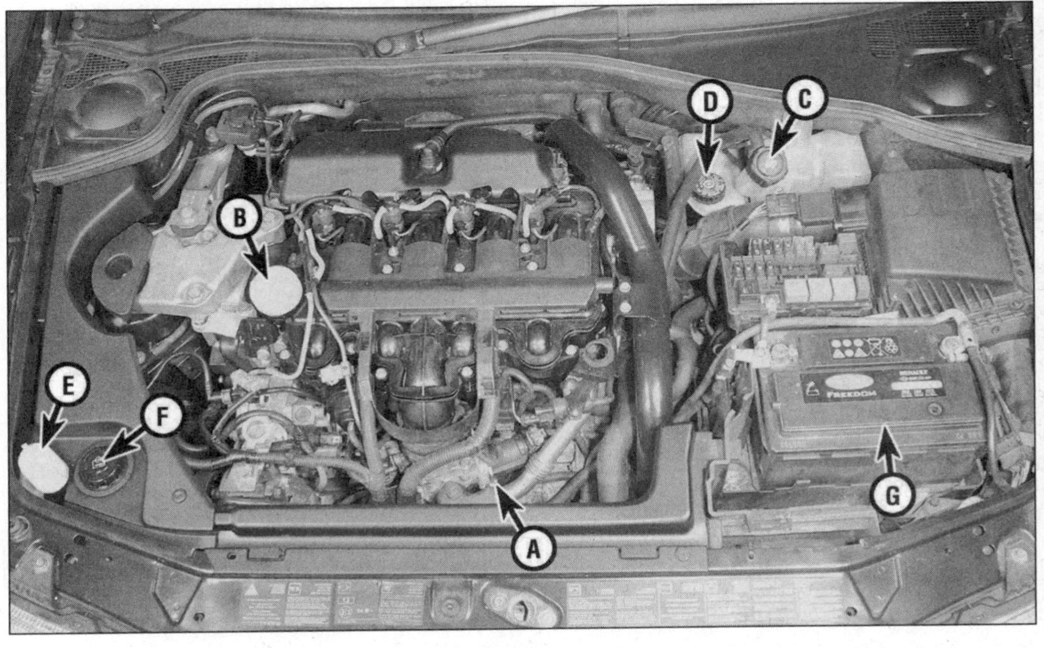

◀ **2.2 litre (G9T) diesel engine (1.9 litre similar)**

A *Engine oil level dipstick*
B *Engine oil filler cap*
C *Coolant expansion tank*
D *Brake fluid reservoir*
E *Screen washer fluid reservoir*
F *Power steering fluid reservoir*
G *Battery*

Engine oil level

Before you start

✔ Make sure that the car is on level ground.

✔ Check the oil level before the car is driven, or at least 5 minutes after the engine has been switched off.

If the oil is checked immediately after driving the vehicle, some of the oil will remain in the upper engine components, resulting in an inaccurate reading on the dipstick.

The correct oil

Modern engines place great demands on their oil. It is very important that the correct oil for your car is used (see *Lubricants and fluids*).

Car care

● If you have to add oil frequently, you should check whether you have any oil leaks. Place some clean paper under the car overnight, and check for stains in the morning. If there are no leaks, then the engine may be burning oil.

● Always maintain the level between the upper and lower dipstick marks. If the level is too low, severe engine damage may occur. Oil seal failure may result if the engine is overfilled by adding too much oil.

1 The dipstick is brightly coloured yellow and is located at the front of the engine on all models except the 1.9 litre diesels. On 1.9 litre diesel engines it is part of the oil filler cap (see *Underbonnet check points* for exact location). Withdraw the dipstick.

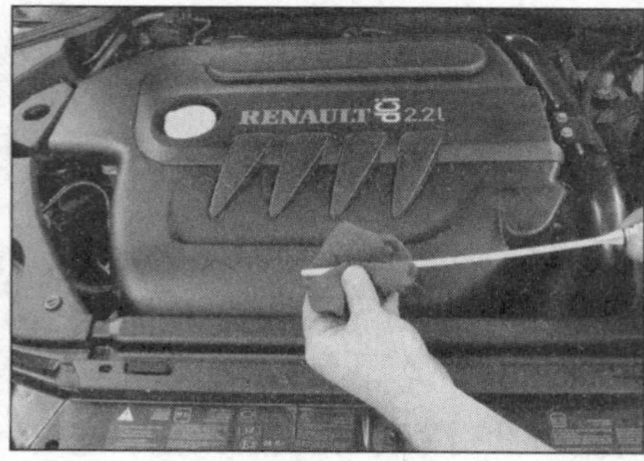

2 Using a clean rag or paper towel, wipe all the oil from the dipstick. Insert the clean dipstick into the tube (or screw the oil filler cap fully on) as far as it will go, then withdraw/unscrew it again.

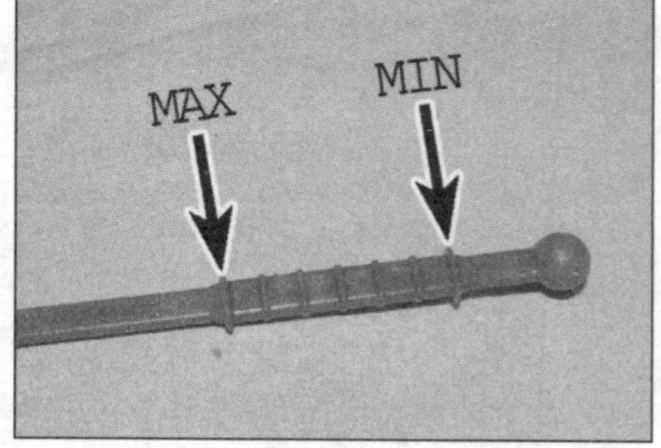

3 Note the oil level on the end of the dipstick, which should be between the upper (MAX) mark and the lower (MIN) mark. Approximately 1.5 to 2.0 litres of oil will raise the level from the lower to the upper mark.

4 Oil is added through the filler cap. Unscrew the filler cap, then top-up the level. A funnel may help to reduce spillage. Add the oil slowly, checking the level on the dipstick often. Do not overfill (see *Car Care*).

Coolant level

Warning: Do not attempt to remove the expansion tank pressure cap when the engine is hot, as there is a very great risk of scalding. Do not leave open containers of coolant about, as it is poisonous.

Car Care

● With a sealed-type cooling system, adding coolant should not be necessary on a regular basis. If frequent topping-up is required, it is likely there is a leak. Check the radiator, all hoses and joint faces for signs of staining or wetness, and rectify as necessary.

● It is important that antifreeze is used in the cooling system all year round, not just during the winter months. Don't top up with water alone, as the antifreeze will become diluted.

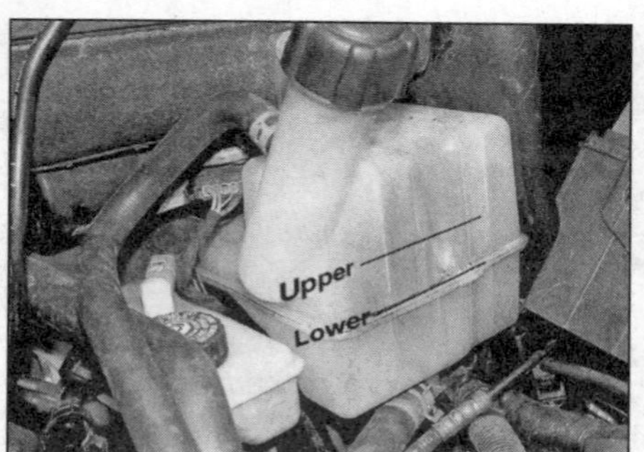

1 The coolant level varies with engine temperature. The level is checked in the expansion tank, which is at the rear left-hand corner of the engine compartment. When the engine is cold, the level should be between the MAX and MIN markings.

2 If topping-up is necessary, wait until the engine is cold, then turn the pressure cap on the expansion tank slowly anti-clockwise, and pause until any pressure remaining in the system is released. Unscrew the cap and lift off.

3 Add coolant to the expansion tank, until the coolant is up to the MAX mark. Refit the cap and tighten it securely. When adding coolant, use the same type as that already in the system.

Power steering fluid level

Before you start

✔ Park the vehicle on level ground.
✔ Set the steering wheel straight-ahead.
✔ The engine should be turned off.

Safety first!

● The need for frequent topping-up indicates a leak, which should be investigated immediately.

Caution: For the check to be accurate, the steering must not be turned once the engine has been stopped.

1 The power steering fluid reservoir is located at the front right-hand side of the engine compartment. The fluid level should be checked with the engine stopped. Before removing the cap for level checking or topping-up, wipe the surrounding area so that dirt does not enter the reservoir.

2 Remove the seal and plastic cover to access the markings on the side of the reservoir. The fluid level should be between the MAX and MIN marks on the side of the reservoir. Unscrew the cap, allowing the fluid to drain from the bottom of the cap as it is removed.

3 Top-up the fluid level to the MAX mark, using the specified type of fluid (do not overfill the reservoir), then refit and tighten the filler cap.

Brake (and clutch) fluid level

Note: *On manual transmission models, the brake fluid reservoir also supplies fluid to the clutch master cylinder.*

Before you start

✔ Make sure that the car is on level ground.

Safety first!

● If the reservoir requires repeated topping-up this is an indication of a fluid leak somewhere in the brake or clutch system, which should be investigated immediately.

● If a leak is suspected, the car should not be driven until the braking system has been checked. Never take any risks where brakes are concerned.

● The fluid level in the reservoir will drop slightly as the brake pads wear down, but the fluid level must never be allowed to drop below the MIN mark.

Warning: Brake fluid can harm your eyes and damage painted surfaces, so use extreme caution when handling and pouring it. Do not use fluid which has been standing open for some time, as it absorbs moisture from the air, which can cause a dangerous loss of braking effectiveness.

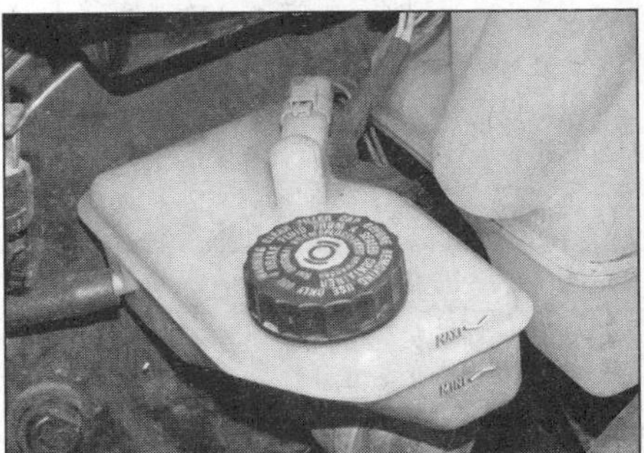

1 The MAX and MIN marks are indicated on the side of the reservoir, which is located at the rear left-hand side of the engine compartment. The fluid level must be kept between these two marks.

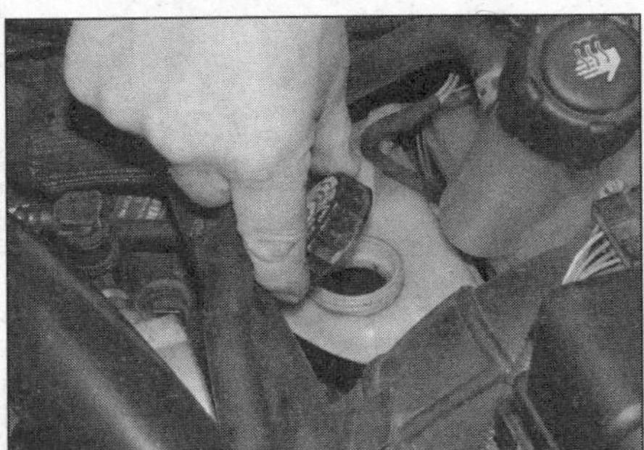

2 If topping-up is necessary, first wipe the area around the filler cap with a clean rag, then remove the cap. When adding fluid, it's a good idea to inspect the reservoir. The system should be drained and refilled if dirt is seen in the fluid (see Chapter 9).

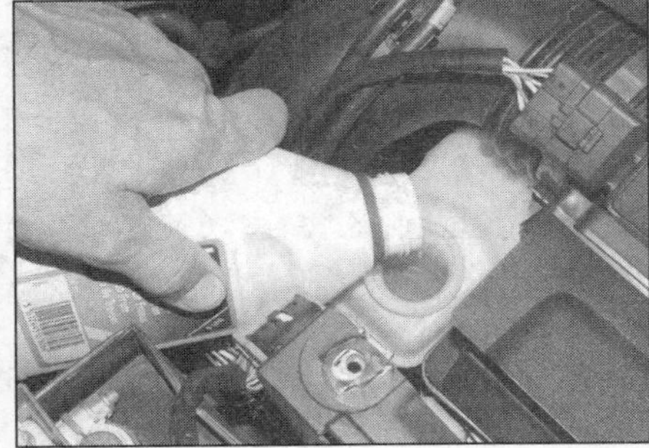

3 Carefully add fluid, avoiding spilling it on surrounding paintwork. Use only the specified hydraulic fluid; mixing different types of fluid can cause damage to the system and/or a loss of braking effectiveness. Bear in mind that the level in the reservoir will raise slightly when the cap/float assembly is refitted. After filling to the correct level, refit the cap securely and reconnect the sensor wires. Wipe off any spilt fluid.

Tyre condition and pressure

It is very important that tyres are in good condition, and at the correct pressure – having a tyre failure at any speed is highly dangerous. Tyre wear is influenced by driving style – harsh braking and acceleration, or fast cornering, will all produce more rapid tyre wear. As a general rule, the front tyres wear out faster than the rears, and some people swap (or 'rotate') tyres from front to rear, to even up wear. However, if this is completely effective, you may incur the expense of replacing four tyres at once!

Note: *The tyre pressure monitoring system on the Laguna will produce an error message if the tyres are rotated.*

Remove any nails or stones embedded in the tread before they penetrate the tyre to cause deflation. If removing a nail reveals a hole, refit the nail to mark the hole's position, then immediately change the wheel and have the tyre repaired.

Regularly check the tyres for damage in the form of cuts or bulges, especially in the sidewalls. Periodically remove the wheels, and clean any dirt or mud from the inside and outside surfaces. Examine the wheel rims for signs of corrosion or damage. Alloy wheels are easily damaged by 'kerbing' whilst parking; steel wheels may also become dented or buckled. A new wheel is very often the only way to overcome severe damage.

New tyres should be balanced when they are fitted, but it may become necessary to re-balance them as they wear, or if the balance weights fitted to the wheel rim should fall off. Unbalanced tyres will wear more quickly, as will the steering and suspension components. Wheel imbalance is normally signified by vibration particularly at a certain speed (typically around 50 mph). If this vibration is felt only through the steering, then it is likely that just the front wheels need balancing. If, however, the vibration is felt through the whole car, the rear wheels could be out of balance. Wheel balancing should be carried out by a tyre dealer or garage.

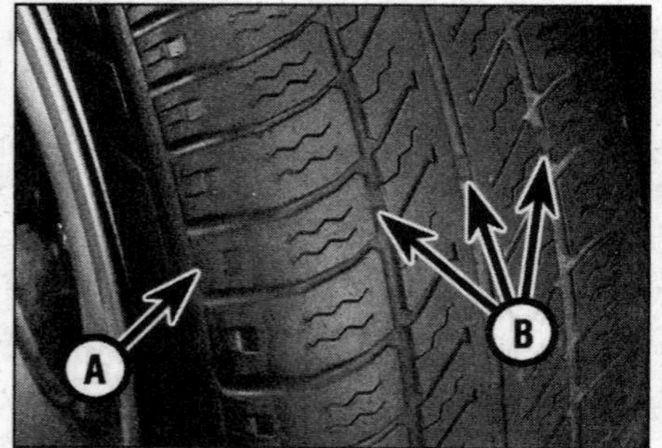

1 ***Tread Depth - visual check***

The original tyres have tread wear safety bands (B), which will appear when the tread depth reaches approximately 1.6 mm. The band positions are indicated by a triangular mark on the tyre sidewall (A).

2 ***Tread Depth - manual check***

Alternatively, tread wear can be monitored with a simple, inexpensive device known as a tread depth indicator gauge.

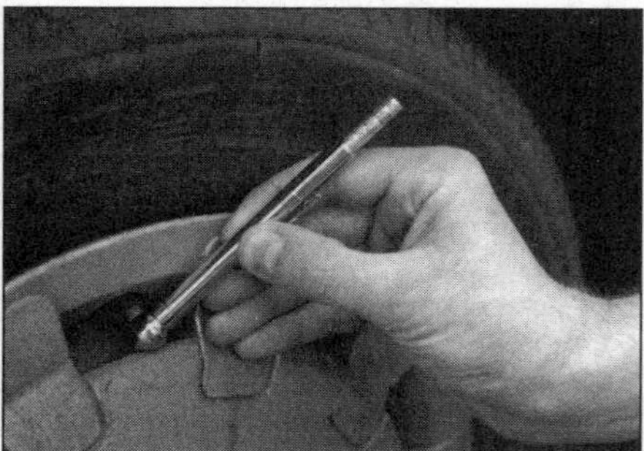

3 ***Tyre Pressure Check***

Check the tyre pressures regularly with the tyres cold. Do not adjust the tyre pressures immediately after the vehicle has been used, or an inaccurate setting will result.

Tyre tread wear patterns

Shoulder Wear

Underinflation (wear on both sides)
Under-inflation will cause overheating of the tyre, because the tyre will flex too much, and the tread will not sit correctly on the road surface. This will cause a loss of grip and excessive wear, not to mention the danger of sudden tyre failure due to heat build-up.
Check and adjust pressures
Incorrect wheel camber (wear on one side)
Repair or renew suspension parts
Hard cornering
Reduce speed!

Centre Wear

Overinflation
Over-inflation will cause rapid wear of the centre part of the tyre tread, coupled with reduced grip, harsher ride, and the danger of shock damage occurring in the tyre casing.
Check and adjust pressures

If you sometimes have to inflate your car's tyres to the higher pressures specified for maximum load or sustained high speed, don't forget to reduce the pressures to normal afterwards.

Uneven Wear

Front tyres may wear unevenly as a result of wheel misalignment. Most tyre dealers and garages can check and adjust the wheel alignment (or "tracking") for a modest charge.
Incorrect camber or castor
Repair or renew suspension parts
Malfunctioning suspension
Repair or renew suspension parts
Unbalanced wheel
Balance tyres
Incorrect toe setting
Adjust front wheel alignment
Note: *The feathered edge of the tread which typifies toe wear is best checked by feel.*

Washer fluid level

● Screenwash additives not only keep the windscreen clean during bad weather, they also prevent the washer system freezing in cold weather – which is when you are likely to need it most. Don't top-up using plain water, as the screenwash will become diluted, and will freeze in cold weather.

Warning: On no account use engine coolant antifreeze in the screen washer system – this may damage the paintwork.

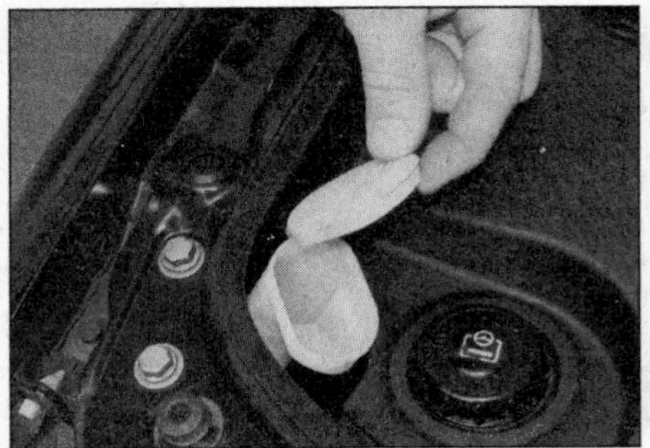

1 The windscreen/tailgate/headlight washer fluid reservoir is located at the right-hand side front of the engine compartment. If topping-up is necessary, open the cap.

2 When topping-up the reservoir a screenwash additive should be added in the quantities recommended on the bottle. The level can safely be filled until the level is visible inside the neck of the reservoir.

Wiper blades

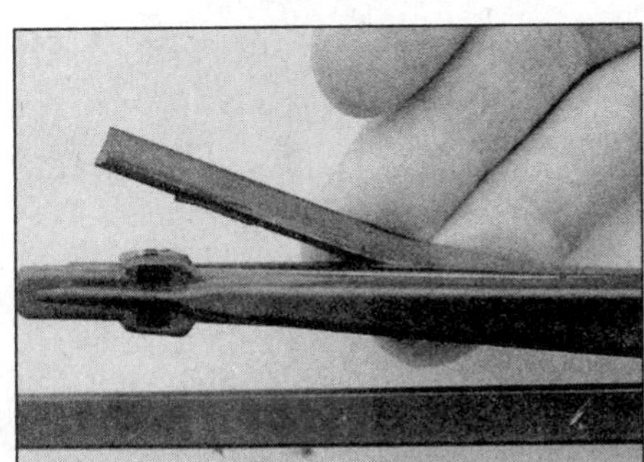

1 Check the condition of the wiper blades; if they are cracked or show any signs of deterioration, or if the glass swept area is smeared, renew them. For maximum clarity of vision, wiper blades should be renewed annually, as a matter of course.

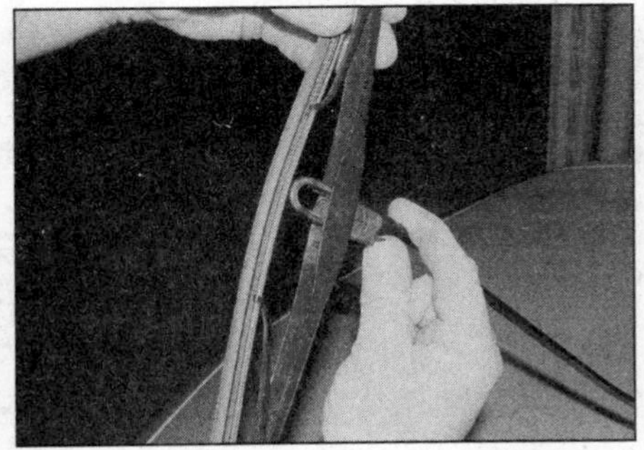

2 To remove a windscreen wiper blade, pull the arm fully away from the screen until it locks. Swivel the blade through 90°, then depress the locking clip at the base of the mounting block, and slide the blade out of the hooked end of the arm.

3 Don't forget to check the tailgate wiper blade as well. Swivelling the blade through 90° then depressing the retaining clips and sliding the blade from the arm will remove the blade.

Bulbs and fuses

✔ Check all external lights and the horn. Refer to the appropriate Sections of Chapter 12 for details if any of the circuits are found to be inoperative.

✔ Visually check all accessible wiring connectors, harnesses and retaining clips for security, and for signs of chafing or damage.

If you need to check your brake lights and indicators unaided, back up to a wall or garage door and operate the lights. The reflected light should show if they are working properly.

1 If a single indicator light, brake light or headlight has failed, it is likely that a bulb has blown and will need to be renewed. Refer to Chapter 12 for details. If both brake lights have failed, it is possible that the brake light switch operated by the brake pedal has failed. Refer to Chapter 9 for details.

2 If more than one indicator light or headlight has failed, it is likely that either a fuse has blown or that there is a fault in the circuit (see Chapter 12). The fuses are behind a panel at the right-hand end of the facia panel. The fuse locations are indicated by symbols on the rear of the cover, which holds the plastic removal tool and spare fuses.

3 Additional fuses and relays are located in a box at the left-hand side of the engine compartment behind the battery. Always fit a new fuse of the same rating, available from car accessory shops. It is important that you find the reason why the fuse failed – see *Electrical fault finding* in Chapter 12.

Battery

Caution: Before carrying out any work on the vehicle battery, read the precautions given in 'Safety first!' at the start of this manual.

✔ Make sure that the battery tray is in good condition, and that the clamp is tight. Corrosion on the tray, retaining clamp and the battery itself can be removed with a solution of water and baking soda. Thoroughly rinse all cleaned areas with water. Any metal parts damaged by corrosion should be covered with a zinc-based primer, then painted.

✔ Periodically (approximately every three months), check the charge condition of the battery as described in Chapter 5A.

✔ If the battery is flat, and you need to jump start your vehicle, see *Roadside Repairs*.

Battery corrosion can be kept to a minimum by applying a layer of petroleum jelly to the clamps and terminals after they are reconnected.

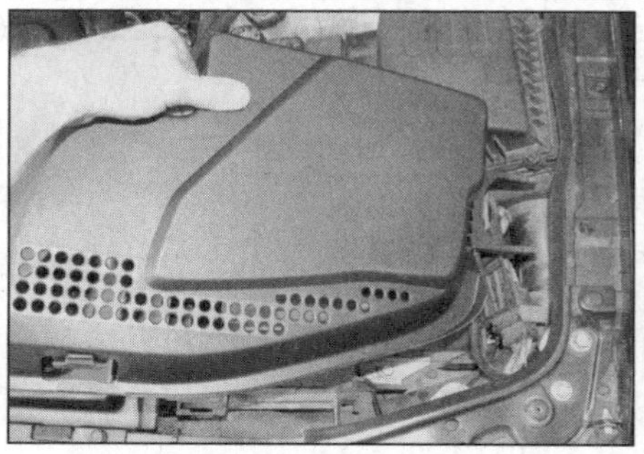

1 The battery is located at the front left-hand corner of the engine compartment; to access the battery, unclip the plastic cover. The exterior of the battery should be inspected periodically for damage such as a cracked case or cover.

2 Check the tightness of the battery cable clamps on the positive and the negative terminals; you should not be able to move them. Each cable should be checked for damaged insulation, cracks and frayed conductors.

3 If corrosion (white fluffy deposits) is evident, remove the cables from the battery terminals, clean them with a small wire brush, then refit them. Automotive stores sell a useful tool for cleaning the battery post and terminals.

4 Note that the battery positive lead terminal has a link wire connected directly to the fuse/relay box.

Lubricants and fluids

Petrol engine	Engine oil, viscosity SAE 5W-30, 5W-40, or 10W-40, to ACEA-A1, A3 or A5
Diesel engine	Engine oil, viscosity SAE 5W-40 or 10W-40, to ACEA-B3 or B4
Cooling system	Ethylene glycol-based antifreeze – RX Glacéol type D coolant
Manual transmission:	
JH3 and JR5 transmissions	Elf Tranself TRJ 75W/80W gear oil
PK6 transmission	Elf Tranself TRP 75W/80W gear oil
Automatic transmission:	
DPO transmission	Elf Renaultmatic D3 SYN (Dexron III)
SU1 transmission	Dexron 2 E standard
Brake and clutch system	Hydraulic fluid to SAE J1703 or DOT 4
Power steering	Elf Renaultmatic D2 or Mobil ATF 220

Tyre pressures (cold)

Note: *Laguna models are equipped with a tyre pressure monitor system; check with handbook or relevant part of this manual for further information. Pressures apply to original-equipment tyres, and may vary if any other make or type of tyre is fitted; check with the tyre manufacturer or supplier for correct pressures if necessary.*

	Front	Rear
Petrol engine models		
Normal use	2.0 bars (29 psi)	2.1 bars (30 psi)
Fully laden or motorway driving	2.3 bars (33 psi)	2.2 bars (32 psi)
Spare	2.3 bars (33 psi)	
Diesel engine models		
1.9 litre models:		
Normal use	2.2 bars (32 psi)	2.1 bars (30 psi)
Fully laden or motorway driving	2.5 bars (36 psi)	2.2 bars (32 psi)
Spare	2.5 bars (36 psi)	
2.2 litre models:		
Normal use	2.3 bars (33 psi)	2.1 bars (30 psi)
Fully laden or motorway driving	2.7 bars (39 psi)	2.2 bars (32 psi)
Spare	2.7 bars (39 psi)	

Chapter 1 Part A: Routine maintenance and servicing – petrol models

Contents

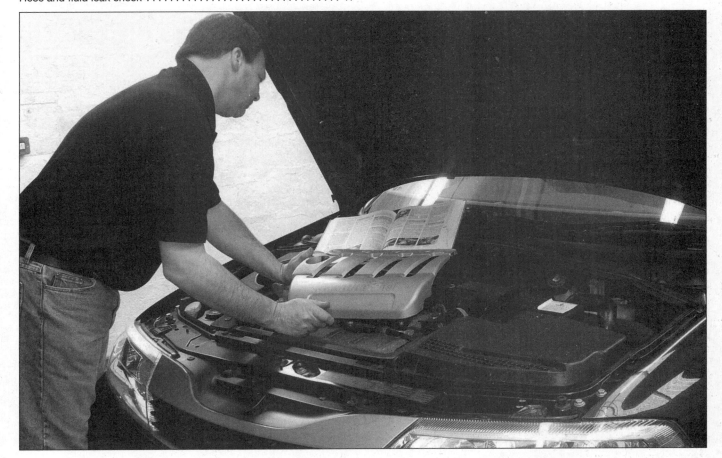

Degrees of difficulty

Easy, suitable for novice with little experience 

Fairly easy, suitable for beginner with some experience

Fairly difficult, suitable for competent DIY mechanic 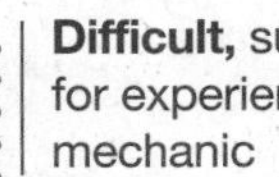

Difficult, suitable for experienced DIY mechanic 

Very difficult, suitable for expert DIY or professional 

Lubricants and fluids

Refer to *Weekly checks* on page 0•17

Capacities

Engine oil (including filter)	
1.6 litre engines (K4M)	4.9 litres
1.8 litre engines (F4P)	5.1 litres
2.0 litre engines (F4R)	5.2 litres
Cooling system	
1.6 and 1.8 litre engines	6.5 litres
2.0 litre engines	6.8 litres
Transmission	
Manual transmission:	
JH3	2.8 litres
JR5	2.5 litres
PK6	2.2 litres
Automatic transmission	
SU1	7.6 litres
DPO	6.0 litres
Fuel tank	70.0 litres

Engine

Auxiliary drivebelt tension	Controlled by automatic tensioner

Cooling system

Antifreeze mixture*:	
35% antifreeze	Protection down to -22°C
50% antifreeze	Protection down to -40°C

* **Note:** *Renault coolant is supplied ready-mixed and does not require further dilution.*

Fuel system

Idle speed (not adjustable – controlled by ECU)	750 ± 50 rpm
Idle mixture CO content	Less than 1.0 % (controlled by ECU)

Ignition system

Firing order	1-3-4-2	
Location of No 1 cylinder	Flywheel end	
Ignition timing	Controlled by ECU – see Chapter 5B	
Spark plugs:	**Type**	**Electrode gap**
1.6 litre	Eyquem RFC 50 LZ 2E	0.9 mm
1.8 litre & 2.0 litre	Champion RFC 87 YCL	0.9 mm

Brakes

Front disc brakes:	
280 mm diameter discs:	
Thickness of brake pads (including backplate)	17.00 mm
Minimum thickness of brake pads (including backplate)	7.00 mm
300 mm diameter discs:	
Thickness of brake pads (including backplate)	17.50 mm
Minimum thickness of brake pads (including backplate)	7.00 mm
Rear disc brakes:	
Pad thickness (including backing):	
New	16.0 mm
Minimum thickness	7.5 mm

Torque wrench settings

	Nm	lbf ft
Ignition coils	15	11
Roadwheel bolts	105	77
Spark plugs	25 to 30	18 to 22

The maintenance intervals in this manual are provided with the assumption that you, not the dealer, will be carrying out the work. These are the minimum maintenance intervals recommended by us for vehicles driven daily. If you wish to keep your vehicle in peak condition at all times, you may wish to perform some of these procedures more often. We encourage frequent maintenance, because it enhances the efficiency, performance and resale value of your vehicle.

If the vehicle is driven in dusty areas, used to tow a trailer, or driven frequently at slow speeds (idling in traffic) or on short journeys, more frequent maintenance intervals are recommended.

When the vehicle is new, a factory-authorised dealer service department should service it, in order to preserve the factory warranty.

Every 250 miles (400 km) or weekly

☐ Refer to *Weekly checks*

Every 9000 miles (15 000 km) or 12 months

☐ Renew the engine oil and filter (Section 3)

Note: *Frequent oil and filter changes are good for the engine and we recommend that the oil and filter be renewed at the interval specified here (or at least once every 12 months), especially if the vehicle is used on a lot of short journeys or covers a small annual mileage.*

Every 18 000 miles (30 000 km) or 2 years

In addition to all the items listed previously, carry out the following:

☐ Check the brake pad thickness – front and rear (Section 4)
☐ Check the operation of the handbrake (Section 5)
☐ Check the operation of the clutch (Section 6)
☐ Check the condition of the auxiliary drivebelts (Section 7)
☐ Check the condition of the seat belts (Section 8)
☐ Check the operation of all electrical systems (Section 9)
☐ Check the condition of the exhaust system and mountings (Section 10)
☐ Check the suspension and steering components (Section 11)
☐ Check the tightness of the roadwheel bolts (Section 12)
☐ Renew the pollen (particle) filter (Section 13)

Every 36 000 miles (60 000 km) or 4 years

In addition to all the items listed previously, carry out the following:

☐ Renew the air filter element (Section 14)
☐ Renew the spark plugs (Section 15)
☐ Check the manual transmission oil level (Section 16)
☐ Check all under bonnet components and hoses for fluid leaks (Section 17)
☐ Check the operation of the air conditioning system (Section 18)
☐ Check the spare fuses are in place (Section 19)
☐ Renew the brake fluid (Section 20)
☐ Carry out a road test (Section 21)
☐ Renew the timing belt (Section 22)*
☐ Renew the coolant (Section 23)

* **Note:** *Although the normal interval for timing belt renewal is 72 000 miles (120 000 km), it is strongly recommended that the interval is halved to 36 000 miles (60 000 km) on vehicles which are subjected to intensive use, ie, mainly short journeys or a lot of stop-start driving. The actual belt renewal interval is therefore very much up to the individual owner, but bear in mind that severe engine damage may result if the belt breaks.*

Underbonnet view of a 1.8 litre model – other models similar

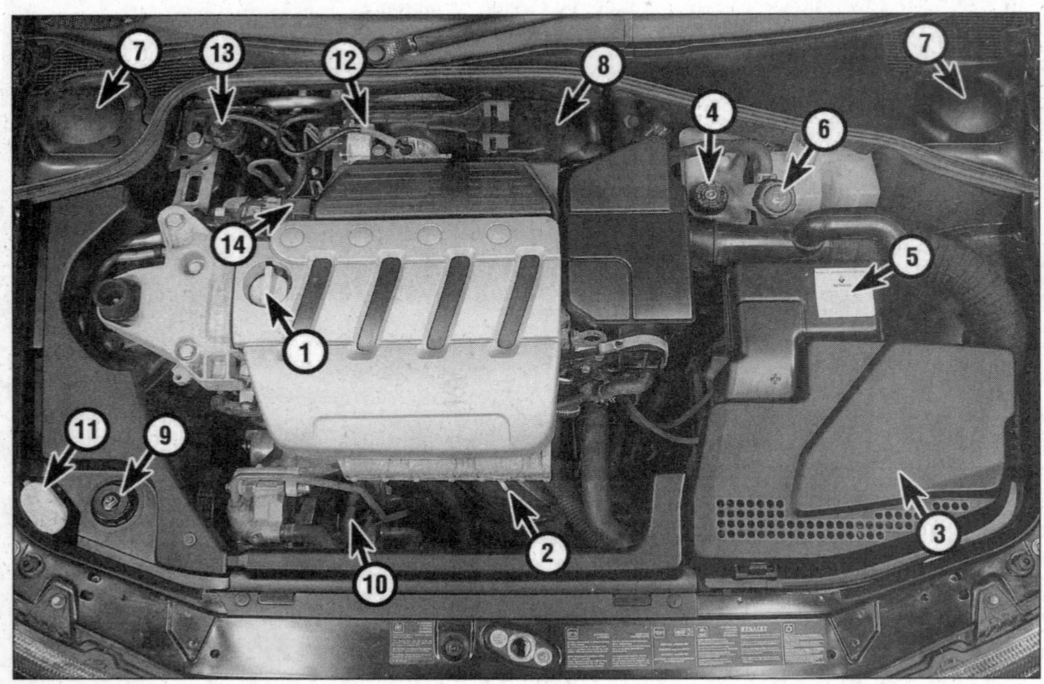

1. *Engine oil filler cap*
2. *Engine oil level dipstick*
3. *Battery*
4. *Brake fluid reservoir*
5. *Relay/fusebox*
6. *Coolant expansion tank*
7. *Suspension strut upper mountings*
8. *Air filter housing*
9. *Power steering fluid reservoir*
10. *Alternator*
11. *Washer fluid reservoir*
12. *Throttle body housing*
13. *Fuel vapour recycling solenoid valve*
14. *Manifold pressure sensor*

Front underbody view of a 1.8 litre model – other models similar

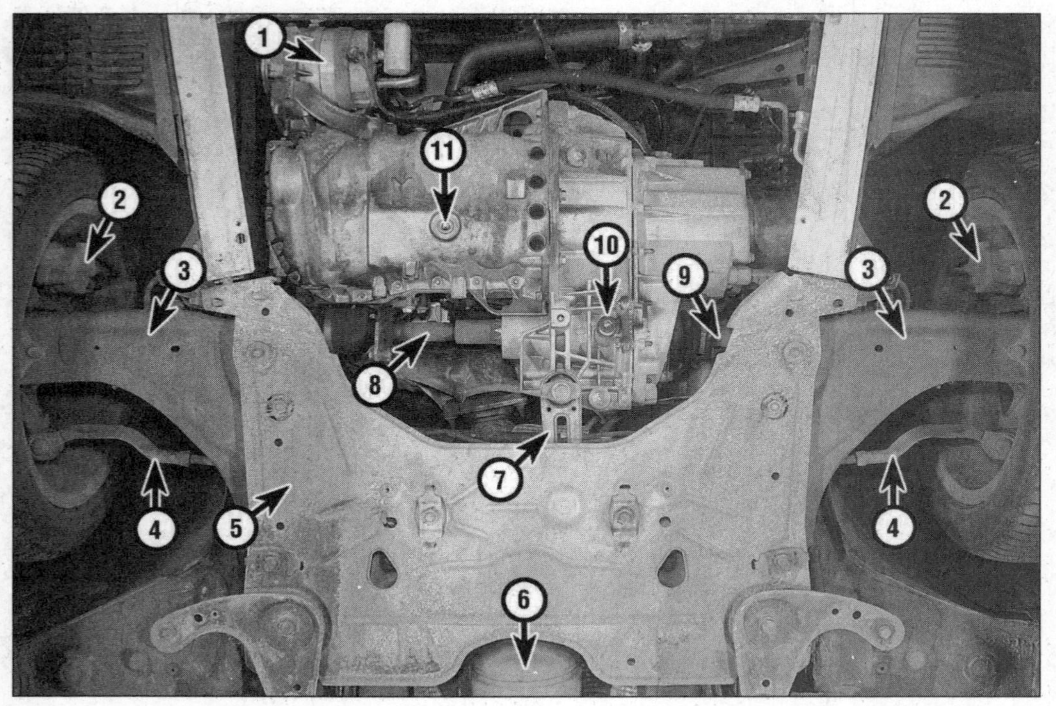

1. *Air conditioning compressor*
2. *Front brake calipers*
3. *Front suspension lower arms*
4. *Track rod arms*
5. *Subframe*
6. *Catalytic converter*
7. *Rear engine mounting link*
8. *Right-hand driveshaft*
9. *Left-hand driveshaft*
10. *Transmission oil drain plug*
11. *Engine oil drain plug*

Rear underbody view of a 1.8 litre model – other models similar

1. *Exhaust expansion box*
2. *Rear suspension mountings*
3. *Rear suspension axle crossmember*
4. *Rear suspension torsion bar*
5. *Rear shock absorbers*
6. *Fuel tank*
7. *Exhaust heat shield*
8. *Fuel vapour charcoal canister*

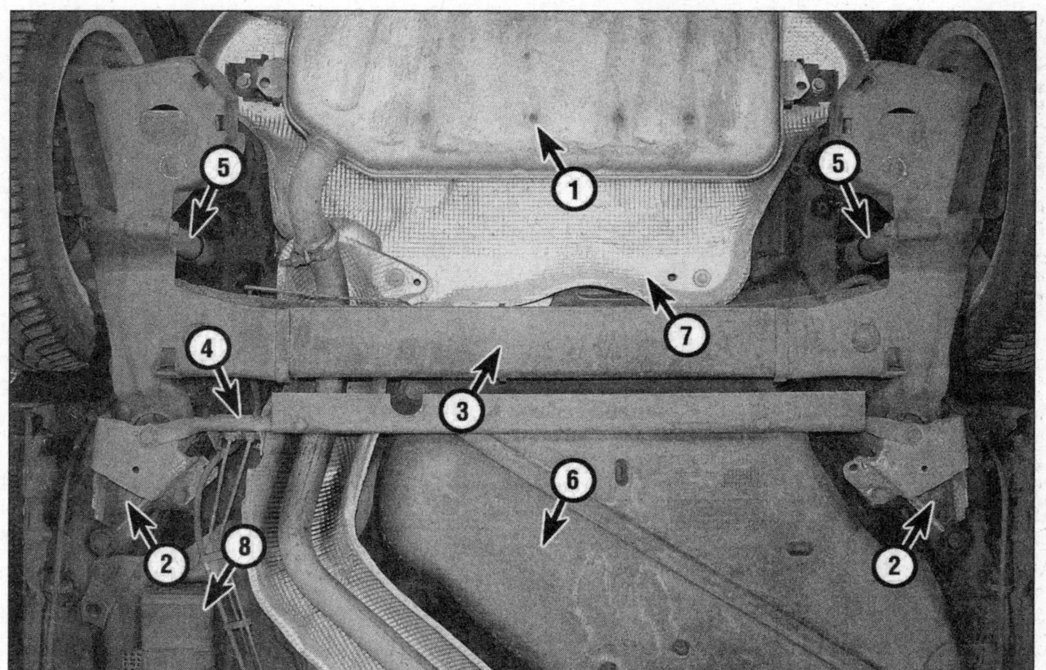

Maintenance procedures

1 Introduction

This Chapter is designed to help the home mechanic maintain his/her vehicle for safety, economy, long life and peak performance.

The Chapter contains a master maintenance schedule, followed by Sections dealing specifically with each task in the schedule. Visual checks, adjustments, component renewal and other helpful items are included. Refer to the accompanying illustrations of the engine compartment and the underside of the vehicle for the locations of the various components.

Servicing your vehicle in accordance with the mileage/time maintenance schedule and the following Sections will provide a planned maintenance programme, which should result in a long and reliable service life. This is a comprehensive plan, so maintaining some items but not others at the specified service intervals will not produce the same results.

As you service your vehicle, you will discover that many of the procedures can – and should – be grouped together, because of the particular procedure being performed, or because of the close proximity of two otherwise-unrelated components to one another. For example, if the vehicle is raised for any reason, the exhaust can be inspected at the same time as the suspension and steering components.

The first step in this maintenance programme is to prepare yourself before the actual work begins. Read through all the Sections relevant to the work to be carried out, then make a list and gather together all the parts and tools required. If a problem is encountered, seek advice from a parts specialist, or a dealer service department.

2 Regular maintenance

If, from the time the vehicle is new, the routine maintenance schedule is followed closely, and frequent checks are made of fluid levels and high-wear items, as suggested throughout this manual, the engine will be kept in relatively good running condition, and the need for additional work will be minimised.

It is possible that there will be times when the engine is running poorly due to the lack of regular maintenance. This is even more likely if a used vehicle, which has not received regular and frequent maintenance checks, is purchased. In such cases, additional work may need to be carried out, outside of the regular maintenance intervals.

If engine wear is suspected, a compression test (refer to Chapter 2A) will provide valuable information regarding the overall performance of the main internal components. Such a test can be used as a basis to decide on the extent of the work to be carried out. If, for example, a compression test indicates serious internal engine wear, conventional maintenance as described in this Chapter will not greatly improve the performance of the engine, and may prove a waste of time and money, unless extensive overhaul work is carried out first.

The following series of operations are those most often required to improve the performance of a generally poor-running engine:

Primary operations

a) Clean, inspect and test the battery (see 'Weekly checks').
b) Check all the engine-related fluids (see 'Weekly checks').
c) Check the condition and tension of the auxiliary drivebelt (Section 7).
d) Check the condition of the air filter element, and renew if necessary (Section 14).
e) Check the fuel filter (Chapter 4A).
f) Check the condition of all hoses, and check for fluid leaks (Section 17).
g) Renew the spark plugs (Section 15)

If the above operations do not prove fully effective, carry out the following secondary operations:

Secondary operations

All items listed under *Primary operations*, plus the following:
a) Check the charging system (Chapter 5A).
b) Check the ignition system (Chapter 5B).
c) Check the fuel system (Chapter 4A).

Every 9000 miles (15 000 km) or 12 months

3 Engine oil and filter renewal

1 Frequent oil and filter changes are the most important preventative maintenance procedures that can be undertaken by the DIY owner. As engine oil ages, it becomes diluted and contaminated, which leads to premature engine wear.

2 Before starting this procedure, gather together all the necessary tools and materials **(see illustration).** Also make sure that you have plenty of clean rags and newspapers handy, to mop-up any spills. Ideally, the engine oil should be warm, as it will drain more easily, and more built-up sludge will be removed with it.

3 Take care not to touch the exhaust or any other hot parts of the engine when working under the vehicle. To avoid any possibility of scalding, and to protect yourself from possible skin irritants and other harmful contaminants in used engine oils, it is advisable to wear gloves when carrying out this work.

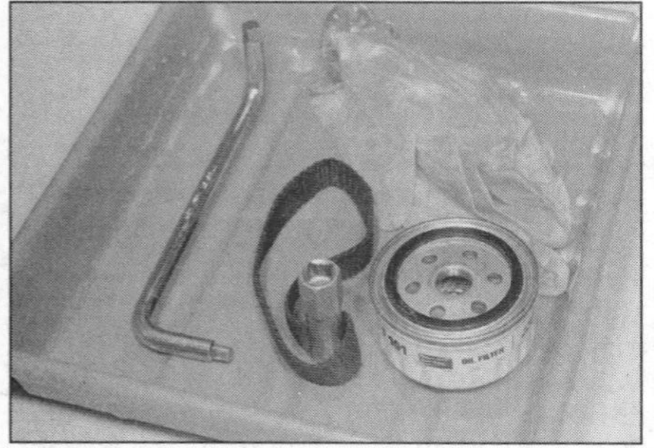

3.2 Tools and materials necessary for the engine oil and filter renewal

3.5 The engine oil drain plug (arrowed) is removed using a square section key

4 Firmly apply the handbrake then jack up the front of the vehicle and support it on axle stands (see *Jacking and vehicle support*). Undo the retaining screws and remove the plastic undertray from underneath the engine/transmission.

5 Remove the oil filler cap, and then slacken the drain plug about half a turn. Position the draining container under the drain plug, and then remove the plug completely **(see Haynes Hint)**. Note that on some engines an 8 mm square section drain plug key will be needed to unscrew the drain plug **(see illustration).**

6 Allow some time for the oil to drain, noting that it may be necessary to reposition the container as the oil flow slows to a trickle.

7 After all the oil has drained; wipe the drain plug and the sealing washer with a clean rag. Examine the condition of the sealing washer, and renew it if it shows signs of scoring or other damage that may prevent an oil-tight seal. Clean the area around the drain plug opening, and refit the plug complete with the washer and tighten it securely.

8 Move the container into position under the oil filter, which is located on the front of the cylinder block.

9 Use an oil filter removal tool to slacken the filter initially, then unscrew it by hand the rest of the way **(see illustration)**. Position it with its open end uppermost to prevent further spillage of oil, then empty the oil from the old filter into the container.

If possible, try to keep the plug pressed into the sump while unscrewing it by hand the last couple of turns. As the plug releases from the threads, move it away sharply so the stream of oil from the sump runs into the container, not up your sleeve.

10 Use a clean rag to remove all oil, dirt and sludge from the filter sealing area on the engine. Check the old filter to make sure that the rubber sealing ring has not stuck to the engine. If it has, carefully remove it.

11 Apply a light coating of clean engine oil to the sealing ring on the new filter, then screw the filter into position on the engine. Tighten the filter firmly by hand only – **do not** use any tools.

12 Refit the undertray and securely tighten its retaining screws. Remove the old oil and all tools from under the vehicle then lower the vehicle to the ground.

13 Fill the engine through the filler hole, using the correct grade and type of oil (refer to *Weekly Checks* for details of topping-up). Pour in half the specified quantity of oil first, and then wait a few minutes for the oil to drain into the sump. Continue to add oil, a small quantity at a time, until the level is up to the lower mark on the dipstick. Adding approximately a further 1.5 litres will bring the level up to the upper mark on the dipstick.

14 Start the engine and run it for a few minutes, while checking for leaks around the oil filter seal and the sump drain plug. Note that there may be a delay of a few seconds before the low oil pressure warning light goes out when the engine is first started, as the oil circulates through the new oil filter and the engine oil galleries before the pressure builds-up.

15 Stop the engine, and wait a few minutes for the oil to settle in the sump once more. With the new oil circulated and the filter now completely full, recheck the level on the dipstick, and add more oil as necessary.

16 Dispose of the used engine oil and filter safely with reference to *General repair procedures* in the Reference section of this manual.

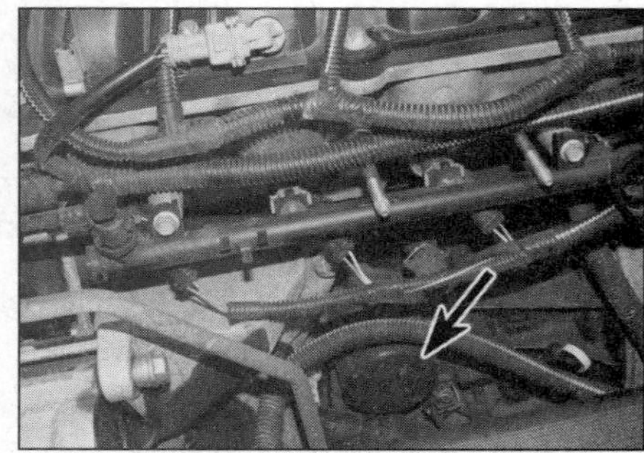

3.9 Oil filter location (arrowed) on the front of the engine – 1.8 litre engine

Every 18 000 miles (30 000 km) or 2 years

4 Brake pad check – front and rear

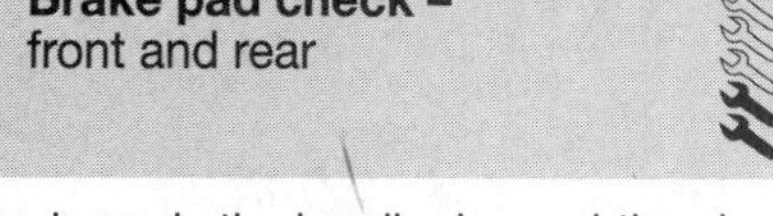

1 Firmly apply the handbrake, and then jack up the front or rear of the car and support it securely on axle stands (see *Jacking and vehicle support*). Remove the roadwheels as required. Remember, the car has disc brakes all round, so all four calipers should be checked.

2 For a quick check, the thickness of friction material remaining on each brake pad can be measured through the aperture in the caliper body **(see Haynes Hint)**. If any pad's friction material is worn to the specified thickness or less, all four pads must be renewed as a set. Pad wear warning contacts may be fitted to the inboard pads, but this should not be used as an excuse for omitting a visual check.

3 For a comprehensive check, the brake pads should be removed and cleaned. This will allow the operation of the caliper to be checked, and the brake disc itself to be fully examined for condition on both sides. Refer to Chapter 9 for further information.

4 On completion refit the roadwheels and lower the car to the ground.

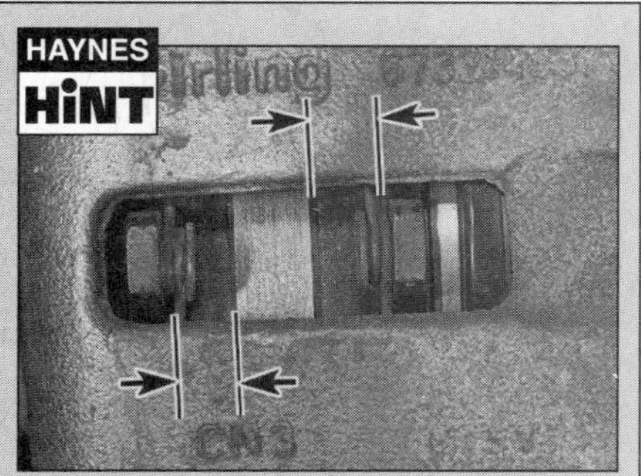

For a quick check, the thickness of friction material remaining on each brake pad can be measured through the aperture in the caliper body.

5 Handbrake check

Note: *The handbrake cable should not be retensioned to correct any fault, and should only be adjusted when fitting new pads, cables or handbrake lever.*

1 The handbrake is kept in adjustment by the self-adjusting action of the rear disc calipers.

2 Chock the front wheels, then jack up the rear of the vehicle, and support securely on axle stands (see *Jacking and vehicle support*).

3 Fully release the handbrake and check that the wheels can be rotated easily by hand. The wheels may drag slightly, but there should be no binding.

4 If the wheels bind, it is likely that the handbrake mechanism or cables are partially seized. If the operation of the mechanism is not satisfactory, proceed as follows.

5 Working inside the vehicle, lift the flap inside the centre console between the front seats, slacken the adjuster nut until there is no tension in the handbrake cables **(see illustration)**.

6 Remove the rear road wheels.

7 Check that the handbrake cables slide freely in their sheaths, and that the operating levers on the calipers move freely (see Chapter 9 for further information).

8 Push the handbrake operating levers on the calipers as far as they will go against their bottom stops.

9 If all the parts move freely, turn the cable adjuster until the handbrake cable end fittings just contact the operating levers on the calipers, without moving the levers **(see illustration)**.

10 Continue to turn the adjuster sleeve until the handbrake operating levers on the calipers begin to move when the handbrake lever is pulled between the first and second notches. There should be no free play in the handbrake cables once the lever is pulled beyond the second notch.

11 Tighten the adjuster locknuts.

12 Refit the roadwheels, and lower the vehicle to the ground.

6 Clutch check

Check that the clutch pedal moves smoothly and easily through its full travel, and that the clutch itself functions correctly, with no trace of slip or drag. If the clutch action is less than precise, this may indicate the need for bleeding the system – it could also indicate the presence of a fluid leak (see Chapter 6).

7 Auxiliary drivebelt check and renewal

Note: *Renault recommends that the auxiliary belt be renewed whenever it is slackened or removed.*

Checking

1 The auxiliary drivebelt is located at the right-hand side of the engine.

2 Numerous different drivebelt configurations may be encountered, depending on engine type and pulley arrangement **(see illustrations)**.

3 Due to their function and material makeup,

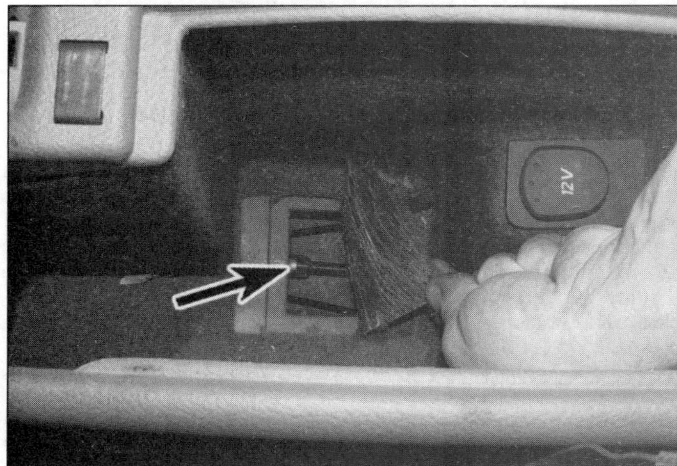

5.5 Handbrake operating rod, slacken the adjuster nut (arrowed)

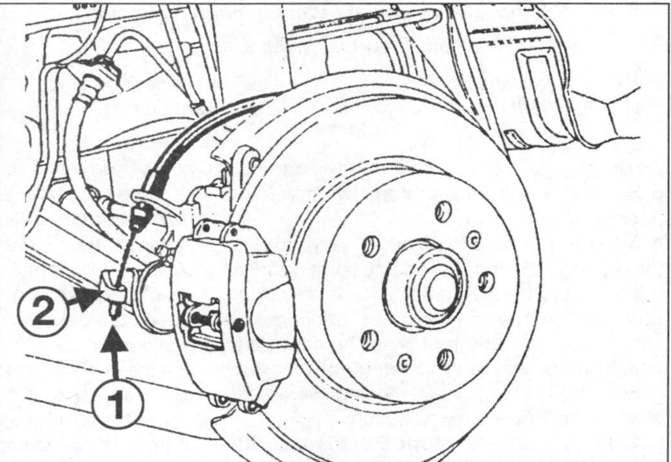

5.9 The handbrake cable end fittings (1) should just contact the operating levers (2)

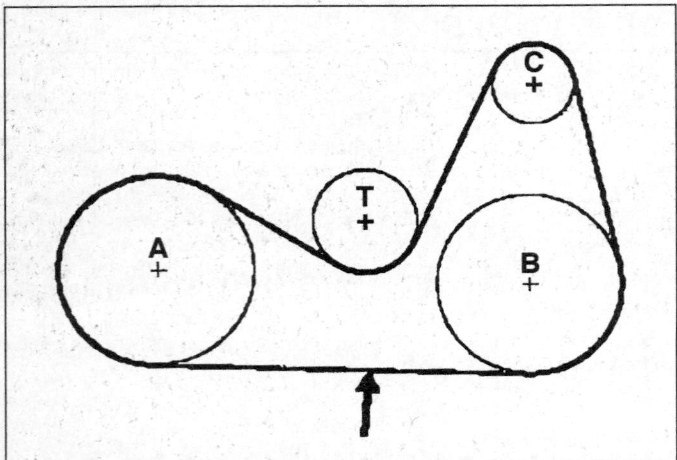

7.2a Auxiliary drivebelt configuration – 1.6 litre engines without air conditioning

Arrow indicates tension checking point

A Crankshaft pulley
B Power steering pump
C Alternator
T Tensioner pulley

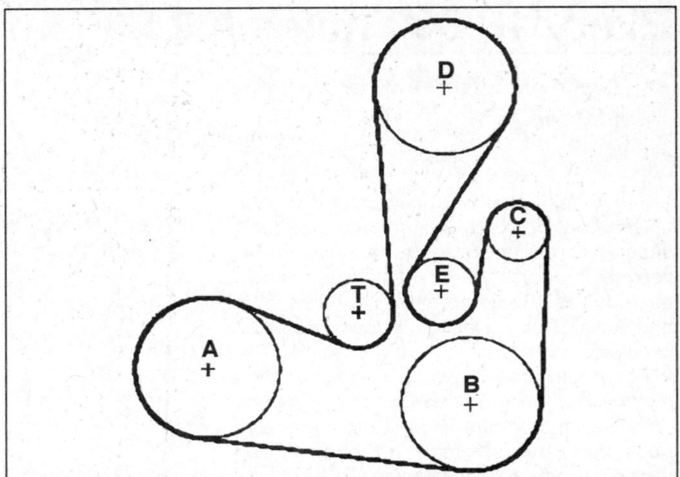

7.2b Auxiliary drivebelt configuration – 1.6 litre engines with air conditioning

A Crankshaft pulley
B Air conditioning compressor
C Alternator
D Power steering pump
E Idler pulley
T Tensioner pulley

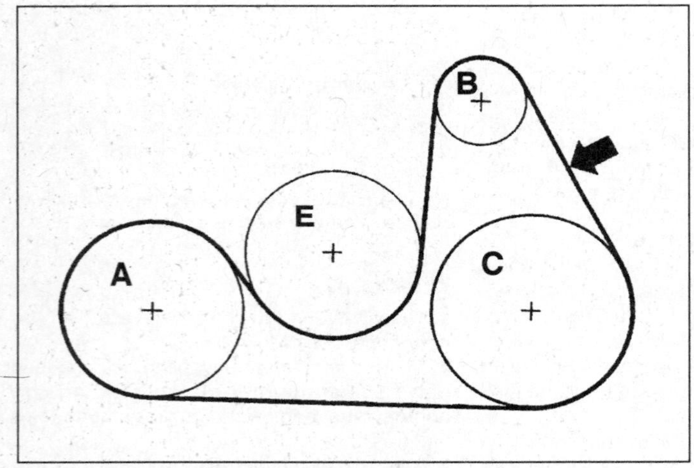

7.2c Auxiliary drivebelt configuration – 1.8 and 2.0 litre engines without air conditioning

Arrow indicates tension checking point

A Crankshaft pulley
B Alternator
C Power steering pump
E Coolant pump

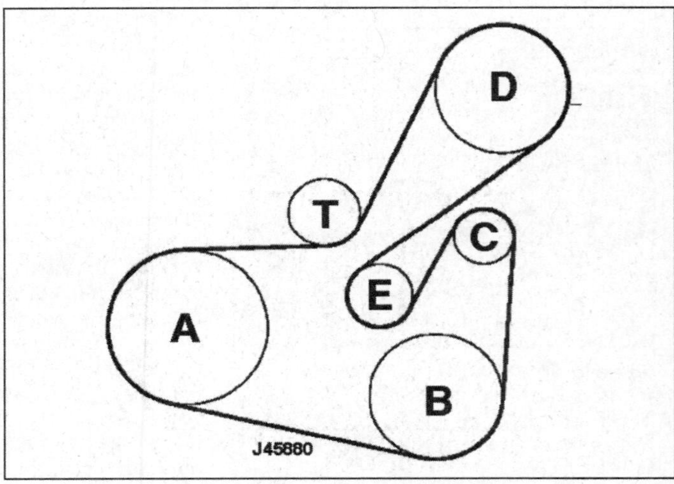

7.2d Auxiliary drivebelt configuration – 1.8 and 2.0 litre engines with air conditioning

A Crankshaft pulley
B Air conditioning compressor
C Alternator
D Power steering pump
E Idler pulley
T Tensioner pulley

drivebelts are prone to failure after a period of time and should therefore be inspected periodically.

4 Since the drivebelt is located very close to the right-hand side of the engine compartment, it is possible to gain better access by raising the front of the vehicle (see *Jacking and vehicle support*) and removing the right-hand wheel, then removing the engine undertray (where applicable), and removing the splash shield from inside the wheel arch.

5 With the engine stopped, inspect the full length of the drivebelt for cracks and separation of the belt plies. It will be necessary to turn the engine (using a spanner or socket and bar on the crankshaft pulley bolt) in order to move the belt around the pulleys so that the belt can be inspected thoroughly. Twist the belt between the pulleys so that both sides can be viewed. Also check for fraying, and glazing which gives the belt a shiny appearance. Check the pulleys for nicks, cracks, distortion and corrosion.

6 If the belt is satisfactory, refit the components removed to access it, then refit the wheel and lower the car to the ground. Tighten the wheel bolts to the specified torque.

Tensioning

7 An automatic tensioner is used to maintain the correct drivebelt tension, and Renault does not give an actual tension value. If problems with belt squeal or slip are encountered, the belt should be renewed. If the problem continues, it may be necessary to renew the tensioner assembly.

Renewal

8 If not already done, apply the handbrake, then jack up the front of the car and support it on axle stands (see *Jacking and vehicle support*). Remove the right-hand wheel, and then remove the engine undertray (where applicable), and the splash shield from inside the wheel arch.

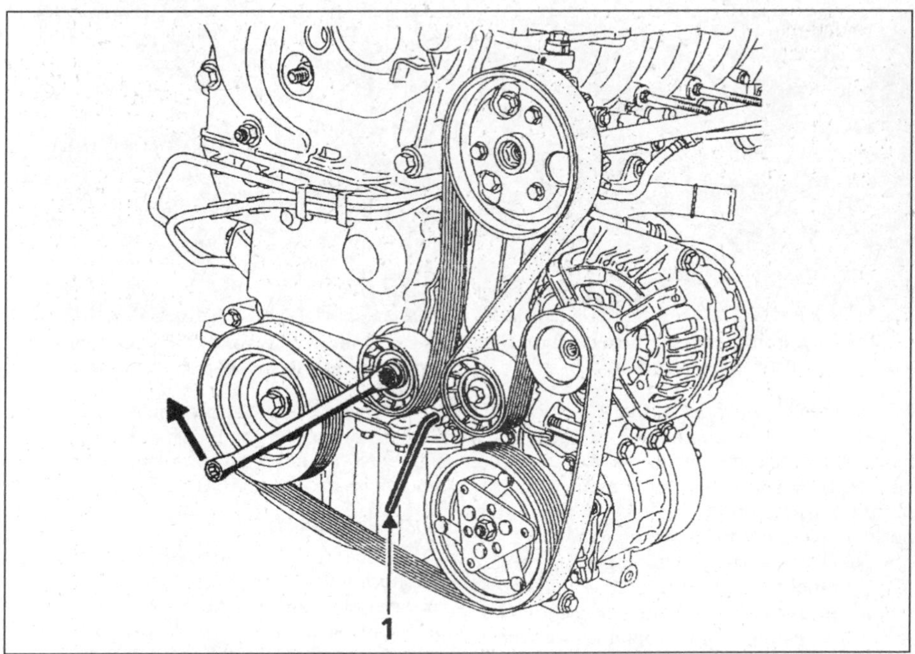

7.10 Releasing the drivebelt tensioner on 1.6 litre engines with air conditioning

Move the tensioner in the direction of the arrow then insert an Allen key (1) to lock the tensioner

9 Before removing the belt, note its fitted position, making sure the run of the belt is straight. The pulleys have six grooves and the belt has five. Depending on model, the inner groove or the outer groove is left unused.

1.6 litre engines

10 Using a 13 mm spanner or socket, turn the tensioner clockwise as shown to release the belt tension **(see illustration)**. Align the holes in the tensioner and bracket and insert a 6 mm Allen key through the holes to lock the tensioner in the released position.

11 Note the routing of the belt, then slip the belt off the pulleys (see paragraph 9).

12 Fit the new belt ensuring that it is routed correctly, then release the tensioner to automatically tension the belt.

1.8 and 2.0 litre engines

13 Using a 16 mm spanner or socket, turn the tensioner clockwise to release the belt tension **(see illustration)**.

14 While the tensioner is held in the clockwise position, slip the belt off the pulleys, noting the routing of the belt.

15 Fit the belt loosely around the main pulleys, making sure that it is correctly located in the grooves (see paragraph 9), then turn the tensioner the same way as previously until the belt can be fitted around the tensioner pulley also.

16 Release the tensioner to automatically tension the belt.

All models

17 Turn the engine through two complete revolutions, using a spanner or socket on the crankshaft pulley bolt. Check that the belt is running properly on its pulleys, and that the tensioner is working correctly (check that the belt is taut, midway along its longest run).

18 On completion, refit the components removed to access the belt, then refit the wheel and lower the car to the ground. Tighten the wheel bolts to the specified torque.

8 Seat belt check

1 Carefully examine the seat belt webbing for cuts, or any signs of serious fraying or deterioration. If the belt is of the retractable type, pull the belt all the way out of the inertia reel, and examine the full extent of the webbing.

2 Fasten and unfasten the belt, ensuring that the locking mechanism holds securely, and releases properly when intended. If the belt is of the retractable type, check also that the retracting mechanism operates correctly when the belt is released.

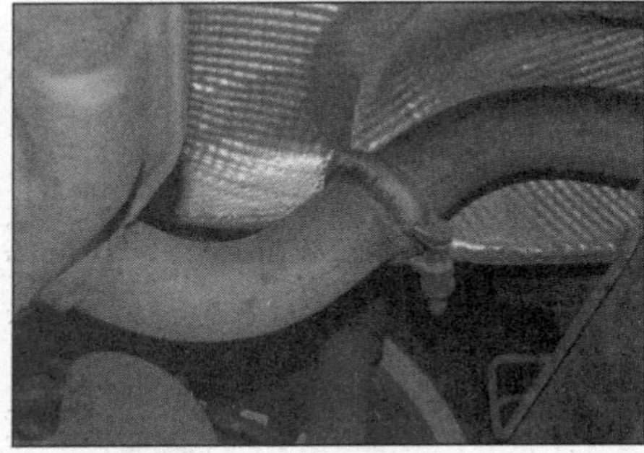

10.2 Check the exhaust system at the joint where it goes over the rear axle

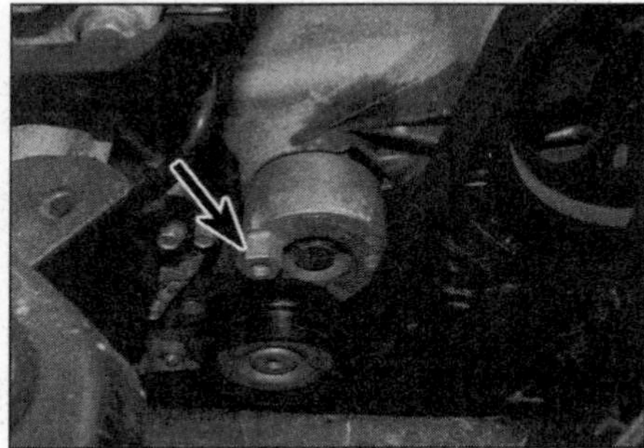

7.13 Use a spanner on the hexagon (arrowed) to release the drivebelt tension – models with air conditioning

3 Check the security of all seat belt mountings and attachments that are accessible without removing any trim or other components.

9 Electrical systems check

1 Check the operation of all electrical equipment, ie, lights, direction indicators, horn, etc. Refer to the appropriate Sections of Chapter 12 for details if any of the circuits are found to be inoperative.

2 Note that stop-light switch adjustment is described in Chapter 9.

3 Visually check all accessible wiring connectors, harnesses and retaining clips for security, and for signs of chafing or damage. Rectify any faults found.

10 Exhaust system check

1 With the engine cold (at least an hour after the vehicle has been driven), check the complete exhaust system from the engine to the end of the tailpipe. The exhaust system is most easily checked with the vehicle raised on a hoist, or suitably supported on axle stands, so that the exhaust components are readily visible and accessible.

2 Check the exhaust pipes and connections for evidence of leaks, severe corrosion and damage. Make sure that all brackets and mountings are in good condition, and that all relevant nuts and bolts are tight. Leakage at any of the joints or in other parts of the system will usually show up as a black sooty stain in the vicinity of the leak **(see illustration)**.

3 Rattles and other noises can often be traced to the exhaust system, especially the brackets and mountings. Try to move the pipes and silencers. If the components are able to come into contact with the body or suspension parts, secure the system with new mountings. Otherwise separate the joints (if possible) and twist the pipes as necessary to provide additional clearance.

11.2a Check the balljoint rubber gaiters (arrowed) . . .

11.2b . . . and the gaiters (arrowed) on the anti-roll bar drop links

11.4 Check for wear in the hub bearings by grasping the wheel and trying to rock it

11 Suspension and steering check

Front suspension and steering

1 Raise the front of the vehicle, and securely support it on axle stands (see *Jacking and vehicle support*).

2 Visually inspect the balljoint dust covers and the steering rack-and-pinion gaiters for splits, chafing or deterioration **(see illustrations)**. Any wear of these components will cause loss of lubricant, together with dirt and water entry, resulting in rapid deterioration of the balljoints or steering gear.

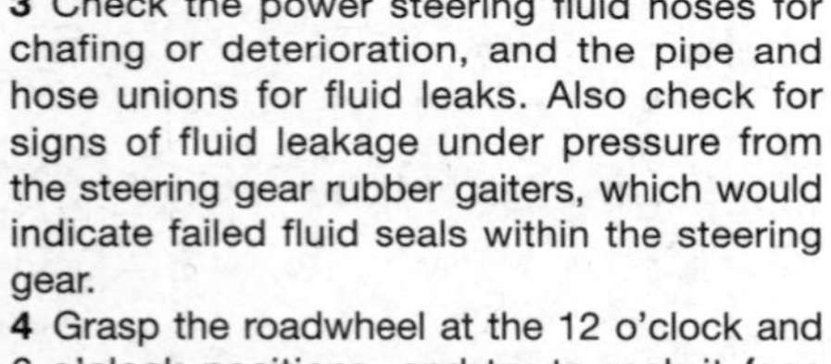

3 Check the power steering fluid hoses for chafing or deterioration, and the pipe and hose unions for fluid leaks. Also check for signs of fluid leakage under pressure from the steering gear rubber gaiters, which would indicate failed fluid seals within the steering gear.

4 Grasp the roadwheel at the 12 o'clock and 6 o'clock positions, and try to rock it **(see illustration)**. Very slight free play may be felt, but if the movement is appreciable, further investigation is necessary to determine the source. Continue rocking the wheel while an assistant depresses the footbrake. If the movement is now eliminated or significantly reduced, it is likely that the hub bearings are at fault. If the free play is still evident with the footbrake depressed, then there is wear in the suspension joints or mountings.

5 Now grasp the wheel at the 9 o'clock and 3 o'clock positions, and try to rock it as before. Any movement felt now may again be caused by wear in the hub bearings or the steering track rod balljoints. If the outer balljoint is worn, the visual movement will be obvious. If the inner joint is suspect, it can be felt by placing a hand over the rack-and-pinion rubber gaiter and gripping the track rod. If the wheel is now rocked, movement will be felt at the inner joint if wear has taken place.

6 Using a large screwdriver or flat bar, check for wear in the suspension mounting bushes by levering between the relevant suspension component and its attachment point. Some movement is to be expected, as the mountings are made of rubber, but excessive wear should be obvious. Also check the condition of any visible rubber bushes, looking for splits, cracks or contamination of the rubber.

7 With the car standing on its wheels, have an assistant turn the steering wheel back-and-forth, about an eighth of a turn each way. There should be very little, if any, lost movement between the steering wheel and roadwheels. If this is not the case, closely observe the joints and mountings previously described. In addition, check the steering column universal joints for wear, and also check the rack-and-pinion steering gear itself.

Rear suspension

8 Chock the front wheels, then jack up the rear of the vehicle and support securely on axle stands (see *Jacking and vehicle support*).

9 Working as described previously for the front suspension, check the rear hub bearings, the suspension bushes and the shock absorber mountings for wear.

Shock absorber

10 Check for any signs of fluid leakage around the shock absorber body, or from the rubber gaiter around the piston rod. Should any fluid be noticed, the shock absorber is defective internally, and should be renewed. **Note:** *Shock absorbers should always be renewed in pairs on the same axle.*

11 The efficiency of the shock absorber may be checked by bouncing the vehicle at each corner. Generally speaking, the body will return to its normal position and stop after being depressed. If it rises and returns on a rebound, the shock absorber is probably suspect. Also examine the shock absorber upper and lower mountings for any signs of wear.

12 Roadwheel bolt check

Note: *A key will be required, to slacken any locking wheel nuts.*

1 Where applicable, remove the wheel trims, and then slacken the roadwheel bolts slightly.

2 Tighten the bolts to the specified torque, using a torque wrench.

13 Pollen (particle) filter renewal

1 The pollen filter (also known as a particle filter) is located inside the vehicle, behind the glove compartment. It is fitted in the air inlet housing, and filters the air to ensure it is completely clean before entering the passenger compartment.

2 Open the glove compartment door and remove the retaining screw from the rear of the pocket **(see illustration)**.

3 Insert a small screwdriver into the slot, release the securing clip and withdraw the pocket from inside of the glove compartment **(see illustrations)**.

13.2 Undo the retaining screw (arrowed)

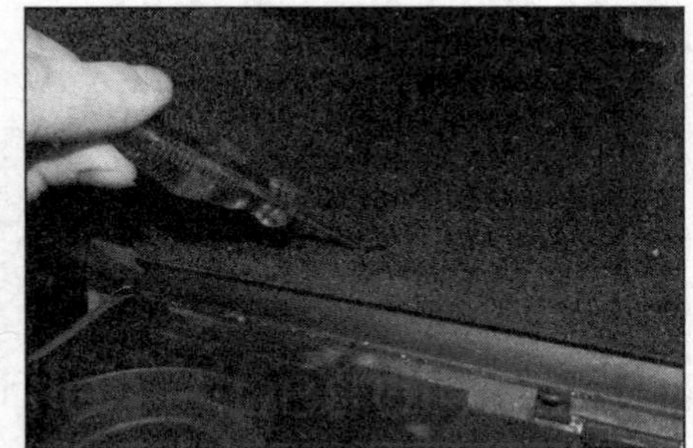

13.3a Press down on the screwdriver . . .

4 Undo the two retaining bolts and withdraw the filter from its housing. Note its fitted position for refitting **(see illustration)**.
5 Refitting is a reversal of removal.

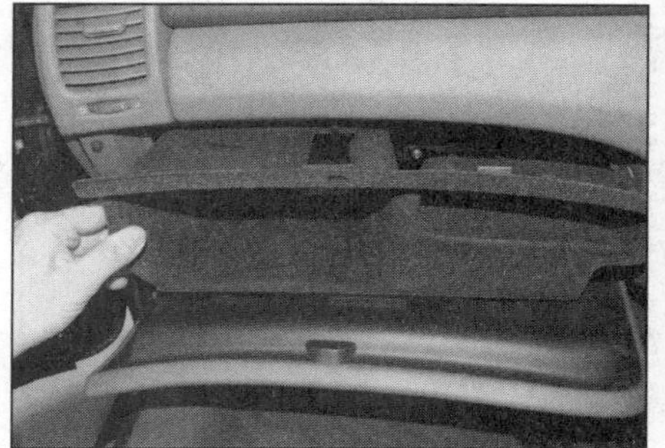
13.3b . . . and withdraw the glove pocket from the facia

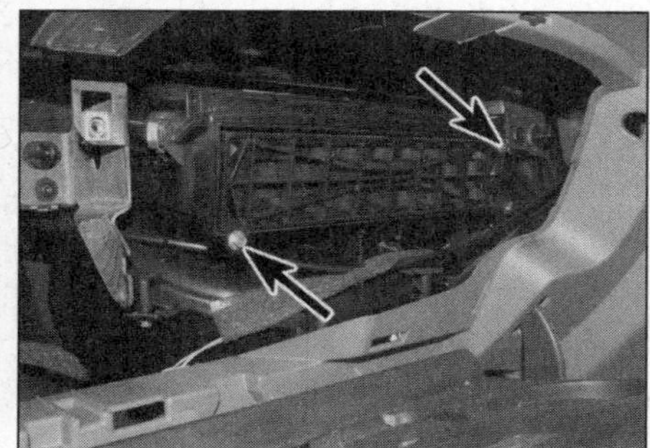
13.4 Undo the two retaining bolts (arrowed)

Every 36 000 miles (60 000 km) or 4 years

14 Air filter element renewal

1 Release the rubber retaining strap and detach the resonator from the air filter housing. Withdraw the resonator from its location **(see illustrations)**. Where necessary, unclip any pipes or cables from the resonator as it is moved to one side.
2 Disconnect the brake servo vacuum pipe from the end of the intake manifold **(see illustration)**.
3 Undo the two screws securing the air filter housing to the intake housing **(see illustration)**.

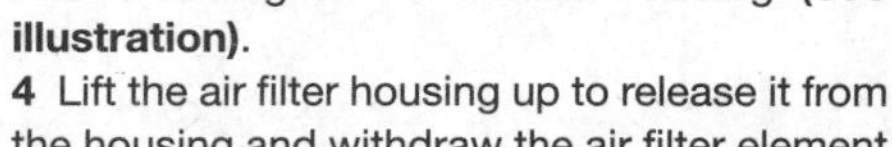

4 Lift the air filter housing up to release it from the housing and withdraw the air filter element **(see illustration)**.
5 Wipe clean the filter housing and fit the new filter. Locate the housing in position and secure with the two screws.
6 Reconnect the brake servo vacuum pipe to the intake manifold.
7 Refit the resonator making sure it is secured in place using the rubber retaining strap. Where applicable, reconnect any pipes or cables in the securing clips.

15 Spark plug renewal

Warning: Voltages produced by an electronic ignition system are considerably higher than those produced by conventional ignition systems. Extreme care must be taken when working on the system with the ignition switched on. Persons with surgically-implanted cardiac pacemaker devices should keep well clear of the ignition circuits, components and test equipment.

14.1a Release the rubber strap . . .

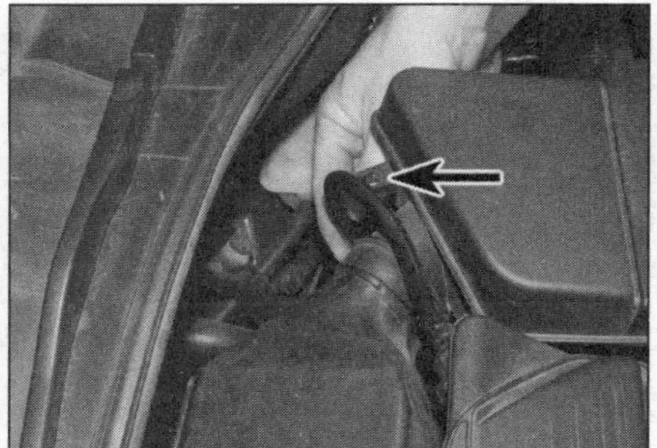
14.1b . . . unclip any pipes from their retaining clips (arrowed) . . .

14.1c . . . and lift out the resonator housing

14.2 Disconnect the brake servo vacuum pipe

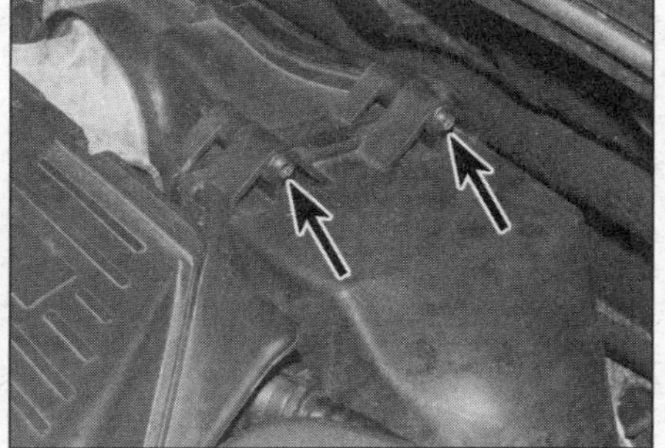
14.3 Undo the two retaining screws (arrowed)

14.4 Unclip the lower part of the air filter cover from the housing

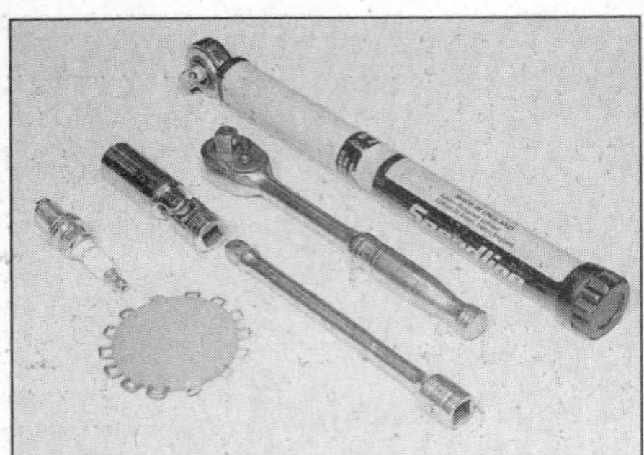

15.2 Tools required for spark plug removal, gap adjustment and refitting

15.3 Unclip the cover from the top of the engine

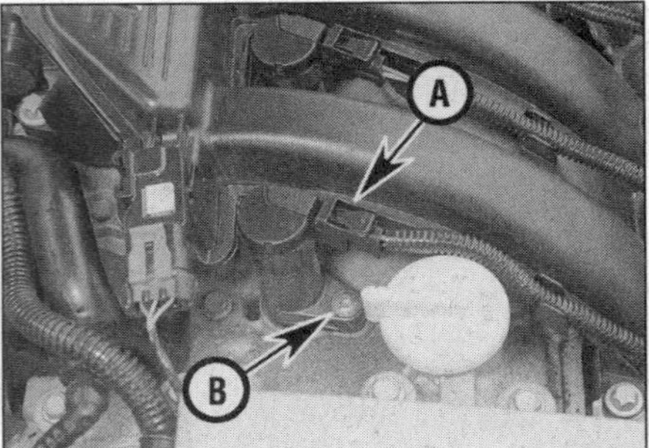

15.4 Ignition coil wiring connector (A) and retaining screw (B)

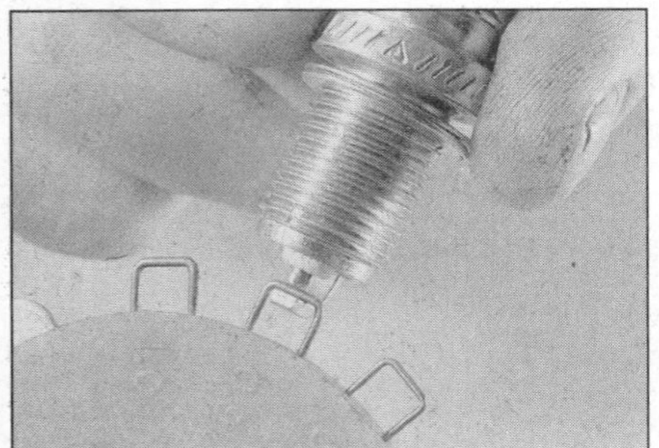

15.12a Measuring the spark plug gap with a wire gauge

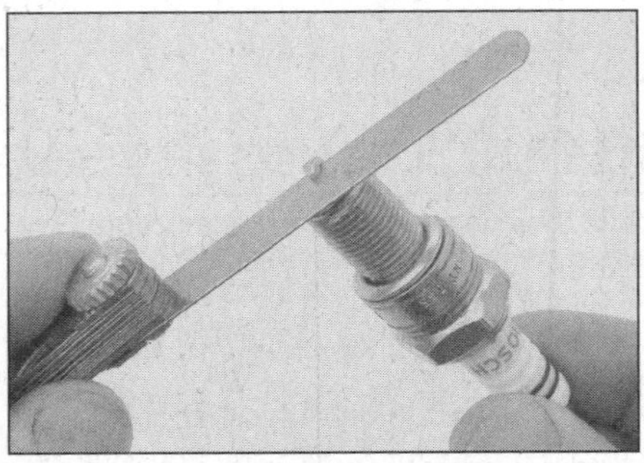

15.12b Measuring the spark plug gap with a feeler blade

1 The correct functioning of the spark plugs is vital for the correct running and efficiency of the engine. It is essential that the plugs fitted are appropriate for the engine (Renault recommendations are at the beginning of this Chapter). If these types are used and the engine is in good condition, the spark plugs should not need attention between scheduled service intervals. Spark plug cleaning is rarely necessary, and should not be attempted unless specialised equipment is available, as damage can easily be caused to the firing ends.

HAYNES HiNT

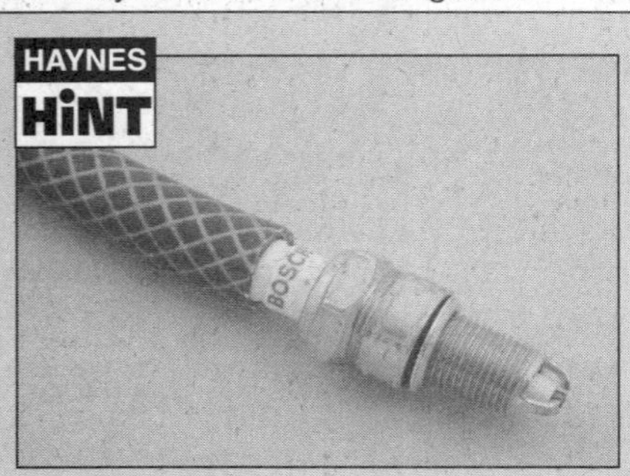

It is very often difficult to insert spark plugs into their holes without cross-threading them. To avoid this possibility, fit a short length of 5/16 inch internal diameter rubber hose over the end of the spark plug. The flexible hose acts as a universal joint to help align the plug with the plug hole. Should the plug begin to cross-thread, the hose will slip on the spark plug, preventing thread damage to the aluminium cylinder head.

2 Spark plug removal and refitting requires a spark plug socket, with an extension which can be turned by a ratchet handle or similar. This socket is lined with a rubber sleeve, to protect the porcelain insulator of the spark plug, and to hold the plug while it is removed or inserted into the spark plug hole. A torque wrench to tighten the plugs to the specified torque will also be required **(see illustration)**.

3 Open the bonnet and remove the plastic engine cover from the top of the cylinder head **(see illustration)**. Note how the ignition coil wiring harnesses are routed and secured by clips along the top of the cylinder head or inlet manifold. To prevent the possibility of mixing up the wiring, it is a good idea to try to work on one spark plug at a time.

4 Each spark plug has a separate ignition coil located over the top of the plug and secured to the cylinder head with retaining screws. Disconnect the wiring connector at the ignition coil, then undo the retaining screw and pull the coil upwards from the spark plug and cylinder head **(see illustration)**.

5 It is advisable to remove the dirt from the spark plug recesses using a clean brush, vacuum cleaner or compressed air before removing the plugs, to prevent dirt dropping into the cylinders.

6 Unscrew the plugs, ensuring that the socket is kept in alignment with each plug – if the socket is forcibly moved to either side, the porcelain top of the plug may be broken off.

7 As each plug is removed, examine it as follows – this will give a good indication of the condition of the engine. If the insulator nose of the spark plug is clean and white, with no deposits, this is indicative of a weak mixture or too hot a plug (a hot plug transfers heat away from the electrode slowly, a cold plug transfers heat away quickly).

8 If the tip and insulator nose are covered with hard black-looking deposits, then this is indicative that the mixture is too rich. Should the plug be black and oily, and then it is likely that the engine is fairly worn, as well as the mixture being too rich.

9 If the insulator nose is covered with light tan to greyish-brown deposits, then the mixture is correct and it is likely that the engine is in good condition.

10 The spark plug electrode gap is of considerable importance as, if it is too large or too small, the size of the spark and its efficiency will be seriously impaired. The gap should be set to the value given in the Specifications at the beginning of this Chapter. Spark plugs with specially-shaped multiple electrodes may be used and it is not necessary or possible to adjust the electrode gap on these types.

11 The centre electrode should never be bent, as this may crack the insulator and cause plug failure, if nothing worse.

12 Special spark plug electrode gap measuring and adjusting tools are available from most motor accessory shops **(see illustrations)**.

13 Before fitting the spark plugs, check that the threaded connector sleeves are tight, and that the plug exterior surfaces and threads are clean.

14 Insert each spark plug into the cylinder head and screw them in by hand, taking extra care to enter the plug threads correctly **(see Haynes Hint)**.

15 When each spark plug is started correctly on its threads, screw it down until it just seats lightly, then tighten it to the specified torque wrench setting.

16 Check the condition of the O-ring seal on the end of each ignition coil and renew them if necessary. Locate the coils over the spark plugs and secure with the retaining screws to the specified torque setting.

17 Connect the ignition coil wiring connectors in their correct order as noted on removal. Where applicable, refit the plastic engine cover.

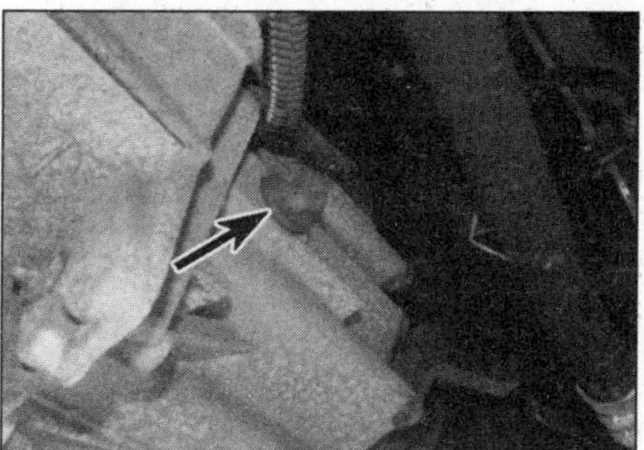

16.3 The filler/level plug (arrowed) is on the front of the transmission

16 Manual transmission oil level check

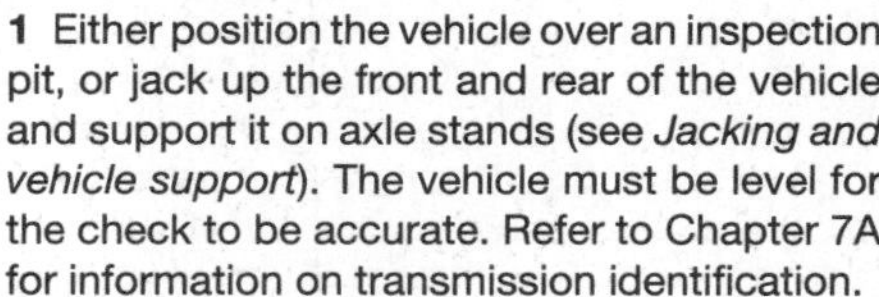

1 Either position the vehicle over an inspection pit, or jack up the front and rear of the vehicle and support it on axle stands (see *Jacking and vehicle support*). The vehicle must be level for the check to be accurate. Refer to Chapter 7A for information on transmission identification.

JH3 and JR5 transmission

2 Undo the retaining screws and remove the undertray from beneath the engine/ transmission.

3 Clean the area around the filler/level plug on the front of the transmission, then slacken and remove the plug from the transmission **(see illustration).** Check the condition of the filler plug seal, and obtain a new one if necessary.

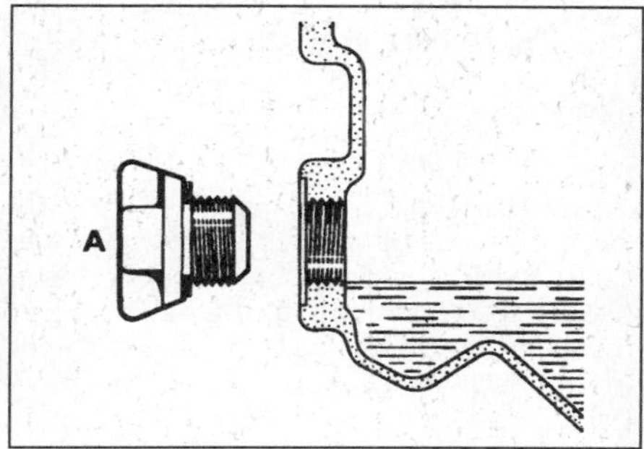

16.5 Manual transmission filler/level plug (A) – correct oil level shown

4 The transmission oil level should be up to the lower edge of the filler/level plug aperture.

5 If necessary, top-up using the specified type of lubricant until the transmission oil level is correct. Fill the transmission until oil starts to flow out and allow excess oil to drain **(see illustration).**

6 Once the transmission oil level is correct, refit the filler/level plug and tighten it securely.

7 Refit the engine undertray then lower the vehicle to the ground. Note that frequent need for topping-up indicates a leakage, possibly through an oil seal. The cause should be investigated and rectified.

PK6 transmission

Note: *This check can only be carried out by using the special Renault tool/dipstick B.Vi.1675.*

8 Clean the area around the transmission oil filler plug that is situated on the left-hand end of the transmission unit, at the front corner **(see illustration).**

9 Slacken and remove the filler plug from the transmission.

10 Insert the dipstick through the filler plug recess. Make sure the slot in the top of the dipstick bracket is located on the rib on the transmission housing.

11 Slide the dipstick out of the filler plug and check the oil level. Note the oil level on the end of the dipstick; it should be between the upper and lower marks. With the oil up to the maximum mark there will be approximately 2.4 litres in the transmission. With the oil up to

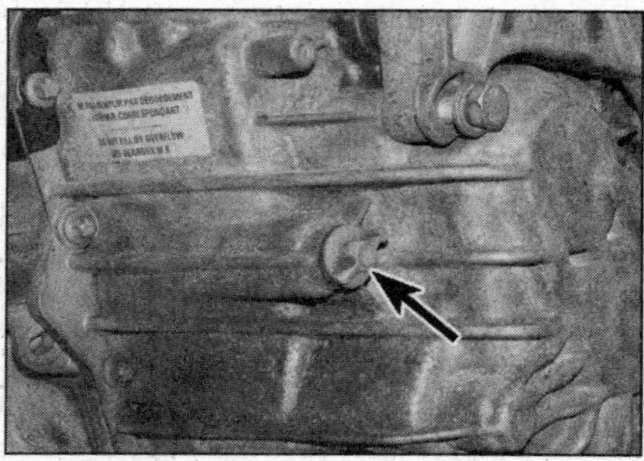

16.8 The filler/level plug (arrowed) is on the left-hand front of the transmission

the minimum mark there will be approximately 2.0 litres in the transmission. The target level is midway between the two.

12 Top-up the transmission oil level with the specified type of lubricant via the filler plughole. Once the level is up to the correct level, refit the filler plug and sealing washer and tighten it securely. Where necessary, refit the undertray and securely tighten its retaining screws. Note that frequent need for topping-up indicates a leakage, possibly through an oil seal. The cause should be investigated and rectified.

17 Hose and fluid leak check

1 Visually inspect the engine joint faces, gaskets and seals for any signs of water or oil leaks. Pay particular attention to the areas around the cylinder head cover, cylinder head, oil filter and sump joint faces. Bear in mind that, over a period of time, some very slight seepage from these areas is to be expected – what you are really looking for is any indication of a serious leak. Should a leak be found, renew the offending gasket or oil seal by referring to the appropriate Chapters in this manual.

17.2 Check the brake hose and metal brake pipes very carefully

2 Also check the security and condition of all the engine-related pipes and hoses, and all braking system pipes and hoses **(see illustration).** Ensure that all cable-ties or securing clips are in place, and in good condition. Clips that are broken or missing can lead to chafing of the hoses, pipes or wiring, which could cause more serious problems in the future.

17.3 Check all hoses for signs of damage and the security of the hose clips

3 Carefully check the radiator hoses and heater hoses along their entire length. Renew any hose that is cracked, swollen or deteriorated. Cracks will show up better if the hose is squeezed. Pay close attention to the hose clips that secure the hoses to the cooling system components. Hose clips can pinch and puncture hoses, resulting in cooling system leaks **(see illustration).**

A leak in the cooling system will usually show up as white- or rust-coloured deposits on the area adjoining the leak.

4 Inspect all the cooling system components (hoses, joint faces, etc) for leaks **(see Haynes Hint)**. Where any problems are found on system components, renew the component or gasket with reference to Chapter 3.

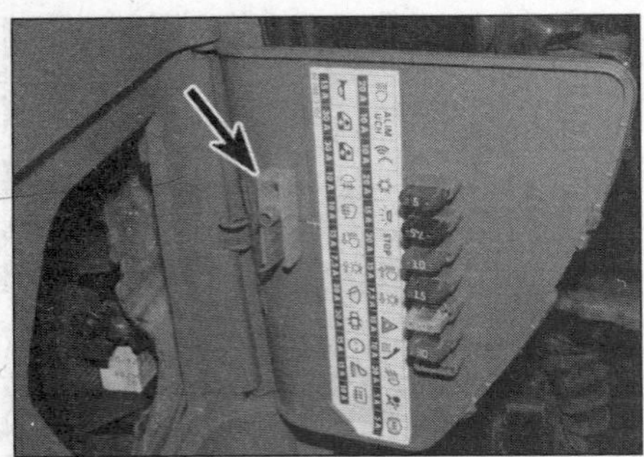

19.1 **Fuse removal tool (arrowed) on inside of cover with spare fuses**

5 With the vehicle raised, inspect the fuel tank and filler neck for punctures, cracks and other damage. The connection between the filler neck and tank is especially critical. Sometimes a rubber filler neck or connecting hose will leak due to loose retaining clamps or deteriorated rubber.

6 Carefully check all rubber hoses and metal fuel lines leading away from the fuel tank. Check for loose connections, deteriorated hoses, crimped lines, and other damage. Pay particular attention to the vent pipes and hoses, which often loop up around the filler neck and can become blocked or crimped. Follow the lines to the front of the vehicle, carefully inspecting them all the way. Renew damaged sections as necessary. Similarly, whilst the vehicle is raised, take the opportunity to inspect all underbody brake fluid pipes and hoses.

7 From within the engine compartment, check the security of all fuel, vacuum and brake hose attachments and pipe unions, and inspect all hoses for kinks, chafing and deterioration.

8 Where applicable, check the condition of the automatic transmission and power steering fluid pipes and hoses.

18 Air conditioning system check

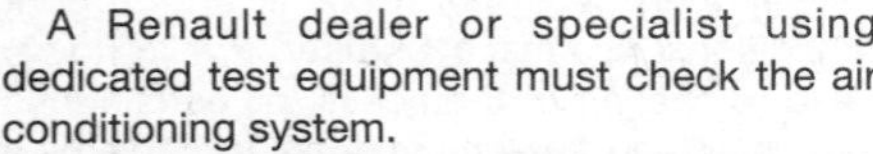

A Renault dealer or specialist using dedicated test equipment must check the air conditioning system.

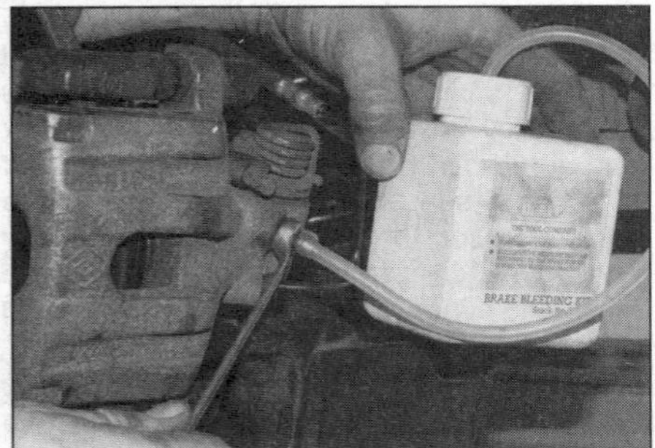

20.2 Change the brake fluid using the same method as for bleeding the brake system

19 Spare fuse check

Check that spare fuses are in place in the locations provided in the fusebox cover (see Chapter 12). It is advisable to carry at least one spare of each rating of fuse fitted **(see illustration).** Spare fuses can be obtained from most car accessory shops, or from a Renault dealer.

20 Brake fluid renewal

Warning: Brake hydraulic fluid can harm your eyes and damage painted surfaces, so use extreme caution when handling and pouring it. Do not use fluid that has been standing open for some time, as it absorbs moisture from the air. Excess moisture can cause a dangerous loss of braking effectiveness.

Caution: On models equipped with ABS, disconnect the battery before carrying out this operation and do not reconnect the battery until after the operation is complete. Failure to do this could lead to air entering the hydraulic unit. If air enters the hydraulic unit pump, it will prove very difficult (in some cases impossible) to bleed the unit. Refer to 'Disconnecting the battery' in the Reference Section.

1 The procedure is similar to that for the bleeding of the hydraulic system as described in Chapter 9, except that the brake fluid reservoir should be emptied by syphoning, using a clean poultry baster or similar before starting, and allowance should be made for the old fluid to be expelled when bleeding a section of the circuit.

2 Working as described in Chapter 9, open the first bleed screw in the sequence **(see illustration)**, and pump the brake pedal gently until nearly all the old fluid has been emptied from the master cylinder reservoir. Top-up to the MAX level with new fluid, and continue pumping until only the new fluid remains in the reservoir, and new fluid can be seen emerging from the bleed screw. Tighten the screw, and top the reservoir level up to the MAX level line.

Old hydraulic fluid is invariably much darker in colour than the new, making it easy to distinguish between the two.

4 When the operation is complete, check that all bleed screws are securely tightened, and that their dust caps are refitted. Wash off all traces of spilt fluid, and recheck the master cylinder reservoir fluid level.

5 Check the operation of the brakes before taking the car on the road.

6 Dispose safely of the used brake fluid with reference to *General repair procedures*.

21 Road test

Instruments and electrical equipment

1 Check the operation of all instruments and electrical equipment.

2 Make sure that all instruments read correctly, and switch on all electrical equipment in turn, to check that it functions properly.

Steering and suspension

3 Check for any abnormalities in the steering, suspension, handling or road 'feel'.

4 Drive the vehicle, and check that there are no unusual vibrations or noises.

5 Check that the steering feels positive, with no excessive 'sloppiness', or roughness, and check for any suspension noises when cornering and driving over bumps.

Drivetrain

6 Check the performance of the engine, clutch, transmission and driveshafts.

7 Listen for any unusual noises from the engine, clutch and transmission.

8 Make sure that the engine runs smoothly when idling, and that there is no hesitation when accelerating.

9 Check that, where applicable, the clutch action is smooth and progressive, that the drive is taken up smoothly, and that the pedal travel is not excessive. Also listen for any noises when the clutch pedal is depressed.

10 Check that all gears can be engaged smoothly without noise, and that the gear lever action is smooth and not abnormally vague or 'notchy'.

11 On automatic transmission models, make sure that all gearchanges occur smoothly, without snatching, and without an increase in engine speed between changes. Check that all of the gear positions can be selected with the vehicle at rest. If any problems are found, they should be referred to a Renault dealer.

12 Listen for a metallic clicking sound from the front of the vehicle, as the vehicle is driven slowly in a circle with the steering on full-lock. Carry out this check in both directions. If a clicking noise is heard, this indicates wear in a driveshaft joint (see Chapter 8).

Braking system

13 Make sure that the vehicle does not pull to one side when braking, and that the wheels do not lock when braking hard.

14 Check that there is no vibration through the steering when braking.

15 Check that the handbrake operates correctly, without excessive movement of the

lever, and that it holds the vehicle stationary on a slope.

16 Test the operation of the brake servo unit as follows. Depress the footbrake four or five times to exhaust the vacuum, and then start the engine. As the engine starts, there should be a noticeable 'give' in the brake pedal as vacuum builds-up. Allow the engine to run for at least two minutes, and then switch it off. If the brake pedal is now depressed again, it should be possible to detect a hiss from the servo as the pedal is depressed. After about four or five applications, no further hissing should be heard, and the pedal should feel considerably harder.

22 Timing belt renewal

Refer to Chapter 2A.

23 Coolant renewal

Warning: Wait until the engine is cold before starting this procedure. Do not allow antifreeze to come in contact with your skin, or with the painted surfaces of the vehicle. Rinse off spills immediately with plenty of water. Never leave antifreeze lying around in an open container, or in a puddle in the driveway or on the garage floor. Children and pets are attracted by its sweet smell, but antifreeze can be fatal if ingested.

Note: *Renault do not specify renewal intervals for the coolant, but it is advisable to drain and refill the system every four years to ensure that the corrosion inhibiting properties of the coolant are maintained.*

Cooling system draining

1 With the engine completely cold, remove the expansion tank filler cap. Turn the cap anti-clockwise, wait until any pressure remaining in the system is released, then unscrew it and lift it off.

2 Where applicable, remove the engine undertray, and then position a suitable container beneath the radiator bottom hose connection. Slacken the hose clip, pull off the hose and allow the coolant to drain into the container.

3 To assist draining, open the cooling system bleed screws. These are located in the radiator, thermostat/coolant housing and heater hose, depending on engine type **(see illustration)**.

4 Flush the system if necessary as described in the following paragraphs, then refit the bottom hose. Use a new hose clip if necessary. Refill the system as described later in this Section.

Cooling system flushing

5 If coolant renewal has been neglected, or if the antifreeze mixture has become diluted, then in time the cooling system may gradually lose efficiency, as the coolant passages become restricted due to rust, scale deposits, and other sediment. Flushing the system clean can restore the cooling system efficiency.

6 The radiator should be flushed independently of the engine, to avoid unnecessary contamination.

Radiator flushing

7 Disconnect the top and bottom hoses and any other relevant hoses from the radiator, with reference to Chapter 3.

8 Insert a garden hose into the radiator top inlet. Direct a flow of clean water through the radiator, and continue flushing until clean water emerges from the radiator bottom outlet.

9 If after a reasonable period, the water still does not run clear, the radiator can be flushed with a good proprietary cleaning agent. It is important that their manufacturer's instructions are followed carefully. If the contamination is particularly bad, insert the hose in the radiator bottom outlet, and reverse-flush the radiator.

Engine flushing

10 To flush the engine, first refit the cylinder block drain plug, and tighten the cooling system bleed screw(s).

11 Remove the thermostat as described in Chapter 3, then temporarily refit the top hose at its engine connection.

12 With the top and bottom hoses disconnected from the radiator, insert a garden hose into the radiator top hose. Direct a clean flow of water through the engine, and continue flushing until clean water emerges from the radiator bottom hose.

13 On completion of flushing, refit the thermostat and reconnect the hoses with reference to Chapter 3.

Cooling system filling

14 Before attempting to fill the cooling system, make sure that all hoses and clips are in good condition, and that the clips are tight. Note that an antifreeze mixture must be used all year round, to prevent corrosion of the engine components. Also check that the cylinder block drain plug is in place and tight.

15 Remove the expansion tank filler cap.

16 Open the cooling system bleed screws (see paragraph 3).

17 Place a container under the vehicle, below the expansion tank, to catch any coolant that may be spilt during the topping-up procedure. Also place a wad of rags around the expansion tank.

18 Slowly fill the system until the coolant level reaches the top of the expansion tank filler neck.

19 Where applicable, close the bleed screws when coolant free from air bubbles emerges.

23.3 Cooling system bleed screw (arrowed) in the heater hose

Close the screws in sequence, starting with the lowest screw in the system.

20 Start the engine, and run it at a fast idle speed (do not exceed 2500 rpm) for approximately 4 minutes. Keep the level topped-up to the top of the expansion tank filler neck.

21 Refit and tighten the expansion tank filler cap.

22 Allow the engine to run for approximately 20 minutes at 2500 rpm (until the cooling fan cuts in and out three times).

23 Stop the engine and check the coolant level, which should be up to the MAX mark on the side of the tank. Check that the expansion tank filler cap is tight.

24 Allow the engine to cool, and then recheck the coolant level with reference to *Weekly checks*. Top-up the level if necessary and refit the expansion tank filler cap. Where applicable, refit the engine undertray.

Antifreeze mixture

25 The antifreeze should always be renewed at the specified intervals. This is necessary not only to maintain the antifreeze properties, but also to prevent corrosion that would otherwise occur as the corrosion inhibitors become progressively less effective.

26 Always use an ethylene glycol-based antifreeze, which is suitable for use in mixed-metal cooling systems. The quantity of antifreeze and levels of protection are given in the Specifications.

27 Before adding antifreeze, the cooling system should be completely drained, preferably flushed, and all hoses checked for condition and security.

28 After filling with antifreeze, a label should be attached to the expansion tank, stating the type and concentration of antifreeze used, and the date installed. Any subsequent topping-up should be made with the same type and concentration of antifreeze.

29 Do not use engine antifreeze in the windscreen/tailgate washer system, as it will cause damage to the vehicle paintwork. A screenwash additive should be added to the washer system in the quantities stated on the bottle.

30 Dispose safely of the used coolant with reference to *General repair procedures*.

Chapter 1 Part B: Routine maintenance and servicing – diesel models

Contents

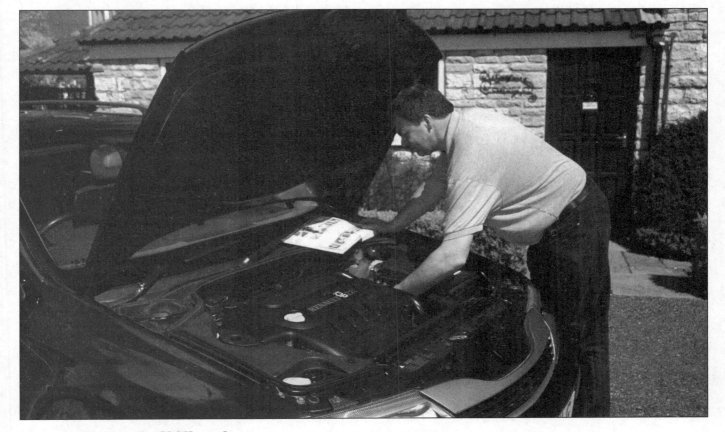

Degrees of difficulty

Easy, suitable for novice with little experience 

Fairly easy, suitable for beginner with some experience

Fairly difficult, suitable for competent DIY mechanic

Difficult, suitable for experienced DIY mechanic 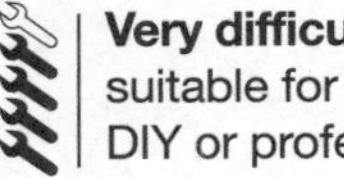

Very difficult, suitable for expert DIY or professional 

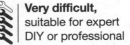

Servicing specifications – diesel models

Lubricants and fluids

Refer to *Weekly checks* on page 0•17

Capacities

Engine oil (Including filter)	
1.9 litre engines (F9Q)	4.8 litres
2.2 litre engines (G9T)	6.3 litres
Difference between MAX and MIN dipstick marks	1.5 to 2.0 litres
Cooling system	7.0 litres
Transmission	
Manual:	
JR5	2.5 litres
PK6	2.2 litres
Automatic:	
SU1	7.6 litres
DPO	6.0 litres
Fuel tank	70.0 litres

Cooling system

Antifreeze mixture*:	
35% antifreeze	Protection down to -23°C
50% antifreeze	Protection down to -40°C

* **Note:** *Renualt coolant is supplied ready-mixed and does not require further dilution*.

Fuel system

Idle speed (non-adjustable)	800 ± 50 rpm

Brakes

Front disc brakes:	
280 mm diameter discs:	
Thickness of brake pads (including backplate)	17.00 mm
Minimum thickness of brake pads (including backplate)	7.00 mm
300 mm diameter discs:	
Thickness of brake pads (including backplate)	17.50 mm
Minimum thickness of brake pads (including backplate)	7.00 mm
Rear disc brakes:	
Pad thickness (including backing):	
New	16.0 mm
Minimum thickness	7.5 mm

Torque wrench settings

	Nm	lbf ft
Auxiliary belt tensioner mounting bolts (later models)	25	18
Roadwheel bolts	105	77

The maintenance intervals in this manual are provided with the assumption that you, not the dealer, will be carrying out the work. These are the minimum maintenance intervals recommended by us for vehicles driven daily. If you wish to keep your vehicle in peak condition at all times, you may wish to perform some of these procedures more often. We encourage frequent maintenance, because it enhances the efficiency, performance and resale value of your vehicle.

If the vehicle is driven in dusty areas, used to tow a trailer, or driven frequently at slow speeds (idling in traffic) or on short journeys, more frequent maintenance intervals are recommended.

When the vehicle is new, a factory-authorised dealer service department should service it, in order to preserve the factory warranty.

Every 250 miles (400 km) or weekly

- [ ] Refer to Weekly checks

Every 9000 miles (15 000 km) or 12 months

- [ ] Renew the engine oil and filter (Section 3)*
- [ ] Drain any water from the fuel filter (Section 4)

*** Note:** *Frequent oil and filter changes are good for the engine and we recommend that the oil and filter be renewed at the interval specified here (or at least once every 12 months), especially if the vehicle is used on a lot of short journeys or covers a small annual mileage.*

Every 18 000 miles (30 000 km) or 2 years

In addition to all the items listed previously, carry out the following:

- [ ] Check the brake pad thickness – front and rear (Section 5)
- [ ] Check the operation of the handbrake (Section 6)
- [ ] Check the operation of the clutch (Section 7)
- [ ] Check the condition of the auxiliary drivebelts (Sections 8 and 9)
- [ ] Check the condition of the seat belts (Section 10)
- [ ] Check the operation of all electrical systems (Section 11)
- [ ] Check the condition of the exhaust system and mountings (Section 12)
- [ ] Check the suspension and steering components (Section 13)
- [ ] Check the tightness of the roadwheel bolts (Section 14)
- [ ] Check the operation of the air conditioning system (Section 15)
- [ ] Renew the air filter element (Section 16)*
- [ ] Renew the fuel filter (Section 17)
- [ ] Check the manual transmission oil level (Section 18)
- [ ] Check all underbonnet components and hoses for fluid leaks (Section 19)
- [ ] Renew the pollen filter (Section 20)

*** Note:** *Although Renault recommend this task to be carried out every 36 000 miles (60 000 km) we recommend that the filter be renewed more frequently, perhaps every 18 000 miles or every two years, especially if the vehicle is used in a dusty environment.*

Every 36 000 miles (60 000 km) or 4 years

In addition to all the items listed previously, carry out the following:

- [ ] Check the spare fuses are in place (Section 21)
- [ ] Carry out a road test (Section 22)
- [ ] Renew the timing belt (Section 23)*
- [ ] Renew the brake fluid (Section 24)
- [ ] Renew the coolant (Section 25)

*** Note:** *Although the normal interval for timing belt renewal is 72 000 miles (120 000 km) for 2.2 litre engines and 45 000 miles (75 000 km) for 1.9 litre engines, it is strongly recommended that the interval is reduced to 36 000 miles (60 000 km) on vehicles which are subjected to intensive use, ie, mainly short journeys or a lot of stop-start driving. The actual belt renewal interval is therefore very much up to the individual owner, but bear in mind that severe engine damage may result if the belt breaks.*

Underbonnet view of a 2.2 litre model – 1.9 litre similar

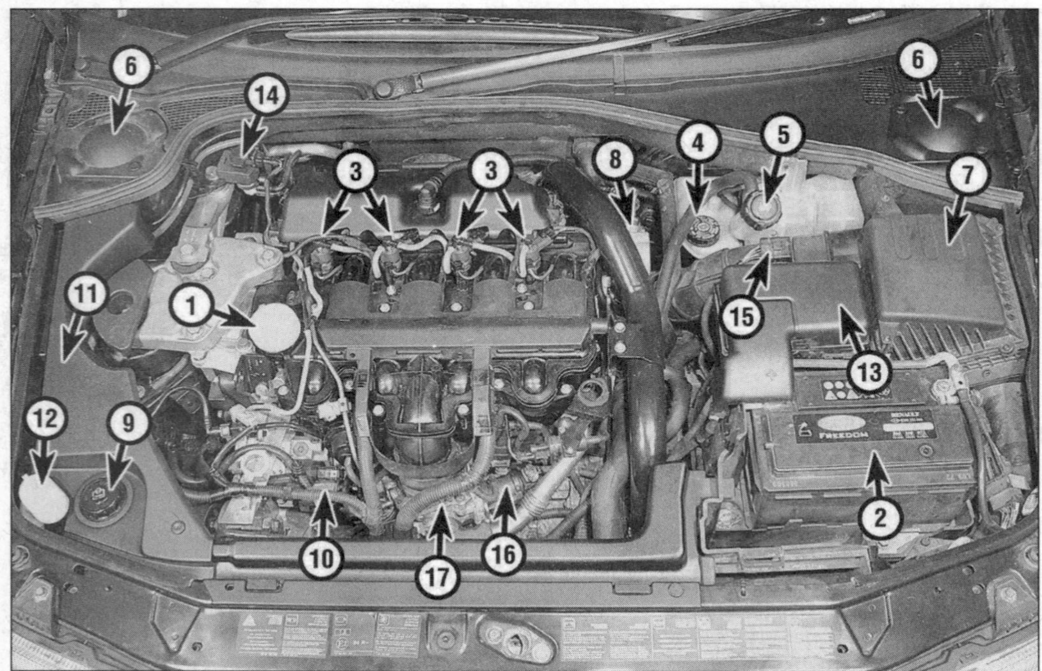

1. *Engine oil filler cap*
2. *Battery*
3. *Injectors*
4. *Brake fluid reservoir*
5. *Coolant expansion tank*
6. *Suspension strut upper mounting*
7. *Air filter housing*
8. *Brake system vacuum pump*
9. *Power steering fluid reservoir*
10. *Fuel injection pump*
11. *Fuel filter and priming bulb (under cover)*
12. *Washer fluid reservoir*
13. *Relay/fusebox*
14. *Turbocharger regulation solenoid*
15. *Airflow meter with air temperature sensor*
16. *Exhaust gas recirculation (EGR) valve*
17. *Engine stop system (damper unit) solenoid valve*

Front underbody view of a 2.2 litre model – 1.9 litre similar

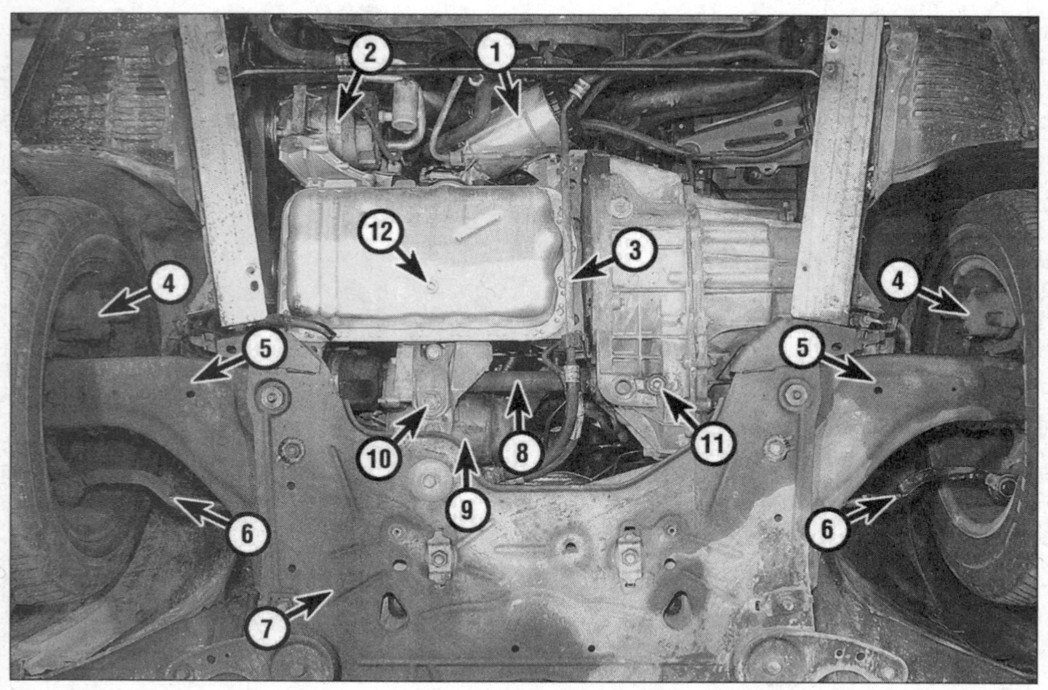

1. *Engine oil cooler/filter*
2. *Air conditioning compressor*
3. *Power steering fluid cooler pipes*
4. *Front brake caliper*
5. *Suspension lower arm*
6. *Track rod arms*
7. *Subframe*
8. *Right-hand driveshaft*
9. *Catalytic converter*
10. *Rear engine mounting link*
11. *Transmission oil drain plug*
12. *Engine oil drain plug*

Rear underbody view of a 2.2 litre model – 1.9 litre similar

1 *Exhaust expansion box*
2 *Rear suspension mountings*
3 *Rear suspension axle crossmember*
4 *Rear suspension torsion bar*
5 *Rear shock absorbers*
6 *Fuel tank*
7 *Heat shield*
8 *Handbrake cables*

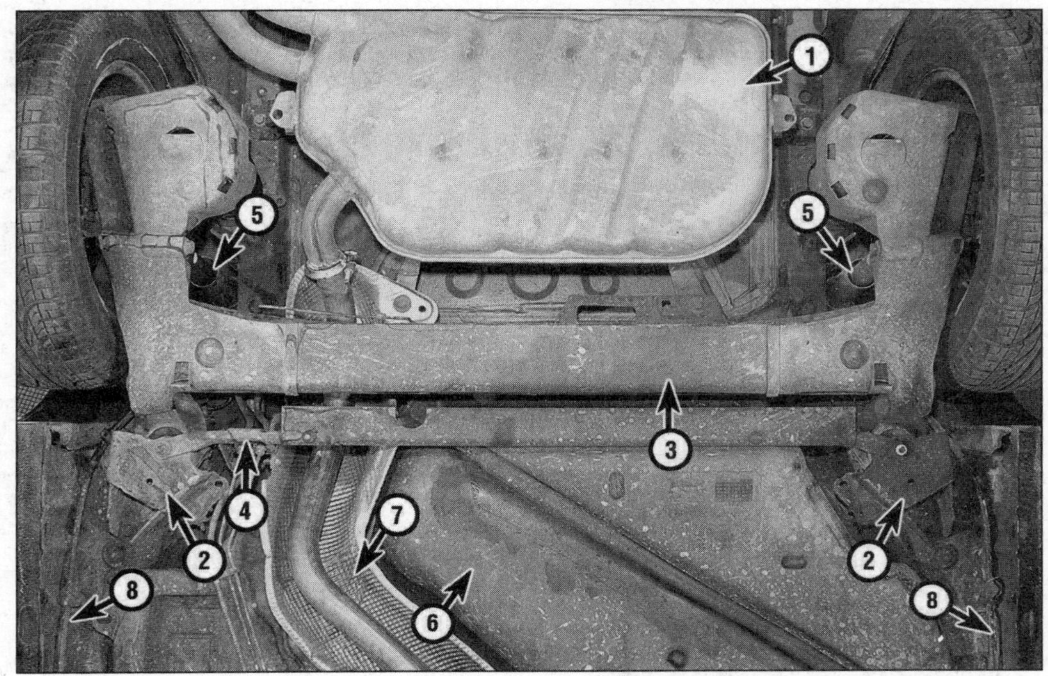

Maintenance procedures

1 Introduction

This Chapter is designed to help the home mechanic maintain his/her vehicle for safety, economy, long life and peak performance.

The Chapter contains a master maintenance schedule, followed by Sections dealing specifically with each task in the schedule. Visual checks, adjustments, component renewal and other helpful items are included. Refer to the accompanying illustrations of the engine compartment and the underside of the vehicle for the locations of the various components.

Servicing your vehicle in accordance with the mileage/time maintenance schedule and the following Sections will provide a planned maintenance programme, which should result in a long and reliable service life. This is a comprehensive plan, so maintaining some items but not others at the specified service intervals will not produce the same results.

As you service your vehicle, you will discover that many of the procedures can – and should – be grouped together, because of the particular procedure being performed, or because of the close proximity of two otherwise-unrelated components to one another. For example, if the vehicle is raised for any reason, the exhaust can be inspected at the same time as the suspension and steering components.

The first step in this maintenance programme is to prepare yourself before the actual work begins. Read through all the Sections relevant to the work to be carried out, then make a list and gather together all the parts and tools required. If a problem is encountered, seek advice from a parts specialist, or a dealer service department.

2 Regular maintenance

If, from the time the vehicle is new, the routine maintenance schedule is followed closely, and frequent checks are made of fluid levels and high-wear items, as suggested throughout this manual, the engine will be kept in relatively good running condition, and the need for additional work will be minimised.

It is possible that there will be times when the engine is running poorly due to the lack of regular maintenance. This is even more likely if a used vehicle, which has not received regular and frequent maintenance checks, is purchased. In such cases, additional work may need to be carried out, outside of the regular maintenance intervals.

If engine wear is suspected, a compression test or leakdown test (refer to Chapter 2B or 2C) will provide valuable information regarding the overall performance of the main internal components. Such a test can be used as a basis to decide on the extent of the work to be carried out. If, for example, a compression test indicates serious internal engine wear, conventional maintenance as described in this Chapter will not greatly improve the performance of the engine, and may prove a waste of time and money, unless extensive overhaul work is carried out first.

The following series of operations are those most often required to improve the performance of a generally poor-running engine:

Primary operations

a) *Clean, inspect and test the battery (see 'Weekly checks').*
b) *Check all the engine-related fluids (see 'Weekly checks').*
c) *Check the condition and tension of the auxiliary drivebelt (Sections 8 and 9).*
d) *Check the condition of the air filter element, and renew if necessary (Section 16).*
e) *Check the fuel filter – drain off any water and renew filter if necessary (Section 17).*
f) *Check the condition of all hoses, and check for fluid leaks (Section 19).*

If the above operations do not prove fully effective, carry out the following secondary operations:

Secondary operations

All items listed under *Primary operations*, plus the following:

a) *Check the charging system (Chapter 5A).*
b) *Check the preheating system (Chapter 5C).*
c) *Check the fuel system (Chapter 4B).*

Every 9000 miles (15 000 km) or 12 months

3 Engine oil and filter renewal

1 Frequent oil and filter changes are the most important preventative maintenance procedures that can be undertaken by the DIY owner. As engine oil ages, it becomes diluted and contaminated, which leads to premature engine wear.

2 Before starting this procedure, gather together all the necessary tools and materials. Also make sure that you have plenty of clean rags and newspapers handy, to mop-up any spills. Ideally, the engine oil should be warm, as it will drain more easily, and more built-up sludge will be removed with it.

HAYNES HiNT

If possible, try to keep the plug pressed into the sump while unscrewing it by hand the last couple of turns. As the plug releases from the threads, move it away sharply so the stream of oil issuing from the sump runs into the container, not up your sleeve.

3 Take care not to touch the exhaust or any other hot parts of the engine when working under the vehicle. To avoid any possibility of scalding, and to protect yourself from possible skin irritants and other harmful contaminants in used engine oils, it is advisable to wear gloves when carrying out this work.

4 Firmly apply the handbrake then jack up the front of the vehicle and support it on axle stands (see *Jacking and vehicle support*). Undo the retaining screws and remove the plastic undertray from underneath the engine/transmission.

5 Remove the oil filler cap. On 1.9 litre engines the dipstick is part of the oil filler cap. On 2.2 litre engines it may be easier to access the dipstick if the plastic engine cover is removed.

6 Slacken the drain plug about half a turn, position the draining container under the drain plug, and then remove the plug completely **(see Haynes Hint)**. Note that on some engines an 8 mm square section drain plug key will be needed to unscrew the drain plug.

7 Allow some time for the oil to drain, noting that it may be necessary to reposition the container as the oil flow slows to a trickle.

8 After all the oil has drained; wipe the drain plug and the sealing washer with a clean rag. Examine the condition of the sealing washer, and renew it if it shows signs of scoring or other damage that may prevent an oil-tight seal. Clean the area around the drain plug opening, and refit the plug complete with the washer and tighten it securely.

9 Move the container into position under the oil filter, which is located on the front of the cylinder block.

1.9 litre engines

10 Use an oil filter removal tool to slacken the filter initially, then unscrew it by hand the rest of the way **(see illustration)**. Position it with its open end uppermost to prevent further spillage of oil, then empty the oil from the old filter into the container.

11 Use a clean rag to remove any oil, dirt and sludge from the filter sealing area on the engine. Check the old filter to make sure that the rubber sealing ring has not stuck to the engine. If it has, carefully remove it.

12 Apply a light coating of clean engine oil to the sealing ring on the new filter, then screw the filter into position on the engine. Tighten the filter firmly by hand only – **do not** use any tools.

2.2 litre engines

13 The filter is a cartridge inside the oil filter housing. Using a special spanner, unscrew the filter housing cap and withdraw the filter cartridge, draining the oil into the container **(see illustration)**.

14 Use a clean rag to remove any oil, dirt and sludge from inside the oil filter housing. Remove any old rubber seals from the oil filter housing and filter cap and fit the new seals, which should be supplied with the filter **(see illustration)**.

15 Apply a light coating of clean engine oil to the sealing rings **(see illustration)**, then insert the filter cartridge. Screw the filter cap into position on the engine. Tighten the filter cap firmly by hand at first, then use spanner to tighten securely

3.10 Oil filter location is on the front of the engine – 1.9 litre engines

3.13 Unscrew the housing cap to remove the oil filter cartridge – 2.2 litre engines

3.14 Fit a new seal to the oil filter housing cap

3.15 Lubricate the seal with some clean engine oil

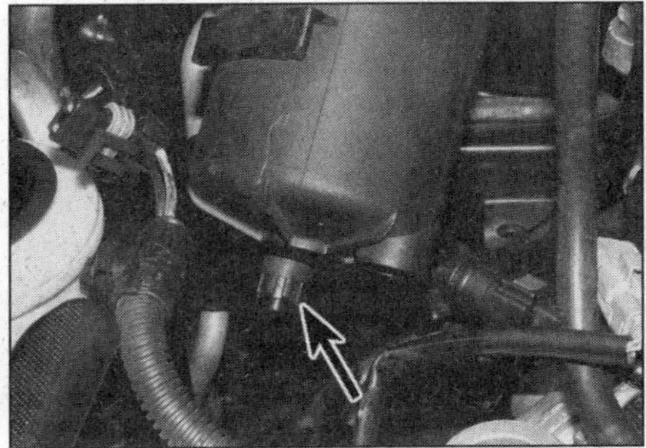

4.1 Water drain screw (arrowed) on the base of the filter housing

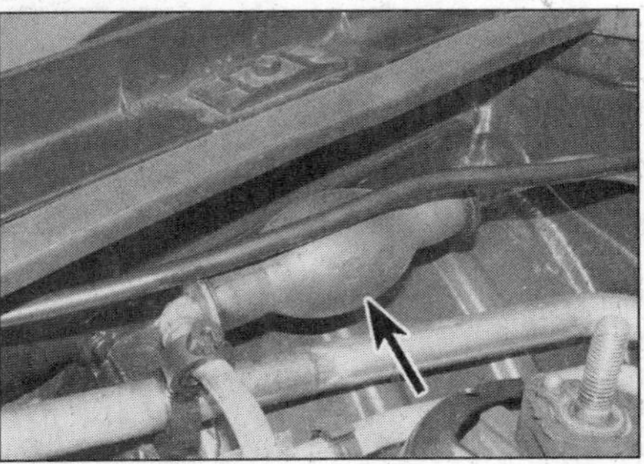

4.3 Hand priming pump (arrowed) on right-hand inner wing panel

All models

16 Refit the undertray and securely tighten its retaining screws. Remove the old oil and all tools from under the vehicle then lower the vehicle to the ground.

17 Fill the engine through the filler hole, using the correct grade and type of oil (refer to *Weekly checks* for details of topping-up). Pour in half the specified quantity of oil first, and then wait a few minutes for the oil to drain into the sump. Continue to add oil, a small quantity at a time, until the level is up to the lower mark on the dipstick. Adding approximately a further 1.5 litre will bring the level up to the upper mark on the dipstick. Refit the oil filler cap.

18 Start the engine and run it for a few minutes, checking that there are no leaks around the oil filter seal and the sump drain plug. Note that when the engine is first started, there will be a delay of a few seconds before the oil pressure warning light goes out while the new filter fills with oil. Do not race the engine while the warning light is on.

19 Stop the engine, and wait a few minutes for the oil to settle in the sump once more. With the new oil circulated and the filter now completely full, recheck the level on the dipstick, and add more oil as necessary.

20 Where applicable, refit the plastic engine cover(s).

21 Dispose of the used engine oil safely with reference to *General repair procedures*.

4 Fuel filter water draining

1 A water drain screw is provided on the base of the fuel filter **(see illustration).**

Wear a pair of light plastic disposable gloves, like those available at the diesel pumps of most filling stations, to protect your hands and have plenty of newspaper or clean rag handy for mopping-up spills. Ensure that diesel fuel does not spill on to the coolant hoses, electrical wiring, alternator, engine mountings or the auxiliary drivebelt – protect them, if necessary.

2 Place a suitable container beneath the drain screw. To make draining easier, a suitable length of tubing can be attached to the outlet on the screw to direct the fuel flow – on some models a drain tube is provided as standard. **Note:** *If desired, access can be improved by unscrewing the nuts securing the filter head to the body and by raising the complete filter assembly to a more convenient position – if this is done, take care not to strain the fuel hoses and electrical wiring.*

3 Loosen the fuel filter bleed screw, then open the drain screw by turning it anti-clockwise. On models where there is no bleed screw, loosen the fuel inlet union on the filter head. On fuel systems with a hand priming pump, this may need to be operated a couple of times to allow the fuel to flow **(see illustration).**

4 Allow the entire contents of the filter to drain into the container, and then securely tighten the drain screw and the bleed screw/fuel filter inlet union (as applicable).

5 Prime and bleed the fuel system as described in Chapter 4B.

6 Dispose of the used fuel safely with reference to *General repair procedures*.

Every 18 000 miles (30 000 km) or 2 years

5 Brake pad check – front and rear

1 Firmly apply the handbrake, and then jack up the front or rear of the car and support it securely on axle stands (see *Jacking and vehicle support*). Remove the roadwheels as required. Remember, the car has disc brakes all round, so all four calipers should be checked.

2 For a quick check, the thickness of friction material remaining on each brake pad can be measured through the aperture in the caliper body **(see Haynes Hint)**. If any pad's friction material is worn to the specified thickness or less, all four pads must be renewed as a set. Pad wear warning contacts may be fitted to the inboard pads, but this should not be used as an excuse for omitting a visual check.

3 For a comprehensive check, the brake pads should be removed and cleaned. This will allow the operation of the caliper to be checked, and the brake disc itself to be fully examined for condition on both sides. Refer to Chapter 9 for further information.

4 On completion refit the roadwheels and lower the car to the ground.

6 Handbrake check

Note: *The handbrake cable should not be retensioned to correct any fault, and should only be adjusted when fitting new pads, cables or handbrake lever.*

1 The handbrake is kept in adjustment by the self-adjusting action of the rear disc calipers.

2 Chock the front wheels, then jack up the

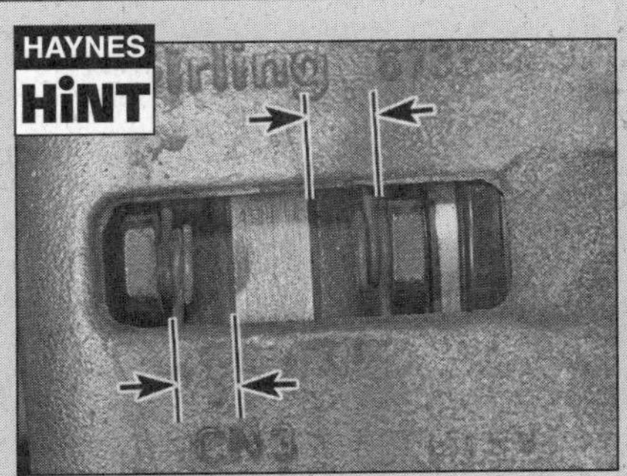

For a quick check, the thickness of friction material remaining on each brake pad can be measured through the aperture in the caliper body.

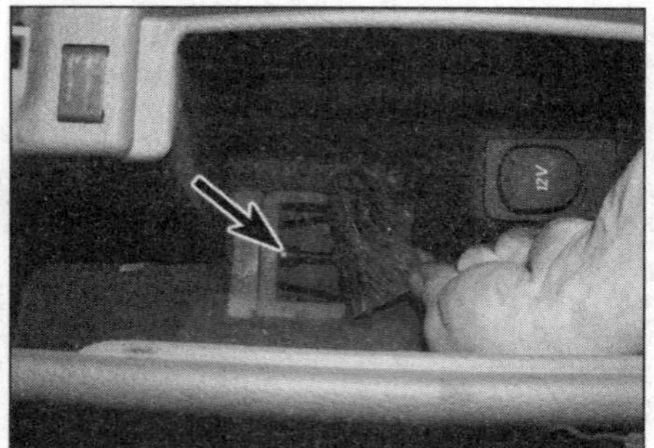

6.5 Handbrake operating rod, slacken the adjuster nut (arrowed)

rear of the vehicle, and support securely on axle stands (see *Jacking and vehicle support*).

3 Fully release the handbrake and check that the wheels can be rotated easily by hand. The wheels may drag slightly, but there should be no binding.

4 If the wheels bind, it is likely that the handbrake mechanism or cables are partially seized. If the operation of the mechanism is not satisfactory, proceed as follows.

5 Working inside the vehicle, lift the flap inside the centre console between the front seats, slacken the adjuster nut until there is no tension in the handbrake cables **(see illustration)**.

6 Remove the rear roadwheels.

7 Check that the handbrake cables slide freely in their sheaths, and that the operating levers on the calipers move freely (see Chapter 9 for further information).

8 Push the handbrake operating levers on the calipers as far as they will go against their bottom stops.

9 If all the parts move freely, turn the cable adjuster until the handbrake cable end fittings just contact the operating levers on the calipers, without moving the levers **(see illustration)**.

10 Continue to turn the adjuster sleeve until the handbrake operating levers on the calipers begin to move when the handbrake lever is pulled between the first and second notches. There should be no free play in the handbrake cables once the lever is pulled beyond the second notch.

11 Tighten the adjuster locknuts.

8.7 Use a spanner on the hexagon (arrowed) to release the tension . . .

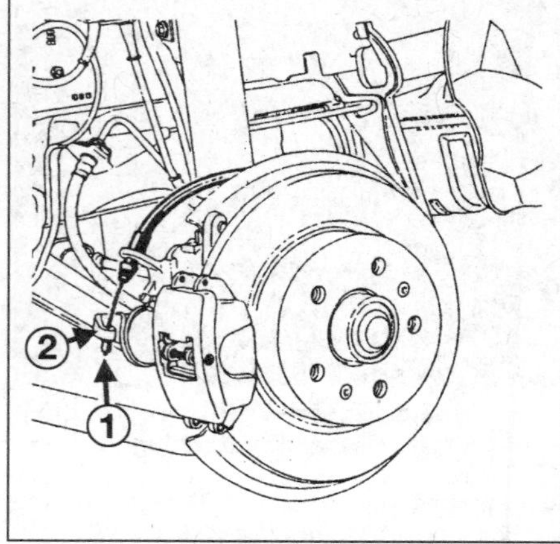

6.9 The handbrake cable end fittings (1) should just contact the operating levers (2)

12 Refit the roadwheels, and lower the vehicle to the ground.

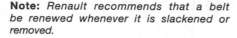

7 Clutch check

Check that the clutch pedal moves smoothly and easily through its full travel, and that the clutch itself functions correctly, with no trace of slip or drag. If the clutch action is less than precise, this may indicate the need for bleeding the system – it could also indicate the presence of a fluid leak (see Chapter 6).

8 Auxiliary drivebelt check and renewal – 1.9 litre engines

Note: *Renault recommends that a belt be renewed whenever it is slackened or removed.*

Checking

1 The auxiliary drivebelt is located at the right-hand side of the engine.

2 Two different drivebelt configurations may be encountered, depending on model.

3 Due to their function and material makeup, drivebelts are prone to failure after a period of time and should therefore be inspected.

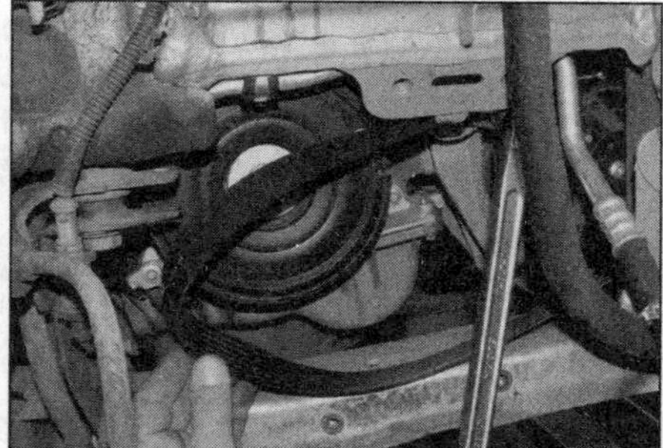
8.8 . . . and remove the belt from the pulleys

4 Since the drivebelt is located very close to the right-hand side of the engine compartment, it is possible to gain better access by raising the front of the vehicle (see *Jacking and vehicle support*) and removing the right-hand wheel, then removing the splash shield from inside the wheel arch.

5 With the engine switched off, inspect the full length of the drivebelt for cracks and separation of the belt plies. It will be necessary to turn the crankshaft (using a socket or spanner on the crankshaft pulley bolt) in order to move the belt from the pulleys so that the full length of the belt can be inspected thoroughly. Twist the belt between the pulleys so that both sides can be viewed. Also check for fraying, and glazing which gives the belt a shiny appearance. Check the pulleys for nicks, cracks, distortion and corrosion.

Tensioning

6 A spring-loaded tensioner is fitted to automatically maintain the correct tension on the belt. If problems with belt squeal or slip are encountered, the belt should be renewed. If the problem continues, it will be necessary to renew the tensioner assembly.

Renewal

Timing belt driven coolant pump

7 To remove the belt use a 16 mm spanner to move the tensioner clockwise (as viewed from the right-hand side of the car) **(see illustration)**.

8 With the tension being held off the belt, note the routing of the belt, and then slip the belt off the pulleys **(see illustration)**.

9 Holding the spanner so that the tensioner is away from the belt, fit the new belt ensuring that it is routed correctly.

10 With the belt in position, carefully release the force on the spanner anti-clockwise so the belt will automatically become tensioned.

11 Refit the roadwheel, and lower the vehicle to the ground.

Auxiliary belt driven coolant pump

Note: *Renault use a special tool for removing and refitting the auxiliary belt (Renault tool Mot. 1676).*

12 Fit Renault tool Mot.1676 to the longest part of the belt between the air conditioning compressor pulley and alternator pulley.

13 With pressure held onto the belt (using tool Mot.1676), fit a locking plate to the spring on the tensioner to hold it in position.

14 With the tension being held off the belt, note the routing of the belt, and then slip the belt off the pulleys.

15 Slacken the two tensioner mounting bolts and slide it upwards in the elongated holes in the bracket. Tighten the mounting bolts finger tight to hold the tensioner in place.

16 Fit the new belt around the pulleys, ensuring that it is routed correctly.

17 Using light thumb pressure, push the tensioner wheel downward against the belt,

9.5 Spring-loaded tensioner . . .

9.6 . . . using an Allen key (arrowed) to lock the tensioner in the released position

9.7 Remove the belt from around the pulleys, noting the routing of the belt

and then tighten the two tensioner mounting bolts to their correct torque setting.

18 Fit the Renault tool to the longest part of the belt between the air conditioning compressor pulley and alternator pulley, and with pressure held onto the belt, remove the locking plate from the spring on the tensioner.

19 Carefully release the force on the tool so the belt will automatically become tensioned.

20 Refit the roadwheel, and lower the vehicle to the ground.

9 Auxiliary drivebelt check and renewal – 2.2 litre engines

Note: *Renault recommends that the belt should be renewed whenever it is slackened or removed.*

Checking

1 The auxiliary drivebelt is located at the right-hand side of the engine.

2 Due to their function and material makeup, drivebelts are prone to failure after a period of time and should therefore be inspected, and if necessary adjusted periodically.

3 Since the drivebelt is located very close to the right-hand side of the engine compartment, it is possible to gain better access by raising the front of the vehicle and removing the right-hand wheel, then removing the splash shield from inside the wheel arch, and the engine undertray.

4 With the engine stopped, inspect the full length of the drivebelt for cracks and separation of the belt plies. It will be necessary to turn the engine (using a spanner or socket and bar on the crankshaft pulley bolt) in order to move the belt from the pulleys so that the belt can be inspected thoroughly. Twist the belt between the pulleys so that both sides can be viewed. Also check for fraying, and glazing which gives the belt a shiny appearance. Check the pulleys for nicks, cracks, distortion and corrosion.

Tensioning

5 A spring-loaded tensioner is fitted to automatically maintain the correct tension on the belt **(see illustration)**. If problems with belt squeal or slip are encountered, the belt should be renewed. If the problem continues, it will be necessary to renew the tensioner assembly.

Renewal

6 To remove the belt, use a spanner to move the tensioner clockwise (as viewed from the right-hand side of the car). A 4 mm Allen key can be inserted into a hole in the tensioner body to hold it in the released position **(see illustration)**.

7 Note the routing of the belt, then slip the belt off the pulleys **(see illustration)**.

8 Fit the new belt ensuring that it is routed correctly.

9 With the belt in position, use the spanner to hold the tensioner in position while the 4 mm Allen key is removed, then carefully release the spanner anti-clockwise so the belt will automatically become tensioned.

10 Refit the wheel arch liner/splash shield and roadwheel, and then lower the vehicle to the ground.

10 Seat belt check

1 Carefully examine the seat belt webbing for cuts, or any signs of serious fraying or deterioration. If the belt is of the retractable type, pull the belt all the way out of the inertia reel, and examine the full extent of the webbing.

2 Fasten and unfasten the belt, ensuring that the locking mechanism holds securely, and releases properly when intended. If the belt is of the retractable type, check also that the retracting mechanism operates correctly when the belt is released.

3 Check the security of all seat belt mountings and attachments that are accessible without removing any trim or other components.

11 Electrical systems check

1 Check the operation of all electrical equipment, ie, lights, direction indicators, horn, etc. Refer to the appropriate Sections of Chapter 12 for details if any of the circuits are found to be inoperative.

2 Note that stop-light switch adjustment is described in Chapter 9.

3 Visually check all accessible wiring connectors, harnesses and retaining clips for security, and for signs of chafing or damage. Rectify any faults found.

12 Exhaust system check

1 With the engine cold (at least an hour after the vehicle has been driven), check the complete exhaust system from the engine to the end of the tailpipe. The exhaust system is most easily checked with the vehicle raised on a hoist, or suitably supported on axle stands, so that the exhaust components are readily visible and accessible.

2 Check the exhaust pipes and connections for evidence of leaks, severe corrosion and damage. Make sure that all brackets and mountings are in good condition, and that all relevant nuts and bolts are tight. Leakage at any of the joints or in other parts of the system will usually show up as a black sooty stain in the vicinity of the leak.

3 Rattles and other noises can often be traced to the exhaust system, especially the brackets and mountings. Try to move the pipes and silencers. If the components are able to come into contact with the body or suspension parts, secure the system with new mountings. Otherwise separate the joints (if possible) and twist the pipes as necessary to provide additional clearance.

13 Suspension and steering check

Front suspension and steering

1 Raise the front of the vehicle, and securely support it on axle stands (see *Jacking and vehicle support*).

2 Visually inspect the balljoint dust covers and the steering rack-and-pinion gaiters for splits, chafing or deterioration **(see illustrations)**.

13.2a Check the balljoint rubber gaiters (arrowed) . . .

13.2b . . . and the gaiters (arrowed) on the anti-roll bar drop links

13.4 Check for wear in the hub bearings by grasping the wheel and trying to rock it

Any wear of these components will cause loss of lubricant, together with dirt and water entry, resulting in rapid deterioration of the balljoints or steering gear.

3 Check the power steering fluid hoses for chafing or deterioration, and the pipe and hose unions for fluid leaks. Also check for signs of fluid leakage under pressure from the steering gear rubber gaiters, which would indicate failed fluid seals within the steering gear.

4 Grasp the roadwheel at the 12 o'clock and 6 o'clock positions, and try to rock it **(see illustration)**. Very slight free play may be felt, but if the movement is appreciable, further investigation is necessary to determine the source. Continue rocking the wheel while an assistant depresses the footbrake. If the movement is now eliminated or significantly reduced, it is likely that the hub bearings are at fault. If the free play is still evident with the footbrake depressed, then there is wear in the suspension joints or mountings.

5 Now grasp the wheel at the 9 o'clock and 3 o'clock positions, and try to rock it as before. Any movement felt now may again be caused by wear in the hub bearings or the steering track rod balljoints. If the outer balljoint is worn, the visual movement will be obvious. If the inner joint is suspect, it can be felt by placing a hand over the rack-and-pinion rubber gaiter and gripping the track rod. If the wheel is now rocked, movement will be felt at the inner joint if wear has taken place.

6 Using a large screwdriver or flat bar, check for wear in the suspension mounting bushes by levering between the relevant suspension component and its attachment point. Some movement is to be expected, as the mountings are made of rubber, but excessive wear should be obvious. Also check the condition of any visible rubber bushes, looking for splits, cracks or contamination of the rubber.

7 With the car standing on its wheels, have an assistant turn the steering wheel back-and-forth, about an eighth of a turn each way. There should be very little, if any, lost movement between the steering wheel and roadwheels. If this is not the case, closely observe the joints and mountings previously described. In addition, check the steering column universal joints for wear, and also check the rack-and-pinion steering gear itself.

Rear suspension

8 Chock the front wheels, then jack up the rear of the vehicle and support securely on axle stands (see *Jacking and vehicle support*).

9 Working as described previously for the front suspension, check the rear hub bearings, the suspension bushes and the shock absorber mountings for wear.

Shock absorber

10 Check for any signs of fluid leakage around the shock absorber body, or from the rubber gaiter around the piston rod. Should any fluid be noticed, the shock absorber is defective internally, and should be renewed. **Note:** *Shock absorbers should always be renewed in pairs on the same axle.*

11 The efficiency of the shock absorber may be checked by bouncing the vehicle at each corner. Generally speaking, the body will return to its normal position and stop after being depressed. If it rises and returns on a rebound, the shock absorber is probably suspect. Also examine the shock absorber upper and lower mountings for any signs of wear.

14 Roadwheel bolt check

Note: *A key will be required, to slacken any locking wheel nuts.*

1 Where applicable, remove the wheel trims, and slacken the roadwheel bolts slightly.

2 Tighten the bolts to the specified torque, using a torque wrench.

15 Air conditioning system check

A Renault dealer using dedicated test equipment must check the air conditioning system.

16 Air filter element renewal

Removal

1 Disconnect the wiring connector from the airflow meter.

2 Slacken the securing clip from the air hose and disconnect it from the filter housing.

3 Undo the four retaining screws from the top of the air cleaner housing **(see illustration)**.

4 Lift out the air filter element and wipe clean the filter housing **(see illustration)**.

Refitting

5 Clean the inside of the air cleaner body and housing/cover, being careful not to get dirt into the inlet duct.

6 Fit the new filter element, making sure it is correctly located, securing it in position with the retaining screws.

7 Refit the air hose to the filter housing and reconnect the wiring connector on the airflow meter.

16.3 Undo the four retaining screws (arrowed) . . .

16.4 . . . and withdraw the air filter element

17.2 Disconnect the wiring connector . . .

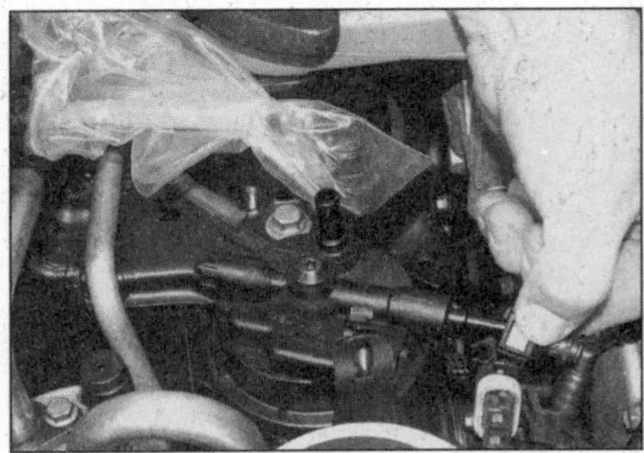
17.3 . . . then the fuel pipes . . .

17.4 . . . and unclip the filter housing from the bracket

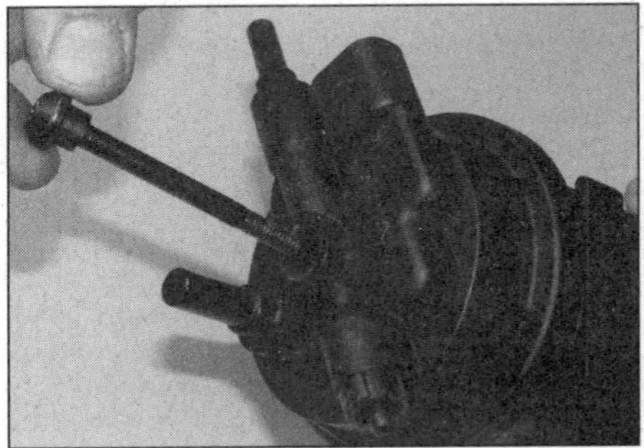

17.5 Remove the centre bolt from the filter housing

17.7 Smear the seal with clean fuel and fit it to the filter housing

17.8 Note the position of the locating peg (arrowed)

17 Fuel filter renewal

Note: *On some models, the filter is part of the filter unit and cannot be renewed separately, check with your local Renault dealer.*

Caution: Do not allow dirt to enter the fuel system during this procedure.

1 Drain the contents of the fuel filter as described in Section 4.

2 Disconnect the fuel heater wiring connector from the top of the filter housing **(see illustration)**.

3 Release the retaining clips and disconnect the fuel lines from the top of the fuel filter housing **(see illustration)**. Take care not to damage the fuel lines as they are removed; cover the ends of the fuel lines to prevent any dirt ingress.

4 Unclip the fuel filter housing from the support bracket on the right-hand inner wing **(see illustration)**.

5 With the fuel filter housing removed from the vehicle, slacken and remove the retaining bolt from the centre of the top of the filter housing **(see illustration)**.

6 Note the fitted position of the top of the filter housing in relation to the lower housing bowl, then release the lower bowl to access the filter. Remove the fuel filter and recover the fuel filter sealing ring, a new seal will be required for refitting.

7 Fit the new filter into the filter housing bowl, then smear the new sealing ring with fuel and fit it to the housing **(see illustration)**.

8 Align the top of the filter housing (in position, noted on removal) and fit the lower bowl to the top of the filter housing **(see illustration)**.

9 Fit a new seal to the retaining bolt and tighten it securely **(see illustration)**.

10 Where applicable, make sure the drain plug in the bottom of the fuel filter housing is tight.

11 Refit the filter housing to its mounting bracket and reconnect the fuel lines to the top of the housing, taking care not to damage the pipes.

12 Reconnect the fuel heater wiring connector to the top of the filter housing.

13 On models with a priming bulb (located on the right-hand front inner wing), fit a piece of clear pipe on the valve on the top of the fuel filter housing and the other end into a container. Open the valve and squeeze the priming bulb a few times, to pump the fuel through. When there is a flow of fuel with no air coming out through the pipe, close the valve **(see illustration)**.

14 On models without a priming bulb fitted, switch the ignition on several times to prime the fuel filter, until it is full of fuel; for further information see Chapter 4B.

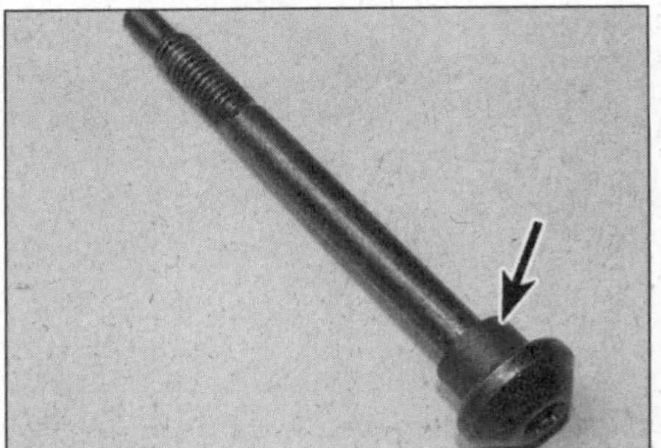
17.9 Lubricate the new seal (arrowed) with clean fuel

18 Manual transmission oil level check

1 Either position the vehicle over an inspection pit, or jack up the front and rear of the vehicle and support it on axle stands (see *Jacking and vehicle support*). The vehicle must be level for the check to be accurate. Refer to Chapter 7A for information on transmission identification.

JR5 transmission

2 Undo the retaining screws and remove

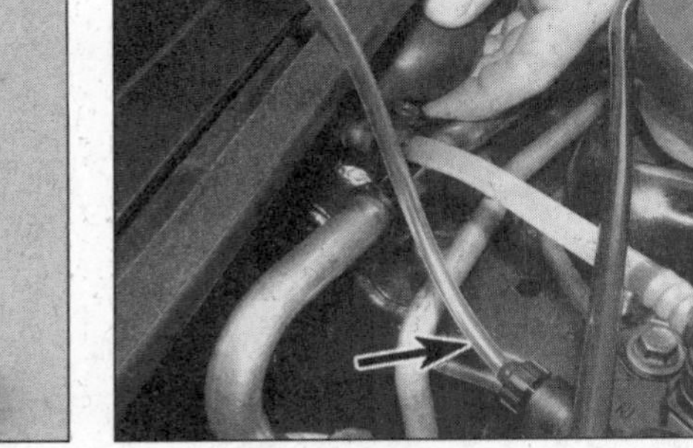
17.13 Clear pipe (arrowed) fitted to filter valve to check for air

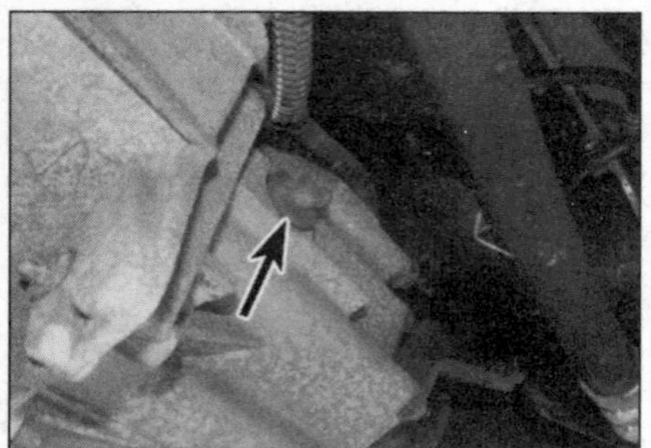
18.3 The filler/level plug (arrowed) is on the front of the transmission

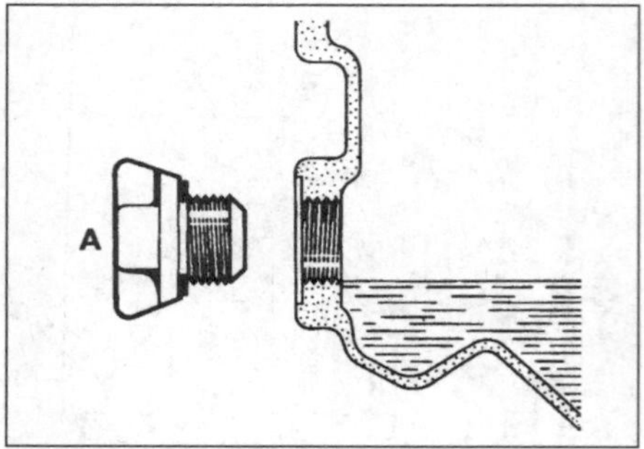

18.5 Manual transmission filler/level plug (A) – correct oil level shown

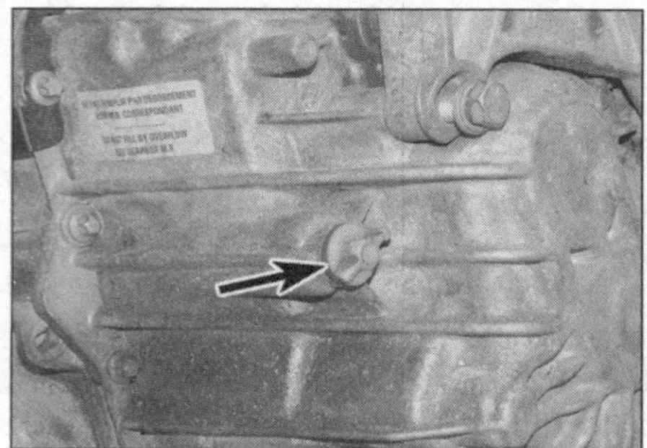
18.8 The filler/level plug (arrowed) is on the left-hand front of the transmission

the undertray from beneath the engine/transmission.

3 Clean the area around the filler/level plug on the front of the transmission, then slacken and remove the plug from the transmission **(see illustration).** Check the condition of the filler plug seal, and obtain a new one if necessary.

4 The transmission oil level should be up to the lower edge of the filler/level plug aperture.

5 If necessary, top-up using the specified type of lubricant until the transmission oil level is correct. Fill the transmission until oil starts to flow out and allow excess oil to drain **(see illustration).**

6 Once the transmission oil level is correct, refit the filler/level plug and tighten it securely.

7 Refit the engine undertray then lower the vehicle to the ground. Note that frequent need for topping-up indicates a leakage, possibly through an oil seal. The cause should be investigated and rectified.

19.2 Check the brake hose and metal brake pipes very carefully

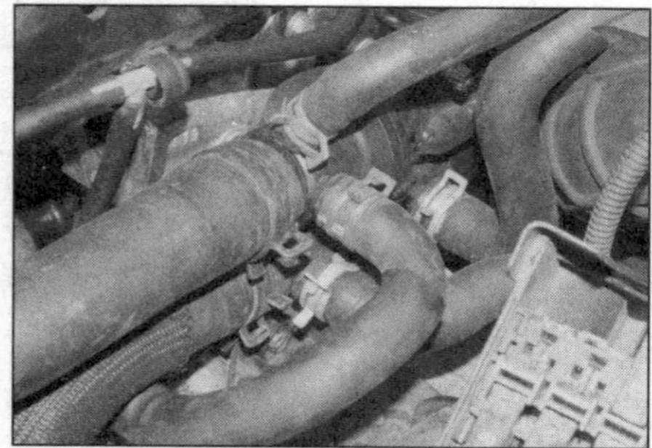
19.3 Check all hoses for signs of damage and the security of the hose clips

PK6 transmission

Note: *This check can only be carried out by using the special Renault tool/dipstick B.Vi.1675.*

8 Clean the area around the transmission oil filler plug that is situated on the left-hand end of the transmission unit, at the front corner **(see illustration).**

9 Slacken and remove the filler plug from the transmission.

10 Insert the dipstick through the filler plug recess. Make sure the slot in the top of the dipstick bracket is located on the rib on the transmission housing.

11 Slide the dipstick out of the filler plug and check the oil level. Note the oil level on the end of the dipstick; it should be between the upper and lower marks. With the oil up to the maximum mark there will be approximately 2.4 litres in the transmission. With the oil up to the minimum mark there will be approximately 2.0 litres in the transmission. The target level is midway between the two.

12 Top-up the transmission oil level with the specified type of lubricant via the filler plughole. Once the level is up to the correct level, refit the filler plug and sealing washer and tighten it securely. Where necessary, refit the undertray and securely tighten its retaining screws. Note that frequent need for topping-up indicates a leakage, possibly through an oil seal. The cause should be investigated and rectified.

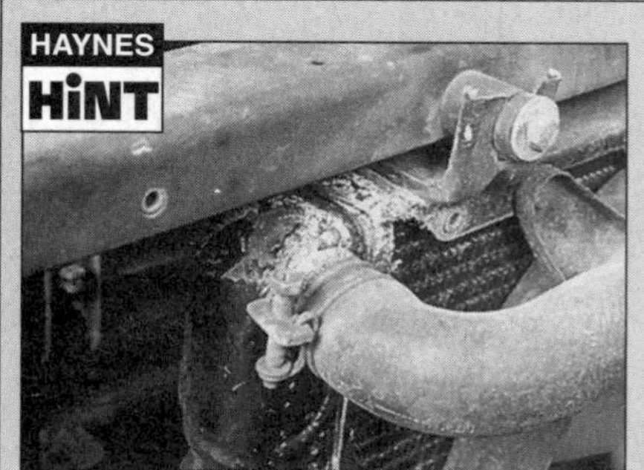

A leak in the cooling system will usually show up as white- or rust-coloured deposits on the area adjoining the leak.

19 Hose and fluid leak check

1 Visually inspect the engine joint faces, gaskets and seals for any signs of water or oil leaks. Pay particular attention to the areas around the cylinder head cover, cylinder head, oil filter and sump joint faces. Bear in mind that, over a period of time, some very slight seepage from these areas is to be expected – what you are really looking for is any indication of a serious leak. Should a leak be found, renew the offending gasket or oil seal by referring to the appropriate Chapters in this manual.

2 Also check the security and condition of all the engine-related pipes and hoses, and all braking system pipes and hoses **(see illustration).** Ensure that all cable-ties or securing clips are in place, and in good condition. Clips that are broken or missing can lead to chafing of the hoses, pipes or wiring, which could cause more serious problems in the future.

3 Carefully check the radiator hoses and heater hoses along their entire length. Renew any hose that is cracked, swollen or deteriorated. Cracks will show up better if the hose is squeezed. Pay close attention to the hose clips that secure the hoses to the cooling system components. Hose clips can pinch and puncture hoses, resulting in cooling system leaks **(see illustration).**

4 Inspect all the cooling system components (hoses, joint faces, etc) for leaks **(see Haynes Hint).** Where any problems are found on system components, renew the component or gasket with reference to Chapter 3.

5 With the vehicle raised, inspect the fuel tank and filler neck for punctures, cracks and other damage. The connection between the filler neck and tank is especially critical. Sometimes a rubber filler neck or connecting hose will leak due to loose retaining clamps or deteriorated rubber.

6 Carefully check all rubber hoses and metal fuel lines leading away from the fuel tank. Check for loose connections, deteriorated hoses, crimped lines, and other damage. Pay particular attention to the vent pipes

and hoses, which often loop up around the filler neck and can become blocked or crimped. Follow the lines to the front of the vehicle, carefully inspecting them all the way. Renew damaged sections as necessary. Similarly, whilst the vehicle is raised, take the opportunity to inspect all underbody brake fluid pipes and hoses.

7 From within the engine compartment, check the security of all fuel, vacuum and brake hose attachments and pipe unions, and inspect all hoses for kinks, chafing and deterioration.

8 Where applicable, check the condition of the automatic transmission and power steering fluid pipes and hoses.

20 Pollen (particle) filter renewal

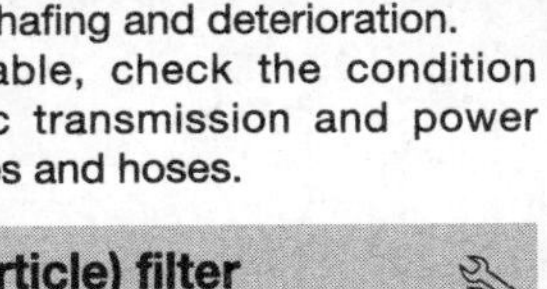

1 The pollen filter (also known as a particle filter) is located inside the vehicle, behind the glove compartment. It is fitted in the air inlet housing, and filters the air to ensure it is completely clean before entering the passenger compartment.

2 Open the glove compartment door and remove the retaining screw from the rear of the pocket **(see illustration).**

3 Release the securing clip and withdraw the pocket from inside of the glove compartment **(see illustrations).**

20.2 Undo the retaining screw (arrowed)

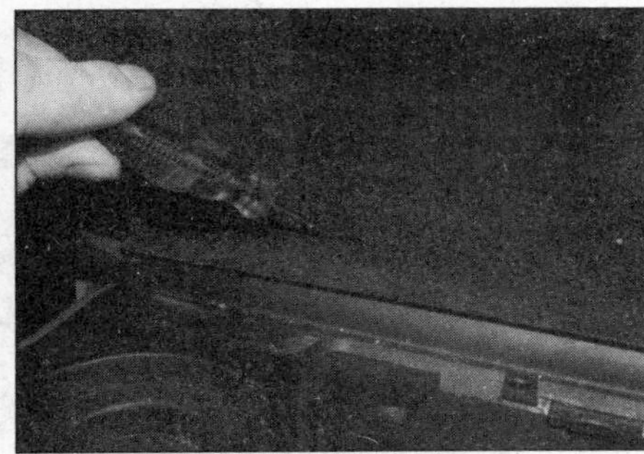

20.3a Press down on the screwdriver . . .

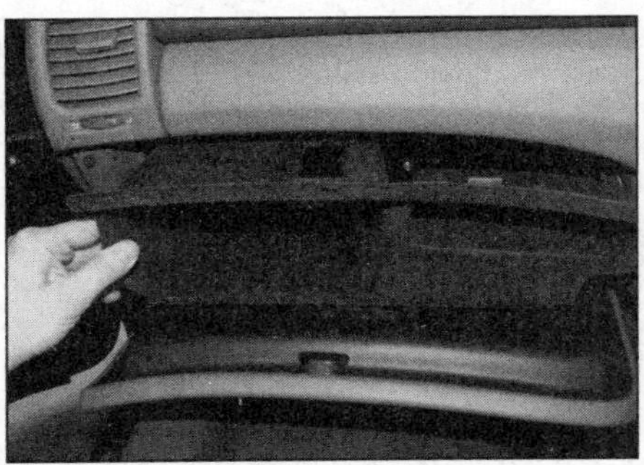

20.3b . . . and withdraw the glove pocket from the facia

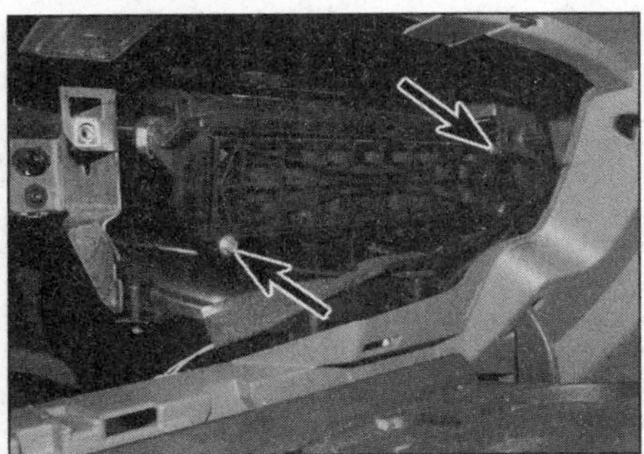

20.4 Undo the two retaining bolts (arrowed)

4 Undo the two retaining screws and withdraw the filter from its housing. Note its fitted position for refitting **(see illustration).**

5 Refitting is a reversal of removal.

Every 36 000 miles (60 000 km) or 4 years

21 Spare fuse check

Check that spare fuses are in place in the locations provided in the fusebox cover (see Chapter 12). It is advisable to carry at least one spare of each rating of fuse fitted **(see illustration).** Spare fuses can be obtained from most car accessory shops, or from a Renault dealer.

22 Road test

Instruments and electrical equipment

1 Check the operation of all instruments and electrical equipment.

2 Make sure that all instruments read correctly, and switch on all electrical equipment in turn, to check that it functions properly.

Steering and suspension

3 Check for any abnormalities in the steering, suspension, handling or road 'feel'.

4 Drive the vehicle, and check that there are no unusual vibrations or noises.

5 Check that the steering feels positive, with no excessive 'sloppiness', or roughness, and check for any suspension noises when cornering and driving over bumps.

Drivetrain

6 Check the performance of the engine, clutch, transmission and driveshafts.

7 Listen for any unusual noises from the engine, clutch and transmission.

8 Make sure that the engine runs smoothly when idling, and that there is no hesitation when accelerating.

9 Check that, where applicable, the clutch action is smooth and progressive, that the drive is taken up smoothly, and that the pedal travel is not excessive. Also listen for any noises when the clutch pedal is depressed.

10 Check that all gears can be engaged smoothly without noise, and that the gear lever action is smooth and not abnormally vague or 'notchy'.

11 On automatic transmission models, make sure that all gearchanges occur smoothly, without snatching, and without an increase in engine speed between changes. Check that all of the gear positions can be selected with the vehicle at rest. If any problems are found, they should be referred to a Renault dealer.

12 Listen for a metallic clicking sound from the front of the vehicle, as the vehicle is driven slowly in a circle with the steering on full-lock. Carry out this check in both directions. If a clicking noise is heard, this indicates wear in a driveshaft joint (see Chapter 8).

Braking system

13 Make sure that the vehicle does not pull to one side when braking, and that the wheels do not lock when braking hard.

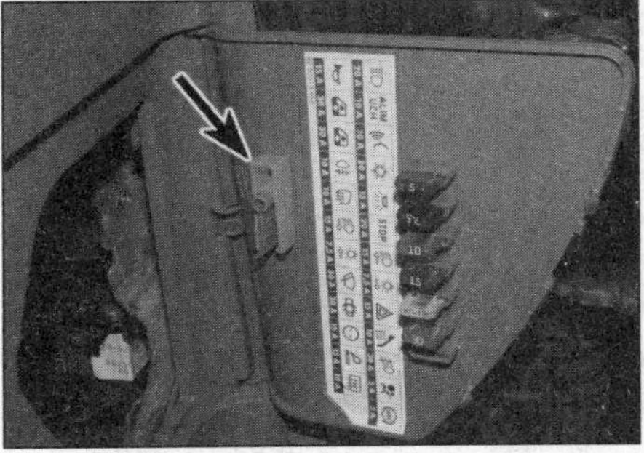

21.1 Fuse removal tool (arrowed) on inside cover with spare fuses

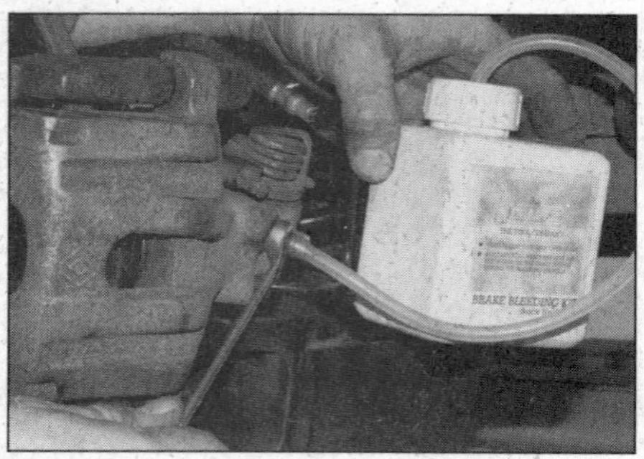

24.2 Change the brake fluid using the same method as for bleeding the brake system

14 Check that there is no vibration through the steering when braking.
15 Check that the handbrake operates correctly, without excessive movement of the lever, and that it holds the vehicle stationary on a slope.
16 Test the operation of the brake servo unit as follows. Depress the footbrake four or five times to exhaust the vacuum, and then start the engine. As the engine starts, there should be a noticeable 'give' in the brake pedal as vacuum builds-up. Allow the engine to run for at least two minutes, and then switch it off. If the brake pedal is now depressed again, it should be possible to detect a hiss from the servo as the pedal is depressed. After about four or five applications, no further hissing should be heard, and the pedal should feel considerably harder.

23 Timing belt renewal

Refer to the relevant Part of Chapter 2.

24 Brake fluid renewal

Warning: Brake hydraulic fluid can harm your eyes and damage painted surfaces, so use extreme caution when handling and pouring it. Do not use fluid that has been standing open for some time, as it absorbs moisture from the air. Excess moisture can cause a dangerous loss of braking effectiveness.

Caution: On models equipped with ABS, disconnect the battery before carrying out this operation and do not reconnect the battery until after the operation is complete. Failure to do this could lead to air entering the hydraulic unit. If air enters the hydraulic unit pump, it will prove very difficult (in some cases impossible) to bleed the unit. Refer to 'Disconnecting the battery' in the Reference Section.

1 The procedure is similar to that for the bleeding of the hydraulic system as described in Chapter 9, except that the brake fluid reservoir should be emptied by syphoning, using a clean poultry baster or similar before starting, and allowance should be made for the old fluid to be expelled when bleeding a section of the circuit.
2 Working as described in Chapter 9, open the first bleed screw in the sequence **(see illustration),** and pump the brake pedal gently until nearly all the old fluid has been emptied from the master cylinder reservoir. Top-up to the MAX level with new fluid, and continue pumping until only the new fluid remains in the reservoir, and new fluid can be seen emerging from the bleed screw. Tighten the screw, and top the reservoir level up to the MAX level line.

Old hydraulic fluid is invariably much darker in colour than the new, making it easy to distinguish between the two.

3 Work through all the remaining bleed screws in the sequence until new fluid can be seen at all of them. Be careful to keep the master cylinder reservoir topped-up to above the MIN level at all times, or air may enter the system and greatly increase the length of the task.
4 When the operation is complete, check that all bleed screws are securely tightened, and that their dust caps are refitted. Wash off all traces of spilt fluid, and recheck the master cylinder reservoir fluid level.
5 Check the operation of the brakes before taking the car on the road.
6 Dispose safely of the used brake fluid with reference to *General repair procedures*.

25 Coolant renewal

Warning: Wait until the engine is cold before starting this procedure. Do not allow antifreeze to come in contact with your skin, or with the painted surfaces of the vehicle. Rinse off spills immediately with plenty of water. Never leave antifreeze lying around in an open container, or in a puddle in the driveway or on the garage floor. Children and pets are attracted by its sweet smell, but antifreeze can be fatal if ingested.

Note: *Renault do not specify renewal intervals for the coolant, but it is advisable to drain and refill the system every four years to ensure that the corrosion inhibiting properties of the coolant are maintained.*

Cooling system draining

1 With the engine completely cold, remove the expansion tank filler cap. Turn the cap anti-clockwise, wait until any pressure remaining in the system is released, then unscrew it and lift it off.
2 Where applicable, remove the engine undertray, and then position a suitable container beneath the radiator bottom hose connection. Slacken the hose clip, pull off the hose and allow the coolant to drain into the container.
3 To assist draining, open the cooling system bleed screws. These are located in the radiator, thermostat/coolant housing and heater hose, depending on engine type **(see illustration).**

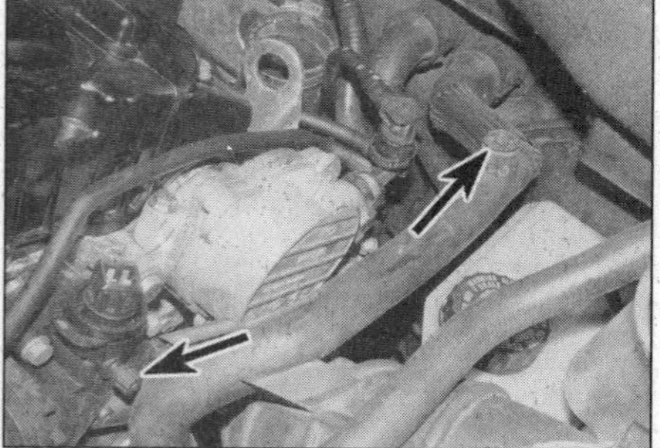

25.3 Cooling system bleed screws (arrowed) in the heater hose and thermostat housing

4 Flush the system if necessary as described in the following paragraphs, then refit the bottom hose. Use a new hose clip if necessary. Refill the system as described later in this Section.

Cooling system flushing

5 If coolant renewal has been neglected, or if the antifreeze mixture has become diluted, then in time the cooling system may gradually lose efficiency, as the coolant passages become restricted due to rust, scale deposits, and other sediment. Flushing the system clean can restore the cooling system efficiency.
6 The radiator should be flushed independently of the engine, to avoid unnecessary contamination.

Radiator flushing

7 Disconnect the top and bottom hoses and any other relevant hoses from the radiator, with reference to Chapter 3.
8 Insert a garden hose into the radiator top inlet. Direct a flow of clean water through the radiator, and continue flushing until clean water emerges from the radiator bottom outlet.
9 If after a reasonable period, the water still does not run clear, the radiator can be flushed with a good proprietary cleaning agent. It is important that their manufacturer's instructions are followed carefully. If the contamination is particularly bad, insert the hose in the radiator bottom outlet, and reverse-flush the radiator.

Engine flushing

10 To flush the engine, first refit the cylinder block drain plug, and tighten the cooling system bleed screw(s).
11 Remove the thermostat as described in Chapter 3, then temporarily refit the top hose at its engine connection.

12 With the top and bottom hoses disconnected from the radiator, insert a garden hose into the radiator top hose. Direct a clean flow of water through the engine, and continue flushing until clean water emerges from the radiator bottom hose.
13 On completion of flushing, refit the thermostat and reconnect the hoses with reference to Chapter 3.

Cooling system filling

14 Before attempting to fill the cooling system, make sure that all hoses and clips are in good condition, and that the clips are tight. Note that an antifreeze mixture must be used all year round, to prevent corrosion of the engine components. Also check that the cylinder block drain plug is in place and tight.
15 Remove the expansion tank filler cap.
16 Open the cooling system bleed screws (see paragraph 3).
17 Place a container under the vehicle, below the expansion tank, to catch any coolant that may be spilt during the topping-up procedure. Also place a wad of rags around the expansion tank.
18 Slowly fill the system until the coolant level reaches the top of the expansion tank filler neck.
19 Where applicable, close the bleed screws when coolant free from air bubbles emerges. Close the screws in sequence, starting with the lowest screw in the system.
20 Start the engine, and run it at a fast idle speed (do not exceed 2500 rpm) for approximately 4 minutes. Keep the level topped-up to the top of the expansion tank filler neck.
21 Refit and tighten the expansion tank filler cap.
22 Allow the engine to run for approximately 20 minutes at 2500 rpm (until the cooling fan cuts in and out three times).
23 Stop the engine and check the coolant level, which should be up to the MAX mark on the side of the tank. Check that the expansion tank filler cap is tight.
24 Allow the engine to cool, and then recheck the coolant level with reference to *Weekly checks*. Top-up the level if necessary and refit the expansion tank filler cap. Where applicable, refit the engine undertray.

Antifreeze mixture

25 The antifreeze should always be renewed at the specified intervals. This is necessary not only to maintain the antifreeze properties, but also to prevent corrosion that would otherwise occur as the corrosion inhibitors become progressively less effective.
26 Always use an ethylene glycol-based antifreeze, which is suitable for use in mixed-metal cooling systems. The quantity of antifreeze and levels of protection are given in the Specifications.
27 Before adding antifreeze, the cooling system should be completely drained, preferably flushed, and all hoses checked for condition and security.
28 After filling with antifreeze, a label should be attached to the expansion tank, stating the type and concentration of antifreeze used, and the date installed. Any subsequent topping-up should be made with the same type and concentration of antifreeze.
29 Do not use engine antifreeze in the windscreen/tailgate washer system, as it will cause damage to the vehicle paintwork. A screenwash additive should be added to the washer system in the quantities stated on the bottle.
30 Dispose safely of the used coolant with reference to *General repair procedures*.

Notes

Chapter 2 Part A:
Petrol engine in-car repair procedures

Contents

Degrees of difficulty

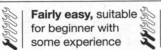

Easy, suitable for novice with little experience	**Fairly easy,** suitable for beginner with some experience	**Fairly difficult,** suitable for competent DIY mechanic	**Difficult,** suitable for experienced DIY mechanic	**Very difficult,** suitable for expert DIY or professional

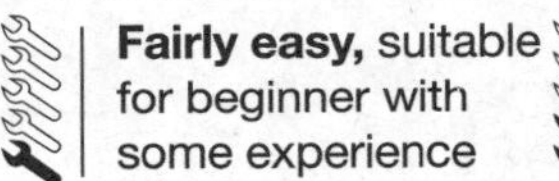

Specifications

General

Type	Four-cylinder, in-line, double overhead camshaft
Designation:	
1.6 litre engines	K4M
1.8 litre engines	F4P
2.0 litre engines	F4R
Bore:	
1.6 litre engines	79.5 mm
1.8 litre engines	82.7 mm
2.0 litre engines	82.7 mm
Stroke:	
1.6 litre engines	80.5 mm
1.8 litre engines	83.0 mm
2.0 litre engines	93.0 mm
Capacity:	
1.6 litre engines	1598 cc
1.8 litre engines	1783 cc
2.0 litre engines	1998 cc
Compression ratio:	
1.6 litre engines	10.0:1
1.8 and 2.0 litre engines	9.8:1
Firing order	1-3-4-2 (No 1 cylinder at flywheel/driveplate end of engine)
Direction of crankshaft rotation	Clockwise, viewed from timing belt end

Camshafts

Drive	Toothed belt
Number of bearings	6
Camshaft bearing journal diameters:	
No 1 to No 5 bearings	24.979 to 25.000
No 6 bearing	27.979 to 28.000
Camshaft endfloat	0.08 to 0.178 mm

Lubrication system

Minimum oil pressure at 80°C:	
At 1000 rpm	1.0 bars (14.5 psi)
At 3000 rpm	3.0 bars (43.5 psi)
Oil pump clearances:	
Gear-to-body:	
Minimum	0.110 mm
Maximum	0.249 mm
Gear endfloat:	
Minimum	0.020 mm
Maximum	0.086 mm

Torque wrench settings

	Nm	lbf ft
1.6 litre engines		
Auxiliary components mounting bracket bolts:		
Bracket-to-engine bolts	44	32
Bracket-to-sump bolt	21	15
Camshaft sprocket nut (without phase-shifter fitted)*:		
Stage 1	30	22
Stage 2	Angle-tighten through 84° ± 4°	
Connecting rod (big-end) caps*	43	32
Crankshaft pulley bolt:		
Stage 1	40	30
Stage 2	Angle-tighten through 115° ± 15°	
Cylinder block TDC blanking plug	20	15
Cylinder head lower section to block:		
Stage 1	20	15
Stage 2	Angle-tighten through 240° ± 6°	
Cylinder head upper section to lower section:		
Stage 1 (bolts 22, 23, 20 and 13 in sequence)	8	6
Stage 2 (bolts 1 to 12, 14 to 19, 21 and 24 in sequence)	15	11
Stage 3 (bolts 22, 23, 20 and 13)	Slacken completely	
Stage 4 (bolts 22, 23, 20 and 13 in sequence)	15	11
Engine/transmission mountings:		
Right-hand engine mounting:		
Acoustic mass unit mounting bolts	21	15
Engine bracket-to-cylinder head bolts	62	46
Tie-rod bracket bolts	105	77
Engine bracket-to-rubber mounting nut	44	32
Rubber mounting-to-body bolts	21	15
Left-hand transmission mounting:		
Mounting bracket-to-transmission bolts	62	46
Mounting stud nut	44	32
Rubber mounting bracket-to-body bolts	62	46
Rear mounting tie-rod link bolts	105	77
Flywheel/driveplate bolts*	55	41
Inlet camshaft sprocket/phase-shifter bolt*	75	55
Inlet camshaft sprocket/phase-shifter plug	15	11
Main bearing cap bolts*:		
Stage 1	25	18
Stage 2	Angle-tighten through 47° ± 5°	
Oil pump:		
Mounting bolts	25	18
Sprocket bolts	10	7
Oil seal housing bolts (timing belt end)	12	9
Oil separator to cylinder head upper section	13	10
Sump bolts:		
Stage 1	8	6
Stage 2	14	10
Timing belt idler pulley bolt	45	33
Timing belt tensioner pulley:		
Pretighten	7	5
Final	27	20
Timing belt upper cover	41	30
Transmission-to-engine bolts	44	32

Torque wrench settings (continued)

	Nm	lbf ft
1.8 and 2.0 litre engines		
Auxiliary components mounting bracket bolts	44	32
Camshaft sprocket nut (without phase-shifter fitted)*:		
Stage 1	30	22
Stage 2	Angle-tighten through 84°	
Connecting rod (big-end) caps*:		
Stage 1	20	15
Stage 2	Angle-tighten through 40° ± 6°	
Crankshaft pulley bolt:		
Stage 1	20	15
Stage 2	Angle-tighten through 115° ± 15°	
Cylinder head lower section to block:		
Stage 1	20	15
Stage 2	Angle-tighten through 165°	
Cylinder head upper section to lower section:		
Stage 1 (bolts 22, 23, 20 and 13 in sequence)	8	6
Stage 2 (bolts 1 to 12, 14 to 19, 21 and 24 in sequence)	12	9
Stage 3 (bolts 22, 23, 20 and 13)	Slacken completely	
Stage 4 (bolts 22, 23, 20 and 13 in sequence)	12	9
Engine/transmission mountings:		
1.8 litre engines:		
Right-hand engine mounting:		
Acoustic mass unit mounting bolts	21	15
Engine bracket-to-cylinder head bolts	62	46
Tie-rod bracket bolts	105	77
Engine bracket-to-rubber mounting nut	44	32
Rubber mounting-to-body bolts	21	15
Left-hand transmission mounting:		
Mounting bracket-to-transmission bolts	62	46
Mounting stud nut	44	32
Rubber mounting bracket-to-body bolts	62	46
Rear mounting tie-rod link bolts	105	77
2.0 litre engines:		
Right-hand engine mounting:		
Mounting bracket-to-cylinder head bolts	62	46
Tie-rod bracket bolts	62	46
Mounting bracket-to-rubber mounting nut	44	32
Rubber mounting bracket-to-body bolts	21	15
Left-hand transmission mounting:		
Mounting bracket-to-transmission bolts	62	46
Mounting stud nut	44	32
Rubber mounting bracket-to-body bolts	62	46
Rear mounting bracket/tie rod:		
Tie-rod link-to-transmission bolt	180	133
Tie-rod link-to-subframe bolt	105	77
Flywheel/driveplate bolts*	55	41
Inlet camshaft sprocket/phase-shifter bolt*	100	74
Inlet camshaft sprocket/phase-shifter plug	25	18
Main bearing cap bolts*	65	48
Oil pump-to-cylinder block bolts	22	16
Oil seal housing bolts (timing belt end)	15	11
Oil separator housing (located on exhaust camshaft cover):		
New bolts (in non-tapped holes)	15	11
New or original bolts (in tapped holes)	10	7
Roadwheel bolts	105	77
Sump bolts:		
Stage 1	8	6
Stage 2	14	10
Timing belt idler pulley bolt	45	33
Timing belt lower cover	20	15
Timing belt tensioner pulley nut	27	20
Timing belt upper cover:		
M10 nuts/bolts	38	28
M8 bolts	18	13
Transmission-to-engine bolts	44	32

** New bolts must be used*

1 General information

This Part of Chapter 2 is devoted to in-car repair procedures for the 1.6, 1.8 and 2.0 litre, 16-valve petrol engines. Similar information covering other engine types can be found in Chapters 2B and 2C. All procedures concerning engine removal and refitting, and engine block/ cylinder head overhaul for petrol and diesel engines can be found in Chapters 2D and 2E.

Refer *to Vehicle identification* in the *Reference Section* of this manual for details of engine code locations.

Most of the operations included in this Chapter are based on the assumption that the engine is still installed in the car. Therefore, if this information is being used during a complete engine overhaul, with the engine already removed, many of the steps included here will not apply.

Engine description

The engines covered in this part of Chapter 2 are of four-cylinder, in-line, double overhead camshaft type, incorporating two inlet valves and two exhaust valves per cylinder. The engines are mounted transversely at the front of the vehicle with the transmission bolted to their left-hand side.

The crankshaft is supported in five shell-type main bearings. Crankshaft endfloat is controlled by thrustwashers fitted to the centre main bearing on 1.6 litre engines, and to No 2 main bearing on 1.8 and 2.0 litre engines.

The connecting rods are attached to the crankshaft by horizontally-split shell-type big-end bearings, and to the pistons by gudgeon pins. On 1.6 litre engines the gudgeon pins are a sliding fit in the pistons and are secured in position with circlips. On 1.8 and 2.0 litre engines, the gudgeon pins are a press-fit in the connecting rods. The aluminium alloy pistons are of the slipper type, and are fitted with three piston rings – two compression rings and a scraper-type oil control ring.

The cylinder head comprises an upper and lower section, mated along the centre line of the camshafts. The upper section of the cylinder head functions as a combined valve cover and camshaft cover, the camshafts run in plain bearings integral to the two cylinder head sections. The camshafts operate the inlet and exhaust valves via roller rocker arms, which are supported at their pivot ends by hydraulic self-adjusting tappets.

Drive to the camshaft is by a toothed timing belt and sprockets with an automatic tensioning mechanism. On later engines, the inlet camshaft sprocket incorporates a phase-shifter, which provides variable valve timing during certain operating conditions. The phase-shifter is activated by the engine management ECU via an electrically-controlled solenoid valve located on the top right-hand side of the cylinder head.

The alternator, power steering pump and air conditioning compressor are all driven from the crankshaft pulley by a multi-ribbed auxiliary drivebelt.

A semi-closed crankcase ventilation system is employed; crankcase fumes are drawn from an oil separator on the cylinder head, and passed via a hose to the inlet manifold.

The lubrication system is of the full-flow, pressure-feed type. Oil is drawn from the sump by a chain-driven gear-type oil pump located beneath the crankshaft. Oil under pressure passes through a filter before being fed to the various shaft bearings and to the valve gear.

Operations with engine in car

The following work can be carried out with the engine in the car:

a) Compression pressure – testing.
b) Timing belt and sprockets – removal and refitting.
c) Camshaft oil seals – renewal.
d) Camshafts, tappets and rocker arms – removal and refitting.
e) Cylinder head – removal and refitting.
f) Cylinder head and pistons – decarbonising.
g) Crankshaft oil seals – renewal.
h) Sump – removal and refitting.
*i) Pistons and connecting rods – removal and refitting.**
j) Oil pump – removal and refitting.
*k) Flywheel/driveplate – removal and refitting.***
l) Engine mountings – removal and refitting.

** Although the operation marked with an asterisk can be carried out with the engine in the car after removal of the sump, it is better for the engine to be removed, in the interests of cleanliness and improved access. For this reason, the procedure is described in Chapter 2D.*

*** On some models it may be necessary to remove the engine and transmission assembly, to make removal of the flywheel easier (see Chapter 2D).*

2 Compression test – description and interpretation

Note: *A compression gauge will be required to carry out this test.*

1 When engine performance is down, or if misfiring occurs which cannot be attributed to the ignition or fuel systems, a compression test can provide diagnostic clues as to the engine's condition. If the test is performed regularly, it can give warning of trouble before any other symptoms become apparent.

2 The engine must be fully warmed-up to normal operating temperature, the battery must be fully-charged, and all the spark plugs must be removed (see Chapter 1A). The aid of an assistant will also be required.

3 Disable the ignition system by disconnecting the crankshaft sensor wiring at the connector located on the left-hand side of the engine. Also disconnect the wiring connectors to each fuel injector to prevent unburned fuel from damaging the catalytic converter.

4 Fit a compression tester to the No 1 cylinder spark plug hole – the type of tester which screws into the plug thread is to be preferred.

5 Have the assistant hold the throttle wide open, and crank the engine on the starter motor; after one or two revolutions, the compression pressure should build-up to a maximum figure, and then stabilise. Record the highest reading obtained.

6 Repeat the test on the remaining cylinders, recording the pressure in each.

7 All cylinders should produce very similar pressures; a difference of more than 2 bars between any two cylinders indicates a fault. Note that the compression should build-up quickly in a healthy engine; low compression on the first stroke, followed by gradually-increasing pressure on successive strokes, indicates worn piston rings. A low compression reading on the first stroke, which does not build-up during successive strokes, indicates leaking valves or a blown head gasket (a cracked cylinder head could also be the cause). Deposits on the undersides of the valve heads can also cause low compression.

8 If the pressure in any cylinder is low, carry out the following test to isolate the cause. Introduce a teaspoonful of clean oil into that cylinder through its spark plug hole, and repeat the test.

9 If the addition of oil temporarily improves the compression pressure, this indicates that bore or piston ring wear is responsible for the pressure loss. No improvement suggests that leaking or burnt valves, or a blown head gasket, may be to blame.

10 A low reading from two adjacent cylinders is almost certainly due to the head gasket having blown between them; the presence of coolant in the engine oil will confirm this.

11 If one cylinder is about 20 percent lower than the others and the engine has a slightly rough idle, a worn camshaft lobe could be the cause.

12 If the compression reading is unusually high, the combustion chambers are probably coated with carbon deposits. If this is the case, the cylinder head should be removed and decarbonised.

13 On completion of the test, refit the spark plugs, and reconnect the ignition system and fuel injectors.

3 Top Dead Centre (TDC) for No 1 piston – locating

Note: *A TDC pin from a Renault dealer (Mot. 1489) or automotive tool shop is required for this operation.*

1 Top Dead Centre (TDC) is the highest point in the cylinder that each piston reaches as the

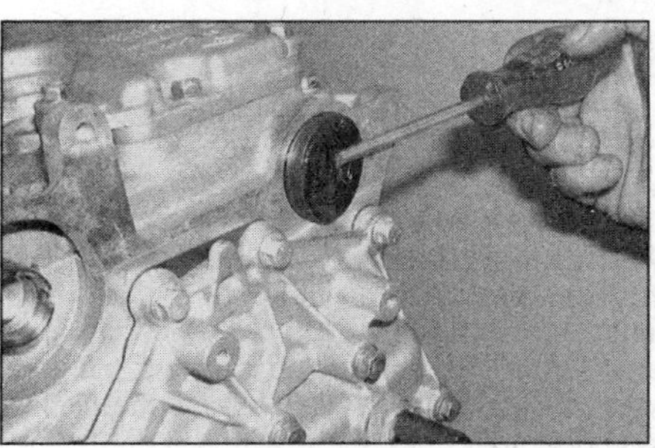
3.7 Using a screwdriver, prise the camshaft sealing caps from the left hand end of the cylinder head

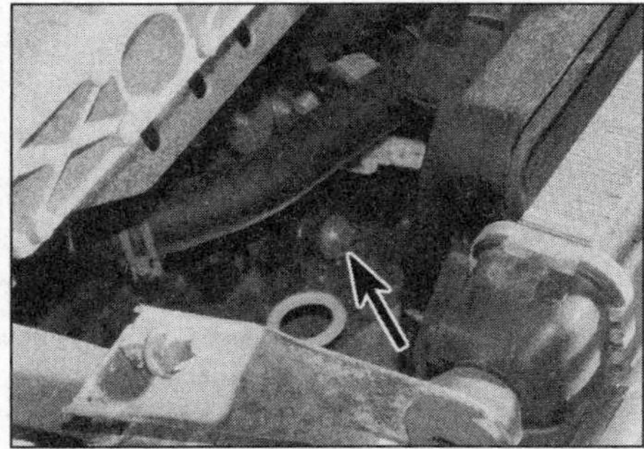
3.8a Unscrew the TDC plug (arrowed) . . .

3.8b . . . obtain the TDC pin tool . . .

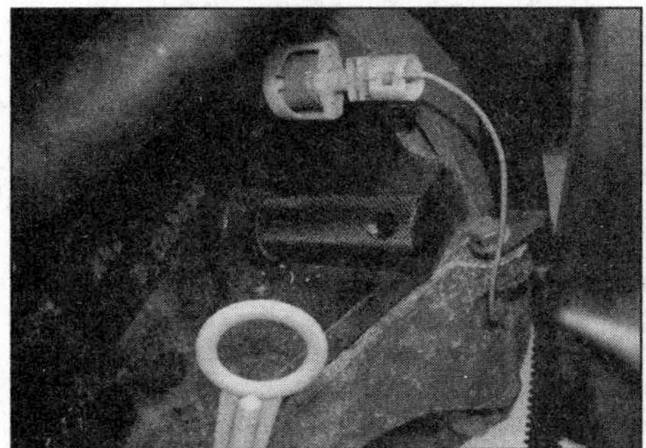
3.8c . . . and screw it into the cylinder block

3.9a The special Renault tool (arrowed) used to lock the camshafts in place

3.9b Home-made tool for locking the camshafts

crankshaft turns. Each piston reaches TDC at the end of the compression stroke, and again at the end of the exhaust stroke. However, for the purpose of timing the engine, TDC refers to the position of No 1 piston at the end of its compression stroke. No 1 piston is at the flywheel (transmission) end of the engine.

2 Apply the handbrake, then jack up the front right-hand side of the car and support it on axle stands. Remove the right-hand roadwheel.

3 Remove the plastic liners from within the right-hand wheel arch to give access to the crankshaft pulley bolt (see Chapter 11).

4 Remove the spark plugs as described in Chapter 1A.

5 The engine must now be turned in order to check that No 1 cylinder (nearest the flywheel) is on the compression stroke (piston rising up the cylinder). As the spark plug holes are deeply recessed, it is not possible to place a finger over them, however, the inverted handle of a screwdriver may be used instead, or alternatively simply listen for air being forced out of the No 1 spark plug hole. Turn the engine in a clockwise direction, using a socket or spanner on the crankshaft pulley bolt, until air is forced from No 1 cylinder; this indicates that No 1 piston is rising on its compression stroke.

6 Remove the air cleaner resonator box or the air inlet duct from the left-hand side of the engine, with reference to Chapter 4A.

7 Using a screwdriver, pierce the centres of the two plastic plugs at the left-hand end of the cylinder head, and pull out the plugs **(see illustration)**. With No 1 piston approaching TDC, the grooves in the ends of the camshafts should be positioned approximately at a 30° angle from the horizontal, with the offset below the centreline, downward ends at the rear of the engine.

8 Unscrew the TDC plug from the left-hand front of the cylinder block, then fully screw in the TDC pin **(see illustrations)**.

9 Carefully turn the crankshaft clockwise until the crankshaft web contacts the TDC pin. At this point, the No 1 piston is at TDC on its compression stroke, and the grooves in the ends of the camshafts will now be positioned horizontally. Renault technicians use a special tool to lock the camshafts in their TDC position. The tool is attached to the left-hand end of the cylinder head to hold the camshafts with their grooves horizontal, and a similar tool may be fabricated from metal plate if necessary **(see illustrations)**.

10 Note that the crankshaft sprocket is not keyed to the crankshaft, therefore if the crankshaft pulley/sprocket is removed it is important to have an accurate method of determining the TDC position of No 1 piston.

4 Timing belt (1.6 litre engines) – removal, inspection and refitting

Note: *This is a complicated operation requiring the use of certain special tools. Read through the entire procedure to familiarise yourself with the work involved then either obtain the manufacturer's special tools or, where applicable, fabricate the home-made alternatives described, before proceeding.*

General information

1 The function of the timing belt is to drive the camshafts and the coolant pump. Should the belt slip or break in service, the valve timing will be disturbed and piston-to-valve contact will occur, resulting in serious engine damage.

2 The timing belt should be renewed at the specified intervals (see Chapter 1A), or earlier if it is contaminated with oil, or if it is at all noisy in operation (a 'scraping' noise due to uneven wear).

3 The manufacturer recommends that the timing belt should be renewed whenever it is removed, and that the timing belt tensioner and idler pulley should also be renewed at the same time. A new crankshaft pulley, retaining bolt will be needed when refitting.

4 Before carrying out this procedure, it will be necessary to obtain a crankshaft TDC positioning pin, and to obtain or fabricate a camshaft holding tool, as described later in this Section. Do not attempt to remove the timing belt unless the special tools or their alternatives are available.

Note: *A Renault TDC pin (Mot. 1489) or approved alternative is required for this operation, and may be obtained from most car accessory shops. Also, a Renault camshaft locking bar (Mot. 1496) or alternative will be required (see text).*

Removal

5 Disconnect the battery negative lead, and move the lead away from the battery (see *Disconnecting the battery*).

6 Apply the handbrake, then jack up the

4.10 Support the right-hand side of the engine with a trolley jack

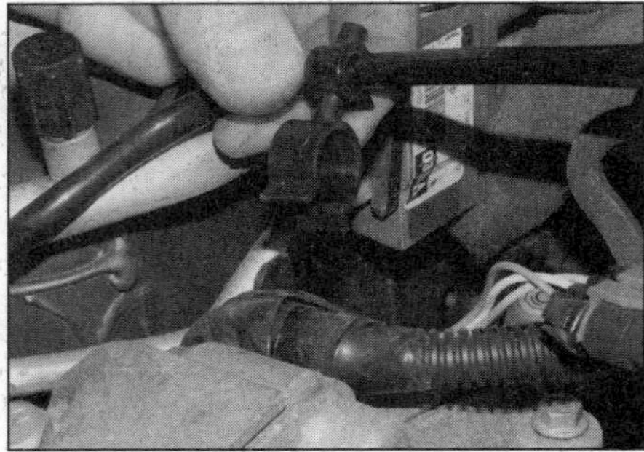
4.13a Unclip the vacuum pipes and wiring loom and move them to one side

4.13b Note how the retaining clips locate in the upper timing cover

4.15a Using a screwdriver, prise the camshaft sealing caps from the left hand end of the cylinder head

front right-hand side of the car and support on axle stands (see *Jacking and vehicle support*). Remove the right-hand roadwheel. Where fitted, remove the engine compartment undertray.

7 Remove the screws and clips securing the right-hand wheel arch liner, referring if necessary to Chapter 11.

8 Remove the auxiliary drivebelt as described in Chapter 1A.

9 Set the engine at TDC for No 1 piston as described in Section 3.

10 Carefully position a trolley jack and a large block of wood under the sump to support the right-hand side of the engine. Raise the jack to just take the weight of the engine **(see illustration)**. If available, an engine support bar can be fitted to take the weight of the engine from above.

11 Remove the clips and take off the trim panels from the right-hand side of the engine compartment.

12 Remove the engine right-hand mounting from the engine and body with reference to Section 13. For improved access it may be necessary to remove the alternator – refer to Chapter 5A.

13 Remove the wiring loom from the right-hand end of the engine by disconnecting it from the inlet manifold and unbolting the support bracket at the right-hand front of the cylinder head. Also unclip and disconnect the vacuum pipe from the inlet manifold. Release the loom from the upper timing cover and position it to one side **(see illustrations)**.

14 Unclip the fuel pipe(s) from the lower timing cover, then remove the air cleaner as described in Chapter 4A.

15 Using a screwdriver, pierce the centres of the two plastic plugs at the left-hand end of the camshafts, and pull the plugs from the cylinder head. With No 1 piston approaching TDC, the grooves in the ends of the camshafts should be as shown **(see illustrations)**.

16 Unscrew the TDC plug from the left-hand front of the cylinder block, then fully screw in the TDC pin **(see illustration)**.

4.15b Turn the crankshaft until the slots in the camshafts are initially positioned at approximately a 30° angle from the horizontal, with the offsets below the centreline

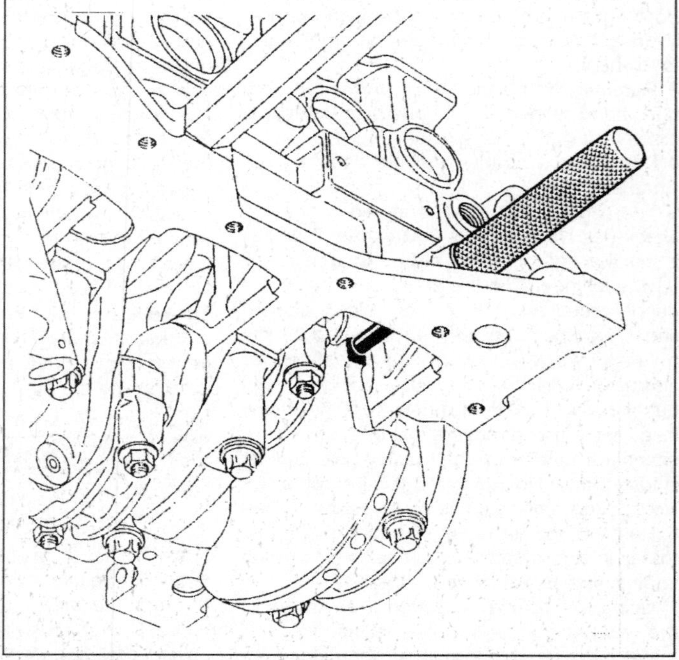
4.16 Fit the TDC pin and turn the crankshaft until it contacts the pin . . .

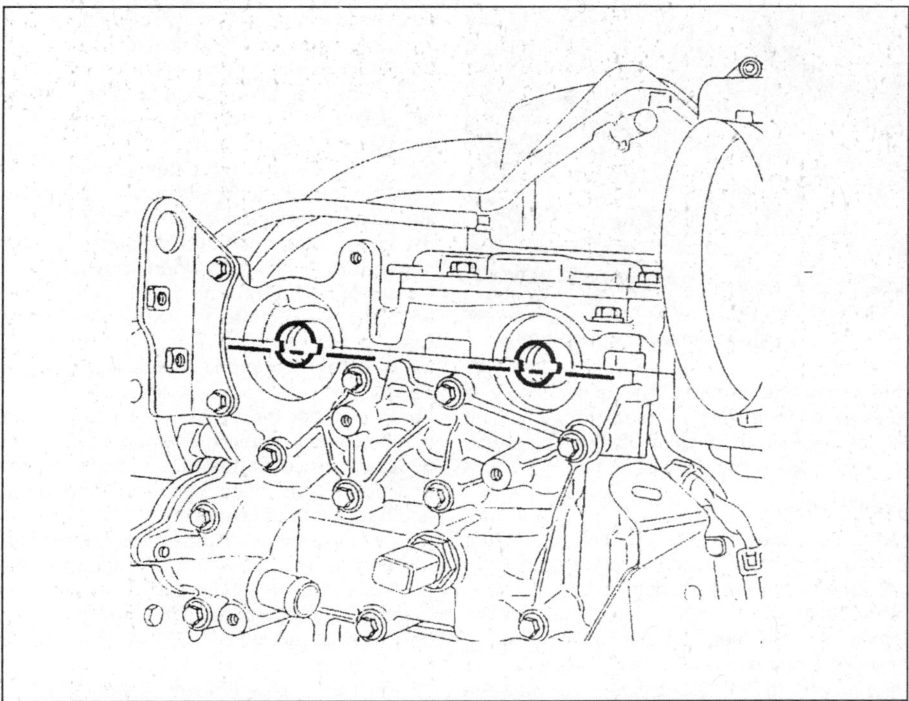

4.17a Check that the camshaft slots are now horizontal with their offsets below the centreline . . .

4.17b . . . engage the camshaft holding tool with the camshaft slots . . .

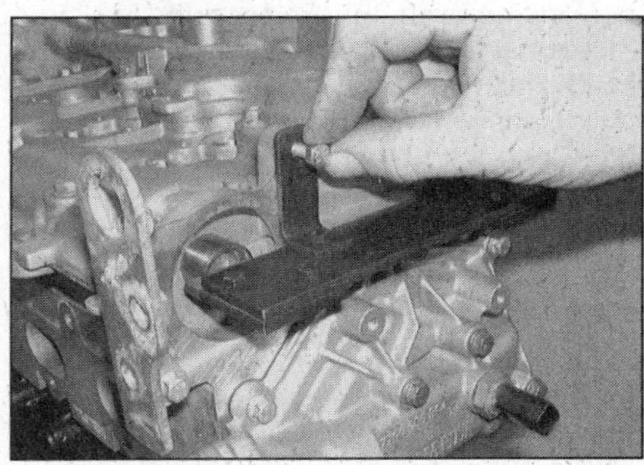

4.17c . . . and secure the tool using a suitable bolt screwed into the cylinder head

17 Carefully turn the crankshaft clockwise until the crankshaft web is in contact with the TDC pin. At this point, the No 1 piston is at TDC on its compression stroke, and the grooves in the ends of the camshafts will now be positioned horizontally. Renault technicians use a special tool to lock the camshafts in their TDC position, however, a length of metal bar may be fabricated **(see illustrations and Tool Tip)**.

TOOL TIP

To make a camshaft holding tool, obtain a length of steel strip and cut it to length so that it will fit across the rear of the cylinder head. Obtain a second length of steel strip of suitable thickness to fit snugly in the slots in the camshafts. Cut the second strip into two lengths and drill accordingly so that they can be bolted to the first strip in the correct position to engage with the camshaft slots. Secure a suitably drilled small piece of steel angle to the first strip so that the tool can be bolted to the threaded hole in the cylinder head upper section.

18 Further confirmation of the TDC position can be gained from the camshaft sprockets. At TDC, the Renault 'diamond' emblem on the exhaust camshaft sprocket and the etched mark on the inlet sprocket (with the VVT unit) will both be facing vertically upwards.

19 Before loosening the crankshaft pulley bolt, note that the crankshaft sprocket is **not** keyed to the crankshaft, therefore if the crankshaft pulley is removed, it is important to have an accurate method of determining the TDC position of No 1 piston. Although the sprocket is not keyed to the crankshaft, there is still a groove in the crankshaft nose, which is at the 12 o'clock position when piston No 1 is at TDC.

20 To prevent the crankshaft from rotating while the pulley bolt is unscrewed, first remove the metal bar from the camshafts then, on manual transmission models, have an assistant engage top gear and firmly depress the brake pedal. Alternatively, and on automatic transmission models, the crankshaft may be held stationary by unbolting the crankshaft speed/position sensor from the top of the transmission and wedging a screwdriver in the starter ring gear teeth through the sensor's opening in the bellhousing.

21 Unscrew the crankshaft pulley bolt, then remove the pulley **(see illustrations)**. **Note:** *The bolt is very tight.*

22 Unbolt the lower timing cover, followed by the upper timing cover **(see illustrations)**.

23 Loosen the timing belt tensioner, then turn the tensioner hub anti-clockwise to release the tension.

24 Note the fitted position of the timing belt and the routing of the belt (a new belt will be

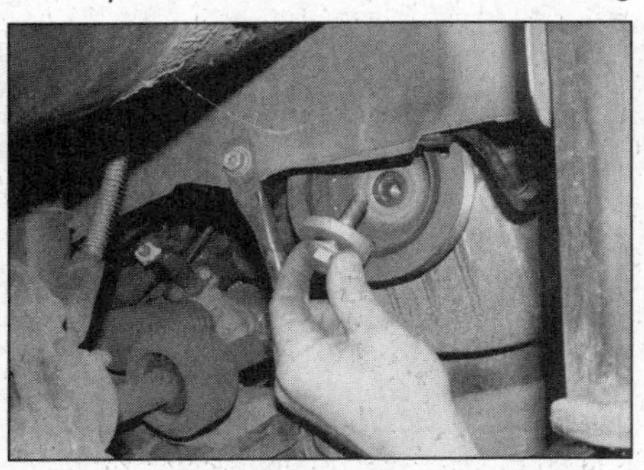

4.21a Unscrew the crankshaft pulley bolt . . .

4.21b . . . and remove the pulley

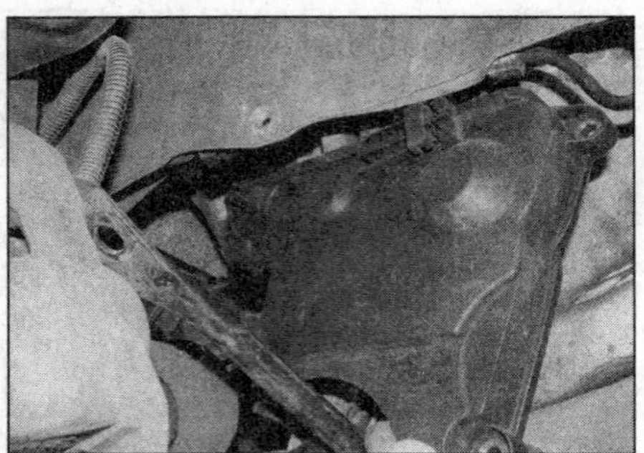
4.22a Remove the lower timing cover . . .

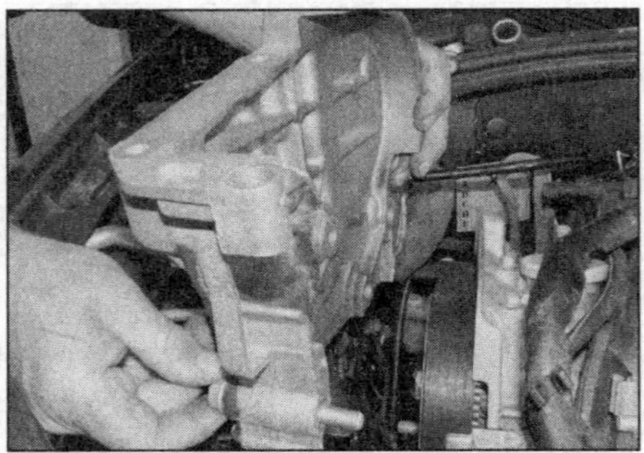
4.22b . . . and the upper timing cover

needed for refitting). Release the belt from the camshaft sprockets, water pump pulley, crankshaft sprocket, tensioner pulley and idler pulley, and remove it from the engine.

25 Clean the sprockets, tensioner and idler and wipe them dry. Also clean the cylinder head and block behind the timing belt running area.

Inspection

Note: *Renault state that the timing belt must be renewed whenever it is removed, and also that the tensioner and idler pulley must be renewed whenever the timing belt is renewed.*

26 Examine the timing belt carefully for any signs of cracking, fraying or general wear, particularly at the roots of the teeth. Renew the belt if there is any sign of deterioration of this nature, or if there is any oil or grease contamination. Renew any leaking oil seals. The belt **must** be renewed if it has completed the maximum mileage given in Chapter 1A.

27 When fitting a new belt, Renault recommend that a new tensioner and idler pulley are also fitted – these are often sold as a kit with a new belt, when purchased from a Renault dealer.

28 Thoroughly clean the nose of the crankshaft and the bore of the crankshaft sprocket, and also the contact surfaces of the sprocket and pulley. This is necessary to prevent the possibility of the sprocket, which is not keyed to the crankshaft, slipping in use and causing engine damage.

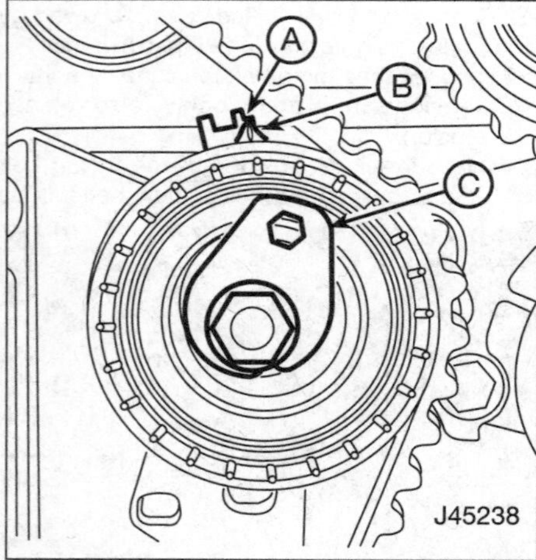

4.32 Timing belt tensioner pulley details

A Shallow notch *C Eccentric adjustment*
B Adjustable index

Refitting

29 Check that the lug on the rear of the tensioner is correctly located in the groove.

30 Check that the camshafts and No 1 piston are still at TDC. Fit the timing belt on the crankshaft sprocket, and then locate it around the water pump and idler, over the camshafts and around the tensioner. Make sure that the belt is taut between the camshaft sprockets.

31 Check that the idler retaining bolt is tightened to the specified torque.

32 Using a 6.0 mm Allen key, turn the index pointer until it is opposite the shallow notch at the front of the fixed notched plate **(see illustration),** and then pretighten the nut to the specified initial torque. Check that the camshafts and crankshaft are still at TDC.

33 Refit the crankshaft pulley and tighten the bolt to the specified torque. This can be done with the timing pin still tight in the cylinder block, and the crankshaft web resting against it. If the original bolt is being re-used, lightly lubricate the threads with engine oil. If a new bolt is being used it should be fitted dry.

34 Remove the locking tool from the camshafts and the TDC pin from the cylinder block. Turn the crankshaft clockwise two complete turns, and then recheck the TDC position and tensioner index setting. If necessary, loosen the nut and use the Allen key to reposition the index pointer in line with the shallow notch. Finally, fully tighten the tensioner to the specified final torque.

4.37 Fit new sealing caps to the cylinder head and tap them into place using a large socket

35 Refit the upper timing cover and lower timing cover, and tighten the bolts securely.

36 Refit the TDC plug to the cylinder block, and tighten it securely.

37 Fit two new plastic plugs in the cylinder head on the left-hand end of the camshafts. Renault technicians use special tools to drive the plugs into position, although suitable sockets or blocks of wood may be used instead **(see illustration)**.

38 Refit the air cleaner with reference to Chapter 4A.

39 Clip the fuel pipes to the lower timing cover.

40 Reconnect the vacuum pipe to the inlet manifold, and attach the wiring loom to the upper timing cover. Refit the support bracket and tighten the bolts, reconnect the wiring and attach it to the support.

41 Refit the engine right-hand mounting to the engine and body with reference to Section 13. Lower the jack and block of wood from the sump (or remove the engine support bar). Where removed, refit the alternator at this stage.

42 Refit the auxiliary drivebelt with reference to Chapter 1A.

43 Refit the right-hand wheel arch liners, and engine compartment undertray, then refit the roadwheel and lower the car to the ground.

44 Reconnect the battery negative lead.

5 Timing belt (1.8 and 2.0 litre engines) – removal and refitting

Note: *This is a complicated operation requiring the use of certain special tools. Read through the entire procedure to familiarise yourself with the work involved then either obtain the manufacturers special tools or, where applicable, fabricate the home-made alternatives described, before proceeding.*

General information

1 The function of the timing belt is to drive the camshafts. Should the belt slip or break in service, the valve timing will be disturbed and piston-to-valve contact will occur, resulting in serious engine damage.

2 The timing belt should be renewed at the specified intervals (see Chapter 1A), or earlier if it is contaminated with oil, or if it is at all noisy in operation (a 'scraping' noise due to uneven wear). Note that the manufacturer recommends that the timing belt should be renewed whenever it is removed, and that the timing belt tensioner and idler pulley should also be renewed at the same time. Additionally, new camshaft sealing caps will be required, and a new crankshaft pulley retaining bolt and camshaft sprocket retaining nuts may be needed, depending on the condition of the components and/or the tensioning method being used when refitting.

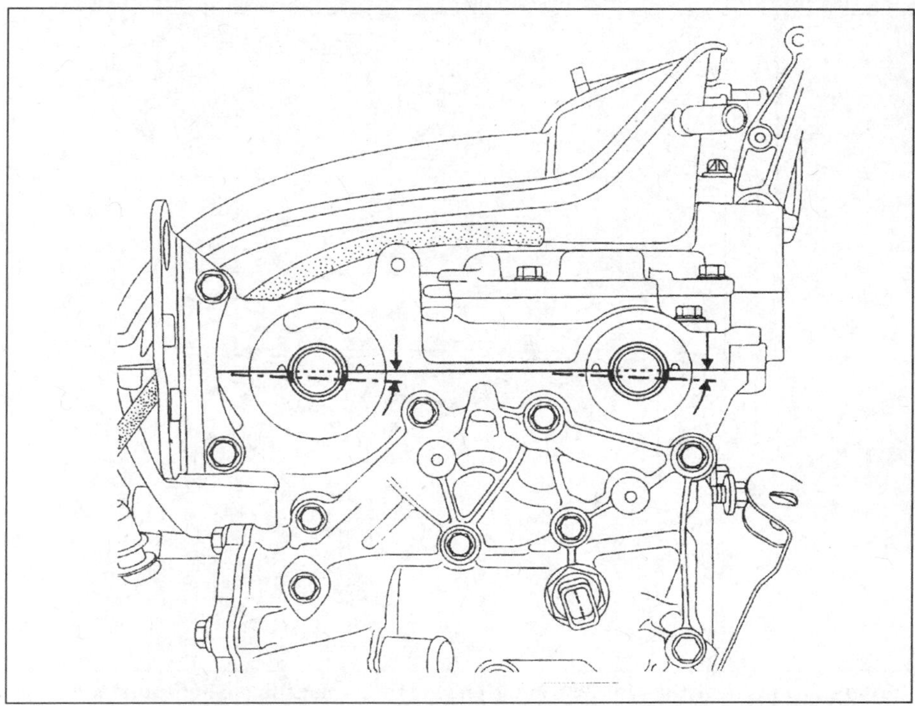

5.14 Turn the crankshaft until the camshaft slots are nearly horizontal, with the offset below the centreline

5.15a Unscrew the plug from TDC pin hole on the left-hand end of the front of the cylinder block . . .

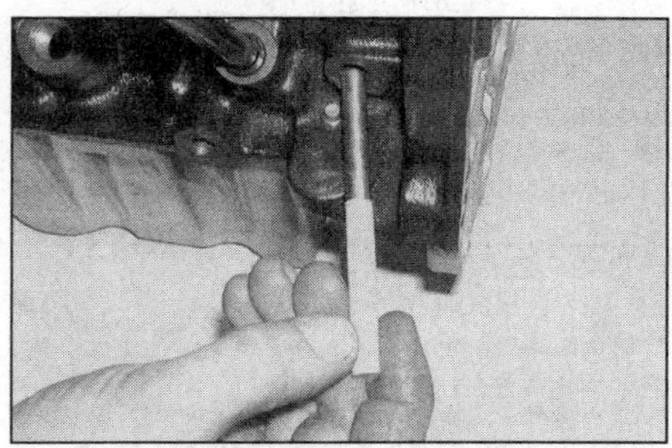

5.15b . . . and insert the special tool or a dowel rod of suitable diameter to be a snug fit in the hole

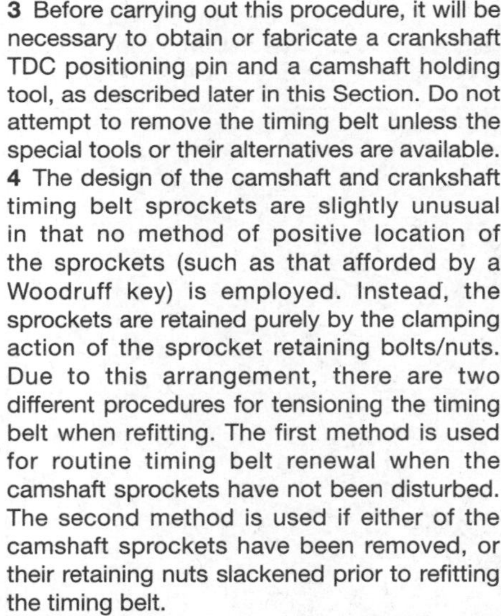

3 Before carrying out this procedure, it will be necessary to obtain or fabricate a crankshaft TDC positioning pin and a camshaft holding tool, as described later in this Section. Do not attempt to remove the timing belt unless the special tools or their alternatives are available.

4 The design of the camshaft and crankshaft timing belt sprockets are slightly unusual in that no method of positive location of the sprockets (such as that afforded by a Woodruff key) is employed. Instead, the sprockets are retained purely by the clamping action of the sprocket retaining bolts/nuts. Due to this arrangement, there are two different procedures for tensioning the timing belt when refitting. The first method is used for routine timing belt renewal when the camshaft sprockets have not been disturbed. The second method is used if either of the camshaft sprockets have been removed, or their retaining nuts slackened prior to refitting the timing belt.

Note: *A Renault TDC pin (Mot. 1054) or approved alternative is required for this operation, and may be obtained from most car accessory shops. Also, a Renault camshaft locking bar (Mot. 1496) or alternative will be required (see text).*

Removal

5 Disconnect the battery negative terminal (refer to *Disconnecting the battery* in the Reference Section of this manual).

6 Apply the handbrake, then jack up the front of the car and support it on axle stands (see *Jacking and vehicle support*). Remove the right-hand front roadwheel, the undo the retaining screws and remove the engine undercover and the front and rear protective covers from the right-hand wheel arch.

7 Remove the auxiliary drivebelt as described in Chapter 1A.

8 Remove the complete air cleaner assembly and inlet ducts as described in Chapter 4A.

9 Position an engine hoist, or an engine lifting beam across the engine compartment, and attach the jib to the right hand engine lifting eyelet. Raise the lifting gear to take up the slack, so that it is just supporting the weight of the engine.

10 Undo the three bolts and one nut securing the right-hand engine mounting bracket to the cylinder head. Similarly, undo the three bolts securing the rubber mounting to the body. Release the relevant cable clips and remove the complete mounting assembly, for further information, see Section 13.

11 Disconnect the wiring connectors at the idle speed stepper motor, throttle position sensor and MAP sensor, then unclip the wiring harness from the upper timing belt cover and move the harness to one side.

12 Release the fuel pipes from the clips on the lower timing belt cover.

13 Prise the sealing caps from the left hand end of the cylinder head, to expose the ends of both camshafts. The caps cannot be re-used, so the easiest way to remove them is to punch a small hole in the centre of each cap and lever them out with a stout screwdriver **(see illustration 4.15a)**.

14 With the help of an assistant to slowly turn the crankshaft using a socket or spanner on the crankshaft pulley bolt, observe the position of the slots in the ends of the camshafts. Turn the crankshaft in a clockwise direction (as viewed from the timing belt end), until the camshaft slots are nearly horizontal, with the offset below the centreline **(see illustration)**.

15 Unscrew the plug from the TDC pin hole on the left-hand end of the front of the cylinder block, located just below the engine identification plate. Insert the crankshaft TDC pin (Renault special tool Mot. 1054) into the hole until it contacts the crankshaft. Alternatively, insert a dowel rod of suitable diameter to be a snug fit in the hole **(see illustrations)**.

16 While maintaining slight pressure on the TDC pin or dowel rod, continue to turn the crankshaft clockwise very slightly until the pin or rod enters the slot provided for this purpose in the crankshaft web. Note that there is a balance hole in the crankshaft web adjacent to the TDC setting slot. If care is not taken, it is very easy for the TDC pin or dowel rod to engage with the balance hole and not the setting slot. If the tool has entered the setting slot, the slots in the ends of the camshafts should now be horizontal (ie, parallel to the join between the upper and lower cylinder head sections) with their offsets below the centreline **(see illustrations)**.

17 Using a socket and extension bar, slacken the crankshaft pulley bolt. Hold the crankshaft stationary while the bolt is unscrewed by engaging a screwdriver with the flywheel ring gear teeth through the opening at the lower

5.16a Turn the crankshaft until the special tool or dowel rod (A) enters the crankshaft setting slot (B) . . .

rear of the cylinder block. Unscrew the bolt and remove the washer and crankshaft pulley.
18 Unscrew the nuts and bolts and remove the lower timing belt cover followed by the upper cover, then collect the spacers from the mounting studs **(see illustrations)**.
19 Slacken the timing belt tensioner pulley centre retaining nut **(see illustration)**
20 Unscrew the mounting bolt and remove the timing belt idler pulley and the spacer **(see illustration)**.
21 Slip the timing belt off the sprockets and remove it **(see illustration)**. Clearance is very limited at the crankshaft sprocket and a

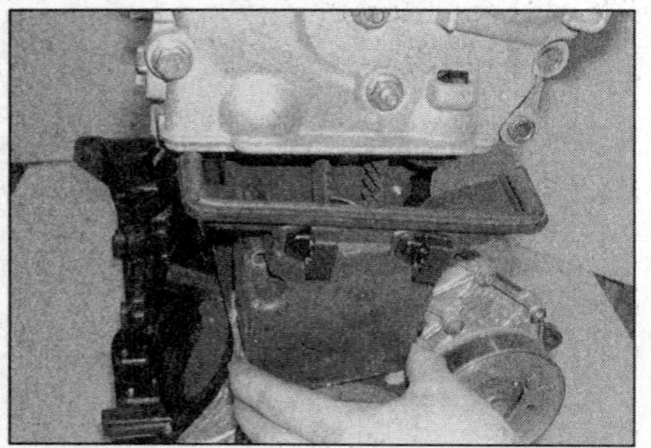
5.18a Unscrew the nuts and bolts and remove the lower timing belt cover . . .

5.18b . . . followed by the upper cover . . .

5.18c . . . then collect the spacers from the studs

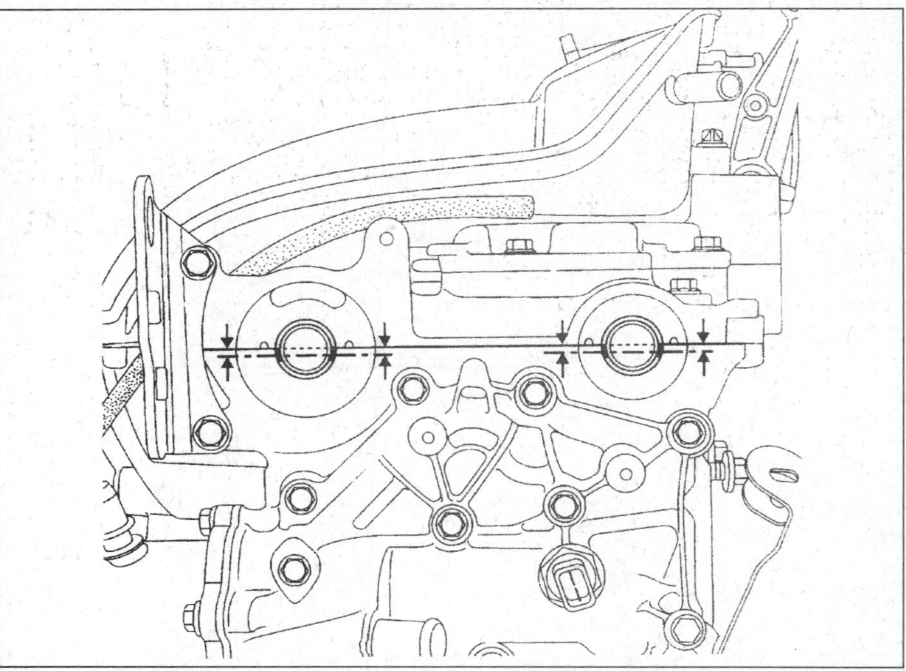
5.16b . . . and check that the slots in the ends of the camshafts are horizontal with their offsets below the centreline

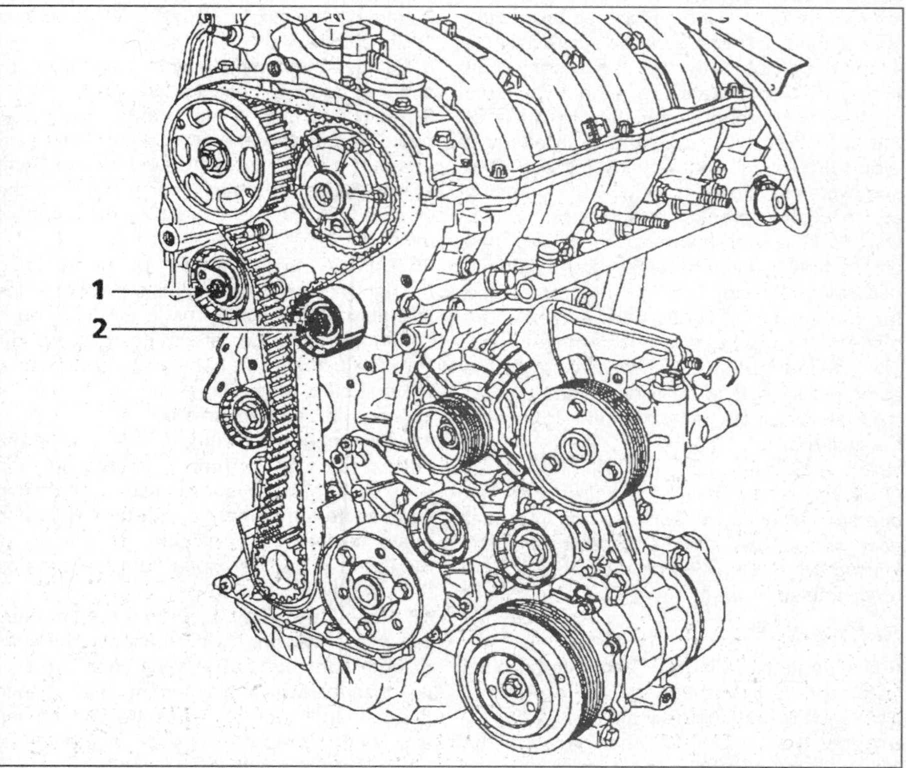

5.19 Timing belt tensioner pulley centre retaining nut (1) and idler pulley bolt (2)

5.20 Unscrew the bolt and remove the timing belt idler pulley and the spacer

5.21 Slip the timing belt off the sprockets and remove it

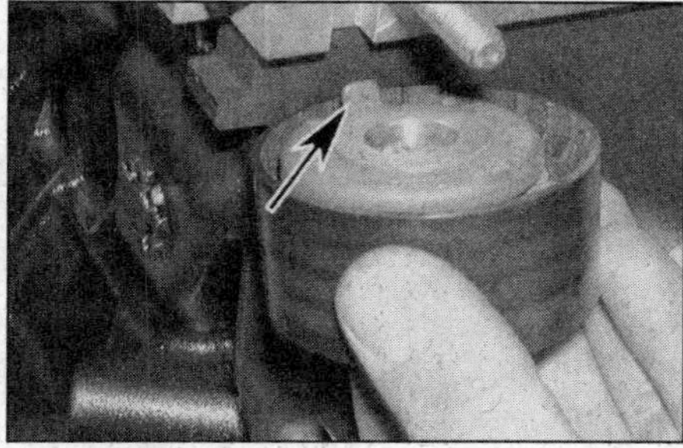
5.24 Fit the new tensioner pulley to the stud ensuring that the lug (arrowed) on the tensioner engages in the cylinder head slot

certain amount of manipulation is necessary. Do not rotate the crankshaft or camshafts with the belt removed, as there is the risk of piston-to-valve contact.

22 Obtain a new timing belt, new tensioner and idler pulleys and new camshaft sealing caps prior to refitting. If method two is being used for the refitting and tensioning procedure, new camshaft sprocket retaining nuts will also be required.

23 Measure the length of the crankshaft pulley retaining bolt, from the underside of the head to the end of the thread. The bolt must be renewed if the length exceeds 49.1 mm.

Note: *To inspect the timing belt for signs of cracking, fraying or general wear, see paragraphs 26 to 28 in Section 4.*

Refitting and tensioning

Method one

Note: *Method one should be used for refitting and tensioning the timing belt when the camshaft sprockets have not been disturbed. If either of the camshaft sprockets have been removed, or their retaining nuts slackened prior to refitting the timing belt, Method two described later in this Section should be used instead.*

24 Fit the new tensioner pulley to the mounting stud ensuring that the lug on the rear of the tensioner body engages in the slot in the cylinder head **(see illustration)**. Screw on the retaining nut, finger tight only at this stage.

25 Check that the crankshaft is still locked with the TDC pin or dowel rod. Slip the crankshaft sprocket off the end of the crankshaft and check that the keyway in the crankshaft is uppermost. Note that although there is a keyway in both the crankshaft and crankshaft sprocket, a Woodruff key is not used.

26 Using a suitable solvent, thoroughly clean the end of the crankshaft, crankshaft sprocket bore, and the crankshaft and sprocket mating faces. It is essential that all traces of oil and grease are removed from these areas to allow the sprocket to be securely clamped when the pulley and retaining bolt are refitted. If the sprocket slips in service, serious engine damage will result.

27 Check that the camshafts are still correctly positioned with the slots parallel to the join between the upper and lower cylinder head sections, with their offsets below the centreline. It may be necessary to turn the camshafts slightly using a spanner on the sprocket retaining nuts, to correctly align the slots.

28 The camshafts must now be retained in this position either by using Renault special tool Mot. 1496, or by fabricating a home-made alternative **(see Tool Tip in Section 4)**.

29 Engage the Renault special tool or the home-made alternative with the slots in the camshafts and secure the tool to the cylinder head using a suitable bolt **(see illustration)**. With the crankshaft against the TDC pin and the camshafts secured with the holding tool, refit the crankshaft sprocket to the end of the crankshaft.

30 Check that the inlet camshaft sprocket/phase-shifter is neither advanced or retarded **(see illustration)**. Locate the new timing belt over the crankshaft and camshaft sprockets, and around the tensioner pulley.

31 Fit the new idler pulley and spacer and

5.29 Engage the camshaft holding tool with the camshaft slots and secure the tool using a suitable bolt screwed into the cylinder head

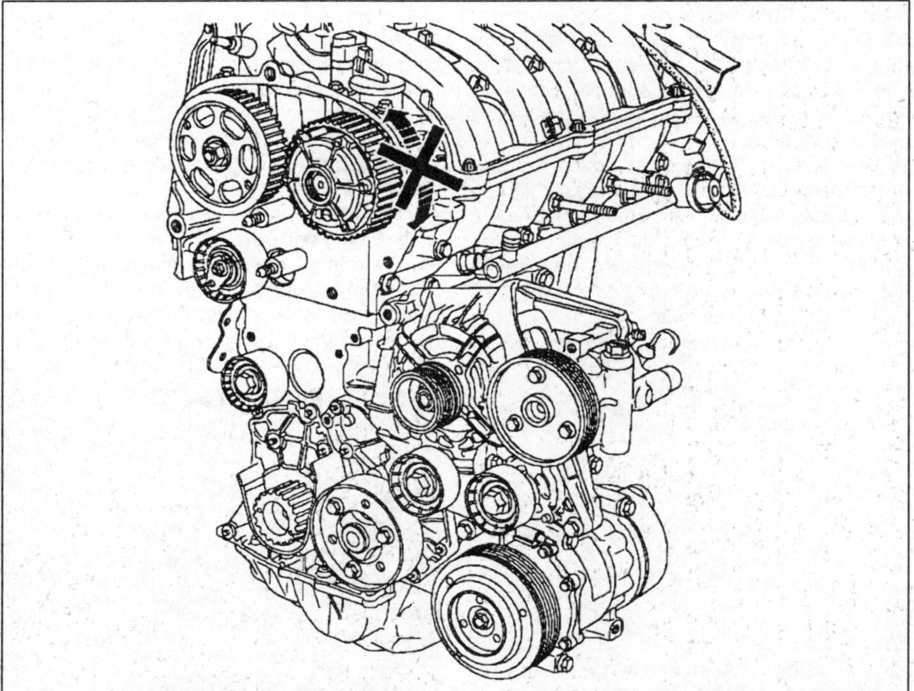
5.30 Check that the sprocket/phase-shifter is neither advanced or retarded before refitting the timing belt

5.31 Fit the new idler pulley and spacer ensuring that the spacer is fitted the correct way round

tighten the retaining bolt to the specified torque. Ensure that the spacer is fitted the correct way round **(see illustration).**

32 Refit the crankshaft pulley and the retaining bolt and washer. If the original bolt is being re-used, lightly lubricate the threads with engine oil. If a new bolt is being used it should be fitted dry. Tighten the bolt so there is approximately 2.0 to 3.0 mm clearance between the bolt and the pulley. The crankshaft sprocket must be free to turn on the crankshaft for the timing belt to be tensioned correctly.

33 Using a 6.0 mm Allen key engaged with the slot in the tensioner pulley arm; rotate the arm clockwise until the indentation on the pulley arm is aligned with the notch on the pulley body **(see illustrations).** Hold the tensioner in this position and initially tighten the retaining nut to 7 Nm (5 lbf ft).

34 Initially tighten the crankshaft pulley retaining bolt to the Stage 1 torque setting as given in the Specifications.

35 Using quick-drying paint, make alignment marks between the camshaft sprockets and cylinder head upper section to use as reference marks in the following procedure **(see illustration).**

36 Remove the TDC pin or dowel rod and the camshaft holding tool, then finally tighten the crankshaft pulley bolt through the Stage 2 angle as given in the Specifications. Lock the crankshaft using a screwdriver engaged with the flywheel ring gear to prevent crankshaft rotation as the bolt is tightened.

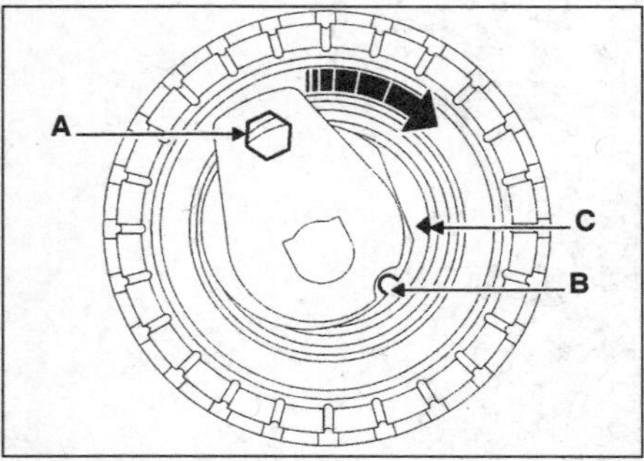

5.33a Using an Allen key in the tensioner arm slot (A) rotate the arm until the indentation (B) is aligned with the notch (C) in the pulley body

37 Turn the crankshaft clockwise through two complete revolutions, but just before completing the second revolution, ie, half a tooth before the previously made reference marks on the sprockets and cylinder head upper section align, refit the TDC pin or dowel rod. Continue turning the crankshaft until the pin or rod fully engage with the crankshaft setting slot.

38 Remove the TDC pin or dowel rod and check that the indentation on the tensioner pulley arm is still aligned with the notch on the pulley body. If not, slacken the tensioner nut and repeat the procedure in paragraphs 33 and 37. If the tensioner pulley is correctly positioned, finally tighten the retaining nut to the specified torque.

39 With the belt correctly tensioned, recheck the timing by once again turning the crankshaft clockwise through two complete revolutions, and stopping just before completing the second revolution, (just before the previously made sprocket reference marks align). Refit the TDC pin or dowel rod then continue turning the crankshaft until the pin or rod fully engages with the crankshaft setting slot.

40 Check that with the crankshaft locked with the TDC pin or dowel rod, it is possible to fit the camshaft holding tool to the slots in the camshafts without force. If the slots are not correctly positioned and the tool will not fit, repeat the complete refitting and tensioning procedure.

41 If the timing is correct, remove the TDC pin and camshaft holding tool and continue with the refitting procedure.

42 Refit new camshaft sealing caps to the left-hand end of the cylinder head and carefully tap them into place using a large socket or similar tool.

43 Apply sealing compound to the TDC pin plug then refit the plug to the cylinder block, tightening it securely.

44 Refit the timing belt upper cover followed by the lower cover and tighten the retaining nuts and bolts to the specified torque, where applicable.

45 Secure the fuel pipes with the clips on the lower timing belt cover.

46 Reconnect the wiring connectors at the idle speed stepper motor, throttle position sensor and MAP sensor, then clip the wiring harness to the upper timing belt cover.

47 Locate the right-hand engine mounting assembly into position and refit the bolts securing the mounting bracket to the cylinder head. Tighten the bolts to the specified torque. Refit the three bolts securing the rubber mounting to the body. Ensure that the movement limiter is positioned centrally over the mounting rubber then tighten the three bolts to the specified torque.

5.33b Hold the tensioner and tighten the retaining nut

48 Remove the engine hoist or lifting beam from the engine compartment.

49 Refit the auxiliary drivebelt as described in Chapter 1A, and the air cleaner components as described in Chapter 4A.

50 Refit the engine undercover and wheel arch covers then refit the right-hand roadwheel. Tighten the wheel bolts to the specified torque.

51 Lower the car to the ground and reconnect the battery.

Method two

Note: *Method two should be used for refitting and tensioning the timing belt if either of the camshaft sprockets have been removed, or their retaining nuts slackened for any reason prior to refitting the belt. If the camshaft sprockets have not been disturbed, Method one described earlier in this Section should be used instead.*

52 Check that the crankshaft is still locked with the TDC pin or dowel rod. Slip the crankshaft sprocket off the end of the crankshaft and check that the keyway in the crankshaft is uppermost. Note that although there is a keyway in both the crankshaft and crankshaft sprocket, a Woodruff key is not used.

53 Using a suitable solvent, thoroughly clean the end of the crankshaft, crankshaft sprocket bore, and the crankshaft and sprocket mating faces. Similarly clean the camshaft ends, camshaft sprocket bores and mating faces. It is essential that all traces of oil and grease are removed from these areas to allow the sprockets to be securely clamped when the pulley and retaining bolt/nuts are refitted. If the sprockets slip in service, serious engine damage will result.

54 Check that the camshafts are still correctly positioned with the slots parallel to the join between the upper and lower cylinder head sections, with their offsets below the centreline. If necessary, temporarily refit the old camshaft sprocket retaining nuts and turn the camshafts slightly, using a spanner on the

5.35 Make alignment marks between the camshaft sprockets and cylinder head upper section to use as reference marks

5.57 Position the sprockets so that the Renault logo (arrowed) is uppermost

nuts, to correctly align the slots.

55 The camshafts must now be retained in this position either by using Renault special tool Mot. 1496, or by fabricating a home-made alternative **(see Tool Tip in Section 4)**.

56 Engage the Renault special tool or the home-made alternative with the slots in the camshafts and secure the tool to the cylinder head using a suitable bolt **(see illustration 5.29)**. With the crankshaft against the TDC pin and the camshafts secured with the holding tool, refit the crankshaft sprocket to the end of the crankshaft.

57 Refit the camshaft sprockets and new retaining nuts. Tighten the nuts so there is approximately 0.5 to 1.0 mm clearance between the nuts and the sprockets, and the sprockets are free to turn. Position the sprockets so that the Renault logo stamped on one of the spokes is vertically uppermost **(see illustration)**.

58 Fit the new tensioner pulley to the mounting stud ensuring that the lug on the rear of the tensioner body engages in the slot in the cylinder head **(see illustration 5.24)**. Screw on the retaining nut, finger tight only at this stage.

59 Check that the inlet camshaft sprocket/phase-shifter is neither advanced or retarded **(see illustration 5.30)**. Locate the new timing belt over the crankshaft and camshaft sprockets, and around the tensioner pulley. Ensure that the camshaft sprockets remain correctly positioned (Renault logo uppermost) as the belt is fitted.

60 Fit the new idler pulley and spacer and tighten the retaining bolt to the specified torque. Ensure that the spacer is fitted the correct way round **(see illustration 5.31)**.

61 Refit the crankshaft pulley and the retaining bolt and washer. If the original bolt is being re-used, lightly lubricate the threads with engine oil. If a new bolt is being used it should be fitted dry. Tighten the bolt so there is approximately 2.0 to 3.0 mm clearance between the bolt and the pulley. The crankshaft and camshaft sprockets must all be free to turn for the timing belt to be tensioned correctly.

62 Using a 6.0 mm Allen key engaged with the slot in the tensioner pulley arm; rotate the arm clockwise until the indentation on the pulley arm is aligned with the notch on the pulley body **(see illustrations 5.33a and 5.33b)**. Hold the tensioner in this position and initially tighten the retaining nut to 7 Nm (5 lbf ft).

63 Turn the exhaust camshaft sprocket through six complete revolutions to initially settle and pretension the timing belt. The sprocket can be turned using a suitable forked tool engaged with the holes in the sprocket **(see Tool Tip)**. During this operation, ensure that the sprocket retaining nuts remain slack to allow the sprockets to turn freely.

64 Check that the indentation on the tensioner pulley arm is still aligned with the notch on the pulley body. If not, slacken the tensioner nut and repeat the procedure in paragraphs 62 and 63. If the tensioner pulley is correctly positioned, finally tighten the retaining nut to the specified torque.

65 Initially tighten the crankshaft pulley retaining bolt to the Stage 1 torque setting as given in the Specifications **(see illustration)**.

66 Using quick-drying paint, make alignment marks between the camshaft sprockets and cylinder head upper section to use as reference marks in the following procedure **(see illustration 5.35)**.

67 Remove the TDC pin or dowel rod and finally tighten the crankshaft pulley bolt through the Stage 2 angle as given in the Specifications **(see illustration)**. Lock the crankshaft using a screwdriver engaged with the flywheel ring gear to prevent crankshaft rotation as the bolt is tightened.

68 Turn the crankshaft clockwise through two complete revolutions, but just before completing the second revolution, ie, half a tooth before the previously made reference marks on the sprockets and cylinder head upper section align, refit the TDC pin or dowel rod. Continue turning the crankshaft until the pin or rod fully engage with the crankshaft setting slot.

69 Tighten both camshaft sprocket retaining nuts to the Stage 1 torque setting, then through the Stage 2 angle as given in the Specifications. The forked tool described in Section 4 can be used to hold the sprockets as the nuts are tightened **(see illustrations)**.

TOOL TiP

To make a camshaft sprocket holding tool, obtain two lengths of steel strip about 6 mm thick by 30 mm wide or similar, one 600 mm long, the other 200 mm long (all dimensions approximate). Bolt the two strips together to form a forked end, leaving the bolt slack so that the shorter strip can pivot freely. At the end of each 'prong' of the fork, drill a suitable hole and fit a nut and bolt to engage with the holes in the sprocket.

5.65 Initially tighten the crankshaft pulley retaining bolt to the Stage 1 torque setting

5.67 Finally tighten the pulley bolt through the Stage 2 angle

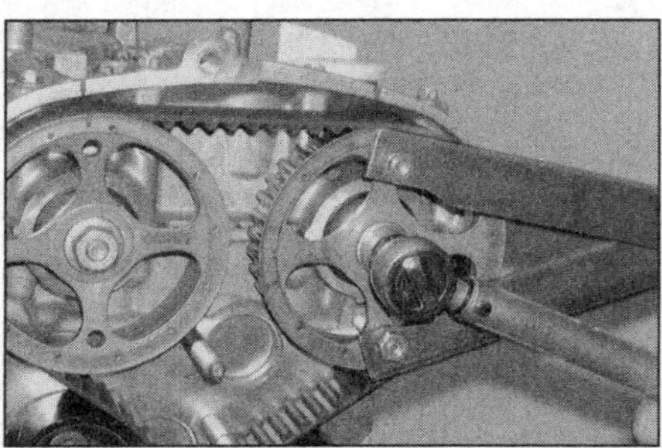

5.69a Tighten both camshaft sprocket retaining nuts to the Stage 1 torque setting . . .

5.69b . . . then through the stage 2 angle

5.71 Hold the tensioner arm and tighten the retaining nut to the specified torque

70 Remove the TDC pin or dowel rod and the camshaft holding tool. Turn the crankshaft clockwise through two complete revolutions, but just before completing the second revolution, ie, half a tooth before the previously made reference marks on the sprockets and cylinder head upper section align, refit the TDC pin or dowel rod. Continue turning the crankshaft until the pin or rod fully engage with the crankshaft setting slot.

71 Remove the TDC pin or dowel rod and check that the indentation on the tensioner pulley arm is still aligned with the notch on the pulley body. If not, slacken the tensioner nut and realign the indentation and notch as described in paragraph 62. Tighten the tensioner nut to the specified torque, then turn the crankshaft through a further two revolutions and recheck the setting **(see illustration)**.

72 With the belt correctly tensioned, recheck the timing by once again turning the crankshaft clockwise through two complete revolutions, and stopping just before completing the second revolution (just before the previously made sprocket reference marks align). Refit the TDC pin or dowel rod, then continue turning the crankshaft until the pin or rod fully engages with the crankshaft setting slot.

73 Check that with the crankshaft locked with the TDC pin or dowel rod, it is possible to fit the camshaft holding tool to the slots in the camshafts without force. If the slots are not correctly positioned and the tool will not fit, repeat the complete refitting and tensioning procedure.

74 If the timing is correct, remove the TDC pin and camshaft holding tool and continue with the refitting procedure.

75 Refit new camshaft sealing caps to the left-hand end of the cylinder head and carefully tap them into place using a large socket or similar tool.

76 Apply sealing compound to the TDC pin plug then refit the plug to the cylinder block, tightening it securely.

77 Refit the timing belt upper cover followed by the lower cover and tighten the retaining nuts and bolts to the specified torque, where applicable.

78 Secure the fuel pipes with the clips on the lower timing belt cover.

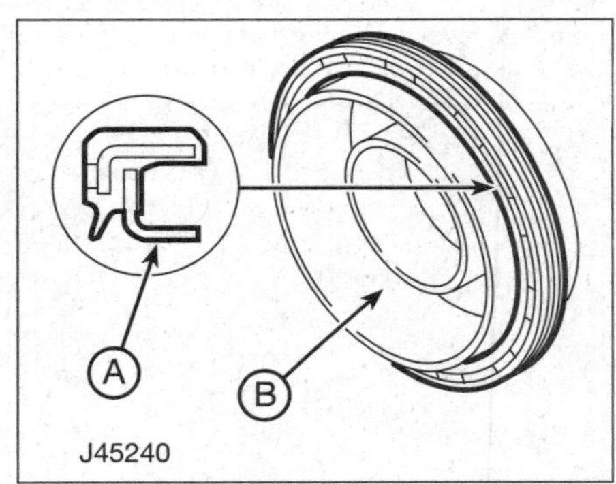

6.0a Camshaft oil seal version 1

A Internal spring
B V-shaped sealing lip

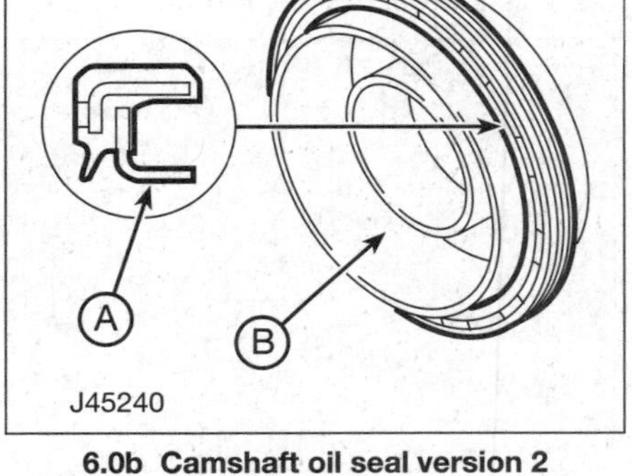

6.0b Camshaft oil seal version 2

A Flat sealing lip
B Fitting protector

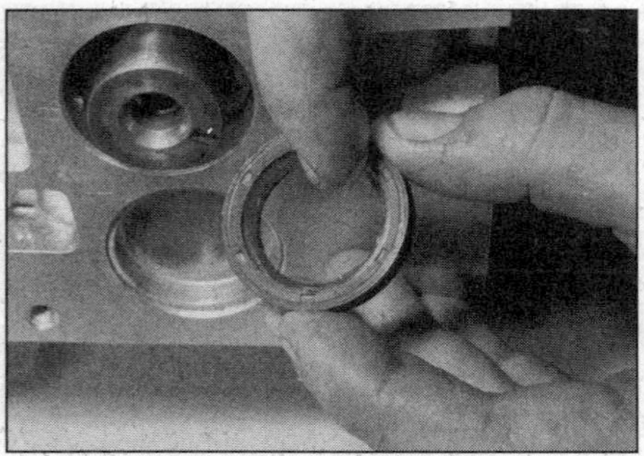

6.4 Smear a small amount of clean oil to the oil seal

6.5 Using a socket to carefully tap the seal into place

79 Reconnect the wiring connectors at the idle speed stepper motor, throttle position sensor and MAP sensor, then clip the wiring harness to the upper timing belt cover.

80 Locate the right-hand engine mounting assembly into position and refit the bolts securing the mounting bracket to the cylinder head. Tighten the bolts to the specified torque. Refit the three bolts securing the rubber mounting to the body. Ensure that the movement limiter is positioned centrally over the mounting rubber then tighten the three bolts to the specified torque.

81 Remove the engine hoist or lifting beam from the engine compartment.

82 Refit the auxiliary drivebelt as described in Chapter 1A, and the air cleaner components as described in Chapter 4A.

83 Refit the engine undercover and wheel arch covers then refit the right-hand roadwheel. Tighten the wheel bolts to the specified torque.

84 Lower the car to the ground and reconnect the battery.

6 Camshaft oil seals – renewal

Note: *There are two versions of camshaft oil seal fitted* ***(see illustrations)****; version 1 has an internal spring and V-shaped sealing lip, version 2 has a flat sealing lip without an internal spring. Version 2 is extremely fragile, and must only be handled by the protector/guide supplied with it. The oil seals are not interchangeable and the fitting procedure for each is different, as described in the following paragraphs.*

1 Remove the camshaft sprocket as described in Section 5.

2 Note the fitted depth of the old oil seal. Using a small screwdriver, prise out the oil seal from the cylinder head taking care not to damage the sealing surface on the camshaft. Alternatively, the oil seal can be removed by drilling two small holes diagonally opposite each other and inserting self-tapping screws in them. A pair of grips can then be used to pull out the oil seals, by pulling on each side in turn.

3 Inspect the seal rubbing surface on the camshaft. If it is grooved or rough in the area where the old seal was fitted, the new seal should be fitted slightly less deeply, so that it rubs on an unworn part of the surface.

Version 1 oil seal

4 Wipe clean the oil seal seating, then smear a little oil on the outer perimeter and sealing lip of the new oil seal **(see illustration)**.

5 Locate the seal squarely in the cylinder head, then drive it into position using a metal tube or socket which has an external diameter slightly less than that of the bore in the cylinder head **(see illustration)**. Alternatively, the oil seal can be pressed into position using a metal tube, washer and nut.

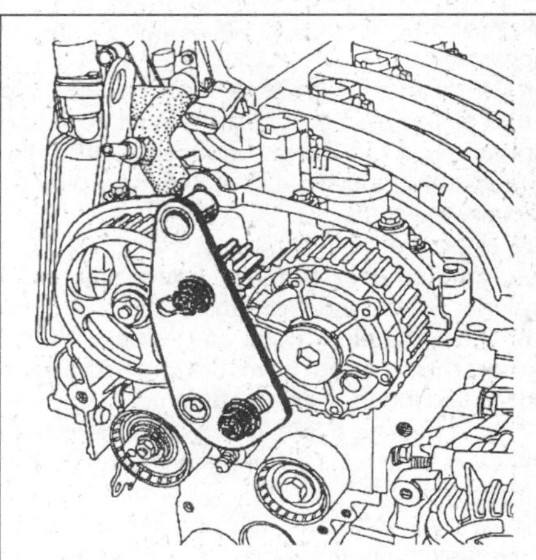

7.5a Renault tool for holding the camshaft sprockets in place

Version 2 oil seal

6 Renault technicians use a special tool (Mot. 1632) to fit the oil seal. The tool consists of a threaded rod, metal tube and nut, and a machined shoulder to locate the protector/guide on. The rod is screwed into the end of the camshaft, and the protector/guide located on the shoulder. The metal tube is then fitted against the oil seal, and the nut tightened to press the seal into the cylinder head/bearing cap. If the Renault tool cannot be obtained, a similar tool can be made out of a threaded rod, metal tube, washer and nut.

7 Wipe clean the oil seal seating, then press the oil seal squarely into position. Note that the Renault tool is designed to locate the seal at the original depth, however, if the camshaft sealing surface is excessively worn, position it less deeply so that it locates on the unworn surface.

8 After fitting the oil seal, remove the protector/guide and tool.

All types

9 Wipe away any excess oil, then refit the camshaft sprocket as described in Section 5.

7 Camshafts, tappets and rocker arms – removal, inspection and refitting

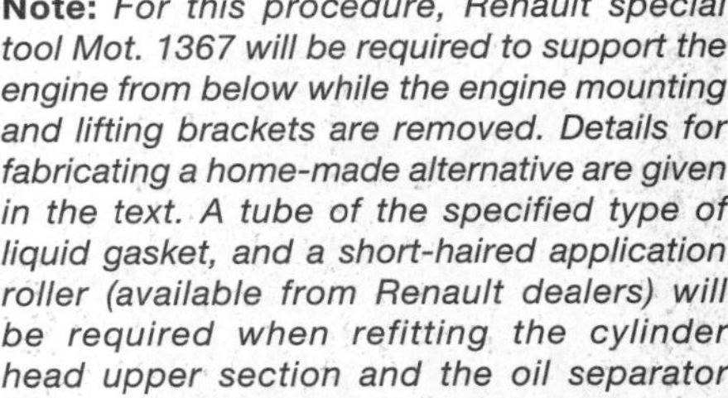

Note: *For this procedure, Renault special tool Mot. 1367 will be required to support the engine from below while the engine mounting and lifting brackets are removed. Details for fabricating a home-made alternative are given in the text. A tube of the specified type of liquid gasket, and a short-haired application roller (available from Renault dealers) will be required when refitting the cylinder head upper section and the oil separator housing. New gaskets, seals and O-rings will also be required for refitting certain other components.*

Note: *The manufacturer recommends that the timing belt should be renewed whenever it is*

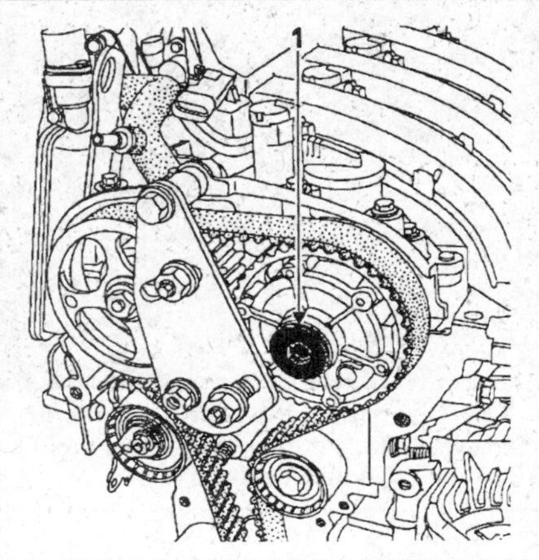

7.5b Remove plug (1) on the inlet camshaft sprocket/phase-shifter

removed, and that the timing belt tensioner and idler pulley should be renewed at the same time.

Removal

1 Disconnect the battery negative terminal (refer to *Disconnecting the battery* in the Reference Section of this manual).

2 Drain the cooling system as described in Chapter 1A.

3 Remove the timing belt as described in Section 4 or Section 5, as applicable.

4 Mark the inlet and exhaust camshaft sprockets for identification when refitting. On all engines, the inlet sprocket is nearest the front of the car.

5 Restrain the camshaft sprockets with a suitable forked tool, which will engage with the sprocket holes **(see Tool Tip in Section 5)**, or alternatively use the Renault special tool. Using a 14 mm hexagon key, unscrew and remove the plug from the inlet camshaft sprocket/phase-shifter **(see illustrations).** Undo the retaining nut from the exhaust camshaft sprocket and the bolt from the inlet camshaft sprocket/phase-shifter, and then remove both sprockets from the camshafts. Note that new sprocket retaining nuts will be required for refitting.

6 The engine must now be supported from below so that the engine hoist or lifting beam used for timing belt removal can be removed for access to the top of the engine. If possible, obtain Renault special tool Mot. 1367, or fabricate a home-made alternative out of square-section steel tube **(see Tool Tip)**.

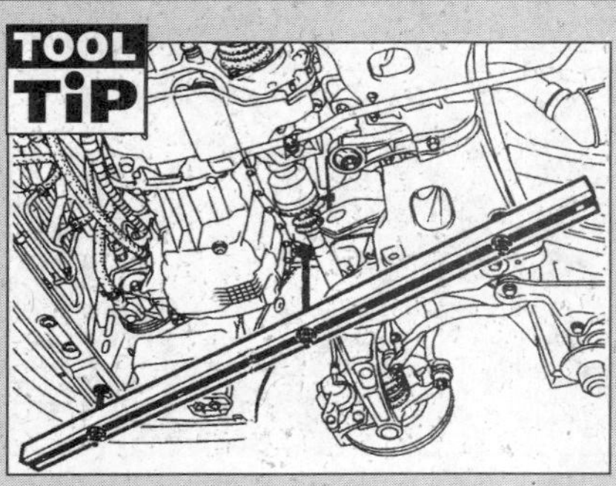

To make an engine support tool, obtain a suitable length of square section steel tube. Drill the tube at both ends so that it can be bolted to the crossmember below the radiator at the front, and to the suspension crossmember at the rear, using suitable nuts, bolts and spacers. Drill a third hole to allow a length of threaded rod to be attached using nuts and washers. The position of the hole should be directly below a suitable location on the engine to allow the upper end of the threaded bar to be attached, either directly with nuts and washers, or by means of a small bracket.

7 Disconnect the wiring connector from the throttle housing.

8 Detach the power steering fluid reservoir from its mounting and move it to one side without disconnecting the fluid hoses.

9 Disconnect the wiring connector at the inlet air temperature sensor on the front of the inlet manifold, and the wiring connectors at each of the four ignition coils **(see illustration)**. Release the ignition coil wiring from the clips on the inlet manifold upper section and move the wiring clear.

10 Undo the nuts securing the fuel injector and fuel rail protective cover at the front of the inlet manifold. Release the wiring harness from the cable clips and remove the cover **(see illustrations)**.

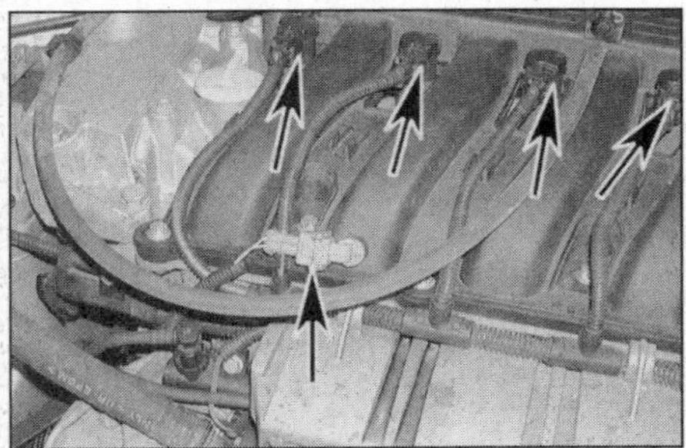

7.9 Disconnect the wiring connectors at the inlet air temperature sensor and at each of the four ignition coils (arrowed)

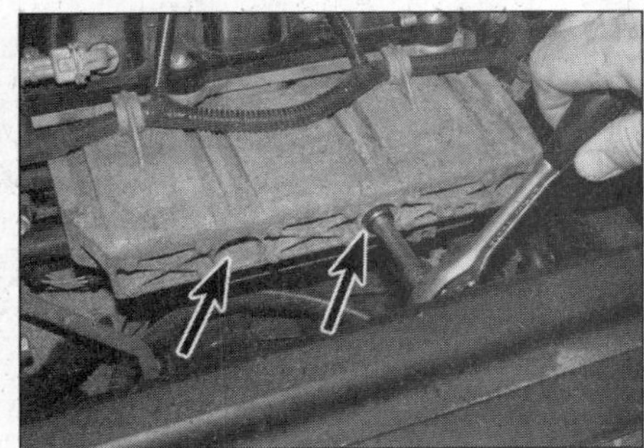

7.10a Undo the two nuts (arrowed) . . .

7.10b . . and remove the protective cover at the front of the inlet manifold

7.12 Disconnect the wiring connector (arrowed) from the variable valve timing control solenoid

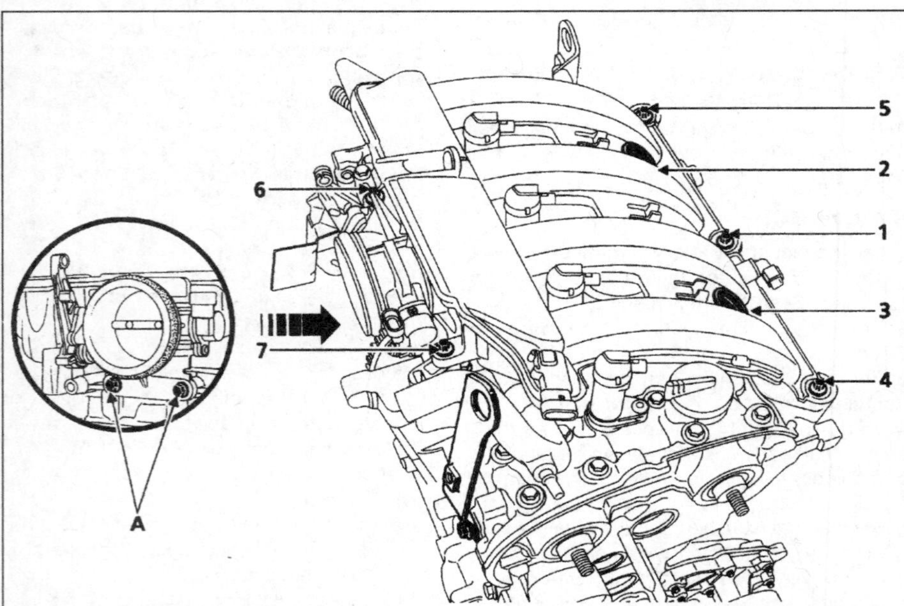

7.13 Inlet manifold upper section and throttle housing attachments

1 to 7 Inlet manifold upper section retaining bolts (numbers also indicate bolt tightening sequence when refitting)
A Throttle housing retaining bolts

11 Undo the bolts and remove the engine lifting brackets from the right-hand and left-hand ends of the cylinder head.

12 Disconnect the brake servo vacuum hose from the inlet manifold upper section. Also disconnect the wiring from the variable valve timing control solenoid valve on the upper section. If necessary, the solenoid valve can be unbolted, and the oil seal removed **(see illustration).**

13 Undo the two bolts at the base of the throttle housing and remove the housing from the inlet manifold upper section **(see illustration)**. Recover the gasket or O-ring as applicable.

14 Undo the five bolts at the front and two bolts at the rear securing the inlet manifold upper section to the lower section and to the oil separator housing. Lift off the manifold and recover the seals.

15 Undo the mounting bolts, and remove the four ignition coils from the spark plugs and cylinder head upper section.

16 Undo the eight bolts and remove the oil separator housing from the cylinder head upper section **(see illustration).**

17 In a progressive sequence, slacken then remove all the bolts securing the cylinder head upper section.

18 Using a soft-faced mallet and a protected screwdriver, gently tap and prise the cylinder head upper section upwards off the lower section **(see illustration).** Note that parting lugs are provided to allow the upper section to be struck or prised against without damage. Do not insert the screwdriver or similar tool into the joint between the two sections as a means of separation. The upper section will be quite tight as it is located on several dowels.

19 Once the upper section is free, lift it squarely from the cylinder head. The camshafts will rise up slightly under the pressure of the valve springs – be careful they don't tilt and jam in either section.

20 Mark the camshafts, inlet and exhaust and lift them out complete with the front oil seals. Be careful of the lobes, which may have sharp edges.

21 Remove the oil seals from the camshafts, noting their fitted positions. Obtain new seals for reassembly.

22 Have ready two suitable boxes divided into sixteen segments each, or some containers or other means of storing and identifying the rocker arms and hydraulic tappets after removal. The box or containers for the hydraulic tappets must be oil tight and deep enough to allow the tappets to be almost totally submerged in oil. Mark the segments in the boxes or the containers with the number for each rocker arm and tappet (ie, 1 to 8 inlet and 1 to 8 exhaust).

23 Lift out the rocker arms and place them in their respective positions in the box or containers **(see illustration).**

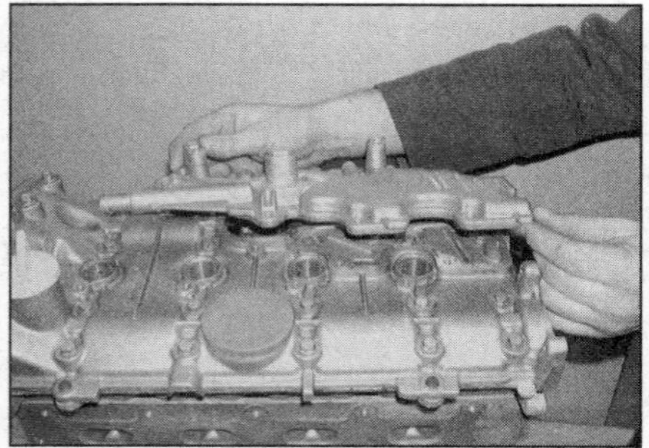

7.16 Undo the eight bolts and remove the oil separator housing

7.18 Gently tap and prise the cylinder head upper section upwards off the lower section

7.23 Lift out the rocker arms and place them in a marked box or containers

7.24 Similarly lift out the tappets and place them upright in a marked box or containers filled with oil

7.36a Refit the camshafts in the cylinder head lower section, with the inlet camshaft at the front of the engine

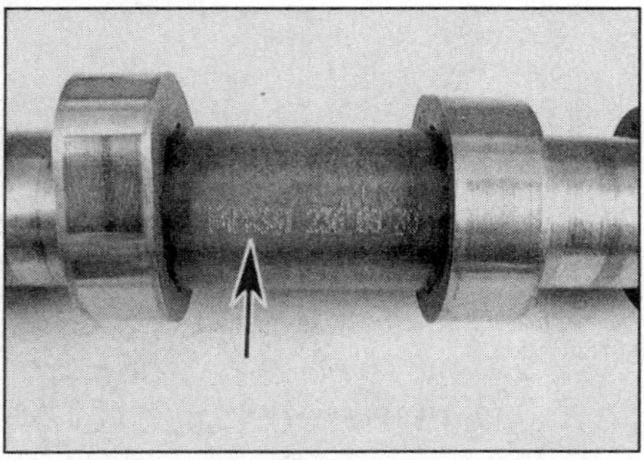

7.36b Camshaft identification code marking A (arrowed). 1.8 litre engine inlet camshaft shown

24 Similarly lift out the tappets and place them upright in their respective positions in the box or containers **(see illustration)**. Once all the tappets have been removed, add clean engine oil to the box or container so that the tappet is submerged.

Inspection

25 Inspect the cam lobes and the camshaft bearing journals for scoring or other visible evidence of wear. Once the surface hardening of the cam lobes has been eroded, wear will occur at an accelerated rate. **Note:** *If these symptoms are visible on the tips of the camshaft lobes, check the corresponding rocker arm, as it will probably be worn as well.*

26 If the camshafts appear satisfactory, measure the bearing journal diameters and compare the figures obtained with those given in the Specifications. If the diameters are not as specified, consult a Renault dealer or engine overhaul specialist. Wear of the camshaft bearings will almost certainly be accompanied by similar wear of the bearings in the cylinder head, which will entail renewal of the cylinder head upper and lower sections together with the camshafts.

27 Inspect the rocker arms and tappets for scuffing, cracking or other damage and renew any components as necessary. Also check the condition of the tappet bores in the cylinder head. As with the camshafts, any wear in this area will necessitate cylinder head renewal.

Refitting

28 Thoroughly clean the sealant from the mating surfaces of the upper and lower cylinder head sections. Use a suitable liquid gasket-dissolving agent (available from Renault dealers) together with a soft putty knife; do not use a metal scraper or the faces will be damaged. As there is no conventional gasket used, the cleanliness of the mating faces is of the utmost importance.

29 Clean off any oil, dirt or grease from both components and dry with a clean lint-free cloth. Ensure that all the oilways are completely clean.

30 To prevent any possibility of the valves contacting the pistons when the camshafts are refitted, remove the TDC pin or dowel rod used to lock the crankshaft, and turn the crankshaft clockwise a quarter turn.

31 Liberally lubricate the tappet bores in the cylinder head lower section with clean engine oil.

32 Prior to refitting each tappet, remove it from its container, place it on the bench the correct way up and press down on the top of the tappet (the stop piston) with your thumb. If it is possible to depress the stop piston then the tappet must be primed by inserting it in a container of diesel fuel before refitting.

33 Insert the tappets into their original bores in the cylinder head lower section unless they have been renewed.

34 Lubricate the rocker arms and place them over their respective tappets and valve stems.

35 Lubricate the camshaft journals in the cylinder head lower section sparingly with oil, taking care not to allow the oil to spill over onto the upper and lower section contact areas.

36 Lay the camshafts in their correct locations in the lower section, remembering that the inlet camshaft must be at the front of the engine. If new camshafts are being fitted, or if the identification marks made during removal have been lost, the camshafts can be identified by referring to the markings located between two of the cam lobes. The markings consist of a series of manufacturer's numbers and letters together with a code to identify the camshaft. On 1.6 litre engines, the two letters at the end of the series denote the camshaft code – AM for inlet camshaft and EM for exhaust camshaft. On 1.8 and 2.0 litre engines, the camshaft code is the fourth digit in the series – A for inlet camshaft and E for exhaust camshaft **(see illustrations)**.

7.37 Position the camshafts so that the slots are horizontal, with the offset below the centreline

37 Turn the camshafts so that the slot in the end of each camshaft is horizontal (ie, parallel to the join between the upper and lower cylinder head sections) with the offset below the centreline **(see illustration)**.

38 Ensure that the mating faces of both cylinder head sections are clean and free of any oil or grease.

39 Using the short-haired roller, apply an even coating of Loctite 518 liquid gasket solution to the mating face of the cylinder head upper section only **(see illustration)**. Ensure that the whole surface is coated to a reddish colour, but take care to keep the solution out of the oilways.

40 With the camshafts correctly positioned, lay the upper section in place on the lower section.

41 Insert all the upper section retaining bolts and progressively tighten them just sufficiently to pull the upper section down into contact with the lower section.

42 The upper section retaining bolts must now be tightened in four stages in the order given in the Specifications **(see illustration)**. First tighten the four bolts indicated in the Specifications in the correct sequence to the setting given (Stage 1). Tighten the remaining bolts in the correct sequence to the setting given (Stage 2). Slacken the original four bolts completely (Stage 3), then finally tighten the original four bolts in the correct sequence to the setting given (Stage 4).

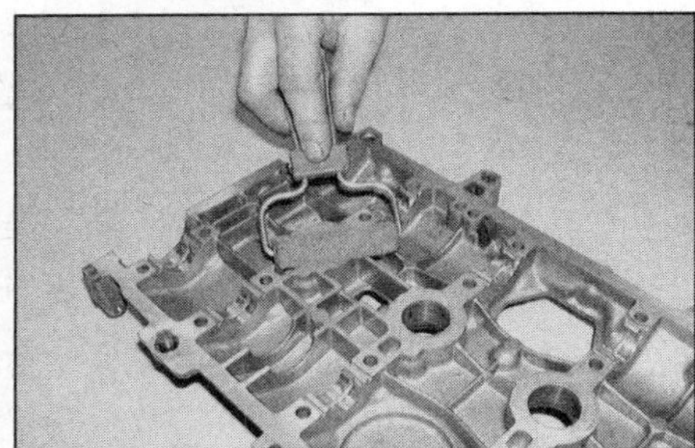

7.39 Apply an even coating of Loctite 518 gasket solution to the mating face of the cylinder head upper section

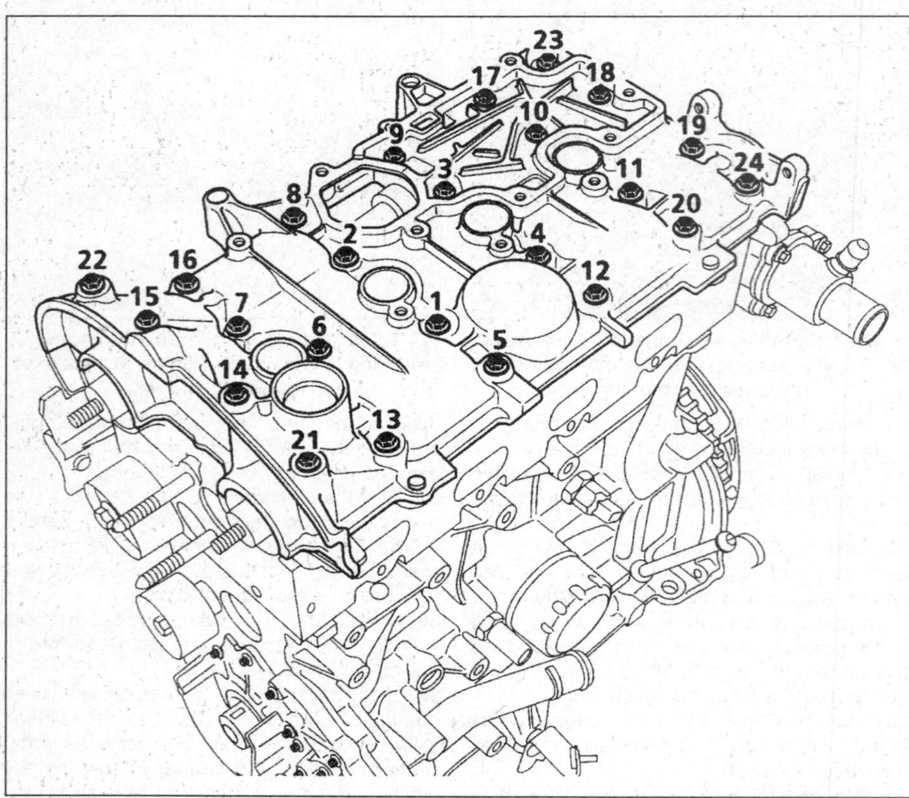

7.42 Cylinder head upper section retaining bolt identification

43 Ensure that the mating faces of oil separator housing and cylinder head upper section are clean and free of any oil or grease.
44 Using the short-haired roller, apply an even coating of Loctite 518 liquid gasket solution to the mating face of the oil separator housing until it is reddish in colour **(see illustration)**.
45 Refit the oil separator housing to the cylinder head upper section. Insert the retaining bolts and tighten them to the specified torque in the sequence shown **(see illustration)**.
46 Lubricate the lips of the two new camshaft oil seals. Fit each seal the correct way round over the camshaft, and tap it home with a large socket or piece of tube until its outer face is flush with the housing; refer to the information in Section 6 for guidance.

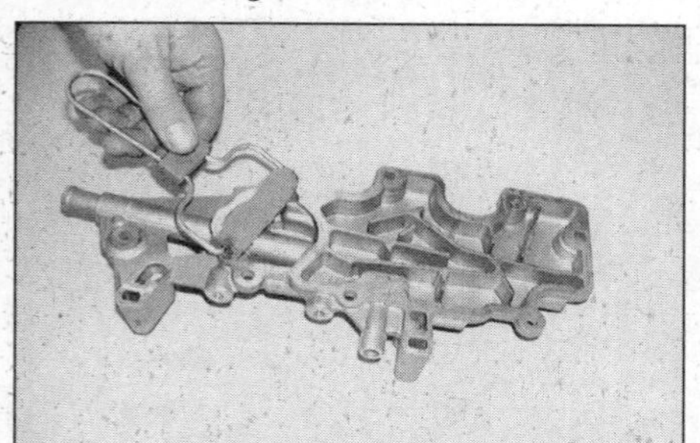
7.44 Apply an even coating of Loctite 518 gasket solution to the mating face of the oil separator housing

47 Refit the four ignition coils to the spark plugs and cylinder head upper section and secure with the retaining bolts tightened securely. Where removed, fit a new oil seal for the variable valve timing control solenoid valve, using a suitable socket and hammer to drive the new seal into position. Refit the solenoid valve and tighten the retaining bolt.
48 Using new seals refit the inlet manifold upper section to the lower section and secure with the seven retaining bolts. Tighten the bolts to the specified torque (see Chapter 4A) in the sequence shown **(see illustration 7.13)**.
49 Using a new gasket or O-ring as applicable, refit the throttle housing to the inlet manifold and secure with the two bolts tightened to the specified torque (see Chapter 4A).

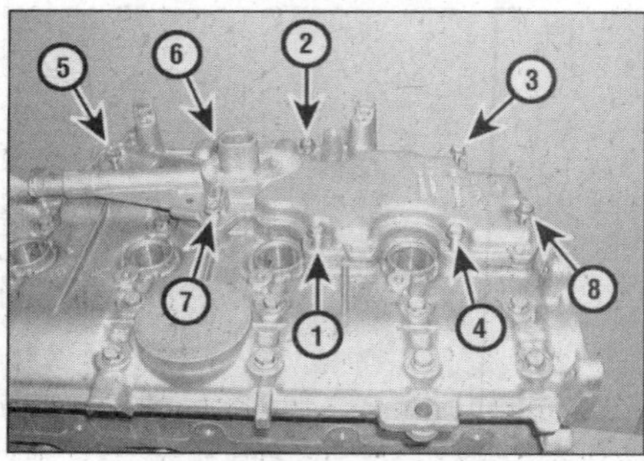

7.45 Oil separator housing retaining bolt tightening sequence

50 Reconnect the brake servo vacuum hose to the inlet manifold.
51 Refit the engine lifting brackets to the right-hand and left-hand ends of the cylinder head. The engine can now be re-attached to the engine hoist or lifting beam allowing the support tool to be removed from below. Alternatively, the tool can be left in position until after the timing belt is refitted.
52 Reconnect the wiring to the four ignition coils and the inlet air temperature sensor on the front of the inlet manifold. Secure the wiring harness with the clips provided on the manifold.
53 Refit the fuel injector and fuel rail protective cover to the front of the inlet manifold, and secure the wiring harness with the cable clips.
54 Refit the power steering fluid reservoir to its mounting.
55 Disconnect the wiring connector to the throttle housing.
56 Turn the crankshaft back a quarter of a turn to the TDC position then, referring to the information given in Section 3, lock the crankshaft with the TDC pin.
57 Refit the timing belt as described in Section 4 or Section 5, as applicable.
58 On completion, refill the cooling system as described in Chapter 1A.

8 Cylinder head – removal and refitting

Removal

1 Remove the camshafts tappets and rocker arms as described in Section 7.
2 Remove the inlet and exhaust manifolds as described in Chapter 4A.
3 Disconnect the radiator top hose, the heater hoses and expansion tank hose from the thermostat housing on the left-hand end of the cylinder head.
4 Disconnect the wiring connector at the coolant temperature sensor on the side of the thermostat housing.
5 Undo the retaining bolts and release the wiring harness support bracket from the left-hand end of the cylinder head.
6 Working in the **reverse** of the sequence shown in **illustration 8.21b**, progressively slacken the cylinder head bolts by half a turn at a time until all the bolts can be unscrewed by hand and removed.
7 Lift the cylinder head upwards and off the cylinder block. If it is stuck, tap it upwards using a hammer and block of wood. Do not try to turn it (it is located by two dowels), nor attempt to prise it free using a screwdriver inserted between the block and head faces. If the locating dowels are a loose fit, remove them and store them with the head for safe-keeping.
8 Remove the cylinder head gasket from the cylinder block.
9 If the cylinder head is to be dismantled for overhaul, refer to Part D of this Chapter.

8.17 Locate a new cylinder head gasket on the cylinder block . . .

8.18 . . . and carefully lower the cylinder head into position

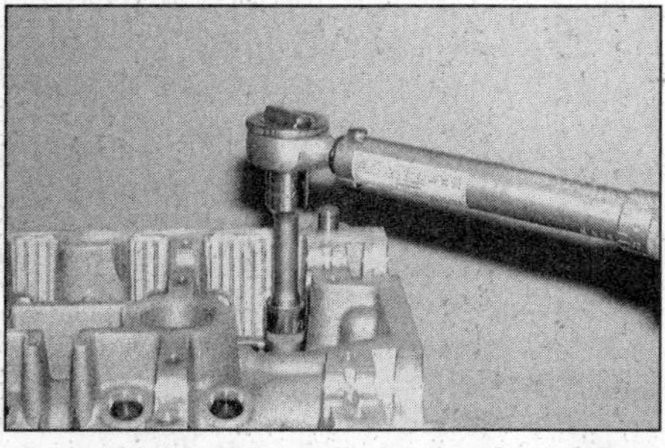

8.21a Tighten the cylinder head retaining bolts to the Stage 1 torque setting using a torque wrench

Preparation for refitting

10 The mating faces of the cylinder head and cylinder block must be perfectly clean before refitting the head. Use a soft putty knife to remove all traces of gasket and carbon; also clean the piston crowns. Take particular care during the cleaning operations, as aluminium alloy is easily damaged. Also, make sure that the carbon is not allowed to enter the oil and water passages – this is particularly important for the lubrication system, as carbon could block the oil supply to the engine's components. Using adhesive tape and paper, seal the water, oil and bolt holes in the cylinder block. To prevent carbon entering the gap between the pistons and bores, smear a little grease in the gap. After cleaning each piston, use a small brush to remove all traces of grease and carbon from the gap, and then wipe away the remainder with a clean rag. Clean all the pistons in the same way.

11 Check the mating surfaces of the cylinder block and the cylinder head for nicks, deep scratches and other damage. If slight, they may be removed carefully with a file, but if excessive, machining may be the only alternative to renewal.

12 If warpage of the cylinder head gasket surface is suspected, use a straight-edge to check it for distortion. Refer to the overhaul information given in Part D of this Chapter if necessary.

13 Examine the cylinder head bolt threads in the cylinder block for damage. If necessary, use the correct-size tap to chase out the threads in the block. Ensure that the bolt holes are clean and free of oil. Syringe or soak up any oil left in the bolt holes. This is most important in order that the correct bolt tightening torque can be applied and to prevent the possibility of the block being cracked by hydraulic pressure when the bolts are tightened.

14 Check the condition of the cylinder head bolts, and particularly their threads, whenever they are removed. Wash the bolts in a suitable solvent, and wipe them dry. Check each bolt for any sign of visible wear or damage, renewing them if necessary.

15 If the bolt condition is satisfactory, measure the length of each bolt from the underside of the head to the end of the thread. If the length of any bolt exceeds 117.7 mm (2.0 litre engines: 118.5 mm), all the bolts must be renewed.

Refitting

16 Ensure that the mating faces of the cylinder block and head are spotlessly clean, that the retaining bolt threads are also clean and dry, and that they screw easily in and out of their locations.

17 Ensure that the locating dowels are correctly fitted to the block and fit a new cylinder head gasket, making sure it is the right way up **(see illustration)**.

18 Carefully lower the cylinder head onto the block, engaging it over the dowels **(see illustration)**.

19 If new cylinder head bolts are being used, they should be fitted dry. If the original bolts are being re-used, lightly oil them, both on their threads and under their heads and allow any excess oil to drain off.

20 Fit the bolts and screw them in until they just contact the cylinder head.

21 Working progressively and in sequence, tighten the cylinder head bolts to their Stage 1 torque setting, using a torque wrench and suitable socket **(see illustrations)**.

22 Once all the bolts have been tightened to their Stage 1 setting, working again in the given sequence, angle-tighten the bolts through the specified Stage 2 angle, using a socket and extension bar. It is recommended

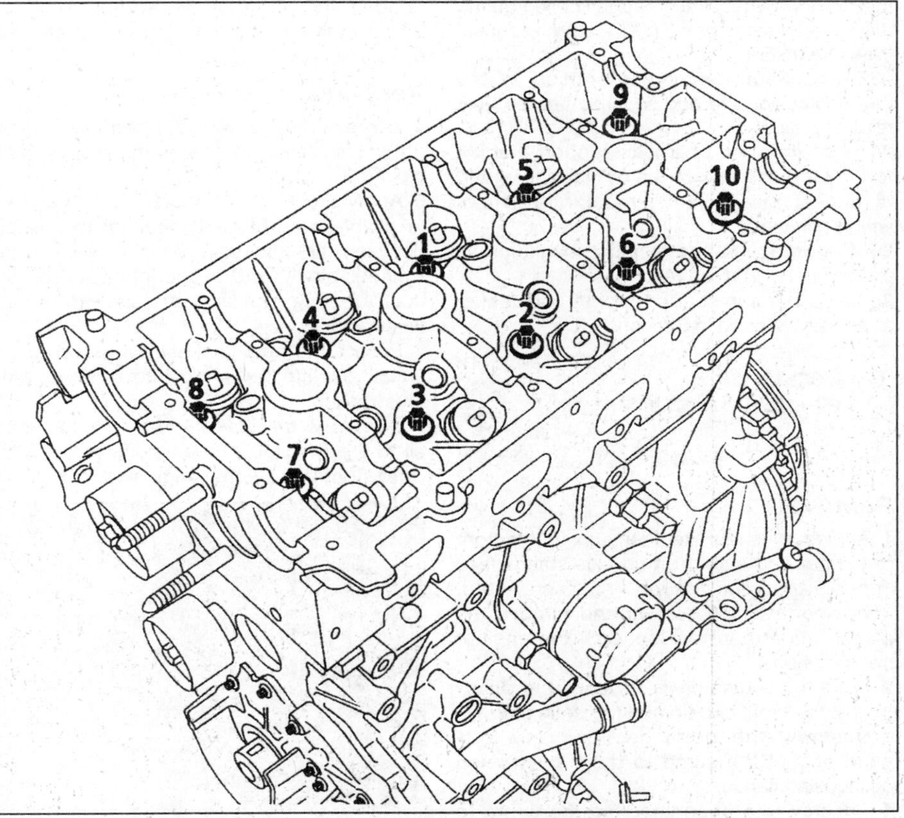

8.21b Cylinder head retaining bolt tightening sequence

8.22 Using an angle tightening gauge to tighten the cylinder head retaining bolts through the Stage 2 angle

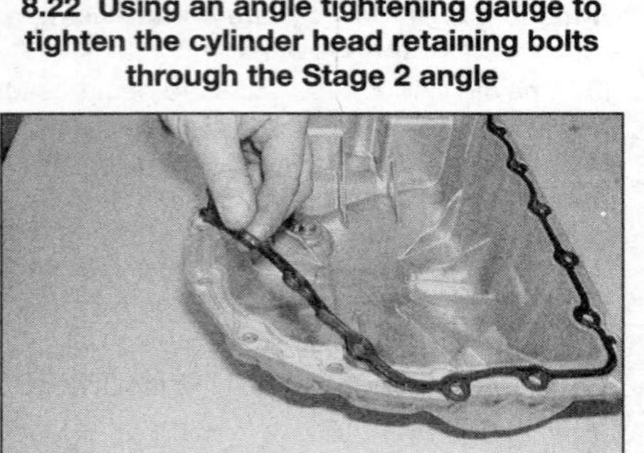

9.7 Locate the new gasket on the top of the sump and lift the sump into position

that an angle-measuring gauge is used during this stage of the tightening, to ensure accuracy **(see illustration)**.

23 Reconnect the coolant hoses to the thermostat housing and securely tighten their retaining clips.

24 Refit the wiring harness support bracket to the left-hand end of the cylinder head and reconnect the coolant temperature sensor wiring connector.

25 Refit the inlet and exhaust manifolds as described in Chapter 4A.

26 Refit the camshafts tappets and rocker arms as described in Section 7.

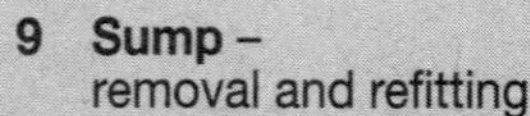

9 Sump – removal and refitting

Removal

1 Apply the handbrake, then jack up the front of the car and support it on axle stands (see *Jacking and vehicle support*). Where fitted, undo the retaining screws and remove the plastic undertray from beneath the engine/transmission.

2 Drain the engine oil as described in Chapter 1A, then refit and tighten the drain plug.

3 Unscrew the bolts securing the left-hand end of the sump to the transmission bellhousing flange.

4 Unscrew the bolts securing the sump to the cylinder block. Tap the sump with a hide or plastic mallet to break the seal, and then remove the sump along with its gasket. Discard the gasket; a new one must be used on refitting.

9.6a Apply a bead of sealant to the join between the crankshaft oil seal housing and cylinder block . . .

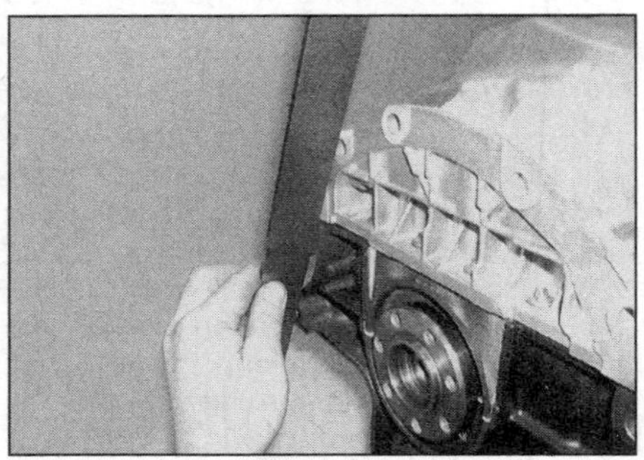

9.8 Use a straight-edge to maintain the alignment between the left-hand end of the sump and cylinder block

Refitting

5 Remove all traces of dirt and oil from the mating surfaces of the sump and cylinder block.

6 Apply a bead of Rhodorseal 5661 sealant (available from Renault dealers) to the join between the crankshaft oil seal housing and cylinder block, and to the join between the main bearing cap and cylinder block **(see illustrations)**.

7 Locate the new gasket on the top of the sump and lift the sump into position **(see illustration)**.

8 Insert the bolts and initially tighten them all to the Stage 1 torque setting given in the Specifications. If the engine is in the car, ensure that the left-hand end of the sump is in contact with the transmission bellhousing flange. If the engine is removed from the car, use a straight-edge to maintain the alignment between the left-hand end of the sump and cylinder block **(see illustration)**.

9 Progressively tighten the bolts to the Stage 2 torque setting in an anti-clockwise spiral pattern starting at the centre and working outwards.

10 Refit the undercover and lower the vehicle to the ground.

11 Fill the engine with fresh oil (it may be useful to renew the oil filter at this stage), with reference to Chapter 1A.

10.2 Unscrew the anti-emulsion plate retaining bolt(s)

9.6b . . . and to the join between the main bearing cap and cylinder block

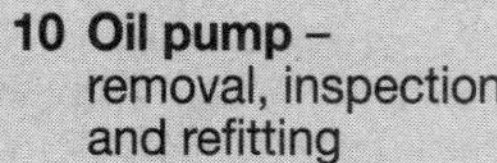

10 Oil pump – removal, inspection and refitting

Removal

1 To remove the oil pump alone, first remove the sump as described in Section 9.

2 Unscrew the oil pump mounting bolts and the additional bolt(s) securing the baffle plate to the crankcase **(see illustration)**.

3 Withdraw the oil pump slightly and remove the baffle plate. Tilt the pump to disengage its sprocket from the drive chain and lift away the pump **(see illustrations)**. If the locating dowels are displaced, refit them in their locations.

4 To remove the pump complete with its drive chain and sprockets, first remove the sump

10.3a Remove the anti-emulsion plate . . .

10.3b . . . then tilt the pump to disengage its sprocket from the drive chain

10.6 Slide the drive sprocket together with the chain from the crankshaft

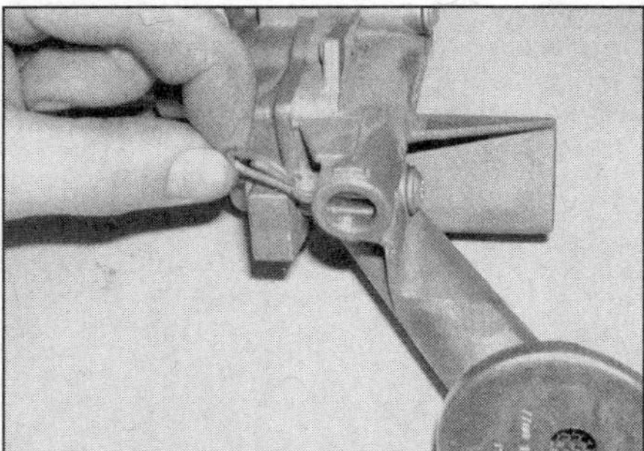
10.7a Extract the oil pressure relief valve retaining clip . . .

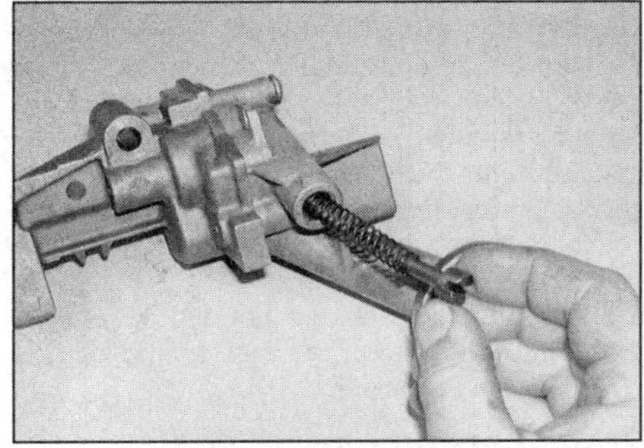
10.7b . . . remove the oil pressure relief valve spring retainer and spring . . .

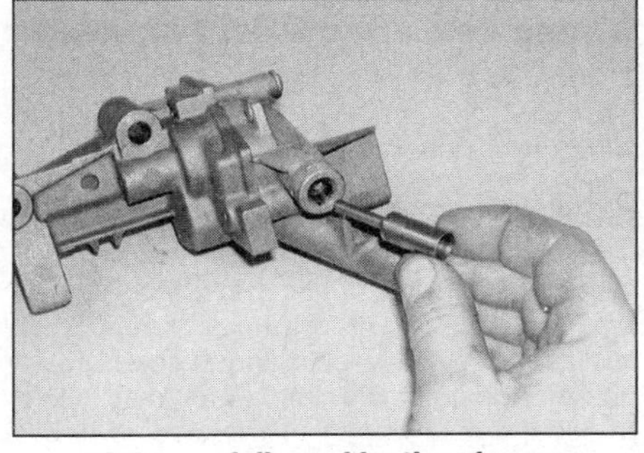
10.7c . . . followed by the plunger

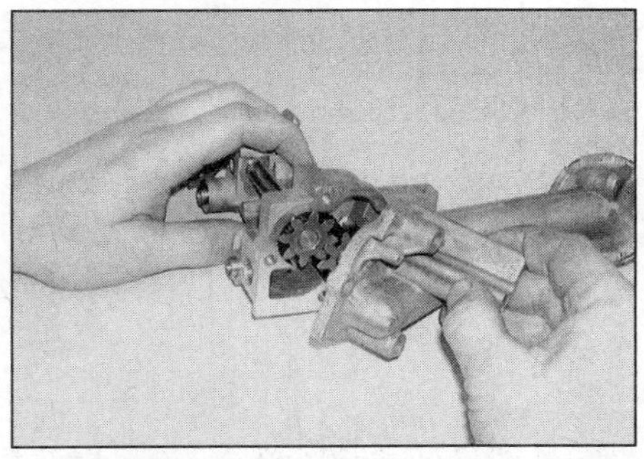
10.8 Unscrew the retaining bolts, and lift off the oil pump cover

as described in Section 9, then remove the crankshaft timing belt end oil seal housing as described in Section 11.

5 Remove the oil pump as described in paragraphs 1 and 2 above.

6 Slide the drive sprocket together with the chain from the crankshaft **(see illustration)**. Note that the drive sprocket is not keyed to the crankshaft, but relies on the pulley bolt being tightened correctly to clamp the sprocket.

Inspection

7 Extract the retaining clip, and remove the oil pressure relief valve spring retainer, spring and plunger **(see illustrations)**.

8 Unscrew the retaining bolts, and lift off the pump cover **(see illustration)**.

9 Carefully examine the gears, pump body and relief valve plunger for any signs of scoring or wear. Renew the pump complete if excessive wear is evident.

10 If the components appear serviceable, measure the clearance between the pump body and the gears using feeler blades. Also measure the gear endfloat, and check the flatness of the end cover **(see illustrations)**. If the clearances exceed the specified tolerances, the pump must be renewed.

11 If the pump is satisfactory, reassemble the components in the reverse order of removal. Fill the pump with oil, then refit the cover and tighten the bolts securely **(see illustration)**.

Refitting

12 Wipe clean the oil pump and cylinder block mating surfaces.

13 Locate the drive sprocket onto the end of the crankshaft, ensuring that it is fitted with the projecting boss facing away from the crankshaft **(see illustration)**. Engage the chain with the sprocket and push the sprocket fully home.

14 Check that the locating dowels are in place either on the pump or on the cylinder block, and then engage the oil pump sprocket with the drive chain. Engage the pump with the dowels, fit the two retaining bolts and tighten them to the specified torque.

10.10a Using feeler blades, measure the clearance between the pump body and the gears . . .

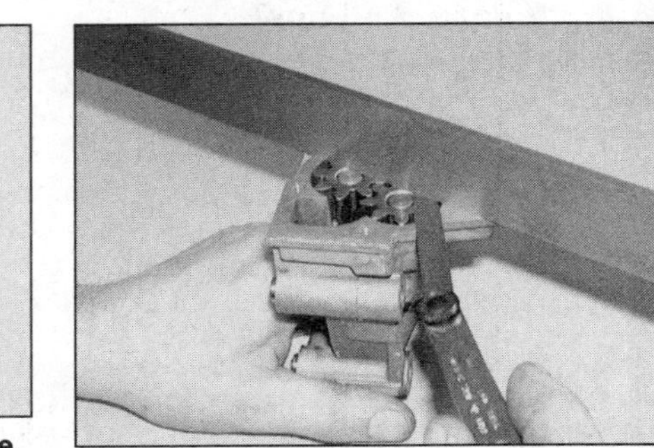
10.10b . . . and measure the gear endfloat

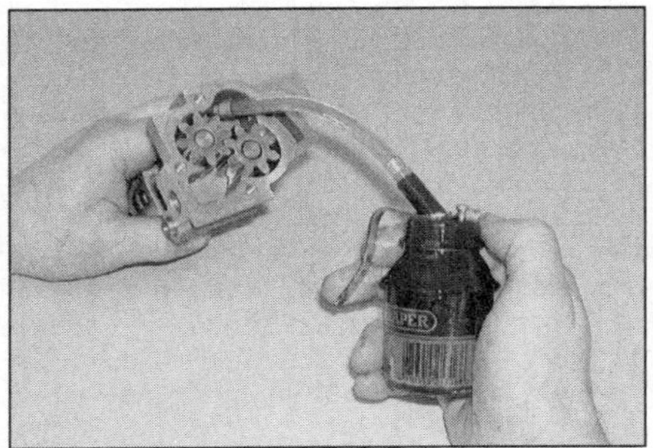
10.11 Fill the pump with oil, then refit the cover

10.13 Ensure that the oil pump drive sprocket is fitted with the projecting boss facing away from the crankshaft

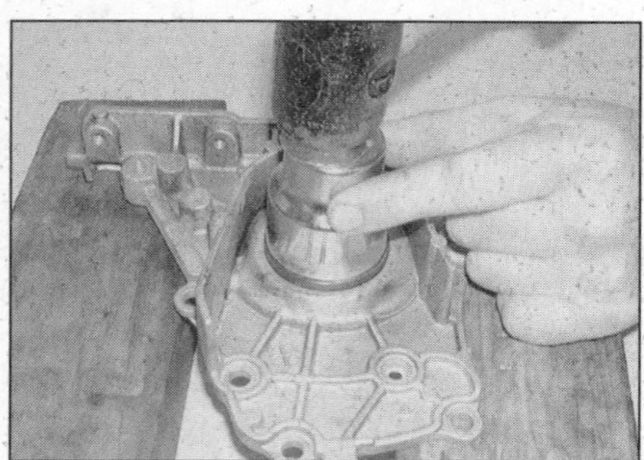

11.12 Use a suitable socket or metal tube to drive the new crankshaft oil seal into the housing

11.19a Lightly coat the oil seal housing mating surface with sealant . . .

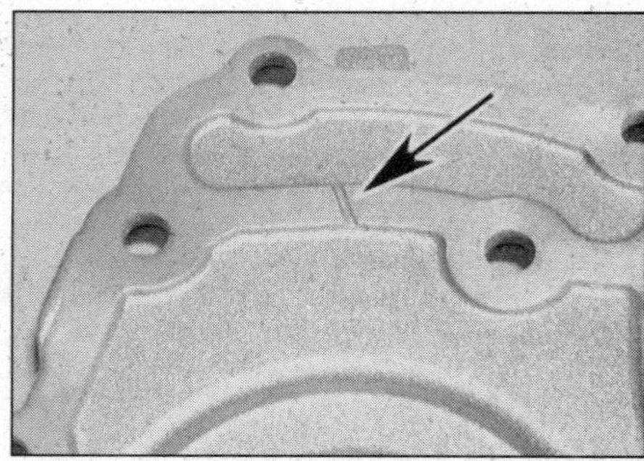

11.19b . . . taking care not to allow the sealant to block the small oil channel (arrowed) at the top of the housing

15 Refit the baffle plate and secure with the retaining bolts.
16 Refit the oil seal housing as described in Section 11.
17 Refit the sump as described in Section 9.

11 Crankshaft oil seals – renewal

Note: *There are two types of seals that may be used on these engines, they are not interchangeable and should only be renewed with the same type.*
a) Early type, which has a spring inside the V-shaped lip of the seal.
b) Later type, which has a flat sealing lip with no spring and comes with a plastic protector, which is also a fitting sleeve.

Timing belt end oil seal

1 Remove the timing belt as described in Section 4 or Section 5, as applicable, then withdraw the sprocket from the end of the crankshaft.
2 Make a note of the correct fitted depth of the seal then punch or drill two small holes opposite each other in the oil seal. Screw a self-tapping screw into each and pull on the screws with pliers to extract the seal.
3 Clean the seal housing and polish off any burrs or raised edges, which may have caused the seal to fail in the first place.
4 Lubricate the lips of the new seal with clean engine oil and ease it into position on the end of the shaft. Press the seal into its housing until it is positioned at the same depth as the original was prior to removal.
5 If necessary, a suitable tubular drift, such as a socket, which bears only on the hard outer edge of the seal, can be used to tap the seal into position. Take great care not to damage the seal lips during fitting and ensure that the seal lips face inwards. Note that if the surface of the shaft was noted to be badly scored, press the new seal slightly further into its housing so that its lip is running on an unmarked area of the shaft.
6 Refit and tension the new timing belt as described in Section 4 or Section 5, as applicable.

Timing belt end oil seal housing

7 Remove the timing belt as described in Section 4 or Section 5, as applicable, then withdraw the sprocket from the end of the crankshaft.
8 Remove the sump as described in Section 9.
9 Unscrew the retaining bolts and withdraw the oil seal housing, noting the locating dowels around its two lower bolt holes. If it is stuck in place, a leverage point is provided on the upper edge (near the timing belt idler pulley) to allow a screwdriver to be used to gently prise the housing free.
10 Note the presence of the oil pump drive chain guide block and of its two locating dowels, Check that the guide block is fit for further use and renew it if there is any doubt about its condition.
11 The oil seal should be renewed whenever the housing is removed. Note the fitted position of the old seal then prise it out with a screwdriver and wipe clean the seating.
12 Lubricate the outer surface of the new seal then locate it squarely on the housing with its closed side facing outwards. Place the housing on blocks of wood, then use a suitable socket or metal tube to drive in the oil seal **(see illustration)**.
13 Clean all traces of sealant from the housing and cylinder block mating faces. Check that the chain guide block is correctly fitted and that the housing locating dowels are in place. Refit the housing as described in the following sub-Sections according to engine type.

1.6 litre engines

14 Apply a 0.6 to 1.0 mm diameter bead of Loctite 518 sealant to the housing mating surface ensuring that the sealant is applied around the inner edges of the bolt holes.
15 Lubricate the lips of the oil seal then locate the housing on the cylinder block.
16 Refit the housing retaining bolts and progressively tighten them in a diagonal sequence to the specified torque.
17 Refit the sump as described in Section 9.
18 Refit and tension the new timing belt as described in Section 4.

1.8 and 2.0 litre engines

19 Lightly coat the housing mating surface with Rhodorseal 5661 sealant (available from Renault dealers). Do not allow the sealant to block the small oil channel at the top of the housing **(see illustrations)**.
20 Lubricate the lips of the oil seal then locate the housing on the cylinder block. Refit the retaining bolts and tighten them progressively to the specified torque.
21 Refit the sump as described in Section 9.
22 Refit and tension the new timing belt as described in Section 5.

Transmission end oil seal

23 Remove the flywheel/driveplate as described in Section 12.
24 Prise out the old oil seal using a small screwdriver, taking care not to damage the surface of the crankshaft. Alternatively, the oil seal can be removed as described in paragraph 2.
25 Inspect the seal-rubbing surface on the crankshaft. If it is grooved or rough in the area where the old seal was fitted, the new seal should be fitted slightly less deeply, so that it rubs on an unworn part of the surface.
26 Wipe clean the oil seal seating, then dip the new seal in fresh engine oil. Locate it over the crankshaft; making sure its sealing lip is facing inwards. Make sure that the oil seal lip is not damaged, as it is located on the crankshaft.
27 Using a metal tube, drive the oil seal squarely into the bore until flush. A block of wood cut to pass over the end of the crankshaft may be used instead.
28 Refit the flywheel/driveplate with reference to Section 12.

12 Flywheel/driveplate – removal, inspection and refitting

Note: *On some models, it may be necessary to completely remove the engine and transmission assembly. New flywheel/driveplate retaining bolts will be required on refitting.*

Removal

1 Remove the transmission as described in Chapter 7A (manual) or 7B (automatic).

2 On manual transmissions, remove the clutch assembly as described in Chapter 6.

3 Prevent the flywheel/driveplate from turning by locking the ring gear teeth with a screwdriver. Alternatively a home-made tool **(see illustration)** can be used. Make alignment marks between the flywheel/driveplate and crankshaft using paint or a suitable marker pen, for refitting.

4 Slacken and remove the flywheel/driveplate retaining bolts and remove the flywheel/driveplate; be careful, as it is very heavy. If the locating dowel (where fitted) is a loose fit in the crankshaft end, remove and store it with the flywheel/driveplate for safe-keeping. Discard the bolts as they should be renewed whenever they are disturbed.

Inspection

5 Examine the flywheel/driveplate for scoring or cracking of the clutch face, and for wear or chipping of the ring gear teeth.

6 If the clutch face is scored, the flywheel may be surface-ground, but renewal is preferable. Seek the advice of a Renault dealer or engine-reconditioning specialist to see if machining is possible.

7 If the ring gear is worn or damaged, it may be possible to renew it separately. This job is best left to an engine specialist; the temperature to which the new ring gear must be heated for installation is critical, if not done accurately the hardness of the teeth will be destroyed.

8 Check the flywheel/driveplate carefully for distortion, and for hairline cracks around the bolt holes, or radiating outwards from the centre. If damage of this sort is found, it must be renewed.

Refitting

9 Clean the mating surfaces of the flywheel/driveplate and crankshaft.

10 Ensure that the locating dowel is in position (where fitted) and offer up the flywheel/driveplate, locating it on the dowel. If the original flywheel/driveplate is being refitted, align the marks made prior to removal.

11 Fit the new retaining bolts, using thread-locking compound. Lock the flywheel using the method employed on dismantling, and tighten the retaining bolts in a diagonal sequence to the specified torque.

12.3 Use a fabricated tool to lock the flywheel ring gear and stop the crankshaft from turning

12 Refit the clutch as described in Chapter 6.

13 Remove the locking tool, and refit the transmission as described in Chapter 7A (manual) or 7B (automatic).

13 Engine mountings – inspection and renewal

Inspection

1 If improved access is required, apply the handbrake, then jack up the front of the car and support it on axle stands (see *Jacking and vehicle support*).

2 Check the mounting rubber to see if it is cracked, hardened or separated from the metal at any point; renew the mounting if any such damage or deterioration is evident.

3 Check that all the mounting's fasteners are securely tightened; use a torque wrench to check if possible.

4 Using a large screwdriver or a crowbar, check for wear in the mounting by carefully levering against it to check for free play. Where this is not possible, enlist the aid of an assistant to move the engine/transmission back-and-forth, or from side-to-side, while you watch the mounting. While some free play is to be expected, even from new components, excessive wear should be obvious. If excessive free play is found, check first that the fasteners are correctly secured, and then renew any worn components as described below.

Renewal

Right-hand mounting

5 Disconnect the battery negative terminal (refer to *Disconnecting the battery* in the Reference Section of this manual).

6 Place a jack beneath the engine, with a block of wood on the jack head (remove the undercover to improve access to the sump). Raise the jack until it is supporting the weight of the engine. Alternately, attach an engine support bar to the lifting brackets and support the weight of the engine with the bar.

7 Where fitted, undo the two retaining bolts and withdraw the acoustic mass unit (metal weight) from the engine mounting assembly.

8 Slacken the two mounting bolts for the tie-rod at the rear of the mounting, remove the front bolt to the engine mounting and swivel the tie-rod to one side **(see illustration)**.

9 Undo the nut securing the rubber mounting to the engine mounting bracket.

10 Slacken and remove the three bolts securing the engine mounting bracket to the cylinder head, and withdraw it from the engine. Where applicable, release any cables or wiring from the top of the engine mounting bracket **(see illustration)**.

11 Unscrew the three retaining bolts and remove the rubber mounting/movement limiter from the body **(see illustration)**.

12 Check carefully for signs of wear or damage on all components, and renew them where necessary.

13 On reassembly, fit the rubber mounting and movement limiter to the body, insert the retaining bolts but tighten them finger tight only at this stage.

14 Refit the upper part of the bracket to the cylinder head, locating it on the stud for the rubber mounting. Tighten the mounting bolts to the cylinder head to the specified torque.

15 Refit the nut securing the rubber mounting to the engine mounting bracket and tighten it to the specified torque.

16 Centralise the rubber mounting/movement limiter, and then tighten the three bolts to the specified torque.

17 Swivel the tie-rod at the rear of the mounting bracket back into place and refit the front bolt to the engine mounting, tighten the bolts to the specified torque.

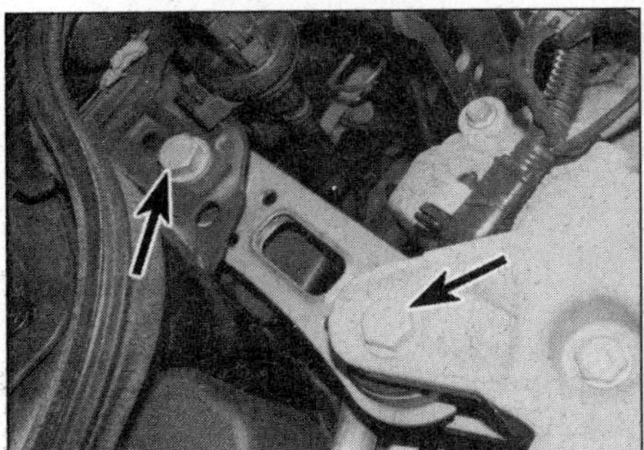

13.8 Slacken the mounting bolts (arrowed)

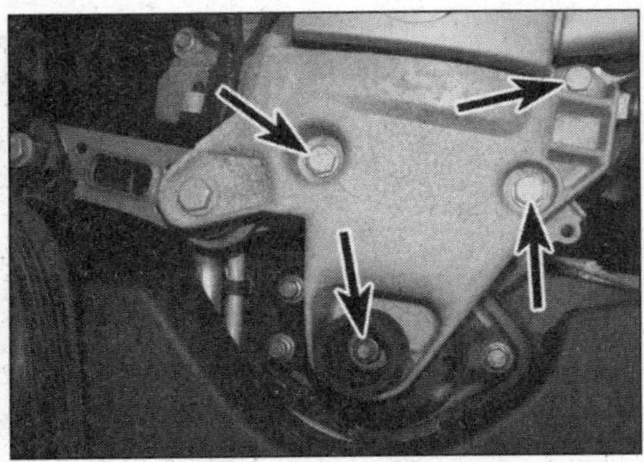

13.9 Remove the mounting bolts and retaining nut (arrowed)

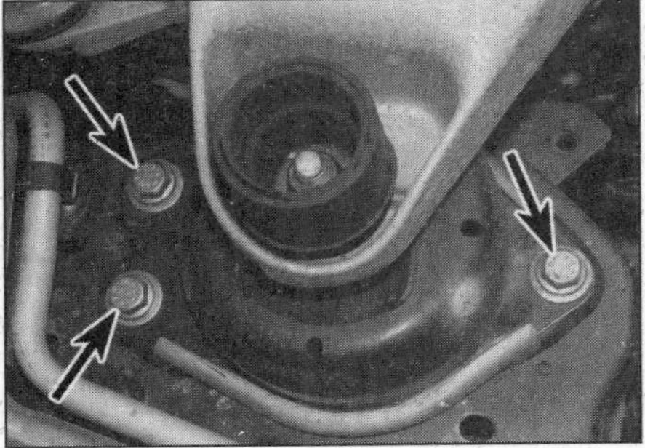

13.11 Undo the three mounting bolts (arrowed)

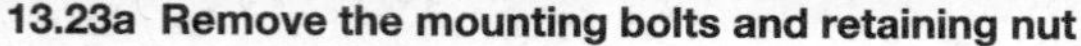
13.23a Remove the mounting bolts and retaining nut

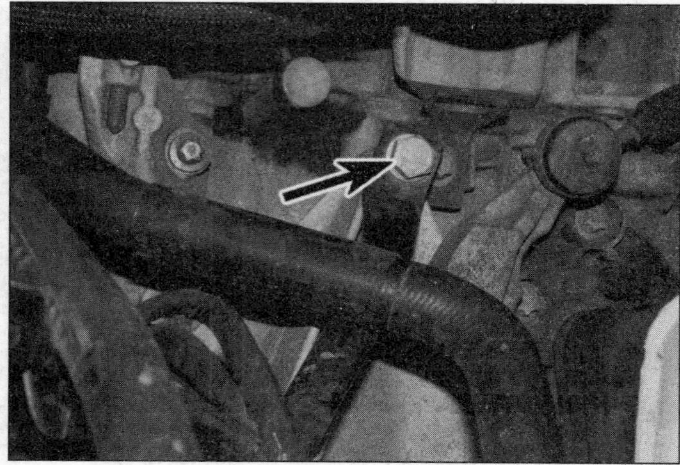
13.23b Undo the stabiliser mounting bolt from the transmission

18 Where applicable, refit the acoustic mass unit (metal weight) to the engine mounting assembly and tighten the retaining bolts to the specified torque.

19 Remove the jack from underneath the engine or the engine support bar (as applicable), and reconnect the battery negative terminal.

Left-hand mounting

20 Disconnect the battery negative terminal (refer to *Disconnecting the battery* in the Reference Section of this manual).

21 Refer to Chapter 4A and remove the air cleaner and inlet components as necessary for access to the mounting.

22 Place a jack beneath the transmission, with a block of wood on the jack head. Raise the jack until it is supporting the weight of the transmission.

23 Slacken and remove the mounting rubber's centre nut, and two retaining bolts and remove the mounting from the engine compartment. Where applicable, undo the mounting bolt and remove the stabiliser bar from the transmission **(see illustrations).**

24 If necessary, undo the retaining bolts and remove the mounting bracket from the top of the transmission housing.

25 Check carefully for signs of wear or damage on all components, and renew them where necessary.

26 Refit the bracket to the transmission, tightening its mounting bolts to the specified torque.

27 Fit the mounting rubber to the bracket and tighten its retaining bolts and centre nut to the specified torque.

28 Refit the air cleaner and inlet components removed for access.

29 Remove the jack from underneath the transmission and reconnect the battery negative terminal.

Rear mounting

30 Disconnect the battery negative terminal (refer to *Disconnecting the battery* in the Reference Section of this manual).

31 If not already done, apply the handbrake, then jack up the front of the car and support it on axle stands (see *Jacking and vehicle support*).

32 Position a jack with a block of wood on its head underneath the sump. Raise the jack until it is supporting the weight of the engine.

33 Slacken and remove the nut and bolt from each end of the mounting link and remove the link from underneath the vehicle. If necessary, undo the retaining nuts and bolts and remove the mounting bracket from the engine/ transmission.

34 Check carefully for signs of wear or damage on all components, and renew them where necessary.

35 On reassembly, fit the mounting bracket (where removed) to the rear of the transmission and tighten its retaining bolts to the specified torque.

36 Fit the mounting link, and tighten both its bolts to their specified torque settings.

37 Lower the vehicle to the ground and reconnect the battery negative terminal.

Chapter 2 Part B:
1.9 litre diesel engine in-car repair procedures

Contents

Degrees of difficulty

Easy, suitable for novice with little experience 

Fairly easy, suitable for beginner with some experience

Fairly difficult, suitable for competent DIY mechanic

Difficult, suitable for experienced DIY mechanic 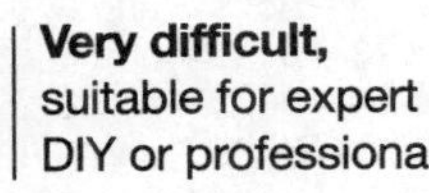

Very difficult, suitable for expert DIY or professional 

Specifications

General

Type	Four-cylinder, in-line, 8-valve single overhead camshaft, direct common-rail injection
Designation	F9Q 750, 751, 752 and 754
Bore	80.0 mm
Stroke	93.0 mm
Capacity	1870 cc
Compression ratio	19:1
Firing order	1-3-4-2 (No 1 cylinder at flywheel/driveplate end of engine)
Direction of crankshaft rotation	Clockwise, viewed from timing belt end

Valve clearances (engine cold)

Inlet	0.15 to 0.25 mm
Exhaust	0.35 to 0.45 mm

Timing belt tension value

Auxiliary belt driven coolant pump:	
Fitting value	68 ± 3 Hz
Minimum operating value	61 ± 5 Hz
Timing belt driven coolant pump:	
Fitting value	88 ± 3 Hz
Minimum operating value	85 ± 3 Hz

Camshaft

Drive	Toothed belt
Endfloat	0.045 to 0.135 mm

Piston

Protrusion	0.56 ± 0.06 mm

Lubrication system

Minimum oil pressure at 80°C:	
At 1000 rpm	1.2 bars (17.4 psi)
At 3500 rpm	3.5 bars (50.8 psi)
Oil pump clearances:	
Gear-to-body:	
Minimum	0.10 mm
Maximum	0.24 mm
Gear endfloat:	
Minimum	0.020 mm
Maximum	0.085 mm

Torque wrench settings

Torque wrench settings	Nm	lbf ft
Camshaft bearing cap beam	20	15
Camshaft sprocket bolt	60	44
Connecting rod (big-end) cap bolts:		
Stage 1	20	15
Stage 2	Angle-tighten through 40° ± 6°	
Crankshaft pulley bolt:		
Stage 1	20	15
Stage 2	Angle-tighten through 115° ± 15°	
Cylinder head bolts*:		
Stage 1 – all bolts	30	22
Stage 2 – all bolts	Angle-tighten through 100° ± 4°	
Stage 3	Wait for at least 3 minutes for the gasket to settle	
Stage 4 – bolts 1 and 2	Slacken fully	
Stage 5 – bolts 1 and 2	25	18
Stage 6 – bolts 1 and 2	Angle-tighten through 213° ± 7°	
Stage 7 – bolts 3 and 4	Slacken fully	
Stage 8 – bolts 3 and 4	25	18
Stage 9 – bolts 3 and 4	Angle-tighten through 213° ± 7°	
Stage 10 – bolts 5 and 6	Slacken fully	
Stage 11 – bolts 5 and 6	25	18
Stage 12 – bolts 5 and 6	Angle-tighten through 213° ± 7°	
Stage 13 – bolts 7 and 8	Slacken fully	
Stage 14 – bolts 7 and 8	25	18
Stage 15 – bolts 7 and 8	Angle-tighten through 213° ± 7°	
Stage 16 – bolts 9 and 10	Slacken fully	
Stage 17 – bolts 9 and 10	25	18
Stage 18 – bolts 9 and 10	Angle-tighten through 213° ± 7°	
Cylinder head cover bolts:		
Stage 1 – centre bolt	12	9
Stage 2 – two outer bolts	12	9
Stage 3 – retighten centre bolt	12	9
Engine/transmission mountings:		
Right-hand engine mounting:		
Acoustic mass unit mounting bolts	21	15
Mounting bracket-to-cylinder head bolts	62	46
Tie-rod bracket bolts	105	77
Mounting bracket-to-rubber mounting nut	44	32
Rubber mounting bracket-to-body bolts	21	15
Left-hand transmission mounting:		
Mounting bracket-to-transmission bolts	105	77
Mounting stud nut	44	32
Rubber mounting bracket-to-body bolts	62	46
Rear mounting bracket/tie rod:		
Tie-rod link-to-subframe bolt	105	77
Tie-rod link-to-mounting bracket	180	133
Mounting bracket-to-transmission bolts	62	46
Flywheel/driveplate bolts*:		
Conventional	50 to 55	37 to 41
Dual mass:		
Stage 1	30	22
Stage 2	Angle-tighten through 56° ± 6°	
Injection pump sprocket nut	70	52
Main bearing caps (tightening order 3, 4, 2, 5, 1):		
Stage 1	20	15
Stage 2	Angle-tighten through 62° ± 4°	
Oil pump bolts	24	18
Roadwheel bolts	105	77
Sump bolts:		
Stage 1	8	6
Stage 2	15	11
Timing belt tensioner nut	50	37
Timing belt tensioner plate bolts	10	7

** New nuts/bolts must be used*

1 General information

How to use this Chapter

This Part of Chapter 2 is devoted to in-car repair procedures for the 1.9 litre diesel engine. Similar information covering the 2.2 litre diesel engines and the petrol engines will be found in Chapters 2A and 2C. All procedures concerning engine removal and refitting, and engine block/cylinder head over-haul for petrol and diesel engines can be found in Chapters 2D and 2E as applicable.

Most of the operations included in Chapter 2B are based on the assumption that the engine is still installed in the car. Therefore, if this information is being used during a complete engine overhaul, with the engine already removed, many of the steps included here will not apply.

Engine description

The engine is of four-cylinder, in-line, single overhead camshaft type, mounted transversely at the front of the vehicle with the transmission bolted to the left-hand side.

The crankshaft is supported in five shell-type main bearings. Thrustwashers are fitted to No 2 main bearing to control crankshaft endfloat.

The connecting rods are attached to the crankshaft by horizontally split shell-type big-end bearings and to the pistons by gudgeon pins. The gudgeon pins are fully-floating and are retained by circlips. The aluminium alloy pistons are of the slipper type and are fitted with three piston rings; two compression rings and a scraper-type oil control ring.

The single overhead camshaft is mounted in five plain bearings machined directly in the aluminium alloy cylinder head and is driven by the crankshaft via a toothed timing belt.

The camshaft operates the valves via inverted bucket-type followers, which operate in bores machined directly in the cylinder head. Valve clearance adjustment is by shims located externally between the followers and the cam lobes or by different thickness followers. The inlet and exhaust valves are mounted vertically in the cylinder head and are each closed by a single valve spring.

The fuel injection pump is driven by the timing belt and is described in further detail in Chapter 4B.

A semi-closed crankcase ventilation system is employed and crankcase fumes are drawn from an oil separator on the cast iron cylinder block and passed via a hose (and in certain cases, a second oil separator) to the inlet tract (see Chapter 4C for further details).

The lubrication system is of the full-flow, pressure-feed type. Oil is drawn from the sump by a chain-driven gear-type oil pump located beneath the crankshaft. Engine oil is fed through an externally-mounted oil filter to the main oil gallery feeding the crankshaft and camshaft. Oil spray jets are fitted to the cylinder block to supply oil to the underside of the pistons. Certain models are fitted with an oil cooler mounted on the cylinder block.

Operations with engine in car

The following operations can be carried out without having to remove the engine from the vehicle:

a) Removal and refitting of the cylinder head.
b) Removal and refitting of the timing belt and sprockets.
c) Renewal of the camshaft oil seals.
d) Removal and refitting of the camshaft.
e) Removal and refitting of the sump.
*f) Removal and refitting of the connecting rods and pistons.**
g) Removal and refitting of the oil pump.
h) Renewal of the crankshaft oil seals.
i) Renewal of the engine mountings.

* **Note:** *Although the operation marked with an asterisk can be carried out with the engine in the car after removal of the sump, it is better for the engine to be removed in the interests of cleanliness and improved access. For this reason, the procedure is described in Chapter 2E.*

2 Compression and leakdown tests – description and interpretation

Compression test

Note: *A compression tester specifically designed for diesel engines must be used for this test, because of the higher pressures involved.*

1 When engine performance is down, or if misfiring occurs which cannot be attributed to a fault in the fuel system, a compression test can provide diagnostic clues as to the engine's condition. If the test is performed regularly it can give warning of trouble before any other symptoms become apparent.

2 The tester is connected to an adapter that screws into the glow plug or injector hole **(see illustration)**. It is unlikely to be worthwhile buying such a tester for occasional use, but it may be possible to borrow or hire one – if not, have the test performed by a garage.

3 Unless specific instructions to the contrary are supplied with the tester, observe the following points:

a) The battery must be in a good state of charge, the air filter must be clean and the engine should be at normal operating temperature
b) All the injectors or glow plugs should be removed before starting the test. If removing the injectors, also remove the fire seal washers (which must be renewed when the injectors are refitted – see Chapter 4B), otherwise they may be blown out
c) Where applicable, it is advisable to disconnect the stop solenoid on the pump to reduce the amount of fuel discharged as the engine is cranked

2.2 Carrying out a compression test

4 The actual compression pressures measured are not as important as the balance between cylinders.

5 The cause of poor compression is less easy to establish on a diesel engine than on a petrol engine. The effect of introducing oil into the cylinders ('wet' testing) is not conclusive, because there is a risk that the oil will sit in the swirl chamber or in the recess on the piston crown instead of passing to the rings. However, the following can be used as a rough guide to diagnosis.

6 All cylinders should produce very similar pressures; any cylinders that have a great difference, indicates the existence of a fault. Note that the compression should build-up quickly in a healthy engine; low compression on the first stroke, followed by gradually increasing pressure on successive strokes, indicates worn piston rings. A low compression reading on the first stroke, which does not build-up during successive strokes, indicates leaking valves or a blown head gasket (a cracked head could also be the cause).

7 A low reading from two adjacent cylinders is almost certainly due to the head gasket having blown between them.

Leakdown test

8 A leakdown test measures the rate at which compressed air fed into the cylinder is lost. It is an alternative to a compression test and in many ways it is better, since the escaping air provides easy identification of where pressure loss is occurring (piston rings, valves or head gasket).

9 The equipment needed for leakdown testing is unlikely to be available to the home mechanic. If poor compression is suspected, have the test performed by a suitably-equipped garage.

3.7 Remove the blanking plug from the cylinder block . . .

3 Top Dead Centre (TDC) for No 1 piston – locating

Caution: Timing pins are intended SOLELY for the purpose of checking the position of the crankshaft during various engine overhaul procedures. DO NOT use them as locking tools to prevent crankshaft rotation while the pulley or flywheel/driveplate bolts are unscrewed or tightened

1 Top Dead Centre (TDC) is the highest point in the cylinder that each piston reaches as the crankshaft turns. Each piston reaches TDC at the end of the compression stroke and again at the end of the exhaust stroke; however, for the purpose of timing the engine, TDC refers to the position of No 1 piston at the end of its compression stroke. No 1 piston is at the flywheel/driveplate end of the engine.

2 When No 1 piston is at TDC, the timing mark on the camshaft sprocket should be aligned with the pointer on the timing belt outer cover (the pulley mark can be viewed through the cut-out in the cover, below the pointer). Additionally, the timing mark on the flywheel/driveplate should be aligned with the TDC mark on the gearbox bellhousing.

3 To align the timing marks, the crankshaft must be turned. This should be done by using a spanner on the crankshaft pulley bolt. Improved access to the pulley bolt can be obtained by jacking up the front right-hand corner of the vehicle and removing the roadwheel and the wheel arch lower liner (secured by plastic clips). If desired, to enable the engine to be turned more easily, remove the glow plugs (Chapter 5C) or the fuel injectors (Chapter 4B).

4 Look through the timing aperture in the gearbox bellhousing and turn the crankshaft until the timing mark on the flywheel/driveplate is aligned with the TDC (0°) mark on the bellhousing.

5 Unscrew the retaining nuts and withdraw the engine sound-insulating cover.

6 Check that the timing mark on the camshaft sprocket is aligned with the pointer on the timing belt outer cover. The engine is now positioned with No 1 piston at TDC on its compression stroke.

7 For absolute accuracy, the crankshaft position should be checked by inserting a timing pin – Renault tool Mot. 1054 **(see Tool Tip)**. To do this, unscrew the blanking plug from the front left-hand end of the cylinder block, next to the base of the oil level dipstick tube **(see illustration)**.

If the special Renault tool mentioned in this Section is not available, an 8 mm diameter rod or drill bit can be used instead. On some engines, however, an 8 mm diameter rod may be too slack a fit in the cylinder block plug aperture for the crankshaft position to be determined accurately – it will therefore be necessary in such cases to have a stepped pin made up, with an 8 mm diameter at its tip to engage in the crankshaft slot and a larger diameter as necessary to fit precisely in the cylinder block aperture.

8 Turn the engine slightly anti-clockwise (against the normal direction of rotation), so that the camshaft sprocket is half a tooth out of alignment with the cover pointer.

9 Insert the timing pin fully into the hole in the front of the engine, then carefully turn the engine clockwise, keeping light pressure on the end of the timing pin. At the TDC position, the pin should enter a slot in the crankshaft web, and the engine should be locked in position (rock the engine very slightly backwards or forwards to achieve engagement). In this position, the camshaft sprocket marks should also come into alignment **(see illustrations)**.

10 Once in place it should be impossible to turn the crankshaft – if the crankshaft will still move to-and-fro slightly, then the timing pin has entered the balance hole instead of the timing slot. **Note:** *Do not attempt to rotate the engine whilst the timing pin is in place. If the engine is to be left in this state for a long period of time, it is a good idea to place warning notices inside the vehicle and in the engine compartment. This will reduce the possibility of the engine being accidentally cranked on the starter motor, which will cause severe damage if done with the timing pin in place.*

11 On completion, remove the timing pin and refit all removed components.

4 Valve clearances – checking and adjustment

Note: *This operation is not part of the maintenance schedule. It should be undertaken if noise from the valve gear becomes evident, or if loss of performance gives cause to suspect that the clearances may be incorrect. A new cylinder head cover gasket may be required on refitting.*

Checking

1 Unscrew the retaining nuts and withdraw the engine sound-insulating cover.

2 Where necessary for improved access, unclip any hoses that are routed across the top of the cylinder head cover and move them to one side out of the way. If fuel lines are disconnected, cover open unions to prevent dirt ingress.

3 Unscrew the bolts from the cylinder head cover and withdraw the cover from the engine. Recover the gasket.

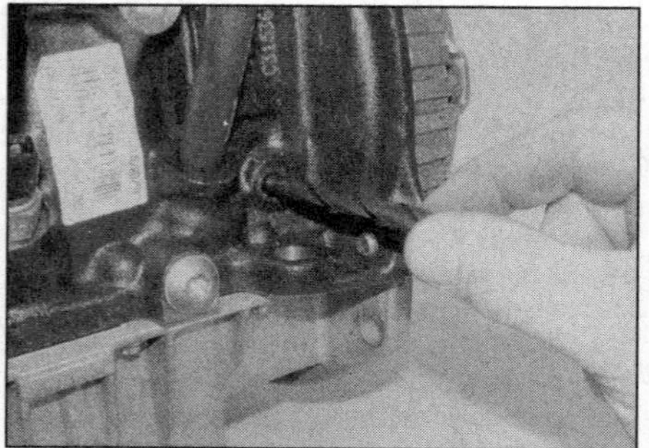

3.9a . . . and insert a suitable drill bit . . .

3.9b . . . or a purpose-made timing pin to check the crankshaft position

3.9c When the crankshaft is at TDC, the pin (arrowed) will go fully home

4 During the following procedure, the crankshaft must be turned, using a spanner on the crankshaft pulley bolt. Improved access to the pulley bolt can be obtained by jacking up the front right-hand corner of the vehicle (see *Jacking and vehicle support*) and removing the roadwheel and the wheel arch lower liner (secured by plastic clips).

5 If desired, to enable the crankshaft to be turned more easily, remove the glow plugs (Chapter 5C) or the fuel injectors (Chapter 4B).

6 Draw the valve positions on a piece of paper, numbering them 1 to 8 from the flywheel/driveplate end of the engine. Identify them as inlet or exhaust (ie, 1I, 2E, 3I, 4E, 5I, 6E, 7I, 8E).

7 Turn the crankshaft until the valves of No 1 cylinder (flywheel/driveplate end) are 'rocking' – the exhaust valve will be closing and the inlet valve will be opening. The piston of No 4 cylinder will be at the top of its compression stroke, with both valves fully closed – the clearances for both valves of No 4 cylinder may now be checked.

8 Insert a feeler gauge of the correct thickness (see Specifications) between the cam lobe and the shim or cam follower and check that it is a firm sliding fit **(see illustration)**. If it is not, use the feeler gauges to ascertain the exact clearance and record this for use when calculating the new shim/follower thickness required. Note that the inlet and exhaust valve clearances are different (see Specifications).

9 With No 4 cylinder valve clearances checked, turn the engine through half a turn so that No 3 valves are 'rocking', then check the valve clearances of No 2 cylinder in the same way. Similarly check the remaining valve clearances in the sequence shown **(see illustration)**.

Note: *On later models, there are NO shims fitted to the cam followers. If the valve clearance is not within tolerance the complete cam follower (bucket) will need to be substituted with one of the correct thickness. Renault parts department can supply 25 different thicknesses of cam followers to suit your requirements.*

Adjustment

Note: *A micrometer will be required for this operation.*

10 Remove the camshaft as described in Section 8, and lift out the followers/shims. Note the fitted position of the followers/shims to calculate the correct thickness for refitting.

11 Where a valve clearance differs from the specified value, then the shim/follower for that valve must be substituted with a thinner or thicker one accordingly. Where shims are fitted, the thickness is normally etched on the shim, but it is prudent to use a micrometer to measure the true thickness of any shim removed, as it may have been reduced by wear **(see illustrations)**. **Note:** *It is permissible to swap the shims around between valves, but not the followers.*

4.8 Measuring a valve clearance

12 The thickness of shim/follower required is calculated as follows. If the measured clearance is less than specified, subtract the measured clearance from the specified clearance and deduct the result from the thickness of the existing shim/follower. For example:

Sample calculation – clearance too small

Clearance measured (A) = 0.15 mm
Desired clearance (B) = 0.20 mm
Difference (B – A) = 0.05 mm
Shim/follower thickness fitted = 3.70 mm
Shim/follower required =
3.70 – 0.05 = 3.65 mm

13 If the measured clearance is greater than specified, subtract the specified clearance from the measured clearance and add the result to the thickness of the existing shim/follower. For example:

Sample calculation – clearance too big

Clearance measured (A) = 0.50 mm
Desired clearance (B) = 0.40 mm
Difference (A – B) = 0.10 mm
Shim/follower thickness fitted = 3.45 mm
Shim/follower required =
3.45 + 0.10 = 3.55 mm

Refitting

14 Where applicable, before refitting the shims, wipe the top of the follower and ensure that all the oil is removed from the shim locating recess in the follower's upper face. Fit the shim to the follower with the projection on the shim engaged with the follower's recess.

VALVES ROCKING ON CYLINDER	CHECK CLEARANCE ON CYLINDER
1	4
3	2
4	1
2	3

4.9 Valve clearance checking sequence

15 When all shims or followers have been selected with the correct thickness, refit the camshaft (and followers, where applicable) as described in Section 8.

Note: *When the camshaft is fitted back in position, check through the valve clearances again to make sure they are within the tolerance given, before refitting all other components.*

16 Refitting is a reversal of removal, but where applicable carry out the following procedures:

a) If not already done, remove the spanner from the crankshaft pulley bolt and the timing pin from the crankshaft.
b) Refit the cylinder head cover, using a new gasket where necessary – tighten the cover retaining bolts evenly to the specified torque wrench setting.
c) Refit the fuel injectors (as described in Chapter 4B) or the glow plugs (Chapter 5C).
d) Reconnect any hoses that were moved for access on removal. If fuel lines were disconnected, reconnect them, then prime and bleed the fuel system as described in Chapter 4B.
e) Refit the engine sound insulating cover.

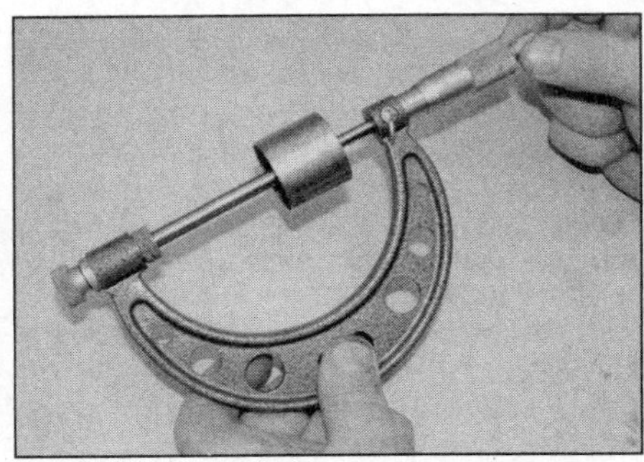

4.11a Checking the follower thickness using a micrometer

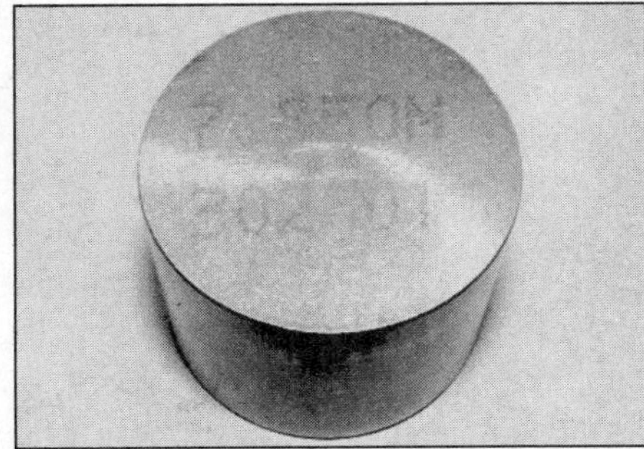

4.11b The follower thickness may still be visible

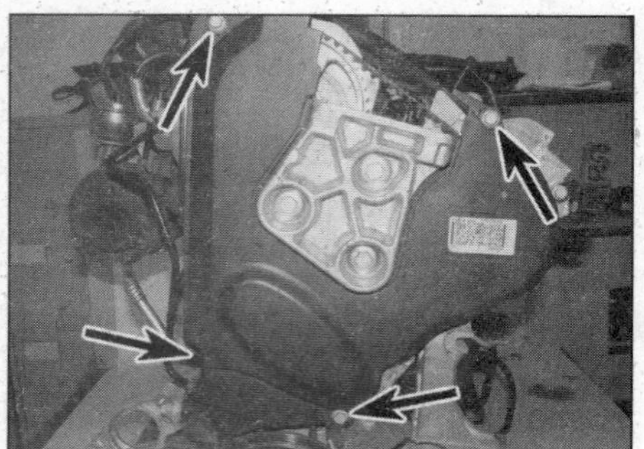

5.11 Remove the four bolts (arrowed) and withdraw the timing belt cover

5 Timing belt – removal and refitting

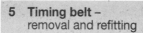

Note: *Renault specifies the use of special electronic tools to correctly set the timing belt tension. If access to this equipment cannot be obtained, an approximate setting can be achieved using the method described below. If this method described is used, the tension must be checked using the special electronic tool at the earliest possible opportunity. Do not drive the vehicle over large distances, or use high engine speeds, until the belt tension is known to be correct. Refer to a Renault dealer for advice.*

Note: *The timing belt should be renewed whenever it is disturbed; never refit a belt that has already been used.*

Removal

1 Disconnect the battery negative terminal (refer to *Disconnecting the battery* in the Reference Section of this manual).

2 Apply the handbrake, then jack up the front of the car and support it on axle stands (see *Jacking and vehicle support*). Remove the right-hand front roadwheel, the undo the retaining screws and remove the engine undercover and the front and rear protective covers from the right-hand wheel arch.

3 Unscrew the retaining nuts/screws and withdraw the engine sound-insulating cover.

4 Remove the auxiliary drivebelt as described in Chapter 1B.

5.13 Loosen the timing belt tensioner nut (arrowed)

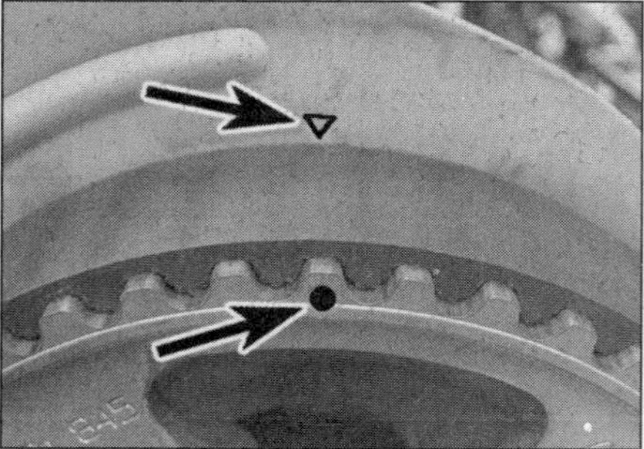

5.12a At TDC the camshaft punch mark on the sprocket aligns with the mark on the backplate

5 Position an engine hoist, or an engine lifting beam across the engine compartment and attach the jib to the right-hand engine lifting eyelet. Raise the lifting gear to take up the slack, so that it is just supporting the weight of the engine.

6 Undo the three bolts securing the right-hand engine-mounting bracket to the cylinder head. Similarly, undo the three bolts securing the rubber mounting to the body, with reference to Section 14. Release the relevant cable clips and remove the complete mounting assembly.

7 Undo the retaining bolts and remove the aluminium side member and body tie-rod on the right-hand side of the car.

8 Unclip the fuel filter from the right-hand inner wing panel and move it to one side, taking care not to damage any of the fuel lines.

9 Using a socket and extension bar, slacken the crankshaft pulley bolt. Hold the crankshaft stationary while the bolt is unscrewed by engaging a screwdriver with the flywheel/driveplate ring gear teeth through the opening at the lower rear of the cylinder block. Unscrew the bolt and remove the washer and crankshaft pulley.

10 Temporarily refit the crankshaft pulley bolt. Turn the crankshaft so that No 1 piston is at TDC on the compression stroke and insert a timing pin to check the crankshaft position, as described in Section 3.

11 Mark the inner timing belt cover in line with the timing mark on the outer cover, then unscrew the securing bolts and withdraw the outer timing belt covers **(see illustration)**.

5.17 M6 bolt (arrowed) fitted to the timing belt inner cover to adjust timing belt tension

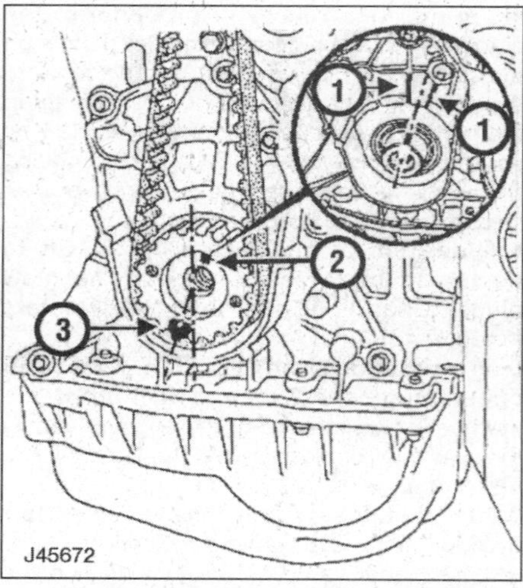

5.12b Crankshaft groove (2) should be between ribs (1) and the timing mark (3) should be one tooth offset at TDC

12 With No 1 piston at TDC on the compression stroke (see paragraph 10), note the position of any timing marks on the camshaft, fuel injection pump and crankshaft sprockets **(see illustrations)**. It may be advisable to make your own marks to aid refitting.

13 Loosen the retaining nut, and then push back the tensioner to relieve the tension on the timing belt **(see illustration)**. Retighten the nut.

14 Release the belt first from the camshaft sprocket, then from the fuel injection pump sprocket, idler pulley and crankshaft sprocket, and remove it from the engine.

15 Do not turn the camshaft or the crankshaft whilst the timing belt is removed, as there is a risk of piston-to-valve contact. If it is necessary to turn the camshaft for any reason, before doing so, remove the timing pin and turn the crankshaft anti-clockwise (viewed from the timing belt end of the engine) by a quarter-turn to position all four pistons halfway down their bores.

16 Clean the sprockets, idler pulley and tensioner and wipe them dry – **do not** apply excessive amounts of solvent to the idler pulley and tensioner otherwise the bearing lubricant may be removed. Also clean the timing belt inner cover and the related surfaces of the cylinder head and block.

Refitting

17 Ensure that the crankshaft is at the TDC position for No 1 cylinder, with the timing pin in place to ensure complete accuracy, as described previously. If the pistons have been positioned halfway down their bores (see paragraph 15), temporarily refit the timing belt outer cover which covers the camshaft sprocket and check that the timing mark on the pulley is aligned with the pointer on the timing belt outer cover, then turn the crankshaft clockwise (viewed from the timing belt end of the engine) until the timing pin can be refitted.

To enable the tensioner to be adjusted, screw a 6 mm bolt into the threaded hole provided in the timing belt inner cover. The bolt will bear against the rear of the tensioner pulley and enable adjustments of the belt tension to be made **(see illustration)**.

18 Where applicable, align any markings on the belt with the timing marks on the crankshaft, camshaft and fuel injection pump sprockets, ensuring that the running direction arrows (where applicable) on the belt are pointing clockwise (viewed from the timing belt end of the engine). Fit the timing belt over the crankshaft sprocket first, followed by the idler pulley, fuel injection pump sprocket, camshaft sprocket and tensioner.

19 Check that all the timing marks are still aligned and remove all slack from the timing belt by tightening the bolt fitted to the timing belt inner cover.

20 The belt tension must now be checked – this can be set or checked accurately **only** by using Renault special tools to pretension the belt and measure its vibration frequency. If this equipment is not available, set the belt's tension as carefully as possible **(see Haynes Hint)**, then take the car to a Renault dealer as soon as possible for the tension to be checked by qualified personnel using the special equipment. Do not take the vehicle on any long journeys or rev the engine to high speeds until the timing belt's tension has been checked and is known to be correct.

With experience, timing belt tension may be judged to be approximately correct when the belt can be twisted 45 to 90° with moderate pressure between the finger and thumb, checking midway between the pulleys on the belt's longest run. If the special tool is not available and there is any doubt about the tension of the timing belt, the vehicle should be taken to a Renault dealer as soon as possible for the tension to be checked by qualified personnel using the special equipment.

21 If the adjustment is incorrect, the tensioner will have to be repositioned by loosening the tensioner nut and by screwing the bolt fitted to the timing belt inner cover in or out.

6.2 Removing the crankshaft sprocket

22 With the correct tension applied, retighten the tensioner nut to the specified torque. This torque is critical, since if the nut were to come loose, considerable engine damage would result. Loosen the bolt fitted to the timing belt inner cover so that it no longer bears on the tensioner roller bracket.

23 Remove the crankshaft timing pin, then refit the crankshaft pulley and securing bolt. Prevent the crankshaft turning using the method described previously and tighten the bolt to the specified torque **(see illustration)**.

24 Check that the crankshaft is still positioned with No 1 piston at TDC (by refitting temporarily the crankshaft timing pin), then remove the timing pin and turn the crankshaft three complete turns in the normal direction of rotation, returning it to the TDC position again. Re-insert the timing pin in the cylinder block.

25 Temporarily refit the timing belt outer cover, which covers the camshaft sprocket, and check that the pulley timing mark still aligns with the pointer on the cover, as noted before removal (see Section 3).

26 Recheck the belt tension as described previously. If the tension is incorrect, the setting and checking procedure must be repeated until the correct tension is achieved.

27 With the belt tensioned correctly, remove the M6 bolt from the timing belt inner cover and remove the timing pin from the cylinder block, if not already done. Refit the blanking plug to the cylinder block and tighten it securely, also tighten the tensioner retaining bolt.

28 Refit the timing belt upper outer covers, ensuring that any brackets secured by the bolts are in position as noted before removal.

29 Locate the right-hand engine mounting assembly into position and refit the bolts securing the mounting bracket to the cylinder head. Tighten the bolts to the specified torque. Refit the three bolts securing the rubber mounting to the body. Ensure that the movement limiter is positioned centrally over the mounting rubber then tighten the three bolts to the specified torque.

It is easy to make up a puller for the crankshaft sprocket using two bolts, a strip of metal and the existing crankshaft pulley bolt. By unscrewing the pulley bolt against the metal strip, the sprocket is drawn off the crankshaft.

5.23 Angle-tighten the crankshaft pulley bolt

30 Remove the engine hoist or lifting beam used to support the engine.

31 Refit the auxiliary drivebelt as described in Chapter 1B.

32 Refit the fuel filter on the right-hand inner wing.

33 Refit the engine sound-insulating cover.

34 Refit the engine compartment under-shield, then refit the wheel arch liner and the roadwheel, and lower the vehicle to the ground.

35 Reconnect the battery negative terminal.

6 Timing belt sprockets and tensioner – removal and refitting

Note: *A new timing belt must be used on refitting.*

Crankshaft sprocket

Removal

1 Remove the timing belt as described in Section 5.

2 It should be possible simply to pull the sprocket off the crankshaft **(see illustration)**. However in some cases a puller may be required to draw off the sprocket – one can easily be made up as shown **(see Tool tip)**.

3 Recover the Woodruff key if it is loose. Examine the oil seal for signs of oil leakage and, if necessary, renew it as described in Section 7.

Refitting

4 Refitting is a reversal of removal. Refit the Woodruff key to the crankshaft keyway and slide on the sprocket, making sure it is correctly engaged with the key and with its flange against the cylinder block/timing belt inner cover.

5 Fit the new timing belt as described in Section 5.

Fuel injection pump sprocket

Note: *Renault special tool Mot. 1200-01 will be required to hold the injection pump sprocket during removal and refitting. A puller will be required to remove the sprocket from the pump shaft, Renault use special tool Mot. 1525 to withdraw the sprocket.*

Removal

6 Remove the timing belt as described in Section 5.

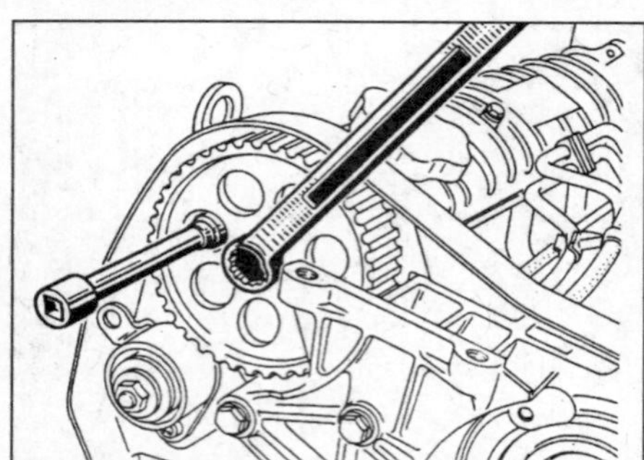

6.13a Using a socket and extension bar to hold the camshaft sprocket

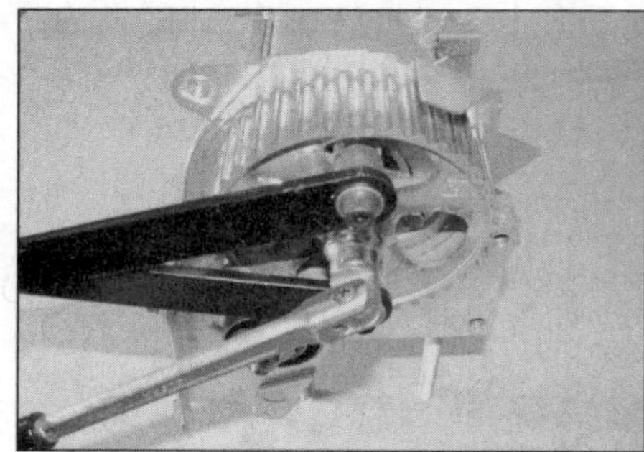

6.13b Using a home-made tool to hold the camshaft sprocket stationary

6.14 Remove the sprocket from the camshaft

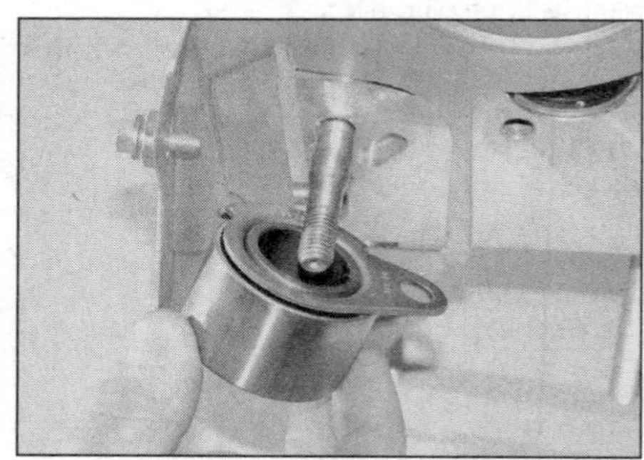

6.21 Removing the tensioner

7 Fit the Renault sprocket holding tool (Mot. 1200-01) to prevent the injection pump sprocket from rotating.

8 Unscrew the sprocket retaining nut, then fit a suitable puller to the sprocket to withdraw it from the pump shaft. Take care not to damage the end of the pump shaft as the sprocket is removed.

9 Remove the sprocket and, where applicable, recover the Woodruff key from the end of the pump shaft if it is loose.

Refitting

10 Refitting is a reversal of removal, bearing in mind the following points:

a) *Tighten the sprocket nut to the specified torque wrench setting.*

b) *Fit and tension the new timing belt as described in Section 5.*

Camshaft sprocket

Note: *A suitable puller will be required for this operation.*

Removal

11 Remove the timing belt as described in Section 5. If it is necessary to turn the camshaft for any reason, before doing so, remove the timing pin and turn the crankshaft anti-clockwise (viewed from the timing belt end of the engine) by a quarter-turn to position all four pistons halfway down their bores.

12 Unscrew the bolts securing the engine right-hand mounting main bracket to the engine and move it to one side. Note this mounting bracket also supports the fuel injection pump, take care not to damage any fuel lines as it is moved.

13 Unscrew the camshaft sprocket bolt. The sprocket can be held using a suitable socket and extension bar engaged with one of the timing belt inner cover securing bolts, or by making up a sprocket holding tool **(see illustrations)**.

14 Remove the bolt, washer and sprocket from the camshaft **(see illustration)**. A suitable puller may be required, in which case ensure that the legs of the puller act on the holes in the sprocket, **not** on the sprocket teeth.

15 Recover the Woodruff key from the end of the camshaft if it is loose – note that on later engines the key is an integral part of the sprocket.

Refitting

16 Refit the Woodruff key (where separate) to the camshaft keyway. Refit the sprocket with its projecting hub towards the cylinder head and ensuring that the key engages correctly with the keyway.

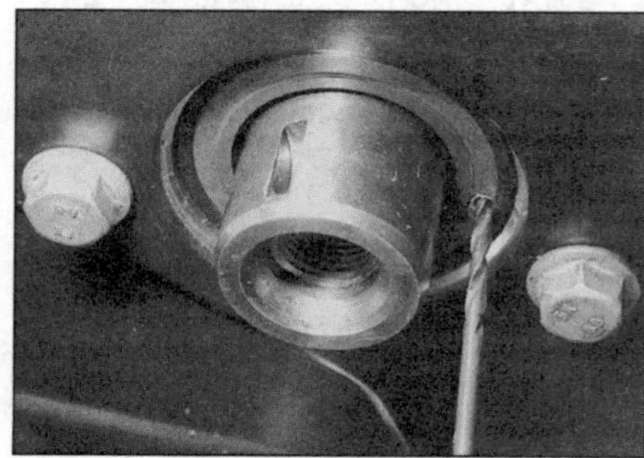

7.3a Drill a small hole . . .

17 Ensure that the washer is in place, then refit the sprocket bolt and tighten it to the specified torque, holding the pulley as during removal.

18 Refit the engine right-hand mountings main bracket to the engine and tighten the securing bolts. Make sure the fuel pump and lines are fitted correctly with reference to Chapter 4B.

19 Fit the new timing belt as described in Section 5.

Tensioner

Removal

20 Remove the timing belt as described in Section 5.

21 Remove the securing nut and its washer, unscrew the retaining bolt, and then withdraw the tensioner assembly **(see illustration)**.

Refitting

22 Refitting is a reversal of removal, but check that the roller spins freely without binding or excessive play. Ensure that the peg on the cylinder block engages with the hole in the tensioner bracket.

23 Fit the new timing belt as described in Section 5.

Idler sprocket

Note: *This type of sprocket is only fitted to engines which have the coolant pump driven by the auxiliary drivebelt.*

Removal

24 Remove the timing belt as described in Section 5.

25 To remove the idler sprocket, undo the retaining bolt and withdraw the sprocket. To remove the idler pulley, unscrew the two securing bolts and withdraw the idler pulley assembly, manipulating it out from the timing belt inner covers.

Refitting

26 Refitting is a reversal of removal, but check that the sprocket/pulley turns freely without binding or excessive play.

27 Fit the new timing belt as described in Section 5.

7 Camshaft oil seals – renewal

Timing belt end oil seal

1 Remove the camshaft sprocket as described in Section 6.

2 Remove the Woodruff key (where separate) from the end of the camshaft, if not already done.

3 Make a note of the fitted depth of the old seal then, using a small screwdriver, prise it out of the cylinder head, taking care not to damage the surface of the camshaft. Alternatively, the oil seal can be removed by drilling a small hole and inserting a self-

7.3b . . . and use a screw and pliers to pull out the seal

7.4 Wrap some insulating tape around the end of the camshaft to prevent damage to the oil seal

7.5 Use a suitable socket to drive the new oil seal into the cylinder head

tapping screw. A pair of grips can then be used to pull out the oil seal, by pulling on the screw **(see illustrations)**. If difficulty is experienced, insert two screws diagonally opposite each other.

4 Wipe clean the oil seal seating in the cylinder head, then dip the new seal in fresh engine oil and locate it over the camshaft with its closed side facing outwards. Make sure that the oil seal lip is not damaged, as it is located on the camshaft **(see illustration)**.

5 Using a tube of suitable diameter, drive the oil seal squarely into the housing to the previously noted depth. A block of wood cut to pass over the end of the camshaft may be used instead **(see illustration)**.

6 Refit the camshaft sprocket as described in Section 6.

Transmission end oil seal

7 No oil seal is fitted to the transmission end of the camshaft. The sealing is provided by a gasket between the cylinder head and the brake vacuum pump housing and, on certain models, by an O-ring fitted between the pump and the housing. The gasket and the O-ring, where applicable, can be renewed after unbolting the pump from the cylinder head (see Chapter 9).

8 Camshaft and followers – removal, inspection and refitting

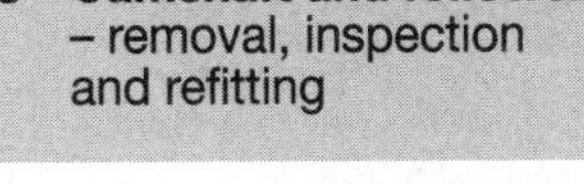

Note: *A new camshaft timing belt end oil seal should be fitted and a new cylinder head cover gasket may be required on refitting. Suitable sealant will be required for the camshaft bearing caps and thread-locking compound for the bearing cap bolts.*

Removal

1 Remove the camshaft sprocket as described in Section 6.

2 Remove the timing belt tensioner as described in Section 6.

3 Unscrew the bolts securing the timing belt upper inner cover to the end of the cylinder head.

4 Manipulate the timing belt inner cover from the camshaft end and withdraw the cover from the engine.

5 Remove the brake vacuum pump from the transmission end of the cylinder head, as described in Chapter 9.

6 Where necessary for improved access, unclip any hoses that are routed across the top of the cylinder head cover and move them to one side out of the way. If any fuel lines are disconnected, cover the open unions to prevent dirt ingress.

7 Unscrew the cylinder head cover bolts and withdraw the cover. Recover the gasket **(see illustrations)**.

8 At this point it may be useful to measure the camshaft endfloat, using a dial gauge. Compare with the value given in the Specifications **(see illustration)**. This will give an indication of the amount of wear present on the thrust surfaces.

9 If the original camshaft is to be refitted, it is advisable to measure the valve clearances at this stage, as described in Section 4, so that any shims/followers required can be obtained before the camshaft is refitted.

10 Check the camshaft bearing cap beam for identification marks and, if none are present, make identifying marks so that it can be refitted in its original position.

11 Progressively slacken the bolts from the bearing cap beam, until the valve spring pressure is relieved. Remove the bolts (noting their locations to ensure correct refitting), and lift the bearing cap beam from the camshaft **(see illustration)**.

12 Lift out the camshaft with the oil seal still in position on the end of the camshaft **(see illustration)**.

13 Remove the followers, (where applicable, keep each follower together with its shim). Place them in a compartmented box, or on a sheet of card marked into eight sections, so that they can be refitted to their original locations. Write down the shim/follower

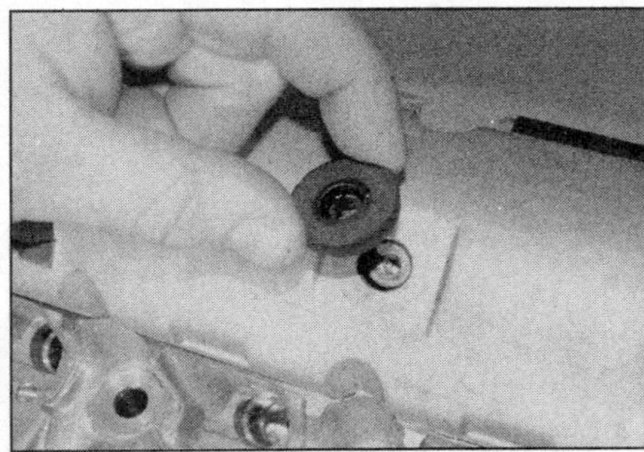

8.7a Remove the sealing washers . . .

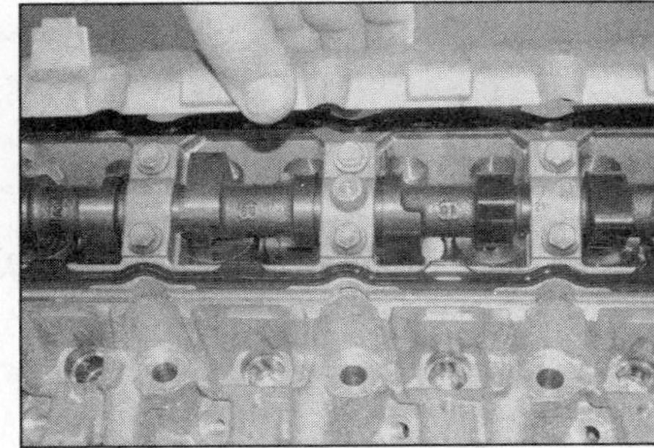

8.7b . . . and the camshaft cover . . .

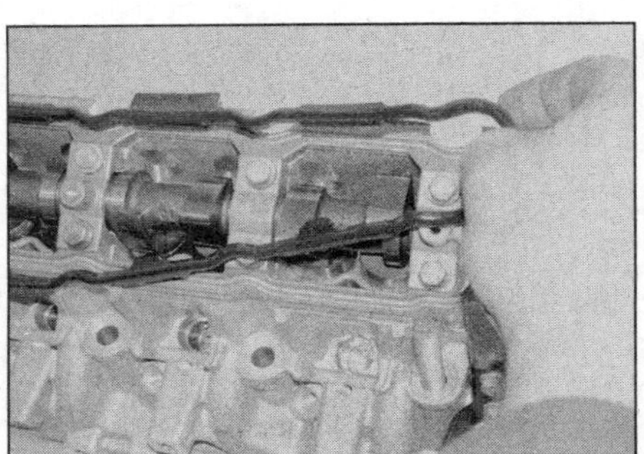

8.7c . . . and recover the rubber gasket

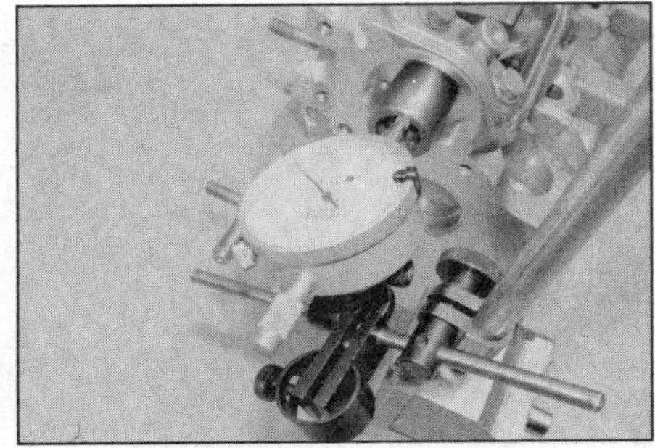

8.8 Measuring camshaft endfloat

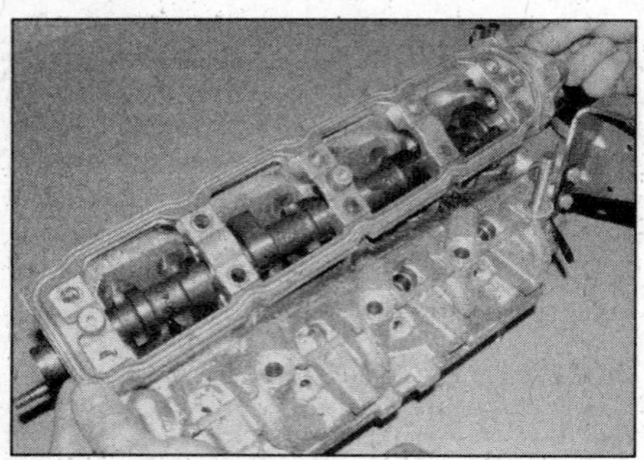
8.11 Lifting the camshaft bearing cap retainer from the cylinder head

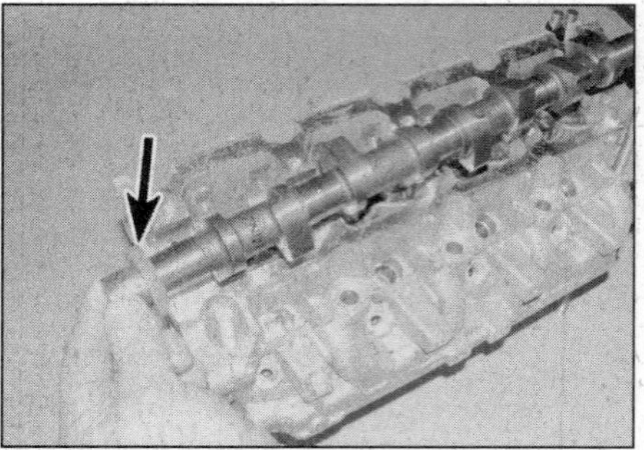
8.12 Lifting out the camshaft with the oil seal (arrowed)

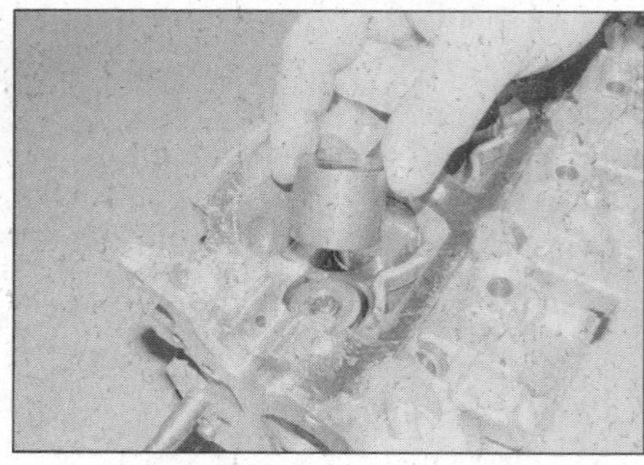
8.13 Lifting out a cam follower

thicknesses – this will be needed later if any of the valve clearances are incorrect. The shim/follower thickness is usually etched on the bottom face of the shim or the top of the follower, but it is prudent to use a micrometer to measure the true thickness of any shim/follower removed, as it may have been reduced by wear **(see illustration)**.

Inspection

14 Examine the camshaft bearing surfaces and cam lobes for wear ridges, pitting or scoring. Renew the camshaft if evident.

15 Renew the oil seal at the timing belt end of the camshaft as a matter of course. Store the camshaft so that its weight is not resting on the seal.

16 Examine the camshaft bearing surfaces in the cylinder head and bearing cap beam. Deep scoring or other damage means that the cylinder head must be renewed.

17 Inspect the followers and shims for scoring, pitting and wear ridges. Renew as necessary.

18 Clean the sealant from the cylinder head to bearing cap beam mating surfaces.

Refitting

19 Ensure that the pistons are positioned halfway down their bores, as described for sprocket removal in Section 6.

20 Refer to paragraphs 9 and 13, and Section 4, to correct the valve clearances. Oil the followers and fit them to the bores from which they were removed **(see illustration)**. Where applicable, fit the correct shim, numbered side downwards, to each follower.

21 Oil the camshaft bearings **(see illustrations)**. Place the camshaft onto the cylinder head. The oil seal can be fitted at this stage, but it must be positioned so that it is flush with the cylinder head face.

22 Apply sealant (Loctite 518, available from Renault dealers) to the cylinder head mating face of the camshaft bearing cap beam **(see illustration)**. Use a roller to get an even layer along its length, making sure no sealant goes inside the camshaft bearing surfaces.

23 Refit the camshaft bearing cap beam **(see illustration)**, ensuring that the camshaft oil seal is correctly located in the end of the cylinder head.

24 Apply a few drops of thread-locking compound to the threads of the bolts for the bearing cap beam. Fit the bolts and tighten them progressively to the specified torque **(see illustration)**.

25 If a new camshaft has been fitted, measure the endfloat using a dial gauge and check that it is within the specified limits.

26 Refit the brake vacuum pump with reference to Chapter 9.

27 Refit the timing belt upper inner cover,

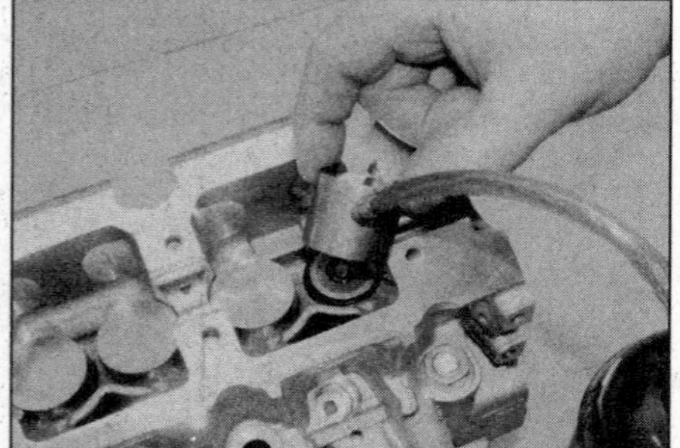
8.20 Oil the followers before refitting

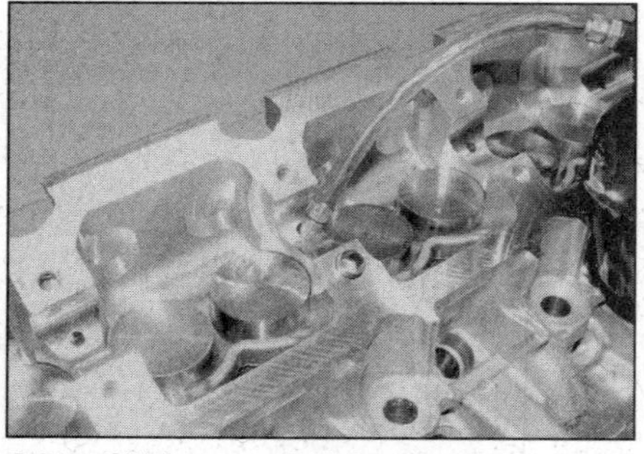
8.21a Oil the camshaft bearing surface . . .

8.21b . . . and refit the camshaft

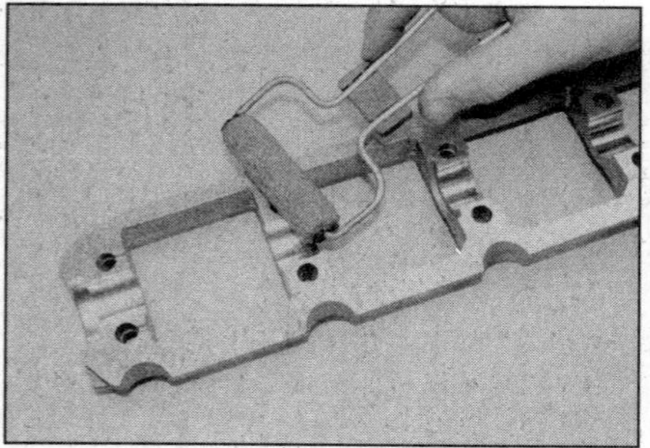
8.22 Applying sealant to the camshaft bearing ladder with a roller

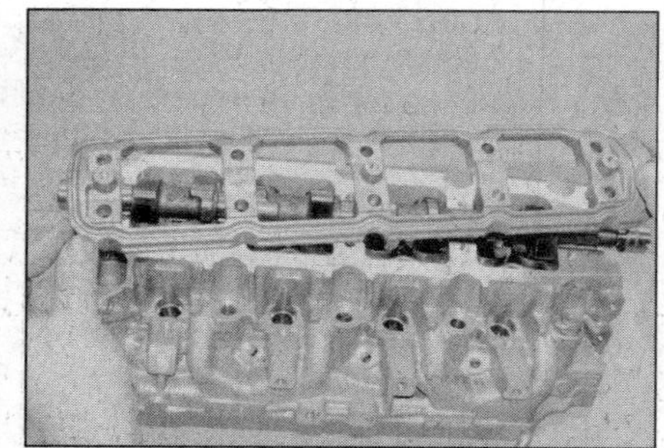
8.23 Refit the camshaft bearing cap beam

8.24 Tighten the bolts progressively to the specified torque

then refit and tighten the bolts securing it to the cylinder head.

28 Refit the timing belt tensioner, ensuring that the peg on the cylinder block engages with the hole in the tensioner bracket.

29 Refit the camshaft sprocket as described in Section 6.

30 Check the valve clearances as described in Section 4 and take any corrective action necessary.

31 Refit the cylinder head cover, using a new gasket – tighten the cover retaining bolts, in the correct sequence, to the specified torque wrench setting.

32 Refit/reconnect any hoses that were moved for access. If fuel lines were disconnected, reconnect them, then prime and bleed the fuel system as described in Chapter 4B.

33 Reconnect the battery negative terminal.

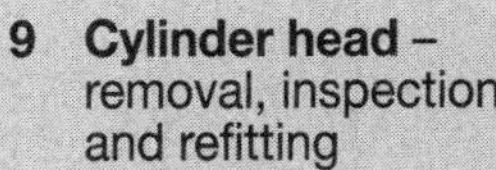

9 Cylinder head – removal, inspection and refitting

Note: *A new cylinder head gasket, cylinder head bolts and a cylinder head cover gasket will be required on refitting.*

Removal

1 The following procedure describes removal and refitting of the cylinder head complete with manifolds and the fuel injection pump.

2 Disconnect the battery negative terminal (refer to *Disconnecting the battery* in the Reference Section of this manual). Unscrew the retaining nuts and withdraw the engine sound-insulating cover.

3 Drain the cooling system as described in Chapter 1B.

4 Remove the auxiliary drivebelt as described in Chapter 1B.

5 Remove the timing belt as described in Section 5 and the timing belt tensioner as described in Section 6.

6 The engine must now be supported from below so that the engine hoist or lifting beam used for timing belt removal can be removed for access to the top of the engine.

7 Disconnect the vacuum hose from the brake vacuum pump **(see illustration)**.

8 Remove the air filter housing, along with the air intake hoses running from the air cleaner

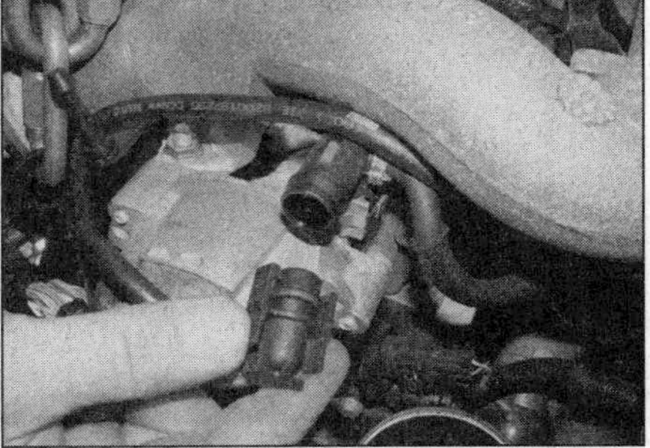

9.7 Disconnect the hose from the brake vacuum pump

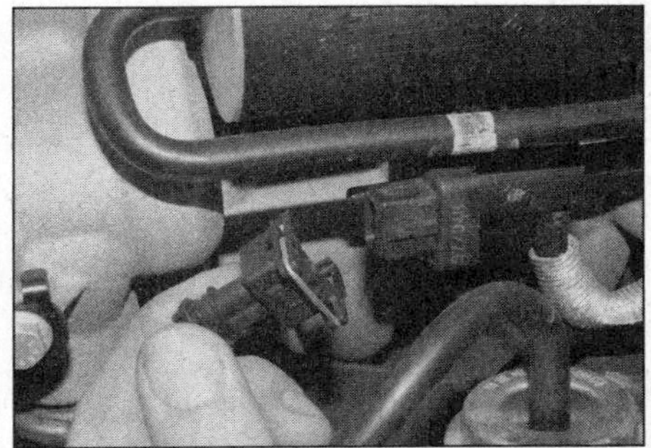

9.10b . . . disconnect the wiring connector . . .

to the inlet manifold, or turbocharger, as applicable (note that, where applicable, the breather hoses which connect to the air intake hoses will also have to be disconnected).

9 Disconnect the air hoses running from the intercooler to the turbocharger and remove them from the engine bay.

10 Undo the two retaining bolts from the vacuum reservoir at the rear of the intake manifold and disconnect the wiring connector below the reservoir. Undo the two mounting bolts and remove the solenoid valve from below the reservoir **(see illustrations)**

11 Slacken and remove the upper mounting bracket bolt from the thermo plunger unit at the rear of the cylinder head at the transmission end.

12 Remove the exhaust front section/catalytic converter as described in Chapter 4B.

13 Slacken and disconnect the oil supply pipe from the top of the turbocharger unit and the

9.10a Undo the two mounting bolts (arrowed) . . .

9.10c . . . and undo the solenoid valve mounting bolts (arrowed)

cylinder block, disconnect the pipe mounting bracket from the rear of the manifold **(see illustrations)**.

14 Disconnect the oil return pipe from the bottom of the turbocharger.

15 Undo the retaining bolts and remove the engine lifting bracket from the timing belt end of the cylinder head.

16 Disconnect the wiring connector from the camshaft sensor, undo the mounting bolt and remove it from the timing belt end of the cylinder head **(see illustration)**

17 Release the retaining clips and disconnect the hoses from the coolant housing on the transmission end of the cylinder head.

18 Disconnect the wiring connector from the temperature switch on the coolant housing.

19 Disconnect the two fuel hoses from the top of the fuel filter assembly. The unions are equipped with quick-release fittings which are intended to be uncoupled using a

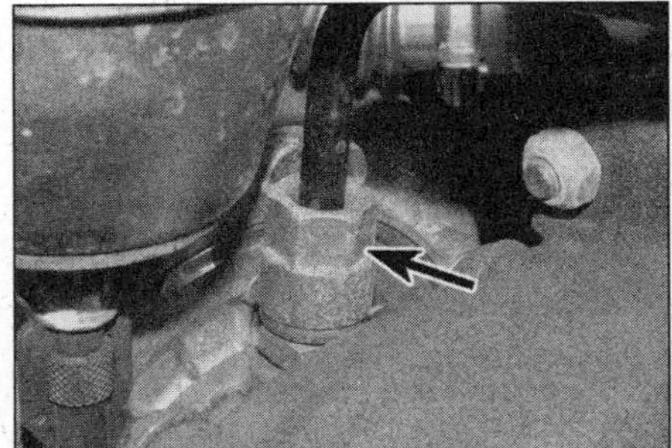

9.13a Oil supply union on the top of the turbo

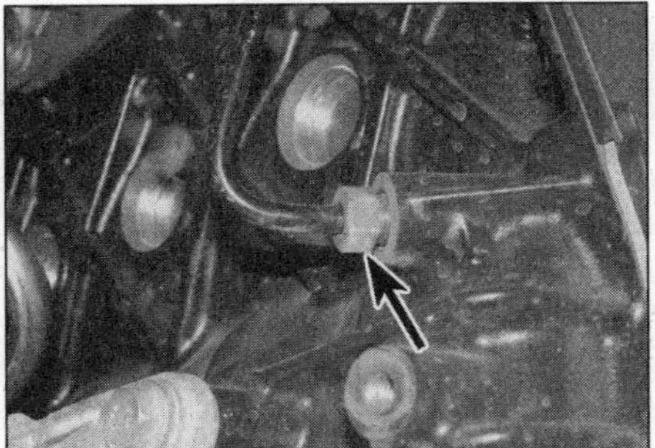

9.13a Turbo oil supply pipe from cylinder block

9.16 Disconnect the wiring connector and undo the bolt (arrowed)

9.21a Disconnect the wiring connectors from the fuel pump pressure regulator . . .

9.21b . . . the fuel rail pressure switch . . .

9.21c . . . and fuel rail temperature sensor

Renault special tool – this is a small forked implement, which is passed between the two outer 'spokes' of the fitting and pressed to disengage the retaining claws. The hose can then be pulled off the union. If the tool is not available, the very careful use of two small electrical screwdrivers should serve to release the union. To stop diesel fuel from spilling, cover the open ends of the hoses.

20 Disconnect the fuel return pipe and release the fuel hoses from any support clips, then position them clear of the cylinder head. Use blanking plugs to seal off any pipes to prevent dirt ingress.

21 Disconnect all relevant wiring from the fuel injection pump and pressure regulator. Label all connections to aid correct refitting **(see illustrations)**.

22 Disconnect the electrical feed wires from the heater plugs and fuel injectors **(see illustration)**.

23 Disconnect the wiring connector to the fuel filter and unclip the harness and move it to one side, noting its fitted position.

24 If not already done, remove the timing pin from the cylinder block and turn the crankshaft anti-clockwise (viewed from the timing belt end of the engine) by a quarter-turn to position all four pistons halfway down their bores.

25 Working in the **reverse** of the sequence shown in illustration 9.39, progressively slacken the cylinder head bolts by half a turn at a time until all bolts can be unscrewed by hand and removed. Note that new bolts must be used for refitting.

26 The cylinder head assembly complete with ancillaries is heavy and it is advisable to attach a hoist and suitable lifting tackle.

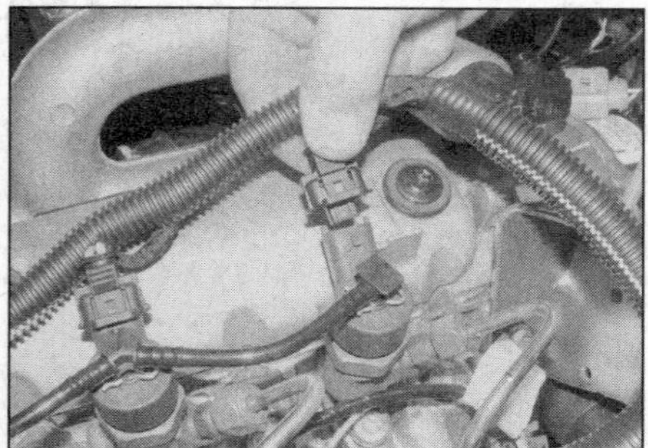

9.22 Disconnecting the wiring connectors from the injectors

27 Lift the cylinder head (complete with manifolds, injection pump and timing belt upper inner cover) upwards and off the cylinder block. If it is stuck, tap it upwards using a hammer and block of wood (taking care not to damage the fuel injection pump). **Do not** try to turn the cylinder head (it is located by two dowels), nor attempt to prise it free using a screwdriver inserted between the block and head faces. If the locating dowels are a loose fit, remove them and store them with the head for safe-keeping **(see illustration)**.

28 If desired, the manifolds, turbocharger and fuel injection pump can be removed from the cylinder head with reference to the relevant Sections of Chapter 4B.

Inspection

29 The mating faces of the cylinder head and block must be perfectly clean before refitting the head. Use a cleaning agent (Renault use a Decapjoint product) to dissolve any remains of gasket still on the mating faces. Take particular care with the aluminium cylinder head, as the soft metal is damaged easily. Also, make sure that debris is not allowed to enter the oil and water channels – this is particularly important for the oil circuit, as carbon could block the oil supply to the camshaft or crankshaft bearings. Using adhesive tape and paper, seal the water, oil and bolt holes in the cylinder block. Clean the piston crowns in the same way.

30 Check the block and head for nicks, deep scratches and other damage. If there is more serious damage, then it may need to be repaired by machining, but this is a specialist job.

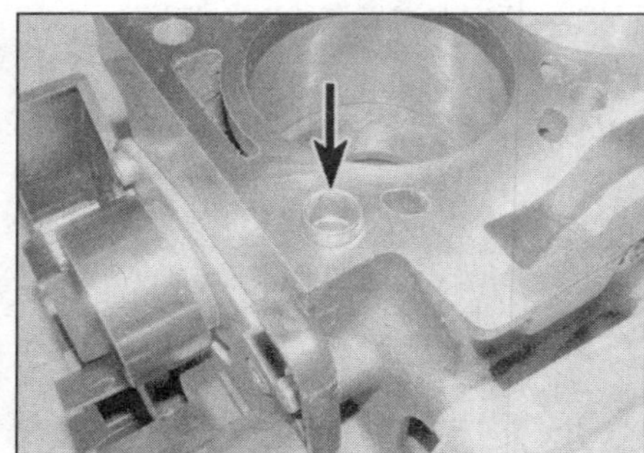

9.27 Cylinder head locating dowel in the cylinder block

31 If warpage of the cylinder head is suspected, use a straight-edge to check it for distortion. Refer to Chapter 2E if necessary.

Warning: If the cylinder head is warped more than the stated specification a new cylinder head will be required, as regrinding of the cylinder head is NOT permitted.

32 Clean out the cylinder head boltholes in the block using a pipe cleaner, or a rag and screwdriver. Make sure that all oil is removed; otherwise there is a possibility of the block being cracked by hydraulic pressure when the bolts are tightened.

33 Examine the cylinder head bolt threads in the cylinder block for damage – if necessary, use the correct-size tap to chase out the threads in the block. Renault recommend that the cylinder head bolts are to be discarded and renewed, regardless of their apparent condition.

Refitting

34 Where applicable, refit the manifolds, turbocharger and fuel injection pump to the cylinder head, with reference to the relevant Sections of Chapter 4B.

35 Turn the crankshaft clockwise (viewed from the timing belt end) until Nos 1 and 4 pistons pass bottom dead centre (BDC) and begin to rise, then position them halfway up their bores (this is to prevent the possibility of piston-to-valve contact). Nos 2 and 3 pistons will also be at their midway positions, but descending their bores. Do not turn the crankshaft again until the timing belt is to be refitted.

36 Ensure that the cylinder head locating dowels are fitted to the cylinder block, then fit the correct gasket the right way round on the cylinder block with the identification mark(s) at the front corner of the engine at the flywheel/ driveplate end.

37 Lower the cylinder head onto the block. Ensure that the timing belt upper inner cover engages correctly with the lower inner cover on the cylinder block. Where applicable, disconnect the lifting tackle and hoist.

38 The new cylinder head bolts must be fitted without oiling them. Insert the bolts, with their washers, and tighten them finger-tight.

39 Tighten the cylinder head bolts to the specified torques in the sequence shown and in the stages given in the Specifications at the beginning of this Chapter **(see illustration)**. The initial stages precompress the gasket and the remaining stages are the main tightening procedure. When angle-tightening the bolts, it is recommended that an angle-tightening gauge be used to ensure accuracy. Note that provided the bolts are tightened exactly as specified, there will be no need to retighten them once the engine has been started and run after reassembly.

Warning: The final tightening stages involve very high forces. Ensure that the tools used are in good condition. If the engine has been removed from the vehicle, it is recommended that the final tightening stages be carried out with the engine refitted to the vehicle (it may be necessary to remove the engine right-hand mounting upper bracket for access to one of the bolts with the engine in the vehicle).

40 Reconnect the wiring connector to the fuel filter and clip the harness back in position as noted on removal.

41 Reconnect the electrical feed wires to the heater plugs and fuel injectors.

42 Reconnect all the relevant wiring to the fuel injection pump and pressure regulator, check the fitted positions as labelled on removal.

43 Remove any blanking plugs and reconnect the fuel return and supply pipes. Locate the fuel pipes in the support clips provided, making sure they are routed correctly.

44 Refit the coolant hoses to the housing on the transmission end of the cylinder head and tighten the retaining clips.

45 Reconnect the wiring connector to the temperature switch on the coolant housing.

46 Refit the camshaft sensor and tighten its mounting bolt.

47 Refit the engine lifting bracket to the cylinder head and tighten its mounting bolts.

48 Reconnect the oil return pipe and the oil supply pipe to the turbocharger unit, refit the supply pipe mounting bracket bolt to the manifold.

49 Refit the exhaust front section/catalytic converter as described in Chapter 4B.

50 Refit the upper mounting bracket bolt for the thermo plunger unit at the rear of the cylinder head.

51 Refit the vacuum reservoir at the rear of the intake manifold and reconnect the wiring connector below the reservoir.

52 Reconnect the air hoses running from the intercooler to the turbocharger.

53 Refit the air filter housing, along with the air intake hoses which were disconnected on removal.

54 Reconnect the vacuum hose to the brake vacuum pump.

55 Refit the timing belt as described in Section 5 and the timing belt tensioner as described in Section 6.

56 Refit the auxiliary drivebelt as described in Chapter 1B.

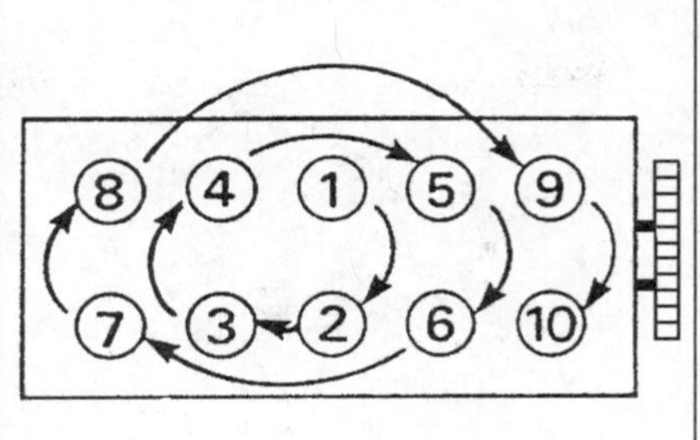

9.39 Cylinder head bolt tightening sequence

57 Refill and bleed the cooling system as described in Chapter 1B.

58 Reconnect the battery negative terminal.

59 Prime and bleed the fuel system as described in Chapter 4B.

60 Follow the procedure described in Chapter 4B, Section 16 (priming the turbocharger oil circuit) before starting the engine.

61 Refit the engine sound-insulating cover.

10 Sump – removal and refitting

Removal

1 Apply the handbrake, then jack up the front of the car and support it on axle stands (see *Jacking and vehicle support*). Undo the retaining screws and remove the plastic undercover from beneath the engine/transmission.

2 Drain the engine oil as described in Chapter 1B, then refit and tighten the drain plug.

3 Unscrew the bolts securing the left-hand end of the sump to the transmission bellhousing flange.

4 Unscrew the bolts securing the sump to the cylinder block. Tap the sump with a hide or plastic mallet to break the seal, and then remove the sump along with its gasket. Discard the gasket; a new one must be used on refitting.

Refitting

5 Remove all traces of dirt and oil from the mating surfaces of the sump and cylinder block.

6 Apply a bead of Rhodorseal 5661 sealant (available from Renault dealers) to the join between the crankshaft oil seal housing and cylinder block, and to the join between the rear main bearing cap and cylinder block **(see illustration)**.

7 Locate the new gasket on the top of the sump and lift the sump into position.

8 Insert the bolts and initially tighten them all to the Stage 1 torque setting given in the Specifications. If the engine is in the car, ensure that the left-hand end of the sump is in contact with the transmission bellhousing flange. If the engine is removed from the car, use a straight-edge to maintain the alignment between the left-hand end of the sump and cylinder block **(see illustration)**.

9 Progressively tighten the bolts to the Stage 2 torque setting in an anti-clockwise spiral pattern starting at the centre and working outwards.

10 Refit the undercover and lower the vehicle to the ground.

11 Fill the engine with fresh oil, with reference to Chapter 1B.

11 Oil pump – removal, inspection and refitting

Removal

1 To remove the oil pump alone, first remove the sump, referring to Section 10.

2 Unscrew bolts securing the anti-emulsion plate to the crankcase and the oil pump mounting bolts **(see illustrations)**. Withdraw the anti-emulsion plate from the cylinder block.

3 Tilt the pump to disengage its sprocket from the drive chain and lift away the pump **(see illustration)**. If the locating dowels are displaced, refit them in their locations.

4 To remove the oil pump complete with its drive chain and sprockets, first remove the sump (Section 10), then unbolt the crankshaft timing belt end oil seal housing, as described in Section 12 **(see illustration)**. Note the presence of the chain guide block and of its two locating dowels.

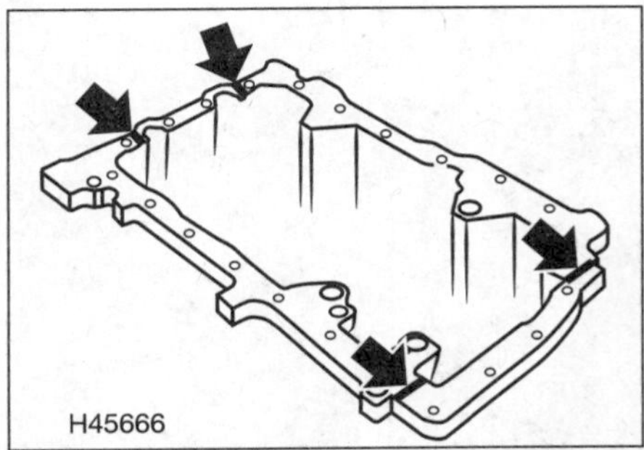

10.6 Apply sealant in the areas shown before refitting the sump

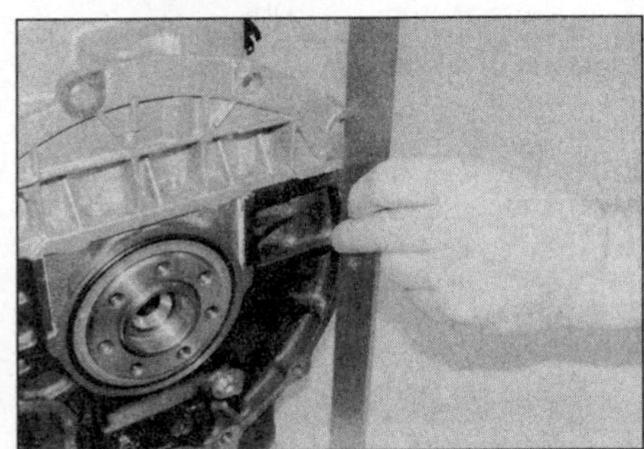

10.8 Use a straight-edge to align the sump and the block

11.2a Unscrew the bolts . . .

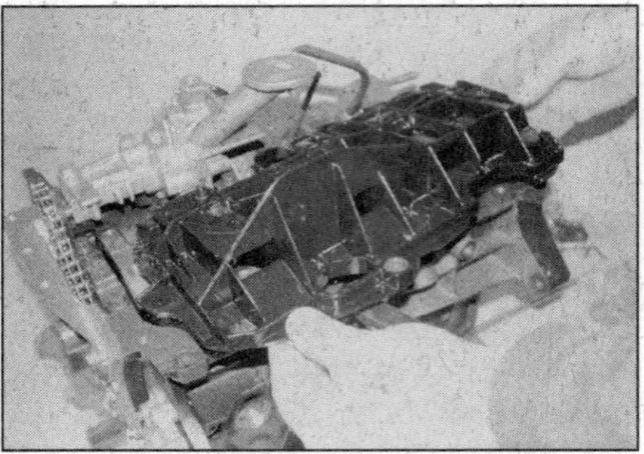

11.2b . . . and remove the anti-emulsion plate . . .

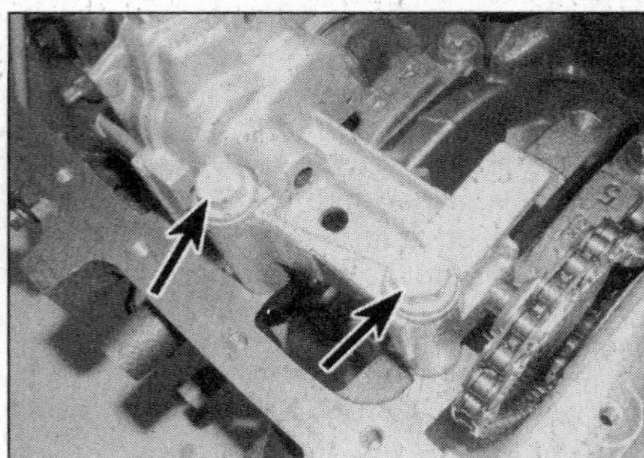

11.2c . . . then undo the pump mounting bolts (arrowed)

11.3 Disengage the oil pump sprocket from the drive chain

11.4 Removing the timing belt end oil seal housing

11.6 Removing the oil pump sprocket drive and chain

5 Unscrew the bolts securing the sprocket to the oil pump hub. Use a screwdriver through one of the holes in the sprocket to hold it stationary.

6 Slide the drive sprocket from the crankshaft and the driven sprocket from the oil pump. Withdraw both sprockets and the chain **(see illustration)**. Note that the drive sprocket is not keyed to the crankshaft, but relies on the pulley bolt being tightened correctly to clamp the sprocket. It is most important that the pulley bolt is correctly tightened otherwise there is the possibility of the oil pump not functioning.

7 Unbolt the oil pump as described in paragraph 2 above.

Inspection

8 Unscrew the retaining bolts and lift off the pump cover. Withdraw the idler gear and the drivegear/shaft. Mark the idler gear before removal, so that it can be refitted in its original position.

9 Extract the retaining clip and remove the oil pressure relief valve spring retainer, spring, spring seat and plunger **(see illustration)**.

10 Clean the components and carefully examine the gears, pump body and relief valve plunger for any signs of scoring or wear. Renew the complete pump assembly if excessive wear is evident (no spare parts are available).

11 If the components appear serviceable, measure the clearance between the pump body and the gears using feeler gauges. Also measure the gear endfloat and check the flatness of the end cover **(see illustrations)**. If the clearances exceed the specified tolerances, the pump must be renewed. There should be no discernible wear or distortion of the end cover.

12 If the pump is satisfactory, reassemble the components in the reverse order of removal **(see illustration)**. Fill the pump with oil, then refit the cover and tighten the bolts securely. Prime the oil pump by filling it with clean engine oil whilst rotating the driveshaft.

11.9 Withdraw the retaining clip and remove the oil pressure relief valve components

11.11a Measuring the oil pump gear-to-body clearance

11.11b Measuring the oil pump gear endfloat

11.11c Checking the flatness of the oil pump cover

Refitting

13 Wipe clean the oil pump and cylinder block mating surfaces.

14 Check that the two locating dowels are fitted in the cylinder block, and then position the oil pump on them and insert the two mounting bolts. Tighten the bolts securely.

15 Engage the sprockets on the chain (if removed), and then refit both sprockets and the chain as an assembly. Slide the drive sprocket fully onto the crankshaft and locate the driven sprocket on the oil pump hub.

16 Align the holes, then insert the sprocket bolts and tighten them securely while holding the sprocket stationary with a screwdriver.

17 Refit the anti-emulsion plate and secure with the retaining bolt(s).

18 Refit the oil seal housing as described in Section 12 – do not forget the chain guide block and its two locating dowels – and the sump (refer to Section 10).

12 Crankshaft oil seals – renewal

Note: *There are two types of seals that may be used on this engine, these are not interchangeable and should only be renewed with the same type.*

a) Early type, which has a spring inside the V-shaped lip of the seal

b) Later type, which has a flat sealing lip with no spring and comes with a plastic protector, which is also a fitting sleeve.

Warning: Renault recommend that the later elastomer seals should only be fitted using a special tool, to prevent any damage to the seal. The seal should not be touched as it is very fragile; when handling only touch the plastic protector sleeve, which is supplied with the seal.

Timing belt end oil seal

1 Remove the crankshaft sprocket, as described in Section 6.

2 Note the fitted position of the old seal, then prise it out of the oil seal housing using a screwdriver or suitable hooked instrument **(see illustration)**. An alternative method of removing the oil seal is to drill carefully two small holes opposite each other in the oil seal and insert self-tapping screws, then pull on the screws with grips. Take care not to damage the surface of the crankshaft or spacer or the seal housing. **Note:** *On some models it may be necessary to remove the timing belt lower inner cover to allow the seal to be withdrawn. If this is the case, remove the idler sprocket and idler pulley (see Section 6) then unbolt the cover.*

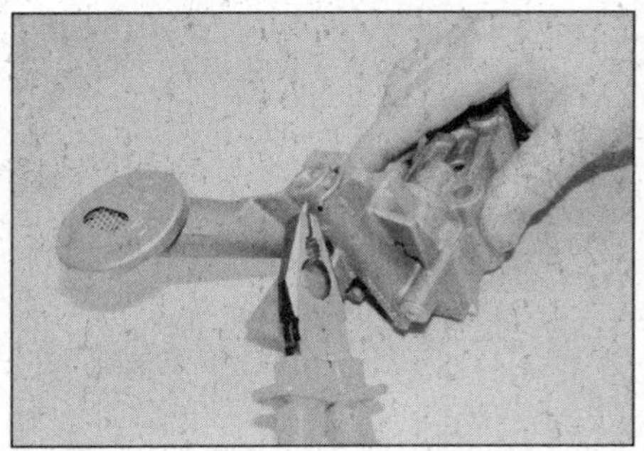

11.12 Bend the end of the retaining clip to ensure it remains in position

3 Clean the seal housing and polish off any burrs or raised edges, which may have caused the seal to fail in the first place. Inspect the seal rubbing surface on the crankshaft. If it is grooved or rough in the area where the old seal was fitted, the new seal should be fitted slightly less deeply, so that it rubs on an unworn part of the crankshaft surface.

4 Wipe clean the oil seal seating, then dip the new seal in fresh engine oil and locate it over the crankshaft with its closed side facing outwards. Make sure that the oil seal lip is not damaged, as it is located on the crankshaft.

5 Using a tube of suitable diameter, drive the oil seal squarely into the housing to the previously noted position – take great care not to damage the seal lips during fitting **(see illustration)**. Note that if the surface of the shaft was noted to be badly scored, press the new seal slightly further into its housing so that its lip is running on an unmarked area of the shaft.

6 Where necessary, refit the timing belt lower inner cover **(see illustration)** and install the idler pulley and idler sprocket as described in Section 6. Refit the crankshaft sprocket as described in Section 6 and fit the new timing belt as described in Section 5.

Timing belt end oil seal housing

7 Remove the timing belt as described in Section 5, and the crankshaft and idler sprockets and the idler pulley with reference to Section 6. Remove the Woodruff key from the crankshaft keyway, and then unbolt the timing belt lower inner cover from the cylinder block.

8 Unscrew the bolts securing the sump to the oil seal housing.

9 Unscrew the retaining bolts and carefully withdraw the oil seal housing, noting the locating dowels around its two lower bolt holes. If it is stuck in place a leverage point is provided on its upper edge (near the timing belt idler pulley) to allow a screwdriver or similar to be used gently to prise the housing away from the cylinder block without risking damage to the delicate mating surfaces of either. If the sump gasket is damaged, the sump will have to be removed to renew it. Note the presence of the oil pump drive chain guide block and of its two locating dowels – check that the guide block is fit for further use and renew it if there is any doubt about its condition.

10 The oil seal should be renewed whenever the housing is removed. Note the fitted position of the old seal, then prise it out with a screwdriver and wipe clean the seating. Smear the outer perimeter of the new seal with fresh engine oil and locate it squarely on the housing with its closed side facing outwards. Place the housing on a block of wood, then use a socket or metal tube to drive in the oil seal.

11 On refitting, clean all traces of sealant from the housing, sump and block mating faces. Check that the chain guide block is correctly fitted and that the housing's locating dowels are in place.

12 Apply a 1.5 mm diameter bead of Rhodorseal 5661 (available from Renault dealers) to the housing's gasket surfaces, around the inner edges of the bolt holes and apply a smear of sealant to the threads of the two bolts (nearest the oil seal) which project inside the cylinder block. Do **NOT** allow sealant to foul the oil gallery at the upper end of the housing. Refit the housing to the

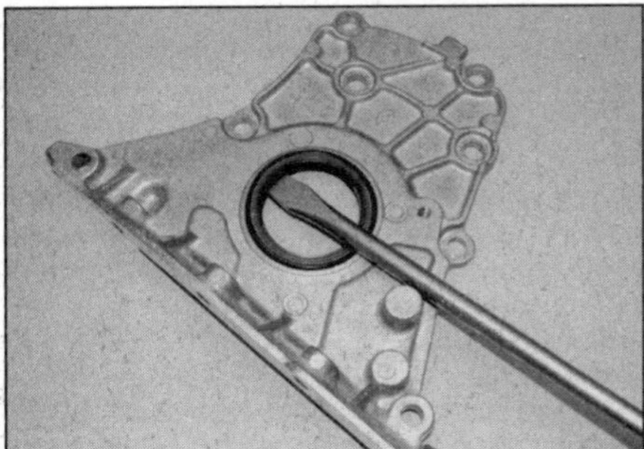

12.2 Removing the timing belt end oil seal with the timing cover removed

12.5 Using a socket to drive in the new oil seal

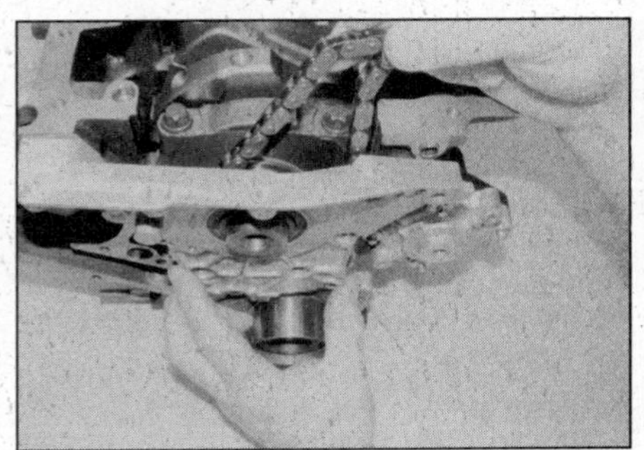

12.6 Refitting the oil seal housing

13.3 The flywheel bolts (arrowed) are unequally spaced for refitting

cylinder block and sump, tightening the bolts securely and evenly. **Note:** *On some models a steel gasket may be fitted, check with your Renault dealer.*

13 Refit the Woodruff key to the crankshaft keyway, then refit the timing belt lower inner cover to the cylinder block, tightening securely its retaining bolts.

14 Refit the crankshaft and idler sprockets and the idler pulley and fit the new timing belt with reference to Sections 6 and 5.

Transmission end oil seal

15 Remove the flywheel/driveplate as described in Section 13.

16 Prise out the old oil seal using a small screwdriver, taking care not to damage the surface of the crankshaft. Alternatively, the oil seal can be removed as described in paragraph 2.

17 Inspect the seal rubbing surface on the crankshaft. If it is grooved or rough in the area where the old seal was fitted, the new seal should be fitted slightly less deeply, so that it rubs on an unworn part of the surface.

18 Wipe clean the oil seal seating, then dip the new seal in fresh engine oil. Locate it over the crankshaft; making sure its sealing lip is facing inwards. Make sure that the oil seal lip is not damaged, as it is located on the crankshaft.

19 Using a metal tube, drive the oil seal squarely into the bore until flush. A block of wood cut to pass over the end of the crankshaft may be used instead.

20 Refit the flywheel/driveplate with reference to Section 13.

13 Flywheel/driveplate – removal, inspection and refitting

Note: *New flywheel/driveplate retaining bolts will be required on refitting. There are two types of flywheel/driveplate fitted to this type of engine, a conventional flywheel/driveplate and a dual mass flywheel/driveplate.*

Removal

1 Remove the transmission as described in Chapter 7A, then remove the clutch assembly as described in Chapter 6.

2 Prevent the flywheel/driveplate from turning by locking the ring gear teeth with a screwdriver. Alternatively a home-made tool similar to that shown in Chapter 2A, Section 12, can be used. Make alignment marks between the flywheel/driveplate and crankshaft using paint or a suitable marker pen.

3 Slacken and remove the flywheel/driveplate retaining bolts and remove the flywheel/driveplate. Do not drop it, as it is very heavy. If the locating dowel (where fitted) is a loose fit in the crankshaft end, remove and store it with the flywheel/driveplate for safe-keeping. Discard the bolts, as they should be renewed whenever they are disturbed. On dual mass type flywheels, make sure the shim is kept located on the two pins in the centre of the flywheel/driveplate **(see illustration)**.

Inspection

Warning: Dual mass flywheels are made up of two parts, NEVER undo the nine retaining bolts around the outer circumference and split the flywheel or it will become ineffective.

4 Check the surface of the flywheel to check if it is worn or burnt with a 'bluish' friction face.

5 Examine the flywheel for scoring of the clutch face, and for wear or chipping of the ring gear teeth. If the clutch face is scored, the flywheel may be surface-ground, but renewal is preferable. Seek the advice of a Renault dealer or engine reconditioning specialist to see if machining is possible. If the ring gear is worn or damaged, the flywheel/driveplate must be renewed, as it is not possible to renew the ring gear separately.

Refitting

6 Clean the mating surfaces of the flywheel/driveplate and crankshaft.

7 Ensure that the locating dowel is in position (where fitted) and offer up the flywheel/driveplate, locating it on the dowel, and fit the new retaining bolts. If the original is being refitted align the marks made prior to removal.

8 Lock the flywheel/driveplate using the method employed on dismantling, and tighten the retaining bolts to the specified torque.

9 Refit the clutch as described in Chapter 6.

10 Remove the locking tool, and refit the transmission as described in Chapter 7A.

14 Engine/transmission mountings – renewal

Inspection

1 If improved access is required, apply the handbrake, then jack up the front of the car and support it on axle stands (see *Jacking and vehicle support*).

2 Check the mounting rubber to see if it is cracked, hardened or separated from the metal at any point; renew the mounting if any such damage or deterioration is evident.

3 Check that all the mounting's fasteners are securely tightened; use a torque wrench to check if possible.

4 Using a large screwdriver or a crowbar, check for wear in the mounting by carefully levering against it to check for free play. Where this is not possible, enlist the aid of an assistant to move the engine/transmission back-and-forth, or from side-to-side, while you watch the mounting. While some free play is to be expected even from new components, excessive wear should be obvious. If excessive free play is found, check first that the fasteners are correctly secured, and then renew any worn components as described below.

Renewal

Right-hand mounting

5 Disconnect the battery negative terminal (refer to *Disconnecting the battery* in the Reference Section of this manual).

6 Place a jack beneath the engine, with a block of wood on the jack head (remove the undercover to improve access to the sump). Raise the jack until it is supporting the weight of the engine. Alternately, attach an engine support bar to the lifting brackets and support the weight of the engine with the bar.

7 Where fitted, undo the two retaining bolts and withdraw the acoustic mass unit (metal weight) from the engine mounting assembly.

8 Slacken the two mounting bolts for the tie-rod at the rear of the mounting, remove the front bolt to the engine mounting and swivel the tie-rod to one side.

9 Undo the nut securing the rubber mounting to the engine mounting bracket.

10 Slacken and remove the three bolts securing the engine mounting bracket to the cylinder head, and withdraw it from the engine. Where applicable, release any cables or wiring from the top of the engine mounting bracket.

11 Unscrew the retaining bolts and remove the rubber mounting and movement limiter from the body.

12 Check carefully for signs of wear or damage on all components, and renew them where necessary.

13 On reassembly, fit the rubber mounting and movement limiter to the body, insert the retaining bolts but tighten them finger tight only at this stage.

14 Refit the upper part of the bracket to the cylinder head, locating it on the stud for the rubber mounting. Tighten the mounting bolts to the cylinder head to the specified torque.

15 Refit the nut securing the rubber mounting to the engine mounting bracket and tighten it to the specified torque.

16 Centralise the movement limiter around the rubber mounting then tighten the three bolts to the specified torque.

17 Swivel the tie-rod at the rear of the mounting bracket back into place and refit the front bolt to the engine mounting, tighten the bolts to the specified torque.

18 Refit the acoustic mass unit to the engine mounting assembly and tighten the retaining bolts to the specified torque.

19 Remove the jack from underneath the engine or the engine support bar (as applicable), and reconnect the battery negative terminal.

Left-hand mounting

20 Disconnect the battery negative terminal (refer to *Disconnecting the battery* in the Reference Section of this manual).

21 Refer to Chapter 4B and remove the air cleaner and inlet components as necessary for access to the mounting.

22 Place a jack beneath the transmission, with a block of wood on the jack head. Raise the jack until it is supporting the weight of the transmission.

23 Slacken and remove the mounting rubber's centre nut, and two retaining bolts and remove the mounting from the engine compartment.

24 If necessary, undo the retaining bolts and remove the mounting bracket from the top of the transmission housing. The mounting stud can be separated from the bracket once its lower retaining nut has been undone.

25 Check carefully for signs of wear or damage on all components, and renew them where necessary.

26 Refit the stud to the mounting bracket and tighten its to the specified torque.

27 Refit the bracket to the transmission, tightening its mounting bolts to the specified torque.

28 Fit the mounting rubber to the bracket and tighten its retaining bolts and centre nut to the specified torque.

29 Refit the air cleaner and inlet components removed for access.

30 Remove the jack from underneath the transmission and reconnect the battery negative terminal.

Rear mounting

31 Disconnect the battery negative terminal (refer to *Disconnecting the battery* in the Reference Section of this manual).

32 If not already done, apply the handbrake, then jack up the front of the car and support it on axle stands (see *Jacking and vehicle support*).

33 Position a jack with a block of wood on its head underneath the sump. Raise the jack until it is supporting the weight of the engine.

34 Slacken and remove the nut and bolt from each end of the mounting link and remove the link from underneath the vehicle. If necessary, undo the retaining nuts and bolts and remove the mounting bracket from the engine/transmission.

35 Check carefully for signs of wear or damage on all components, and renew them where necessary.

36 On reassembly, fit the mounting bracket (where removed) to the rear of the transmission and tighten its retaining bolts to the specified torque.

15.4a Remove the oil filter mounting stud . . .

15.4b . . . then withdraw the oil cooler and recover the sealing ring

37 Fit the mounting link, and tighten both its bolts to there specified torque settings.

38 Lower the vehicle to the ground and reconnect the battery negative terminal.

15 Oil cooler – removal and refitting

Removal

1 Drain the cooling system as described in Chapter 1B.

2 Remove the oil filter (refer to Chapter 1B).

3 Loosen the clips and disconnect the coolant hoses from the oil cooler.

4 Unscrew the oil filter mounting stud, which also secures the oil cooler, and withdraw the oil cooler from the engine. Recover the sealing ring **(see illustrations)**.

Refitting

5 Refitting is a reversal of removal, but use a new sealing ring.

16 Oil pressure switch – removal and refitting

1 The oil pressure switch is a vital early warning of low oil pressure. The switch operates the oil warning light on the instrument panel – the light should come on with the ignition, and go out almost immediately when the engine starts.

2 If the light does not come on, there could be a fault on the instrument panel, the switch wiring, or the switch itself. If the light does not go out, low oil level, worn oil pump (or sump pick-up blocked), blocked oil filter, or worn main bearings could be to blame – or again, the switch may be faulty.

3 If the light comes on while driving, the best advice is to turn the engine off immediately, and not to drive the car until the problem has been investigated – ignoring the light could mean expensive engine damage.

Removal

4 The oil pressure switch is located on the front face of the engine, next to the oil filter.

5 Jack up the front of the car, and support it on axle stands (see *Jacking and vehicle support*) – to improve access, remove the oil filter, referring to Chapter 1B if necessary.

6 Disconnect the wiring plug from the switch **(see illustration)**.

7 Unscrew the switch from the block, and remove it together with its sealing washer. There should only be a very slight loss of oil when this is done.

Inspection

8 Examine the switch for signs of cracking or splits. If the top part of the switch is loose, this is an early indication of impending failure.

9 Check that the wiring terminals at the switch are not loose, then trace the wire from the switch connector until it enters the main loom – any wiring defects will give rise to apparent oil pressure problems.

Refitting

10 Refitting is the reverse of the removal procedure, noting the following points:

a) *Clean the switch threads before fitting. Tighten the switch securely.*
b) *Reconnect the switch connector, making sure it clicks home properly. Ensure that the wiring is routed away from any hot or moving parts.*
c) *Lower the car to the ground, then check the engine oil level and top-up if necessary (see 'Weekly checks').*
d) *Check for signs of oil leaks once the engine has been restarted and warmed-up to normal operating temperature.*

16.6 Disconnect the oil pressure switch wiring plug

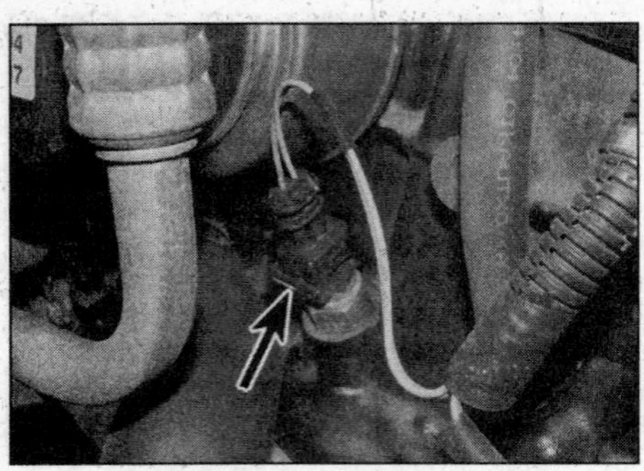

17.2a Disconnect the oil level sensor wiring plug . . .

17.2b . . . then unscrew and withdraw the sensor from the block

17 Oil level sensor – removal and refitting

Removal

1 The sensor is fitted at the front of the engine, next to the oil filter. Access to the sensor may be easiest from under the vehicle, jack up the front of the car, and support it on axle stands (see *Jacking and vehicle support*). Undo the retaining bolts and remove the engine undertray.

2 Disconnect the wiring plug, then unscrew and withdraw the sensor from the engine block **(see illustrations)**.

Refitting

3 Refitting is a reversal of removal. Tighten the sensor securely, to prevent leaks.

Chapter 2 Part C:
2.2 litre diesel engine in-car repair procedures

Contents

Degrees of difficulty

Easy, suitable for novice with little experience 	**Fairly easy,** suitable for beginner with some experience	**Fairly difficult,** suitable for competent DIY mechanic	**Difficult,** suitable for experienced DIY mechanic	**Very difficult,** suitable for expert DIY or professional 

Specifications

General

Type	Four-cylinder, in-line, double overhead camshaft, 16-valve
Designation	G9T 702/703
Bore	87.0 mm
Stroke	92.0 mm
Capacity	2188 cc
Compression ratio	18:1
Firing order	1-3-4-2 (No 1 cylinder at flywheel/driveplate end of engine)
Direction of crankshaft rotation	Clockwise, viewed from timing belt end

Camshafts

Drive	Toothed belt
Number of bearings on each	6
Camshaft endfloat	0.05 to 0.13 mm

Lubrication system

Minimum oil pressure at 80°C:	
At 1000 rpm	1.6 bars (23.2 psi)
At 3000 rpm	4.0 bars (58.0 psi)

Torque wrench settings

	Nm	lbf ft
Auxiliary drivebelt idler pulley nut	45	33
Auxiliary drivebelt tensioner pulley bolt	21	15
Balance shaft unit mounting bolts:		
Stage 1	15	11
Stage 2	Angle-tighten through 38° ± 6°	
Blanking plug in cylinder block (for TDC access)	22	16

Torque wrench settings (continued)

	Nm	lbf ft
Brake vacuum pump mounting bolts	23	17
Camshaft bearing cap bolts:		
Caps 1 and 6	12	9
Caps 2, 3, 4 and 5	10	7
Camshaft sprocket hub bolt	60	44
Camshaft sprocket bolts	10	7
Connecting rod (big-end) cap bolts:		
Stage 1	25	18
Stage 2	Angle-tighten through 60° ± 6°	
Crankshaft pulley bolt:		
Stage 1	50	37
Stage 2	Angle-tighten through 90° ± 6°	
Cylinder block main bearing casting bolts:		
Large (12 mm) inner bolts*:		
Stage 1	20	15
Stage 2	Angle-tighten through 150° ± 10°	
Smaller (8 mm) outer bolts	20	15
Cylinder head bolts**:		
Stage 1	30	22
Stage 2	Angle-tighten through 300° ± 6°	
Cylinder head cover/inlet manifold bolts	12	9
Cylinder head mounting block bolts (timing belt cover end)	25	18
Engine/transmission mountings:		
Right-hand engine mounting:		
Mounting bracket-to-cylinder head bolts	62	46
Tie rod bracket bolts	105	77
Mounting bracket-to-rubber mounting nut	44	32
Rubber mounting bracket-to-body bolts	21	15
Left-hand transmission mounting:		
Mounting bracket-to-transmission bolts	105	77
Mounting stud nut	44	32
Rubber mounting bracket-to-body bolts	62	46
Rear mounting bracket/tie rod:		
Tie rod link-to-transmission bolt	180	133
Tie rod link-to-subframe bolt	105	77
Flywheel/driveplate bolts*:		
Standard:		
Stage 1	20	15
Stage 2	Angle-tighten through 45° ± 6°	
Dual mass:		
Stage 1	25	18
Stage 2	Angle-tighten through 50° ± 6°	
Intermediate shaft mounting bolts:		
Stage 1	25	18
Stage 2	Angle-tighten through 30° ± 6°	
Oil baffle plate bolts	10	7
Oil filter housing mounting bolts	22	16
Oil dipstick guide mounting bolts		
Lower bolt	25	18
Upper bolt	10	7
Oil pump mounting bolts		
M6 bolts	10	7
M8 bolts	25	18
Piston base cooling jets **(Note: left-handed thread)**	20	15
Roadwheel bolts	105	77
Rocker shaft retaining bolts	13	10
Sump bolts:		
Stage 1	5	4
Stage 2	9	7
Timing belt cover bolts	10	7
Timing belt tensioner pulley bolt	25	18
Timing belt lower pulley bolt	30	22
Timing gear cover bolts:		
M6 bolts	12	9
M8 bolts	30	22

** New bolts must be used.*

*** Renew the head bolts and refer to the specific instructions contained in Section 9 when tightening the cylinder head bolts.*

1 General information

How to use this Chapter

This Part of Chapter 2 is devoted to in-car repair procedures for the 2.2 litre diesel engine. Similar information covering the 1.9 litre diesel engines and the petrol engines will be found in Chapters 2A and 2B. All procedures concerning engine removal and refitting, and engine block/cylinder head overhaul for petrol and diesel engines can be found in Chapters 2D and 2E as applicable.

Most of the operations included in Chapter 2C are based on the assumption that the engine is still installed in the car. Therefore, if this information is being used during a complete engine overhaul, with the engine already removed, many of the steps included here will not apply.

Engine description

The 2.2 litre diesel engine is a four-cylinder overhead camshaft 16-valve design, mounted transversely at the front of the vehicle with the transmission bolted to the left-hand side. The power steering pump, alternator and air conditioning compressor are driven by the auxiliary drivebelt. The brake servo vacuum pump is driven directly by the exhaust camshaft at the flywheel/driveplate end.

On all engines, the crankshaft is supported in five shell-type main bearings. Thrustwashers are fitted to No 2 main bearing to control crankshaft endfloat. The connecting rods are attached to the crankshaft by horizontally split shell-type big-end bearings, and to the pistons by gudgeon pins. The gudgeon pins are a sliding fit in the connecting rods and are retained by circlips. The aluminium alloy pistons are of the slipper type, and are fitted with three piston rings – two compression rings and a scraper-type oil control ring.

The double overhead camshafts are mounted in the cylinder head, and are driven by a toothed timing belt via an intermediate shaft gear driven from the crankshaft. The fuel injection pump and coolant pump are also gear driven from the crankshaft.

The camshaft operates the 16 valves, which are mounted in the cylinder head, through rocker arms situated directly above the camshaft.

Engine lubrication is by pressure feed from a gear-type oil pump, the pump is chain driven off the timing belt end of the crankshaft. Engine oil is fed through an externally mounted oil filter and oil cooler to the main oil gallery feeding the crankshaft and camshaft. The oil cooler helps keep the oil temperature constant under arduous operating conditions.

Operations with engine in car

The following operations can be carried out without having to remove the engine from the vehicle:

a) Removal and refitting of the cylinder head.
b) Removal and refitting of the timing belt and sprockets.
c) Removal and refitting of the camshaft and rocker shafts.
d) Removal and refitting of the sump.
*e) Removal and refitting of the big-end bearings, connecting rods, and pistons.**
f) Removal and refitting of the oil pump.
g) Renewal of the engine/transmission mountings.
h) Removal and refitting of the flywheel/driveplate.

** Although the operation marked with an asterisk can be carried out with the engine in the car after removal of the sump, it is better for the engine to be removed, in the interests of cleanliness and improved access. For this reason, the procedure is described in Chapter 2E.*

2 Compression test – description and interpretation

Refer to Chapter 2B, Section 2.

3 Top Dead Centre (TDC) for No 1 piston – locating

1 Top dead centre (TDC) is the highest point in the cylinder that each piston reaches as the crankshaft turns. Each piston reaches TDC at the end of the compression stroke and again at the end of the exhaust stroke. However, for the purpose of timing the engine, TDC refers to the position of No 1 piston at the end of its compression stroke.

2 Disconnect the battery negative terminal (refer to *Disconnecting the battery* in the Reference Section of this manual).

3 Apply the handbrake, and then jack up the front of the car and support it on axle stands (see *Jacking and vehicle support*). Remove the right-hand roadwheel.

4 Undo the retaining screws and remove the engine undertray and the plastic covers from within the right-hand wheel arch, to gain access to the crankshaft pulley bolt.

5 Place a jack beneath the engine, with a block of wood on the jack head. Raise the jack until it is supporting the weight of the engine. Alternatively, attach and support bar to the engine and use the bar to support the weight of the engine/transmission.

6 Slacken and remove the retaining nut and bolts and remove the upper right-hand engine mounting as described in Section 14 of this Chapter.

7 Unclip the turbocharger adjustment solenoid valve from its mounting bracket **(see illustration)**.

8 Undo the retaining bolts and remove the upper mounting bracket from the top of the cylinder head to gain access to the camshaft sprockets **(see illustration)**.

9 The crankshaft must now be turned until the index mark on the crankshaft pulley is aligned on the vertical axis of the engine **(see illustration)**. Using a spanner or socket on the crankshaft pulley bolt can turn the crankshaft. Note that the crankshaft must always be turned in a clockwise direction (viewed from the right-hand side of vehicle).

10 Unscrew the access plug from the transmission end of the front of the cylinder block, and insert the timing pin (Renault tool Mot. 1536). Engage the timing pin in the access hole provided in the cylinder block **(see illustrations)**.

11 With the timing pin held in place it will be necessary to rotate the crankshaft slightly in a clockwise direction (viewed from the right-hand side of vehicle), until it stops against the timing pin.

3.7 Unclip the solenoid valve from bracket (arrowed)

3.8 Removing the upper timing belt cover

3.9 The markings (arrowed) must align vertically

3.10a Unscrew the blanking plug/bolt . . .

3.10b . . . and insert the timing pin

3.12 Renault camshaft locking plates (arrowed)

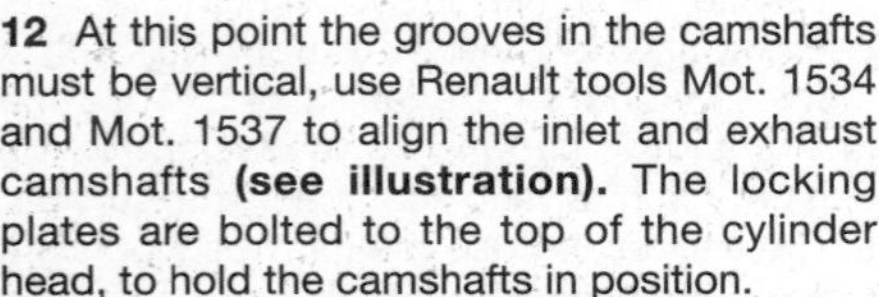

12 At this point the grooves in the camshafts must be vertical, use Renault tools Mot. 1534 and Mot. 1537 to align the inlet and exhaust camshafts **(see illustration).** The locking plates are bolted to the top of the cylinder head, to hold the camshafts in position.

13 The engine is now positioned with No 1 piston at TDC on its compression stroke. For further information on setting the timing up see timing belt removal and refitting in Section 6.

Note: *Do not attempt to rotate the engine whilst the crankshaft is locked in position. If the engine is to be left in this state for a long period of time, it is a good idea to place warning notices inside the vehicle, and in the engine compartment. This will reduce the possibility of the engine being accidentally cranked on the starter motor, which is likely to cause damage with the timing rod in place.*

4.5 Removing the crankshaft pulley

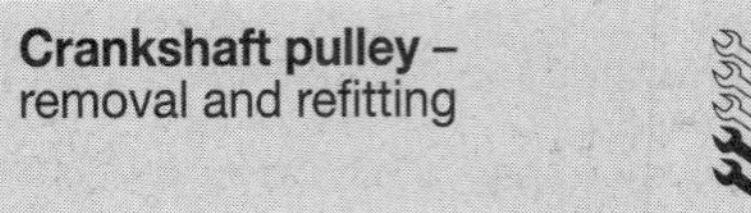

4 Crankshaft pulley – removal and refitting

Removal

1 Disconnect the battery negative terminal (refer to *Disconnecting the battery* in the Reference Section of this manual). Apply the handbrake, and then jack up the front of the car and support it on axle stands (see *Jacking and vehicle support*). Remove the right-hand roadwheel.

2 Unbolt and remove the plastic undertray from the beneath the engine/transmission and the plastic cover from within the right-hand wheel arch.

3 Remove the auxiliary drivebelt as described in Chapter 1B.

4 Slacken the crankshaft pulley retaining bolt. To prevent crankshaft rotation whilst the retaining bolt is slackened, select top gear and have an assistant apply the brakes firmly. If this fails to prevent rotation, lock the flywheel/driveplate ring gear; the starter motor may need to be removed to access the flywheel/driveplate ring gear. *Do not* be tempted to use the crankshaft timing pin to prevent the crankshaft from rotating (see Section 3).

5 Remove the retaining bolt and pulley from the end of the crankshaft **(see illustration)**.

Refitting

6 Remove all traces of locking compound from the crankshaft threads.

7 Clean the threads of the crankshaft pulley retaining bolt and apply a few drops of locking compound (Renault recommend the use of Loctite Autoform).

8 Refit the pulley to the crankshaft and screw in the retaining bolt. Tighten the bolt first to the specified Stage 1 torque and then through the specified Stage 2 angle, using the method employed on removal to prevent rotation.

9 Refit the auxiliary drivebelt as described in Chapter 1B.

5 Timing belt cover – removal and refitting

Removal

1 Disconnect the battery negative terminal (refer to *Disconnecting the battery* in the Reference Section of this manual).

2 Apply the handbrake, then jack up the front of the car and support it on axle stands (see *Jacking and vehicle support*). Remove the right-hand front roadwheel.

3 Undo the retaining screws and remove the engine undertray and the plastic protective covers from the inside the right-hand wheel arch

4 Place a jack beneath the engine, with a block of wood on the jack head. Raise the jack until it is supporting the weight of the engine. Alternatively, attach and support bar to the engine and use the bar to support the weight of the engine/transmission.

5 Slacken and remove the retaining nut and bolts and remove the right-hand engine mounting bracket as described in Section 14 of this Chapter.

6 Unclip the turbocharger adjustment solenoid valve from its mounting bracket.

7 Undo the retaining bolts and remove the upper mounting bracket from the top of the camshaft sprockets **(see illustration)**. Note the lifting eye on the front of the cylinder head may need to be slackened or removed

8 Slacken and remove the retaining bolts from the timing belt cover and mounting bracket, and remove the timing belt cover from the engine **(see illustration)**.

5.7 Lift of the upper mounting bracket . . .

5.8 . . . and withdraw the timing belt cover

6.3 Camshaft locking tools bolted (arrowed) to cylinder head

Refitting

9 Refitting is a reverse of the removal procedure, ensuring that the cover is correctly seated before tightening the retaining bolts securely.

6 Timing belt – removal and refitting

Note: *The timing belt should be renewed whenever it is disturbed; never refit a belt that has already been used. It is recommended that the timing belt, tensioner and idler pulley should be renewed altogether as a kit.*

Removal

1 Remove the timing belt cover as described in Section 5.

2 Position number 1 cylinder at TDC on its compression stroke, as described in Section 3.

3 Check the crankshaft and camshafts are locked in position using the Renault tools noted in Section 3 **(see illustration)**.

4 Slacken the three securing bolts on the exhaust camshaft sprocket.

5 Undo the tensioner pulley retaining bolt and remove it from the cylinder block **(see illustration)**. A new tensioner will be required when refitting.

6 Remove the three bolts from the exhaust camshaft sprocket and remove it, slipping the timing belt off with the sprocket and removing them from the engine. If signs of oil contamination are found, trace the source of the oil leak and rectify it. Wash down the engine timing belt area and all related components, to remove all traces of oil. Check that the idler pulley rotates freely, without any sign of roughness. If necessary, renew as described in Section 7.

Refitting

7 Clean the sprockets and tensioners, and wipe them dry. Do not apply excessive amounts of solvent to the tensioner wheels; otherwise the bearing lubricant may be contaminated. Also clean the front of the cylinder head and block.

8 Ensure that the crankshaft is at the TDC position for No 1 cylinder and is locked in this position using the timing pin through the access hole in the crankcase and that the camshafts are correctly positioned (see Section 3 of this Chapter).

6.5 Remove the tensioner securing bolt (arrowed)

9 Slacken the three retaining bolts on the inlet camshaft sprocket and align the sprocket so that the bolts are centred in their holes **(see illustration)**. The holes in the inlet and exhaust camshaft sprockets are elongated to allow for adjustment.

10 Fit the new tensioner pulley, making sure the slot in the back of the tensioner lines up with the locating peg on the cylinder block **(see illustration)**. Tighten the securing bolt hand tight at this time.

11 Offer up the new belt making sure the arrows marked on the belt (where applicable) are pointing in the direction of rotation. Starting with the lower sprocket, align the new belt and route the belt around the idler pulley, over the inlet camshaft sprocket and then guide it around the tensioner pulley.

6.9 Slacken the three camshaft sprocket bolts (arrowed)

12 With the exhaust camshaft sprocket located inside the timing belt, slide the sprocket onto the end hub of the exhaust camshaft **(see illustration)**. Tighten the retaining bolts hand tight at this moment; try to keep the bolts to the centre of the elongated holes so as to allow for any further adjustment. Ensure that any marks on the timing belt are correctly aligned and slide the belt fully into position.

13 Using a 6.0 mm Allen key engaged with the slot in the tensioner pulley arm; rotate the arm anti-clockwise until the top edge of the moving plate on the camshaft locking tool is aligned with the top edge of the fixed plate on the tool **(see illustrations)**.

14 Hold the tensioner in this position and tighten the retaining bolt to 25 Nm (18 lbf ft). The pointer on the tension wheel should be aligned with the upper edge of the fixed backplate **(see illustration)**

6.10 Make sure the locating peg (arrowed) is located

6.12 Refit the exhaust sprocket complete with timing belt

6.13a Turn the tensioner so that the pointer (arrowed) . . .

6.13b . . . aligns the top of the moving plate (arrowed)

6.14 Pointer should be aligned with upper edge (arrowed)

6.18 Inlet camshaft tool bolted in position

6.19 Exhaust camshaft tool bolted in position

6.20 Align the tab on the end of the plate with the upper edge of the locking tool

6.21 Pointer should be aligned in the middle of the groove (arrowed)

15 Check that the inlet and exhaust camshaft sprocket retaining bolts are centred in their holes, and then tighten them to 10 Nm (7 lbf ft).

16 Remove the crankshaft timing pin and the camshaft locking plates, then using a suitable socket and extension bar on the crankshaft pulley bolt, rotate the crankshaft through two complete rotations in a clockwise direction (viewed from the right-hand end of the engine). *Do not* at any time rotate the crankshaft anti-clockwise.

17 With the engine back to TDC, refit the timing pin to the cylinder block to check the crankshaft is back in position.

18 Fit the locking plate (Renault tool Mot. 1534) to the inlet camshaft and tighten by hand at this time. Slacken the three camshaft sprocket securing bolts by one turn each. Turn the camshaft centre hub using a 16 mm spanner until the locking plate is located correctly, then tighten the locking plate mounting bolt to hold the inlet camshaft in position **(see illustration)**.

19 Fit the locking plate (Renault tool Mot. 1537) to the exhaust camshaft and tighten by hand at this time. Slacken the three camshaft sprocket securing bolts by one turn each. Turn the camshaft centre hub using a 16 mm spanner until the locking plate is located correctly, then tighten the locking plate mounting bolt to hold the exhaust camshaft in position **(see illustration)**.

20 Slacken the tensioner securing bolt, while holding a 6.0 mm Allen key engaged with the slot in the tensioner pulley arm; rotate the arm clockwise until the tab on the top edge of the moving plate on the camshaft locking tool is aligned with the top edge of the fixed plate on the tool **(see illustration)**.

21 Hold the tensioner in this position and tighten the retaining bolt to 25 Nm (18 lbf ft). The pointer on the tension wheel should be aligned in the centre of the groove in the fixed backplate **(see illustration)**

22 Retighten the inlet and exhaust camshaft sprocket securing bolts back to 10 Nm (7 lbf ft). Make sure they are not on their full limit at the edge of the elongated holes.

23 Remove the crankshaft timing pin from the cylinder block and refit the blanking plug, use sealant on the threads and tighten to the specified torque setting.

24 Remove the camshaft locking plates from the camshafts.

25 Refit the timing belt covers as described in Section 5.

26 Refit the undertray and the protective covers from inside the wheel arch, then fit the roadwheel.

27 Remove the jack/engine support bar (as applicable).

28 Lower the vehicle to the ground and tighten the wheel bolts to the specified torque. Reconnect the battery.

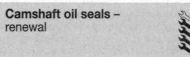

7 Camshaft oil seals – renewal

Timing belt end oil seals

Note: *A new timing belt must be used on refitting.*

1 Remove the timing belt as described in Section 6.

2 With the camshaft sprocket removed, slacken the centre bolt on the camshaft sprocket hub, then undo the retaining bolt and remove the camshaft locking tool **(see illustration)**.

3 Remove the camshaft sprocket centre hub from the end of the camshaft and make a note of the correct fitted depth of the seal **(see illustration)**.

4 Punch or drill two small holes opposite each other in the oil seal, take care not to scratch or damage the surface area of the camshaft. Screw a self-tapping screw into each and pull on the screws with pliers to extract the seal **(see illustration)**.

5 Clean the seal housing and polish off any

7.2 Undo the retaining bolt (arrowed) and remove the camshaft locking tool

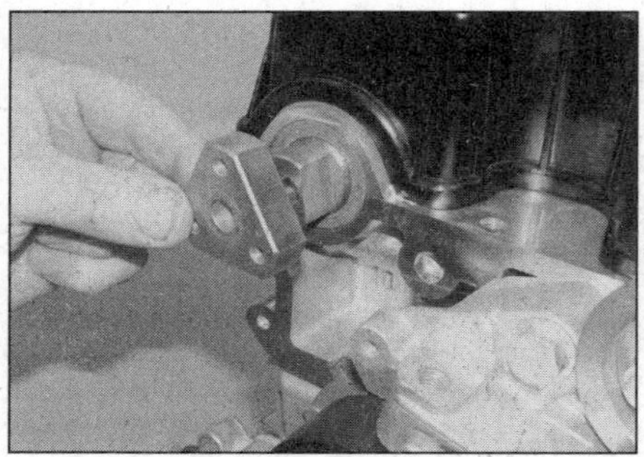
7.3 Remove the camshaft sprocket centre hub

7.4 Using a thin piece of metal sheet (arrowed) to protect the camshaft surface

7.6a Insulating tape wrapped around camshaft to prevent damage to seal

7.6b Using a socket to tap the seal into position

burrs or raised edges which may have caused the seal to fail in the first place.

6 Lubricate the lips of the new seal with clean engine oil and ease it into position on the end of the shaft. Press the seal into its housing until it is positioned at the same depth as the original was prior to removal. If necessary, a suitable tubular drift, such as a socket, which bears only on the hard outer edge of the seal, can be used to tap the seal into position **(see illustrations)**. Take great care not to damage the seal lips during fitting and ensure that the seal lips face inwards. Note that if the surface of the shaft was noted to be badly scored, press the new seal slightly further into its housing so that its lip is running on an unmarked area of the shaft.

7 Refit the camshaft sprocket and timing belt as described in Section 6.

8 This procedure shows the exhaust camshaft oil seal being renewed, carry out the same procedures to replace the inlet camshaft oil seal.

Transmission end oil seal

9 The braking system vacuum pump is mounted directly on the end of the exhaust camshaft. If oil is leaking remove the pump and investigate the cause as described in Chapter 9.

8 Camshaft and rocker shafts – removal, inspection and refitting

Note: *New camshaft oil seals and a new timing belt must be used on refitting.*

Removal

1 Remove the inlet manifold/camshaft cover as described in Chapter 4B.

2 Remove the timing belt as described in Section 6.

3 Undo the retaining bolts and remove the brake vacuum pump from the flywheel/driveplate end of the exhaust camshaft **(see illustration).**

4 Note the fitted position of the rocker shafts, undo the retaining bolts and remove them from the top of the cylinder head **(see illustrations). Note:** *The exhaust rocker shaft has a flat piece going to the end of the shaft on the timing belt side.*

5 The camshaft bearing caps should be numbered 1 to 6 from the flywheel/driveplate end of the engine. If the caps are not already numbered, identify them, numbering them from the flywheel/driveplate end of the engine. **Note:** *If not already removed, undo the retaining bolts and remove the camshaft locking tools from the timing belt end of the camshafts, see Section 6.*

6 Slacken and remove the camshaft bearing cap bolts, noting their correct fitted locations, then remove the bearing caps from the cylinder head. If the cap locating dowels (where applicable) are a loose fit, remove them and store them with the caps for safe-keeping.

7 Note the fitted position of the camshafts, with the flats on the timing belt end of the camshafts being in the vertical position **(see illustration).** Lift the camshaft from the cylinder head. Remove the oil seals from the timing belt end of the camshaft and discard: they must be renewed.

8.3 Removing the brake vacuum pump

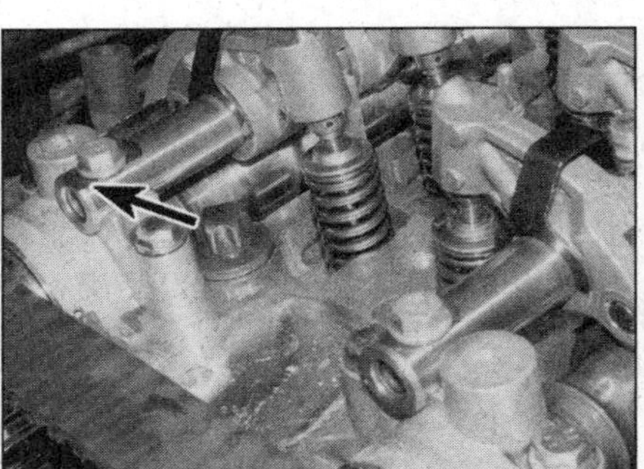
8.4b The exhaust rocker shaft has a flat (arrowed) on the timing belt end when fitted

Inspection

8 Examine the camshaft bearing surfaces and cam lobes for signs of wear ridges and scoring. Renew the camshaft if any of these conditions are apparent. Examine the condition of the bearing surfaces, both on the camshaft journals and in the cylinder head/bearing caps. If the head bearing surfaces are worn excessively, the cylinder head will need to be renewed.

9 Examine the rocker arm bearing surfaces that contact the camshaft lobes for wear ridges and scoring. Renew any rocker on which these conditions are apparent. If a bearing surface is badly scored, also examine the corresponding lobe on the

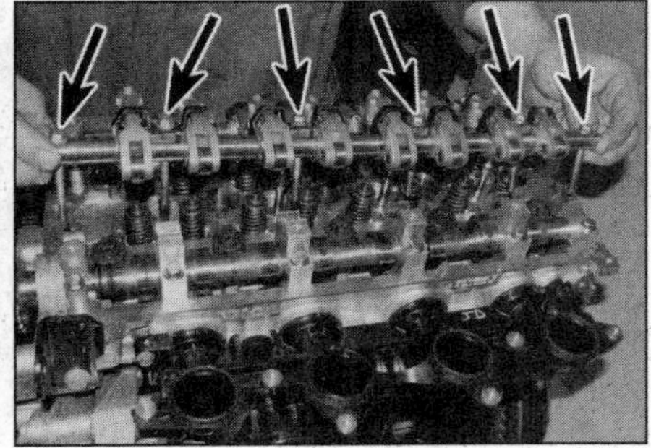
8.4a Undo the retaining bolts (arrowed) and remove the rocker shaft

8.7 Flat (arrowed) should be vertical

8.9a Remove the mounting bolt from the rocker shaft . . .

8.9b . . . release the retaining clip . . .

8.9c . . . remove the spacer from between the rockers . . .

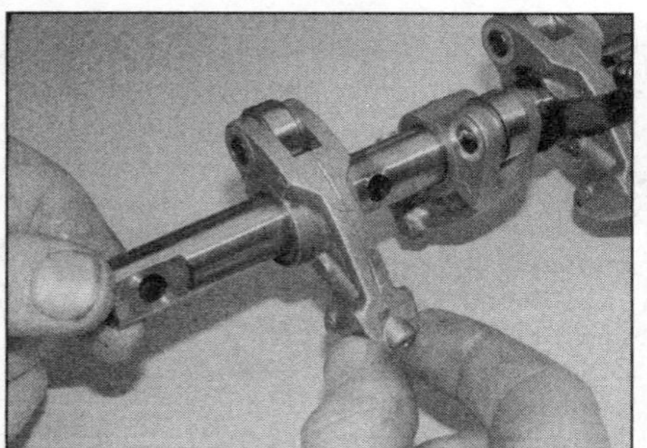
8.9d . . . and slide the rocker off the shaft

8.11 Only tighten the outer bearing caps (arrowed) at this point

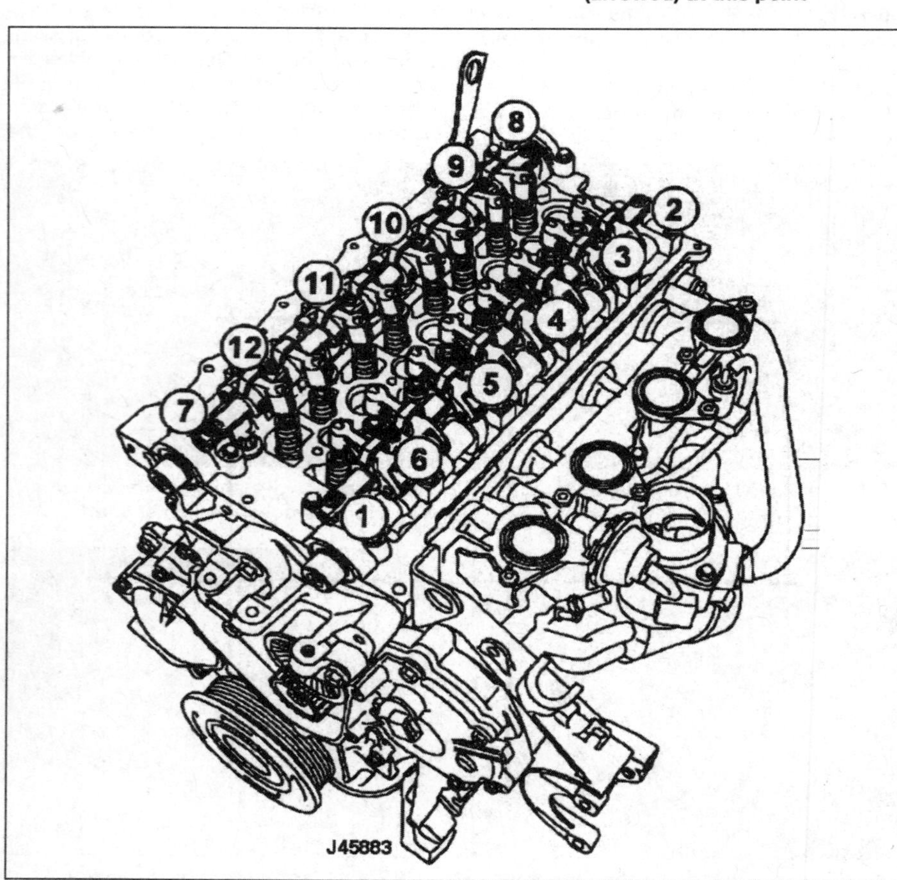

8.14 Tightening sequence for the rocker shafts

camshaft for wear, as it is likely that both will be worn. Renew worn components as necessary **(see illustrations).**

Refitting

10 Lubricate the cam lobes and bearing journals with clean engine oil of the specified grade and fit the camshaft to the head.

11 Refit the camshaft bearing caps in the same order as noted on removal, making sure they are fitted in their original locations and the correct way around. At this point, only tighten camshaft bearing caps 1 and 6 on the inlet and exhaust camshafts to the specified torque setting **(see illustration).**

12 With the engine still in the TDC position (see Section 3) align the camshafts as noted on removal. Use the locking tools (as described in Section 6), which are fitted to the timing belt end of the cylinder head to hold the camshafts in position.

13 Remove the crankshaft timing pin and rotate the crankshaft backwards through 90° (a quarter of a turn) so that all the pistons are positioned halfway up their bores. This will prevent the valves being forced against the pistons as the camshaft cap bolts are tightened.

14 Lubricate the rocker shafts and rocker arms with clean engine oil. Refit the rocker shafts to the cylinder head, making sure they are fitted in their original locations, see paragraph 4. Tighten the mounting bolts to the specified torque setting, in the correct sequence starting with the inlet rocker shaft **(see illustration).**

15 Now tighten the inner camshaft bearing caps 2, 3, 4 and 5 to the specified torque setting in the correct sequence **(see illustration opposite).**

16 Carefully rotate the crankshaft through 90° in the correct direction of rotation, to bring No 1 and 4 cylinders back to TDC, and refit the crankshaft timing pin (see Section 3).

17 Fit a new camshaft oil seals as described in Sections 7.

18 Refit the brake vacuum pump as described in Chapter 9.

19 Refit the inlet manifold/camshaft cover as described in Chapter 4B.

20 Refit the timing belt as described in Section 6.

21 On completion check the engine oil level as described in *Weekly checks*. Start the engine and check for any noises. **Note:** *Do not run the engine at high speeds until the correct oil pressure has been reached.*

9 Cylinder head – removal and refitting

Note 1: *New cylinder head bolts and a new timing belt will be required on refitting.*

Note 2: *Before restarting the engine, it may be necessary to use a diagnostic tool to clear any faults that may be stored in the injection ECU.*

Caution: Be careful not to allow dirt into the injection pump or injector pipes during this procedure. Cover or plug the open ends as they are disconnected.

Removal

1 Disconnect the battery negative terminal (refer to *Disconnecting the battery* in the Reference Section of this manual), then drain the cooling system with reference to Chapter 1B.

2 Remove the timing belt with reference to Section 6.

3 With the engine supported from below, the top of the engine can now be easily accessed.

4 Remove the air cleaner assembly and air inlet pipes as described in Chapter 4B.

5 Slacken the retaining clips and remove the turbocharger intercooler pipes from the top left-hand side of the cylinder head **(see illustrations)**.

6 Undo the retaining bolts and remove the EGR pipe from the front of the engine **(see illustration)**.

7 Slacken the retaining clips from the connection pipe between the inlet manifold and air vent unit **(see illustration)**.

8 Undo the three retaining bolts and remove the wiring harness protector cover from the top of the cylinder head cover **(see illustration)**. Remove any absorbent soundproofing pads from the cylinder head cover; if these are saturated in diesel or oil then they may need to be renewed.

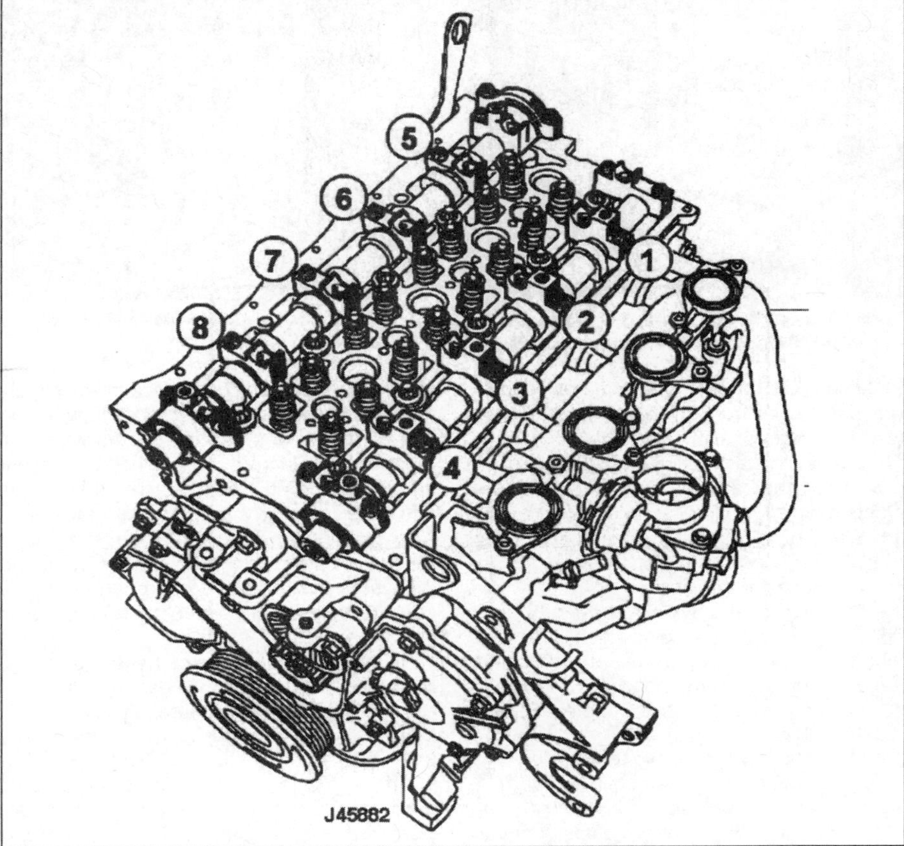

8.15 Tightening sequence for inner camshaft bearing caps

9.5a Slacken the retaining clips . . .

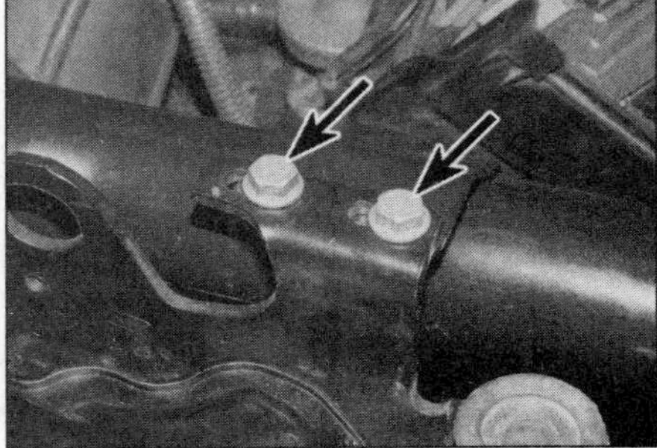

9.5b . . . and undo the mounting bolts (arrowed)

9.6 Removing the EGR pipe

9.7 Slacken the retaining clip from the air vent unit

9.8 Undo the three bolts arrowed

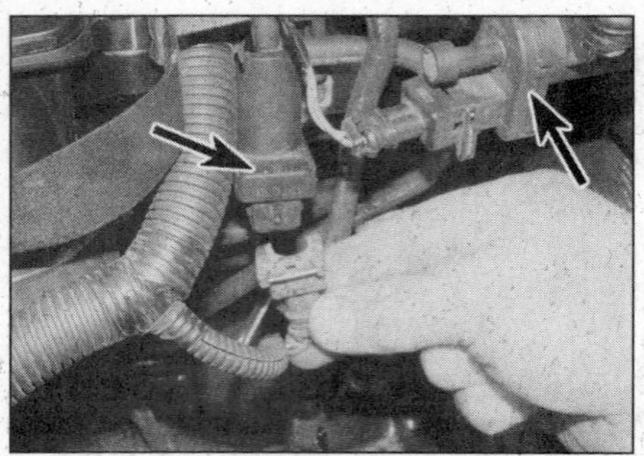

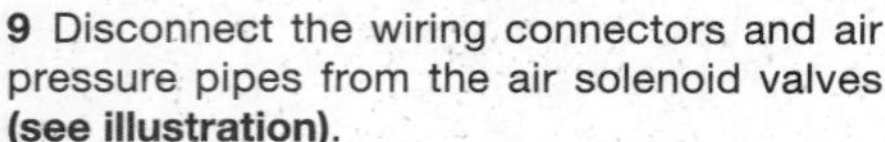

9.9 Disconnect the wiring and air pipes from the solenoid valves (arrowed)

9.10 Disconnect the pipes arrowed

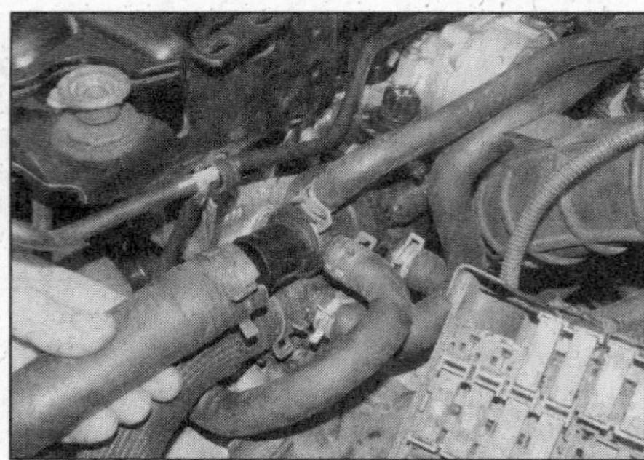

9.11 Disconnect the coolant hoses from the coolant housing

9 Disconnect the wiring connectors and air pressure pipes from the air solenoid valves **(see illustration)**.

10 Disconnect the fuel pipes and the vacuum pipe from the rear of the fuel pump **(see illustration)**.

11 Slacken the retaining clips and disconnect the coolant hoses at the left-hand end of the cylinder head **(see illustration)**.

12 Disconnect the wiring connector from coolant temperature sender, which is screwed into the coolant outlet housing on the left-hand end of the cylinder head.

13 Working as described in Chapter 4B, carry out the following.

- *a) Undo the union nuts and remove the metal pipes linking the pump to the injectors and fuel rail.*
- *b) Disconnect the fuel return pipes from the injectors and the fuel rail.*
- *c) Remove the inlet manifold/camshaft cover and fuel rail.*
- *d) Remove the fuel injectors.*
- *e) Remove the turbocharger unit.*

14 Remove the rocker shafts as described in Section 8.

15 Progressively slacken the cylinder head bolts by half a turn at a time until all bolts can be unscrewed by hand and removed.

16 Lift the cylinder head upwards and off the cylinder block. If it is stuck, tap it upwards using a hammer and block of wood. *Do not* try to rotate it (it is located by two dowels), nor attempt to prise it free using a screwdriver inserted between the block and head faces. If the locating dowels are a loose fit, remove them and store them with the head for safe-keeping. As the head is removed, check around the cylinder head to make sure everything has been disconnected.

Inspection

17 The mating faces of the cylinder head and block must be perfectly clean before refitting the head. Use a scraper (taking care not to damage the surface of the had) to remove all traces of gasket and carbon, and also clean the tops of the pistons. Take particular care with the aluminium cylinder head, as the soft metal is damaged easily. Also, make sure that debris is not allowed to enter the oil and water channels – this is particularly important for the oil circuit, as carbon could block the oil supply to the camshaft or crankshaft bearings. Using adhesive tape and paper, seal the water, oil and bolt holes in the cylinder block. To prevent carbon entering the gap between the pistons and bores, smear a little grease in the gap. After cleaning the piston, rotate the crankshaft so that the piston moves down the bore, and then wipe out the grease and carbon with a cloth rag. Clean the piston crowns in the same way.

18 Check the block and head for nicks, deep scratches and other damage. If slight, they may be removed carefully with a file. More serious damage may be repaired by machining, but this is a specialist job.

19 If warpage of the cylinder head is suspected, use a straight-edge to check it for distortion. Refer to Chapter 2E if necessary.

20 Ensure that the cylinder head bolt holes in the crankcase are clean and free of oil. Syringe or soak up any oil left in the bolt holes. This is most important in order that the correct bolt tightening torque can be applied and to prevent the possibility of the block being cracked by hydraulic pressure when the bolts are tightened.

21 Examine the cylinder head bolt threads in the cylinder block for damage. If necessary, use the correct-size tap to chase out the threads in the block, and use a die to clean the threads on the bolts. The cylinder head bolts must be discarded and renewed, regardless of their apparent condition.

22 Check the correct cylinder head gasket is available; there are two different thickness of gasket offered.

- *a) No holes = 1.16 ± 0.05 mm*
- *b) Two holes = 1.21 ± 0.05 mm*

Refitting

23 Ensure that the mating faces of the cylinder block and head are spotlessly clean, that the retaining bolt threads are also clean and dry, and that they screw easily in and out of their locations.

24 Check that No 1 piston is still at TDC, and that the camshafts are correctly positioned.

Caution: If the camshaft and/or crankshaft are incorrectly positioned, there is a risk of valves being forced into pistons as the head is refitted.

25 Ensure that the locating dowels are correctly fitted to the block and fit a new cylinder head gasket, making sure it is the right way up.

26 Carefully lower the cylinder head onto the block, engaging it over the dowels. If the swirl chambers are a loose fit, take care to ensure that they stay correctly positioned as the head is lowered into position.

27 Working progressively, starting from the centre bolts and working outwards in a spiral motion, tighten the cylinder head bolts to their Stage 1 torque setting, using a torque wrench and suitable socket.

28 Once all bolts are tightened to the Stage 1 specified torque setting, working in the same way, tighten each bolt through its specified final Stage 2 angle, using a socket and extension bar. It is recommended that an angle-measuring gauge be used during this stage of the tightening, to ensure accuracy.

29 Refit the rocker shafts as described in Section 8.

30 Working as described in Chapter 4B, carry out the following.

- *a) Reconnect the metal fuel pipes linking the pump to the injectors and fuel rail.*
- *b) Reconnect the fuel return pipes to the injectors and the fuel rail.*
- *c) Refit the inlet manifold/camshaft cover.*
- *d) Refit the fuel injectors.*
- *e) Refit the turbocharger unit.*

31 Refit the coolant hoses to the coolant housing on the left-hand side of the cylinder head.

32 Reconnect the wiring connector to the coolant temperature sender, which is screwed into the coolant outlet housing on the left-hand end of the cylinder head.

33 Reconnect the fuel pipes to the rear of the fuel pump.

34 Reconnect the wiring connectors and air pressure pipes to the air solenoid valves.

35 Refit the wiring harness protector cover to the top of the cylinder head cover and tighten the three retaining bolts.

36 Tighten the two retaining clips that attach the connection pipe between the inlet manifold and air vent unit.

37 Refit the EGR pipe to the air vent unit and the front of the engine.

38 Refit the turbocharger intercooler pipes to

the top left-hand side of the cylinder head and tighten the retaining clips.

39 Refit the air cleaner assembly and air inlet pipes as described in Chapter 4B.

40 Refit the timing belt with reference to Section 6.

41 Reconnect the battery negative terminal, and then refill the cooling system with reference to Chapter 1B.

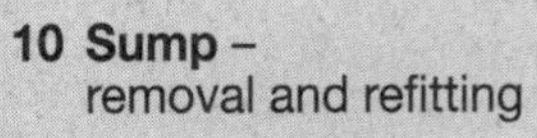

10 Sump – removal and refitting

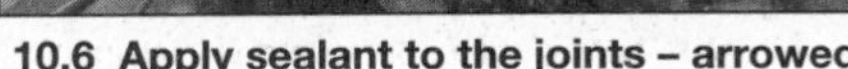

10.6 Apply sealant to the joints – arrowed

10.7 Fit the gasket to the sump

Removal

1 Apply the handbrake, then jack up the front of the car and support it on axle stands (see *Jacking and vehicle support*). Undo the retaining screws and remove the plastic undertray from beneath the engine/transmission.

2 Drain the engine oil as described in Chapter 1B, then refit and tighten the drain plug, using a new sealing washer.

3 Where applicable, unscrew the bolts from the air conditioning and power steering pipe mounting brackets, unclip the pipes and move them to one side.

4 Unscrew and remove the bolts securing the sump to the crankcase. Tap the sump with a hide or plastic mallet to break the seal, and then remove the sump along with its gasket. Discard the gasket; a new one must be used on refitting.

Refitting

5 Remove all traces of dirt and oil from the mating surfaces of the sump and cylinder block.

6 Apply sealant (Rhodorseal 5661) to the front edge of the mating surface, where the timing cover meets the cylinder block **(see illustration).**

7 Locate the new gasket on the top of the sump and lift the sump into position **(see illustration).**

8 Insert the bolts and tighten them in the correct sequence to the specified torque **(see illustration).**

9 If removed, refit the air conditioning and power steering pipes mounting bracket.

10 Refit the undertray and lower the vehicle to the ground.

11 Fill the engine with fresh oil, with reference to Chapter 1B.

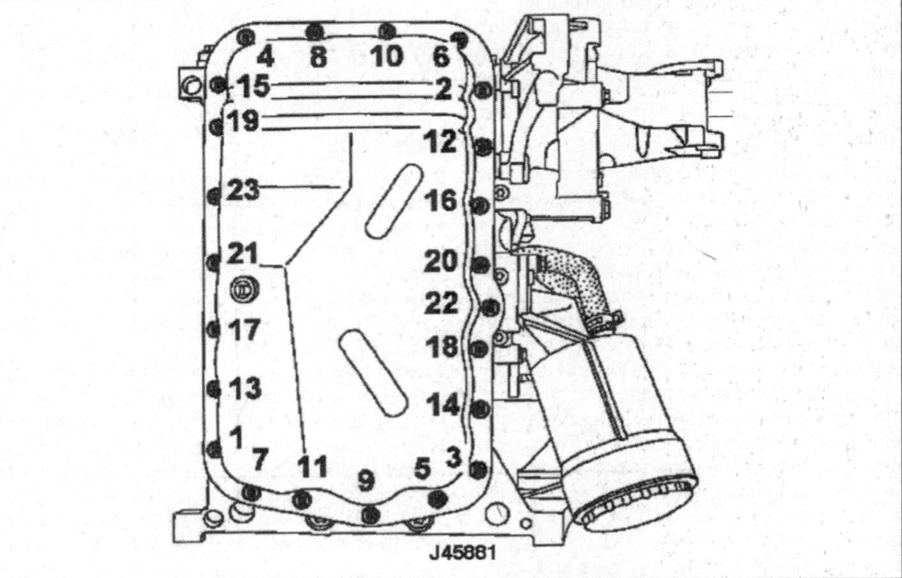

10.8 Tightening sequence for the sump

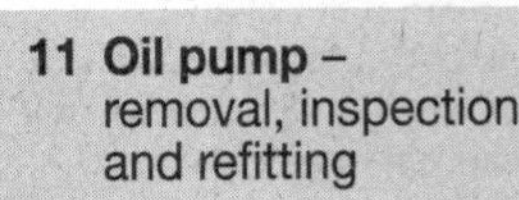

11 Oil pump – removal, inspection and refitting

Removal

Oil pump

1 Remove the sump as described in Section 10.

2 Unscrew the oil pump retaining bolts and withdraw the pump, tilt the pump to disengage its sprocket from the drive chain and lift away the pump from the crankcase **(see illustrations).**

Drive chain and sprockets

Note: *A new timing belt and timing cover oil seals will be required on refitting. It is also recommended that the crankshaft oil seal be renewed.*

3 To remove the oil pump complete with its drive chain and sprockets, first remove the sump (Section 10), then remove the timing gear housing/cover from the cylinder block as described in Chapter 2E.

4 Unbolt the oil pump from the cylinder block as described in paragraph 2 above.

11.2a Undo the bolts – arrowed . . .

11.2b . . . and withdraw the pump from the chain

11.5 Withdraw the chain and sprocket from the crankshaft

11.6a Undo the bolts and split the pump

11.6b Remove the gears to check for wear

5 Slide the drive sprocket from the crankshaft, complete with oil pump drive chain **(see illustration)**. Note the fitted position of the drive sprocket, with the oil splash shield facing outwards.

Inspection

6 Unscrew the retaining bolts and lift off the pump cover. Withdraw the gears to check for wear, mark the position of the gears before removal, so that they can be refitted in their original position **(see illustrations)**.
7 Clean the components and carefully examine the gears and pump body for any signs of scoring or wear. Renew the complete pump assembly if excessive wear is evident (no spare parts are available).
8 If the components appear serviceable, measure the clearance between the pump body and the gears using feeler gauges. Also measure the gear endfloat and check the flatness of the end cover, see Chapter 2B, Section 11. If the clearances are excessive, the pump must be renewed. There should be no discernible wear or distortion of the end cover.
9 If the pump is satisfactory, reassemble the components in the reverse order of removal. Fill the pump with oil, then refit the cover and tighten the bolts securely. Prime the oil pump by filling it with clean engine oil whilst rotating the sprocket.

Refitting

10 Wipe clean the oil pump and cylinder block mating surfaces.
11 Engage the crankshaft sprocket on the chain (if removed), and then refit both sprocket and the chain to the crankshaft. Make sure the crankshaft sprocket is fitted the correct way, see paragraph 5.
12 Manoeuvre the pump into position and engage it with the drive chain. Position the oil pump on the crankcase and insert the mounting bolts, tighten the bolts to the specified torque setting.
13 Refit the timing gear housing/cover to the cylinder block as described in Chapter 2E.
14 Ensure that the pump pick-up filter is clean and unblocked and the oil pump is primed with clean engine oil.
15 Refit the sump as described in Section 10.

12 Flywheel/driveplate – removal, inspection and refitting

Removal

1 Remove the transmission as described in Chapter 7A, then remove the clutch assembly as described in Chapter 6.
2 Prevent the flywheel/driveplate from turning by locking the ring gear teeth with a screwdriver. Make alignment marks between the flywheel/driveplate and crankshaft using paint or a suitable marker pen.
3 Slacken and remove the flywheel/driveplate retaining bolts and remove the flywheel/driveplate. Do not drop it, as it is very heavy. If the locating dowel (where fitted) is a loose fit in the crankshaft end, remove and store it with the flywheel/driveplate for safe-keeping. Discard the bolts, as they should be renewed whenever they are disturbed.

Inspection

4 Examine the flywheel for scoring of the clutch face, and for wear or chipping of the ring gear teeth. If the clutch face is scored, the flywheel may be surface-ground, but renewal is preferable. Seek the advice of a Renault dealer or engine-reconditioning specialist to see if machining is possible. If the ring gear is worn or damaged, the flywheel/driveplate must be renewed, as it is not possible to renew the ring gear separately.

13.4 Carefully fit the seal over the end of the crankshaft

Refitting

5 Clean the mating surfaces of the flywheel/driveplate and crankshaft.
6 Ensure that the locating dowel is in position (where fitted) and offer up the flywheel/driveplate, locating it on the dowel, and fit the new retaining bolts. If the original is being refitted align the marks made prior to removal.
7 Lock the flywheel/driveplate using the method employed on dismantling, and tighten the retaining bolts to the specified torque.
8 Refit the clutch as described in Chapter 6.
9 Remove the locking tool, and refit the transmission as described in Chapter 7A.

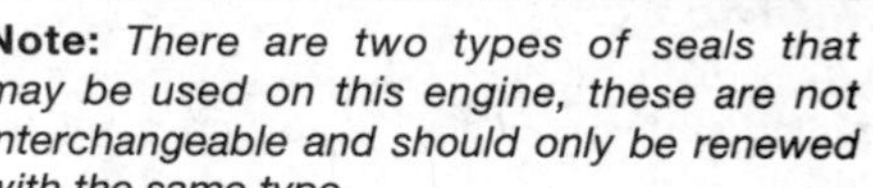

13 Crankshaft oil seals – renewal

Note: *There are two types of seals that may be used on this engine, these are not interchangeable and should only be renewed with the same type.*
a) Early type, which has a spring inside the V-shaped lip of the seal.
b) Later type, which has a flat sealing lip with no spring and comes with a plastic protector, which is also a fitting sleeve. On this type, Do NOT remove the sleeve from the inside of the sealuntil the seal is seated in place.

Timing belt end oil seal

1 Remove the crankshaft pulley as described in Section 4.
2 Make a note of the correct fitted depth of the seal then punch or drill two small holes opposite each other in the oil seal. Screw a self-tapping screw into each and pull on the screws with pliers to extract the seal.
3 Clean the seal housing and polish off any burrs or raised edges, which may have caused the seal to fail in the first place.
4 On early type seals (see note at beginning of Section), lubricate the seal with some clean engine oil then carefully press the seal into its housing over the end of the crankshaft, until it is positioned at the same depth as the original **(see illustration)**.
5 On later type seals (see note at beginning of

Section), DO NOT lubricate the seal. Carefully press the seal complete with protective sleeve into its housing until it is positioned at the same depth as the original. With the oil seal in position, slide the sleeve from the end of the crankshaft to remove it.

6 If necessary, a suitable tubular drift, such as a socket, which bears only on the hard outer edge of the seal can be used to tap the seal into position. Take great care not to damage the seal lips on the end of the crankshaft during fitting and ensure that the seal lips face inwards. Note that if the surface of the shaft was noted to be badly scored, press the new seal slightly further into its housing so that its lip is running on an unmarked area of the shaft.

7 Refit the crankshaft sprocket as described in Section 7.

Transmission end oil seal

8 Remove the flywheel/driveplate as described in Section 12.

9 Prise out the old oil seal using a small screwdriver, taking care not to damage the surface of the crankshaft. Alternatively, the oil seal can be removed as described in paragraph 2.

10 Wipe clean the oil seal seating and inspect the seal rubbing surface on the crankshaft. If it is grooved or rough in the area where the old seal was fitted, the new seal should be fitted slightly less deeply, so that it rubs on an unworn part of the surface.

11 On early type seals (see note at beginning of Section), lubricate the seal with some clean engine oil then carefully press the seal into its housing over the end of the crankshaft, until it is positioned at the same depth as the original.

12 On later type seals (see note at beginning of Section), DO NOT lubricate the seal. Carefully press the seal complete with protective sleeve into its housing until it is positioned at the same depth as the original. With the oil seal in position, slide the sleeve from the end of the crankshaft to remove it.

13 If necessary, a suitable tubular drift, such as a socket, which bears only on the hard outer edge of the seal can be used to tap the seal into position. Take great care not to damage the seal lips on the end of the crankshaft during fitting and ensure that the seal lips face inwards.

14 Refit the flywheel/driveplate as described in Section 12.

14 Engine/transmission mountings – inspection and renewal

Inspection

1 If improved access is required, apply the handbrake, then jack up the front of the car and support it on axle stands (see *Jacking and vehicle support*).

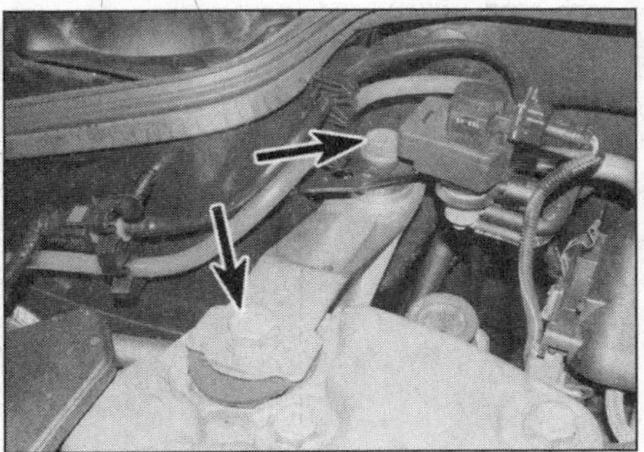

14.7 Slacken the two mounting bolts – arrowed

2 Check the mounting rubber to see if it is cracked, hardened or separated from the metal at any point; renew the mounting if any such damage or deterioration is evident.

3 Check that all the mounting's fasteners are securely tightened; use a torque wrench to check if possible.

4 Using a large screwdriver or a crowbar, check for wear in the mounting by carefully levering against it to check for free play. Where this is not possible, enlist the aid of an assistant to move the engine/transmission back-and-forth, or from side-to-side, while you watch the mounting. While some free play is to be expected even from new components, excessive wear should be obvious. If excessive free play is found, check first that the fasteners are correctly secured, and then renew any worn components as described below.

Renewal

Right-hand mounting

5 Disconnect the battery negative terminal (refer to *Disconnecting the battery* in the Reference Section of this manual).

6 Place a jack beneath the engine, with a block of wood on the jack head (remove the undercover to improve access to the sump). Raise the jack until it is supporting the weight of the engine. Alternately, attach an engine support bar to the lifting brackets and support the weight of the engine with the bar.

7 Slacken the two mounting bolts for the tie-rod at the rear of the mounting, and then remove the front bolt to the engine mounting **(see illustration)**.

14.9 Removing the engine upper mounting bracket

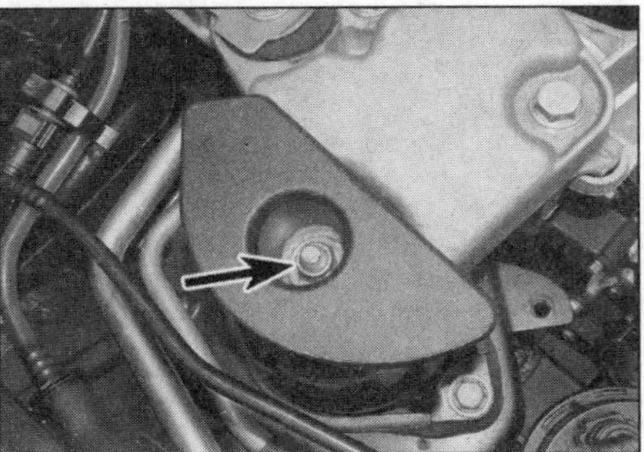

14.8 Undo the nut (arrowed) and remove the acoustic mass

8 Undo the nut securing the rubber mounting to the engine mounting bracket and withdraw the acoustic mass unit (metal weight) from the engine mounting assembly **(see illustration)**.

9 Slacken and remove the three bolts securing the engine mounting bracket to the cylinder head, and withdraw it from the engine **(see illustration)**. Where applicable, release any cables or wiring from the top of the engine mounting bracket.

10 Unscrew the three retaining bolts and remove the engine rubber mounting from the body **(see illustration)**.

11 Check carefully for signs of wear or damage on all components, and renew them where necessary.

12 On reassembly, fit the engine rubber mounting to the body, insert the retaining bolts but tighten them finger tight only at this stage.

13 Refit the upper part of the bracket to the cylinder head, locating it on the stud for the rubber mounting. Tighten the mounting bolts to the cylinder head to the specified torque.

14 Refit the acoustic mass unit (metal weight) and nut securing the rubber mounting to the engine mounting bracket and tighten it to the specified torque.

15 Centralise the engine rubber mounting then tighten the three bolts to the specified torque.

16 Move the tie-rod at the rear of the mounting bracket back into place and refit the front bolt to the engine mounting, tighten the bolts to the specified torque.

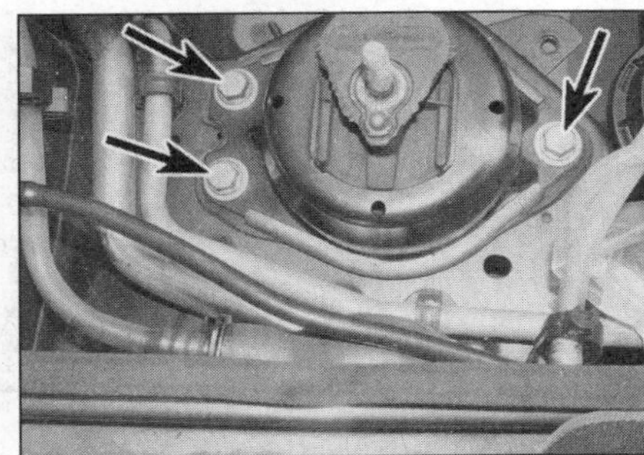

14.10 Remove the mounting bolts – arrowed

14.19 Location of left-hand engine/ transmission mounting

14.21a Using a puller to release the centre stud from the mounting

14.21b Remove the mounting from the mounting bracket

17 Remove the jack from underneath the engine or the engine support bar (as applicable), and reconnect the battery negative terminal.

Left-hand mounting

18 Disconnect the battery negative terminal (refer to *Disconnecting the battery* in the Reference Section of this manual).

19 Refer to Chapter 4B and remove the air cleaner and inlet components as necessary for access to the mounting **(see illustration)**.

20 Place a jack beneath the transmission, with a block of wood on the jack head. Raise the jack until it is supporting the weight of the transmission.

21 Slacken and remove the mounting rubber's centre nut, and two outer retaining bolts and remove the mounting from the engine compartment. This mounting can be a tight fit on the transmission centre stud; a puller may be necessary to withdraw it **(see illustrations)**.

22 If necessary, undo the retaining bolts and remove the mounting bracket from the top of the transmission housing **(see illustration)**. The transmission will need to be lowered to access the mounting bracket retaining bolts.

23 Check carefully for signs of wear or damage on all components, and renew them where necessary.

24 Refit the bracket to the transmission, tightening its mounting bolts to the specified torque.

25 Fit the mounting rubber to the bracket and tighten its retaining bolts and centre nut to the specified torque.

26 Refit the air cleaner and inlet components removed for access.

27 Remove the jack from underneath the transmission and reconnect the battery negative terminal.

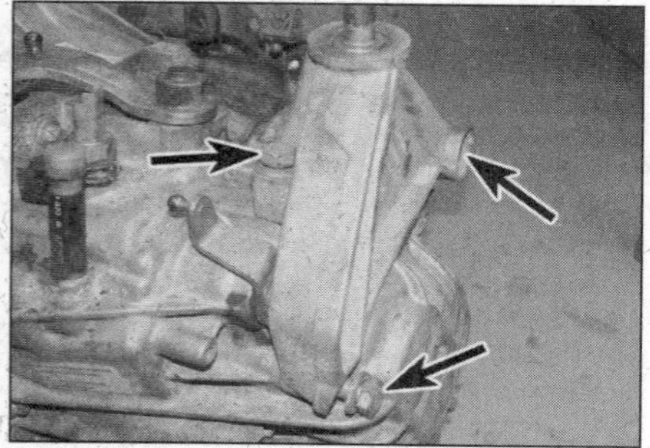

14.22 Mounting bracket retaining bolts – arrowed

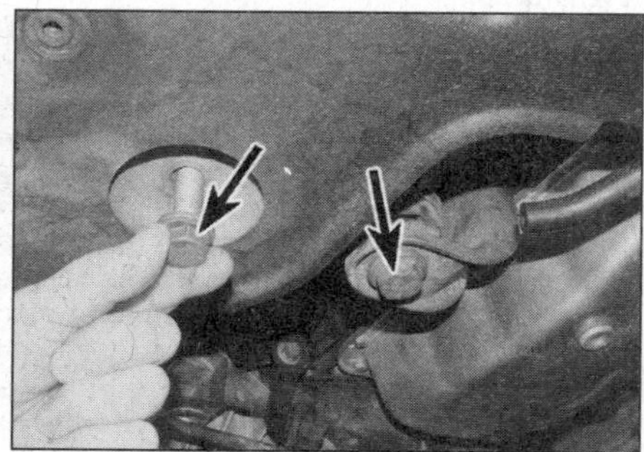

14.31a Undo the two mounting bolts – arrowed . . .

14.31b . . . and remove the mounting link arm

14.32 Remove the mounting bolts – arrowed

Rear mounting

28 Disconnect the battery negative terminal (refer to *Disconnecting the battery* in the Reference Section of this manual).

29 If not already done, apply the handbrake, then jack up the front of the car and support it on axle stands (see *Jacking and vehicle support*).

30 Position a jack with a block of wood on its head underneath the sump. Raise the jack until it is supporting the weight of the engine.

31 Slacken and remove the nut and bolt from each end of the mounting link and remove the link from underneath the vehicle **(see illustrations)**.

32 If necessary, undo the retaining bolts and remove the mounting bracket from the engine/ transmission **(see illustration)**. It will be necessary to remove the right-hand driveshaft (as described in Chapter 8) to access the mounting bolts

33 Check carefully for signs of wear or damage on all components, and renew them where necessary.

34 On reassembly, fit the mounting bracket (where removed) to the rear of the transmission and tighten its retaining bolts to the specified torque. Refit the driveshaft as described in Chapter 8.

35 Fit the mounting link, and tighten both its bolts to there specified torque settings.

36 Lower the vehicle to the ground and reconnect the battery negative terminal.

15 Oil cooler – removal and refitting

Note: *The oil cooler is part of the oil filter housing, it would be a good practice to renew the oil and oil filter, whenever the oil cooler is removed.*

Removal

1 Apply the handbrake, then jack up the front of the car and support it on axle stands (see *Jacking and vehicle support*). Undo the retaining screws and remove the engine undertray to gain access to the oil cooler, which is part of the oil filter housing and is mounted on the front of the cylinder block.

15.4 Disconnect the coolant hoses from the filter housing

2 Drain the engine oil and remove the oil filter as described in Chapter 1B, then refit and tighten the drain plug.

3 Drain the cooling system as described in Chapter 1B. Alternatively, clamp the oil cooler coolant hoses as close to the cooler as possible, and be prepared for some coolant loss as the hoses are disconnected.

4 Slacken the retaining clips and disconnect the hoses from the oil cooler **(see illustration)**.

5 Disconnect the wiring connector from the oil pressure switch **(see illustration)**.

6 Undo the retaining bolt and disconnect the earth cable from the oil filter housing **(see illustration)**.

7 Remove the oil cooler/filter housing mounting bolts and withdraw it, along with its seal/gasket **(see illustration)**. Discard all seals/gaskets; new ones must be used on refitting.

Refitting

8 Fit a new seal/gasket to the oil cooler/filter housing, then offer the cooler to the cylinder block **(see illustration)**. Ensure that the cooler is correctly positioned then refit the mounting bolts and tighten it securely.

9 Refit the earth cable to the oil filter housing and tighten the securing bolt.

10 Reconnect the wiring connector to the oil pressure switch.

11 Reconnect the coolant hoses to the oil cooler/filter housing, making sure the retaining clips are secure.

12 Fit a new oil filter and refill the engine with oil as described in Chapter 1B.

13 Refill or top-up the cooling system as described in Chapter 1B or *Weekly checks* (as applicable). Start the engine, and check the oil cooler/filter housing for signs of leakage.

16 Oil pressure switch – removal and refitting

1 The oil pressure switch is a vital early warning of low oil pressure. The switch operates the oil warning light on the instrument panel – the light should come on with the ignition, and go out almost immediately when the engine starts.

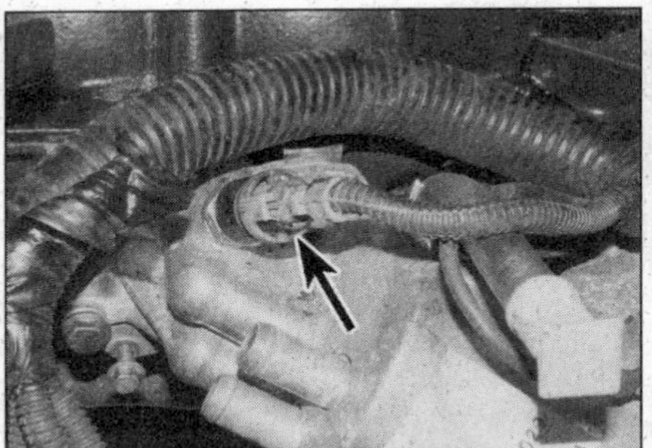

15.5 Disconnect the wiring connector – arrowed

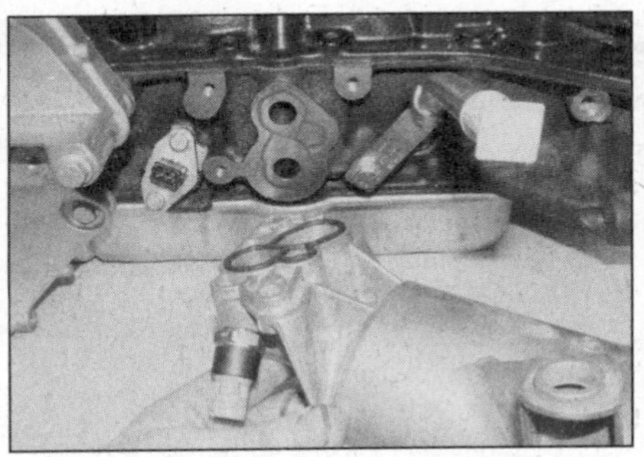

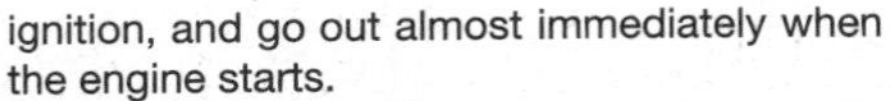

15.7 Removing oil cooler/filter housing from cylinder block

2 If the light does not come on, there could be a fault on the instrument panel, the switch wiring, or the switch itself. If the light does not go out, low oil level, worn oil pump (or sump pick-up blocked), blocked oil filter, or worn main bearings could be to blame – or again, the switch may be faulty.

3 If the light comes on while driving, the best advice is to turn the engine off immediately, and not to drive the car until the problem has been investigated – ignoring the light could mean expensive engine damage.

Removal

4 The oil pressure switch is located on the front of the engine, in the oil filter housing **(see illustration)**.

5 It may be easier to access the switch from underneath the vehicle, jack up the front of the car, and support it on axle stands (see *Jacking and vehicle support*). Undo the retaining bolts and remove the engine undertray.

6 Disconnect the wiring plug from the switch.

7 Unscrew the switch from the housing, and remove it together with its sealing washer. There should only be a very slight loss of oil when this is done.

Inspection

8 Examine the switch for signs of cracking or splits. If the top part of the switch is loose, this is an early indication of impending failure.

9 Check that the wiring terminals at the switch

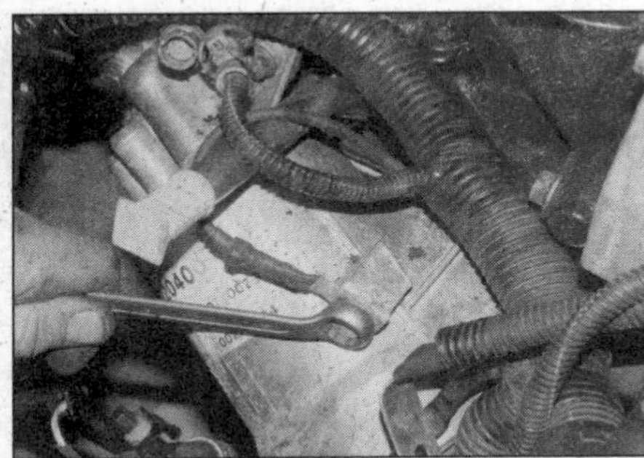

15.6 Undo the earth cable securing bolt

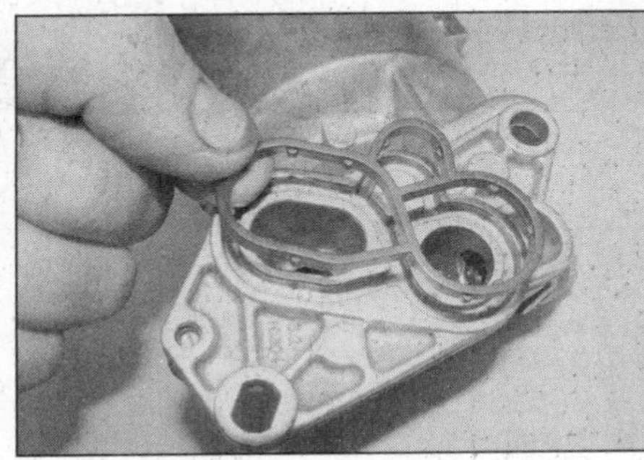

15.8 Fit new seal/gasket to housing

are not loose, then trace the wire from the switch connector until it enters the main loom – any wiring defects will give rise to apparent oil pressure problems.

Refitting

10 Refitting is the reverse of the removal procedure, noting the following points:

a) Clean the switch threads before fitting. Tighten the switch securely.

b) Reconnect the switch connector, making sure it clicks home properly. Ensure that the wiring is routed away from any hot or moving parts.

c) Lower the car to the ground, then check the engine oil level and top-up if necessary (see 'Weekly checks').

d) Check for signs of oil leaks once the engine has been restarted and warmed-up to normal operating temperature.

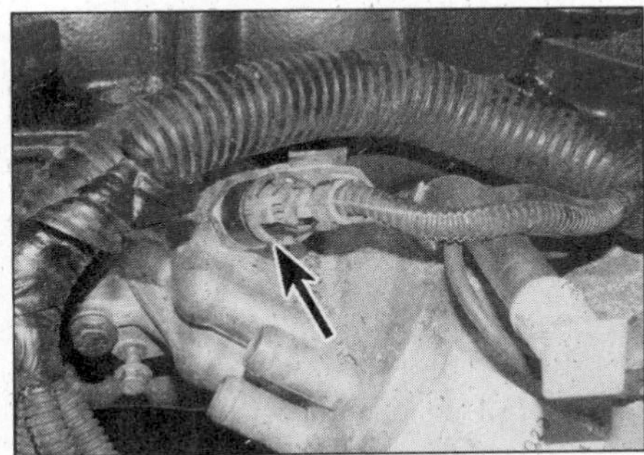

16.4 Oil pressure switch – arrowed

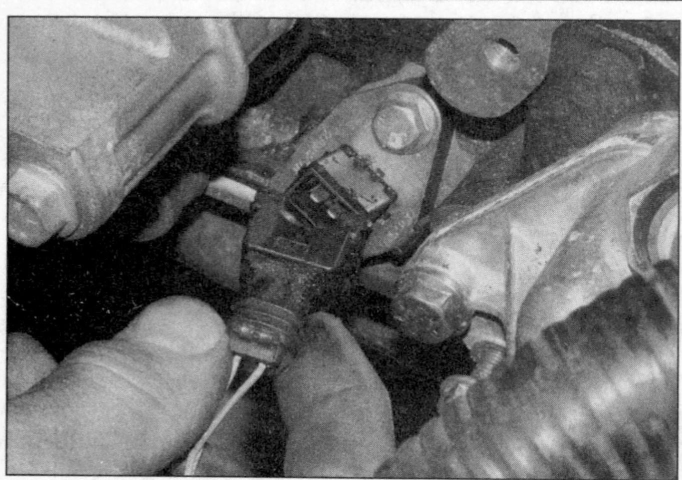

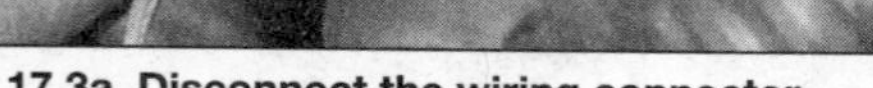

17.3a Disconnect the wiring connector . . .

17.3b . . . and undo the retaining bolts (arrowed

17 Oil level sensor – removal and refitting

Removal

1 The sensor is fitted at the front of the engine, next to the oil filter housing.

2 Access to the sensor may be easiest from under the vehicle, jack up the front of the car, and support it on axle stands (see *Jacking and vehicle support*). Undo the retaining bolts and remove the engine undertray.

3 Disconnect the wiring plug, then unscrew the two retaining bolts and withdraw the sensor from the engine block **(see illustrations)**. It will be necessary to carefully turn the sensor anti-clockwise, while withdrawing it from the cylinder block.

Warning: Do not force the sensor as it is turned, otherwise damage will occur.

Refitting

4 Refitting is a reversal of removal. Tighten the sensor securely, to prevent leaks.

Chapter 2 Part D: Petrol engine removal and overhaul procedures

Contents

Degrees of difficulty

Easy, suitable for novice with little experience	**Fairly easy,** suitable for beginner with some experience	**Fairly difficult,** suitable for competent DIY mechanic	**Difficult,** suitable for experienced DIY mechanic	**Very difficult,** suitable for expert DIY or professional 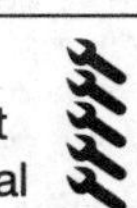

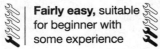

Specifications

1.6 litre engines

Cylinder head		
Maximum gasket face distortion	0.05 mm	
Cylinder head height	137.0 mm	
Valve seat angle (included)	89°	
Valve seat width:		
Inlet	1.3 to 2.7 mm	
Exhaust	1.4 to 2.7 mm	
Valves	**Inlet**	**Exhaust**
Valve head diameter	32.58 to 32.82 mm	27.84 to 28.08 mm
Valve stem diameter	5.474 to 5.494 mm	5.463 to 5.483 mm
Valve length	109.32 mm	107.64 mm
Valve seat angle (included)	89°	89°
Valve springs		
External diameter	27.0 mm	
Free length	41.30 mm	
Cylinder block		
Cylinder bore diameter:		
Class A	79.50 to 79.51 mm	
Class B	79.51 to 79.52 mm	
Class C	79.52 to 79.53 mm	
Pistons		
Piston diameter:		
Class A	79.47 to 79.48 mm	
Class B	79.48 to 79.49 mm	
Class C	79.49 to 79.50 mm	
Piston-to-bore clearance	0.02 to 0.04 mm	
Piston rings		
End gap (measured in cylinder):		
Top compression	0.15 to 0.35 mm	
Second compression	0.40 to 0.60 mm	
Oil control	0.20 to 0.90 mm	
Ring gap spacing	120°	

1.6 litre engines (continued)

Crankshaft

Endfloat	0.045 to 0.85 mm
Main bearing journal diameter:	
Class A	47.990 to 47.997 mm
Class B	47.997 to 48.003 mm
Class C	48.003 to 48.010 mm
Big-end bearing journal diameter	43.96 to 43.98 mm

Torque wrench settings

Refer to Chapter 2A Specifications

1.8 and 2.0 litre engines

Cylinder head

Maximum gasket face distortion	0.05 mm
Cylinder head height	138.15 mm
Valve seat angle (included)	89°
Valve seat width:	
Inlet	1.3 to 2.7 mm
Exhaust	1.4 to 2.7 mm

Valves	Inlet	Exhaust
Valve head diameter	33.38 to 33.62 mm	28.88 to 29.12 mm
Valve stem diameter	5.462 to 5.480 mm	5.438 to 5.456 mm
Valve length	109.93 to 110.23 mm	108.72 to 109.02 mm
Valve seat angle (included)	90°	90°

Valve springs

External diameter	27.0 mm
Free length	41.30 mm

Cylinder block

Cylinder bore diameter:	
Class 2 (or B)	82.710 to 82.720 mm
Class 3 (or C)	82.720 to 82.730 mm

Pistons

Piston diameter:	
Class 2 (or B)	82.680 to 82.690 mm
Class 3 (or C)	82.690 to 82.700 mm
Piston-to-bore clearance	0.02 to 0.04 mm

Piston rings

End gap (measured in cylinder):	
Top compression	0.20 to 0.35 mm
Second compression	0.40 to 0.60 mm
Oil control	0.25 to 0.75 mm
Ring gap spacing	120°

Crankshaft

Endfloat	0.07 to 0.23 mm
Main bearing journal diameter	54.785 to 54.805
Big-end bearing journal diameter	47.980 to 48.000 mm

Torque wrench settings

Refer to Chapter 2A Specifications

1 General information

Included in this Part of Chapter 2 are details of removing the engine/transmission from the car and general overhaul procedures for the cylinder head, cylinder block and all other engine internal components.

The information given ranges from advice concerning preparation for an overhaul and the purchase of parts, to detailed step-by-step procedures covering removal, inspection, renovation and refitting of engine internal components.

After Section 5, all instructions are based on the assumption that the engine has been removed from the car. For information concerning in-car engine repair, as well as the removal and refitting of those external components necessary for full overhaul, refer to Part A of this Chapter and to Section 4. Ignore any preliminary dismantling operations described in Part A that are no longer relevant once the engine has been removed from the car.

Apart from torque wrench settings, which are given at the beginning of Part A, all specifications relating to engine overhaul are at the beginning of this Chapter.

2 Engine/transmission removal – preparation and precautions

If you have decided that an engine must be removed for overhaul or major repair work, several preliminary steps should be taken.

Locating a suitable place to work is extremely important. Adequate workspace, along with storage space for the car, will be needed. If a workshop or garage is not available, at the very least, a flat, level, clean work surface is required.

If possible, clear some shelving close to the work area and use it to store the engine components and ancillaries as they are removed and dismantled. In this manner the components stand a better chance of staying clean and undamaged during the overhaul. Laying out components in groups together with their fixing bolts, screws, etc, will save time and avoid confusion when the engine is refitted.

Clean the engine compartment and engine/transmission before beginning the removal procedure; this will help visibility and help to keep tools clean.

The help of an assistant should be available; there are certain instances when one person cannot safely perform all of the operations required to remove the engine from the vehicle. Safety is of primary importance, considering the potential hazards involved in this kind of operation. A second person should always be in attendance to offer help in an emergency. If this is the first time you have removed an engine, advice and aid from someone more experienced would also be beneficial.

Plan the operation ahead of time. Before starting work, obtain (or arrange for the hire of) all of the tools and equipment you will need. Access to the following items will allow the task of removing and refitting the engine/transmission to be completed safely and with relative ease: an engine hoist – rated in excess of the combined weight of the engine/transmission, a heavy-duty trolley jack, complete sets of spanners and sockets as described in the reference section of this manual, wooden blocks, and plenty of rags and cleaning solvent for mopping-up spilled oil, coolant and fuel. A selection of different sized plastic storage bins will also prove useful for keeping dismantled components grouped together. If any of the equipment must be hired, make sure that you arrange for it in advance, and perform all of the operations possible without it beforehand; this may save you time and money.

Plan on the vehicle being out of use for quite a while, especially if you intend to carry out an engine overhaul. Read through the whole of this Section and work out a strategy based on your own experience and the tools, time and workspace available to you. Some of the overhaul processes may have to be carried out by a Renault dealer or an engineering works – these establishments often have busy schedules, so it would be prudent to consult them before removing or dismantling the engine, to get an idea of the amount of time required to carry out the work.

During the engine removal procedure, it is advisable to make notes of the locations of all brackets, cable ties, earthing points, etc, as well as how the wiring harnesses, hoses and electrical connections are attached and routed around the engine and engine compartment. An effective way of doing this is to take a series of photographs of the various components before they are disconnected or removed. A digital or simple inexpensive disposable camera is ideal for this and the resulting photographs will prove invaluable when the engine is refitted.

Always be extremely careful when lifting the engine/transmission assembly from the engine bay. Serious injury can result from careless actions. If help is required, it is better to wait until it is available rather than risk personal injury and/or damage to components by continuing alone. By planning ahead and taking your time, a job of this nature, although major, can be accomplished successfully and without incident.

3 Engine and transmission – removal, separation, connection and refitting

Note: *The engine is removed upwards from the car as a complete unit with the transmission; the two are then separated for overhaul.*

Removal

1 Set the bonnet in the upright position (by tying it to the radio aerial) or, to improve access, remove it completely as described in Chapter 11.

2 Remove the battery as described in Chapter 5A, then remove the battery tray.

3 Undo the retaining screws or unclip (depending on model) and lift off the plastic covers from the top of the engine.

4 Apply the handbrake, then jack up the front of the car and support it on axle stands (see *Jacking and vehicle support*). Remove both front roadwheels.

5 Undo the retaining screws and remove the plastic undertray from beneath the engine/transmission. Also remove the plastic covers from the left- and right-hand wheel arches.

6 If the engine is to be dismantled, working as described in Chapter 1A, drain the engine oil. Clean and refit the drain plug, tightening it securely.

7 Drain the transmission oil as described in Chapter 7A or 7B. Refit the drain and filler plugs, and tighten them securely.

8 Drain the cooling system as described in Chapter 1A.

9 Working as described in Chapter 8, disconnect and remove the left-hand driveshaft from the transmission. **Note:** *Do not allow the shaft to hang down under its own weight as this could damage the constant velocity joints/gaiters.*

10 Remove the complete right-hand driveshaft assembly as described in Chapter 8.

11 Remove the air cleaner assembly and air inlet ducts as described in Chapter 4A.

12 Remove the auxiliary drivebelt as described in Chapter 1A.

13 Release the retaining clip and disconnect the clutch hydraulic hose from the transmission as described in Chapter 6 and position it clear. Cover or cap the ends of the pipe and connector to prevent any dirt ingress **(see illustration)**.

14 Disconnect the gearchange linkage from the transmission as described in Chapter 7A or 7B.

15 Referring to Chapter 4A, carry out the following operations.

a) Disconnect the fuel hoses from the fuel rail and release them from the clips/support brackets. Move the hoses clear.

b) Disconnect the wiring connectors from the throttle housing, starter motor and alternator.

c) Remove the exhaust system front pipe/catalytic converter.

d) Disconnect the camshaft position sensor wiring connector.

e) Disconnect any vacuum hoses and wiring connectors from sensors around the engine, making note of there fitted position.

f) Disconnect the relevant vacuum hoses from the inlet manifold.

16 Remove the headlights as described in Chapter 12.

17 Remove the front bumper as described in Chapter 11.

18 Disconnect the bonnet release cable from the bonnet lock on the front body panel.

19 Undo the bolts securing the wiring harness support brackets to the front body panel.

20 Undo the retaining bolts securing the power steering pump to its mounting bracket, with reference to Chapter 10, and then move it to one side.

21 Referring to the procedures described in Chapter 3, remove the electric cooling fans and the radiator, including the air conditioning condenser. Note that once the front body panel has been released, it should be removed completely (do not lay it across the top of the engine).

3.13 Fit protective cap (arrowed) over the ends of the hose

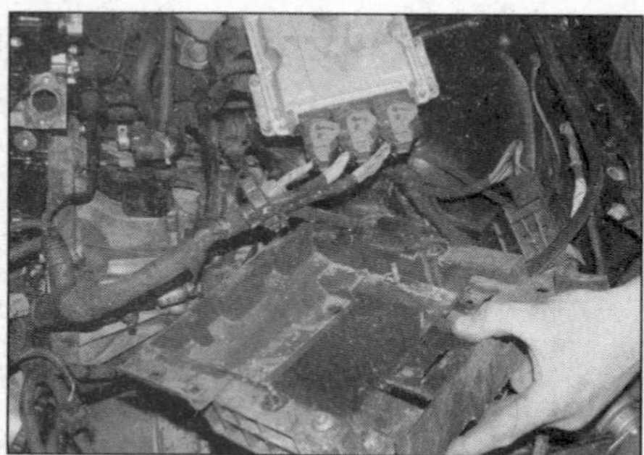

3.24 Move the ECU and tray to one side

22 Disconnect the coolant hoses from the expansion tank, then disconnect the heater hoses, and remaining coolant hoses from the engine. Release any support clips as necessary then move all the hoses clear of the engine.
23 Undo the retaining nuts/bolts and free the power steering pipes from the mounting brackets on the transmission. Check that the pipes are released from all the relevant retaining clips and are positioned clear of the engine/transmission.
24 Trace the engine wiring harness and disconnect any wiring still attached to the engine/transmission assembly. With reference to Chapter 4A, move the ECU and tray to one side, making sure it is in a safe position **(see illustration).**
25 Undo the securing bolts and release the applicable earth cables from the engine and transmission units, similarly disconnect any earth cables from the subframe.
26 Manoeuvre the engine hoist into position, and attach it to the lifting brackets bolted onto the cylinder head. Raise the hoist until it is supporting the weight of the engine.
27 On models equipped with air conditioning, disconnect the compressor clutch wiring connector then unbolt the compressor from the auxiliary components mounting bracket on the engine. Carefully move the compressor, away from the front of the engine and support it on the front lower crossmember **(see illustration)**. It may be necessary to disconnect additional retaining clips or mountings to allow the assembly to be moved clear. Take care not to place excess strain on the various pipes and hoses and ensure that all the components are well supported or tied clear of the engine. *Do not* disconnect the refrigerant lines from the compressor (refer to the warnings given in Chapter 3).

3.27 Cable tie (arrowed) holding compressor in position

28 From underneath the vehicle, undo the retaining bolts and remove the rear mounting link, connecting the engine/transmission mounting to the body.
29 Unscrew the nut from the transmission left-hand mounting stud then undo the bolts securing the rubber mounting assembly and remove it from the vehicle body.
30 Undo the retaining bolts and remove the right-hand engine mounting acoustic tie-rod.
31 Undo the mounting bolts and nut securing the right-hand engine mounting bracket and remove it from the vehicle. Slacken the rubber mounting bolts to the body to allow for settlement movement when refitting.
32 Make a final check that any components which would prevent the removal of the engine/transmission from the car have been removed or disconnected. Ensure that components such as the gearchange linkage/ cables and driveshafts are secured so that they cannot be damaged on removal.
33 With the help of an assistant, raise the hoist and lift the engine/transmission slightly, ensuring that nothing is trapped or damaged. Once the engine is high enough, turn it slightly as necessary and withdraw it forwards, out of the engine compartment and clear of the car.

Separation

34 With the engine/transmission assembly removed, support the assembly on suitable blocks of wood, on a workbench (or failing that, on a clean area of the workshop floor).
35 Undo the retaining bolts, and remove the starter motor from the transmission, noting the correct fitted position of the locating dowel (see Chapter 5A).
36 On automatic models, the torque converter is attached to the driveplate by three nuts, which are accessed either behind the driveplate lower cover plate or through the starter motor aperture. Turn the engine as required to position the nuts in the aperture, then unscrew and remove them. **Note:** *The nuts must be renewed every time they are removed.* Where applicable, unbolt the access plate from the bottom of the transmission.
37 Ensure that both engine and transmission are adequately supported, then slacken and remove the remaining bolts securing the transmission housing to the engine. Note the correct fitted positions of each bolt (and the relevant brackets) as they are removed, to use as a reference on refitting.
38 Carefully withdraw the transmission from the engine, ensuring that the weight of the transmission is not allowed to hang on the input shaft while it is engaged with the clutch friction plate. On automatic models, as the transmission is removed, make sure the torque converter is kept pushed fully onto the transmission shaft.
39 Once the transmission is free, remove the locating dowels from the engine or transmission, and keep them in a safe place.
40 On automatic models, secure the torque converter in position by bolting a length of metal bar to one of the housing bolt holes, or by tying one of the studs to the TDC sensor aperture on the top of the housing.

Connection

41 If the engine and transmission have not been separated, proceed as described from paragraph 49 onwards.
42 Ensure that the locating dowels are correctly positioned prior to installation.
43 On manual models, ensure that the clutch friction plate and transmission input shaft splines are clean and dry. Do not apply grease to the splines as they have a special low-friction nickel coating. Make sure the clutch release mechanism components are correctly fitted (see Chapter 6).
44 On automatic models, remove the retaining bar or wire used to hold the torque converter in place. Ensure that the torque converter is pushed fully onto the transmission. Apply a smear of high melting point grease (Renault recommend the use of Molykote BR2) to the converter-centring ring.
45 Carefully offer the transmission to the engine, until the locating dowels are engaged. Don't allow the weight of the transmission to hang on the input shaft as it is engaged with the clutch friction plate/torque converter. Support the transmission to hold it in position.
46 On automatic models, align the torque converter studs with the driveplate holes as the transmission is refitted. Apply thread-locking compound (Renault recommend the use of Loctite Frenbloc) to the new retaining nuts and tighten them to the specified torque.
47 Refit the transmission housing-to-engine bolts, ensuring that all the necessary brackets are correctly positioned, and tighten them to the specified torque setting.
48 Refit the starter motor making sure its locating dowel is correctly positioned and securely tighten its retaining bolts (see Chapter 5A).

Refitting

49 Reconnect the hoist and lifting tackle to the engine lifting brackets. With the aid of an assistant, lift the assembly into the engine compartment, and manoeuvre it as necessary to clear the surrounding components, as during removal.
50 With the engine/transmission in position, refit the left-hand rubber mounting and tighten the retaining bolts to the specified torque. Fit the nut to the mounting stud tightening it by hand only at this stage.
51 Refit the right-hand mounting and engine bracket assembly. Tighten the bracket to engine bolts to the specified torque, but only tighten the rubber mounting bolts to the body by hand at this stage.
52 Refit the rear mounting link and support rod and lightly tighten the retaining bolts.

53 Rock the engine to settle it on its mountings. Centralise the right-hand mounting movement limiter, then tighten the three rubber mounting bolts to the specified torque. Go around and tighten all the remaining mounting nuts and bolts to their specified torque settings and detach the hoist from the engine.

54 The remainder of the refitting procedure is a direct reversal of the removal sequence, noting the following points:

a) *Ensure that the wiring loom is correctly routed and retained by all the relevant retaining clips; all connectors should be correctly and securely reconnected.*
b) *Prior to refitting the driveshafts to the transmission, renew the driveshaft oil seal(s) as described in Chapter 7A or 7B.*
c) *Ensure that all disturbed hoses are correctly reconnected, and securely retained by their retaining clips.*
d) *Bleed the clutch fluid as described in Chapter 6.*
e) *Refill the engine and transmission with the correct quantity and type of oil, as described in Chapters 1A and 7A or 7B.*
f) *Refill the cooling system as described in Chapter 1A.*

4 Engine overhaul – preliminary information

It is much easier to dismantle and work on the engine if it is mounted on a portable engine stand. These stands can often be hired from a tool hire shop. Before the engine is mounted on a stand, the flywheel should be removed so that the stand bolts can be tightened into the end of the cylinder block.

If a stand is not available, it is possible to dismantle the engine with it suitably supported on a sturdy, workbench or on the floor. Be careful not to tip or drop the engine when working without a stand.

If you intend to obtain a reconditioned engine, all ancillaries must be removed first, to be transferred to the new engine (just as they will if you are doing a complete engine overhaul yourself). These components include the following.

a) *Engine mountings and brackets (Chapter 2A).*
b) *Alternator including auxiliary components mounting bracket (Chapter 5A).*
c) *Starter motor (Chapter 5A).*
d) *The ignition system and HT components including all sensors, coil modules and spark plugs (Chapters 1A and 5B).*
e) *Exhaust manifold (Chapter 4A).*
f) *Inlet manifold with fuel injection components (Chapter 4A).*
g) *All electrical switches, actuators and sensors and the engine wiring harness (Chapters 4A, 4C and 5B).*
h) *Coolant pump, thermostat, hoses, and distribution pipe (Chapter 3).*
i) *Clutch components (Chapter 6).*
j) *Flywheel (Chapter 2A).*
k) *Oil filter (Chapter 1A).*
l) *Dipstick, tube and bracket.*

Note: *When removing the external components from the engine, pay close attention to details that may be helpful or important during refitting. Note the fitting positions of gaskets, seals, washers, bolts and other small items.*

If you are obtaining a short engine (cylinder block, crankshaft, pistons and connecting rods all assembled), then the cylinder head, timing belt (together with tensioner, tensioner and idler pulleys and covers) and auxiliary drivebelt tensioner will have to be removed also.

If a complete overhaul is planned, the engine can be dismantled in the order given below.

a) *Inlet and exhaust manifolds.*
b) *Timing belt, sprockets, tensioner, pulleys and covers.*
c) *Cylinder head.*
d) *Flywheel.*
e) *Sump.*
f) *Oil pump.*
g) *Pistons/connecting rods.*
h) *Crankshaft.*

5 Cylinder head – dismantling, cleaning, inspection and reassembly

Note: *New and reconditioned cylinder heads are available from the manufacturer and from engine overhaul specialists. Specialist tools are required for the dismantling and inspection procedures, and new components may not be readily available. It may, therefore, be more practical and economical for the home mechanic to purchase a reconditioned head rather than dismantle, inspect and recondition the original head.*

Dismantling

1 Remove the cylinder head as described in Part A of this Chapter.

2 According to components still fitted, remove the thermostat housing (Chapter 3), the spark plugs (Chapter 1A) and any other unions, pipes, sensors or brackets as necessary.

3 Place the cylinder head on wooden blocks and tap each valve stem smartly, using a light hammer and drift, to free the spring and associated items.

4 Fit a deep reach type valve spring compressor to each valve in turn and compress each spring until the collets are exposed. Lift out the collets; a small screwdriver, a magnet or a pair of tweezers may be useful. Carefully release the spring compressor and remove it.

5 Remove the valve spring upper seat and the valve spring. Pull the valve out of its guide.

6 Pull off the valve stem oil seal with a pair of long-nosed pliers. Alternatively, a valve stem oil seal removal tool can be obtained from automotive accessory shops. The tool is basically a pair of pliers with specially shaped ends that grip the seal.

7 It is essential that each valve is stored together with its collets, spring and seats. The valves should also be kept in their correct sequence, unless they are so badly worn or burnt that they are to be renewed. If they are going to be kept and used again, place each valve assembly in a labelled polythene bag or similar container.

8 Continue removing all the remaining valves in the same way.

Cleaning

9 Thoroughly clean all traces of old gasket material and sealing compound from the cylinder head upper and lower mating surfaces. Use a suitable liquid gasket-dissolving agent (available from Renault dealers) together with a soft putty knife; do not use a metal scraper or the faces will be damaged.

10 Remove the carbon from the combustion chambers and ports, then clean all traces of oil and other deposits from the cylinder head, paying particular attention to the bearing journals, tappet bores, valve guides and oil ways.

11 Wash the head thoroughly with paraffin or a suitable solvent. Take plenty of time and do a thorough job. Be sure to clean all oil holes and galleries very thoroughly and then dry the head completely.

12 Scrape off any heavy carbon deposits that may have formed on the valves, then use a power-operated wire brush to remove deposits from the valve heads and stems.

Inspection

Note: *Be sure to perform all the following inspection procedures before concluding that the services of an engineering works are required. Make a list of all items that require attention.*

Cylinder head

13 Inspect the head very carefully for cracks, evidence of coolant leakage, and other damage. If cracks are found, a new cylinder head should be obtained.

14 Use a straight-edge and feeler blade to check that the cylinder head gasket surface is not distorted. If it is, it may be possible to resurface it; consult your dealer or engine overhaul specialist **(see illustration)**.

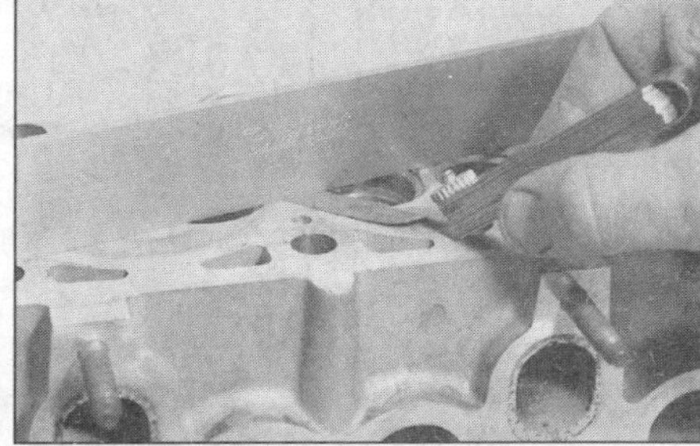

5.14 Use a straight-edge and feeler blade to check for distortion of the cylinder head gasket surface

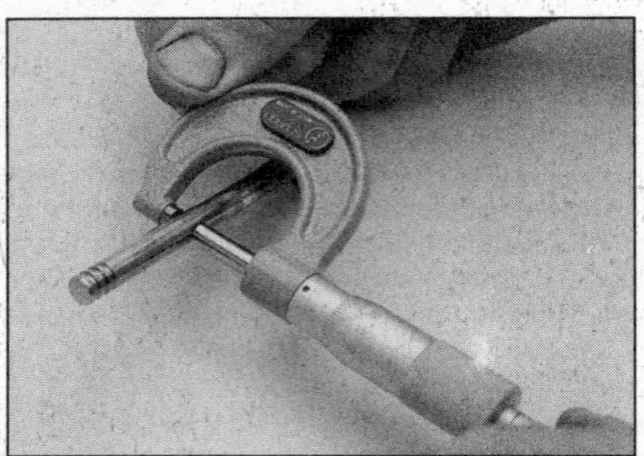
5.21 Measure the valve stem diameter using a micrometer

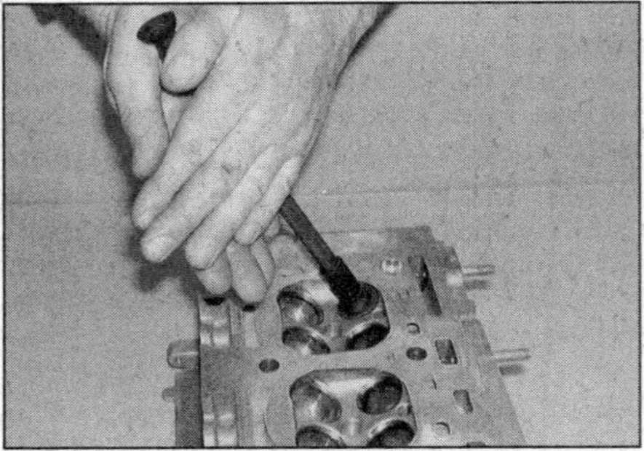
5.24 With a semi-rotary action, grind the valve head to its seat

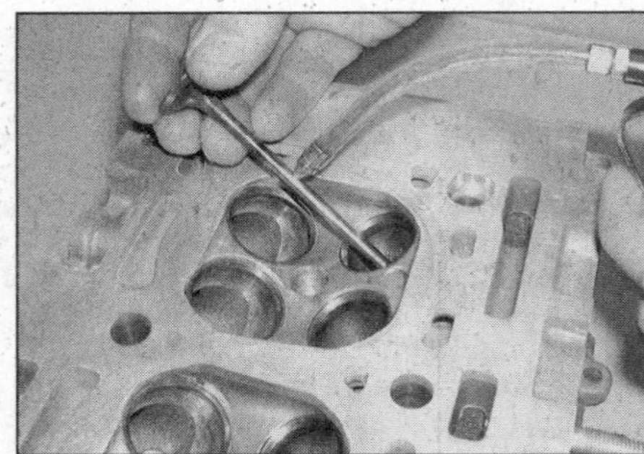
5.30 Oil the stem of the valve and insert it into the guide

15 Examine the valve seats in each of the combustion chambers. If they are severely pitted, cracked or burned, then they will need to be renewed or recut by an engine overhaul specialist. If they are only slightly pitted, this can be removed by grinding-in the valve heads and seats with fine valve-grinding compound, as described below.

16 If the valve guides appear worn, indicated by a side-to-side motion of the valve, new guides must be fitted. The renewal of valve guides should be carried out by an engine overhaul specialist.

17 If the valve seats are to be recut, this must be done *only after* the guides have been renewed.

18 The threaded holes in the cylinder head must be clean to ensure accurate torque readings when tightening fixings during reassembly. Carefully run the correct size tap (which can be determined from the size of the relevant bolt which fits in the hole) into each of the holes to remove rust, corrosion, thread sealant or other contamination, and to restore damaged threads. If possible, use compressed air to clear the holes of debris produced by this operation. Do not forget to clean the threads of all bolts and nuts as well.

19 Any threads which cannot be restored in this way can often be reclaimed by the use of thread inserts. If any threaded holes are damaged, consult your dealer or engine overhaul specialist and have them install any thread inserts where necessary.

Valves

20 Examine the head of each valve for pitting, burning, cracks and general wear, and check the valve stem for scoring and wear ridges. Rotate the valve, and check for any obvious indication that it is bent. Look for pits and excessive wear on the tip of each valve stem. Renew any valve that shows any such signs of wear or damage.

21 If the valve appears satisfactory at this stage, measure the valve stem diameter at several points, using a micrometer **(see illustration)**. Any significant difference in the readings obtained indicates wear of the valve stem. Should any of these conditions be apparent, the valve(s) must be renewed.

22 If the valves are in satisfactory condition, they should be ground (lapped) into their respective seats, to ensure a smooth gas-tight seal. If the seat is only lightly pitted, or if it has been recut, fine grinding compound *only* should be used to produce the required finish. Coarse valve-grinding compound should *not* be used unless a seat is badly burned or deeply pitted; if this is the case, the cylinder head and valves should be inspected by an expert, to decide whether seat recutting, or even the renewal of the valve or seat insert, is required.

23 Valve grinding is carried out as follows. Place the cylinder head upside-down on a bench, with a block of wood at each end to give clearance for the valve stems.

24 Smear a trace of (the appropriate grade) valve-grinding compound on the seat face, and press a suction grinding tool onto the valve head. With a semi-rotary action, grind the valve head to its seat, lifting the valve occasionally to redistribute the grinding compound **(see illustration)**. A light spring placed under the valve head will greatly ease this operation.

25 If coarse grinding compound is being used, work only until a dull, matt even surface is produced on both the valve seat and the valve, then wipe off the used compound, and repeat the process with fine compound. When a smooth unbroken ring of light grey matt finish is produced on both the valve and seat, the grinding operation is complete. *Do not* grind in the valves any further than absolutely necessary, or the seat will be prematurely sunk into the cylinder head.

26 When all the valves have been ground-in, carefully wash off *all* traces of grinding compound, using paraffin or a suitable solvent, before reassembly of the cylinder head.

Valve components

27 Examine the valve springs for signs of damage and discoloration, and also measure their free length.

28 Stand each spring on a flat surface, and check it for squareness. If any of the springs are damaged, distorted, or have lost their tension, obtain a complete set of new springs. It is normal to fit new springs as a matter of course if a major overhaul is being carried out.

29 Renew the valve stem oil seals regardless of their apparent condition.

Reassembly

30 Oil the stem of the first valve to be fitted and insert it into the corresponding guide **(see illustration)**.

31 The new valve stem oil seals should be supplied with a plastic fitting sleeve to protect the seal when it is fitted over the valve **(see illustration)**. If not, wrap a thin piece of polythene around the valve stem allowing it to extend about 10 mm above the end of the valve stem.

32 With the fitting sleeve, or polythene in place around the valve, fit the valve stem oil seal and push it onto the valve guide by hand as far as it will go with a suitable socket or piece of tube **(see illustrations)**. The lower valve spring seat is integral with the stem oil seal and the internal diameter of the socket or tube used for fitting must be large enough to fit over the oil seal portion and contact the

5.31 Fit a protective sleeve over the valve stem to aid fitting the valve stem oil seal

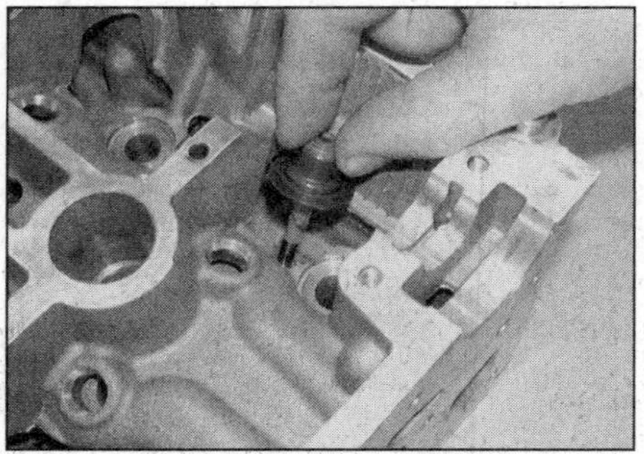
5.32a Fit the valve stem oil seal . . .

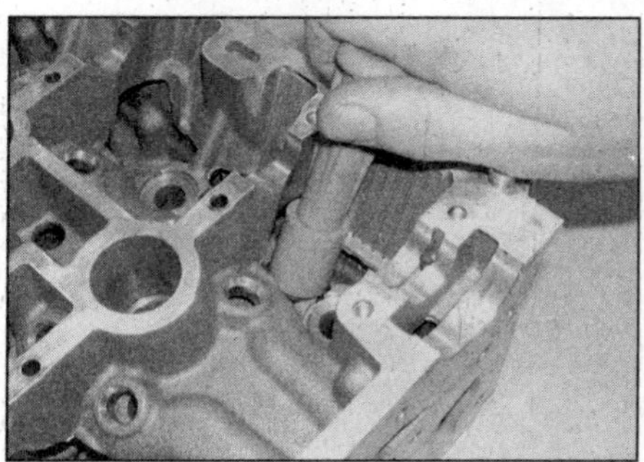

5.32b . . . and push it onto the valve guide with a suitable socket or tube

5.33a Fit the valve spring . . .

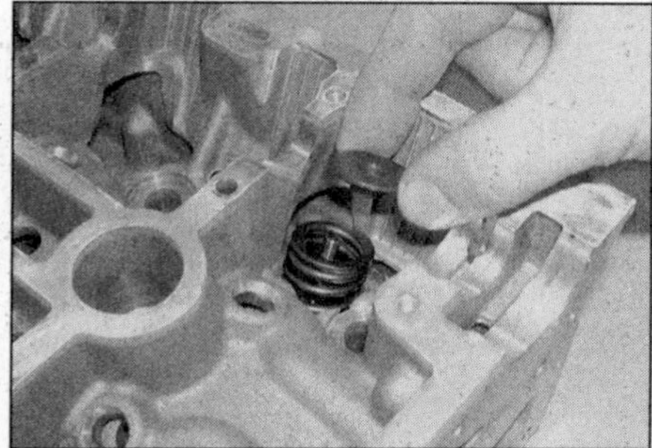

5.33b . . . followed by the upper spring seat . . .

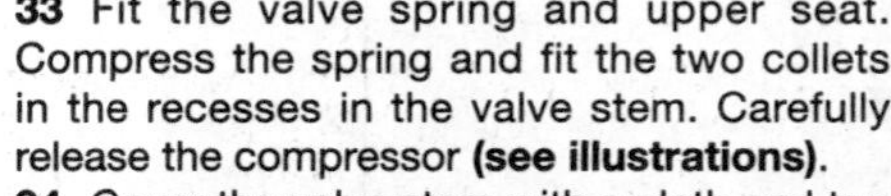

spring seat. Once the seal is seated, remove the protective sleeve or polythene.

33 Fit the valve spring and upper seat. Compress the spring and fit the two collets in the recesses in the valve stem. Carefully release the compressor **(see illustrations)**.

34 Cover the valve stem with a cloth and tap it smartly with a light hammer to verify that the collets are properly seated.

35 Repeat these procedures on all the other valves.

36 Refit the remainder of the disturbed components then refit the cylinder head as described in Part A of this Chapter.

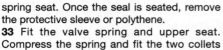

5.33c . . . then compress the spring using the spring compressors . . .

5.33d . . . and fit the two collets in the recesses in the valve stem, using a small screwdriver or similar

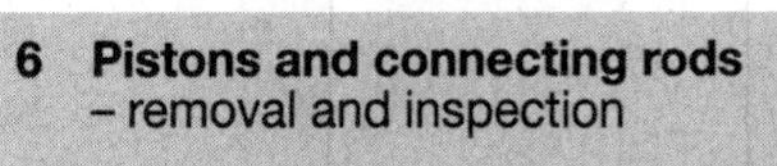

6 Pistons and connecting rods – removal and inspection

Removal

1 Remove the cylinder head, sump, oil pump and flywheel as described in Part A of this Chapter.

2 Feel inside the tops of the bores for a pronounced wear ridge. It is recommended that you remove such a ridge (with a scraper or ridge reamer) before attempting to remove the pistons, as the pistons rings may jam beneath the ridge making removal difficult. Note that a ridge large enough to cause complications such as this will almost certainly mean that further attention to the cylinder block is necessary.

3 Check that there are identification numbers or marks on each connecting rod and cap; paint suitable marks if necessary, so that each rod can be refitted in the same position and the same way round.

4 Remove the two connecting rod nuts/bolts. Tap the cap with a soft-faced hammer to free it. Remove the bearing cap, and note that on 1.8 and 2.0 litre engines the lower bearing shell does not have locating tabs **(see illustration)**. Make a careful note of the position of the shell in the bearing cap – during refitting the shell must be refitted to the cap in exactly the same position; no alignment markings or locating tabs are provided. **Note:** *On all engines, new big-end bearing cap nuts or bolts (as applicable) will be needed for reassembly.*

5 Push the connecting rod and piston up and out of the bore, noting that on 1.8 and 2.0 litre engines, like the lower bearing shell, the upper bearing shell has no locating tabs or alignment markings. Make a careful note of the position of the shell in the connecting rod – during refitting the shell must be refitted to the rod in exactly the same position.

6 Refit the cap to the connecting rod, the correct way round, so that they do not get mixed up. On some models, serrations are used on the bearing cap and connecting rod mating surfaces to ensure that the cap can only be fitted the correct way around **(see illustration)**.

7 Check to see if there is an arrow on the top of the piston, which should be pointing toward the flywheel or timing belt end of the cylinder block depending on engine **(see illustration)**. If no arrow can be seen, make a suitable direction mark yourself.

8 Repeat the operations on the remaining connecting rods and pistons.

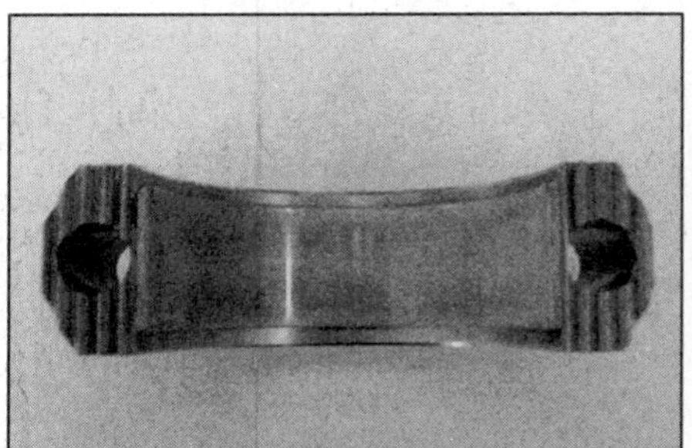

6.4 On 1.8 and 2.0 litre engines, the big-end bearing shells do not have locating tabs

6.6 The serrations on the bearing cap and connecting rod mating surfaces ensure the cap can only be fitted the correct way

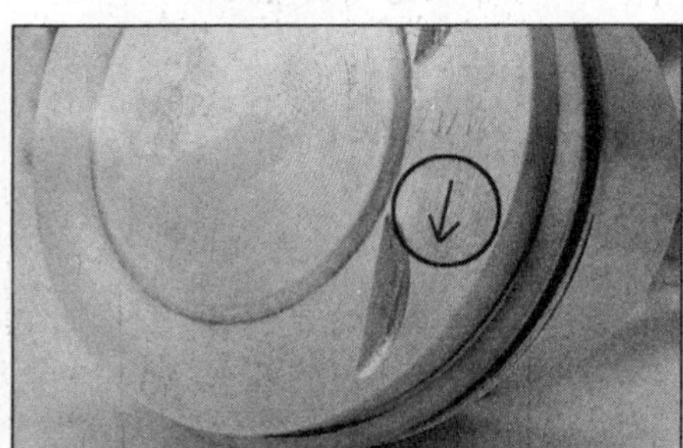

6.7 The arrow points toward the flywheel on 1.6 and 1.8 litre engines, and toward the timing belt on 2.0 litre engines

6.10 Removing the piston rings using a feeler blade

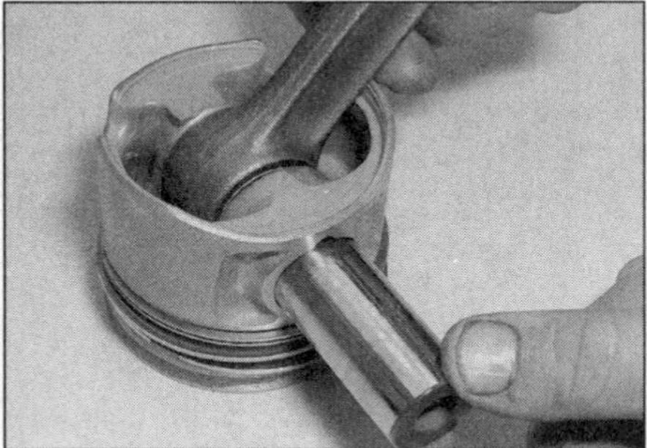

6.21 Push the gudgeon pin out of the piston and connecting rod

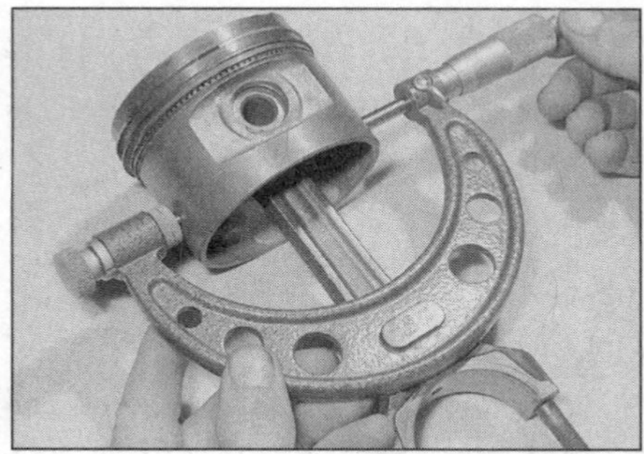

6.22 Measure the diameter of each piston using a micrometer (see text)

Inspection

9 Before the inspection process can be carried out, the piston/connecting rod assemblies must be cleaned, and the original piston rings removed from the pistons.

10 Carefully expand the old rings and remove them from the top of the pistons. The use of two or three old feeler blades will be helpful in preventing the rings dropping into empty grooves **(see illustration)**. Be careful not to scratch the pistons with the ends of the ring. The rings are brittle and will snap if they are spread too far. They are also very sharp – protect your hands and fingers.

11 Scrape all traces of carbon from the top of the piston. A hand-held wire brush (or a piece of fine emery cloth) can be used, once the majority of the deposits have been scraped away.

12 Remove the carbon from the ring grooves in the piston, using an old ring. Break the ring in half to do this (be careful not to cut your fingers – piston rings are sharp). Be careful to remove only the carbon deposits – do not remove any metal, and do not nick or scratch the sides of the ring grooves.

13 Once the deposits have been removed, clean the piston/rod assemblies with paraffin or a suitable solvent, and dry thoroughly. Make sure the oil return holes in the ring grooves are clear.

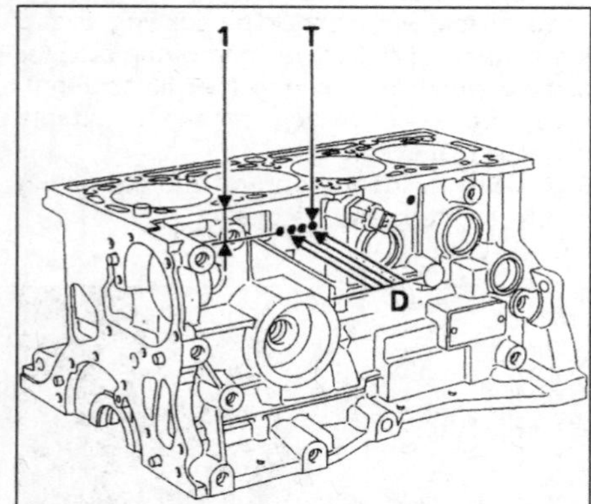

6.23 Piston/cylinder bore class group markings (1.6 litre engines)

1 Distance from block mating surface to centre of class group identification holes
D Position of class group identification holes for each cylinder
T Class group identification holes

14 If the pistons and cylinder bores are not damaged or worn excessively, and if the cylinder block does not need further attention, the original pistons can be refitted. Normal piston wear appears as even vertical wear on the piston thrust surfaces, and slight looseness of the top ring in its groove. New piston rings should always be used when the engine is reassembled.

15 Carefully inspect each piston for cracks around the skirt, around the gudgeon pin holes, and at the ring lands (between the ring grooves).

16 Look for scoring and scuffing on the piston skirt, holes in the piston crown, and burned areas at the edge of the crown. If the skirt is scored or scuffed, the engine may have been suffering from overheating and/or abnormal combustion, which caused excessively-high operating temperatures. The cooling and lubrication systems should be checked thoroughly. Scorch marks on the sides of the piston show that blow-by has occurred. A hole in the piston crown or burned areas at the edge of the piston crown, indicates that abnormal combustion (pre-ignition, knocking, or detonation) has been occurring. If any of the above problems exist, the causes must be investigated and corrected, or the damage will occur again. The causes may include inlet air leaks, incorrect fuel/air mixture or an emission control system fault.

17 Corrosion of the piston, in the form of pitting, indicates that coolant has been leaking into the combustion chamber and/or the crankcase. Again, the cause must be corrected, or the problem may persist in the rebuilt engine.

18 Examine each connecting rod carefully for signs of damage, such as cracks around the big-end and small-end bearings. Check that the rod is not bent or distorted. Damage is highly unlikely, unless the engine has been seized or badly overheated. Detailed checking of the connecting rod assembly can only be carried out by an engine overhaul specialist with the necessary equipment.

19 On 1.6 litre engines the gudgeon pins are an interference fit in the connecting rod small-end bearing. Therefore, piston and/or connecting rod renewal should be entrusted to a Renault dealer or engine repair specialist, who will have the necessary tooling to remove and install the gudgeon pins.

20 On 1.8 and 2.0 litre engines, the gudgeon pins are of the floating type, secured in position by two circlips. Where necessary, the pistons and connecting rods can be separated as follows.

21 Make a note of any identification marks on the connecting rod, in relation to the arrow on the piston crown, so that the connecting rod and piston can be refitted the correct way round on reassembly. Remove one of the circlips, which secure the gudgeon pin and push the gudgeon pin out of the piston and connecting rod **(see illustration)**.

22 The diameter of the pistons should now be measured with a micrometer using the procedures described in the following sub-Sections, according to engine type **(see illustration)**.

1.6 litre engines

23 Using a micrometer, measure the diameter of all four pistons at a point 42 mm from the top of the crown, at right angles to the gudgeon pin axis. Compare the measurements obtained with those listed in the Specifications. Note that three standard size piston and cylinder bore classes are available, A, B and C – the class letter being stamped on the piston crown. The class of the corresponding cylinder bore can be determined from the group of four small identification holes drilled into the side of the block. The distance from the block mating surface to the centre of the holes identifies the class of the bore. Class A holes are drilled 17 mm down from the mating surface, class B holes 27 mm and class C holes 37 mm **(see illustration)**. If new pistons are to be obtained, they must be of the same class as the cylinder bore to which they will be fitted.

1.8 and 2.0 litre engines

24 Using a micrometer, measure the diameter of all four pistons at a point 43.8 mm from the top of the crown, at right angles to the gudgeon pin axis. Compare the measurements obtained with those listed in the Specifications. Note that two standard size piston and cylinder bore classes are available, identified as 2 and 3 (or B and C) – the class number being stamped on the piston crown. The class of the corresponding cylinder bore can be determined from the small identification holes drilled into the side of the block, one adjacent to each cylinder. The distance from the block mating surface to the centre of the holes identifies the class of the bore. Class 2 (or B) holes are drilled 13 mm down from the mating surface and class 3 (or C) holes 19 mm **(see illustration)**. If new pistons are to be obtained, they must be of the same class as the cylinder bore to which they will be fitted.

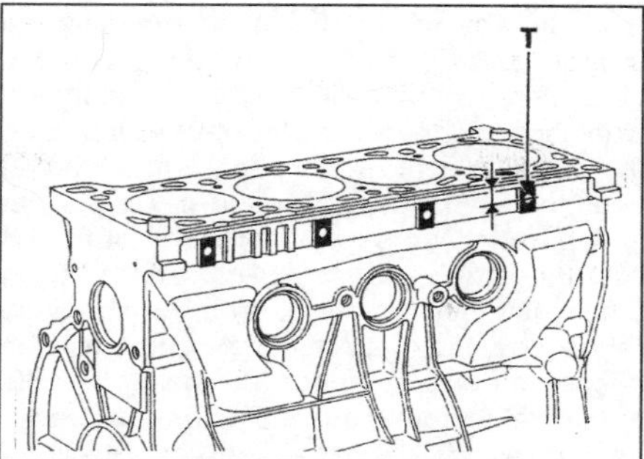

6.24 Piston/cylinder bore class group markings (1.8 and 2.0 litre engines)

T Class group identification holes
Arrows indicate distance from block mating surface to centre of holes

All engines

25 If the diameter of any of the pistons is out of the tolerance band listed for its particular class, then all four pistons must be renewed. Record the measurements and use them to check the piston-to-bore clearance when the cylinder bores are measured later in this Chapter.

26 On 1.8 and 2.0 litre engines, check the fit of the gudgeon pin in the connecting rod bush and in the piston. If there is perceptible play, a new bush or an oversize gudgeon pin must be fitted. Consult a Renault dealer or engine reconditioning specialist.

27 Examine all components and obtain any new parts required. If new pistons are purchased, they will be supplied complete with gudgeon pins and circlips. Circlips can also be purchased separately.

28 Oil the gudgeon pin. Reassemble the connecting rod and piston, making sure the rod is the right way round, and secure the gudgeon pin with the circlip. Position the circlip so that it's opening is facing upward.

29 Repeat these operations for the remaining pistons.

7 Crankshaft – removal and inspection

Note: *If no work is to be done on the pistons and connecting rods, then removal of the cylinder head and pistons will not be necessary. Instead, the pistons need only be pushed far enough up the bores so that they are positioned clear of the crankpins.*

Removal

1 With reference to Part A of this Chapter, and earlier Sections of this part as applicable, carry out the following:

a) *Remove the sump.*
b) *Remove the oil pump drive chain and sprockets.*
c) *Remove the clutch components and flywheel.*
d) *Remove the pistons and connecting rods (refer to the Note above).*

2 Before the crankshaft is removed, it is advisable to check the endfloat. Mount a dial gauge with the stem in line with the crankshaft and just touching the crankshaft nose.

3 Push the crankshaft fully away from the gauge, and zero it. Next, lever the crankshaft towards the gauge as far as possible, and check the reading obtained. The distance that the crankshaft moved is its endfloat; if it is greater than specified, check the crankshaft thrust surfaces for wear. If no wear is evident, new thrustwashers should correct the endfloat.

4 Continue with the removal procedure as described in the following sub-Sections according to engine type.

1.6 litre engines

5 Unscrew and remove the main bearing cap retaining bolts and withdraw the caps, noting that the caps are numbered 1 to 5 from the transmission (flywheel) end of the engine.

TOOL TiP

To make a main bearing cap removal tool for 1.8 litre engines, obtain a length of steel strip about 6 mm thick by 30 mm wide, and long enough to straddle the main bearing cap. Drill three holes in the strip as shown. Attach two suitable lengths of threaded rod, using two nuts each, to the outer two holes in the strip, or alternatively two old cylinder head bolts can be used instead. Make a lifting plate by cutting a second length of steel strip, long enough to fit over the bearing cap. Drill a hole in the centre, then mark and drill a hole each side so that the plate can be bolted to the holes in the cap. Attach a threaded rod to the lifting plate using two nuts and screw on another nut at the top.

Recover the lower main bearing shells, and tape them to their respective caps for safe-keeping.

6 Carefully lift out the crankshaft, taking care not to displace the upper main bearing shells, and discard the oil seal.

7 Recover the upper bearing shells from the cylinder block, and tape them to their respective caps for safe-keeping. Remove the thrustwasher halves from the side of crankcase main bearing, and store them with the bearing cap.

1.8 and 2.0 litre engines

8 No 1 main bearing cap (nearest the flywheel end of the engine) is sealed to the sides of the cylinder block with a semi-permanent silicone based sealant. As there is very little clearance between the crankshaft and cylinder block in this area in which to tap or prise the cap free, it will be necessary to use Renault special tool Mot. 1423 for removal. Alternatively, fabricate a home-made alternative **(see Tool tip)**.

9 Unscrew and remove the main bearing cap retaining bolts and carefully withdraw all the caps except No 1. The caps are numbered 1 to 5 from the transmission (flywheel) end of the engine. Note that the main bearing shells do not have locating tabs. If possible (assuming that the shell remains in the cap as the cap is removed) make a careful note of the position of the shell in the bearing cap and its fitted direction – during refitting the shell must be refitted to the cap in exactly the same position; no alignment markings or locating tabs are provided. Recover the lower main bearing shells if they remained on the crankshaft, and tape all the shells to their respective caps for safe-keeping.

10 Position the removal tool on the cylinder block and attach the lifting plate to the two threaded holes in No 1 main bearing cap using suitable bolts. Turn the nut on the threaded centre rod of the tool to withdraw the bearing cap from the cylinder block **(see illustration)**. Remove the tool, recover the lower main bearing shell (if still on the crankshaft) and tape it to the cap.

11 Carefully lift out the crankshaft, taking care not to displace the upper main bearing shells, and discard the oil seal.

12 Again, make a careful note of the fitted positions of the bearing shells and recover

7.10 Using the home-made tool to remove No 1 main bearing cap (1.8 litre engines)

7.18 Use a micrometer to measure the crankshaft journal diameters

the upper shells from the cylinder block. Tape them the correct way round to their respective caps for safe-keeping. Remove the thrust washer halves from the side of crankcase main bearing, and store them with the bearing cap.

Inspection

13 Clean the crankshaft using paraffin or a suitable solvent, and dry it, preferably with compressed air if available. Be sure to clean the oil holes with a pipe cleaner or similar probe to ensure that they are not obstructed.

Warning: Wear eye protection when using compressed air.

14 Check the main and big-end bearing journals for uneven wear, scoring, pitting and cracking.

15 Big-end bearing wear is accompanied by distinct metallic knocking when the engine is running (particularly noticeable when the engine is pulling from low speed) and some loss of oil pressure.

16 Main bearing wear is accompanied by severe engine vibration and rumble – getting progressively worse as engine speed increases – and again by loss of oil pressure.

17 Check the bearing journal for roughness by running a finger lightly over the bearing surface. Any roughness (which will be accompanied by obvious bearing wear) indicates that the crankshaft requires regrinding (where possible) or renewal.

18 Using a micrometer, measure the diameter of the main and big end journals, and compare the results with the Specifications **(see illustration)**. By measuring the diameter at a number of points around each journal's circumference, you will be able to determine whether or not the journal is out-of-round. Take the measurement at each end of the journal, near the webs, to determine if the journal is tapered. Compare the results obtained with those given in the Specifications. If the crankshaft journals are outside the tolerance range specified, a new crankshaft will be needed as only standard size bearing shells are available from the manufacturer. However, seek the advice of an engine overhaul specialist first, as to whether regrinding may be possible and whether suitable bearing shells can be supplied to match.

19 Check the oil seal contact surfaces at each end of the crankshaft for wear and damage. If either seal has worn a deep groove in the surface of the crankshaft, consult an engine overhaul specialist; repair may be possible, otherwise a new crankshaft will be required.

8.1 Piston oil spray jets are fitted to the base of each cylinder on 1.8 litre engines

8 Cylinder block/crankcase – cleaning and inspection

Cleaning

1 Prior to cleaning, remove all external components and senders, and any gallery plugs or caps that may be fitted. On 1.8 and 2.0 litre engines, piston oil spray jets are fitted to the base of each cylinder **(see illustration)**. Numerous special tools are required to remove and refit these jets and if there is any doubt about their condition, have the jets renewed by an engine overhaul specialist.

2 If any of the castings are extremely dirty, all should be steam-cleaned.

3 After the castings are returned from steam cleaning, clean all oil holes and oil galleries one more time. Flush all internal passages with warm water until the water runs clear. If you have access to compressed air, use it to speed the drying process, and to blow out all the oil holes and galleries.

Warning: Wear eye protection when using compressed air.

4 If the castings are not very dirty, you can do an adequate cleaning job with hot soapy water (as hot as you can stand!) and a stiff brush. Take plenty of time, and do a thorough job. Regardless of the cleaning method used, be sure to clean all oil holes and galleries very thoroughly, and to dry all components completely. Apply clean engine oil to the cylinder bores to prevent rusting.

5 The threaded holes in the cylinder block must be clean to ensure accurate torque readings when tightening fixings during reassembly. Carefully run the correct size tap (which can be determined from the size of the relevant bolt which fits in the hole) into each of the holes to remove rust, corrosion, thread sealant or other contamination, and to restore damaged threads. If possible, use compressed air to clear the holes of debris produced by this operation. Do not forget to clean the threads of all bolts and nuts as well.

6 Any threads, which cannot be restored in this way, can often be reclaimed by the use of thread inserts. If any threaded holes are damaged, consult your dealer or engine overhaul specialist and have them install any thread inserts where necessary.

7 If the engine is not going to be reassembled right away, cover it with a large plastic bag to keep it clean; protect the machined surfaces, as described above, to prevent rusting.

Inspection

8 Visually check the castings for cracks and corrosion. Look for stripped threads in the threaded holes. If there has been any history of internal coolant leakage, it may be worthwhile having an engine overhaul specialist check the cylinder block/crankcase for cracks with special equipment. If defects are found, have them repaired, if possible, or renew the assembly.

9 Check the condition of the cylinder head and sump or intermediate section mating surfaces. Check the surfaces for any possible distortion using the straight-edge and feeler blade method described earlier for cylinder head inspection. If distortion is slight, consult an engine overhaul specialist as to the best course of action.

10 Check each cylinder bore for scuffing and scoring. Check for signs of a wear ridge at the top of the cylinder, indicating that the bore is excessively worn.

11 If the necessary measuring equipment is available, measure the diameter of each cylinder at the top (just under the ridge area), centre and bottom of the cylinder bore, parallel to the crankshaft axis using a cylinder bore gauge. Next, measure the bore diameter at the same three locations across the crankshaft axis. Note the measurements obtained. Have this work carried out by an engine overhaul specialist if you do not have access to the measuring equipment needed.

12 To obtain the piston-to-bore clearance, measure the piston diameter as described earlier in this Chapter, and subtract the piston diameter from the largest bore measurement.

13 Repeat these procedures for the remaining pistons and cylinder bores.

14 Compare the results with the Specifications at the beginning of this Chapter; if any measurement is beyond the dimensions specified for that class, or if any bore measurement is significantly different from the others (indicating that the bore is tapered or oval), the piston or bore is excessively-worn. Note that each cylinder bore is identified by a class marking stamped into side or rear of the cylinder block. Refer to the information contained in Section 7 for details of interpretation of the class markings.

15 If any of the cylinder bores are badly scuffed or scored, or if they are excessively-worn, out-of-round or tapered, the usual course of action would be to have the cylinder block/crankcase rebored, and to fit new, oversized, pistons on reassembly. Check for availability of parts, seek the advice of a Renault dealer or engine overhaul specialist on the best course of action.

16 If the bores are in reasonably good condition and not excessively worn, then it may only be necessary to renew the piston rings.

17 If this is the case, the bores should be honed, to allow the new rings to bed in correctly and provide the best possible seal. Honing is an operation that will be carried out for you by an engine-reconditioning specialist.

18 After all machining operations are completed; the entire block/crankcase must be washed very thoroughly with warm soapy water to remove all traces of abrasive grit produced during the machining operations. When the cylinder block/crankcase is completely clean, rinse it thoroughly and dry it, then lightly oil all exposed machined surfaces, to prevent rusting.

19 The final step is to renew the main bearing cap retaining bolts. As with all bolts that are tightened to a very high torque setting or through a torque angle, they are prone to stretch, often up to the extent of their elastic limit. It is virtually impossible to judge the strain that this imposes on a particular bolt, and if any are in any way flawed, breakage when retightening, or failure in service could be the result.

9 Main and big-end bearings – inspection and selection

Inspection

1 Even though the main and big end bearing shells should be renewed during the engine overhaul, the old shells should be retained for close examination, as they may reveal valuable information about the condition of the engine.

2 Bearing failure occurs because of lack of lubrication, the presence of dirt or other foreign particles, overloading the engine, and corrosion **(see illustration)**. Regardless of the cause of bearing failure, the cause must be corrected (where applicable) before the engine is reassembled, to prevent it from happening again.

3 When examining the bearing shells, remove them from the cylinder block/crankcase and main bearing caps, and from the connecting rods and the big-end bearing caps, and then lay them out on a clean surface in the same general position as their location in the engine. This will enable you to match any bearing problems with the corresponding crankshaft journal. *Do not* touch any of the shell's bearing surfaces with your fingers while checking it, or the delicate surface may be scratched.

4 Dirt or other foreign matter gets into the engine in a variety of ways. It may be left in the engine during assembly, or it may pass through filters or the crankcase ventilation system. It may get into the oil, and from there into the bearings. Metal chips from machining operations and normal engine wear are often present. Abrasives are sometimes left in engine components after reconditioning, especially when parts are not thoroughly cleaned using the proper cleaning methods. Whatever the source, these foreign objects often end up embedded in the soft bearing material, and are easily recognised. Large particles will not embed in the material, and will score or gouge the shell and journal. The best prevention for this cause of bearing failure is to clean all parts thoroughly, and to keep everything spotlessly clean during engine assembly. Frequent and regular engine oil and filter changes are also recommended.

5 Lack of lubrication (or lubrication breakdown) has a number of inter-related causes. Excessive heat (which thins the oil), overloading (which squeezes the oil from the bearing face) and oil leakage (from excessive bearing clearances, worn oil pump or high engine speeds) all contribute to lubrication breakdown. Blocked oil passages, which usually are the result of misaligned oil holes in a bearing shell, will also starve a bearing of oil, and destroy it. When lack of lubrication is the cause of bearing failure, the bearing material is wiped or extruded from the shell's steel backing. Temperatures may increase to the point where the steel backing turns blue from overheating.

6 Driving habits can have a definite effect on bearing life. Full-throttle, low-speed operation (labouring the engine) puts very high loads on bearings, which tends to squeeze out the oil film. These loads cause the shells to flex, which produces fine cracks in the bearing face (fatigue failure). Eventually, the bearing material will loosen in pieces, and tear away from the steel backing.

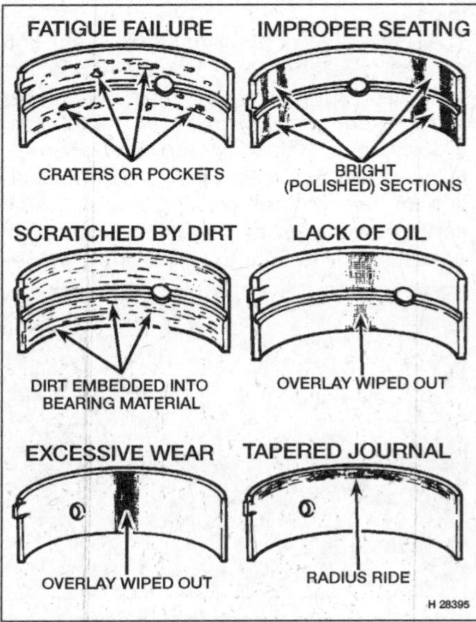

9.2 Typical bearing failures

7 Short-distance driving leads to corrosion of bearings, because insufficient engine heat is produced to drive off condensed water and corrosive gases. These products collect in the engine oil, forming acid and sludge. As the oil is carried to the engine bearings, the acid attacks and corrodes the bearing material.

8 Incorrect shell refitting during engine assembly will lead to bearing failure as well. Tight-fitting shells leave insufficient bearing running clearance, and will result in oil starvation. Dirt or foreign particles trapped behind a bearing shell result in high spots on the bearing, which lead to failure.

9 *Do not* touch any shell's bearing surface with your fingers during reassembly; there is a risk of scratching the delicate surface, or of depositing particles of dirt on it.

Selection

10 Although there are different crankshaft main bearing journal diameter classes, the main bearing shells supplied by the manufacturer are available in one standard size only. The big-end bearing shells are also only supplied in one standard size. As an actual running clearance dimension for the bearings is not specified, the only safe course of action is to fit new main and big-end bearing shells whenever an overhaul is being undertaken. Assuming that the relevant crankshaft journals are all within tolerance, the running clearances will then be correct. Before obtaining new bearing shells, consult a Renault dealer or engine reconditioning specialist as to the latest recommendations concerning bearing shell selection.

10 Engine overhaul – reassembly sequence

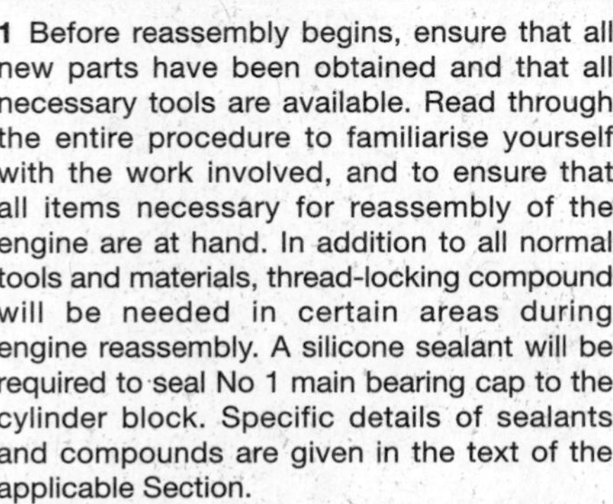

1 Before reassembly begins, ensure that all new parts have been obtained and that all necessary tools are available. Read through the entire procedure to familiarise yourself with the work involved, and to ensure that all items necessary for reassembly of the engine are at hand. In addition to all normal tools and materials, thread-locking compound will be needed in certain areas during engine reassembly. A silicone sealant will be required to seal No 1 main bearing cap to the cylinder block. Specific details of sealants and compounds are given in the text of the applicable Section.

2 In order to save time and avoid problems, engine reassembly can be carried out in the following order:

a) Crankshaft.
b) Pistons/connecting rods.
c) Oil pump drive chain and sprockets.
d) Sump.
e) Flywheel.

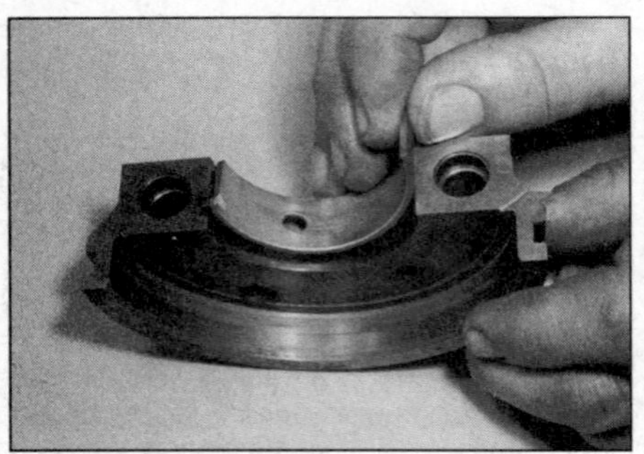
11.3 Fitting a shell to No 1 main bearing cap

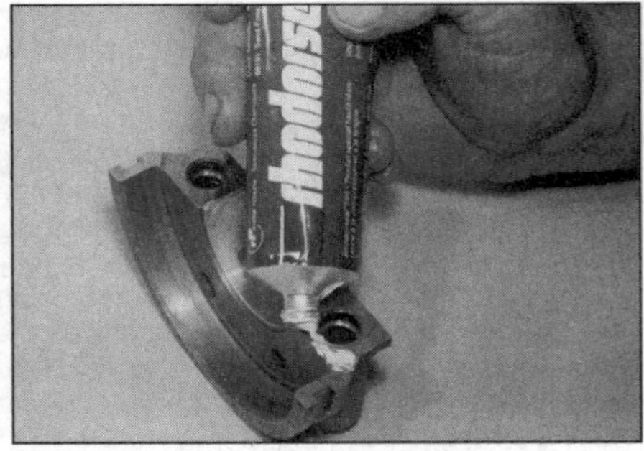

11.7a Apply a thin coating of sealant to the mating surface of No 1 main bearing cap . . .

11.7b . . . then fit the cap to the block

f) Cylinder head.
g) Camshaft and tappets.
h) Timing belt, tensioner, sprockets and idler pulleys.
i) Engine external components.

3 At this stage, all engine components should be absolutely clean and dry, with all faults repaired. The components should be laid out (or in individual containers) on a completely clean work surface.

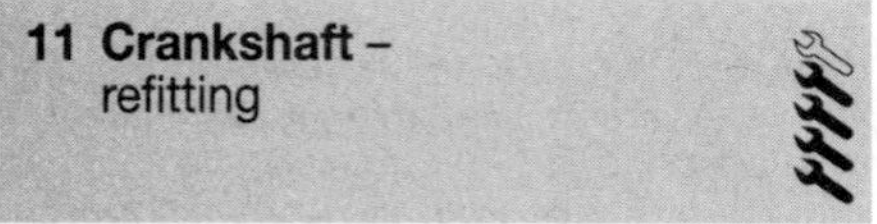

11 Crankshaft – refitting

Note: *To obtain the correct main bearing running clearance, new main bearing shells should always be fitted regardless of the condition of the original ones.*

1 Crankshaft refitting is the first stage of engine reassembly following overhaul. It is assumed at this point that the cylinder block/crankcase and crankshaft have been cleaned, inspected and repaired or reconditioned as necessary. Position the cylinder block on a clean level work surface, with the crankcase facing upwards. The crankshaft can now be refitted as described in the following sub-Sections according to engine type.

1.6 litre engines

2 Clean the backs of the bearing shells and the bearing locations in both the cylinder block and the main bearing caps. If new shells are being fitted, ensure that all traces of the protective grease are cleaned off using paraffin. Wipe dry the shells and caps with a lint-free cloth.

3 Press the bearing shells into their locations, noting that the shells with the oil groves are fitted to the cylinder block and to main bearing caps 2 and 4. The shells without oil grooves are fitted to main bearing caps 1, 3 and 5 **(see illustration)**. Ensure that the tab on each shell engages in the notch in the cylinder block or main bearing cap. If the original bearing shells are being used they must be refitted in their original locations.

4 Using a little grease, stick the thrustwashers to each side of the centre main bearing upper location; ensure that the oilway grooves on each thrustwasher face outwards (away from the cylinder block).

5 Liberally lubricate each bearing shell in the cylinder block with clean engine oil then lower the crankshaft into position ensuring that the bearing shells and thrustwashers remain correctly seated.

6 Ensure that the cap locating dowels are in position and fit main bearing caps 2 to 5 to their correct locations and the correct way round.

7 Apply a thin coating of Rhodorseal 5661 sealant (available from Renault dealers) to the mating surface of No 1 main bearing cap, taking great care not to block the oil return grooves, then fit the cap **(see illustrations)**.

8 Insert the new main bearing cap bolts and tighten them to the specified Stage 1 torque setting using a torque wrench. Once all the bolts have been tightened to their Stage 1 setting, angle-tighten the bolts through the specified Stage 2 angle, using a socket and extension bar. It is recommended that an angle-measuring gauge is used during this stage of the tightening, to ensure accuracy.

9 Check that the crankshaft is free to turn without stiffness or tight spots.

10 Check the crankshaft endfloat with reference to Section 7.

11 Lubricate the oil seal location, the crankshaft, and a new oil seal. Fit the seal, lips inwards, and use a piece of tube (or the old seal, inverted) to tap it into place until flush.

12 Continue with the engine reassembly procedures as described in the relevant Sections of this Chapter and Chapter 2A.

1.8 and 2.0 litre engines

13 Before refitting the crankshaft a decision must be made as to the method to be used when fitting the main bearing shells to the cylinder block and bearing caps. Renault specify the use of special tool Mot. 1493 to accurately position the bearing shells in their locations. However, with care, it is possible to position the shells in their locations equally accurately without the tool. In the following procedure, both methods are described.

14 To seal the contact surfaces of No 1 main bearing cap to the cylinder block, a tube of Rhodorseal 5661 sealant, together with a hardening agent and application syringe will be required. This is available as a kit from Renault dealers **(see illustration)**.

15 Clean the backs of the bearing shells and the bearing locations in both the cylinder block and the main bearing caps. If new shells are being fitted, ensure that all traces of the protective grease are cleaned off using paraffin. Wipe dry the shells, block and caps with a lint-free cloth.

16 Lay out the bearing shells ready for fitting, noting that the shells with the oil groves are fitted to the cylinder block, and the shells without oil grooves are fitted to the main bearing caps. If the original bearing shells are being used they must be refitted in their original locations and in their original fitted direction as noted during removal.

17 If the Renault special tool is being used, place the tool over the bearing location in the

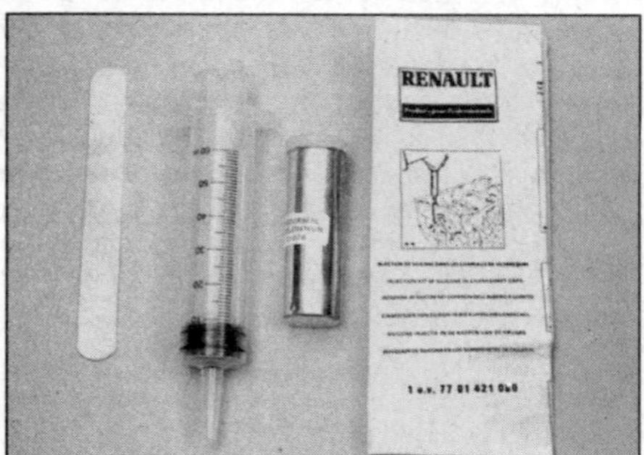

11.14 Renault sealing kit for No 1 main bearing cap

11.17a If the Renault tool is being used to fit the main bearing shells to the block, place the tool over the bearing location . . .

11.17b . . . insert the bearing shell into the tool . . .

11.17c . . . and press one end of the shell until the other end contacts the tool

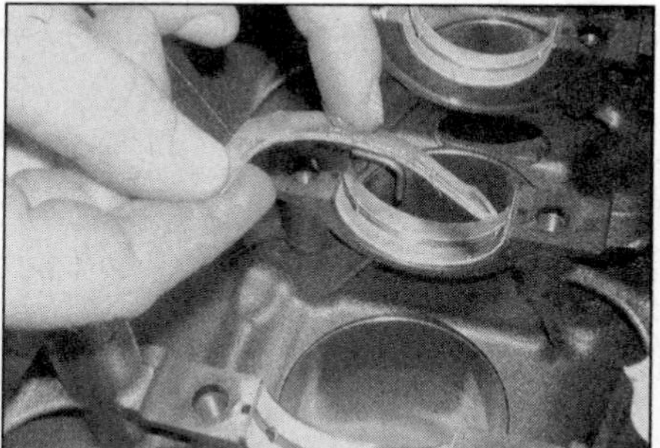

11.19a Smear a little grease on the crankshaft thrustwashers . . .

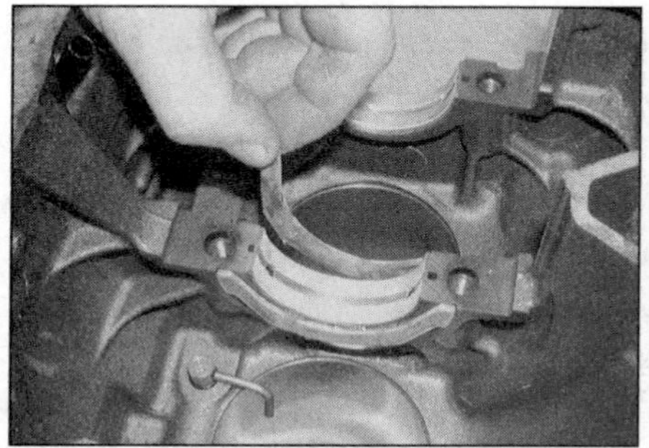

11.19b . . . and stick them to No 2 main bearing upper location

11.20a Liberally lubricate the upper main bearing shells . . .

11.20b . . . then lower the crankshaft into position

cylinder block and insert the bearing shell into the tool. Hold the tool and press one end of the bearing shell until the shell seats fully in its location and its other end contacts the stop on the tool **(see illustrations)**. Refit all the remaining shells to the cylinder block in the same way.

18 If the bearing shells are being fitted without the tool, press them into position in the cylinder block so that they are exactly centred in their locations and their edges are flush with the surface of the block.

19 Using a little grease, stick the thrustwashers to each side of No 2 main bearing upper location; ensure that the oilway grooves on each thrustwasher face outwards (away from the cylinder block) **(see illustrations)**.

20 Liberally lubricate each bearing shell in the cylinder block with clean engine oil then lower the crankshaft into position ensuring that the bearing shells and thrustwashers remain correctly seated **(see illustrations)**.

21 Fit the bearing shells to the main bearing caps using the same method as for the shells in the block **(see illustrations)**.

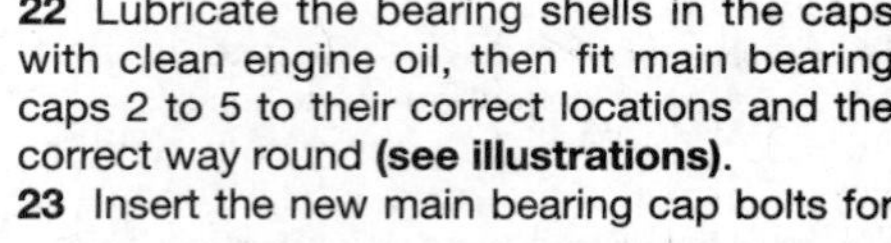

22 Lubricate the bearing shells in the caps with clean engine oil, then fit main bearing caps 2 to 5 to their correct locations and the correct way round **(see illustrations)**.

23 Insert the new main bearing cap bolts for

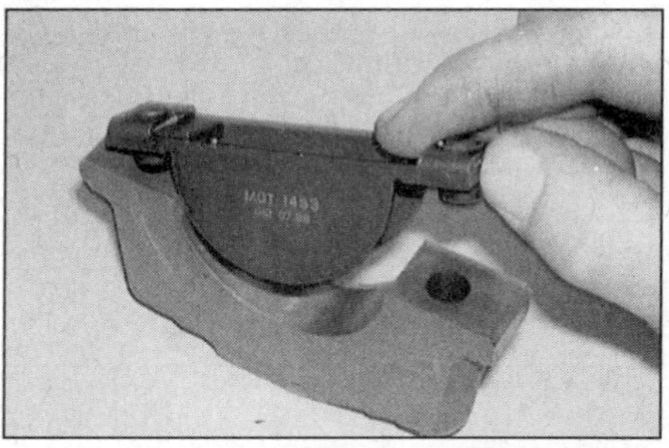

11.21a If the special tool is being used to fit the main bearing shells to the caps, fit the tool in the cap . . .

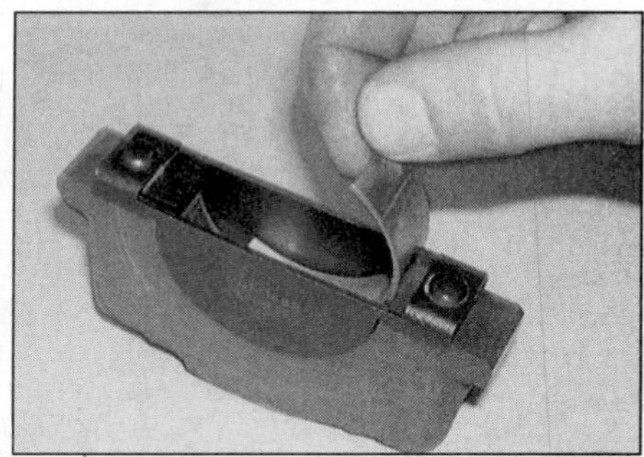

11.21b . . . insert the bearing shell into the tool . . .

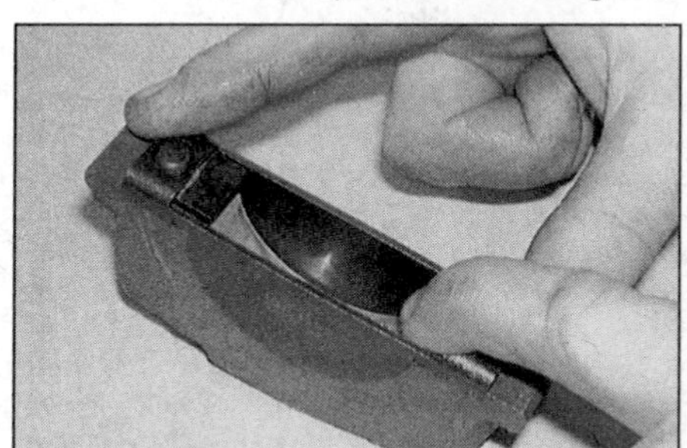

11.21c . . . then hold the tool and press one end of the shell until the other end contacts the tool

11.22a Liberally lubricate the bearing shells . . .

11.22b . . . then fit main bearing caps 2 to 5

11.23 Insert the new bolts for bearing caps 2 to 5 and tighten them to the specified torque

11.26a Apply a thin coating of sealant to No 1 main bearing cap lower mating surface in the cylinder block . . .

11.26b . . . then fit No 1 main bearing cap

caps 2 to 5 and tighten them to the specified torque **(see illustration)**.

24 Check that the crankshaft is free to turn without stiffness or tight spots, then check the crankshaft endfloat with reference to Section 7.

25 Thoroughly clean the contact surfaces of No 1 main bearing cap and its location in the cylinder block with methylated spirit and allow to dry thoroughly.

26 Apply a thin coating of Rhodorseal 5661 sealant to the bearing cap lower mating surface in the cylinder block, then fit the cap **(see illustrations)**. Insert the new main bearing cap bolts and tighten them to the specified torque.

27 Mix approximately half of the 100 g tube of Rhodorseal 5661 sealant together with half the hardener as described in the instructions supplied with the kit. Using the syringe supplied, inject the mixture into the grooves on each side of the bearing cap, until it can be seen to flow out slightly on both sides of the grooves **(see illustration)**. Using a clean cloth, wipe away any surplus mixture from the inside and outside of the cylinder block.

28 Allow the sealant to dry for a few minutes, and then cut away any surplus sealant from the sump mating face **(see illustration)**.

29 Check that the crankshaft is free to turn without stiffness or tight spots.

30 Lubricate the oil seal location, the crankshaft, and a new oil seal. Fit the seal, lips inwards, and use a piece of tube (or the old seal, inverted) to tap it into place until flush.

31 Continue with the engine reassembly procedures as described in the relevant Sections of this Chapter and Chapter 2A.

12 Pistons and piston rings – assembly

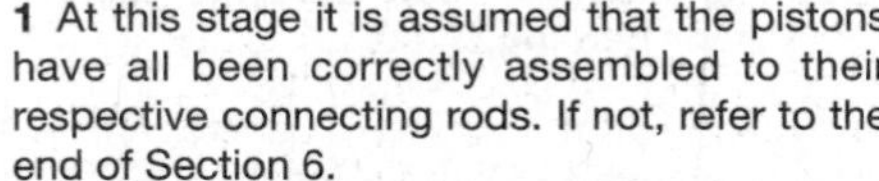

1 At this stage it is assumed that the pistons have all been correctly assembled to their respective connecting rods. If not, refer to the end of Section 6.

2 Before the rings can be fitted to the pistons, the end gaps must be checked with the rings inserted into the cylinder bores.

3 Lay out the piston assemblies and the new ring sets so the components are kept together in their groups, during and after end gap checking. Position the cylinder block on the work surface, on its side, allowing access to the top and bottom of the bores.

4 Take the No 1 piston top ring and insert it into the top of the first cylinder. Push it down the bore using the top of the piston; this will ensure that the ring remains square with the cylinder walls. Position the ring near the bottom of the cylinder bore, at the lower limit of ring travel.

5 Measure the ring gap using feeler blades.

6 Repeat the procedure with the ring at the top of the cylinder bore, at the upper limit of its travel and compare the measurements with the figures given in the Specifications.

7 If new rings are being fitted it is unlikely that the end gaps will be too small. If a measurement is found to be undersize, there is the risk that the ring ends may contact each other during engine operation, possibly resulting in engine damage. If the gaps are too small, check that you have the correct rings for your engine and for the cylinder bore size.

8 It is equally unlikely that the end gap will be too large. If the gaps are too large, again, check that you have the correct rings for your engine and for the cylinder bore size.

9 Repeat the checking procedure for each ring in the first cylinder, and then for the rings in the remaining cylinders. Remember to keep rings, pistons and cylinders matched up.

10 Once the ring end gaps have been checked, the rings can be fitted to the pistons. **Note:** *Always follow any instructions supplied with the new piston ring sets – different manufacturers may specify different*

11.27 Using the syringe, inject the mixture into the grooves on each side of No 1 main bearing cap, until it flows out on both sides

11.28 When dry, cut away any surplus sealant from the sump mating face

procedures. Do not mix up the top and second compression rings, as they have different cross-sections.

11 The oil control ring (lowest on the piston) is installed first. It is composed of three separate components. Slip the expander into the groove, then install the lower side rail into the groove between the expander and the ring land, and then install the upper side rail in the same manner.

12 Install the second ring next. **Note:** *The second ring and top ring are different, and can be identified by their cross-sections.* Making sure the ring is the correct way up, fit the ring into the middle groove on the piston, taking care not to expand the ring any more than is necessary **(see illustration)**.

13 Install the top ring in the same way; making sure the ring is the correct way up. Where the ring is symmetrical, fit it with its identification marking facing upwards **(see illustration)**.

14 When all the rings are in position arrange the ring gaps 120° apart.

15 Repeat the above procedure for the remaining pistons and rings.

13 Pistons and connecting rod assemblies – refitting

1.6 litre engines

1 Before refitting the piston/connecting rod assemblies, the cylinder bores must be perfectly clean, the top edge of each cylinder must be chamfered, and the crankshaft must be in place.

2 Remove the big-end bearing cap from No 1 cylinder connecting rod, and remove the original bearing shells.

3 Clean the backs of the big-end bearing shells and the recesses in the connecting rods and big-end caps. If new shells are being fitted, ensure that all traces of the protective grease are cleaned off using paraffin. Wipe the shells and connecting rods dry with a lint-free cloth.

4 Press the bearing shells into the connecting rods and caps in their correct positions. Make sure that the location tabs are engaged with the cut-outs in the connecting rods.

5 Position the piston ring gaps in their correct positions around the piston, lubricate the piston and rings with clean engine oil, and attach a piston ring compressor to the piston. Leave the piston crown protruding slightly, to guide the piston into the cylinder bore. The rings must be compressed until they're flush with the piston.

6 Rotate the crankshaft until No 1 big-end journal is at BDC (Bottom Dead Centre), and apply a coat of engine oil to the cylinder walls.

7 Arrange the No 1 piston/connecting rod assembly so that the arrow on the piston crown points toward the flywheel end of the engine. Gently insert the assembly into the No 1 cylinder bore, and rest the bottom edge of the ring compressor on the cylinder block **(see illustration)**.

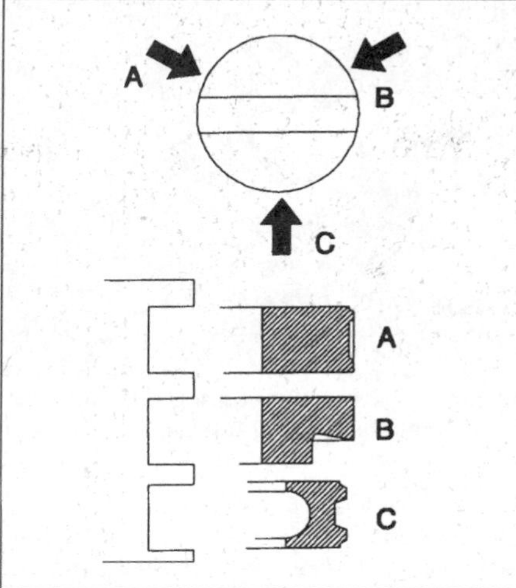

12.12 Piston ring identification and end gap positioning (2.0 litre engines)

8 Tap the top edge of the ring compressor to make sure it's contacting the block around its entire circumference.

9 Gently tap on the top of the piston with the end of a wooden hammer handle, whilst guiding the connecting rod big-end onto the crankpin **(see illustration)**. The piston rings may try to pop out of the ring compressor just before entering the cylinder bore, so keep some pressure on the ring compressor. Work slowly, and if any resistance is felt as the piston enters the cylinder, stop immediately. Find out what is binding (usually a ring), and fix it before proceeding. *Do not*, for any reason, force the piston into the cylinder – you might break a ring and/or the piston.

10 Make sure the bearing surfaces are perfectly clean, and then apply a uniform layer of clean engine oil to both of them. You may have to push the piston back up the cylinder bore slightly to expose the bearing surface of the shell in the connecting rod.

11 Slide the connecting rod back into place on the big-end journal and refit the big-end bearing cap. Lubricate the threads of the studs, fit the new nuts and tighten them to the specified torque

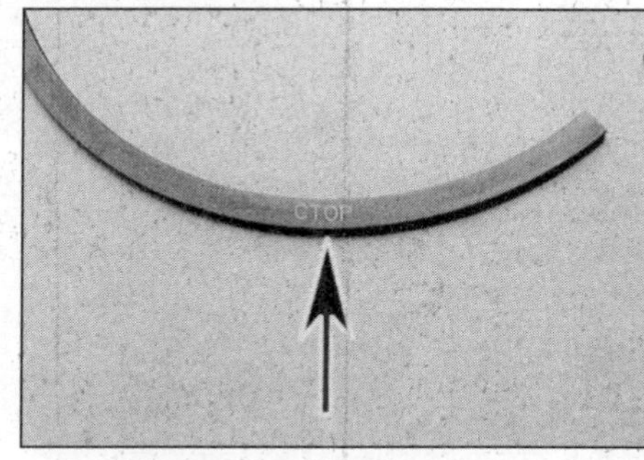
12.13 Piston ring identification marking (arrowed)

12 Repeat the entire procedure for the remaining piston/connecting rod assemblies. The important points to remember are:

a) *Keep the backs of the bearing shells and their locations in the connecting rods and caps perfectly clean when assembling them.*
b) *Make sure you have the correct piston/rod assembly for each cylinder.*
c) *The arrow on the piston crown must face the flywheel end of the engine.*
d) *Lubricate the cylinder bores with clean engine oil.*
e) *Lubricate the bearing surfaces before fitting the big-end bearing caps.*

13 After all the piston/connecting rod assemblies have been properly installed, rotate the crankshaft a number of times by hand, to check for any obvious binding.

1.8 and 2.0 litre engines

14 A decision must first be made as to the method to be used when fitting the big-end bearing shells to the connecting rods and caps. Renault specify the use of special tool Mot. 1492 to accurately position the bearing shells in the rod and cap. However, with care, it is possible to position the shells in their locations equally accurately without the tool. If the special tools are being used, follow the instructions supplied with the tool to fit the

13.7 Insert the piston/connecting rod assembly into the cylinder bore, and rest the bottom edge of the ring compressor on the block

13.9 Tap on the top of the piston with the end of a wooden hammer handle, whilst guiding the connecting rod big-end onto the crankpin

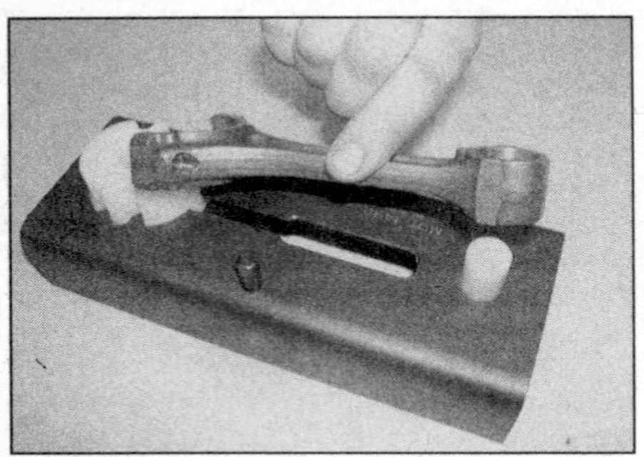

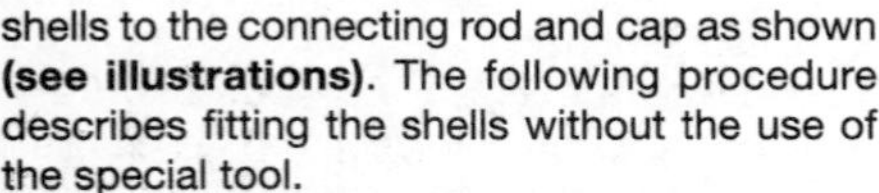

13.14a On 1.8 litre engines, if the special tool is being used to fit the big-end bearing shells to the connecting rods, place the rod on the tool . . .

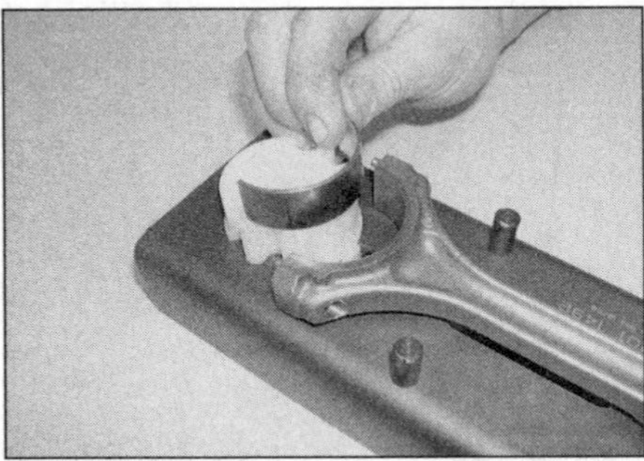

13.14b . . . insert the bearing shell into the sliding part of the tool . . .

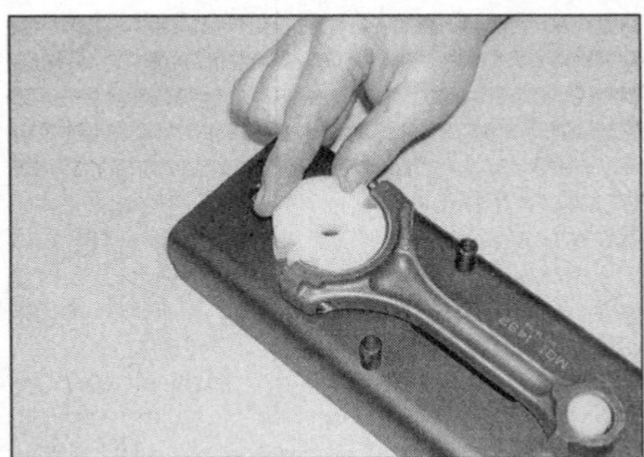

13.14c . . . then push the tool sliding part and bearing shell into the connecting rod. Fit the shells to the caps in the same way

shells to the connecting rod and cap as shown **(see illustrations)**. The following procedure describes fitting the shells without the use of the special tool.

15 Before refitting the piston/connecting rod assemblies, the cylinder bore must be perfectly clean, the top edge of each cylinder must be chamfered, and the crankshaft must be in place.

16 Remove the original bearing shells (observing the notes in Section 6, relating to the position of the shells in the bearing cap and connecting rod) and wipe the bearing recesses of the connecting rod and cap with a clean, lint-free cloth. They must be kept spotlessly clean. Ensure that new big-end bearing cap retaining bolts are available.

17 Clean the back of the new upper bearing shell, fit it to No 1 connecting rod, then fit the other shell of the bearing to the big-end bearing cap. Position the shells in the rod and cap so that they are exactly centred in their locations and their edges are flush with the rod and cap mating surfaces. If the original bearing shells are being used they must be refitted in exactly the same position as noted during removal.

18 Position the piston ring gaps in their correct positions around the piston, lubricate the piston and rings with clean engine oil, and attach a piston ring compressor to the piston **(see illustration)**. Leave the piston crown protruding slightly, to guide the piston into the cylinder bore. The rings must be compressed until they're flush with the piston.

19 Rotate the crankshaft until No 1 big-end journal is at BDC (Bottom Dead Centre), and apply a coat of engine oil to the cylinder walls. Note that, No 1 cylinder is at the flywheel end of the cylinder block.

20 Arrange the No 1 piston/connecting rod assembly so that the arrow on the piston crown points toward the flywheel end. Gently insert the assembly into the No 1 cylinder bore, and rest the bottom edge of the ring compressor on the cylinder block.

21 Tap the top edge of the ring compressor to make sure it's contacting the block around its entire circumference.

22 Gently tap on the top of the piston with the end of a wooden hammer handle, whilst guiding the connecting rod big-end onto the crankpin with the aid of a long screwdriver **(see illustrations)**. The piston rings may try to pop out of the ring compressor just before entering the cylinder bore, so keep some pressure on the ring compressor. Work slowly, and if any resistance is felt as the piston enters the cylinder, stop immediately. Find out what is binding (usually a ring), and fix it before proceeding. *Do not*, for any reason, force the piston into the cylinder – you might break a ring and/or the piston. Take care also not to let the connecting rod foul the piston oil spray jets, as it approaches the crankshaft.

23 Make sure the bearing surfaces are perfectly clean, and then apply a uniform layer of clean engine oil to both of them **(see illustration)**. You may have to push the piston back up the cylinder bore slightly to expose the bearing surface of the shell in the connecting rod.

24 Slide the connecting rod back into place on the big-end journal and refit the big-end bearing cap. Lubricate the bolt threads, fit the new bolts and tighten them to the specified Stage 1 torque setting, then through the specified Stage 2 angle. It is recommended that an angle-measuring gauge is used during this stage of the tightening, to ensure accuracy **(see illustrations)**.

25 Repeat the entire procedure for the remaining piston/connecting rod assemblies.

Caution: Do not rotate the crankshaft until the first pair of big-end bearing caps have been tightened to their final torque settings, or the bearing shells may be dislodged.

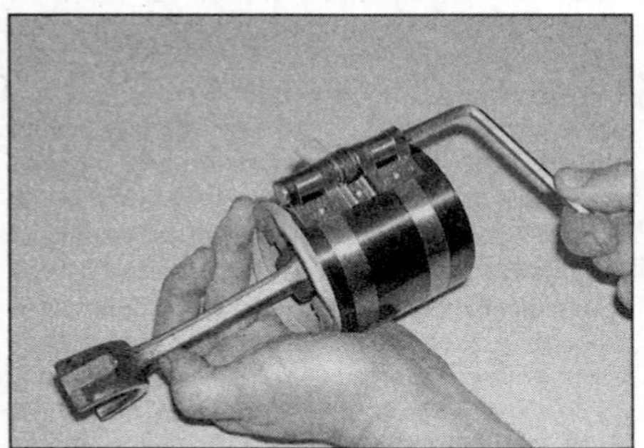

13.18 Attach a ring compressor to the piston

13.22b Guide the connecting rod big-end onto the crankpin with the aid of a long screwdriver

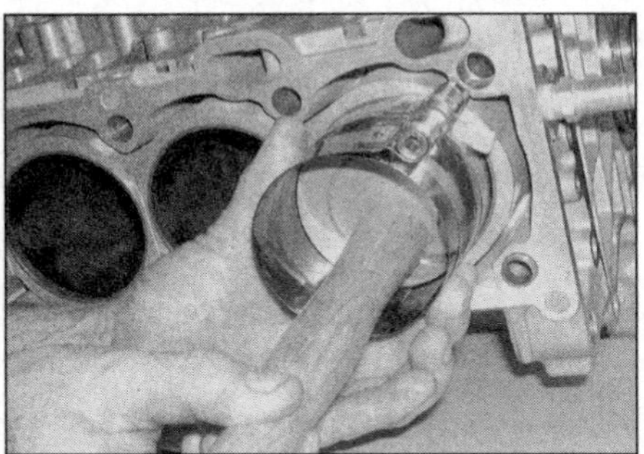

13.22a Gently tap on the top of the piston with the end of a wooden hammer handle

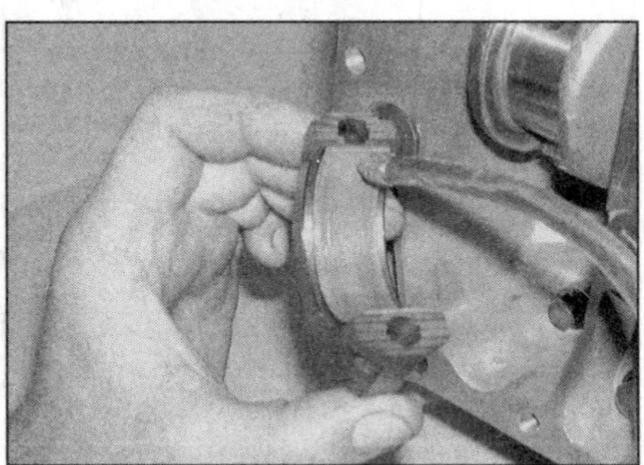

13.23 Apply clean engine oil to the bearing cap surfaces

26 The important points to remember are:

a) Keep the backs of the bearing shells and their locations in the connecting rods and caps perfectly clean when assembling them.

b) Ensure that the bearing shells are correctly positioned on the rods and caps.

c) Make sure you have the correct piston/rod assembly for each cylinder.

d) The arrow on the piston crown must face the flywheel end of the engine.

e) Lubricate the cylinder bores with clean engine oil.

f) Lubricate the bearing surfaces before fitting the big-end bearing caps.

27 After all the piston/connecting rod assemblies have been properly installed, rotate the crankshaft a number of times by hand, to check for any obvious binding.

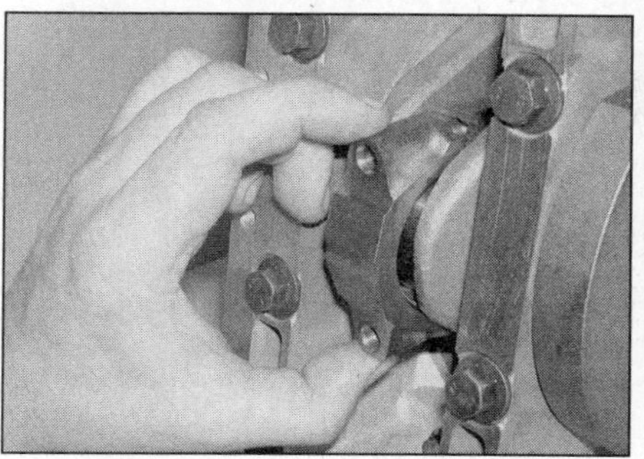

13.24a Refit the big-end bearing cap . . .

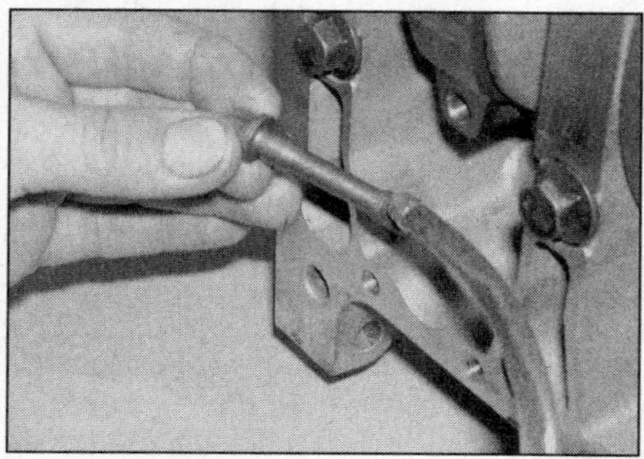

13.24b . . . lubricate the threads of the new bearing cap bolts . . .

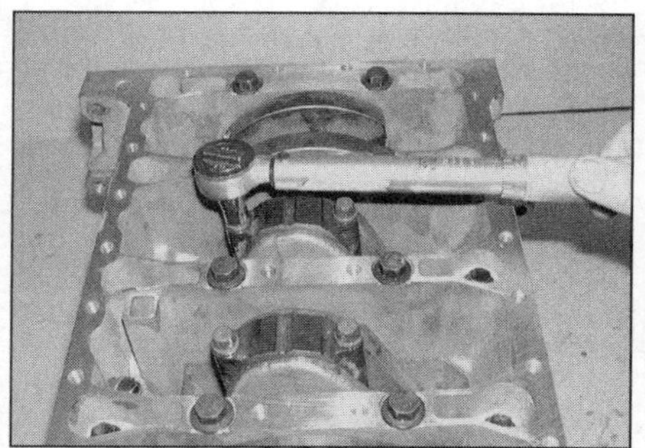

13.24c . . . tighten them to the first stage torque . . .

13.24d . . . then angle-tighten them through the second stage angle

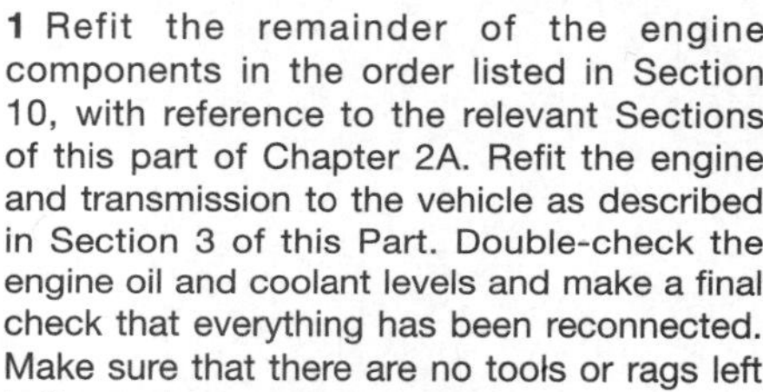

14 Engine – initial start-up after overhaul and reassembly

1 Refit the remainder of the engine components in the order listed in Section 10, with reference to the relevant Sections of this part of Chapter 2A. Refit the engine and transmission to the vehicle as described in Section 3 of this Part. Double-check the engine oil and coolant levels and make a final check that everything has been reconnected. Make sure that there are no tools or rags left in the engine compartment.

2 Remove the spark plugs and disable the ignition system by disconnecting the crankshaft sensor wiring at the connector. Disconnect the fuel injector wiring connectors to prevent fuel being injected into the cylinders.

3 Turn the engine over on the starter motor until the oil pressure warning light goes out. If the light fails to extinguish after several seconds of cranking, check the engine oil level and oil filter security. Assuming these are correct, check the security of the oil pressure sensor wiring – do not progress any further until you are sure that oil is being pumped around the engine at sufficient pressure.

4 Refit the spark plugs and HT leads, and reconnect the crankshaft sensor and fuel injector wiring connectors.

5 Start the engine, noting that this also may take a little longer than usual, due to the fuel system components being empty.

6 While the engine is idling, check for fuel, coolant and oil leaks. Don't be alarmed if there are some odd smells and smoke from parts getting hot and burning off oil deposits. Note also that it may initially be a little noisy until the hydraulic tappets fill with oil.

7 Keep the engine idling until hot water is felt circulating through the top hose, check that it idles reasonably smoothly and at the usual speed, then switch it off.

8 After a few minutes, recheck the oil and coolant levels, and top-up as necessary (see Chapter 1A).

9 If new components such as pistons, rings or crankshaft bearings have been fitted, the engine must be run-in for the first 500 miles (800 km). Do not operate the engine at full-throttle, or allow it to labour in any gear during this period. It is recommended that the oil and filter be changed at the end of this period.

Notes

Chapter 2 Part E:
Diesel engine removal and overhaul procedures

Contents

Section number

Degrees of difficulty

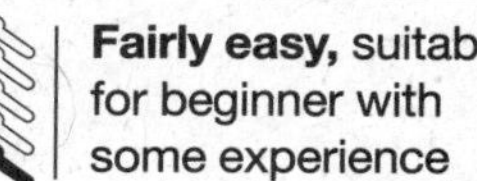

Easy, suitable for novice with little experience	**Fairly easy,** suitable for beginner with some experience	**Fairly difficult,** suitable for competent DIY mechanic	**Difficult,** suitable for experienced DIY mechanic	**Very difficult,** suitable for expert DIY or professional

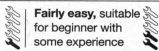

Specifications

1.9 litre engines

Cylinder head		
Maximum gasket face distortion	0.05 mm	
Cylinder head height	162.75 ± 1.75 mm	
Valve seat angle	89.5°	
Valve seat width	1.8 mm	
Valves	**Inlet**	**Exhaust**
Valve head diameter	35.200 to 35.450 mm	32.500 to 35.750 mm
Valve stem diameter	6.974 to 6.996 mm	6.960 to 6.982 mm
Valve length	110.79 to 111.19 mm	110.59 to 110.79 mm
Valve lift (max)	8.866 mm	10.344 mm
Valve springs		
Free length	44 to 48 mm	
External diameter	29.5 mm	
Internal diameter	21.5 ± 0.1 mm	
Pistons		
Piston diameter (nominal)	79.866 ± 0.0075 mm	
Piston rings		
Thickness:		
Top compression	2.5 mm	
Second compression (sealing)	2.0 mm	
Oil control (scraper)	3.0 mm	
End gap (measured in cylinder):		
Top compression	0.2 to 0.35 mm	
Second compression (sealing)	0.7 to 0.9 mm	
Oil control (scraper)	0.25 to 0.5 mm	

1.9 litre engines (continued)

Crankshaft	
Main bearing journal diameter:	
Size group 1 (blue)	54.785 to 54.795 mm
Size group 2 (red)	54.795 to 54.805 mm
Main bearing running clearance	0.027 to 0.086 mm
Big-end bearing journal diameter:	
Standard	48.01 mm +0.01 mm
Big-end bearing running clearance	0.027 to 0.086 mm
Crankshaft endfloat	0.067 to 0.233 mm

Torque wrench settings

Refer to Chapter 2B Specifications

2.2 litre engines

Cylinder head		
Maximum gasket face distortion	0.05 mm	
Cylinder head height	90.2 ± 0.08 mm	
Valve seat angle (included)	89°30'	
Valves	**Inlet**	**Exhaust**
Valve head diameter	30.6 ± 0.12 mm	29.5 ± 0.12 mm
Valve stem diameter	5.9675 ± 0.0125 mm	5.9575 ± 0.0075 mm
Valve length	123.2 ± 0.15 mm	123 ± 0.15 mm
Valve lift (max)	7.8 mm	7.8 mm
Valve springs		
Free length	46.7 mm	
External diameter	20.9 mm	
Internal diameter	14.1 ± 0.2 mm	
Cylinder block		
Maximum gasket face distortion	0.06 mm	
Gudgeon pin		
Length	64.7 to 65 mm	
External diameter	30.994 to 31 mm	
Internal diameter	15.13 ± 0.1 mm	
Pistons		
Piston diameter (nominal)	86.799 to 86.813 mm	
Piston protrusion	0.334 to 0.464 mm	
Piston rings		
Thickness:		
Top compression	3.0 mm	
Second compression (sealing)	1.75 mm	
Oil control (scraper)	2.50 mm	
End gap (measured in cylinder):		
Top compression	0.2 to 0.35 mm	
Second compression (sealing)	0.5 to 0.7 mm	
Oil control (scraper)	0.25 to 0.5 mm	
Crankshaft		
Main bearing journal diameter	57.98 to 58.00 mm	
Main bearing running clearance	0.036 to 0.071 mm	
Big-end bearing journal diameter	47.99 to 48.03 mm	
Big-end bearing running clearance	0.027 to 0.086 mm	
Crankshaft endfloat	0.060 to 0.232 mm	

Torque wrench settings

Refer to Chapter 2C Specifications

1 General information

Included in this Part of Chapter 2 are details of removing the engine/transmission from the car and general overhaul procedures for the cylinder head, cylinder block and all other engine internal components.

The information given ranges from advice concerning preparation for an overhaul and the purchase of parts, to detailed step-by-step procedures covering removal, inspection, renovation and refitting of engine internal components.

After Section 5, all instructions are based on the assumption that the engine has been removed from the car. For information concerning in-car engine repair, as well as the removal and refitting of those external components necessary for full overhaul, refer to Parts B and C of this Chapter and to Section 5. Ignore any preliminary dismantling operations described in Parts B or C that are no longer relevant once the engine has been removed from the car.

Apart from torque wrench settings, which are given at the beginning of Parts B or C (as applicable), all specifications relating to engine overhaul are at the beginning of this Part of Chapter 2.

2 Engine overhaul – general information

It is not always easy to determine when, or if, an engine should be completely overhauled, as a number of factors must be considered.

High mileage is not necessarily an indication that an overhaul is needed, while low mileage does not preclude the need for an overhaul. Frequency of servicing is probably the most important consideration. An engine which has had regular and frequent oil and filter changes, as well as other required maintenance, should give many thousands of miles of reliable service. Conversely, a neglected engine may require an overhaul very early in its life.

Excessive oil consumption is an indication that piston rings, valve seals and/or valve guides are in need of attention. Make sure that oil leaks are not responsible before deciding that the rings and/or guides are worn. Perform a compression test, as described in Part B of this Chapter, to determine the likely cause of the problem.

Check the oil pressure with a gauge fitted in place of the oil pressure switch, and compare it with that specified. If it is extremely low, the main and big-end bearings, and/or the oil pump, are probably worn out.

Loss of power, rough running, knocking or metallic engine noises, excessive valve gear noise, and high fuel consumption may also point to the need for an overhaul, especially if they are all present at the same time. If a complete service does not remedy the situation, major mechanical work is the only solution.

An engine overhaul involves restoring all internal parts to the specification of a new engine. During an overhaul, the pistons and the piston rings are renewed. New main and big-end bearings are generally fitted; if necessary, the crankshaft may need to be renewed also. The valves are serviced as well, since they are usually in less-than-perfect condition at this point. While the engine is being overhauled, other components, such as the starter and alternator, can be overhauled as well. The end result should be an as-new engine that will give many trouble-free miles. **Note:** *Critical cooling system components such as the hoses, thermostat and coolant pump should be renewed when an engine is overhauled. The radiator should be checked carefully, to ensure that it is not clogged or leaking. Also, it is a good idea to renew the oil pump whenever the engine is overhauled.*

Before beginning the engine overhaul, read through the entire procedure, to familiarise yourself with the scope and requirements of the job. Overhauling an engine is not difficult if you follow carefully all of the instructions, have the necessary tools and equipment, and pay close attention to all specifications. It can, however, be time-consuming. Plan on the car being off the road for a minimum of two weeks, especially if parts must be taken to an engineering works for repair or reconditioning. Check on the availability of parts and make sure that any necessary special tools and equipment are obtained in advance. Most work can be done with typical hand tools, although a number of precision measuring tools are required for inspecting parts to determine if they must be renewed. Often the engineering works will handle the inspection of parts and offer advice concerning reconditioning and renewal. **Note:** *Always wait until the engine has been completely dismantled, and until all components (especially the cylinder block and the crankshaft) have been inspected, before deciding what service and repair operations must be performed by an engineering works. The condition of these components will be the major factor to consider when determining whether to overhaul the original engine, or to buy a reconditioned unit. Do not, therefore, purchase parts or have overhaul work done on other components until they have been thoroughly inspected.* As a general rule, time is the primary cost of an overhaul, so it does not pay to fit worn or sub-standard parts.

As a final note, to ensure maximum life and minimum trouble from a reconditioned engine, everything must be assembled with care, in a spotlessly-clean environment.

3 Engine removal – methods and precautions

If you have decided that the engine must be removed for overhaul or major repair work, several preliminary steps should be taken.

Locating a suitable place to work is extremely important. Adequate workspace, along with storage space for the car, will be needed. If a workshop or garage is not available, at the very least, a flat, level, clean work surface is required.

Cleaning the engine compartment and engine/transmission before beginning the removal procedure will help keep tools clean and organised.

An engine hoist or A-frame will also be necessary. Make sure the equipment is rated in excess of the combined weight of the engine and transmission. Safety is of primary importance, considering the potential hazards involved in lifting the engine/transmission out of the car.

If this is the first time you have removed an engine, an assistant should ideally be available. Advice and aid from someone more experienced would also be helpful. There are many instances when one person cannot simultaneously perform all of the operations required when lifting the engine out of the vehicle.

Plan the operation ahead of time. Before starting work, arrange for the hire of or obtain all of the tools and equipment you will need. Some of the equipment necessary to perform engine/transmission removal and installation safely and with relative ease (in addition to an engine hoist) is as follows: a heavy duty trolley jack, complete sets of spanners and sockets as described in the reference section of this manual, wooden blocks, and plenty of rags and cleaning solvent for mopping-up spilled oil, coolant and fuel. If the hoist must be hired, make sure that you arrange for it in advance, and perform all of the operations possible without it beforehand. This will save you money and time.

Plan for the car to be out of use for quite a while. An engineering works will be required to perform some of the work, which the do-it-yourself person cannot accomplish without special equipment. These places often have a busy schedule, so it would be a good idea to consult them before removing the engine, in order to accurately estimate the amount of time required to rebuild or repair components that may need work.

During the engine removal procedure, it is advisable to make notes of the locations of all brackets, cable ties, earthing points, etc, as well as how the wiring harnesses, hoses and electrical connections are attached and routed around the engine and engine compartment. An effective way of doing this is to take a series of photographs of the various components before they are disconnected or removed. A digital or simple inexpensive disposable camera is ideal for this and the resulting photographs will prove invaluable when the engine is refitted.

Always be extremely careful when lifting the engine/transmission assembly from the engine bay. Serious injury can result from careless actions. If help is required, it is better to wait until it is available rather than risk personal injury and/or damage to components by continuing alone. By planning ahead and taking your time, a job of this nature, although major, can be accomplished successfully and without incident.

4 Engine and transmission – removal, separation, connection and refitting

Caution: Be careful not to allow dirt into the injection pump or injector pipes during this procedure.

Note: *The engine is removed upwards from the engine compartment as a complete*

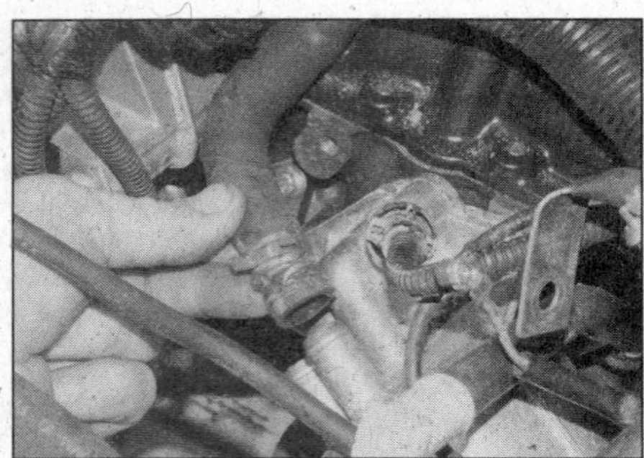
4.13 Disconnect the coolant hoses from the oil cooler – 2.2 litre shown

unit with the transmission; the two are then separated for overhaul.

Removal

1 Apply the handbrake, then jack up the front of the car and support it on axle stands (see *Jacking and vehicle support*). Remove both front roadwheels.

2 Set the bonnet in the upright position or, to improve access, remove it completely as described in Chapter 11.

3 Undo the retaining screws and remove the plastic undertray from beneath the engine/ transmission. Also remove the plastic covers from the left- and right-hand wheel arches. Undo the retaining screws or unclip (depending on model) and lift off the plastic covers from the top of the engine.

4 If the engine is to be dismantled, working as described in Chapter 1B, first drain the oil and remove the oil filter. Clean and refit the drain plug, tightening it securely.

5 Remove the battery and battery tray as described in Chapter 5A.

6 Remove the air cleaner assembly and associated components as described in Chapter 4B.

7 Drain the transmission oil as described in Chapter 7A or 7B. Refit the drain and filler plugs, and tighten them securely.

8 On models equipped with air conditioning, remove the auxiliary drivebelt (see Chapter 1B).

9 Drain the cooling system as described in Chapter 1B. Slacken the retaining clips and disconnect the coolant hoses from the left-hand end of the cylinder head.

4.22 Move the ECU and tray to one side

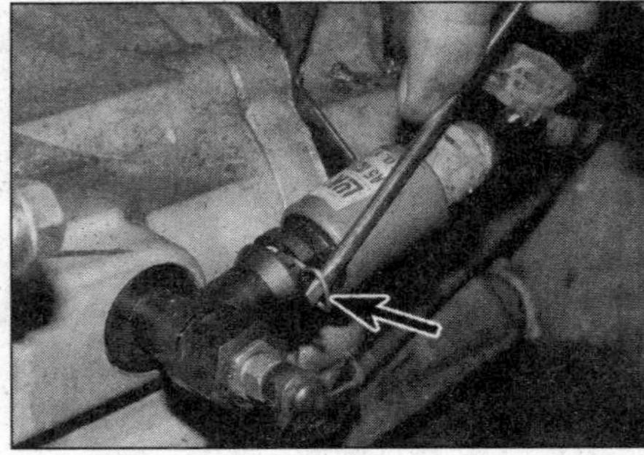
4.19 Release the retaining clip (arrowed) from the clutch fluid pipe

10 Remove the front bumper as described in Chapter 11.

11 Referring to the procedures described in Chapter 3, remove the electric cooling fans and the radiator, including air conditioning condenser. Note that once the front body panel has been released, it should be removed completely (do not lay it across the top of the engine).

12 On models where the coolant pump is driven by the auxiliary drivebelt, slacken the clip(s) and disconnect the hoses from the rear of the coolant pump.

13 Release the retaining clips and disconnect the hoses from the oil cooler **(see illustration)**.

14 Referring to Chapter 3, disconnect the coolant hoses from the expansion tank and heater matrix union then unbolt the hose mounting brackets from the top of the transmission and remove the hose assemblies from the engine compartment, where necessary, disconnecting the wiring connector from the coolant temperature sender as the hoses are removed.

15 Referring to Chapter 4B, carry out the following operations.

a) Disconnect the wiring connectors from the throttle housing, starter motor and alternator.

b) Disconnect the fuel feed and return hoses from the injection pump. Free the hose from its clip on the manifold.

c) Disconnect any vacuum hoses and wiring connectors from sensors around the engine, making note of there fitted position.

d) Remove the exhaust system front pipe/ catalytic converter.

4.24 Air conditioning compressor cable tied to the crossmember

16 Release the retaining clip and disconnect the vacuum hose from the brake servo unit and (where necessary) the vacuum solenoid valve.

17 Undo the retaining bolts securing the power steering pump to its mounting bracket, with reference to Chapter 10, and then move it to one side.

18 Undo the retaining nuts/bolts and free the power steering pipes from the mounting brackets on the transmission. Check that the pipes are released from all the relevant retaining clips and are positioned clear of the engine/transmission.

19 Release the retaining clip and disconnect the clutch hydraulic hose from the transmission as described in Chapter 6 and position it clear. Cover or cap the ends of the pipe and connector to prevent any dirt ingress **(see illustration).**

20 Disconnect the gearchange linkage from the transmission as described in Chapter 7A or 7B.

21 Working as described in Chapter 8, disconnect and remove the driveshafts from the transmission. **Note:** *Do not allow the shaft to hang down under its own weight as this could damage the constant velocity joints/gaiters.*

22 Trace the engine wiring harness and disconnect any wiring still attached to the engine/transmission assembly. With reference to Chapter 4B, move the ECU and tray to one side, making sure it is in a safe position **(see illustration).**

23 Undo the securing bolts and release the applicable earth cables from the engine and transmission units, similarly disconnect any earth cables from the subframe.

24 On models equipped with air conditioning, disconnect the compressor clutch wiring connector then unbolt the compressor from the auxiliary components mounting bracket on the engine. Carefully move the compressor away from the front of the engine and support it on the front lower crossmember **(see illustration)**. It may be necessary to disconnect additional retaining clips or mountings to allow the assembly to be moved clear. Take care not to place excess strain on the various pipes and hoses and ensure that all the components are well supported or tied clear of the engine. *Do not* disconnect the refrigerant lines from the compressor (refer to the warnings given in Chapter 3).

25 Manoeuvre the engine hoist into position, and attach it to the lifting brackets bolted onto the cylinder head. Raise the hoist until it is supporting the weight of the engine.

26 From underneath the vehicle, undo the retaining bolts and remove the rear mounting link, connecting the engine/transmission mounting to the body.

27 Unscrew the nut from the transmission left-hand mounting stud then undo the bolts securing the rubber mounting assembly and remove it from the vehicle body.

28 Undo the retaining bolts and remove the right-hand engine mounting acoustic tie-rod.
29 Undo the mounting bolts and nut securing the right-hand engine mounting bracket and remove it from the vehicle. Slacken the rubber mounting bolts to the body to allow for settlement movement when refitting.
30 Make a final check that any components which would prevent the removal of the engine/transmission from the car have been removed or disconnected. Ensure that components such as the gearchange linkage/cables and driveshafts are secured so that they cannot be damaged on removal.
31 With the help of an assistant, raise the hoist and lift the engine/transmission slightly, ensuring that nothing is trapped or damaged. Once the engine is high enough, turn it slightly as necessary and withdraw it forwards, out of the engine compartment and clear of the car.

Separation

34 With the engine/transmission assembly removed, support the assembly on suitable blocks of wood, on a workbench (or failing that, on a clean area of the workshop floor).
35 Undo the retaining bolts, and remove the starter motor from the transmission, noting the correct fitted position of the locating dowel (see Chapter 5A).
36 On Automatic models, the torque converter is attached to the driveplate by three nuts, which are accessed either behind the driveplate lower cover plate or through the starter motor aperture. Turn the engine as required to position the nuts in the aperture, then unscrew and remove them. **Note:** *The nuts must be renewed every time they are removed.* Where applicable, unbolt the access plate from the bottom of the transmission.
37 Ensure that both engine and transmission are adequately supported, then slacken and remove the remaining bolts securing the transmission housing to the engine. Note the correct fitted positions of each bolt (and the relevant brackets) as they are removed, to use as a reference on refitting.
38 Carefully withdraw the transmission from the engine, ensuring that the weight of the transmission is not allowed to hang on the input shaft while it is engaged with the clutch friction plate. On automatic models, as the transmission is removed, make sure the torque converter is kept pushed fully onto the transmission shaft.
39 Once the transmission is free, remove the locating dowels from the engine or transmission, and keep them in a safe place.
40 On automatic models, secure the torque converter in position by bolting a length of metal bar to one of the housing bolt holes, or by tying one of the studs to the TDC sensor aperture on the top of the housing.

Connection

41 If the engine and transmission have not been separated, proceed as described from paragraph 49 onwards.
42 Ensure that the locating dowels are correctly positioned prior to installation.
43 On manual models, ensure that the clutch friction plate and transmission input shaft splines are clean and dry. Do not apply grease to the splines as they have a special low-friction nickel coating. Make sure the clutch release mechanism components are correctly fitted (see Chapter 6).
44 On automatic models, remove the retaining bar or wire used to hold the torque converter in place. Ensure that the torque converter is pushed fully onto the transmission. Apply a smear of high melting point grease (Renault recommend the use of Molykote BR2) to the converter-centring ring.
45 Carefully offer the transmission to the engine, until the locating dowels are engaged. Ensure that the weight of the transmission is not allowed to hang on the input shaft as it is engaged with the clutch friction plate/torque converter. Support the transmission to hold it in position.
46 On automatic models, align the torque converter studs with the driveplate holes as the transmission is refitted. Apply thread-locking compound (Renault recommend the use of Loctite Frenbloc) to the new retaining nuts and tighten them to the specified torque.
47 Refit the transmission housing-to-engine bolts, ensuring that all the necessary brackets are correctly positioned, and tighten them to the specified torque setting.
48 Refit the starter motor making sure its locating dowel is correctly positioned and securely tighten its retaining bolts (see Chapter 5A).

Refitting

49 Reconnect the hoist and lifting tackle to the engine lifting brackets. With the aid of an assistant, lift the assembly into the engine compartment, and manoeuvre it as necessary to clear the surrounding components, as during removal.
50 With the engine/transmission in position, refit the left-hand rubber mounting and tighten the retaining bolts to the specified torque. Fit the nut to the mounting stud tightening it by hand only at this stage.
51 Refit the right-hand mounting and engine bracket assembly. Tighten the bracket to engine bolts to the specified torque, but only tighten the rubber mounting bolts by hand at this stage.
52 Refit the rear mounting link and support rod and lightly tighten the retaining bolts.
53 Rock the engine to settle it on its mountings. Centralise the right-hand mounting movement limiter, then tighten the three rubber mounting bolts to the specified torque. Go around and tighten all the remaining mounting nuts and bolts to their specified torque settings and detach the hoist from the engine.
54 The remainder of the refitting procedure is a direct reversal of the removal sequence, noting the following points:

a) Ensure that the wiring loom is correctly routed and retained by all the relevant retaining clips; all connectors should be correctly and securely reconnected.
b) Prior to refitting the driveshafts to the transmission, renew the driveshaft oil seal(s) as described in Chapter 7A or 7B.
c) Ensure that all disturbed hoses are correctly reconnected, and securely retained by their retaining clips.
d) Adjust the clutch cable as described in Chapter 6.
e) Refill the engine and transmission with the correct quantity and type of oil, as described in Chapters 1B and 7A or 7B.
f) Refill the cooling system as described in Chapter 1B.

5 Engine overhaul – dismantling sequence

It is much easier to dismantle and work on the engine if it is mounted on a portable engine stand. These stands can often be hired from a tool hire shop. Before the engine is mounted on a stand, the flywheel should be removed so that the stand bolts can be tightened into the end of the cylinder block.

If a stand is not available, it is possible to dismantle the engine with it suitably-supported on a sturdy, workbench or on the floor. Be careful not to tip or drop the engine when working without a stand.

If you intend to obtain a reconditioned engine, all ancillaries must be removed first, to be transferred to the new engine (just as they will if you are doing a complete engine overhaul yourself). These components include the following.

a) Engine mountings and brackets (Chapter 2B or 2C).
b) Alternator including auxiliary components mounting bracket (Chapter 5A).
c) Power steering pump and bracket(s) (Chapter 10).
d) Coolant pump, thermostat and housing, and coolant outlet chamber/elbow (Chapter 3).
e) Oil filter (Chapter 1B).
f) Oil cooler housing (Chapter 2B or 2C)
g) Braking system vacuum pump (Chapter 9).
h) Dipstick tube.
i) Fuel system components (Chapter 4B).
j) Wiring harness and all electrical switches and sensors.
k) Inlet and exhaust manifolds (Chapter 4B).
l) Clutch components (Chapter 6).
m) Flywheel (Chapter 2B or 2C).

Note: *When removing the external components from the engine, pay close attention to details that may be helpful or important during refitting. Note the fitting positions of gaskets, seals, washers, bolts and other small items.*

If you are obtaining a short engine (cylinder block, crankshaft, pistons and connecting rods

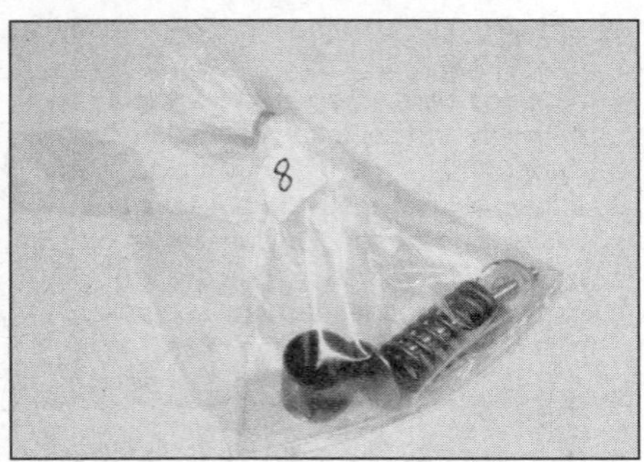

6.7 Place each valve and its associated components in a labelled polythene bag

all assembled), then the cylinder head, timing belt (together with tensioner, tensioner and idler pulleys and covers) and auxiliary drivebelt tensioner will have to be removed also.

If a complete overhaul is planned, the engine can be dismantled in the order given below.

a) Inlet and exhaust manifolds.
b) Timing belt, sprockets, tensioner, pulleys and covers.
c) Cylinder head.
d) Flywheel.
e) Sump.
f) Oil pump.
g) Pistons/connecting rods.
h) Crankshaft.

6 Cylinder head - dismantling

Note: *New and reconditioned cylinder heads are available from the manufacturer, and from engine overhaul specialists. Be aware that some specialist tools are required for the dismantling and inspection procedures, and new components may not be readily available. It may therefore be more practical and economical for the home mechanic to purchase a reconditioned head, rather than dismantle, inspect and recondition the original head.*

1 Remove the cylinder head as described in Chapter 2B or 2C (as applicable).

2 Remove the camshaft, rockers, followers and shims/hydraulic tappets (as applicable) as described in Chapter 2B or 2C.

3 Place the cylinder head on wooden blocks and tap each valve stem smartly, using a light hammer and drift, to free the spring and associated items.

4 Using a valve spring compressor, compress each valve spring in turn until the split collets can be removed. Lift out the collets; a small screwdriver, a magnet or a pair of tweezers may be useful. Carefully release the spring compressor and remove it.

5 Remove the valve spring upper seat and the valve spring. Pull the valve out of its guide.

6 Pull off the valve stem oil seal with a pair of long-nosed pliers. Alternatively, a valve stem oil seal removal tool can be obtained from automotive accessory shops. The tool is basically a pair of pliers with specially shaped ends that grip the seal.

7 It is essential that each valve is stored together with its collets, spring and seats **(see illustration)**. The valves should also be kept in their correct sequence, unless they are so badly worn or burnt that they are to be renewed. If they are going to be kept and used again, place each valve assembly in a labelled polythene bag or similar container.

8 Continue removing all the remaining valves in the same way.

7 Cylinder head and valves - cleaning and inspection

1 Thorough cleaning of the cylinder head and valve components, followed by a detailed inspection, will enable you to decide how much valve service work must be carried out during the engine overhaul. **Note:** *If the engine has been severely overheated, it is best to assume that the cylinder head is warped - check carefully for signs of this.*

Cleaning

2 Scrape away all traces of old gasket material from the cylinder head.

3 Scrape away the carbon from the combustion chambers and ports, then wash the cylinder head thoroughly with paraffin or a suitable solvent.

4 Scrape off any heavy carbon deposits that may have formed on the valves, then use a power-operated wire brush to remove deposits from the valve heads and stems.

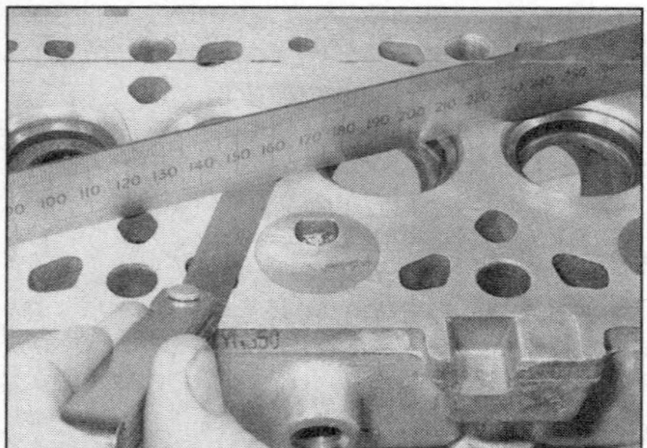

7.6 Checking the cylinder head gasket surface for distortion

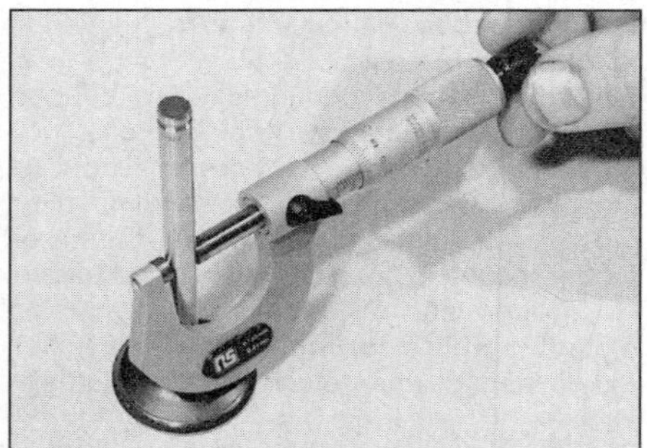

7.12 Measuring a valve stem diameter

Inspection

Note: *Be sure to perform all the following inspection procedures before concluding that the services of a machine shop or engine overhaul specialist are required. Make a list of all items that require attention.*

Cylinder head

5 Inspect the head very carefully for cracks, evidence of coolant leakage, and other damage. If cracks are found, a new cylinder head should be obtained.

6 Use a straight-edge and feeler blade to check that the cylinder head surface is not distorted **(see illustration)**. Renault state that no resurfacing of the cylinder head surface is possible.

7 Examine the valve seats in each of the combustion chambers. If they are severely pitted, cracked, or burned, they will need to be recut by an engine overhaul specialist. If they are only slightly pitted, this can be removed by grinding-in the valve heads and seats with fine valve-grinding compound, as described below.

8 Check the valve guides for wear by inserting the relevant valve, and checking for side-to-side motion of the valve. A very small amount of movement is acceptable. If the movement seems excessive, remove the valve. Measure the valve stem diameter (see below), and renew the valve if it is worn. If the valve stem is not worn, the wear must be in the valve guide, and the guide must be renewed. The renewal of valve guides is best carried out by a Renault dealer, or engine overhaul specialist, who will have the necessary tools available.

9 If renewing the valve guides, the valve seats should be reground only *after* the guides have been fitted.

10 Inspect the swirl chambers for burning or damage such as cracking. Small cracks in the chambers are acceptable; renewal of the chambers will only be required if chamber tracts are badly burned and disfigured, or if they are no longer a tight fit in the cylinder head. If there is any doubt as to the swirl chamber condition, seek the advice of a Renault dealer or a suitable repairer who specialises in diesel engines.

Valves

11 Examine the head of each valve for pitting, burning, cracks, and general wear. Check the valve stem for scoring and wear ridges. Rotate the valve, and check for any obvious indication that it is bent. Look for pits or excessive wear on the tip of each valve stem. Renew any valve that shows any such signs of wear or damage.

12 If the valve appears satisfactory at this stage, measure the valve stem diameter at several points using a micrometer **(see illustration)**. Any significant difference in the readings obtained indicates wear of the valve stem. Should any of these conditions be apparent, the valve(s) must be renewed.

13 If the valves are in satisfactory condition,

they should be ground (lapped) into their respective seats, to ensure a smooth, gas-tight seal. If the seat is only lightly pitted, or if it has been recut, fine grinding compound *only* should be used to produce the required finish. Coarse valve-grinding compound should *not* be used, unless a seat is badly burned or deeply pitted. If this is the case, the cylinder head and valves should be inspected by an expert, to decide whether seat recutting, or even the renewal of the valve or seat insert (where possible) is required.

14 Valve grinding is carried out as follows. Place the cylinder head upside-down on a bench.

15 Smear a trace of (the appropriate grade of) valve-grinding compound on the seat face, and press a suction grinding tool onto the valve head. With a semi-rotary action, grind the valve head to its seat, lifting the valve occasionally to redistribute the grinding compound **(see illustration)**. A light spring placed under the valve head will greatly ease this operation.

16 If coarse grinding compound is being used, work only until a dull, matt even surface is produced on both the valve seat and the valve, then wipe off the used compound, and repeat the process with fine compound. When a smooth unbroken ring of light grey matt finish is produced on both the valve and seat, the grinding operation is complete. *Do not* grind-in the valves any further than absolutely necessary, or the seat will be prematurely sunk into the cylinder head.

17 When all the valves have been ground-in, carefully wash off *all* traces of grinding compound using paraffin or a suitable solvent, before reassembling the cylinder head.

Valve components

18 Examine the valve springs for signs of damage and discoloration and also measure their free length using vernier calipers or a steel rule or by comparing the existing spring with a new component.

19 Stand each spring on a flat surface, and check it for squareness. If any of the springs are damaged, distorted or have lost their tension, obtain a complete new set of springs. It is normal to renew the valve springs as a matter of course if a major overhaul is being carried out.

20 Renew the valve stem oil seals regardless of their apparent condition.

8 Cylinder head – reassembly

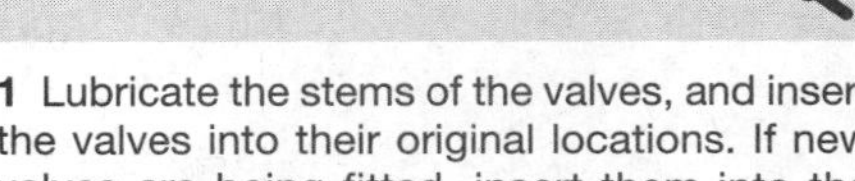

1 Lubricate the stems of the valves, and insert the valves into their original locations. If new valves are being fitted, insert them into the locations to which they have been ground.

2 Refit the spring seat then, working on the first valve, dip the new valve stem seal in fresh engine oil. Carefully locate it over the valve and onto the guide. Take care not to damage the

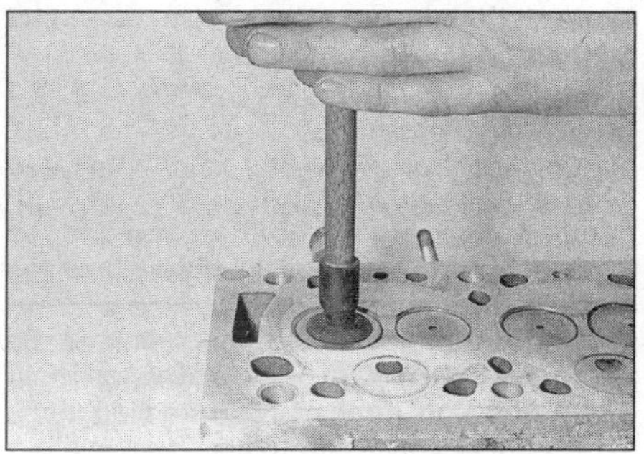

7.15 Grinding-in a valve

seal as it is passed over the valve stem. Use a suitable socket or metal tube to press the seal firmly onto the guide **(see illustration)**.

3 Locate the valve spring on top of its seat, and then refit the spring retainer **(see illustrations)**.

4 Compress the valve spring, and locate the split collets in the recess in the valve stem **(see illustration)**. Release the compressor, then repeat the procedure on the remaining valves.

5 With all the valves installed, place the cylinder head on blocks on the bench and, using a hammer and interposed block of wood, tap the end of each valve stem to settle the components.

6 Refit the camshaft, followers and shims/hydraulic tappets (as applicable) as described in Chapter 2B or 2C.

7 The cylinder head can then be refitted as described in Chapter 2B or 2C.

9 Piston/connecting rod assemblies – removal

Note: *New connecting rod big-end cap bolts will be required on refitting.*

1 Remove the cylinder head, sump and oil pump as described in Part B or C of this Chapter as applicable.

2 If there is a pronounced wear ridge at the top of any bore, it may be necessary to remove it with a scraper or ridge reamer, to avoid piston damage during removal. Such a ridge indicates excessive wear of the cylinder bore.

3 Using quick-drying paint, mark each connecting rod and big-end bearing cap with its respective cylinder number on the flat machined surface provided; if the engine has been dismantled before, note carefully any identifying marks made previously **(see illustration)**. Note that No 1 cylinder is at the transmission (flywheel) end of the engine.

4 Turn the crankshaft to bring pistons 1 and 4 to BDC (bottom dead centre).

5 Unscrew the bolts from No 1 piston big-end bearing cap. Take off the cap, noting its correct fitted position, and recover the bottom half bearing shell. If the bearing shells are to be re-used, tape the cap and the shell together.

6 Using a hammer handle, push the piston up through the bore, and remove it from the top of the cylinder block. Recover the bearing shell, and tape it to the connecting rod for safe-keeping.

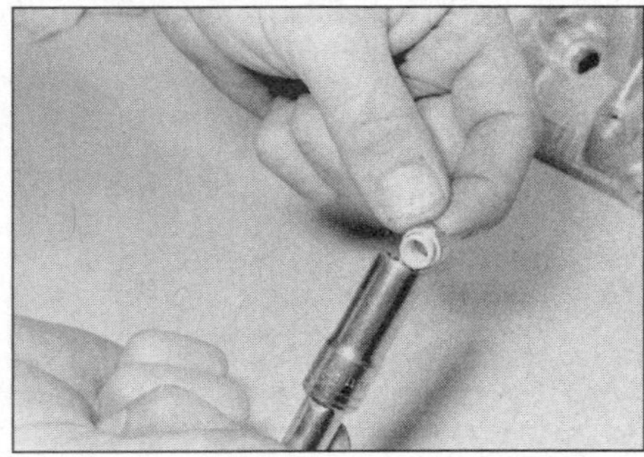

8.2 Press on the new valve guide oil seal using a socket

8.3a Fit the valve spring . . .

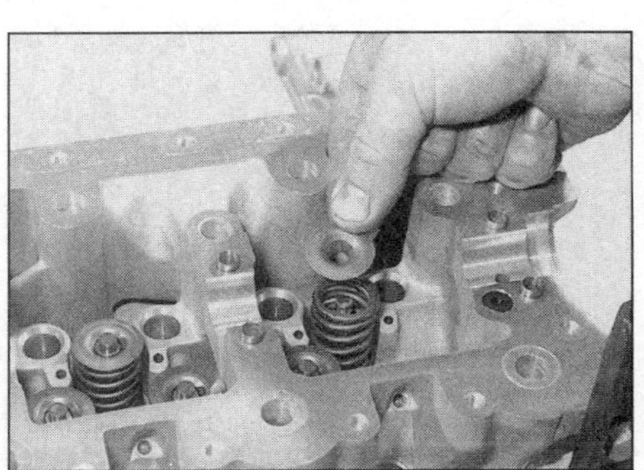

8.3b . . . and the spring retainer . . .

8.4 . . . then compress the valve and fit the collets

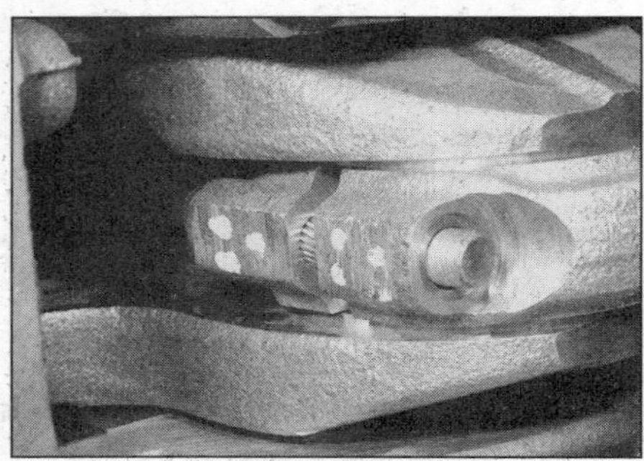

9.3 Identify the connecting rods and bearing caps using quick-drying paint

7 Loosely refit the big-end cap to the connecting rod, and secure with the bolts – this will help to keep the components in their correct order.

8 Remove No 4 piston assembly in the same way.

9 Turn the crankshaft through 180° to bring pistons 2 and 3 to BDC (bottom dead centre), and remove them in the same way.

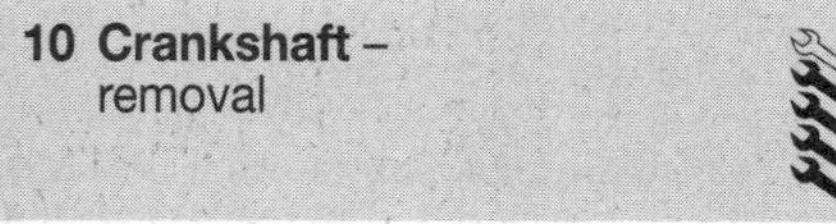

10 Crankshaft – removal

1.9 litre engines

1 Remove the timing belt, the crankshaft sprocket, the oil pump and the flywheel as described in Part B of this Chapter. If the piston and connecting rod assemblies are also to be removed, remove the cylinder head.

2 Check the crankshaft endfloat as described in Section 13, then proceed as follows.

3 Remove the piston and connecting rod assemblies as described in Section 9. If no work is to be done on the pistons and connecting rods, unbolt the caps and push the pistons far enough up the bores that the connecting rods are positioned clear of the crankshaft journals.

4 Undo the retaining bolts and remove the timing belt lower cover from the cylinder block.

5 Slacken and remove the retaining bolts securing the crankshaft front oil seal housing to the cylinder block and remove the housing from the crankshaft end. If the cover locating dowels are a loose fit, remove and store them with the cover for safe-keeping.

6 The main bearing caps should be numbered 1 to 5 from the transmission (flywheel) end of the engine **(see illustration)**. If not, mark them accordingly using quick-drying paint in the same way as the connecting rods.

7 Unscrew and remove the main bearing cap retaining bolts, and withdraw the caps **(see illustration)**. Recover the lower main bearing shells, and tape them to their respective caps for safe-keeping. Note that No 1 main bearing cap is sealed to the sides of the cylinder block with a semi-permanent silicone-based sealant. As there is very little clearance between the crankshaft and cylinder block in this area in which to tap or prise the cap free, it may be necessary to use Renault special tool Mot. 1423 for removal. Alternatively, fabricate a home-made alternative as shown in Chapter 2D, Section 7.

8 Carefully lift out the crankshaft, taking care not to displace the upper main bearing shells, and discard the oil seal **(see illustration)**.

9 Recover the upper bearing shells from the cylinder block, and tape them to their respective caps for safe-keeping. Remove the thrustwasher halves from the side of crankcase main bearing, and store them with the bearing cap.

2.2 litre engines

Note: *New cylinder block casting main bearing bolts and will be required on refitting.*

10 Remove the balance shaft unit, oil pump, drive chain and sprockets, the flywheel and the rear mounting bracket as described in Chapter 2C. If the piston and connecting rod assemblies are also to be removed, remove the cylinder head.

11 Check the crankshaft endfloat as described in Section 13, then proceed as follows.

12 On models without a balancer shaft assembly fitted, undo the retaining bolts and remove the anti-emulsion plate.

13 Slacken and remove the smaller outer bolts securing the main bearing casting to the cylinder block **(see illustration)**.

14 Working in a diagonal sequence, evenly and progressively slacken the ten large main bearing casting retaining bolts by a turn at a time. Once all the bolts are loose, remove them from the casting. Discard the bolts; new ones must be used on refitting **(see illustration)**.

15 With all the retaining bolts removed, carefully lift the main bearing casting away from the base of the cylinder block and recover the sealing ring from the oilway. Recover the lower main bearing shells, and tape them to their respective locations in the casting. If the locating dowels are a loose fit, remove them and store them with the casting for safe-keeping.

16 Remove the piston and connecting rod assemblies as described in Section 9. If no work is to be done on the pistons and connecting rods, unbolt the caps and push the pistons far enough up the bores so that the connecting rods are positioned clear of the crankshaft journals.

17 Lift out the crankshaft, and discard the oil seal.

10.6 The main bearing caps should be numbered 1 to 5 from the transmission (flywheel) end of the engine

10.7 Unscrew and remove the main bearing cap retaining bolts, and withdraw the caps

10.8 Lifting the crankshaft from the crankcase

10.13 Slacken and remove the smaller outer main bearing casting bolts . . .

10.14 . . . then unscrew and remove the ten larger inner bolts

18 Recover the upper main bearing shells, and store them along with the relevant lower bearing shell. Also recover the two thrustwashers (one fitted either side of No 2 main bearing) from the cylinder block.

11 Cylinder block – cleaning and inspection

Cleaning

1 Remove all external components and electrical switches/sensors from the block. For complete cleaning, the core plugs should ideally be removed. Drill a small hole in the plugs, and then insert a self-tapping screw into the hole. Pull out the plugs by pulling on the screw with a pair of grips, or by using a slide hammer.

2 Undo the retaining bolts and remove the piston oil jet spray tubes from inside the cylinder block.

3 Scrape all traces of gasket from the cylinder block, and from the main bearing casting (where fitted), taking care not to damage the gasket/sealing surfaces.

4 Remove all oil gallery plugs (where fitted). The plugs are usually very tight – they may have to be drilled out, and the holes retapped. Use new plugs when the engine is reassembled.

5 If any of the castings are extremely dirty, all should be steam-cleaned.

6 After the castings are returned, clean all oil holes and oil galleries one more time. Flush all internal passages with warm water until the water runs clear. Dry thoroughly, and apply a light film of oil to all mating surfaces, to prevent rusting. Also oil the cylinder bores. If you have access to compressed air, use it to speed up the drying process, and to blow out all the oil holes and galleries.

Warning: Wear eye protection when using compressed air.

7 If the castings are not very dirty, you can do an adequate cleaning job with hot (as hot as you can stand), soapy water and a stiff brush. Take plenty of time, and do a thorough job. Regardless of the cleaning method used, be sure to clean all oil holes and galleries very thoroughly, and to dry all components well. Protect the cylinder bores as described above, to prevent rusting.

8 All threaded holes must be clean, to ensure accurate torque readings during reassembly. To clean the threads, run the correct-size tap into each of the holes to remove rust, corrosion, thread sealant or sludge, and to restore damaged threads. If possible, use compressed air to clear the holes of debris produced by this operation.

Warning: Wear eye protection when cleaning out these holes in this way.

9 Apply suitable sealant to the new oil gallery plugs, and insert them into the holes in the block. Tighten them securely. Similarly apply a suitable sealant to new core plugs and tap them into the block using a socket or tube.

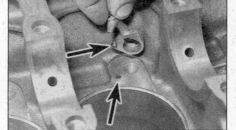

11.10a Refit the piston oil jets, making sure the locating pegs are correctly located in the block holes (arrowed) . . .

11.10b . . . and refit the retaining bolts – 1.9 litre shown

10 Refit the piston oil jet spray tubes to the cylinder block, making sure their locating pegs are correctly engaged, and securely tighten the retaining bolts **(see illustrations)**.

11 If the engine is not going to be reassembled right away, cover it with a large plastic bag to keep it clean; protect all mating surfaces and the cylinder bores as described above, to prevent rusting.

Inspection

12 Visually check the castings for cracks and corrosion. Look for stripped threads in the threaded holes. If there has been any history of internal water leakage, it may be worthwhile having an engine overhaul specialist check the cylinder block with special equipment. If defects are found, have them repaired if possible, or renew the assembly.

13 Check the each cylinder bore for scuffing and scoring. Check for signs of a wear ridge at the top of the cylinder, indicating that the bore is excessively worn.

14 Oversize pistons are not available for any of the diesel engines. If the bores are worn, it will be necessary to obtain a new cylinder block, together with new standard size pistons.

15 Seek the advice of a Renault dealer or engine overhaul specialist regarding standard size cylinder bore size groups and the availability of matching pistons.

12 Piston/connecting rod assemblies – inspection

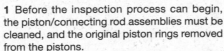

1 Before the inspection process can begin, the piston/connecting rod assemblies must be cleaned, and the original piston rings removed from the pistons.

2 Carefully expand the old rings over the top of the pistons. The use of two or three old feeler blades will be helpful in preventing the rings dropping into empty grooves. Be careful not to scratch the piston with the ends of the ring. The rings are brittle, and will snap if they are spread too far. They're also very sharp – protect your hands and fingers. Note that the third ring may incorporate an expander. Always remove the rings from the top of the piston. Keep each set of rings with its piston if the old rings are to be re-used.

3 Scrape away all traces of carbon from the top of the piston. A hand-held wire brush (or a piece of fine emery cloth) can be used, once the majority of the deposits have been scraped away, the piston identification markings should be visible.

4 Remove the carbon from the ring grooves in the piston, using an old ring. Break the ring in half to do this (be careful not to cut your fingers – piston rings are sharp). Be careful to remove only the carbon deposits – do not remove any metal, and do not nick or scratch the sides of the ring grooves.

5 Once the deposits have been removed, clean the piston/connecting rod assembly with paraffin or a suitable solvent, and dry thoroughly. Make sure that the oil return holes in the ring grooves are clear.

6 If the pistons and cylinder bores are not damaged or worn excessively, the original pistons can be refitted. Normal piston wear shows up as even vertical wear on the piston thrust surfaces, and slight looseness of the top ring in its groove. New piston rings should always be used when the engine is reassembled.

7 Carefully inspect each piston for cracks around the skirt, around the gudgeon pin holes, and at the piston ring 'lands' (between the ring grooves).

8 Look for scoring and scuffing on the piston skirt, holes in the piston crown, and burned areas at the edge of the crown. If the skirt is scored or scuffed, the engine may have been suffering from overheating, and/or abnormal combustion, which caused excessively high operating temperatures. The cooling and lubrication systems should be checked thoroughly. Scorch marks on the sides of the pistons show that blow-by has occurred. A hole in the piston crown, or burned areas at the edge of the piston crown, indicates that abnormal combustion has been occurring. If any of the above problems exist, the causes must be investigated and corrected, or the damage will occur again. The causes may include incorrect injection pump timing, or a faulty injector.

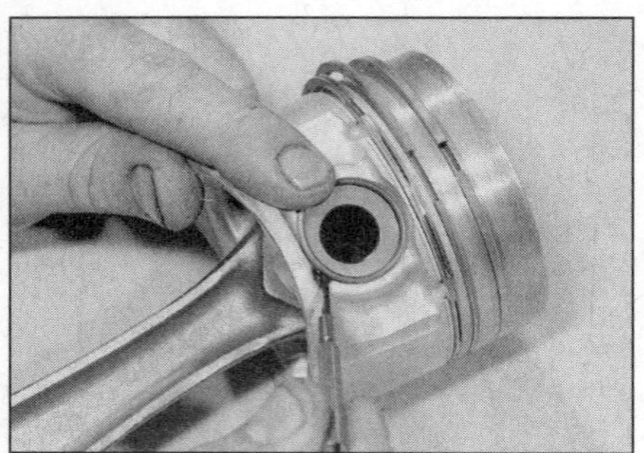

12.12a Carefully prise out the circlip . . .

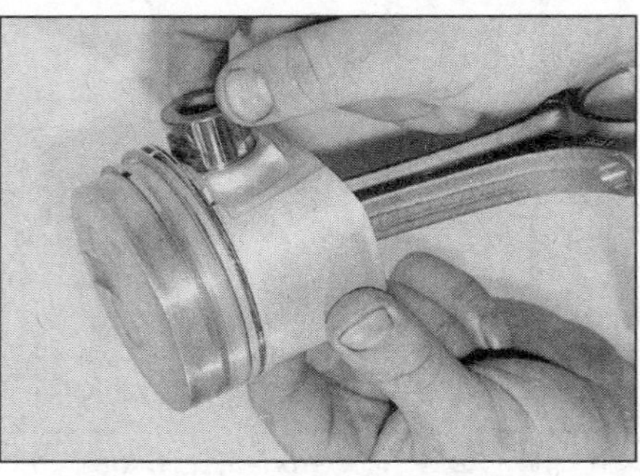

12.12b . . . then press out the gudgeon pin and separate the piston and connecting rod

9 Corrosion of the piston, in the form of pitting, indicates that coolant has been leaking into the combustion chamber and/ or the crankcase. Again, the cause must be corrected, or the problem may persist in the rebuilt engine.

10 Examine each connecting rod carefully for signs of damage, such as cracks around the big-end and small-end bearings. Check that the rod is not bent or distorted. Damage is highly unlikely, unless the engine has been seized or badly overheated. Detailed checking of the connecting rod assembly can only be carried out by a Renault dealer or engine repair specialist with the necessary equipment.

11 The gudgeon pins are of the floating type, secured in position by two circlips. If necessary, the pistons and connecting rods can be separated as follows.

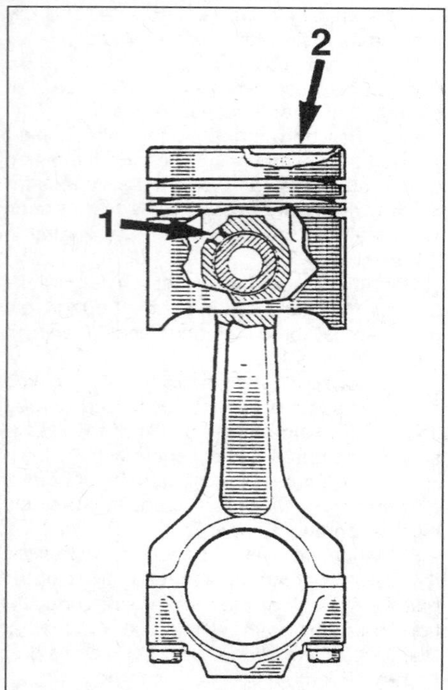

12.17 On 1.9 litre engines, oil hole (1) in connecting rod small-end should face away from combustion chamber (2) in piston crown

12 Using a small flat-bladed screwdriver, prise out the circlips, and push out the gudgeon pin **(see illustrations)**. Hand pressure should be sufficient to remove the pin. Identify the piston and rod to ensure correct reassembly. Discard the circlips – new ones *must* be used on refitting.

13 Examine the gudgeon pin and connecting rod small-end bearing for signs of wear or damage. Wear will mean both the pin and connecting rod will have to be renewed.

14 The connecting rods themselves should not be in need of renewal, unless seizure or some other major mechanical failure has occurred. Check the alignment of the connecting rods visually, and if the rods are not straight, take them to an engine overhaul specialist for a more detailed check.

15 Examine all components, and renew any worn parts. If new pistons are purchased, they will be supplied complete with gudgeon pins and circlips. Circlips can also be purchased individually.

16 If the pistons and/or connecting rods are to be renewed, seek the advice of a Renault dealer or engine overhaul specialist regarding cylinder bore/piston size groups.

17 On 1.9 litre engines, locate the piston on the connecting rod so that the oil hole in the rod faces away from the combustion chamber in the piston crown **(see illustration)**. Apply a smear of clean engine oil to the gudgeon pin. Slide it into the piston and through the connecting rod small-end. Check that the piston pivots freely on the rod, then secure the gudgeon pin in position with two new circlips. Ensure that each circlip is correctly located in its groove in the piston.

18 On 2.2 litre engines, locate the piston on the connecting rod so that the oil hole in the rod faces the rear (exhaust side) of the engine. Apply a smear of clean engine oil to the gudgeon pin. Slide it into the piston and through the connecting rod small-end. Check that the piston pivots freely on the rod, then secure the gudgeon pin in position with two new circlips. Ensure that each circlip is correctly located in its groove in the piston with the gap at the top.

13 Crankshaft – inspection

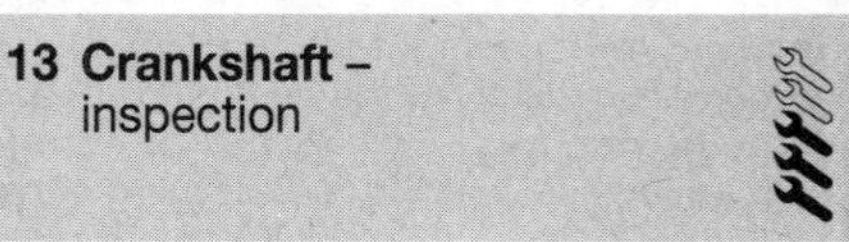

Checking endfloat

1 If the crankshaft endfloat is to be checked, this must be done when the crankshaft is still installed in the cylinder block, but is free to move (see Section 10).

2 Check the endfloat using a dial gauge in contact with the end of the crankshaft. Push the crankshaft fully one way, and then zero the gauge. Push the crankshaft fully the other way, and check the endfloat **(see illustration)**. The result can be compared with the specified amount, and will give an indication as to whether new thrustwashers are required.

3 If a dial gauge is not available, feeler blades can be used. First push the crankshaft fully towards the flywheel end of the engine, then use feeler blades to measure the gap between the web of the crankpin and the thrustwasher **(see illustration)**.

Inspection

4 Clean the crankshaft using paraffin or a suitable solvent, and dry it, preferably with compressed air if available. Be sure to clean the oil holes with a pipe cleaner or similar probe, to ensure that they are not obstructed.

Warning: Wear eye protection when using compressed air.

5 Check the main and big-end bearing journals for uneven wear, scoring, pitting and cracking.

13.2 Measuring the crankshaft endfloat using a dial gauge

13.3 Measuring the crankshaft endfloat using a feeler blade

6 Big-end bearing wear is accompanied by distinct metallic knocking when the engine is running (particularly noticeable when the engine is pulling from low speed) and some loss of oil pressure.

7 Main bearing wear is accompanied by severe engine vibration and rumble – getting progressively worse as engine speed increases – and again by loss of oil pressure.

8 Check the bearing journal for roughness by running a finger lightly over the bearing surface. Any roughness (which will be accompanied by obvious bearing wear) indicates that the crankshaft requires renewal.

9 Using a micrometer, measure the diameter of the main and big-end bearing journals, and compare the results with the Specifications. By measuring the diameter at a number of points around each journal's circumference, you will be able to determine whether or not the journal is out-of-round. Take the measurement at each end of the journal, near the webs, to determine if the journal is tapered. Compare the results obtained with those given in the Specifications.

10 Check the oil seal contact surfaces at each end of the crankshaft for wear and damage. If the seal has worn a deep groove in the surface of the crankshaft, consult an engine overhaul specialist; repair may be possible, but otherwise a new crankshaft will be required.

11 As no oversize bearing shells are produced by Renault, if the crankshaft has worn beyond the specified limits, it will have to be renewed; it cannot be reground. Consult your Renault dealer or engine specialist for further information on parts availability.

14 Main and big-end bearings – inspection and selection

Inspection

1 Even though the main and big-end bearings should be renewed during the engine overhaul, the old bearings should be retained for close examination, as they may reveal valuable information about the condition of the engine.

2 Bearing failure can occur due to lack of lubrication, the presence of dirt or other foreign particles, overloading the engine, or corrosion **(see illustration)**. Regardless of the cause of bearing failure, the cause must be corrected (where applicable) before the engine is reassembled, to prevent it from happening again.

3 When examining the bearing shells, remove them from the cylinder block, the main bearing caps, the connecting rods and the connecting rod big-end bearing caps. Lay them out on a clean surface in the same general position as their location in the engine. This will enable you to match any bearing problems with the corresponding crankshaft journal.

4 Dirt and other foreign matter gets into the engine in a variety of ways. It may be left in the engine during assembly, or it may pass through filters or the crankcase ventilation system. It may get into the oil, and from there into the bearings. Metal chips from machining operations and normal engine wear are often present. Abrasives are sometimes left in engine components after reconditioning, especially when parts are not thoroughly cleaned using the proper cleaning methods. Whatever the source, these foreign objects often end up embedded in the soft bearing material, and are easily recognised. Large particles will not embed in the bearing, and will score or gouge the bearing and journal. The best prevention for this cause of bearing failure is to clean all parts thoroughly, and keep everything spotlessly clean during engine assembly. Frequent and regular engine oil and filter changes are also recommended.

5 Lack of lubrication (or lubrication breakdown) has a number of interrelated causes. Excessive heat (which thins the oil), overloading (which squeezes the oil from the bearing face) and oil leakage (from excessive bearing clearances, worn oil pump or high engine speeds) all contribute to lubrication breakdown. Blocked oil passages, which usually are the result of misaligned oil holes in a bearing shell, will also oil-starve a bearing, and destroy it. When lack of lubrication is the cause of bearing failure, the bearing material is wiped or extruded from the steel backing of the bearing. Temperatures may increase to the point where the steel backing turns blue from overheating.

6 Driving habits can have a definite effect on bearing life. Full-throttle, low-speed operation (labouring the engine) puts very high loads on bearings, tending to squeeze out the oil film. These loads cause the bearings to flex, which produces fine cracks in the bearing face (fatigue failure). Eventually, the bearing material will loosen in pieces, and tear away from the steel backing.

7 Short-distance driving leads to corrosion of bearings, because insufficient engine heat is produced to drive off the condensed water and corrosive gases. These products collect in the engine oil, forming acid and sludge. As the oil is carried to the engine bearings, the acid attacks and corrodes the bearing material.

8 Incorrect bearing installation during engine assembly will lead to bearing failure as well. Tight-fitting bearings leave insufficient bearing running clearance, and will result in oil starvation. Dirt or foreign particles trapped behind a bearing shell result in high spots on the bearing, which lead to failure.

Selection

9 The main and big-end bearing shells supplied by the manufacturer are only available in one standard size. Therefore, if the relevant crankshaft journals are all within tolerance, and new bearing shells are fitted, the bearing running clearances should then be correct. Before obtaining new bearing shells, consult a Renault dealer or engine reconditioning specialist as to the latest recommendations concerning bearing shell selection.

15 Engine overhaul – reassembly sequence

1 Before reassembly begins, ensure that all new parts have been obtained, and that all necessary tools are available. Read through the entire procedure to familiarise yourself with the work involved, and to ensure that all items necessary for reassembly of the engine are at hand. In addition to all normal tools and materials, thread-locking compound will be needed. A suitable tube of liquid sealant will also be required for the joint faces that are fitted without gaskets. It is recommended that Renault's own product(s) are used, which are specially formulated for this purpose; the relevant product names are quoted in the text of each Section where they are required.

2 In order to save time and avoid problems, engine reassembly can be carried out in the following order:

a) Crankshaft.
b) Piston/connecting rod assemblies.
c) Oil pump.
d) Sump.
e) Flywheel.
f) Cylinder head.
g) Timing belt tensioner and sprockets, and timing belt.
h) Engine external components.

3 At this stage, all engine components should be absolutely clean and dry, with all faults repaired. The components should be laid out (or in individual containers) on a completely clean work surface.

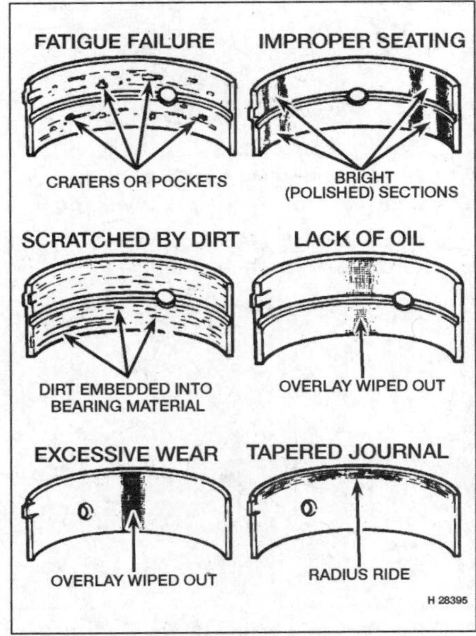

14.2 Typical bearing failures

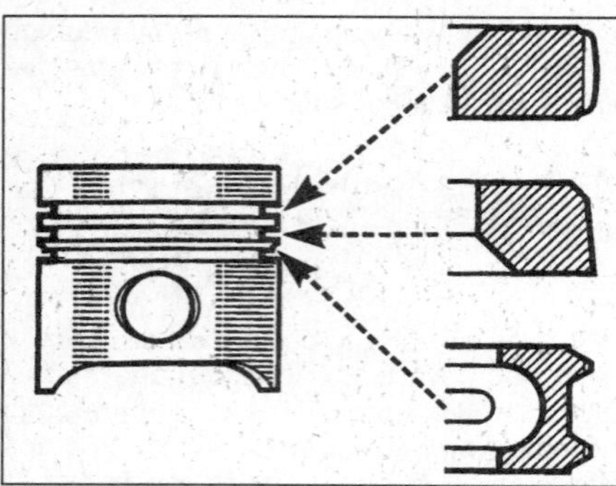

16.2 Piston ring fitting diagram

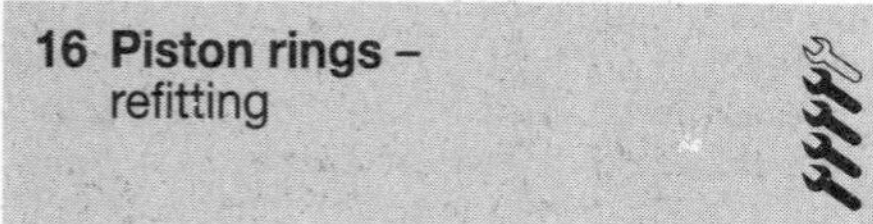

16 Piston rings – refitting

1 Before refitting the rings to the pistons, check their end gaps by inserting each of them in their cylinder bores. Use the piston to make sure that they are square. Renault rings are supplied pregapped; no attempt should be made to adjust the gaps by filing.

2 Refit the piston rings as follows. Where the original rings are being refitted, use the marks or notes made on removal, to ensure that each ring is refitted to its original groove and the same way up. New rings generally have their top surfaces identified by markings (often an indication of size, such as STD, or the word TOP) – the rings must be fitted with such markings uppermost **(see illustration)**. **Note:** *Always follow any instructions supplied with the new piston ring sets – different manufacturers may specify different procedures. Do not mix up the top and second compression rings, as they have different cross-sections.*

3 The oil control ring (lowest one on the piston) should be installed first, and is composed of three separate elements. Slip the spacer/ expander into the groove. Next, install the lower side rail. Place one end of the side rail into the groove between the spacer/expander and the ring land, hold it firmly in place, and slide a finger around the piston while pushing the rail into the groove. Next, install the upper side rail in the same manner. After the three oil ring components have been installed, check that both the upper and lower side rails can be turned smoothly in the ring groove.

4 The second compression (middle) ring is installed next, followed by the top compression ring – ensure their marks are uppermost. Do not expand either ring any more than necessary to slide it over the top of the piston.

5 With all the rings in position, space the ring gaps (including the elements of the oil control ring) uniformly around the piston at 120° intervals. Repeat the procedure for the remaining pistons and rings.

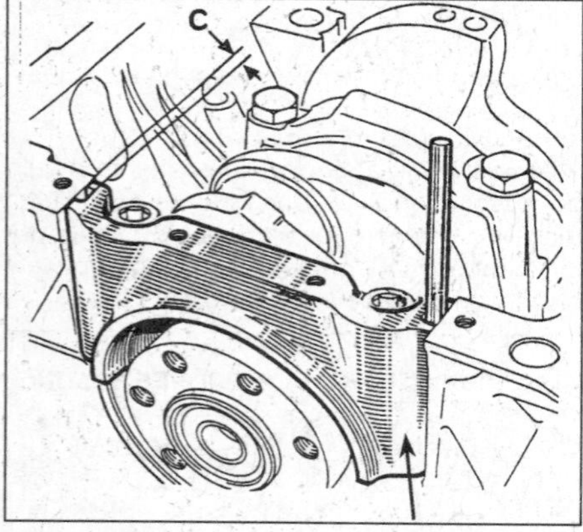

17.2a Measuring No 1 main bearing cap side seal groove using a dowel rod

Bearing cap (arrowed)
C Seal groove measurement

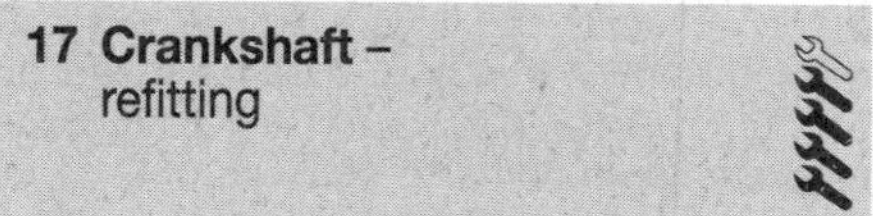

17 Crankshaft – refitting

Note: *To obtain the correct main bearing running clearance, new main bearing shells should always be fitted regardless of the condition of the original ones.*

1 Crankshaft refitting is the first stage of engine reassembly following overhaul. It is assumed at this point that the cylinder block/ crankcase and crankshaft have been cleaned, inspected and repaired or reconditioned as necessary. Position the cylinder block on a clean level work surface, with the crankcase facing upwards. The crankshaft can now be refitted as described in the following sub-Sections according to engine type.

1.9 litre engines

2 Before fitting the crankshaft and main bearings, decide whether the No 1 main bearing cap is to be sealed using butyl seals or silicone sealant. If butyl seals are to be used, it is necessary to determine the correct thickness of the seals to obtain from Renault. To do this, place the bearing cap in position without any seals and secure it with the two retaining bolts. Locate a twist drill, dowel rod or any other suitable implement which will just fit in the side seal groove **(see illustration)**. Now measure the implement – this dimension is the side seal groove size. If the dimension is less than or equal to 5 mm, a 5.10 mm thick side seal is needed. If the dimension is more than 5 mm, a 5.4 mm thick side seal is required. If No 1 main bearing cap is to be fitted using sealant, a tube of Rhodorseal 5661 sealant, together with a hardening agent and application syringe, will be required. This is available as a kit from Renault dealers **(see illustration)**.

3 Clean the backs of the bearing shells and the bearing locations in both the cylinder block and the main bearing caps. If new shells are being fitted, ensure that all traces of the protective grease are cleaned off using paraffin. Wipe dry the shells, block and caps with a lint-free cloth.

4 Lay out the bearing shells ready for fitting, noting that the shells with the oil holes are fitted to the cylinder block. If the original bearing shells are being used they must be refitted in their original locations and in their original fitted direction as noted during removal.

5 Press the bearing shells into their locations, ensuring that the tab on each shell engages in the notch in the cylinder block or main bearing cap.

6 Using a little grease, stick the thrustwashers to each side of the main bearing upper location; ensure that the oilway grooves on each thrustwasher face outwards (away from the cylinder block) **(see illustration)**.

7 Liberally lubricate each bearing shell in the cylinder block with clean engine oil then lower the crankshaft into position ensuring that the bearing shells and thrustwashers remain correctly seated.

8 Ensure that the cap locating dowels are in position and fit the main bearing caps numbers 2 to 5. Ensure that the caps are fitted in their correct locations and the correct way round. Insert the bearing cap bolts and tighten them to the specified torque setting **(see illustration)**.

9 Check that the crankshaft is free to turn without stiffness or tight spots, then check the crankshaft endfloat with reference to Section 13.

10 Thoroughly clean the contact surfaces of No 1 main bearing cap and its location in the

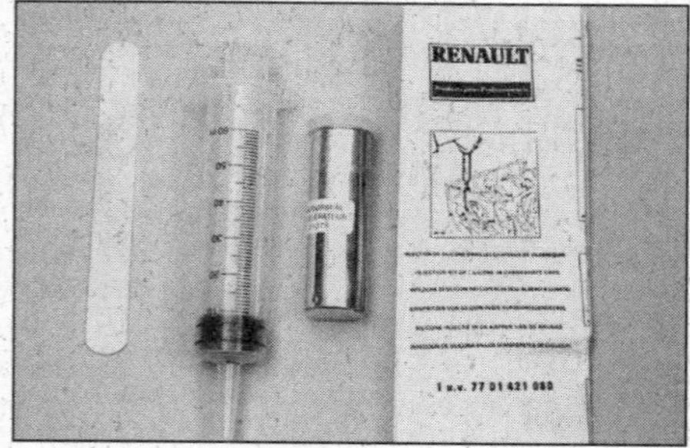

17.2b Renault sealing kit for No 1 main bearing cap grooves. Full instructions are supplied with the kit

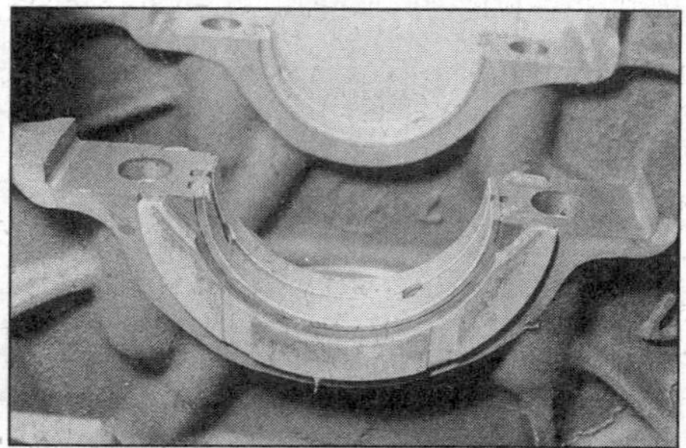

17.6 Stick the thrustwasher halves to the cylinder block using grease, making sure their oil grooves are facing outwards

17.8 Fit bearing caps numbers 2 to 5 and tighten the retaining bolts to the specified torque

cylinder block with methylated spirit and allow to dry thoroughly **(see illustration)**.

11 If fitting butyl seals to No 1 bearing cap, fit the seals with their grooves facing outwards. Position the seals so that approximately 0.2 mm of seal protrudes at the bottom-facing side (the side towards the crankcase). Apply a thin coating of Rhodorseal 5661 sealant to the bearing cap lower mating surface in the cylinder block, and lubricate the seals with a little oil **(see illustrations)**. When the cap is being fitted, use the bolts as a guide by just starting them in their threads, then pressing the cap firmly into position. When the cap is almost fully home, check that the seals still protrude slightly at the cylinder block mating face.

12 Screw in the main bearing cap bolts and tighten them to the specified torque. Trim the protruding ends of the butyl seals flush with the surface of the cylinder block sump mating face.

13 If No 1 main bearing cap is to be fitted using sealant, apply a thin coating of Rhodorseal 5661 sealant to the bearing cap lower mating surface in the cylinder block, then fit the cap. Insert the main bearing cap bolts and tighten them to the specified torque.

14 Mix approximately half of the 100 g tube of Rhodorseal 5661 sealant together with half the hardener as described in the instructions supplied with the kit. Using the syringe supplied, inject the mixture into the grooves on each side of the bearing cap, until it can be seen to flow out slightly on both sides of the grooves. Using a clean cloth, wipe away any

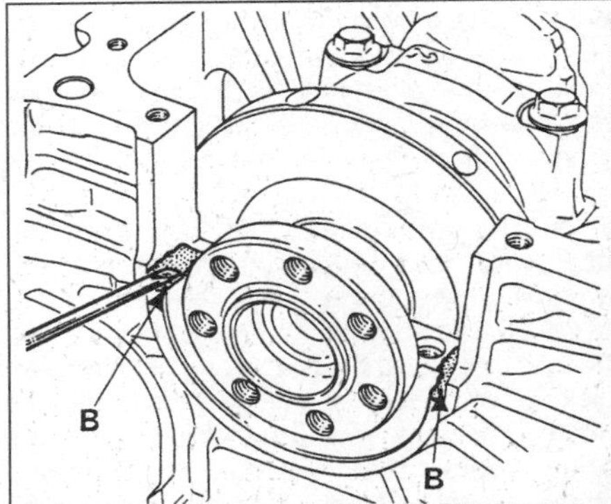

17.11c Apply sealant to No 1 bearing cap lower mating surface (B) in the cylinder block

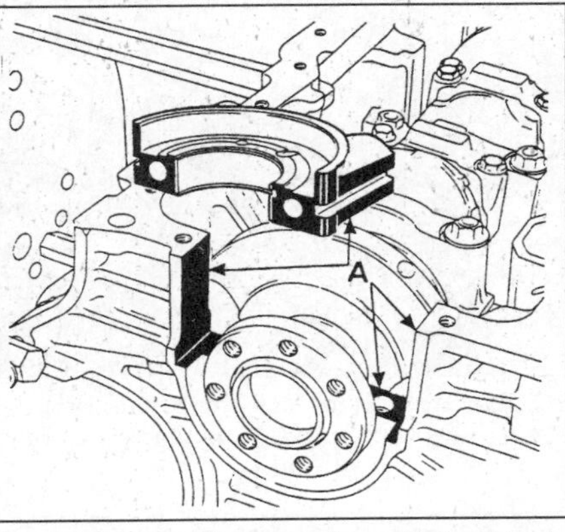

17.10 Thoroughly clean the cylinder block and No 1 main bearing cap mating faces (A)

surplus mixture from the inside and outside of the cylinder block.

15 Allow the sealant to dry for a few minutes, then cut away any surplus sealant from the sump mating face.

16 Fit a new seal to the crankshaft timing belt end oil seal housing and refit the housing with reference to Chapter 2B.

17 Fit a new crankshaft flywheel end oil seal, with reference to Chapter 2B.

18 Where applicable, refit the timing belt lower inner cover.

19 Refit the piston/connecting rod assemblies, oil pump, flywheel, cylinder head, timing belt sprockets and fit a new timing belt as described in Chapter 2B.

2.2 litre engines

20 Clean the backs of the bearing shells and the bearing locations in both the cylinder block and the main bearing casting. If new shells are being fitted, ensure that all traces of the protective grease are cleaned off using paraffin. Wipe dry the shells, block and casting with a lint-free cloth.

21 Lay out the bearing shells ready for fitting, noting that the shells with the oil holes are fitted to the cylinder block. If the original bearing shells are being used they must be refitted in their original locations and in their original fitted direction as noted during removal.

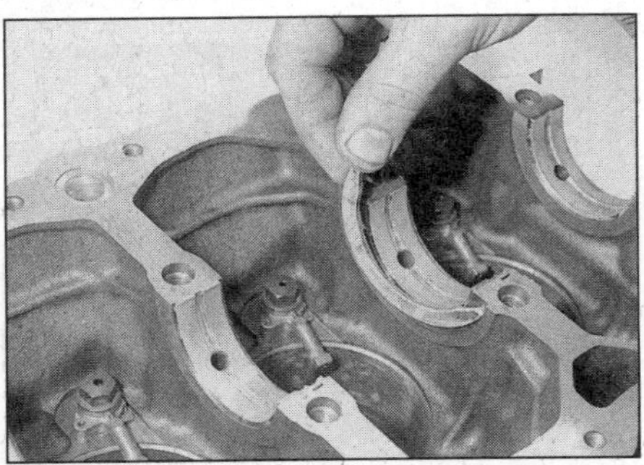
17.23 Fit the thrustwasher halves to the side of No 2 main bearing

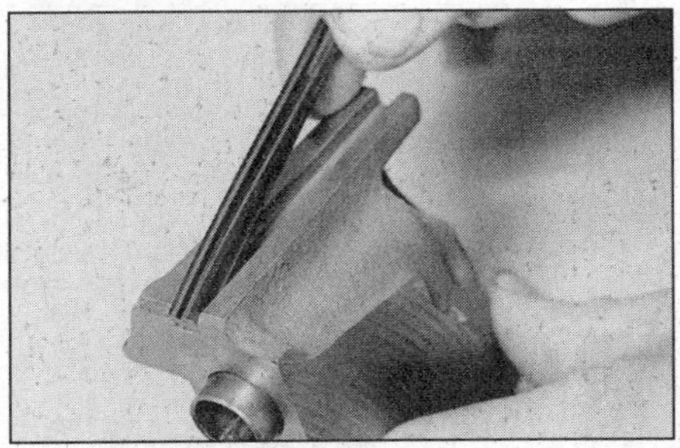
17.11a Fit the sealing strips to No 1 bearing cap so that its groove is facing away from the cap . . .

17.11b . . . and position the strip so that it protrudes above the cap mating surface by approximately 0.2 mm

22 Press the bearing shells into their locations, ensuring that the tab on each shell engages in the notch in the cylinder block or main bearing casting.

23 Using a little grease, stick the thrustwashers to each side of the main bearing upper location; ensure that the oilway grooves on each thrustwasher face outwards (away from the cylinder block) **(see illustration)**.

24 Liberally lubricate each bearing shell in the cylinder block with clean engine oil then lower the crankshaft into position ensuring that the bearing shells and thrustwashers remain correctly seated.

25 Ensure that the mating surfaces of the cylinder block and main bearing casting are clean and dry. Apply a bead of Loctite 518 sealant approximately 0.6 to 1.0 mm wide to the mating surface of the block as shown **(see illustration)**.

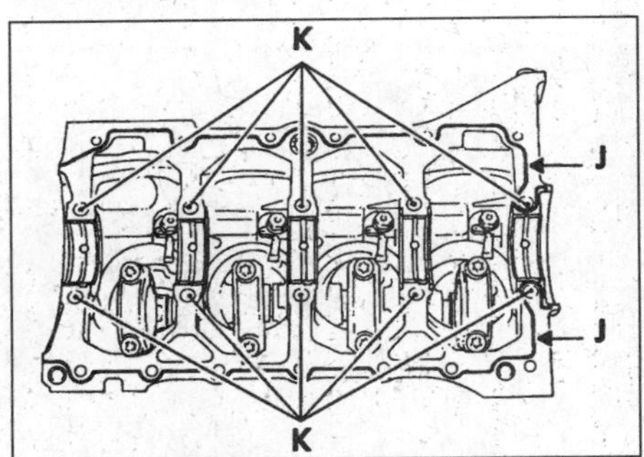

17.25 Apply a bead of sealant (J) to the cylinder block mating surface (K shows the locations of the ten main bearing bolts)

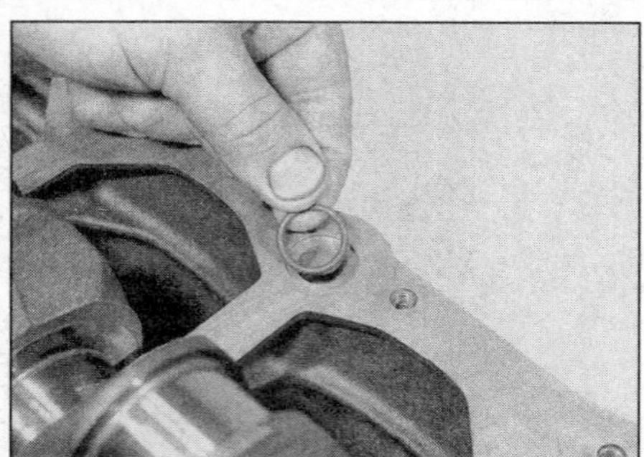
17.26 Fit a new sealing ring to the cylinder block oilway recess

17.29b . . . and then through the specified Stage 2 angle

26 Fit a new sealing ring to the cylinder block oilway **(see illustration)**.

27 Ensure that the locating dowels are in position then carefully lower the main bearing casting onto the block.

28 Fit the ten new large casting bolts and screw in the smaller (8 mm) bolts, tightening all bolts lightly only.

18.5 Tap the piston into the bore using a hammer handle

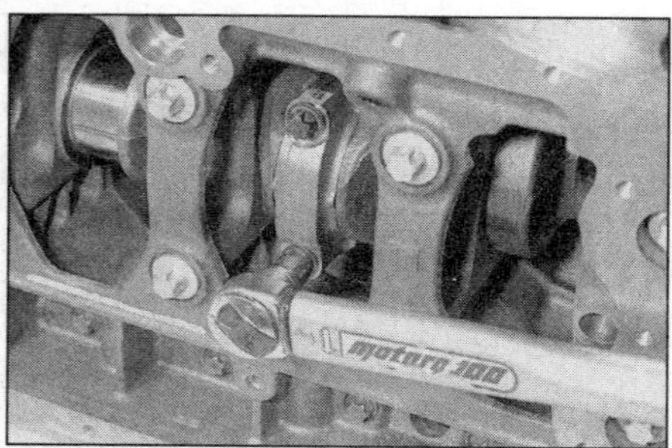
18.8a Fit the new bearing cap bolts and tighten them first to the Stage 1 torque setting . . .

17.29a Tighten the ten inner main bearing bolts first to the specified Stage 1 torque setting . . .

17.30 With the large inner bolts tightened correctly, tighten the smaller outer bolts to the specified torque

29 Working in a diagonal sequence, starting at the centre and working outwards, tighten the ten large (inner) main bearing casting bolts to their specified Stage 1 torque setting. Once all bolts have been tightened, go around in the same sequence and tighten the bolts through the specified Stage 2 angle, using a socket and extension bar. It is recommended that an angle-measuring gauge is used during this stage of the tightening, to ensure accuracy **(see illustrations)**.

30 Once the casting large bolts are correctly tightened, go around and tighten the smaller bolts to the specified torque setting **(see illustration)**.

31 Check that the crankshaft is free to turn without stiffness or tight spots, then check the crankshaft endfloat with reference to Section 13.

32 Refit/reconnect the piston/connecting rod assemblies to the crankshaft as described in Section 18.

33 Fit a new crankshaft oil seal as described in Chapter 2C.

34 Fit a new sealing ring to the oil return pipe upper section then refit the pipe and securely tighten its retaining bolt. Refit the lower section to the base of the main bearing casting and securely tighten its retaining bolt.

35 Refit the oil pump and drive chain (renew the crankshaft oil seal), flywheel, cylinder head, timing belt sprockets and fit a new timing belt as described in Chapter 2C.

18.8b . . . and then through the Stage 2 angle setting

18 Piston/connecting rod assemblies – refitting

Note: *To obtain the correct big-end bearing running clearance, new bearing shells should always be fitted regardless of the condition of the original ones.*

1 Clean the backs of the big-end bearing shells and the recesses in the connecting rods and big-end caps. If new shells are being fitted, ensure that all traces of the protective grease are cleaned off using paraffin. Wipe the shells and connecting rods dry with a lint-free cloth.

2 Press the big-end bearing shells into the connecting rods and caps in their correct positions. Make sure that the location tabs are engaged with the cut-outs in the connecting rods.

3 Lubricate the bores; the pistons and piston rings then lay out each piston/connecting rod assembly in its respective position.

4 Starting with assembly number 1, make sure that the piston rings are still spaced as described in Section 16, then clamp them in position with a piston ring compressor.

5 Insert the piston/connecting rod assembly into the top of cylinder No 1. Ensure that the combustion chamber recess on the piston crown is towards the front (oil filter side) of the cylinder block. Using a block of wood or hammer handle against the piston crown, tap the assembly into the cylinder until the piston crown is flush with the top of the cylinder/liner **(see illustration)**.

6 Taking care not to mark the cylinder bore, liberally lubricate the crankpin and both bearing shells, then pull the piston/connecting rod assembly down the bore and onto the crankpin. Refit the big-end bearing cap to the connecting rod.

7 On 1.9 litre engines, fit the new bearing cap bolts and tighten them evenly and progressively to the specified torque.

8 On 2.2 litre engines, fit the new bearing cap bolts and tighten them evenly and progressively to the Stage 1 torque setting. Once both bolts have been tightened to the Stage 1 setting, angle-tighten them through the specified Stage 2 angle, using a socket and extension bar. It is recommended that an angle-measuring gauge is used during this stage of the tightening, to ensure accuracy **(see illustrations)**.

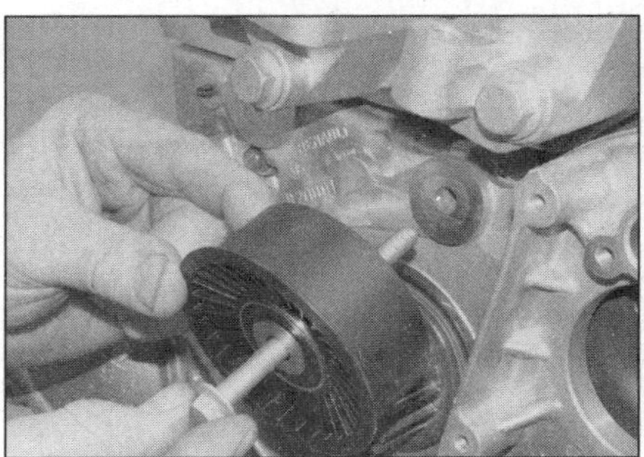

19.3 Remove the idler pulley from the timing gear cover

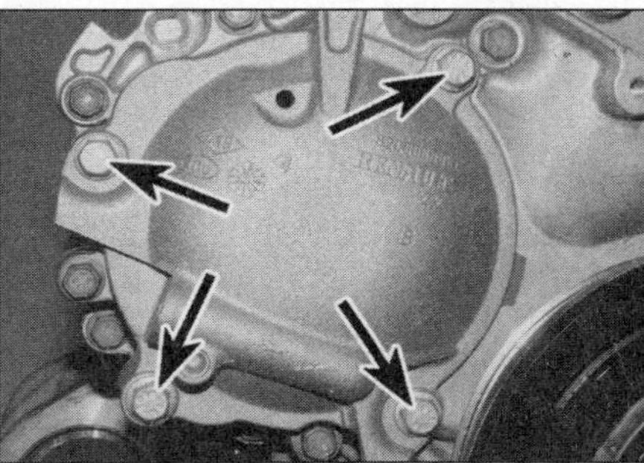

19.4 Undo the bolts (arrowed) to remove cover

19.5a Remove the timing gear cover . . .

9 Refit the remaining three piston and connecting rod assemblies in the same way.

10 Rotate the crankshaft, and check that it turns freely, with no signs of binding or tight spots.

11 Refit the oil pump, sump and the cylinder head as described in Part B or C of this Chapter.

19 Timing gear sprockets (2.2 litre engines) – removal, inspection and refitting

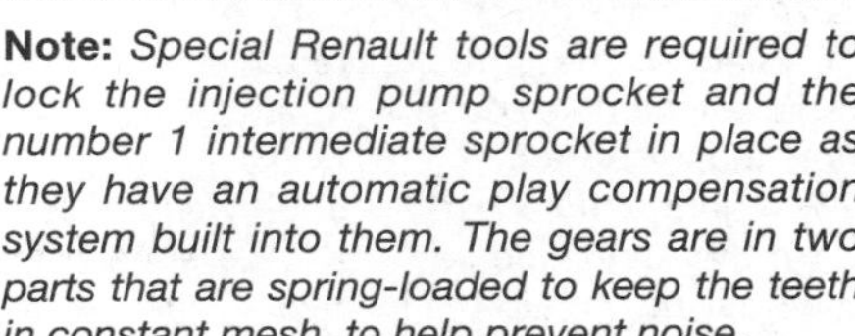

Note: *Special Renault tools are required to lock the injection pump sprocket and the number 1 intermediate sprocket in place as they have an automatic play compensation system built into them. The gears are in two parts that are spring-loaded to keep the teeth in constant mesh, to help prevent noise.*

Removal

1 Remove the timing belt and tensioner as described in Chapter 2C, Section 6.

2 Remove the crankshaft pulley as described in Chapter 2C, Section 4.

3 Undo the retaining bolt and remove the idler pulley from the timing gear cover **(see illustration).**

4 Undo the retaining bolts and remove the coolant pump cover **(see illustration).** Discard the gasket; a new one will be required for refitting.

5 Working your way around the outer edge of the casing, undo the retaining bolts and remove the timing gear cover. Discard the gasket/seal a new one will be required for refitting **(see illustrations)**.

High-pressure pump sprocket

6 Mark or note the position of the sprocket before removing and use this when refitting. Slacken the sprocket retaining nut and remove it from the pump shaft **(see illustration).**

7 Screw locking pin (Renault special tool Mot. 1538) into the sprocket to lock the automatic play compensation system **(see illustration).**

8 Fit the sprocket extractor (Renault special tool Mot. 1548) to the sprocket and tighten the centre bolt to remove the sprocket from the pump shaft **(see illustrations)**.

9 If the sprocket is removed without the special tools, then the sprocket will need to be spring-loaded for refitting. Renault use a special tool (Mot. 1540) to achieve this **(see illustration)**. The load on the spring is not excessive and can be accomplished by manufacturing a suitable home-made tool.

Intermediate sprocket No 1

10 Fit the sprocket locking tool (Renault special tool Mot. 1539) to the sprocket and

19.5b . . . and remove the gasket/seal

19.6 Remove the sprocket retaining nut

19.7 Screw the locking pin into the sprocket

19.8a Fit the sprocket extractor . . .

19.8b . . . and tighten the centre bolt (arrowed)

19.9 Renault tool for loading the tension on the sprockets

19.10 Fit the locking tool to the intermediate sprocket

19.11 Remove the sprocket retaining bolt

19.12 Remove the sprocket complete with locking tool

19.13a Remove the shim/washer . . .

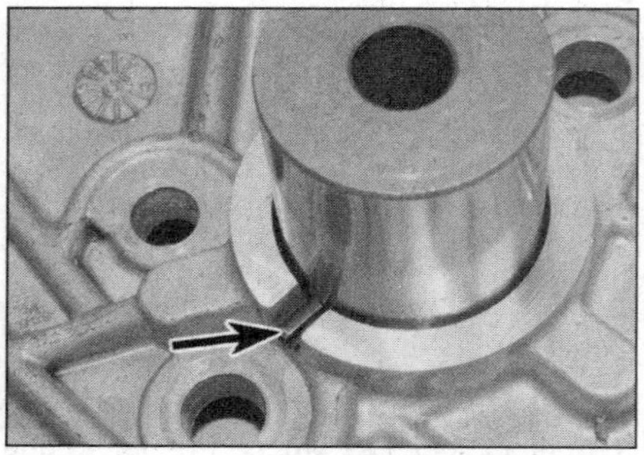

19.13b . . . note locating peg (arrowed)

tighten the locking tabs to hold it in place **(see illustration)**.

11 Slacken the sprocket retaining bolt and remove it from the centre of the locking tool **(see illustration)**.

12 Withdraw the intermediate sprocket complete with locking tool from the shaft **(see illustration)**.

13 Where required, remove the washer/shim from the shaft and withdraw the shaft from the housing, noting the location of the roll-pin **(see illustrations)**.

14 If the sprocket is removed without the special tools, then the sprocket will need to be spring-loaded for refitting. Renault use a special tool (Mot. 1540) to achieve this **(see illustrations)**. The load on the spring is not excessive and can be accomplished by manufacturing a suitable home-made tool.

Intermediate sprocket No 2

15 Using a screwdriver, remove the plastic cover from inside the centre of the sprocket **(see illustration)**. A new cover seal will be required for refitting.

16 Slacken the sprocket retaining bolt and remove it complete with intermediate sprocket **(see illustrations)**.

17 Where required, remove the washer/shim from the shaft and withdraw the shaft from the housing, noting the location of the roll-pin **(see illustrations)**.

19.14a Load the tension on the intermediate sprocket . . .

19.14b . . . then fit the locking tool

19.15 Pierce the seal with a screwdriver to remove

19.16a Slacken the retaining bolt . . .

19.16b . . . and remove intermediate sprocket

19.17a Remove the shim/washer from the spigot shaft

Crankshaft sprocket

18 Slide the sprocket off the end of the crankshaft, and then remove the locking key from the slot in the end of the crankshaft **(see illustrations)**.

Coolant pump sprocket

19 Refer to coolant pump removal and refitting procedure in Chapter 3.

Inspection

20 Inspect the teeth of the sprockets for signs of nicks and damage. The teeth are not prone to wear, and should normally last the life of the engine.

21 Check for any wear on the shafts and the locating pins on the intermediate sprocket spigots.

22 Check that intermediate sprocket No 1 and the high-pressure pump sprocket are in their tensioned position before refitting (see paragraphs 9 and 14).

23 With all the sprockets removed from the engine the inner housing/casing can be unbolted from the cylinder block **(see illustration)**.

Refitting

24 Refitting is a reversal of removal, bearing in mind the following points:

a) See Chapter 4B for further information on fuel pump sprocket.

b) Make sure the intermediate sprocket spigot shafts are located correctly in the rear housing.

c) Fit the washer/shims to the intermediate sprocket spigot shafts.

d) Lubricate all parts with clean engine oil as it is assembled.

e) Refit the locking key in the end of the crankshaft before refitting the crankshaft sprocket.

f) See Chapter 3 for further information on coolant pump sprocket.

20 Engine – initial start-up after overhaul

1 With the engine refitted in the vehicle,

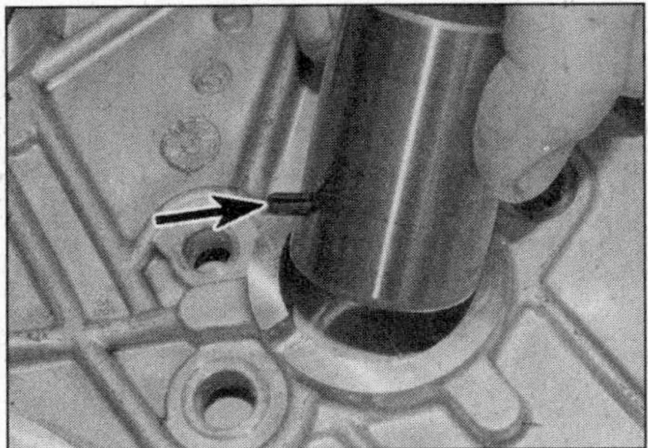

19.17b Check the roll-pin (arrowed)

19.18a Remove the crankshaft sprocket . . .

19.18b . . . and retrieve the locking key

19.23 Removing the timing gear inner housing/casing

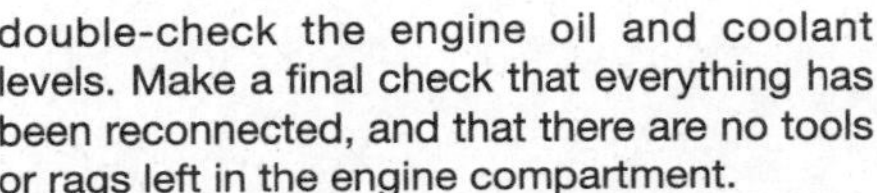

double-check the engine oil and coolant levels. Make a final check that everything has been reconnected, and that there are no tools or rags left in the engine compartment.

2 Disconnect the wiring from the stop solenoid on the injection pump (see Chapter 4B), then turn the engine on the starter motor until the oil pressure warning light goes out. Reconnect the wire to the stop solenoid.

3 Prime the fuel system as described in Chapter 4B.

4 Fully depress the accelerator pedal, turn the ignition key and wait for the preheating warning light to go out.

5 Start the engine, noting that this may take a little longer than usual, due to the fuel system components having been disturbed.

6 While the engine is idling, check for fuel, water and oil leaks. Don't be alarmed if there are some odd smells and smoke from parts getting hot and burning off oil deposits.

7 Assuming all is well; keep the engine idling until hot water is felt circulating through the top hose, then switch off the engine.

8 After a few minutes recheck the oil and coolant levels as described in *Weekly checks*, and top-up as necessary.

9 If they were tightened as described, there is no need to retighten the cylinder head bolts once the engine has first run after reassembly.

10 If new pistons, rings or crankshaft bearings have been fitted, the engine must be treated as new, and run-in for the first 500 miles (800 km). *Do not* operate the engine at full-throttle, or allow it to labour at low engine speeds in any gear. It is recommended that the oil and filter be changed at the end of this period.

Chapter 3
Cooling, heating and air conditioning systems

Contents

Degrees of difficulty

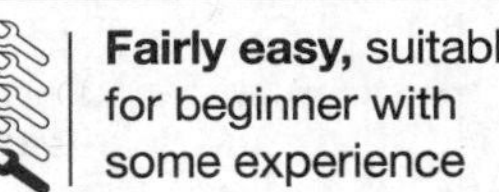

Easy, suitable for novice with little experience	**Fairly easy,** suitable for beginner with some experience	**Fairly difficult,** suitable for competent DIY mechanic	**Difficult,** suitable for experienced DIY mechanic	**Very difficult,** suitable for expert DIY or professional

Specifications

General

Cooling system type	Pressurised sealed system, with front-mounted radiator and electric cooling fan
Cooling system pressure:	
Brown cap	1.2 bar
Black cap with yellow hand mark	1.4 bar

Thermostat

Opening temperatures:	
Starts to open	89°C
Fully open	99°C

Air conditioning

Compressor type	Delphi Harrison V5e
Oil type	Planetelf PAG 488
Oil quantity	220 cm^3 ± 15
Refrigerant type	R 134a
Refrigerant quantity	650g ± 35

Torque wrench settings	Nm	lbf ft
Air conditioning compressor mounting bolts	21	15
Air conditioning support bracket mounting bolts	44	32
Roadwheel bolts	105	77
1.6 litre petrol engines		
Coolant pump bolts:		
Stage 1	8	6
Stage 2 (M6 bolts)	11	8
Stage 3 (M8 bolts)	22	16
1.8 and 2.0 litre engines		
Auxiliary belt tensioner (auxiliary belt driven coolant pumps)	25	18
Coolant pump bolts	9	7
Coolant pump (auxiliary belt driven)	17	13
Coolant pump pulley (auxiliary belt driven)	20	15
1.9 litre diesel engines		
Auxiliary belt tensioner (auxiliary belt driven coolant pumps)	25	18
Coolant pump (timing belt driven)	10	7
Coolant pump (auxiliary belt driven)	17	13
Coolant pump pulley (auxiliary belt driven)	20	15
2.2 litre diesel engines		
Coolant pump	10	7
Coolant pump cover bolts	10	7
Coolant pump sprocket nut	50	37

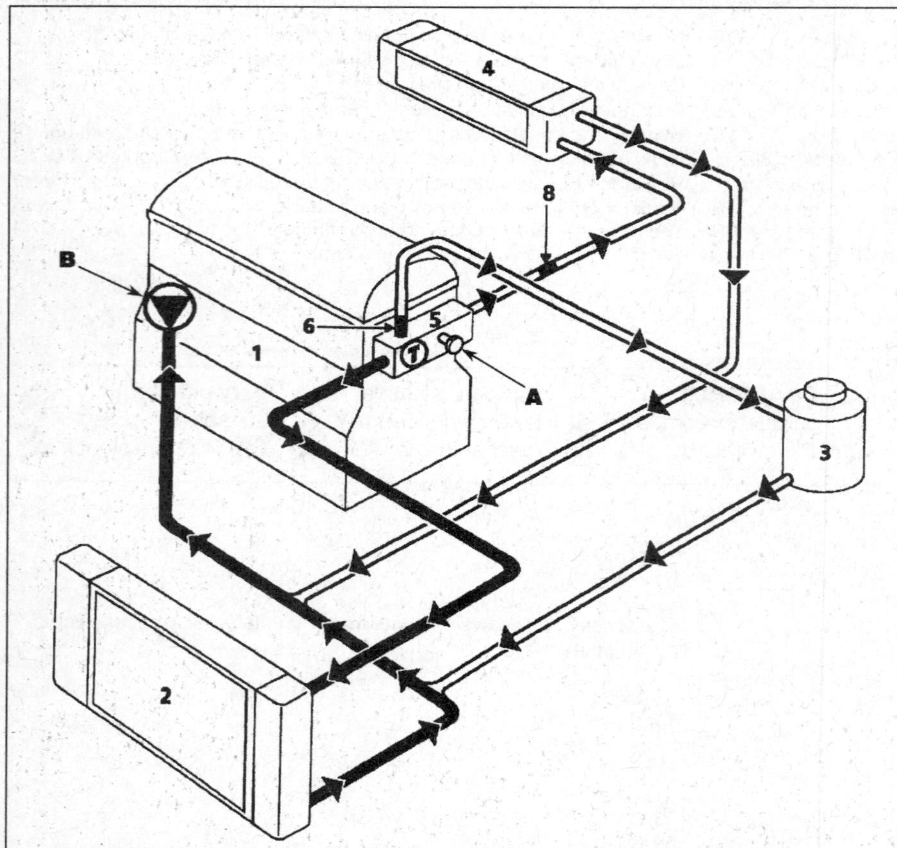

1.1a Cooling system schematic – petrol engines (manual transmission)

1 Cylinder block
2 Radiator
3 Expansion bottle
4 Heater matrix/radiator
5 Coolant/thermostat housing
6 3mm diameter restrictor
7 Oil heat exchanger
8 8.5mm diameter restrictor
9 10mm diameter restrictor
10 11mm diameter by-pass
11 Thermoplunger mounting
A Bleed screws
B Water pump
T Thermostat

1 General information and precautions

The cooling system is of pressurised type, comprising a coolant pump driven by the timing belt or the auxiliary drivebelt (depending on engine type), an aluminium crossflow radiator, expansion tank, electric cooling fan(s), a thermostat, heater matrix, and all associated hoses and switches **(see illustrations)**.

The system functions as follows. Cold coolant in the bottom of the radiator passes through the bottom hose to the coolant pump, where it is pumped around the cylinder block and head passages, and through the oil cooler(s) (where fitted). After cooling the cylinder bores, combustion surfaces and valve seats, the coolant reaches the underside of the thermostat, which is initially closed. The coolant passes through the heater, and is returned via the cylinder block to the coolant pump.

When the engine is cold, the coolant circulates only through the cylinder block, cylinder head, and heater. When the coolant reaches a predetermined temperature, the thermostat opens, and the coolant passes through the top hose to the radiator. As the coolant circulates through the radiator, it is cooled by the inrush of air when the car is in forward motion. The airflow is supplemented by the action of the electric cooling fan(s) when necessary. Upon reaching the bottom of the radiator, the coolant has now cooled, and the cycle is repeated.

When the engine is at normal operating temperature, the coolant expands, and some of it is displaced into the expansion tank.

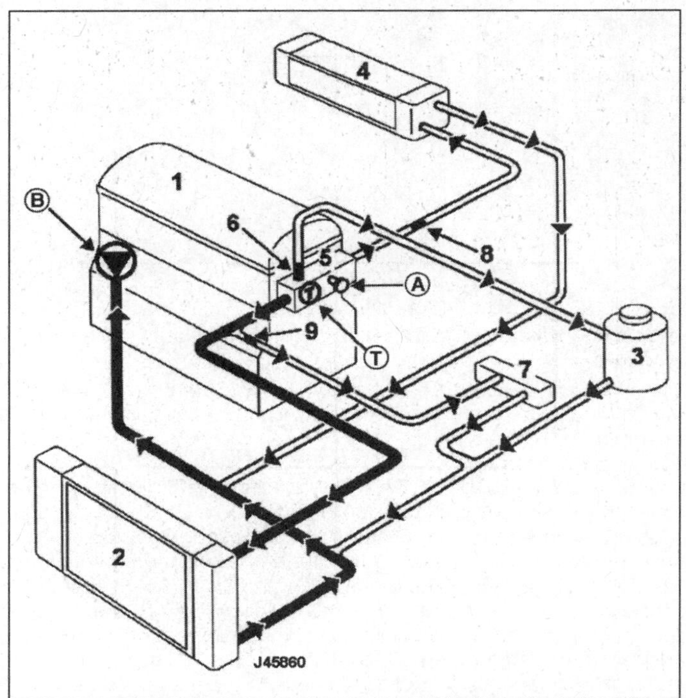

1.1b Cooling system schematic – petrol engines (automatic transmission)
See illustration 1.1a for key

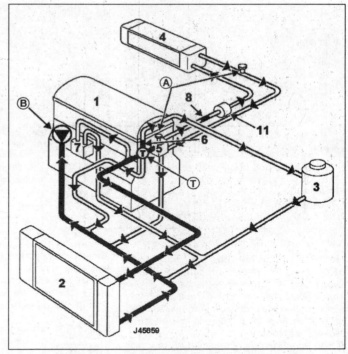

1.1c Cooling system schematic – 1.9 litre diesel engines
See illustration 1.1a for key

Coolant collects in the tank, and is returned to the radiator when the system cools.

On models fitted with engine oil cooler, the coolant also passes through the oil cooler. Similarly, coolant also passes through the automatic transmission fluid cooler and the turbocharger, where applicable.

Precautions

Warning: Do not attempt to remove the expansion tank filler cap, or to disturb any part of the cooling system, while the engine is hot, as there is a high risk of scalding. If the expansion tank filler cap must be removed before the engine and radiator have fully cooled (even though this is not recommended), the pressure in the cooling system must first be relieved. Cover the cap with a thick layer of cloth, to avoid scalding, and slowly unscrew the filler cap until a hissing sound is heard. When the hissing has stopped, indicating that the pressure has reduced, slowly unscrew the filler cap until it can be removed; if more hissing sounds are heard, wait until they have stopped before unscrewing the cap completely. At all times, keep well away from the filler cap opening, and protect your hands.

Warning: Do not allow antifreeze to come into contact with your skin, or with the painted surfaces of the vehicle. Rinse off spills immediately, with plenty of water. Never leave antifreeze lying around in an open container, or in a puddle in the driveway or on the garage floor. Children and pets are attracted by its sweet smell, but antifreeze can be fatal if ingested.

Warning: If the engine is hot, the electric cooling fan may start rotating even if the engine is not running. Be careful to keep your hands, hair and any loose clothing well clear when working in the engine compartment.

Warning: Refer to Section 10 for precautions to be observed when working on models equipped with air conditioning.

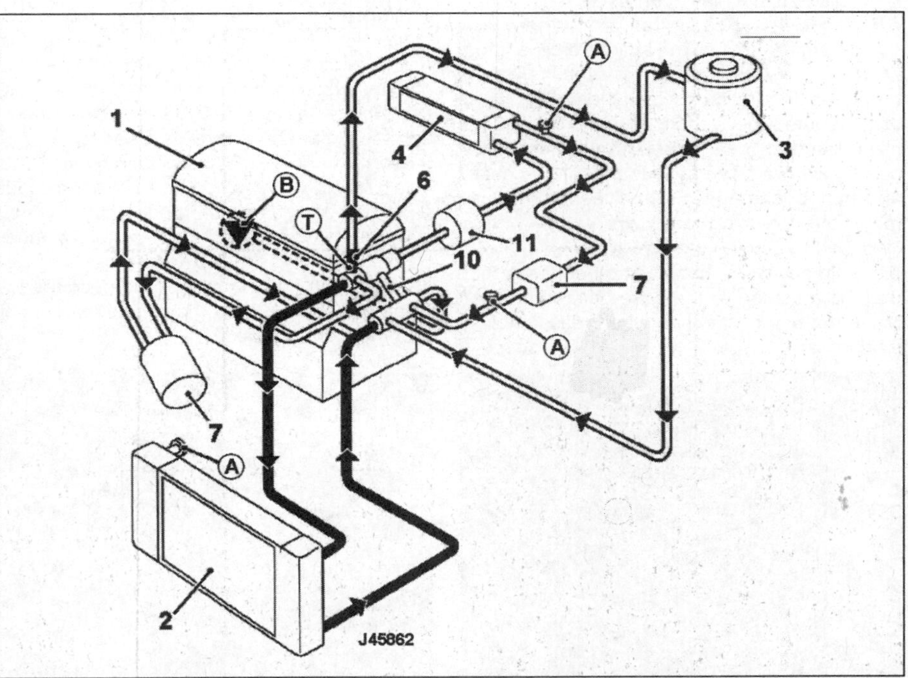

1.1d Cooling system schematic – 2.2 litre diesel engines (manual transmission)
See illustration 1.1a for key

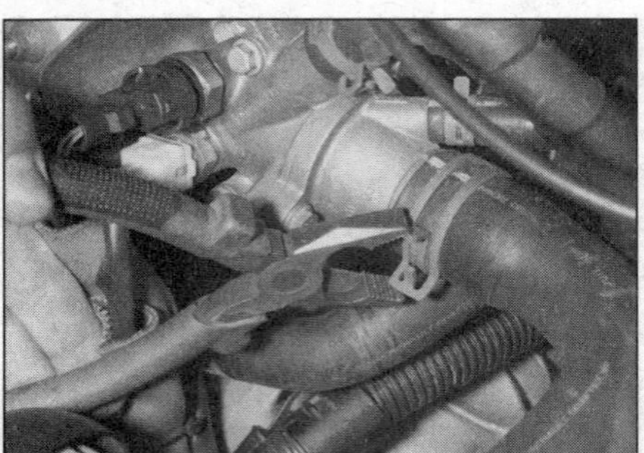

2.4 Using a pair of pliers to release the hose spring clip

2.12a Twist the connector (arrowed) anti-clockwise to release

2.12b Twist in the direction of the arrow to release

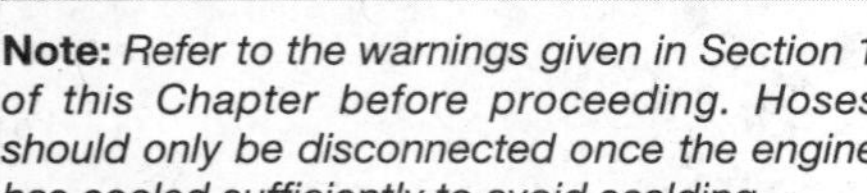

2 Cooling system hoses – disconnection and renewal

Note: *Refer to the warnings given in Section 1 of this Chapter before proceeding. Hoses should only be disconnected once the engine has cooled sufficiently to avoid scalding.*

1 If the checks described in the relevant part of Chapter 1 reveal a faulty hose, it must be renewed as follows.

2 The number, routing and pattern of hoses will vary according to model, but the same basic procedure applies. Before commencing work, make sure that the new hoses are to hand, along with new hose clips if needed. It is good practice to renew the hose clips at the same time as the hoses.

3 First drain the cooling system (see the relevant part of Chapter 1). If the coolant is not due for renewal, it may be re-used, providing it is collected in a clean container.

4 Release the hose clips from the hose concerned. Almost all the standard clips fitted at the factory are the spring type, released by squeezing its tangs together with pliers, at the same time working the clip away from the hose stub **(see illustration)**. These clips can be awkward to use, can pinch old hoses, and may become less effective with age, so may have been updated with Jubilee clips (released by turning the screw).

5 Unclip any wires, cables or other hoses that may be attached to the hose being removed. Make notes for reference when reassembling if necessary.

6 Note that the coolant unions are fragile (many are made of plastic); do not use excessive force when attempting to remove the hoses. If a hose proves to be difficult to remove, try to release it by rotating the hose ends before attempting to free it – if this fails, try gently prising up the end of the hose with a small screwdriver to 'break' the seal. Do not apply too much force, and take care not to damage the pipe stubs or hoses.

If the hose is stiff, use a little soapy water as a lubricant, or soften the hose by soaking it with hot water. If all else fails, cut the coolant hose with a sharp knife, then slit it so that it can be peeled off in two pieces. Although this may prove expensive if the hose is otherwise undamaged, it is preferable to buying a new radiator.

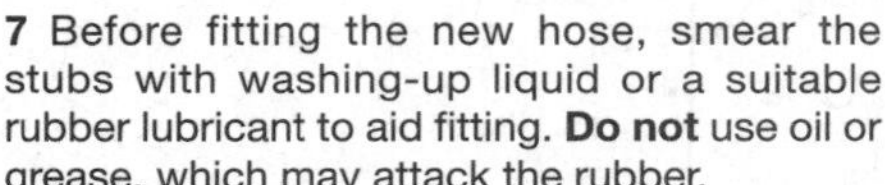

7 Before fitting the new hose, smear the stubs with washing-up liquid or a suitable rubber lubricant to aid fitting. **Do not** use oil or grease, which may attack the rubber.

8 Fit the hose clips over the ends of the hose, and then fit the hose over its stubs.

9 Work the hose into position, checking that it is correctly routed. When satisfied, slide each clip back along the hose until it passes over the flared end of the relevant inlet/outlet, before tightening the clip securely.

10 Refill the cooling system as described in Chapter 1A or 1B. Run the engine, and check that there are no leaks.

11 Recheck the tightness of the hose clips on any new hoses after a few hundred miles.

Heater matrix hose connector

12 Twist the connector anti-clockwise (blue plastic collar) to release the locking tabs, and then pull the hose connector back to release it from the heater matrix pipes **(see illustrations)**.

13 Clean the collar on the hose and check the condition of the seals, renew if necessary.

14 When reconnecting, press the connector into position until the locking tabs engages.

3 Radiator – removal, inspection and refitting

Removal

1 Apply the handbrake, then jack up the front of the vehicle and support securely on axle stands (see *Jacking and vehicle support*).

2 Disconnect the battery negative terminal (refer to *Disconnecting the battery* in the Reference Section of this manual).

3 Remove the undertray from below the engine/transmission, then drain the cooling system as described in the relevant part of Chapter 1.

4 Remove the battery and battery tray, with reference to Chapter 5A **(see illustration)**.

5 Unclip the power steering reservoir from its mounting point and move it to one side **(see illustration)**.

6 Remove the front bumper and radiator grille panel as described in Chapter 11.

7 Remove the both headlight units as described in Chapter 12.

8 Unscrew the bolts at each end, and the central bolt securing the upper front crossmember panel, then lift it away from the body panels, and lay it carefully across the engine (support the panel on rags to prevent the possibility of damage to other components in the engine compartment) **(see illustration)**.

9 Release the securing clips, and disconnect the top and bottom coolant hoses from the radiator **(see illustration)**. **Note:** *The bottom hose may have already been disconnected to drain the cooling system.*

10 Disconnect the wiring plug(s) from the

3.4 Removing the battery tray

3.5 Unclip the PAS reservoir from its mounting bracket

3.8 Remove the upper crossmember from the top of the radiator

3.9 Releasing the radiator top hose

3.10 Disconnect the cooling fan wiring connector

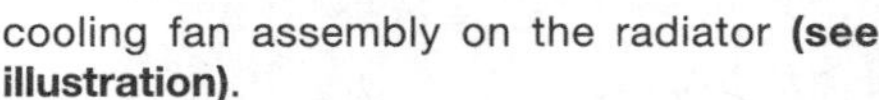

cooling fan assembly on the radiator **(see illustration)**.

11 On models with air conditioning, release the retaining clips (one at each side) and lift the condenser to disconnect it from the radiator/intercooler. Cable tie the condenser to the crossmember, taking care not to damage it **(see illustrations)**.

12 On turbo models, undo the retaining clips and disconnect the air hoses/ducts from the intercooler and move them to one side. Release the clips, one at each side that hold the radiator to the intercooler. The intercooler can then be withdrawn from in between the radiator and condenser **(see illustrations)**.

13 Release the two R clips and remove the washers from the lower locating pegs on the bottom of the radiator, there is one at each side of the radiator. Lift the radiator to release the lower locating lugs from the body front panel. Withdraw the radiator upwards from the front of the vehicle **(see illustration)**.

Inspection

14 If the radiator has been removed due to suspected blockage, reverse-flush it as described in the relevant part of Chapter 1. Clean dirt and debris from the radiator fins, using a low-pressure air line (in which case, wear eye protection) or a soft brush. Be careful, as the fins are sharp, and can be easily damaged.

15 If necessary, a radiator specialist can perform a 'flow test' on the radiator, to establish whether an internal blockage exists.

3.11a Release the securing clips . . .

3.11b . . . and remove the condenser from the intercooler

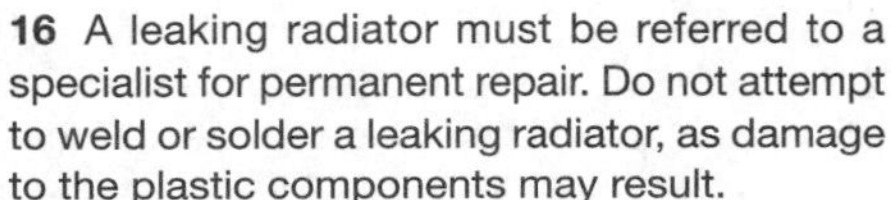

16 A leaking radiator must be referred to a specialist for permanent repair. Do not attempt to weld or solder a leaking radiator, as damage to the plastic components may result.

17 If the radiator is to be sent for repair or renewed, remove all hoses, and the cooling fan switch (where fitted).

18 Inspect the condition of the radiator mounting rubbers, and renew them if necessary.

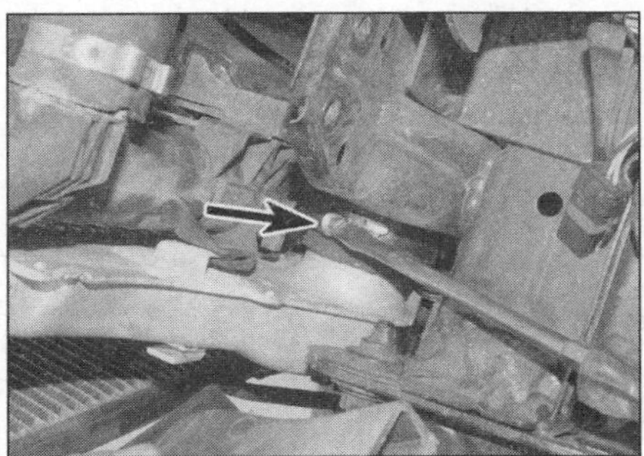

3.12a Undo the securing clip (arrowed) and disconnect the hose

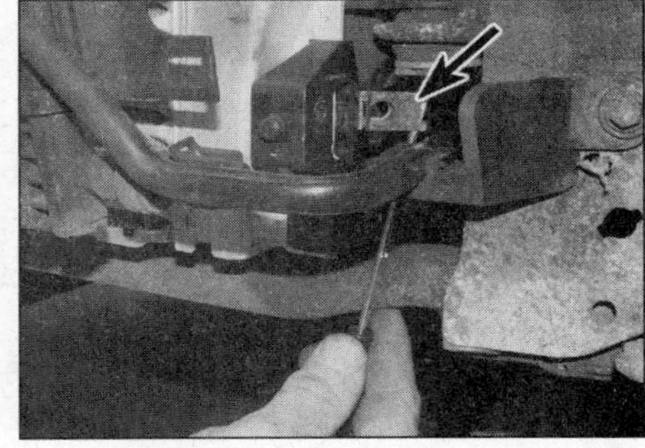

3.12b Release the securing clip (arrowed) . . .

3.12c . . . and withdraw the intercooler from the radiator

3.13a Release the R clips . . .

3.13b . . . then lift and remove the radiator

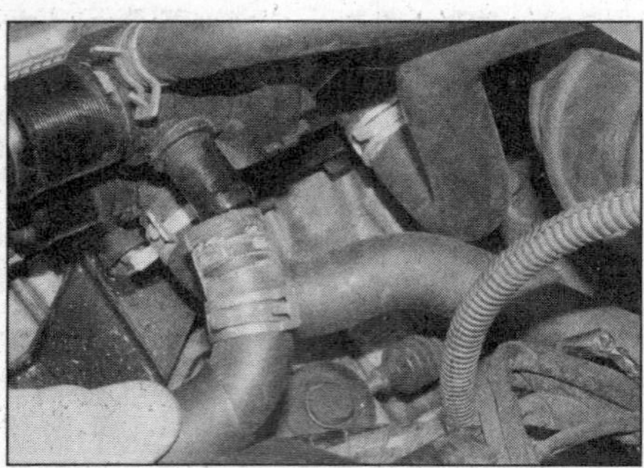
4.5 Removing the hoses from coolant/ thermostat housing – 2.2 diesel shown

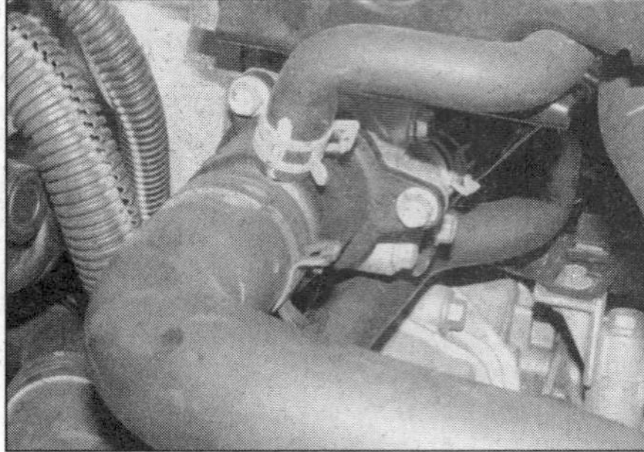
4.6a Thermostat housing on petrol engines . . .

4.6b . . . and removing the housing on 1.9 diesel engine

Refitting

19 Refitting is a reversal of removal, bearing in mind the following points:

a) *Take care not to damage the radiator fins (nor the condenser/intercooler, where applicable) during refitting.*
b) *Refit the front bumper (see Chapter 11).*
c) *Refit the headlights (see Chapter 12).*
d) *On completion, refill the cooling system as described in Chapter 1A or 1B.*

4 Thermostat – removal, testing and refitting

Note: *On some engine types, the thermostat is part of the coolant housing and cannot be removed separately. The complete coolant housing/thermostat will need to be renewed as a unit.*

4.7 Removing the thermostat sealing ring – 2.2 diesel shown

Removal

1 The thermostat is located in a housing bolted to the left-hand side of the cylinder head above the transmission on all engines.
2 Where applicable to improve access, remove the air cleaner assembly as described in Chapter 4A or 4B.
3 Partially drain the cooling system to below the level of the thermostat housing, as described in Chapter 1A or 1B.
4 Where necessary, release any relevant wiring and hoses from the retaining clips, and position clear of the thermostat housing to improve access.
5 Disconnect the coolant hose(s) from the thermostat housing cover **(see illustration)**.
6 Unscrew the securing bolts/nuts, and carefully withdraw the thermostat housing cover, along with the thermostat **(see illustrations)**.
7 Note the fitted position of the thermostat, then (where applicable) lift it from the cover/housing, and recover the sealing ring/gasket **(see illustration)**.

Testing

8 A rough test of the thermostat may be made by suspending it with a piece of string in a container full of water. Heat the water to bring it to the boil – the thermostat must open by the time the water boils. If not, renew it.
9 If a thermometer is available, the precise opening temperature of the thermostat may be determined; compare with the figures given in the Specifications. The opening temperature is also marked on the thermostat.
10 A thermostat that fails to close, as the cooling system gets cooler must also be renewed.

Refitting

11 Refitting is a reversal of removal, bearing in mind the following points:

a) *Examine the sealing ring/gasket for signs of damage or deterioration, and if necessary, renew.*
b) *Where applicable, ensure that the thermostat is fitted the correct way round, with the spring facing into the housing.*
c) *On completion, refill the cooling system as described in Chapter 1A or 1B.*

5 Radiator cooling fan – removal and refitting

Removal

1 Disconnect the battery negative terminal (refer to *Disconnecting the battery* in the Reference Section of this manual).
2 The cooling fan is attached to the rear of the radiator. Depending on engine type, it may be possible to unclip the fan from the radiator and manoeuvre it out from the engine bay. If necessary remove the radiator as described in Section 3, to gain better access to the fan assembly.
3 Disconnect the wiring plug(s) from the fan motor and resistor/relay (where fitted), and unclip the wiring from the shroud **(see illustration)**.
4 Release the retaining clips at either side of the shroud and lift the fan assembly to withdraw it from the radiator **(see illustration)**.

5.3 Disconnect the wiring plug from the cooling fan

5.4a Release the securing clip (arrowed) . . .

5.4b . . . and withdraw the fan/shroud from the radiator

5 If required, the fan motor can then be unbolted and removed from the plastic fan shroud **(see illustration).**

Refitting

6 Refit by reversing the removal operations.

6 Cooling system electrical switches - testing, removal and refitting

Radiator cooling fan switch

General information

1 The operation of the radiator fan is controlled by the fuel injection ECU. On models with air conditioning, the fan has a slow- and high-speed setting, controlled when the air conditioning is switched on. **Note:** *If there is a fault on the slow-speed circuit, the fan will run at the high-speed setting.*

a) Slow speed – if the coolant temperature is greater than 99°C, the fan will operate at its slow speed. When the coolant temperature is lower than 96°C, the fan stops operating.

b) High speed – if the coolant temperature is greater than 102°C, the fan will operate at its high speed. When the coolant temperature is lower than 99°C, the fan stops operating.

c) The coolant temperature warning light will illuminate if the temperature is greater than 114°C. When the coolant temperature drops below 111°C, the light will go out.

Radiator cooling fan resistor/relay

Removal and refitting

2 The resistor/relay is located in the shroud around the cooling fan; disconnect the wiring connector, release the retaining clip and remove the resistor/relay from the shroud **(see illustration).**

Coolant temperature sender

General information

3 The temperature sender is located in the thermostat housing at the left-hand of the cylinder head **(see illustrations).**

4 The temperature gauge is fed with a stabilised voltage from the instrument panel feed (via the ignition switch and a fuse). The sender controls the gauge earth. The sender contains a thermistor – an electronic component whose electrical resistance decreases at a predetermined rate as its temperature rises. When the coolant is cold, the sender resistance is high, current flow through the gauge is reduced, and the gauge needle points towards the blue (cold) end of the scale. As the coolant temperature rises and the sender resistance falls, current flow increases, and the gauge needle moves towards the upper end of the scale. If the sender is faulty, it must be renewed.

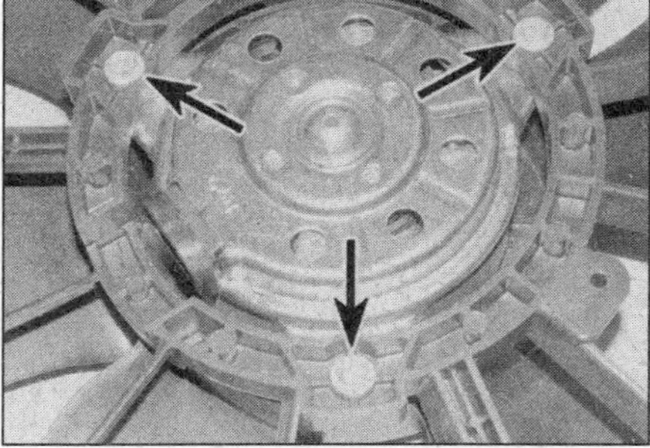

5.5 Undo the retaining bolts (arrowed)

5 On models with a temperature warning light, the light is fed with a voltage from the instrument panel. The sender controls the light earth. The sender is effectively a switch, which operates at a predetermined temperature to earth the light and complete the circuit. If the light is fitted in addition to a gauge, the senders for the gauge and light are incorporated in a single unit, with two wires, one each for the light and gauge earths.

Testing

6 If the gauge develops a fault, first check the other instruments; if they do not work at all, check the instrument panel electrical feed. If the readings are erratic, there may be a fault in the voltage stabiliser, which will necessitate renewal of the stabiliser (the stabiliser is integral with the instrument panel printed circuit board – see Chapter 12). If the fault lies in the temperature gauge alone, check it as follows.

7 If the gauge needle remains at the cold end of the scale when the engine is hot, disconnect the sender wiring plug, and earth the relevant wire to the engine. If the needle then deflects when the ignition is switched on, the sender unit is proved faulty, and should be renewed. If the needle still does not move, remove the instrument panel (Chapter 12) and check the continuity of the wire between the sender unit and the gauge, and the feed to the gauge unit. If continuity is shown, and the fault still exists, then the gauge is faulty, and the gauge unit should be renewed.

8 If the gauge needle remains at the hot end of the scale when the engine is cold, disconnect the sender wire. If the needle then returns to the cold end of the scale when the ignition is switched on, the sender unit is proved faulty, and should be renewed. If the needle still does not move, check the remainder of the circuit as described previously.

9 The same basic principles apply to testing the warning light. The light should illuminate when the relevant sender wire is earthed.

Removal and refitting

10 Partially drain the cooling system to below the level of the thermostat housing, as described in Chapter 1A or 1B.

11 Disconnect the wiring connector, then (depending on model) either release the securing clip and withdraw the temperature sensor from the coolant housing, or unscrew it from the housing to remove **(see illustrations).**

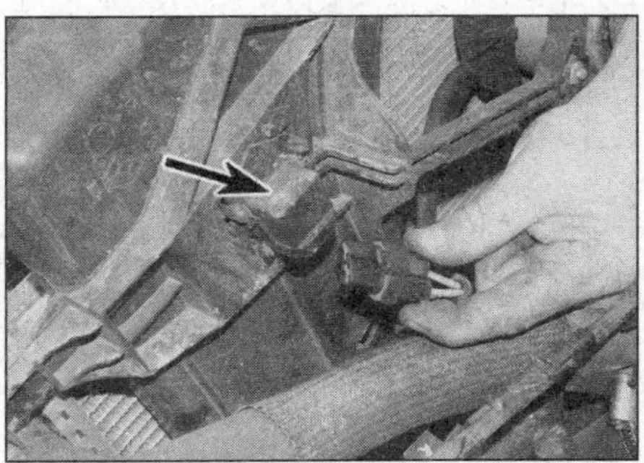

6.2 Disconnect the wiring plug from the resistor/relay (arrowed)

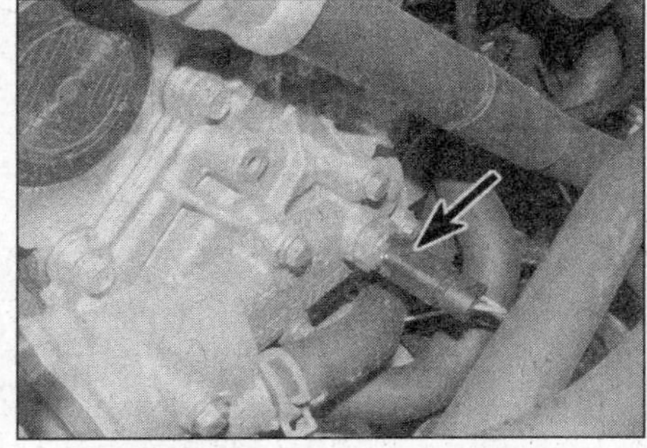

6.3a Temperature sender unit (arrowed) – 1.6 litre petrol engine

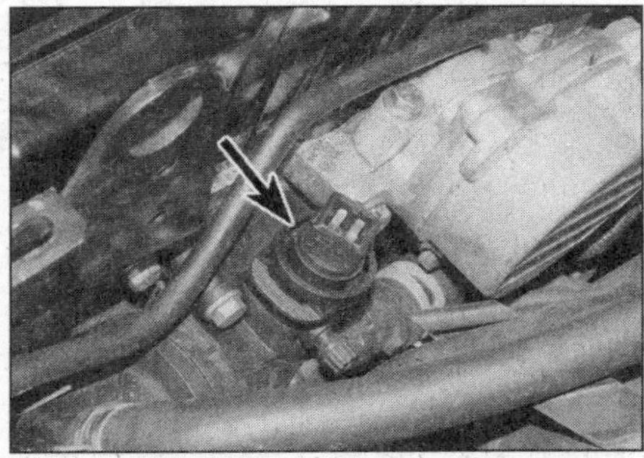

6.3b Temperature sender unit (arrowed) – 2.2 litre diesel engine

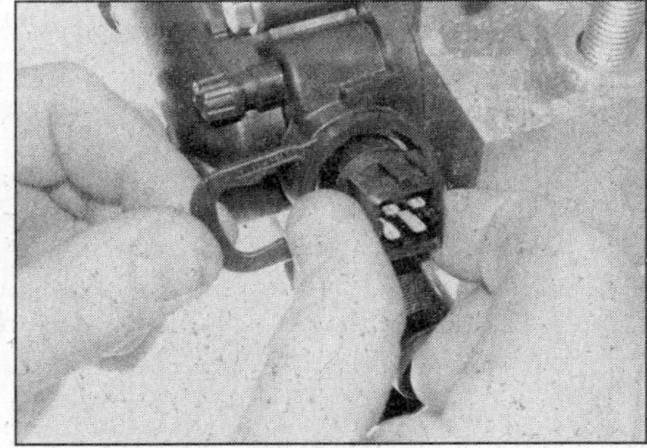

6.11a Unclip the temperature sender . . .

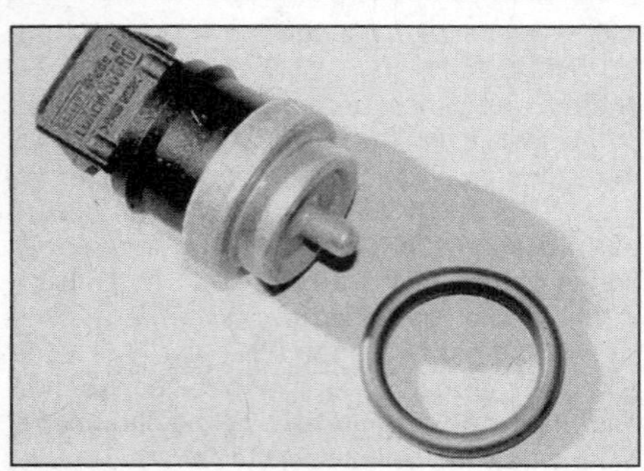

6.11b . . . and fit a new sealing ring – diesel shown

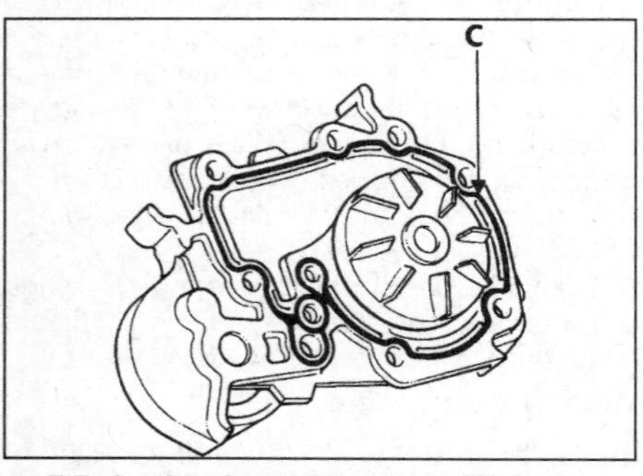

7.7 Apply a bead of sealant (C) to the coolant pump mating face

12 Refit the temperature sensor into the coolant housing using a reversal of the removal procedure. Make sure it is either securely held by the clip, or screwed in tightly enough to prevent leaks.

13 Top-up or refill the cooling system, with reference to *Weekly checks,* Chapter 1A or 1B.

Coolant temperature sensors – fuel system

14 Various sensors may be fitted to both petrol and diesel engines, depending on engine type. Refer to the relevant part of Chapter 4 for details of the sensor locations and function. Removal and refitting is as described previously in this Section, paragraphs 10 to 13.

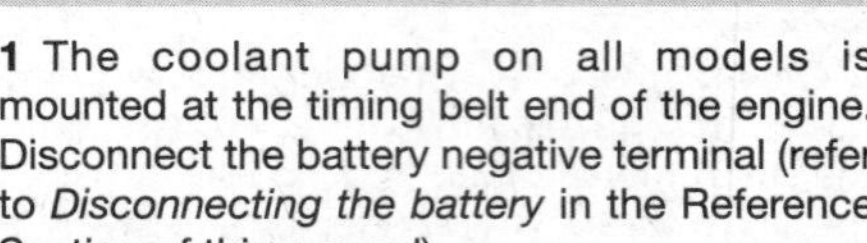

7 Coolant pump – removal and refitting

1 The coolant pump on all models is mounted at the timing belt end of the engine. Disconnect the battery negative terminal (refer to *Disconnecting the battery* in the Reference Section of this manual).

2 Drain the cooling system as described in Chapter 1A or 1B.

1.6 litre petrol engine

Note: *A tube of Loctite 518 sealant will be required on refitting.*

3 Remove the timing belt and timing belt tensioner as described in Chapter 2A.

4 Working in the **reverse** of the tightening sequence shown in illustration 7.9, undo the eight coolant pump retaining bolts, noting the locations of the different size bolts.

5 Withdraw the pump from the block, tapping it with a soft-faced mallet if it is stuck.

6 Commence refitting by thoroughly cleaning the mating faces of the pump and the cylinder block, ensuring that all traces of sealant are removed.

7 Apply a 0.6 to 1.0 mm wide band of Loctite 518 sealant to the pump mating face **(see illustration)**.

8 Locate the pump in position and refit the retaining bolts to their correct locations. Note that a suitable thread sealant should be applied to the threads of bolts 1 and 4.

9 Working in the sequence shown tighten all the bolts to the specified Stage 1 torque setting **(see illustration)**. Again working in sequence tighten the M6 bolts to the torque setting given for Stage 2, then tighten the M8 bolts to the setting given for Stage 3.

10 Refit the timing belt tensioner and timing belt as described in Chapter 2A, it is recommended that a new belt is fitted

11 On completion, refill the cooling system as described in Chapter 1A.

1.8 and 2.0 litre petrol engine and 1.9 litre diesel engine

Timing belt driven coolant pump

Note: *A new seal/gasket will be required on refitting.*

12 Remove the auxiliary drivebelt as described in Chapter 1A or 1B.

13 Remove the timing belt as described in Chapter 2A or 2B.

14 Working in the **reverse** of the tightening sequence shown **(see illustration)**, unscrew the bolts securing the pump to the cylinder block, and withdraw the pump from the block. If the pump is stuck, tap it using a soft-faced mallet. Recover the gasket/seal and discard it; a new one must be used on refitting.

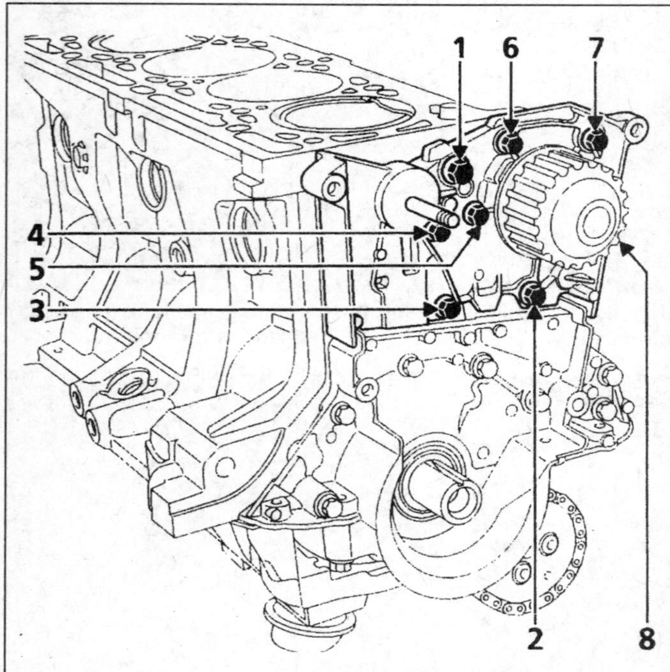

7.9 Coolant pump retaining bolt tightening sequence

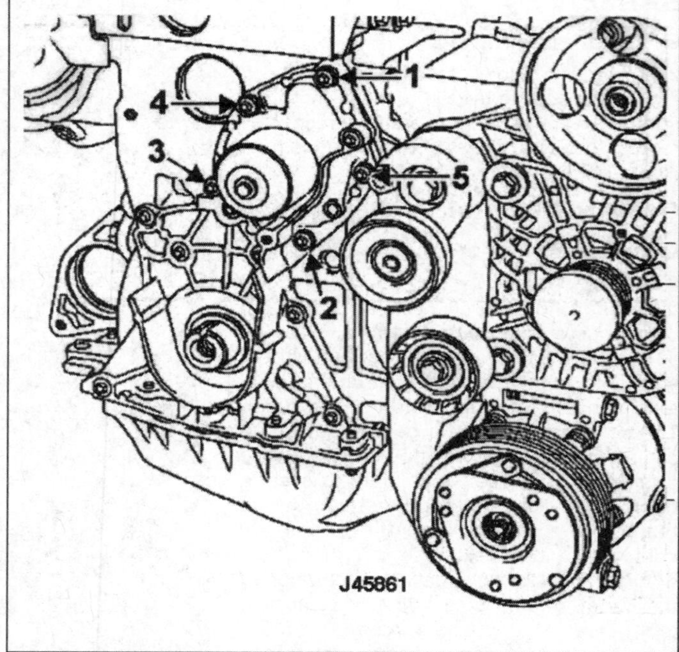

7.14 Coolant pump retaining bolt tightening sequence

7.34 Removing the engine mounting

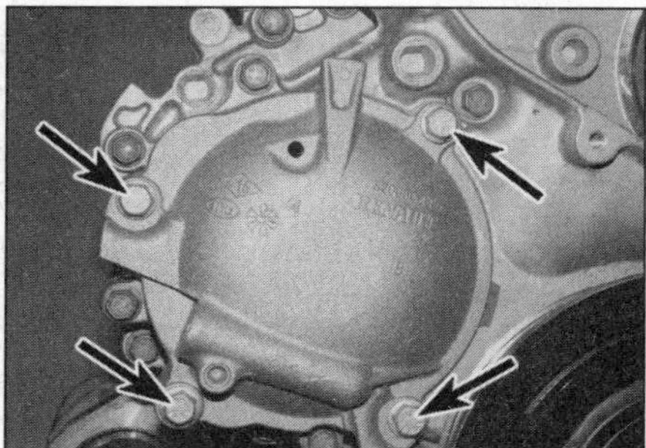
7.35 Undo the four retaining bolts (arrowed)

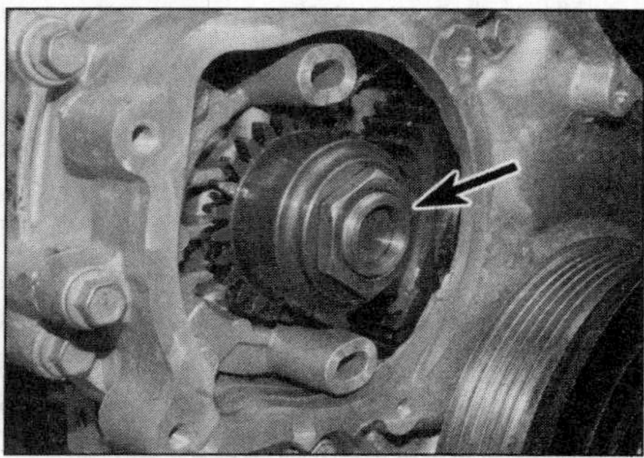
7.36 Remove the sprocket retaining nut – arrowed

15 Commence refitting by thoroughly cleaning the mating faces of the pump and the cylinder block, then fitting a new gasket/seal.

16 Locate the pump in position and refit the retaining bolts to their correct locations. Note that a suitable thread sealant should be applied to the threads of bolts 1, 3 and 4 **(see illustration 7.14)**.

17 Working in the sequence shown in illustration 7.14 tighten all the bolts to the specified torque setting.

18 Refit the timing belt as described in Chapter 2A or 2B, it is recommended that a new belt is fitted

19 On completion, refill the cooling system as described in Chapter 1A or 1B.

Auxiliary belt driven coolant pump

Note: *A new seal/gasket will be required on refitting.*

20 Slacken the three coolant pump pulley securing bolts by one full turn, do not remove at this point.

21 Remove the auxiliary drivebelt as described in Chapter 1B.

22 Undo the retaining bolts and remove the auxiliary belt automatic tensioner from the mounting bracket.

23 The three coolant pump pulley bolts can now be removed, and the pulley withdrawn from the pump.

24 Unscrew the bolts securing the pump to the cylinder block, and withdraw the pump from the block. If the pump is stuck, tap it using a soft-faced mallet. Recover the gasket/seal and discard it; a new one must be used on refitting.

25 Commence refitting by thoroughly cleaning the mating faces of the pump and the cylinder block, then fitting a new gasket/seal.

26 Locate the pump in position and refit the retaining bolts to their correct locations. Tighten all the bolts to the specified torque setting.

27 Refit the coolant pump pulley and tighten the retaining bolts to the specified torque setting.

28 Refit the auxiliary belt automatic tensioner and tighten the retaining bolts to the specified torque setting

29 Refit the auxiliary belt as described in Chapter 1B, it is recommended that a new belt is fitted.

30 On completion, refill the cooling system as described in Chapter 1B.

2.2 litre diesel engine

Note: *A new gasket and seal will be required on refitting.*

31 Apply the handbrake, and then jack up the front of the car and support it on axle stands (see *Jacking and vehicle support*). Remove the right-hand roadwheel.

32 Undo the retaining screws and remove the engine undertray and the plastic covers from within the right-hand wheel arch, to gain access to the engine.

33 Place a jack beneath the engine, with a block of wood on the jack head. Raise the jack until it is supporting the weight of the engine. Alternatively, attach and support bar to the engine and use the bar to support the weight of the engine/transmission.

34 Slacken and remove the retaining nut and bolts and remove the upper right-hand engine mounting bracket **(see illustration)**.

35 Lower the engine slightly to gain access to the coolant pump cover bolts, slacken the retaining bolts and remove the cover **(see illustration)**. Remove gasket, a new one will be required for refitting.

36 Slacken and remove the coolant pump sprocket retaining nut **(see illustration)**.

37 A puller will be required to remove the sprocket, fit the puller to the sprocket and withdraw it from the coolant pump shaft **(see illustrations)**.

38 Unscrew the securing bolts, and withdraw the coolant pump from the cylinder block **(see illustrations)**.

39 Commence refitting by thoroughly cleaning the mating faces of the pump and block.

40 Fit a new seal in position on the pump, then refit the pump and securely tighten the bolts **(see illustration)**.

7.37a Using a puller to release the sprocket . . .

7.37b . . . and then remove it from the pump

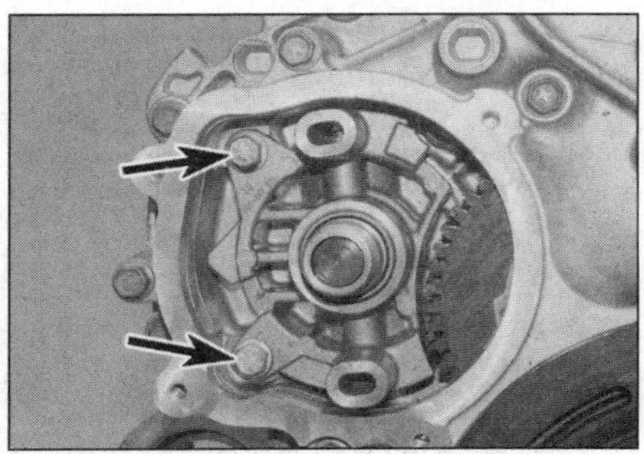
7.38a Undo the two retaining bolts (arrowed) . . .

7.38b . . . and remove the coolant pump from the housing

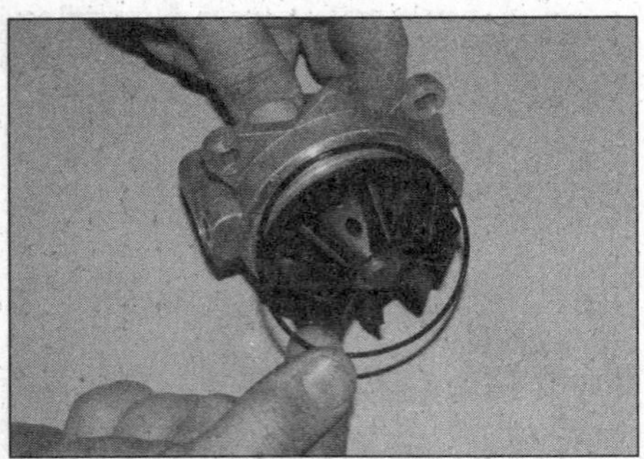
7.40 Fitting a new seal to the coolant pump

Warning: Make sure the coolant pump is sealed correctly and there is no coolant leak. If the pump does leak coolant, it will escape into the engine oil.

41 Refit the coolant pump sprocket and tighten retaining nut to the specified torque setting.

42 Refit the coolant pump cover and tighten retaining nut to the specified torque setting. Renew gasket.

43 Refit the right-hand engine mounting with reference to Chapter 2C.

44 Refit the undertray and the protective covers from inside the wheel arch, then fit the roadwheel.

45 Remove the jack/engine support bar (as applicable).

46 Lower the vehicle to the ground and tighten the wheel bolts to the specified torque. Reconnect the battery.

47 On completion, refill the cooling system as described in Chapter 1B. Check and top-up engine oil as required.

8 Heating and ventilation system – general information

The heating/ventilation system consists of a four-speed blower motor (housed behind the facia), a control unit mounted in the facia, face level vents in the centre and at each end of the facia, and air ducts to the front and rear footwells.

The facia-mounted controls operate flap valves to deflect and mix the air flowing through the various parts of the heating/ventilation system. The flap valves are contained in the air distribution housing, which acts as a central distribution unit, passing air to the various ducts and vents.

Cold air enters the system through the grille at the top of the engine compartment scuttle. If required, the airflow is boosted by the blower motor, and then flows through the various ducts, according to the settings of the controls. Stale air is expelled via the vents in the rear of the vehicle. If warm air is required, the cold air is passed over the heater matrix, which is heated by the engine coolant. A recirculation position button on the blower motor switch enables the outside air supply to be closed off, while the air inside the vehicle is recirculated. This can be useful to prevent unpleasant odours entering from outside the vehicle, but should only be used briefly, as the recirculated air inside the vehicle will soon become stale.

Models with manual air conditioning have a conventional heater/ventilation control unit, with a button that is used to switch on the air conditioning or, on higher specification models, a fully-electronic automatic air conditioning is fitted, with an electronic control panel. Further details of the air conditioning system can be found in Section 10.

9 Heating and ventilation system components – removal and refitting

Conventional control unit

1 Remove the Renault card reader panel, by unclipping it and withdrawing it from the facia.

2 Unclip the control panel cover from the facia panel.

3 Remove the two securing screws from the bottom of the control panel, lift the control panel and twist it backwards, then withdraw it from the facia.

4 Working at the rear of the control panel, disconnect the control cables, and the wiring plug(s), noting their locations, then remove the control unit.

5 Refitting is a reversal of removal, but before reconnecting the cables, position the air distribution unit flaps against their stops, and position the heater/ventilation control knobs at their anti-clockwise stops. Check the operation of the heater controls before refitting the control unit securing screws.

Electronic control unit

6 Remove the Renault card reader panel, by unclipping it and withdrawing it from the facia **(see illustration).**

7 Unclip the heater control panel from the facia and disconnect the wiring plugs from the rear of the unit **(see illustrations)**. Once the wiring plugs have been disconnected, the unit can be removed.

Heater/ventilation control cables

8 Remove the heater/ventilation control unit as described previously in this Section.

9 Unclip both trims from each side of the centre console in the front passenger footwells **(see illustration)**.

10 Working from the driver's side, undo the retaining bolts and remove the side protection plate from the air distribution unit **(see illustration)**.

11 Disconnect the end of the relevant cable from the lever on the air distribution unit, then withdraw the cable, noting its routing to aid refitting.

12 Refitting is a reversal of removal, bearing in mind the following points.

a) *Before refitting the cables, position the air distribution unit flaps against their stops,*

9.6 Withdraw the card reader from the facia

9.7a Remove the control panel from the facia . . .

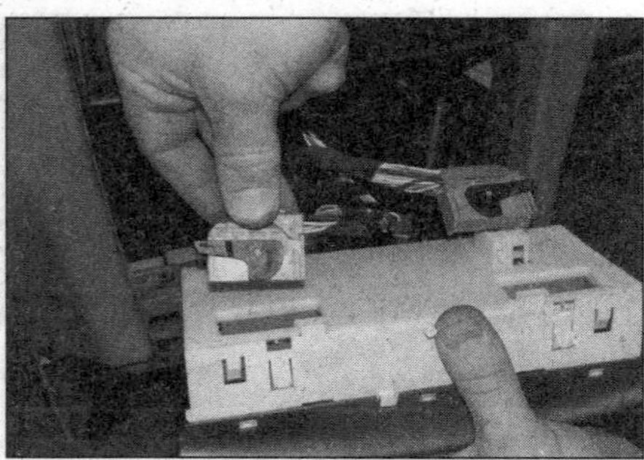
9.7b . . . and disconnect the wiring connectors

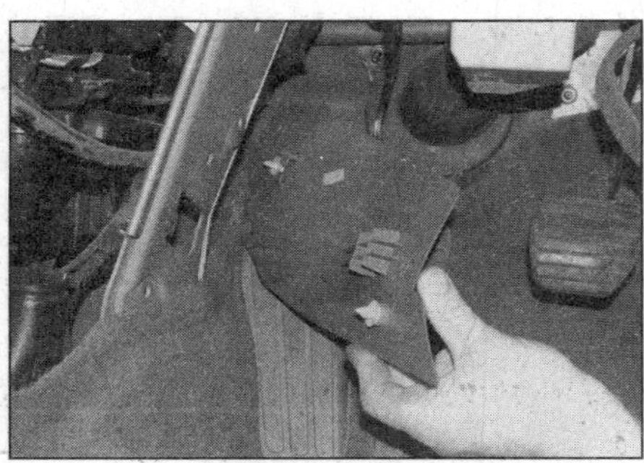
9.9 Unclip the trim panels from the footwell

and position the heater/ventilation control knobs at their anti-clockwise stops.
b) Route the cable(s) as noted before removal.
c) Check the operation of the heater controls before refitting the control unit securing screws.

Heater matrix

13 Drain the cooling system as described in the relevant part of Chapter 1.

14 Remove the facia panel as described in Chapter 11.

15 Unclip the footwell air vent ducts from the air distribution housing **(see illustration)**.

16 Undo the mounting bolts/nuts and remove the protection plate from the driver's side of the air distribution housing **(see illustration)**. Release the wiring clip from the protection plate.

17 Unclip the wiring harness retaining clip from the passenger side of the air distribution housing **(see illustration)**.

18 Working under the air distribution housing, remove the four bolts that hold the lower housing onto the heater unit and withdraw it from the passenger footwell **(see illustrations)**.

19 Insert a small screwdriver into the locking collar and twist it to release the locking collars from the two coolant pipes **(see illustrations)**.

20 Release the two coolant pipes from the heater matrix; a container will be required to catch any coolant which is still in the heater system **(see illustration)**. New seals will be required when refitting.

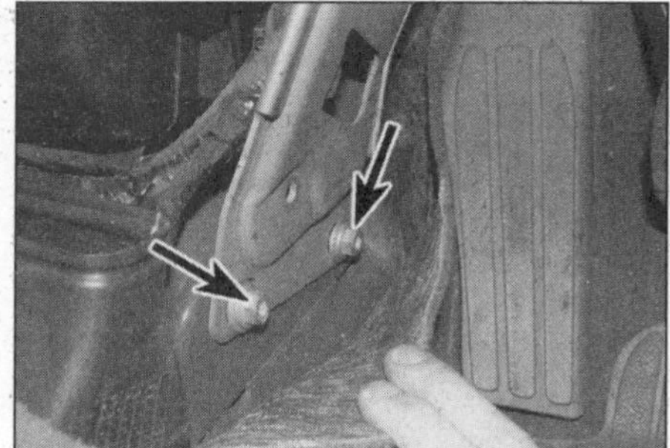

9.10 Undo the two lower bolts (arrowed)

9.15 Unclip the air ducting from the housing

9.16 Remove the protection plate from the driver's side

9.17 Release the wiring clips from the housing

21 Carefully manipulate the heater matrix from under the air distribution housing, and then withdraw the matrix, taking care not to spill any remaining coolant inside the vehicle **(see illustration)**.

22 Refitting is a reversal of removal, bearing in mind the following points.

a) Ensure that the foam insulation strips are in place when fitting the matrix to the air distribution unit.

9.18a Undo the retaining bolts . . .

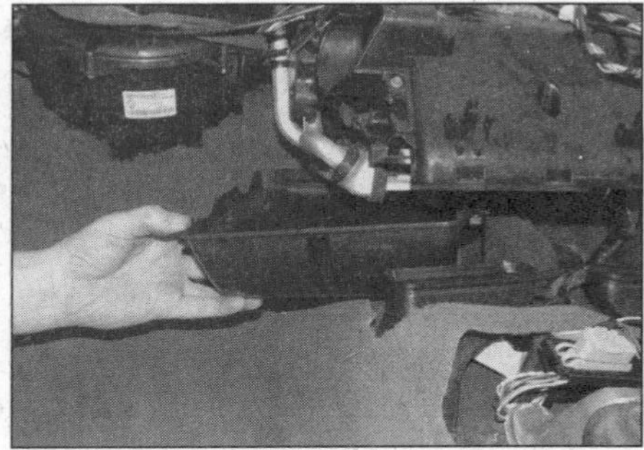

9.18b . . . and withdraw the lower housing

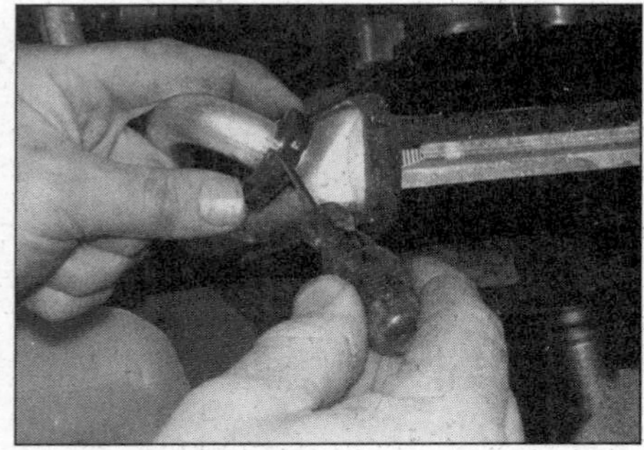

9.19a Release the securing clip . . .

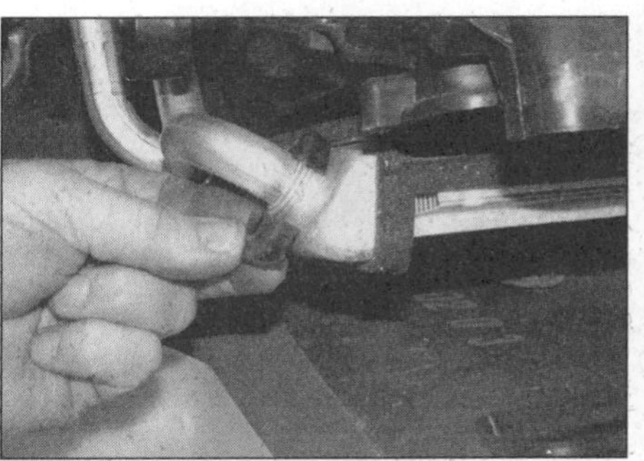

9.19b . . . and remove the locking collar

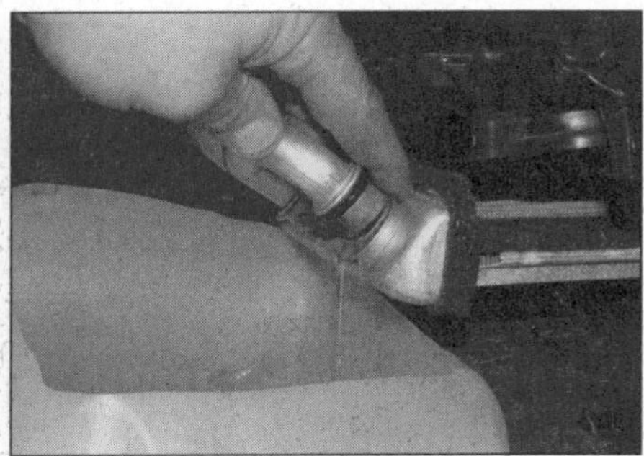

9.20 Catching the excess coolant in a container

9.21 Withdrawing the heater matrix from the housing

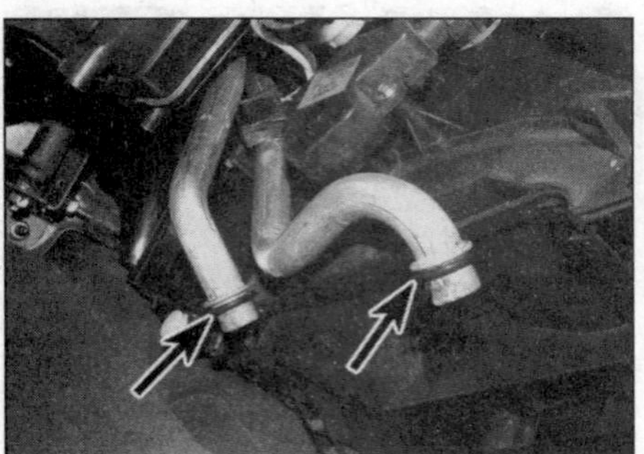
9.22 Fit new seals (arrowed) to the coolant pipes

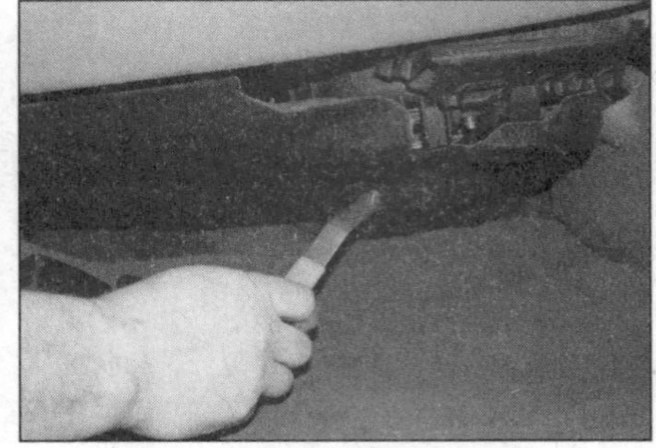
9.24a Release the retaining clip . . .

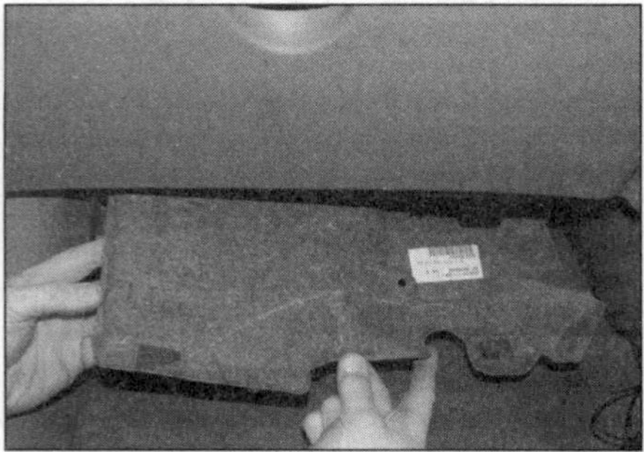
9.24b . . . and remove the lower trim panel

b) Make sure new seals are fitted to the coolant pipes ***(see illustration).***
c) Refit the facia panel as described in Chapter 11.
d) On completion, refill the cooling system as described in the relevant part of Chapter 1.

Heater blower motor

23 Disconnect the battery negative terminal (refer to *Disconnecting the battery* in the Reference Section of this manual).
24 Working inside the passenger compartment, remove the passenger's side lower soundproofing trim from under the facia panel **(see illustrations)**.
25 Disconnect the wiring block connector and unclip the wiring loom from the heater blower assembly **(see illustration).**
26 Undo the retaining bolt, twist the motor cover clockwise, and then lower the motor/cover assembly from the air distribution unit. Disconnect the heater motor wiring connector **(see illustrations)**.
27 Refitting is a reversal of removal.

Heater blower motor resistor

28 Disconnect the battery negative terminal (refer to *Disconnecting the battery* in the Reference Section of this manual).
29 The resistor is located in the blower motor housing; remove the heater blower motor as described previously.
30 Undo the two retaining bolts and remove the resistor from the heater housing **(see illustrations)**.
31 Refitting is a reversal of removal.

10 Air conditioning system – general information and precautions

General information

An air conditioning system is available on some models. It enables the temperature of incoming air to be lowered; it also dehumidifies the air, which makes for rapid demisting and increased comfort. Two types of air conditioning are fitted – manual and automatic (climate control).

The cooling side of the system works in the same way as a domestic refrigerator. Refrigerant gas is drawn into a belt-driven compressor, and passes into a condenser in front of the radiator, where it loses heat and

9.25 Disconnect the wiring connector

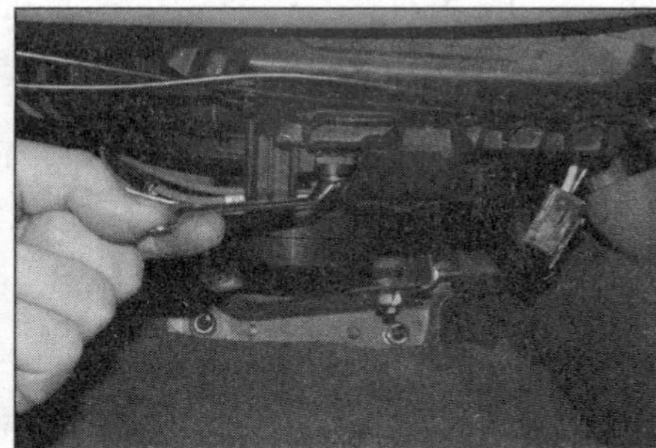
9.26a Undo the retaining bolts . . .

9.26b . . . and withdraw the blower motor

9.26c If required, disconnect the wiring connector

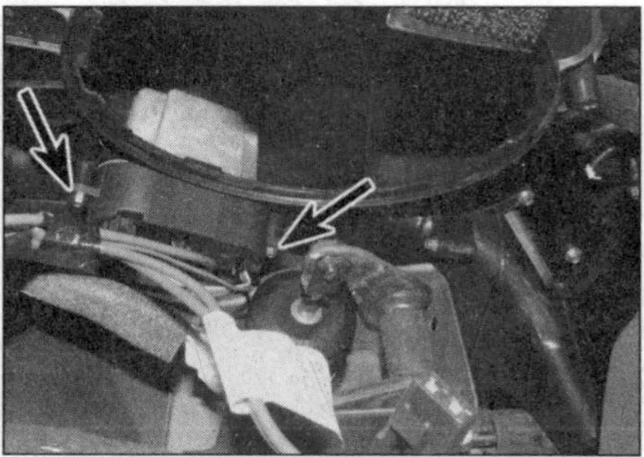
9.30a Undo the two retaining bolts (arrowed) . . .

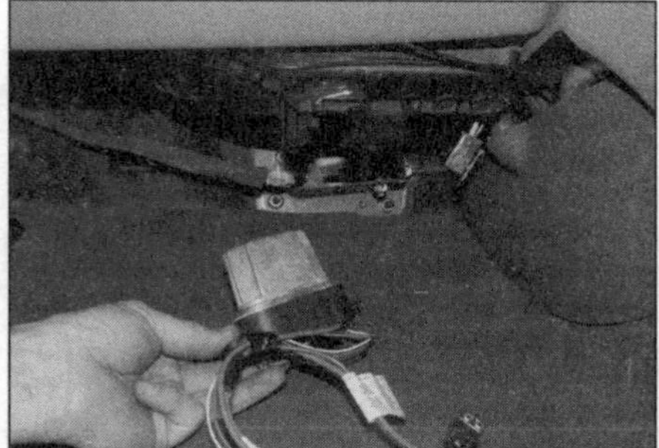
9.30b . . . and withdraw the resistor unit from the housing

becomes liquid. The liquid passes through an expansion valve to an evaporator, where it changes from liquid under high pressure to gas under low pressure. This change is accompanied by a drop in temperature, which cools the evaporator. The refrigerant returns to the compressor and the cycle begins again.

Air blown through the evaporator passes to the air distribution unit, where it is mixed with hot air blown through the heater matrix, to achieve the desired temperature in the passenger compartment. On models with climate control, an auxiliary electric heater is fitted, to provide 'instant' heat from cold, and to assist in maintaining the temperature that has been selected. Otherwise, the heating side of the system works in the same way as on models without air conditioning.

Precautions

Warning: The refrigerant is potentially dangerous, and should only be handled by qualified persons. If it is splashed onto the skin, it can cause frostbite. It is not itself poisonous, but in the presence of a naked flame (including a cigarette) it forms a poisonous gas.

Uncontrolled discharging of the refrigerant is dangerous, and damaging to the environment. It follows that a Renault dealer or an air conditioning specialist must only carry out any work on the air conditioning system that involves opening the refrigerant circuit.

Do not operate the air conditioning system if it is known to be short of refrigerant; the compressor may be damaged **(see Tool tip)**.

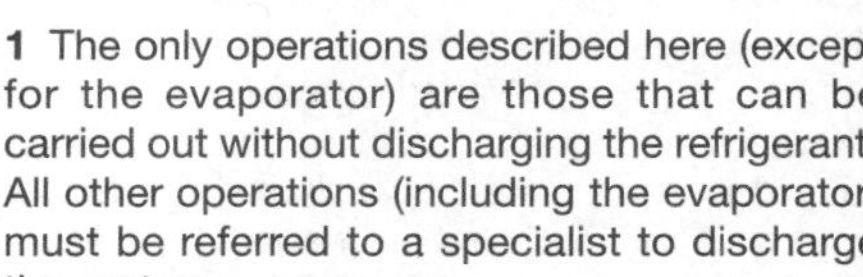

11 Air conditioning system components – removal and refitting

1 The only operations described here (except for the evaporator) are those that can be carried out without discharging the refrigerant. All other operations (including the evaporator) must be referred to a specialist to discharge the system.

Compressor

2 If necessary, the compressor can be unbolted and moved aside, without disconnecting its flexible hoses, after removing the drivebelt (see Chapter 1A or 1B) and disconnecting the wiring plug **(see illustrations)**.

Compressor drivebelt

3 Refer to the auxiliary drivebelt procedures in Chapter 1A or 1B.

Condenser

4 The condenser is fitted to the front of the radiator (or intercooler on turbo models). To remove the condenser follow the procedures as described in Section 3 for the removal and refitting of the radiator.

5 To remove the condenser completely requires that the system is discharged before unscrewing the unions, but with care, the condenser can be lifted from its clips on the radiator and moved aside without disturbing the unions.

6 Protect the condenser while removed by wrapping it in a piece of cardboard. Make sure the refrigerant pipes are not damaged or put under any strain when the condenser is moved to one side.

Pressure switch

Note: *The tri-function pressure switch is located in the bottom left-hand corner of the condenser* ***(see illustration)*** *to protect the refrigerant circuit. This can be removed without draining the system, as it is mounted on a 'Schrader' valve (automatic shut-off valve). Based on the pressure sensor information, the engine ECU controls the radiator cooling fan. The switch has a low pressure cut-off at 2 bars and a high pressure cut-off at 27 bars, this informs the injection computer of the pressure in the refrigerant circuit.*

7 Remove the front bumper for access to the sensor, as described in Chapter 11.

8 Disconnect the wiring connector from the sensor.

9 Slacken and remove the pressure sensor from the condenser.

10 Refitting is a reversal of removal. Check the condition of the sensor seal, and fit a new one if necessary.

Heating/ventilation control motors

Note: *On models with automatic air conditioning (climate control), electric motors are used instead of the cables used on basic models. Control cables are still used on models with manual air conditioning.*

11 Depending on model, there can be six control motors fitted to the air distribution housing.

1) Recirculation motor.
2) De-icing distribution motor.
3) Lower blown air distribution motor.
4) Right-hand mixing motor.
5) Left-hand mixing motor.
6) Air quality sensor.

TOOL TiP

Many car accessory shops sell one-shot air conditioning recharge aerosols. These generally contain refrigerant, compressor oil, leak sealer and system conditioner. Some also have a dye to help pinpoint leaks.

Warning: These products must only be used as directed by the manufacturer, and do not remove the need for regular maintenance.

11.2a Slacken and remove the lower mounting bolt (arrowed) . . .

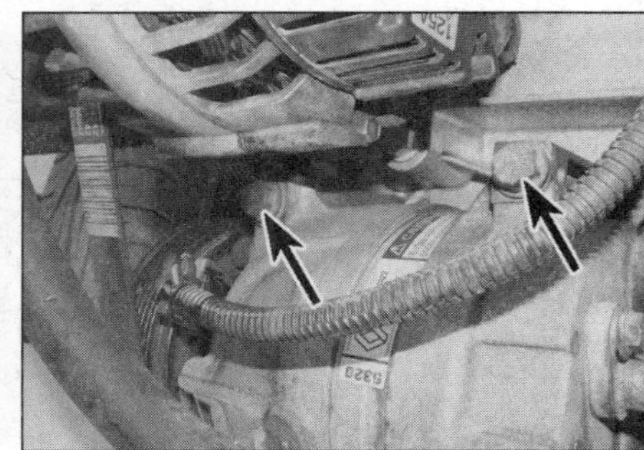

11.2b . . . the upper two mounting bolts (arrowed) . . .

11.2c . . . then cable-tie the compressor to the front crossmember

11.7 Pressure switch (arrowed) fitted to bottom of condenser

11.13a Left – air quality sensor. Right – recirculation motor

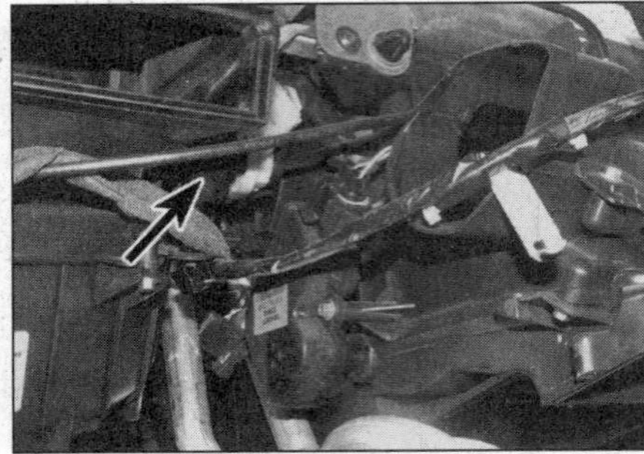

11.13b De-icing distribution motor (arrowed) – left-hand mixing motor below

11.13c Right-hand mixing motor

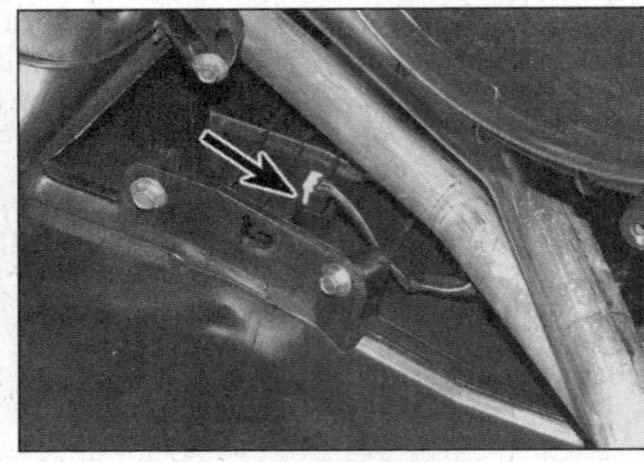

11.15 Evaporator sensor – arrowed

12 To access the motors the facia will need to be removed, as described in Chapter 11.

13 In each case, disconnect the wiring plug, then remove the two mounting bolts and withdraw the motor **(see illustrations).**

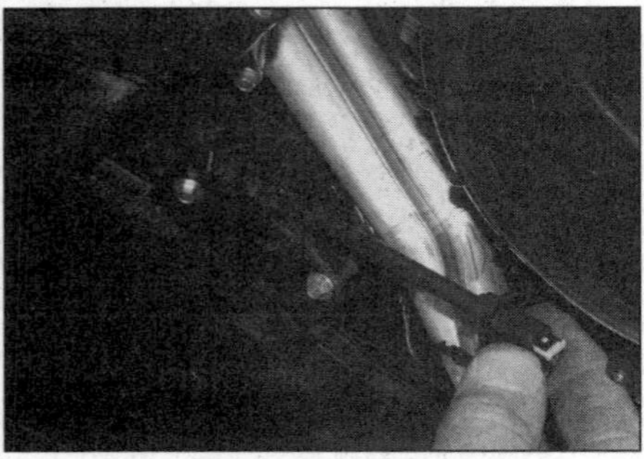

11.17 Turn and withdraw the evaporator sensor

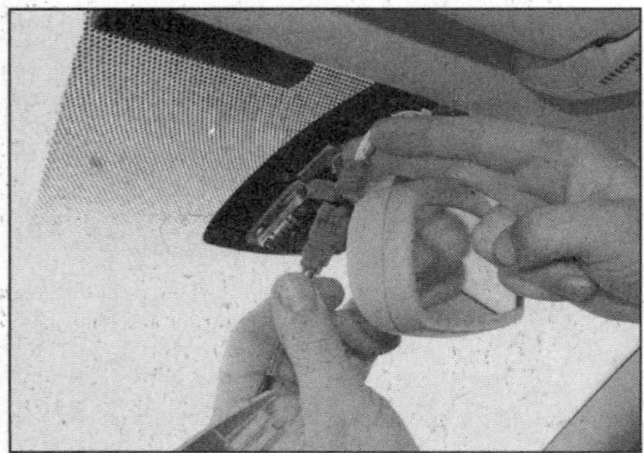

11.21a Disconnect the wiring connector . . .

14 Refitting is a reversal of removal. If nothing has been disturbed while the motor was removed, it should fit straight back on – however, if necessary, turn the heater flap spindle until the mark corresponds to that on the motor.

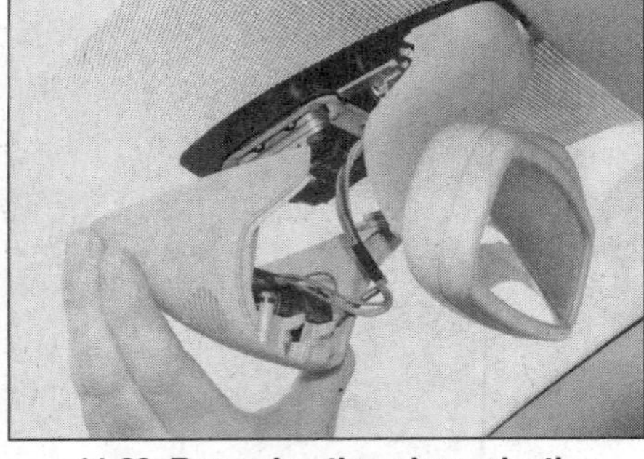

11.20 Removing the mirror plastic surround

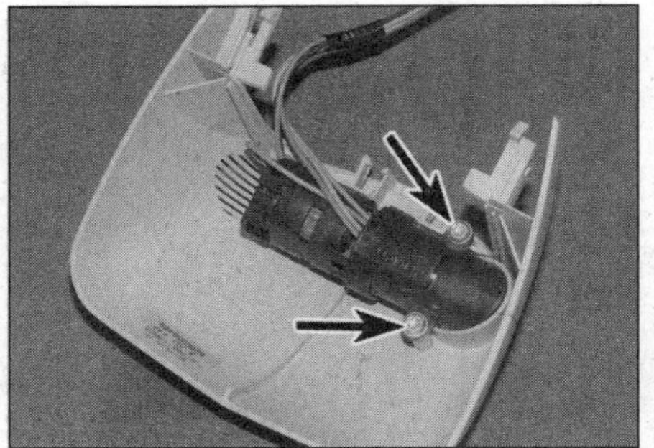

11.21b . . . and undo the two retaining screws – arrowed

Evaporator sensor

15 The sensor is located below the coolant pipes to the heater matrix on the left-hand side of the air distribution housing, behind the facia panel, it provides temperature information at the outlet of the evaporator **(see illustration)**.

16 Unclip the trim from the passenger footwell at the side of the centre console.

17 Disconnect the wiring connector, and then turn the sensor through 90° to remove it from the air distribution housing **(see illustration).**

18 Refitting is a reversal of removal.

Interior temperature/ humidity sensor

19 On models with automatic air conditioning (climate control), two sensors monitor the passenger compartment temperature and humidity, and whether the car is parked in strong sunlight, in order to maintain the selected temperature as closely as possible.

20 The sensor is located in front of the interior mirror. Using a small screwdriver, carefully prise off the mirror surround front section. Slide the mirror surround rear cover downwards to remove **(see illustration)**.

21 Disconnect the sensor wiring plug, then unscrew the two sensor mounting bolts and remove the sensor **(see illustrations)**.

22 Refitting is a reversal of removal.

Interior sun sensor

23 Using a small screwdriver, and taking care to protect the facia, prise up the sensor from the top of the facia panel **(see illustration)**.

24 Disconnect the wiring plug from the sensor as it is removed.

25 Refitting is a reversal of removal.

Exterior temperature sensor

26 The exterior temperature sensor is located in the right-hand exterior mirror **(see illustration)**.

27 Remove the mirror glass and the mirror front shell as described in Chapter 11.

28 Unclip the sensor from its mounting on the mirror body.

29 No wiring plug is provided, so the two sensor wires have to be cut to remove the sensor. When doing this, leave as much wire

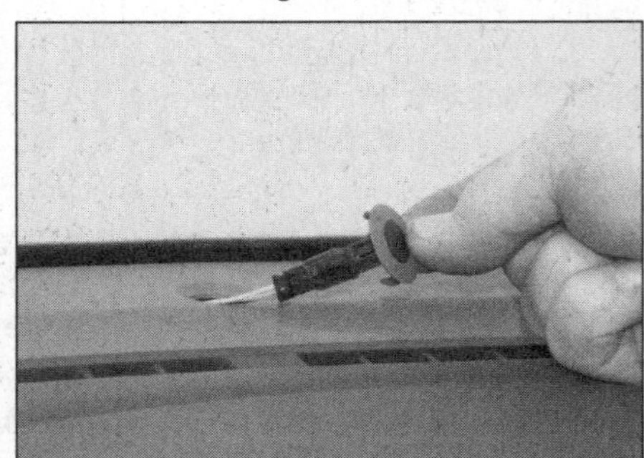

11.23 Prise the sensor from the top of the facia

11.26 Exterior temperature sensor – arrowed

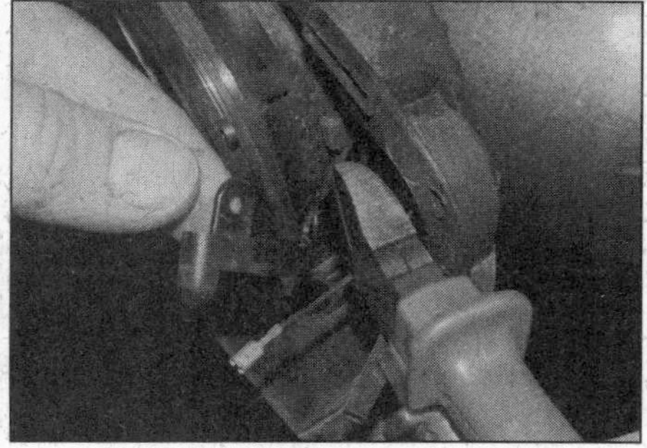
11.29 Cutting the sensor wiring

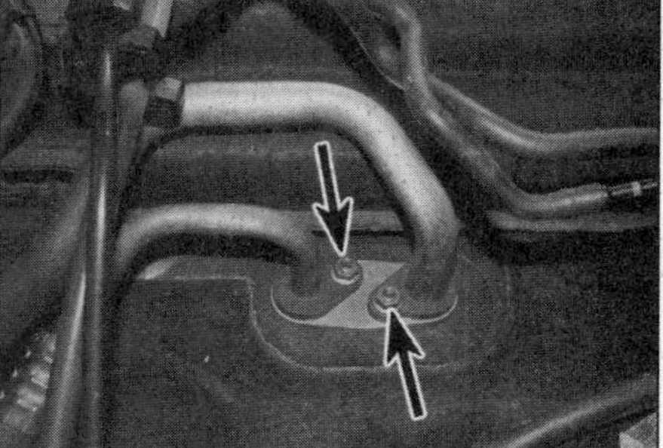
11.31a Undo the two retaining nuts (arrowed) . . .

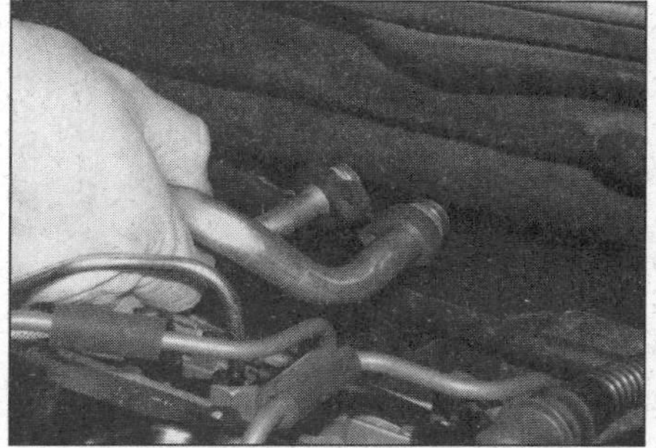
11.31b . . . and disconnect the air conditioning pipes

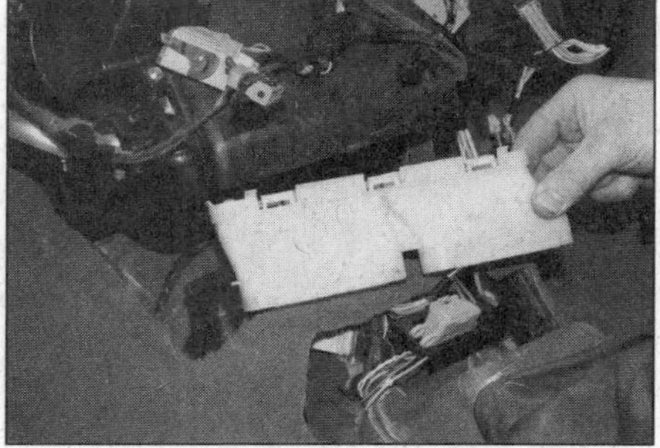
11.35 Unclip the air duct from the heater unit

11.36 Undo the retaining nuts (arrowed) and lower the steering column

as possible on the car, to make fitting the new sensor easier **(see illustration)**.

30 Refitting is a reversal of removal. Solder the new sensor wires to the old ones, observing the wire colour coding, and insulate the two joints with tape or heat-shrink tubing.

Evaporator

Warning: Do not attempt to open the refrigerant circuit yourself, refer to the precautions at the end of Section 10.

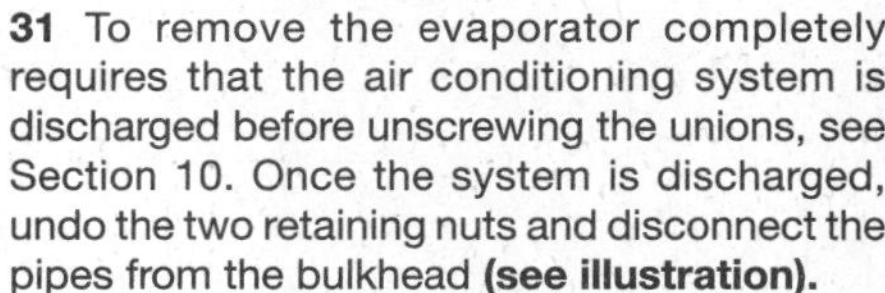

31 To remove the evaporator completely requires that the air conditioning system is discharged before unscrewing the unions, see Section 10. Once the system is discharged, undo the two retaining nuts and disconnect the pipes from the bulkhead **(see illustration).**

32 Drain the cooling system as described in the relevant part of Chapter 1.

33 Remove the facia panel as described in Chapter 11.

34 Undo the mounting bolts/nuts and remove the protection plate from the driver's side of the air distribution housing **(see illustration 9.16)**. Release the wiring clip from the protection plate.

35 Unclip the footwell air vent ducts from the air distribution housing **(see illustration).**

36 Undo the retaining nuts and disconnect the steering column from the crossmember **(see illustration)**, see Chapter 10 for further information.

37 Working your way along the crossmember you will need to disconnect any clips or screws, which will be securing other components and wiring loom to the crossmember. Make a note of the fitted position of these clips and screws for refitting **(see illustrations).**

38 Remove the plastic blanking plug from the right-hand front door pillar and undo the end mounting bolt from the crossmember **(see illustrations).** This bolt will not be able to be removed completely, unless the door hinge is removed. Slide the bolt out and leave it in place, take care not to shut the door while this bolt is left in this position.

11.37a Undo the retaining screws . . .

11.37b . . . and release the retaining clips

11.38a Remove the plastic blanking plug . . .

11.38b . . . and undo the mounting bolt

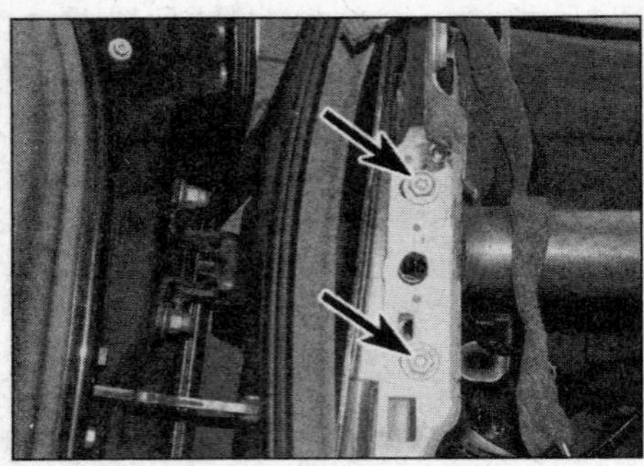
11.39a Undo the bolts (arrowed) from the left-hand side of the crossmember . . .

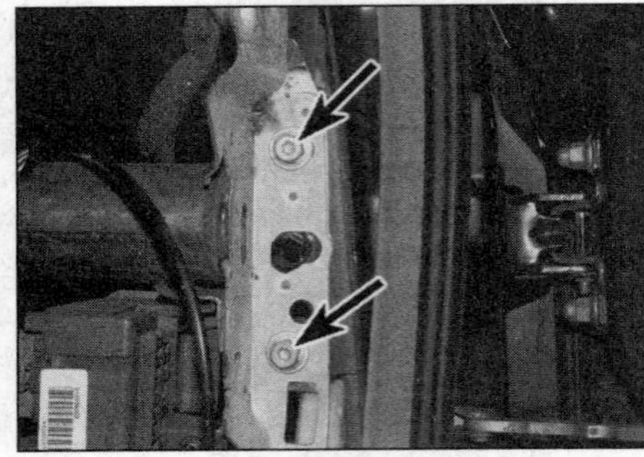
11.39b . . . and the bolts (arrowed) from the right-hand side

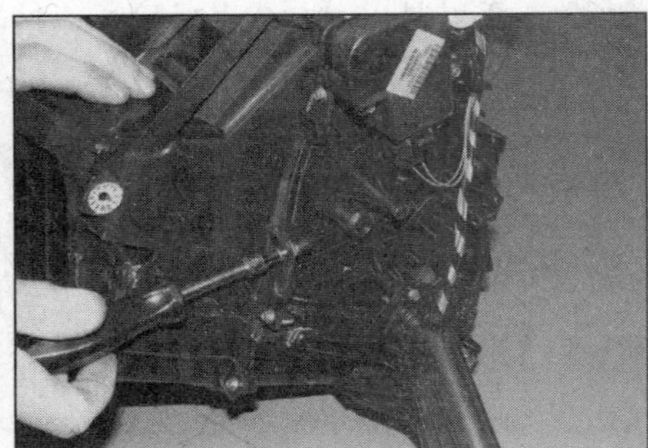
11.41a Undo the retaining bolts . . .

11.41b . . . split the housing . . .

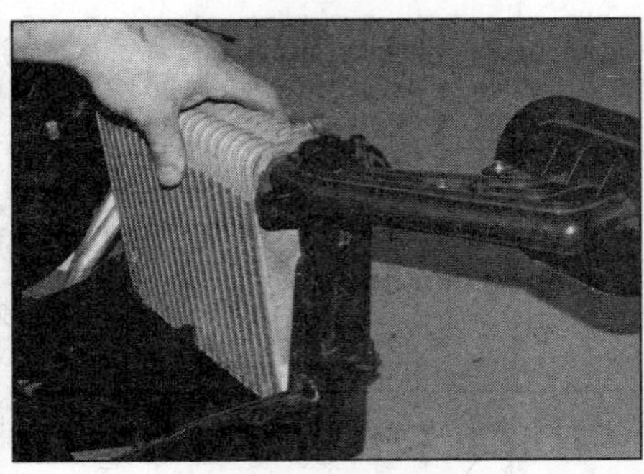
11.41c . . . and withdraw the evaporator

11.41d Note the locating peg – arrowed

39 Undo the retaining bolts from each side of the reinforcement crossmember and remove it from across the top of the air distribution housing **(see illustrations).**

40 Remove the air distribution housing from inside the vehicle, check for anything still connected to the housing as it is being removed.

41 Working your way around the housing, undo the retaining bolts and split the air distribution unit, then withdraw the evaporator from the housing **(see illustrations).**

42 Refitting is a reversal of removal.

Chapter 4 Part A:
Fuel/exhaust systems – petrol engine models

Contents

Degrees of difficulty

Easy, suitable for novice with little experience	**Fairly easy,** suitable for beginner with some experience	**Fairly difficult,** suitable for competent DIY mechanic	**Difficult,** suitable for experienced DIY mechanic	**Very difficult,** suitable for expert DIY or professional

Specifications

System type

Type	Sagem S2000 sequential multi-point injection

Fuel system data

Fuel pump type (including filter)	Electric, immersed in tank
Fuel pressure regulator control pressure	3.5 ± 0.06 bars
Fuel pump flow output (minimum)	80 to 120 litres/hour
Specified idle speed (not adjustable – controlled by ECU)	750 ± 50 rpm
Idle mixture CO content	less than 1.0 % (controlled by ECU)
Air temperature sensor resistance:	
At -10°C	9539 ± 915 ohms
At 25°C	2051 ± 123 ohms
Coolant temperature sensor resistance:	
At 25°C	2252 ± 112 ohms
At 80°C	280 ± 8 ohms
Crankshaft sensor	200 to 270 ohms at 23°C
Injector resistance	14.5 ± 0.7 ohms at 20°C
Throttle potentiometer:	
Voltage	5.0 volts
Resistance	1000 ± 250 ohms

Recommended fuel

Minimum octane rating	95 or 98 RON unleaded. Leaded fuel or LRP must **not** be used

Torque wrench settings

	Nm	lbf ft
Air filter intake housing to inlet manifold	10	7
Exhaust manifold bolts	18	13
Exhaust manifold heat shield bolts	10	7
Exhaust manifold strut bolt	8	6
Fuel rail mounting bolts	10	7
Fuel rail protector cover nut	25	18
Inlet manifold lower section bolts	21	15
Inlet manifold upper section bolts	10	7
Knock (pinking) sensor	30	22
Oxygen (lambda) sensor	45	33
Throttle housing bolts	10	7

1 General information and precautions

The fuel system consists of a fuel tank that is mounted under the rear of the car with an electric fuel pump and fuel filter immersed in it, and a fuel feed line leading to the fuel rail on the engine. A further line from the fuel tank leads to the charcoal canister located beneath the vehicle. Unlike earlier models, there is no return line to the fuel tank. The fuel pump supplies fuel to the fuel rail, which acts as a reservoir for the four fuel injectors that inject fuel into the inlet tracts. The fuel pressure regulator is located in the base of the fuel pump in the fuel tank.

The amount of fuel supplied by the injectors is precisely controlled by the Electronic Control Unit (ECU), located under the battery tray. The unit uses the signals from the crankshaft position sensor and the camshaft position sensor to trigger each injector separately in cylinder firing order (sequential injection), with benefits in terms of better fuel economy and leaner exhaust emissions.

The ECU is the heart of the entire engine management system controlling the fuel injection, ignition and emissions control systems. The module receives information from various sensors, which is then computed and compared with preset values stored in its memory, to determine the required period of injection.

A crankshaft position sensor generates information on crankshaft position and engine speed. The inductive head of the sensor runs just above the engine flywheel and scans a series of protrusions on the flywheel periphery. As the crankshaft rotates, the sensor transmits a pulse to the system's ignition module every time a protrusion passes it. There is one missing protrusion in the flywheel periphery at a point corresponding to 90° BTDC. The ignition module recognises the absence of a pulse from the crankshaft position sensor at this point to establish a reference mark for crankshaft position. Similarly, the time interval between absent pulses is used to determine engine speed. This information is then fed to the ECU for further processing.

The camshaft position sensor is located in the cylinder head so that it registers with a lobe on the camshaft. The sensor functions in the same way as the crankshaft position sensor, producing a series of pulses; this gives the ECU a reference point to enable it to determine the firing order, and operate the injectors in the appropriate sequence.

The coolant temperature sensor supplies engine temperature information. The sensor is an NTC (Negative Temperature Coefficient) thermistor – that is, a semi-conductor whose electrical resistance decreases as its temperature increases. The sensor provides the ECU with a constantly varying (analogue) voltage signal, corresponding to the temperature of the engine coolant. This is used to refine the calculations made by the module, when determining the correct amount of fuel required to achieve the ideal air/fuel mixture ratio.

Inlet air temperature information is provided by another NTC sensor fitted to the inlet manifold. The MAP (manifold absolute pressure) sensor is located on the inlet manifold or throttle housing, and provides the ECU with information on engine load.

The engine features a throttle that is electronically-controlled – an accelerator cable is not fitted. Instead, a throttle position sensor fitted to the accelerator pedal provides the ECU with the throttle-opening signal, and this is relayed to a motor-driven throttle valve. This system also enables the ECU to control the engine idle speed, varying the throttle opening as required by changes in engine temperature and load.

Roadspeed information is provided by the anti-lock braking system (ABS) wheel sensors.

An oxygen sensor in the exhaust system provides the module with constant feedback – 'closed-loop' control – that enables it to adjust the mixture to provide the best possible operating conditions for the catalytic converter. A further sensor is fitted, downstream of the converter, to monitor the converter's operation, and this provides an even finer degree of emission control.

Both the idle speed and mixture are under the control of the ECU, and cannot be adjusted.

Precautions

Warning: Many of the procedures in this Chapter require the removal of fuel lines and connections, which may result in some fuel spillage. Before carrying out any operation on the fuel system, refer to the precautions given in 'Safety first!' at the beginning of this manual, and follow them implicitly. Petrol is a highly dangerous and volatile liquid, and the precautions necessary when handling it cannot be overstressed. Always work in a well-ventilated area.

Note 1: *Residual pressure will remain in the fuel lines long after the car was last used. When disconnecting any fuel line, first depressurise the fuel system as described in Section 6. Even after this is done, fuel will still be present – always have clean rag handy to catch any spillage.*

Note 2: *Before disconnecting any of the fuel injection system sensor wiring plugs, ensure at least that the ignition is switched off (ideally, disconnect the battery). If a sensor is disconnected while 'live', it could result in a fault code being logged in the system memory, and may even cause damage to the component concerned.*

2 Air filter assembly and inlet housing – removal and refitting

Removal

1 Unclip the air inlet pipe from the air resonator **(see illustration)**.

2 Release the rubber securing strap and withdraw the air resonator from the filter housing **(see illustration)**.

3 Disconnect the brake servo vacuum hose from the end of the inlet manifold **(see illustration)**.

4 Disconnect the oxygen (lambda) sensor wiring connector mounting bracket to facilitate removal of the air filter housing.

5 Undo the two screws and detach the air filter housing and filter from the inlet housing **(see illustration)**.

6 Undo the two bolts securing the inlet housing to the inlet manifold, these are

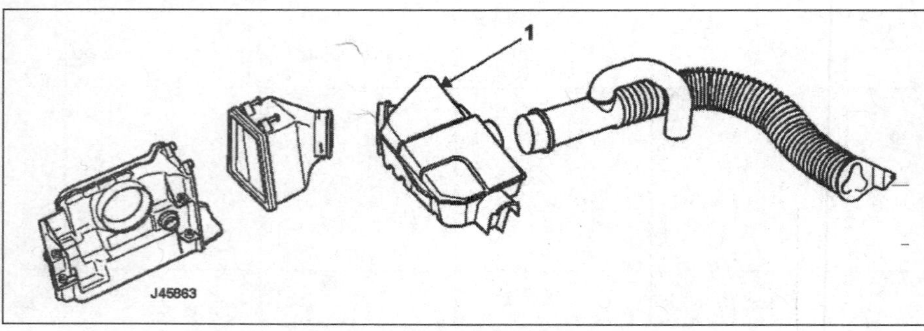

2.1 Air intake system includes a resonator (1)

2.2 Remove the air resonator

2.3 Disconnect the brake vacuum hose

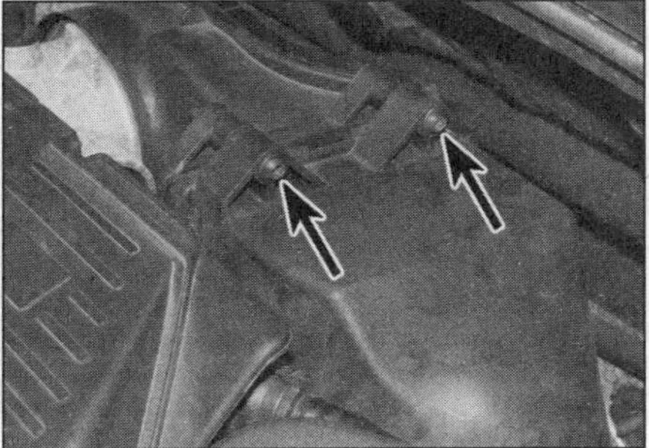

2.5 Undo the two screws – arrowed

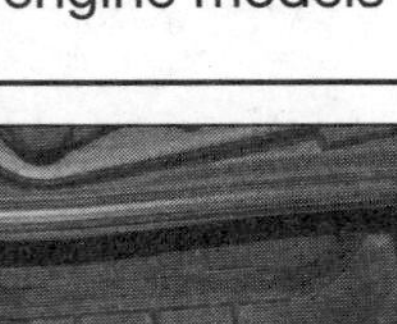

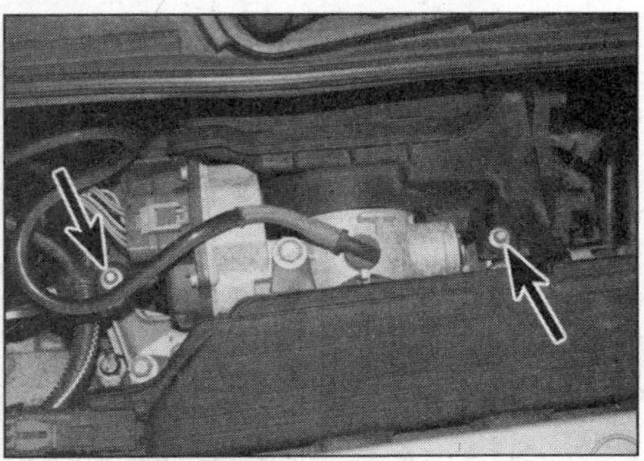

2.6 Undo the two bolts – arrowed

viewed from the top of the inlet housing **(see illustration)**.

7 Withdraw the housing from the manifold by rotating it through 90 degrees and manoeuvring it out towards the left-hand side of the engine compartment.

Refitting

8 Refitting is the reverse of removal, making sure all the ducts and wiring connectors are securely reconnected. Check all seals and renew if necessary.

3 Accelerator pedal – removal and refitting

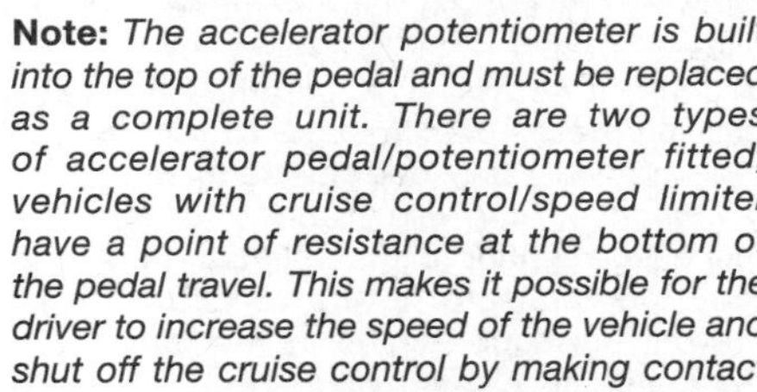

Note: *The accelerator potentiometer is built into the top of the pedal and must be replaced as a complete unit. There are two types of accelerator pedal/potentiometer fitted; vehicles with cruise control/speed limiter have a point of resistance at the bottom of the pedal travel. This makes it possible for the driver to increase the speed of the vehicle and shut off the cruise control by making contact at the end of the pedal travel. When fitting a new accelerator potentiometer, make sure the correct one is used.*

Removal

1 Release the retaining clips and remove the lower cover panel from under the facia panel in the driver's side footwell.

2 Reach up behind the facia and disconnect the wiring connector from the accelerator pedal.

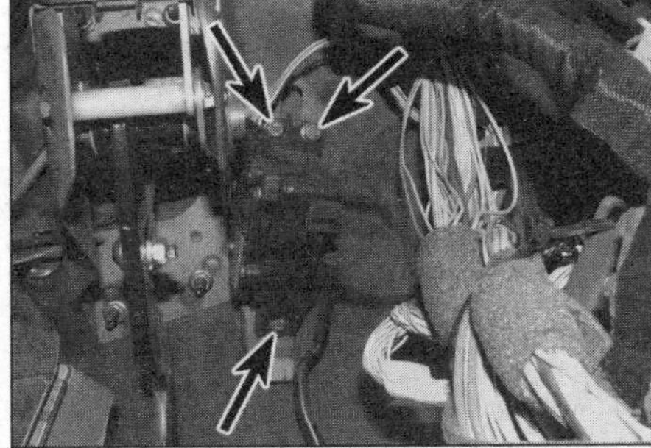

3.3 Undo the retaining bolts – arrowed

3 Slacken and remove the pedal pivot retaining bolts and remove the pedal from underneath the facia **(see illustration)**.

4 Examine the pedal assembly for signs of wear and renew as necessary.

Refitting

5 Refitting is a reversal of the removal procedure, applying a little multi-purpose grease to the pedal pivot point.

4 Unleaded petrol – general information and usage

Note: *The information given in this Chapter is correct at the time of writing. If updated information is thought to be required, check with a Renault dealer. If travelling abroad, consult one of the motoring organisations (or a similar authority) for advice on the fuel available.*

1 All petrol models are designed to run on fuel with an octane rating of 95 or 98 (RON). All models have a catalytic converter, and so must be run on unleaded fuel **only**. Under no circumstances should leaded fuel (UK 4-star) or LRP be used, as this may damage the converter.

5 Fuel injection systems – checking

Note: *Refer to the warning note in Section 1 before proceeding.*

1 If a fault appears in the fuel injection system, first ensure that all the system wiring connectors are securely connected and free of corrosion – also refer to paragraphs 6 to 9 below. Then ensure that the fault is not due to poor maintenance; ie, check that the air filter element is clean, the spark plugs are in good condition and correctly gapped, the cylinder compression pressures are correct, the ignition system wiring is in good condition and securely connected, and the engine breather hoses are clear and undamaged, referring to Chapters 1A, 2A and 5B.

2 If these checks fail to reveal the cause of the problem, the car should be taken to a Renault dealer for testing. A diagnostic connector is fitted behind the ashtray at the front of the centre console, into which dedicated electronic test equipment can be plugged **(see illustration).** The test equipment is capable of 'interrogating' the engine management system ECU electronically and accessing its internal fault log (reading fault codes).

3 Fault codes can only be extracted from the ECU using a dedicated fault code reader. A Renault dealer will obviously have such a reader, but they are also available from other suppliers. It is unlikely to be cost-effective for the private owner to purchase a fault code reader, but a well-equipped local garage or auto-electrical specialist will have one.

4 Using this equipment, faults can be pinpointed quickly and simply, even if their occurrence is intermittent. Testing all the system components individually in an attempt to locate the fault by elimination is a time-consuming operation that is unlikely to be fruitful (particularly if the fault occurs dynamically), and carries a high risk of damage to the ECU's internal components.

5 Experienced home mechanics equipped with an accurate tachometer and a carefully-calibrated exhaust gas analyser may be able to check the exhaust gas CO content and the engine idle speed; if these are found to be out of specification, then the car must be taken to a Renault dealer for assessment. Neither the air/fuel mixture (exhaust gas CO content) nor the engine idle speed are manually adjustable; incorrect test results indicate the need for maintenance (possibly injector cleaning) or a fault within the fuel injection system.

5.2 Diagnostic connector (arrowed) behind the ashtray

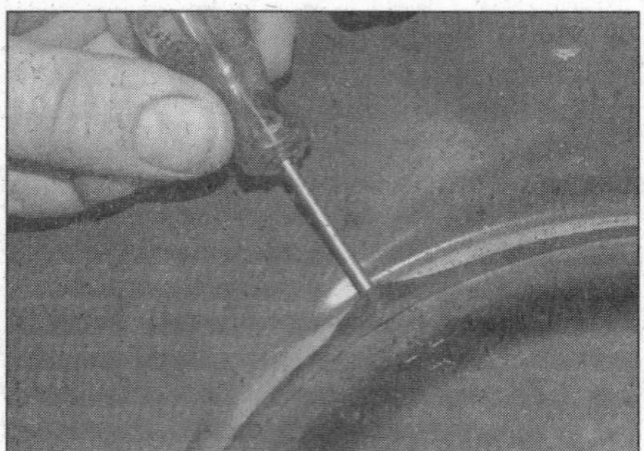
7.3a Use a screwdriver – note position of arrow . . .

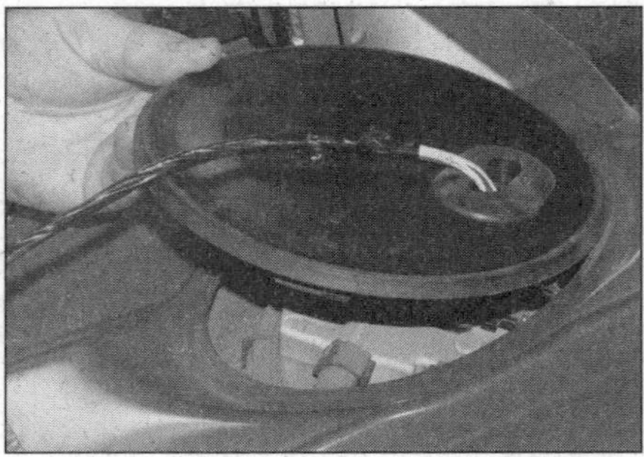
7.3b . . . and unclip the cover from the floor panel

7.4 Disconnect the wiring connector from the sender unit

6 Certain faults, such as failure of one of the engine management system sensors, will cause the system to revert to a backup (or 'limp-home') mode. This is intended to be a 'get-you-home' facility only – the engine management warning light will come on when this mode is in operation.

7 In this mode, the signal from the defective sensor is substituted with a fixed value (it would normally vary), which may lead to loss of power, poor idling, and generally poor running, especially when the engine is cold.

8 However, the engine may in fact run quite well in this situation, and the only clue (other than the warning light) would be that the exhaust CO emissions (for example) would be higher than they should be.

9 Bear in mind that, even if the defective sensor is correctly identified and renewed, the engine will not return to normal running until the fault code is erased, taking the system out of back-up mode. This also applies even if the cause of the fault was a loose connection or damaged piece of wire – until the fault code is erased, the system will continue in back-up mode.

6 Fuel injection system – depressurisation

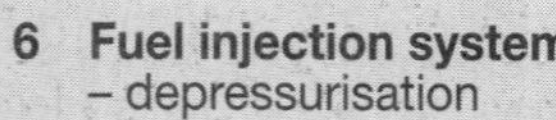

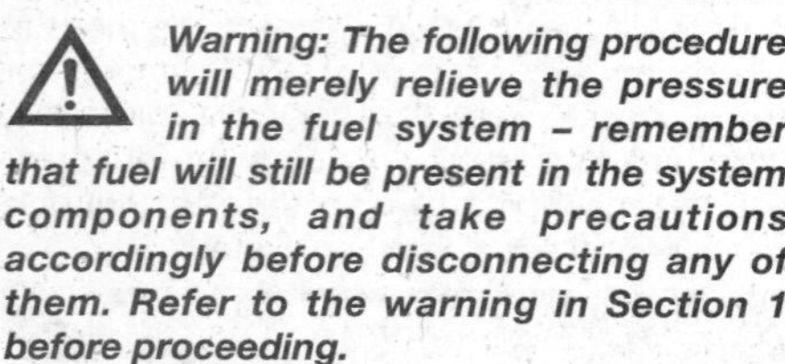

Warning: The following procedure will merely relieve the pressure in the fuel system – remember that fuel will still be present in the system components, and take precautions accordingly before disconnecting any of them. Refer to the warning in Section 1 before proceeding.

1 The fuel system referred to in this Section is defined as the tank-mounted fuel pump, the fuel filter, the fuel injector(s) and the pressure regulator in the injector housing/fuel rail, and the metal pipes and flexible hoses of the fuel lines between these components. All these contain fuel, which will be under pressure while the engine is running, and/or while the ignition is switched on. The pressure will remain for some time after the ignition has been switched off, and it must be relieved in a controlled fashion when any of these components are disturbed for servicing work.

2 Whichever depressurisation method is used, bear in mind the following points:

a) Plug the disconnected pipe ends, to minimise fuel loss and prevent the entry of dirt into the fuel system.

b) Note that, once the fuel system has been depressurised and drained (even partially), it will take significantly longer to restart the engine – perhaps several seconds of cranking – before the system is refilled and pressure restored.

Method 1

3 The simplest depressurisation method is to disconnect the fuel pump electrical supply by removing the fuel pump fuse (refer to the wiring diagrams or the label on the relevant fusebox for exact location) and starting the engine; allow the engine to idle until it stops through lack of fuel. Turn the engine over once or twice on the starter to ensure that all pressure is released, then switch off the ignition; do not forget to refit the fuse when work is complete.

Method 2

4 Disconnect the battery negative terminal (refer to *Disconnecting the battery* in the Reference Section of this manual).

5 Place a suitable container beneath the connection or union to be disconnected, and have a large rag ready to soak up any escaping fuel not being caught by the container. Slowly loosen the connection or union nut to avoid a sudden release of pressure, and position the rag around the connection, to catch any fuel spray that may be expelled.

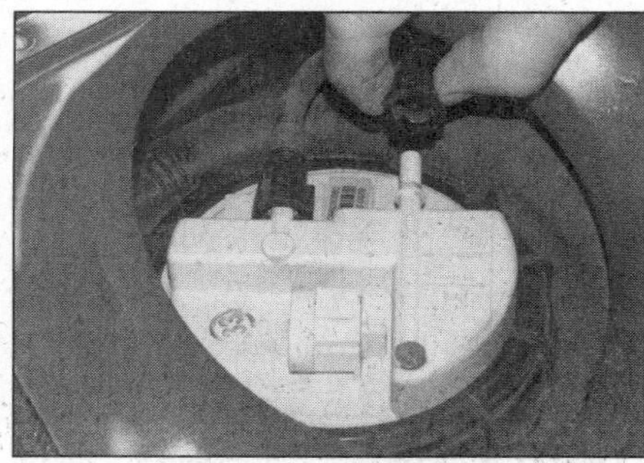
7.5 Release the fuel lines – noting their fitted position

7 Fuel gauge sender unit – removal and refitting

Warning: Refer to the warning in Section 1 before proceeding.

Note: *The fuel gauge sender unit also incorporates the fuel pump.*

Removal

1 Disconnect the battery negative terminal (refer to *Disconnecting the battery* in the Reference Section of this manual).

2 Open the right-hand rear passenger door and lift up the rear seat cushion, pull back the carpet to reveal the fuel gauge sender unit access cover.

3 Using a screwdriver, carefully prise the plastic access cover from the floor to expose the fuel sender unit **(see illustrations).**

4 Disconnect the wiring connector from the fuel gauge sender unit **(see illustration)**, and tape the connector to the vehicle body, to prevent it disappearing behind the tank.

5 Depending on model, there may be two fuel hoses attached to the sender unit, mark the fuel hoses for identification purposes. The hoses have quick-release fittings to ease removal **(see illustration)**. To disconnect each hose, slide out the locking tab (where fitted) from the collar then, bearing in mind the information in Section 6, depress the collar and detach the hose from the sender unit. Disconnect hoses from the top of the sender unit, noting the correct fitted position of the sealing rings and plug the hose ends to minimise fuel loss.

6 Noting the alignment marks on the sender unit cover and fuel tank, unscrew the locking ring and remove it from the tank **(see illustrations)**. This is best accomplished by the special Renault tool that fits the locking ring or a home-made equivalent. If special tool is not available use a screwdriver on the raised ribs of the locking ring. Carefully tap the screwdriver to turn the ring anti-clockwise until it can be unscrewed by hand.

7 Note the position of the sender unit, then carefully lift the fuel sender assembly out of the fuel tank, taking great care not to damage the fuel level gauge sender, or to spill fuel onto

the interior of the vehicle. Recover the rubber sealing ring and discard it – a new one must be used on refitting **(see illustration)**.

8 Note that the fuel pump/fuel gauge sender unit is only available as a complete assembly – no components are available separately.

Refitting

9 Ensure that the fuel sender/pump pick-up filter is clean and free of debris. Fit the new sealing ring to the top of the fuel tank **(see illustration)**.

10 Carefully manoeuvre the sender/pump assembly into the fuel tank, aligning it into the position noted on removal.

11 Align the mark on the fuel sender cover with the alignment marks on the fuel tank, then refit the locking ring. Securely tighten the locking ring, and then recheck that the sender/pump cover and tank marks are all correctly aligned. **Note:** *If available, use the special Renault service tool (Mot. 1397) to tighten the locking ring.*

12 Ensure that the sealing rings are in position and reconnect the hoses to the top of the fuel sender unit, using the marks made on removal to ensure that they are correctly reconnected. Check the end fittings are clipped securely in position and (where necessary) refit the locking tabs to the collars.

13 Reconnect the wiring connector.

14 Reconnect the battery negative terminal, and start the engine. Check the fuel sender/pump unit hose unions for signs of leakage.

15 If all is well, refit the plastic access cover and fold the carpet and rear seat cushion down into position.

8 Fuel pump – removal and refitting

The fuel pump is an integral part of the fuel gauge sender unit assembly (see Section 7).

9 Fuel tank – removal and refitting

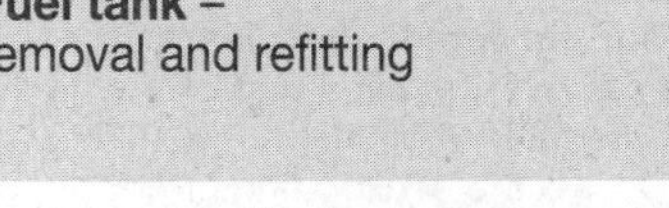

Warning: Refer to the warning in Section 1 before proceeding.

Removal

1 Before removing the fuel tank, all fuel must be drained from the tank. Since a fuel tank drain plug is not provided, it is therefore preferable to carry out the removal operation when the tank is nearly empty. Before proceeding, disconnect the battery negative terminal (refer to *Disconnecting the battery* in the Reference Section of this manual), and syphon or hand-pump the remaining fuel from the tank.

2 Disconnect the fuel pipes and wiring from the fuel gauge sender unit as described in Section 7.

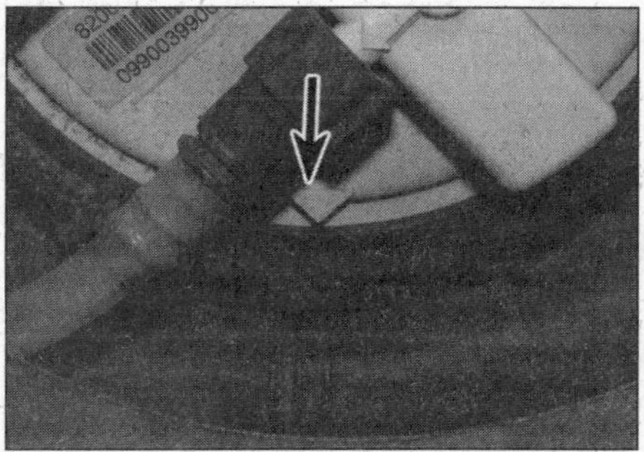

7.6a Alignment marks arrowed

3 To remove the fuel tank, first jack up the rear of the car, and support it on axle stands (see *Jacking and vehicle support*). Make sure it is a sufficient height to be able to withdraw the fuel tank from under the vehicle.

4 Remove the exhaust system and relevant heat shield(s) as described in Section 14.

5 Remove the right-hand rear wheel then undo the retaining screws and remove the plastic wheel arch liner.

6 Slacken the retaining clip at the bottom of the filler neck and disconnect it from the tank. Position a container below the filler neck to catch any fuel still in the fuel tank.

7 Release the quick-release fitting and disconnect the anti-blowback pipe at its connection situated just in front of the filler neck.

8 Place a trolley jack with a flat block of wood inserted beneath the tank, then raise the jack until it is supporting the weight of the tank.

9 Slacken and remove the fuel tank mounting bolts.

10 Slowly lower the fuel tank out of position, disconnecting any other relevant vent pipes as they become accessible (where necessary), and remove the tank from underneath the vehicle. The aid of an assistant will be required for this procedure.

11 If the tank is contaminated with sediment or water, remove the fuel pump/sender unit (Section 7), and swill the tank out with clean fuel. The tank is injection-moulded from a synthetic material – if seriously damaged it should be renewed. However, in certain cases, it may be possible to have small leaks or minor damage repaired. Seek the advice

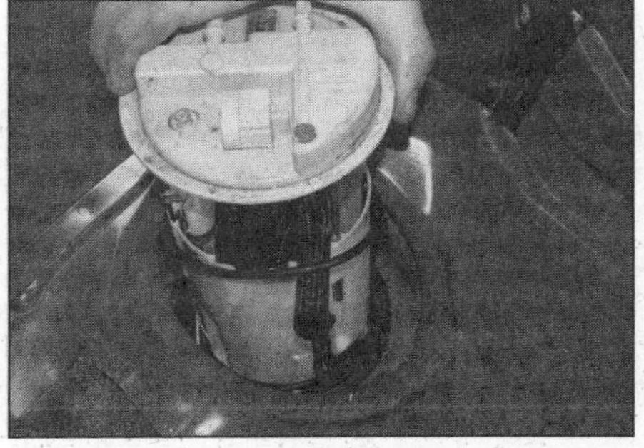

7.7 Withdraw the fuel sender/pump from the tank

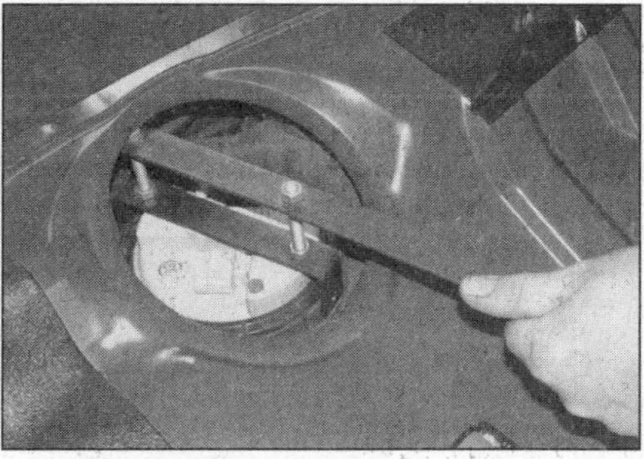

7.6b Using a home-made tool to remove the locking ring

of a specialist before attempting to repair the fuel tank.

Refitting

12 Refitting is the reverse of the removal procedure, noting the following points:

a) *When lifting the tank back into position, take care to ensure that none of the hoses become trapped between the tank and vehicle body. Also ensure that the filler neck is correctly located as the tank is raised into position.*

b) *Ensure that all pipes and hoses are correctly routed. Make sure the sealing rings are in position in the quick-release fittings prior to fitting and make sure they are securely clipped in position.*

c) *On completion, refill the tank with a small amount of fuel, and check for signs of leakage prior to taking the vehicle out on the road.*

10 Throttle body/housing – removal and refitting

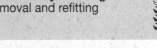

Warning: Refer to the warning in Section 1 before proceeding.

Note: *This is a motorised throttle body and it cannot be separated from the motor, if faulty the complete motorised throttle body has to be renewed as a unit.*

Removal

1 Depressurise the fuel system with reference to Section 6.

7.9 Fitting new sealing ring

2 Disconnect the battery negative terminal (refer to *Disconnecting the battery* in the Reference Section of this manual).

3 Where applicable, remove the plastic cover from the top of the engine.

4 Remove the air filter air inlet housing as described in Section 2.

5 Disconnect the wiring connector from the potentiometer on the side of the throttle housing **(see illustration)**.

6 Disconnect the fuel vapour rebreathing pipe from the solenoid valve on the right-hand rear of the engine compartment.

7 Undo the retaining bolts and remove the throttle housing from the inlet manifold. Recover the housing seal/gasket, noting that a new one will be required for refitting.

Refitting

8 Refitting is a reversal of the removal procedure, noting the following points:

a) *Ensure that all mating surfaces are clean and dry.*

b) *Use a new seal/gasket and tighten the housing retaining bolts to the specified torque.*

c) *Refit the air cleaner inlet housing or air inlet duct with reference to Section 2.*

d) *Ensure that all hoses are correctly reconnected and, where necessary, are securely held in position by the retaining clips.*

e) *Ensure that all wiring is correctly routed, and that the connectors are securely reconnected.*

f) *If a new throttle body has been fitted, it will need to be initialised and set up using Renault diagnostic equipment before it will function correctly.*

11 Fuel pump/fuel pressure – checking

Note: *Refer to the warning note in Section 1 before proceeding.*

Fuel pump

1 Switch on the ignition, and listen for the fuel pump (the sound of an electric motor running, audible from beneath the rear seats). Assuming there is sufficient fuel in the tank, the

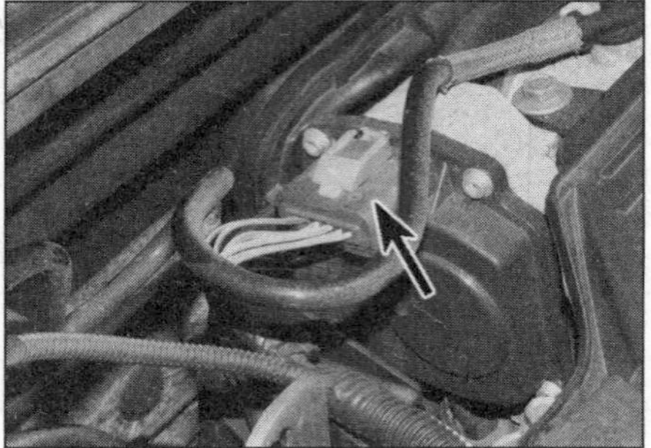

10.5 Disconnect the wiring connector – arrowed

pump should start and run for approximately one or two seconds, then stop, each time the ignition is switched on. **Note:** *If the pump runs continuously all the time the ignition is switched on, the electronic control system is running in the back-up (or 'limp-home') mode. This almost certainly indicates a fault has been logged in the ECU fault memory, and the car should therefore be taken to a Renault dealer for a full test of the complete system, using the correct diagnostic equipment; do not waste time or risk damaging the components by trying to test the system without such facilities.*

2 If the pump does not run at all, check the fuse, relay and wiring (see Chapter 12).

Fuel pressure

3 A fuel pressure gauge will be required for this check, and should be connected in the fuel line at the front of the inlet manifold, where the fuel supply pipe joins the fuel rail. Always follow the gauge maker's instructions.

4 Start the engine and allow it to idle for a few seconds. Note the gauge reading as soon as the pressure stabilises, and compare it with the regulated fuel pressure figure listed in the Specifications.

a) *If the pressure is high, check for a restricted fuel return line. If the line is clear, this indicates a fuel pressure regulator fault.*

b) *If the pressure is low, this may indicate a blocked or kinked fuel line, blocked fuel filter, failing fuel pump, or again, a pressure regulator fault.*

5 The fuel pump, filter and pressure regulator are contained in a single unit, immersed in the fuel tank. It appears that a fault in any one of the three will require a complete new unit, but check for spares availability.

6 Carefully disconnect the fuel pressure gauge, depressurising the system first as described in Section 6. Be sure to cover the fitting with a rag before slackening it. Mop up any spilt petrol.

7 Run the engine, and check that there are no fuel leaks.

12 Fuel injection system components – removal and refitting

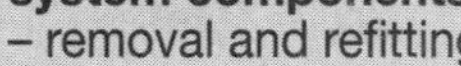

Note: *Refer to the warning note in Section 1 before proceeding.*

Fuel rail and injectors

Note: *If a faulty injector is suspected, before condemning the injector, it is worth trying the effect of one of the proprietary injector-cleaning treatments.*

Removal

1 Disconnect the battery negative terminal (refer to *Disconnecting the battery* in the Reference Section of this manual).

2 Undo the two retaining nuts and remove the fuel rail protector cover from the front of the inlet manifold **(see illustration)**.

3 Depressurise the fuel system with reference to Section 6, and then disconnect the fuel pipe from the end of the fuel rail **(see illustration)**. **Note:** *There will still be fuel in the fuel pipe and fuel rail, place some rags around the connection to soak up any residual fuel. Cover the alternator below the fuel pipe to protect it from any spilt fuel.*

4 Disconnect the wiring plugs from the injectors and the knock sensor, then move the wiring loom to one side.

5 Unscrew and remove the two mounting bolts, and carefully ease the fuel rail, together with the injectors from the inlet manifold **(see illustration)**.

6 Note the fitted positions of the injectors then remove the clips and ease the injectors from the fuel rail.

7 Remove the sealing rings from the grooves at each end of the injectors and obtain new ones.

12.2 Removing the fuel rail protector

12.3 Disconnect the fuel pipe – arrowed

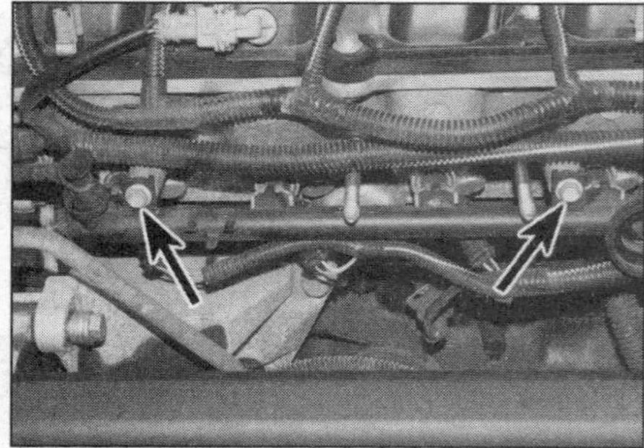

12.5 Undo the two fuel rail mounting bolts – arrowed

Refitting

8 Refitting is a reversal of the removal procedure, noting the following points:

a) *Renew all sealing rings, using a smear of clean engine oil to aid installation.*

b) *Refit the fuel rail assembly, making sure the sealing rings remain correctly positioned, and tighten the retaining bolts to the specified torque.*

c) *On completion start the engine and check for fuel leaks.*

Fuel pressure regulator

Note: *The following procedure is for a fuel pressure regulator, which is located on the end of the fuel rail. On some models the pressure regulator is part of the fuel pump/sender unit, which is inside the fuel tank (see Sections 7 and 8).*

Removal

9 Disconnect the battery negative terminal (refer to *Disconnecting the battery* in the Reference Section of this manual).

10 Remove the rail protector cover from the top of the inlet manifold.

11 Depressurise the fuel system with reference to Section 6.

12 Disconnect the vacuum pipe, release the retaining clip and withdraw the regulator from the fuel rail.

Refitting

13 Refitting is a reversal of the removal procedure, noting the following points:

a) *Renew sealing ring, using a smear of clean engine oil to aid installation.*

b) *On completion start the engine and check for fuel leaks.*

Inlet air temperature sensor

Removal

14 The air temperature sensor is located on the front of the inlet manifold **(see illustration)**.

15 Where applicable, remove the plastic cover from the top of the engine.

16 Disconnect the wiring plug from the sensor, then twist and remove the sensor from the inlet manifold.

Refitting

17 Refitting is a reversal of removal. Check the condition of the sensor's O-ring seal, and if necessary fit a new one.

Coolant temperature sensor

18 The sensor is located on the thermostat housing at the left-hand end of the cylinder head **(see illustration)**, above the transmission bellhousing. Refer to Chapter 3 for removal and refitting details.

Knock sensor

19 The knock sensor (where fitted) is located on the front of the cylinder block **(see illustration)**. Refer to Chapter 5B for the removal and refitting procedures.

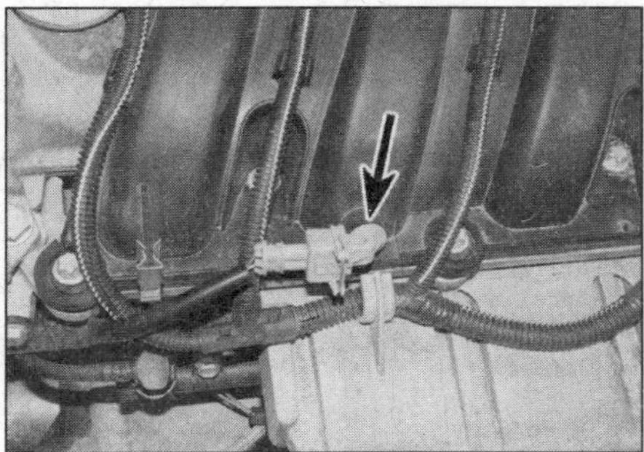

12.14 Air temperature sensor – arrowed

Manifold absolute pressure (MAP) sensor

Removal

20 The MAP sensor is mounted on the rear of the upper section of the inlet manifold **(see illustration)**.

21 Disconnect the wiring and (where applicable) the vacuum hose from the sensor.

22 Unscrew the mounting bolts and remove the sensor.

Refitting

23 Refitting is a reversal of removal.

Fuel system and fuel pump relays

24 The fuses and relays are located in the engine compartment, behind the battery. Unclip the plastic cover to access the fuses and relays – see Chapter 12 for more details.

Crankshaft speed/ position sensor

Removal

25 The sensor is mounted on the top of the transmission bellhousing at the left-hand end of the cylinder block.

26 Remove the air cleaner resonator box or air hoses, as necessary, to improve access, referring to Section 2.

27 Remove the battery and battery tray as described in Chapter 5A.

28 Trace the wiring back from the sensor to the wiring connector, and disconnect it from the main harness.

12.20 Manifold pressure sensor – 1.8 litre engine shown

12.18 Coolant temperature sensor – 1.8 litre engine shown

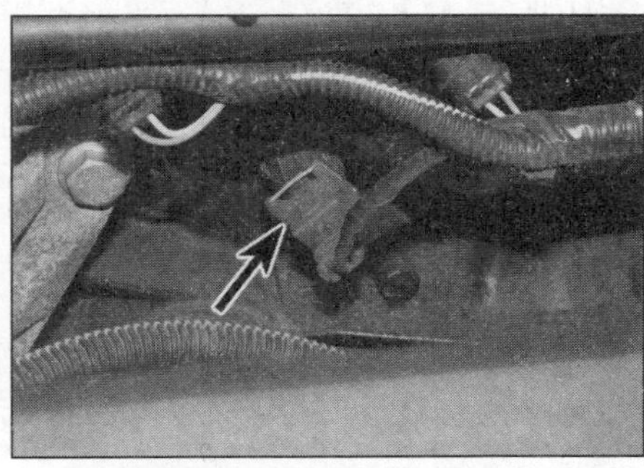

12.19 Knock sensor – 1.8 litre engine shown

29 Unscrew the retaining bolt and remove the sensor.

Refitting

30 Refitting is a reversal of removal. Ensure that the sensor retaining bolt is securely tightened – note that only the special shouldered bolts originally fitted must be used to secure the sensor; these bolts locate the sensor precisely to give the correct air gap between the sensor tip and the flywheel/ driveplate.

Variable valve timing (dephaser) solenoid

Removal

31 Where fitted, the solenoid is mounted on top of the engine, near the timing belt end. Unclip and remove the engine top cover for access **(see illustration)**.

12.31 Camshaft solenoid valve – 1.8 litre engine shown

12.35 Remove the battery tray . . .

12.36 . . . and the mounting bracket . . .

12.37 . . . then withdraw the ECU

32 Disconnect the wiring plug, then unscrew the mounting bolt and withdraw the solenoid from the top of the engine.

Refitting

33 Refitting is a reversal of removal. Ensure that the mounting bolt and the wiring plug are secure.

Electronic control unit (ECU)

Note: *The ECU is electronically-coded to match the engine immobiliser and certain other engine components. If the ECU is being removed in order to fit a new unit, it is highly recommended that a Renault dealer should carry out this work.*

Caution: The ECU wiring plugs should only be disconnected after the disconnecting battery. If the ECU is unplugged 'live', it could be damaged.

Removal

34 Unclip and remove the engine compartment upper cover.

35 Remove the battery and battery tray as described in Chapter 5A **(see illustration)**.

36 Undo the retaining bolts and remove the bracket from across the top of the ECU **(see illustration).**

37 Remove the mounting bolts and withdraw the ECU from its mounting bracket **(see illustration)**.

38 Slide back the locking catches, and disconnect the wiring plug connectors from the ECU.

Refitting

39 Refitting is a reversal of removal. Ensure that the ECU wiring plugs are securely reconnected.

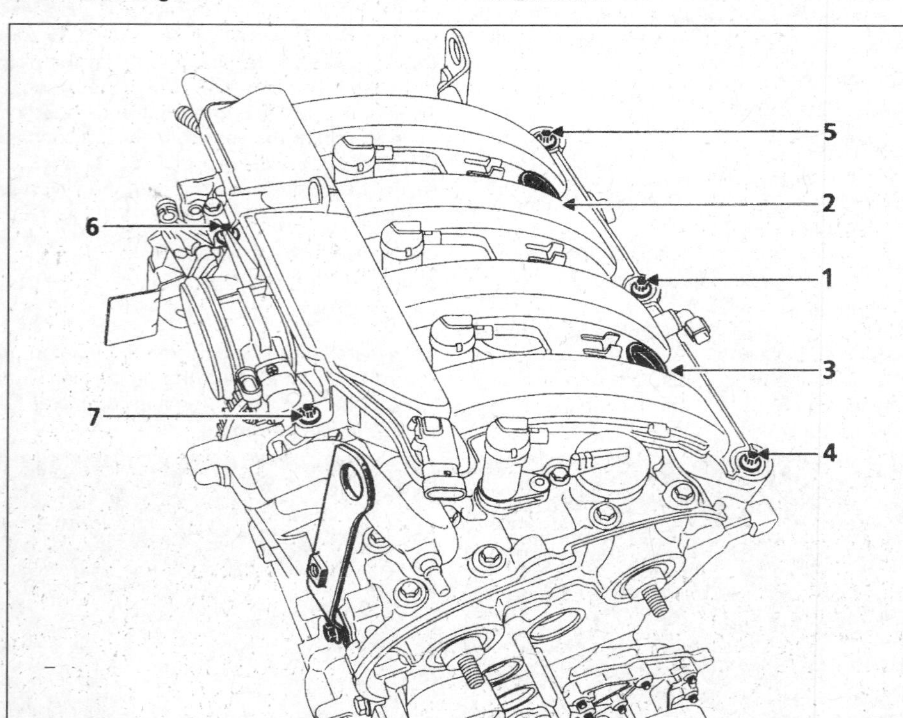

13.5 Inlet manifold upper section

1 to 7 Inlet manifold upper section retaining bolts (numbers also indicate bolt tightening sequence when refitting)

13 Manifolds – removal and refitting

Inlet manifold

Removal

1 Disconnect the battery negative terminal (refer to *Disconnecting the battery* in the Reference Section of this manual).

2 To remove the manifold plastic upper section first remove the throttle body housing as described in Section 10.

3 Disconnect the wiring connectors at the absolute air pressure (MAP) sensor.

4 Disconnect the wiring connector at the inlet air temperature sensor on the front of the inlet manifold, and the wiring connectors at each of the four ignition coils. Release the ignition coil wiring from the clips on the inlet manifold upper section and move the wiring to one side.

5 Undo the five bolts at the front and two bolts at the rear securing the inlet manifold upper section to the lower section and to the oil separator housing **(see illustration)**. Lift off the manifold upper section and recover the seals.

6 To remove the manifold lower section, first remove the upper section as previously described.

7 Remove the fuel rail and injectors as described in Section 12.

8 Undo the bolts securing the lower manifold to the cylinder head and the bolt securing the manifold to the upper timing cover at the right-hand side of the engine. Withdraw the manifold from its location and manoeuvre it out from behind the auxiliary components mounting bracket. Recover the gasket.

Refitting

9 Refitting is a reverse of the removal procedure noting the following points.

a) *Ensure that the manifold and cylinder mating surfaces are clean and dry and fit a new gasket or seals as applicable.*
b) *Fit all the bolts in the lower section finger tight first. Tighten the bolt at the timing belt end first, ensuring that the projections on the top of the manifold inner side are*

level with the cylinder head upper section, then tighten all the bolts to the specified torque setting.
c) *Refit the fuel rail and injector assembly as described in Section 12.*
d) *Tighten the manifold upper section retaining bolts in the sequence shown in illustration 13.5.*
e) *Ensure that all relevant hoses and wiring connections are reconnected to their original positions, and are securely held (where necessary) by their retaining clips.*
f) *Refit the throttle body housing as described in Section 10.*
g) *Refit the air cleaner assembly and inlet ducts as described in Section 2.*

Exhaust manifold

Removal

10 Disconnect the battery negative terminal (refer to *Disconnecting the battery* in the Reference Section of this manual).
11 Remove the plastic cover from the top of the engine.
12 Remove the air cleaner assembly and inlet ducts as described in Section 2.
13 Disconnect the oxygen (lambda) sensor wiring at the connector located at the left-hand end of the cylinder head. Unscrew the sensor and remove it from the top of the exhaust manifold.
14 Undo the retaining bolts and remove the exhaust manifold heat shield.
15 Apply the handbrake, then jack up the front of the car and support it on axle stands (see *Jacking and vehicle support*). Remove the engine undertray.
16 Undo the retaining nuts and bolts and separate the exhaust system front pipe from the manifold. Move the front pipe away from the manifold slightly and suitably support it. Recover the flange gasket.
17 Unbolt the support strut from the base of the manifold.
18 Undo the bolts securing the manifold to the cylinder head **(see illustration)**. Pivot the manifold through approximately 45° and manipulate it from its location and out towards the right-hand side.

Refitting

19 Refitting is a reverse of the removal procedure noting the following points.
a) *Ensure that the manifold and cylinder mating surfaces are clean and dry and fit a new gasket or seals as applicable.*
b) *Refit the manifold and tighten the retaining nuts/bolts in the correct sequence to the specified torque, see illustration 13.18.*
c) *Ensure that the heat shield is correctly located between the manifold and oxygen sensor.*
d) *Use a new gasket on the manifold-to-front pipe flange joint.*

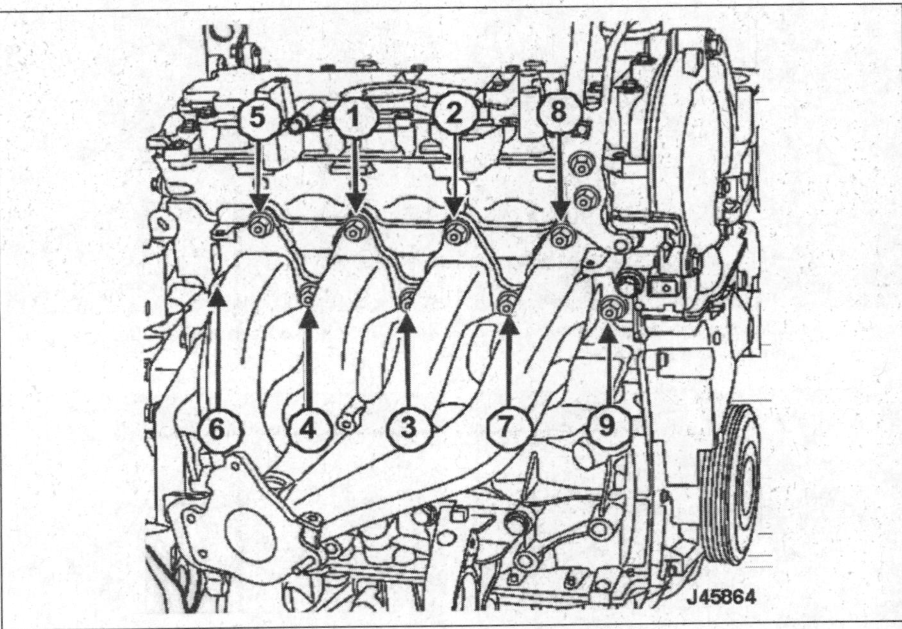

13.18 Exhaust manifold retaining bolts – tightening sequence

14 Exhaust system – general information, removal and refitting

General information

1 On new vehicles the exhaust system consists of two sections:
1) *The front pipe, catalytic converter and intermediate pipe.*
2) *The rear silencer/tailpipe.*

2 The front pipe joints are secured by nuts and bolts, the front pipe being of the flexible pipe to allow for movement in the exhaust system. A clamping ring secures the joint between the front and rear sections. The system is suspended throughout its entire length by rubber mountings.
3 Although on new vehicles the catalytic converter and intermediate pipe are in the same exhaust section, when replacement is needed they are renewed individually, which requires the original exhaust section to be cut into two halves (see paragraph 9).

Removal

4 To remove the system or part of the system, first jack up the front or rear of the car, and support it on axle stands (see *Jacking and vehicle support*). Alternatively, position the car over an inspection pit, or on car ramps.

Original front pipe, catalytic converter and intermediate pipe section

5 Where there is a oxygen sensor fitted to the front pipe, trace the wiring back from the sensor and disconnect it at the wiring connector **(see illustration)**. Free the wiring from any relevant retaining clips so the sensor is free to be removed with the front pipe.
6 Slacken and remove the nuts and bolts securing the front flexible pipe flange joint to the manifold **(see illustration)**.
7 Have an assistant support the front end of the pipe then slacken the mounting clamp

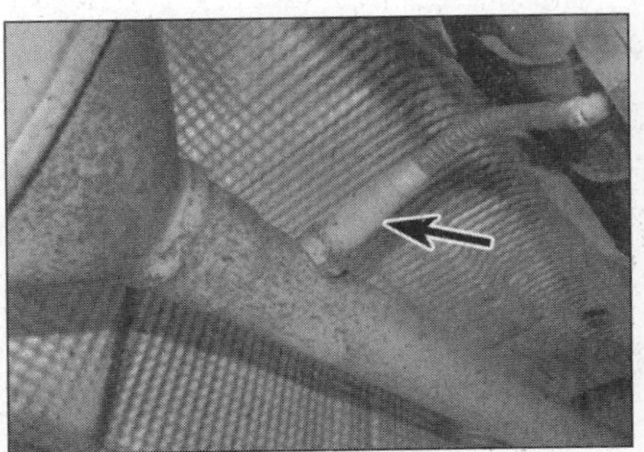

14.5 Oxygen/lambda sensor – arrowed

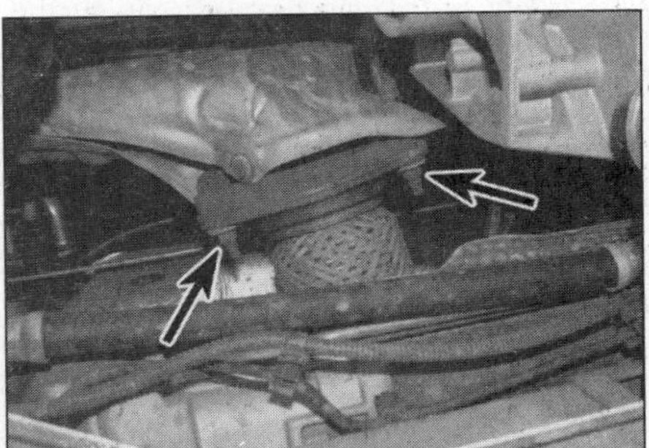

14.6 Undo the front pipe retaining nuts – arrowed

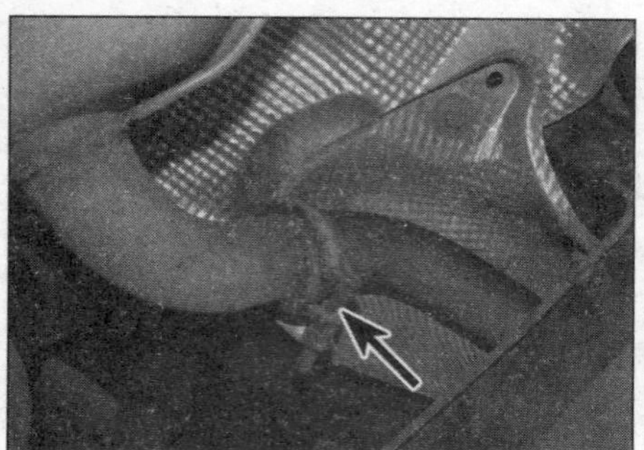

14.7 Slacken the clamp (arrowed) to remove the exhaust

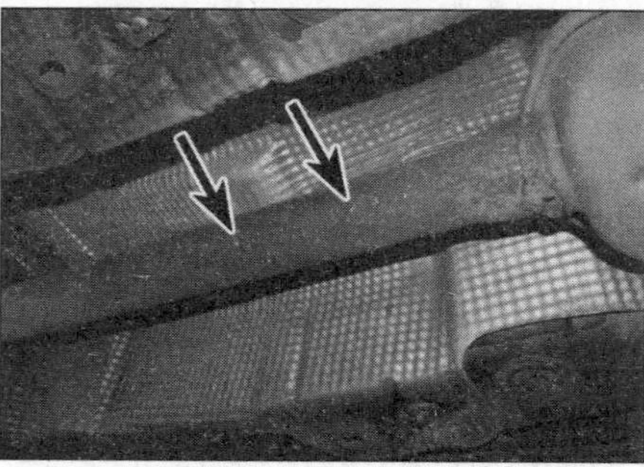

14.9 Punch marks (arrowed) 80 mm apart

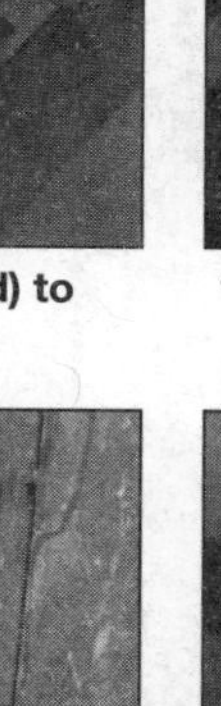

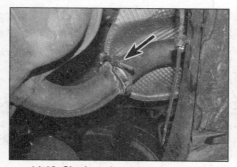

14.16 Slacken the clamp (arrowed)

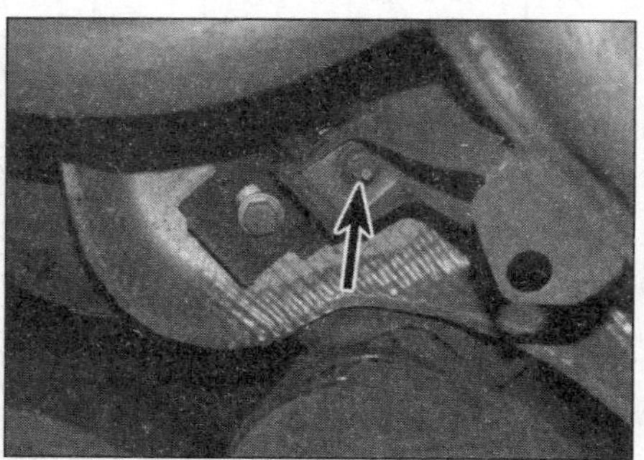

14.17 Undo the exhaust mounting retaining nut – arrowed

nuts and detach the intermediate pipe from the rear silencer/tailpipe **(see illustration)**.

8 Unhook the section from its mounting rubber(s) and remove it from the underneath the vehicle.

9 If the section has been removed to enable it to be cut in half, locate the cutting area, which is situated on the straight section of pipe approximately midway between the catalytic converter and silencer. The cutting point is marked with two circular punch marks on the side of the pipe **(see illustration)**. The punch marks are 80 mm apart and the exhaust section should be cut at the mid-point between the two punch marks. Renault supply a special after-sales sleeve, which is used for rejoining the front and intermediate sections. **Note:** *Ensure that the exhaust pipe is cut squarely or it will be difficult to obtain a gas-tight seal when the exhaust is refitted.*

Replacement catalytic converter

10 Slacken and remove the nuts securing the front pipe/catalytic converter to the manifold. Remove the bolts, then separate the flange joint and recover the gasket.

11 Slacken the clamping sleeve nut and bolt and slide the sleeve along the intermediate pipe.

12 Remove the catalytic converter and clamping sleeve. Discard the clamping sleeve; it must be renewed whenever it is disturbed.

Replacement intermediate pipe

13 Slacken the clamping ring nuts and detach the intermediate pipe from the rear silencer/tailpipe.

14 Slacken the clamping sleeve nut and bolt and slide the sleeve along the catalytic converter.

15 Remove the intermediate pipe and clamping sleeve. Discard the clamping sleeve; it must be renewed whenever it is disturbed.

Rear silencer/tailpipe

16 Slacken the clamping ring nuts and detach the intermediate pipe from the rear silencer/tailpipe **(see illustration)**.

17 Undo the mounting nuts at each side of the rear silencer and free it from its mounting rubbers, remove it from underneath the vehicle **(see illustration)**.

Heat shield(s)

18 The heat shields are secured to the underside of the body by various nuts, clips and bolts. Each shield can be removed once the relevant exhaust section has been removed. If a shield is being removed to gain access to a component located behind it, it may prove sufficient in some cases to remove the retaining nuts and/or bolts, and simply lower the shield, without disturbing the exhaust system.

Refitting

19 Each section is refitted by reversing the removal sequence, noting the following points:

a) Ensure that all traces of corrosion have been removed from the flanges, and renew all necessary gaskets.

b) Inspect the rubber mountings for signs of damage or deterioration, and renew as necessary.

c) When refitting the front flexible pipe to the manifold, ensure that a new gasket is fitted.

d) When reconnecting the intermediate pipe to rear silencer/tailpipe joint, apply a smear of exhaust system jointing paste to the flange joint, to ensure a gas-tight seal. Tighten the clamping ring nuts evenly and progressively so that the clearance between the clamp halves remains equal on either side.

e) On models with a replacement catalytic converter/intermediate pipe section, apply a smear of exhaust system jointing paste (Renault recommend the use of Sodicam) to the inside of the new clamping ring. With the catalytic converter and intermediate pipe correctly located at their outer ends, make sure both inner ends of the cut pipe are positioned squarely against the stop of the clamping sleeve. Position the sleeve bolt vertically on the left-hand side of the pipe and securely tighten the nut until it is heard to click; the clamp bolt has a groove in it to ensure that the nut is correctly tightened (equivalent to a tightening torque of around 25 Nm).

f) Prior to tightening the exhaust system fasteners, ensure that all rubber mountings are correctly located, and that there is adequate clearance between the exhaust system and vehicle underbody.

Chapter 4 Part B:
Fuel/exhaust systems – diesel engine models

Contents

Degrees of difficulty

Easy, suitable for novice with little experience	**Fairly easy,** suitable for beginner with some experience	**Fairly difficult,** suitable for competent DIY mechanic	**Difficult,** suitable for experienced DIY mechanic	**Very difficult,** suitable for expert DIY or professional

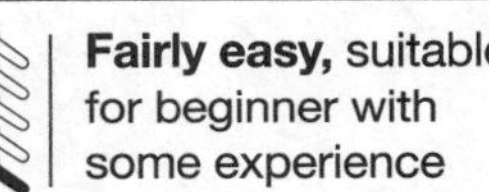

Specifications

General

System type	Rear-mounted fuel tank, high-pressure pump with common-rail, direct injection, turbocharger
Type	Bosch CP3
Firing order	1-3-4-2 (No 1 cylinder at flywheel end of engine)

Fuel system data

Idle speed	800 ± 50 rpm
Maximum with no load on engine:	
1.9 litre engine	4850 ± 150 rpm
2.2 litre engines	4200 ± 150 rpm
Maximum with load on engine:	
1.9 litre engine	4500 ± 100 rpm
2.2 litre engines	4800 ± 150 rpm
High-pressure pump:	
Type	Bosch
Operating pressure	300 to 1350 bar
Direction of rotation	Clockwise viewed from sprocket end
Injectors:	
Type	Bosch solenoid injector
Solenoid resistance	< 0.2 ohms
Operating pressure	1350 bar
Maximum pressure	1525 bar
Glow plug:	
Type	Beru
Resistance (connector removed)	0.6 ohms
Thermoplungers resistance (at 20 degrees C)	0.45 ± 0.05 ohms

Torque wrench settings

	Nm	lbf ft
1.9 litre engines		
Catalytic converter-to-turbocharger nuts	26	19
EGR valve mounting bolts	8	6
Fuel rail high-pressure pipe union nut	25	18
Fuel rail mounting bolts	22	16
Fuel rail pressure sensor	35	26
Injection pump pressure regulator bolts	6	4
Injection pump right-hand mounting bolts	30	22
Injection pump sprocket nut	70	52
Injector clamp bolts	25	18
Injector high-pressure fuel pipe union nuts	25	18
Inlet/exhaust manifold nuts	28	21
Oil feed pipe-to-turbocharger union	25	18
Oil return pipe-to-turbocharger bolts	12	9
Throttle valve unit (damper unit) bolts	8	6
Turbocharger mounting nuts	24	18
2.2 litre engines		
Catalytic converter-to-expansion chamber nuts	21	15
Catalytic converter-to-turbocharger nuts	44	32
Exhaust heat shield bolts	10	7
Exhaust manifold nuts	27	20
Exhaust manifold studs	8	6
Fuel high-pressure pipe union nuts	25	18
Fuel rail mounting bolts	23	17
Fuel rail pressure sensor	35	26
Heater plugs	15	11
Injection pump mounting bolts	32	24
Injection pump pressure regulator bolts	6	4
Injection pump sprocket nut	90	66
Injection pump-to-cylinder block support bracket bolt	30	22
Injector nuts*:		
Timing belt side	6	4
Flywheel side:		
Stage 1	6	4
Stage 2	Angle-tighten through 360° ± 30°	
Injector studs*	2	1.5
Lower inlet manifold (plenum chamber) bolts	12	9
Oil return pipe bolt	9	7
Oil supply pipe to turbocharger	15	11
Oil supply union to cylinder block	42	31
Turbocharger mounting nuts	26	19
Upper inlet manifold/rocker cover bolts**	12	9

** New bolts/nuts must be used.*

*** Refer to the specific instructions in the text when tightening the inlet manifold bolts.*

1 General information and precautions

General information

The fuel system consists of a rear-mounted fuel tank, a fuel filter with integral water separator, and a high-pressure pump with common-rail injection system, electronic injectors and associated components.

The main components of the system are:

a) Electronic control unit (ECU).
b) High-pressure pump.
c) Fuel filter.
d) Injector rail.
e) Four electronic solenoid injectors.
f) Airflow meter.
g) Fuel temperature sensor.
h) Coolant temperature sensor.
i) Cylinder reference sensor.
j) Engine speed sensor.
k) Turbocharging pressure sensor.
l) EGR valve.

The common-rail injection system operates as follows. Fuel is drawn from the fuel tank to the high-pressure pump by a low-pressure transfer pump integrated in the high-pressure pump. Before reaching the high-pressure pump, the fuel passes through a fuel filter where foreign matter and water are removed. As the fuel passes through the filter, it is heated by an electric heater. On reaching the high-pressure pump, the fuel is pressurised according to demand, and accumulates in the injection common-rail. The pressure in the rail is accurately maintained using a pressure sensor in the rail and a pressure regulator under the control of the engine management ECU. This arrangement keeps heat generation to a minimum, and improves engine output. The rail pressure is also maintained by the injectors themselves; short electrical pulses which are not long enough to open the injector, allow fuel into the return (leak-off) circuit, and also the normal pulses which open the injectors cause a reduction in pressure. The ECU determines the exact timing and duration of the injection period according to engine operating conditions.

The four fuel injectors inject a homogeneous spray of fuel into the combustion chambers located in the cylinder head. The injectors operate sequentially according to the firing order of the cylinders, and each injector needle is lubricated by fuel, which accumulates in the spring chamber. Each injector has its own unique flow characteristics, which are used by the system ECU to calculate the exact quantity of fuel to inject.

In terms of the sensors used by the ECU to control a modern common-rail diesel system, these engines are very similar to their petrol equivalents. The ECU determines engine speed and position from a TDC sensor fitted to the transmission bellhousing which detects a reference tooth on the flywheel ring gear, and signals the ECU. A similar sensor is fitted to monitor the camshaft, to give a reference for No 1 cylinder. Further sensors are used to monitor airflow into the engine, air temperature, and turbocharging pressure. On the fuel side, fuel pressure, temperature and flow rate are all monitored, according to model, via sensors on the high-pressure pump and/or the fuel rail. As with the petrol-engine models, an 'electronic' throttle is fitted, with an accelerator position sensor instead of the mechanical cable previously used.

Provided that the specified maintenance is carried out, the fuel injection equipment will give long and trouble-free service. The main potential cause of damage to the high-pressure pump and injectors is dirt or water in the fuel. It is highly recommended that a set of fuel line plugs is obtained – these are available from motor accessory shops and better motor factors.

Servicing of the high-pressure pump, injectors, and electronic equipment and sensors is very limited for the home mechanic, and any dismantling or adjustment other than that described in this Chapter must be entrusted to a Renault dealer or fuel injection specialist.

If a fault appears in the injection system, first ensure that all the system wiring connectors are securely connected and free of corrosion. Should the fault persist, the car should be taken to a Renault dealer or specialist who can test the system on a diagnostic tester. The tester will locate the fault quickly and simply, alleviating the need to test all the system components individually, which is a time-consuming operation that carries a risk of damaging the ECU. It is advisable to have any faulty components renewed by the dealer as in many instances the tester is required to reprogram the ECU in the event of component or sensor renewal.

Precautions

Warning: It is necessary to take certain precautions when working on the fuel system components, particularly the fuel injectors and high-pressure pump. Before carrying out any operations on the fuel system, refer to the precautions given in 'Safety first!' at the beginning of this manual. Allow the engine to cool for 5 to 10 minutes to ensure the fuel pressure and temperature are at a minimum.

Warning: Exercise extreme caution when working on the high-pressure fuel system. Do not attempt to test the fuel injectors or disconnect the high-pressure lines with the engine running. Never expose the hands or any part of the body to injector spray, as the high working pressure can cause the fuel to penetrate the skin, with possibly fatal results. You are strongly advised to have any work which involves testing the injectors under pressure carried out by a dealer or fuel injection specialist.

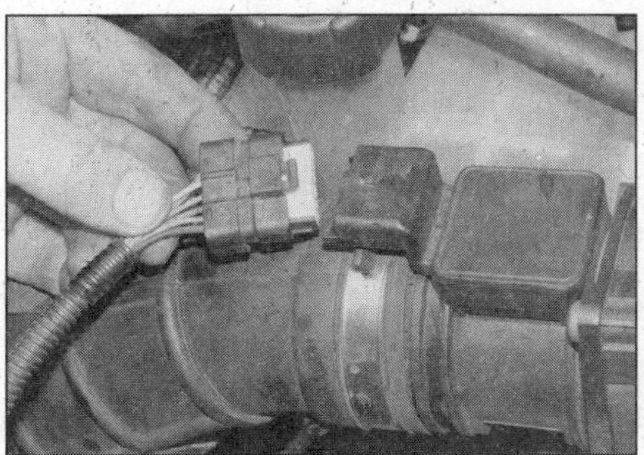

2.2 Disconnect the airflow/temperature sensor wiring connector

2.3 Release the securing clip and disconnect the hose

2 Air cleaner assembly and inlet ducts – removal and refitting

Removal

1 Unclip the plastic covers from the engine, battery and the fuse/relay box in the engine compartment.

2 Disconnect the wiring connector from the airflow sensor **(see illustration)**.

3 Slacken the hose clips and disconnect the air inlet hoses from the air cleaner housing **(see illustration)**.

4 Undo the four retaining screws from the top of the air cleaner housing and remove the air filter element **(see illustration)**.

5 Lift the lower part of the filter housing, which is located in rubber grommets in the inner wing panel, and remove it from the vehicle **(see illustration)**

6 With the air cleaner housing removed, the air inlet hoses and plastic ducts can be individually removed after slackening the retaining clips and undoing the relevant retaining bolts.

2.4 Undo the retaining screws – arrowed

2.5 Air filter housing locating grommets – arrowed

Refitting

7 Refitting is the reverse of removal, making sure all the hoses and ducts are securely reconnected.

3 Accelerator pedal – removal and refitting

Refer to Chapter 4A, Section 3.

4 Fuel system – priming and bleeding

Note: *Refer to the precautions in Section 1 before proceeding.*

Warning: Do not attempt to bleed the system by loosening any of the unions on the high-pressure circuit. Disconnecting any of the system sensors, or the fuel injectors, will result in a fault code being logged by the system ECU, which must then be cleared by a Renault dealer.

1 After disconnecting part of the fuel supply system or running out of fuel, it is necessary to prime the system and bleed off any air that may have entered the system components.

2 On most models, there is a pump to enable the system to be bled, this consists of a hand-operated priming bulb located next to the filter assembly on the right-hand side inner wing

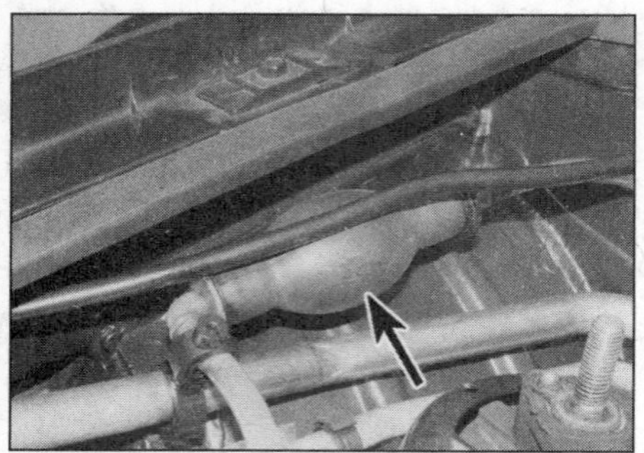

4.2 Hand priming pump (arrowed)

panel **(see illustration)**. **Note:** *On models with no hand-operated priming pump, the ignition will need to be switched on and off (in 5 second bursts) several times for the pump to prime the filter. On these models, there is a low-pressure pump between the intake assembly and the fuel filter.*

3 Squeeze the priming bulb several times to purge the low-pressure circuit of air.

4 Attempt to start the engine normally, however, do not operate the starter motor for more than 5 seconds. If necessary, operate the starter motor in 4 to 5 second bursts followed by pauses of 8 to 10 seconds. As soon as the engine starts, let it run at fast idle speed until a regular idle speed is reached.

5 Fuel gauge sender unit – removal and refitting

Refer to Chapter 4A, Section 7.

6 Fuel tank – removal and refitting

Refer to Chapter 4A, Section 9.

7 Idle speed – general

1 The engine management ECU uses the following inputs to calculate the recommended idle speed according to the varying load on the engine by peripheral electrical or mechanical components.

a) Engine coolant temperature.
b) Battery voltage.
c) The gear selected.
d) Electrical consumers (heater fan, climate control system, thermo-plungers, etc).

2 At normal engine temperature with no electrical consumers switched on and neutral selected, the engine idle speed will be in the range specified.

3 If the accelerator pedal sensor is faulty, the ECU will override the idle speed to 1200 rpm, and the injection warning light will be illuminated on the instrument panel.

4 If the information from the brake switch and the accelerator pedal sensor does not correspond then the idle speed will be raised to 1250 rpm and the warning light will be illuminated.

5 Should the idle speed be repeatedly incorrect, the car should be taken to a Renault dealer who will have the necessary diagnostic equipment to pinpoint the faulty component responsible.

8 Engine stop system – description, removal and refitting

Description

1 This system is designed to stop the engine quickly, once the ignition has been switched off. It consists of a throttle valve (also called a damper unit), solenoid valve, diaphragm and a vacuum reservoir. On 1.9 litre engines it is located on the left-hand rear of the engine, where the air intake hose connects. On 2.2 litre engines it is located on the front of the engine, where the air intake hose connects.

2 When the ignition is switched off, the solenoid valve is operated to allow a vacuum to the diaphragm unit. The diaphragm unit then closes the throttle valve, preventing any air into the engine, which stops the engine immediately.

3 Before removing any items, disconnect the battery negative terminal (refer to *Disconnecting the battery* in the Reference Section of this manual).

1.9 litre engines

Throttle valve housing (damper unit)

4 Slacken the retaining clip and disconnect the air intake hose from the throttle/damper unit.

5 Disconnect the vacuum pipe from the diaphragm unit.

6 Undo the retaining bolts and withdraw the throttle valve unit from the intake manifold, recover the gasket/seal (as applicable).

7 Refitting is a reversal of removal, using a new gasket/seal and tightening to the specified torque.

Solenoid valve

8 The solenoid valve is located below the vacuum tank on the rear of the intake manifold. Disconnect the wiring connector and the vacuum pipe(s) from the solenoid valve.

9 Undo the retaining bolt and withdraw the valve from the intake manifold **(see illustration).**

10 Refitting is a reversal of removal.

Diaphragm unit

11 The diaphragm unit is part of the throttle valve housing and cannot be removed separately see paragraphs 4 to 6.

Vacuum reservoir/canister

12 The vacuum tank is located on the rear of the intake manifold. Disconnect the vacuum pipes from the each side of the reservoir/canister **(see illustration)**.

13 Undo the retaining bolts and withdraw the vacuum reservoir from the intake manifold.

14 Refitting is a reversal of removal.

2.2 litre engines

Throttle valve housing (damper unit)

15 Slacken the retaining clip and disconnect the air intake hose from the bottom of the throttle/damper unit **(see illustration)**.

16 Disconnect the vacuum pipe from the diaphragm unit **(see illustration)**.

17 Undo the retaining bolts and disconnect

8.9 Undo the valve retaining bolts – arrowed

8.12 Undo the vacuum tank retaining bolts – arrowed

8.15 Release the securing clip (arrowed) and disconnect the hose

the EGR pipe from the front of the throttle valve housing, recover the gasket/seal **(see illustration)**.

18 Disconnect the wiring connector from the EGR valve on the side of the throttle valve housing **(see illustration)**.

19 Undo the retaining bolts and remove the mounting bracket between the power steering pump bracket and the throttle valve housing **(see illustration)**.

20 Slacken the retaining clip on the air intake hose at the top of the throttle/damper unit **(see illustration)**.

21 Undo the three mounting bolts from the throttle valve housing and withdraw it from the cylinder block. Disconnect the vacuum pipes from the rear of the throttle housing **(see illustrations)**.

22 To remove the throttle flap and diaphragm assembly, undo the four retaining bolts and remove the upper part of the throttle valve housing **(see illustration)**. A new gasket will be required for refitting.

23 Refitting is a reversal of removal, using new gaskets/seals where required.

Solenoid valve

24 The solenoid valve is located to the right of the throttle valve housing (as viewed from the front). Disconnect the wiring block connector from the solenoid valve **(see illustration)**.

25 Undo the retaining bolts and withdraw the valve from the mounting bracket, disconnect the vacuum pipes as it is removed **(see illustration)**.

26 Refitting is a reversal of removal.

8.16 Disconnect the vacuum pipe

8.17 A new gasket will be needed

8.18 Disconnect the EGR valve wiring connector – arrowed

8.19 Undo the bracket securing bolts – arrowed

Diaphragm unit

27 The diaphragm unit is part of the throttle flap see paragraph 22.

Vacuum reservoir/canister

28 The vacuum reservoir is located at the rear of the throttle valve housing. Remove

8.20 Release the securing clip from the upper hose

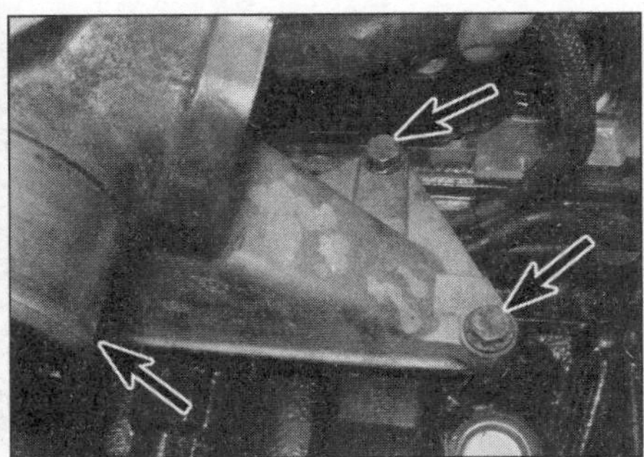

8.21a Undo the three mounting bolts arrowed (one is hidden) . . .

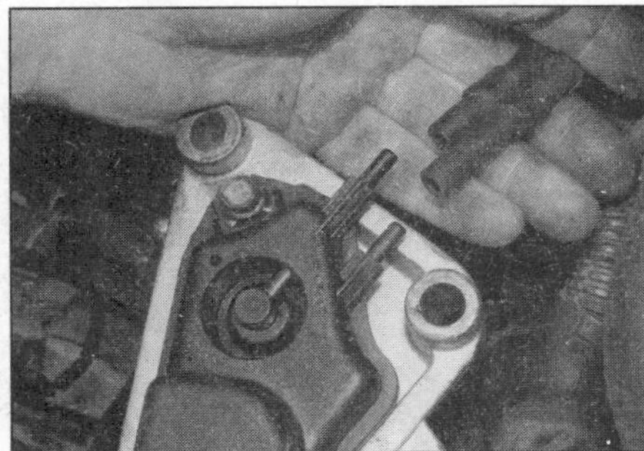

8.21b . . . and disconnect the vacuum pipes

8.22 Removing the upper part of the throttle housing

8.24 Disconnecting the wiring connector from the solenoid valve

8.25 Undo the valve mounting bolts – arrowed

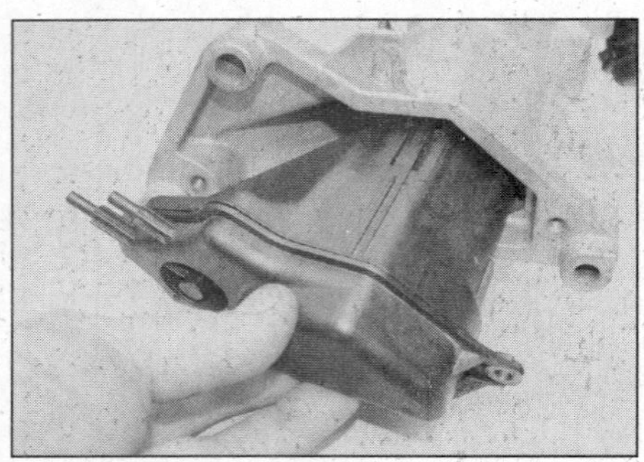

8.29 Withdraw the vacuum reservoir from the throttle valve housing

the throttle valve housing as described in paragraphs 15 to 21.

29 Undo the retaining bolts and withdraw the vacuum reservoir from the rear of the throttle valve housing **(see illustration)**.

30 Refitting is a reversal of removal.

9 Fuel system sensors and components – removal and refitting

Note: *Refer to the precautions in Section 1 before proceeding.*

1 Disconnect the battery negative lead (refer to *Disconnecting the battery* in the Reference Chapter).

Fuel pump pressure regulator

2 Remove the plastic covers from the top of the engine.

3 Disconnect the battery negative lead, and move the lead away from the battery (see *Disconnecting the battery*).

4 Disconnect the wiring plug from the fuel pressure regulator located on the rear of the high-pressure pump **(see illustration)**.

5 Clean the area around the base of the regulator, then remove the three regulator mounting bolts **(see illustration)**.

6 Ease the regulator out of position (any resistance is due to the O-ring seals) without using any tools. Once the regulator is free, recover any O-ring seals that were left behind – new seals should be obtained for refitting.

7 Fit the new seals, lubricated with clean diesel fuel, to the regulator.

8 Wash the regulator mating face and mounting aperture on the pump with clean diesel fuel, then wipe clean – it is most important that no dirt is introduced into the pump during refitting.

9 Offer up the regulator, and push it gently into position, twisting it slightly to help enter the O-rings. Once it is fully home, refit the bolts and tighten by hand initially.

10 Tighten the three bolts evenly to the specified torque.

11 Reconnect the regulator wiring plug and the battery negative lead.

12 On completion, start the engine and check for signs of leakage before refitting the engine covers.

Fuel rail pressure sensor

13 The fuel rail pressure sensor is screwed directly into the fuel rail.

14 Remove the plastic covers from the top of the engine. On 2.2 litre models, disconnect the breather pipe and unclip the fuel rail protector cover **(see illustration)**.

15 Disconnect the wiring plug from the pressure sensor, then unscrew and remove it from the rail **(see illustrations).** Recover the sealing washer – a new one must be used when refitting. If the sensor is to be removed for a long period, cap the open connection on the fuel rail to prevent dirt entry.

16 Refitting is a reversal of removal. Use a new sealing washer, and tighten the sensor to the specified torque. On completion, and before refitting the engine top cover, run the engine and check for signs of fuel leakage.

Fuel temperature sensor

17 The fuel temperature sensor is only fitted to some 1.9 litre models. It is clipped to the front of the fuel rail, and is tapped into the low-pressure fuel return circuit.

18 Remove the engine top cover.

19 Squeeze and disconnect the connector on the top of the sensor **(see illustration).**

20 The two remaining sensor pipes are heat-shrunk plastic, and may prove difficult to remove without causing damage. If suitable pieces of rubber joining sleeve can be found, the plastic could be cut off, providing the sensor stubs underneath are not damaged – the rubber sleeves can then be used when refitting, providing careful checks are made for signs of leaks. If the sensor is not being renewed, trace the pipes to the quick-release connector on the pump, and to the rubber

9.4 Disconnect the wiring connector from the pressure regulator

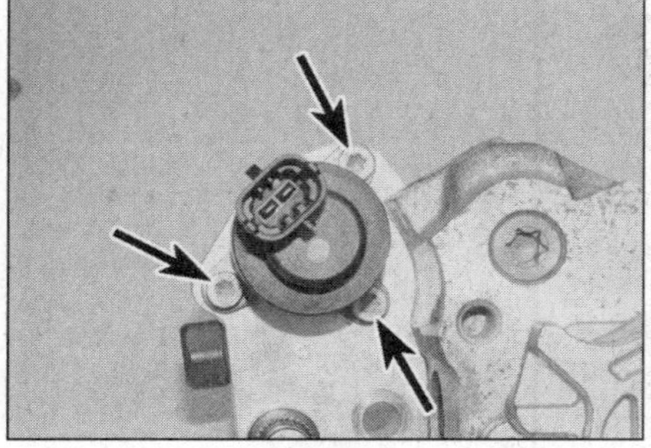

9.5 Undo the regulator mounting bolts – arrowed

9.14 Unclip the protective cover – 2.2 litre engines

9.15a Disconnecting the wiring connector on 1.9 litre engines . . .

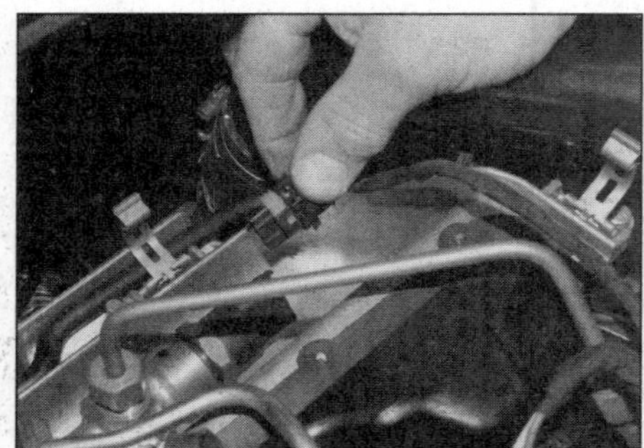

9.15b . . . and on 2.2 litre engines

9.19 Disconnect the fuel temperature sensor wiring connector – 1.9 litre engine

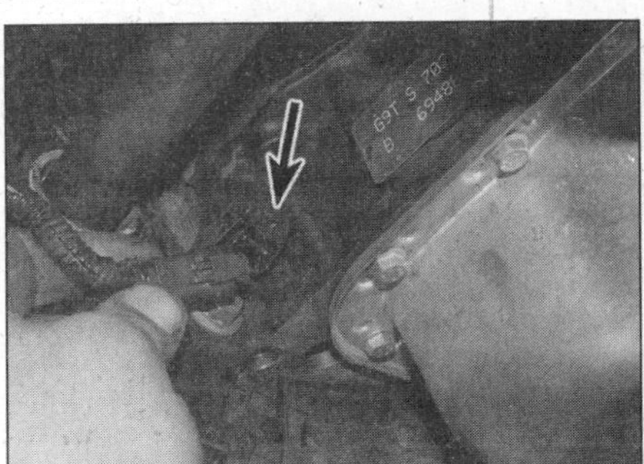
9.27 Crankshaft sensor – arrowed

9.32a Disconnect the wiring connector . . .

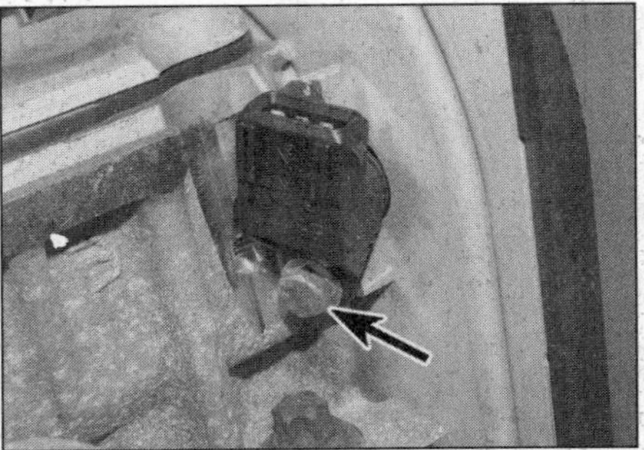
9.32b . . . and undo the retaining bolt – arrowed

sleeve on the leak-off pipes, and disconnect there.

21 Unclip the sensor from the fuel rail, and remove it.

22 Refitting is a reversal of removal. Check for signs of leakage from any of the pipes that have been disturbed.

Crankshaft speed/position sensor

1.9 litre engines

23 Remove the battery and battery tray as described in Chapter 5A, and the injection ECU as described below.

24 The sensor is located on the front of the transmission bellhousing. Disconnect the wiring plug, then remove the sensor mounting bolt and withdraw it.

25 Check the sensor for signs of damage, and clean it before refitting. Refitting is a reversal of removal.

2.2 litre engines

26 Apply the handbrake, then jack up the front of the car and support it on axle stands (see *Jacking and vehicle support*). Remove the engine undertray.

27 The sensor is located on the rear of the engine cylinder block at the flywheel end. Disconnect the wiring plug, then release the retaining clip and remove the sensor **(see illustration)**.

28 Check the sensor for signs of damage, and clean it before refitting. Refitting is a reversal of removal.

Accelerator pedal position sensor

29 Refer to Section 3.

Cylinder (camshaft) position sensor – 1.9 litre engines

30 The camshaft position sensor is fitted to the rear of the cylinder head, at the timing belt end.

31 Remove the plastic cover from the top of the engine.

32 Disconnect the wiring plug from the position sensor, then unscrew the mounting bolt underneath, and withdraw it from the engine **(see illustrations)**. Check the condition of the sensor seal and, if necessary, fit a new one.

33 Refitting is a reversal of removal.

Cylinder (fuel pump) position sensor – 2.2 litre engines

34 The fuel pump position sensor is fitted to the timing cover on the right-hand side of the engine.

35 Remove the plastic covers from the right-hand side of the engine compartment.

36 Disconnect the wiring plug from the position sensor, then unscrew the mounting bolt, and withdraw it from the engine **(see illustrations)**. Check the condition of the sensor seal, and if necessary, fit a new one.

37 Refitting is a reversal of removal.

Turbocharging pressure sensor

38 The turbocharging pressure sensor is fitted to the air duct, which runs from the intercooler to the throttle damper valve unit.

39 Disconnect the wiring plug from one side of the sensor, then slide back the locking clip at the opposite end. Carefully pull the sensor out of the duct, noting that it has a small O-ring seal, and remove it. Check the condition of the sensor seal and, if necessary, fit a new one.

40 Refitting is a reversal of removal.

Turbocharger pressure regulating solenoid

41 The pressure regulating solenoid valve is fitted to the right-hand rear corner of the engine compartment.

42 Unhook the solenoid from the mounting bracket **(see illustration).**

43 Disconnect the solenoid wiring plug and the two vacuum hoses from the valve (noting their positions for refitting), and remove the valve.

44 Refitting is a reversal of removal.

Airflow and air temperature sensor

45 The airflow meter fitted to the main air cleaner body has an integral air temperature sensor.

46 Remove the upper section of the air cleaner assembly as described in Section 2.

47 Remove the two mounting screws, and withdraw the airflow meter from the air cleaner. Check the condition of the sealing ring, and renew if necessary **(see illustrations)**.

9.36a Disconnect the wiring connector . . .

9.36b . . . undo the retaining bolt and remove the sensor

9.42 Remove the pressure regulating solenoid from its mounting bracket

9.47a Remove the screws – arrowed

9.47b Renew the sealing ring if necessary

9.51 Remove the securing bracket . . .

9.52 . . . and withdraw the ECU

48 Refitting is a reversal of removal.

Electronic control unit (ECU)

Note: *The ECU is electronically-coded to match the engine immobiliser and certain other engine components. If the ECU is being removed in order to fit a new unit, it is highly recommended that a Renault dealer should carry out this work.*

Caution: The ECU wiring plugs should only be disconnected after the disconnecting battery. If the ECU is unplugged 'live', it could be damaged.

49 Unclip and remove the engine compartment upper cover.

50 Remove the battery and battery tray as described in Chapter 5A.

51 Undo the retaining bolts and remove the bracket from across the top of the ECU **(see illustration).**

52 Remove the mounting bolts and withdraw the ECU from its mounting bracket **(see illustration).**

53 Slide back the locking catches, and disconnect the wiring plug connectors from the ECU.

54 Refitting is a reversal of removal. Ensure that the ECU wiring plugs are securely reconnected.

10 Fuel injection pump – removal and refitting

Caution: Be careful not to allow dirt into the injection pump or injector pipes during this procedure. New sealing rings should be used on the fuel pipe banjo unions when refitting.

1.9 litre engines

Note: *Refer to the precautions in Section 1 before proceeding.*

Removal

1 Disconnect the battery negative lead (refer to *Disconnecting the battery* in the Reference Chapter).

2 Loosen the right-hand front wheel bolts, then jack up the front of the car and support on axle stands. Remove the right front wheel, engine undertray and wheel arch liner.

3 Remove the auxiliary drivebelt as described in Chapter 1B, and the timing belt with reference to Chapter 2B.

4 Disconnect the crankcase breather hose that runs across the top of the engine, and move it to one side.

5 Disconnect the wiring plugs from the following fuel system components **(see illustrations)**:

a) The fuel filter (see Chapter 1B).
b) The glow plugs.
c) The fuel pressure regulator (back of the pump).
d) The fuel pressure sensor (at the pump end of the fuel rail).

10.5a Disconnect the wiring connectors from the fuel filter . . .

10.5b . . . the glow plugs (arrowed) . . .

10.5c . . . the fuel pressure regulator . . .

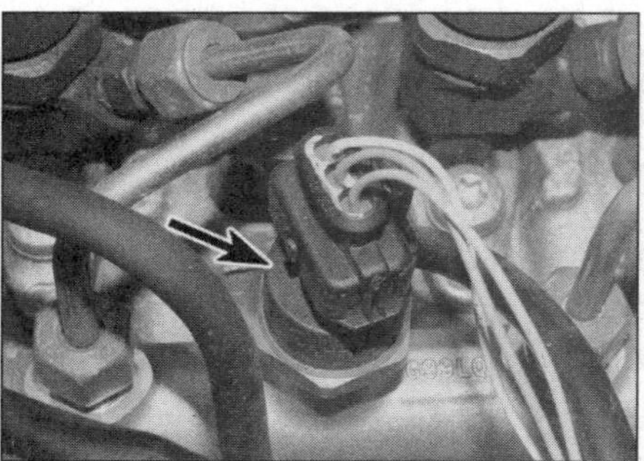
10.5d . . and the fuel pressure sensor

6 Disconnect the fuel supply and return pipes from the injection pump **(see illustration)**. Unclip or undo the pipes as necessary, once disconnected. Cap or plug the open connections, to reduce fuel loss, and to prevent the entry of dirt.

7 Loosen the fuel rail mounting bolts by a few turns, so that the rail is still fitted, but loose **(see illustration)**.

8 Unscrew the unions and remove the pump-to-rail high-pressure fuel pipe. Again, cap or

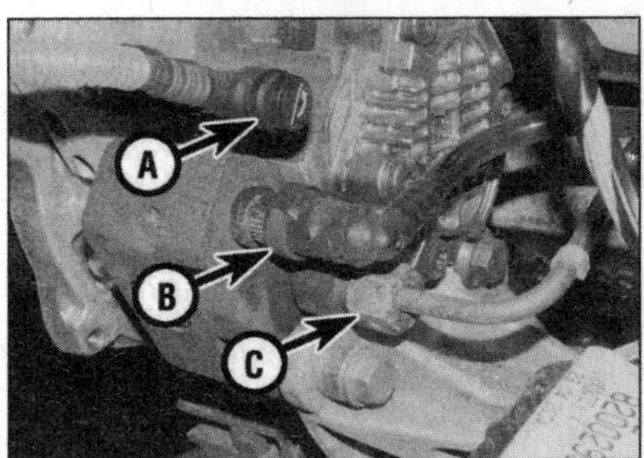

10.6 Supply pipe from fuel filter (A), fuel rail return pipe (B) and pump to fuel rail (C)

10.7 One of the fuel rail mounting bolts – arrowed

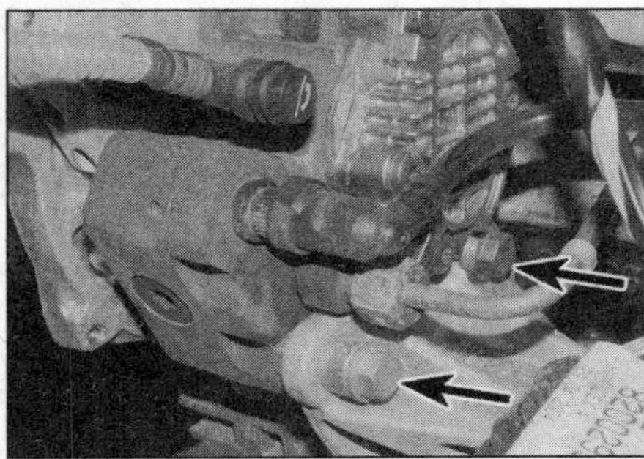

10.9 Injection pump rear mounting bolts

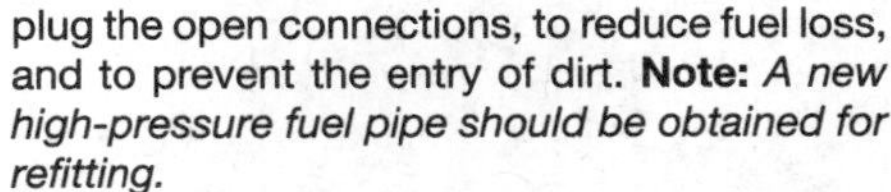

plug the open connections, to reduce fuel loss, and to prevent the entry of dirt. **Note:** *A new high-pressure fuel pipe should be obtained for refitting.*

9 Remove the two mounting bolts from the rear of the pump **(see illustration)**, then the three from the front support (which forms the mounting point for the engine right-hand mounting), and carefully lift the pump out with the front support attached.

10 Separating the pump from the front support means removing the pump sprocket to access the support bolts. Removing the pump sprocket will require a suitable puller (the sprocket is located on a taper), and some means of holding the sprocket while the nut is loosened. Once the sprocket has been removed, three further bolts secure the front support. It may be preferable to entrust this part of the job to a Renault dealer or well-equipped workshop.

Refitting

11 Refitting is a reversal of removal, noting the following points:

a) *Fit a new high-pressure pipe as follows. Some pipes may be supplied with a sachet of lubricant, which should be used on the union nut threads before fitting – if no lubricant is provided, none should be applied. Finger-tighten the nuts before tightening them to the specified torque. Take care not to place the new high-pressure pipe under any stress when the unions are tightened.*

b) *Tighten all nuts and bolts to the specified torque.*

c) *Fit a new timing belt as described in Chapter 2B.*

d) *On completion, prime and bleed the fuel system as described in Section 4. Run the engine, and check for fuel leaks.*

2.2 litre engines

Note: *The following procedure describes pump removal and refitting using the special Renault injection pump sprocket holding tool (Mot. 1548). This tool holds the sprocket securely in position whilst the pump is removed; keeping the timing belt correctly tensioned, and so removes the need to disturb the timing belt. If the procedure is to be attempted without the special tool, great care must be taken to ensure that the pump sprocket is held firmly in position so that it does not move in relation to the timing belt. If the sprocket moves or the timing belt tension is released it will be necessary to remove the timing belt cover and check the position of the sprocket timing marks prior to starting the engine.*

Removal

12 Disconnect the battery negative terminal (refer to *Disconnecting the battery* in the Reference Section of this manual).

13 Position number 1 cylinder at TDC on its compression stroke and lock the crankshaft in position as described in Chapter 2C, Section 3. **Do not** attempt to rotate the engine once the crankshaft is locked in position.

14 Remove the throttle valve damper unit as described is Section 8.

15 Disconnect the wiring connector from the fuel high-pressure regulator **(see illustration)**.

16 Disconnect the fuel supply and return pipes from the injection pump **(see illustration)**. Unclip the pipes as necessary, once disconnected. Cap or plug the open connections, to reduce fuel loss, and to prevent the entry of dirt.

17 Undo the retaining bolts from the lower rear mounting bracket and remove it from the engine **(see illustration)**.

18 Release the breather pipe, then unclip the plastic cover from above the fuel rail and move it to one side **(see illustration)**.

19 Disconnect the fuel high-pressure pipe from the fuel rail and release it from its mounting bracket to remove **(see illustrations)**. Cap or plug the open connections, to reduce fuel loss, and to prevent the entry of dirt.

10.15 Fuel pressure regulator – arrowed

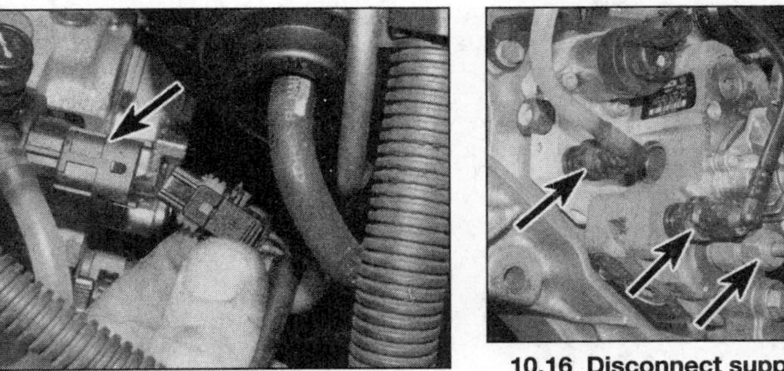

10.16 Disconnect supply pipe from fuel filter, fuel rail return pipe and pump-to-fuel rail pipe

10.17 Injection pump rear mounting bracket bolts – arrowed

10.18 Unclip the protective cover from above the fuel rail

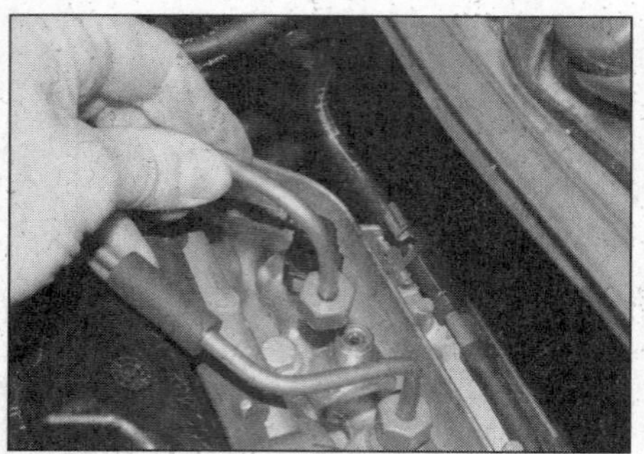
10.19a Undo the fuel pipe union from the fuel rail . . .

10.19b . . . and undo the mounting bracket retaining bolt – arrowed

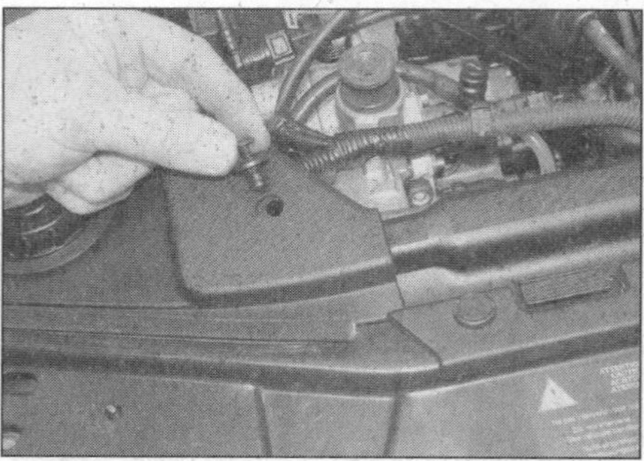
10.20a Release the retaining clips . . .

10.20b . . . remove the PAS filler cap and seal . . .

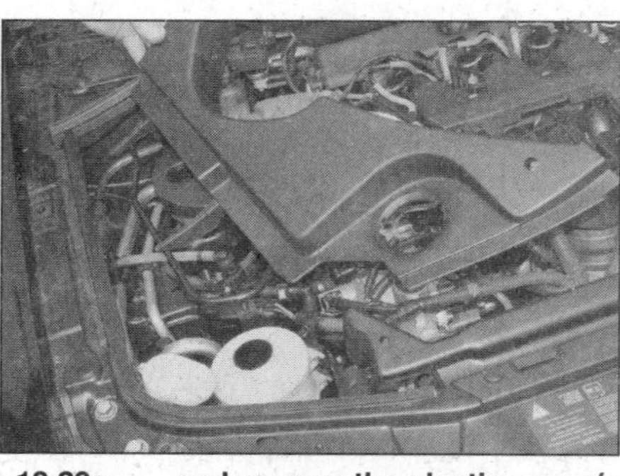
10.20c . . . and remove the plastic cover/shield

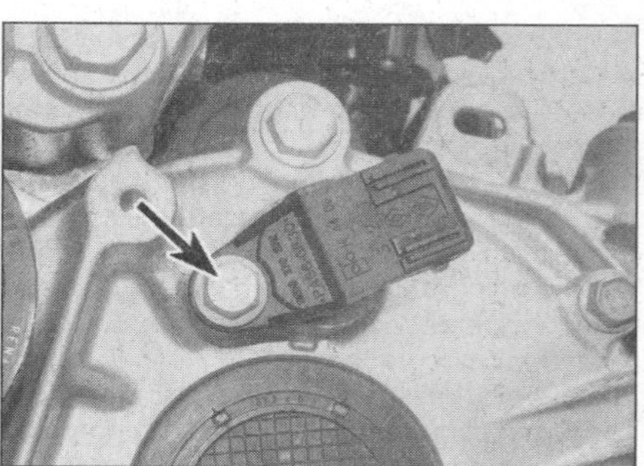
10.22 Undo the sensor retaining bolt – arrowed

20 Release the retaining clip, remove the power steering reservoir cap and withdraw the plastic cover/shield **(see illustrations).**

21 Unclip the fuel filter from its mounting bracket and move it to one side, then undo the retaining bolts from the mounting bracket and remove it from the inner wing panel.

22 Disconnect the wiring connector, then undo the retaining bolt and remove the position sensor from the timing belt cover **(see illustration).** Recover the O-ring seal to prevent it falling inside the timing cover.

23 Using a screwdriver, pierce a hole in the pump hub plastic plug and remove it from the timing cover. A new one will be required for refitting **(see illustration).**

24 With the engine still at TDC and the setting pin removed, hold the crankshaft in position, using a spanner on the crankshaft pulley retaining bolt. Slacken and remove the pump hub central mounting nut **(see illustration).**

25 Bolt the Renault injection pump sprocket holding tool (Mot. 1548 – see **Note** at the start of this Section) in position on the engine timing cover **(see illustration)**. In the absence of the special Renault tool, a suitable alternative could be fabricated, to prevent the pump sprocket from moving.

26 Slacken the three retaining bolts from the rear of the pump by a three or four turns, do not remove the bolts completely at this point **(see illustration)**.

27 Tighten the centre bolt of the Renault special tool, to release the taper on the pump shaft from the sprocket **(see illustration)**.

28 Once the sprocket is free from the pump shaft, the three mounting bolts (which have already been slackened – paragraph 26) can be removed and the pump assembly withdrawn **(see illustration)**.

Refitting

29 Refitting is a reversal of removal, noting the following points:

a) Fit a new high-pressure pipe as follows. Some pipes may be supplied with a sachet of lubricant, which should be used

10.23 Pierce hole with screwdriver to remove plug

10.24 Remove the pump sprocket retaining nut

10.25 Renault special injection pump sprocket holding tool

10.26 Slacken the pump retaining bolts – arrowed

on the union nut threads before fitting – if no lubricant is provided, none should be applied. Finger-tighten the nuts before tightening them to the specified torque. Take care not to place the new high-pressure pipe under any stress when the unions are tightened.

b) Tighten all nuts and bolts to the specified torque.

*c) Fit a new O-ring seal to the pump housing **(see illustration).***

*d) Fit a new plastic pump hub seal/plug to the timing gear cover **(see illustration).***

e) On completion, prime and bleed the fuel system as described in Section 4. Run the engine, and check for fuel leaks.

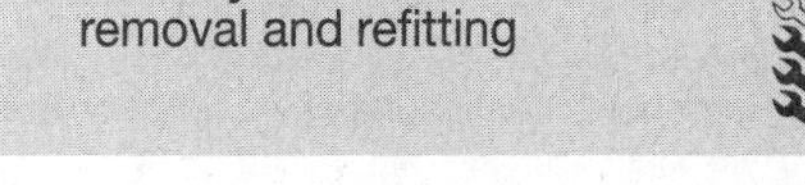

11 Fuel injectors – removal and refitting

Note: *Refer to the precautions in Section 1 before proceeding.*

Testing

1 Injectors deteriorate with prolonged use, and it is reasonable to expect them to need reconditioning or renewal after 60 000 miles (100 000 km) or so. Accurate testing, overhaul and calibration of the injectors must be left to a specialist.

Removal

Note: *Take care not to allow dirt into the injectors or fuel pipes during this procedure; clean around the area before commencing work. Note that all high-pressure pipes and return pipes that are removed must be renewed as a matter of course. The injector flame shield washers must also be renewed. On 2.2 litre models, new injector retaining studs, spacers and nuts will also be required.*

2 To gain access to the injectors, remove the engine upper cover.

3 Carefully clean around the injectors and injector pipe union nuts.

4 Disconnect the wiring connectors from the fuel injectors **(see illustration)**.

5 Note the fitted position and disconnect the leak-off pipes from the injectors **(see illustrations)**.

6 Slacken the union nuts securing the injector pipes to the fuel rail whilst being prepared for some fuel spillage. Note carefully the locations of the pipe clamps, for use when refitting new pipes.

7 Unscrew the union nuts and disconnect the pipes from the injectors, then completely remove the pipes. On 2.2 litre engines, counter-hold the unions on the injectors when unscrewing the union nuts. Cover the ends of the injectors, to prevent dirt ingress **(see illustration)**.

8 On 1.9 litre engines, unscrew the bolt securing each injector clamp plate, lift off the clamp plates and withdraw the injectors.

10.27 Tightening the centre bolt to release the pump shaft from the sprocket

10.28 Remove the bolts and carefully withdraw the pump

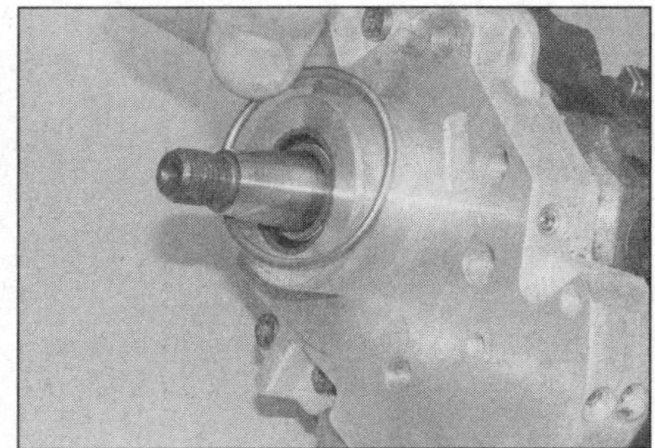

10.29a Fit new seal to the pump housing

10.29b Fit new seal/plug to the timing gear cover

Recover the flame shield washer between the injectors and the cylinder head.

9 On 2.2 litre engines, unscrew the injector clamp retaining nuts and remove the injectors **(see illustrations)**. Renault uses a special puller (tool Mot. 1549) to remove the injectors from the cylinder head. The injectors can be a tight fit in the cylinder head and need to be withdrawn vertically with the aid of a puller. A releasing agent can be used around the

11.4 Disconnect the wiring connectors from the injectors

11.5a Release the retaining clips – one arrowed . . .

11.5b . . . and remove the leak-off pipes

11.7 Use caps to cover the ends of the fuel pipes

11.9a Undo the retaining nuts – arrowed . . .

11.9b . . . and withdraw the injectors

11.11a Fit new injector retaining studs . . .

11.11b . . . and spacers

injectors to aid removal. Recover the washers from the cylinder head. New injector retaining studs, spacers and nuts will be required for refitting.

Refitting

10 Obtain new sealing washers and new fuel pipes for refitting.

11 On 2.2 litre engines, fit new injector retaining studs and spacers, coat the threads with oil and tighten them as tight as possible by hand **(see illustrations).**

12 Take care not to drop the injectors, or allow the needles at their tips to become damaged **(see illustration)**. The injectors are precision-made to fine limits, and must not be handled roughly. In particular, never mount them in a bench vice.

13 Fit new washers between the injectors and the cylinder head **(see illustration)**, insert the injectors then fit the mounting clamp plates.

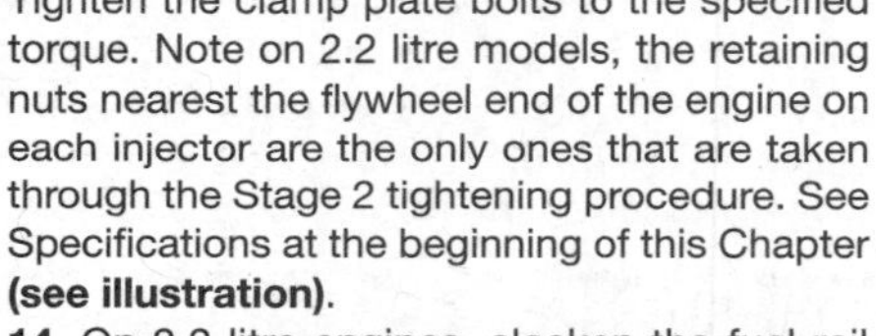

11.12 Check the seals (arrowed) on injectors

Tighten the clamp plate bolts to the specified torque. Note on 2.2 litre models, the retaining nuts nearest the flywheel end of the engine on each injector are the only ones that are taken through the Stage 2 tightening procedure. See Specifications at the beginning of this Chapter **(see illustration)**.

14 On 2.2 litre engines, slacken the fuel rail mounting bolts before refitting the fuel pipes.

15 Fit new injector pipes, and tighten the union nuts on the injectors and the fuel rail by hand at first. Make sure the pipe clamps are in their previously noted positions. Bearing in mind the high vibration levels with a diesel engine, if the clamps are wrongly positioned or missing, problems may be experienced with pipes breaking or splitting. With all the pipes in place tighten them to the specified torque setting.

16 On 2.2 litre engines, with the fuel pipes all in position tighten the fuel rail mounting bolts to the specified torque.

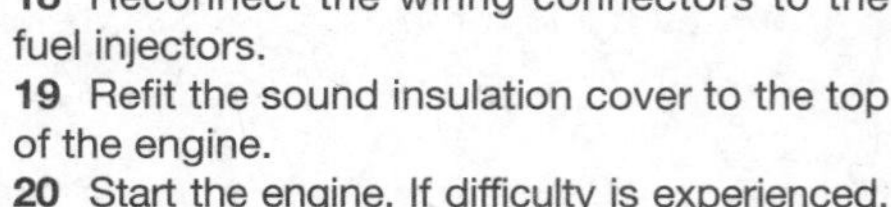

17 Renew the injector leak-off pipes, and refit in the noted position.

18 Reconnect the wiring connectors to the fuel injectors.

19 Refit the sound insulation cover to the top of the engine.

20 Start the engine. If difficulty is experienced, bleed the fuel system as described in Section 4.

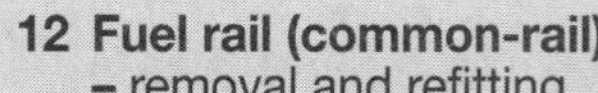

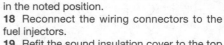

12 Fuel rail (common-rail) – removal and refitting

Note: *Refer to precautions in Section 1 before proceeding. After switching off the engine, allow several minutes for the fuel pressure to subside before disconnecting any of the high-pressure fuel pipes. Take care not to allow dirt into the fuel pipes during this procedure; clean around the area before commencing work. Note that all high-pressure pipes removed must be renewed as a matter of course.*

Removal

1 Disconnect the battery negative lead (refer to *Disconnecting the battery* in the Reference Chapter).

2 Remove the plastic engine covers from the top of the engine.

3 On 2.2 litre models, disconnect the breather pipe, release the securing clips and remove the fuel rail protective cover **(see illustrations).** Where fitted, remove the absorbent soundproofing material from around the fuel rail.

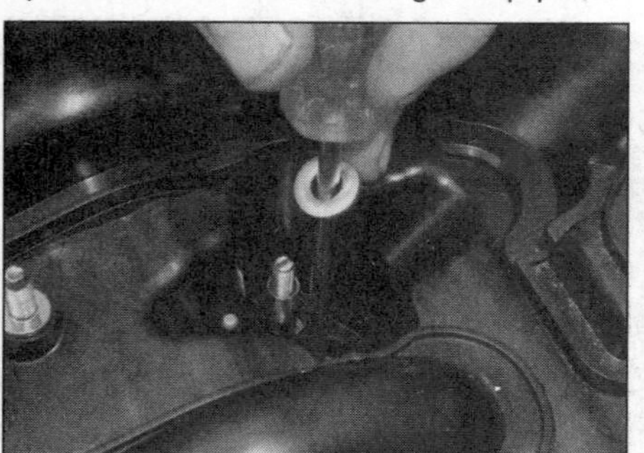

11.13a Using a long thin screwdriver to slide the new washers into place

11.13b Only the retaining nuts arrowed are taken to the stage 2 angle tightening

12.3a Disconnect the breather pipe . . .

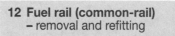

12.3b . . . and unclip the protective cover

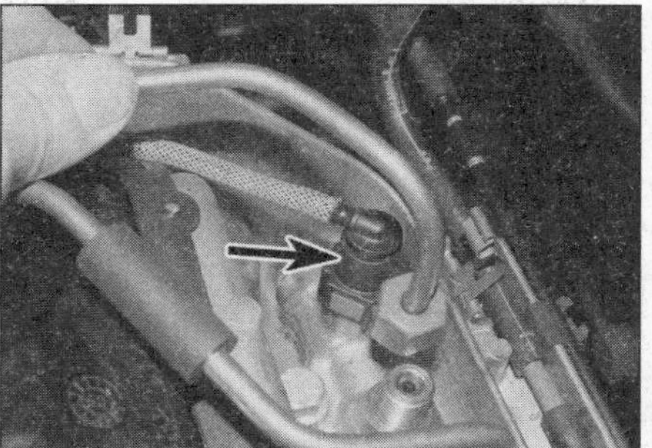
12.5a Disconnect the fuel supply and return pipe – arrowed

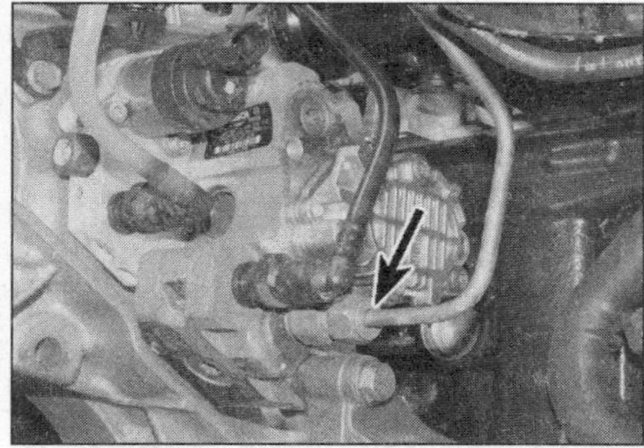
12.5b Disconnect the fuel supply pipe – arrowed

4 Disconnect the wiring connectors from the fuel rail pressure switch and the injectors.

5 Disconnect the fuel supply and return pipes from the fuel rail and high-pressure pump and remove, new ones will be required for refitting **(see illustrations)**.

6 Release the fuel pipes and unclip any wiring from retaining clips, note their position for refitting **(see illustration)**.

7 While holding the injectors with one spanner, unscrew the high-pressure pipe union nuts with a further spanner. As a precaution against remaining pressure in the pipes, first wrap some cloth/rag around the union. Take care not to damage the leak-off stubs on the injectors. Similarly, unscrew the union nuts from the fuel rail, and then remove the pipes (new ones will be required for refitting).

8 Cover or plug all fuel apertures to prevent entry of dust and dirt into the fuel system **(see illustration)**.

9 Unbolt and remove the fuel rail **(see illustration)**.

10 To remove the protector tray from below the fuel rail, release the pipe from along the securing clips, undo the mounting bolts and withdraw the tray from the rear of the engine **(see illustrations)**. Release the drain pipe from the end of the tray as it is removed.

Refitting

11 Refitting is a reversal of removal, noting the following points:

a) *Tighten all nuts and bolts to the specified torque.*

b) *Fit a new high-pressure pipes, some may be supplied with a sachet of lubricant, which should be used on the union nut threads before fitting – if no lubricant is provided, none should be applied. Finger-tighten the nuts before tightening them to the specified torque. Take care not to place the new high-pressure pipes under any stress when the unions are tightened.*

c) *When tightening the pipe union nuts onto the injectors, counter-hold the injectors with a further spanner.*

d) *Where applicable, refit the absorbent soundproofing material around the fuel rail, if it is contaminated with diesel it will need to be renewed.*

e) *On completion, prime and bleed the fuel system as described in Section 4. Run the engine, and check for fuel leaks.*

13 Inlet and exhaust manifolds (1.9 litre engines) – removal and refitting

Removal

1 The inlet and exhaust manifolds cannot be removed individually. Although the manifolds

12.6 Release the pipes from the mounting bracket

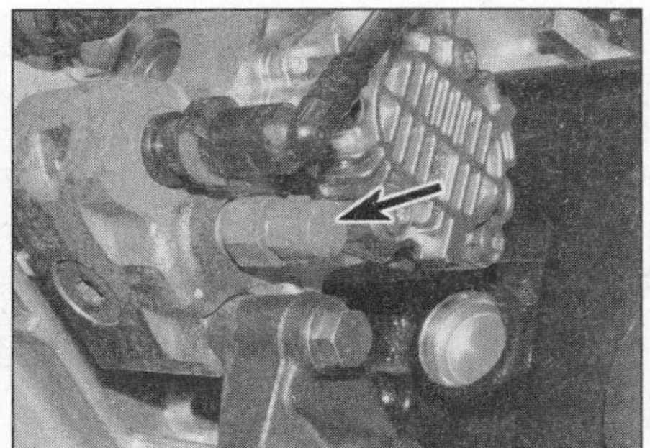
12.8 Cap fitted to prevent dirt ingress

12.9 Fuel rail mounting bolts – arrowed

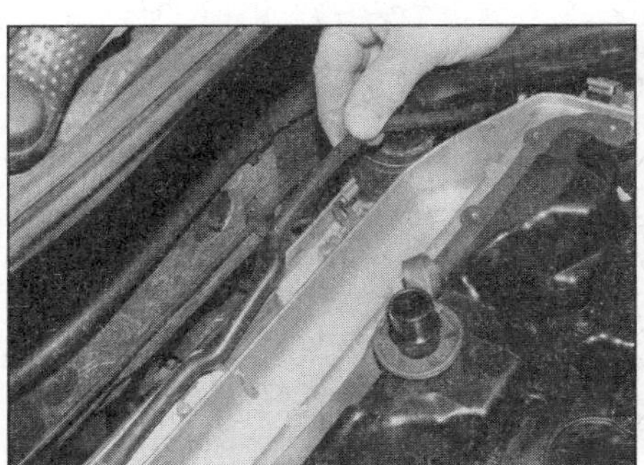
12.10a Unclip the pipe . . .

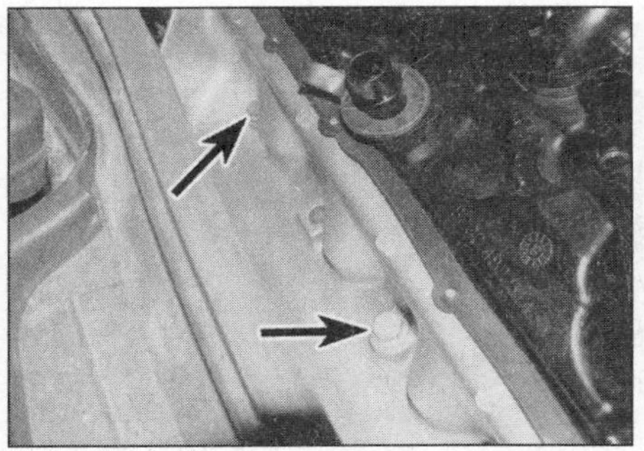
12.10b . . . undo the fuel tray mounting bolts – arrowed . . .

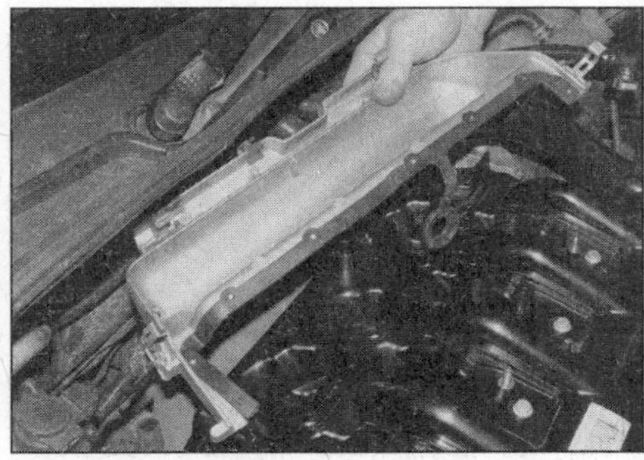
12.10c . . . and remove the fuel tray

13.5 Disconnect the EGR valve wiring connector

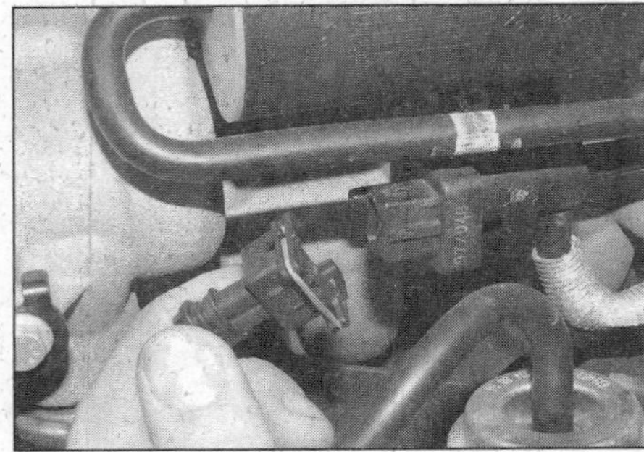
13.6 Disconnect the vacuum control solenoid wiring connector

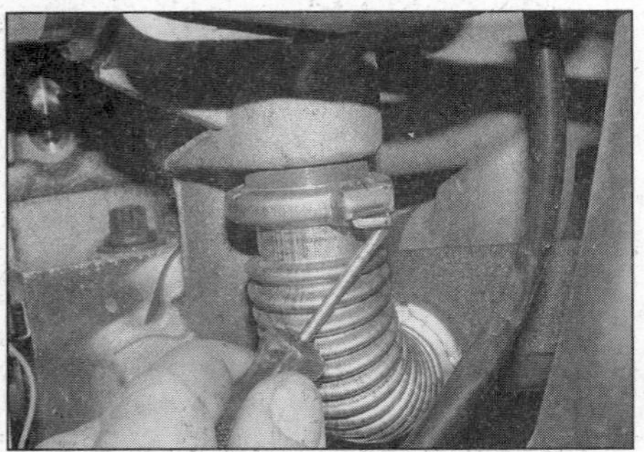
13.9 Releasing the EGR pipe securing clip

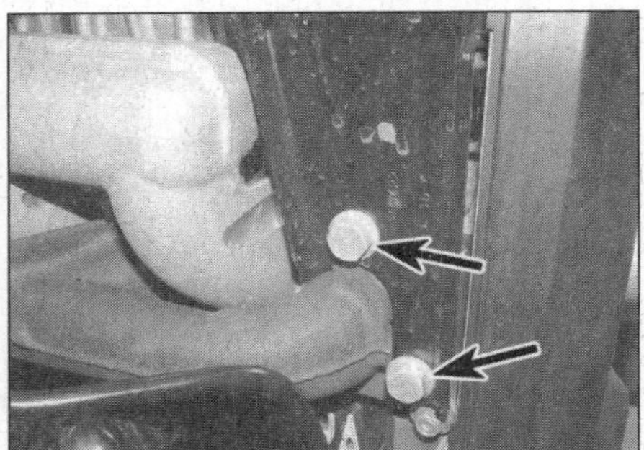
13.10 Undo the lifting bracket mounting bolts – arrowed

are separate, the same nuts retain them, since the stud holes are split between the manifold flanges.

2 Disconnect the battery negative terminal (refer to *Disconnecting the battery* in the Reference Section of this manual).

3 To gain access to the manifolds, remove the engine upper cover(s).

4 Slacken the retaining clip and disconnect the air intake hose from the throttle valve unit (damper unit) on the inlet manifold.

5 Disconnect the wiring connector from the EGR valve, undo the retaining bolts and remove the EGR valve from the manifold **(see illustration).**

6 Remove the two small Allen screws securing the vacuum reservoir to the rear of the inlet manifold. Move the reservoir clear, disconnecting as few of the hoses as possible. Remove two further screws, then disconnect the wiring plug and remove the vacuum control solenoid fitted below the reservoir **(see illustration)**.

7 Unbolt the vacuum hose support bracket from the rear of the inlet manifold, then unclip the rest of the hoses from the front and top, noting how they are fitted and routed. Also unclip the engine breather hose from the inlet manifold.

8 Undo the upper mounting bracket bolt from the thermoplunger mounting bracket.

9 Slacken the retaining clips and disconnect the EGR pipe from the exhaust manifold to the inlet manifold **(see illustration).** The pipe can be removed, as required, when the manifolds are free to move and be separated. Note that new clips may be required when refitting.

10 Undo the retaining bolts and remove the engine lifting bracket from the timing belt end of the cylinder head **(see illustration).**

11 Note the location of any wiring connectors or vacuum/breather hoses attached to the manifolds, and disconnect them.

14.1 Remove the retaining bolt and two nuts (arrowed)

14.6 Slacken the retaining clips – arrowed

12 Apply the handbrake, then jack up the front of the car and support it on axle stands (see *Jacking and vehicle support*). Remove the engine undertray.

13 Remove the turbocharger as described in Section 16.

14 Progressively unscrew the nuts securing the inlet and exhaust manifolds and withdraw them from the cylinder head. Recover the manifold gasket. A new gasket will be required for refitting.

Refitting

15 Refitting is a reversal of removal, bearing in mind the following points.

a) *Ensure that the cylinder head and manifold mating surfaces are clean and use a new gasket. Tighten all fixings to the specified torque.*
b) *Where applicable, refit the EGR recirculation valve (using a new gasket) and pipe with reference to Chapter 4C.*
c) *Refit the turbocharger as described in Section 16.*
d) *Ensure that any vacuum/breather hoses are correctly reconnected as noted before removal.*
e) *Ensure that any wiring or hose brackets/ clips are positioned as noted before removal.*

14 Inlet and exhaust manifolds (2.2 litre engines) – removal and refitting

Inlet manifold

Note: *The upper part of the inlet manifold is part of the rocker/camshaft cover.*

Removal

1 Disconnect the battery negative terminal (refer to *Disconnecting the battery* in the Reference Section of this manual). Remove the engine covers and release the retaining clips and remove the wiring harness cover from the front of the inlet manifold **(see illustration).**

2 Remove the injectors as described in Section 11.

3 Remove the fuel rail as described in Section 12.

4 Disconnect the wiring connectors from the heater plugs and the EGR valve on the throttle housing/damper unit.

5 Unclip the wiring harness from across the top of the manifold/rocker cover and move it to one side, note the routing of the harness for refitting.

6 Slacken the retaining clip from the connection hose between the throttle housing/ damper unit and the manifold/rocker cover **(see illustration).**

7 Remove the right-hand engine mounting as described in Chapter 2C, Section 14.

8 Evenly and progressively slacken and remove the bolts securing the manifold upper section to the cylinder head and lower inlet chamber.

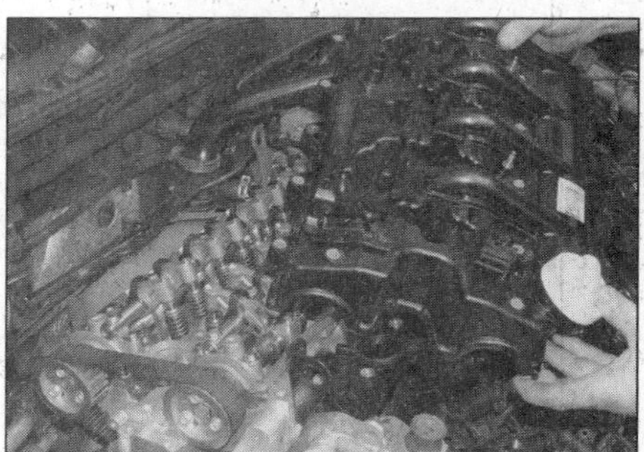

14.9 Removing the upper manifold/cover from the engine

14.11 Removing the lower section of the manifold from the cylinder head

14.12a Apply sealant in the positions arrowed . . .

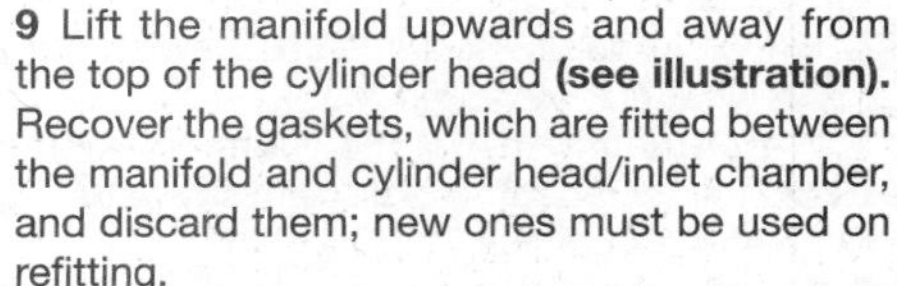

9 Lift the manifold upwards and away from the top of the cylinder head **(see illustration).** Recover the gaskets, which are fitted between the manifold and cylinder head/inlet chamber, and discard them; new ones must be used on refitting.

10 To remove the lower inlet manifold (plenum chamber), remove the throttle valve housing/ damper unit as described in Section 8. Disconnect any connectors attached to the lower inlet manifold and move them to one side, noting their fitted position.

11 Slacken and remove the retaining bolts and remove the lower section of the inlet manifold (plenum chamber) from the front of the cylinder head **(see illustration)**.

Refitting

12 Refitting is the reverse of removal noting the following.

a) *Apply sealant (Rhodorseal 5661) to the corners of the camshaft bearing caps, at both ends of the cylinder head* ***(see illustrations).***
b) *If the lower inlet chamber has been removed, use new gaskets/seals and tighten the bolts to the specified torque.*
c) *Ensure that the upper inlet manifold/ rocker cover and cylinder head mating surfaces are clean and dry and fit the new gaskets/seals* ***(see illustration).***
d) *Install the manifold and tighten its retaining bolts to the specified torque, in the recommended order* ***(see illustration).*** *Apply a drop of loctite to the threads on the inlet manifold bolts 1, 2, 4, 6, 8, 10, 12 and 13 before fitting.*
e) *Use new seal for EGR pipe, ensuring that the mating surfaces are clean and dry, and securely tighten its retaining bolts.*
f) *Refit the engine mounting, throttle valve housing, fuel rail and injectors using the relevant Sections as reference.*

Exhaust manifold

Removal

13 Remove the turbocharger as described in Section 16.

14 Undo the retaining bolts and remove the heat shield from the exhaust manifold **(see illustration)**.

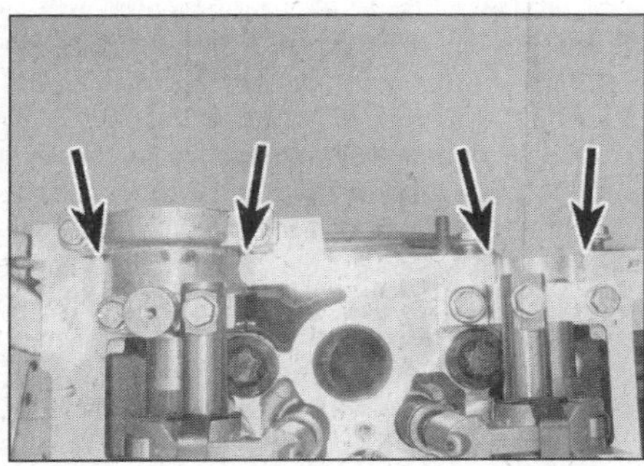

14.12b . . . at both ends of the cylinder head

14.12c Fit new gaskets to the inlet manifold/rocker cover

15 Slacken and remove the manifold retaining nuts and remove the exhaust manifold from the engine compartment. Recover the manifold gasket and discard it; a new one must be used on refitting **(see illustration)**.

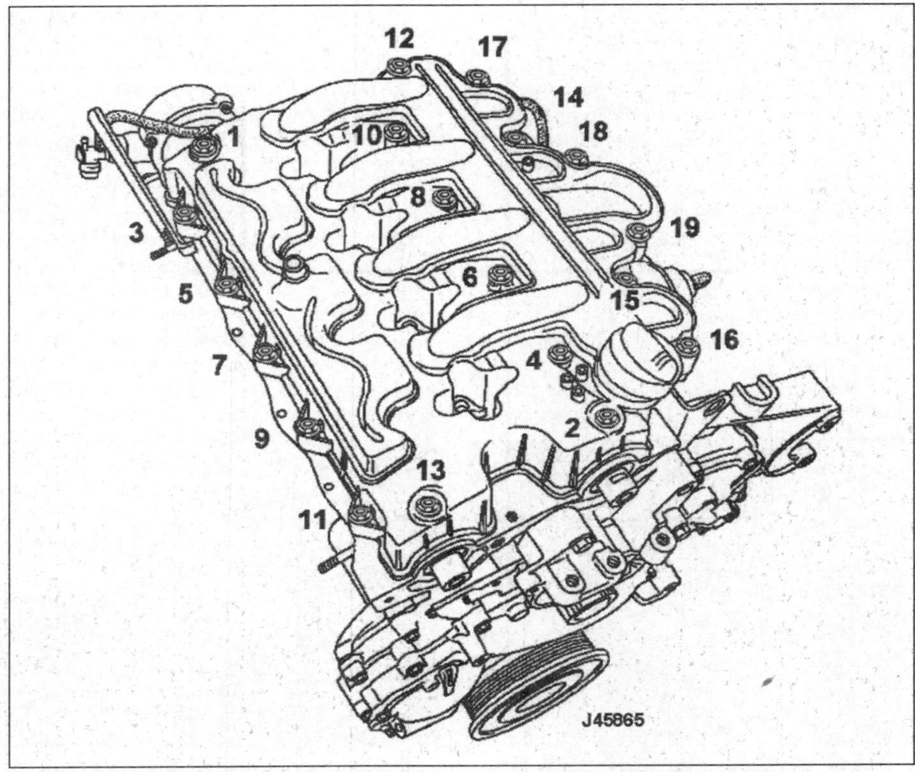

14.12d Tightening sequence of the inlet manifold/rocker cover

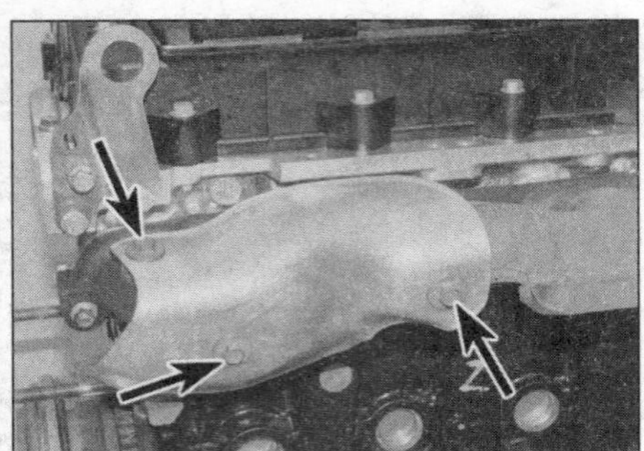
14.14 Undo the heat shield bolts – arrowed

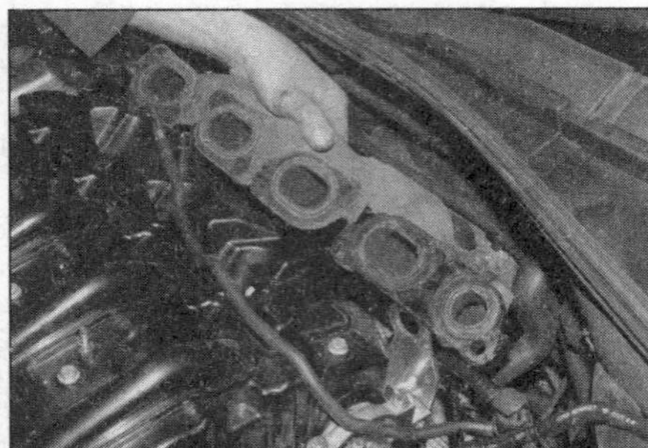
14.15 Remove the exhaust manifold

Refitting

16 Refitting is the reverse of removal, using a new gasket(s) and tightening the manifold retaining nuts to the specified torque, starting from the middle and working your way outwards.

15 Turbocharger – description and precautions

Description

A turbocharger increases engine efficiency by raising the pressure in the inlet manifold above atmospheric pressure. Instead of the air simply being sucked into the cylinders, it is forced in. Additional fuel is supplied by the injection pump in proportion to the increased air intake.

Energy for the operation of the turbocharger comes from the exhaust gas. The gas flows through a specially-shaped housing (the turbine housing) and in so doing, spins the turbine wheel. The turbine wheel is attached to a shaft, at the end of which is another vaned wheel known as the compressor wheel. The compressor wheel spins in its own housing and compresses the inducted air on the way to the inlet manifold.

Between the turbocharger and the inlet manifold, the compressed air passes through an intercooler. This is an air-to-air heat exchanger, mounted in front of the radiator, and supplied with cooling air ducted through the front of the car. The purpose of the intercooler is to remove from the inducted air some of the heat gained in being compressed. Because cooler air is denser, removal of this heat further increases engine efficiency.

Boost pressure (the pressure in the inlet manifold) is limited by a wastegate, which diverts the exhaust gas away from the turbine wheel in response to a pressure-sensitive actuator. Turbocharging pressure is controlled by a solenoid valve mounted at the right-hand rear corner of the engine compartment, with a pressure sensor located in the air duct, which runs from the intercooler to the throttle damper valve unit – refer to Section 9.

The turbo shaft is pressure-lubricated by an oil feed pipe from the main oil gallery. The shaft 'floats' on a cushion of oil. A drain pipe returns the oil to the sump.

Precautions

- The turbocharger operates at extremely high speeds and temperatures. Certain precautions must be observed to avoid premature failure of the turbo or injury to the operator.
- Do not race the engine immediately after start-up, especially if it is cold. Give the oil a few seconds to circulate.
- Always allow the engine to return to idle speed before switching it off – do not blip the throttle and switch off, as this will leave the turbo spinning without lubrication.
- Allow the engine to idle for several minutes before switching off after a high-speed run.
- Observe the recommended intervals for oil and filter changing, and use a reputable oil of the specified quality. Neglect of oil changing, or use of inferior oil, can cause carbon formation on the turbo shaft and subsequent failure.

Warning: Do not operate the turbo with any parts exposed. Foreign objects falling onto the rotating vanes could cause excessive damage and (if ejected) personal injury.

16 Turbocharger – removal and refitting

Note: *New turbocharger-to-exhaust manifold nuts must be used on refitting. If a new turbocharger is to be fitted, new exhaust elbow-to-turbocharger nuts and new oil feed copper gasket will be required.*

1 Whilst the engine is still warm, spray the turbocharger mounting bolts with a penetrating oil to ease removal.

2 Ensure that the engine has cooled sufficiently to avoid burns.

3 Disconnect the battery negative terminal (refer to *Disconnecting the battery* in the Reference Section of this manual).

4 Remove the plastic covers from the top of the engine.

5 Apply the handbrake, then jack up the front of the vehicle, and support securely on axle stands (see *Jacking and vehicle support*). Where applicable, remove the engine undertray.

6 Working under the vehicle, remove the exhaust front section/catalytic converter with reference to Section 18.

Removal

1.9 litre engines

7 Unscrew the turbocharger oil return pipe union from the outlet on the underside of the turbocharger. Be prepared for some oil spillage.

8 Slacken and remove the lower retaining nut for the turbocharger-to-manifold.

9 Working inside the engine compartment, disconnect the vacuum pipes, undo the retaining bolts and withdraw the vacuum reservoir and stop system solenoid from the intake manifold, as described in Section 8.

10 Disconnect the rubber vacuum pipe from the wastegate pressure regulator valve.

11 Unscrew the union nut, and disconnect the oil feed pipe from the top of the turbocharger. It may be necessary to unbolt the feed pipe-retaining clip from the inlet manifold **(see illustrations)**.

12 Slacken the retaining clips and disconnect the air intake and outlet hoses from the turbocharger.

13 Unscrew the two upper turbocharger-to-manifold nuts, slide the turbocharger from the manifold studs and manipulate it from its location.

2.2 litre engines

Note: *A new oil supply pipe will be required for refitting. The pipe can only be removed*

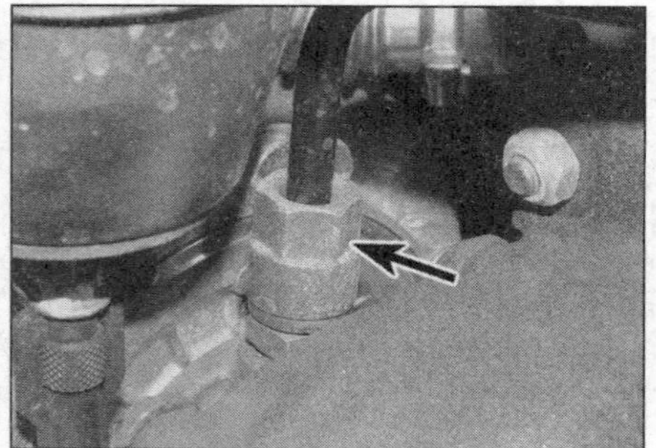
16.11a Disconnect the oil feed pipe from the top of the turbo (arrowed) . . .

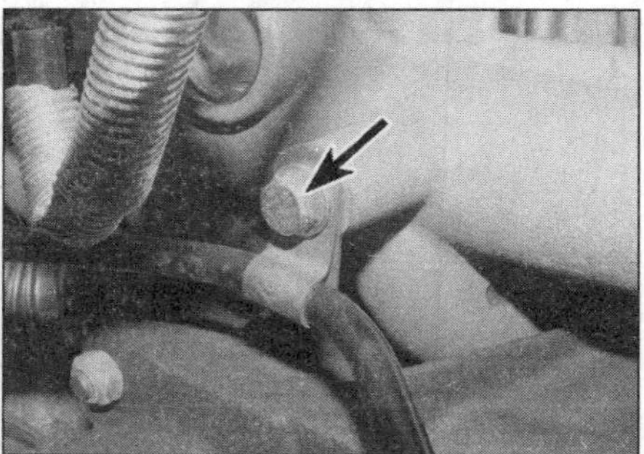
16.11b . . . and remove retaining clip bolt – arrowed

16.15 Disconnect the air intake hose

16.17a Slacken the retaining clip . . .

16.17b . . . and remove the turbo outlet hose mounting bolts – arrowed

with the turbocharger, as there is no access to the union nut on the turbocharger while it is in place.

14 Remove the fuel rail and protector tray as described in Section 12.

15 Slacken the retaining clip and disconnect the air intake to the turbocharger **(see illustration)**.

16 Disconnect the rubber vacuum pipe from the wastegate pressure regulator valve.

17 Slacken the retaining clip and remove the air outlet hose from the turbocharger and the metal outlet pipe from the left-hand end of the cylinder head **(see illustrations)**.

18 Undo the turbocharger oil return pipe union from the outlet on the underside of the turbocharger. Be prepared for some oil spillage **(see illustrations)**.

19 Unscrew the union nut, and disconnect the oil feed pipe from the cylinder block **(see illustration)**. The oil supply pipe cannot be disconnected from the turbocharger end until the turbo is removed from the vehicle.

20 Unscrew the three turbocharger-to-manifold nuts, slide the turbocharger from the manifold studs and manipulate it from its location **(see illustration)**.

Refitting

21 Refitting is a reversal of removal, but renew any damaged hose clamps, and use new turbocharger-to-exhaust manifold nuts which should be tightened to the specified torque.

22 Tighten the oil feed and return pipe-to-turbocharger union nuts to the specified torque using new gaskets/seals **(see illustrations)**.

23 On 2.2 litre models, the oil supply pipe itself should be renewed along with new seals. Fit the new supply pipe to the turbocharger before it is fitted to the manifold, making sure it is parallel between the faces of the turbocharger **(see illustration)**.

24 On completion, the following procedure must be observed before starting the engine.

16.18a Undo the mounting bolts – arrowed . . .

16.18b . . . and withdraw the return pipe from the cylinder block

16.19 Disconnect the oil feed pipe from the cylinder block

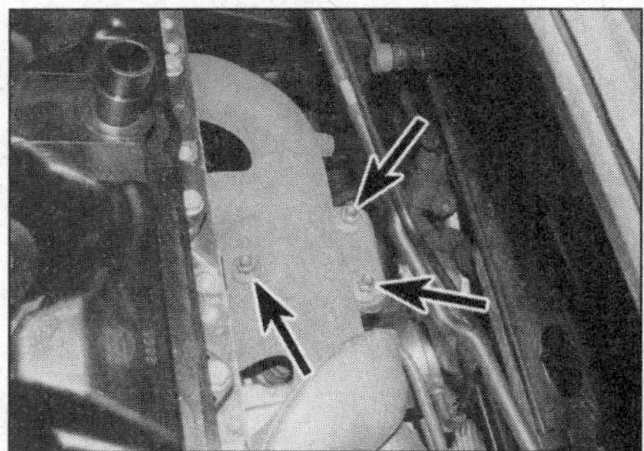
16.20 Undo the turbo mounting nuts – arrowed

16.22a Fit new gaskets to the turbo pipes . . .

16.22b . . . and new oil seals – arrowed

16.23 Fit new supply pipe (arrowed) to the turbo before refitting

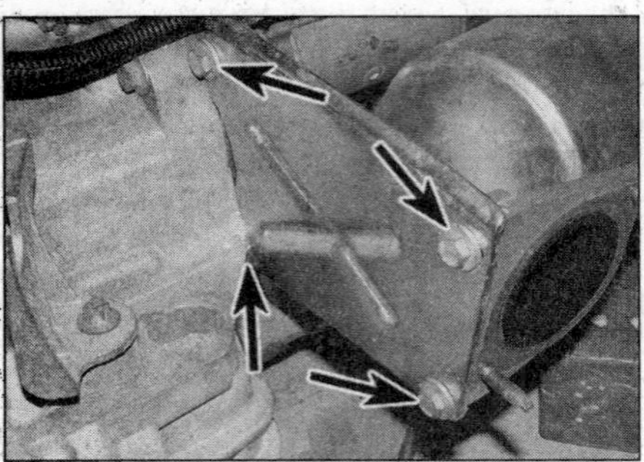

18.11a Undo the mounting plate bolts (arrowed) – 1.9 litre engine

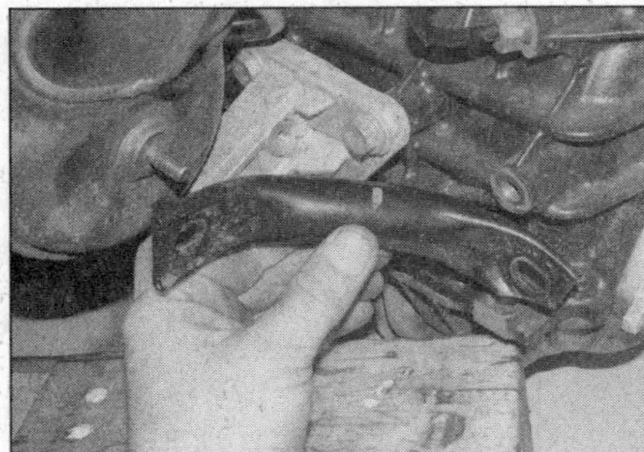

18.11b Remove the stay bracket – 1.9 litre engine

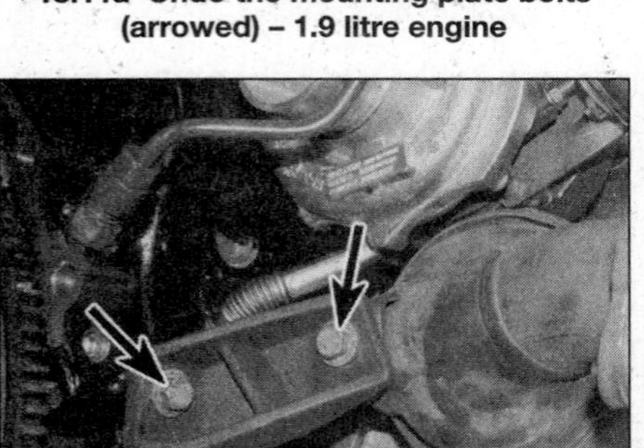

18.11c Left-hand stay bracket bolts (arrowed) – 2.2 litre engine

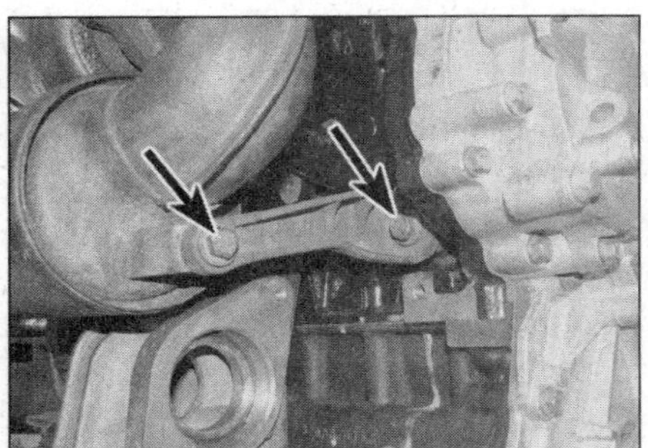

18.11d Right-hand stay bracket bolts (arrowed) – 2.2 litre engine

a) To ensure an immediate oil supply to the turbo before the engine is started, Renault specify that the engine first be prevented from firing by disconnecting the fuel pressure regulator on the high-pressure pump. Crank the engine for several seconds, then reconnect the components and start as normal. However, doing this may introduce a fault code in the engine ECU, which would then have to be cleared by using specialist diagnostic equipment.

b) Run the engine at idle speed, and check the turbocharger oil unions for leakage. Rectify any problems without delay.

c) After the engine has been run, check the engine oil level, and top-up if necessary.

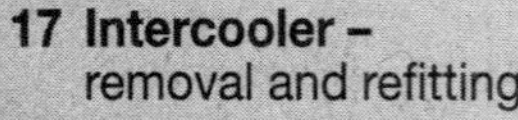

17 Intercooler – removal and refitting

Removal

1 The intercooler is located at the front of the car between the cooling system radiator and the air conditioning condenser. To remove the intercooler, refer to Chapter 3, Section 3 for the radiator removal and refitting procedures. **Note:** *There is no need to drain the cooling system, as the radiator does not need to be removed completely. Once access is gained, the intercooler can be unbolted and withdrawn from between the radiator and the condenser, taking care not to damage any other components.*

Refitting

2 Refitting is a reversal of removal.

18 Exhaust system – general information, removal and refitting

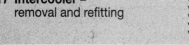

General information

1 The exhaust system consists of three sections:

1) Catalytic converter
2) Front pipe and intermediate pipe.
3) Rear silencer/tailpipe

2 The catalytic converter and front pipe joints are secured by nuts and bolts, the front pipe being of the flexible pipe, to allow for movement in the exhaust system. A clamping ring secures the joint between the front and rear sections. The system is suspended throughout its entire length by rubber mountings.

3 Ensure that the exhaust has cooled sufficiently to avoid burns.

Removal

4 To remove the system or part of the system, first jack up the front or rear of the car, and support it on axle stands (see *Jacking and vehicle support*). Alternatively, position the car over an inspection pit, or on car ramps.

Front and intermediate pipe sections

5 Where there is an oxygen (lambda) sensor fitted to the front pipe, trace the wiring back from the sensor and disconnect it at the wiring connector. Free the wiring from any relevant retaining clips so the sensor is free to be removed with the front pipe.

6 Slacken and remove the nuts and bolts securing the front flexible pipe flange joint to the catalytic converter.

7 Have an assistant support the front end of the pipe then slacken the mounting clamp nuts and detach the intermediate pipe from the rear silencer/tailpipe.

8 Unhook the section from its mounting rubber(s) and remove it from the underneath the vehicle.

Catalytic converter

9 To make it easier for the catalytic converter to be removed, it may be necessary to remove the right-hand driveshaft as described in Chapter 8.

10 Slacken and remove the nuts securing the front flexible pipe to the catalytic converter. Remove the bolts, then separate the flange joint and recover the gasket.

11 Undo the retaining bolts and remove the stay brackets from each side of the catalytic converter **(see illustrations).**

12 Slacken and remove the nuts securing the catalytic converter to the turbo. Withdraw the converter from under the car **(see illustrations)**, recover the gasket – a new one will be needed for refitting.

Rear silencer/tailpipe

13 Slacken the clamping ring nuts and detach the intermediate pipe from the rear silencer/tailpipe.

14 Undo the mounting bolts at each side of the rear silencer and free it from its mounting

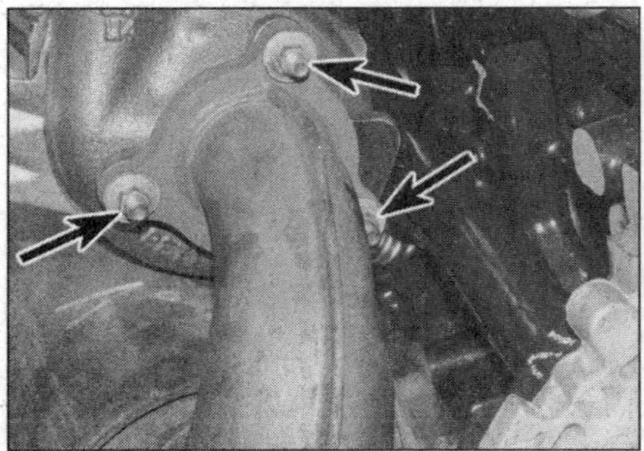

18.12a Undo the mounting bolts – arrowed . . .

18.12b . . . and withdraw the catalytic converter – 2.2 litre engine

rubbers, remove it from underneath the vehicle.

Heat shield(s)

15 The heat shields are secured to the underside of the body by various nuts and bolts. Each shield can be removed once the relevant exhaust section has been removed. If a shield is being removed to gain access to a component located behind it, it may prove sufficient in some cases to remove the retaining nuts and/or bolts, and simply lower the shield, without disturbing the exhaust system.

Refitting

16 Each section is refitted by reversing the removal sequence, noting the following points:

a) Ensure that all traces of corrosion have been removed from the flanges, and renew all necessary gaskets.

b) Inspect the rubber mountings for signs of damage or deterioration, and renew as necessary.

c) When refitting the front flexible pipe to the catalytic converter, ensure that a new gasket is fitted.

d) When reconnecting the intermediate pipe to rear silencer/tailpipe joint, apply a smear of exhaust system jointing paste to the flange joint, to ensure a gas-tight seal. Tighten the clamping ring nuts evenly and progressively so that the clearance between the clamp halves remains equal on either side.

e) Prior to tightening the exhaust system fasteners, ensure that all rubber mountings are correctly located, and that there is adequate clearance between the exhaust system and vehicle underbody.

18.12c Removing the catalytic converter – 1.9 litre engine

Chapter 4 Part C: Emission control systems

Contents

Degrees of difficulty

Easy, suitable for novice with little experience 	**Fairly easy,** suitable for beginner with some experience 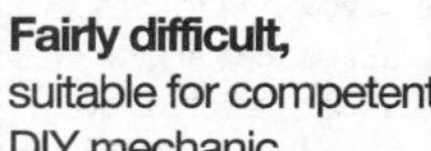	**Fairly difficult,** suitable for competent DIY mechanic	**Difficult,** suitable for experienced DIY mechanic 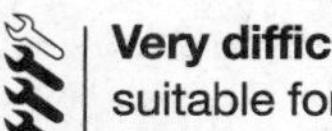	**Very difficult,** suitable for expert DIY or professional

Specifications

Torque wrench settings	Nm	lbf ft
EGR solenoid valve mounting bolts	8	6
Oxygen (lambda) sensor	45	33

1 General information

All petrol engine models have the ability to use unleaded petrol and also have various other features built into the fuel system to help minimise harmful emissions. On top of this, all models are equipped with the crankcase emission control system described below. All models are also equipped with a catalytic converter and an evaporative emission control system.

All diesel engine models are also designed to meet the strict emission requirements and are equipped with a crankcase emission control system. In addition to this certain models may also be fitted with a catalytic converter to reduce exhaust emissions. To further reduce emissions, they are also equipped with an exhaust gas recirculation (EGR) system.

The emission control systems function as follows.

Petrol models

Crankcase emission control

To reduce the emission of unburned hydrocarbons from the crankcase into the atmosphere, the engine is sealed and the blow-by gases and oil vapour are drawn from inside the crankcase, through a wire mesh oil separator, into the inlet tract to be burned by the engine during normal combustion.

Under conditions of high manifold depression (idling, deceleration) the gases will be sucked positively out of the crankcase. Under conditions of low manifold depression (acceleration, full-throttle running) the gases are forced out of the crankcase by the (relatively) higher crankcase pressure; if the engine is worn, the raised crankcase pressure (due to increased blow-by) will cause some of the flow to return under all manifold conditions.

Exhaust emission control

To minimise the amount of pollutants which escape into the atmosphere, all models are fitted with a catalytic converter in the exhaust system. The system is of the closed-loop type, in which one or two oxygen sensors in the exhaust system provides the fuel injection/ignition system ECU with constant feedback, enabling the ECU to adjust the mixture to provide the best possible conditions for the converter to operate.

The oxygen (lambda) sensors have a heating element built-in that is controlled by the ECU through the oxygen sensor relay to quickly bring the sensor's tip to an efficient operating temperature. The sensor's tip is sensitive to oxygen and sends the ECU a varying voltage depending on the amount of oxygen in the exhaust gases; if the inlet air/fuel mixture is too rich, the exhaust gases are low in oxygen so the sensors sends a low-voltage signal, the voltage rising as the mixture weakens and the amount of oxygen rises in the exhaust gases. Peak conversion efficiency of all major pollutants occurs if the inlet air/fuel mixture is maintained at the chemically correct ratio for the complete combustion of petrol of 14.7 parts (by weight) of air to 1 part of fuel (the 'stoichiometric' ratio). The sensor output voltage alters in a large step at this point, the ECU using the signal change as a reference point and correcting the inlet air/fuel mixture accordingly by altering the fuel injector pulse width.

Evaporative emission control

To minimise the escape into the atmosphere of unburned hydrocarbons, an evaporative emissions control system is also fitted to all models. The fuel tank filler cap is sealed and a charcoal canister is mounted behind the right-hand front wing. The canister collects the petrol vapours generated in the tank when the car is parked and stores them until they can be cleared from the canister (under the control of the fuel injection/ignition system ECU) via the purge valve into the inlet tract to be burned by the engine during normal combustion.

To ensure the engine runs correctly when it is cold and/or idling and to protect the catalytic converter from the effects of an over-rich mixture, the purge control valve is not opened by the ECU until the engine has warmed-up, and the engine is under load; the valve solenoid is then modulated on and off to allow the stored vapour to pass into the inlet tract.

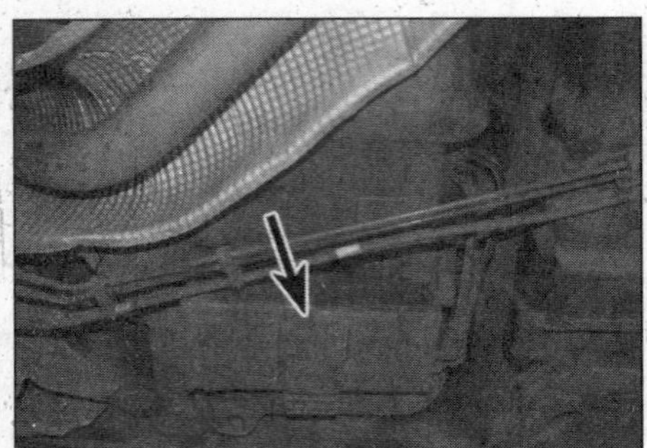
2.3 Charcoal (fuel vapour) canister – arrowed

Diesel models

Crankcase emission control

Refer to petrol models.

Exhaust emission control

To minimise the level of exhaust pollutants released into the atmosphere, a catalytic converter is fitted in the exhaust system. The catalytic converter consists of a canister containing a fine mesh impregnated with a catalyst material, over which the hot exhaust gases pass. The catalyst speeds up the oxidation of harmful carbon monoxide, unburnt hydrocarbons and soot, effectively reducing the quantity of harmful products released into the atmosphere via the exhaust gases.

Exhaust gas recirculation system

This system is designed to recirculate small quantities of exhaust gas into the inlet tract, and therefore into the combustion process. This process reduces the level of oxides of nitrogen present in the final exhaust gas which is released into the atmosphere.

The volume of exhaust gas recirculated is controlled by signals supplied to the injection computer. An electrically-operated EGR solenoid valve is fitted to the inlet manifold/ throttle body housing to regulate the quantity of exhaust gas recirculated.

The injection computer receives information from the following components:

a) Coolant temperature sensor.
b) Air temperature sensor.
c) Atmospheric pressure sensor.
d) Accelerator pedal position potentiometer.

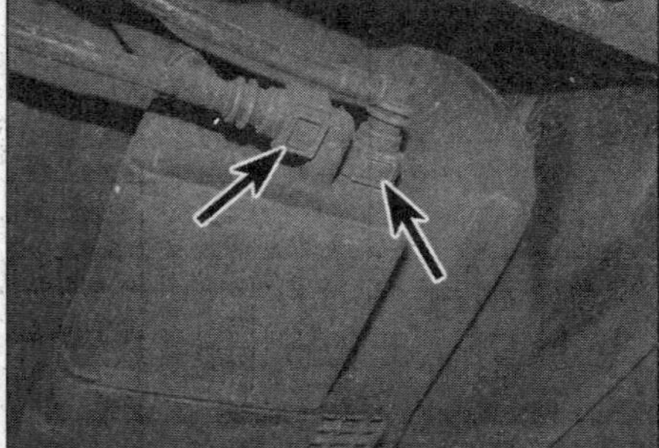
2.5 Release the two quick-release fittings – arrowed

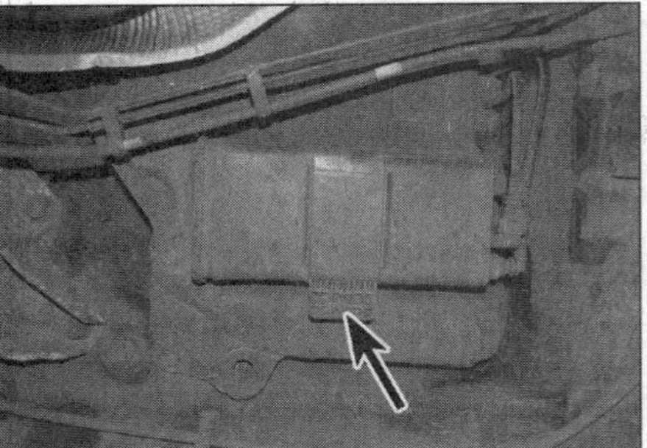
2.4 Undo the retaining screw – arrowed

e) Engine speed sensor.
f) Airflow meter.
g) Injection flow rate.
h) Turbocharging pressure sensor or solenoid valve.

If any faults develop in these components the supply to the EGR solenoid valve is stopped.

The EGR function is disabled if:

a) The battery voltage is less than 9 volts.
b) The engine speed is less than 700 rpm (1.9 litre engines).
c) The engine speed is above 900 rpm when the pedal is released (2.2 litre engines).
d) The vehicle speed is below 7 mph (1.9 litre engines).
e) The vehicle speed is below 3 mph and the engine speed is less than 900 rpm for 40 seconds (2.2 litre engines).

2 Petrol engine emission control systems – testing and component renewal

Crankcase emission control

1 The components of this system require no attention other than to check that the hose(s) are clear and undamaged at regular intervals. **Note:** *When removing hoses to check for condition or blockage, make sure their fitted positions are noted for reassembly.*

Evaporative emission control

Testing

2 If the system is thought to be faulty, disconnect the hoses from the charcoal canister and purge control valve and check that they are clear by blowing through them. If the purge control valve(s) or charcoal canister is thought to be faulty, they must be renewed.

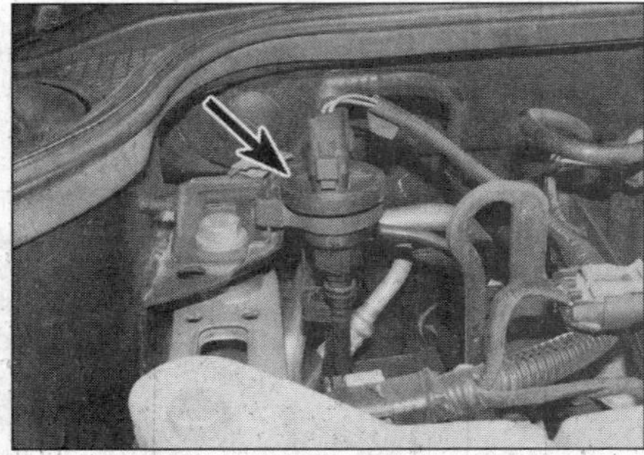
2.7 Purge (fuel vapour) valve – arrowed

Charcoal (fuel vapour) canister renewal

3 The charcoal canister is located under the fuel tank on the rear passenger side of the vehicle **(see illustration)**. To gain access to the canister, firmly apply the handbrake then jack up the rear of the car and support it on axle stands (see *Jacking and vehicle support*).

4 Slacken and remove the retaining screw and lower the canister from the fuel tank **(see illustration)**.

5 The hoses are equipped with quick-release fittings depress the centre collar of the fitting with a small flat-bladed screwdriver then detach the hoses from the canister **(see illustration)**. Make a note of the location of the hoses for refitting.

6 Refitting is a reverse of the removal procedure, ensuring that the hoses are correctly reconnected.

Purge (fuel vapour) valve renewal

7 The purge valve is mounted onto the right-hand rear of the engine compartment bulkhead, next to the suspension mounting turret **(see illustration)**.

8 To renew the purge valve, disconnect the battery negative terminal then depress the retaining clip and disconnect the wiring connector from the valve.

9 Disconnect the hoses from the valve, noting their correct fitted locations then release the valve from its retaining clip and remove it from the engine compartment.

10 Refitting is a reversal of the removal procedure, ensuring that the valve is fitted the correct way around and the hoses are securely connected.

Exhaust emission control

Testing

11 The performance of the catalytic converter can be checked by measuring the exhaust gases using an exhaust gas analyser.

12 If the CO level at the tailpipe is too high, the vehicle should be taken to a Renault dealer so that the complete fuel injection and ignition systems, including the oxygen sensor, can be thoroughly checked using the special diagnostic equipment. Once these have been checked and are known to be free from faults, the fault must be in the catalytic converter, which must be renewed.

Catalytic converter renewal

13 Refer to Chapter 4A, Section 14.

Oxygen (lambda) sensor renewal

Note 1: *The oxygen sensor is delicate and will not work if it is dropped or knocked, if its power supply is disrupted, or if any cleaning materials are used on it. Some engines are fitted with an 'upstream' oxygen sensor screwed into the exhaust manifold.*

14 Firmly apply the handbrake then jack up the front of the vehicle and support it on axle stands (see *Jacking and vehicle support*).

15 Trace the wiring back from the oxygen sensor, which is screwed into the exhaust front pipe or exhaust manifold and disconnect its wiring connector, freeing the wiring from any relevant retaining clips or ties.

16 Unscrew the sensor and remove it from the exhaust system front pipe or manifold **(see illustration)**.

17 Refitting is a reverse of the removal procedure. Prior to installing the sensor apply a smear of high-temperature grease to the sensor threads. Tighten the sensor to the specified torque and ensure that the wiring is correctly routed and in no danger of contacting either the exhaust system or engine.

3 Diesel engine emission control systems – testing and component renewal

Crankcase emission control

1 The components of this system require no attention other than to check that the hose(s) are clear and undamaged at regular intervals.

2 If the system is thought to be faulty, first check that the hoses are unobstructed and not damaged.

3 On high-mileage cars, particularly when regularly used for short journeys, a sludge-like deposit may be evident inside the system hoses and oil separators. If excessive deposits are present, the relevant component(s) should be removed and cleaned.

4 Periodically inspect the system components for security and damage, and renew them as necessary.

Exhaust emission control

Testing

5 The performance of the catalytic converter can be checked by measuring the exhaust gases using an exhaust gas analyser which is suitable for diesel engines.

Catalytic converter renewal

6 Refer to Chapter 4B, Section 18.

Exhaust gas recirculation system

Testing

7 Testing of the system should be entrusted to a Renault dealer, who will have the specialist diagnostic equipment to carry out any tests.

Solenoid valve renewal – 1.9 litre engines

8 Disconnect the battery negative terminal (refer to *Disconnecting the battery* in the Reference Section of this manual).

9 The EGR valve is mounted on the left-hand end of the inlet manifold, below the throttle/damper unit.

10 Slacken the retaining clip and disconnect the air intake hose from the throttle/damper unit, to gain better access.

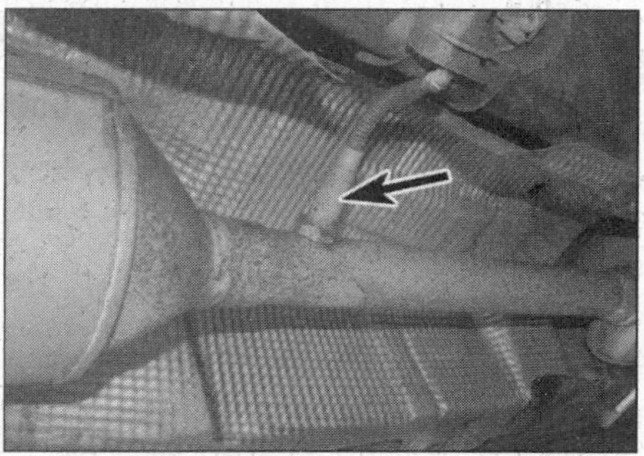

2.16 Oxygen sensor location – arrowed

11 Disconnect the wiring connector from the EGR valve.

12 Slacken and remove the retaining bolts and free the valve from the inlet manifold **(see illustration)**. Recover the gasket and discard it; a new one must be used on refitting.

13 Refitting is the reverse of removal, using new gaskets and ensuring that the bolts are securely tightened.

Solenoid valve renewal – 2.2 litre engine

14 Disconnect the battery negative terminal (refer to *Disconnecting the battery* in the Reference Section of this manual).

15 The EGR valve is mounted on the side of the throttle/damper unit on the inlet manifold at the front of the engine.

16 Undo the two retaining bolts and disconnect the EGR pipe from the throttle/damper unit to gain better access **(see illustration)**.

17 Slacken and remove the retaining bolts and free the valve from the throttle/damper unit. Recover the gasket and discard it; a new one must be used on refitting **(see illustration)**.

18 Refitting is the reverse of removal, using new gaskets and ensuring that the valve is clean and the bolts are securely tightened **(see illustration)**.

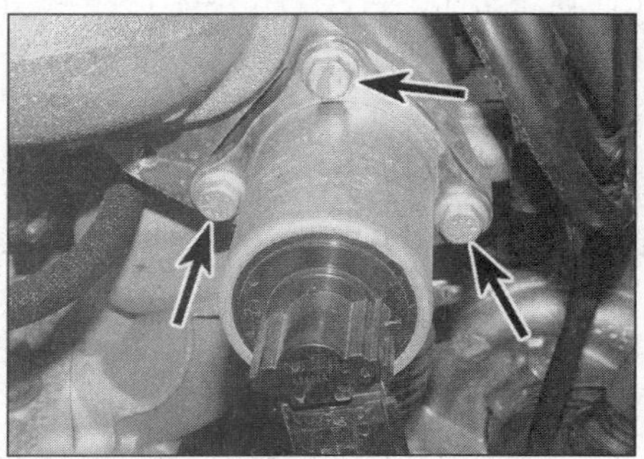

3.12 Undo the EGR valve mounting bolts – arrowed

3.16 Remove the EGR pipe and gasket

3.17 Withdraw the valve from the throttle/damper unit

3.18 Fit new gasket to the EGR valve

4 Catalytic converter – general information and precautions

General information

The catalytic converter reduces harmful exhaust emissions by chemically converting the more poisonous gases to ones which (in theory at least) are less harmful. The chemical reaction is known as an 'oxidising' reaction, or one where oxygen is 'added'.

Inside the converter is a honeycomb structure, made of ceramic material and coated with the precious metals palladium, platinum and rhodium (the 'catalyst' which promotes the chemical reaction). The chemical reaction generates heat, which itself promotes the reaction – therefore, once the car has been driven several miles, the body of the converter will be very hot.

The ceramic structure contained within the converter is understandably fragile, and will not withstand rough treatment. Since the converter runs at a high temperature, driving through deep standing water (in flood conditions, for example) is to be avoided, since the thermal stresses imposed when plunging the hot converter into cold water may well cause the ceramic internals to fracture, resulting in a 'blocked' converter – a common cause of failure. A converter that has been damaged in this way can be checked by shaking it (do not strike it) – if a rattling noise is heard, this indicates probable failure.

Precautions

The catalytic converter is a reliable and simple device which needs no maintenance in itself, but there are some facts of which an owner should be aware if the converter is to function properly for its full service life.

Petrol models

a) *DO NOT use leaded petrol (or lead-replacement petrol, LRP) in a car equipped with a catalytic converter – the lead (or other additives) will coat the precious metals, reducing their converting efficiency and will eventually destroy the converter.*
b) *Always keep the ignition and fuel systems well maintained in accordance with the manufacturer's schedule.*
c) *If the engine develops a misfire, do not drive the car at all (or at least as little as possible) until the fault is cured.*
d) *DO NOT push- or tow-start the car – this will soak the catalytic converter in unburned fuel, causing it to overheat when the engine does start.*
e) *DO NOT switch off the ignition at high engine speeds.*
f) *DO NOT use fuel or engine oil additives – these may contain substances harmful to the catalytic converter.*
g) *DO NOT continue to use the car if the engine burns oil to the extent of leaving a visible trail of blue smoke.*
h) *Remember that the catalytic converter operates at very high temperatures. DO NOT, therefore, park the car in dry undergrowth, over long grass or piles of dead leaves after a long run.*
i) *Remember that the catalytic converter is FRAGILE – do not strike it with tools during servicing work.*
j) *In some cases a sulphurous smell (like that of rotten eggs) may be noticed from the exhaust. This is common to many catalytic converter-equipped cars and once the car has covered a few thousand miles the problem should disappear.*
k) *The catalytic converter, used on a well-maintained and well-driven car, should last at least 100 000 miles – if the converter is no longer effective it must be renewed.*
l) *If a substantial loss of power is experienced, remember that this could be due to the converter being blocked. This can occur simply as a result of high mileage, but may be due to the ceramic element having fractured and collapsed internally (see paragraph 3). A new converter is the only cure in this instance.*
m) *As mentioned above, driving through deep water should be avoided if possible. The sudden cooling effect may fracture the ceramic honeycomb, damaging it beyond repair.*

Diesel models

The catalytic converter fitted to diesel models is simpler than that fitted to petrol models, but it still needs to be treated with respect to avoid problems:

a) *DO NOT use fuel or engine oil additives – these may contain substances harmful to the catalytic converter.*
b) *DO NOT continue to use the car if the engine burns (engine) oil to the extent of leaving a visible trail of blue smoke.*
c) *Remember that the catalytic converter operates at very high temperatures. DO NOT, therefore, park the car in dry undergrowth, over long grass or piles of dead leaves after a long run.*
d) *As mentioned above, driving through deep water should be avoided if possible. The sudden cooling effect will fracture the ceramic honeycomb, damaging it beyond repair.*
e) *Remember that the catalytic converter is FRAGILE – do not strike it with tools during servicing work, and take care handling it when removing it from the car for any reason.*
f) *If a substantial loss of power is experienced, remember that this could be due to the converter being blocked. This can occur simply as a result of high mileage, but may be due to the ceramic element having fractured and collapsed internally (see paragraph 3). A new converter is the only cure in this instance.*
g) *The catalytic converter, used on a well-maintained and well-driven car, should last at least 100 000 miles – if the converter is no longer effective, it must be renewed.*

Chapter 5 Part A: Starting and charging systems

Contents

Degrees of difficulty

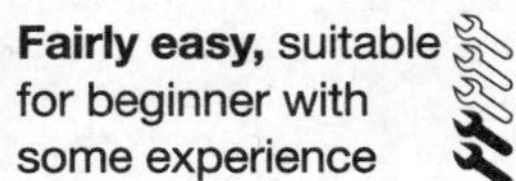

Easy, suitable for novice with little experience	**Fairly easy,** suitable for beginner with some experience	**Fairly difficult,** suitable for competent DIY mechanic	**Difficult,** suitable for experienced DIY mechanic	**Very difficult,** suitable for expert DIY or professional

Specifications

Battery

Type	Lead-acid, low-maintenance or 'maintenance-free'
Charge condition:	
Poor	11.5 volts
Normal	12.0 volts
Good	12.7 volts

Alternator

Type:	
1.6 and 1.8 litre petrol engine	Valeo SG10 – 120A or SG12 – 125A
2.0 litre petrol engine	Valeo SG9 – 125A or SG12 – 125A
Diesel engine	Valeo SG 12 – 125A
Regulated voltage	13.5 to 14.8 volts

Starter motor

Type:	
1.6 and 1.8 litre petrol engine	Bosch 0 001 060 17 or 0 001 060 22
2.0 litre petrol engine	Bosch 0 001 106 023
1.9 litre diesel engine	Valeo D7R44, D7R47 or D7R49
2.2 litre diesel engine	Valeo D7RP53

Torque wrench settings

	Nm	lbf ft
Alternator mounting bolts	21	15
Alternator support bracket mounting bolts	44	32
Starter motor mounting bolts	44	32

1 General information and precautions

General information

The engine electrical system consists mainly of the charging and starting systems. Because of their engine-related functions, these components are covered separately from the body electrical devices such as the lights, instruments, etc (which are covered in Chapter 12). On petrol engine models refer to Part B for information on the ignition system, and on diesel models refer to Part C for information on the preheating system.

The electrical system is of the 12-volt negative earth type.

The battery is of the low maintenance or 'maintenance-free' (sealed for life) type and is charged by the alternator, which is belt-driven from the crankshaft pulley.

The starter motor is of the pre-engaged type incorporating an integral solenoid. On starting, the solenoid moves the drive pinion into engagement with the flywheel ring gear before the starter motor is energised. Once the engine has started, a one-way clutch prevents the motor armature being driven by the engine until the pinion disengages from the flywheel.

Precautions

Further details of the various systems are given in the relevant Sections of this Chapter. While some repair procedures are given, the usual course of action is to renew the component concerned. The owner whose interest extends beyond mere component renewal should obtain a copy of the *Automotive Electrical & Electronic Systems Manual*, available from the publishers of this manual.

It is necessary to take extra care when working on the electrical system to avoid damage to semi-conductor devices (diodes and transistors), and to avoid the risk of personal injury. In addition to the precautions given in *Safety first!* at the beginning of this manual, observe the following when working on the system:

- *Always remove rings, watches, etc, before working on the electrical system*. Even with the battery disconnected, capacitive discharge could occur if a component's live terminal is earthed through a metal object. This could cause a shock or nasty burn.
- *Do not reverse the battery connections*. Components such as the alternator, electronic control units, or any other components having semi-conductor circuitry could be irreparably damaged.
- If the engine is being started using jump leads and a slave battery, connect the batteries *positive-to-positive* and *negative-to-negative* (see *Jump starting*). This also applies when connecting a battery charger.
- Never disconnect the battery terminals, the alternator, any electrical wiring or any test instruments when the engine is running.
- Do not allow the engine to turn the alternator when the alternator is not connected.
- Never test for alternator output by 'flashing' the output lead to earth.
- Never use an ohmmeter of the type incorporating a hand-cranked generator for circuit or continuity testing.
- Always ensure that the battery negative lead is disconnected when working on the electrical system.
- Before using electric-arc welding equipment on the car, disconnect the battery, alternator and components such as the fuel injection/ignition electronic control unit to protect them from the risk of damage.
- Several systems fitted to the vehicle require battery power to be available at all times, either to ensure their continued operation (such as the clock) or to maintain security codes which would be wiped if the battery were to be disconnected. To ensure that there are no unforeseen consequences of this action, Refer to *Disconnecting the battery* in the Reference Section of this manual for further information.

2 Electrical fault finding – general information

Refer to Chapter 12.

3 Battery – testing and charging

Testing

Standard and low maintenance battery

1 If the vehicle covers a small annual mileage, it is worthwhile checking the specific gravity of the electrolyte every three months, to determine the state of charge of the battery. Use a hydrometer to make the check, and compare the results with the following table. The temperatures quoted in the table are ambient (air) temperatures. Note that the specific gravity readings assume an electrolyte temperature of 15°C (60°F); for every 10°C (18°F) below 15°C (60°F), subtract 0.007. For every 10°C (18°F) above 15°C (60°F), add 0.007.

	Above 25°C (77°F)	Below 25°C (77°F)
Fully-charged	1.210 to 1.230	1.270 to 1.290
70% charged	1.170 to 1.190	1.230 to 1.250
Discharged	1.050 to 1.070	1.110 to 1.130

2 If the battery condition is suspect, first check the specific gravity of electrolyte in each cell. A variation of 0.040 or more between any cells indicates loss of electrolyte or deterioration of the internal plates.

3 If the specific gravity variation is 0.040 or more, the battery should be renewed. If the cell variation is satisfactory but the battery is discharged, it should be charged as described later in this Section.

Maintenance-free battery

4 In cases where a 'sealed for life' maintenance-free battery is fitted, topping-up and testing of the electrolyte in each cell is not possible. The condition of the battery can therefore only be tested using a battery condition indicator or a voltmeter.

5 Certain models may be fitted with a Delco type maintenance-free battery, with a built-in charge condition indicator. The indicator is located in the top of the battery casing, and indicates the condition of the battery from its colour. If the indicator shows green, then the battery is in a good state of charge. If the indicator turns darker, eventually to black, then the battery requires charging, as described later in this Section. If the indicator shows clear/yellow, then the electrolyte level in the battery is too low to allow further use, and the battery should be renewed. **Do not** attempt to charge, load or jump start a battery when the indicator shows clear/yellow.

All battery types

6 If testing the battery using a voltmeter, connect the voltmeter across the battery and compare the result with those given in the Specifications under 'charge condition'. The test is only accurate if the battery has not been subjected to any kind of charge for the previous six hours. If this is not the case, switch on the headlights for 30 seconds, then wait four to five minutes before testing the battery after switching off the headlights. All other electrical circuits must be switched off, so check that the doors and tailgate are fully shut when making the test.

7 If the voltage reading is less than 12.0 volts, then the battery is discharged, whilst a reading of 12.2 to 12.4 volts indicates a partially-discharged condition.

8 If the battery is to be charged, remove it from the vehicle (Section 4) and charge it as described later in this Section.

Charging

Note: *The following is intended as a guide only. Always refer to the manufacturer's recommendations (often printed on a label attached to the battery) before charging a battery.*

Standard and low maintenance battery

9 Charge the battery at a rate of 3.5 to 4 amps and continue to charge the battery at this rate until no further rise in specific gravity is noted over a four hour period.

10 Alternatively, a trickle charger charging at the rate of 1.5 amps can safely be used overnight.

11 Specially rapid 'boost' charges that are claimed to restore the power of the battery in 1 to 2 hours are not recommended, as they can cause serious damage to the battery plates through overheating.

12 While charging the battery, note that the

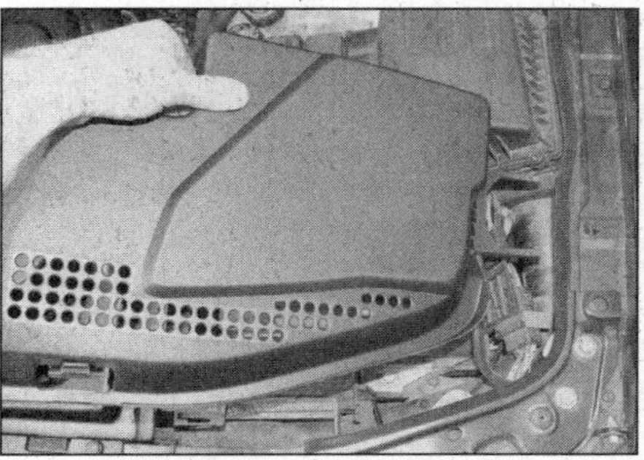
4.2 Remove the cover from the battery

4.3 Disconnect the earth cable from the battery

4.4 Remove the cover from the fuse/relay box

4.5 Disconnect the positive link cable from the fuse/relay box

4.6 Undo the battery securing clamp

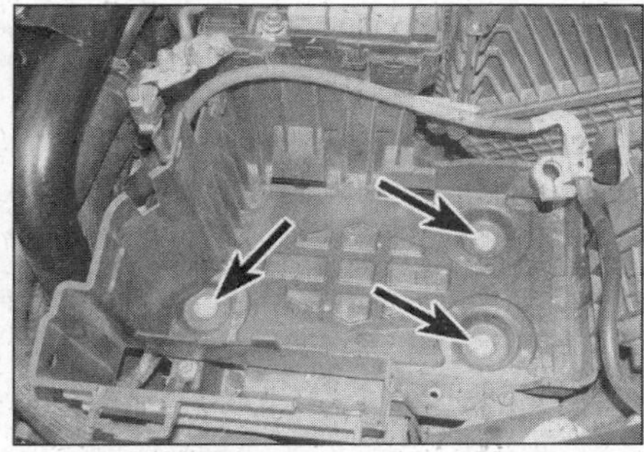
4.8a Undo the retaining bolts – arrowed

temperature of the electrolyte should never exceed 37.8°C (100°F).

Maintenance-free battery

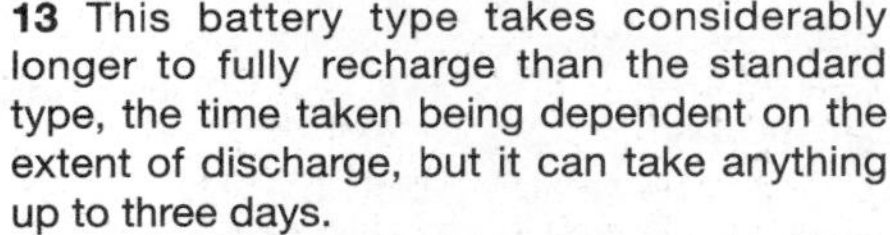
13 This battery type takes considerably longer to fully recharge than the standard type, the time taken being dependent on the extent of discharge, but it can take anything up to three days.

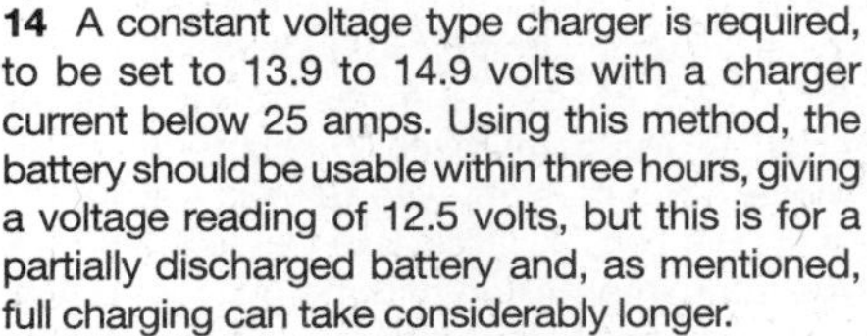
14 A constant voltage type charger is required, to be set to 13.9 to 14.9 volts with a charger current below 25 amps. Using this method, the battery should be usable within three hours, giving a voltage reading of 12.5 volts, but this is for a partially discharged battery and, as mentioned, full charging can take considerably longer.

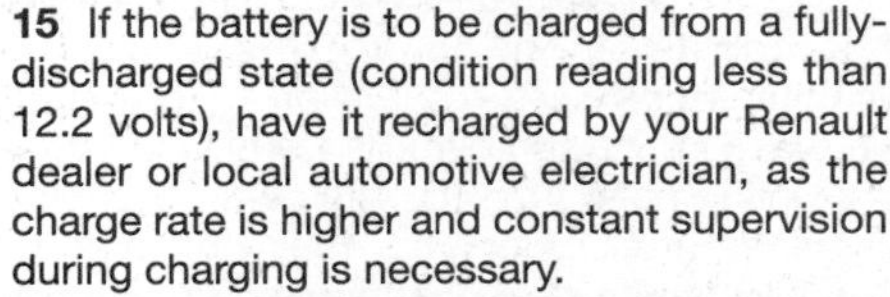
15 If the battery is to be charged from a fully-discharged state (condition reading less than 12.2 volts), have it recharged by your Renault dealer or local automotive electrician, as the charge rate is higher and constant supervision during charging is necessary.

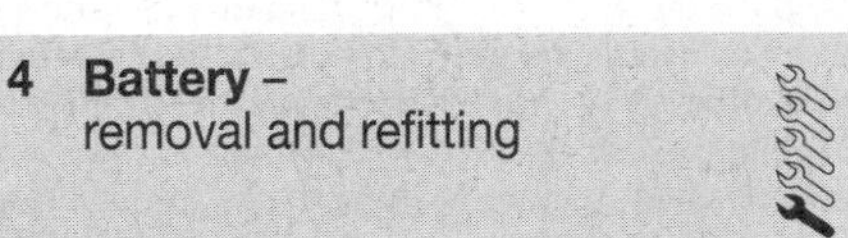
4 Battery – removal and refitting

Note: *Refer to 'Disconnecting the battery' in the Reference Section of this manual before proceeding.*

Removal

1 The battery is located on the left-hand side front of the engine compartment.

2 Open the bonnet and unclip the plastic cover from the front left-hand corner of the engine bay **(see illustration)**.

3 Slacken the clamp nut and disconnect the negative (earth) terminals from the battery **(see illustration)**.

4 Unclip the cover from the battery positive terminal and fuse/relay box **(see illustration)**.

5 Disconnect the positive terminal lead from the battery in the same way as the negative, it will be necessary to undo the retaining nut and disconnect the positive link cable from the relay box **(see illustration)**.

6 Unscrew the securing bolt and remove battery securing clamp **(see illustration)**. On certain automatic transmission models, it will be necessary to unclip the transmission ECU from the front of the battery to gain access to the clamp.

7 The battery can then be lifted out of the engine compartment.

8 To remove the battery tray (to access the injection ECU), remove the three security bolts/screws from the base of the tray. Using a large screwdriver with a socket head remove the securing bolts, if the bolts are tight, they may need to be drilled out **(see illustrations)**.

9 Before withdrawing the tray from the vehicle, release the retaining clips and disconnect the relay/fuse box from the rear of the battery

4.8b Using a socket screwdriver head to remove the bolts

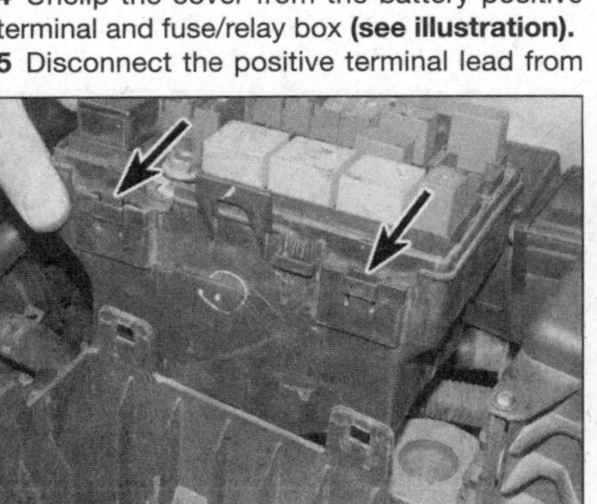
4.9a Release the fuse/relay box retaining clips (arrowed) . . .

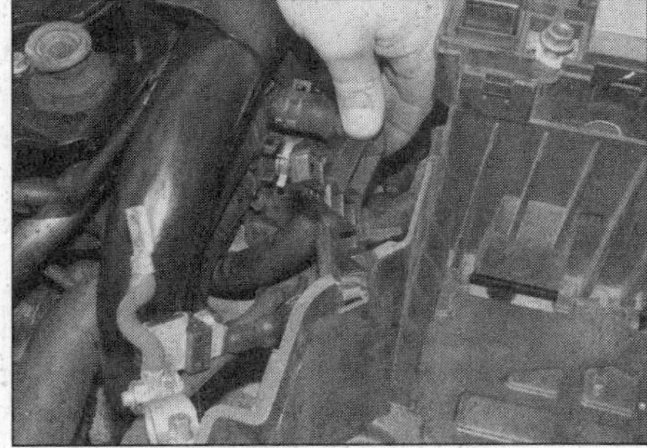
4.9b . . . unclip the positive cable wiring bracket . . .

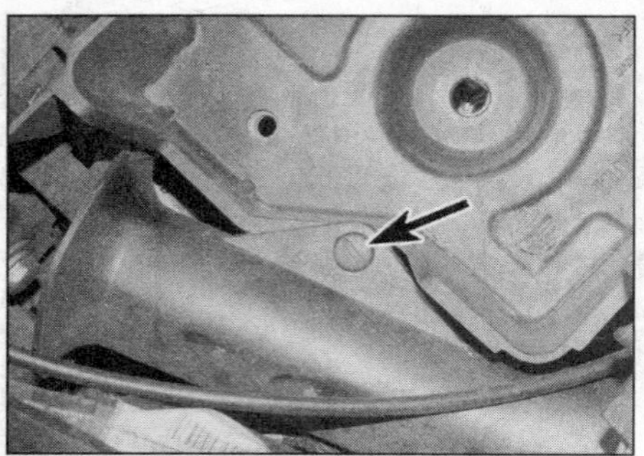

4.9c . . . release the air intake securing clip – arrowed . . .

4.9d . . . and unhook the wiring loom bracket (arrowed) from the battery tray

tray. Where necessary (depending on model), unclip any other retaining clips from the side of the battery tray **(see illustrations)**.

Refitting

10 Refitting is a reversal of removal. Smear petroleum jelly on the terminals when reconnecting the leads to reduce corrosion. Always reconnect the positive lead first, and the negative lead last.

5 Charging system – testing

Note: *Refer to the warnings given in 'Safety first!' and in Section 1 of this Chapter before starting work.*

1 If the ignition warning light fails to illuminate when the ignition is on, first check the alternator wiring connections for security. If satisfactory, check that the warning light bulb has not blown, and that the bulbholder is secure in its location in the instrument panel. If the light still fails to illuminate, check the continuity of the warning light feed wire from the alternator to the bulbholder. If all is satisfactory, the alternator is at fault and should be renewed or taken to an auto-electrician for testing and repair.

2 If the ignition warning light illuminates when the engine is running, stop the engine and check that the auxiliary drivebelt is correctly tensioned (see the relevant part of Chapter 1) and that the alternator connections are secure. If all is so far satisfactory, have the alternator checked by an auto-electrician for testing and repair.

3 If the alternator output is suspect even though the warning light functions correctly, the regulated voltage may be checked as follows.

4 Connect a voltmeter across the battery terminals and start the engine.

5 Increase the engine speed until the voltmeter reading remains steady; the reading should be approximately 13.2 to 14.8 volts, and no more than 14.8 volts.

6 Switch on as many electrical accessories (eg, the headlights, heated rear window and heater blower) as possible, and check that the alternator maintains the regulated voltage at around 13.2 to 14.8 volts.

7 If the regulated voltage is not as stated, the fault may be due to worn brushes, weak brush springs, a faulty voltage regulator, a faulty diode, a severed phase winding, or worn or damaged slip-rings. The alternator should be renewed or taken to an auto-electrician for testing and repair.

6 Alternator drivebelt – removal, refitting and tensioning

Refer to the procedure given for the auxiliary drivebelt in the relevant part of Chapter 1.

7 Alternator – testing, removal and refitting

Testing

1 If the alternator is thought to be suspect, it should be removed from the vehicle and taken to an auto-electrician for testing on specialist equipment. However, check on the cost of repairs before proceeding, as it may prove more economical to obtain a new or exchange alternator. If the brushes/regulator pack is at fault, it is possible to renew it quite easily, see Section 8.

Removal

2 Disconnect the battery negative terminal (refer to *Disconnecting the battery* in the Reference Section of this manual).

3 Remove the auxiliary drivebelt as described in the relevant part of Chapter 1.

4 Disconnect the electrical wiring connectors from the rear of the alternator **(see illustration)**.

7.4 Disconnect the wiring connectors (arrowed) from the alternator

5 Undo the retaining bolt and remove the auxiliary belt idler pulley from by the alternator lower mounting bolt **(see illustration)**.

7.5 Removing the idler pulley from the mounting bracket

6 On 2.2 diesel engines, undo the air conditioning compressor retaining bolts and move it to one side, with reference to Chapter 3, Section 11. Use cable ties to attach it to the subframe, taking care not to damage the pipes; it may be necessary to disconnect the electrical wiring connectors from the compressor.

7 Slacken and remove the lower and upper mounting bolts from the alternator. On some engines, the upper bolt does not need to be fully removed as the mounting bracket is slotted to allow the bolt to be removed with the alternator **(see illustration)**.

7.7 Locating slot (arrowed) for upper mounting bolt

8 With spacers fitted to its mounting lugs, the alternator may prove difficult to remove from the mounting bracket. Take care when prising the alternator out from the mounting bracket to avoid damaging it, or any surrounding components. Support the alternator from underneath to prevent it falling, and then remove the alternator from the engine.

Refitting

9 Refitting is a reversal of removal. Refer to the relevant part of Chapter 1A or 1B for details of fitting (and tensioning, where necessary) the auxiliary drivebelt. Note that the alternator mounting holes are fitted with adjustable spacers, which are clamped to the mounting bracket when the bolts are tightened. This makes the task of refitting the alternator difficult; tap the spacers out slightly to provide additional clearance **(see illustration).**

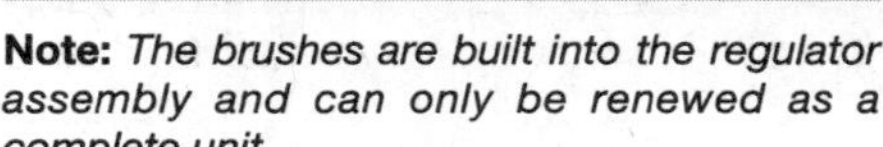

8 Alternator brushes/regulator – removal and refitting

Note: *The brushes are built into the regulator assembly and can only be renewed as a complete unit.*

Removal

1 Disconnect the battery negative terminal (refer to *Disconnecting the battery* in the Reference Section of this manual).

2 Remove the alternator from the engine as described in previous Section.

3 Undo the retaining screws and remove the rear plastic cover from the alternator **(see illustration).**

4 Slide the protective sleeve which covers the brushes and the slip-rings out from the rear of the alternator **(see illustration).**

5 Undo the three retaining bolts and withdraw the brushes/regulator assembly from the alternator **(see illustration).**

6 Check the carbon brushes and slip-rings for wear, make sure the brushes are able to slide freely in their guides without any sign of binding.

Refitting

7 Refitting is a reversal of removal

9 Starting system – testing

Note: *Refer to the precautions given in 'Safety first!' and in Section 1 of this Chapter before starting work.*

1 If the starter motor fails to operate, the following possible causes may be to blame.

a) The battery is faulty.

b) The electrical connections between the switch, solenoid, battery and starter motor are somewhere failing to pass the necessary current from the battery through the starter to earth.

c) The solenoid is faulty.

d) The starter motor is mechanically or electrically defective.

7.9 Tap the spacers outwards to allow for fitting

2 To check the battery, switch on the headlights. If they dim after a few seconds, this indicates that the battery is discharged – recharge (see Section 3) or renew the battery. If the headlights glow brightly, operate the ignition switch and observe the lights. If they dim, then this indicates that current is reaching the starter motor; therefore the fault must lie in the starter motor. If the lights continue to glow brightly (and no clicking sound can be heard from the starter motor solenoid), this indicates that there is a fault in the circuit or solenoid – see following paragraphs. If the starter motor turns slowly when operated, but the battery is in good condition, then this indicates that either the starter motor is faulty, or there is considerable resistance somewhere in the circuit.

3 If a fault in the circuit is suspected, disconnect the battery leads (including the earth connection to the body), the starter/solenoid wiring and the engine/transmission earth strap. Thoroughly clean the connections, and reconnect the leads and wiring, then use a voltmeter or test lamp to check that full battery voltage is available at the battery positive lead connection to the solenoid, and that the earth is sound. Smear petroleum jelly around the battery terminals to prevent corrosion – corroded connections are amongst the most frequent causes of electrical system faults.

4 If the battery and all connections are in good condition, check the circuit by disconnecting the wire from the solenoid blade terminal. Connect a voltmeter or test lamp between the wire end and a good earth (such as the battery negative terminal), and check that the wire is live when the starter button is pressed. If it is, then the circuit is sound – if not the circuit wiring can be checked as described in Chapter 12.

5 The solenoid contacts can be checked by connecting a voltmeter or test lamp between the battery positive feed connection on the starter side of the solenoid, and earth. When the starter button is pressed, there should be a reading or lighted bulb, as applicable. If there is no reading or lighted bulb, the solenoid is faulty and should be renewed.

6 If the circuit and solenoid are proved sound, the fault must lie in the starter motor. In this event, it may be possible to have the starter motor overhauled by a specialist, but check on the cost of spares before proceeding, as it may prove more economical to obtain a new or exchange motor.

10 Starter motor – removal and refitting

Removal

1 Disconnect the battery negative terminal (refer to *Disconnecting the battery* in the Reference Section of this manual).

2 Where applicable, remove the engine covers and engine undertray from the vehicle to gain better access.

Petrol engine models

3 Remove the air cleaner assembly and inlet ducts as described in Chapter 4A.

4 Slacken and remove the retaining nuts and disconnect the wiring from the starter motor solenoid. Recover the washers under the nuts.

5 Slacken and remove the bolts securing the starter motor to the transmission housing.

6 Remove the motor upwards and out of position, noting the position of the locating dowel.

8.3 Remove the rear cover . . .

8.4 . . . withdraw the slip-ring and brushes cover . . .

8.5 . . . then remove the brushes/regulator unit

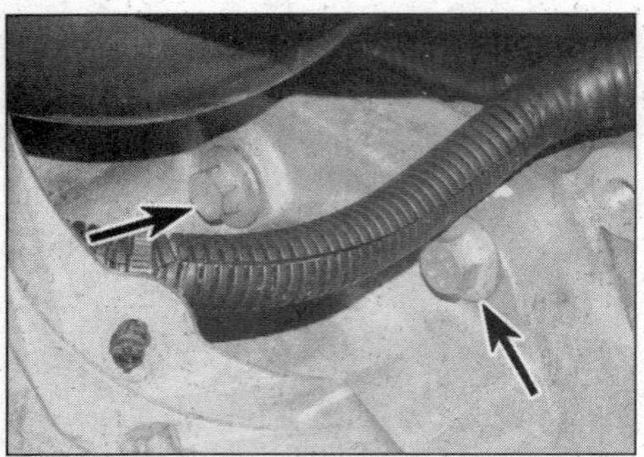
10.12a Remove the bolts from the transmission side . . .

10.12b . . . and the bolt from the engine side . . .

10.12c . . . and withdraw the starter motor

1.9 litre diesel engine models

7 Remove the air cleaner assembly and inlet ducts as described in Chapter 4B.

8 Remove the exhaust front pipe/catalytic converter as described in Chapter 4B.

9 Slacken the retaining clips and remove the air hoses from the turbocharger to the intercooler, with reference to Chapter 4B.

10 Slacken and remove the retaining nuts and disconnect the wiring from the starter motor solenoid. Recover the washers under the nuts.

11 Undo the retaining bolt and remove the earth strap from the starter motor housing.

12 Undo the starter motor mounting bolts then remove the motor downwards and out of position, noting the position of the locating dowel **(see illustrations)**.

2.2 litre diesel engine models

13 Slacken the retaining clips and remove the air hoses from the turbocharger to the intercooler, with reference to Chapter 4B.

14 Slacken the retaining clip and disconnect the hose from the bottom of the air inlet damper valve unit on the front of the engine **(see illustration)**.

15 Undo the retaining nuts and disconnect the wiring connectors from the starter solenoid. Recover any washers from under the nuts **(see illustration)**.

16 Undo the retaining bolt and remove the earth strap from the top starter motor **(see illustration)**.

17 Slacken and remove the three bolts securing the starter motor to the transmission housing and remove the motor from the engine compartment **(see illustration)**. Noting the position of the locating dowel.

Refitting

18 Refitting is a reversal of removal. There is a locating dowel, either fitted to the transmission bellhousing or the starter motor bolt hole, to ensure that the starter motor is centralised. Make sure this is correctly positioned before refitting the starter motor.

11 Starter motor – testing and overhaul

If the starter motor is thought to be suspect, it should be removed from the vehicle and taken to an auto-electrician for testing. Most auto-electricians will be able to supply and fit brushes at a reasonable cost. However, check on the cost of repairs before proceeding, as it may prove more economical to obtain a new or exchange motor.

12 Ignition card reader – removal and refitting

Removal

1 Disconnect the battery negative terminal (refer to *Disconnecting the battery* in the Reference Section of this manual).

2 Unclip the ashtray from the centre console **(see illustration)**.

3 Carefully unclip and withdraw the card reader from the facia panel, disconnect the wiring connector from the rear of the card reader as it is removed **(see illustrations)**.

10.14 Slacken the retaining clip (arrowed) and remove the hose

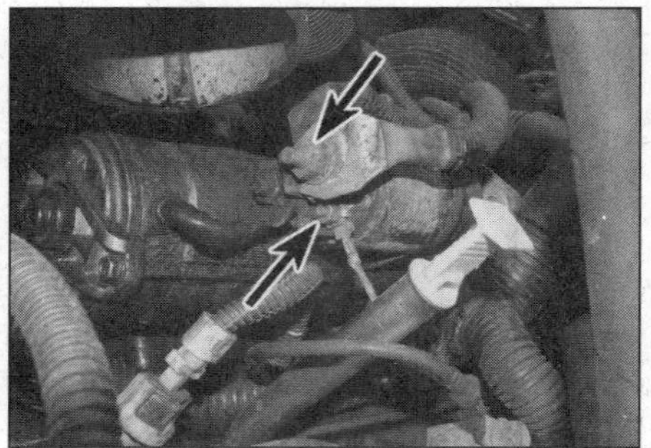

10.15 Undo the retaining nuts – arrowed

10.16 Undo the earth strap retaining bolt – arrowed

10.17 Withdraw the starter motor from the transmission

12.2 Remove the ashtray

12.3a Unclip the card reader from the facia . . .

12.3b . . . and disconnect the wiring connector

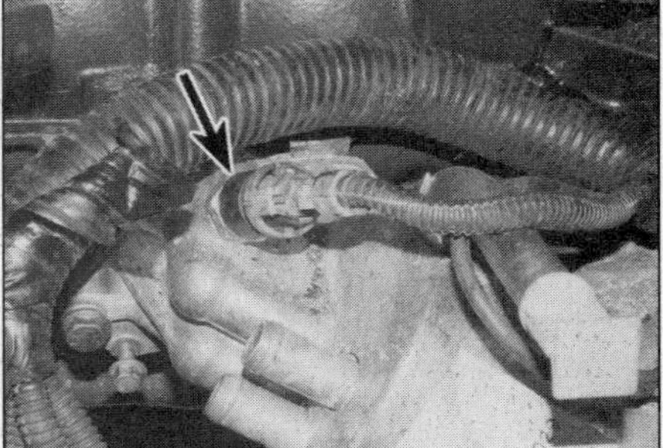

13.1 Oil pressure switch (arrowed) – 2.2 litre diesel engine

Refitting

4 Refitting is the reverse of removal.

13 Oil pressure warning light switch – removal and refitting

Removal

1 The switch is located at the front of the cylinder block. On petrol engine models the switch is on the right-hand end of the cylinder block. On diesel engine models the switch is located in the centre of the cylinder block in the filter housing **(see illustration)**. If access is poor, it may be necessary to improve access by removing the starter motor.

2 Disconnect the battery negative terminal (refer to *Disconnecting the battery* in the Reference Section of this manual).

3 Depress the retaining tabs and disconnect the wiring from the switch.

4 Unscrew the switch from the cylinder block, and recover the sealing washer. Be prepared for oil spillage, and if the switch is to be left removed from the engine for any length of time, plug the hole in the cylinder block.

Refitting

5 Examine the sealing washer for damage or deterioration and if necessary renew.

6 Refit the switch, complete with washer, and tighten it securely. Reconnect the wiring connector.

7 If necessary, top-up the engine oil as described in *Weekly checks*.

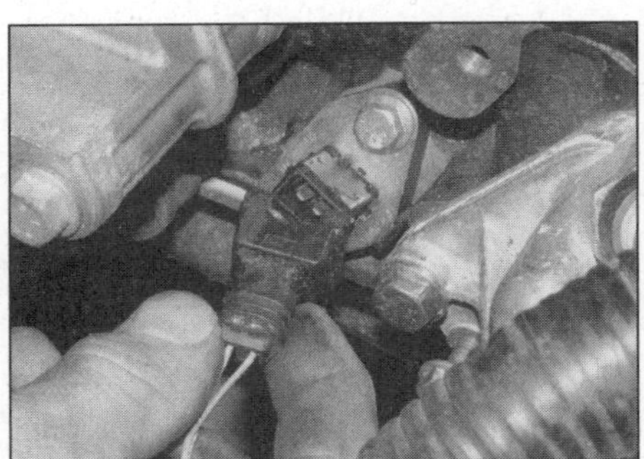

14.3 Disconnect the wiring connector from the sensor

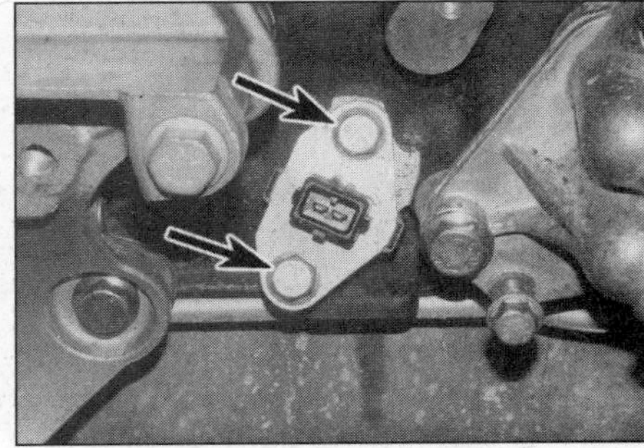

14.5 Undo the oil level sensor bolts (arrowed) – 2.2 litre engine

14 Oil level sensor – removal and refitting

Removal

1 The sensor is located on the front side of the cylinder block.

2 To gain access to the sensor, firmly apply the handbrake then jack up the front of the vehicle and support it on axle stands (see *Jacking and vehicle support*). Undo the retaining screws and remove the plastic undertray from beneath the engine/transmission.

3 Disconnect the wiring connector from the oil level sensor **(see illustration)**.

4 On petrol engine models, unscrew the sensor and withdraw it from the block.

5 On diesel engine models, undo the retaining bolts and carefully withdraw the sensor from the block **(see illustration)**. Recover the sensor sealing ring and discard it, a new one should be used on refitting.

Refitting

6 Refitting is the reverse of removal. On petrol engine models apply a smear of sealant to the threads of the sensor prior to refitting, and on diesel engine models using a new sensor sealing ring.

Notes

Chapter 5 Part B: Ignition system – petrol engine models

Contents

Degrees of difficulty

Easy, suitable for novice with little experience 	**Fairly easy,** suitable for beginner with some experience	**Fairly difficult,** suitable for competent DIY mechanic	**Difficult,** suitable for experienced DIY mechanic	**Very difficult,** suitable for expert DIY or professional 

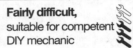

Specifications

General

Ignition system type	Fully electronic, computer-controlled, with four individual ignition coils, one on each spark plug
Firing order	1-3-4-2
Location of No 1 cylinder	Flywheel end

Ignition system data

Ignition timing	Controlled by the ECU – see text
Ignition HT coil resistances:	
Primary windings	0.5 ohms
Secondary windings	10 to 12 kohms

Torque wrench settings

	Nm	lbf ft
Ignition coil bolts	15	11
Knock 'pinking' sensor	30	22
Spark plugs	25 to 30	18 to 22

1 General information and precautions

General information

The ignition system is integrated with the fuel injection system to form a combined engine management system under the control of one ECU (see Chapter 4A for further information). All engines are fitted with a distributorless ignition system.

The ignition system uses one coil for each cylinder, with each coil mounted on the relevant spark plug. The coils are fed in series, two at a time, and the system operates on the 'wasted spark' principle, where each plug sparks twice for every cycle of the engine, once on the compression stroke and once on the exhaust stroke.

The camshaft/crankshaft position/speed sensor (see Chapter 4A) is used to determine piston position as well as engine speed.

The power module for the ignition is integrated in the engine management ECU. The ECU uses the inputs from the sensors to calculate the required ignition advance setting and coil-charging time – an integral amplifier circuit within the ECU switches the ignition coil primary (LT) circuit.

The knock sensor (where fitted) is mounted

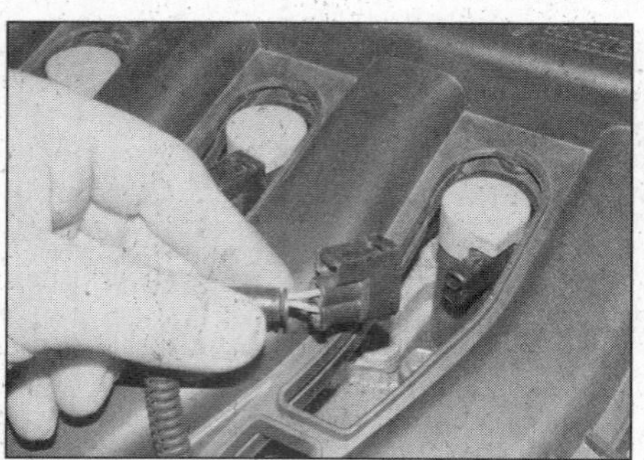

3.3 Disconnect the wiring connector from each coil

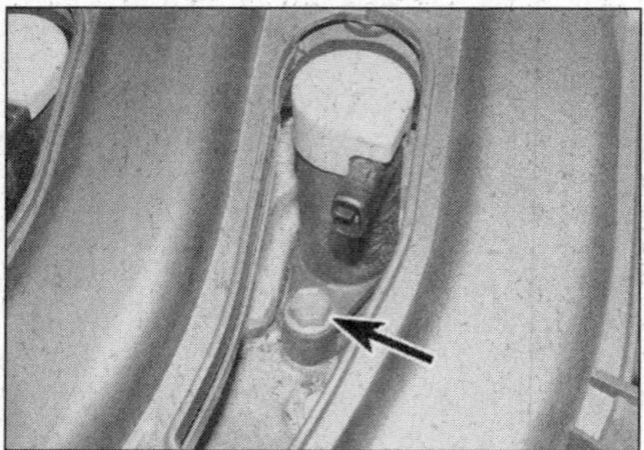

3.4a Unscrew the mounting bolt – arrowed . . .

3.4b . . . and withdraw the coil from the engine

on the cylinder block to inform the ECU when the engine is 'pinking'. Its sensitivity to a particular frequency of vibration allows it to detect the impulses which are caused by the shock waves set up when the engine starts to 'pink' (pre-ignite). The knock sensor sends an electrical signal to the ECU that retards the ignition advance setting until the pinking ceases – the ignition timing is then gradually returned to the 'normal' setting. This maintains the ignition timing as close to the knock threshold as possible – the most efficient setting for the engine under normal running conditions.

Precautions

The following precautions must be observed to prevent damage to the ignition system components and to reduce risk of personal injury.

a) *Ensure the ignition is switched off before disconnecting any of the ignition wiring.*
b) *Ensure that the ignition is switched off before connecting or disconnecting any ignition test equipment, such as a timing light.*
c) *Do not earth the coil primary or secondary circuits.*

Warning: Voltages produced by an electronic ignition system are considerably higher than those produced by conventional ignition systems. Extreme care must be taken when working on the system with the ignition switched on. Persons with surgically implanted cardiac pacemaker devices should keep well clear of the ignition circuits, components and test equipment

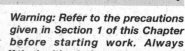

2 Ignition system – testing

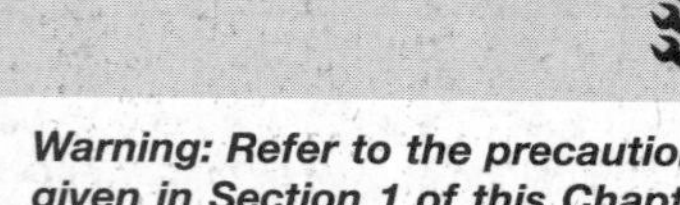

Warning: Refer to the precautions given in Section 1 of this Chapter before starting work. Always switch off the ignition before disconnecting or connecting any component and when using a multi-meter to check resistances.

1 The components of ignition systems are normally very reliable; most faults are far more likely to be due to loose or dirty connections, or to 'tracking' of HT voltage due to dirt, dampness or damaged insulation than to the failure of any of the system's components. Always check all wiring thoroughly before condemning an electrical component and work methodically to eliminate all other possibilities before deciding that a particular component is faulty.

2 The old practice of checking for a spark by holding the live end of a spark plug HT lead (or in this case, the individual coils) a short distance away from the engine is not recommended; not only is there a high risk of a powerful electric shock, but the coil or ECU may be damaged. However, if necessary each plug can be checked individually by removing it, then reconnecting the coil and connecting the body of the spark plug to a suitable earthing point on the engine using a battery jumper lead. It is important to make a good earth connection if using this method. Never try to 'diagnose' misfires by pulling off one coil at a time.

Engine will not start

3 If the engine either will not turn over at all, or only turns very slowly, first check the battery and starter motor as described in Chapter 5A.

4 Use an ohmmeter to check the resistances of the coils, and compare with the information given in the Specifications.

5 If these checks fail to reveal the cause of the problem, the vehicle should be taken to a Renault dealer for testing. A wiring block connector is incorporated in the engine management circuit, into which a special electronic diagnostic tester can be plugged. The tester will locate the fault quickly and simply, alleviating the need to test all the system components individually, which is a time-consuming operation that carries a high risk of damaging the ECU. If necessary, the system wiring and wiring connectors can be checked as described in Chapter 12, ensuring that the ECU wiring connector is first disconnected with the ignition switched off.

Engine misfires

6 An irregular misfire suggests either a loose connection or intermittent fault in the primary circuit, or an HT fault between the coils and spark plugs.

7 With the ignition switched off, check carefully through the system ensuring that all connections are clean and securely fastened.

8 Check that the HT coils and their associated wiring connections are clean and dry.

9 Regular misfiring of one cylinder may be due to a faulty spark plug, faulty injector, a faulty coil or loss of compression in the relevant cylinder. Regular misfiring of all the cylinders suggests a fuel supply fault, such as a clogged fuel filter or faulty fuel pump.

3 Ignition HT coils – removal, testing and refitting

Removal

1 Disconnect the battery negative terminal (refer to *Disconnecting the battery* in the Reference Section of this manual).

2 Remove the plastic covers from the top of the engine.

3 Carefully disconnect the wiring terminals from each of the coils, taking care not to damage them on removal **(see illustration).**

4 Undo the retaining bolt and withdraw the coil from the top of the spark plug **(see illustrations).**

Testing

5 Each coil can be tested as described in the previous Section, using an ohmmeter to check for the resistances given in the Specifications.

6 Further testing of the ignition system should be carried out by a Renault dealer using specialised equipment connected to the engine management diagnostic socket.

Refitting

7 Refitting is a reversal of removal, noting the following points:

a) *Check the condition of the O-ring seals at the base of the coil mounting and renew if necessary.*
b) *Before refitting the coils over the plugs, Renault recommend that the rubber boots are first lightly lubricated inside, using fluorine grease (part number 82 00 168 855).*
c) *Tighten the mounting bolts to the specified torque, and ensure that the wiring connectors are correctly and securely refitted.*

4 Knock sensor – removal and refitting

Removal

1 The knock sensor is located on the front of the cylinder block below the fuel rail **(see illustration)**.

2 To remove the sensor, first disconnect the wiring, and then unscrew it from the cylinder block.

Refitting

3 Refitting is a reversal of removal. Ensure that the sensor and its seating on the cylinder block or head are completely clean and tighten the sensor to the specified torque wrench setting. It is essential that these measures are scrupulously observed, as if the sensor is not correctly secured to a clean mating surface it may not be able to detect the impulses caused by pre-ignition. If this were to happen, the correction of ignition timing would not take place, with the consequent risk of severe engine damage.

5 Ignition timing – checking and adjustment

With the type of ignition fitted, the ignition timing is constantly being monitored and adjusted by the engine management ECU, and nominal checking values cannot be given. Therefore, it is not possible for the home mechanic to check the ignition timing. The only way in which the ignition timing can be checked is using special electronic test equipment, connected to the engine management system diagnostic connector (refer to Chapter 4A). No adjustment of the ignition timing is possible. Should the ignition timing be incorrect, then a fault must be present in the engine management system.

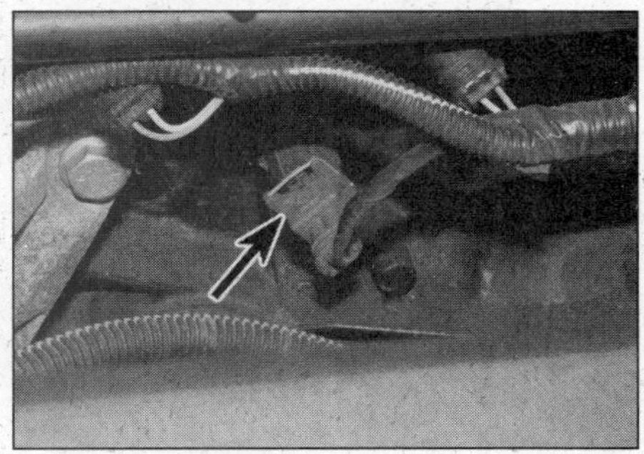

4.1 Knock sensor location – arrowed

Chapter 5 Part C:
Pre/post-heating system – diesel engine models

Contents

Degrees of difficulty

Easy, suitable for novice with little experience 	**Fairly easy,** suitable for beginner with some experience	**Fairly difficult,** suitable for competent DIY mechanic	**Difficult,** suitable for experienced DIY mechanic	**Very difficult,** suitable for expert DIY or professional 

Specifications

Glow plugs

Type:	
1.9 litre	Beru or Champion
2.2 litre	Beru
Resistance (with connector removed)	0.6 ohms

Torque wrench setting

	Nm	lbf ft
Glow plugs	15	11

1 General information

The pre/post-heating system consists of glow plugs screwed into the combustion chambers, a control unit mounted under the left-hand front wheel arch (see Section 4), and a coolant temperature sensor located on the thermostat housing (see Chapter 3). The control unit is activated by the engine management ECU (see Chapter 4B).

The glow plugs are supplied with current from the control unit in several phases, namely variable preheating, fixed preheating, starting heating, and post-heating (while the engine is running).

The variable preheating phase occurs when the ignition is switched on. During this phase the preheating warning light is illuminated on the instrument panel for no more than 15 seconds. The period of preheating depends on the temperature of the coolant and battery voltage.

The fixed preheating phase occurs immediately after the variable phase finishes. After the warning light has extinguished, and the driver has started the engine, the glow plugs remain supplied with a current for a fixed period of 10 seconds.

During the period when the starter motor is in operation, the glow plugs are continuously supplied with current.

The post-heating phase occurs immediately after the engine has been started, and the period of post-heating depends on the temperature of the coolant. The maximum period of variable post-heating is 60 seconds, at which point the system is switched off. Post-heating will cease if the coolant temperature exceeds 30°C.

2 Pre/post-heating system – testing

1 If the system malfunctions, testing is ultimately by substitution of known good units, but some preliminary checks may be made as follows.

2 Connect a voltmeter or 12 volt test lamp between the glow plug supply cable and earth (engine or vehicle metal). Make sure that the live connection is kept clear of the engine and bodywork.

3 Have an assistant switch on the ignition, and check that voltage is applied to the glow plugs. Note the time for which the warning light is lit, and the total time for which voltage is applied before the system cuts out. Switch off the ignition and compare to the times given in the previous Section.

4 If there is no supply at all, the relay, ECU or associated wiring is at fault, see Chapter 12.

5 To locate a defective glow plug, disconnect the main supply cable and the interconnecting wire or strap from the top of the glow plugs. Be careful not to drop the nuts and washers.

6 Use a continuity tester, or a 12 volt test lamp connected to the battery positive terminal, to check for continuity between each glow plug terminal and earth. The resistance of a glow plug in good condition is very low (less than 1 ohm), so if the test lamp does not light or the continuity tester shows a high resistance, the glow plug is certainly defective.

7 If an ammeter is available, the current draw of each glow plug can be checked. After an initial surge of 15 to 20 amps, each plug should draw 10 amps. Any plug that draws much more or less than this is probably defective.

8 As a final check, the glow plugs can be removed and inspected as described in the following Section.

9 If the pre/post-heating system is faulty, first check the wiring to each individual component. If this does not locate the fault, ideally each component should be substituted with known good units until the fault is located. If this is not possible, take the vehicle to a Renault dealer or diesel specialist who will have the diagnostic equipment necessary to pinpoint the fault quickly.

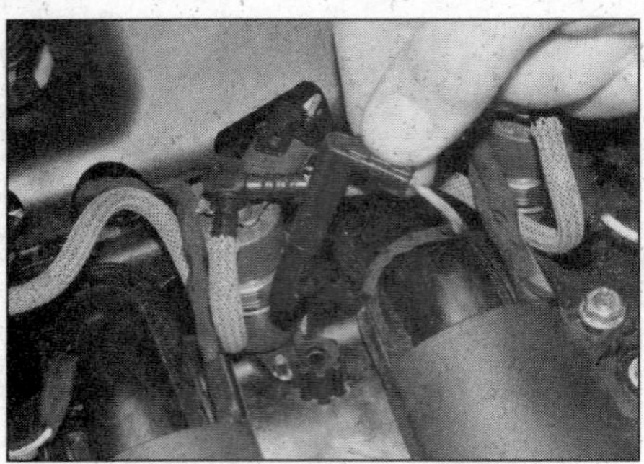
3.3a Disconnect the glow plug wiring connector – 2.2 litre engine

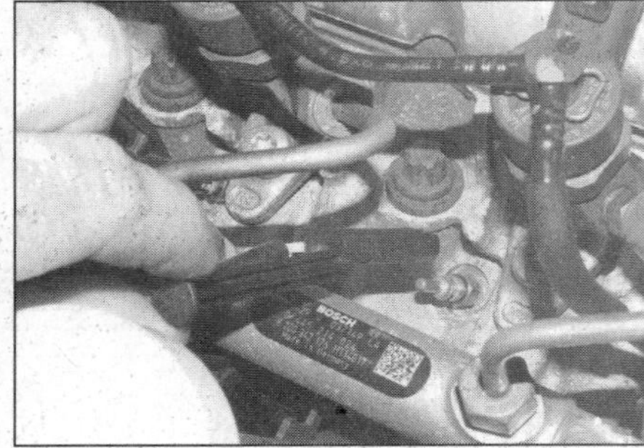
3.3a Disconnect the glow plug wiring connector – 1.9 litre engine

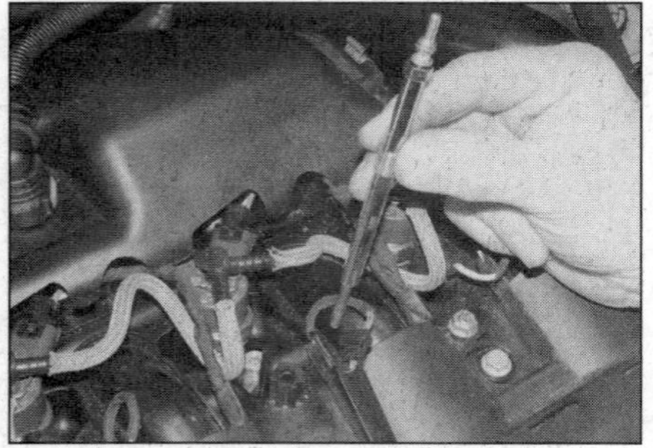
3.4a Removing the glow plug – 2.2 litre engine

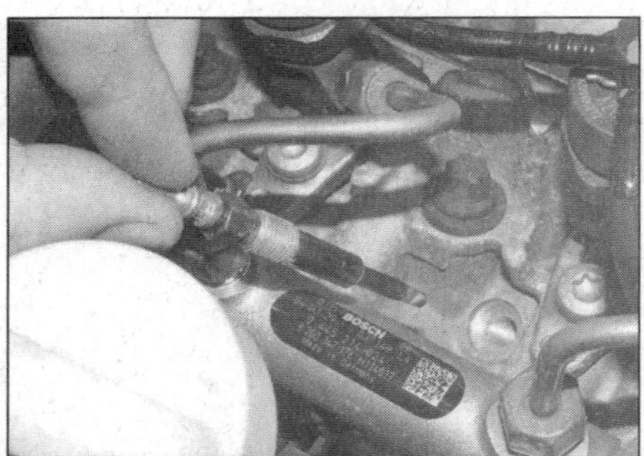
3.4b Removing the glow plug – 1.9 litre engine

3 Glow plugs – removal, inspection and refitting

Caution: If the preheating system has just been energised, or if the engine has been running, the glow plugs will be very hot.

Removal

1 Disconnect the battery negative terminal (refer to *Disconnecting the battery* in the Reference Section of this manual).

2 Remove the plastic covers from the top of the engine.

3 Unclip the electrical connector from the top of the relevant glow plug **(see illustrations)**, and then clean around the outside of the glow plug, to prevent dirt entering the cylinder.

4 Unscrew the glow plug and remove it from the cylinder head **(see illustrations)**.

5 Carry out the same procedure for all four glow plugs. If leaving glow plugs out for a while, blank of the holes in the cylinder head to prevent any contamination.

Inspection

6 Inspect each glow plug for physical damage. Burnt or eroded glow plug tips can be caused by a bad injector spray pattern. Have the injectors checked if this sort of damage is found.

7 If the glow plugs are in good physical condition, check them electrically using a 12 volt test lamp or continuity tester as described in the previous Section.

8 The glow plugs can be energised by applying 12 volts to them to verify that they heat up evenly and in the required time. Observe the following precautions.

a) Support the glow plug by clamping it carefully in a vice or self-locking pliers. Remember it will become red-hot.

b) Make sure that the power supply or test lead incorporates a fuse or overload trip to protect against damage from a short-circuit.

c) After testing, allow the glow plug to cool for several minutes before attempting to handle it.

9 A glow plug in good condition will start to glow red at the tip after drawing current for 5 seconds or so. Any plug that takes much longer to start glowing, or which starts glowing in the middle instead of at the tip, is defective.

Refitting

10 Refit by reversing the removal operations. Apply a smear of copper-based anti-seize compound to the plug threads and tighten the glow plugs to the specified torque. Do not over-tighten, as this can damage the glow plug element.

4 Pre/post-heating system control unit – removal and refitting

1 The pre/post-heating system control unit is an electronic relay, which is controlled by the injection computer. It has a 9-pin wiring connector that has a separate power circuit to each glow plug. The control unit is mounted on the brake ABS unit mounting bracket, which is located under the left-hand front wheel arch, behind the splash shield **(see illustration)**.

Wiring connector allocation

Track	Description
1	Supply to plug 3.
2	Supply to plug 4.
3	Positive battery feed.
4	Not used.
5	Not used.
6	Supply to plug 1.
7	Supply to plug 2.
8	Control from injection computer.
9	Fault finding.

Removal

2 Disconnect the battery negative terminal (refer to *Disconnecting the battery* in the Reference Section of this manual).

3 Raise the front of the vehicle, and securely support it on axle stands (see *Jacking and vehicle support*). It is possible to gain better access by removing the left-hand front wheel.

4 Undo the retaining screws and remove the splash shield from inside the wheel arch.

5 Disconnect the wiring connector from the unit and remove the unit from under the front wing.

6 Slacken and remove the retaining bolt securing the unit to the body **(see illustration)**.

Refitting

7 Refitting is a reversal of removal, ensuring that the wiring connectors are securely connected.

4.1 Pre/post-heating control unit (arrowed) location

4.6 Pre/post-heating control unit mounting bolt – arrowed

Chapter 6
Clutch

Contents

Degrees of difficulty

Easy, suitable for novice with little experience 

Fairly easy, suitable for beginner with some experience

Fairly difficult, suitable for competent DIY mechanic

Difficult, suitable for experienced DIY mechanic

Very difficult, suitable for expert DIY or professional 

Specifications

General

Type	Single dry friction plate, with diaphragm spring pressure plate, hydraulically-operated release bearing

Friction plate

Diameter:	
Petrol engines	215.0 mm
Diesel engines	228.0 mm
Friction material thickness (new):	
Petrol engines	6.8 mm
Diesel engines	8.4 mm

Torque wrench settings

	Nm	lbf ft
Pedal mounting bracket nuts	34	25
Slave cylinder/release bearing bolts	9	7
Pressure plate cover to flywheel:		
Petrol engines	20	15
Diesel engines	12	9

2.2 Disconnect linkage rod – arrowed

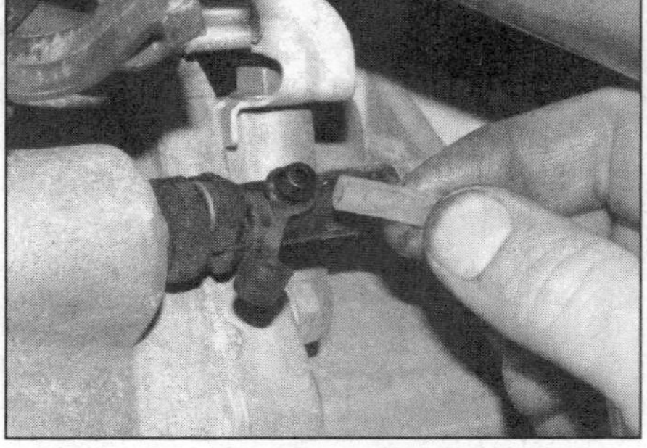

2.3 Connect a piece of tubing over the bleed nipple

2.6 Disconnect the pipes from the master cylinder – arrowed

1 General information

The clutch consists of a friction plate, a pressure plate assembly and a release bearing; all of these components are contained in the large cast-aluminium alloy bellhousing, sandwiched between the engine and the transmission. The release mechanism is hydraulic, operated by a master cylinder and a slave cylinder, which is part of the release bearing. The hydraulic master cylinder is located in the pedal bracket on the bulkhead, and the clutch fluid reservoir is shared with the brake fluid reservoir on the top of the brake master cylinder. Inside the reservoir each circuit has its own compartment, so that in the event of fluid loss in the clutch circuit, the brake circuit remains fully operational.

The friction plate is fitted between the engine flywheel and the clutch pressure plate, and is allowed to slide on the transmission input shaft splines.

The pressure plate assembly is bolted to the engine flywheel. When the engine is running, drive is transmitted from the crankshaft, via the flywheel, to the friction plate (these components being clamped securely together by the pressure plate assembly) and from the friction plate to the transmission input shaft.

To interrupt the drive, the spring pressure must be relaxed by the hydraulically-operated release mechanism. Depressing the clutch pedal operates the master cylinder, which in turn operates the slave cylinder and presses the release bearing against the pressure plate spring fingers. This causes the springs to deform and releases the clamping force on the pressure plate.

When the pedal is released, the diaphragm spring forces the pressure plate into contact with the friction linings on the friction plate. The disc is now firmly sandwiched between the pressure plate and the flywheel, thus transmitting engine power to the transmission.

Wear of the friction material on the friction plate is automatically compensated for by the operation of the hydraulic system. As the friction material on the friction plate wears, the pressure plate moves towards the flywheel causing the clutch diaphragm spring inner fingers to move outwards. When the clutch pedal is released, excess fluid is expelled through the master cylinder into the fluid reservoir.

Warning: Hydraulic fluid is poisonous; wash off immediately and thoroughly in the case of skin contact, and seek immediate medical advice if any fluid is swallowed or gets into the eyes. Certain types of hydraulic fluid are flammable, and may ignite when allowed into contact with hot components; when servicing any hydraulic system, it is safest to assume that the fluid is flammable, and to take precautions against the risk of fire as though it is petrol that is being handled. Hydraulic fluid is also an effective paint stripper, and will attack plastics; if any is spilt, it should be washed off immediately, using copious quantities of fresh water. Finally, it is hygroscopic (it absorbs moisture from the air) – old fluid may be contaminated and unfit for further use. When topping-up or renewing the fluid, always use the recommended type, and ensure that it comes from a freshly-opened sealed container.

2 Clutch master cylinder – removal and refitting

Note: *Refer to the warning in Section 1 before proceeding.*

Removal

1 Disconnect the battery negative terminal (refer to *Disconnecting the battery* in the Reference Section of this manual).

2 Working inside the vehicle in the driver's side footwell, unclip the trim panel from above the clutch pedal. Disconnect the balljoint connector from the top of the clutch pedal **(see illustration).**

3 Unscrew the brake fluid reservoir cap, then connect a piece of tubing which is a tight fit over the clutch bleed nipple located on the pipe at the front of the transmission **(see illustration)**. Place the other end of the tube into a container large enough to hold the contents of the brake fluid reservoir.

4 Open the bleed nipple, and let the fluid drain out of the clutch hydraulic system into the container. Let the fluid flow until the clutch part of the reservoir is empty. Depress the clutch pedal a few times to empty the master cylinder and pipes.

5 Place some absorbent cloth below the pipe connections on the master cylinder, to soak up any fluid still in the system.

6 Disconnect the supply pipe from the reservoir and the feed pipe to the slave cylinder from the master cylinder **(see illustration)**. To release the slave cylinder feed pipe, withdraw the retaining clip, and disconnect the pipe. Cap or tape over the open pipe connections, to prevent further loss of fluid.

7 Release the master cylinder from the bulkhead by turning it a quarter-turn clockwise, and remove it.

Refitting

8 Refitting is a reversal of removal, noting the following points:

a) Check the condition of the pipe seals, and renew if necessary.
b) Ensure that all fluid hose connections are clean, and are securely made.
c) Fill and bleed the clutch system on completion, as described in Section 5.
d) Check the clutch system is operating correctly with no leaks.
e) Check the operation of the brakes, and if necessary, bleed the system as described in Chapter 9.

3 Clutch slave cylinder – removal and refitting

Note: *Refer to the warning in Section 1 before proceeding.*

Removal

1 Remove the transmission as described in Chapter 7A.

2 On 5-speed transmissions, undo the two retaining bolts to split the slave cylinder from the connecting pipe in the transmission housing.

3 On 6-speed transmissions pull out the retaining clip to split the slave cylinder from the connecting pipe in the transmission housing **(see illustration)**.

4 Inside the bellhousing, unscrew and remove the two mounting bolts (5-speed transmissions) or three mounting bolts (6-speed transmissions) then withdraw the slave cylinder/release bearing over the transmission input shaft **(see illustration)**.

Refitting

5 Refitting is a reversal of removal, noting the following points:

a) Renew the slave cylinder/release bearing seal.

b) Tighten the flange bolts securely (5-speed transmissions).

c) Make sure the retaining clip is located securely (6-speed transmissions).

d) Tighten the release bearing mounting bolts to the specified torque.

e) Refit the transmission as described in Chapter 7A.

f) On completion, bleed the clutch as described in Section 5.

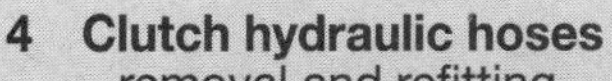

4 Clutch hydraulic hoses – removal and refitting

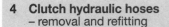

Note: *Refer to the warning in Section 1 before proceeding.*

Removal

1 Disconnect the battery negative terminal (refer to *Disconnecting the battery* in the Reference Section of this manual).

2 To improve access, remove the air cleaner and inlet ducts as described in Chapter 4A or 4B, as applicable.

3 Unscrew the brake fluid reservoir cap and empty the system of fluid as described in Section 2, paragraphs 3 to 5.

4 At the slave cylinder end, carefully prise out the securing clip (do not remove the clip completely), pull on the pipe to release it from the slave cylinder connecting pipe. Cap or tape over the slave cylinder connection, to prevent further fluid loss **(see illustrations)**.

5 Trace the pipe back to the bulkhead connections, releasing it from the mounting clips.

6 Place some absorbent cloth below the pipe connections on the master cylinder. Remove the clips from the master cylinder unions, and disconnect the pipes **(see illustration)**. Cap or tape over the open pipe connections, to prevent further loss of fluid. The pipe can now be removed from the vehicle.

7 To remove the supply pipe from the reservoir to the master cylinder. Pull the pipe of the connection at the reservoir and off the master cylinder **(see illustration).** Cap or tape over the open pipe connections to prevent further loss of fluid.

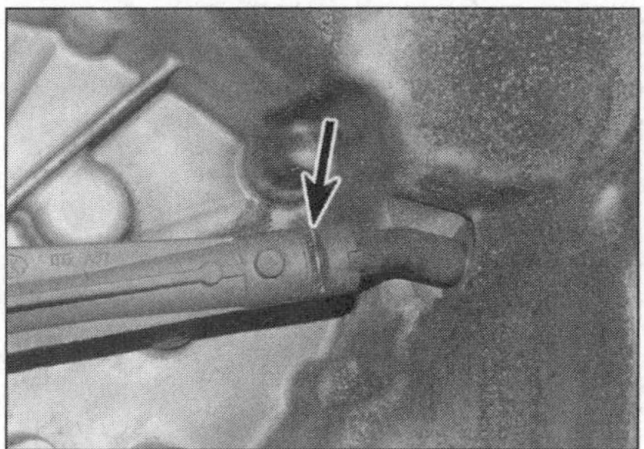

3.3 Release the retaining clip – arrowed

Refitting

8 Refitting is a reversal of removal, noting the following points:

a) Make sure the retaining clips are located securely in the hose connections.

b) Fill and bleed the clutch system on completion, as described in Section 5.

c) Check the operation of the brakes and, if necessary, bleed the system as described in Chapter 9.

d) Refit the air cleaner and inlet ducts as described in Chapter 4A or 4B, as applicable.

5 Clutch hydraulic system – bleeding

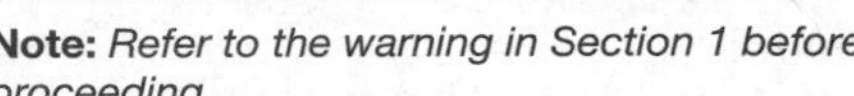

Note: *Refer to the warning in Section 1 before proceeding.*

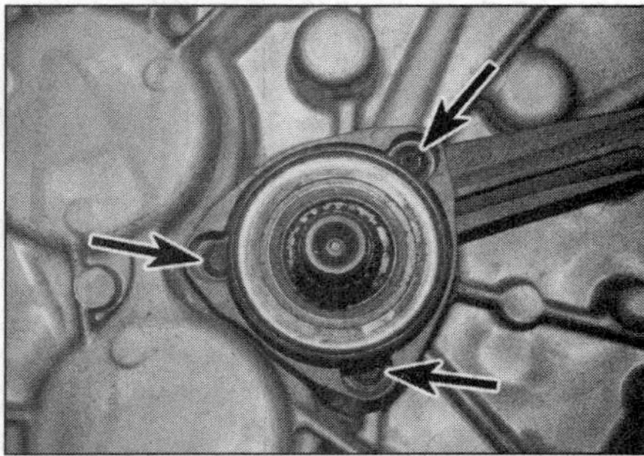

3.4 Undo the slave cylinder mounting bolts – arrowed

1 The correct operation of any hydraulic system is only possible after removing all air from the components and circuit; this is achieved by bleeding the system.

2 During the bleeding procedure, add only clean, unused hydraulic fluid of the recommended type; never re-use fluid that has already been bled from the system. Ensure that sufficient fluid is available before starting work.

3 If there is any possibility of incorrect fluid being already in the system, the hydraulic circuit must be flushed completely with uncontaminated, correct fluid.

4 If hydraulic fluid has been lost from the system, or air has entered because of a leak, ensure that the fault is cured before continuing further.

5 The bleed nipple is fitted to the slave cylinder at the front of the transmission bellhousing **(see illustration)**.

6 Disconnect the battery negative terminal

4.4a Release the retaining clip . . .

4.4b . . . and cap the end to prevent dirt ingress

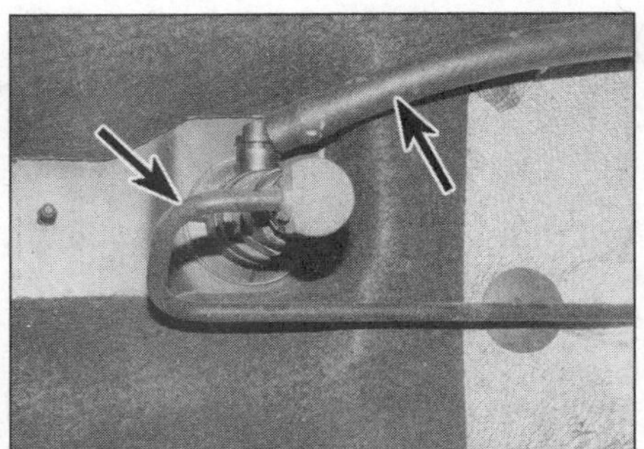

4.6 Disconnect the pipes (arrowed) from the master cylinder

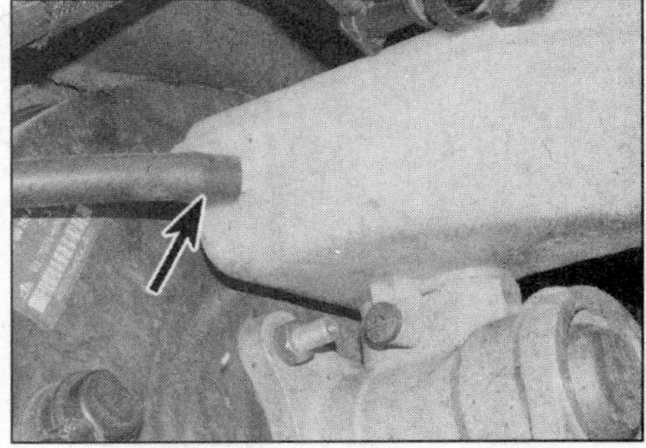

4.7 Disconnect the supply pipe (arrowed) from the reservoir

5.5 Clutch slave cylinder bleed nipple – arrowed

(refer to *Disconnecting the battery* in the Reference Section of this manual).

7 To improve access, remove the air cleaner and inlet ducts as described in Chapter 4A or 4B, as applicable.

8 Unscrew the brake fluid reservoir cap, and top-up the fluid level to the MAX mark. Keep an eye on the fluid level as bleeding progresses, and keep it topped-up above the MIN mark throughout.

9 Referring to Section 2, paragraphs 3 and 4, connect a piece of tube to the bleed nipple, and open the circuit as described – bleeding and filling the system is done by gravity.

10 If the system is known to be empty (or if new parts have been fitted), have an assistant hold the clutch pedal depressed until the flow of bubbles seen in the pipe ceases. Depress and release the clutch pedal a few times, to purge the air from the master cylinder and pipes. Top-up the fluid level as necessary.

11 When no more bubbles are seen in the fluid, release the clutch pedal, and then press the slave cylinder pipe firmly back into place.

12 Top-up the fluid level to the MAX mark, and refit the reservoir cap.

13 Check the operation of the clutch – any lack of response indicates the need for further bleeding.

14 If the clutch system was emptied, check the brakes for any sign of 'sponginess' in the pedal, which would mean the brakes also require bleeding, as described in Chapter 9.

15 Discard any hydraulic fluid that has been bled from the system; it will not be fit for re-use.

16 If the clutch is not operating correctly after repeated bleeding, the master cylinder or slave cylinder may be faulty. If new parts are fitted, it may be that there is an air-lock in the system; disconnect the hoses from each component in turn to check there is fluid at that point. Place some absorbent cloth below the pipe connections as they are removed, to soak up the fluid that escapes. The system will then need further bleeding. **Note:** *If any fluid is spilt, it should be washed off immediately, using copious quantities of fresh water.*

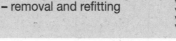

6 Clutch pedal assembly – removal and refitting

Removal

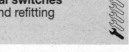

1 Disconnect the battery negative terminal (refer to *Disconnecting the battery* in the Reference Section of this manual).

2 Working inside the vehicle in the driver's side footwell, unclip the trim panel from above the clutch pedal. Disconnect the ball-joint connector from the top of the clutch pedal **(see illustration).**

3 Remove the clutch pedal switches as described in Section 7.

4 Undo the retaining nuts and remove the clutch pedal mounting bracket assembly from the bulkhead **(see illustrations).**

5 To remove the pedal from the mounting bracket, undo the retaining nut and withdraw the pivot bolt **(see illustration).** Note the position of any springs and spacers as the pedal is removed from the mounting bracket.

Refitting

6 Refitting is a reversal of removal, noting the following points:

a) Ensure the switches are located correctly and the wiring connectors are secure.

b) Tighten the pedal mounting bracket nuts to the specified torque setting.

c) Check the clutch pedal is operating correctly and not fouling any other components and wiring.

7 Clutch pedal switches – removal and refitting

1 Two clutch pedal switches are fitted, one at the top of the pedal bracket, which has a blue connector and a lower one on the front of the pedal itself, which has a grey connector **(see illustrations).**

6.2 Disconnect linkage rod – arrowed

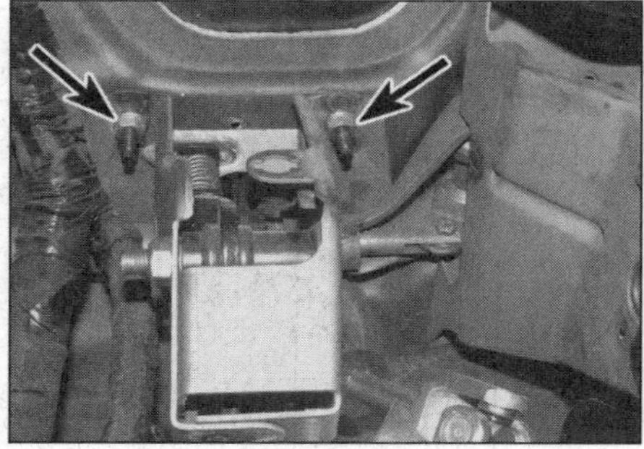

6.4a Undo the upper mounting bolts (arrowed) . . .

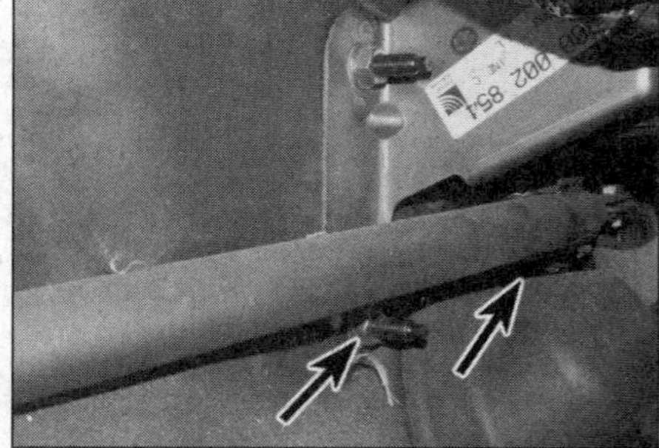

6.4b . . . and the lower mounting bolts – arrowed

6.5 Clutch pedal pivot mounting bolt – arrowed

7.1a Upper clutch pedal switch (arrowed) – viewed with facia removed

7.1b Lower front clutch pedal switch (arrowed)

2 The signals from both switches may be used by the engine ECU to permit smoother gearchanging, and to enable other related control functions, such as idle speed control when the pedal is depressed.

Removal

3 Working inside the vehicle in the driver's side footwell, unclip the trim panel from above the clutch pedal.

4 Disconnect the wiring plugs from the relevant switch.

5 Twist the switch through a quarter-turn, and remove it from the pedal mounting bracket.

Refitting

6 Refitting is a reversal of removal, noting the following point:

a) *Before refitting the switches, pull out the switch plungers by a few clicks – either during refitting, or when the pedal is first used, the switches will then self-adjust correctly* ***(see illustration)****.*

8 Clutch assembly – removal, inspection and refitting

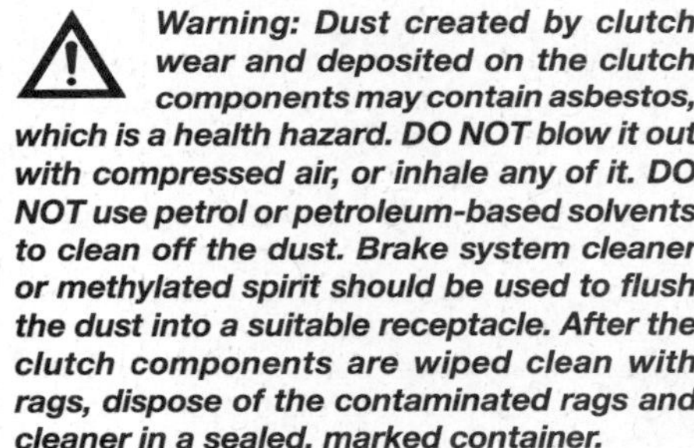

Warning: Dust created by clutch wear and deposited on the clutch components may contain asbestos, which is a health hazard. DO NOT blow it out with compressed air, or inhale any of it. DO NOT use petrol or petroleum-based solvents to clean off the dust. Brake system cleaner or methylated spirit should be used to flush the dust into a suitable receptacle. After the clutch components are wiped clean with rags, dispose of the contaminated rags and cleaner in a sealed, marked container.

Note: *Although some friction materials may no longer contain asbestos, it is safest to assume that they do, and to take precautions accordingly.*

Removal

1 Unless the complete engine/transmission is to be removed from the car and separated for major overhaul (see the relevant part of Chapter 2), the clutch can be reached by removing the transmission as described in Chapter 7A.

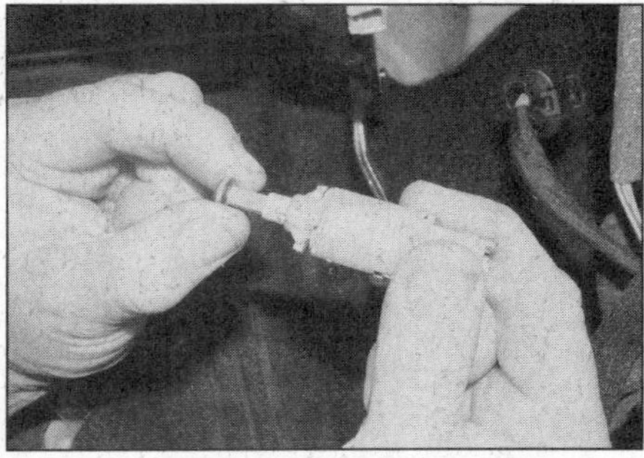

7.6 Pull out the switch plunger before refitting

2 Before disturbing the clutch, use paint or a marker pen to mark the relationship of the pressure plate assembly to the flywheel **(see illustration).**

3 To prevent the flywheel from turning, position a screwdriver over the dowel on the cylinder block and engage it with one of the teeth on the starter ring gear **(see illustration).**

4 Working in a diagonal sequence, slacken the pressure plate cover bolts by half a turn at a time, until spring pressure is released and the bolts can be unscrewed by hand.

5 Carefully prise the pressure plate assembly off its locating dowels, and collect the friction plate, noting which way round the friction plate is fitted **(see illustrations). Note:** *Be prepared to catch the friction plate, which may drop out when the pressure plate assembly is removed.*

Inspection

Note: *Due to the amount of work necessary to remove and refit clutch components, it is usually considered good practice to renew the clutch friction plate, pressure plate assembly and release bearing as a matched set, even if only one of these is actually worn enough to require renewal. It is also worth considering the renewal of the clutch components on a preventive basis if the engine and/or transmission have been removed for some other reason.*

6 With the clutch assembly removed, clean off all traces of dust using a dry cloth, working in a well-ventilated atmosphere. When cleaning clutch components, read first the warning at the beginning of this Section.

7 Examine the friction plate linings for signs of wear, damage or oil contamination. If the friction material is cracked, burnt, scored or damaged, or if it is contaminated with oil or grease (shown by shiny black patches), the friction plate must be renewed **(see illustration)**. Check the depth of the rivets below the friction material surface. If any are at or near the surface of the friction material, then the friction plate must be renewed.

8 If the friction material is still serviceable, check that the centre boss splines are unworn, that the torsion springs are in good condition and securely fastened, and that all the rivets are tight. If any wear or damage is found, the friction plate must be renewed.

9 If the friction material is fouled with oil, this must be due to an oil leak from the crankshaft oil seal, from the sump-to-cylinder block joint, or from the transmission input shaft. Renew the seal or repair the joint, as appropriate, as

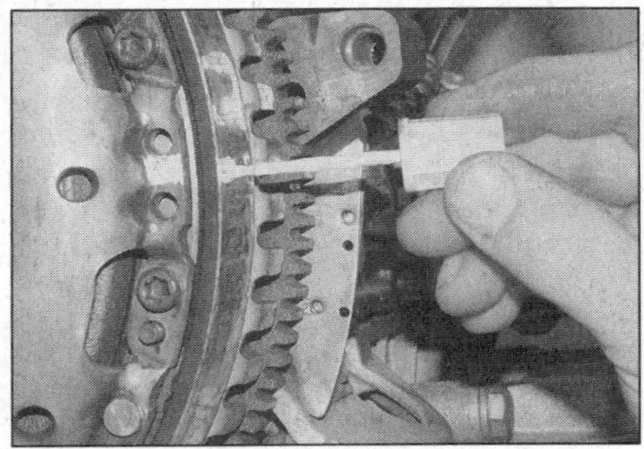

8.2 Mark the relationship of the pressure plate cover to the flywheel

8.3 Using a screwdriver in the ring gear teeth while unscrewing the pressure plate cover bolts

8.5a Withdraw the pressure plate assembly . . .

8.5b . . . and the friction plate, noting which way round it is fitted

8.7 Inspect the friction disc linings (A), springs (B – where applicable) and splines (C)

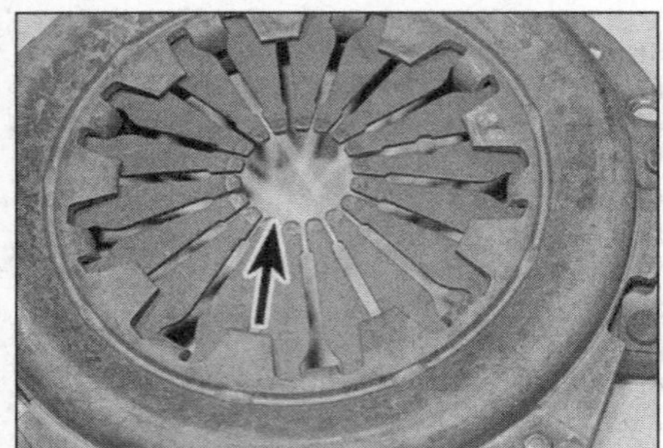

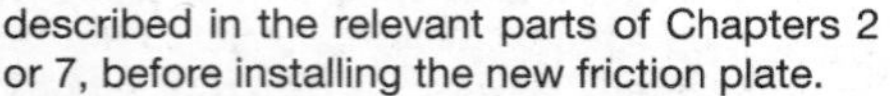

8.10 Check the diaphragm spring fingers for wear, especially at the tips

8.11 Check the machined face (arrowed) of the pressure plate

8.14 Mount a large bolt and washer into a vice, then fit the pressure plate over it

described in the relevant parts of Chapters 2 or 7, before installing the new friction plate.

10 Check the pressure plate assembly for obvious signs of wear or damage; shake it to check for loose rivets or worn or damaged fulcrum rings, and check that the drive straps securing the pressure plate to the cover do not show signs of overheating (such as a deep yellow or blue discoloration). If the diaphragm spring is worn or damaged, or if its pressure is in any way suspect, the pressure plate assembly should be renewed **(see illustration).**

11 Examine the machined bearing surfaces of the pressure plate and of the flywheel; they should be clean, completely flat, and free from scratches or scoring **(see illustration)**. If either is discoloured from excessive heat, or shows signs of cracks, it should be renewed – although minor damage of this nature can sometimes be polished away using emery paper.

12 Check that the release bearing contact surface rotates smoothly and easily, with no sign of noise or roughness. Also check that the surface itself is smooth and unworn, with no signs of cracks, pitting or scoring. If there is any doubt about its condition, the bearing must be renewed.

Refitting

6-speed transmissions

13 The clutch pressure plate assembly on models with the 6-speed transmission is unusual, in that there is a pre-adjustment mechanism to compensate for wear in the friction plate. This mechanism must be reset before refitting the pressure plate. A new plate may be supplied preset, in which case this procedure can be ignored.

14 A large-diameter bolt (M14 at least) long enough to pass through the pressure plate, a matching nut, and several large-diameter washers, will be needed for this procedure. Mount the bolt head in the jaws of a sturdy bench vice, with one large washer fitted **(see illustration).**

15 Offer the plate over the bolt, friction plate surface facing down, and locate it centrally over the bolt and washer – the washer should bear on the centre hub.

16 Fit several further large washers over the bolt, so that they bear on the ends of the spring fingers, then add the nut and tighten by hand to locate the washers **(see illustration).**

17 The purpose of the procedure is to turn the plate's internal adjuster disc so that the three small green coil springs visible on the plate's outer surface are fully compressed. Tighten the nut just fitted until the adjuster disc is free to turn. Using a pair of thin-nosed or circlip pliers in one of the three windows on the top surface, open the jaws of the pliers to turn the adjuster disc anti-clockwise, so that the springs are fully compressed **(see illustrations).**

18 Hold the pliers in this position, and then unscrew the centre nut. Once the nut is released, the adjuster disc will be gripped in position, and the pliers can be removed. Take the pressure plate from the vice, and it is ready to fit.

All transmissions

19 On reassembly, ensure that the disc contact surfaces of the flywheel and pressure plate are completely clean, smooth, and free from oil or grease. Use solvent to remove any protective grease from new components.

20 Fit the friction plate so that its spring hub assembly faces away from the flywheel (5-speed transmissions); on 6-speed transmissions, the friction plate has a protruding small-diameter centre bush which locates into the crankshaft spigot bearing. There may also be a marking showing which way round the plate is to be refitted. Depending on the type of centralising tool being used, the friction plate may be held in position at this stage.

21 Refit the pressure plate assembly, aligning the marks made on dismantling (if the original pressure plate is re-used), and locating the pressure plate on its locating dowels. Fit the pressure plate cover bolts, but tighten them only finger-tight, so that the friction plate can still be moved.

22 The friction plate must now be centralised, so that when the transmission is refitted its input shaft will pass through the splines at the centre of the friction plate.

23 Centralisation can be achieved by passing a screwdriver or other long bar through the friction plate and into the hole in the crankshaft; the friction plate can then be moved around until it is centred on the crankshaft hole.

24 Alternatively, a clutch-aligning tool can be used to eliminate the guesswork; these can be obtained from most accessory shops.

8.16 Fit large washers and a nut to the bolt, and hand-tighten

8.17a Tighten the nut until the spring adjuster is free to turn . . .

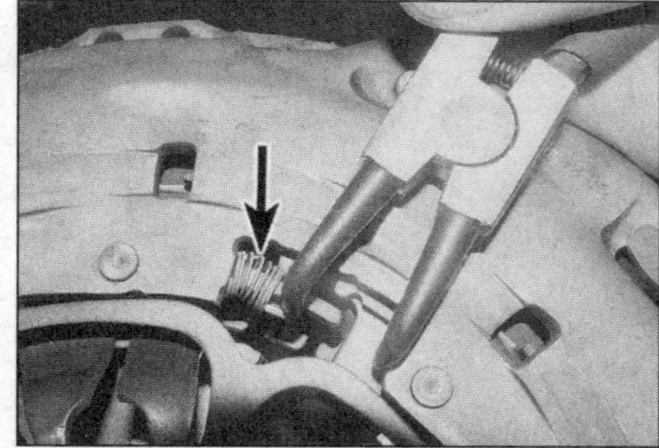

8.17b . . . then open up the jaws of suitable pliers to compress the springs

8.24 Using a clutch alignment tool to centralise the friction plate

8.25a Centralise the pressure plate on the disc . . .

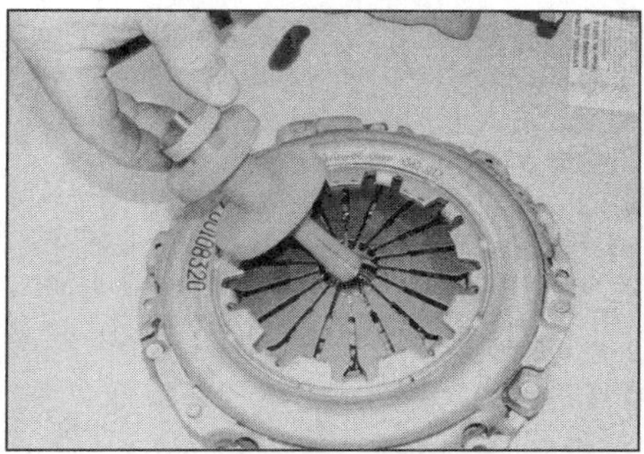

8.25b . . . fit the tool and tighten to clamp the friction plate to the pressure plate . . .

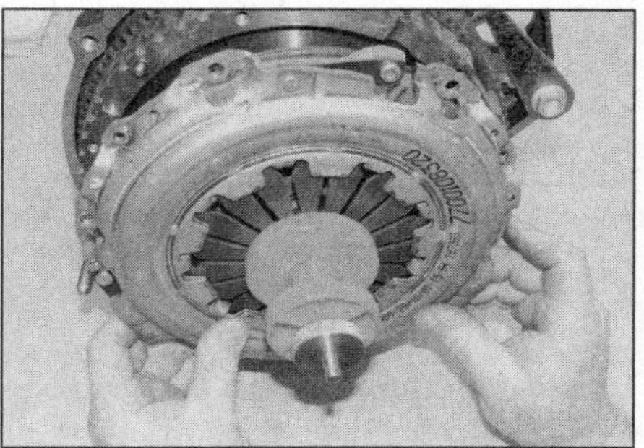

8.25c . . . then locate the assembly on the flywheel

8.26 Hold the flywheel stationary while tightening the clutch cover bolts

The normal type consists of a spigot bar with several different adapters, but a home-made aligning tool can be fabricated from a length of metal rod or wooden dowel which fits closely inside the crankshaft hole, and has insulating tape wound around it to match the diameter of the friction plate splined hole **(see illustration)**.

25 A more recent type of aligning tool works by clamping the friction plate to the pressure plate before locating the two items on the flywheel **(see illustrations)**.

26 When the friction plate is centralised, tighten the pressure plate cover bolts evenly and in a diagonal sequence to the specified torque setting **(see illustration)**.

27 Ensure that the clutch friction plate and transmission input shaft splines are clean and dry. Do not apply grease to the splines as they have a special low-friction nickel coating.

28 Refit the transmission as described in Chapter 7A.

9 Clutch release bearing – removal, inspection and refitting

Removal

1 For access to the clutch release bearing, the transmission must be removed as described in Chapter 7A.

2 The clutch release bearing is part of the slave cylinder assembly and cannot be renewed separately. Remove the slave cylinder as described in Section 3.

Inspection

3 Note that it is often considered worthwhile to renew the release bearing as a matter of course regardless of its condition, considering the amount of work necessary to access it. Check that the contact surface rotates smoothly and easily, with no sign of noise or roughness, and that the surface itself is smooth and unworn, with no signs of cracks, pitting or scoring. If there is any doubt about its condition, the bearing (and slave cylinder) must be renewed.

Refitting

4 Refit the slave cylinder as described in Section 3.

5 Refit the transmission with reference to Chapter 7A.

Chapter 7 Part A:
Manual transmission

Contents

Degrees of difficulty

Easy, suitable for novice with little experience

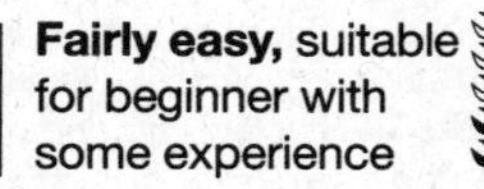

Fairly easy, suitable for beginner with some experience

Fairly difficult, suitable for competent DIY mechanic

Difficult, suitable for experienced DIY mechanic

Very difficult, suitable for expert DIY or professional

Specifications

General

Type	Manual, five or six forward speeds and reverse. Synchromesh on all forward speeds
Designation:	
Petrol engine models:	
1.6 litre engines	JH3
1.8 litre engines	JR5
2.0 litre engines	JR5 or PK6
Diesel engine models:	
1.9 litre engines	JR5 or PK6
2.2 litre engines	PK6

Note: *Transmission code is stamped on a plate attached to the transmission (see Section 1).*

Lubrication

Type	See *Lubricants and fluids*
Capacity	See Chapter 1A or 1B

Torque wrench settings

Torque wrench settings	Nm	lbf ft
Engine-to-transmission bolts/nuts	44	32
Engine/transmission mountings	See the relevant part of Chapter 2	
Roadwheels bolts	105	77
Starter motor mounting bolts	44	32
Sidemember bolts	44	32
Sidemember-to-tie-rod bolts	44	32
Transmission mounting:		
Mounting bracket-to-transmission bolts	62	46
Mounting stud nut	44	32
Rubber mounting bracket-to-body bolts	62	46
Transmission filler plug:		
PK6	2	1.5
JH3 and JR5	2	1.5
Transmission drain plug:		
PK6	18	13
JH3 and JR5	22	16

2.3a Transmission filler/level plug (arrowed) – 5-speed transmission

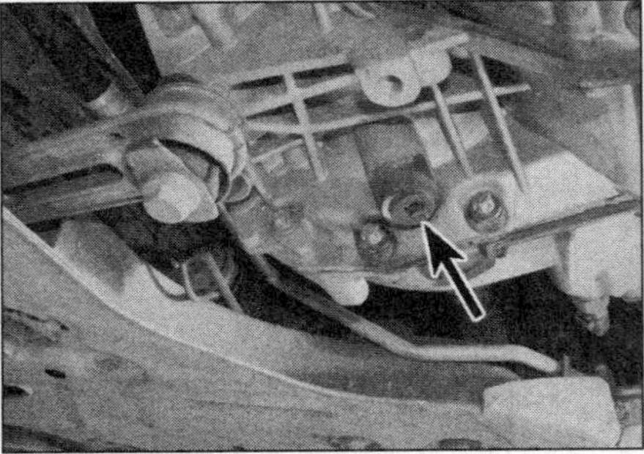

2.3b Transmission drain plug (arrowed) – 5-speed transmission

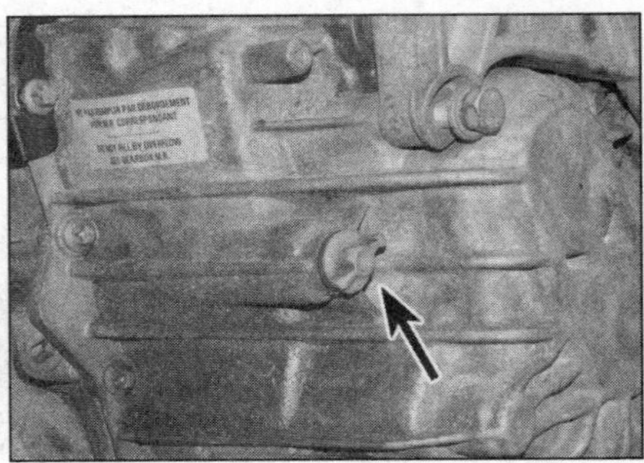

2.3c Transmission filler/level plug (arrowed) - 6-speed transmission

1 General information

The transmission is contained in a cast-aluminium alloy casing bolted to the engine's left-hand end, and consists of the gearbox and final drive differential – often called a transaxle. Throughout this Chapter, the operations often differ depending on which type of transmission is fitted. The transmission type is stamped on an identification plate which is attached to the transmission, either on the top of the casing or on the underside.

Drive is transmitted from the crankshaft via the clutch to the input shaft, which has a splined extension to accept the clutch friction plate, and rotates in sealed ball-bearings. From the input shaft, drive is transmitted to the output shaft, which rotates in a roller bearing at its right-hand end, and a sealed ball-bearing at its left-hand end. From the output shaft, the drive is transmitted to the differential crownwheel, which rotates with the differential case and planetary gears, thus driving the sun gears and driveshafts. The rotation of the planetary gears on their shaft allows the inner roadwheel to rotate at a slower speed than the outer roadwheel when the car is cornering.

The input and output shafts are arranged side-by-side, parallel to the crankshaft and driveshafts, so that their gear pinion teeth are in constant mesh. In the neutral position, the output shaft gear pinions rotate freely, so that drive cannot be transmitted to the crownwheel.

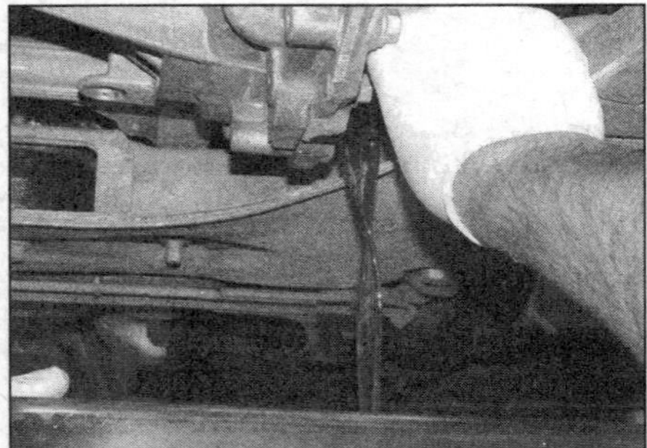

2.5 Unscrew the drain plug and allow the oil to drain

The gear selection is via a floor-mounted lever and dual cable arrangement. The transmission selector rod(s) causes the appropriate selector fork to move its respective synchro-sleeve along the shaft to lock the gear pinion to the synchro-hub. Since the synchro-hubs are splined to the output shaft, this locks the pinion to the shaft so that drive can be transmitted. To ensure that gearchanging can be made quickly and quietly, a synchromesh system is fitted to all forward gears, consisting of baulk rings and spring-loaded fingers, as well as the gear pinions and synchro-hubs. The synchromesh cones are formed on the mating faces of the baulk rings and gear pinions.

2 Transmission – draining and refilling

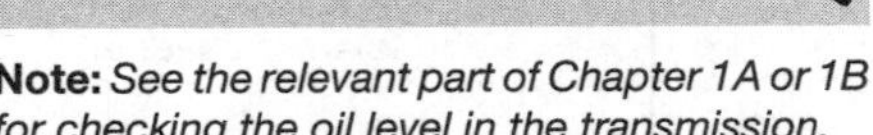

Note: *See the relevant part of Chapter 1A or 1B for checking the oil level in the transmission.*

1 This operation is much quicker and more efficient if the car is first taken on a journey of sufficient length to warm the engine/transmission up to operating temperature.

2 Park the car on level ground, switch off the ignition and apply the handbrake firmly. For improved access, jack up the front of the car and support it on axle stands (see *Jacking and vehicle support*). The car must be lowered to the ground and level, to ensure accuracy, when refilling and checking the oil level.

3 Undo the retaining screws and remove the undertray from beneath the engine/transmission. Remove all dirt from around the drain and filler/level plugs then unscrew from the front face of the transmission (JH3 and JR5 transmissions) or from the left-hand end of the transmission (PK6 transmission). Recover the sealing washer **(see illustrations)**.

4 Position a suitable container under the drain plug situated on the base of the transmission housing.

5 Unscrew the drain plug and allow the oil to drain completely into the container **(see illustration)**. If the oil is hot, take precautions against scalding. Clean both the filler/level and the drain plugs, being especially careful to wipe any metallic particles off the magnetic inserts. Discard the original sealing washers; they should be renewed whenever they are disturbed.

6 When the oil has finished draining, clean the drain plug threads and those of the transmission casing, fit a new sealing washer and refit the drain plug, tightening it securely. It the car was raised for the draining operation, now lower it to the ground. Where necessary, refit the undertray to the vehicle.

7 Refilling the transmission is an extremely awkward operation. Above all, allow plenty of time for the oil level to settle properly before checking it. Note that the car must be parked on flat level ground when checking the oil level.

8 Refill the transmission with the exact amount of the specified type of oil (see *Weekly checks*) then check the oil level as described in the relevant part of Chapter 1. When the level is correct, refit the filler or filler level plug with a new sealing washer and tighten securely.

Note: *If the correct amount was poured into the transmission and a large amount flows out on checking the level, refit the filler or filler/level plug and take the car on a short journey so that the new oil is distributed fully around the transmission components, then check the level again on your return.*

3 Gearchange mechanism (PK6 transmission) – adjustment

Gear control adjustment

1 On PK6 transmissions, if a stiff, sloppy or imprecise gearchange leads you to suspect that a fault exists within the mechanism, first unclip the gear lever gaiter and pull it upwards to release it from the centre console.

2 With the gear lever at rest in the neutral position, a spacer (strip of metal or similar) will be required to check the clearance between the gear lever and the stop housing **(see illustration)**.

3 The clearance should be between 6.1 mm and 7.3 mm. If the clearance is not correct, adjust the gear control cable at the transmission end.

Gear control cable adjustment

4 Open the bonnet and locate the gear control cable linkage on the top of the transmission.

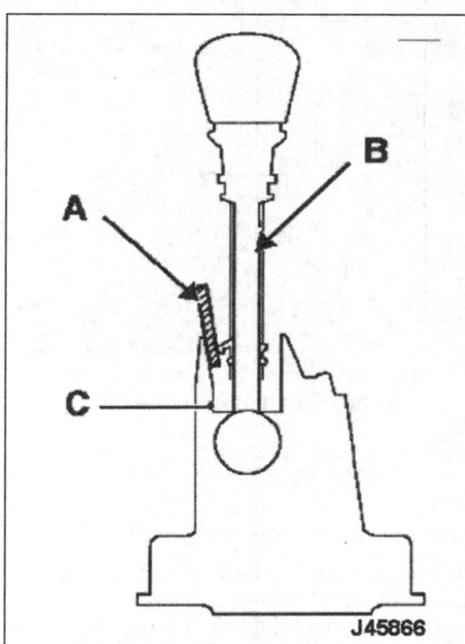

3.2 Gear control adjustment – PK6 transmission

A Feeler gauge
B Gear lever
C Gear control upper stop

To improve access, remove the air cleaner and inlet ducts as described in Chapter 4A or 4B, as applicable.

5 Release the securing clip from the end of the cable **(see illustration)**, then insert a 6.7 mm thickness spacer (strip of metal or similar) in between the gear lever and the stop housing inside the vehicle.

6 Making sure the gear lever and gear linkage on the transmission are still both in the neutral position, refit the yellow clip back into the transmission end of the gear control cable.

7 Remove the thickness gauge, then move the gear lever through all the gears to check that they can all be selected.

8 Use the thickness gauge to check that the clearance is within the tolerance specified.

9 If clearance is correct, refit the gear lever gaiter back in place in the centre console.

10 If this does not cure the fault, check the selector cables and lever for any wear or damage.

4 Gearchange mechanism – removal and refitting

Removal

1 Working inside the vehicle, remove the centre console as described in Chapter 11.

2 Remove the foam soundproofing from around the gear lever, and then ensure that the gear lever is in the neutral position **(see illustration)**.

3 To improve access to the top of the transmission, remove the air cleaner housing and inlet ducts as described in Chapter 4A or 4B, as applicable.

4 To release the cables from their operating levers on top of the transmission, press the securing catch and lift the cable ends off the lever **(see illustration)**. On the 6-speed transmission, take care not to disturb the locking clip just behind the cable end fitting on the selector cable **(see illustration 3.5)**.

5 Work back along the cables to the clips that secure them into the mounting bracket on the transmission. Release the retaining clips and lift the cables from the bracket **(see illustration)**.

6 Firmly apply the handbrake, and then jack up the front of the vehicle and support it securely on axle stands (see *Jacking and vehicle support*).

7 Referring to Chapter 4A or 4B as necessary, disconnect the exhaust pipe at the front joint, and move the exhaust aside. Remove the fasteners securing the front heat shield, and withdraw it to access the bottom of the gear control mechanism.

8 Working inside the vehicle, unscrew the four mounting bolts from the base of the gear lever **(see illustration)**.

9 Lower the mechanism out from under the car, while an assistant feeds the gear cables down from the engine compartment.

Refitting

10 Refitting is a reversal of removal. On 6-speed transmissions, if necessary, check the cable adjustment as described in Section 3.

5 Oil seals – renewal

Right-hand driveshaft oil seal

1 Apply the handbrake, then jack up the front

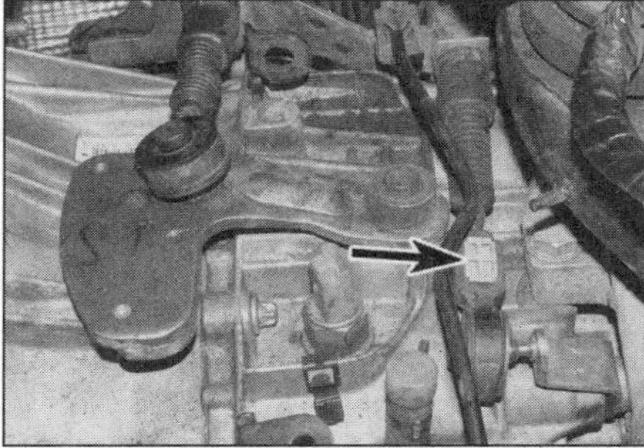

3.5 Gear control cable locking clip – arrowed

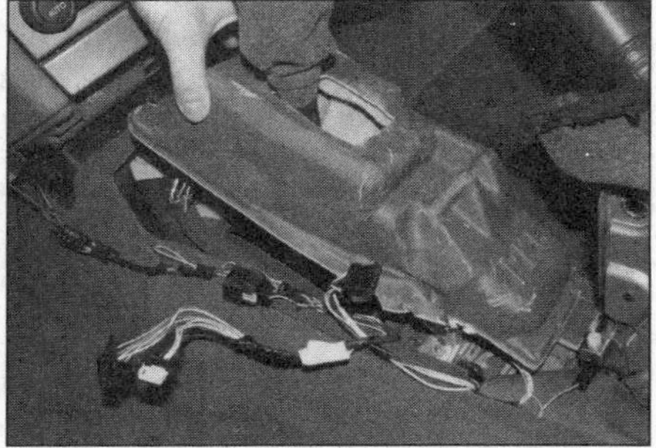

4.2 Remove the soundproofing from around the gear control unit

4.4 Press the centre locking clip to release the cable

4.5 Release the clips to disengage the outer cable

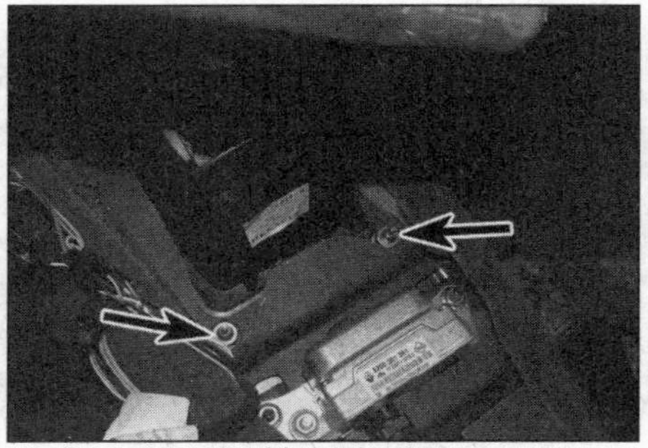

4.8a Undo the rear gear control unit mounting bolts (arrowed) . . .

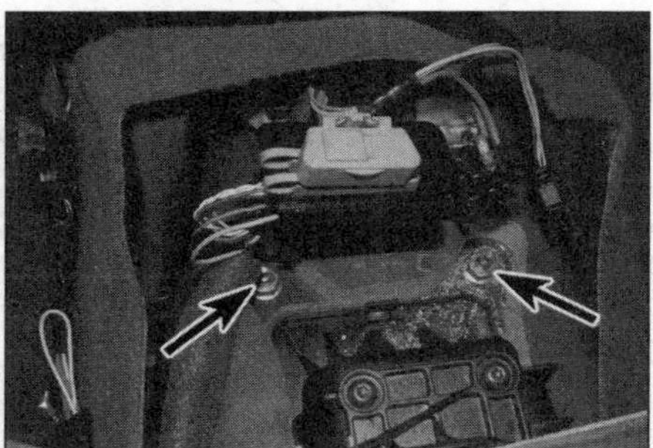

4.8b . . . and the front mounting bolts – arrowed

5.7 Tap the right-hand seal with a small drift to remove it

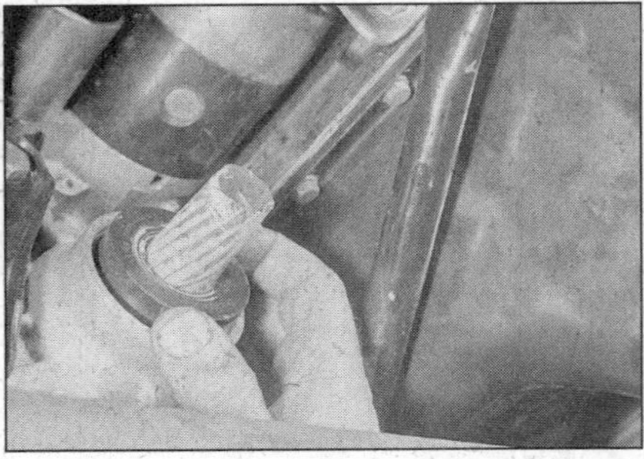
5.8a Locate the new oil seal over the shaft splines . . .

5.8b . . . and press the seal into position using a socket or metal tube

of the car and support it on axle stands (see *Jacking and vehicle support*). Remove the right-hand wheel.

2 Drain the transmission oil (see Section 2).

3 Referring to Chapter 8, disconnect the driveshaft from the transmission. Note that it is not necessary to remove the driveshaft completely; the shaft can be left attached to the hub assembly and slid off from the differential gear splines as the hub assembly is pulled outwards. **Note:** *Do not allow it to hang down under its own weight as this could damage the constant velocity joints/gaiters.*

4 Wipe clean the area around the differential oil seal.

5 Where applicable, remove the O-ring from the splined gear shaft.

6 Measure the seal's fitted depth below the casing edge. This is necessary to determine the correct fitted position of the new oil seal if the special Renault fitting tool is not being used.

7 Free the old oil seal, either by levering it out, or, using a small drift to tap the outer edge of the seal inwards so that the opposite edge of the seal tilts out of the casing **(see illustration)**. A pair of pliers or grips can then be used to pull out the oil seal. Take care not to damage the splines of the differential side gear.

8 Wipe clean the oil seal seating in the casing. Press the new seal squarely into the transmission; making sure its sealing lip is facing inwards, until it is positioned at the same depth as the original was prior to removal **(see illustrations)**. If necessary the seal can be tapped into position using a piece of metal tube or a socket, which bears only on the hard outer edge of the seal. **Note:** *The new seal may have a protective sleeve fitted; leave this in place until the driveshaft is fitted.*

9 Carefully refit the driveshaft assembly as described in Chapter 8. With the driveshaft in place slide the protective sleeve from inside the oil seal and clip it into position in the groove in the driveshaft. **Note:** *If there is no groove in the driveshaft for the protective sleeve to locate, then the protective sleeve will need to be destroyed, to remove it from the shaft.*

10 Where applicable, slide a new O-ring into position on the splines of the shaft.

11 Refill the transmission with oil as described in Section 2.

12 Refit the roadwheel and lower the car to the ground and tighten the roadwheel bolts to the specified torque.

Left-hand driveshaft oil seal

13 On the left-hand side of the transmission there is no oil seal. The driveshaft gaiter forms the seal. If oil is leaking from the left-hand driveshaft to the transmission joint, renew the gaiter as described in Chapter 8.

Input shaft oil seal

JH3 transmission

14 On the JH3 type transmission, it is not possible to renew the input shaft oil seal without first dismantling the transmission. The guide tube assembly is a press-fit in the housing and is removed inwards. Oil seal renewal should therefore be entrusted to a Renault dealer or transmission overhaul specialist.

JR5 and PK6 transmission

15 Remove the transmission as described in Section 7.

16 Slacken and remove the retaining bolts and remove the clutch slave cylinder/release bearing as described in Chapter 6.

17 Note the correct fitted position of the seal then carefully punch or drill two small holes opposite each other in the oil seal. Screw a self-tapping screw into each, and pull on the screws with pliers to extract the seal.

Warning: Take care not to damage or scratch the shaft or seal surface on removal.

18 Clean the seal housing, and polish off any burrs or raised edges, which may have caused the seal to fail in the first place.

19 Wrap tape around the end of the input shaft and slide the new seal into position, making sure its sealing lip is facing inwards. Press the seal squarely into the transmission housing, if necessary, using a suitable tubular drift which bears only on the hard outer edge of the seal.

20 Remove the tape from the input shaft then refit the slave cylinder/release bearing assembly as described in Chapter 6.

21 Refit the transmission (see Section 7).

6 Reversing light switch – testing, removal and refitting

6.1a Reversing light switch location – 5-speed transmission

6.1b Reversing light switch location – 6-speed transmission

Testing

1 The reversing light circuit is controlled by a plunger-type switch. On 5-speed transmissions, it is screwed into the left-hand side of the transmission casing, next to the driveshaft inner joint. On 6-speed transmissions, it is on the top of the transmission casing **(see illustrations)**. If a fault develops in the circuit, first ensure that the circuit fuse has not blown.

2 To test the switch, disconnect the wiring connector, and use a multi-meter (set to the resistance function) or a battery-and-bulb test circuit to check that there is continuity between the switch terminals only when reverse gear is selected. If this is not the case, and there are no obvious breaks or other damage to the wires, the switch is faulty, and must be renewed.

Removal

5-speed models

3 Firmly apply the handbrake then jack up the front of the vehicle and support it on axle stands (see *Jacking and vehicle support*).

4 To improve access, undo the retaining screws and remove the plastic undertray and/or protective cover from underneath the transmission (as applicable).

6-speed models

5 To improve access to the top of the transmission, remove the air cleaner and inlet ducts as described in Chapter 4A or 4B, as applicable.

All models

6 Disconnect the wiring connector **(see illustration)**, and then unscrew it from the transmission casing along with its sealing washer. **Note:** *On 5-speed models there may be oil loss, have a container ready to catch the transmission fluid and top-up as necessary.*

Refitting

7 Fit a new sealing washer to the switch, then screw it back into the transmission housing and tighten it securely.

8 Reconnect the wiring connector, and test the operation of the circuit.

9 Refit the protective cover and/or undercover (as applicable) and lower the vehicle to the ground.

10 On 5-speed models, if any oil was lost when the switch was removed, check the oil level as described in the relevant part of Chapter 1.

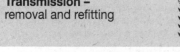

7 Transmission – removal and refitting

Note 1: *This Section describes the removal of the transmission leaving the engine in position in the car. Alternatively, the engine and transmission can be removed together, as described in Chapter 2D or 2E, and then separated on the bench.*

Note 2: *On models with the 6-speed transmission, it may be necessary to remove the front suspension subframe as described in Chapter 10.*

Removal

1 Remove the battery, fuse/relay box and battery tray as described in Chapter 5A, Section 4.

2 Remove the injection ECU from below the battery tray as described in Chapter 4A, Section 12, then undo the mounting bolts and lift out the ECU mounting bracket **(see illustration)**.

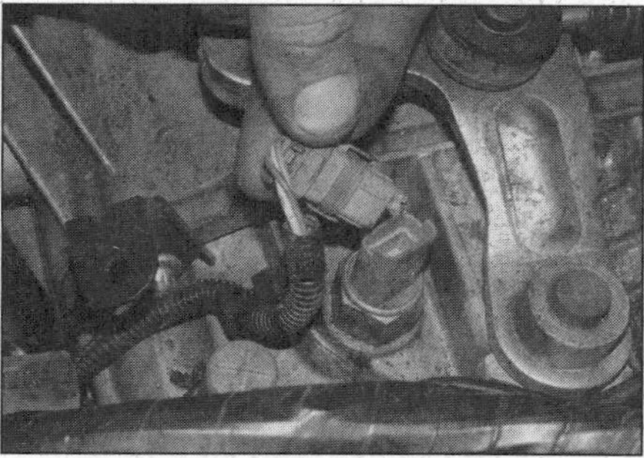

6.6 Disconnecting the wiring connector – 6-speed transmission

3 Remove the air cleaner housing and inlet ducts as described in Chapter 4A or 4B, as applicable.

4 Firmly apply the handbrake then jack up the front of the vehicle and support it on axle stands (see *Jacking and vehicle support*). **Note:** *When jacking the vehicle and supporting it on axle stands, make sure there is enough room to get the transmission out from under the vehicle.*

5 Remove both front roadwheels then undo the retaining screws and remove the plastic cover from under the engine/transmission and the left-hand front wheel arch liner.

6 Drain the transmission oil as described in Section 2.

7 Disconnect the gearchange mechanism from the transmission as described in Section 4.

8 Disconnect the wiring connector from the reversing light switch.

9 Remove the left-hand driveshaft as described in Chapter 8.

10 Referring to Chapter 8, disconnect the right-hand driveshaft from the transmission. Note that it is not necessary to remove the driveshaft completely; the shaft can be left attached to the hub assembly and released from the transmission as the hub assembly is pulled outwards. **Note:** *Do not allow it to hang down under its own weight as this could damage the constant velocity joints/gaiters.*

11 Where applicable, remove the crankshaft speed/position sensor as described in Chapter 4A, Section 12.

12 Undo the retaining bolts and remove the strut/bar from between the exhaust and the transmission housing.

13 Referring to the relevant Part of Chapter 2, slacken and remove the engine/transmission rear lower mounting connecting link nuts and bolts and remove the link from the vehicle **(see illustrations)**.

14 Undo the retaining bolts and disconnect the exhaust front pipe, moving it to one side **(see illustration).**

15 Undo the retaining bolt securing the power steering pipes to the end of the transmission. Position the pipes clear of the transmission so they will not hinder removal.

16 Where applicable, unscrew the nut securing the wiring harness earth lead to the chassis leg on the transmission side.

17 Remove the starter motor as described in Chapter 5A. Undo the retaining nut/bolt and detach the earth strap from the transmission.

7.2 Remove the ECU and plastic tray

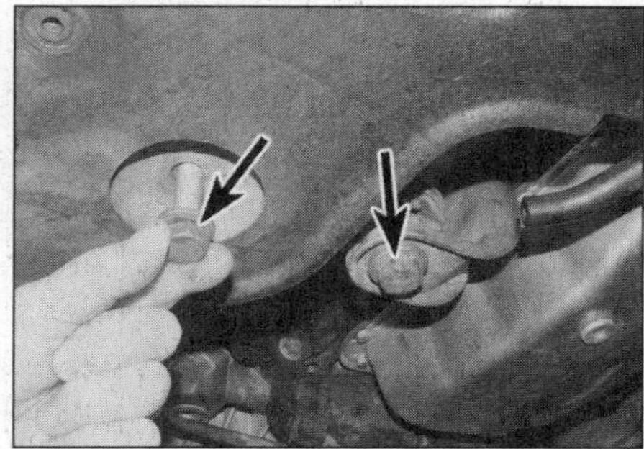

7.13a Undo the mounting bolts (arrowed) . . .

7.13b . . . and remove the rear lower mounting link

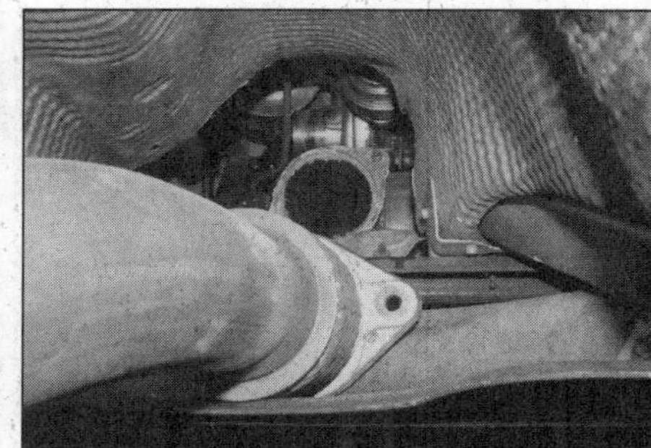

7.14 Disconnect the exhaust front pipe

7.18 Remove the air duct from the intercooler – turbo models

7.21 Remove the bar between the two sidemembers

7.22a Undo the front mounting bolts (arrowed) from the sidemember . . .

7.22b . . . and the tie-rod mounting bolts – arrowed

18 Where applicable, loosen the hose clip and disconnect the air duct from the turbocharger and remove it from the engine compartment **(see illustration)**.

19 Where applicable, undo the retaining bolts and nuts and free the coolant pipe/ wiring support brackets from the top of the transmission housing.

20 Using the information in Chapter 6, first drain the clutch system via the bleed nipple, then disconnect the hydraulic fluid pipe from the slave cylinder.

7.23 Engine support bar fitted across the top of the engine

7.24 Remove the mounting

7.25a Remove the upper bracket mounting bolt – arrowed . . .

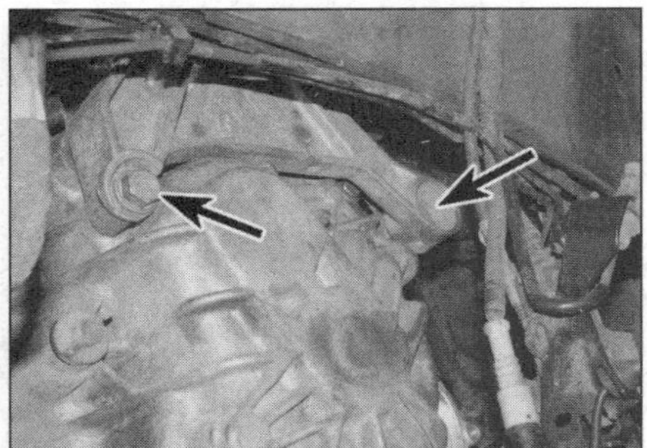
7.25b . . . and the lower mounting bracket bolts – arrowed

21 Undo the mounting bolts and remove the transverse bar from between the two sidemembers **(see illustration)**.

22 Undo the mounting bolts and remove the left-hand sidemember and tie-rods **(see illustrations)**.

23 Place a jack with a block of wood beneath the engine, to take the weight of the engine. Alternatively, attach a hoist or support bar to the engine lifting eyes to take the engine weight **(see illustration)**. Also place a trolley jack and block of wood beneath the transmission, and raise the jack to take the weight of the transmission.

24 With the weight of the transmission now supported, the engine left-hand mounting must be unscrewed and removed **(see illustration)**. Note that, especially with the 6-speed unit, it will be necessary to lower the engine/transmission at the transmission end during the removal procedure.

25 Slacken and remove the upper bolt from the mounting bracket, then lower the transmission slightly and undo the two bolts securing the lower part of the mounting bracket to the transmission housing, then manoeuvre it out of position **(see illustrations)**.

26 With the jack positioned beneath the transmission taking the weight, slacken and remove the remaining nuts and bolts securing the transmission housing to the engine. Work your way around the circumference of the transmission housing, noting the correct fitted positions of each nut/bolt, and the necessary brackets, as they are removed (this will be useful as a reference on refitting). Make a final check that all components have been disconnected, and are positioned clear of the transmission so that they will not hinder the removal procedure.

27 With the nuts/bolts removed, move the trolley jack and transmission to the left, to free it from its locating dowels. Once the transmission is free, lower the jack and manoeuvre the unit out from under the car. Remove the locating dowels from the transmission or engine if they are loose, and keep them in a safe place.

Refitting

28 The transmission is refitted by a reversal of the removal procedure, bearing in mind the following points:

a) *Ensure that the clutch friction plate and transmission input shaft splines are clean and dry. Do not apply grease to the splines as they have a special low-friction nickel coating.*
b) *Ensure that the locating dowels are correctly positioned prior to installation and make sure the clutch release mechanism components are correctly fitted (see Chapter 6).*
c) *Tighten all nuts and bolts to the specified torque (where given).*
d) *Refit the driveshafts as described in Chapter 8.*
e) *Bleed the clutch system as described in Chapter 6.*

f) Check the gearchange and where applicable adjust the mechanism as described in Section 3.

g) On completion, refill the transmission with the specified type and quantity of lubricant, as described in Section 2.

8 Transmission overhaul - general information

Overhauling a manual transmission is a difficult and involved job for the DIY home mechanic. In addition to dismantling and reassembling many small parts, clearances must be precisely measured and, if necessary, changed by selecting shims and spacers. Internal transmission components are also often difficult to obtain, and in many instances, extremely expensive. Because of this, if the transmission develops a fault or becomes noisy, the best course of action is to have the unit overhauled by a specialist repairer, or to obtain an exchange reconditioned unit.

Nevertheless, it is not impossible for the more experienced mechanic to overhaul the transmission, provided the special tools are available, and the job is done in a deliberate step-by-step manner, so that nothing is overlooked.

The tools necessary for an overhaul include internal and external circlip pliers, bearing pullers, a slide hammer, a set of pin punches, a dial test indicator, and possibly a hydraulic press. In addition, a large, sturdy workbench and a vice will be required.

During dismantling of the transmission, make careful notes of how each component is fitted, to make reassembly easier and more accurate.

Before dismantling the transmission, it will help if you have some idea what area is malfunctioning. Certain problems can be closely related to specific areas in the transmission, which can make component examination and renewal easier. Refer to the *Fault finding* Section at the end of this manual for more information.

Chapter 7 Part B: Automatic transmission

Contents

Degrees of difficulty

Easy, suitable for novice with little experience 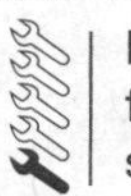

Fairly easy, suitable for beginner with some experience

Fairly difficult, suitable for competent DIY mechanic

Difficult, suitable for experienced DIY mechanic

Very difficult, suitable for expert DIY or professional 

Specifications

General

Type	Electronically-controlled with four or five forward speeds and reverse. Final drive/differential integral with transmission
Designation:	
4-speed	DPO
5-speed	SU1

Ratios

DPO transmission:	
1st	2.72:1
2nd	1.50:1
3rd	1.00:1
4th	0.71:1
Reverse	2.45:1
SU1 transmission:	
1st	4.68:1
2nd	2.94:1
3rd	1.92:1
4th	1.30:1
5th	1.00:1
Reverse	3.18:1

Lubrication

Type	See *Lubricants and fluids*
Capacity (from dry):	
SU1	7.6 litres
DPO	6.0 litres
Drain and refill initial quantity (see text):	
SU1	3.3 litres
DPO	3.5 litres

Torque wrench settings

Torque wrench settings	Nm	lbf ft
All transmissions		
Driveplate-to-torque converter nuts	35	26
Engine-to-transmission bolts/nuts	44	32
Roadwheel bolts	105	77
Starter motor mounting bolts	44	32
Sidemember bolts	44	32
Sidemember-to-tie-rod bolts	44	32
Transmission mounting:		
Mounting bracket-to-transmission bolts	62	46
Mounting stud nut on body	45	33

Torque wrench settings (continued)

	Nm	lbf ft
DPO type transmission		
Drain plug	25	18
Exchanger flow control solenoid	10	7
Input and output speed sensor bolts	10	7
Line pressure sensor	8	6
Multi-function switch mounting bolts	10	7
Selector lever mounting bolts	10	7
Sump retaining bolts	10	7
SU1 type transmission		
Dipstick guide tube mounting bolt	5	4
Input and output speed sensor bolts	6	4
Multi-function switch mounting bolts	25	18
Selector lever mounting bolts	15	11
Sump retaining bolts	12	9

1 General information

Two different types of automatic transmission are available on Laguna models. Either a four-speed (DPO) or a five-speed (SU1) type of transmission is available depending on engine type. Both units are electronically-controlled, fully-automatic transmissions operating on similar principles, but with more features incorporated into the DPO unit, see Section 6.

The transmission consists of a torque converter, an epicyclic geartrain, hydraulically-operated clutches and brakes, sensors and an electronic control unit (ECU).

The torque converter provides a fluid coupling between engine and transmission, which acts as an automatic clutch, and also provides a degree of torque multiplication when accelerating. On the DPO type transmission the torque converter incorporates a lock-up function whereby the engine and transmission can be directly coupled by means of a small clutch unit inside the torque converter. The lock-up function is only activated when the engine is running and is controlled by the transmission ECU, according to vehicle operating conditions.

The epicyclic geartrain provides the forward gears or reverse gear, depending on which of its component parts are held stationary or allowed to turn. The components of the geartrain are held or released by brakes and clutches, which are activated by a hydraulic control unit. A fluid pump within the transmission provides the necessary hydraulic pressure to operate the brakes and clutches.

Impulses from switches and sensors connected to the transmission throttle and selector linkages are directed to the ECU computer module, which determines the ratio to be selected from the information received. The computer activates solenoid valves, which in turn open or close ducts within the hydraulic control unit. This causes the clutches and brakes to hold or release the various components of the geartrain, and provide the correct ratio for the particular engine speed or load. The information from the computer module can be overridden by use of the selector lever, and a particular gear can be held if required, regardless of engine speed. On the DPO transmission, the selector lever also incorporates a shift-lock feature, which prevents the selector lever being moved from the P position unless the brake pedal is depressed.

The automatic transmission fluid is cooled by passing the fluid through a cooler at the rear of the transmission on DPO units and at the front of the transmission on SU1 units. Coolant from the cooling system also passes through the cooler, to cool the fluid.

Due to the complexity of the automatic transmission, any repair or overhaul work must be left to a Renault dealer with the necessary special equipment for fault diagnosis and repair. The contents of the following Sections are therefore confined to supplying general information, and any service information and instructions that can be used by the owner.

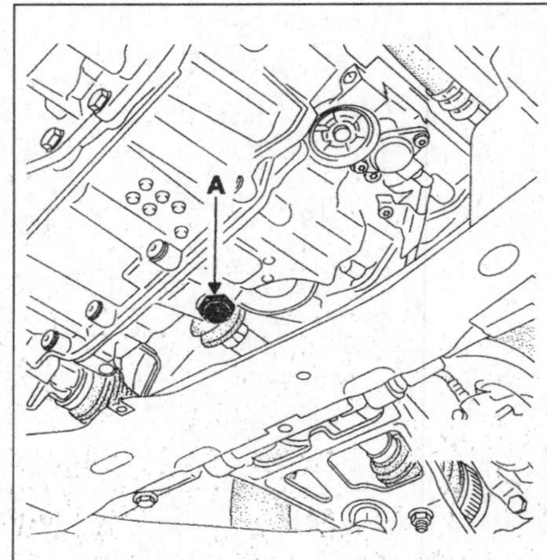

2.4a Combined drain plug and level-checking plug unit (A) on the DPO transmission

2 Automatic transmission fluid - draining and refilling

Note 1: *The transmission is a 'sealed-for-life' unit and fluid renewal is not required as a service item. The following procedure should only be necessary if there is any reason to believe that the fluid may be contaminated, or if repair work requiring the fluid to be drained is to be carried out. The transmission fluid filling and level-checking procedure is particularly complicated, and the home mechanic would be well advised to take the vehicle to a Renault dealer to the draining and refilling work carried out. To ensure accuracy, special test equipment is necessary to measure the fluid temperature when carrying out the level check. However, the following procedure is given for those who may have access to this equipment.*

DPO type transmission

Draining

1 Take the vehicle on a short run, to warm the transmission up to normal operating temperature.

2 Park the car on level ground, then switch off the ignition and apply the handbrake firmly. Jack up the front of the car and support it securely on axle stands (see *Jacking and Vehicle Support*). Note that, when refilling and checking the fluid level, the car must be level to ensure accuracy.

3 Undo the retaining screws and remove the plastic undertray from beneath the engine/transmission.

4 Position a suitable container under the transmission. Unscrew the transmission drain plug and allow the fluid to drain completely into the container. Note that the drain plug and level-checking plug are incorporated into one unit – the drain plug is the larger of the two hexagonal headed plugs forming the draining/level-checking unit **(see illustrations)**.

Warning: If the fluid is hot, take precautions against scalding.

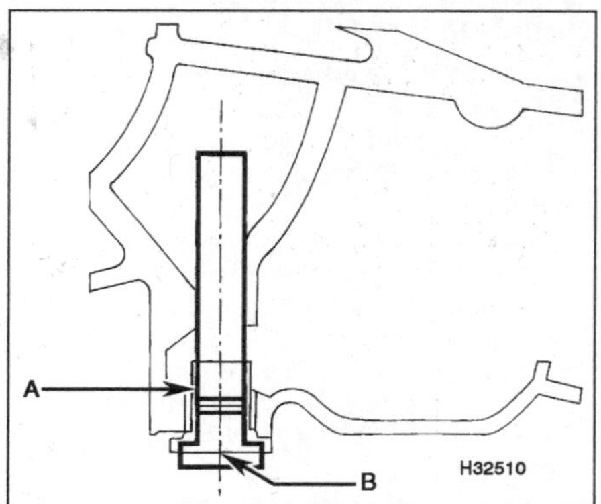

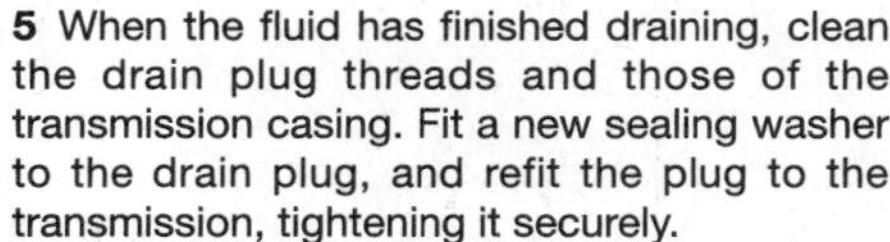
2.4b Cross-section of the combined drain/ level plug - DPO transmission

A Drain plug
B Level (overflow) plug

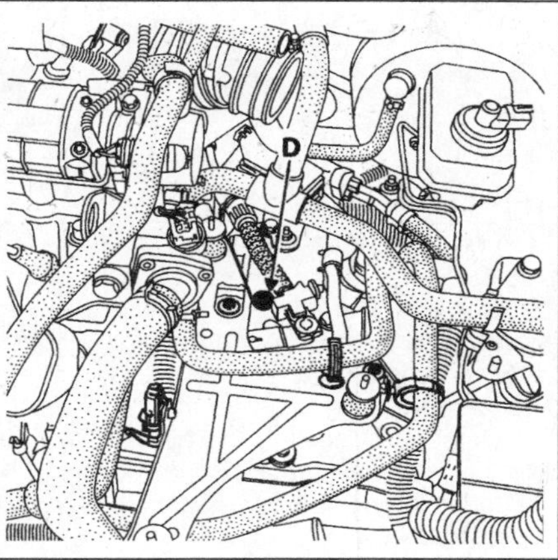

2.6 Transmission fluid filler plug (D) - DPO transmission

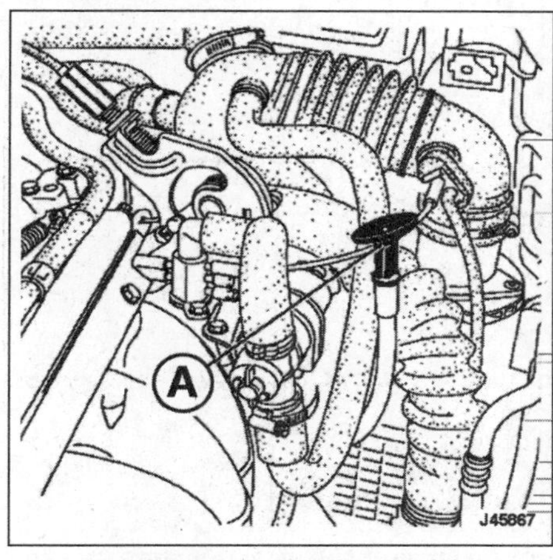

2.11 Transmission dipstick (A) - SU1 transmission

5 When the fluid has finished draining, clean the drain plug threads and those of the transmission casing. Fit a new sealing washer to the drain plug, and refit the plug to the transmission, tightening it securely.

Refilling

6 Remove the air cleaner assembly as described in Chapter 4A or 4B, then unscrew the filler plug from the top of the transmission **(see illustration)**. Add 3.5 litres of the specified fluid to the transmission via the filler plug opening, using a clean funnel with a fine-mesh filter, and then refit the plug.

7 With the selector lever in Park, run the engine at idle speed until the fluid temperature reaches 60°C. **Note:** *Diagnostic equipment will be required to check the temperature of the fluid, see your Renault dealer.*

8 With the engine still running, unscrew the level plug from the centre of the draining/level-checking unit. Allow the excess fluid to run out into a calibrated container drop-by-drop, and then refit the plug. The amount of fluid should be more than 0.1 litres; if it is not, the fluid level in the transmission is incorrect.

9 If the level is incorrect, add an extra 0.5 litre of the specified fluid to the transmission, as described in paragraph 6. Allow the transmission to cool down to 50°C, and then repeat the checking procedure again as described in the previous paragraphs. Repeat the procedure as required until more than the specified amount of fluid is drained as described in the previous paragraphs, indicating that the transmission fluid level is correct, and then securely tighten the level plug. Refit the engine undertray and the air cleaner assembly.

10 Diagnostic equipment will be required to enter the date of oil change and reset the oil-ageing counter in the electronic control unit. See your Renault dealer as soon as possible for final check.

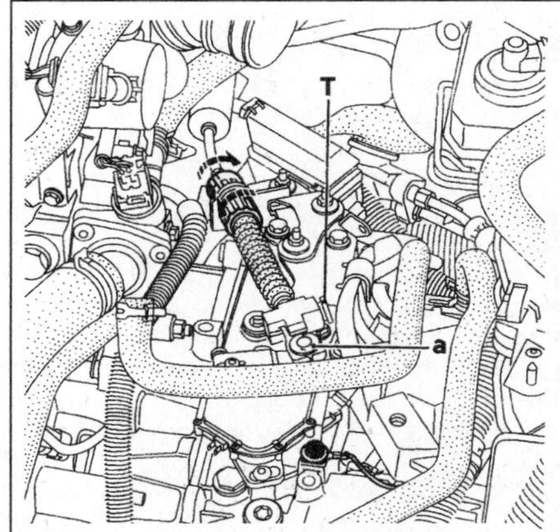

3.4 Selector cable fitting details - DPO transmission

a End fitting on multi-function switch
T Adjuster tab

Arrows indicate method of releasing locking rings from cable support bracket

SU1 type transmission

Draining

11 The SU1 transmission will need specialised equipment to drain the transmission fluid as it can only be drained by suction, via the dipstick tube **(see illustration)**.

Refilling

12 Fill the transmission with the specified oil through the dipstick tube, refill with the same quantity of oil retrieved when draining to obtain an approximate level (approximately 3.3 litres), use a clean funnel with a fine-mesh filter, and then refit the dipstick.

13 With the selector lever in Park, run the engine at idle speed until the fluid temperature reaches 80°C. **Note:** *Diagnostic equipment will be required to check the temperature of the fluid, see your Renault dealer.*

14 With the engine still running, remove the dipstick and check the level of the fluid on the dipstick, it should be between the two upper graduations on the 80°C side of the dipstick, top-up as necessary

15 Diagnostic equipment will be required to enter the date of oil change and reset the oil-ageing counter in the electronic control unit. See your Renault dealer as soon as possible for a final check.

3 Selector cable - adjustment

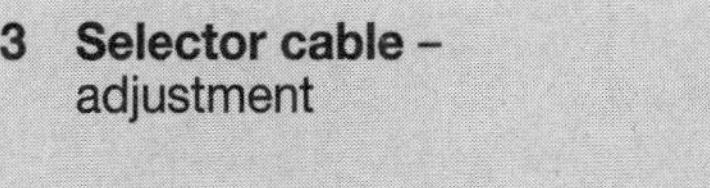

1 Move the selector lever inside the car to the N position.

2 Disconnect the selector cable end fitting from the multi-function switch on top of the transmission. To improve access to the cable, remove the air cleaner housing as described in Chapter 4A or 4B.

3 Check that the multi-function switch is in the N position, and if necessary set it accordingly.

4 Depress the tab on the side of the cable end fitting and retain it in the released position **(see illustration)**.

5 Reconnect the selector cable to the multi-function switch then release the tab on the end fitting to lock the cable. Refit the air cleaner housing as described in Chapter 4A or 4B.

6 Check that the selector lever moves freely, and that the starter motor will only operate with P or N selected. Also check that the Park function operates correctly.

4 Selector cable - removal and refitting

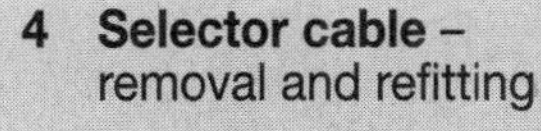

Removal

1 Remove the selector lever assembly as described in Section 5.

2 Release the outer cable retaining clip then detach the inner cable balljoint and free the cable from the selector lever assembly.

3 Examine the cable, looking for worn end fittings or a damaged outer casing, and for signs of fraying of the inner wire. Check the

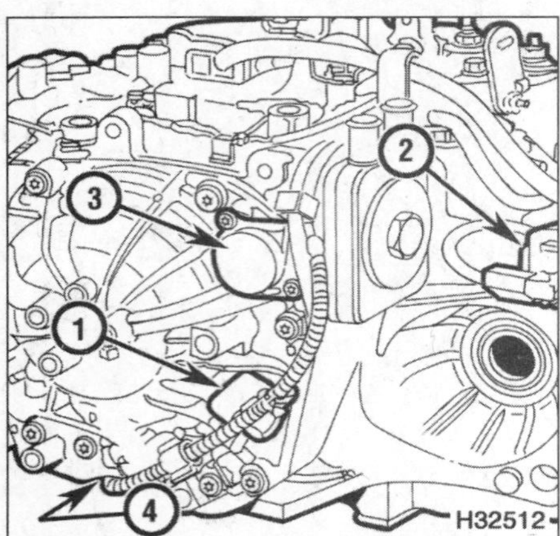

6.2a Sensor locations – DPO transmission

1 *Input speed sensor*
2 *Output speed sensor*
3 *Fluid cooler flow control solenoid*
4 *Line pressure sensor*

cable's operation; the inner wire should move smoothly and easily through the outer casing. If the adjuster mechanism is thought to be faulty the cable must be renewed.

Refitting

4 Refitting is the reverse of removal.

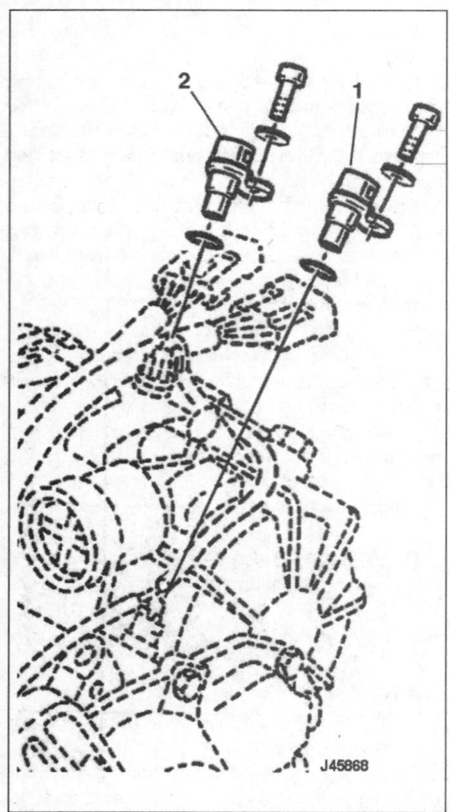

6.2b Sensor locations – SU1 transmission

1 *Input speed sensor*
2 *Output speed sensor*

5 Selector lever assembly – removal and refitting

Removal

1 Working inside the vehicle, remove the centre console as described in Chapter 11.

2 Where applicable, remove the foam soundproofing from around the selector lever, and then ensure that the gear lever is in the neutral position.

3 To improve access to the top of the transmission, remove the air cleaner housing and inlet ducts as described in Chapter 4A or 4B, as applicable.

4 Disconnect the selector cable end fitting from the multi-function switch on top of the transmission. Release the outer cable from the support bracket by turning the two locking rings in opposite directions **(see illustration 3.4)**. Do not move the orange ring as the locking rings are released. Note that if the orange ring breaks during removal, this will not adversely affect the operation of the cable and is not grounds for cable renewal.

5 Firmly apply the handbrake, and then jack up the front of the vehicle and support it securely on axle stands (see *Jacking and vehicle support*).

6 Referring to Chapter 4A or 4B as necessary, disconnect the exhaust pipe at the front joint, and move the exhaust aside. Remove the fasteners securing the front heat shield, and withdraw it to access the bottom of the gear control mechanism.

7 Working inside the vehicle, unscrew the four mounting bolts from the base of the lever assembly.

8 Lower the lever assembly out from under the car, release the cable sealing grommet from the bulkhead then withdraw the cable, releasing it from all the relevant retaining clips and guides, and remove it from inside the vehicle.

6.4 Transmission wiring harness modular connector (3) and mounting plate bolts (1) – DPO transmission

Refitting

9 Refitting is the reverse of removal, noting the following points.

a) *Examine the selector lever assembly for signs of wear or damage and renew if necessary.*
b) *Prior to refitting, apply a smear of multi-purpose grease to the sliding surfaces of the selector lever mechanism.*
c) *Refit the air cleaner assembly as described in Chapter 4A or 4B, as applicable.*
d) *Ensure that the outer cable sealing grommet is correctly located in the bulkhead.*
e) *On completion check the operation of the selector lever and, if necessary, adjust the cable as described in Section 3.*

6 Electronic control unit (ECU) and sensors – general information

General information

The transmission electronic control unit (ECU) is located between the battery and the passenger side headlamp. To remove the transmission ECU, remove the battery plastic cover and first disconnect the battery negative terminal (refer to *Disconnecting the battery* in the Reference Section of this manual). Unclip the ECU from the battery tray and disconnect the wiring block connector.

There are a number of sensors fitted to the transmission unit; these sensors can all be removed without draining the fluid from the transmission **(see illustrations).** Always disconnect the battery negative terminal before disconnecting any electrical connections (refer to *Disconnecting the battery* in the Reference Section of this manual).

Before removing the sensors it may be necessary to remove other components, such as the front wheel and wheel arch liner, air cleaner assembly and air ducts; see the relevant Chapters.

Before removing any of the sensors, first disconnect the modular wiring block connector from the top of the transmission **(see illustration).**

Undo the retaining bolt from the relevant sensor/solenoid and withdraw it from the transmission housing, recover the O-ring seal/gasket. When refitting the sensor/solenoid, fit a new O-ring seal/gasket and tighten the retaining bolt to the specified torque setting.

7 Oil seals – renewal

Differential oil seals

1 Disconnect the battery negative terminal (refer to *Disconnecting the battery* in the Reference Section of this manual).

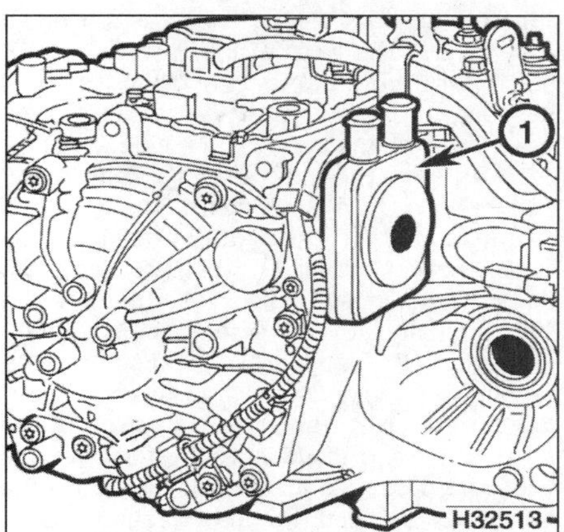

8.1a Location of the fluid cooler (1) on the DPO transmission

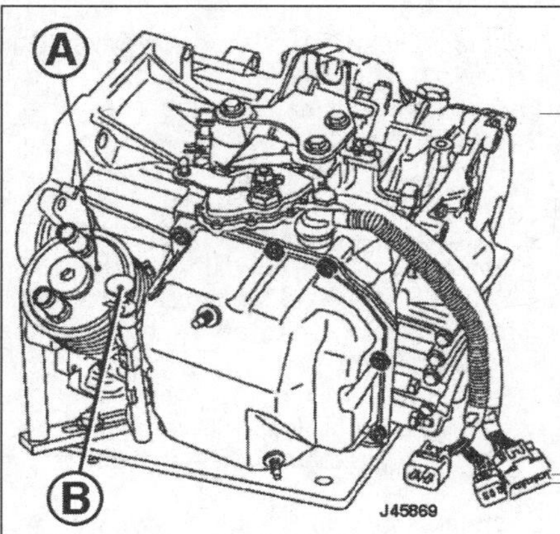

8.1b Location of the fluid cooler (A) and dipstick (B) on the SU1 transmission

2 Apply the handbrake, then jack up the front of the car and support it on axle stands (see *Jacking and vehicle support*). Remove the relevant roadwheel.

3 Drain the transmission fluid as described in Section 2.

4 Referring to Chapter 8, disconnect the driveshaft assembly from the transmission on the side being worked on. Note that it is not necessary to remove the driveshaft completely, the shaft can be left attached to the hub assembly and freed from the transmission as the hub assembly is pulled outwards. **Note:** *Do not allow it to hang down under its own weight as this could damage the constant velocity joints/gaiters.*

5 Note the fitted depth of the old seal, then carefully lever the seal out of position using a flat-bladed screwdriver. **Note:** *When removing the seal, make sure the spring (where applicable) from inside the seal does not drop into the transmission.*

6 Wipe clean the oil seal seating in the casing and apply a smear of oil to the seal lip. Making sure the seal lip is facing inwards, carefully ease the new seal into position over the differential shaft. Press the seal squarely into the transmission until it is positioned at the same depth as the original was prior to removal. If necessary the seal can be tapped into position using a piece of metal tube or a socket which bears only on the hard outer edge of the seal.

7 Carefully refit the driveshaft assembly without damaging the seals, as described in Chapter 8.

8 Refill the transmission with new fluid as described in Section 2.

9 Refit the roadwheel, lower the car to the ground and tighten the wheel bolts to the specified torque.

Torque converter seal

10 Remove the transmission from the engine as described in Section 10.

11 Remove the retaining strap and carefully slide the torque converter off the transmission shaft. Be prepared for fluid loss as the converter is removed.

12 Using a flat-bladed screwdriver, carefully lever the seal out from the centre of the torque converter, taking great care not to mark the metal bush.

13 Press the new seal squarely into position making sure its sealing lip is facing inwards.

14 Lubricate the lip of the seal with clean transmission fluid and carefully slide the converter onto the transmission shaft.

15 Make sure the torque converter is correctly engaged with the transmission shaft splines then refit the transmission as described in Section 10.

8 Fluid cooler – removal and refitting

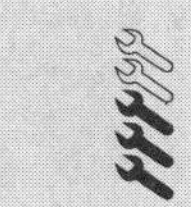

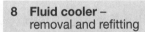

Removal

1 The fluid cooler is located on the rear left-hand side on DPO units, and on the front of the transmission next to the dipstick on SU1 units **(see illustrations)**. To gain access to the cooler, remove the air cleaner and inlet ducts/ hoses as described in Chapter 4A or 4B.

2 To minimise coolant loss, clamp the coolant hoses on either side of the fluid cooler. Alternately, drain the cooling system as described in Chapter 1A or 1B.

3 Loosen the clips and disconnect the hoses from the fluid cooler – be prepared for some coolant spillage. Wash off any spilt coolant immediately with cold water, and dry the surrounding area before proceeding further.

4 Slacken and remove the mounting bolt(s), and remove the fluid cooler from the transmission. There will be some loss of fluid, so some clean rags should be placed around the cooler to absorb spillage. Make sure that dirt is prevented from entering the hydraulic system.

5 Remove the sealing ring from each mounting bolt and the sealing rings fitted between the cooler and transmission. Discard all sealing rings; new ones must be used on refitting.

Refitting

6 Lubricate the new seals with clean automatic transmission fluid, then fit the two new seals to the base of the fluid cooler, and a new seal to each mounting bolt.

7 Locate the fluid cooler on the top of transmission housing, ensuring its lower seals remain in position. Refit the mounting bolt(s) and tighten them securely.

8 Reconnect the coolant hoses to the fluid cooler, and securely tighten their retaining clips. Remove the hose clamps.

9 Refit the air cleaner housing and inlet ducts/ hoses as described in Chapter 4A or 4B.

10 On completion, top-up the cooling system and check the automatic transmission fluid level as described in *Weekly checks* and Section 2.

9 Multi-function switch – removal, refitting and adjustment

Removal

1 The multi-function switch informs the electronic control unit of the selector lever position, prevents the starter motor operating when the transmission is in gear and also controls the reversing lights. The switch is located on the top of the transmission.

2 Inside the car, set the selector lever in the N position – keep it in this position throughout.

3 Disconnect the battery negative terminal (refer to *Disconnecting the battery* in the Reference Section of this manual).

4 To gain better access to the switch unit, remove the air cleaner and inlet ducts/hoses as described in Chapter 4A or 4B.

5 Disconnect the selector cable end fitting from the multi-function switch lever **(see illustration 3.4)**.

DPO transmission

6 Pull out the locking tab and disconnect the transmission wiring harness modular connector **(see illustration 6.4)**.

7 Undo the three mounting bolts and release the modular connector mounting plate from the top of the transmission.

8 Undo the two multi-function switch mounting bolts and lift off the switch. Trace the switch wiring back to the modular connector plate and disconnect the 12-pin socket from the connector plate **(see illustration)**. Remove the multi-function switch from the transmission.

SU1 transmission

9 Remove the battery, fuse/relay box and battery tray as described in Chapter 5A.

10 Remove the injection ECU from below the battery tray as described in Chapter 4A or 4B, then undo the mounting bolts and lift out the ECU mounting bracket.

11 Withdraw the dipstick and guide tube from the transmission housing, retrieve the seal; a new one will be required for refitting.

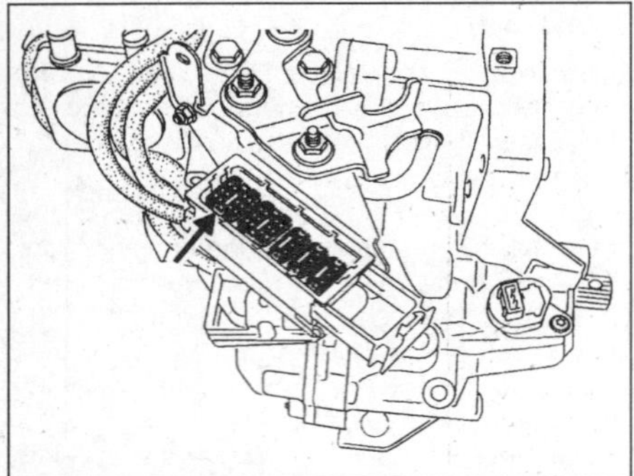

9.8 Multi-function switch wiring socket (arrowed) in the modular connector plate – DPO transmission

12 Mark the selector lever in relation to its splined shaft, then slacken its fasteners, noting its fitted position. Always counter-hold the lever with a spanner, whilst slackening the retaining nut as damage to the transmission may occur. Remove the nut and locking washer, and then remove the lever from the switch unit.

13 Undo the two multi-function switch mounting bolts and withdraw the switch from the transmission. Trace the wiring from the multi-function switch down to the left-hand side of the transmission and disconnect the wiring block connectors.

Refitting and adjustment

14 Reconnect the multi-function switch wiring connectors.

15 Position the multi-function switch on the transmission and refit the two mounting bolts, finger tight only at this stage.

16 On SU1 transmissions, a Renault special tool (No B.Vi. 1403) is required to lock the switch into position. Using the marks noted on removal, refit the lever and switch unit into position and then tighten the retaining bolts and nut.

17 Reconnect the selector cable end fitting to the multi-function switch lever.

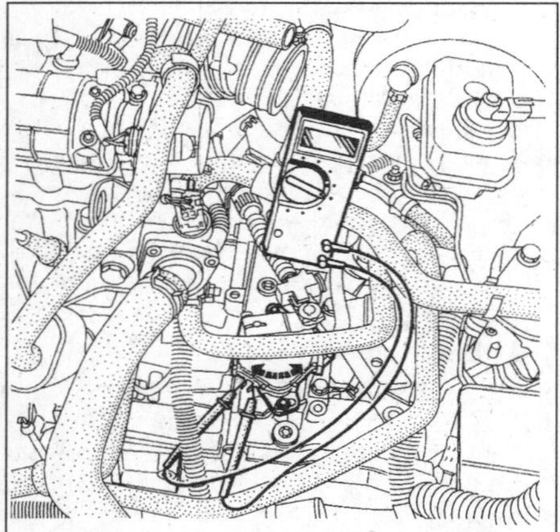

9.18 Using an ohmmeter to set the multi-function switch position – DPO transmission

18 On DPO transmissions, with the gear selector lever and multi-function switch in position N, connect an ohmmeter across the two test terminals on the side of the multi-function switch **(see illustration)**. Turn the switch body until the internal switch contacts close and 0 ohms is indicated on the ohmmeter. Hold the switch body in this position and tighten the two retaining bolts.

19 Refit the air cleaner and inlet ducts/hoses as described in Chapter 4A or 4B, then reconnect the battery.

20 Refit the battery, fuse/relay box and battery tray as described in Chapter 5A.

21 Refit the injection ECU as described in Chapter 4A or 4B.

22 Check that the starter motor will only operate with P or N selected.

23 For further adjustment of the selector cable see Section 3.

10 Automatic transmission – removal and refitting

Note: *If a new transmission and/or torque converter are being fitted, note that a Renault dealer must reset the ECU auto-adaptive values. On models with the SU1 transmission, it will be necessary to remove the front suspension subframe first as described in Chapter 10.*

Removal

1 Disconnect the battery negative terminal (refer to *Disconnecting the battery* in the Reference Section of this manual),

2 Remove the automatic transmission ECU from the battery tray as described in Section 6 of this Chapter.

3 Remove the battery, fuse/relay box and battery tray as described in Chapter 5A.

4 Remove the injection ECU from below the battery tray as described in Chapter 4A or 4B, then undo the mounting bolts and lift out the ECU mounting bracket.

5 Remove the air cleaner housing and inlet ducts/hoses as described in Chapter 4A or 4B.

6 Firmly apply the handbrake then jack up the front of the vehicle and support it on axle stands (see *Jacking and vehicle support*). Remove both front roadwheels then undo the retaining screws and remove the plastic undertray and left-hand wheel arch liner.

7 Remove the starter motor as described in Chapter 5A.

8 Drain the transmission fluid as described in Section 2.

9 Remove the both of the driveshafts as described in Chapter 8.

10 Undo the retaining bolts and disconnect the exhaust front pipe, moving it to one side and disconnect the oxygen sensor wiring connector.

11 Undo the retaining bolt securing the power steering pipes to the end of the transmission. Position the pipes clear of the transmission so they will not hinder removal.

12 Where applicable, unscrew the nut securing the wiring harness earth lead to the chassis leg on the transmission side.

13 Remove the crankshaft sensor as described in Chapter 4A or 4B.

14 Either drain the cooling system as described in Chapter 1A or 1B, or clamp the hoses to minimise coolant loss then release the retaining clips and detach the coolant hoses from the transmission fluid cooler. Mop up any spilt coolant.

15 On the DPO transmissions, pull out the locking tab and disconnect the transmission wiring harness modular connector. Protect the connector by placing it in a plastic bag. On the SU1 transmissions, trace the wiring from the multi-function switch down to the left-hand side of the transmission and disconnect the wiring block connectors.

16 Disconnect the selector cable from the transmission and position it clear of the unit (see Section 5, paragraph 4).

17 Undo the mounting bolts and remove the transverse bar from under the vehicle, between the two side members.

18 Undo the mounting bolts and remove the left-hand sidemember and tie-rods.

19 Place a jack with a block of wood beneath the engine, to take the weight of the engine. Alternatively, attach a hoist or support bar to the engine lifting eyes to take the engine weight. Also place a trolley jack and block of wood beneath the transmission, and raise the jack to take the weight of the transmission.

20 Slacken and remove the bolts securing the rear mounting to the transmission and position the mounting clear of the transmission.

21 Where applicable, undo the retaining bolts and remove the driveplate lower cover plate from the base of the transmission housing. On some models the plate has support struts attached to it, these will have to be unbolted from the side of the cylinder block.

22 The torque converter is attached to the driveplate by three nuts, which are accessed either behind the driveplate lower cover plate or through the starter motor aperture. Turn the engine as required to position the nuts in the aperture, then unscrew and remove them. **Note:** *The nuts must be renewed every time they are removed.* Where applicable, unbolt the access plate from the bottom of the transmission.

23 With the weight of the transmission now supported, the engine left-hand mounting must be unscrewed and removed. Note that, it will be necessary to lower the engine/transmission at the transmission end during the removal procedure.

24 Slacken and remove the upper bolt(s) from the mounting bracket, then lower the transmission slightly and undo the bolt(s) securing the lower part of the mounting bracket to the transmission housing, then manoeuvre it out of position.

25 With the jack positioned beneath the

transmission taking the weight, slacken and remove the remaining nuts and bolts securing the transmission housing to the engine. Work your way around the circumference of the transmission housing, noting the correct fitted positions of each nut/bolt, and the necessary brackets, as they are removed (this will be useful as a reference on refitting). Make a final check that all components have been disconnected, and are positioned clear of the transmission so that they will not hinder the removal procedure.

26 With the bolts removed, make sure the torque converter is pushed fully onto the transmission shaft then move the trolley jack and transmission to the left, to free it from its locating dowels.

27 Once the transmission is free, lower the jack and manoeuvre the unit out from under the car. Remove the locating dowels from the transmission or engine if they are loose, and keep them in a safe place.

28 Secure the torque converter in position by bolting a length of metal bar to one of the housing holes, or by tying one of the studs to the crankshaft sensor aperture on the top of the housing **(see illustration)**.

Refitting

29 The transmission is refitted by a reversal of the removal procedure, bearing in mind the following points

a) Remove the retaining bar and ensure that the torque converter is pushed fully onto the transmission. Apply a smear of high-melting point grease (Renault recommend the use of Molykote BR2) to the converter centring ring.

b) Ensure the locating dowels are correctly positioned prior to installation and clean the torque converter-to-driveplate stud threads.

c) Aligning the torque converter studs with the driveplate holes as the transmission is refitted. Apply thread-locking compound (Renault recommend the use of Loctite Frenbloc) to the new retaining nuts and tighten them to the specified torque.

d) Tighten all nuts and bolts to the specified torque (where given).

e) Refit the driveshafts as described in Chapter 8.

f) Connect the selector cable and adjust as described in Sections 3 and 4.

g) On completion, top-up/refill the transmission and final drive (as applicable) with the specified type and quantity of lubricant, as described in Section 2.

11 Automatic transmission overhaul – general information

In the event of a fault occurring with the transmission, it is first necessary to determine whether it is of an electrical, mechanical or hydraulic nature, and to do this special test equipment is required. It is therefore essential to have the work carried out by a Renault dealer if a transmission fault is suspected.

Do not remove the transmission from the car for possible repair before professional fault diagnosis has been carried out, since most tests require the transmission to be in the vehicle. Diagnostic equipment should be connected to the vehicle to determine the fault before any work is carried out.

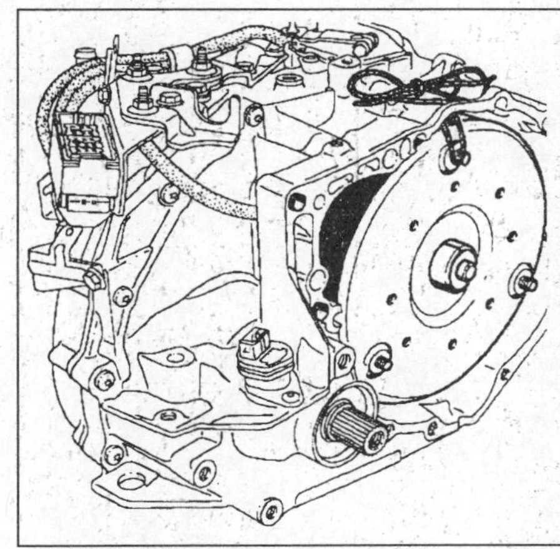

10.28 Using a piece of string to secure the torque converter in the transmission bellhousing

Chapter 8
Driveshafts

Contents

Degrees of difficulty

Easy, suitable for novice with little experience 

Fairly easy, suitable for beginner with some experience

Fairly difficult, suitable for competent DIY mechanic

Difficult, suitable for experienced DIY mechanic

Very difficult, suitable for expert DIY or professional 

Specifications

General

Type	Steel shafts with constant velocity (CV) joint at each end
Lubrication	Special grease supplied in sachets with gaiter kits – joints are otherwise prepacked with grease, and sealed

Torque wrench settings

	Nm	lbf ft
Driveshaft nut*	280	207
Driveshaft support bearing bolts (right-hand side)	30	22
Left-hand driveshaft inner gaiter retaining plate bolts	30	22
Roadwheel bolts	105	77
Track rod end balljoint nut	37	27

** Use new nuts.*

1 General information

1 Drive is transmitted from the differential to the front wheels by means of two driveshafts of unequal length. Constant velocity (CV) joints are fitted to each end of the driveshafts, to ensure the smooth and efficient transmission of power at all suspension and steering angles.

2 Both driveshafts are fitted with ball-and-cage-type constant velocity (CV) joints at their outer ends **(see illustration)**. Each joint has an outer member, which is splined at its outer end to accept the wheel hub, and is threaded so that the hub can be fastened by a large nut. The inner joint of the driveshafts are of the spider and yoke-type CV joint.

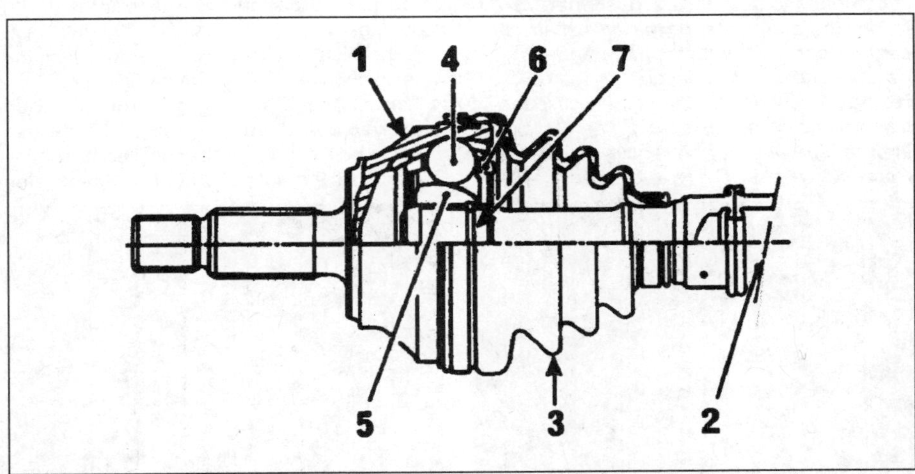

1.2 Sectional view of the ball-and-cage type constant velocity joint

1 Outer member
2 Driveshaft
3 Gaiter
4 Ball-bearing
5 Inner member
6 Ball cage
7 Circlip

3 The right-hand driveshaft is a two-piece shaft, which is supported by an intermediate

2.3 Using a fabricated tool to hold the front hub stationary whilst the driveshaft nut is slackened

2.5a Using a balljoint separator . . .

2.5b . . . to release the track rod end

bearing, located at the rear of the cylinder block. The inner section of the right-hand driveshaft is a connecting shaft, which is splined into the differential sunwheel. The inner and outer sections are joined together at the intermediate support bearing by a spider-and-yoke-type CV joint.

4 On manual transmission models, the left-hand side, inner end of the driveshaft also engages with a spider-type joint, but the yoke in which the tripod is free to slide is an integral part of the differential sunwheel. The inner gaiter is secured to the transmission casing via a retaining plate and bolts, and to a ball-bearing on the driveshaft via a retaining clip. The bearing allows the driveshaft to turn within the gaiter, which does not revolve.

5 On models with automatic transmission, the left-hand inner CV joint is also a spider-and-yoke-type joint, but it is a splined fit into the differential sunwheel.

2 Right-hand driveshaft – removal and refitting

Note 1: *The driveshaft can be removed as a complete assembly, as described in the following paragraphs, or the driveshaft outer section can be removed independently, as described later in this Section.*

Note 2: *A new driveshaft nut, new suspension strut-to-hub carrier nuts, and a new track rod end balljoint nut may be required on refitting. Some Molykote BR2 type of grease will be required to coat the inner end of the driveshaft splines. A balljoint separator tool will also be required for this operation.*

2.6 Tapping the upper suspension strut-to-hub carrier bolt from the hub carrier

Complete driveshaft

Removal

1 Apply the handbrake, then jack up the front of the vehicle and support securely on axle stands (see *Jacking and vehicle support*). Remove the relevant front roadwheel.

2 If the driveshaft nut has been loosened, proceed to paragraph 4, otherwise proceed as follows.

3 Refit at least two roadwheel bolts to the front hub, and tighten them securely. Have an assistant firmly depress the brake pedal to prevent the front hub from rotating, then using a socket and a long extension bar, slacken and remove the driveshaft retaining nut. Alternatively, a tool can be fabricated from two lengths of steel strip (one long, one short) and a nut and bolt; the nut and bolt forming the pivot of a forked tool. Bolt the tool to the hub using two wheel bolts, and hold the tool to prevent the hub from rotating as the driveshaft retaining nut is undone **(see illustration).** This nut is very tight; make sure that there is no risk of pulling the car off the axle stands. (If the roadwheel trim allows access to the driveshaft nut, the initial slackening can be done with the wheels chocked and on the ground.)

4 Unbolt the brake caliper from the hub carrier as described in Chapter 9. Note that there is no need to disconnect the fluid hose – suspend the caliper from the suspension strut using wire or string, ensuring that the hose is not strained. Unclip the hose from any securing brackets.

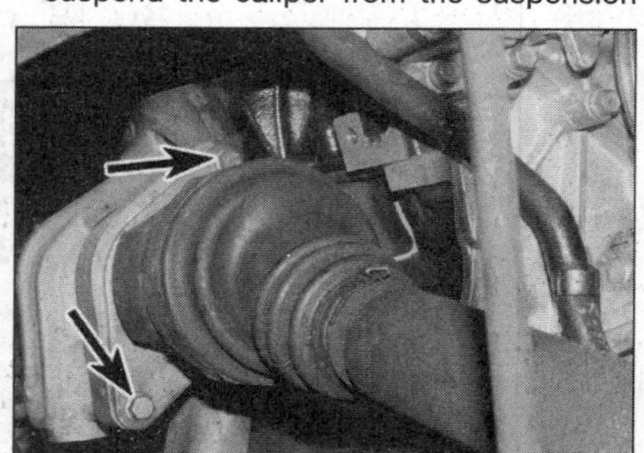
2.8 Undo the intermediate bracket mounting bolts – arrowed

5 Slacken and partially unscrew the track rod end balljoint nut (unscrew the nut as far as the end of the threads on the balljoint to prevent damage to the threads as the joint is released), then release the balljoint using a balljoint separator tool **(see illustrations)**. Remove the nut, and discard it – a new nut must be used on refitting.

6 Unscrew the nut from the end of the upper suspension strut-to-hub carrier bolt. Note that the bolt is splined into the hub carrier. Temporarily screw the nut onto the end of the bolt to protect the bolt threads, and then tap the bolt from the hub carrier, using a soft-faced hammer **(see illustration)**. Noting the direction the bolt is fitted, withdraw the bolt.

7 Similarly, unscrew the lower suspension strut-to-hub carrier nut, and tap the bolt to free the splines from the hub carrier. Do not remove the bolt at this stage.

8 Working at the inner end of the driveshaft, unscrew the two bolts securing the driveshaft inner section retaining plate to the engine intermediate mounting bracket/bearing carrier **(see illustration)**.

9 Unscrew the driveshaft nut from the hub carrier end of the driveshaft and recover the washer. Discard the nut; a new one must be used on refitting.

10 The driveshaft must now be released from the hub carrier. It should be possible to release the driveshaft by tapping the end of the driveshaft using a soft-faced hammer, or a hammer and a soft metal drift – **do not** strike the end of the driveshaft hard, as this may cause damage to the joints.

11 Unscrew the nut from the lower suspension strut-to-hub carrier bolt, and withdraw the bolt (noting the direction the bolt is fitted) to enable the hub carrier to be pivoted downwards. Pivot the hub carrier downwards as necessary until the end of the driveshaft can be withdrawn from the hub **(see illustration).**

12 Place a container beneath the transmission end of the driveshaft to catch escaping oil/fluid, which may be released as the end of the driveshaft, is withdrawn.

13 Pull the driveshaft from the transmission

2.11 Pivot the hub downwards to release the driveshaft

and the engine mounting bracket/bearing carrier.

Refitting

14 Before refitting, thoroughly clean the mating faces of the driveshaft bearing and bearing carrier, making sure it is well-greased. Check the condition of the oil seal contact face on the driveshaft – if the driveshaft surface is excessively worn or deeply grooved, the driveshaft inner section should be renewed (as described later in this Section).

15 It is recommended that the differential output oil seal is renewed before refitting the driveshaft (see Chapter 7A).

16 Thoroughly clean the driveshaft splines, and the apertures in the transmission and hub assembly. Apply some Molykote BR2 type of grease to the driveshaft inner splines and shoulders. Check that all gaiter clips are securely fastened.

17 Slide the inner end of the driveshaft into position in the transmission, and engage the intermediate bearing with the engine mounting bracket/bearing carrier, then secure with the retaining plate, and securely tighten the bolts.

18 Engage the outer end of the driveshaft with the hub assembly.

19 Refit the lower suspension strut-to-hub carrier bolt (noting that the bolts fits from the front of the vehicle), and screw a new nut onto the bolt. Do not screw the nut fully onto the bolt at this stage.

20 Screw the **new** driveshaft nut onto the end of the driveshaft as far as possible by hand, ensuring that the washer is in place, and then tighten the nut until the end of the driveshaft is fully engaged with the hub. Do not fully tighten the nut at this stage.

21 Refit the upper suspension strut-to-hub carrier bolt (noting that the bolts fits from the front of the vehicle), and screw a new nut onto the bolt. Tap the bolts into position in the hub carrier (until the splines are engaged and the underside of the bolt head touches the suspension strut, then tighten the upper and lower suspension strut-to-hub carrier nuts to the specified torque (Chapter 10).

22 Reconnect the track rod end to the hub carrier, and tighten a new balljoint nut to the specified torque (Chapter 10).

23 Refit the brake caliper, with reference to Chapter 9.

24 Use the method employed on removal to prevent the hub from rotating, and tighten the driveshaft retaining nut to the specified torque. Check that the hub rotates freely.

25 Where applicable, tear off the protective cover from the outer driveshaft joint gaiter. Do not use a sharp tool, which may damage the gaiter.

26 Refit the roadwheel, then lower the vehicle to the ground and tighten the roadwheel bolts to the specified torque.

27 On completion, check the transmission oil/fluid level using the information in the relevant part of Chapter 1 or Chapter 7.

Driveshaft outer section

Removal

Note: *A sachet of the appropriate grease and new retaining clip (available from a Renault dealer) will be required to pack the driveshaft joint on refitting.*

28 Proceed as described in paragraphs 1 to 7.

29 Working at the inner end of the driveshaft, cut the inner driveshaft gaiter securing clip, and slide the gaiter back from the joint.

30 Proceed as described in paragraphs 9 to 11.

31 Carefully withdraw the driveshaft outer section spider joint from the driveshaft yoke inner section. Be prepared to hold the rollers in place, otherwise they may fall off the tripod ends as the driveshaft outer section is withdrawn. If necessary, secure the rollers in place using tape. The rollers are matched to the tripod stems, and it is important that they are not interchanged.

Refitting

32 Wipe clean the driveshaft inner section and the joint spider, then pack about half of the sachet of new grease into the inner yoke and around the joint spider. Insert the driveshaft outer section joint spider into the driveshaft inner section yoke, keeping the driveshaft horizontal as far as possible.

33 Pack the remainder of the grease evenly into the joint gaiter. Slide the gaiter over the end of the driveshaft inner section, and then secure the gaiter with a new retaining clip.

34 Engage the outer end of the driveshaft with the hub assembly.

35 Refit the lower suspension strut-to-hub carrier bolt (noting that the bolts fits from the front of the vehicle), and screw a new nut onto the bolt. Do not screw the nut fully onto the bolt at this stage.

36 Proceed as described in paragraphs 20 to 27.

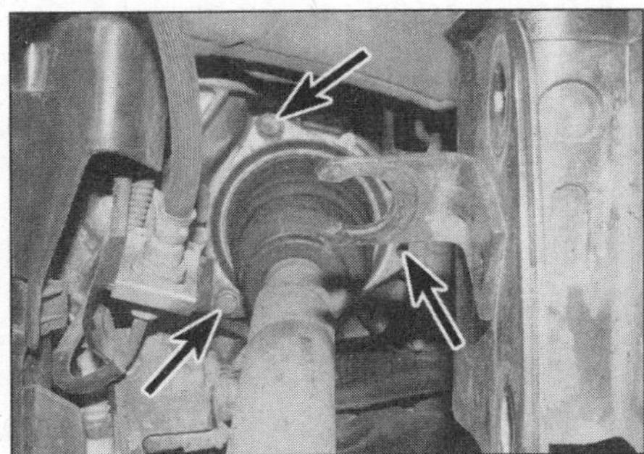
3.3 Undo the gaiter retaining plate bolts – arrowed

3 Left-hand driveshaft – removal and refitting

Note: *A new driveshaft nut, new suspension strut-to-hub carrier nuts, and a new track rod end balljoint nut may be required on refitting. Some Molykote BR2 type of grease will be required to coat the inner end of the driveshaft splines. A balljoint separator tool will also be required for this operation.*

Manual transmission models

Removal

1 Drain the transmission oil, as described in Chapter 7A.

2 Proceed as described in Section 2, paragraphs 1 to 7.

3 Working at the transmission end of the driveshaft, unscrew the three bolts securing the gaiter retaining plate to the transmission casing **(see illustration)**.

4 Proceed as described in Section 2, paragraphs 9 to 12.

5 Pull the driveshaft from the transmission, and then withdraw the assembly from under the vehicle.

Refitting

Note: *If a new driveshaft is being fitted, it may be supplied with a protective cardboard cover fitted over the outer driveshaft gaiter. In this case, do not remove the cover until the completion of the refitting procedure.*

6 Wipe clean the side of the transmission. Insert the driveshaft joint spider into the sunwheel yoke, keeping the driveshaft horizontal as far as possible **(see illustration)**.

7 Align the gaiter retaining plate with its bolt holes in the transmission casing, then refit the retaining plate bolts, and tighten them to the specified torque. Ensure the gaiter is not twisted.

3.6 Keeping the driveshaft horizontal while refitting

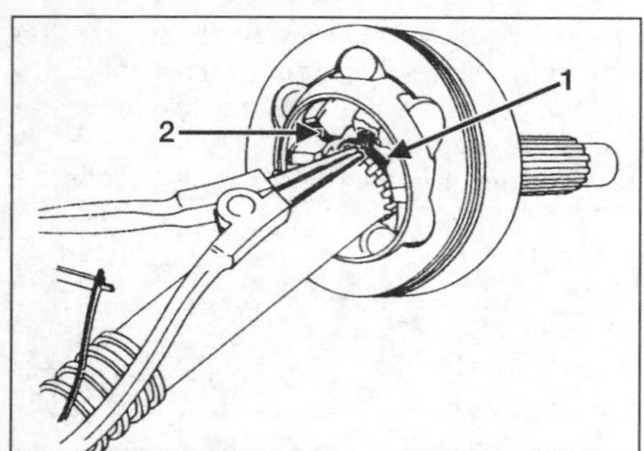

4.4 Open the circlip (1) and tap the exposed face of the ball hub (2) to free the joint

8 Engage the outer end of the driveshaft with the hub assembly.

9 Refit the lower suspension strut-to-hub carrier bolt (noting that the bolts fits from the front of the vehicle), and screw a new nut onto the bolt. Do not screw the nut fully onto the bolt at this stage.

10 Proceed as described in Section 2, paragraphs 20 to 27.

Automatic transmission models

Removal

11 Proceed as described in Section 2, paragraphs 1 to 12 (ignoring paragraph 8).

12 Pull the driveshaft from the transmission and withdraw it from under the vehicle.

Refitting

13 Proceed as described in Section 2, paragraphs 14 to 27 (ignore the reference to the intermediate bearing mounting which is only fitted to the right-hand driveshaft).

4 Driveshaft rubber gaiters – renewal

Note: *Check with your local Renault dealer or motor factors, to ensure that the appropriate gaiter repair kit is available before starting work.*

Outer joint

1 Remove the driveshaft as described in Section 2 or 3, as applicable.

2 Cut through the gaiter retaining clips, then slide the gaiter down the shaft to expose the outer constant velocity joint.

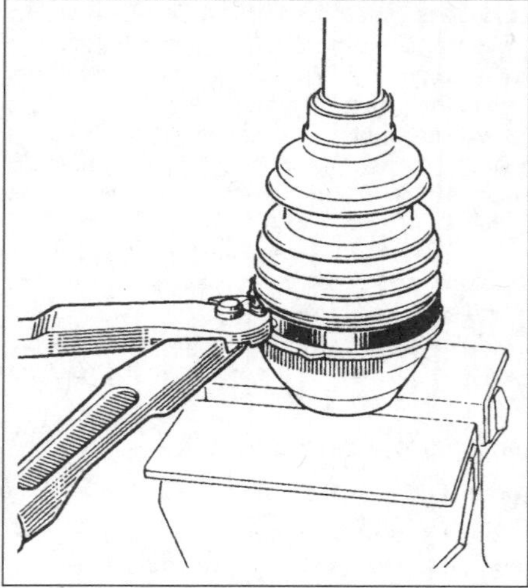

4.9 Securing the gaiter retaining clip using crimping pliers

3 Scoop out as much grease as possible from the joint.

4 Using circlip pliers, expand the joint internal circlip **(see illustration)**. At the same time, tap the exposed face of the ball hub with a mallet to separate the joint from the driveshaft. Slide off the gaiter.

5 With the constant velocity joint removed from the driveshaft, clean the joint using paraffin, or a suitable solvent, and dry it thoroughly. Carry out a visual inspection of the joint.

6 Move the inner splined driving member from side-to-side, to expose each ball in turn at the top of its track. Examine the balls for cracks, flat spots or signs of surface pitting.

7 Inspect the ball tracks on the inner and outer members. If the tracks have widened, the balls will no longer be a tight fit. At the same time, check the ball cage windows for wear or cracking between the windows.

8 If any of the constant velocity joint components are found to be worn or damaged, it will be necessary to renew the joint (check on the availability of components with a Renault dealer). If the joint is in satisfactory condition, obtain a repair kit from your Renault dealer consisting of a new gaiter, rubber collar, clips, and the correct type and quantity of grease.

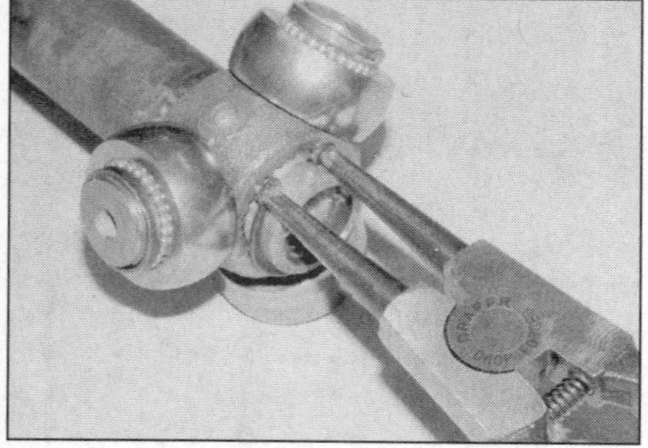

4.18a Remove the circlip . . .

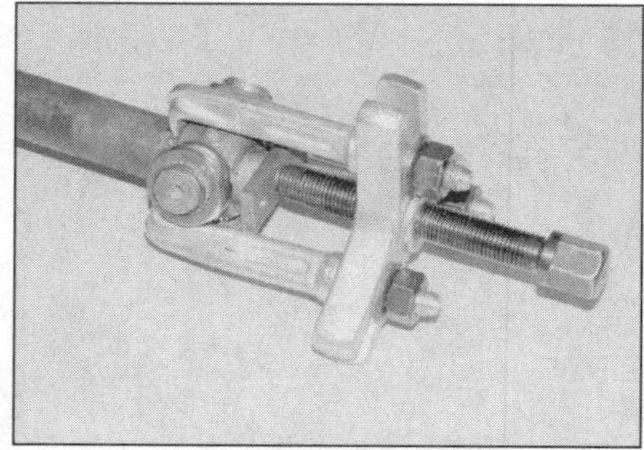

4.18b . . . and withdraw the joint, using a puller

9 Tape over the splines on the end of the driveshaft, then slide the smaller retaining clip and the gaiter onto the shaft. Locate the inner end of the gaiter in the groove on the driveshaft, and secure it in position with the retaining clip. A special tool is available to compress the retaining clip, but a satisfactory result can be achieved by carefully using a pair of side-cutters – take care not to cut the clip **(see illustration)**.

10 Remove the tape, then slide the constant velocity joint coupling onto the driveshaft until the internal circlip locates in the driveshaft groove.

11 Check that the circlip holds the joint securely on the driveshaft, then pack the joint with the grease supplied. Work the grease well into the ball tracks, and fill the gaiter with any excess.

12 Locate the outer lip of the gaiter in the groove on the joint outer member. With the coupling aligned with the driveshaft, lift the lip of the gaiter to equalise the air pressure. Secure the gaiter in position with the large retaining clip.

13 Check that the constant velocity joint moves freely in all directions, then refit the driveshaft to the vehicle as described in Section 2 or 3, as applicable.

Right-hand inner joint

14 Remove the right-hand driveshaft as described in Section 2.

15 Using a pair of snips, cut through the gaiter securing clips (note that it may be necessary to saw through the larger clip).

16 Slide back the gaiter, and wipe out as much grease as possible from the joint.

17 Slide the outer member off the end of the spider-tripod joint. Be prepared to hold the rollers in place, otherwise they may fall off the tripod ends as the outer member is withdrawn. If necessary, secure the rollers in place using tape after removal of the outer member. The rollers are matched to the tripod stems, and it is important that they are not interchanged.

18 The tripod joint can now be removed. Remove the circlip securing the tripod to the end of the driveshaft **(see illustrations)**. Make alignment marks between the tripod and the shaft for use when refitting.

19 If the tripod is tight, draw the tripod off the driveshaft end using a puller. Ensure that the legs of the puller are located behind the tripod inner member and do not contact the joint rollers. Alternatively, support the tripod inner member, and press the shaft out using a hydraulic press, again ensuring that no load is applied to the joint rollers.

20 With the joint spider removed, slide the gaiter and inner retaining collar off the end of the driveshaft.

21 Wipe clean the joint components, taking care not to remove the alignment marks made on dismantling. **Do not** use paraffin or other solvents to clean this type of joint.

22 Examine the tripod joint, rollers and outer member for any signs of scoring or wear.

Check that the rollers move smoothly on the tripod stems. If wear is evident, the tripod joint and roller assembly can be renewed, but it is not possible to obtain a new outer member (check with a Renault dealer on the availability of spares). Obtain a repair kit consisting of a gaiter, retaining clip, metal insert and joint cover, and the correct type and amount of special grease.

23 Tape over the driveshaft splines, and slide the gaiter (complete with the retaining clips) onto the driveshaft.

24 Remove the tape, then, aligning the marks made on dismantling, engage the tripod joint with the driveshaft splines. Use a hammer and soft metal drift to tap the joint onto the shaft, taking great care not to damage the driveshaft splines or joint rollers. Alternatively, support the driveshaft, and press the joint into position using a hydraulic press and suitable tubular spacer which bears only on the joint inner member.

25 Secure the tripod joint in position with the circlip, ensuring that it is correctly located in the driveshaft groove.

26 Evenly distribute the special grease contained in the repair kit around the tripod joint and inside the outer member. Pack the gaiter with the remainder of the grease.

27 Slide the outer member into position over the tripod joint.

28 Engage the inside of the gaiter with the groove in the outer member. Using a blunt rod, carefully lift the inner lip of the gaiter to equalise the air pressure.

29 With the rod in position, slide the outer end of the gaiter on the driveshaft until the dimension from the inner machined face of the outer member to the outer end of the driveshaft gaiter is as shown **(see illustration)**. Hold the gaiter in this position and withdraw the rod.

30 Fit the small retaining clip to the outer end of the gaiter. Remove any slack in the gaiter retaining clip by carefully compressing the raised section of the clip. In the absence of the special tool, a pair of side-cutters may be used – take care not to cut the clip.

31 Similarly fit the larger retaining clip to the gaiter and secure the gaiter in position in the outer member groove, as described previously.

32 Check that the constant velocity joint moves freely in all directions, then refit the driveshaft as described in Section 2.

Left-hand inner joint

Manual transmission

Note: *This procedure can only be carried out using the Renault special tool (T.Av. 1244 for 6-speed transmissions and T.Av. 944 for 5-speed transmissions). At the time of writing, no measurement was available. Before removing the bearing and gaiter, make a note of the measurement as a guide for refitting.*

33 Remove the left-hand driveshaft as described in Section 3.

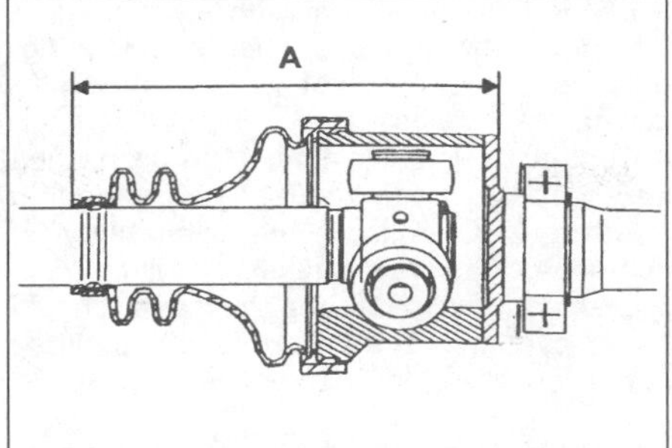

4.29 Slide the gaiter until the dimension is as shown

A = 156.0 ± 1.0 mm

34 Using circlip pliers, extract the circlip securing the tripod joint to the driveshaft. Note that on some models, the joint may be staked in position; if so, relieve the stakings using a file.

35 Using a dab of paint or a hammer and punch, mark the tripod joint in relation to the driveshaft, to use as a guide to refitting.

36 The tripod joint can now be removed. If it is tight, draw the joint off the driveshaft end using a puller. Ensure that the legs of the puller are located behind the joint inner member and do not contact the joint rollers. Alternatively, support the inner member of the tripod joint and press the shaft out of the joint, again ensuring that no load is applied to the joint rollers.

37 The gaiter and bearing assembly is removed in the same way, either by drawing the bearing off the driveshaft, or by pressing the driveshaft out of the bearing. Remove the retaining plate; noting which way round it is fitted. Check the measurement of the fitted position of the bearing as a guide for refitting.

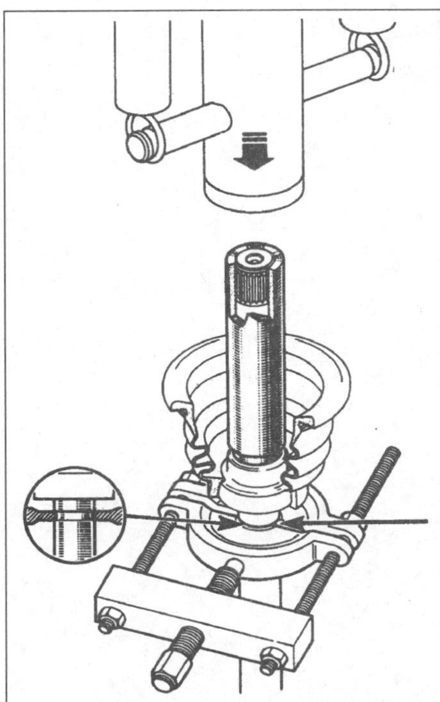

4.41a Pressing the inner bearing/gaiter onto the driveshaft – inset shows clamp located in driveshaft groove

38 Obtain a new gaiter, which is supplied complete with the small bearing.

39 Owing to the lip-type seal used in the bearing, the bearing and gaiter must be pressed into position. If a hammer and tubular drift are used to drive the assembly onto the driveshaft, there is a risk of distorting the seal.

40 Refit the retaining plate to the driveshaft, ensuring that it is fitted the correct way round.

41 Support the driveshaft, and press the gaiter bearing onto the shaft, using the Renault special tool (see note above), which bears only on the bearing inner race. Position the bearing so that the end of the Renault tool is level with the end of the shaft **(see illustrations)**. If no tool is available fit the bearing and gaiter to the measurement noted on removal.

42 Align the marks made on dismantling, and engage the tripod joint with the driveshaft splines. Use a hammer and soft metal drift to tap the joint onto the shaft, taking care not to damage the driveshaft splines or joint rollers. Alternatively, support the driveshaft, and press the joint into position using a tubular spacer that bears only on the joint inner member.

43 Secure the tripod joint in position with the circlip, ensuring that it is correctly located in the driveshaft groove.

44 Refit the driveshaft to the vehicle as described in Section 3.

Automatic transmission

45 Remove the left-hand driveshaft as described in Section 3.

46 Follow the procedures as described in paragraphs 15 to 31, noting the following differences:

a) *Paragraph 17. On automatic models there are metal plates which need bending outwards to allow the spider joint to slide out of the yoke.*
b) *Paragraph 29. On automatic models the measurement of A = 153.5 ± 1.0 mm.*
c) *When re-assembling the driveshaft, the metal plates which were bent out*

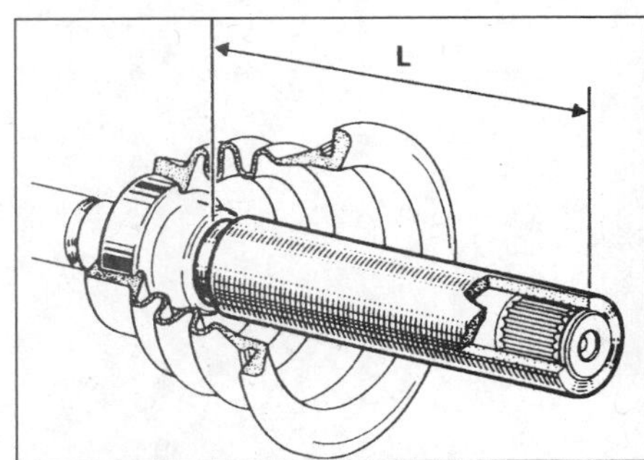

4.41b Fitting dimension for the driveshaft inner bearing/gaiter

L = Length obtained using Renault special tool T.Av. 944 – 5-speed transmissions
L = Length obtained using Renault special tool T.Av. 1244 – 6-speed transmissions

on removal will need to be carefully hammered back down into position.

47 Check that the constant velocity joint moves freely in all directions, then refit the driveshaft as described in Section 3.

5 Driveshaft overhaul – general information

1 If any of the checks described in the relevant part of Chapter 1 reveal wear in a driveshaft joint, first remove the roadwheel trim or centre cap (as appropriate) and check that the driveshaft retaining nut is still correctly tightened; if in doubt, use a torque wrench to check it. Refit the centre cap or trim, and repeat the check on the other driveshaft.

2 Road test the vehicle, and listen for a metallic clicking from the front as the vehicle is driven slowly in a circle on full-lock. If a clicking noise is heard, this indicates wear in the outer constant velocity joint.

3 If vibration, consistent with roadspeed, is felt through the vehicle when accelerating, there is a possibility of wear in the inner constant velocity joints.

4 Constant velocity joints can be dismantled and inspected for wear as described in Section 4. Check on the availability of components before dismantling a joint.

5 On models with ABS, the sensor ring should be removed from the old driveshaft and fitted to the new one. See Chapter 9.

6 Right-hand driveshaft intermediate bearing – renewal

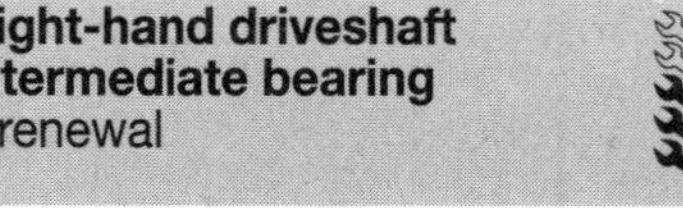

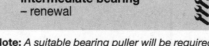

Note: *A suitable bearing puller will be required to draw the bearing off the driveshaft end.*

1 Remove the right-hand driveshaft as described in Section 2.

2 Check that the bearing outer race rotates smoothly and easily, without any signs of roughness or undue free play between the inner and outer races. If necessary, renew the bearing as follows.

3 If desired, remove the driveshaft inner section, with reference to Section 2.

4 Where applicable, remove the bearing retaining circlip.

5 Using a long-reach universal bearing puller, carefully draw the bearing off the inner end of the driveshaft.

6 Thoroughly clean the contact faces of the driveshaft and the new bearing.

7 Apply a smear of grease to the inner race of the new bearing, then fit the bearing over the end of the driveshaft.

8 Using hammer and a suitable piece of tubing, which bears only on the bearing inner race, tap the new bearing into position on the driveshaft until it contacts the locating shoulder on the shaft.

9 Where applicable, fit the bearing retaining circlip.

10 Check that the bearing rotates freely, then refit the driveshaft as described in Section 2.

Chapter 9
Braking system

Contents

Degrees of difficulty

Easy, suitable for novice with little experience	**Fairly easy,** suitable for beginner with some experience	**Fairly difficult,** suitable for competent DIY mechanic	**Difficult,** suitable for experienced DIY mechanic	**Very difficult,** suitable for expert DIY or professional

Specifications

General

System type	Servo-assisted hydraulic circuit, split diagonally with anti-lock braking system (ABS). Front and rear disc brakes on all models. On diesel models, vacuum provided by engine-driven pump. Cable-operated handbrake acting on rear brakes

Front brakes

280 mm diameter discs:	
Thickness (new)	24.00 mm
Minimum disc thickness	21.50 mm
Thickness of brake pads (including backplate)	17.00 mm
Minimum thickness of brake pads (including backplate)	7.00 mm
300 mm diameter discs:	
Thickness (new)	26.00 mm
Minimum. disc thickness	23.50 mm
Thickness of brake pads (including backplate)	17.50 mm
Minimum. thickness of brake pads (including backplate)	7.00 mm
Maximum disc run-out	0.07 mm

Rear disc brakes

Disc thickness:	
Diameter	274 mm or 300 mm
Thickness (New)	11.00 mm
Minimum thickness	8.50 mm
Maximum disc run-out	0.07 mm
Pad thickness (including backing):	
New	16.00 mm
Minimum thickness	7.50 mm

Torque wrench settings

Torque wrench settings	Nm	lbf ft
Brake disc securing screws	15	11
Brake fluid hose and pipe unions	14	10
Fluid bleed screws	7	5
Front brake caliper guide pin bolts	7	5
Front brake caliper mounting bracket-to-hub carrier bolts	105	77
Master cylinder-to-vacuum servo nuts	21	15
Rear brake caliper guide pin bolts	7	5
Rear brake caliper mounting bracket-to-hub carrier bolts	105	77
Rear hub nut	280	207
Vacuum servo bolts	29	21
Wheel bolts	105	77

1 General information

The braking system is of the servo-assisted, dual-circuit hydraulic type. The arrangement of the hydraulic system is such that each circuit operates one front and one rear brake from a tandem master cylinder. Under normal circumstances, both circuits operate in unison. However, in the event of hydraulic failure in one circuit, full braking force will still be available at two wheels.

All models have disc brakes all round, and ABS is fitted as standard. The front disc brakes are actuated by single-piston sliding type calipers, which ensure that equal pressure is applied to each disc pad. The rear disc brakes are actuated by single-piston sliding calipers, which incorporate mechanical handbrake mechanisms.

On all models, the handbrake provides an independent mechanical means of rear brake application.

On diesel engines, there is insufficient vacuum in the inlet manifold to operate the braking system servo effectively at all times. To overcome this problem, a vacuum pump is fitted to the engine, to provide sufficient vacuum to operate the servo unit. The vacuum pump is driven directly from the camshaft.

Note: *When servicing any part of the system, work carefully and methodically; also observe scrupulous cleanliness when overhauling any part of the hydraulic system. Always renew components (in axle sets, where applicable) if in doubt about their condition, and use only genuine Renault parts, or at least those of known good quality. Note the warnings given in 'Safety first!' and at relevant points in this Chapter concerning the dangers of asbestos dust and hydraulic fluid. Always work on one side of the brake system at a time, if in any doubt when refitting components, the other side can then be used as reference.*

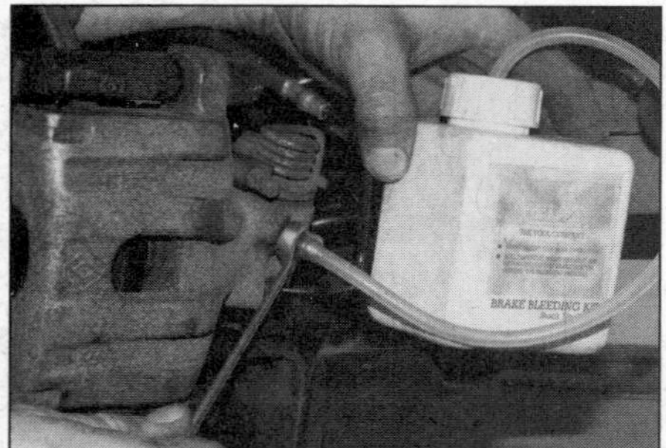

2.14 Bleeding the rear brake caliper

2 Hydraulic system – bleeding

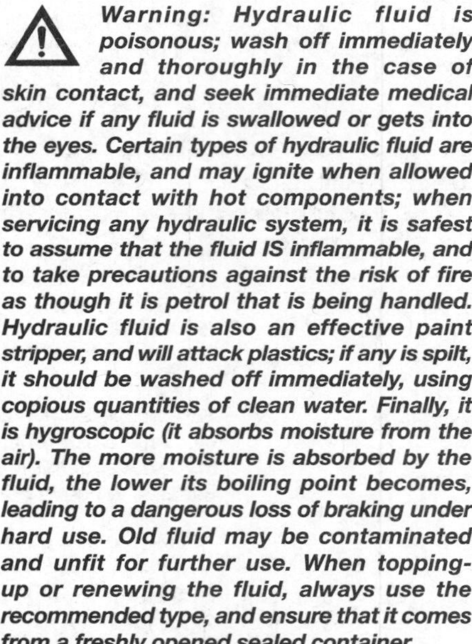

Warning: Hydraulic fluid is poisonous; wash off immediately and thoroughly in the case of skin contact, and seek immediate medical advice if any fluid is swallowed or gets into the eyes. Certain types of hydraulic fluid are inflammable, and may ignite when allowed into contact with hot components; when servicing any hydraulic system, it is safest to assume that the fluid IS inflammable, and to take precautions against the risk of fire as though it is petrol that is being handled. Hydraulic fluid is also an effective paint stripper, and will attack plastics; if any is spilt, it should be washed off immediately, using copious quantities of clean water. Finally, it is hygroscopic (it absorbs moisture from the air). The more moisture is absorbed by the fluid, the lower its boiling point becomes, leading to a dangerous loss of braking under hard use. Old fluid may be contaminated and unfit for further use. When topping-up or renewing the fluid, always use the recommended type, and ensure that it comes from a freshly opened sealed container.

General

1 The correct functioning of the brake hydraulic system is only possible after removing all air from the components and circuit; this is achieved by bleeding the system.

2 During the bleeding procedure, add only clean, fresh hydraulic fluid of the specified type; never re-use fluid that has already been bled from the system. Ensure that sufficient fluid is available before starting work.

3 If there is any possibility of incorrect fluid being used in the system, the brake lines and components must be completely flushed with uncontaminated fluid and new seals fitted to the components.

4 If brake fluid has been lost from the master cylinder due to a leak in the system, ensure that the cause is traced and rectified before proceeding further.

5 Park the vehicle on level ground, switch off the ignition and select first gear. Chock the wheels and release the handbrake.

6 Check that all pipes and hoses are secure, unions tight, and bleed screws closed. Remove the dust caps and clean any dirt from around the bleed screws.

7 Unscrew the brake fluid reservoir cap, and top-up the reservoir to the MAX level line. Refit the cap loosely, and remember to maintain the fluid level at least above the MIN level line throughout the procedure, otherwise there is a risk of further air entering the system.

8 There is a number of one-man, do-it-yourself, brake bleeding kits currently available from motor accessory shops. It is recommended that one of these kits is used wherever possible, as they greatly simplify the bleeding operation, and also reduce the risk of expelled air and fluid being drawn back into the system. If such a kit is not available, the basic (two-man) method must be used, which is described in detail below.

9 If a kit is to be used, prepare the vehicle as described previously, and follow the kit manufacturer's instructions, as the procedure may vary slightly according to the type being used; generally, they are as outlined below in the relevant sub-section.

10 Whichever method is used, the correct sequence must be followed to ensure that the removal of all air from the system.

Bleeding sequence

11 If the hydraulic system has only been partially disconnected and suitable precautions were taken to minimise fluid loss, it should only be necessary to bleed that part of the system (ie, the relevant caliper, or the primary or secondary circuit).

12 If the complete system is to be bled, then it should be done in the following sequence:

a) Rear right-hand brake.
b) Front left-hand brake.
c) Rear left-hand brake.
d) Front right-hand brake.

Bleeding

Basic (two-man) method

13 Collect a clean glass jar and a suitable length of plastic or rubber tubing, which is a tight fit over the bleed screw, and a ring spanner to fit the screws. The help of an assistant will also be required.

14 If not already done, remove the dust cap from the bleed screw of the first wheel to be bled and fit the bleed tube to the screw **(see illustration).**

15 Immerse the other end of the bleed tube in the jar, which should contain enough fluid to cover the end of the tube.

16 Ensure that the reservoir fluid level is maintained at least above the MIN level line throughout the procedure.

17 Open the bleed screw approximately half a turn, and have your assistant depress the brake pedal with a smooth steady stroke down to the floor, and then hold it there. When the flow of fluid through the tube stops, tighten the bleed screw and have your assistant release the pedal slowly.

18 Repeat this operation (paragraph 17) until clean brake fluid, free from air bubbles, can be seen flowing from the end of the tube.

19 When no more air bubbles appear, tighten the bleed screw, remove the bleed tube and refit the dust cap. Repeat these procedures on the remaining calipers in sequence until all air is removed from the system and the brake pedal feels firm again.

Using a one-way valve kit

20 As their name implies, these kits consist of a length of tubing with a one-way valve fitted, to prevent expelled air and fluid being drawn back into the system; some kits incorporate a translucent container, which can be positioned so that the air bubbles can be more easily seen flowing from the end of the tube.

21 The kit is connected to the bleed screw, which is then opened. The user returns to the driver's seat, depresses the brake pedal with a smooth steady stroke, and slowly releases it; this is repeated until the expelled fluid is clear of air bubbles.

22 Note that these kits simplify work so much that it is easy to forget the reservoir fluid level; ensure that this is maintained at least above the MIN level line at all times.

Using a pressure-bleeding kit

23 These kits are usually operated by the reserve of pressurised air contained in the spare tyre. However, note that it will probably be necessary to reduce the pressure to a lower level than normal; refer to the instructions supplied with the kit.

24 By connecting a pressurised, fluid-filled container to the fluid reservoir, bleeding is then carried out by simply opening each bleed screw in turn (in the specified sequence) and allowing the fluid to run out, rather like turning on a tap, until no air bubbles can be seen in the expelled fluid.

25 This method has the advantage that the large reservoir of fluid provides an additional safeguard against air being drawn into the system during bleeding.

26 Pressure bleeding is particularly effective when bleeding 'difficult' systems, or when bleeding the complete system at the time of routine fluid renewal. It is also the method recommended by Renault if the hydraulic system has been drained either wholly or partially.

All methods

27 When bleeding is completed, check and top-up the fluid level in the reservoir.

28 Check the feel of the brake pedal. If it feels at all spongy, air must still be present in the system, and further bleeding is indicated. Failure to bleed satisfactorily after a reasonable repetition of the bleeding operations may be due to worn master cylinder seals.

29 Discard brake fluid which has been bled from the system; it will not be fit for re-use.

ABS braking system

Warning: To bleed the ABS system it is necessary to use Renault diagnostic equipment. If only a brake caliper or hose has been removed (and suitable precautions have been taken to minimise fluid loss), it is possible to bleed the hydraulic system conventionally as described in the following paragraphs. If the system is being bled for any other reason (master cylinder removal or hydraulic unit removal), bleeding should be entrusted to a Renault dealer equipped with the necessary diagnostic equipment.

General

30 Refer to paragraphs 1 to 10.

Bleeding a brake caliper

31 Provided that the system has only been partially disconnected and suitable precautions were taken to minimise fluid loss, it should only be necessary to bleed that part of the system (ie, the relevant caliper or hose), as follows.

32 Bleed the caliper in the conventional way, as described previously for the conventional braking system (two-man method, or using a one-way valve kit).

33 Fill the reservoir with brake fluid.

34 With the end of the bleed tube immersed in the jar, proceed as follows.

a) Open the bleed screw.
b) Depress the brake pedal and hold it down.
c) Close the bleed screw.
d) Release the brake pedal.
e) Wait for three seconds.
f) Repeat the steps a) to e) at least ten times, until fluid emerges free from air bubbles.

35 With the bleed screw closed, pump the brake pedal three times in succession.

36 Repeat the steps a) to d) in paragraph 34.

37 Check the brake fluid level, and top-up if necessary (see *Weekly checks*).

38 If the braking system performance is not satisfactory after bleeding, the vehicle should be taken to a Renault dealer to have the system bled using the appropriate diagnostic equipment.

3 Hydraulic pipes and hoses – inspection and renewal

Note: *Before starting work, refer to the warning at the beginning of Section 2 concerning the dangers of hydraulic fluid.*

Inspection

1 The hydraulic pipes, hoses, hose connections and pipe unions should be regularly examined.

2 First check for signs of leakage at the pipe unions, and then examine the flexible hoses for signs of cracking, chafing and fraying.

3 The brake pipes should be examined carefully for signs of dents, corrosion or other damage. Corrosion should be scraped off and, if the depth of pitting is significant, the pipes renewed. This is particularly likely in those areas underneath the vehicle body where the pipes are exposed and unprotected.

Removal

4 If any pipe or hose is to be renewed, minimise fluid loss by removing the fluid reservoir cap and then tightening it down onto a piece of polythene (taking care not to damage the level sender unit) to obtain an airtight seal. Alternatively, flexible hoses can be sealed, if required, using a proprietary brake hose clamp; metal brake pipe unions can be plugged (if care is taken not to allow dirt into the system) or capped immediately they are disconnected. Place a wad of rag under any union that is to be disconnected, to catch any spilt fluid. If a section of pipe is to be removed from the master cylinder, the reservoir should be emptied by syphoning out the fluid or drawing out the fluid with a pipette.

5 If a flexible hose is to be disconnected, unscrew the brake pipe union nut before removing the spring clip that secures the hose to its mounting bracket **(see illustration)**.

6 To unscrew the union nuts, it is preferable to obtain a brake pipe spanner of the correct size (11 mm/13 mm split ring); these are available from motor accessory shops. Failing this, a close-fitting open-ended spanner will be required, though if

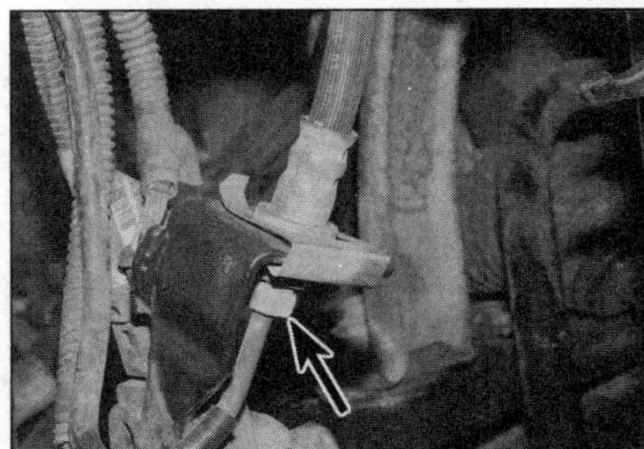

3.5 Unscrew the union nut (arrowed) before removing the spring clip

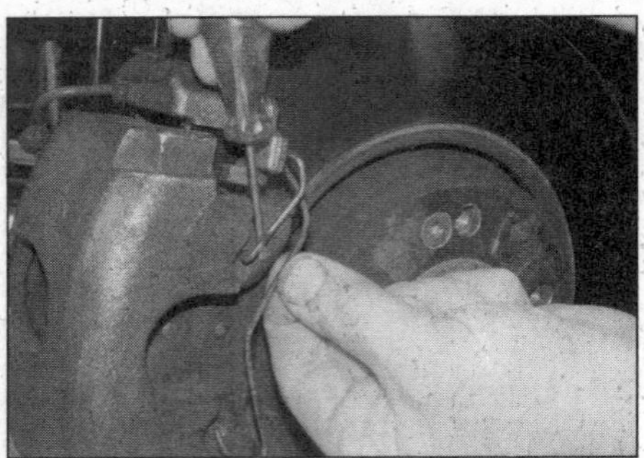
4.2a Release the spring clip . . .

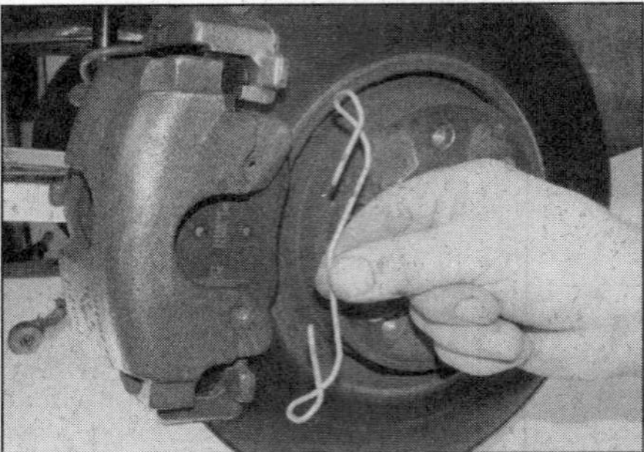
4.2b . . . and remove it from the caliper

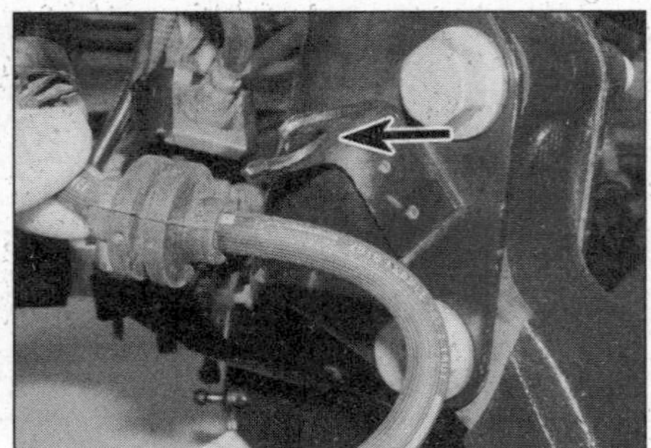
4.3 Unclip the brake hose from the bracket – arrowed

the nuts are tight or corroded, their flats may be rounded off if the spanner slips. In such a case, a self-locking wrench is often the only way to unscrew a stubborn union, but it follows that the pipe and the damaged nuts must be renewed on reassembly. Always clean a union and surrounding area before disconnecting it. If disconnecting a component with more than one union, make a careful note of the connections before disturbing any of them.

7 If a brake pipe is to be renewed, it can be obtained, cut to length and with the union nuts and end flares in place, from Renault dealers. All that is then necessary is to bend it to shape, following the line of the original, before fitting it to the vehicle. Alternatively, most motor accessory shops can make up brake pipes from kits, but this requires very careful measurement of the original to ensure that the new one is of the correct length. The safest answer is usually to take the original to the shop as a pattern.

Refitting

8 On refitting, do not overtighten the union nuts. The specified torque wrench settings (where given) are not high, and it is not necessary to exercise brute force to obtain a sound joint.

9 Ensure that the pipes and hoses are correctly routed with no kinks, and that they are secured in the clips or brackets provided. In the case of flexible hoses, make sure that they cannot contact other components during movement of the steering and/or suspension assemblies.

10 After fitting, remove the polythene from the reservoir (or remove the plugs or clamps, as applicable), and bleed the hydraulic system as described in Section 2. Wash off any spilt fluid, and check carefully for fluid leaks.

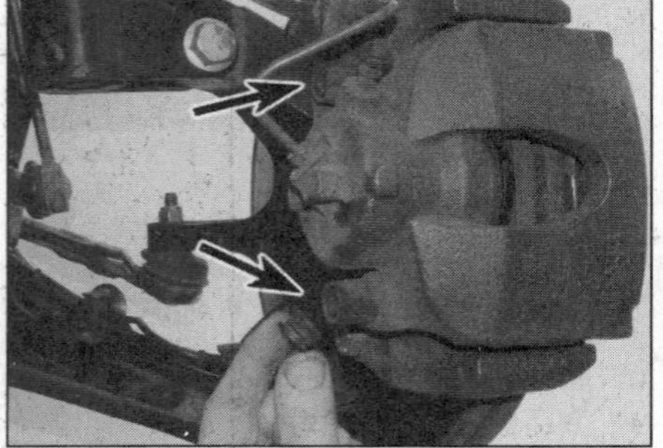
4.4 Remove the plastic plugs from the guide pin bolts – arrowed

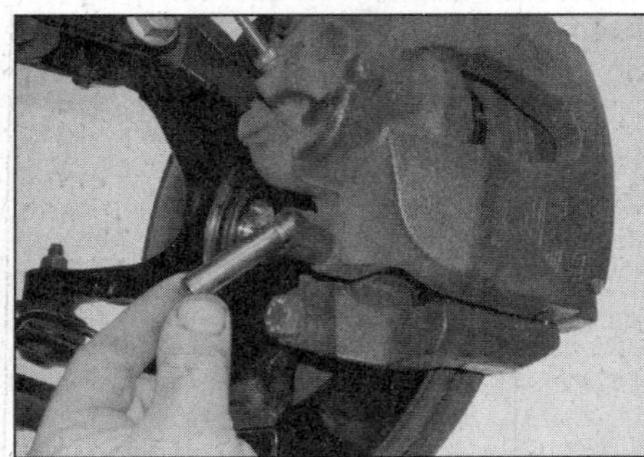
4.5 Removing the lower guide pin bolt

4.6a Withdraw the brake caliper . . .

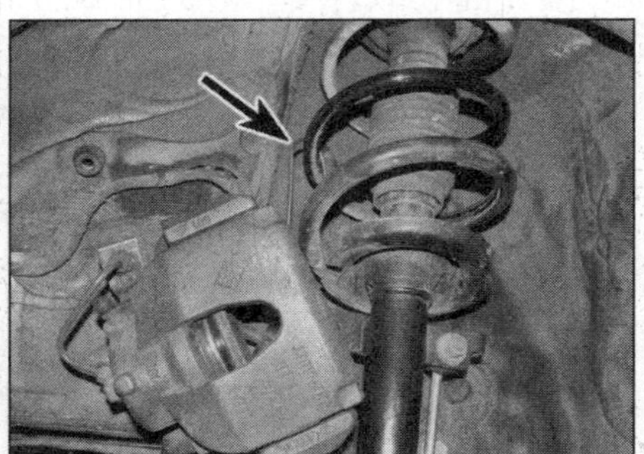
4.6b . . . and hang it on a piece of bent wire – arrowed

4 Front brake pads – renewal

Warning: Disc brake pads must be renewed on both front wheels at the same time – never renew the pads on only one wheel, as uneven braking may result. Also, the dust created by wear of the pads may contain asbestos, which is a health hazard. Never blow it out with compressed air and don't inhale any of it. An approved filtering mask should be worn when working on the brakes. DO NOT use petroleum-based solvents to clean brake parts. Use brake cleaner or methylated spirit only.

1 Apply the handbrake then jack up the front of the vehicle and support it securely on axle stands (see *Jacking and vehicle support*). Remove the front roadwheels.

2 Use a thin screwdriver to unclip and release the spring clip from the caliper mounting bracket **(see illustrations).** Note the spring clips fitted position for refitting.

3 Unclip the brake hose from the mounting bracket on the lower part of the strut **(see illustration).**

4 Unclip the two plastic plugs from the end of the guide pin bolts **(see illustration).**

5 Unscrew the two caliper guide pin bolts from the rear of the caliper **(see illustration).**

6 With the guide pin bolts removed, lift the caliper away from the brake disc and move it to one side. The inner brake pad has a clip attached to it that locates in the caliper piston, so the pad will come away with the caliper **(see illustrations).** Do not let the brake caliper hang on the brake hose; fasten it up using a piece of wire.

7 Withdraw the two brake pads, one from the carrier bracket and one from the caliper. If required, the thickness of the pads can be checked at this stage using a steel rule **(see illustration).**

8 Before refitting the pads, check that the guide pins are free to slide in the caliper and check that the rubber dust excluders around the guide pins are undamaged. Brush the dust and dirt from the caliper and piston but do not inhale it, as it is injurious to health. Inspect the

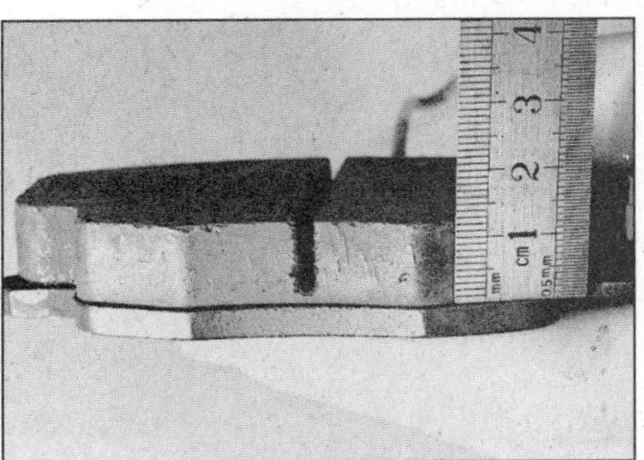
4.7 Measuring brake pad friction material thickness

dust excluder around the piston for damage and inspect the piston for evidence of fluid leaks, corrosion or damage. If attention to any of these components is necessary, refer to Section 8.

9 Make sure that the caliper piston is fully retracted in its bore. If not, fit the bleed bottle and tube to the bleed screw, open the bleed screw and carefully draw the piston in, preferably using a G-clamp or, alternatively, using a flat bar or screwdriver as a lever **(see illustration)**. As the piston is retracted, the fluid will be pushed out of the bleed screw and into a bleed bottle. Tighten the bleed screw when the piston is fully retracted. See Section 2 for further information.

10 To refit the brake pads, place them in position on the carrier bracket and in the caliper piston **(see illustrations)**.

11 Position the caliper in place over the brake disc, then fit the guide pin bolts starting with the lowest one first. Tighten the bolt to the specified torque.

12 Refit the two plastic plugs to the ends of the guide pin bolts.

13 Reconnect the brake hose to the mounting bracket on the lower part of the strut. **Note:** *Make sure the brake hose and ABS sensor wiring are secure and will not foul any other components.*

14 Refit the spring clip to the caliper mounting bracket, making sure it is fitted correctly as noted on removal **(see illustration).**

15 Refit the roadwheel, then repeat the renewal procedure on the remaining front brake.

5.2a Using a pair of pliers, disconnect the handbrake inner cable from the lever on the caliper . . .

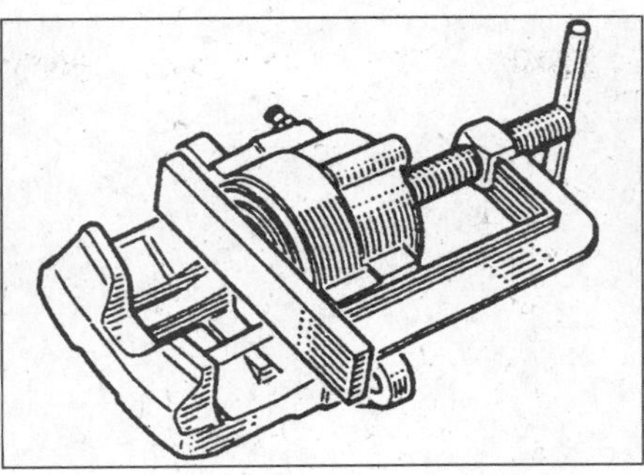
4.9 Using a G-clamp to retract a front caliper piston into its bore

4.10b . . . and the inner pad to the caliper piston

16 On completion, check the fluid level in the reservoir, and then depress the brake pedal two or three times to bring the pads into contact with the disc.

17 Lower the vehicle to the ground and tighten the roadwheels to the specified torque setting.

5 Rear brake pads – renewal

Warning: Disc brake pads must be renewed on both rear wheels at the same time – never renew the pads on only one wheel, as uneven braking may result. Also, the dust created by wear of the pads may contain asbestos, which is a health hazard. Never blow it out with compressed air and don't inhale any of it. An approved filtering mask should be worn when working on the brakes. DO NOT use petroleum-based solvents to clean brake parts. Use brake cleaner or methylated spirit only.

5.2b . . . then slide the outer cable from the support bracket on the caliper

4.10a Fit the outer brake pad to the mounting bracket . . .

4.14 Check the fitted position of the spring clip

1 Chock the front wheels, engage reverse gear (or P on models with automatic transmission) and release the handbrake. Jack up the rear of the vehicle and support it securely on axle stands (see *Jacking and vehicle support*). Remove the relevant roadwheel.

2 Using a pair of pliers, disconnect the handbrake inner cable from the lever on the caliper, then slide the outer cable from the support bracket on the caliper **(see illustrations)**. If any difficulty is experienced in releasing the inner cable from the lever, slacken the adjuster nut on the handbrake operating rod with reference to Section 16 and 17.

3 Use a thin screwdriver to unclip and release the spring clip from the caliper mounting bracket **(see illustration).** Note the spring clips fitted position for refitting.

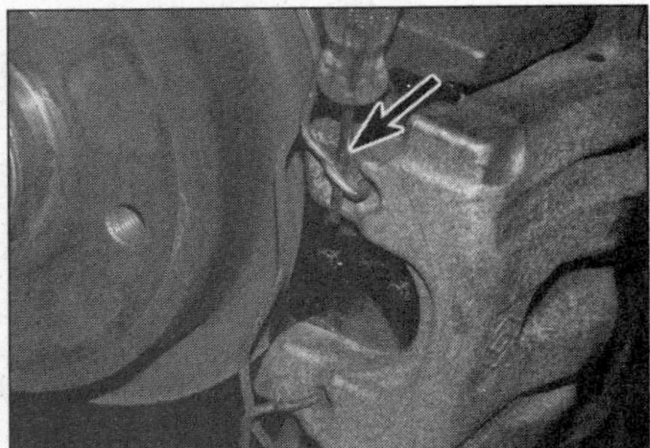
5.3 Release the spring clip with a thin screwdriver – arrowed

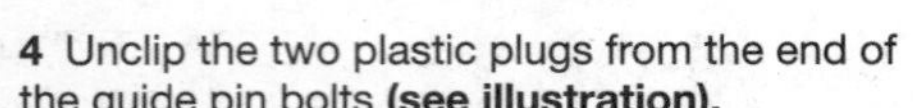

5.4 Removing the plastic plug from the lower guide pin bolt

5.5 Removing the upper guide pin bolt

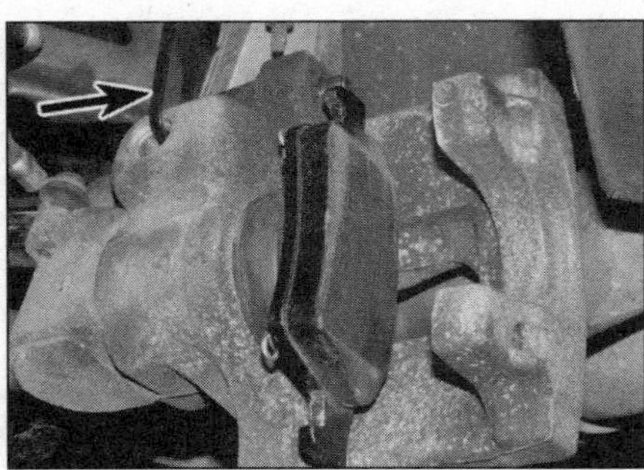

5.6 Withdraw the brake caliper and hang it on a cable tie – arrowed

4 Unclip the two plastic plugs from the end of the guide pin bolts **(see illustration).**

5 Unscrew the two caliper guide pin bolts from the rear of the caliper **(see illustration)**.

6 With the guide pin bolts removed, carefully lift the caliper away from the brake disc and move it to one side. The inner brake pad has a clip attached to it that locates on the caliper piston, so the pad will come away with the caliper **(see illustration)**. Do not let the brake caliper hang on the brake hose/pipe; fasten it up using a piece of wire.

7 Withdraw the two brake pads, one from the carrier bracket and one from the caliper. If required, the thickness of the pads can be checked at this stage using a steel rule **(see illustration 4.7)**.

8 Before refitting the pads, check that the guide pins are free to slide in the caliper and check that the rubber dust excluders around the guide pins are undamaged. Brush the dust and dirt from the caliper and piston but do not inhale it, as it is injurious to health. Inspect the dust excluder around the piston for damage and inspect the piston for evidence of fluid leaks, corrosion or damage. If attention to any of these components is necessary, refer to Section 9.

9 The caliper piston must now be fully retracted into the cylinder. Fit the bleed bottle and tube to the bleed screw, open the bleed screw and turn the piston clockwise, whilst simultaneously pressing the piston into the cylinder, until the piston continues to turn but will not go in any further. A special tool is available to retract the piston, but it should be possible to carry out the job using a pair of circlip pliers **(see illustration)**. As the piston is pressed in, the fluid will be forced out of the bleed screw and into a bleed bottle. Tighten the bleed screw, when the piston is fully retracted. See Section 2 for further information.

10 To refit the brake pads, place them in position on the carrier bracket and on the caliper piston **(see illustrations)**.

11 Position the caliper in place over the brake disc, then fit the guide pin bolts starting with the lowest one first. Tighten the bolt to the specified torque.

12 Refit the two plastic plugs to the ends of the guide pin bolts.

13 Refit the spring clip to the caliper mounting bracket, making sure it is fitted correctly as noted on removal **(see illustration).**

14 Reconnect the handbrake cable to the lever on the caliper, refer to Sections 15 and 16 for further information **Note:** *Make sure the brake pipe on the rear of the caliper is no closer than 20 mm from the brake caliper* ***(see illustration).***

15 Refit the roadwheel, then repeat the renewal procedure on the remaining rear brake.

16 On completion, check the fluid level in the reservoir, and then depress the brake pedal two or three times to bring the pads into contact with the disc.

17 If the handbrake adjustment was disturbed to allow disconnection of the handbrake cable, adjust the handbrake as described in the relevant part of Chapter 1.

18 Lower the vehicle to the ground and tighten the roadwheels to the specified torque setting.

5.9 Using circlip pliers to retract the caliper piston

5.10a Fit the outer brake pad to the mounting bracket . . .

5.10b . . . and the inner pad to the caliper piston

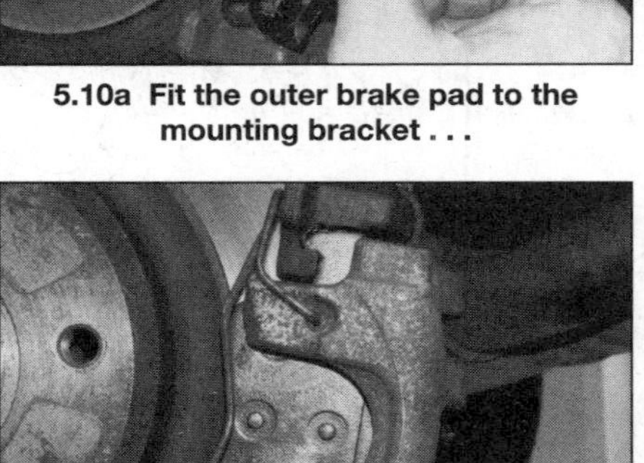

5.13 Check the fitted position of the spring clip

5.14 Make sure the brake pipe (arrowed) is no closer than 20 mm from the caliper body

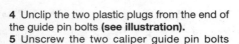

6 Front brake disc – inspection, removal and refitting

Note: *Before starting work, refer to the warning at the beginning of Section 4 concerning the dangers of asbestos dust. If either disc requires renewal, both should be renewed at the same time, to ensure even and consistent braking. In principle, new pads should be fitted also.*

Inspection

1 Apply the handbrake, then jack up the front of the vehicle and support it securely on axle stands (see *Jacking and vehicle support*). Remove the appropriate front roadwheel.

2 Slowly rotate the brake disc so that the full area of both sides can be checked; remove the brake pads, as described in Section 4, if better access is required to the inboard surface. Light scoring is normal in the area swept by the brake pads, and can be removed using emery tape. If heavy scoring is found, the disc must be renewed.

3 It is normal to find a lip of rust and brake dust around the disc's perimeter; this can be scraped off if required. If, however, a lip has formed due to wear of the brake pad swept area, the disc thickness must be measured using a micrometer **(see illustration)**. Take measurements at several places around the disc at the inside and outside of the pad swept area; if the disc has worn at any point to the specified minimum thickness or less, it must be renewed.

4 If the disc is thought to be warped, it can be checked for run-out, ideally by using a dial gauge mounted on any convenient fixed point, while the disc is slowly rotated **(see illustration)**. In the absence of a dial gauge, use feeler blades to measure (at several points all around the disc) the clearance between the disc and a fixed point such as the caliper mounting bracket. If the measurements obtained are at the specified maximum or beyond, the disc is excessively warped, and must be renewed; however, it is worth checking first that the hub bearing is in good condition (Suspension and steering check in the relevant part of Chapter 1, and Chapter 10). Also try the effect of removing the disc and turning it through 180° to reposition it on the hub; if run-out is still excessive, the disc must be renewed.

5 Check the disc for cracks (especially around the wheel bolt holes), and for any other wear or damage. Renew the disc if necessary.

Removal

Note: *Suitable thread-locking compound will be required to coat the threads of the brake caliper mounting bracket bolts on refitting.*

6 If not already done, proceed as described in paragraph 1.

7 Unscrew the two bolts securing the brake caliper mounting bracket to the hub carrier,

6.3 Checking the disc thickness with a micrometer

6.4 Checking disc run-out using a dial gauge

and slide the caliper assembly, complete with pads, off the disc (if necessary, pull the caliper body outwards, away from the centre of the car – this will push the piston back into its bore to allow the pads to pass over the disc) **(see illustration)**. Using a piece of wire or string, tie the caliper to the front suspension coil spring, to avoid placing any strain on the hydraulic brake hose or pad wear sensor wiring.

8 If the same disc is to be refitted, use chalk or paint to mark the relationship of the disc to the hub.

9 Remove the screws securing the brake disc to the hub **(see illustration)**, and remove the disc. If it is tight, lightly tap its rear face with a hide or plastic mallet.

Refitting

10 Ensure that the mating surfaces of the disc and hub are clean and flat.

11 Offer the disc into position (where applicable, align the marks made on the disc and hub before removal), then refit and securely tighten the disc securing screw(s).

12 If a new disc has been fitted, use a suitable solvent to wipe any preservative coating from the disc before refitting the caliper.

13 Thoroughly clean the caliper mounting bracket bolt threads, and then apply locking fluid to the bolt threads.

14 Slide the caliper and pad assembly into position over the disc, ensuring that the pads are correctly located, and then refit the caliper mounting bracket bolts, and tighten to the specified torque.

6.7 Slide the complete caliper assembly from the brake disc

15 Refit the roadwheel, then lower the vehicle to the ground and tighten the roadwheel bolts to the specified torque.

16 On completion, depress the brake pedal several times to bring the brake pads into contact with the disc.

7 Rear brake disc – inspection, removal and refitting

Note: *Before starting work, refer to the warning at the beginning of Section 4 concerning the dangers of asbestos dust. If either disc requires renewal, both should be renewed at the same time, to ensure even and consistent braking. In principle, new pads should be fitted also.*

Inspection

1 Chock the front wheels, engage reverse gear (or P on models with automatic transmission) and release the handbrake. Jack up the rear of the vehicle and support it securely on axle stands (see *Jacking and vehicle support*). Remove the relevant roadwheel.

2 Proceed as described for the inspection of the front brake discs, paragraphs 1 to 5, in Section 6.

Removal

3 Remove the brake pads as described in Section 5.

4 Unscrew the two bolts securing the brake caliper mounting bracket to the hub

6.9 Remove the brake disc retaining screws – arrowed

7.4 Removing the brake caliper mounting bracket

7.5 Tap the cap from the centre of the brake disc

7.6a Slacken the rear hub nut . . .

7.6b . . . and discard it – fit a new nut on reassembly

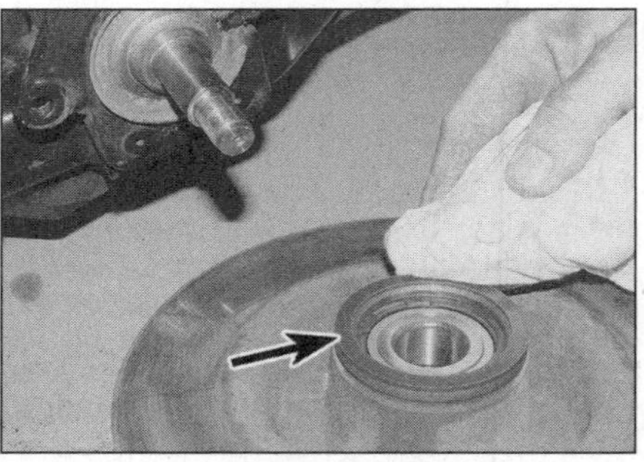
7.9 Clean around the ABS magnetic ring before refitting

carrier, and remove it clear of the disc **(see illustration)**.

5 Using a hammer and suitable chisel (or large flat-bladed screwdriver), carefully tap and prise the cap from the centre of the brake disc **(see illustration)**.

6 Using a socket and long bar, slacken and remove the rear hub nut – this will be very tight, so ensure that the car is well supported, and that only good quality, close-fitting tools are used **(see illustrations)**. Discard the hub nut; a new one must be used on refitting.

7 It should now be possible to withdraw the brake disc and hub bearing assembly from the stub axle by hand. If the disc is tight, tap the periphery of the disc using a hide or plastic mallet.

Refitting

8 If a new disc is being fitted, use a suitable solvent to wipe any preservative coating from the disc before refitting. Note that new discs may be supplied with new wheel bearings already fitted; see Chapter 10, for further information on rear wheel bearings.

9 Before refitting the disc, carefully clean the ABS magnetic ring on the back of the hub bearing **(see illustration)**.

10 Slide the disc back into position on the stub axle and fit the new rear hub nut; tighten it to the specified torque. Tap the cap back into place, in the centre of the disc (if the cap is in poor condition a new one should be fitted).

11 Apply a few drops of locking fluid onto the threads of the caliper mounting bracket bolts. Offer up the bracket and refit the bolts, tightening them to the specified torque.

12 Refit the brake pads as described in Section 5.

13 Refit the roadwheel, then lower the vehicle to the ground and tighten the roadwheel bolts to the specified torque.

14 On completion, depress the brake pedal several times to bring the brake pads into contact with the disc.

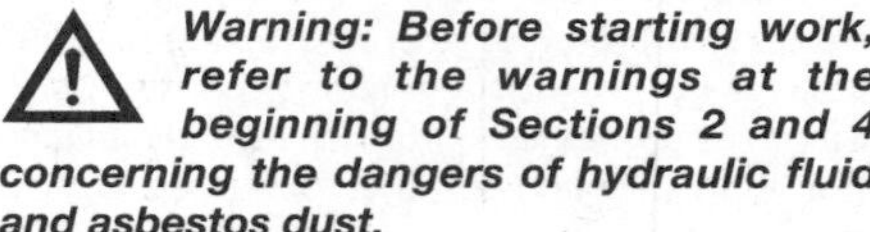

8 Front brake caliper – removal, overhaul and refitting

Warning: Before starting work, refer to the warnings at the beginning of Sections 2 and 4 concerning the dangers of hydraulic fluid and asbestos dust.

Removal

1 Apply the handbrake, then jack up the front of the vehicle and support it securely on axle stands (see *Jacking and vehicle support*). Remove the appropriate roadwheel.

2 Minimise fluid loss by using a brake hose clamp or a similar tool with protected jaws to clamp the flexible hose leading to the caliper.

3 Clean the area around the pipe union on the caliper, and then slacken and remove the brake pipe union nut **(see illustration)**. Use a rag around the brake pipe union to catch any fluid loss, cap the end of the pipe to prevent dirt ingress.

4 Remove the brake caliper as described in paragraphs 2 to 6, of Section 4.

Overhaul

Note: *Make sure an appropriate overhaul kit can be obtained before dismantling the caliper.*

5 With the caliper on the bench, wipe away all traces of dust and dirt, but *avoid inhaling the dust, as it is injurious to health.*

6 Using a small flat-bladed screwdriver, carefully prise the dust seal retaining clip out of the caliper bore.

7 Withdraw the partially-ejected piston from the caliper body and remove the dust seal. The piston can be withdrawn by hand, or if necessary forced out by applying compressed air to the union bolt hole.

Caution: The piston may be ejected with some force. Only low pressure should be required, such as is generated by a foot pump. If the piston is forced out using compressed air, place a wooden block between the caliper body and the piston to prevent the possibility of damage to the piston as it is ejected.

8 Extract the piston hydraulic seal using a blunt instrument such as a knitting needle or a feeler blade, taking care not to damage the caliper bore.

9 Where applicable, withdraw the guide pins from the caliper and remove the rubber gaiters.

10 Thoroughly clean all components using only methylated spirit, isopropyl alcohol or clean hydraulic fluid as a cleaning medium. Never use mineral-based solvents, such as petrol or paraffin, which will attack the hydraulic system rubber components.

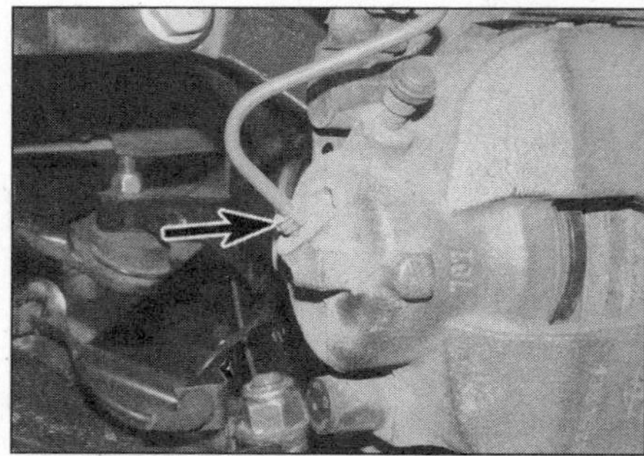
8.3 Undo the front brake pipe union nut – arrowed

Dry the components immediately, using compressed air or a clean, lint-free cloth. Use compressed air to blow clear the fluid passages.

11 Check all components and renew any that are worn or damaged. Check particularly the cylinder bore and piston; if they are scratched, worn or corroded in any way, they must be renewed (note that this means the renewal of the complete body assembly). Similarly, check the condition of the guide pins and their bores; they should be undamaged and (when cleaned) a reasonably tight sliding fit in the caliper mounting bracket bores. If there is any doubt about the condition of a component, renew it.

12 If the assembly is fit for further use, obtain the appropriate repair kit; the components are available from Renault dealers, in various combinations.

13 Renew all rubber seals, dust covers and caps disturbed on dismantling as a matter of course; these should never be re-used.

14 Before starting reassembly, ensure that all components are absolutely clean and dry.

15 Dip the piston and the new piston (fluid) seal in clean hydraulic fluid. Smear clean fluid on the cylinder bore surface.

16 Fit the new piston (fluid) seal, using only the fingers to manipulate it into the cylinder bore groove. Fit the new dust seal to the piston. Refit the piston to the cylinder bore using a twisting motion, ensuring that the piston enters squarely into the bore. Press the piston fully into the bore, then press the dust seal into the caliper body.

17 Install the dust seal retaining clip, ensuring that it is correctly seated in the caliper groove.

18 Apply the grease supplied in the repair kit (or a good quality high-temperature brake grease or anti-seize compound) to the guide pins. Fit the pins to the caliper mounting bracket. Fit the new rubber gaiters, ensuring that they are correctly located in the grooves on both the pin and mounting bracket.

Refitting

19 Refit the brake pads and caliper as described in Section 4.

20 Where applicable, remove the cap from the end of the brake pipe and fit the brake pipe union to the caliper. Tighten the brake pipe union nut to the specified torque.

21 Remove the clamp from the caliper fluid hose.

22 Apply the footbrake several times to position the pads against the discs.

23 Bleed the hydraulic system as described in Section 2. Providing the precautions described were taken to minimise brake fluid loss, it should only be necessary to bleed the relevant front brake.

24 Refit the roadwheel, then lower the vehicle to the ground and tighten the roadwheel bolts to the specified torque.

9 Rear brake caliper – removal, overhaul and refitting

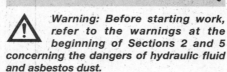

Warning: Before starting work, refer to the warnings at the beginning of Sections 2 and 5 concerning the dangers of hydraulic fluid and asbestos dust.

Removal

1 Chock the front wheels, engage reverse gear (or P on models with automatic transmission) and release the handbrake. Jack up the rear of the vehicle and support it securely on axle stands (see *Jacking and vehicle support*). Remove the relevant roadwheel.

2 Minimise fluid loss by using a brake hose clamp or a similar tool with protected jaws, to clamp the flexible hose leading to the caliper.

3 Clean the area around the pipe union on the caliper, and then slacken and remove the brake pipe union nut **(see illustration)**. Use a rag around the brake pipe union to catch any fluid loss, cap the end of the pipe to prevent dirt ingress.

4 Remove the brake caliper as described in paragraphs 2 to 6, of Section 5.

Overhaul

5 At the time of writing, no information was available for the overhaul of the rear brake calipers. The only parts available are guide pins and dust covers/gaiters. Consult a Renault dealer regarding the availability of spare parts.

Refitting

6 Refit the brake pads and caliper as described in Section 5.

7 Where applicable, remove the cap from the end of the brake pipe and fit the brake pipe union to the caliper. Tighten the brake pipe union nut to the specified torque.

8 Remove the clamp from the caliper fluid hose.

9 Apply the footbrake several times to position the pads against the discs.

10 Bleed the hydraulic system as described in Section 2. Providing the precautions described were taken to minimise brake fluid loss, it should only be necessary to bleed the relevant rear brake.

9.3 Undo the rear brake pipe union nut – arrowed

11 Refit the roadwheel, then lower the vehicle to the ground and tighten the roadwheel bolts to the specified torque.

10 Master cylinder – removal, overhaul and refitting

Note: *Before starting work, refer to the warnings at the beginning of Section 2 concerning the dangers of hydraulic fluid.*

Note: *A new master cylinder-to-servo seal will be required on refitting.*

Removal

1 Remove the retaining nut and move the coolant expansion bottle to one side **(see illustration)**.

2 Remove the air intake pipe from across the front of the brake master cylinder **(see illustration)**. Refer to Chapter 4A or 4B, depending on model, for further information.

3 Syphon the fluid from the master cylinder reservoir. Use a syringe, a clean battery hydrometer or a poultry baster to do this, **never** use the mouth to suck the fluid out through a tube.

4 Disconnect the wiring connector for the low fluid level warning light and disconnect the supply pipe to the clutch master cylinder. Plug the end of the supply pipe to the clutch master cylinder to prevent fluid leaking **(see illustration)**.

10.1 Remove the coolant bottle retaining nut – arrowed

10.2 Withdraw the air intake resonator from the engine bay – 1.8 litre engine

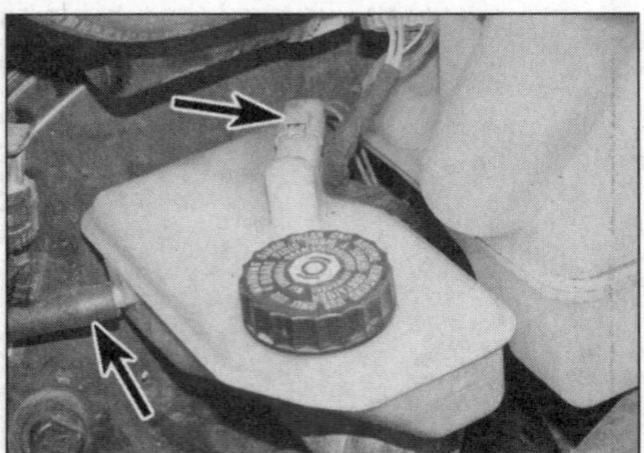

10.4 Disconnect the wiring connector and the clutch supply hose – arrowed

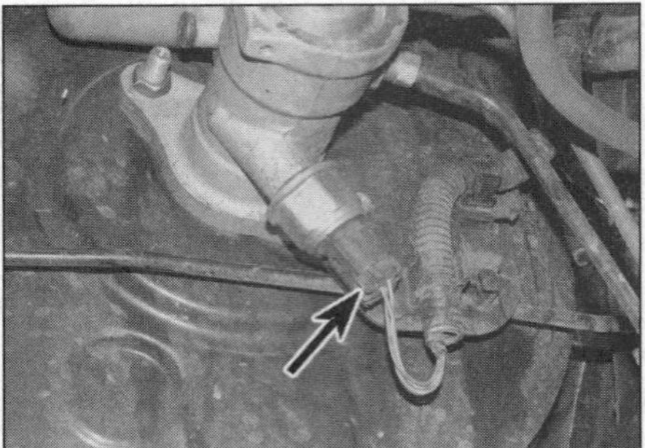

10.5 Disconnect the wiring connector (arrowed) from the pressure switch

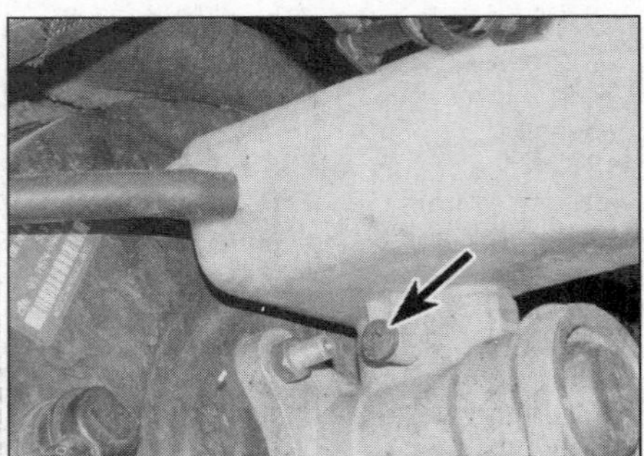

10.9 Undo the retaining screw – arrowed

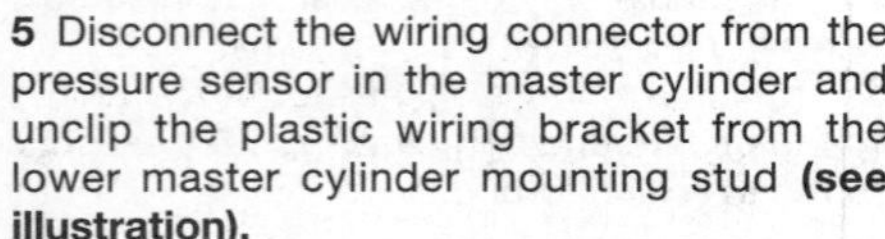

5 Disconnect the wiring connector from the pressure sensor in the master cylinder and unclip the plastic wiring bracket from the lower master cylinder mounting stud **(see illustration).**

6 Note the locations of the hydraulic pipes and then disconnect them from the master cylinder by unscrewing the unions. Place a wad of rag under the master cylinder to catch any fluid, which may drain out.

7 Unscrew the nuts securing the master cylinder to the front face of the vacuum servo, and withdraw the master cylinder.

8 Recover the seal from between the master cylinder and the servo; a new one will be required for refitting.

Overhaul

9 A faulty master cylinder cannot be overhauled, as no spare parts are available. If the master cylinder is faulty or worn, the complete assembly must be renewed. To remove the reservoir from the master cylinder, remove the securing screw **(see illustration).**

Refitting

10 Remove all traces of dirt from the master cylinder and servo unit mating surfaces. Fit a new seal to the groove on the master cylinder body.

11 Fit the master cylinder to the servo, ensuring that the servo pushrod enters the master cylinder bore centrally. Refit the master cylinder mounting nuts, and tighten them to the specified torque.

12 Wipe clean the brake pipe unions, and then refit them to the master cylinder ports. Tighten the union nuts to the specified torque.

13 Further refitting is a reversal of removal, noting the following points:

a) *Refit the clutch master cylinder supply pipe and bleed the clutch as described in Chapter 6.*
b) *Make sure the wiring connectors are secured.*
c) *On completion, fill the reservoir with fresh fluid and bleed the brakes as described in Section 2.*
d) *Check the operation of the brakes before taking the car out on the road.*

11 Vacuum servo unit – testing, removal and refitting

Testing

1 Operation of the servo can be checked in the following way.

2 With the engine stopped, depress the brake pedal several times. The pedal travel should remain the same each time the pedal is depressed.

3 Depress the brake pedal fully and hold it down, then start the engine. It should be possible to feel the pedal move down slightly.

4 Hold the pedal depressed with the engine running, then switch off the engine, whilst still holding the pedal depressed. The pedal should not rise nor fall.

5 Start the engine and run it for at least a minute. Stop the engine, and then depress the brake pedal several times. The pedal travel should decrease with each application, and it should be possible to detect a 'hissing' sound from the servo as the pedal is depressed. After about four or five depressions of the pedal, no further hissing should be heard, and the pedal should feel considerably firmer.

6 If the foregoing tests do not prove satisfactory, check the servo vacuum hose and non-return valve for security and leakage at the valve grommet.

7 If the brake servo operates properly in the test, but still gives less effective service on the road, the air filter through which air flows into the servo should be inspected. A dirty filter will reduce the effectiveness of the servo.

8 The servo unit itself cannot be repaired and therefore renewal is necessary if the unit proves to be faulty.

Removal

9 Remove the master cylinder, as described in Section 10.

10 Disconnect the vacuum non-return valve from the servo unit, with reference to Section 12.

11 To give better access, remove the heater blower motor as described in Chapter 3.

12 Working in the passenger's footwell, disconnect the servo pushrod from the brake pedal linkage by releasing the spring clip and pulling out the clevis pin **(see illustration).**

13 Again working in the passenger's footwell, unscrew the brake servo mounting nuts **(see illustration)**.

14 Withdraw the servo from the engine compartment.

Refitting

15 Before refitting the servo, check that the length of the servo pushrod is as specified **(see illustration)**. The length is measured from the rear face of the servo to the centre of the hole in the pushrod clevis. If necessary,

11.12 Release the spring clip (arrowed) from the servo pushrod

11.13 Undo the servo mounting nuts – arrowed

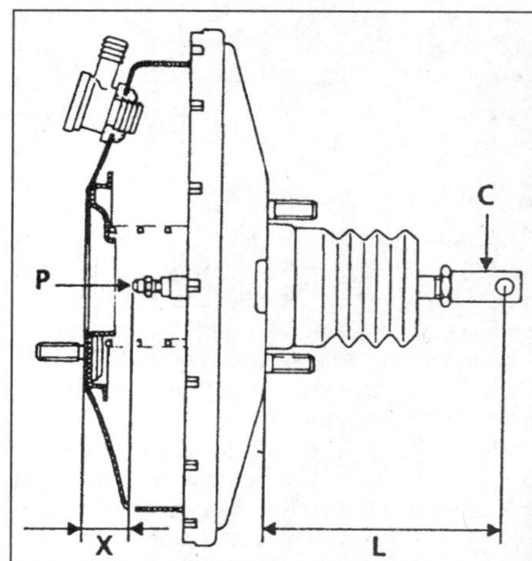

11.15 Vacuum servo operating rod and pushrod setting

C Servo pushrod
P Servo operating rod
X Cannot be adjusted
L = 122.0 mm – right-hand-drive models
L = 165.5 mm – left-hand-drive models

adjust the length of the pushrod by loosening the locknut and turning the clevis. Tighten the locknut on completion.

16 Refitting is a reversal of removal, but refit the master cylinder with reference to Section 10.

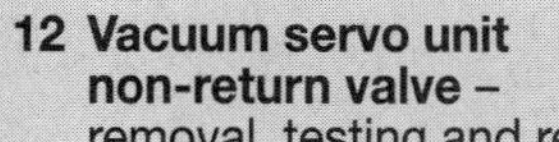

12 Vacuum servo unit non-return valve – removal, testing and refitting

Removal

1 Referring to Chapter 4A or 4B if necessary, remove the air cleaner duct for access to the servo unit vacuum hose **(see illustration)**.

2 Withdraw the valve from its rubber sealing grommet, using a pulling and twisting motion **(see illustration)**. Remove the grommet from the servo.

3 To remove the hose completely, squeeze the tabs at the other end of the hose, and disconnect it from the inlet manifold or vacuum pump **(see illustrations)**.

Testing

4 Examine the check valve for signs of damage, and renew if necessary. The valve may be tested by blowing through it in both directions. Air should flow through the valve in one direction only – when blown through from the servo unit end of the valve. Renew the valve if this is not the case.

5 Examine the rubber sealing grommet and flexible vacuum hose for signs of damage or deterioration, and renew as necessary.

Refitting

6 Fit the sealing grommet into position in the servo unit.

12.1 Withdraw the air intake resonator from the engine bay – 1.8 litre engine

12.2 The valve is located in the front of the servo – arrowed

12.3a Disconnect the servo hose from the vacuum pump on diesels . . .

12.3b . . . or the inlet manifold on petrol engines

7 Ease the check valve into position, taking care not to displace or damage the grommet. Reconnect the vacuum hose to the inlet manifold or vacuum pump.

8 On completion, start the engine and check that there are no air leaks. Check the operation of the brakes before taking the car onto the road.

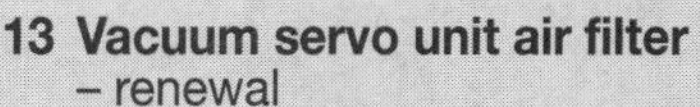

13 Vacuum servo unit air filter – renewal

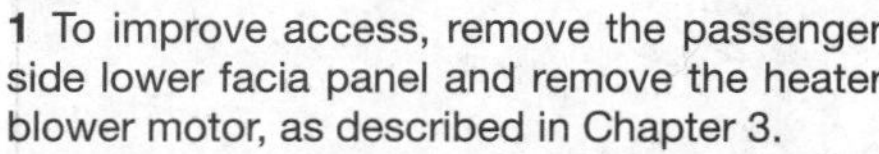

1 To improve access, remove the passenger side lower facia panel and remove the heater blower motor, as described in Chapter 3.

2 Pull back the dust excluder from the rear of the servo, and slide it up the pushrod **(see illustration)**.

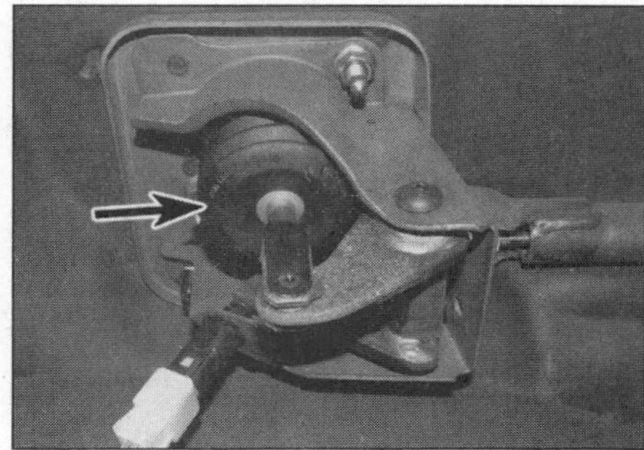

13.2 Pull back the rubber gaiter – arrowed

3 Using a scriber or similar pointed tool, prise the filter from its housing, and cut it to allow it to pass over the pushrod **(see illustration)**.

4 Cut the new filter, and push it into position, ensuring that it is correctly seated.

5 Push the dust excluder into position.

6 Refit the heater blower motor, as described in Chapter 3.

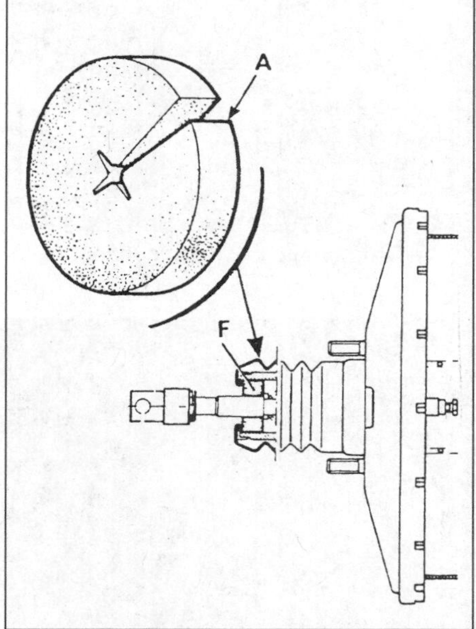

13.3 Vacuum servo air filter location (F)

Cut the new filter at A to enable fitting

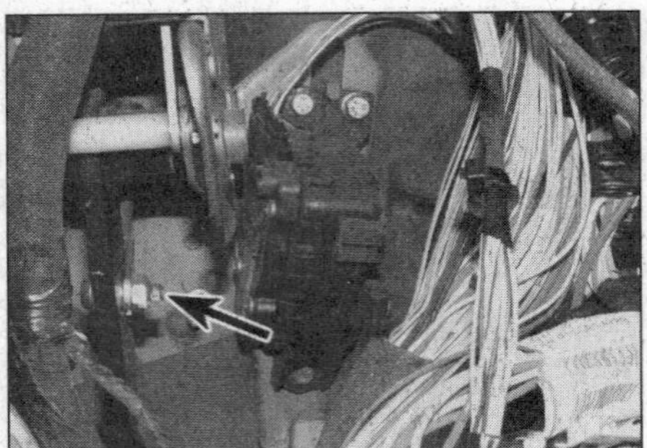
14.2 Undo the pivot bolt – arrowed

14.3 Undo the brake pedal assembly mounting nuts – arrowed

14 Brake pedal – removal and refitting

Removal

1 Renault recommends removing the facia panel (Chapter 11) and the steering column (Chapter 10) to improve access to the brake pedal. Although this would make it a lot easier to get at, it appears perfectly possible to remove the brake pedal with these components in place.

2 Undo the bolt which secures the pedal-to-cross-shaft **(see illustration)**, then slide out the bolt and disconnect the pedal from the shaft.

3 Unscrew the mounting nuts securing the pedal-mounting bracket to the bulkhead **(see illustration)**, and then remove the pedal assembly, twisting it sideways to release it.

4 Check the condition of the clevis pin and its spring clip – these are vital components connecting the brake pedal to the cross-shaft, and if their condition is at all suspect, new parts should be fitted.

Refitting

5 Refitting is a reversal of removal, noting the following points:

a) Tighten the pedal mounting bracket nuts securely.
b) Ensure that the pedal-to-cross-shaft clevis pin's spring clip is securely refitted.
c) Check the operation of the brakes before taking the car out on the road.

15 Brake pedal cross-shaft – removal and refitting

Removal

1 Remove the brake pedal assembly as described in Section 14. As with brake pedal removal, it should not be necessary to remove the facia panel (Chapter 11) for this operation, although it would make access easier.

2 Remove the heater blower motor, as described in Chapter 3.

3 Working in the passenger footwell, disconnect the wiring plug from the brake light switch on the bracket for the servo operating lever. Turn the brake light switch 90° anti-clockwise and remove it **(see illustrations)**.

4 Remove the brake vacuum servo unit as described in Section 11. It may be possible to move this away from the bulkhead without disconnecting the brake pipes and master cylinder.

5 With the servo unit disconnected from the bulkhead, remove the remaining nuts from the cross-shaft mounting bracket.

6 Slacken and remove the pivot bolt at the brake pedal end of the cross-shaft **(see illustration)**, and withdraw the shaft out through the passenger side of the vehicle.

7 Examine the shaft, and all related components, very carefully. If there are signs of damage to any component, new parts should be fitted – never take risks where brakes are concerned.

Refitting

8 Refitting is a reversal of removal, noting the following points:

a) Check the brake light switches are securely fitted.
b) Tighten all fasteners securely, or to the specified torque.
c) Refit the heater blower motor as described in Chapter 3, and the brake pedal assembly as described in Section 14.
d) Check the operation of the brakes before taking the car out on the road.

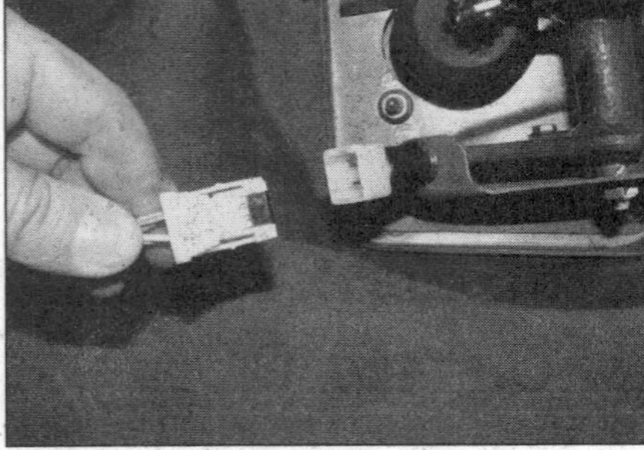
15.3a Disconnect the wiring connector . . .

15.3b . . . twist the switch anti-clockwise and remove

15.6 Undo the pivot bolt (arrowed) from the end of the cross-shaft

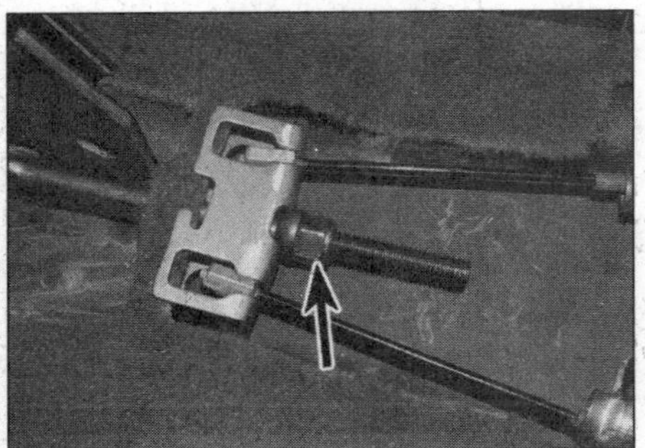
16.2 Remove the adjusting nut (arrowed) from the operating rod

16 Handbrake lever – removal and refitting

Removal

1 Working inside the vehicle, remove the centre console, as described in Chapter 11.

2 Unscrew the adjuster nut, and disconnect the operating rod from the cable equaliser **(see illustration)**.

3 Disconnect the wiring connector from the switch **(see illustration)**, then pull back the carpet/sound insulation from around the base of the handbrake lever to expose the handbrake lever securing nuts.

4 Unscrew the bolts securing the handbrake

16.3 Disconnect the switch wiring connector – arrowed

lever assembly to the floor, and then withdraw the handbrake lever/rod assembly **(see illustration)**.

Refitting

5 Refitting is a reversal of removal, but on completion check the handbrake cable adjustment, as described in the relevant part of Chapter 1.

17 Handbrake cables – removal and refitting

Removal

1 There are two handbrake cables, one cable running from each rear brake assembly to the cable equaliser under the centre console.

2 Chock the front wheels, engage reverse gear (or P on models with automatic transmission) and release the handbrake. Jack up the rear of the car and support it securely on axle stands (see *Jacking and vehicle support*). Remove the rear wheels.

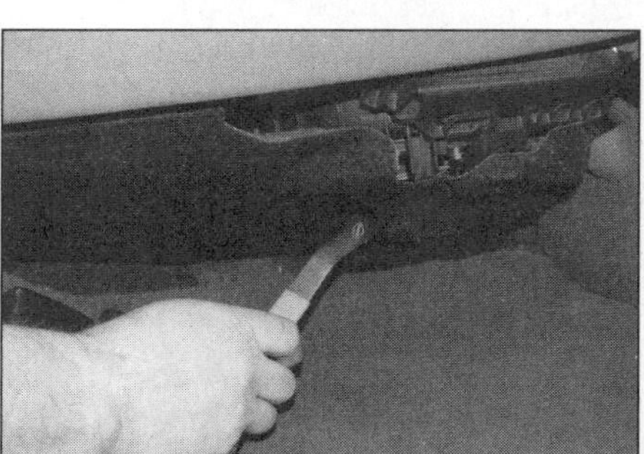

18.1a Release the retaining clip . . .

18.2 Brake light switch (arrowed) in passenger footwell

16.4 Undo the handbrake lever assembly mounting nuts – arrowed

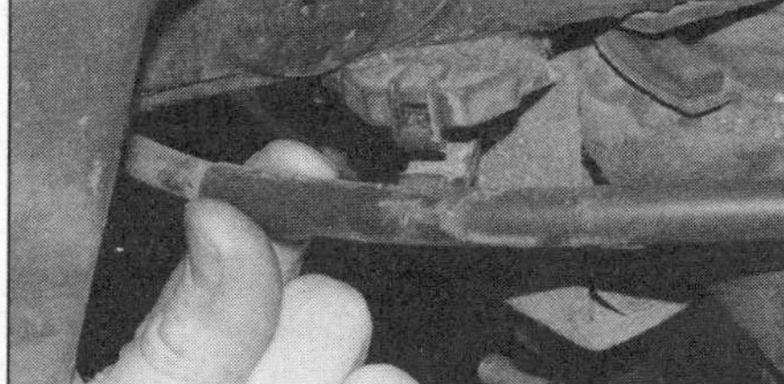

17.6a Release the handbrake from the retaining clips . . .

18.1b . . . and withdraw the trim panel

18.3 Twist the brake light switch anti-clockwise to remove

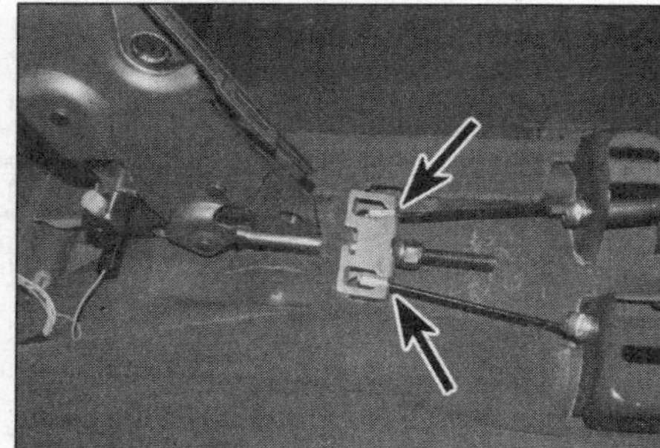

17.4 Disengage the handbrake cables (arrowed) from the equaliser

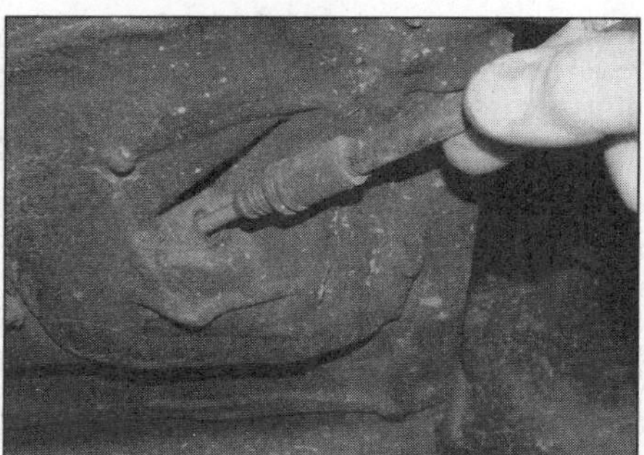

17.6b . . . and withdraw from the floor panel

3 Working inside the vehicle, remove the centre console, as described in Chapter 11.

4 Slacken the adjuster nut, and disengage the cables from the cable equaliser **(see illustration)**.

5 Using a pair of pliers, disconnect the handbrake inner cable from the lever on the caliper, then slide the outer cable from the support bracket on the caliper **(see illustrations 5.2a and 5.2b)**.

6 Release the cable from the clips on the body and suspension components, and withdraw the outer cable from the floor panel **(see illustrations)**.

Refitting

7 Refitting is a reversal of removal, but lightly grease the ends of the inner cable, and on completion, check the cable adjustment as described in the relevant part of Chapter 1.

18 Stop-light switch – removal, refitting and adjustment

Removal

1 Release the retaining clips and remove the trim panel from under the glovebox **(see illustrations)**.

2 The stop-light switch is located on the passenger side end of the brake pedal cross-shaft, and is accessed from the front passenger footwell **(see illustration)**.

3 Disconnect the wiring plug from the brake light switch, then turn the switch 90° anti-clockwise and remove it **(see illustration)**.

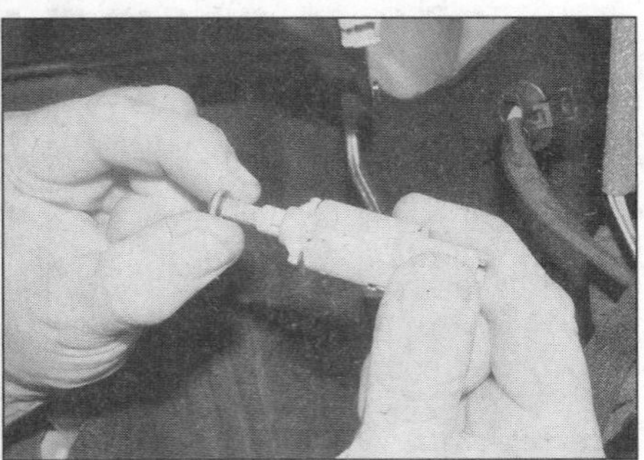

18.4 Reset the switch plunger by pulling it out by a few clicks

Refitting and adjustment

4 Refitting is a reversal of removal. Before fitting the switch, the plunger should be reset as follows. Pull the plunger out firmly – it should extend on its ratchet mechanism by several clicks **(see illustration)**. When the switch is refitted and the pedal pressed for the first few times, the plunger will be pushed back in automatically to the correct setting.

5 On completion, check the operation of the stop-lights.

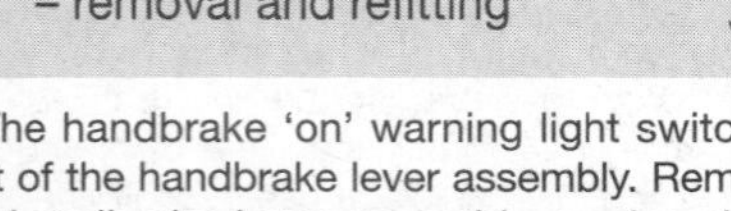

19 Handbrake 'on' warning light switch – removal and refitting

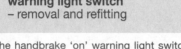

The handbrake 'on' warning light switch is part of the handbrake lever assembly. Remove the handbrake lever assembly as described in Section 16. On some models, it may be possible to undo the retaining bolts and remove the switch from the mounting bracket.

20 Anti-lock braking system (ABS) – general information

The purpose of the system is to prevent the wheel(s) locking during heavy braking. This is achieved by automatic release of the brake on the relevant wheel before it can lock up, followed by rapid reapplication of the brake.

The main components of the system are four wheel sensors (one per wheel), and a modulator block which contains the ABS computer, the hydraulic solenoid valves and accumulators, and an electrically-driven return pump.

The solenoids are controlled by the computer, which receives signals from the wheel sensors. The sensors detect the speed of rotation of a reluctor ring, attached to the wheel hub. By comparing the speed signals from the four wheels, the computer can determine when a wheel is decelerating at an abnormal rate, and can therefore predict when a wheel is about to lock. During normal operation, the system functions in the same way as a non-ABS braking system.

If the computer senses that a wheel is about to lock, the ABS system enters the 'pressure-maintain' phase. The computer operates the relevant solenoid valve in the modulator block; this isolates the brake on the wheel in question from the master cylinder, effectively sealing-in the hydraulic pressure.

If the speed of rotation of the wheel continues to decrease at an abnormal rate, the ABS system then enters the 'pressure-decrease' phase. The return pump operates and pumps the hydraulic fluid back into the master cylinder, releasing pressure on the brake. When the speed of rotation of the wheel returns to an acceptable rate, the pump stops and the solenoid valve opens, allowing hydraulic pressure to return and reapply the brake. This cycle can be carried out at up to 10 times a second.

The action of the solenoid valves and return pump creates pulses in the hydraulic circuit. When the ABS system is functioning, these pulses can be felt through the brake pedal.

Some models are also equipped with an additional safety feature built into the ABS system, called EBD (Electronic Brake force Distribution), which automatically apportions braking effort between the front and rear wheels. The EBD function is built into the system's software, and the intention is to limit braking effort (fluid pressure) to the rear wheels, to prevent them locking up under heavy braking.

Another feature of the ABS is Brake Assist, which monitors how rapidly the brake pedal is pressed, and determines whether an emergency stop is required – in this case, maximum braking effort is applied more quickly than the driver would normally be able to, unaided.

The Electronic Stability Programme (ESP) is available as an option. This system uses the ABS to prevent wheel spin or skidding during acceleration or cornering, by selectively and partially applying the brakes individually or in pairs, to either 'steer' the car, or slow the front wheels (traction control). An accelerometer, lateral sensor is mounted under the driver's seat, which informs the system ECU of the lateral (sideways) forces acting on the car, indicating the direction and speed of cornering. An integral steering angle sensor in the steering system is used to indicate the amount of steering lock applied. A front-wheel-drive car will typically understeer (run wide) if excess power is used when cornering on a slippery road – if the yaw sensor detects this condition, one or more brakes will be applied to help turn the car, and engine power will be momentarily reduced. Similarly, the traction control function uses the front wheel sensors to detect abnormally-fast wheel rotation, relative to the vehicle speed – when wheel spin is occurring, the engine power will be reduced, and the front brakes applied slightly

The operation of the ABS system is entirely dependent on electrical signals. To prevent the system responding to any inaccurate signals, a built-in safety circuit monitors all signals received by the computer. If an inaccurate signal or low battery voltage is detected, the ABS system is automatically shut-down, and the warning light on the instrument panel is illuminated to inform the driver that the ABS system is not operational. Normal braking is unaffected, apart from the loss of the Electronic Brake force Distribution function (which may result in premature rear wheel lock-up under braking).

If a fault does develop in the ABS system, the car must be taken to a Renault dealer for fault diagnosis and repair. Check first, however, that the problem is not due to loose or damaged wiring connections, or badly routed wiring picking up false signals from the ignition system.

21 Anti-lock braking system (ABS) components – removal and refitting

Front wheel sensor

Removal

1 Disconnect the battery negative terminal (refer to *Disconnecting the battery* in the Reference Section of this manual).

2 Apply the handbrake, then jack up the front of the vehicle and support securely on axle stands (see *Jacking and vehicle support*). To improve access, remove the relevant roadwheel.

3 Locate the sensor wiring connector, clipped to the front subframe, and then separate the two halves of the connector. Release the wiring from any clips and support brackets **(see illustrations)**.

21.3a Sensor wiring connector – arrowed

21.3b Disconnect the sensor wiring connector

4 The sensor can then be unclipped from the retaining clip/ring on the hub carrier **(see illustration)**.

Refitting

5 Refitting is a reversal of removal, but ensure that the wiring plugs are correctly reconnected and the sensor located in its retaining clip.

Rear wheel sensor

Removal

6 Remove the rear brake disc as described in Section 7.

7 The sensor can then be unclipped from the retaining clip on the hub carrier **(see illustration)**.

8 Trace the sensor wiring back along the rear suspension arm and unclip it from any securing clips, and then separate the two halves of the connector.

Refitting

9 Refitting is a reversal of removal, but ensure that the wiring plugs are correctly reconnected and the sensor located in its retaining clip.

Front wheel sensor ring

10 The sensor ring is part of the wheel bearing, remove and refit the front wheel bearing including sensor retaining ring as described in Chapter 10 **(see illustration)**.

Rear wheel sensor ring

11 The sensor ring is integral with the rear wheel bearing, and cannot be removed separately. Refer to Chapter 10 for details of rear wheel bearing removal and refitting.

Electronically-controlled hydraulic unit

Removal

12 The control unit is located under the left-hand side of the vehicle, in front of the wheel, behind the wheel arch liner **(see illustration)**. To make access easier, remove the front bumper as described in Chapter 11.

13 Disconnect the battery negative terminal (refer to *Disconnecting the battery* in the Reference Section of this manual).

14 To improve access, apply the handbrake, then jack up the front of the vehicle and support securely on axle stands (see *Jacking and vehicle support*).

15 Remove the left-hand front wheel, then undo the securing screws, and withdraw the plastic splash shield to expose the control unit.

16 On diesel models, undo the retaining bolt and remove the pre/post-heating unit from the hydraulic unit mounting bracket **(see illustration)**.

17 Release the securing clip, and disconnect the wiring plug from the side of the electronic control unit **(see illustration)**.

18 Place a suitable container beneath the hydraulic assembly to catch escaping fluid as the pipes are disconnected.

19 Note the locations of the fluid pipes (mark them if necessary), then unscrew the union nuts, and disconnect the six fluid pipes from the hydraulic unit. Unclip the two pipes from the securing clips on the side of the mounting bracket **(see illustration)**.

20 Unscrew the two tie-rod upper mounting bolts and slacken the two front aluminium sidemember mounting bolts **(see illustrations)**. Do not remove the two front sidemember mounting bolts, just slacken them a few turns to allow the sidemember to drop down.

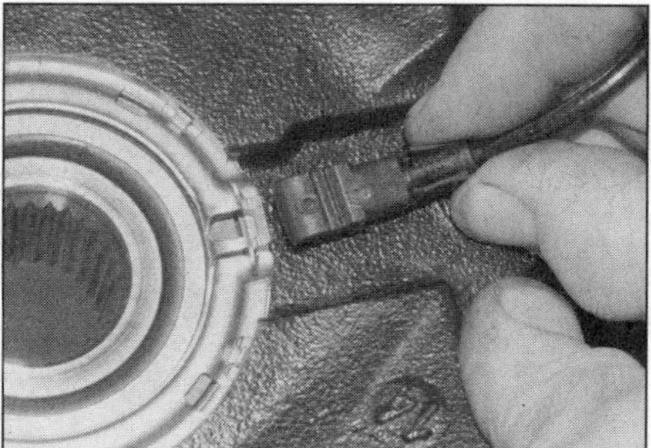

21.4 Disconnect the front wheel sensor from the retaining clip

21.7 Disconnect the rear wheel sensor from the retaining clip

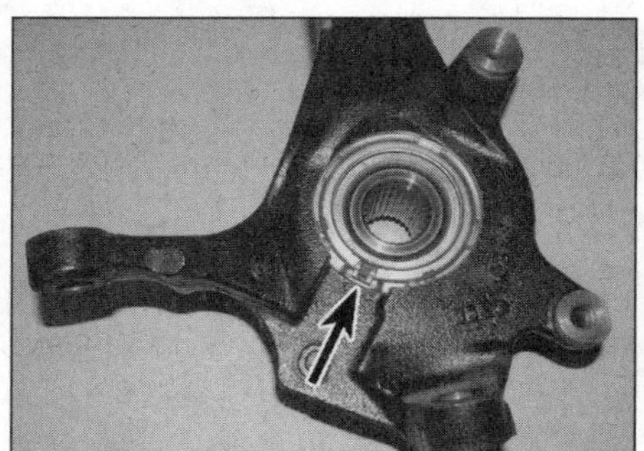

21.10 The sensor and retaining ring (arrowed) are part of the bearing assembly

21.12 Location of the brake hydraulic unit – arrowed

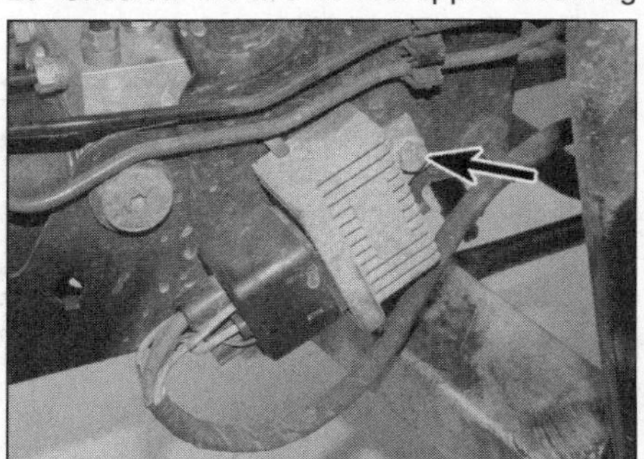

21.16 Undo the retaining bolt – arrowed

21.17 Release the securing clip (arrowed) and disconnect the wiring connector

21.19 Unclip the brake pipes from the clips – arrowed

21.20a Remove the two retaining bolts (arrowed) . . .

21.20b . . . and slacken the two front mounting bolts – arrowed

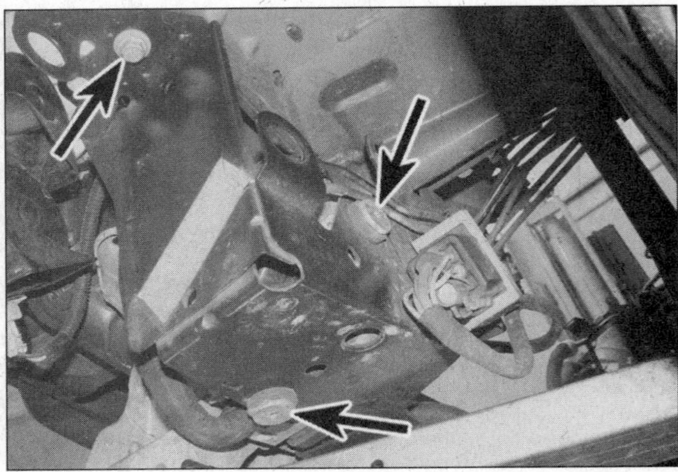
21.21 Undo the brake unit mounting bracket bolts – arrowed

21 Unscrew the mounting bolts securing the ABS control assembly to the body and mounting bracket **(see illustration)**, the number of bolts may vary depending on model.

22 Withdraw the hydraulic unit, and plug or cover the open ends of the pipes and the apertures in the hydraulic unit to prevent dirt entry and further fluid loss.

Caution: Do not attempt to dismantle the hydraulic unit assembly. Overhaul of the unit is a complex job, and should be entrusted to a Renault dealer or brake specialist.

Refitting

23 Refitting is a reversal of removal, bearing in mind the following points.

a) Take great care not to allow dirt to enter the hydraulic circuit as the pipes are reconnected.
b) Ensure that the pipes are reconnected to their correct locations as noted before removal.
c) Ensure that the wiring plug is correctly reconnected.
d) Tighten the electronic control unit securing bolts securely. Do not overtighten the bolts.
e) Before connecting the battery, bleed the complete brake system as described in Section 2.
f) If you have any problems with bleeding the system, have the system checked by a suitably-equipped Renault dealer or brake specialist.

22.6a Disconnect the servo hose from the vacuum pump – 1.9 litre engine

22.6b Disconnect the servo hose from the vacuum pump – 2.2 litre engine

22.7a Remove the pump mounting bolts (arrowed) – 1.9 litre engine

22.7b Removing the vacuum pump – 2.2 litre engine

22 Brake vacuum pump (diesel engine models) – testing, removal and refitting

Testing

Note: *A vacuum gauge will be required.*

1 The operation of the braking system vacuum pump can be checked using a vacuum gauge.

2 Disconnect the vacuum pipe from the pump, and connect the gauge to the pump union using a suitable length of hose.

3 Start the engine and allow it to idle, and then measure the vacuum created by the pump. As a guide, after one minute, a minimum of approximately 500 mm Hg should be recorded. If the vacuum registered is significantly less than this, it is likely that the pump is faulty. However, seek the advice of a Renault dealer before condemning the pump.

Removal

4 Unclip and remove the engine cover.

5 If required, to give better access to the vacuum pump, remove the air intake hoses and intercooler hoses as described in Chapter 4B.

6 Squeeze together the tabs on the hose end fitting, and disconnect the vacuum hose from the pump **(see illustrations)**.

7 Slacken and remove the two mounting bolts securing the pump to the end of the cylinder head **(see illustrations)**, then remove the pump. Recover the pump gasket/O-ring seal and discard it; a new one should be used on refitting.

Refitting

8 Ensure that the pump and cylinder head mating surfaces are clean and dry, and fit the new gasket/O-ring seal to the head **(see illustrations)**.

9 Manoeuvre the pump into position aligning the drive dog with the slot in the end of the camshaft. Refit the pump to the cylinder head, ensuring that the gasket/O-ring remains correctly seated, then refit the pump mounting bolts and tighten them securely.

10 Reconnect the vacuum hose to the pump, making sure that it is securely clipped into position.

11 If removed, refit the air intake hose and intercooler hoses, as described in Chapter 4B. Refit the engine cover.

12 On completion, check the operation of the brakes.

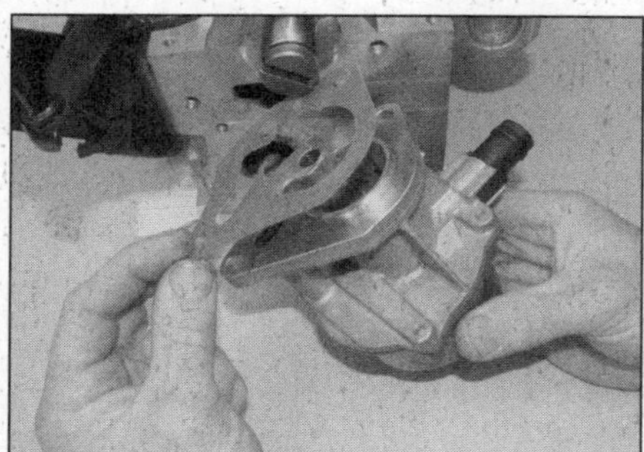

22.8a Fit new gasket when refitting the vacuum pump – 1.9 litre engine

22.8b Fit new O-ring seal when refitting the vacuum pump – 2.2 litre engine

Notes

Chapter 10
Suspension and steering

Contents

Section number

Degrees of difficulty

Easy, suitable for novice with little experience 	**Fairly easy,** suitable for beginner with some experience	**Fairly difficult,** suitable for competent DIY mechanic	**Difficult,** suitable for experienced DIY mechanic	**Very difficult,** suitable for expert DIY or professional

Specifications

Front suspension

Type	Independent, by MacPherson struts, with coil springs and integral shock absorbers. Anti-roll bar fitted to all models
Hub bearing free play	0 to 0.05 mm

Rear suspension

Type	Semi-independent 'flexible' beam axle, telescopic shock absorbers and separate coil springs. Rear anti-roll bars on all models
Hub bearing free play	0 to 0.05 mm

Steering

Type	Rack-and-pinion with collapsible safety column. Variable hydraulic power steering fitted to all models

Wheel alignment

Front wheel toe-setting	0°10' ± 10' (1.0 ± 1.0 mm) toe-in

Torque wrench settings

	Nm	lbf ft
Front suspension		
Aluminium sidemembers	44	32
Aluminium sidemembers tie-rod bolts	44	32
Anti-roll bar clamp bolts	21	15
Anti-roll bar drop link nuts	44	32
Driveshaft nut	280	207
Front subframe mounting bolts	105	77
Lower arm balljoint nut	110	81
Lower arm-to-subframe mounting bolts	180	133
Suspension strut piston rod nut	62	46
Suspension strut-to-hub carrier nuts and bolts	180	133
Suspension strut upper mounting bolts	21	15
Tie-rod between subframe and body:		
Subframe bolt	105	77
Body bolt	62	46
Rear suspension		
Axle mounting bolts	80	59
Hub nut	280	207
Shock absorber securing bolts (upper and lower)	105	77
Stub axle securing bolts	105	77
Steering		
Steering column intermediate shaft-to-steering gear pinion clamp bolt and nut	21	15
Steering column securing mounting nuts	21	15
Steering pump and support bracket mounting bolts	21	15
Steering rack/gear securing nuts	180	133
Steering wheel securing bolt	44	32
Track rod end balljoint-to-hub carrier nut	37	27
Track rod end clamp bolt	20	15
Track rod inner balljoint	50	37
Roadwheels		
Roadwheel bolts	105	77

1 General information

The independent front suspension is of the MacPherson strut type, incorporating coil springs and integral telescopic shock absorbers. The MacPherson struts are located by transverse lower suspension arms, which utilise rubber inner mounting bushes and incorporate a balljoint at the outer ends. The front hub carriers, which carry the wheel bearings, brake calipers and the hub/disc assemblies, are bolted to the MacPherson struts and connected to the lower arms via the balljoints. A front anti-roll bar is fitted to all models. The anti-roll bar is rubber-mounted onto the subframe, and connects both the suspension struts.

The rear suspension consists of a semi-independent 'flexible' beam axle, also known as an H axle, telescopic shock absorbers and separate coil springs. Rear anti-roll bars on all models.

The steering column is connected by a universal joint to an integral intermediate shaft, which has a second universal joint at its lower end. The lower universal joint is attached to the steering gear pinion by means of a clamp bolt and nut.

The steering gear is mounted onto the front subframe. It is connected by two track rods and balljoints to steering arms projecting rearwards from the hub carriers. The track rod ends are threaded to enable wheel alignment adjustment.

Power-assisted steering is fitted as standard on all models. The power steering pump is belt-driven from the crankshaft pulley.

2 Front hub assembly - removal and refitting

Note: *A new driveshaft nut will be required on refitting, and all Nyloc-type self-locking nuts should be renewed. A balljoint separator tool will be required for this operation.*

Removal

1 Apply the handbrake, then jack up the front of the vehicle and support securely on axle stands (see *Jacking and vehicle support*).

2 It is advisable to remove the ABS wheel sensor, as described in Chapter 9, to avoid any possibility of damage during the removal procedure.

3 If the driveshaft nut has been loosened, proceed to paragraph 5, otherwise proceed as follows.

4 Refit at least two roadwheel bolts to the front hub, and tighten them securely. Have an assistant firmly depress the brake pedal to prevent the front hub from rotating then, using a socket and a long extension bar, slacken the driveshaft retaining nut. Alternatively, a tool can be fabricated from two lengths of steel strip (one long, one short) and a nut and bolt; the nut and bolt forming the pivot of a forked tool. Bolt the tool to the hub using two wheel bolts, and hold the tool to prevent the hub from rotating as the driveshaft retaining nut is undone **(see illustration)**. This nut is very tight; make sure that there is no risk of pulling the car off the axle stands. (If the roadwheel

2.4 Using a fabricated tool to hold the front hub stationary whilst the driveshaft retaining nut is slackened

2.7 Using a balljoint splitter on the track rod arm

2.8 Tapping out the upper suspension strut-to-hub carrier bolt

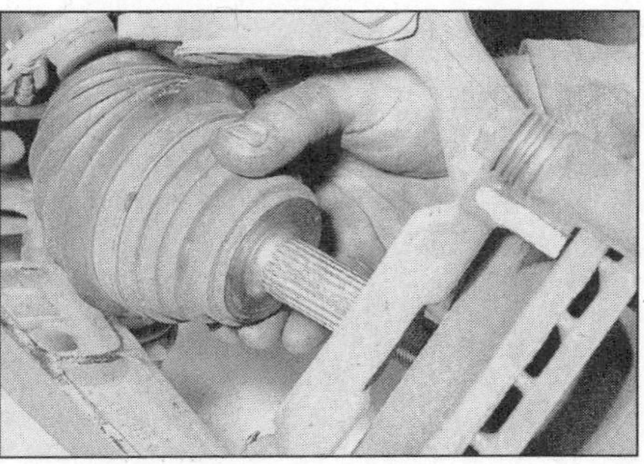

2.12 Releasing the end of the driveshaft from the hub carrier

trim allows access to the driveshaft nut, the initial slackening can be done with the wheels chocked and on the ground.)

5 If the hub bearings are to be disturbed, remove the brake disc as described in Chapter 9. If not, unbolt the brake caliper and move it to one side, as described in Chapter 9. Note that there is no need to disconnect the fluid hose – tie the caliper to the front suspension coil spring, using a piece of wire or string to avoid straining the brake hose.

6 Slacken and partially unscrew the lower arm balljoint nut (unscrew the nut as far as the end of the threads on the balljoint to prevent damage to the threads as the joint is released), then release the balljoint using a balljoint separator tool. Remove the nut and discard it – a new nut must be used on refitting.

7 Similarly, release the balljoint and disconnect the track rod from the steering arm on the hub carrier **(see illustration)**.

8 Unscrew the nut from the upper suspension strut-to-hub carrier bolt as far as the end of the bolt threads, then tap the end of the bolt (using the nut to protect the threads) to release the splines from the hub carrier. Withdraw the bolt, and discard the nut – a new nut must be used on refitting **(see illustration)**.

9 Similarly, unscrew the lower suspension strut-to-hub carrier nut, and tap the bolt to free the splines from the hub carrier. Do not remove the bolt at this stage.

10 Unscrew the driveshaft nut from the end of the driveshaft. Recover the washer. Discard the nut – a new one must be used on refitting.

11 The driveshaft must now be released from the hub carrier. It should be possible to release the driveshaft by tapping the end of the driveshaft using a soft-faced hammer, or a hammer and a soft metal drift – **do not** strike the end of the driveshaft hard, as this may cause damage to the joints.

12 Pull the hub assembly from the lower arm balljoint, and tilt it until the splined end of the driveshaft can be released from it **(see illustration)**.

13 Support the end of the driveshaft by suspending it using wire or string – do not allow the end of the driveshaft to hang down under its own weight, as this may damage the CV joints.

14 Remove the lower suspension strut-to-hub carrier bolt, and withdraw the hub carrier.

Refitting

15 Thoroughly clean the hub assembly end of the driveshaft and the splines in the hub.

16 Coat the hub end of the driveshaft with grease (Renault recommend the use of Molykote BR2), then engage the end of the driveshaft with the hub.

17 Refit the lower suspension strut-to-hub assembly bolt (noting that the bolts fits from the front of the vehicle), and screw a new nut onto the bolt. Do not tap the bolt into position or screw the nut fully onto the bolt at this stage.

18 Reconnect the lower arm balljoint to the hub assembly, making sure the balljoint shield is in place first **(see illustration)**.

19 Fit a new balljoint nut and tighten to the specified torque, an Allen key can be used to hold the balljoint in position **(see illustration)**.

20 Screw the **new** driveshaft nut onto the end of the driveshaft as far as possible by hand, ensuring that the washer is in place, and then tighten the nut until the end of the driveshaft is fully engaged with the hub. Do not fully tighten the nut at this stage.

21 Refit the upper suspension strut-to-hub carrier bolt (noting that the bolts fits from the front of the vehicle), and screw a new nut onto the bolt. Tap the upper and lower bolts into position to engage the splines with the hub carrier, and then tighten the upper and lower suspension strut-to-hub carrier nuts to the specified torque.

22 Reconnect the track rod end to the hub carrier, and tighten a new balljoint nut to the specified torque.

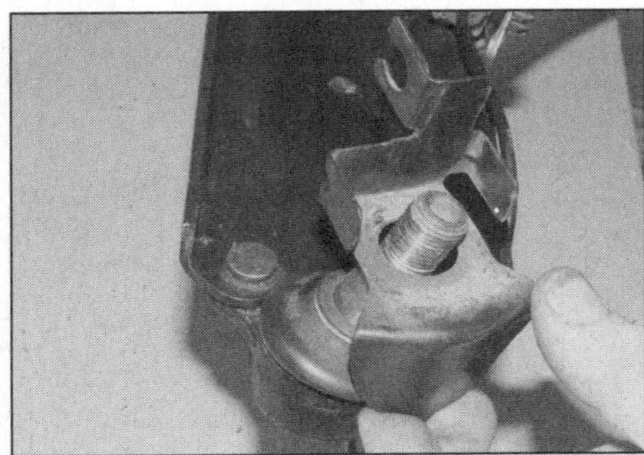

2.18 Make sure the balljoint shield is fitted

23 Where applicable, refit the brake disc, and then refit the brake caliper, with reference to Chapter 9.

24 Use the method employed on removal to prevent the hub from rotating, and tighten the driveshaft retaining nut to the specified torque. Check that the hub rotates freely.

25 Where applicable, refit the ABS wheel sensor, with reference to Chapter 9.

26 Refit the roadwheel, then lower the vehicle to the ground and tighten the roadwheel bolts to the specified torque.

3 Front hub bearing – checking and renewal

Note: *The bearing is a sealed, pre-adjusted and prelubricated, double-row ball type, and is intended to last the car's entire service life without maintenance or attention. Do not attempt to remove the bearing unless absolutely necessary, as it will be damaged during the removal operation. Never overtighten the driveshaft nut in an attempt to 'adjust' the bearing.*

Note: *A press will be required to dismantle and rebuild the assembly; if such a tool is not available, a large bench vice and suitable spacers (such as large sockets) will serve as an adequate substitute. The bearing's inner races are an interference fit on the hub; if the inner race remains on the hub when it is pressed out of the hub carrier, a suitable knife-edged bearing puller will be required to remove it.*

2.19 Using an Allen key to counter-hold the balljoint

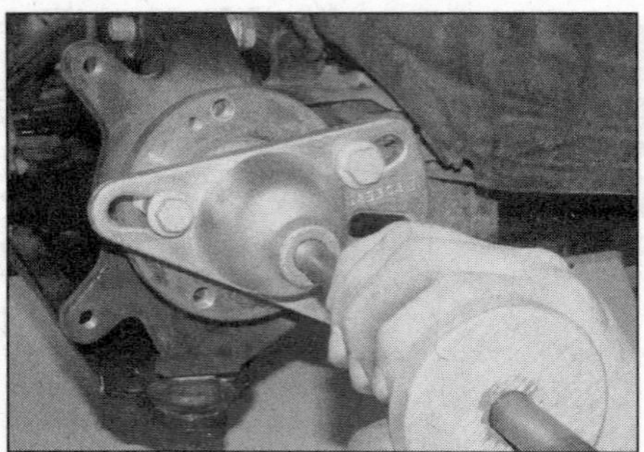

3.6a Using a slide hammer . . .

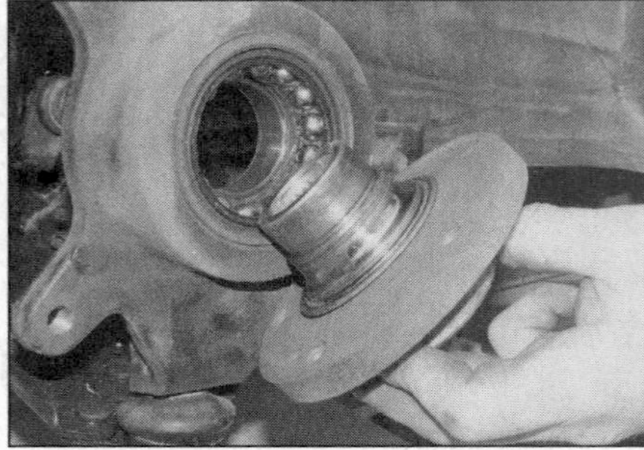

3.6b . . . to withdraw the hub flange

3.8 Using a press to remove the bearing from the hub

Checking

1 Wear in the front hub bearings can be checked for as described in Chapter 1A or 1B. However, the most common first symptom of bearing wear is a rumbling noise, noted at a particular roadspeed, or when the offending wheel is loaded-up during cornering. In this case, besides rocking the wheel, spin it and listen carefully, to distinguish between the sound of the brake pads rubbing the disc, and the rumble of bearing wear. Compare the sound with the other front wheel to confirm.

2 Wheel bearings do not have to be renewed in pairs. However, if the bearing on one side has worn, it may only be a short while before the other one needs renewal.

Renewal

Note: *A new driveshaft nut will be required on refitting, and all Nyloc-type self-locking nuts should be renewed. A balljoint separator tool will be required for this operation.*

3 Apply the handbrake, then jack up the front of the vehicle and support securely on axle stands (see *Jacking and vehicle support*). Remove the appropriate front wheel.

4 Refit at least two roadwheel bolts to the front hub, and tighten them securely. Have an assistant firmly depress the brake pedal to prevent the front hub from rotating then, using a socket and a long extension bar, slacken and remove the driveshaft retaining nut. Alternatively, a tool can be fabricated from two lengths of steel strip (one long, one short) and a nut and bolt; the nut and bolt forming the pivot of a forked tool. Bolt the tool to the hub using two wheel bolts, and hold the tool to prevent the hub from rotating as the driveshaft retaining nut is undone **(see illustration 2.4)**. This nut is very tight; make sure that there is no risk of pulling the car off the axle stands. (If the roadwheel trim allows access to the driveshaft nut, the initial slackening can be done with the wheels chocked and on the ground.)

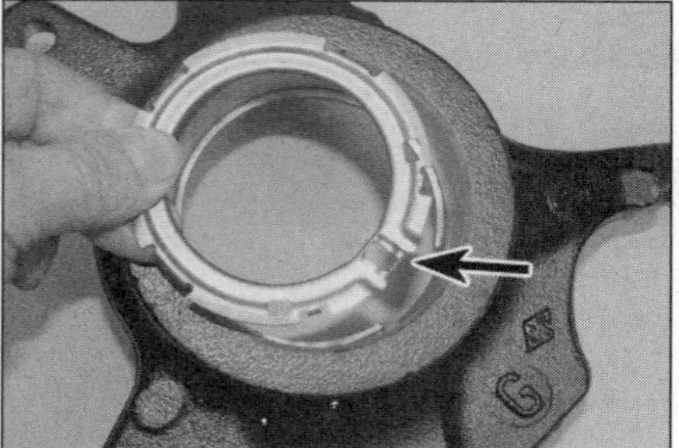

3.10 Align the ABS sensor retaining clip (arrowed) correctly

3.11 Plastic cover to protect the ABS magnetic ring

3.12 Using a press to fit the bearing into the hub carrier

3.13 Using a press to refit the flange into the bearing/hub carrier

5 Remove the brake disc as described in Chapter 9.

6 Fit a slide hammer/puller onto the hub flange and pull the hub flange out of the bearing **(see illustrations)**. If the bearing outboard inner race remains on the hub, remove it using a suitable bearing puller (see note above).

7 Remove the remainder of the hub carrier as described in Section 2, paragraphs 6 to 14.

8 Securely support the face of the hub carrier. Using a suitable tubular spacer, which bears only on the inner race of the bearing, press the complete bearing out of the housing in the hub carrier **(see illustration)**.

9 Thoroughly clean the hub and hub carrier, removing all traces of dirt and grease. Polish away any burrs or raised edges which might hinder reassembly. Check for cracks or any other signs of wear or damage, and renew the components if necessary. As noted above, the bearing must be renewed whenever they are disturbed. A bearing kit, which consists of the bearing and ABS sensor ring is available from Renault dealers.

10 Fit the new ABS sensor-retaining ring, making sure it is fitted the correct way around and the sensor-retaining clip is in the correct direction **(see illustration)**.

11 On reassembly, check that the new bearing is not damaged; the bearing has a magnetic ring on the inner side to operate the ABS sensor and is packed with a plastic cover to protect it **(see illustration)**. Remove the plastic cover and apply a light film of oil to the bearing outer race and to the hub flange shaft.

Caution: When fitting the bearing, take care not to damage the magnetic sensor ring built into the inner face of the bearing.

12 Securely support the hub carrier, and locate the bearing in its housing. Press the bearing into position, ensuring that it enters the housing squarely, using a suitable tubular spacer which bears only on the outer race. Press the bearing into position until it contacts the shoulder in the hub carrier **(see illustration)**. **Note:** *Make sure the ABS sensor retaining ring has not moved before completely pressing the bearing home.*

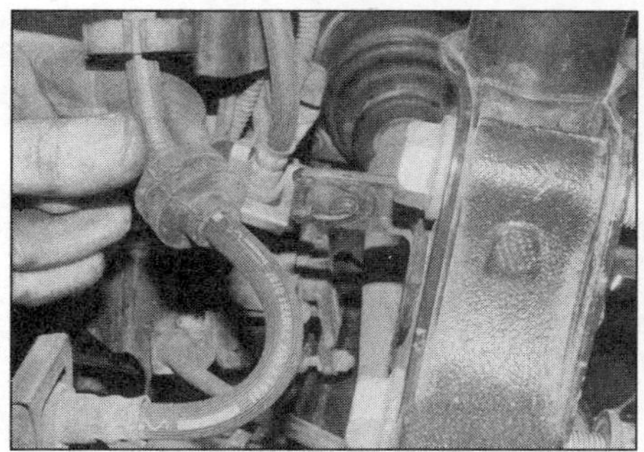

4.2 Unclipping the brake hose from the strut

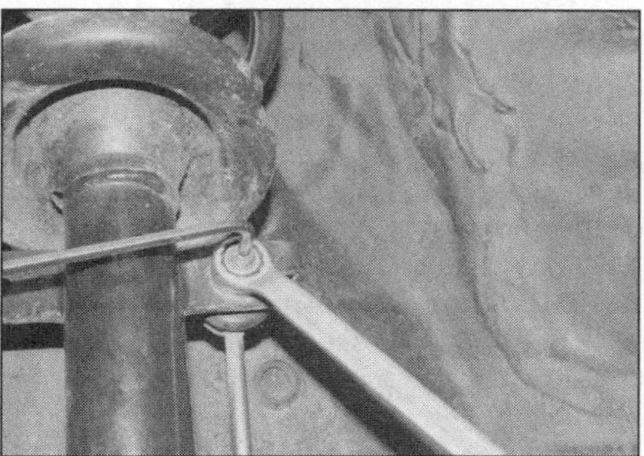

4.3 Unscrewing the anti-roll bar drop link-to-suspension strut nut

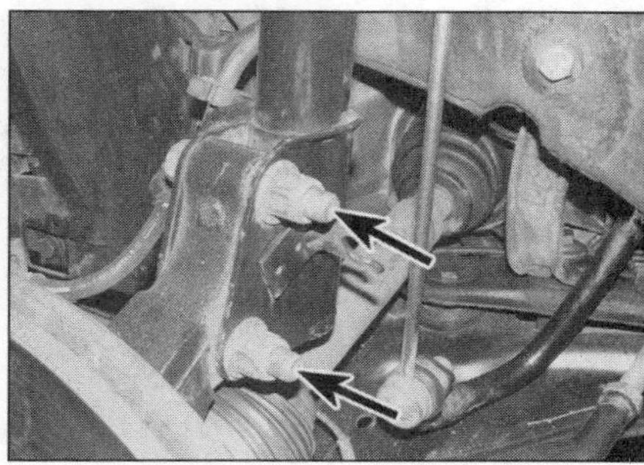

4.4 Strut lower mounting bolts – arrowed

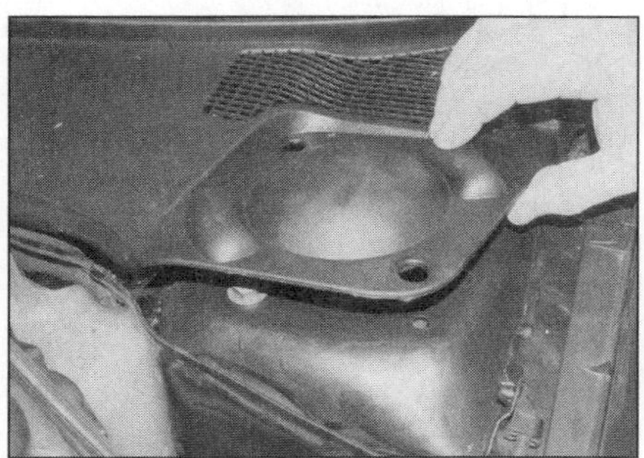

4.5 Remove the plastic trim cover

4.6 Remove the centre retaining nut and the outer mounting bolts – arrowed

13 Securely support the hub carrier and support the bearing inner race from underneath (taking care not to damage the ABS sensor retaining ring) and press the hub flange into the hub carrier/bearing. Press the flange down until the bearing seats against the face of the flange **(see illustration)**. Check that the hub flange rotates freely. Wipe off any excess oil or grease.

14 Refit the hub carrier as described in Section 2.

4 Front suspension strut – removal, overhaul and refitting

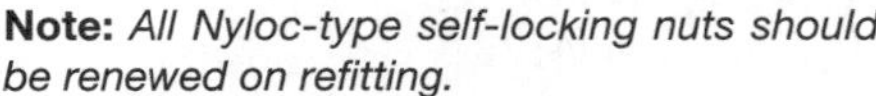

Note: *All Nyloc-type self-locking nuts should be renewed on refitting.*

Removal

1 Apply the handbrake, then jack up the front of the vehicle and support it securely on axle stands (see *Jacking and vehicle support*). Remove the appropriate roadwheel.

2 Unclip the brake fluid pipe and the brake pad wear indicator wiring from the brackets at the lower end of the suspension strut **(see illustration)**. Similarly, release the ABS sensor wiring from its clips on the suspension strut.

3 Unscrew the nut securing the anti-roll bar drop link to the suspension strut – if necessary, the drop link pin can be counter-held using an Allen key. Discard the nut – a new one must be used on refitting **(see illustration)**.

4 Unscrew the nut from the upper suspension strut-to-hub carrier bolt as far as the end of the bolt threads, then tap the end of the bolt (using the nut to protect the threads) to release the splines from the hub carrier **(see illustration)**. Withdraw the bolt, and discard the nut – a new nut must be used on refitting. Repeat the procedure on the lower suspension strut-to-hub carrier bolt, and then support the hub carrier with an axle stand, to prevent putting a strain on the driveshaft.

5 From within the engine compartment, release the securing clips and remove the plastic trim cover **(see illustration).**

6 Unscrew the centre retaining nut and upper rubber stop, then undo the two outer mounting bolts securing the strut upper mounting to the turret **(see illustration)**. Support the strut as the bolts are removed, to prevent it from dropping.

7 Release the strut from the stub axle carrier, and withdraw it from under the wheel arch, take care not to damage the driveshaft gaiter.

8 Once the strut has been removed, make sure the hub carrier is supported to prevent damage to the driveshaft.

Overhaul

Note: *Spring compressor tools will be required for this operation.*

9 With the strut removed from the car, clean away all external dirt then mount the strut upright in a vice.

10 Fit the spring compressor tool and compress the coil spring until all tension is relieved from the upper mounting **(see illustration)**.

11 Where applicable, withdraw the plastic cap from the piston rod nut, then counter-hold the piston rod with an Allen key or a hexagon bit, and unscrew the nut with a ring spanner.

12 Note the orientation and location of all components to aid refitting.

13 Lift off the washer, upper mounting, and spring seat assembly.

14 Lift off the spring and compressor tool. Do not remove the tool from the spring unless the spring is to be renewed.

15 Remove the convoluted dust cover/gaiter, bump stop, and the lower spring seat and bearing components.

16 With the strut assembly now completely dismantled, examine all the components for wear, damage or deformation and check the bearing for smoothness of operation. Renew any of the components as necessary.

17 Examine the strut for signs of fluid leakage. Check the strut piston rod for signs of pitting along its entire length and check the strut body for signs of damage or elongation of the mounting bolt holes. Test the operation of the strut, while holding it in an upright position, by moving the piston rod through a full stroke and then through short strokes of 50 to 100 mm. In both cases the resistance felt should be smooth and continuous. If the resistance is jerky, or uneven, or if there is any visible sign of wear or damage to the strut, renewal is necessary.

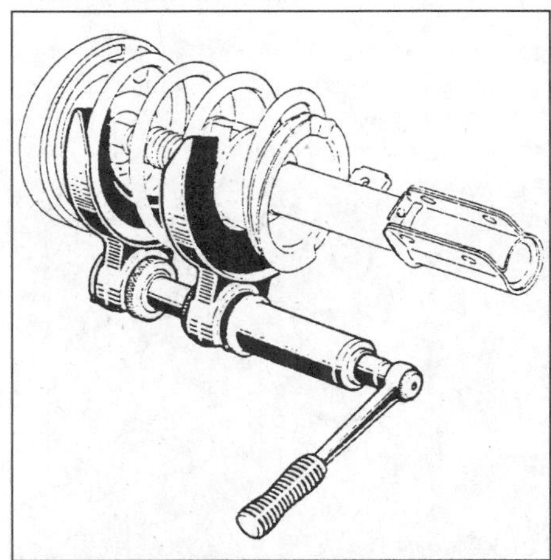

4.10 Spring compressor tool in position on the suspension strut coil spring

5.2 Lower arm mounting bolts (arrowed) – accessed from the top of the subframe

18 If any doubt exists about the condition of the coil spring, gradually release the spring compressor, and check the spring for distortion and signs of cracking. Since Renault specifies no minimum free length, the only way to check the tension of the spring is to compare it to a new component. Renew the spring if it is damaged or distorted, or if there is any doubt as to its condition.

19 Inspect all other components for signs of damage or deterioration, and renew any that are suspect.

20 Reassembly is a reversal of dismantling, bearing in mind the following points.

a) *If a new strut is being fitted, prime the strut before refitting the spring, by compressing and extending the piston rod several times.*
b) *Ensure that all components are correctly orientated and positioned, as noted before dismantling.*
c) *Make sure that the spring ends are correctly located in the upper and lower seats.*
d) *Tighten the piston rod nut to the specified torque.*

Refitting

21 Manoeuvre the strut assembly into position, taking care not damage the driveshaft gaiter. Ensure that the locating pins on the top mounting engage with the corresponding holes in the turret.

22 Refit the bolts and nut securing the upper mounting to the turret, but do not fully tighten them at this stage.

23 Engage the hub carrier with the lower end of the strut, taking care not to damage the driveshaft gaiter, then insert the two hub carrier-to-suspension strut mounting bolts from the front side of the strut. Tap the bolts into position to engage the splines with the hub carrier, and then fit the new nuts to the rear of the bolts, and tighten them to the specified torque.

24 Tighten the strut upper mounting bolts and centre retaining nut to the specified torque, then refit the plastic cover trim to the top of the strut.

25 Reconnect the anti-roll bar drop link to the suspension strut, then fit a new nut and tighten to the specified torque (again, counter-hold the drop link pin if necessary).

26 Clip the wiring and the brake pipe into the appropriate brackets on the strut.

27 Refit the roadwheel, then lower the vehicle to the ground and tighten the roadwheel bolts to the specified torque.

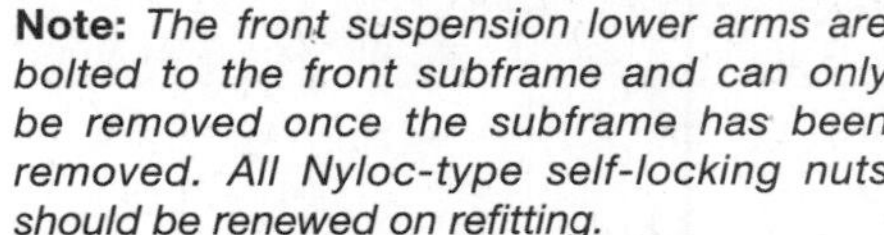

5 Front suspension lower arm – removal, overhaul and refitting

Note: *The front suspension lower arms are bolted to the front subframe and can only be removed once the subframe has been removed. All Nyloc-type self-locking nuts should be renewed on refitting.*

Removal

1 Remove the front subframe as described in Section 7.

2 Working at the inner end of the lower arms, loosen the bolts securing the lower arm to the subframe. If necessary, counter-hold the nuts **(see illustration)**.

3 Withdraw the securing bolts, and nuts (recover the locking plates if they are loose), and manipulate the lower arm out from the subframe.

Overhaul

4 At the time of writing, no lower arm components were available separately. If the bushes or lower balljoint are worn, a complete new arm should be fitted. Check with a Renault dealer or reputable motor factors to see whether this is still the case, as repair kits may become available over time.

Refitting

5 Manipulate the lower arm into position then fit the new mounting nuts and bolts. Where applicable, ensure that the locking plates are in position under the mounting nuts Tighten the bolts to the specified torque.

6 Refit the front subframe as described in Section 7.

6 Front anti-roll bar components – removal and refitting

Anti-roll bar

Note: *The front anti-roll bar is bolted to the top of the front subframe and can only be accessed once the subframe has been lowered by approximately 20 cm. All Nyloc-type self-locking nuts should be renewed on refitting.*

Removal

1 Lower the front subframe, follow the procedure for removing the front subframe as described in Section 7. There should be no need to disconnect the power steering pipes and wiring. As the subframe is lowered, check for any cables, pipes or hoses that may get damaged.

2 Unscrew the four bolts securing the two anti-roll bar clamps to the subframe.

3 Remove the anti-roll bar from the subframe.

Refitting

4 Refitting is a reversal of removal, but renew any Nyloc-type self-locking nuts, and tighten all fixings to the specified torque.

Drop link

Note: *New drop link securing nuts should be used on refitting.*

Removal

5 Apply the handbrake, then jack up the front of the car and support it on axle stands (see *Jacking and vehicle support*). If desired, remove the roadwheel to improve access.

6 Slacken and remove the upper and lower drop link securing nuts, and withdraw the drop link. If necessary, counter-hold the drop link pins using an Allen key **(see illustrations)**.

7 Examine the link for signs of damage or wear, paying particular attention to the

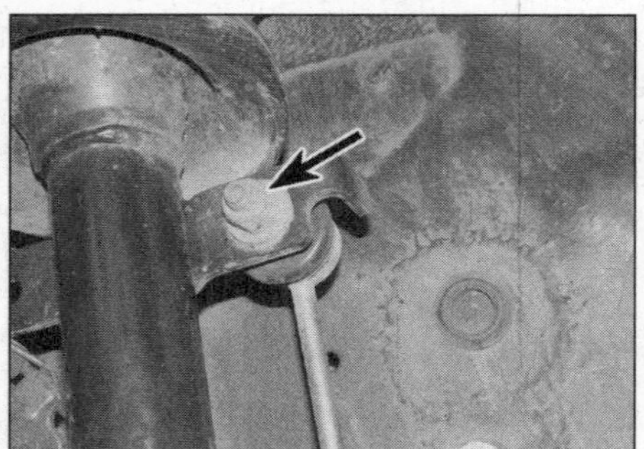

6.6a Remove the upper balljoint securing nut (arrowed) . . .

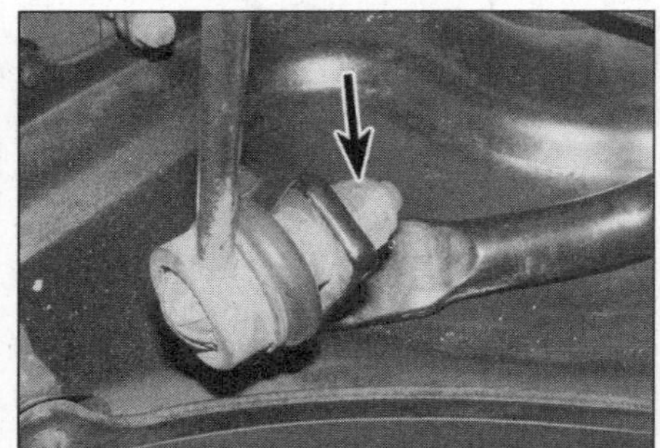

6.6b . . . and the lower balljoint securing nut – arrowed

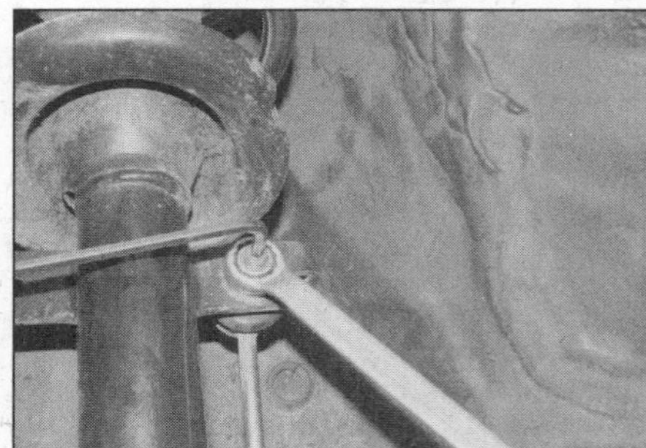

6.6c Using an Allen key to counter-hold the balljoint

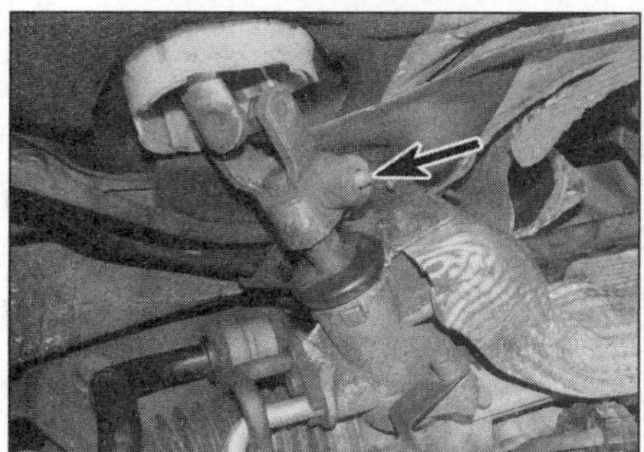
7.4 Remove the steering column lower pinch-bolt – arrowed

7.6 Undo the drop-links lower mounting nut – arrowed

7.9 Unscrew the through-bolt (arrowed) securing the rear engine mounting to the subframe

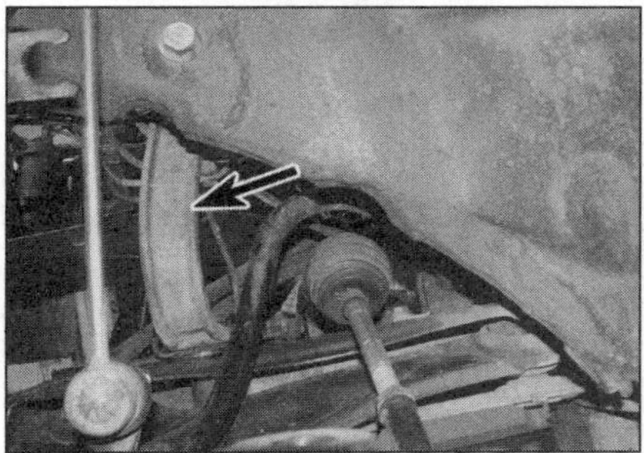
7.10 Remove the subframe tie-rods – left-hand side arrowed

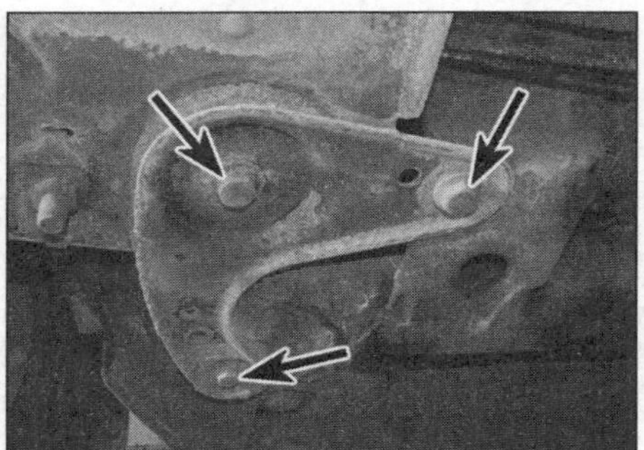
7.12 Undo the bracing plate/subframe mounting bolts – arrowed

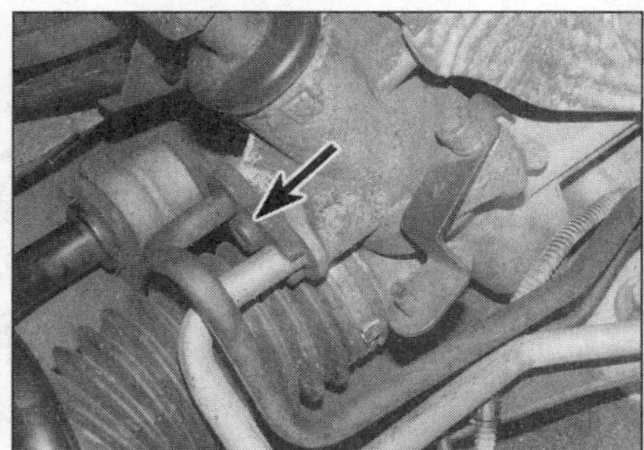
7.15 Undo the power steering pipe retaining bolt – arrowed

balljoints. It is not possible to renew the bushes independently, and if the balljoints are worn, the complete link must be renewed.

Refitting

8 Refitting is a reversal of removal, but use new securing nuts, and tighten the nuts to the specified torque.

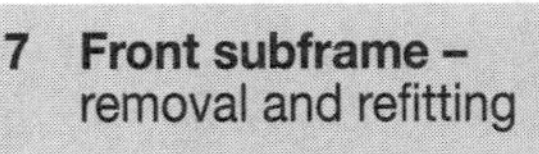

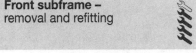

7 Front subframe – removal and refitting

Note: *New subframe securing bolts must be used on refitting. All Nyloc-type self-locking nuts should be renewed on refitting. A balljoint separator tool will be required for this operation.*

Removal

1 Apply the handbrake, then jack up the front of the vehicle and support it securely on axle stands (see *Jacking and vehicle support*). Remove the roadwheels.

2 Disconnect the battery negative terminal (refer to *Disconnecting the battery* in the Reference Section of this manual).

3 Fit clamps to the power steering fluid hoses as close as possible to the fluid reservoir. This will help to minimise fluid loss during subsequent operations.

4 Unscrew the steering column-to-steering gear pinion pinch-bolt and nut **(see illustration)**.

5 Remove the track rod ends as described in Section 20.

6 Working on each side of the vehicle in turn, unscrew the nuts securing the anti-roll bar drop links to the anti-roll bar **(see illustration)**. If necessary, counter-hold the drop link pins using an Allen key.

7 Again working on each side of the vehicle, slacken and partially unscrew the lower arm balljoint nut (unscrew the nut as far as the end of the threads on the balljoint to prevent damage to the threads as the joint is released), then release the balljoint using a balljoint separator tool. Remove the nut, and discard it – a new nut must be used on refitting.

8 Release the ABS sensor wiring from any clips on the lower arm and subframe. Note the routing of the wiring to aid refitting.

9 Working under the vehicle, unscrew the through-bolt and nut securing the rear engine mounting to the subframe **(see illustration)**.

10 Position a jack under the centre of the subframe, and raise the jack to support the subframe. Undo the mounting bolts and remove the tie-rods from each side of the subframe **(see illustration)**.

11 Unscrew the securing bolts, and remove the aluminium sidemembers from each side of the vehicle.

12 Unscrew the securing bolts, and remove the bracing plates from the rear of the subframe **(see illustration)**.

13 Loosen the subframe bolts, and lower the subframe slightly (supporting with the jack), release any pipes or wiring from along the top of the subframe.

14 Reach up above the steering gear, and check the steering column lower joint is disengaging from the steering rack. Disconnect any sensor wiring connector and/or the variable power steering solenoid wiring connectors from the steering rack.

15 Place a container beneath the steering gear, then unscrew the retaining bolt/plate and disconnect the fluid pipes from the steering gear **(see illustration)**. Be prepared for some fluid spillage as the pipes are disconnected, and plug the pipe and steering gear openings to minimise fluid loss and to prevent the entry of dirt into the system. Unclip the power steering pipes from the retaining clips.

16 Ensure that the subframe is adequately supported, then unscrew the securing bolts completely, lower the subframe on the jack and withdraw the assembly, complete with the steering gear, from under the vehicle. **Note:** *When lowering the subframe, take care not to damage the brake pipes.*

Refitting

17 Refitting is a reversal of removal, bearing in mind the following points.

a) If the steering gear has been removed from the subframe, refit it with reference to Section 16.
b) Use new subframe securing bolts, and tighten all fixings to the specified torque.
c) Ensure that all wiring is correctly routed as noted before removal.
d) Use new lower arm balljoint nuts, and renew any Nyloc-type self-locking nuts disturbed during the removal procedure.
e) Refit the track rod ends (see Section 20).
f) Ensure that the steering column lower joint is securely attached to the pinion housing on the steering gear.
g) On completion, bleed the power steering

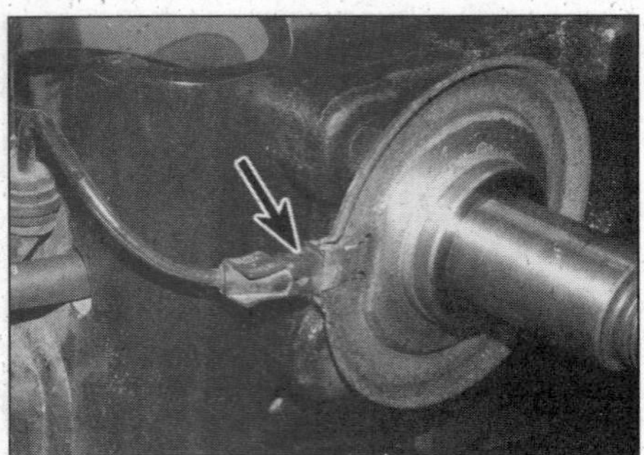

8.2 Disconnect the speed sensor (arrowed) from the retaining clip

hydraulic system as described in Section 18, and check the front wheel alignment as described in Section 21.

8 Rear stub axle assembly – removal and refitting

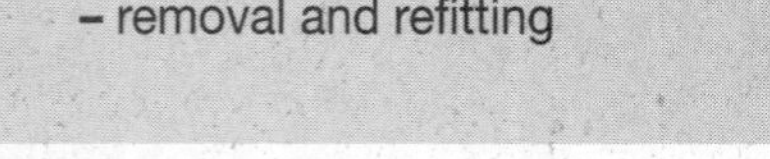

Note: *A new rear hub nut will be required on refitting.*

Removal

1 Remove the rear brake disc as described in Chapter 9.

2 Disconnect the wheel sensor from the retaining clip on the bearing shield on the stub axle **(see illustration)**.

3 Undo the four mounting bolts at the rear of the stub axle and remove the stub axle from the rear axle.

Refitting

4 Refitting is a reversal of removal. For further information, see Chapter 9 for refitting the rear brake disc.

9 Rear hub bearings – checking and renewal

Note: *The bearing is a sealed, pre-adjusted and prelubricated, double-row ball type, and is intended to last the car's entire service life without maintenance or attention. Do not attempt to remove the bearing unless absolutely necessary, as it will be damaged during the removal operation. Never overtighten the hub nut in an attempt to 'adjust' the bearing. A press will be required to remove the bearing; if such a tool is not available, a large bench vice and suitable spacers (such as large sockets) will serve as an adequate substitute.*

Checking

1 Wear in the rear hub bearings can be checked for as described in Chapter 1A or 1B. However, the most common first symptom of bearing wear is a rumbling noise, noted at a particular roadspeed, or when the offending wheel is loaded-up during cornering. In this case, besides rocking the wheel, spin it and listen carefully, to distinguish between the sound of the brake pads rubbing the disc, and the rumble of bearing wear. Compare the sound with the other rear wheel to confirm.

2 Wheel bearings do not have to be renewed in pairs. However, if the bearing on one side has worn, it may only be a short while before the other one needs renewal.

Removal

3 Remove the rear brake disc as described in Chapter 9. **Note:** *New rear discs supplied by Renault dealers may come with new wheel bearings already fitted, but wheel bearing kits should also be available. Check for the availability of parts before stripping.*

4 To remove the bearing, the retaining circlip must first be removed, which requires the use of a sturdy pair of circlip pliers **(see illustrations)**. A new circlip should be used when refitting – one is usually supplied in the bearing kits supplied by Renault dealers.

5 Care must be taken during bearing renewal, as there is a magnetic (reluctor) ring fitted to the rear of the disc which must not be damaged. Mount the disc over the open jaws of a sturdy bench vice, with the magnetic ring facing upwards **(see illustration)**.

6 After applying a generous amount of spray lubricant, we were able to pull the bearing out, using two blocks of wood, together with a large nut and bolt, and several washers/ spacers **(see illustration)**.

7 Tighten the nut and bolt to apply pressure to the bearing – this, and a few hammer blows, should be enough to get the bearing moving, and extract it **(see illustration)**.

Refitting

8 Using emery paper, clean off any burrs or raised edges from the hub, which might stop the components going back together – take

9.4a Insert a pair of circlip pliers into the holes . . .

9.4b . . . then compress the circlip to remove

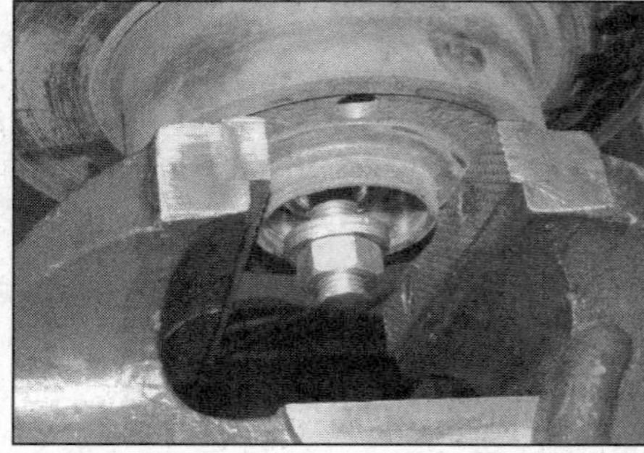

9.5 Mount the disc over the open jaws of a vice . . .

9.6 . . . then fit a large bolt, nut, spacers and two blocks of wood . . .

9.7 . . . to extract the bearing

9.8a Clean off any burrs from the bearing location

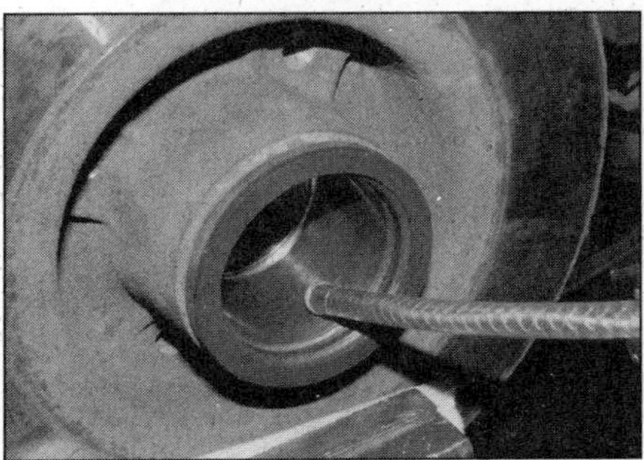
9.8b Lightly oil the bearing location

9.9a Offer the bearing into place . . .

9.9b . . . then tap it gently to start it into the hub

9.10a Fit the same nut, bolt and spacers used for removal . . .

9.10b . . . then tighten the nut/bolt to press the bearing into place

9.11 Fit the new bearing retaining circlip

care not to damage the magnetic ring. Clean and lightly lubricate the bearing location in the hub **(see illustrations)**.

9 Offer the bearing into position, and using a suitable spacer, tap it gently around its edge to start it squarely into the disc/hub **(see illustrations)**.

10 Using the same nut/bolt and spacers as for removal, tighten the nut and bolt to press the bearing into place **(see illustrations)**.

11 The bearing is fully seated when the circlip groove is visible. Fit the new circlip using suitable circlip pliers to retain the bearing **(see illustration)**.

12 Refit the brake disc as described in Chapter 9.

10 Rear shock absorber – removal, testing and refitting

Removal

1 Chock the front wheels and engage reverse gear (or P on automatic transmission models). Jack up the rear of the vehicle and support it securely on axle stands (see *Jacking and vehicle support*). Remove the appropriate rear roadwheel.

2 Using a jack, raise the trailing arm slightly until the shock absorber is slightly compressed. Remove the lower mounting bolt **(see illustration)**.

3 Working at the top end of the shock absorber, unscrew the upper securing bolt **(see illustration)**.

4 Withdraw the shock absorber from under the vehicle **(see illustration)**.

Testing

5 Examine the shock absorber for signs of fluid leakage. Check the piston for signs of pitting along its visible length, and check the shock absorber body for signs of damage. Test the operation of the shock absorber (mounting it in a vice if necessary), while holding it in an upright position, by moving the piston through a full stroke and then through short strokes of 50 to 100 mm. In both cases the resistance felt should be smooth and continuous. If the resistance is jerky, or uneven, or if there is any visible sign of wear or damage to the shock absorber, renewal is necessary. Note that the mounting bushes are not available separately. Shock absorbers should always be renewed in pairs.

Refitting

6 Prior to refitting the shock absorber, mount it upright in a vice, and operate it fully through several strokes in order to prime it. (This is

10.2 Remove the lower mounting bolt

10.3 Remove the upper mounting bolt

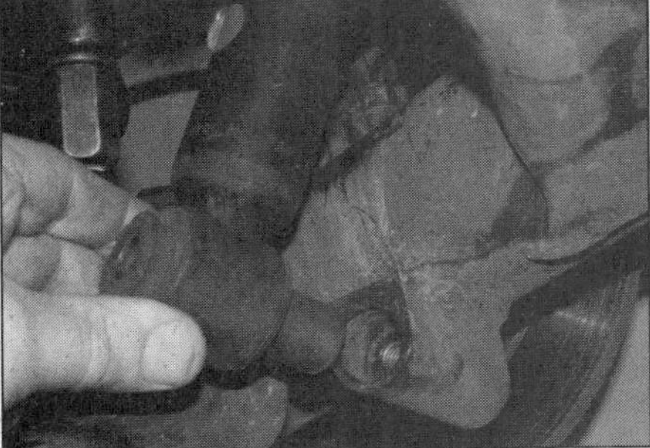
10.4 Withdrawing the lower part of the shock absorber

12.3 Disconnect the speed sensors – left-hand side arrowed

necessary even if a new unit is being fitted, as it may have been stored horizontally, and so need priming). Apply a smear of multi-purpose grease to the shock absorber mounting bolts.

7 Refitting is a reversal of removal, but delay tightening the shock absorber mounting bolts until the vehicle is on the ground, then tighten the bolts to the specified torque.

11 Rear coil spring – removal and refitting

Removal

1 Disconnect the shock absorber lower mounting on the side concerned as described in Section 10.

2 Before removing the spring, mark it for position relative to the car – the spring should already have a paint code mark on it, which can be used to ensure it is orientated properly when refitting.

3 Carefully lower the jack supporting the trailing arm, and remove the coil spring and its lower mounting rubber from the trailing arm. Lever the trailing arm down slightly if necessary to remove the spring.

4 Check the condition of the lower mounting rubber, and renew if necessary. If new springs are being fitted, note that these should always be fitted in pairs.

5 If required, the spring upper mounting/bump stop can be unclipped from the body, and a new one fitted.

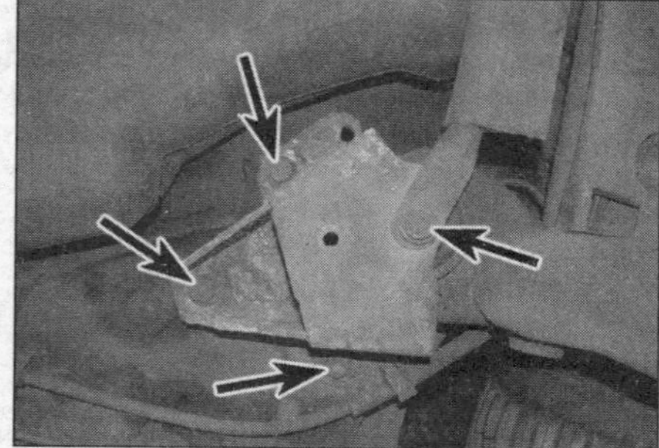

12.9 Axle mounting retaining bolts (arrowed) – right-hand side shown

12.5 Undo the brake pipe unions – arrowed

Refitting

6 Refitting is a reversal of removal, remembering the following points:

a) Align the spring as noted before removal, so that it sits properly in the trailing arm.

b) Refit the shock absorber lower mounting as described in Section 10, noting that the bolt should not be tightened until the car is resting on its wheels.

12 Rear axle assembly – removal and refitting

Note: *Renewal of the rear axle bushes requires the use of a press. Check on parts availability before removing the rear axle for bush renewal.*

Removal

1 Chock the front wheels and engage reverse gear (or P on automatic models). Loosen the rear wheel bolts, then jack up the rear of the car and support it on axle stands. Remove both rear roadwheels.

2 If a new rear axle is to be fitted, remove the brake discs as described in Chapter 9. Otherwise, to make refitting the axle easier, remove the rear brake pads and tie up the calipers as described in Chapter 9.

3 Disconnect the wiring plugs from the ABS rear wheel sensors (behind the discs, facing forwards) **(see illustration)**. Trace the wiring back, and unclip it from the axle.

4 Unhook the handbrake cable ends from the operating levers on the calipers, then unclip the cable outers from the calipers. Trace the cables back, and ensure they are disconnected from the clips relevant to the rear axle.

5 Use a brake hose clamp or a similar tool with protected jaws to clamp the brake flexible hoses at the nearest convenient point. Disconnect the rear brake pipes at the flexible hose unions which are clipped to the axle crossmember **(see illustration)**. Plug or tape over the union ends to prevent dirt entry. Wash off any spilt fluid immediately.

6 Disconnect the rear shock absorber lower mountings as described in Section 10.

7 Remove the rear springs as described in Section 11.

8 On models with xenon headlights, it may be necessary to disconnect the wiring from, and to unbolt, the ride height level sensor attached to the rear axle.

9 Clean the area under the car around the axle mounting plates, and mark their positions relative to the floor using paint. Loosen the axle mounting plate bolts either side **(see illustration)**.

10 With the aid of an assistant, position two sturdy jacks under the ends of the axle, and just take its weight.

11 Remove the three mounting plate bolts each side progressively, then, with an assistant on hand to steady the axle on the jacks, lower the axle out from under the car. Check along the length of the axle, to make sure there are no cables or pipes still attached.

12 If a new axle is being fitted, remove the brake pipes from the original and fit them to the new axle. Also transfer the brake assemblies using the information in Chapter 9.

Refitting

13 Refitting is a reversal of removal, noting the following points:

a) Align the axle mounting plates with the marks made prior to removal, then tighten the bolts to the specified torque.

b) Refit the springs and reconnect the shock absorbers as described in Sections 11 and 10.

c) Refit the brake components, then on completion bleed the braking system as described in Chapter 9.

d) On completion, it may be advisable to have the rear wheel alignment checked by a Renault dealer or competent specialist. On models with xenon headlights, the headlight system should also be set up by a Renault dealer on completion.

13 Vehicle ride height – checking and adjustment

General information

1 The vehicle ride height measurements are used to ensure accuracy when checking the front suspension and steering angles. This is since the angles will vary slightly according to the ride height of the vehicle. The ride height measuring points are as shown. The front and rear ride heights can also be calculated as follows.

Note: *From January 2003 the underbody height designations changed from:*

H1 = R1
H2 = W1
H4 = R2
H5 = W2

Checking

2 To accurately check the ride height, position the unladen vehicle on a level surface, with the tyres correctly inflated and the fuel tank full.

Ride height

3 To check the front ride height, measure and record the dimensions H1/R1 (centre of the wheel axis to the ground) and H2/W1 (subframe to the ground) on both sides of the vehicle. Subtract H2/W1 from H1/R1 to find the underbody height-checking dimension.
4 To check the rear ride height, measure and record the dimensions H4/R2 (centre of the wheel axis to the ground) and H5/W2 (centre of the rear trailing arm bush to the ground) on both sides of the vehicle. Subtract H5/W2 from H4/R2 to find the underbody height-checking dimension.
5 Note that the difference between the heights on each side must not exceed 5 mm, with the driver's side slightly higher than the passenger side.
6 Check with your local Renault dealer to check that these dimensions are within the range given for your vehicle. **Note:** *The specification varies according to the model and engine type of the vehicle and was not available to us at the time of writing.*
7 If the ride height differs greatly from that specified, examine the suspension components for signs of wear or damage.
8 If further checks or adjustments are required, take your vehicle to your local Renault dealer who will have the specialised equipment to do this.

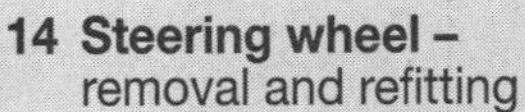

14 Steering wheel – removal and refitting

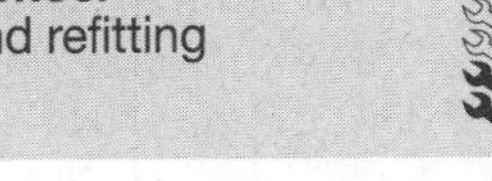

Warning: Refer to the precautions given in Chapter 12 about airbags before proceeding.

Note: *A new steering wheel securing bolt must be used on refitting and tightened to the specified torque setting.*

Removal

1 Remove the airbag (see Chapter 12).
2 Ensure that the front wheels are in the straight-ahead position, with the steering column lock engaged.
3 Slacken and remove the steering wheel securing bolt **(see illustration)**.
4 Depending on model, disconnect the wiring connectors mounted in the steering wheel **(see illustration)**.
5 Mark the steering wheel and the steering column shaft in relation to each other, then lift the steering wheel off the column splines. Carefully feed the wiring down through the centre of the steering wheel on removal.

Refitting

6 Refitting is a reversal of removal, noting the following points.

a) Ensure that the front wheels are still in the straight-ahead position, with the steering column lock engaged.
b) Align the marks made on the steering wheel and column shaft before removal.

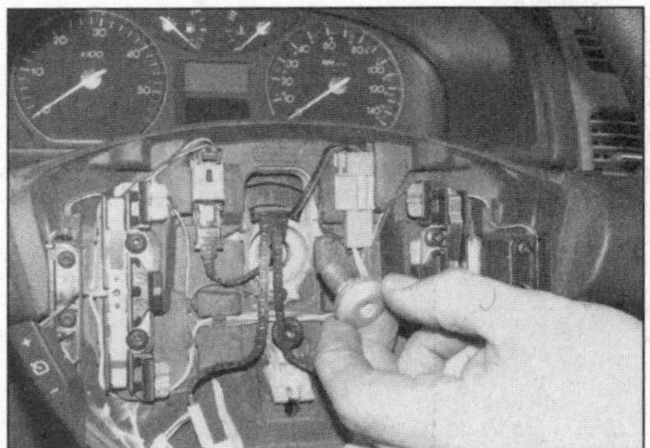

14.3 Slacken and remove the steering wheel bolt

c) Tighten a new steering wheel securing bolt to the specified torque.
d) Reconnect the wiring connectors in the steering wheel securely.
e) Refit the airbag as described in Chapter 12.

15 Steering column and intermediate shaft – removal, inspection and refitting

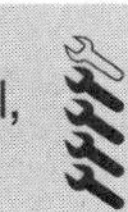

Removal

1 Disconnect the battery negative lead.
2 Remove the steering wheel as described in Section 14.
3 Remove the steering column switch assembly as described in Chapter 12.
4 Remove the driver's side facia lower trim panel as described in Chapter 11.

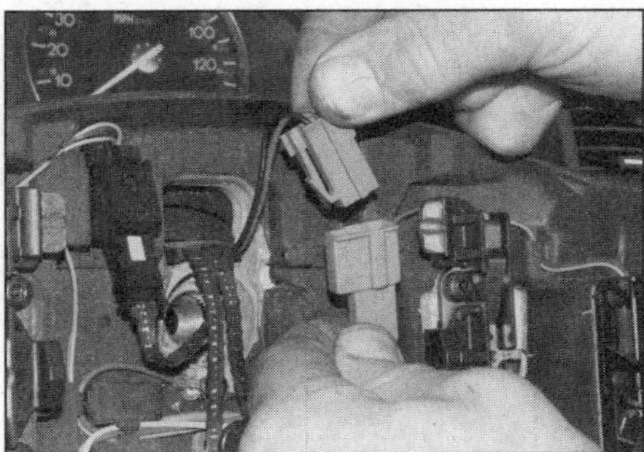

14.4 Disconnect the wiring connectors

5 Remove the instrument panel as described in Chapter 12.
6 Working inside the engine bay, unscrew the steering column-to-steering gear pinion pinch-bolt and nut **(see illustration)**.
7 Working back inside the vehicle, disconnect the wiring connector from the steering column lock. Unclip the wiring harness so that the column is free to be removed **(see illustration)**.
8 Pull back the floor covering at the base of the steering column and free the rubber gaiter from the floor panel.
9 The column is mounted to the facia crossmember by two nuts accessible through the instrument panel aperture; the column is then hooked into the lower part of the crossmember. Undo the two upper retaining nuts, and then lift the column upwards to release it from the crossmember and remove it from the car **(see illustrations)**.

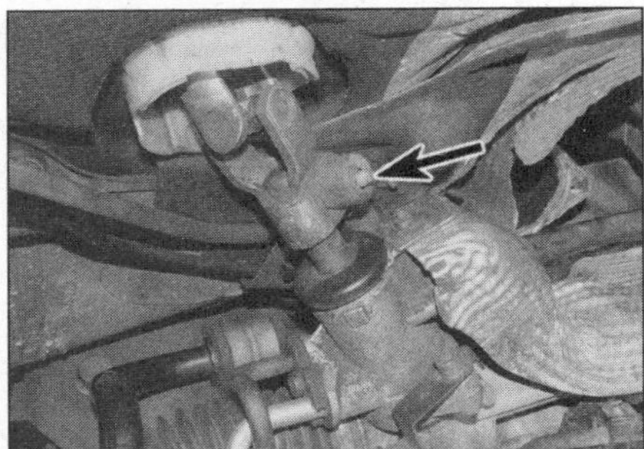

15.6 Undo the lower steering column pinch-bolt – arrowed

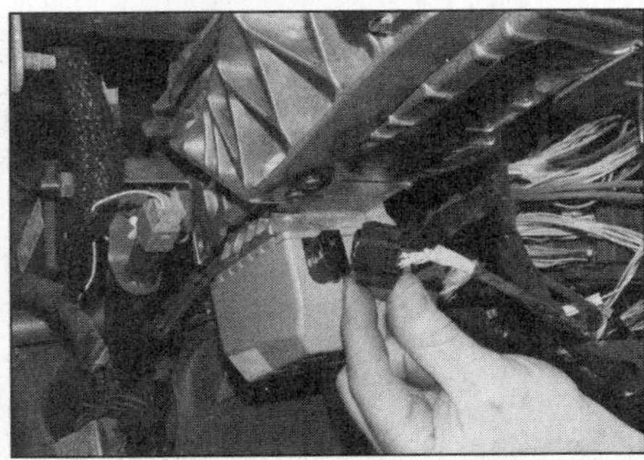

15.7 Disconnect the wiring connector from the steering lock

15.9a Undo the mounting nuts – arrowed . . .

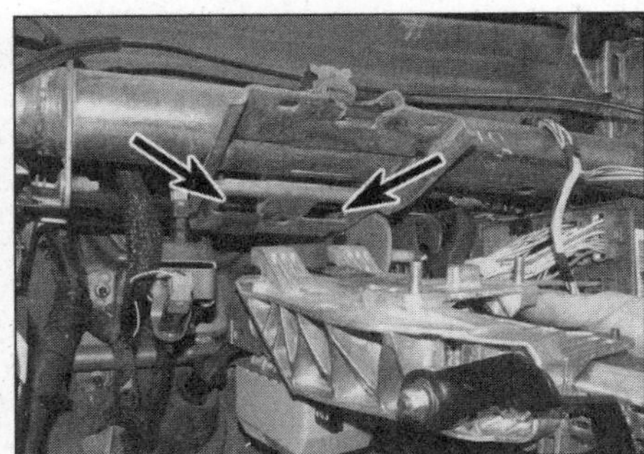

15.9b . . . and unhook the steering column from the mounting bracket – arrowed

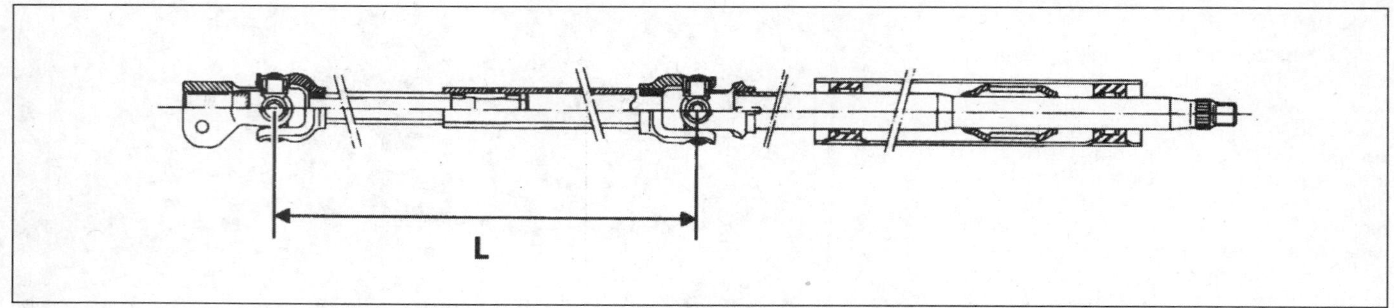

15.11 Steering column intermediate shaft checking dimension (L)

Right-hand drive models: L = 321.1 ± 1 mm *Left-hand drive models: L = 329.5 ± 1 mm*

Inspection

10 Check the steering shaft for signs of free play in the column bushes, and check the universal joints for signs of damage or roughness in the joint bearings. If damage or wear is found on the steering shaft universal joints or shaft bushes, the column must be renewed as an assembly.

11 The intermediate shaft attached to the bottom of the steering column incorporates a telescopic safety feature. In the event of a front-end crash, the shaft collapses and prevents the steering wheel injuring the driver. Before refitting the steering column, the length of the intermediate shaft must be checked **(see illustration).** If the length is shorter than specified, the complete steering column must be renewed. Damage to the intermediate shaft is also implied if it is found that the clamp bolt at its base cannot be inserted freely when refitting the column.

Steering lock

12 The (electric) steering column lock is attached using a bolt with a **left-hand thread**. The lock can be removed with the column in place, as described in Chapter 12.

Refitting

13 Refitting is a reversal of removal, noting the following points:

a) Tighten the steering column mounting nuts to the recommended torque specified.

b) Check that all wiring connectors are securely connected.

c) Fit a new nut and bolt when reconnecting the steering column universal joint.

16 Steering gear assembly – removal, overhaul and refitting

Note: *New steering gear securing nuts must be used on refitting.*

Removal

1 Remove the front subframe as described in Section 7.

2 Unbolt the exhaust heat shield from the top of the steering rack **(see illustration)**.

3 Mark the position of the steering gear mounting lugs on the subframe, so that the steering gear can be refitted in exactly the same position.

4 Unscrew the mounting bolts, and remove the steering gear from the subframe **(see illustration)**.

Overhaul

5 Renewal procedures for the gaiters and the track rod ends are given in Sections 17 and 20 respectively.

6 Examine the steering gear assembly for signs of wear or damage. Check that the rack moves freely over the full length of its travel, with no signs of roughness or excessive free play between the steering gear pinion and rack. Internal wear or damage can only be cured by renewing the steering gear assembly.

7 Note that the steering gear is supplied as an assembly complete with track rods, but the track rod ends will have to be removed from the old assembly and transferred to the new steering gear, as described in Section 20.

Refitting

8 Refit the steering gear to the subframe, ensuring that the lugs are aligned with the marks made on the subframe before removal. Fit new securing nuts, and tighten to the specified torque.

9 Refit the heat shield.

10 Refit the subframe as described in Section 7.

17 Steering gear rubber gaiters – renewal

1 Remove the track rod end as described in Section 20.

2 Mark the fitted position of the gaiter on the track rod. Release the retaining clips, and slide the gaiter off the steering gear housing and track rod end.

3 Thoroughly clean the track rod and the steering gear housing, using fine abrasive paper to polish off any corrosion, burrs or sharp edges which might damage the sealing lips of the new gaiter on installation.

4 Where applicable, recover the grease from inside the old gaiter. If it is uncontaminated with dirt or grit, apply it to the track rod inner balljoint. If the old grease is contaminated, or it is suspected that some has been lost, apply some new molybdenum disulphide grease.

5 Grease the inside of the new gaiter. Carefully slide the gaiter onto the track rod, and locate it on the steering gear housing. Align the outer edge of the gaiter with the mark made on the track rod prior to removal, and then secure it in position with new retaining clips.

6 Refit the track rod end as described in Section 20.

18 Power steering hydraulic system – bleeding

1 This procedure will only be necessary when any part of the hydraulic system has been

16.2 Undo the heat shield securing bolts – arrowed

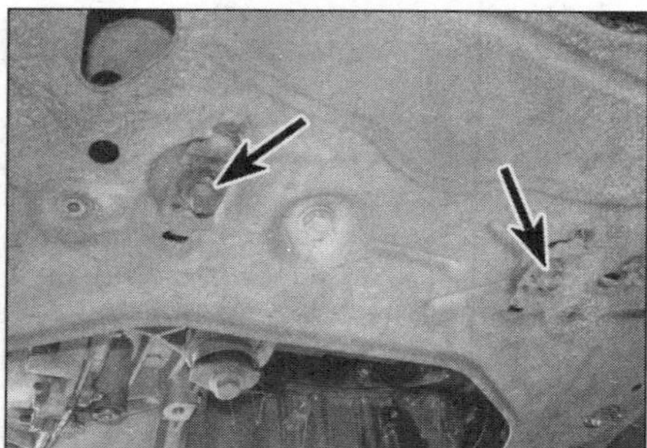

16.4 Steering rack mounting bolts – arrowed

disconnected, or if air has entered because of leakage.

2 Remove the fluid reservoir filler cap, and top-up the fluid level to the maximum mark, using only the specified fluid. Refer to *Lubricants and fluids* for fluid specifications, and to *Weekly checks* for details of the fluid reservoir markings.

3 With the engine stopped, slowly move the steering from lock-to-lock several times to expel trapped air, then top-up the level in the fluid reservoir. Repeat this procedure until the fluid level in the reservoir does not drop any further.

4 Start the engine. Slowly move the steering from lock-to-lock several times to expel any air remaining in the system. Repeat this procedure until bubbles cease to appear in the fluid reservoir.

5 If, when turning the steering, an abnormal noise is heard from the fluid pipes, it indicates that there is still air in the system. Check this by turning the wheels to the straight-ahead position and switching off the engine. If the fluid level in the reservoir rises, air is still present in the system, and further bleeding is necessary.

6 Once all traces of air have been removed, stop the engine and allow the system to cool. Once cool, check that the fluid level is up to the maximum mark on the power steering fluid reservoir; top-up if necessary.

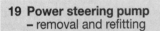

19 Power steering pump - removal and refitting

Removal

1 Disconnect the battery negative terminal (refer to *Disconnecting the battery* in the Reference Section of this manual).

2 Apply the handbrake, then jack up the front of the vehicle (see *Jacking and vehicle support*), and remove the right-hand roadwheel.

3 Where applicable, remove the securing screws, and withdraw the engine undershield. Remove the splash shield from under the wheel arch.

4 Where applicable, slacken the three power steering pump pulley securing bolts.

5 Remove the auxiliary drivebelt as described in Chapter 1A or 1B.

6 Detach the power steering fluid reservoir from its mounting bracket and move it to one side without disconnecting the fluid hoses.

7 Fit clamps to the power steering fluid hoses, as close as possible to the fluid reservoir to minimise fluid loss during the following operations.

8 The alternator is positioned directly below the power steering pump unit; cover the alternator with a plastic sheet or similar to prevent the entry of power steering fluid when the hoses are disconnected.

9 Slacken the retaining clips, and disconnect the fluid supply and feed hoses from the pump **(see illustration)**. If necessary, to disconnect the feed pipe, unscrew the union nut and recover the O-ring. Be prepared for some fluid spillage as the hoses/pipes are disconnected; plug the hose/pipe and pump openings to minimise fluid loss and to prevent the entry of dirt into the system.

19.9 Disconnect the supply pipe and feed hose from the pump

19.12 removing the pump pulley – 2.2 litre diesel engine

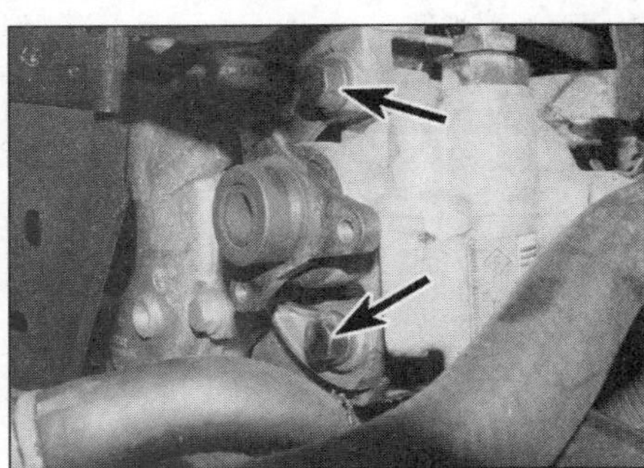

19.13a Undo the front mounting bolts (arrowed) . . .

19.13b . . . and the rear mounting bolt – arrowed

10 Where applicable, release the fluid hoses/pipes from any clips or brackets to enable the hoses/pipes to be moved to one side, clear of the pump.

11 Depending on model, bearing in mind the information given on depressurising the fuel system in Chapter 4A, and taking suitable safety precautions, it may be necessary to disconnect the fuel supply hose from the end of the fuel rail to access the upper pump mounting bolt.

12 Where applicable, unscrew the three securing bolts, and remove the power steering pump pulley **(see illustration)**.

13 Unscrew the two front mounting bolts and the rear mounting bolt, then withdraw the power steering pump from its mounting bracket **(see illustrations)**. On models where the pulley has not been removed, work through the openings in the pump pulley to unscrew the two front mounting bolts.

20.2 Count the exposed threads and slacken the locking nut

Refitting

14 Refitting is a reversal of removal, bearing in mind the following points.

a) Where applicable, use a new O-ring when reconnecting the feed pipe union.

b) Refit the auxiliary drivebelt as described in Chapter 1A or 1B.

c) On completion, reconnect the battery then remove the hose clamps, and bleed the power steering hydraulic system as described in Section 18.

20 Track rod end - removal and refitting

Note: *A balljoint separator tool will be required for this operation. A new balljoint nut will be required on refitting.*

Removal

1 Apply the handbrake, then jack up the front of the vehicle and support it securely on axle stands (see *Jacking and vehicle support*). Remove the appropriate front roadwheel.

2 Count the number of exposed threads on the end of the track rod to use as a guide when refitting, and then slacken the track rod end locking nut **(see illustration)**.

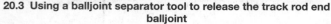

20.3 Using a balljoint separator tool to release the track rod end balljoint

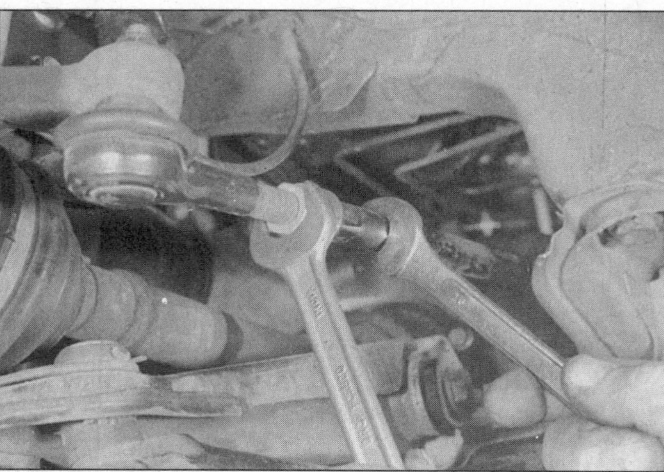
20.6 Hold the track rod end while tightening the locking nut

3 Remove the nut securing the track rod end to the hub carrier. Release the balljoint tapered shank using a universal balljoint separator. If the track rod end is to be re-used, protect the threaded end of the shank by screwing the nut back on a few turns before using the separator **(see illustration)**.

4 Counting the **exact** number of turns necessary to do so, unscrew the track rod end from the track rod. Counter-hold the track rod using a spanner on the flats provided.

5 Carefully clean the balljoint and the threads. Renew the track rod end if the balljoint movement is sloppy or if it is too stiff, if it is excessively worn, or if it is damaged in any way. Carefully check the shank taper and threads. If the gaiter is damaged, the complete track rod end must be renewed; it is not possible to obtain the gaiter separately.

Refitting

6 Screw the track rod end into the track rod by the number of turns noted on removal and tighten the locking nut **(see illustration)**. This should leave the same number of threads exposed on the end of the track rod as noted before removal.

7 Refit the balljoint shank to the hub carrier, and tighten the new retaining nut to the specified torque. If difficulty is experienced due to the balljoint shank rotating, jam it by exerting pressure on the top of the balljoint.

8 Refit the roadwheel, lower the vehicle to the ground and tighten the roadwheel bolts to the specified torque.

9 Check the front wheel alignment as described in Section 21, then tighten the track rod end clamp-bolt.

21 Wheel alignment and steering angles – general information

General information

1 A car's steering and suspension geometry is defined in four basic settings – all angles are expressed in degrees (toe settings are also expressed as a measurement); the relevant settings are camber, castor, steering axis inclination and toe-setting. With the exception of toe-setting, none of these settings are adjustable.

Front wheel toe setting

Checking

2 Due to the special measuring equipment necessary to check the wheel alignment, and the skill required to use it properly, the checking and adjustment of these settings is best left to a Renault dealer or similar expert. Most tyre-fitting shops now possess sophisticated checking equipment.

3 For accurate checking, the vehicle must be at the kerb weight specified in *Dimensions and weights*.

4 Before starting work, check first that the tyre sizes and types are as specified, then check tyre pressures and tread wear. Also check roadwheel run-out, the condition of the hub bearings, the steering wheel free play and the condition of the front suspension components (see the relevant part of Chapter 1). Correct any faults found.

5 Park the vehicle on level ground, with the front roadwheels in the straight-ahead position. Rock the rear and front ends to settle the suspension. Release the handbrake and roll the vehicle backwards approximately 1 metre, then forwards again, to relieve any stresses in the steering and suspension components.

6 Two methods are available to the home mechanic for checking the front wheel toe setting. One method is to use a gauge to measure the distance between the front and rear inside edges of the roadwheels. The other method is to use a scuff plate, in which each front wheel is rolled across a movable plate which records any deviation, or scuff, of the tyre from the straight-ahead position as it moves across the plate. Such gauges are available in relatively inexpensive form from accessory outlets. It is up to the owner to decide whether the expense is justified, in view of the small amount of use such equipment would normally receive.

7 Prepare the vehicle as described in paragraphs 3 to 5 above.

8 If the measurement procedure is being used, carefully measure the distance between the front edges of the roadwheel rims and the rear edges of the rims. Subtract the rear measurement from the front measurement, and check that the result is within the specified range. If not, adjust the toe setting as described in paragraph 10.

9 If scuff plates are to be used, roll the vehicle backwards, check that the roadwheels are in the straight-ahead position, then roll it across the scuff plates so that each front roadwheel passes squarely over the centre of its respective plate. Note the angle recorded by the scuff plates. To ensure accuracy, repeat the check three times, and take the average of the three readings. If the roadwheels are running parallel, there will of course be no angle recorded; if a deviation value is shown on the scuff plates, compare the reading obtained for each wheel with that specified. If the value recorded is outside the specified tolerance, the toe setting is incorrect, and must be adjusted as follows.

Adjustment

10 Apply the handbrake, then jack up the front of the vehicle and support it securely on axle stands (see *Jacking and vehicle support*). Turn the steering wheel onto full-left lock, and record the number of exposed threads on the end of the right-hand track rod. Now turn the steering onto full-right lock, and record the number of threads on the left-hand side. If there are the same number of threads visible on both sides, then subsequent adjustment should be made equally on both sides. If there are more threads visible on one side than the other, it will be necessary to compensate for this during adjustment. **Note:** *It is important*

to ensure that, after adjustment, the same number of threads are visible on the end of each track rod.

11 First clean the track rod threads; if they are corroded, apply penetrating fluid before starting adjustment. Release the steering gear rubber gaiter outboard clips, then peel back the gaiters and apply a smear of grease, so that both gaiters are free and will not be twisted or strained as their respective track rods are rotated.

12 Use a straight-edge and a scriber or similar to mark the relationship of each track rod to the track rod end. Working on each track rod end in turn, unscrew its clamp bolt.

13 Alter the length of the track rods, bearing in mind the note in paragraph 10, by screwing them into or out of the track rod ends. Rotate the track rod using an open-ended spanner fitted to the flats provided. If necessary, counter-hold the track rod end using a second spanner **(see illustration)**. Shortening the track rods (screwing them into their track rod ends) will reduce toe-in and increase toe-out. Note that one full turn of the track rods will alter the toe-setting by 30' (3.0 mm).

14 When the setting is correct, hold the track rods and securely tighten the track rod end clamp bolts. Check that the balljoints are seated correctly in their sockets, and count the exposed threads on the ends of the track rods. If the number of threads exposed is not the same on both sides, then the adjustment has not been made equally, and problems will be encountered with tyre scrubbing in turns; also, the steering wheel spokes will no longer be horizontal when the wheels are in the straight-ahead position.

15 When the track rod lengths are the same, lower the vehicle to the ground and recheck the toe setting; readjust if necessary. When the setting is correct, tighten the track rod end clamp bolts. Ensure that the steering gear rubber gaiters are seated correctly and are not twisted or strained, then secure them in position with new retaining clips.

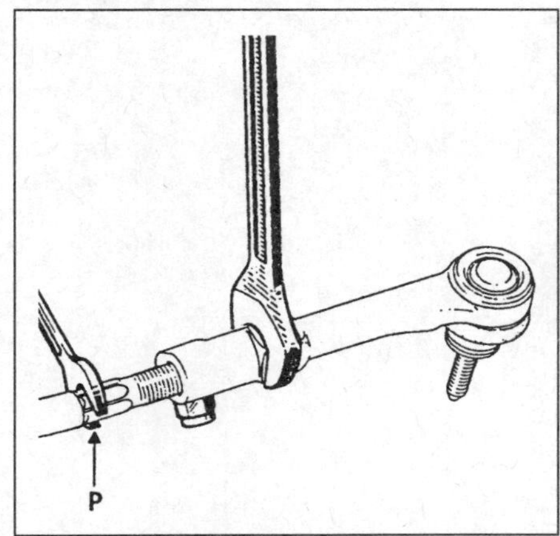

21.13 Counter-hold the track rod end and rotate the track rod using the flats (P) provided

Chapter 11
Bodywork and fittings

Contents

Degrees of difficulty

Easy, suitable for novice with little experience 

Fairly easy, suitable for beginner with some experience

Fairly difficult, suitable for competent DIY mechanic

Difficult, suitable for experienced DIY mechanic

Very difficult, suitable for expert DIY or professional 

Specifications

Torque wrench setting	Nm	lbf ft
Seat belt anchor bolts	25	18

1 General information

The bodyshell is of five-door Hatchback or Estate (Sport Tourer) configuration, and is made of pressed-steel sections. Most components are welded together, but some use is made of structural adhesives. The front wings are bolted on and are manufactured from a polymer compound, which can withstand an impact of up to 10 mph (16 km/h) without sustaining permanent damage.

The bonnet, doors and some other vulnerable panels are made of zinc-coated metal, and are further protected by being coated with an anti-chip primer prior to being sprayed.

Extensive use is made of plastic materials, mainly in the interior, but also in exterior components. The front and rear bumpers and the front grille are injection-moulded from a synthetic material, which is very strong, and yet light. Plastic components such as wheel arch liners are fitted to the underside of the vehicle, to improve the body's resistance to corrosion.

2 Maintenance – bodywork and underframe

The general condition of a vehicle's bodywork is the one thing that significantly affects its value. Maintenance is easy, but needs to be regular. Neglect, particularly after minor damage, can lead quickly to further deterioration and costly repair bills. It is important also to keep watch on those parts of the vehicle not immediately visible, for instance the underside, inside all the wheel arches, and the lower part of the engine compartment.

The basic maintenance routine for the bodywork is washing – preferably with a lot of water, from a hose. This will remove all the loose solids, which may have stuck to the vehicle. It is important to flush these off in such a way as to prevent grit from scratching the finish. The wheel arches and underframe need washing in the same way, to remove any accumulated mud that will retain moisture and tend to encourage rust. Oddly enough, the best time to clean the underframe and wheel arches is in wet weather, when the mud is thoroughly wet and soft. In very wet weather, the underframe is usually cleaned of large accumulations automatically, and this is a good time for inspection.

Periodically, except on vehicles with a wax-based underbody protective coating, it is a good idea to have the whole of the underframe of the vehicle steam-cleaned, engine compartment included, so that a thorough inspection can be carried out to see what minor repairs and renovations are necessary. Steam cleaning is available at many garages, and is necessary for the removal of the accumulation of oily grime, which sometimes is allowed to become thick in certain areas. If steam cleaning facilities are not available, there are one or two excellent grease solvents available, which can be brush-applied; the dirt can then be simply hosed off. Note that these methods should not be used on vehicles with wax-based underbody protective coating, or the coating will be removed. Such vehicles should be inspected annually, preferably just prior to winter, when the underbody should be washed down, and any damage to the wax coating repaired. Ideally, a completely fresh coat should be applied. It would also be worth considering the use of such wax-based protection for injection into door panels, sills, box sections, etc, as an additional safeguard against rust damage, where such protection is not provided by the vehicle manufacturer.

After washing paintwork, wipe off with a chamois leather to give an unspotted clear finish. A coat of clear protective wax polish will give added protection against chemical pollutants in the air. If the paintwork sheen has dulled or oxidised, use a cleaner/polisher combination to restore the brilliance of the shine. This requires a little effort, but such dulling is usually caused because regular washing has been neglected. Care needs to be taken with metallic paintwork, as special non-abrasive cleaner/polisher is required to avoid damage to the finish. Always check that the door and ventilator opening drain holes and pipes are completely clear, so that water can be drained out. Brightwork should be treated in the same way as paintwork. Windscreens and windows can be kept clear of the smeary film that often appears, by the use of proprietary glass cleaner. Never use any form of wax or other body or chromium polish on glass.

3 Maintenance – upholstery and carpets

Mats and carpets should be brushed or vacuum-cleaned regularly, to keep them free of grit. If they are badly stained, remove them from the vehicle for scrubbing or sponging, and make quite sure they are dry before refitting. Seats and interior trim panels can be kept clean by wiping with a damp cloth. If they do become stained (which can be more apparent on light-coloured upholstery), use a little liquid detergent and a soft nail brush to scour the grime out of the grain of the material. Do not forget to keep the headlining clean in the same way as the upholstery. When using liquid cleaners inside the vehicle, do not over-wet the surfaces being cleaned. Excessive damp could get into the seams and padded interior, causing stains, offensive odours or even rot. If the inside of the vehicle gets wet accidentally, it is worthwhile taking some trouble to dry it out properly, particularly where carpets are involved. Do not leave oil or electric heaters inside the vehicle for this purpose.

4 Minor body damage – repair

Minor scratches

If the scratch is very superficial, and does not penetrate to the metal of the bodywork, repair is very simple. Lightly rub the area of the scratch with a paintwork renovator, or a very fine cutting paste, to remove loose paint from the scratch, and to clear the surrounding bodywork of wax polish. Rinse the area with clean water.

Apply touch-up paint to the scratch using a fine paintbrush; continue to apply fine layers of paint until the surface of the paint in the scratch is level with the surrounding paintwork. Allow the new paint at least two weeks to harden, and then blend it into the surrounding paintwork by rubbing the scratch area with a paintwork renovator or a very fine cutting paste. Finally, apply wax polish.

Where the scratch has penetrated right through to the metal of the bodywork, causing the metal to rust, a different repair technique is required. Remove any loose rust from the bottom of the scratch with a penknife, and then apply rust-inhibiting paint, to prevent the formation of rust in the future. Using a rubber or nylon applicator, fill the scratch with bodystopper paste. If required, this paste can be mixed with cellulose thinners, to provide a very thin paste that is ideal for filling narrow scratches. Before the stopper-paste in the scratch hardens, wrap a piece of smooth cotton rag around the top of a finger. Dip the finger in cellulose thinners, and quickly sweep it across the surface of the stopper-paste in the scratch; this will ensure that the surface of the stopper-paste is slightly hollowed. The scratch can now be painted over as described earlier in this Section.

Dents

When deep denting of the vehicle's bodywork has taken place, the first task is to pull the dent out, until the affected bodywork almost attains its original shape. There is little point in trying to restore the original shape completely, as the metal in the damaged area will have stretched on impact, and cannot be reshaped fully to its original contour. It is better to bring the level of the dent up to a point which is about 3 mm below the level of the surrounding bodywork. In cases where the dent is very shallow anyway, it is not worth trying to pull it out at all. If the underside of the dent is accessible, it can be hammered out gently from behind, using a mallet with a wooden or plastic head. Whilst doing this, hold a suitable block of wood firmly against the outside of the panel, to absorb the impact from the hammer blows and thus prevent a large area of the bodywork from being 'belled-out'.

Should the dent be in a section of the bodywork, which has a double skin, or some other factor making it inaccessible from behind, a different technique is called for. Drill several small holes through the metal inside the area – particularly in the deeper section. Then screw long self-tapping screws into the holes, just sufficiently for them to gain a good purchase in the metal. Now the dent can be pulled out by pulling on the protruding heads of the screws with a pair of pliers.

The next stage of the repair is the removal of the paint from the damaged area, and from an inch or so of the surrounding 'sound' bodywork. This is accomplished most easily by using a wire brush or abrasive pad on a power drill, although it can be done just as effectively by hand, using sheets of abrasive paper. To complete the preparation for filling, score the surface of the bare metal with a screwdriver or the tang of a file, or alternatively, drill small holes in the affected area. This will provide a really good 'key' for the filler paste.

To complete the repair, see the Section on filling and respraying.

Rust holes or gashes

Remove all paint from the affected area, and from an inch or so of the surrounding 'sound' bodywork, using an abrasive pad or a wire brush on a power drill. If these are not available, a few sheets of abrasive paper will do the job most effectively. With the paint removed, you will be able to judge the severity of the corrosion, and therefore decide whether to renew the whole panel (if this is possible) or to repair the affected area. New body panels are not as expensive as most people think, and it is often quicker and more satisfactory to fit a new panel than to attempt to repair large areas of corrosion.

Remove all fittings from the affected area, except those that will act as a guide to the original shape of the damaged bodywork (eg headlamp shells etc). Then, using tin snips or a hacksaw blade, remove all loose metal and any other metal badly affected by corrosion. Hammer the edges of the hole inwards, in order to create a slight depression for the filler paste.

Wire-brush the affected area to remove the powdery rust from the surface of the remaining metal. Paint the affected area with rust-inhibiting paint; if the back of the rusted area is accessible, treat this also.

Before filling can take place, it will be necessary to block the hole in some way. This can be achieved by the use of aluminium or plastic mesh, or aluminium tape.

Aluminium or plastic mesh, or glass-fibre matting is probably the best material to use for a large hole. Cut a piece to the approximate size and shape of the hole to be filled, then position it in the hole so that its edges are below the level of the surrounding bodywork. It can be retained in position by several blobs of filler paste around its periphery.

Aluminium tape should be used for small or very narrow holes. Pull a piece off the roll, trim it to the approximate size and shape required, then pull off the backing paper (if used) and stick the tape over the hole; it can be overlapped if the thickness of one piece is insufficient. Burnish down the edges of the tape with the handle of a screwdriver or similar, to ensure that the tape is securely attached to the metal underneath.

Filling and respraying

Before using this Section, see the Sections on dent, deep scratch, rust holes and gash repairs.

Many types of body filler are available, but generally speaking, those proprietary kits which contain a tin of filler paste and a tube of resin hardener are best for this type of repair. A wide, flexible plastic or nylon applicator will be found invaluable for imparting a smooth and well-contoured finish to the surface of the filler.

Mix up a little filler on a clean piece of card or board – measure the hardener carefully (follow the maker's instructions on the pack), otherwise the filler will set too rapidly or too slowly. Using the applicator, apply the filler paste to the prepared area; draw the applicator across the surface of the filler to achieve the correct contour and to level the surface. As soon as a contour that approximates to the correct one is achieved, stop working the paste – if you carry on too long, the paste will become sticky and begin to 'pick-up' on the applicator. Continue to add thin layers of filler paste at 20-minute intervals, until the level of the filler is just proud of the surrounding bodywork.

Once the filler has hardened, the excess can be removed using a metal plane or file. From then on, progressively finer grades of abrasive paper should be used, starting with a 40-grade production paper, and finishing with a 400-grade wet-and-dry paper. Always wrap the abrasive paper around a flat rubber, cork, or wooden block – otherwise the surface of the filler will not be completely flat. During the smoothing of the filler surface, the wet-and-dry paper should be periodically rinsed in water. This will ensure that a very smooth finish is imparted to the filler at the final stage.

At this stage, the 'dent' should be surrounded by a ring of bare metal, which in turn should be encircled by the finely 'feathered' edge of the good paintwork. Rinse the repair area with clean water, until all of the dust produced by the rubbing-down operation has gone.

Spray the whole area with a light coat of primer – this will show up any imperfections in the surface of the filler. Repair these imperfections with fresh filler paste or body stopper, and once more smooth the surface with abrasive paper. If body stopper is used, it can be mixed with cellulose thinners, to form a really thin paste that is ideal for filling small holes. Repeat this spray-and-repair procedure until you are satisfied that the surface of the filler, and the feathered edge of the paintwork, are perfect. Clean the repair area with clean water, and allow to dry fully.

The repair area is now ready for final spraying. Paint spraying must be carried out in a warm, dry, windless and dust-free atmosphere. This condition can be created artificially if you have access to a large indoor working area, but if you are forced to work in the open, you will have to pick your day very carefully. If you are working indoors, dousing the floor in the work area with water will help to settle the dust which would otherwise be in the atmosphere. If the repair area is confined to one body panel, mask off the surrounding panels; this will help to minimise the effects of a slight mis-match in paint colours. Bodywork fittings (eg chrome strips, door handles etc) will also need to be masked off. Use genuine masking tape, and several thicknesses of newspaper, for the masking operations.

Before commencing to spray, agitate the aerosol can thoroughly, and then spray a test area (an old tin, or similar) until the technique is mastered. Cover the repair area with a thick coat of primer; the thickness should be built up using several thin layers of paint, rather than one thick one. Using 400-grade wet-and-dry paper, rub down the surface of the primer until it is really smooth. While doing this, the work area should be thoroughly doused with water, and the wet-and-dry paper periodically rinsed in water. Allow to dry before spraying on more paint.

Spray on the top coat, again building up the thickness by using several thin layers of paint. Start spraying at the top of the repair area, and then, using a side-to-side motion, work downwards until the whole repair area and about 2 inches of the surrounding original paintwork is covered. Remove all masking material 10 to 15 minutes after spraying on the final coat of paint.

Allow the new paint at least two weeks to harden, then, using a paintwork renovator or a very fine cutting paste, blend the edges of the paint into the existing paintwork. Finally, apply wax polish.

Plastic components

With the use of more and more plastic body components by the vehicle manufacturers (eg bumpers. spoilers, and in some cases major body panels), rectification of more serious damage to such items has become a matter of either entrusting repair work to a specialist in this field, or renewing complete components. Repair of such damage by the DIY owner is not really feasible, owing to the cost of the equipment and materials required for effecting such repairs. The basic technique involves making a groove along the line of the crack in the plastic, using a rotary burr in a power drill. The damaged part is then welded back together, using a hot air gun to heat up and fuse a plastic filler rod into the groove. Any excess plastic is then removed, and the area rubbed down to a smooth finish. It is important that a filler rod of the correct plastic is used, as body components can be made of a variety of different types (eg polycarbonate, ABS, polypropylene).

Damage of a less serious nature (abrasions, minor cracks etc) can be repaired by the DIY owner using a two-part epoxy filler repair. Once mixed in equal, this is used in similar fashion to the bodywork filler used on metal panels. The filler is usually cured in twenty to thirty minutes, ready for sanding and painting.

If the owner is renewing a complete component himself, or if he has repaired it with epoxy filler, he will be left with the problem of finding a suitable paint for finishing which is compatible with the type of plastic used. At one time, the use of a universal paint was not possible, owing to the complex range of plastics encountered in body component applications. Standard paints, generally speaking, will not bond to plastic or rubber satisfactorily, but suitable paints to match any plastic or rubber finish, can be obtained from dealers. However, it is now possible to obtain a plastic body parts finishing kit that consists of a pre-primer treatment, a primer and coloured top coat. Full instructions are normally supplied with a kit, but basically, the method of use is to first apply the pre-primer to the component concerned, and allow it to dry for up to 30 minutes. Then the primer is applied, and left to dry for about an hour before finally applying the special-coloured top coat. The result is a correctly coloured component, where the paint will flex with the plastic or rubber, a property that standard paint does not normally possess.

5 Major body damage – repair

Where serious damage has occurred, or large areas need renewal due to neglect, it means that complete new panels will need welding-in, and this is best left to professionals. If the damage is due to impact, it will also be necessary to check completely the alignment of the bodyshell, and this can only be carried out accurately by a Renault dealer using special jigs. If the body is left misaligned, it is primarily dangerous, as the car will not handle properly, and secondly, uneven stresses will be imposed on the steering, suspension and possibly transmission, causing abnormal wear, or complete failure, particularly to such items as the tyres.

6 Bumpers – removal and refitting

Front bumper

Removal

1 To improve access, apply the handbrake, then jack up the front of the vehicle and support securely on axle stands (see *Jacking and vehicle support*). Remove the roadwheels.

2 Disconnect the battery negative terminal (refer to *Disconnecting the battery* in the Reference Section of this manual).

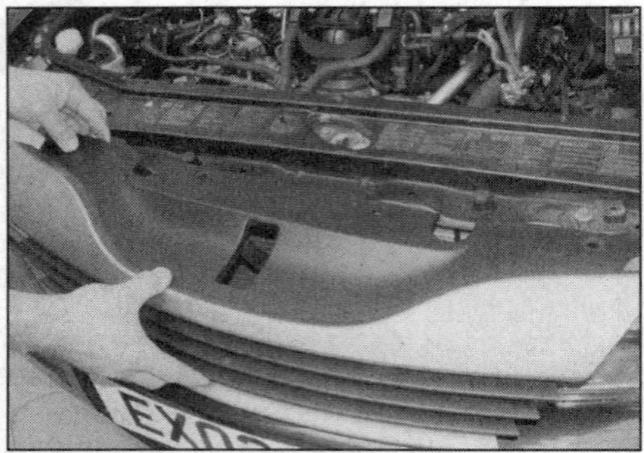
6.3 Remove the grille from the bumper

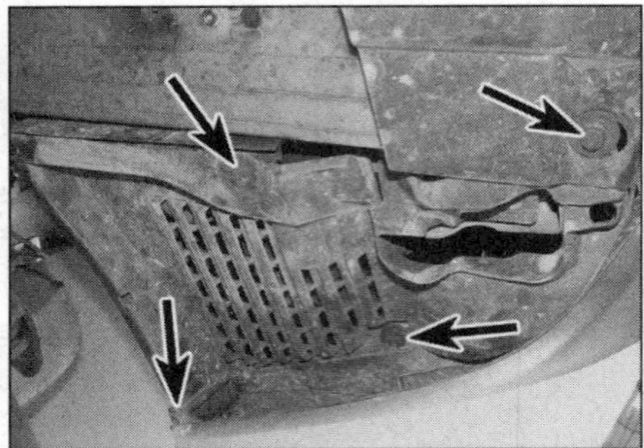
6.5 Remove the splash shield retainers (arrowed) from each side of the bumper

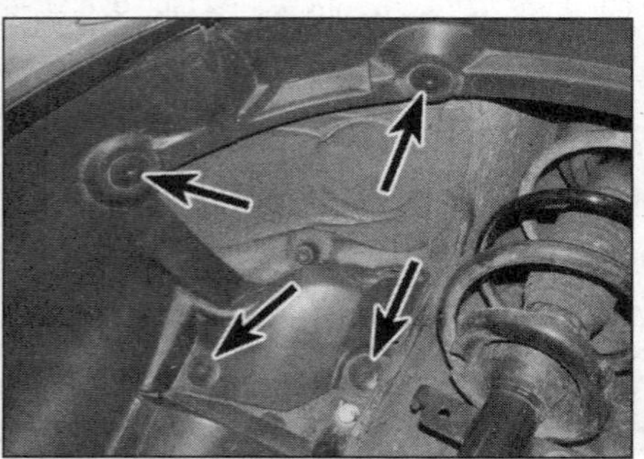
6.6 Unclip the plastic plugs – arrowed

6.7 Unscrew the bumper securing bolts – arrowed

3 Release the four upper retaining clips and unclip the grille from the top of the bumper **(see illustration)**.

4 Remove the engine undertray and unscrew the two securing screws from the centre of the lower edge of the bumper.

5 Working at the bottom of the bumper on each side of the vehicle, remove the securing screws, plastic plug and retaining bolt from the plastic under-wing splash shields **(see illustration)**.

6 Working under the wheel arches, release the plastic retaining plugs securing the wheel arch liners, then unclip the wheel arch liners from the wheel arches for access to the bumper side securing bolts **(see illustration)**.

7 Unscrew the bumper side securing bolts, one at each end of the bumper **(see illustration)**.

8 On models with front foglights mounted in the bumper, working at the rear of the light units, disconnect the wiring plugs and, where applicable, release the wiring from the clips at the rear of the bumper **(see illustration)**.

9 On models with front headlight washer jets, working at the rear of the bumper, disconnect the washer hose **(see illustration)**.

10 With the aid of an assistant, pull the bumper forwards from the body front panel and check that everything is disconnected. Remove the bumper.

Refitting

11 Refitting is a reversal of removal, but where applicable ensure that the foglight wiring plugs and the headlight washer hose are reconnected securely. Make sure that the bumper side locating lugs engage correctly with the clips on the body.

Rear bumper

Removal – Hatchback models

12 To improve access, chock the front wheels and engage reverse gear (or P on automatic transmission models). Jack up the rear of the vehicle and support it securely on axle stands (see *Jacking and vehicle support*).

13 Working in the luggage compartment, remove the securing screws, and remove the both rear light units **(see illustrations)**.

14 Unscrew the now-exposed upper bumper left and right-hand side retaining screws **(see illustration)**.

15 Working under the rear of the bumper, release the three lower bumper securing clips **(see illustration)**.

16 Working at each side of the bumper, remove the screws securing the splash shields/wheel arch liners to the rear and bottom edges of the bumper, and remove the splash shields/wheel arch liners **(see illustration)**.

17 Working at each side of the bumper, remove the securing clip that secures each

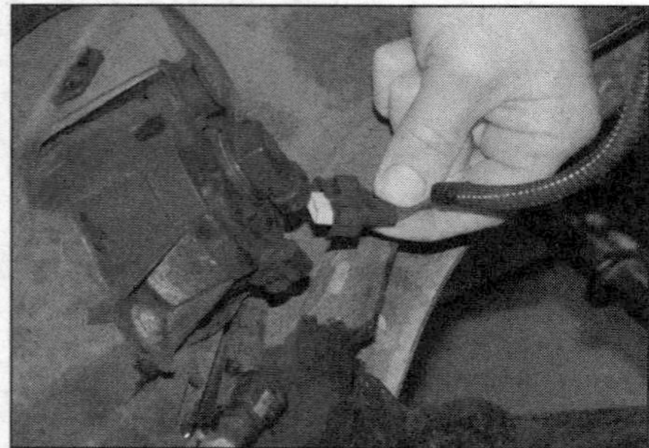
6.8 Disconnect the wiring connectors from the rear of the foglights

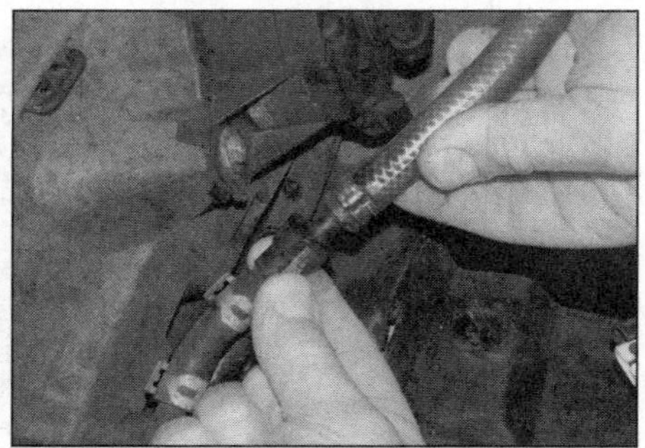
6.9 Disconnect the headlight washer hose

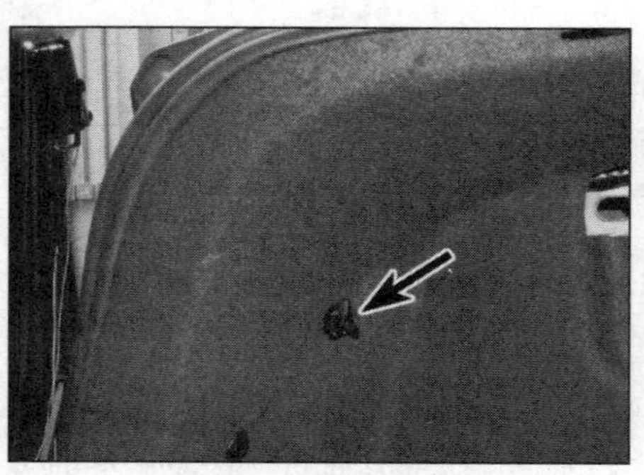
6.13a Remove the securing nut (arrowed) . . .

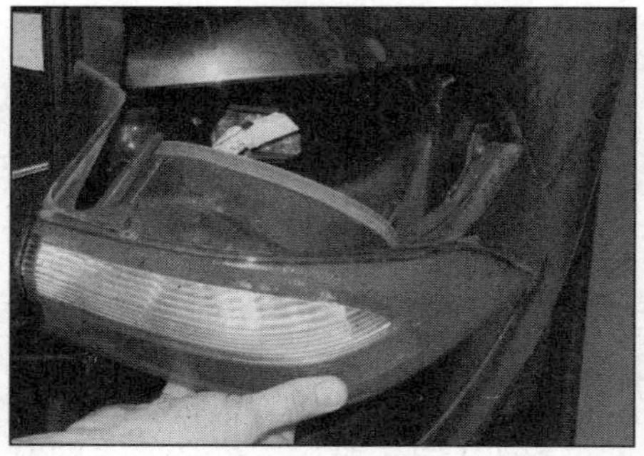
6.13b . . . and remove the rear light units

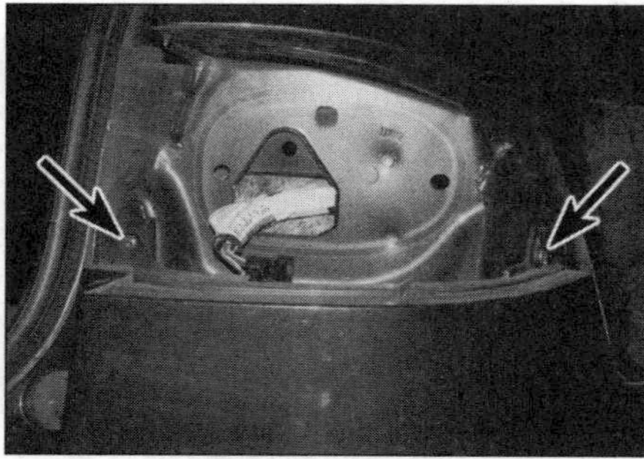
6.14 Undo the bumper upper retaining screws – arrowed

6.15 Release the lower bumper securing clips

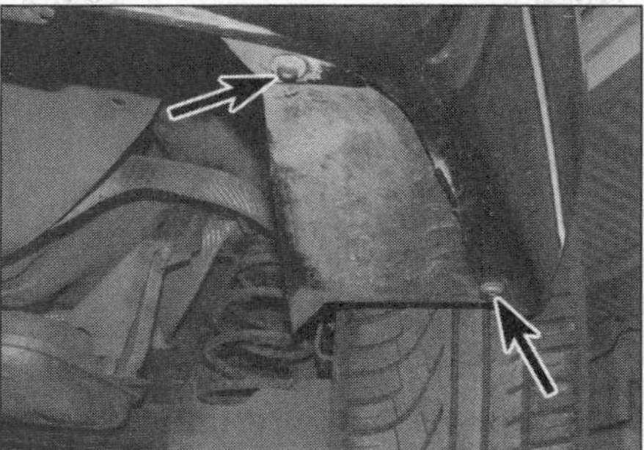
6.16 Remove the lower splash shield retaining screws - arrowed

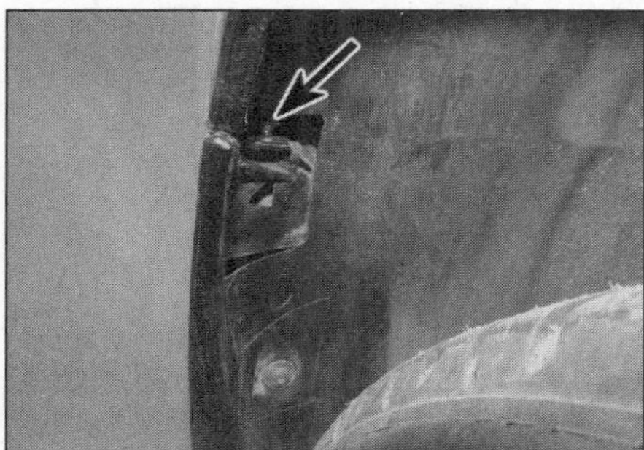
6.17a Release the centre pin of the retaining clip (arrowed) . . .

side of the bumper to the rear wing panel **(see illustrations)**.

18 Disconnect the wiring connector from the upper left-hand rear of the bumper, in the bottom of the rear light recess **(see illustration)**.

19 With the aid of an assistant, pull the bumper rearwards, away from the body, to disengage the side securing lugs, and then withdraw the bumper from the rear of the vehicle. Make sure that everything is disconnected as it is removed.

Removal - Estate models

20 To improve access, chock the front wheels and engage reverse gear (or P on automatic transmission models). Jack up the rear of the vehicle and support it securely on axle stands (see *Jacking and vehicle support*).

21 Working in the luggage compartment, remove the securing screws, and remove the both rear light units as described in Chapter 12.

22 Unscrew the now-exposed upper bumper left and right-hand side retaining screws **(see illustration)**.

23 Unclip the plastic covers, then undo the two upper retaining screws on the top edge of the bumper **(see illustrations)**.

24 Working under the rear of the bumper, release the three lower bumper securing clips **(see illustration)**.

25 Working at each side of the bumper, remove the screws securing the splash shields/wheel arch liners to the rear and bottom edges of the bumper, and remove the splash shields/wheel arch liners **(see illustration)**.

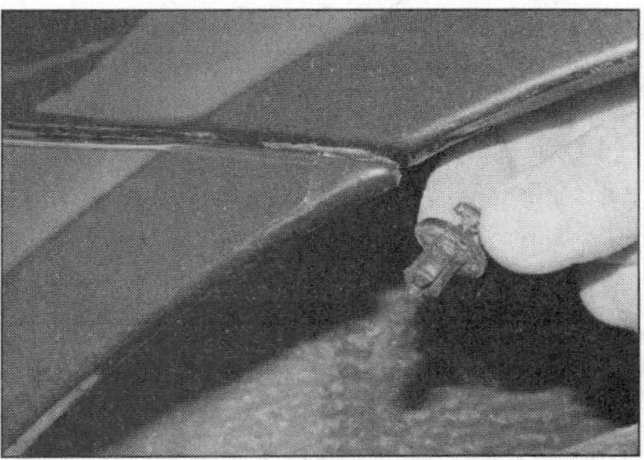
6.17b . . . and withdraw the clip from the wing panel

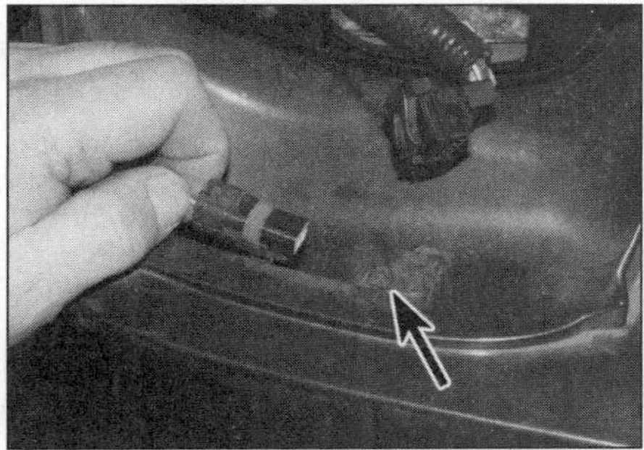
6.18 Disconnect the wiring connector - arrowed

26 Working at each side of the bumper, remove the securing clip that secures each side of the bumper to the rear wing panel **(see illustration)**.

27 With the aid of an assistant, pull the bumper rearwards, away from the body, disengage the side securing lugs and then withdraw the bumper from the rear of the

6.22 Undo the bumper upper retaining screws - arrowed

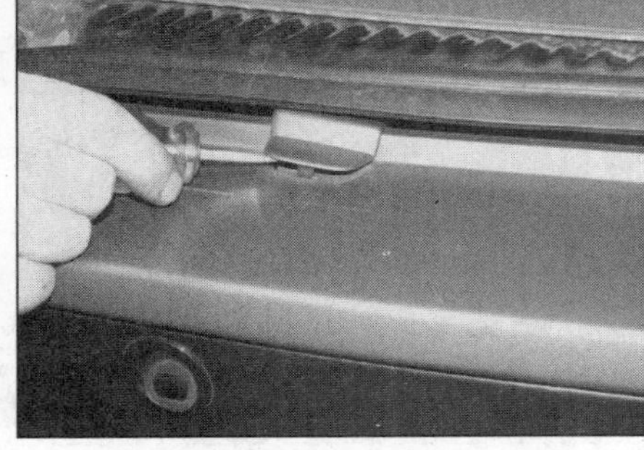
6.23a Release the plastic covers . . .

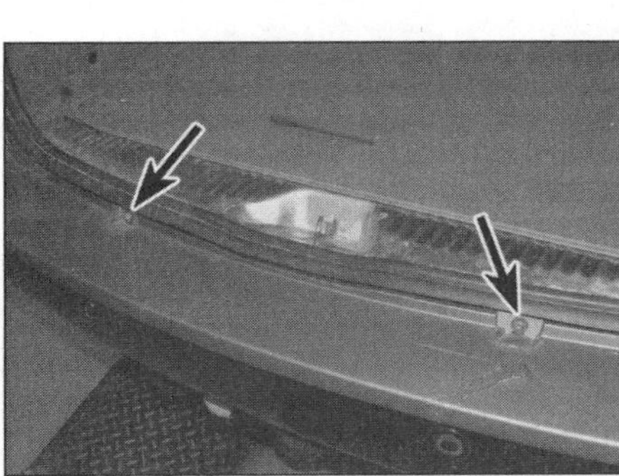
6.23b . . . and remove the retaining screws - arrowed

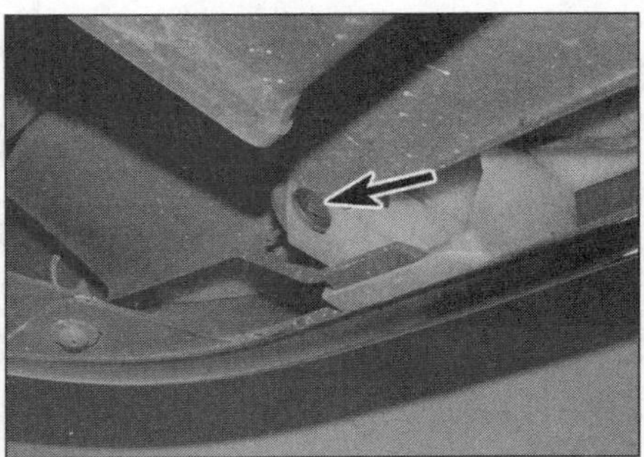
6.24 Release the lower bumper securing clips

6.25 Remove the lower splash shield retaining screws - arrowed

6.26 Release the centre pin and withdraw the clip from the wing panel

vehicle. Disconnect the parking sensor wiring connector as the bumper is removed **(see illustration)**.

Refitting

28 Refitting is a reversal of removal, but ensure that the bumper side locating lugs engage correctly with the clips on the body and, where applicable, make sure that the parking sensor wiring connector is connected securely.

7 Radiator grille panel – removal and refitting

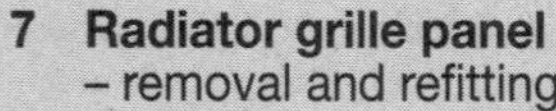

Removal

1 Open the bonnet and remove the four upper retaining clips **(see illustration)**.

7.1 Release the securing clips – arrowed

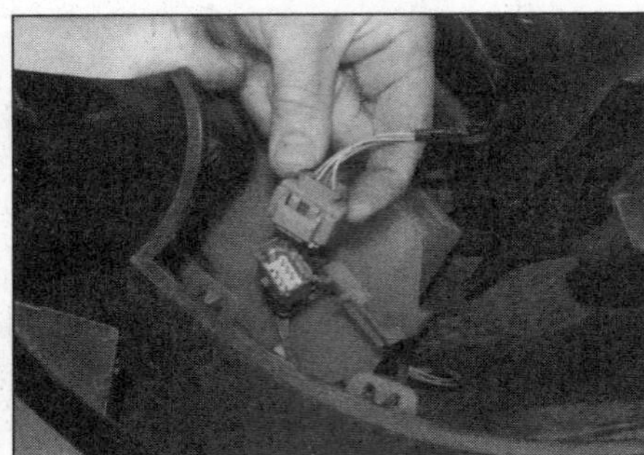

6.27 Disconnect the wiring sensor

2 Unclip the grille at the centre from the top of the bumper and withdraw it upwards **(see illustration)**.

Refitting

3 Refitting is a reversal of removal, but make sure that the grille has located correctly in the lower retaining clip.

8 Bonnet – removal, refitting and adjustment

Removal

1 Open the bonnet, and support it in the open position using the bonnet stay.

2 Using a pencil, or felt-tipped pen, mark the outline of each bonnet hinge relative to the bonnet, to use as a guide on refitting.

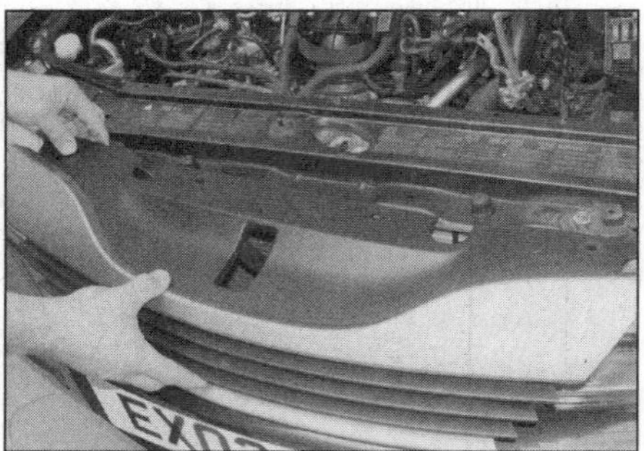

7.2 Withdraw the grille from the bumper

3 Unclip the rubber grommet and disconnect the windscreen washer hose **(see illustration)**.

4 Have an assistant support the bonnet, then working at each side of the bonnet in turn, unscrew the bolts securing the hinge to the bonnet **(see illustration)**. To prevent any damage to the bonnet, place rags under each rear corner of the bonnet before removing the mounting bolts.

5 Unclip the bonnet stay then, with the aid of the assistant, lift the bonnet from the vehicle.

Refitting and adjustment

6 With the aid of an assistant, offer up the bonnet and loosely fit the securing bolts. Align the hinges with the marks made on removal, and then tighten the securing bolts securely.

7 Reconnect the windscreen washer hose and secure into position with the rubber grommet.

8 Close the bonnet and check for alignment with the surrounding body panels. If necessary, slacken the hinge bolts, and re-align the bonnet within the elongated holes to suit. Once the bonnet is correctly aligned, tighten the hinge bolts securely.

9 Once the bonnet is correctly aligned, check that the bonnet fastens and releases in a satisfactory manner. If adjustment is necessary, slacken the bonnet lock striker securing bolts, and adjust the position of the strikers to suit (see Section 10). Once the lock operation is satisfactory, securely tighten the striker securing bolts.

9 Bonnet release cable – removal and refitting

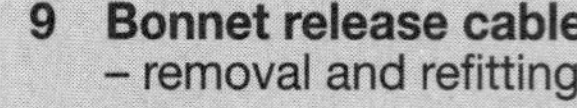

Note: *The bonnet release cable is clipped to the reinforcing crossmember behind the facia panel **(see illustration)**. To remove the cable it may be necessary to remove the facia panel as described later in this Chapter. If a new cable is going to be fitted, the old cable could stay in place and a new one rerouted to prevent the facia being removed.*

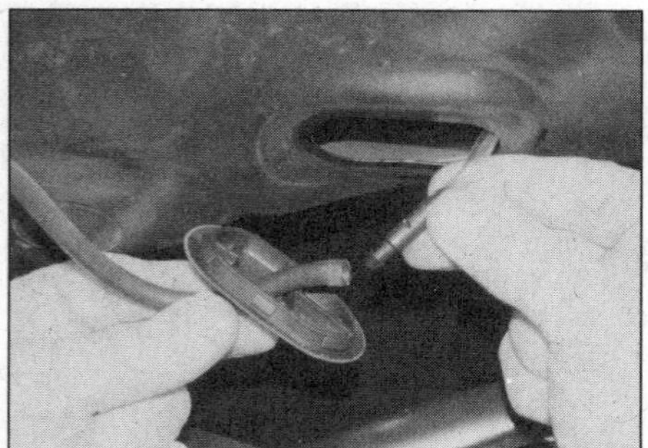

8.3 Disconnect the washer hose

8.4 Undo the bonnet mounting bolts – arrowed

9.0 Unclipping the bonnet cable from the reinforcing crossmember – facia removed

Removal

1 With the bonnet open, release the retaining clips and remove the plastic trim from across the front panel **(see illustrations 10.1a and 10.1b)**.

2 Disconnect the bonnet release cable from the lock mechanism **(see illustration 10.2)**.

3 Working in the passenger compartment on the driver's side, reach up behind the facia and locate the bonnet release handle. Pull the handle up and undo the securing bolt **(see illustration)**.

4 Working under the facia panel, release the cable from any clips and brackets, noting its routing. See note at the beginning of this Section.

5 On the front passenger side of the vehicle, pull the cable through the bulkhead into the passenger compartment **(see illustration)** and, where applicable, untie the string from the end of the cable **(see Haynes Hint)**.

To aid refitting, tie a length of string to the end of the cable in the engine compartment. Pull the end of the string through into the passenger compartment as the cable is removed, then untie the string from the end of the release cable and leave it in position. The string can then be used to pull the cable back through into the engine compartment on refitting.

Refitting

6 Refitting is a reversal of removal but, where applicable, use the string to pull the cable through the bulkhead into the engine compartment, and ensure that the cable is routed as noted before removal.

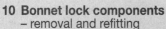

10 Bonnet lock components – removal and refitting

Bonnet lock

Removal

1 With the bonnet open, release the retaining clips and remove the plastic trim from across the front panel **(see illustrations)**.

2 Disconnect the bonnet release cable from the lock mechanism **(see illustration)**.

3 Unscrew the two bolts securing the lock to the body front panel.

4 Withdraw the lock from under the body front panel.

Refitting

5 Refitting is a reversal of removal.

6 On completion, check the operation of the lock. If necessary, adjust the position of the lock striker within the elongated holes in the bonnet to achieve satisfactory lock operation.

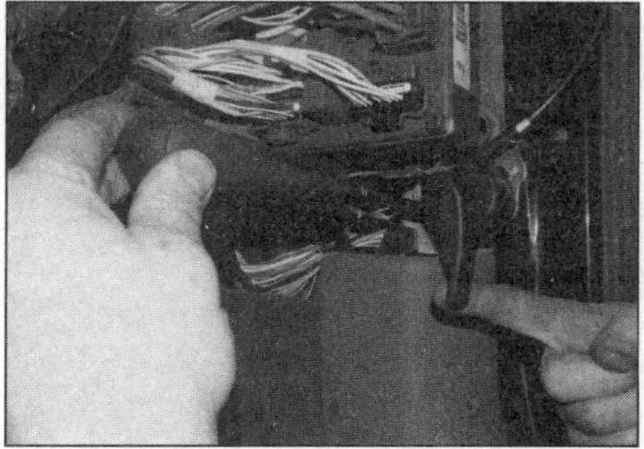

9.3 Pull on the handle and undo the mounting bolt

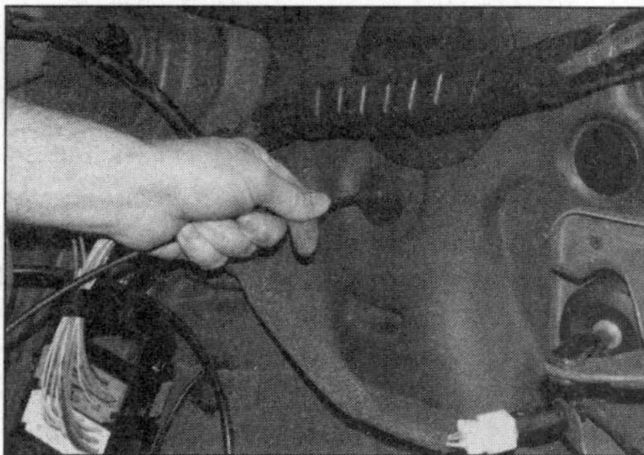

9.5 Pull the bonnet release cable through the bulkhead

Note also that the operation of the lock can be adjusted by altering the thickness of the shims fitted under the lock strikers.

Bonnet lock striker

Removal

7 With the bonnet open, mark the position of the striker using paint or a felt-tipped pen, to aid alignment on refitting.

8 Unbolt the striker from the bonnet, and recover the spacer shim.

Refitting

9 Refitting is a reversal of removal, but align the striker with the marks made before removal.

10 On completion, check the operation of the lock. If necessary, adjust the position of the lock striker within the elongated holes in the bonnet to achieve satisfactory lock operation.

Note also that the operation of the lock can be adjusted by altering the thickness of the shims fitted under the lock strikers.

11 Door – removal, refitting and adjustment

Removal

1 Disconnect the battery negative terminal (refer to *Disconnecting the battery* in the Reference Section of this manual).

2 Open the door, then pull back the securing clip, and disconnect the door wiring connector. **Note:** *Depending on whether it is the front or rear door, the securing clip may slide up or down* ***(see illustrations)***.

10.1a Release the retaining clips . . .

10.1b . . . and withdraw the plastic trim cover

10.2 Disconnect the bonnet release cable from the mechanism – arrowed

11.2a Slide the clip downwards to disconnect the wiring connector – rear door

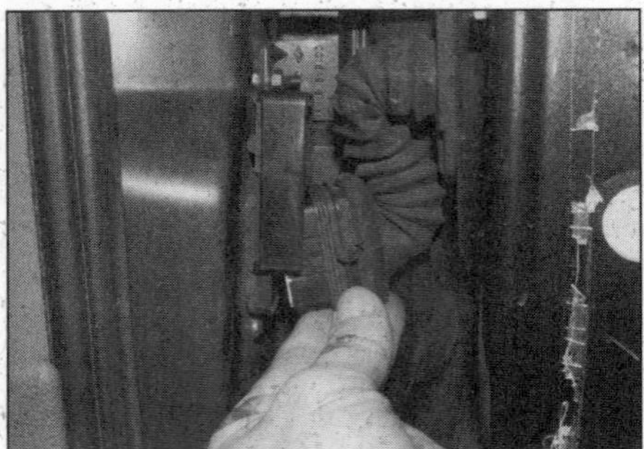

11.2b Slide the clip upwards to disconnect the wiring connector – front door

11.3 Undo the door check strap bolt – arrowed

11.5 Undo the door hinge retaining nuts – arrowed

11.9 Striker securing bolts – arrowed

3 Unscrew the bolt securing the door check strap to the door pillar **(see illustration)**.

4 Support the door on blocks of wood, with rags positioned under the door to protect the paintwork.

5 Have an assistant steady the door, then remove the securing nuts from the upper and lower door hinges **(see illustration)**.

6 Carefully lift the door from the vehicle, taking care not to damage the paintwork.

7 To remove the hinges from the pillar undo the retaining nuts from the rear of the pillar. On front doors, remove the inner wheel arch liner to access the securing nuts and, on the rear doors, remove the inner pillar trim panel as described in Section 25.

Refitting and adjustment

8 Refitting is a reversal of removal, but check that the door is correctly aligned with the surrounding bodywork. Adjustment is made by altering the position of the hinges within the elongated bolt holes.

9 Check that the striker enters the lock centrally when the door is closed, and if necessary loosen the striker and reposition it until satisfactory lock operation is obtained **(see illustration)**.

12 Door inner trim panel – removal and refitting

Removal

Front door

1 Disconnect the battery negative terminal (refer to *Disconnecting the battery* in the Reference Section of this manual).

2 Carefully prise the mirror trim plate from the front corner of the door **(see illustration)**.

3 Using a small screwdriver, unclip the plastic plug and remove the pull handle retaining screw **(see illustrations)**.

4 Unclip the electric mirror switch from the grab handle and disconnect the wiring connector.

5 Remove the electric window switch panel as described in Chapter 12, Section 4.

6 Working at the lower edge of the door trim panel, unscrew the trim panel securing screws **(see illustration)**.

7 Using a suitable forked tool, work around the edge of the door trim panel, and release the panel securing clips **(see illustration)**. A knife may be needed to cut the mastic sealer around the outer edge.

8 Pull the panel upwards from the door, disconnect the wiring connectors for the speaker and door open warning light as the panel is removed.

12.2 Prise the mirror trim plate from the door

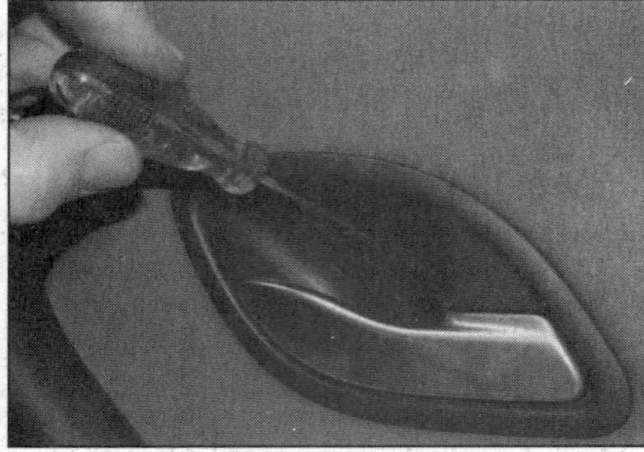

12.3a Unclip the plastic plug . . .

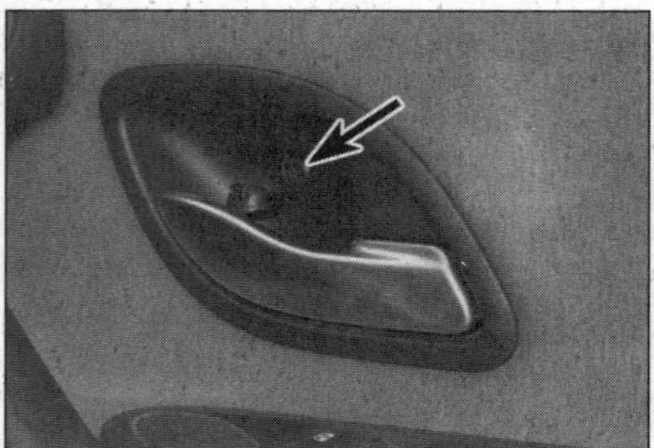

12.3b . . . and remove the retaining screw – arrowed

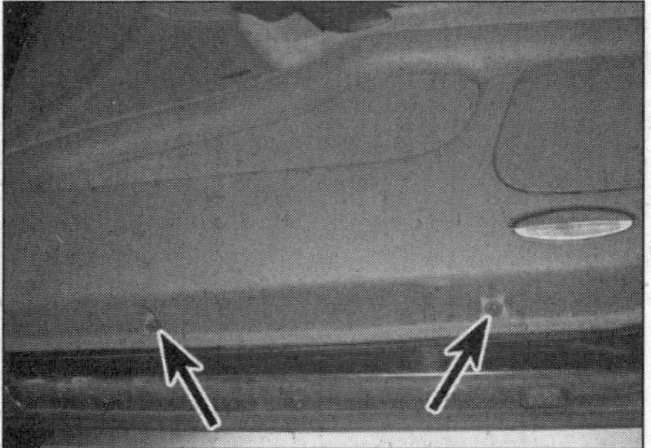

12.6 Remove the two lower panel securing screws – arrowed

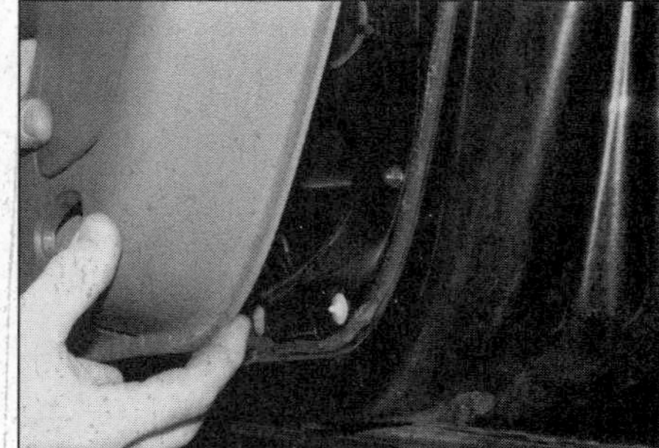

12.7 Unclip the panel from the door frame

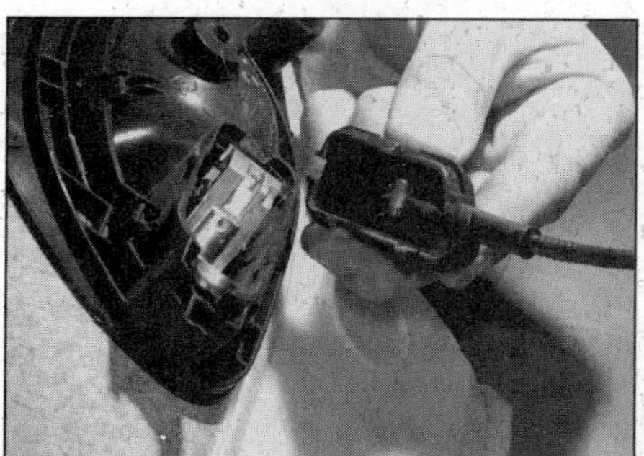
12.9 Unclip the cable from the door pull handle

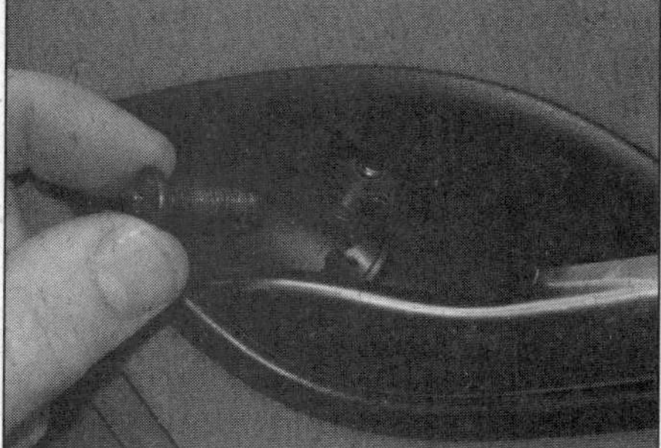
12.11 Removing the door pull handle retaining screw

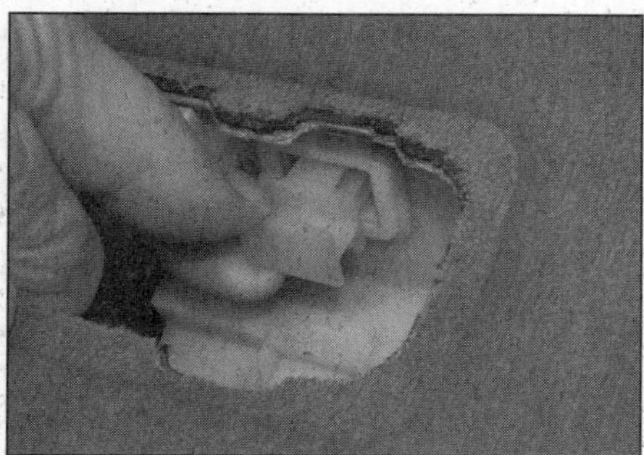
12.12 Pull out the securing clip

9 Also, as the panel is withdrawn from the door, unclip the door lock release cable from the door pull handle **(see illustration)**.

Rear door

10 Disconnect the battery negative terminal (refer to *Disconnecting the battery* in the Reference Section of this manual).

11 Using a small screwdriver, unclip the plastic plug and remove the pull handle retaining screw **(see illustration)**.

12 On models with electric windows, remove the electric window switch panel as described in Chapter 12, Section 4. With the switch panel removed, pull out the door panel securing clip **(see illustration)**.

13 On models with manual windows, note the position of the window regulator handle with the window shut, and then remove the regulator handle. If necessary, use a forked tool, together with a piece of cloth to protect the door trim, to release the handle from the spindle.

14 Working at the lower edge of the door trim panel, unscrew the trim panel securing screws **(see illustration)**.

15 Using a suitable forked tool, work around the edge of the door trim panel, and release the panel securing clips. A knife may be needed to cut the mastic sealer around the outer edge.

16 Pull the panel upwards from the door, disconnect the wiring connectors for the speaker and door open warning light as the panel is removed.

17 Also as the panel is withdrawn from the door, unclip the door lock release cable from the door pull handle **(see illustration 12.9)**.

Refitting

18 Refitting is a reversal of removal, bearing in mind the following points.

a) *Note that Renault recommends that the door panel sealing mastic should be renewed.*
b) *Before refitting, check whether any of the trim panel securing clips were broken on removal, and renew them as necessary.*
c) *Where applicable, ensure that any wiring is connected or fed through the holes in the trim panel as it is refitted.*
d) *Make sure the door lock release cable is connected securely to the door pull handle.*
e) *On the rear door trims, push the securing clip in to secure the door trim panel **(see illustration)**.*

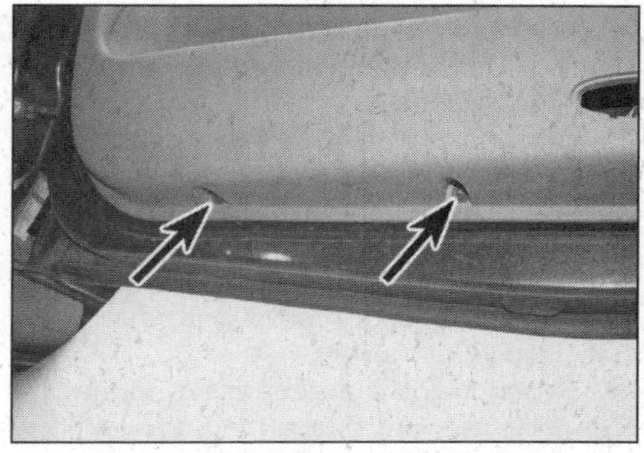
12.14 Remove the two lower panel securing screws – arrowed

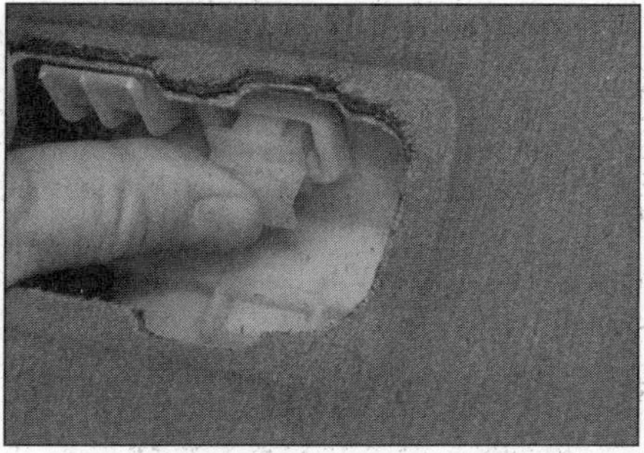
12.18 Press the securing clip back into position

13 Door handles and lock components – removal and refitting

Door interior handle

1 The interior handle is part of the door trim panel, remove the door inner trim panel as described in Section 12.

Front door lock cylinder

Note: *There is a door lock cylinder only fitted to the passenger side front door, the driver's side door has a dummy lock housing.*

Removal

2 On the passenger side front door, unclip the door lock cover **(see illustration)**.

3 Open the door and remove the plastic grommet from the rear edge of the door, then slacken the securing screw **(see illustration)**. This screw does not need to be completely removed.

4 The lock (passenger side) or dummy lock housing (driver's side) can now be withdrawn from the door handle **(see illustration)**.

Refitting

5 Refitting is a reversal of the removal procedure.

Front door exterior handle

Removal

6 Remove the door lock cylinder as described previously in this Section.

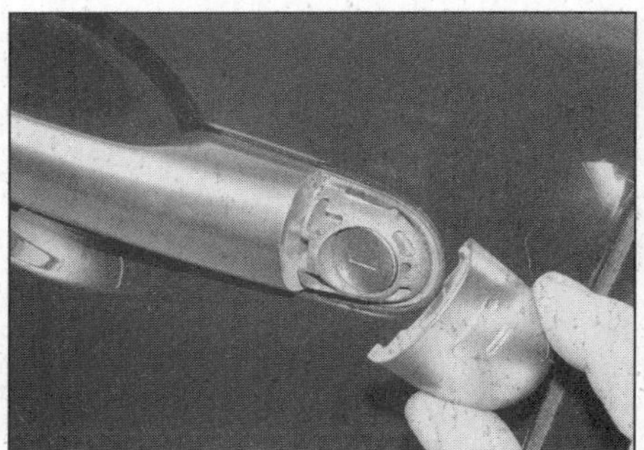
13.2 Unclip the lock barrel cover – passenger side only

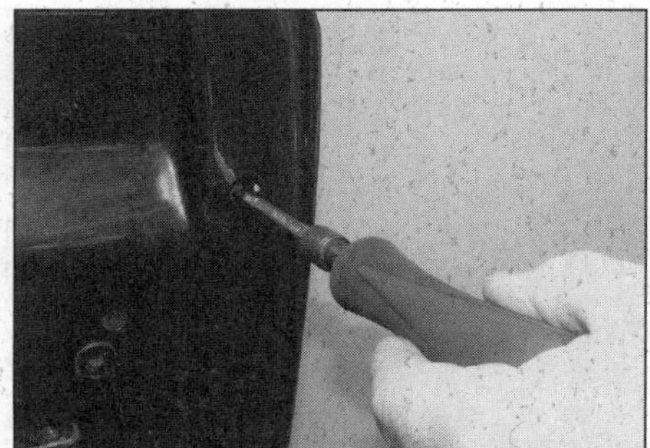
13.3 Slacken the securing screw

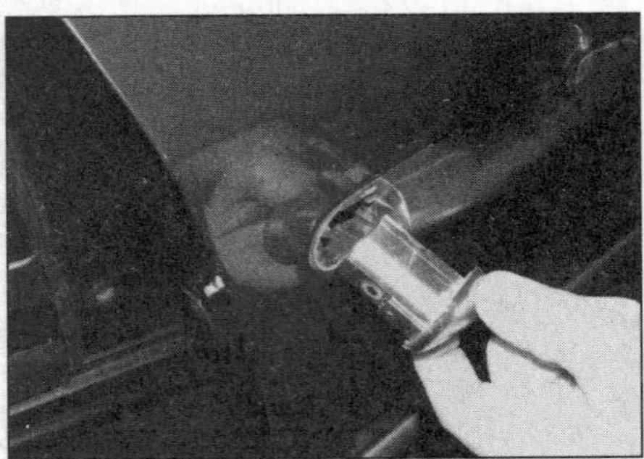
13.4 Withdrawing the dummy lock housing from the driver's door

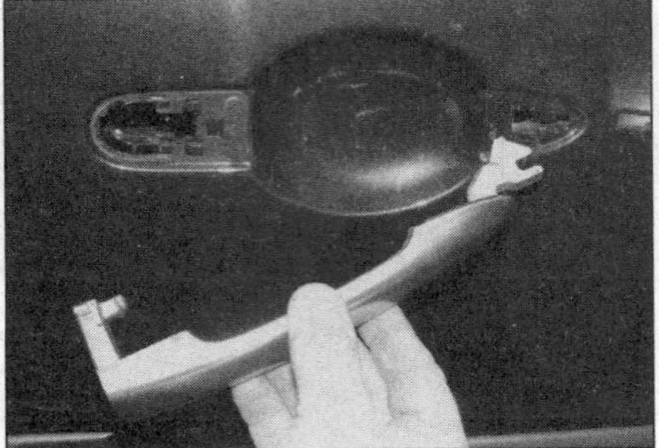
13.7 Removing the outer door handle from the door

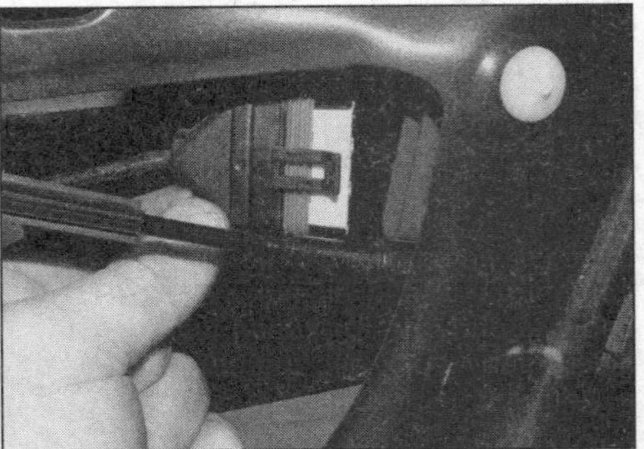
13.11 Disconnecting the door lock wiring connector

7 Slide the handle towards the rear edge of the door, then pull the handle outwards to release it from the door panel **(see illustration)**.

Refitting

8 Refitting is a reversal of the removal procedure.

Rear door exterior handle

9 The removal and refitting procedures are as described previously for the front door exterior handle.

Door lock

Removal

10 Remove the door inner trim panel as described in Section 12.

11 Disconnect the wiring connector from the door lock assembly **(see illustration)**.

12 Remove the door lock cylinder and exterior handle as described previously in this Section. Unclip the seal from the door panel **(see illustration)**.

13 Working at the rear edge of the door, unscrew the three lock securing screws **(see illustrations)**.

14 Using a small screwdriver, release the two lugs and push the lock housing to the rear edge of the door to unclip it from the door panel **(see illustration)**.

15 Reach inside the door and withdraw the lock assembly out through the door aperture **(see illustration)**.

16 If required, the lock operating cable can be unclipped from the door catch mechanism **(see illustration)**.

Refitting

17 Refitting is a reversal of the removal procedure.

14 Door window glass and regulator – removal and refitting

Front door window glass

Removal

1 Remove the door inner trim panel as described in Section 12.

2 Position the window glass in the down position and remove the two retaining clips from the window risers at the lower edge of the glass **(see illustrations)**.

3 Unclip the inner weatherstrip from the lower edge of the window aperture.

4 Unclip the glass from the risers and slide the glass upwards, lift the glass out through the inside of the window aperture by tilting it forwards.

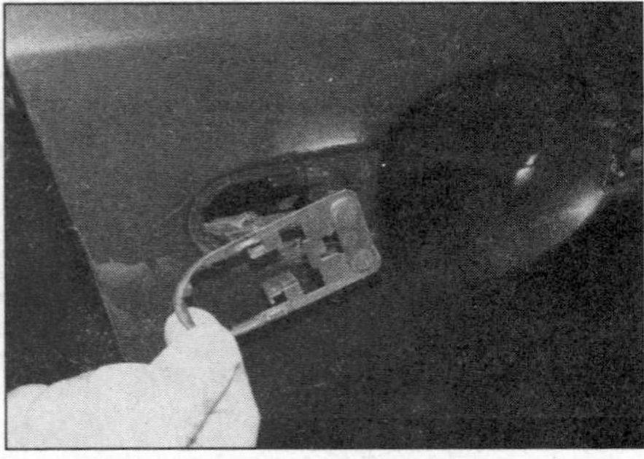
13.12 Unclip the seal from the door panel

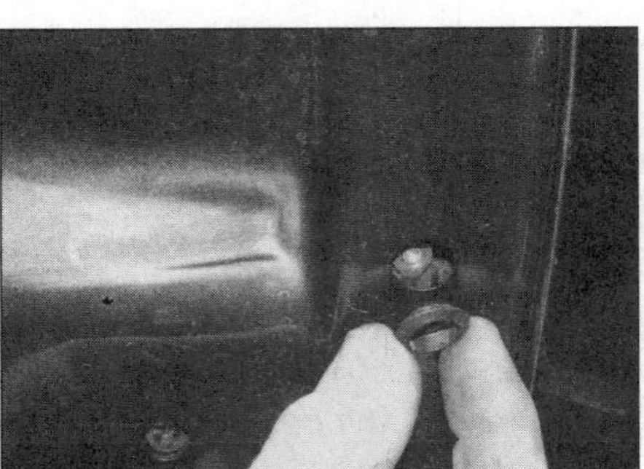
13.13a Unclip the plastic grommet . . .

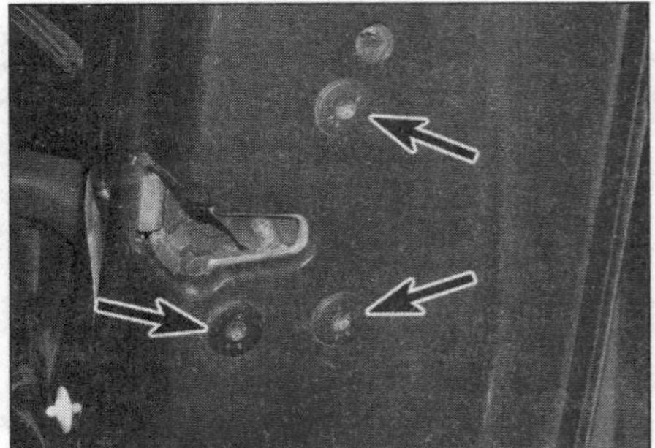
13.13b . . . and undo the lock securing screws – arrowed

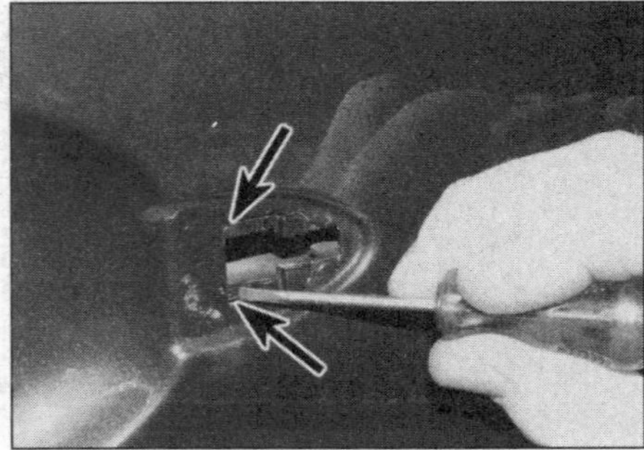
13.14 Release the two lugs – arrowed

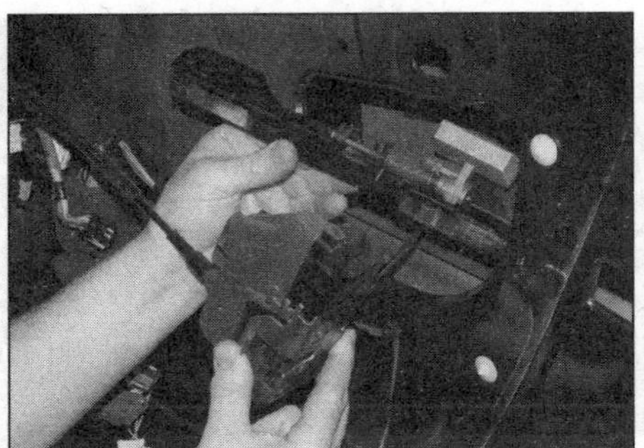
13.15 Removing the door lock assembly

13.16 Unclip the cable from the door catch assembly

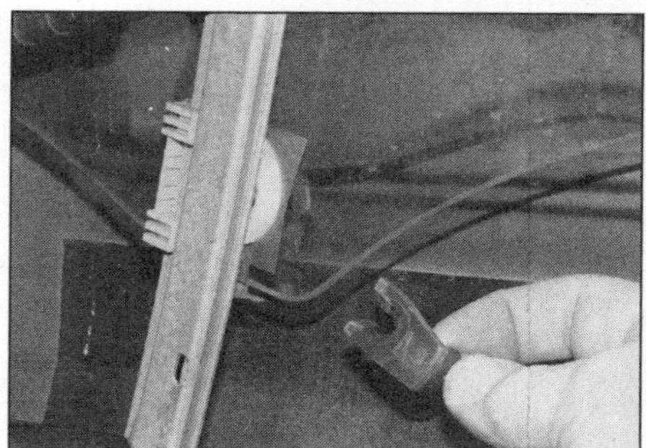
14.2a Release the front securing clip . . .

14.2b . . . and the rear securing clip – arrowed

14.8 Undo the channel mounting bolts – arrowed

Refitting

5 Refitting is a reversal of removal, but ensure that the weatherstrip is securely refitted, and refit the door inner trim panel with reference to Section 12.

Rear door window glass

Removal

6 Proceed as described in paragraphs 1 to 3. **Note:** *There is only one retaining clip securing the glass to one riser on the rear doors.*
7 Unclip the glass from the riser and slide it downwards to the bottom of the inner door shell.
8 Remove the two lower mounting bolts from the window channel upright **(see illustration)**.
9 Peel back the window channel rubber and remove the retaining screw from the top edge of the channel **(see illustrations)**.
10 Twist the channel and withdraw it forwards and out from the window aperture.
11 The sliding glass can now be lifted out through the window aperture by tilting it forwards.
12 The fixed window glass can now be removed by sliding it forwards.

Refitting

13 Refitting is a reversal of removal, but ensure that the weatherstrip is securely refitted. Check that the door trim holding clips are secure before refitting the fixed window glass **(see illustration)**.

Front door window regulator

Removal

14 Remove the door inner trim panel as described in Section 12.
15 Position the window glass in the down position and remove the two retaining clips from the window risers at the lower edge of the glass **(see illustrations 14.2a and 14.2b)**.
16 Unclip the glass from the risers and slide it up to the top of the window frame. The window glass can be supported at the top of the window frame by using strong adhesive tape.
17 Disconnect the wiring connector from the window regulator assembly **(see illustration)**.
18 Release the window regulator operating cable securing clips from the inner door panel **(see illustration)**.
19 Unscrew the five mounting bolts securing the assembly to the door panel, and then withdraw the regulator and risers out through the door aperture **(see illustrations)**.

Refitting

20 Refitting is a reversal of removal, but

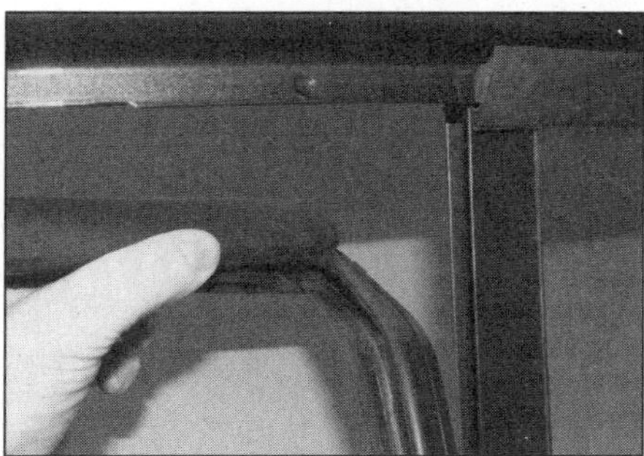
14.9a Peel back the window channel . . .

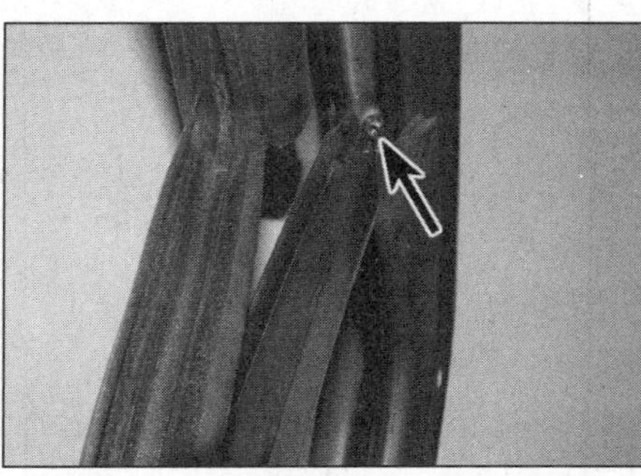
14.9b . . . and undo the upper retaining screw – arrowed

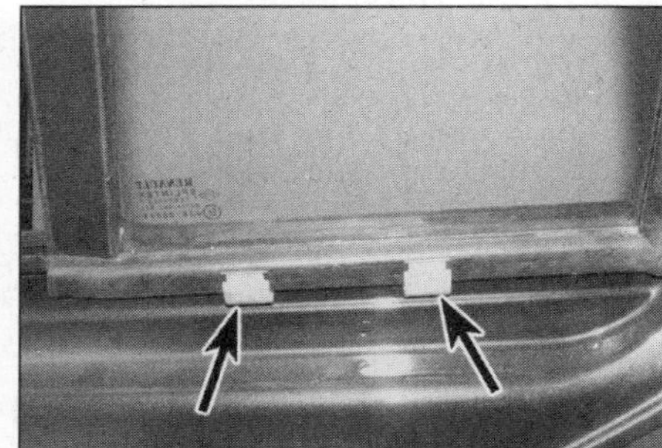
14.13 Door trim holding clips – arrowed

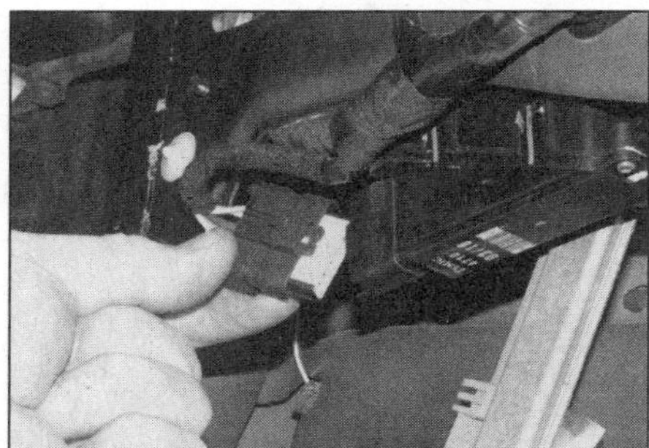
14.17 Disconnect the regulator wiring connector

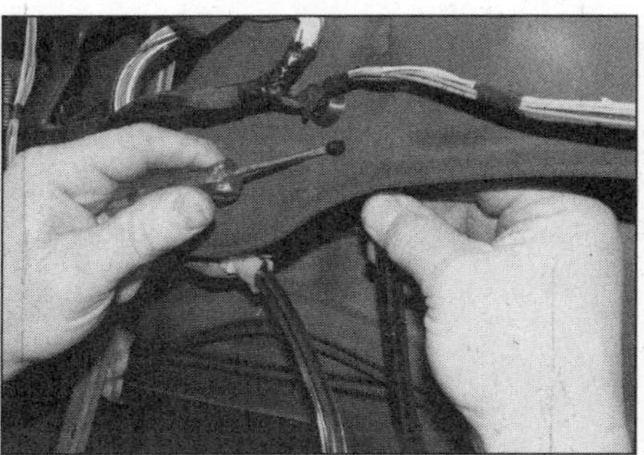
14.18 Unclip the cables from the door panel

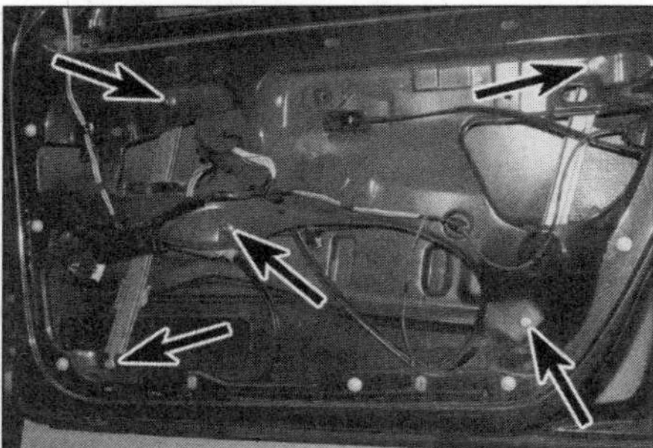
14.19a Undo the five mounting bolts (arrowed) . . .

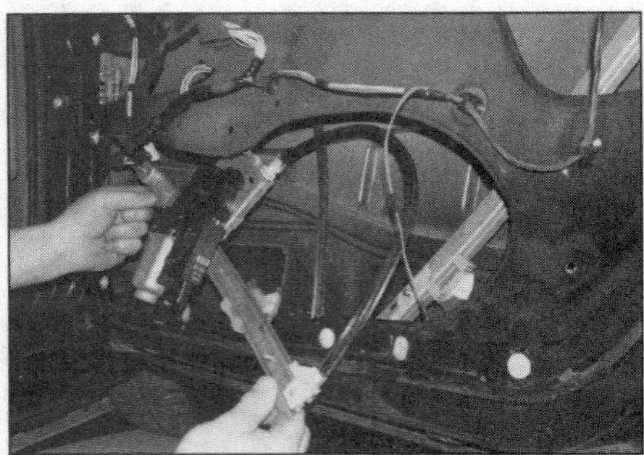

14.19b . . . and withdraw the regulator assembly out of the door

14.22 Remove the window glass securing clip

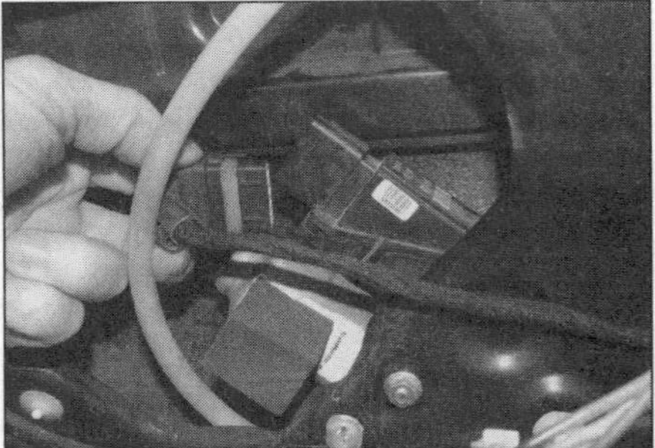

14.24 Disconnect the regulator wiring connector

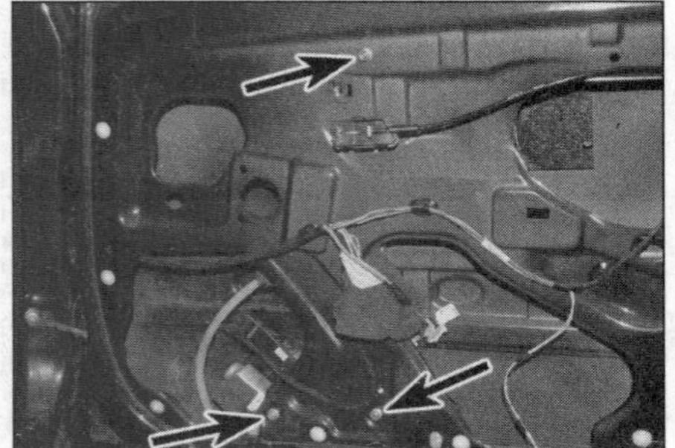

14.25a Undo the three mounting bolts (arrowed) . . .

14.25b . . . and withdraw the regulator assembly out of the door

ensure that the weatherstrip is securely refitted, and refit the door inner trim panel with reference to Section 12.

Rear door window regulator

Removal

21 Remove the door inner trim panel as described in Section 12.

22 Position the window glass in the down position and remove the retaining clip from the window riser at the lower edge of the glass **(see illustration)**.

23 Unclip the glass from the riser and slide it up to the top of the window frame. The window glass can be supported at the top of the window frame by using strong adhesive tape.

24 Disconnect the wiring connector from the window regulator assembly **(see illustration)**.

25 Unscrew the three mounting bolts securing the assembly to the door panel, and then withdraw the regulator and risers out through the door aperture **(see illustrations)**.

Refitting

26 Refitting is a reversal of removal, but ensure that the weatherstrip is securely refitted, and refit the door inner trim panel with reference to Section 12.

15 Tailgate and support struts – removal, refitting and adjustment

Tailgate – Hatchback models

Removal

1 Disconnect the battery negative terminal (refer to *Disconnecting the battery* in the Reference Section of this manual).

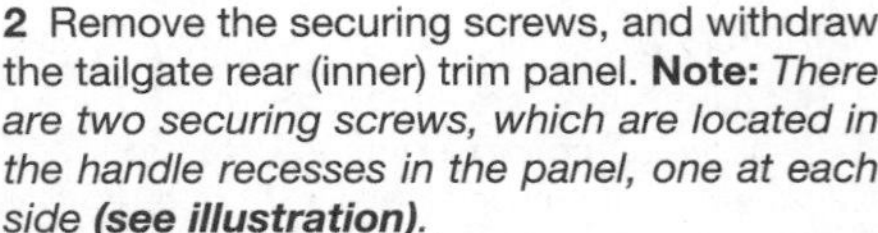

2 Remove the securing screws, and withdraw the tailgate rear (inner) trim panel. **Note:** *There are two securing screws, which are located in the handle recesses in the panel, one at each side **(see illustration)**.*

3 Carefully unclip the trim panel from along the upper edge of the tailgate, and then unclip the left and right-hand trim panels **(see illustrations)**.

4 Disconnect the wiring from all electrical components mounted in the tailgate.

5 Release the wiring from any clips inside the tailgate.

6 Pull the wiring grommet from the apertures in the tailgate.

7 If the original tailgate is to be refitted, tie a length of string to the ends of all relevant wiring, then feed the wiring through the top of the tailgate. Untie the string, leaving it in position in the tailgate to assist refitting.

8 With the aid of an assistant, support the tailgate, then prise out the support strut spring clips, and pull the struts from the balljoints on the tailgate **(see illustration)**.

9 Unscrew the nut on each side of the tailgate, securing the hinge in position.

10 Unscrew the bolt on each side securing the tailgate to the hinge, and then carefully lift the tailgate from the vehicle.

Refitting and adjustment

11 If a new tailgate is to be fitted, transfer all serviceable components (lock components, wiper motor, etc) to it.

12 Refitting is a reversal of removal, bearing in mind the following points.

a) If the original tailgate is refitted, draw

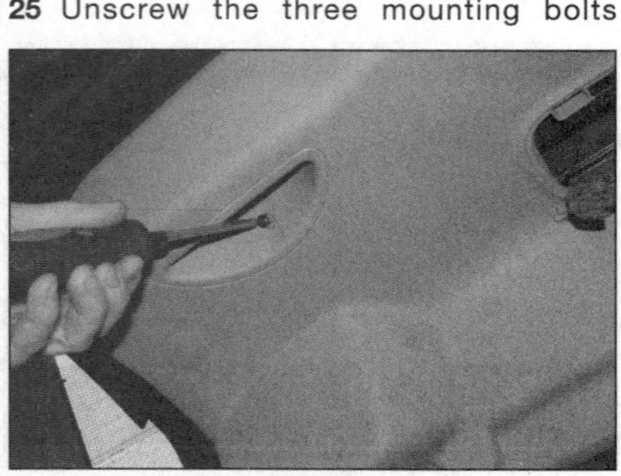

15.2 Undo the retaining screws

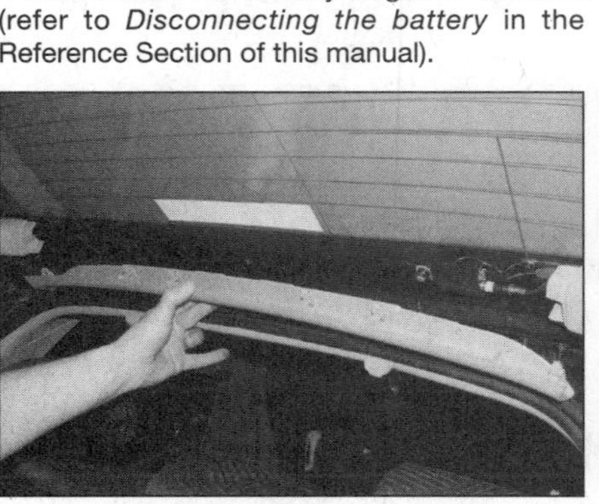

15.3a Unclip the upper trim panel . . .

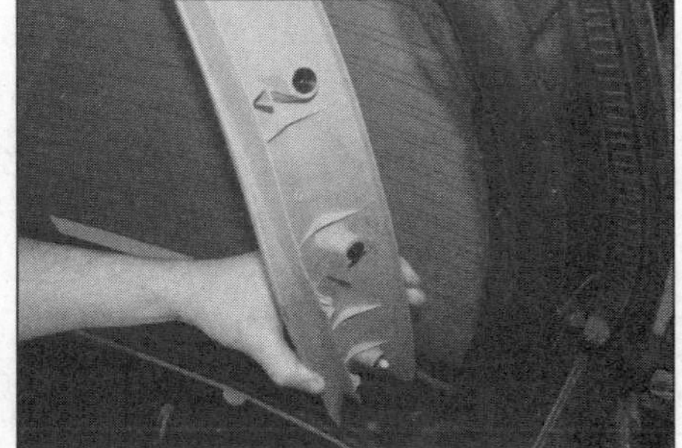

15.3b . . . and then the two side trim panels

15.8 Releasing the spring clips on the strut balljoint

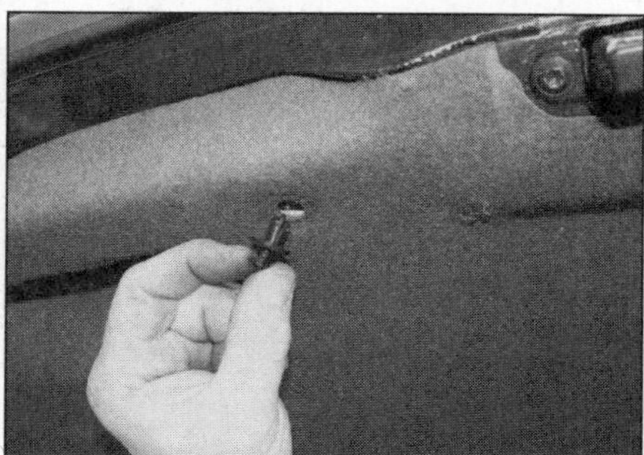
15.14a Remove the retaining clips . . .

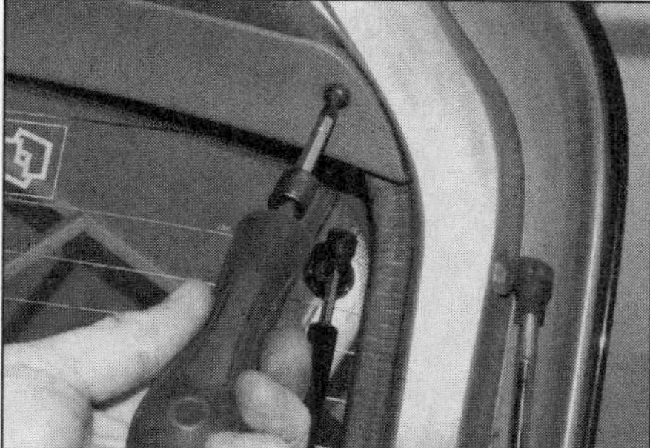
15.14b . . . and the securing screws

15.16 Unclip the wiring grommets from the tailgate

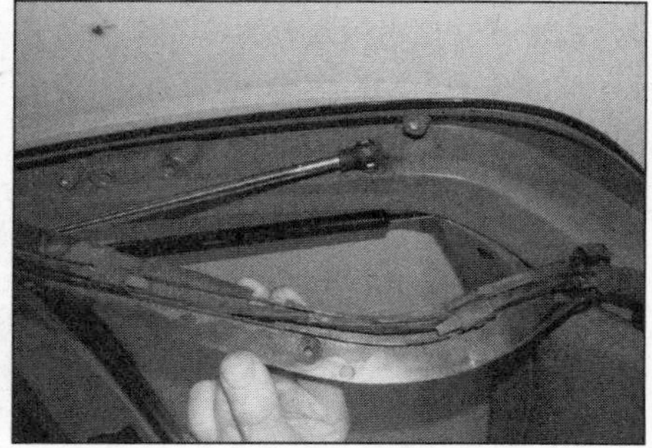
15.17 Remove the wiring loom from along the side of the tailgate

15.20 Remove the cover and undo the securing nut – arrowed

the wiring through the tailgate using the string.

b) If necessary, adjust the plastic buffers to obtain a good fit when the tailgate is shut. The position of the buffers can be altered by loosening the securing screws.

c) If necessary, adjust the position of the tailgate lock striker within its elongated holes to achieve satisfactory lock operation (remove the luggage compartment rear trim panel for access to the lock striker).

Tailgate – Estate models

Removal

13 Disconnect the battery negative terminal (refer to *Disconnecting the battery* in the Reference Section of this manual).

14 Remove the retaining clips and the securing screws, and withdraw the tailgate inner trim panel **(see illustrations)**.

15 Disconnect the wiring from all electrical components mounted in the tailgate. Release the wiring from any clips inside the tailgate.

16 Pull the wiring grommets from the apertures at each side of the tailgate **(see illustration)**.

17 Unscrew the wiring loom plastic trim from along the left-hand side of the tailgate **(see illustration)**.

18 If the original tailgate is to be refitted, tie a length of string to the ends of all relevant wiring, then feed the wiring through the top of the tailgate. Untie the string, leaving it in position in the tailgate to assist refitting.

19 With the aid of an assistant, support the tailgate, then prise out the support strut spring clips, and pull the struts from the balljoints on the tailgate.

20 Remove the plastic covers, and then unscrew the nuts on each side securing the tailgate hinge, then carefully lift the tailgate from the vehicle **(see illustration)**.

Refitting and adjustment

21 If a new tailgate is to be fitted, transfer all serviceable components (lock components, wiper motor, etc) to it.

22 Refitting is a reversal of removal, bearing in mind the following points.

a) If the original tailgate is refitted, draw the wiring through the tailgate using the string.

b) If necessary, adjust the plastic buffers to obtain a good fit when the tailgate is shut. The position of the buffers can be altered by loosening the securing screws.

c) If necessary, adjust the position of the tailgate lock striker within its elongated holes to achieve satisfactory lock operation (remove the luggage compartment rear trim panel for access to the lock striker).

Tailgate glass – Estate models

Removal

23 Open the tailgate and undo the spoiler upper retaining screws at each side of the tailgate **(see illustration)**.

24 Unclip the plastic cover from the centre of the tailgate and disconnect the wiring block connector and the washer pipe **(see illustrations)**. Feed the wiring and the washer pipe out from the top of the tailgate.

25 Close the tailgate and open the tailgate glass.

26 With the aid of an assistant, support the

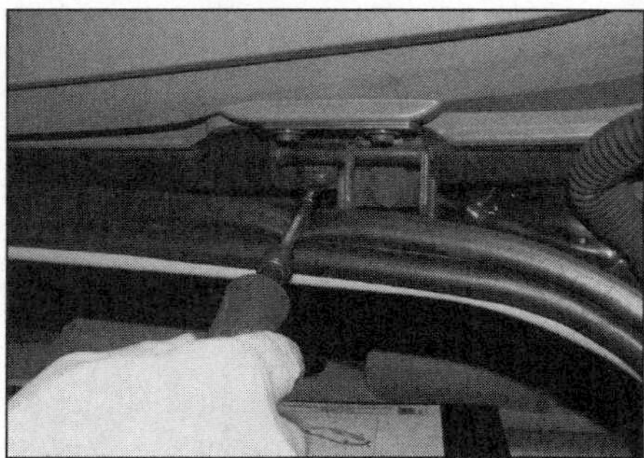
15.23 Undo the spoiler upper retaining screws

15.24a Disconnect the wiring connector and the washer pipe . . .

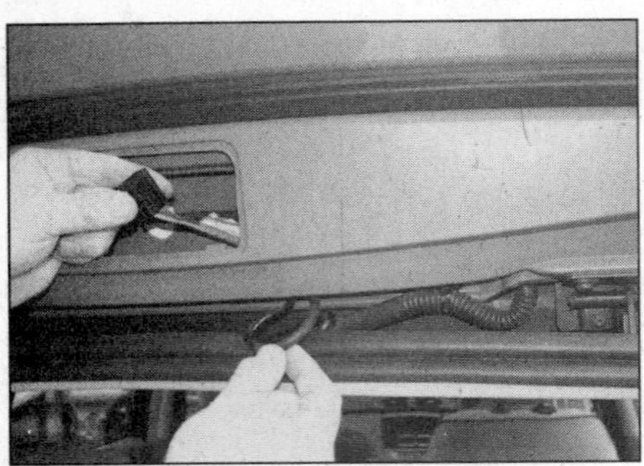
15.24b ... and pull them out from the top of the tailgate

15.26 Releasing the spring clips on the strut balljoint

15.27 Undo the retaining screws – arrowed

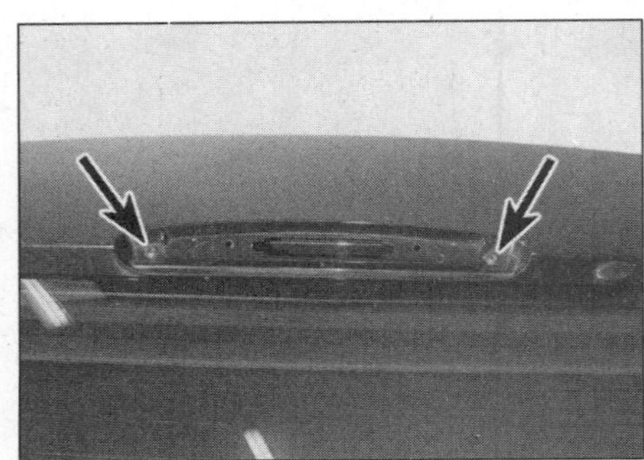
15.28 Undo the two retaining screws – arrowed

tailgate glass, then prise out the support strut spring clips, and pull the struts from the balljoints on the glass **(see illustration)**.

27 Remove the retaining screws, and then carefully lift the tailgate glass from the vehicle **(see illustration)**. **Note:** *As the glass is removed, the spoiler will also be removed with it; feed the wiring and washer pipe away from the tailgate as the glass is removed.*

28 To remove the spoiler from the tailgate glass completely, remove the high-level brake light as described in Chapter 12, Section 7. Then undo the two securing screws from behind the light unit **(see illustration)**.

Refitting and adjustment

29 Refitting is a reversal of the removal procedure.

Support strut

Removal

30 With the aid of an assistant, support the tailgate in the open position.

31 Using a suitable flat-bladed screwdriver, release the spring clip, and pull the support strut from its balljoint on the tailgate **(see illustration 15.26)**.

32 Similarly, release the strut from the balljoint on the body, and withdraw the strut from the vehicle.

Refitting

33 Refitting is a reversal of removal, but ensure that the spring clips are correctly engaged.

16 Tailgate lock components – removal and refitting

Hatchback models

Release switch

1 Disconnect the battery negative terminal (refer to *Disconnecting the battery* in the Reference Section of this manual).

2 Remove the securing screws, and withdraw the tailgate rear (inner) trim panel. **Note:** *there are two securing screws, which are located in the handle recesses in the panel one at each side* ***(see illustration)****.*

3 Slacken the two retaining nuts and remove the lower retaining bolt from the lock cover-protector **(see illustration)**.

4 Release the securing clip and disconnect the wiring connector from the release switch **(see illustration)**.

5 Working through the aperture in the tailgate, undo the release switch mounting bracket nuts **(see illustration)**.

6 From outside the tailgate, withdraw the tailgate release switch from the tailgate **(see illustration)**.

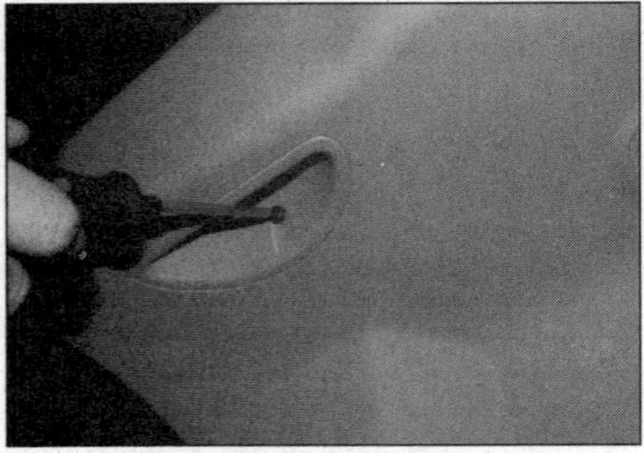
16.2 Undo the rear trim securing screws

16.3 Slacken the upper two nuts and remove the lower bolt

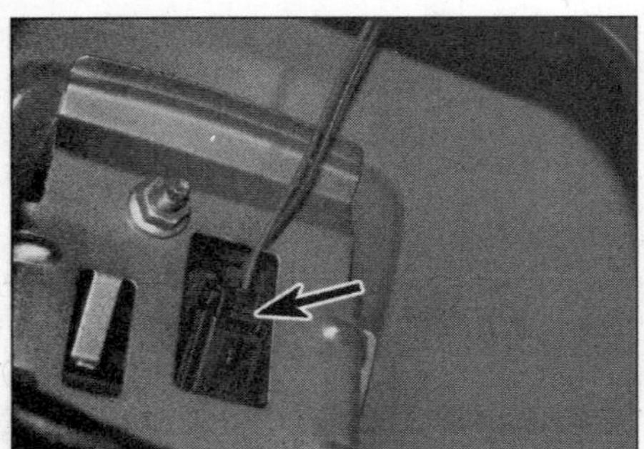
16.4 Disconnect the wiring connector – arrowed

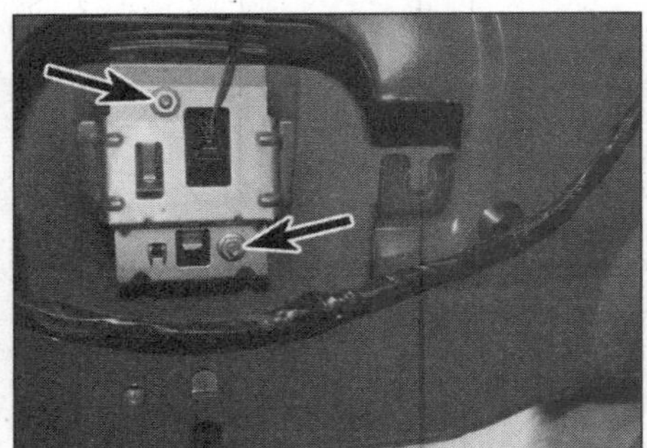
16.5 Undo the release switch mounting plate bolts – arrowed

16.6 Withdraw the release switch from the tailgate

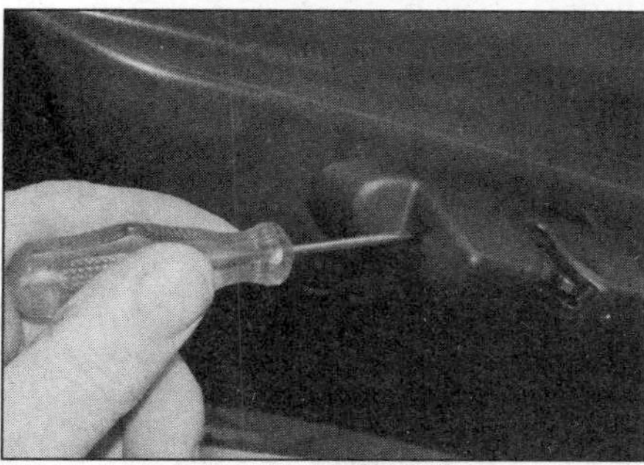

16.9a Release the securing clips . . .

16.9b . . . and withdraw the protective cover

16.10a Undo the catch mounting bolts . . .

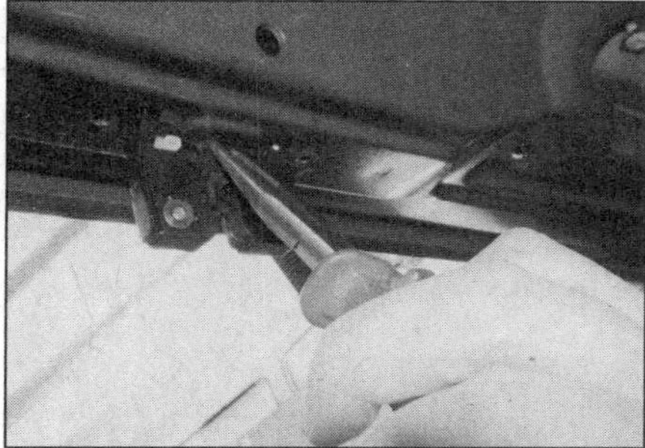

16.10b . . . and release the locking clip

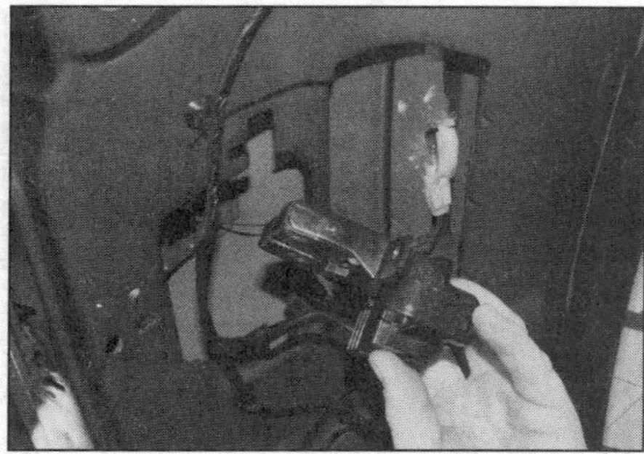

16.11 Withdraw the locking catch from the tailgate

16.13 Remove the rear trim panel

7 Refitting is a reversal of removal, but check the operation of the lock on completion.

Locking catch

8 Proceed as described in paragraphs 1 to 3.

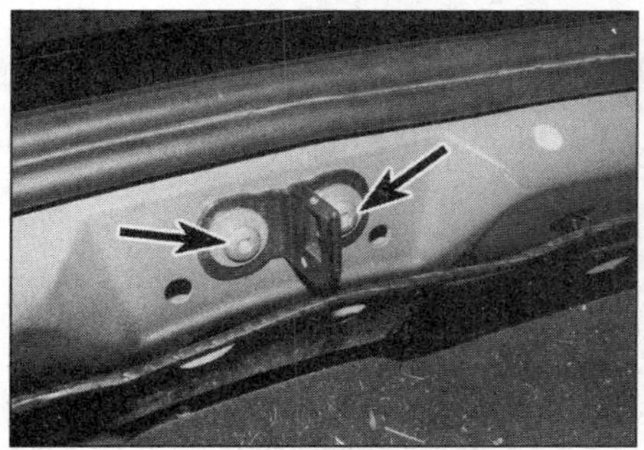

16.14 Undo the two retaining bolts – arrowed

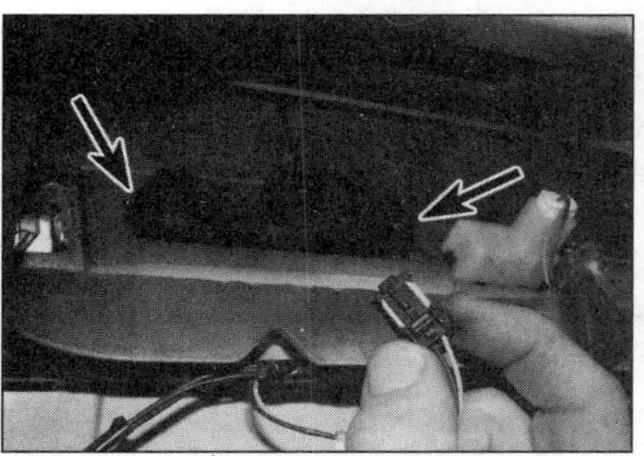

16.18 Release the securing clips – arrowed

9 Working on the lower edge of the tailgate, unclip the plastic protective cover from the locking catch **(see illustrations)**.

10 Undo the two retaining bolts from the locking catch and, using a pair of pliers,

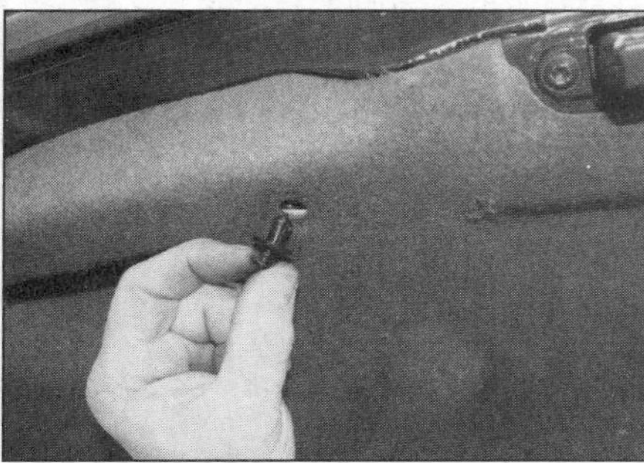

16.17 Remove the retaining clips

16.19 Withdraw the release switch from the tailgate

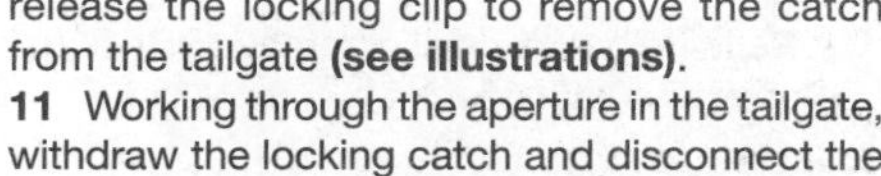

release the locking clip to remove the catch from the tailgate **(see illustrations)**.

11 Working through the aperture in the tailgate, withdraw the locking catch and disconnect the wiring connector **(see illustration)**.

12 Refitting is a reversal of removal, but check the operation of the lock before refitting the tailgate trim panel.

Lock striker

13 Working in the luggage compartment, remove the securing screws and clips, and withdraw the luggage compartment rear trim panel **(see illustration)**.

14 Unscrew the securing bolts **(see illustration)**, and remove the striker.

15 Refitting is a reversal of removal, but check the operation of the lock on completion, and if necessary adjust the position of the lock striker within its elongated holes to achieve satisfactory lock operation.

Estate (Sport Tourer) models

Release switch

16 Disconnect the battery negative terminal (refer to *Disconnecting the battery* in the Reference Section of this manual).

17 Remove the retaining clips and screws, and withdraw the tailgate rear (inner) trim panel **(see illustration)**.

18 Disconnect the wiring connector from the release switch and release the securing clips **(see illustration)**.

19 From outside the tailgate, withdraw the tailgate release switch from the tailgate **(see illustration)**.

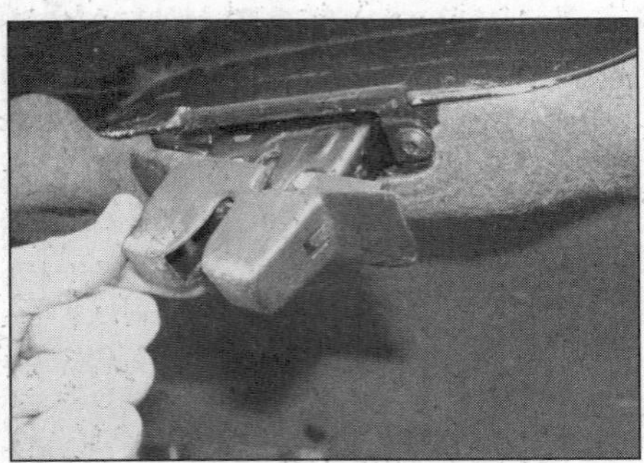
16.22 Remove the protective cover from the catch

16.23 Undo the catch mounting bolts – arrowed

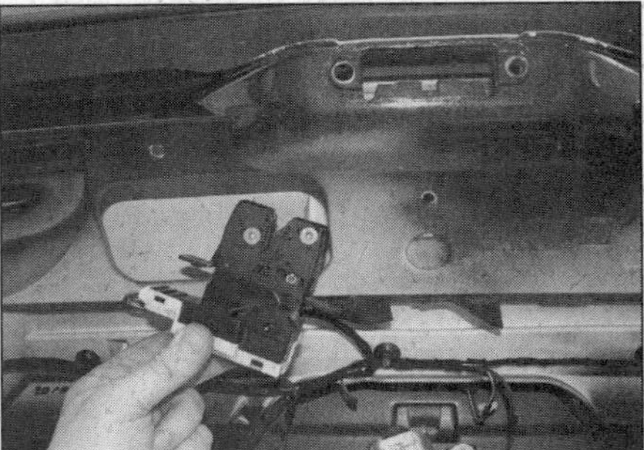
16.24 Withdraw the locking catch from the tailgate

16.26 Remove the rear trim panel

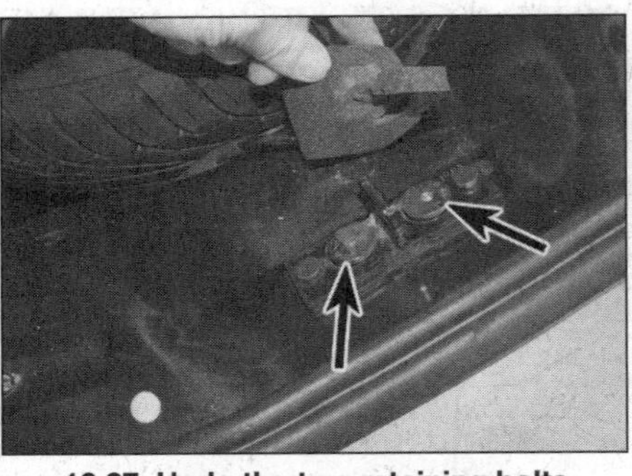
16.27 Undo the two retaining bolts – arrowed

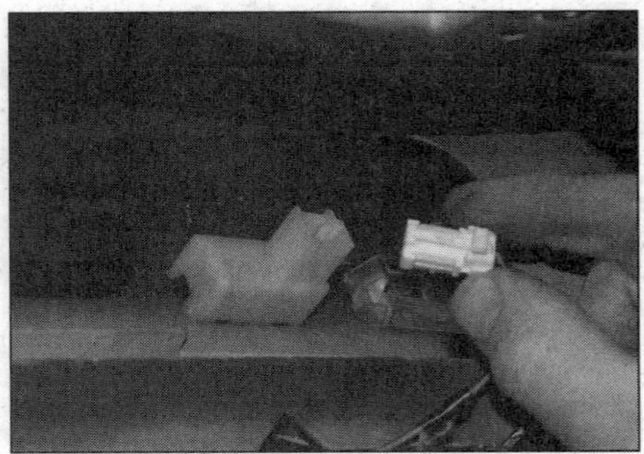
16.31 Disconnect the release switch wiring connector

20 Refitting is a reversal of removal, but check the operation of the lock on completion.

Locking catch

21 Proceed as described in paragraphs 16 and 17.

22 Working on the lower edge of the tailgate, release the retaining clips and unclip the plastic protective cover from the locking catch **(see illustration)**.

23 Undo the two retaining bolts from the locking catch on the lower edge of the tailgate **(see illustration)**.

24 Working through the aperture in the tailgate, withdraw the locking catch and disconnect the wiring connector **(see illustration)**.

25 Refitting is a reversal of removal, but check the operation of the lock before refitting the tailgate trim panel.

Lock striker

26 Working in the luggage compartment, remove the securing bolts, and withdraw the luggage compartment rear trim panel **(see illustration)**.

27 Remove the foam packing and unscrew the securing bolts **(see illustration)**, and remove the striker.

28 Refitting is a reversal of removal, but check the operation of the lock on completion, and if necessary adjust the position of the lock striker within its elongated holes to achieve satisfactory lock operation.

Window release switch

29 Disconnect the battery negative terminal (refer to *Disconnecting the battery* in the Reference Section of this manual).

30 Remove the retaining clips, and withdraw the tailgate rear (inner) trim panel **(see illustration 16.17)**.

31 Working through the aperture in the tailgate, disconnect the wiring connector from the release switch **(see illustration)**.

32 From outside the tailgate, withdraw the tailgate release switch from the tailgate **(see illustration)**.

33 Refitting is a reversal of removal, but check the operation of the lock on completion.

Window locking catch

34 With the tailgate window open, release the securing clips and remove the tailgate upper trim panel **(see illustration)**.

35 Working inside the tailgate, disconnect the wiring connector from the locking catch **(see illustration)**.

36 Undo the two retaining screws from the locking catch and withdraw it from the tailgate.

37 Refitting is a reversal of removal, but

16.32 Withdraw the release switch from the tailgate

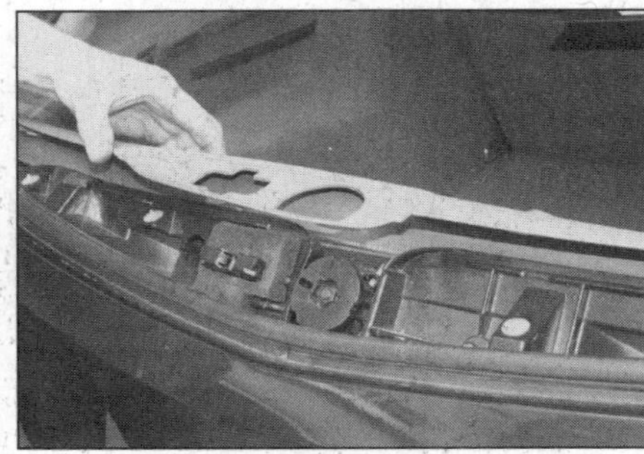
16.34 Unclip the trim from the tailgate

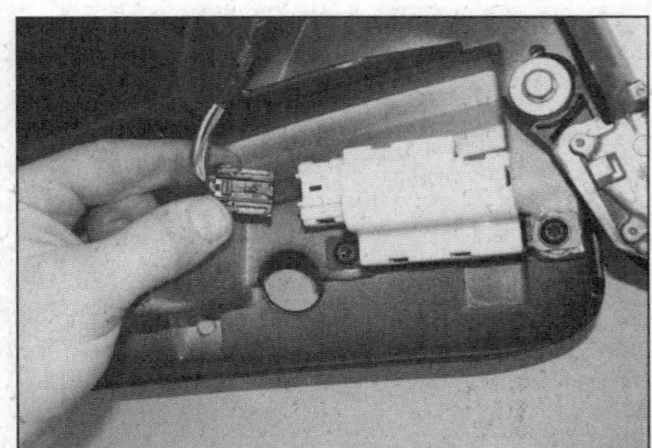
16.35 Disconnect the wiring connector

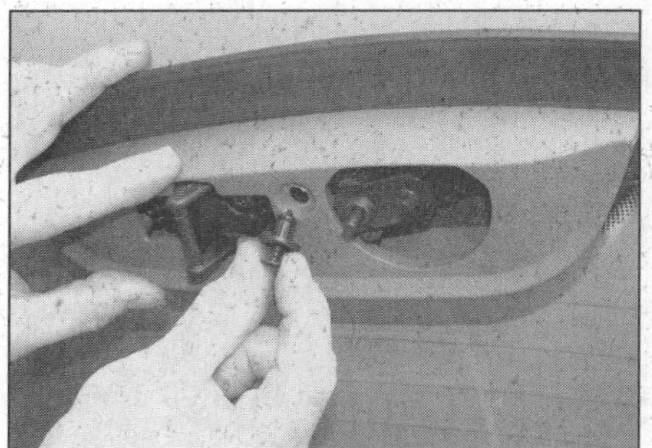
16.38 Release the securing clip

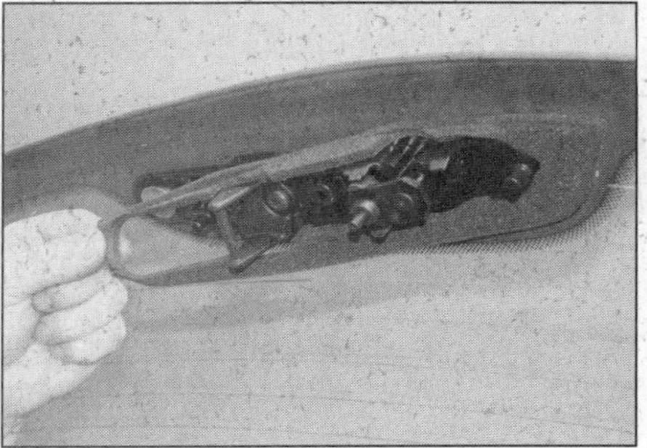
16.39 Peel back the foam gasket

16.40 Undo the lock striker mounting bolts – arrowed

check the operation of the lock before refitting the tailgate trim panel.

Window lock striker

38 With the tailgate window open, release the securing clip and remove the lock striker trim panel **(see illustration)**.

39 Peel off the foam gasket from around the lock striker mounting bracket **(see illustration)**.

40 Undo the retaining screws and remove the lock striker from the mounting bracket **(see illustration)**.

41 Refitting is a reversal of removal, but check the operation of the lock on completion, and if necessary adjust the position of the lock striker within its elongated holes to achieve satisfactory lock operation.

17 Central locking system components – removal and refitting

The central locking is controlled by the multi-timer unit, which Renault calls a UCH. This is attached to the fuse and relay box, which is located inside the vehicle, under the right-hand side of the facia (as seen from the driver's seat). If there is a fault with this unit, it will require checking with Renault diagnostic equipment.

The door tailgate lock motors and switches are an integral part of the lock assemblies – see Sections 13 and 16 of this Chapter.

18 Electric window components – general information

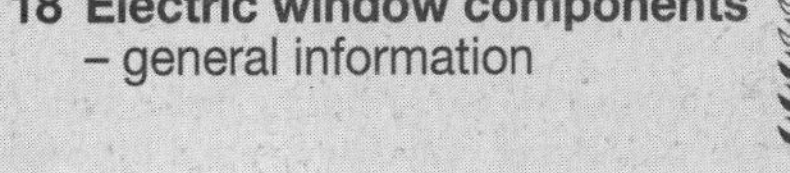

Window switches

1 Refer to Chapter 12, Section 4.

Window regulator motors

2 The motors are integral with the regulator mechanism, and cannot be renewed independently, the complete door regulator assembly must be renewed as described in Section 14.

Electronic control unit

3 The electric windows are controlled by the multi-timer unit, which Renault calls a UCH. This is attached to the fuse and relay box, which is located inside the vehicle, under the right-hand side of the facia (as seen from the driver's seat). If there is a fault with this unit, it will require checking with Renault diagnostic equipment.

19 Exterior mirrors and associated components – removal and refitting

Mirror

Removal

1 Disconnect the battery negative terminal (refer to *Disconnecting the battery* in the Reference Section of this manual).

2 Working at the inside edge of the door, unclip the mirror inner trim panel from the door **(see illustration)**.

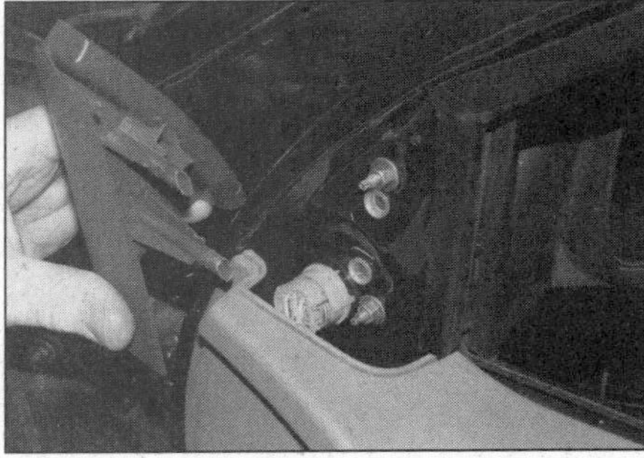
19.2 Removing the mirror inner trim cover

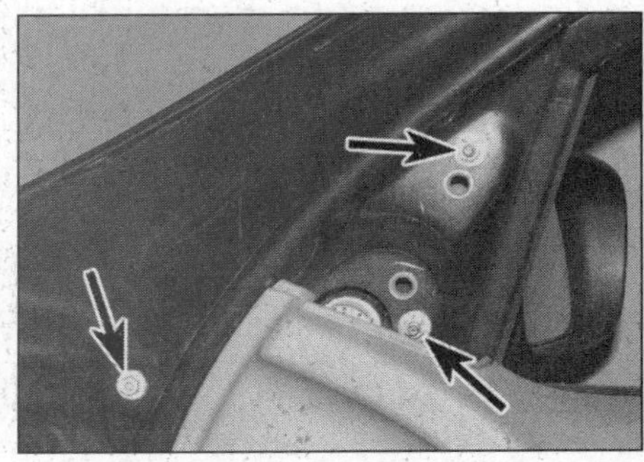
19.4 Undo the securing bolt and nuts – arrowed

3 Disconnect the mirror wiring connector **(see illustration)**.

4 Support the mirror, and then unscrew the two nuts and the bolt (at the front edge of the door) securing the mirror to the door **(see illustration)**. **Note:** *Take great care not to drop the nuts into the door behind the trim panel.*

5 Remove the mirror assembly from the door frame.

Refitting

6 Refitting is a reversal of the removal procedure.

Mirror glass

Removal

7 Tilt the mirror assembly outwards (towards the front of the vehicle).

8 Using a flat-bladed tool, carefully prise behind the top edge of the mirror glass **(see illustration)**. Support the glass, lever the tool

19.3 Disconnecting the mirror wiring connector

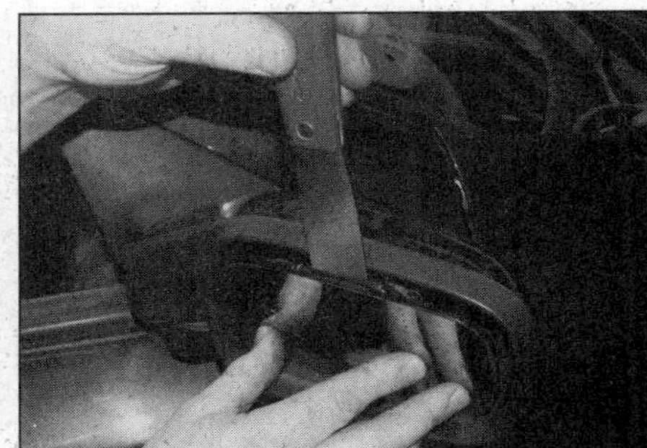
19.8 Carefully prise the mirror glass to release the clips

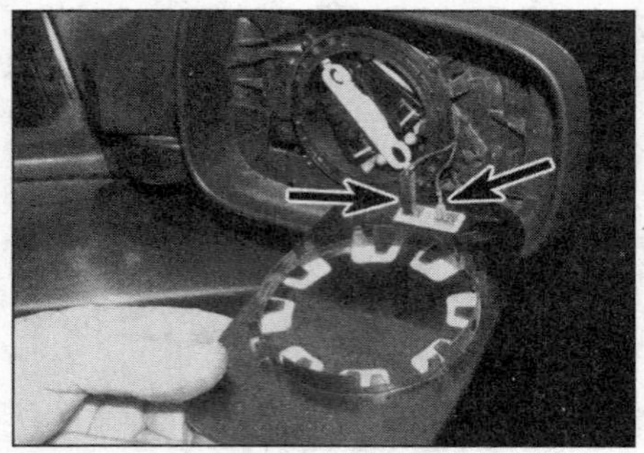
19.9 Disconnect the wiring connectors – arrowed

19.13a Release the retaining clips . . .

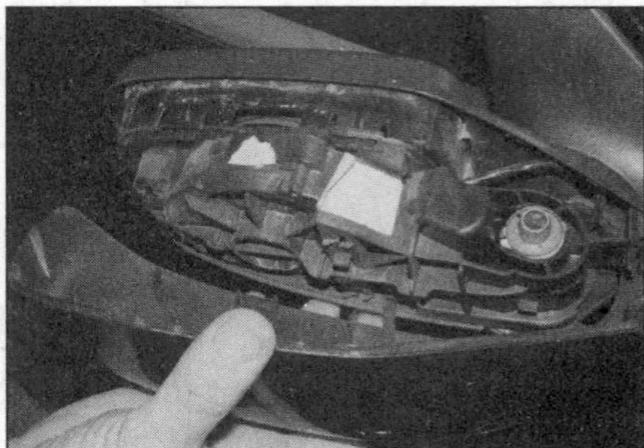
19.13b . . . and withdraw the rear cover

forwards and the mirror glass will unclip from the mirror assembly. Take care not to drop the mirror glass as the clip is released.

9 Withdraw the glass and, disconnect the heating element wires from the rear of the glass **(see illustration)**.

Refitting

10 Reconnect the wires to the rear of the glass.

11 To refit the glass, press the glass into position until it engages securely, taking care not to damage the glass.

Mirror rear cover

Removal

12 Remove the mirror glass, as described previously in this Section.

13 Using a small screwdriver, from inside the mirror aperture, release the retaining tabs, and then carefully prise the shell from the mirror **(see illustrations)**.

Refitting

14 Refitting is a reversal of removal.

20 Windscreen, tailgate and fixed side window glass – general information

These areas of glass are secured by the tight fit of the weatherstrip in the body aperture, and are bonded in position with a special adhesive. Renewal of such fixed glass is a difficult, messy and time-consuming task, which is considered beyond the scope of the home mechanic. It is difficult, unless one has plenty of practice, to obtain a secure, waterproof fit. Furthermore, the task carries a high risk of breakage; this applies especially to the laminated glass windscreen. In view of this, owners are strongly advised to have this sort of work carried out by one of the many specialist windscreen fitters.

21 Sunroof – general information

This type of sunroof is a complex piece of equipment, consisting of a large number of components. It is strongly recommended that the sunroof mechanism is not disturbed unless absolutely necessary. If the sunroof mechanism is faulty, or requires overhaul, consult a Renault dealer for advice. Even removing the sunroof motor requires that the headlining be taken down, which is not a job to be taken on lightly.

22 Body exterior fittings – removal and refitting

Radiator grille panel

1 Refer to Section 7.

Rear spoiler (Hatchback)

Removal

2 Open the tailgate, and then unscrew the spoiler securing bolts, two on each side of the tailgate **(see illustration)**.

3 Lift the spoiler from the tailgate.

Refitting

4 Refitting is a reversal of removal.

Scuttle cover panels

Removal

5 Remove the wiper arms as described in Chapter 12. A lever may be required for wiper arm removal.

6 Unclip the weatherstrip from the edge of the scuttle panel **(see illustration)**.

7 Release the securing clips, two at each side, securing the scuttle cover panel to the suspension turrets **(see illustration)**.

8 Starting with the right-hand side scuttle panel, lift it upwards in the top corner to release the retaining clip. Then pull the panel forwards to release the rear clips securing the panel under the windscreen **(see illustrations)**. Take care not to break the clips.

9 Now lift the left-hand side panel upwards

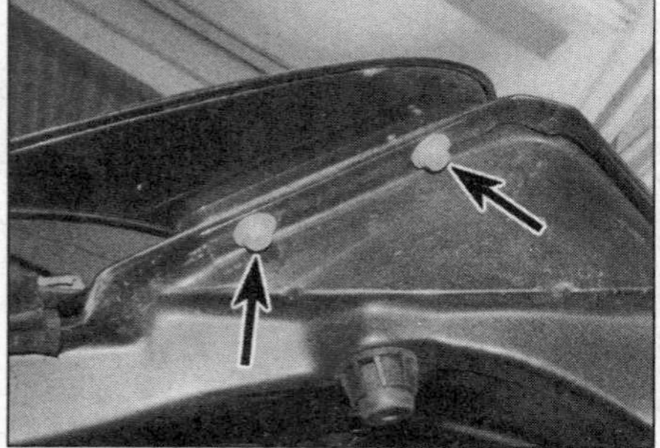
22.2 Undo the spoiler mounting bolts – arrowed

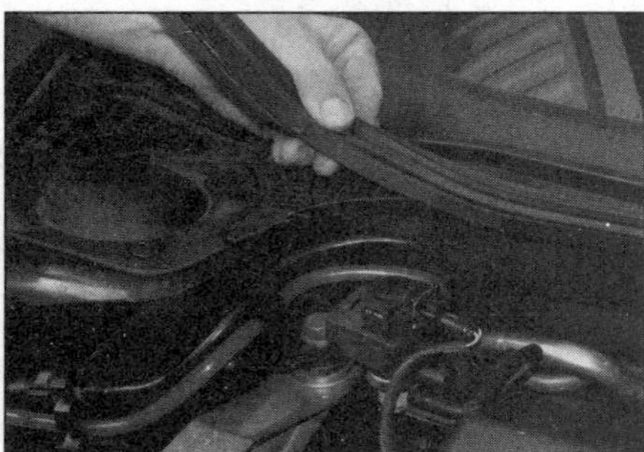
22.6 Peel back the weatherstrip and remove it from the car

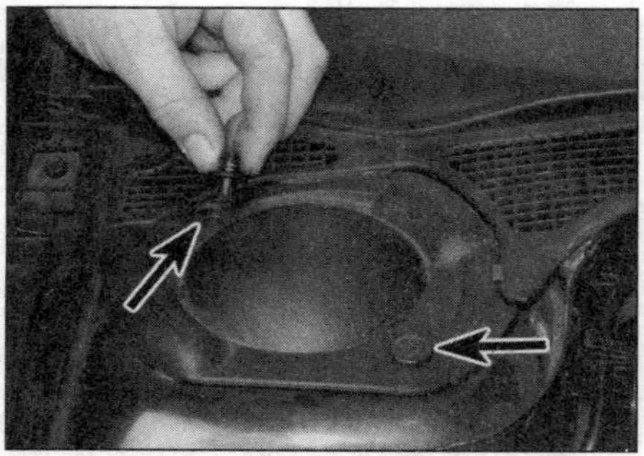
22.7 Remove the securing clips – arrowed

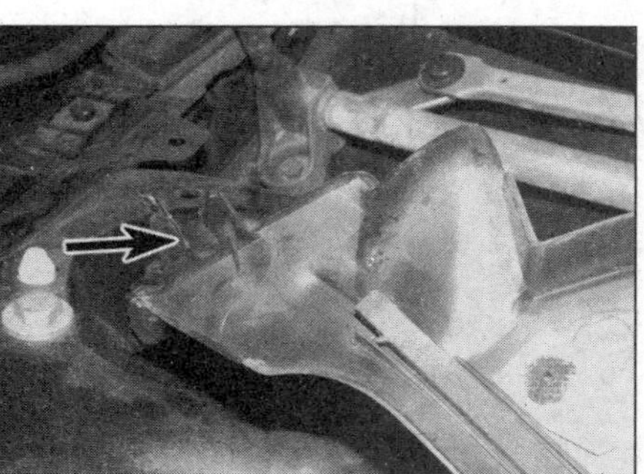
22.8a Rear corner retaining clip

in the top corner to release the retaining clip. Then pull the panel forwards to release the rear clips securing the panel under the windscreen **(see illustration)**. Take care not to break the clips.

Refitting

10 Refitting is a reversal of removal, ensuring that the panel securing clips are securely engaged under the windscreen.

Wheel arch liners, mud shields and engine undertray

11 The wheel arch liners and engine undertray (where applicable) are secured by a combination of self-tapping screws, and push-fit clips. Removal is self-evident, and normally the clips can be released by pulling the liner away from the wheel arch.

12 The mud shields are secured in a similar manner, although certain panels may be secured using pop-rivets. Where applicable, drill out the pop-rivets, and use new rivets on refitting.

Rubbing strips

Note: *Take care not to damage the paintwork when removing the rubbing strips.*

Front door

13 Open the door, and remove the indicator side repeaters from the front of the rubbing strip **(see illustration)**.

14 Working outside the door, unclip the end of the rubbing strip and slide it towards the rear of the door.

15 When refitting a rubbing strip, align the clips in the strip with the corresponding holes in the door. Push the strip towards the front of the door to engage the holes. Refit the indicator side repeater.

Rear door

16 Open the front door first, insert a slim screwdriver in through the grommet, and locate the small hole inside the door, corresponding to the top of the rubbing strip. Push inwards to release the locking clip.

17 Slide the moulding towards the front of the car to remove it.

18 When refitting a rubbing strip, first pull out the locking clip fitted at the front of the door. Align the clips in the strip with the corresponding holes in the door. Push the strip rearwards to engage the holes. Refit the grommet on completion.

Badges

19 The various badges may be secured with adhesives. To remove them, either soften the adhesive using a hot-air gun or hairdryer (taking care to avoid damage to the paintwork), or separate the badge from the body by 'sawing' through the adhesive using a length of nylon cord. **Note:** *Some badges are located by pegs in plastic grommets – these will need to be carefully prised from the bodywork.*

20 Clean off all traces of adhesive using white spirit, then wash the area with warm

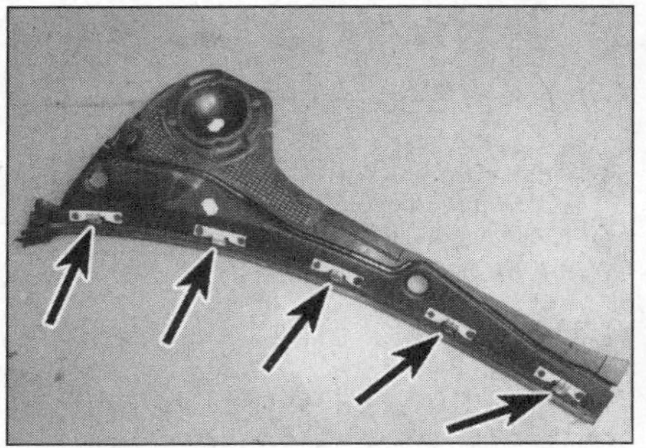

22.8b Lower windscreen retaining clips

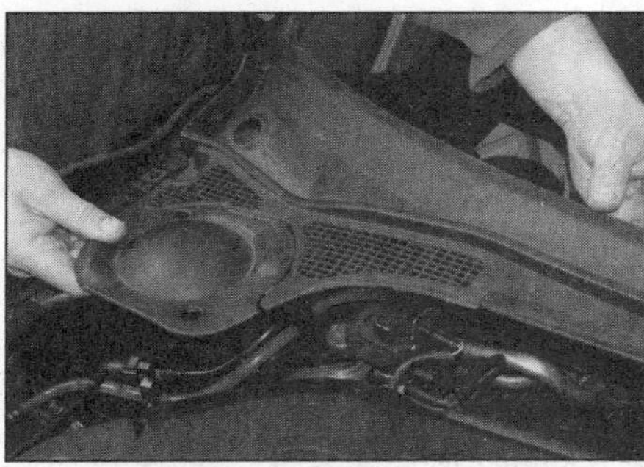

22.8c Remove the right-hand scuttle panel

22.9 Remove the left-hand scuttle panel

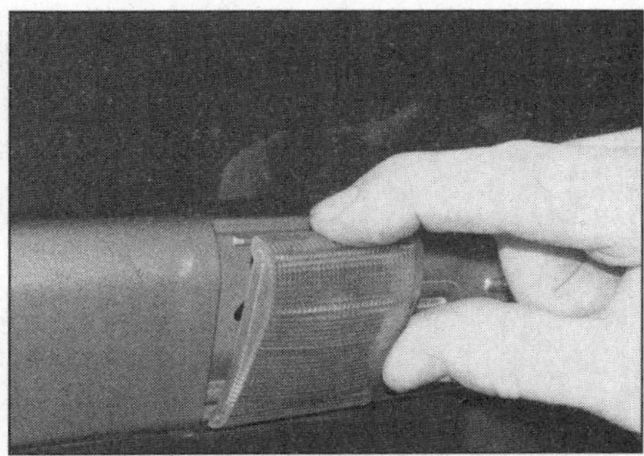

22.13 Unclip the indicator side repeater

soapy water to remove all traces of spirit, and allow to dry. Ensure that the surface to which the new badge is to be fastened is completely clean, and free from grease and dirt.

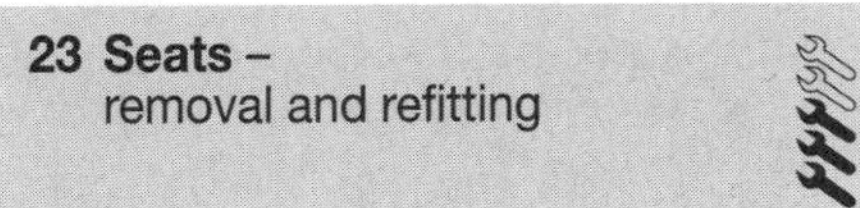

23 Seats – removal and refitting

Front seat

Warning: Observe the following precautions before attempting to remove the seat.

a) Remove the ignition key card.

b) Disconnect the battery negative terminal (refer to 'Disconnecting the battery' in the Reference Section of this manual), and wait for five minutes before carrying out any further work.

Removal

1 Slide the seat as far forward as possible.

2 Disconnect the battery negative terminal (refer to *Disconnecting the battery* in the Reference Section of this manual), and observe the precautions given at the start of this Section.

3 Apply the handbrake, then jack up the front of the vehicle and support securely on axle stands (see *Jacking and vehicle support*).

4 Working under the vehicle, unscrew the four seat securing nuts, to access the two inner nuts, unclip the plastic grommets from the floor panel **(see illustrations)**.

5 Working inside the vehicle, release the seat belt from the seat stalk by disengaging it from the locking clip, using a thin screwdriver **(see illustration)**.

6 Carefully lift out the seat, and remove it from inside the vehicle. **Note:** *As the seat is lifted from the floor panel the wiring block*

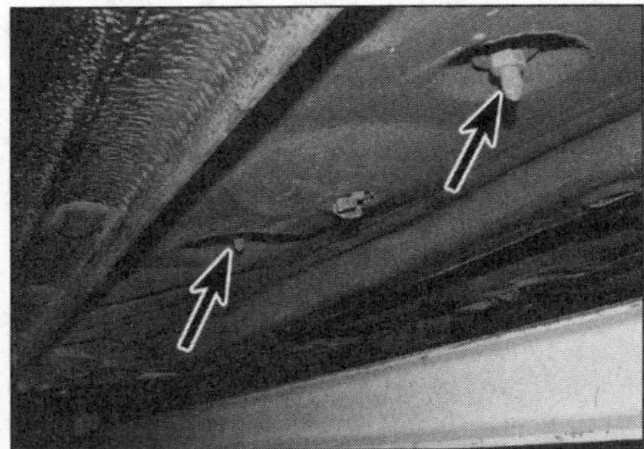

23.4a Undo the outer securing nuts (arrowed) . . .

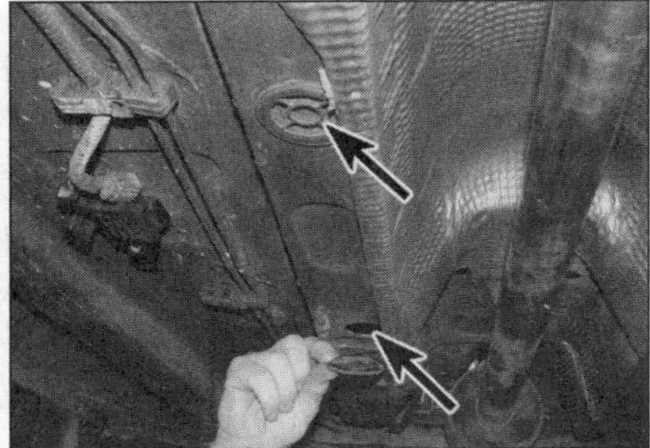

23.4b . . . and the inner securing nuts – under the grommets

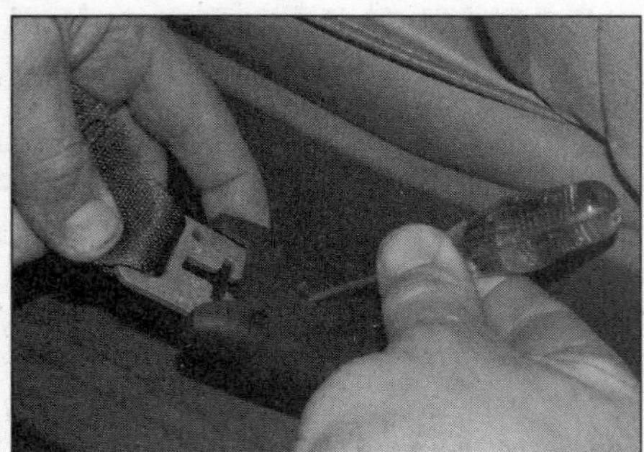

23.5 Releasing the seat belt locking clip

23.6a Sliding wiring block connector . . .

23.6b . . . and fixed wiring block connector

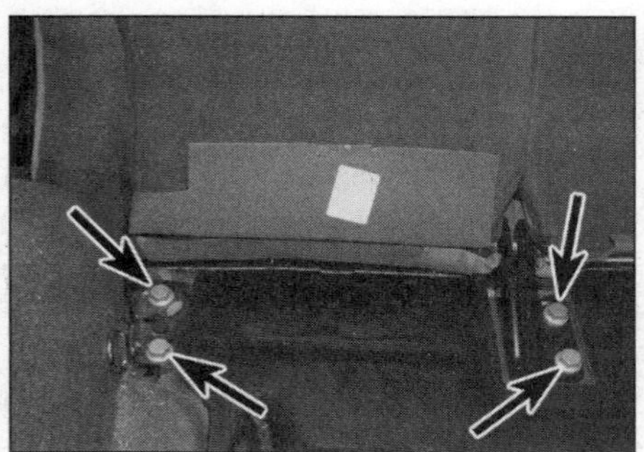

23.9 Rear seat back mounting bolts - arrowed

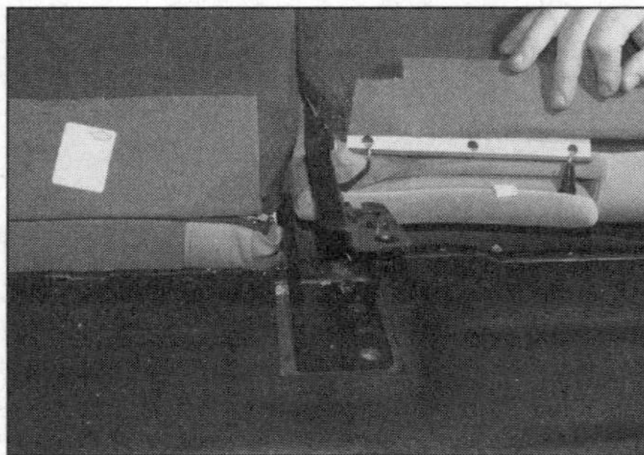

23.10 Removing the right-hand side seat back

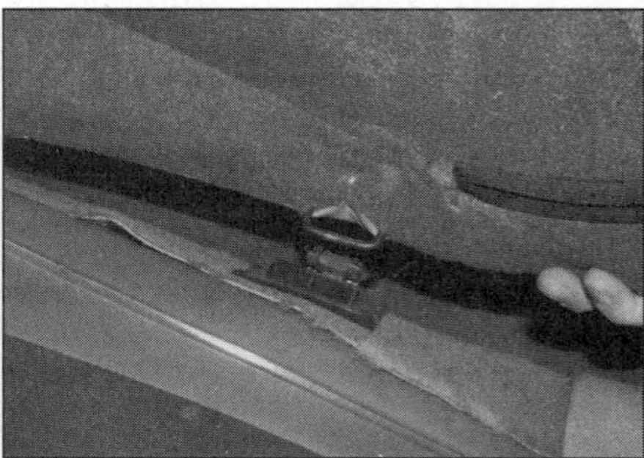

23.12 Carefully pull the hinge from the retaining clip

*connector will automatically be disconnected **(see illustrations)**.*

Refitting

7 Refitting is a reversal of removal, but ensure that the locking clip on the seat stalk engages the seat belt securely and the wiring block connector slides into position correctly.

Rear seat back

Removal

8 Fold the rear seat cushion forwards.

9 Working at the bottom of the seat back, remove the securing bolts **(see illustration)**.

10 Remove the seat back from the car, note the right-hand side will need to be removed first to allow the left-hand side to be removed **(see illustration)**.

Refitting

11 Refitting is a reversal of removal.

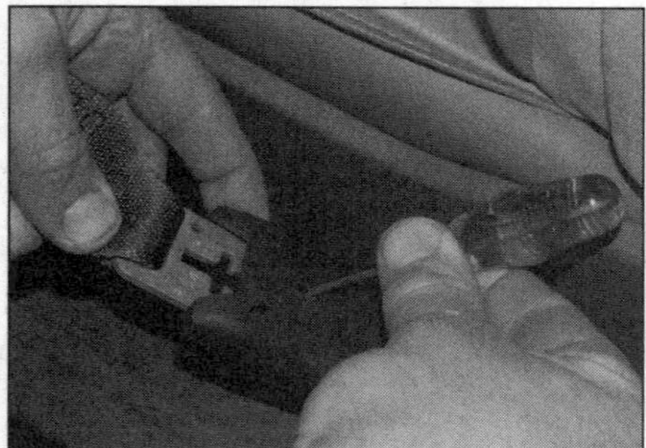

24.8 Releasing the seat belt locking clip

Rear seat cushion

Removal

12 Fold the seat cushion forwards, then slide the metal hinge from the plastic retaining clips by pulling the cushion upwards to release it **(see illustration)**. Take care not to damage the plastic retaining clips as the hinge is removed.

Refitting

13 Refitting is a reversal of removal.

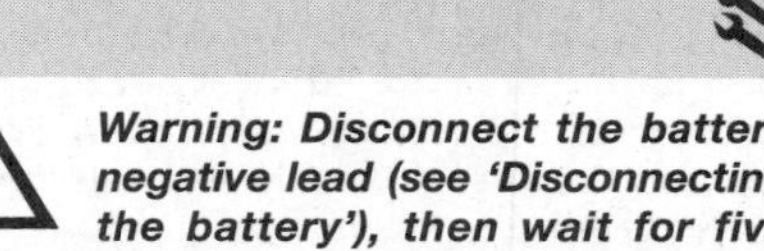

24 Seat belt components - removal and refitting

Warning: Disconnect the battery negative lead (see 'Disconnecting the battery'), then wait for five minutes before proceeding. If this waiting period is not observed, there is danger of activating the seat belt tensioners.

Note: *If the car has been in an accident, all affected seat belt components must be renewed.*

Seat belt tensioners

Information and precautions

1 Seat belt pretensioners are fitted to remove any slack from the front and outer rear seat belts in the event of a frontal impact. The system is designed to reduce the chances of injury by pulling your body back into the seat.

2 The system consists of two special seat belt tensioner/stalk assemblies mounted directly on the front seats, or on the outer rear belt inertia reels, connected to the airbag control unit.

3 Each tensioner/stalk assembly consists of a special buckle attached to a cable. The end of the cable is attached to a piston inside the tensioner cylinder.

4 In the event of a severe frontal impact, the seat belt tensioners will be triggered by the airbag control unit (for more information on the airbag system, refer to Chapter 12).

5 When a tensioner ignition module is triggered, a small capsule is energised, which rapidly releases gas into the tensioner cylinder. As the gas is released, the piston is forced along the cylinder, pulling the cable (approximately 70 mm) and hence the seat belt stalk, which in turn removes any slack from the seat belt, pulling the belt tight against the wearer. The rear belt reels contain similar systems, to spin the reel and retract the belt.

6 Once a seat belt tensioner has been triggered, it must be renewed.

7 Take care, when working on the car, not to expose the pretensioner system components to excess heat, impact, or even magnetic field, as this may cause inadvertent triggering or a malfunction in an accident.

Front belt

8 Using a small screwdriver in the hole provided, depress the catch to release the belt from the buckle on the outside of the seat **(see illustration)**.

9 Remove the B-pillar trim panels as described in Section 25.

10 Unscrew the inertia reel mounting bolt,

then unhook and lift out the belt reel **(see illustration)**.

11 Unscrew the upper mounting bolt, and remove the seat belt from the car **(see illustration)**.

12 Refitting is a reversal of removal. Tighten the belt mountings to the specified torque.

Front belt height adjuster

13 Remove the B-pillar trim panel, as described in Section 25.

14 To remove the adjuster completely, unscrew the seat belt upper mounting bolt.

15 Unscrew the adjuster upper bolt, then lift the height adjuster to unhook the lower mounting, and withdraw the adjuster from the pillar **(see illustrations)**.

16 Refitting is a reversal of removal. Tighten the mountings to the specified torque.

Front belt tensioners

17 Remove the front seat as described in Section 23.

18 Disconnect the wiring plug from the belt tensioner.

19 Unscrew the tensioner mounting bolt, and remove the tensioner from the seat, unclipping the operating cable as required **(see illustration)**.

20 Refitting is a reversal of removal. Ensure the wiring plugs are securely reconnected before refitting the battery lead, and tighten the mounting bolts to the specified torque.

Rear side belt

21 Remove the rear sill and wheel arch trim panels as described in Section 25.

22 Unscrew the seat belt lower anchor bolt **(see illustration)**.

23 Where the seat belt passes through the C-pillar trim panel, remove the trim panel as described in Section 25.

24 Unscrew the seat belt upper mounting bolt (Estate models have a height adjuster fitted, see paragraphs 13 to 16 for removal procedure of the height adjuster) **(see illustrations)**.

25 Remove further side trim panels as necessary, as described in Section 25, to access the inertia reel. Disconnect the belt tensioner wiring plug. Unscrew the inertia reel mounting bolt, then unhook and lift out the reel **(see illustration)**. Remove the seat belt from the car.

24.10 Inertia reel mounting bolt – arrowed

24.11 Upper seat belt mounting bolt – arrowed

24.15a Unscrew the two mounting bolts (arrowed) . . .

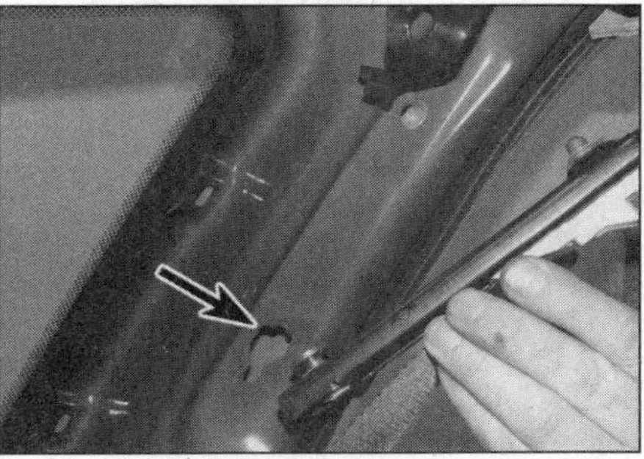

24.15b . . . and lift the adjuster from the slotted lower mounting – arrowed

26 Refitting is a reversal of removal. Tighten the mountings to the specified torque.

Rear centre belt

27 Tilt the rear seat cushion forward to access the seat belt stalk retaining bolts.

28 Remove the bolt from the centre belt buckle, which also secures the belt lower mounting – note the fitted order of the components.

29 The belt's inertia reel is contained inside the seat backrest, which can be removed as

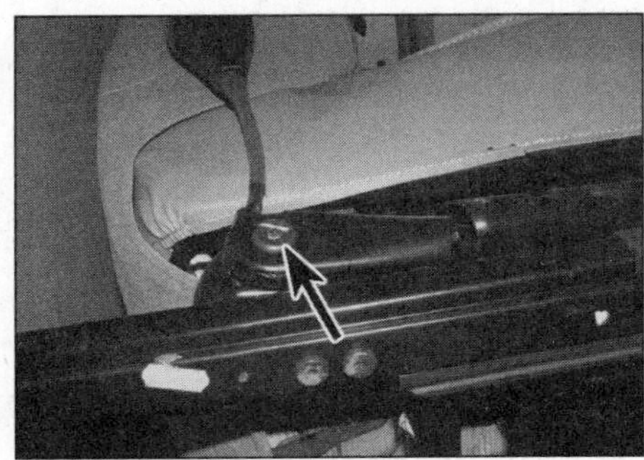

24.19 Tensioner mounting bolt – arrowed

24.22 Rear seat belt lower mounting bolt – arrowed

24.24a Upper mounting bolt (arrowed) – Hatchback model

24.24b Upper mounting bolt (arrowed) – Estate model

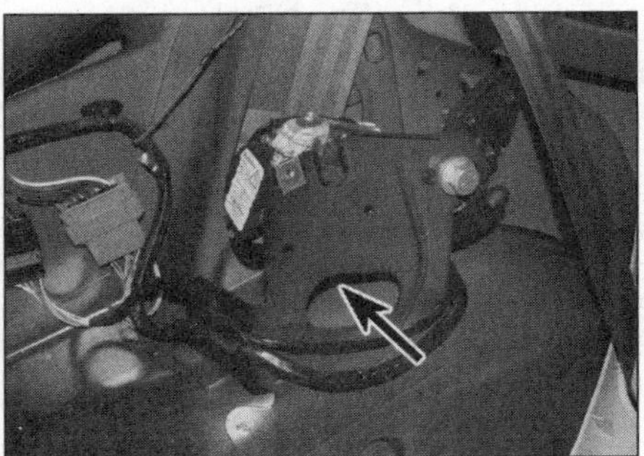

24.25 Inertia reel mounting bolt (arrowed) – through aperture

25.9 Pull the trim upwards to disengage from the facia

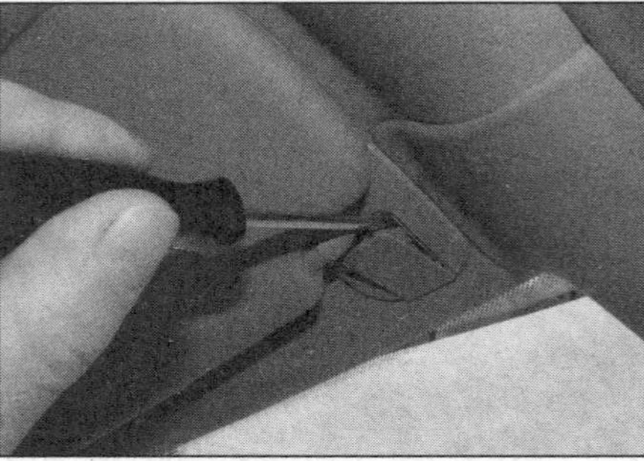
25.11 Prise out the cover panel

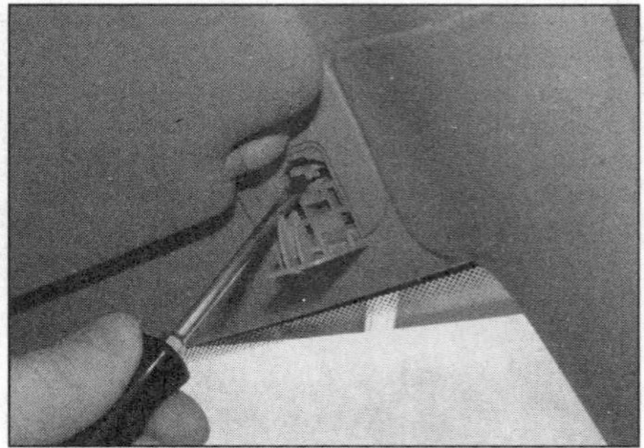
25.12a Release the locking clip . . .

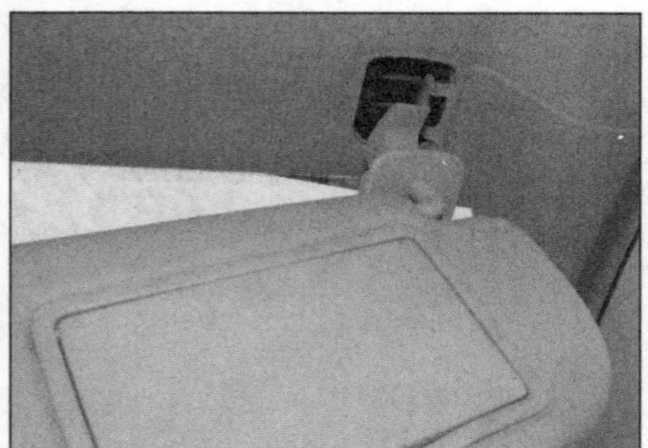
25.12b . . . and withdraw the sun visor

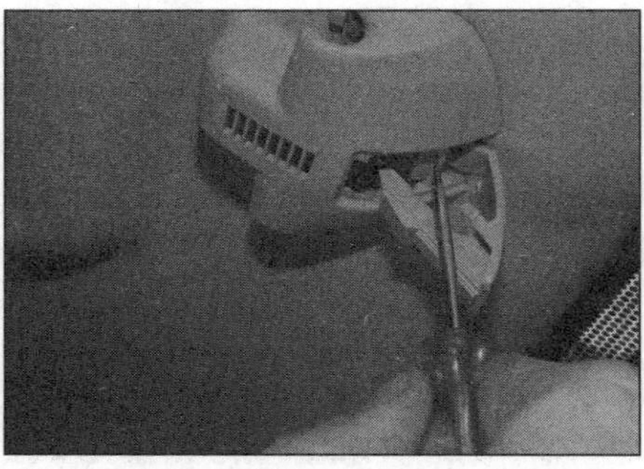
25.13a Prise out the cover panel, release the locking clip . . .

25.13b . . . and withdraw the centre mounting

described in Section 23. The seat has a zip fastener around the edge of the backrest, to 'open' the seat for access to the internal components. However, this zip has no 'handle', so cannot be opened without the use of a Renault tool. For this reason, take the backrest to your dealer for work on the centre belt.

30 Refitting is a reversal of removal. Tighten the lower mounting to the specified torque.

25 Interior trim – removal and refitting

General information

1 The interior trim panels are all secured using either plastic clips built into the panel, or screws.

2 Before removing a panel, study it carefully, noting how it is secured. Often, other panels or ancillary components (such as seat belt mountings, grab handles, etc) must be removed before a particular panel can be withdrawn.

3 Once any such components have been removed, check that there are no other panels overlapping the one to be removed. Usually, the sequence to be followed will become obvious on close inspection.

4 Remove all obvious fasteners, such as screws, which may have plastic covers fitted. If the panel cannot be freed, it is probably secured by hidden clips or fasteners on the rear of the panel. Such fasteners are usually situated around the edge of the panel, and can be prised up to release them. Note that plastic clips can break quite easily, so it is advisable to have a few new clips of the correct type available for refitting. Generally, the best way of releasing such clips is to use a wide flat-bladed tool, designed for the purpose – these are available from tool suppliers such as Draper. If this is not available, an old, broad-bladed screwdriver with the edges rounded-off and wrapped in insulating tape will serve as a good substitute.

5 The following paragraphs and the accompanying illustrations describe removal and refitting of all the major trim panels. Note that the type and number of fasteners used often varies during the production run of a particular model, so differences may be found to the procedures provided.

6 When removing a panel, **never** use excessive force, or the panel may be damaged.

25.15 Unclip the top of the lower panel

Always check carefully that all fasteners have been removed or released before attempting to withdraw a panel.

7 When refitting, secure the fasteners by pressing them firmly into place. Ensure that all disturbed components are correctly secured, to prevent rattles.

A-pillar trim panel

8 Remove the sun visor on the side concerned, as described in paragraphs 11 to 14, in this Section. Pull the rubber weatherstrip down from the door aperture, adjacent to the trim panel.

9 Pull the top of the trim panel outwards at the top to release the securing clip, and then pull upwards to release the trim from the top of the facia panel **(see illustration)**. Remove the panel from the car.

10 Refitting is a reversal of removal.

Sun visors

11 Prise down the cover panel using a small screwdriver **(see illustration)**.

12 Release the retaining tab inside, and withdraw the sun visor mounting from the headlining **(see illustrations)**.

13 A similar method is used to remove the sun visor centre mounting **(see illustrations)**.

14 Refitting is a reversal of removal.

B-pillar trim panels

Lower panel

15 Pull the lower trim panel outwards to release it from the upper trim panel **(see illustration)**.

16 Slide the lower trim panel upwards

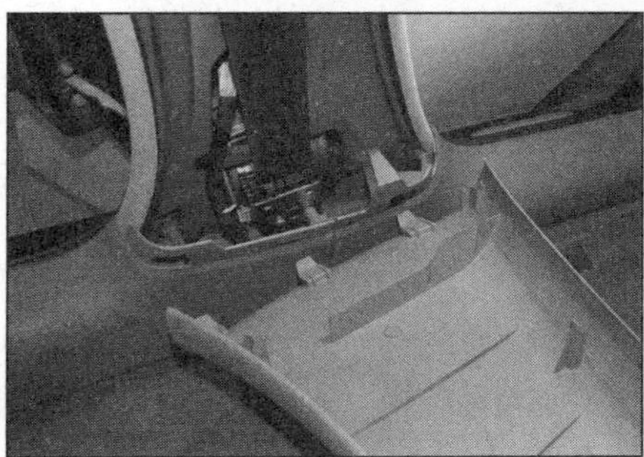

25.16 Unclip the trim panel from the sill trim panels

25.19 Release the two retaining clips

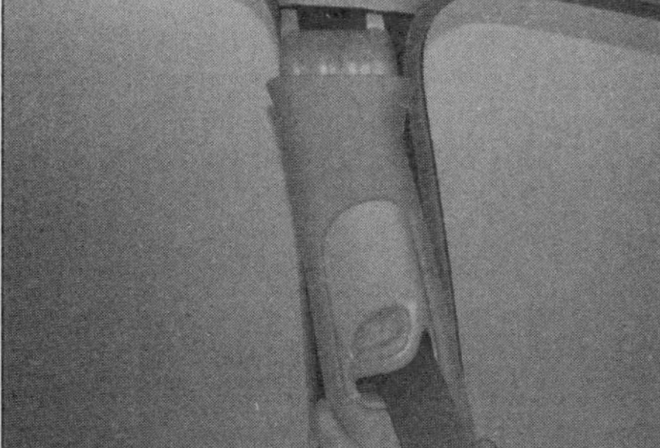

25.20a Slide the trim panel downwards

25.20b Pass the seat belt through the trim panel

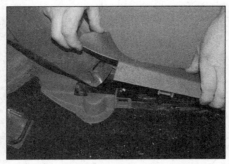

25.25a Unclip the rear of the sill trim panel . . .

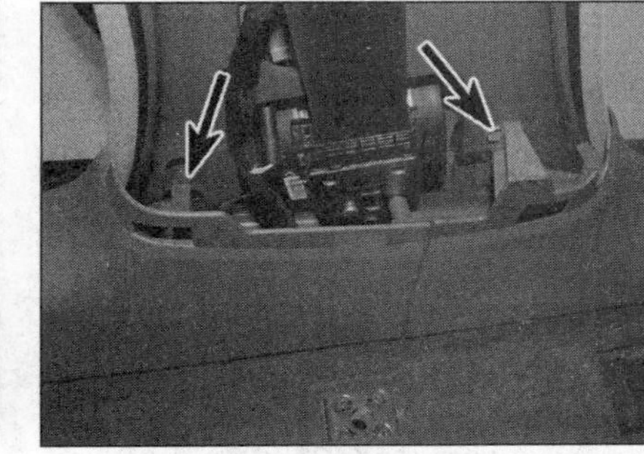

25.25b . . then unclip the rear sill trim from the front sill trim

to release it from the sill trim panels **(see illustration)**.

17 Refitting is a reversal of removal.

Upper panel

18 Remove the lower B-pillar trim panel as described in paragraphs 15 to 17, previously in this Section.

19 Pull back the rubber weatherstrip in front of and behind the panel as necessary, then squeeze together the retaining clips at the base of the panel, and pull the panel out from the pillar **(see illustration)**.

20 Withdraw the panel downwards to release the retaining clips at the top of the trim panel – it will still be 'attached' to the front seat belt, which can be disconnected from the seat **(see illustration 23.5)**, and passed through the trim panel **(see illustrations)**.

21 Refitting is a reversal of removal, making sure the seat belt height adjuster is located correctly in the rear of the trim panel.

Sill trim panels

Rear

22 Remove the lower B-pillar trim panel as described in paragraphs 15 to 17, previously in this Section.

23 Remove the rear seat cushion as described in Section 23, paragraph 12.

24 Move the front seat as far forward as possible.

25 The rear sill trim panel can now be unclipped at the rear of the panel and then at the front, disengaging it from the front sill trim panel **(see illustrations)**.

26 Refitting is a reversal of removal.

Front

27 Remove the lower B-pillar trim panel as described in paragraphs 15 to 17, previously in this Section.

28 Unclip the rear sill trim panel from the front sill trim panel as described in paragraph 25 of this section **(see illustrations 25.25a and 25.25b)**.

29 Move the front seat as far back as possible.

30 Working along the length of the sill panel, starting from the rear, release the retaining clips and withdraw the sill trim panel from the vehicle.

31 Refitting is a reversal of removal.

Parcel shelf trim panel

32 Remove the parcel shelf itself. Where applicable, prise out and disconnect the boot light from the panel **(see illustration)**. On some models it may be necessary to disconnect the wiring connector from the 12 volt supply connector.

33 Release the catch and tilt the seat backs forward.

34 Undo the retaining screw from the rear trim panel, on Estate models the screw is behind a plastic cover **(see illustrations)**.

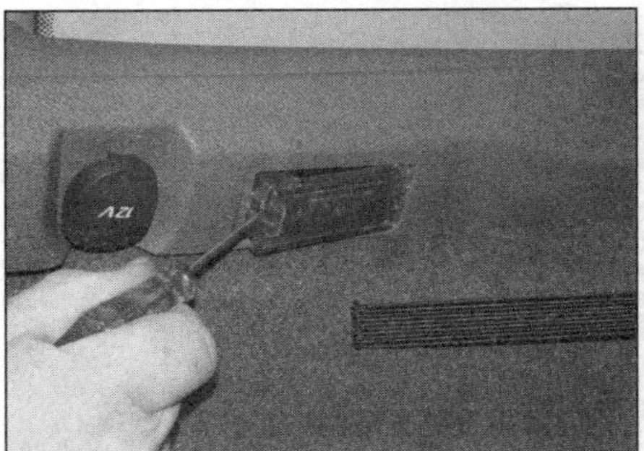

25.32 Prise out the boot light from the trim panel

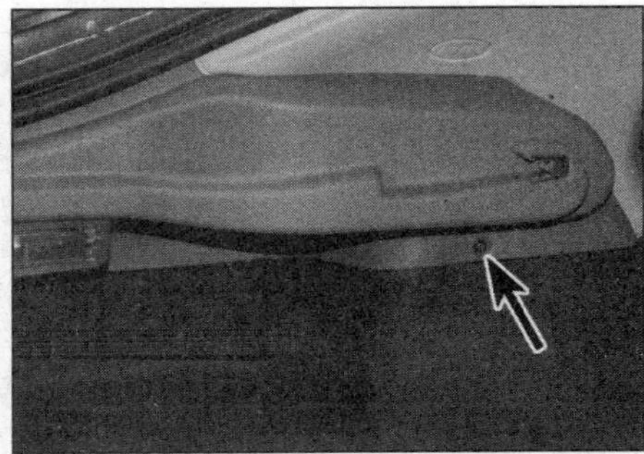

25.34a Undo the retaining screw (arrowed) – Hatchback model

25.34b Unclip the plastic cover . . .

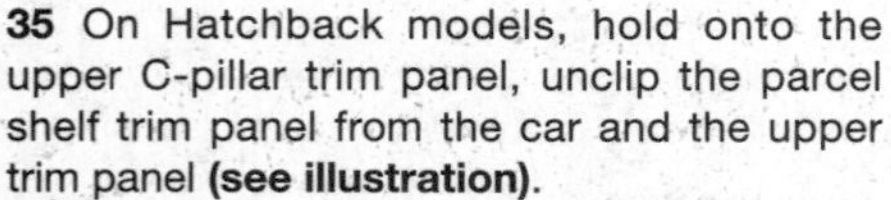

25.34c . . . and remove the retaining screw – arrowed

25.35 Unclipping the shelf trim panel – Hatchback model

25.36a Unclipping the shelf trim panel from the C-pillar . . .

35 On Hatchback models, hold onto the upper C-pillar trim panel, unclip the parcel shelf trim panel from the car and the upper trim panel **(see illustration)**.

36 On Estate models, unclip the parcel shelf trim panel from the C-pillar and the upper trim quarter panel will be removed with it **(see illustrations)**.

37 Refitting is a reversal of removal.

Rear wheel arch trim panel

38 Remove the rear sill trim panel as described in paragraphs 22 to 26, previously in this Section.

39 Remove the rear seat as described in Section 23.

40 Release the retaining clips and withdraw the wheel arch trim panel from the vehicle **(see illustration)**.

41 Refitting is a reversal of removal.

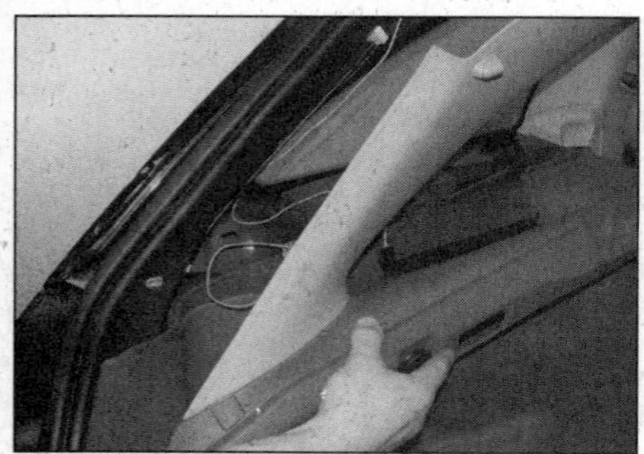

25.36b . . . and withdraw the complete panel – Estate model

25.43a C-pillar trim panel – Hatchback model

C-pillar trim panel

Note: *On models with the optional rear side airbags (identifiable by a label on the panel), be aware that the airbag unit is directly behind the trim panel (Hatchback models) or towards the top (Estate models). Unless the airbag is to be removed, as described in Chapter 12, no action is required.*

42 Remove the parcel shelf trim panel as described in paragraphs 32 to 36, previously in this Section.

43 Unclip the panel and remove it **(see illustrations)**. The panel will be 'attached' by the rear seat belt, which can be released by unbolting the seat belt lower mounting (see Section 24)

44 Refitting is a reversal of removal.

Boot carpet side panel

45 Remove the parcel shelf trim panel as described in paragraphs 32 to 36, previously in this Section.

46 The carpet trim panel sits underneath the trim panels just removed, and is hooked over the seat backrest catches. Release the carpet and remove it **(see illustration)**.

47 Refitting is a reversal of removal.

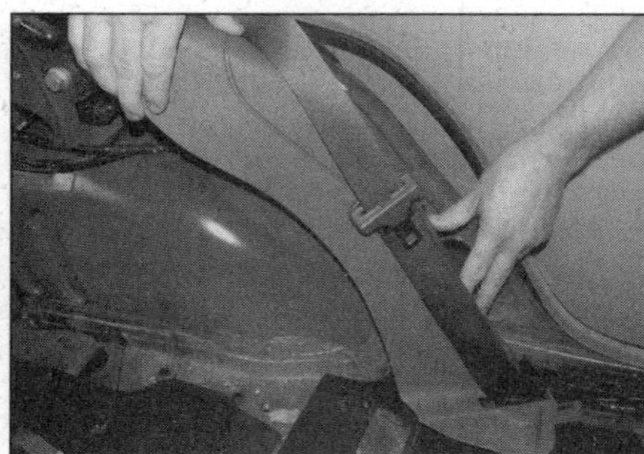

25.40 Unclipping the wheel arch trim

25.43b Unclipping C-pillar trim panel – Estate model

Carpets

48 The carpet is held in position by the sill trim panels, and other surrounding panels and components.

49 Carpet removal and refitting is reasonably straightforward, but very time-consuming, due to the fact that many of the adjoining trim panels must be removed first. It will also be necessary to remove components such as the seats and their mountings, the centre console, etc.

Grab handles

50 Using a small screwdriver, prise out the retaining peg at each end of the grab handle **(see illustrations)**.

51 Lower the grab handle from the headlining and remove it **(see illustration)**.

52 Refitting is a reversal of removal.

Headlining

Warning: Disconnect the battery negative lead (see 'Disconnecting the battery'), then wait for five minutes before proceeding. If this waiting period is not observed, there is danger of activating the side curtain airbags, which are located in the headlining.

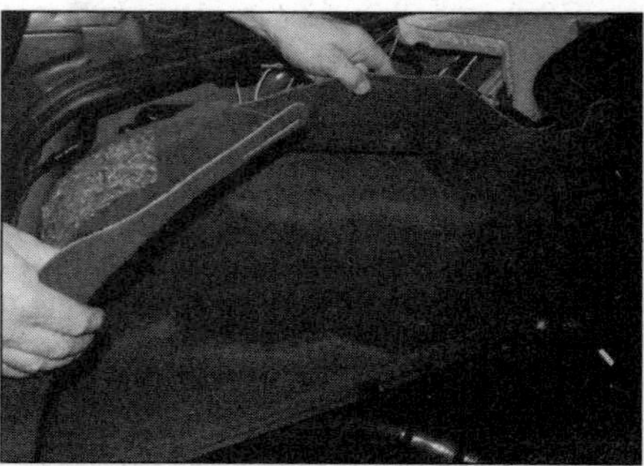

25.46 Removing the boot carpet side trim – Hatchback model

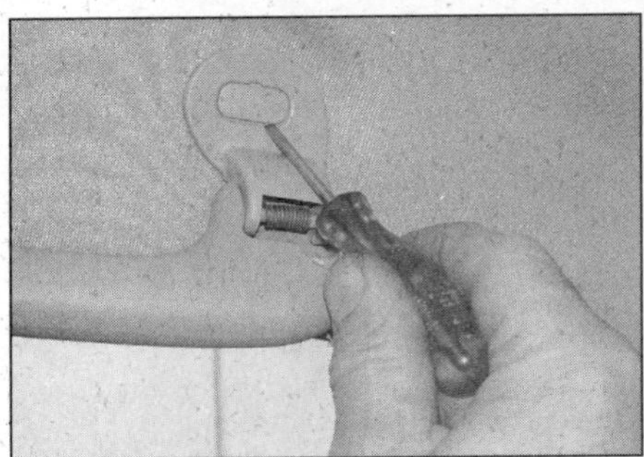
25.50a Using a small screwdriver . . .

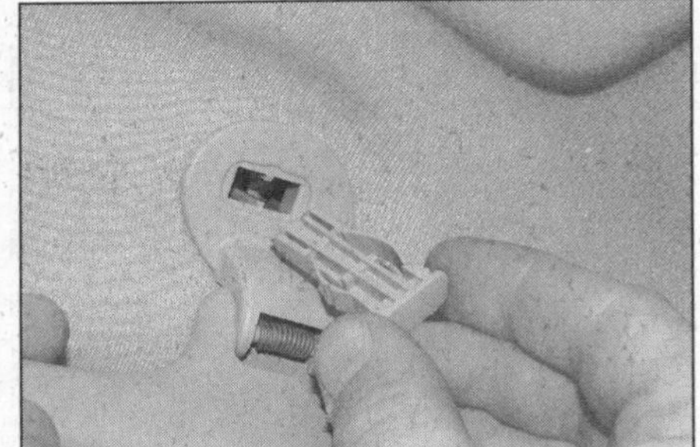
25.50b . . . prise out the grab handle retaining pegs

25.51 Remove the grab handle from the headlining

53 The headlining is held in place by the grab handles, sun visors, sunroof trim, door pillar trim panels, rear quarter trim panels, weatherseals, etc. When all the fittings have been removed or prised clear, it can then be withdrawn out through the tailgate aperture. Disconnect the wiring plugs for the side curtain airbags as they become accessible.

54 Note that headlining removal requires considerable skill and patience if it is to be carried out without damage, and is therefore best entrusted to an expert.

26 Centre console – removal and refitting

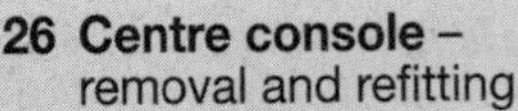

Removal

1 Disconnect the battery negative terminal (refer to *Disconnecting the battery* in the Reference Section of this manual).

2 Push the front seats as far forward as possible, then unscrew the two centre console rear securing screws, one screw on each side of the console **(see illustration)**.

3 Unclip the gear lever gaiter surround/lever trim plate from the top of the centre console **(see illustration)**.

4 Unclip the handbrake lever gaiter surround from the top of the centre console **(see illustration)**.

5 Unclip the ashtray from its housing **(see illustration)**.

6 Carefully prise the switch panel from the top of the console to release the retaining clips along its length. Disconnect the wiring plugs as the panel is removed **(see illustrations)**.

7 Working at the front of the console, unscrew the two securing screws **(see illustration)**.

8 Disconnect the wiring connectors that go over the crossmembers inside the centre console **(see illustration)**.

9 Working at the front of the console, pull the edges of the console outwards to release the

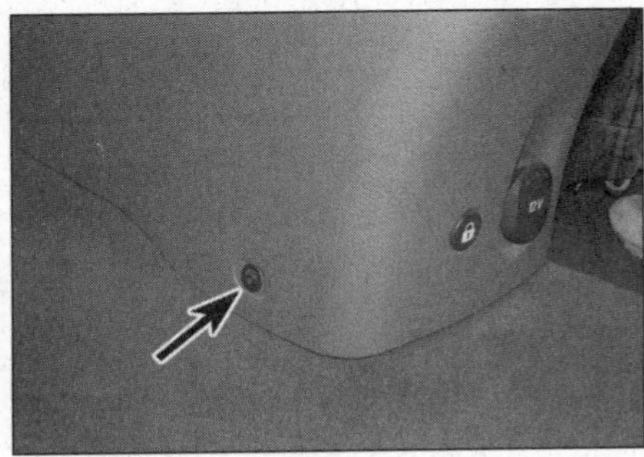
26.2 Centre console rear retaining screw – one side shown

26.3 Unclip the gear lever gaiter

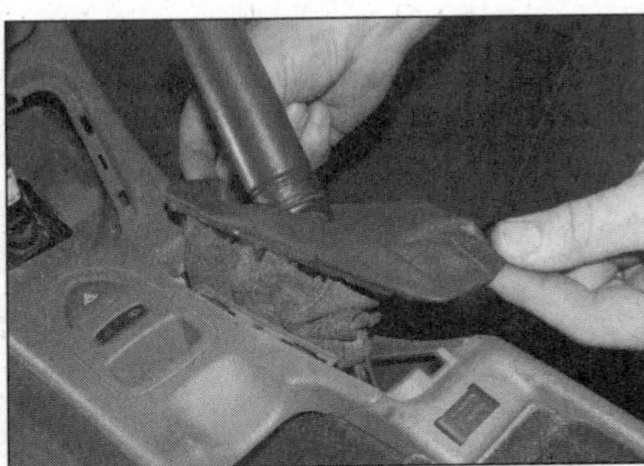
26.4 Unclip the handbrake lever gaiter

26.5 Withdraw the ashtray from the facia

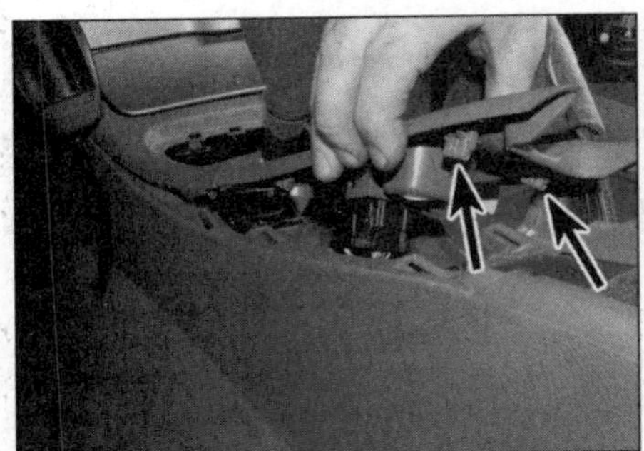
26.6a Switch panel upper retaining clips – arrowed

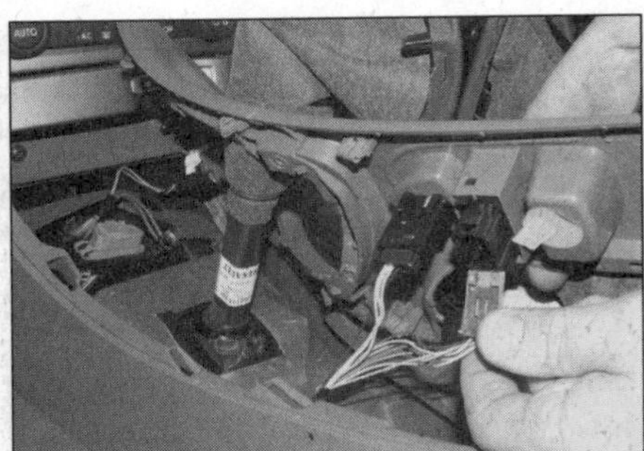
26.6b Disconnect the wiring connectors on removal

26.7 Undo the two front securing screws – arrowed

26.8 Disconnect the wiring connectors inside the centre console

securing lugs, then pull the console rearwards to free it from its mountings.

10 Pull the handbrake lever fully up, then withdraw the console over the gear lever and the handbrake lever **(see illustration)**.

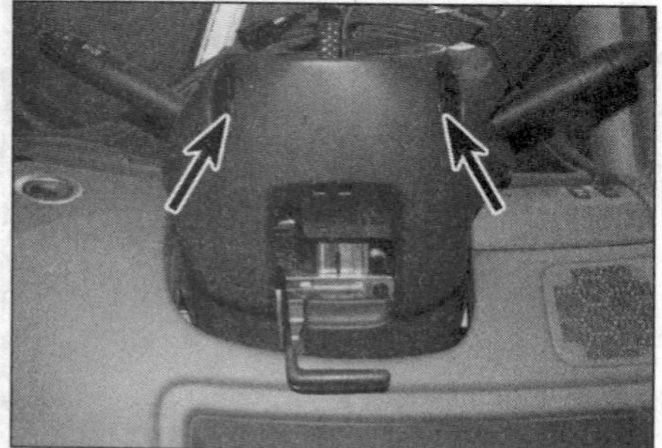
27.2a Undo the retaining screws (arrowed) . . .

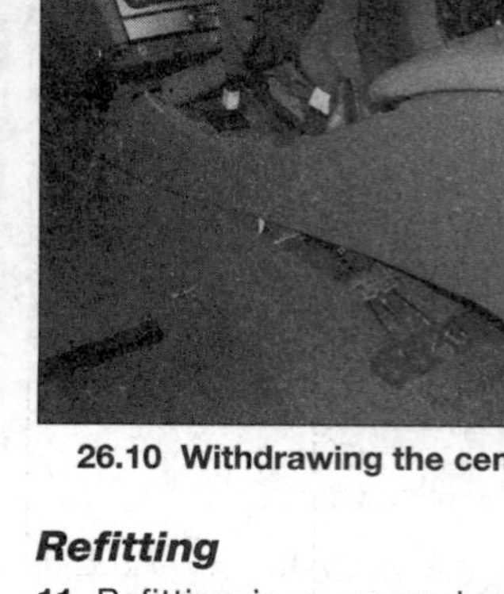
26.10 Withdrawing the centre console

Refitting

11 Refitting is a reversal of the removal procedure.

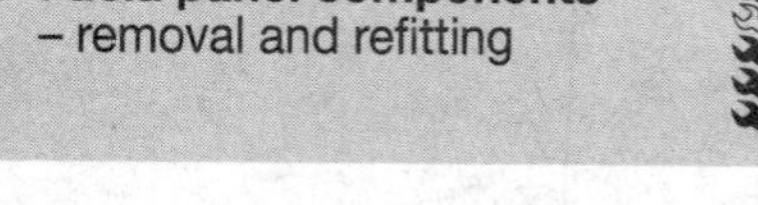

27 Facia panel components – removal and refitting

Steering column shrouds

Removal

1 Remove the steering wheel as described in Chapter 10.

2 Working under the steering column, move the steering height adjuster handle downwards, then remove the securing screws and withdraw the lower steering column shroud **(see illustrations)**.

3 Lift the upper steering column shroud away from the steering column, release the three retaining clips at the rear of the trim panel and withdraw it from the steering column **(see illustration)**.

Refitting

4 Refitting is a reversal of removal, but refit the steering wheel as described in Chapter 10.

Glovebox

Removal

5 Open the glovebox and remove the upper securing screw **(see illustration)**.

6 Using a small screwdriver, release the securing clip and withdraw the glovebox from the facia **(see illustrations)**.

Refitting

7 Refitting is a reversal of removal.

Complete facia assembly

Removal

8 Disconnect the battery negative terminal (refer to *Disconnecting the battery* in the Reference Section of this manual).

9 Remove the steering wheel as described in Chapter 10, and the steering column shrouds as described previously in this Section.

10 Remove the centre console as described in Section 26.

11 Remove the radio/cassette player as described in Chapter 12.

12 Remove the ignition card reader as described in Chapter 5A, Section 12.

13 Remove the heater control panel as described in Chapter 3, Section 9.

14 Undo the facia retaining screw from the rear of the radio/cassette aperture **(see illustration)**.

27.2b . . . and withdraw the lower trim panel

27.3 Release the retaining clips – arrowed

27.5 Undo the retaining screw – arrowed

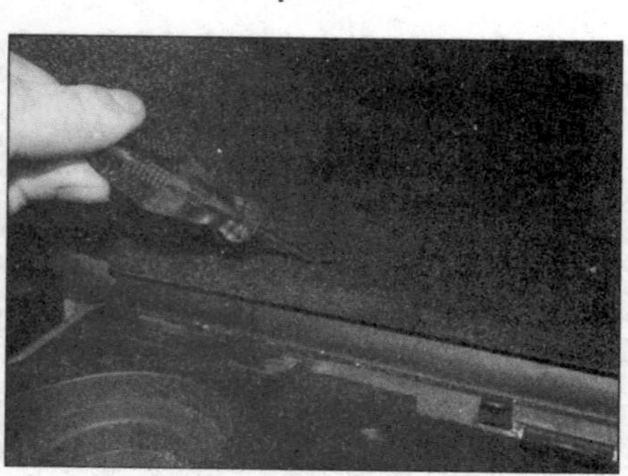
27.6a Release the securing clip . . .

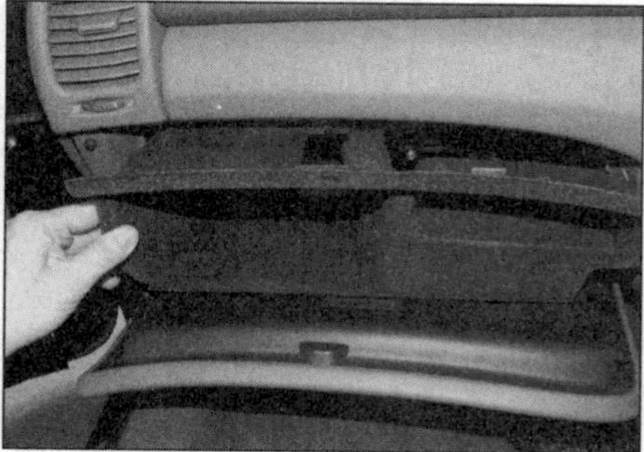
27.6b . . . and withdraw the glovebox

27.14 Undo the facia centre retaining screw – arrowed

15 Unclip the upper display from the top of the facia panel; disconnect the wiring connectors as it is removed **(see illustrations)**.
16 Carefully unclip the sensor from the centre of the facia by the windscreen and disconnect the wiring connector **(see illustration)**.
17 Remove the glovebox as described in paragraphs 5 and 6, previously in this Section. Then unclip the glovebox light and disconnect the wiring connector **(see illustration)**.
18 The passenger airbag stays attached to the facia panel as it is removed. Trace the wiring back from the passenger airbag unit and disconnect the wiring block connector in the left-hand corner of the facia panel **(see illustration)**.
19 Remove the switch/stalk assembly from the top of the steering column as described in Chapter 12.
20 Remove the instrument panel as described in Chapter 12.
21 Undo the steering column upper mounting nuts and remove the facia retaining screw **(see illustration)**.
22 Fully open the front doors, and unclip the trim panels from the right and left-hand side of the facia panel. On the left-hand side panel, disconnect the wiring connector from the airbag isolation switch **(see illustrations)**.
23 Undo the retaining screws from the ends of the facia panel, two at each side **(see illustration)**.
24 Remove the A-pillar trim panels as described in Section 25.
25 Working on each side of the facia in turn, carefully unclip the covers from the speakers (tweeters) in the top of the facia panel, then unclip the speaker and disconnect the wiring connector **(see illustrations)**.
26 Undo the facia retaining screw from inside the glovebox aperture **(see illustration)**.
27 With the aid of an assistant, pull the

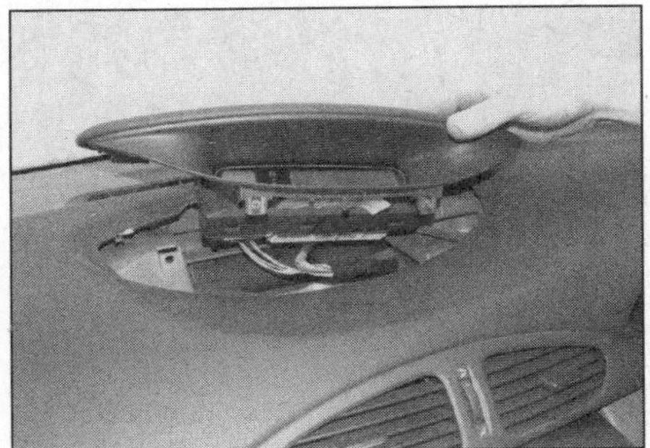
27.15a Unclip the display from the facia . . .

27.15b . . . and disconnect the wiring connectors

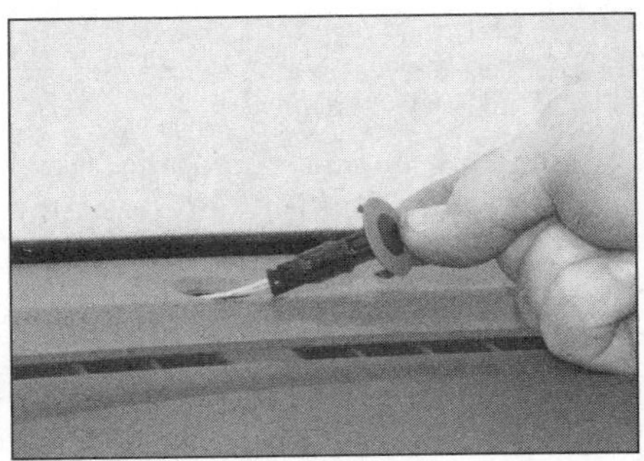
27.16 Unclipping the sensor from the facia

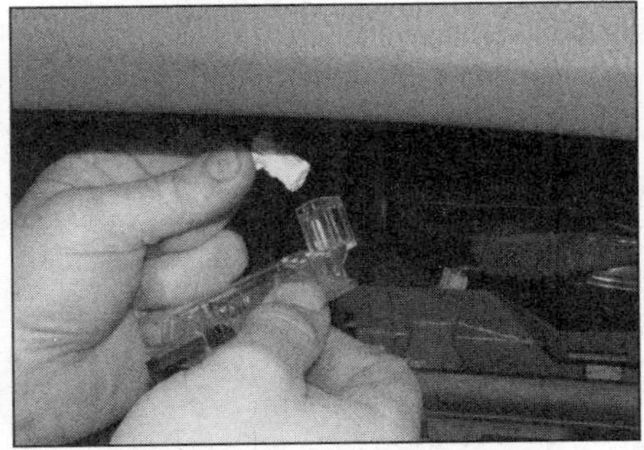
27.17 Remove the glovebox light

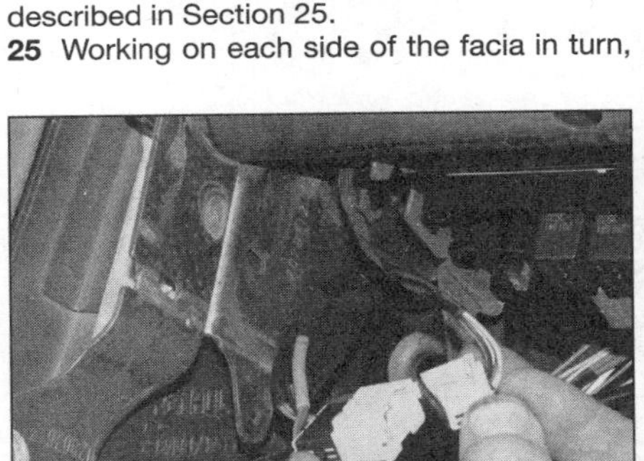
27.18 Disconnect the passenger airbag wiring connector

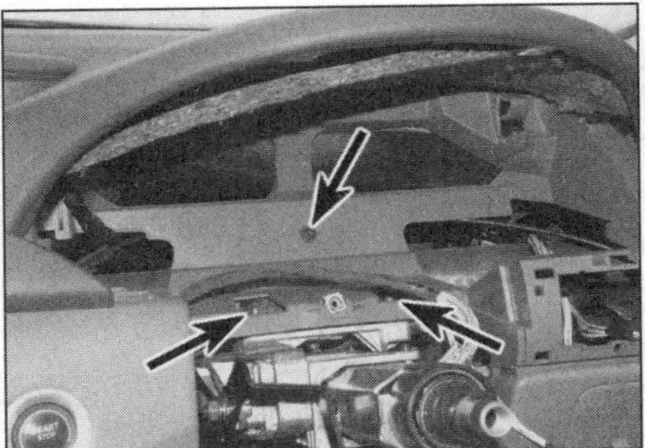
27.21 Undo the mounting nuts and the retaining screw – arrowed

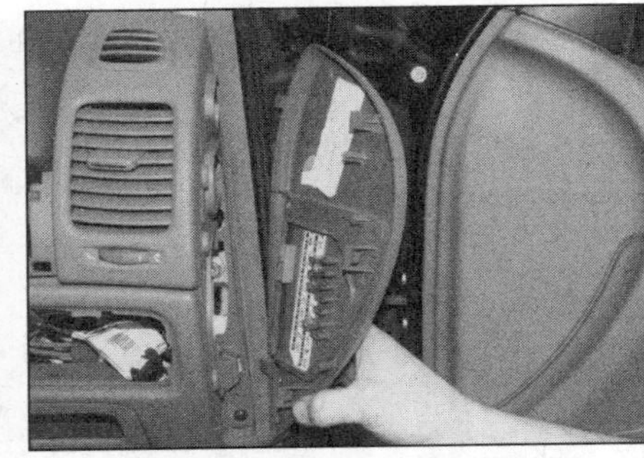
27.22a Unclip the facia end trim panels . . .

27.22b . . . and disconnect the wiring connectors

27.23 Undo the facia end retaining screws – right-hand side shown

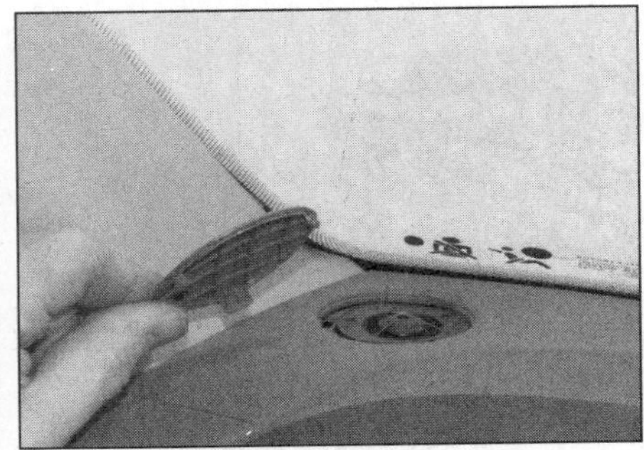
27.25a Unclip the speaker cover . . .

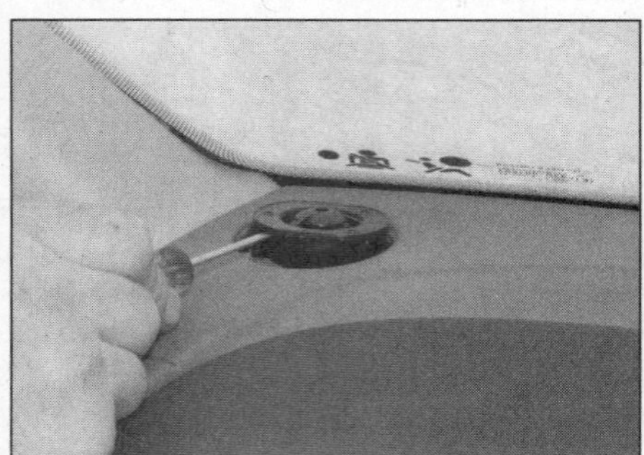
27.25b . . . then remove the speaker

27.26 Undo the facia retaining screw – arrowed

27.27 Retaining clip (arrowed) in the top corners of the facia panel

top corner edges of the facia upwards **(see illustration)**, then pull the facia forwards, and disconnect any remaining wiring. Release the wiring harnesses from any clips and brackets on the facia, and take careful note of the wiring harness routing to aid refitting. Withdraw the facia through one of the front door apertures.

28 To remove the reinforcement crossmember see the heater matrix removal procedure, in Chapter 3.

Refitting

29 Refitting is a reversal of removal, bearing in mind the following points.

- *a) Ensure that the facia is correctly centred in the passenger compartment.*
- *b) Ensure that all wiring harnesses are correctly routed as noted before removal, and ensure that all wiring connectors are securely reconnected.*
- *c) Where applicable, refer to the relevant Chapters for the refitting procedures.*
- *d) Ensure that the facia panel is located securely at the upper corners of the facia panel.*
- *e) Where applicable, have the airbag system checked by a Renault dealer before refitting the airbag units – refer to Chapter 12 for details.*

Chapter 12
Body electrical system

Contents

Degrees of difficulty

Easy, suitable for novice with little experience 	**Fairly easy,** suitable for beginner with some experience	**Fairly difficult,** suitable for competent DIY mechanic	**Difficult,** suitable for experienced DIY mechanic	**Very difficult,** suitable for expert DIY or professional 

Specifications

General

System type	12 volt negative earth

Fuses

Refer to label on fusebox cover

Bulbs

	Type	Wattage
Direction indicator (orange-coloured)	PY21W	21
Direction indicator side repeater (wedge-base)	W5W	5
Front foglight	H11	55
Front sidelight (wedge-base)	W5W	5
Headlight with halogen bulbs:		
Main beam	H1*	55
Dip beam	H7*	55
Headlight with xenon bulbs:		
Main beam	H1*	55
Dip beam	D2R*	37
High-level brake light	LEDs (no bulbs fitted)	
Interior lights:		
Wedge	W5W	5
Festoon	C5W	5
Festoon	C7W	7
Number plate light (festoon)	C5W	5
Rear foglight (driver's side only)	P21W	21
Reversing light	P21W	21
Stop/tail	P21/5W	21/5

* **Note:** *As the headlights have plastic lenses,* ***anti-UV type bulbs*** *are used (the headlight may be damaged if any other type of bulb is used).*

Torque wrench settings

	Nm	lbf ft
Airbag electronic control unit nuts	8	6
Airbag securing screws	5	4

1 General information and precautions

The electrical system is of 12 volt negative earth type. Power for the lights and all electrical accessories is supplied by a lead-acid type battery, which is charged by the alternator.

This Chapter covers repair and service procedures for the various electrical components not associated with engine. Information on the battery, alternator and starter motor can be found in Chapter 5A.

It should be noted that, prior to working on any component in the electrical system, the battery negative terminal should first be disconnected, to prevent the possibility of electrical short-circuits and/or fires.

Precautions

Warning: Before carrying out any work on the electrical system, read through the precautions given in 'Safety first!' at the beginning of this manual, and in Chapter 5A.

Warning: Models are equipped with an airbag system. When working on the electrical system, refer to the precautions given in Section 23 to avoid the possibility of personal injury.

Caution: Before proceeding, refer to 'Disconnecting the battery' in the Reference Section of this manual for further information.

2 Electrical fault finding – general information

Note: *Refer to the precautions given in 'Safety first!' and in Section 1 of this Chapter before starting work.*

General

1 A typical electrical circuit consists of an electrical component; any switches, relays, motors, fuses, fusible links or circuit breakers related to that component, and the wiring and connectors which link the component to both the battery and the chassis. To help to pinpoint a problem in an electrical circuit, wiring diagrams are included at the end of this Chapter.

2 Before attempting to diagnose an electrical fault, first study the appropriate wiring diagram, to obtain a more complete understanding of the components included in the particular circuit concerned. The possible sources of a fault can be narrowed down by noting whether other components related to the circuit are operating properly. If several components or circuits fail at one time, the problem is likely to be related to a shared fuse or earth connection.

3 Multiplex wiring makes traditional electrical fault finding more difficult, as inter-related circuits are connected together as required by the multi-timer unit. This factor makes tracing faults from one end of the car to the other almost impossible, with the added factor that the multi-timer unit may also be at fault, in not switching/connecting the circuits correctly. Once testing has passed beyond the basic stage, it may be more time-efficient to have the fault diagnosed by a Renault dealer.

Warning: Since this is a multiplex wiring system, every circuit in the car passes through at least one 'ECU'. For this reason, it is inadvisable to use any kind of self-powered test equipment, as this may cause damage to the electronic modules fitted.

4 Electrical problems usually stem from simple causes, such as loose or corroded connections, a faulty earth connection, a blown fuse, a melted fusible link, or a faulty relay (refer to Section 3 for details of testing relays). Visually inspect the condition of all fuses, wires and connections in a problem circuit before testing the components. Use the wiring diagrams to determine which terminal connections will need to be checked, in order to pinpoint the trouble-spot.

5 The basic tools required for electrical fault finding include a circuit tester or voltmeter (a 12 volt bulb with a set of test leads can also be used for certain tests); a self-powered test light (sometimes known as a continuity tester); an ohmmeter (to measure resistance); a battery and set of test leads; and a jumper wire, preferably with a circuit breaker or fuse incorporated, which can be used to bypass suspect wires or electrical components. Before attempting to locate a problem with test instruments, use the wiring diagram to determine where to make the connections.

6 To find the source of an intermittent wiring fault (usually due to a poor or dirty connection, or damaged wiring insulation), a 'wiggle' test can be performed on the wiring. This involves wiggling the wiring by hand, to see if the fault occurs as the wiring is moved. It should be possible to narrow down the source of the fault to a particular section of wiring. This method of testing can be used in conjunction with any of the tests described in the following sub-Sections.

7 Apart from problems due to poor connections, two basic types of fault can occur in an electrical circuit – open-circuit or short-circuit.

8 Open-circuit faults are caused by a break somewhere in the circuit, which prevents current from flowing. An open-circuit fault will prevent a component from working, but will not cause the relevant circuit fuse to blow.

9 Short-circuit faults are caused by a 'short' somewhere in the circuit, which allows the current flowing in the circuit to 'escape' along an alternative route, usually to earth. Short-circuit faults are normally caused by a breakdown in wiring insulation, which allows a feed wire to touch either another wire, or an earthed component such as the bodyshell. A short-circuit fault will normally cause the relevant circuit fuse to blow.

Finding an open-circuit

10 To check for an open-circuit, connect one lead of a circuit tester or voltmeter to either the negative battery terminal or a known good earth.

11 Connect the other lead to a connector in the circuit being tested, preferably nearest to the battery or fuse.

12 Switch on the circuit, bearing in mind that some circuits are live only when the ignition switch is moved to a particular position.

13 If voltage is present (indicated either by the tester bulb lighting or a voltmeter reading, as applicable), this means that the section of the circuit between the relevant connector and the battery is problem-free.

14 Continue to check the remainder of the circuit in the same fashion.

15 When a point is reached at which no voltage is present, the problem must lie between that point and the previous test point with voltage. Most problems can be traced to a broken, corroded or loose connection.

Finding a short-circuit

16 To check for a short-circuit, first disconnect the load(s) from the circuit (loads are the components which draw current from a circuit, such as bulbs, motors, heating elements, etc).

17 Remove the relevant fuse from the circuit, and connect a circuit tester or voltmeter to the fuse connections.

18 Switch on the circuit, bearing in mind that some circuits are live only when the ignition switch is moved to a particular position.

19 If voltage is present (indicated either by the tester bulb lighting or a voltmeter reading, as applicable), this means that there is a short-circuit.

20 If no voltage is present, but the fuse still blows with the load(s) connected, this indicates an internal fault in the load(s).

Finding an earth fault

21 The battery negative terminal is connected to 'earth' – the metal of the engine/transmission and the car body – and most systems are wired so that they only receive a positive feed, the current returning via the metal of the car body. This means that the component mounting and the body form part of that circuit. Loose or corroded mountings can therefore cause a range of electrical faults, ranging from total failure of a circuit, to a puzzling partial fault. In particular, lights may shine dimly (especially when another circuit sharing the same earth point is in operation), motors (eg, wiper motors or the radiator cooling fan motor) may run slowly, and the operation of one circuit may have an apparently unrelated effect on another. Note that on many vehicles, earth straps are used between certain components, such as the engine/transmission and the body, usually where there is no metal-to-metal contact between components, due to flexible rubber mountings, etc.

22 To check whether a component is properly earthed, disconnect the battery, and connect one lead of an ohmmeter to a known good earth point. Connect the other lead to the wire or earth connection being tested. The resistance reading should be zero; if not, check the connection as follows.

23 If an earth connection is thought to be faulty, dismantle the connection, and clean back to bare metal both the bodyshell and the wire terminal or the component earth connection mating surface. Be careful to remove all traces of dirt and corrosion, and then use a knife to trim away any paint, so that a clean metal-to-metal joint is made. On reassembly, tighten the joint fasteners securely; if a wire terminal is being refitted, use serrated washers between the terminal and the bodyshell, to ensure a clean and secure connection. When the connection is remade, prevent the onset of corrosion in the future by applying a coat of petroleum jelly or silicone-based grease, or by spraying on (at regular intervals) a proprietary ignition sealer.

3 Fuses and relays – general information

Fuses

1 Fuses are designed to break a circuit when a predetermined current is reached, in order to protect the components and wiring that could be damaged by excessive current flow. Any excessive current flow will be due to a fault in the circuit, usually a short-circuit (see Section 2).

2 The main fuses are located in the fusebox, in the right-hand side of the facia panel **(see illustration).**

3 A blown fuse can be recognised from its melted or broken wire.

4 To remove a fuse, first ensure that the relevant circuit is switched off.

5 Using the plastic tool provided on the fusebox cover, pull the fuse from its location **(see illustration)**. Spare fuses are also provided on the fusebox cover.

6 Before renewing a blown fuse, trace and rectify the cause, and always use a fuse of the correct rating. Never substitute a fuse of a higher rating, or make temporary repairs using wire or metal foil; more serious damage, or even fire, could result.

7 Additional fuses are located in the engine compartment fusebox. First, remove the plastic cover to access the fuses and relays **(see illustrations)**.

8 Note that the fuses are colour-coded. Refer to the label on the fusebox cover for details of the circuits protected.

3.2 Main fusebox located in end of facia panel

Relays

9 A relay is an electrically-operated switch, which is used for the following reasons:

a) A relay can switch a heavy current remotely from the circuit in which the current is flowing, allowing the use of lighter-gauge wiring and switch contacts.

b) A relay can receive more than one control input, unlike a mechanical switch.

c) A relay can have a timer function – for example, the intermittent wiper relay.

10 As a result of the switching functions contained within the multi-timer unit, fewer relays are fitted than normal. Those that are fitted are located by the two main fuseboxes in the passenger and engine compartments. Refer to the wiring diagrams at the end of this Chapter for more information.

11 If a circuit or system controlled by a relay develops a fault, and the relay is suspect, operate the system. If the relay is functioning, it should be possible to hear it 'click' as it is energised. If this is the case, the fault lies with the components or wiring of the system. If the relay is not being energised, then either the relay is not receiving a main supply or a switching voltage, or the relay itself is faulty. Testing is by the substitution of a known good unit, but be careful – while some relays are identical in appearance and in operation, others look similar but perform different functions.

Multi-timer Unit

12 The interior multi-timer unit (also known as the UCH, or Unité de Commande d'Habitacle) is located under the facia panel, on the driver's side. For further information on the multi-timer unit, see Section 26.

3.7a Unclip the plastic cover . . .

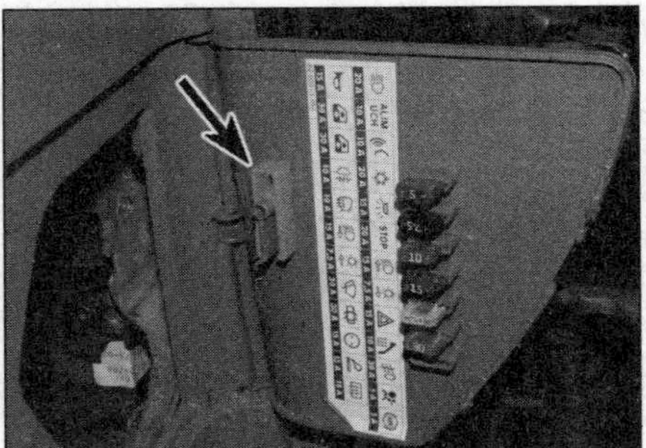

3.5 Plastic tool (arrowed) used to remove fuses

4 Switches – removal and refitting

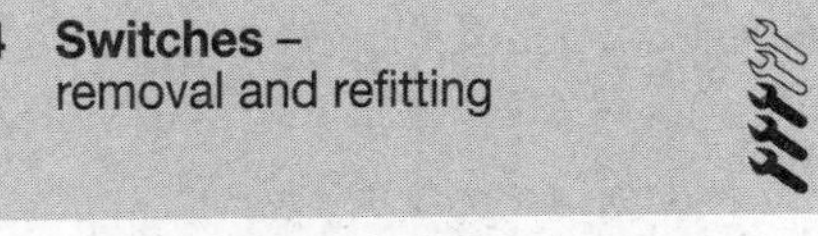

Note: *Before removing any switch, at least make sure the ignition is off (remove the keycard). Ideally, disconnect the battery negative lead, and position the lead away from the battery (also see 'Disconnecting the battery').*

Ignition card reader

1 Refer to Chapter 5A.

Starter/stop button

2 Taking care not to damage the facia panel, carefully unclip the starter/stop button from the facia.

3 Disconnect the wiring plug from the back of the starter button.

4 Refitting is a reversal of removal.

Steering column combination switches

Note: *The steering column switches are mounted on, and connected through, a module fitted behind the steering wheel, which also contains the airbag rotary connector. To renew an individual switch, see the following procedure.*

5 Remove the steering wheel as described in Chapter 10.

6 Remove the steering column shrouds, with reference to Chapter 11, Section 27.

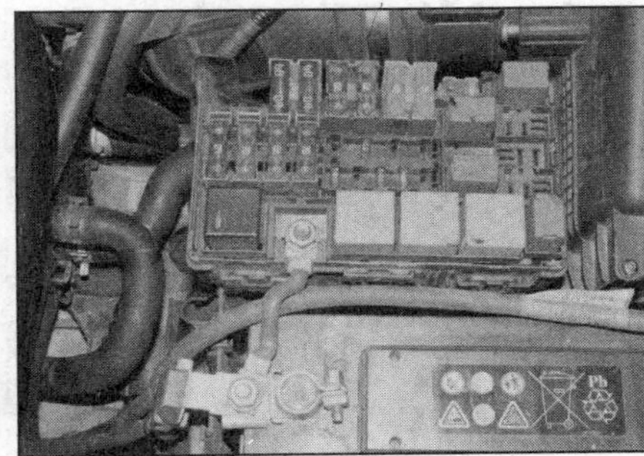

3.7b . . . to access the engine compartment fusebox

4.7a Releasing the clips (arrowed) on the light switch . . .

4.7b . . . and disconnect the wiring connector

4.8a Releasing the clips on the wiper switch

4.8b . . . and disconnect the wiring connector

7 To remove the lighting stalk, release the upper and lower securing clips and slide the switch out from the rotary switch assembly **(see illustrations).** Disconnect the switch wiring connector.

8 To remove the wiper control stalk, release the upper and lower locking clips and slide the switch out from the rotary switch assembly **(see illustrations).** Disconnect the switch wiring connector.

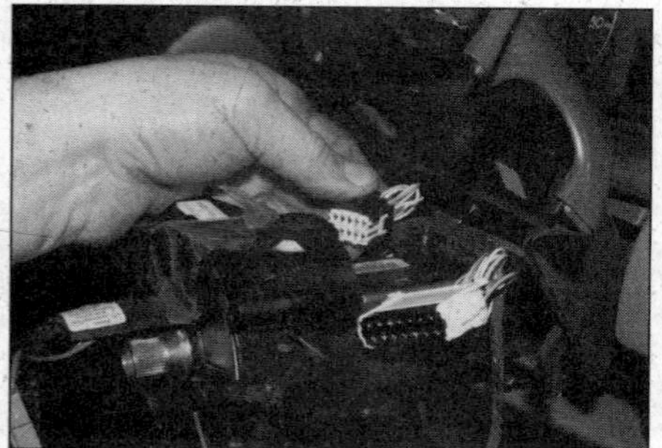

4.12a Remove the upper wiring connector(s) . . .

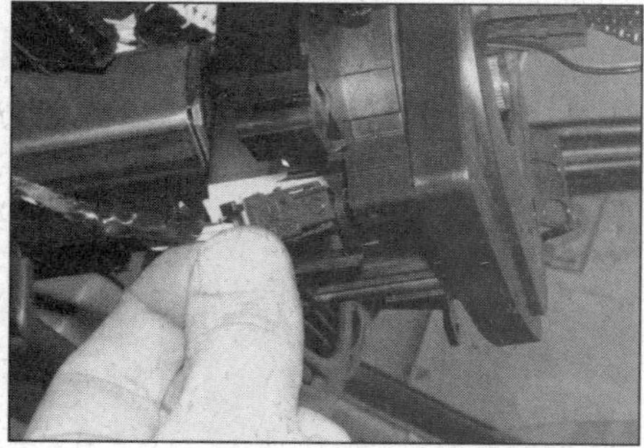

4.12b . . . and the lower wiring connector(s)

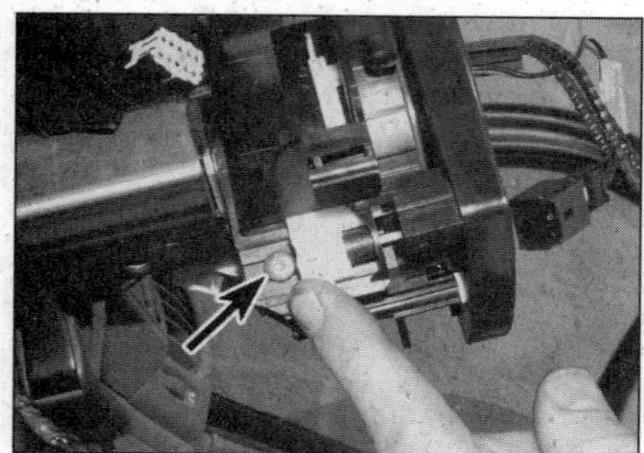

4.13a Slacken the retaining screw (arrowed) . . .

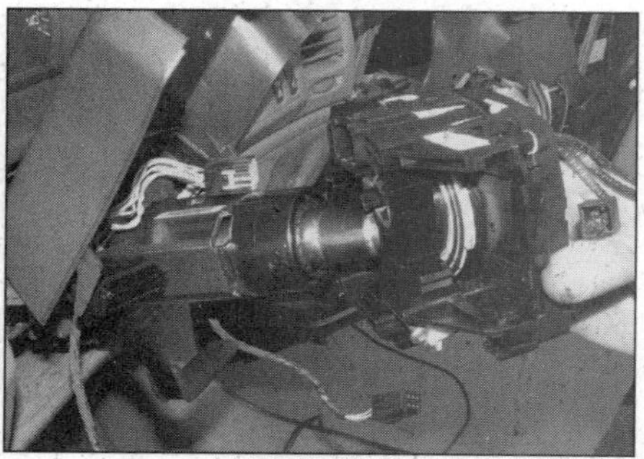

4.13b . . . and withdraw the rotary switch

9 Refitting is a reversal of removal, but ensure that the steering wheel is refitted as described in Chapter 10.

Steering column rotary airbag/cruise control switch

10 The rotary switch is used to provide an electrical connection between the steering column and the steering wheel on models with an airbag and/or cruise control. The rotary switch can be removed with the lighting and wiper control stalks still attached or remove the stalks first, as described previously in this Chapter.

11 Ensure that the front wheels are in the straight-ahead position, then remove the steering wheel as described in Chapter 10, and the steering column shrouds as described in Chapter 11, Section 27.

12 Disconnect the wiring plugs from the rear of the switch assembly **(see illustrations).** If the lighting switch, wiper control and radio switch is still attached, the wiring connectors will need to be removed.

13 Slide the plastic cover upwards and slacken the retaining screw, and then withdraw the switch assembly from the column **(see illustrations).**

14 Refitting is a reversal of removal, bearing in mind the following points.

a) Ensure that the front wheels are in the straight-ahead position.

b) If a new switch assembly is being fitted, it will be supplied ready-centred, and held in position by an adhesive label which will tear the first time the steering wheel is turned – do not remove the label before the steering wheel is refitted.

c) If the switch assembly has been removed without the front wheels in the straight-ahead position, the switch ribbon cable can be centred manually by moving it whilst pressing the centre section of the switch. Note that with the front wheels in the straight-ahead position, the switch hub on the steering column locks in position – make sure that the switch hub is locked, and that the arrows at the top of the rotary switch are aligned, then refit the rotary switch.

d) Where applicable, feed the horn wiring through the centre of the switch as it is refitted.

e) Refit the steering wheel as described in Chapter 10.

Radio remote control switch

15 Remove the steering wheel as described in Chapter 10.

16 Remove the steering column shrouds, with reference to Chapter 11, Section 27.

17 Disconnect the wiring plug from the switch assembly **(see illustration).**

18 Unscrew the switch securing screw, and withdraw the switch from the rotary switch assembly **(see illustration).**

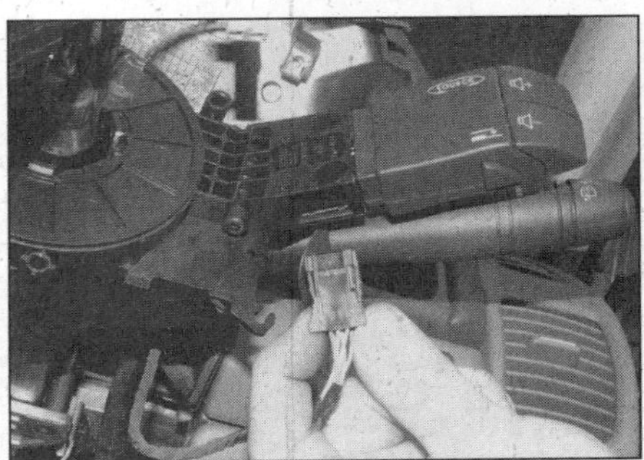
4.17 Disconnect the wiring connector

4.18 Unscrew the switch securing bolt – arrowed

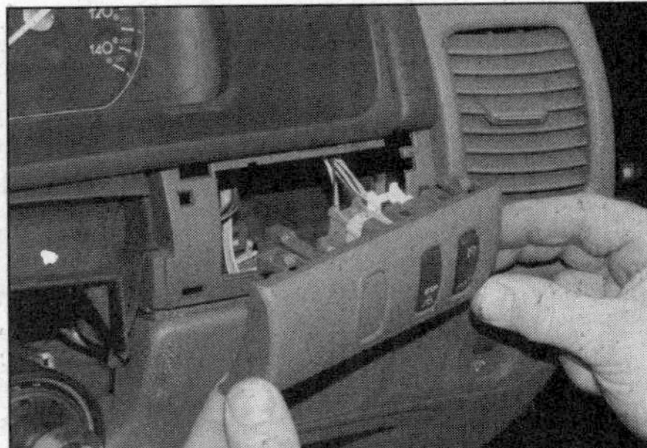
4.20a Unclip the switch panel . . .

4.20b . . . and disconnect the wiring connectors

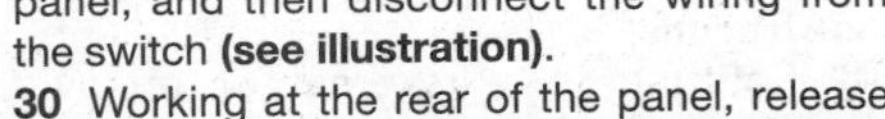
4.21 Unclip the switches from the rear of the panel

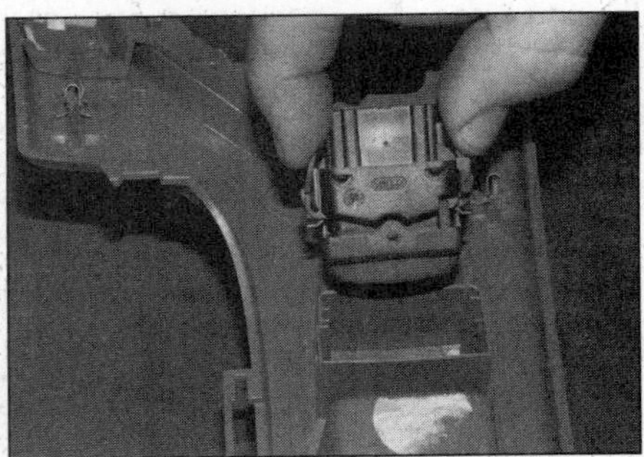
4.24 Unclip the switches from the rear of the panel

19 Refitting is a reversal of removal, but ensure that the wiring is routed as noted before removal.

Facia-mounted switches

20 Unclip the switch panel from the facia panel. Pull the panel downwards to release the upper securing lugs, then disconnect the wiring from the switches and withdraw the panel **(see illustrations).**

21 Working at the rear of the panel, release the locking clips and then withdraw the switch from the panel **(see illustration)**.

22 Refitting is a reversal of removal.

Centre console switches

23 Carefully prise the switch panel assembly from the top of the centre console, with reference to Chapter 11, Section 26.

24 Working at the rear of the panel, release the locking clips and then withdraw the switch from the panel **(see illustration)**.

25 Refitting is a reversal of removal.

Hazard warning light switch

26 Carefully prise the switch panel assembly from the top of the centre console, with reference to Chapter 11, Section 26.

27 Working at the rear of the panel, release the locking clips and push the switch out through the top of the panel **(see illustrations)**.

28 Refitting is a reversal of removal.

Instrument panel illumination/ headlight adjuster switch

29 Unclip the switch panel from the facia panel, and then disconnect the wiring from the switch **(see illustration)**.

30 Working at the rear of the panel, release the locking clips and then withdraw the switch from the panel **(see illustration)**.

31 Refitting is a reversal of removal.

Door-mounted switches

32 Release the securing clips and remove the switch panel from the top of the armrest.

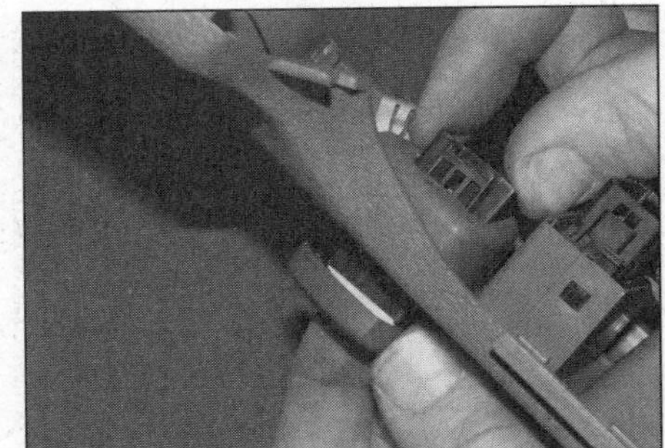
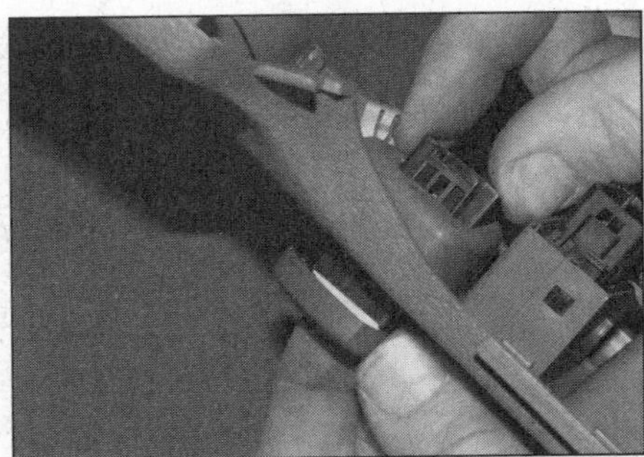
4.27a Unclip the retaining clips . . .

4.27b . . . and push the switch out of the panel

4.29 Unclip the switch panel and disconnect the wiring connector

4.30 Unclip the switch from the rear of the panel

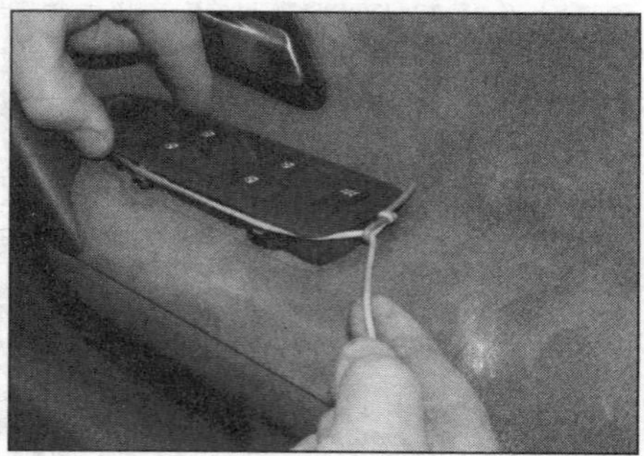
4.32a Using a piece of wire to release the securing clips . . .

4.32b . . . and withdraw the switch panel

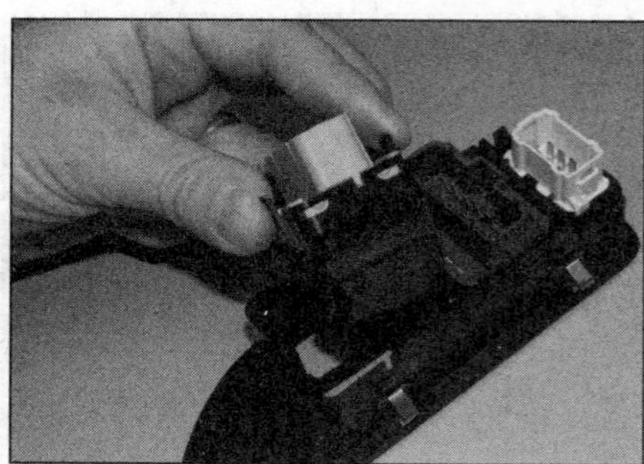
4.34 Unclip the switches from the rear of the panel

Using a piece of thin cable or string, wrap it around the switch panel and pull it to release the securing clips **(see illustrations)**.

33 Disconnect the wiring connectors from the switches in the panel, and withdraw the panel.

34 Working at the rear of the panel, release the securing clips and withdraw the switch from the panel **(see illustration)**.

35 Refitting is a reversal of removal.

Sunroof switch

36 Prise the switch panel out of the headlining, and disconnect the wiring plug from it **(see illustrations)**.

37 Use a small screwdriver, release the tabs around the switch body, and remove it from the panel.

38 Refitting is a reversal of removal.

Interior light switches

39 The interior/courtesy lights are operated by the interior multi-timer unit (see Section 26), using information from the central locking system.

Passenger airbag selector switch

Warning: Disconnect the battery negative lead (see 'Disconnecting the battery'), then wait for five minutes before proceeding. If this waiting period is not observed, there is danger of activating the passenger airbag.

40 Unclip the facia end cover panel at the passenger side and disconnect the wiring plug from the switch **(see illustration)**.

41 Release the retaining clips and push the switch through the 'front' of the panel **(see illustrations)**.

42 Refitting is a reversal of removal. Reconnect the switch before reconnecting the battery.

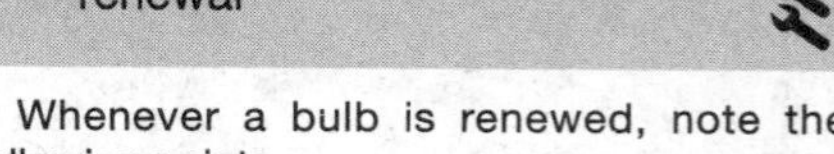
5 Bulbs (exterior lights) – renewal

1 Whenever a bulb is renewed, note the following points.

a) *Disconnect the battery negative terminal (refer to 'Disconnecting the battery' in the Reference Section of this manual), before starting work.*
b) *Remember that, if the light has just been in use, the bulb may be extremely hot.*
c) *Always check the bulb contacts and holder, ensuring that there is clean metal-to-metal contact between the bulb and its live(s) and earth. Clean off any corrosion or dirt before fitting a new bulb.*
d) *Wherever bayonet-type bulbs are fitted, ensure that the live contact(s) bear firmly against the bulb contact.*
e) *Always ensure that the new bulb is of the correct rating, and that it is completely clean before fitting it; this applies particularly to headlight/foglight bulbs (see below).*

Headlight (halogen)

Note: *On models with automatic transmission, it will be necessary to release the transmission electronic control unit for access to the left-hand side headlight unit. To do this, detach the retaining strap, or lift the retaining hook, as applicable, and move the unit to one side.*

2 Working in the engine compartment, to access the headlight bulbs, remove the relevant round cover from the back of the light

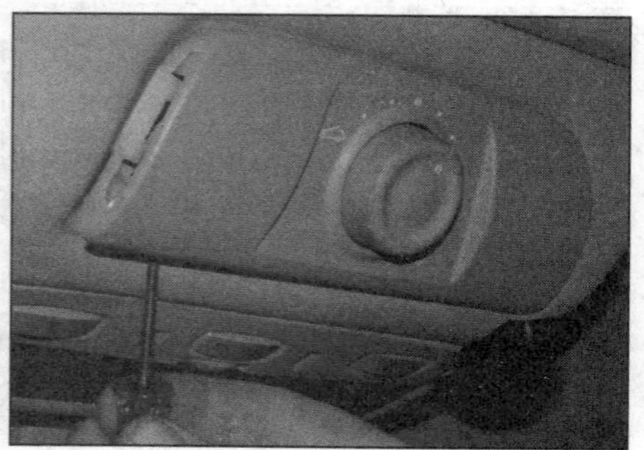
4.36a Carefully prise the switch panel . . .

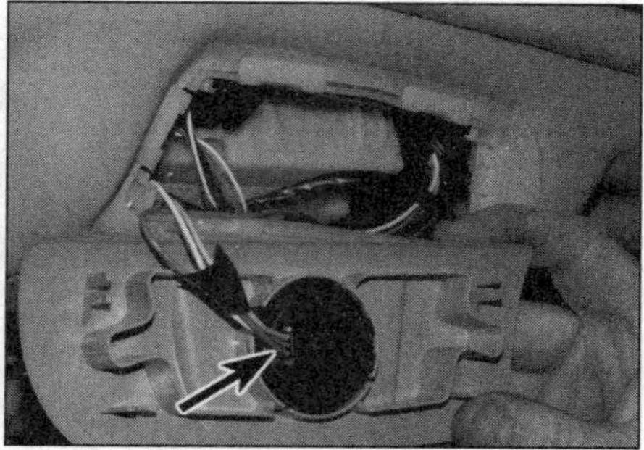
4.36b . . . and disconnect the wiring connector – arrowed

4.40 Unclip the facia end trim panel

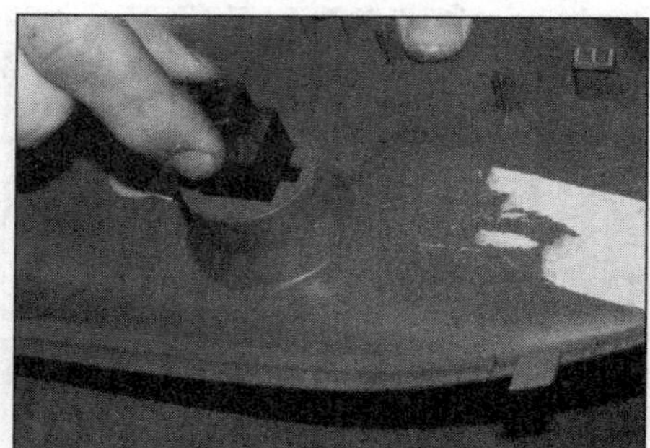
4.41a Push the switch through . . .

4.41b . . . and withdraw it from the panel

5.2 Rotate the cover anti-clockwise to remove – main beam shown

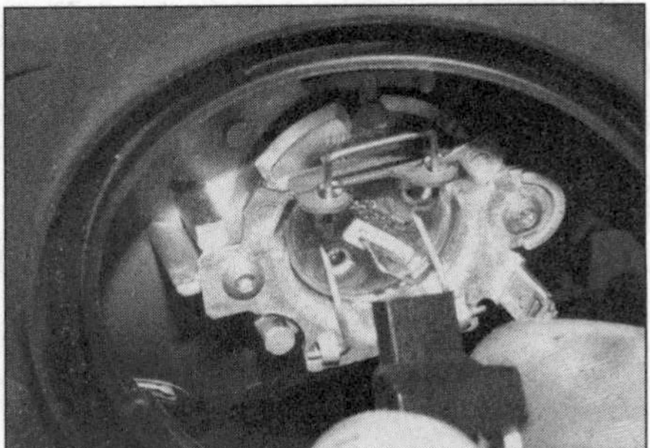
5.3a Disconnect the wiring connector . . .

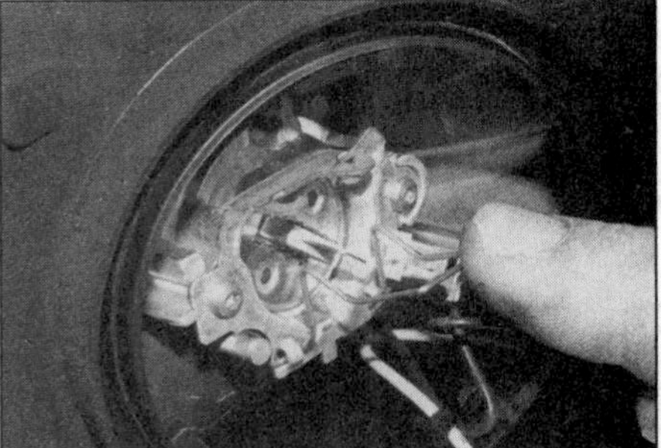
5.3b . . . release the retaining clip . . .

5.3c . . . and withdraw the bulb

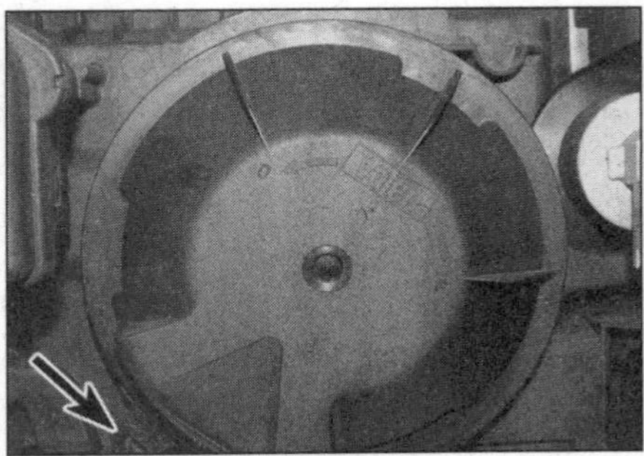
5.7 Check for retaining screw in slot – arrowed

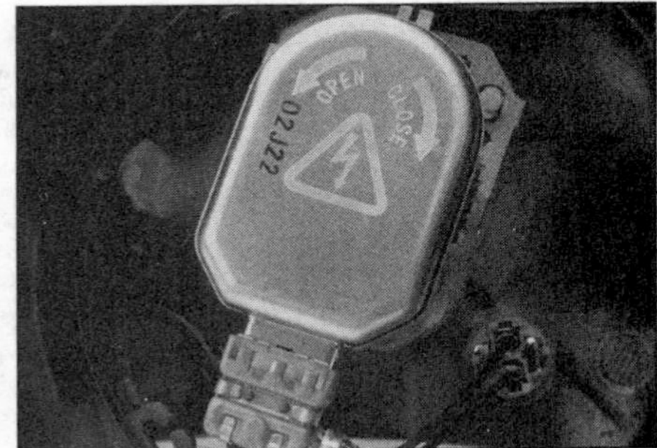

5.8a Turn the unit anti-clockwise . . .

unit – the inner cover is for the main beam bulb **(see illustration)**, with the outer cover for the dipped beam (and sidelight).

3 Bulb removal itself is the same for either bulb, though the bulbs themselves are different. Disconnect the wiring plug from the bulb, then unhook the wire, retaining clip, fold it down, and withdraw the bulb **(see illustrations)**.

4 When handling the new bulb, use a tissue or clean cloth to avoid touching the glass with the fingers; moisture and grease from the skin can cause blackening and rapid failure of this type of bulb.

5 Refitting is a reversal of removal.

Headlight (xenon)

Note: *Renewal of the main beam bulb is as described for the halogen light previously in this Section – for renewal of the xenon dipped beam bulb, proceed as follows.*

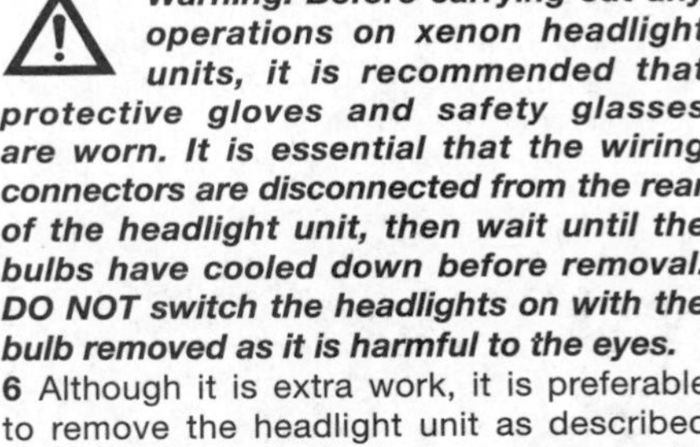

Warning: Before carrying out any operations on xenon headlight units, it is recommended that protective gloves and safety glasses are worn. It is essential that the wiring connectors are disconnected from the rear of the headlight unit, then wait until the bulbs have cooled down before removal. DO NOT switch the headlights on with the bulb removed as it is harmful to the eyes.

6 Although it is extra work, it is preferable to remove the headlight unit as described in Section 7. However, bulb renewal may be possible with the headlight in place.

7 Rotate the plastic cover in an anti-clockwise direction to remove the cover from the rear of the headlight unit. Note on some models it may be necessary to remove the retaining screw from the lower part of the cover **(see illustration)**.

8 Turn the high-voltage unit on the rear of the bulb anti-clockwise about an eighth of a turn, and withdraw it from the bulb **(see illustrations)**.

9 To remove the high-voltage unit from the vehicle, disconnect the wiring connector and put it safely to one side **(see illustration)**.

10 Release the wire clip retaining the bulb, then turn the bulb anti-clockwise about an eighth of a turn and withdraw it from the light unit. The external conductor of the bulb is fragile, take care not to damage or knock it **(see illustrations)**.

11 When handling the new bulb, use a tissue or clean cloth to avoid touching the glass with the fingers; moisture and grease from the skin can cause blackening and rapid failure of this type of bulb.

12 Refitting is a reversal of removal.

13 Renault recommend that the xenon headlight system should be re-initialised by a dealer following bulb renewal.

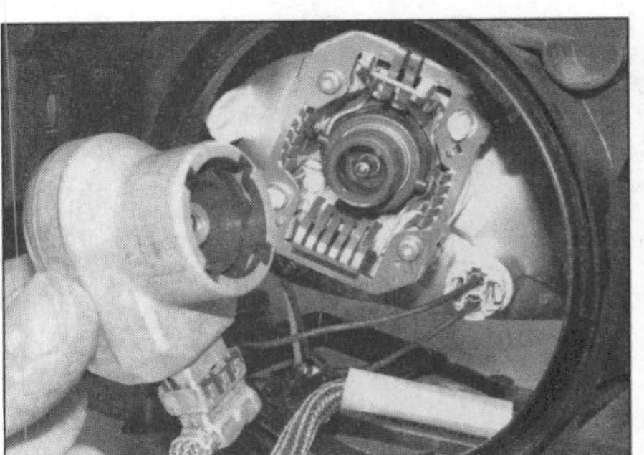
5.8b . . . and remove it from the bulb

5.9 Disconnect the wiring connector

5.10a Release the wire retaining clip . . .

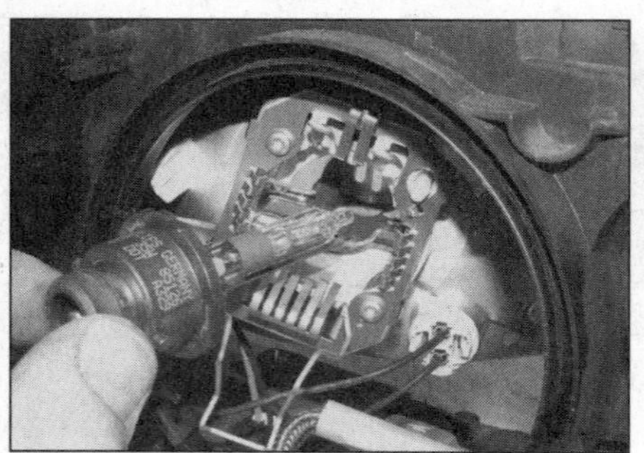

5.10b . . . and withdraw the bulb

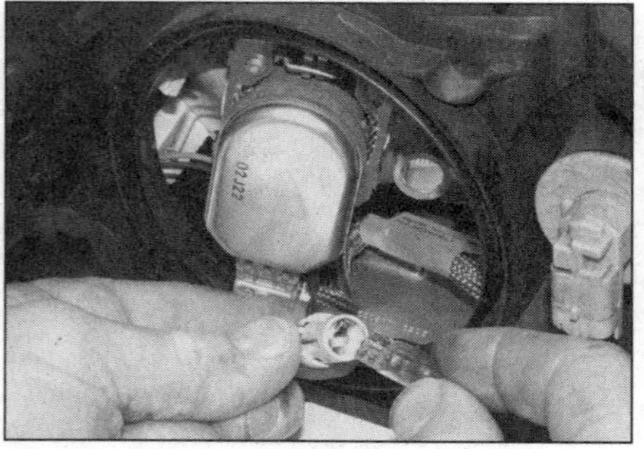

5.16 . . . and withdraw the bulb

Front sidelight

14 Remove the dipped beam cover from the rear of the headlight unit, as described previously in this Section.

5.15 Remove the bulbholder . . .

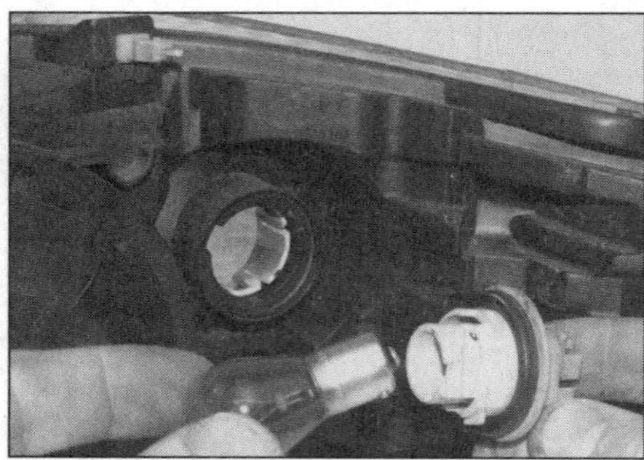

5.19 Indicator bulb removal

15 Withdraw the bulbholder from the rear of the headlight assembly **(see illustration)**.

16 The bulb is a push-fit (capless) in the bulbholder **(see illustration)**.

17 Refitting is a reversal of removal.

Front direction indicator light

18 Twist the bulbholder anti-clockwise and withdraw it from the rear of the headlight unit.

19 The bulb is a bayonet-fit in the bulbholder **(see illustration)**.

20 Refitting is a reversal of removal.

Front direction indicator side repeater light

21 Carefully prise the light unit from the door trim panel **(see illustration)**.

22 Twist the bulbholder anti-clockwise, and withdraw it from the light unit **(see illustration)**.

23 The bulb is a push-fit in the bulbholder **(see illustration)**.

24 Fit the new bulb and refit the light unit using a reversal of the removal procedure.

Front foglight

25 Undo the retaining screws and remove the splash shield from below the foglight unit **(see illustration)**.

26 Reach up behind the foglight and disconnect the wiring connector **(see illustration)**.

27 Working at the rear of the light unit, twist the cover anti-clockwise and remove it **(see illustration)**.

28 Remove the bulb by pulling it out of its holder.

29 When handling the new bulb, use a tissue or clean cloth to avoid touching the glass with the fingers; moisture and grease from the skin can cause blackening and rapid failure of this type of bulb. If the glass is accidentally

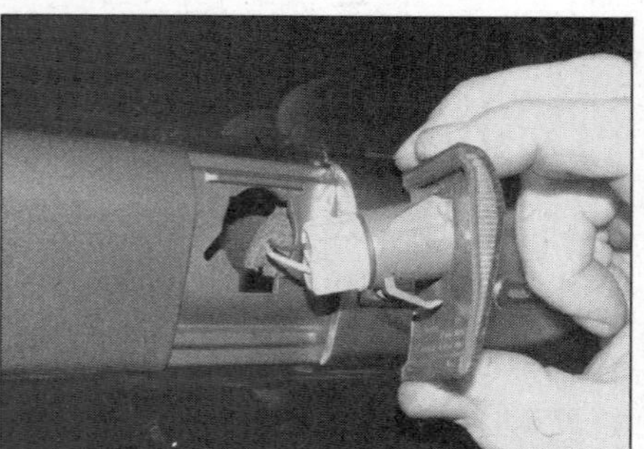

5.21 Unclip the side repeater

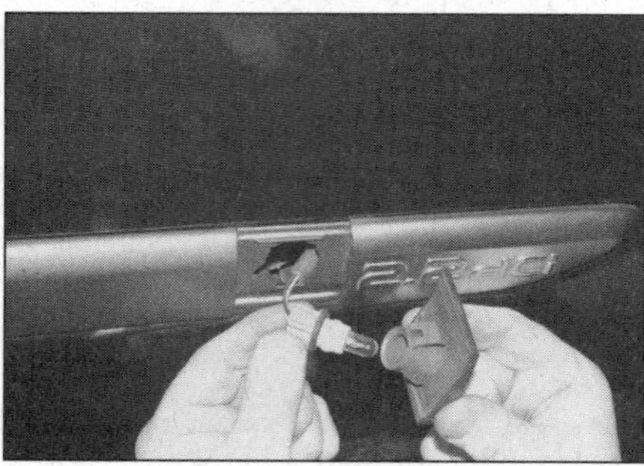

5.22 Remove the bulbholder

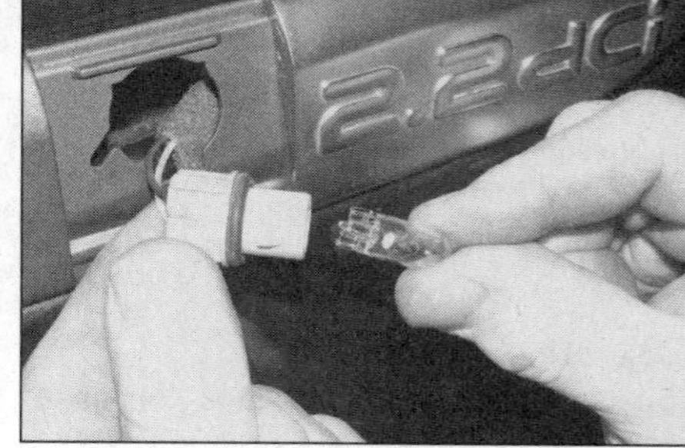

5.23 Pull the bulb out of the bulbholder

5.25 Remove the splash shield – arrowed

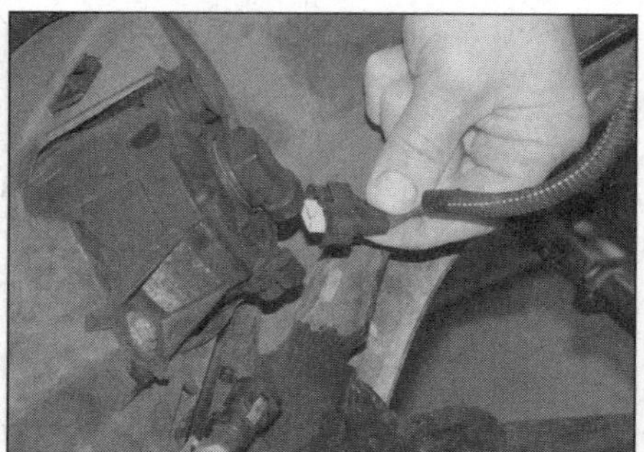

5.26 Disconnect the wiring connector from the foglight

5.27 Remove the bulb and holder from the light unit

touched, wipe it clean using methylated spirit.

30 Install the new bulb, ensuring that it locates correctly in the light unit.

31 Refitting is a reversal of removal.

Rear wing-mounted lights

Hatchback

32 Open the tailgate and undo the plastic retaining nut from inside the rear of the luggage compartment **(see illustration)**.

33 Remove the rear light unit and disconnect the wiring block connector **(see illustration).**

34 Depress the retaining clips, and withdraw the bulbholder from the rear of the light unit **(see illustration)**.

35 The bulbs are a bayonet-fit in the bulbholder **(see illustration)**.

36 Refitting is a reversal of removal, but ensure that the light unit is correctly seated in the rear wing panel.

Estate

37 Open the tailgate, then release the retaining clip, and remove the cover panel from the rear of the luggage compartment for access to the light assembly **(see illustration)**.

38 Carefully pull out the sound insulation to expose the bulbholder **(see illustration)**.

39 Depress the retaining clips, and withdraw the bulbholder from the rear of the light unit **(see illustration)**.

40 The bulbs are a bayonet-fit in the bulbholder **(see illustration)**.

41 Refitting is a reversal of removal, but ensure that the sound insulation and trim are correctly fitted to the rear of the light unit.

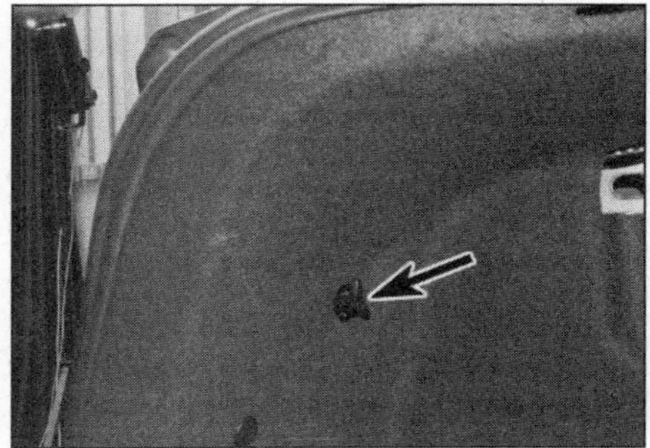

5.32 Undo the plastic securing nut – arrowed

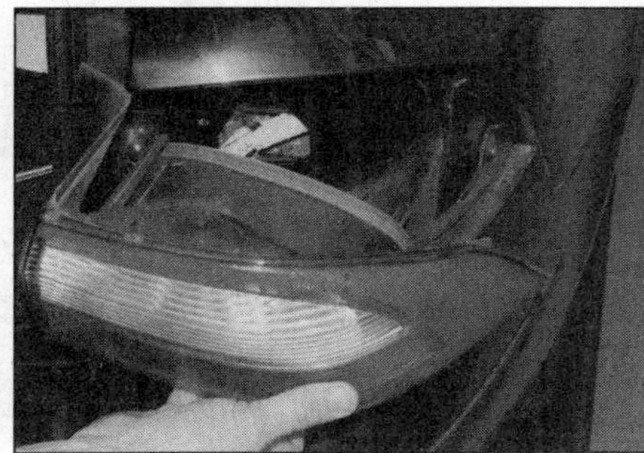

5.33 Withdraw the light unit from the wing panel

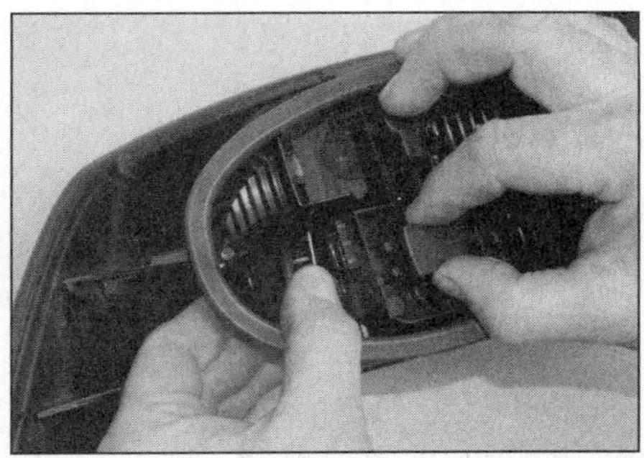

5.34 Release the bulbholder from the light unit

5.35 Twist and remove the bulb

Tailgate-mounted rear lights

42 Open the tailgate and remove the plastic plug from inside the tailgate trim panel, undo the retaining bolt **(see illustrations)**.

43 Remove the rear light unit and disconnect the wiring block connector **(see illustration).**

44 Depress the retaining clips, and withdraw the bulbholder from the rear of the light unit **(see illustration)**.

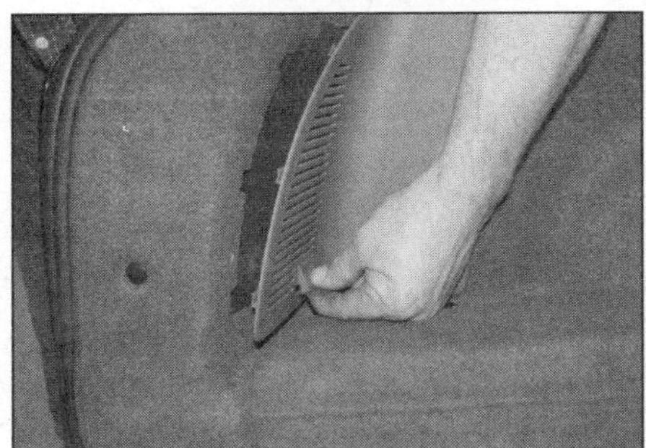

5.37 Unclip the plastic trim from the rear of the light unit

5.38 Pull out the soundproofing

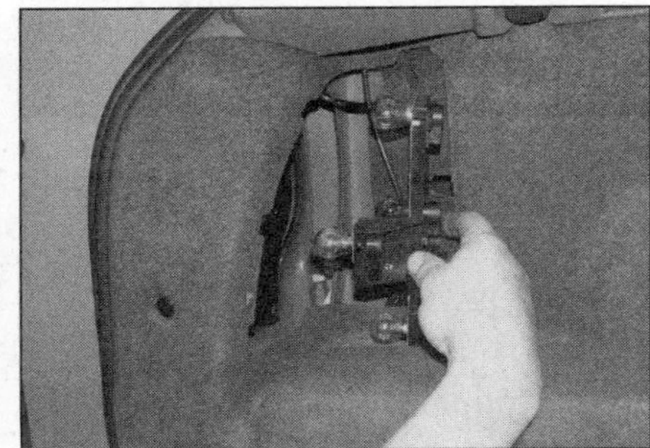

5.39 Unclip the bulbholder from the light unit

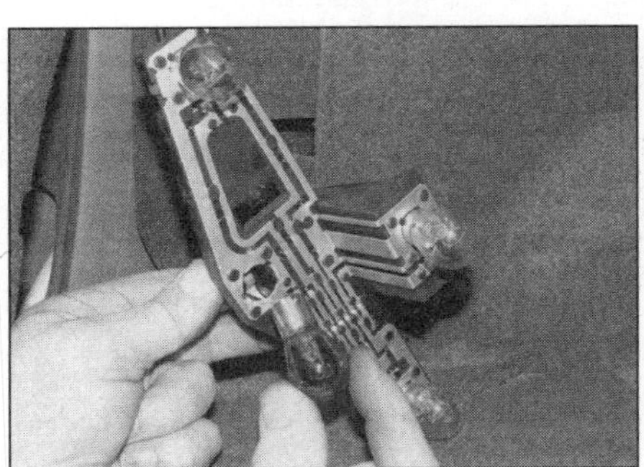

5.40 Twist and remove the bulb

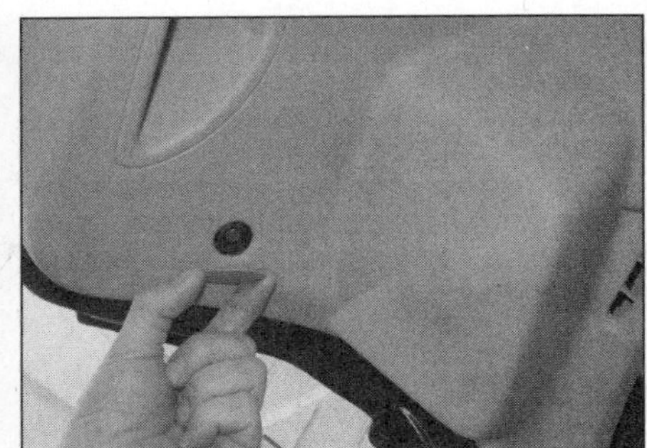

5.42a Remove the plastic plug . . .

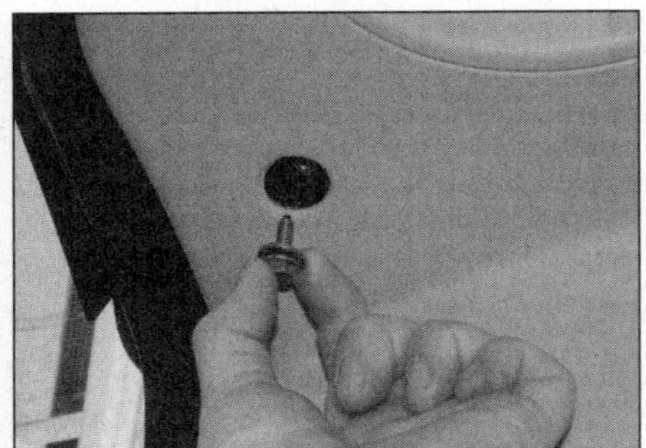

5.42b . . . and remove the securing bolt

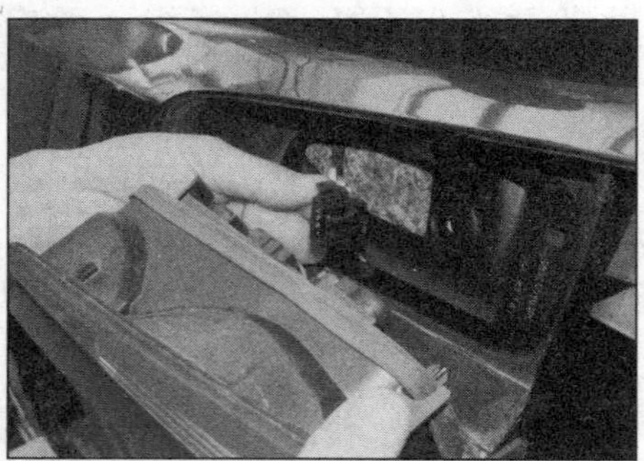
5.43 Disconnect the wiring connector

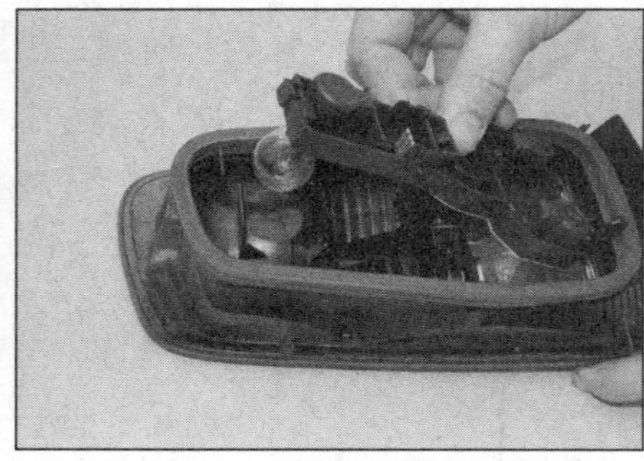
5.44 Release the bulbholder from the light unit

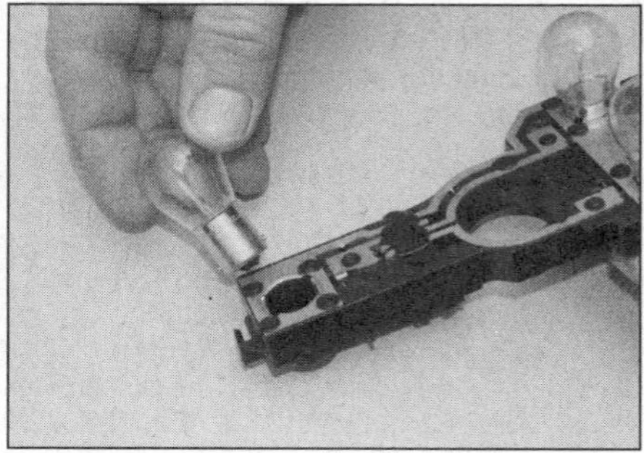
5.45 Twist and remove the bulb

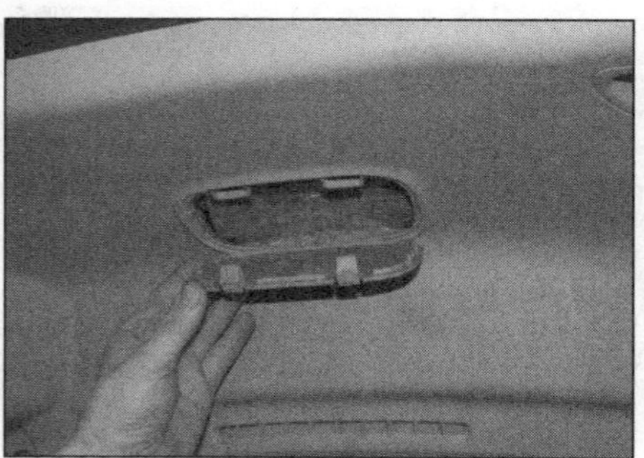
5.47 Unclip the cover panel

5.48 Release the securing clip (arrowed) and pivot outwards

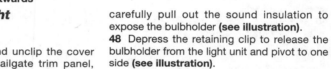

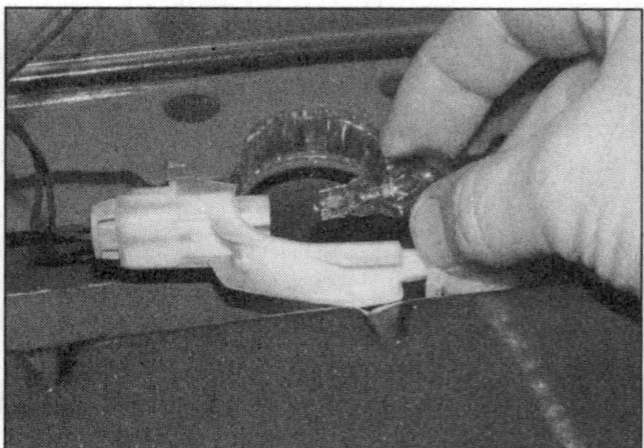
5.49 Withdraw the bulb from the holder

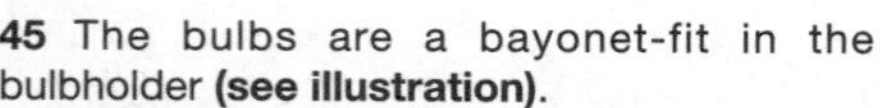
45 The bulbs are a bayonet-fit in the bulbholder **(see illustration)**.

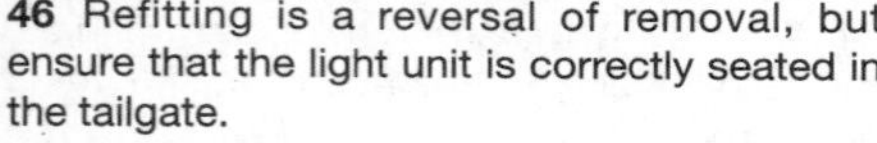
46 Refitting is a reversal of removal, but ensure that the light unit is correctly seated in the tailgate.

High-level stop-light

Hatchback

47 Open the tailgate, and unclip the cover from the centre of the tailgate trim panel, carefully pull out the sound insulation to expose the bulbholder **(see illustration)**.

48 Depress the retaining clip to release the bulbholder from the light unit and pivot to one side **(see illustration)**.

49 The bulb is a push-fit in the bulbholder **(see illustration)**.

50 Refitting is a reversal of removal, but ensure that the sound insulation and trim are correctly fitted to the tailgate trim panel.

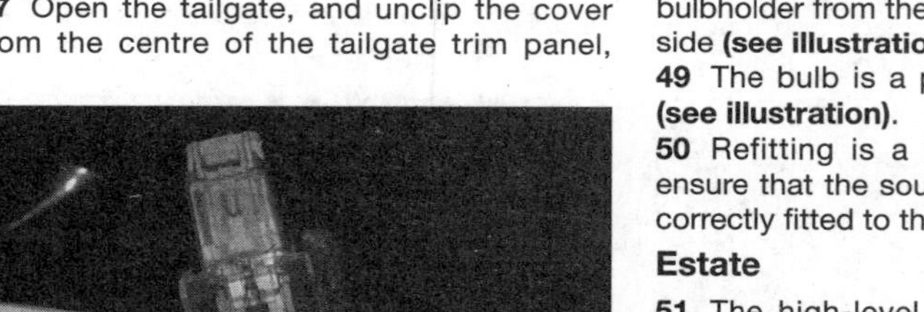

Estate

51 The high-level stop-light on the Estate model is a sealed unit with LEDs and does not have bulbs you can renew. To remove the complete high-level light unit see Section 7.

Number plate light

52 Press the tab on the side of the bulbholder and withdraw the light unit from above the number plate **(see illustration)**.

53 On Estate models, withdraw the capless bulb from the rear of the number plate light unit **(see illustration)**

54 On hatchback models, disconnect the wiring connector, remove the lens from the bulbholder and withdraw the festoon bulb from the contacts **(see illustrations)**.

55 Refitting is a reversal of removal.

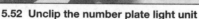

5.52 Unclip the number plate light unit

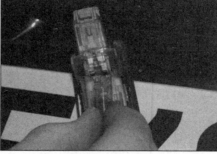

5.53 Pull the capless bulb from its holder

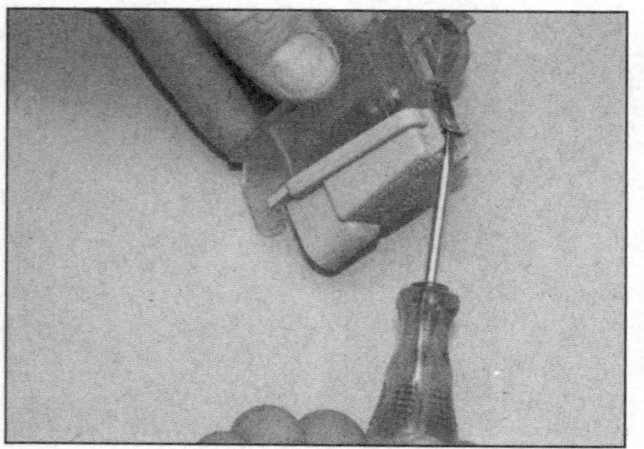
5.54a Release the securing clip . . .

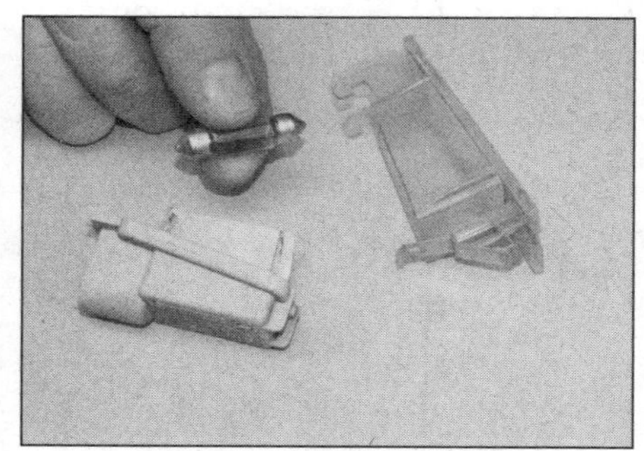
5.54b . . . and remove the bulb

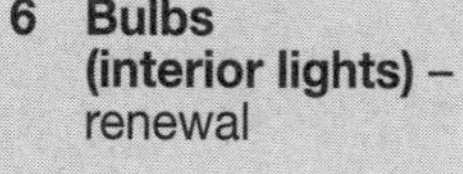

6 Bulbs (interior lights) – renewal

General

1 Refer to Section 5, paragraph 1.

6.2a Unclip the front light lens cover

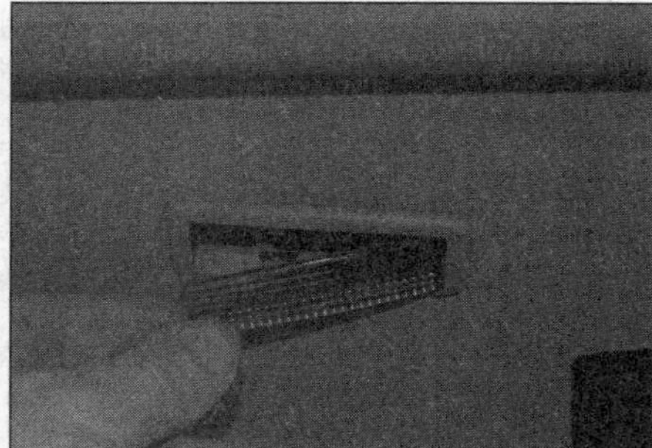
6.2b Unclip the light lens cover

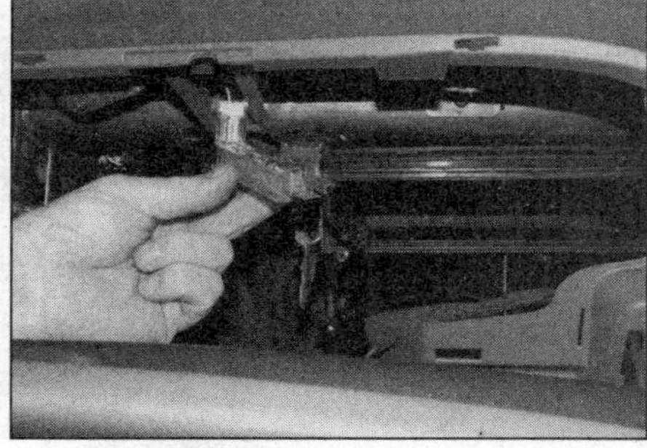
6.7 Unclip the glovebox light from the facia

Courtesy light and map reading light

2 Carefully prise the light unit lens/cover from the light unit **(see illustrations)**.

3 The centre bulb is a festoon bulb, which can be unclipped from the bulbholder in the light unit.

4 The outer bulbs are bayonet fit bulbs that can be twisted and removed from the bulbholder in the light unit.

5 Refitting is a reversal of removal.

Glovebox light

6 Open the glovebox lid and if required remove the glovebox pocket from the facia panel as described in Chapter 11, Section 27.

7 Unclip the light unit from the facia panel **(see illustration)** and remove the bulb from the spring contacts.

8 Refitting is a reversal of removal.

Luggage compartment light

9 Open the tailgate, then depress the retaining clip, and prise out the light unit **(see illustration)**.

10 Unclip the lens from the base of the light unit, then pull the bulb from the spring contacts **(see illustration)**.

11 Refitting is a reversal of removal.

Instrument panel illumination and warning light bulbs

12 The instrument panel is a 'solid-state' type, which means the 'bulbs' are non-renewable LEDs. The instrument panel is removed as described in Section 10.

Pushbutton switch illumination bulbs

13 The bulbs are integral with the switches, and cannot be renewed independently.

Cigarette lighter illumination bulb

14 Remove the complete cigarette lighter assembly as described in Section 12.

15 Unclip the cover from the bulb, the pull the bulb from the bulbholder.

16 Refitting is a reversal of removal.

Heater/ventilation control unit illumination bulbs

17 The heater control panel is a 'solid-state' type, which means the 'bulbs' are non-renewable LEDs. The heater control panel is removed as described in Chapter 3.

6.9 Unclip the light unit from the trim panel

6.10 Remove the lens from the base of the light unit

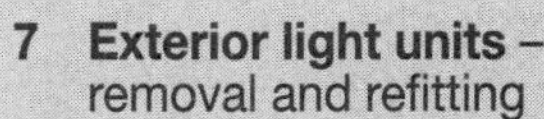

7 Exterior light units – removal and refitting

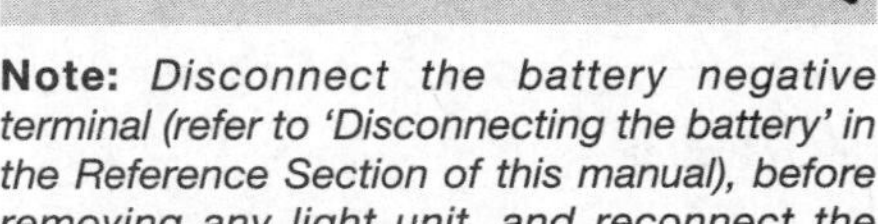

Note: *Disconnect the battery negative terminal (refer to 'Disconnecting the battery' in the Reference Section of this manual), before removing any light unit, and reconnect the lead after refitting the unit.*

Headlight

Warning: Before carrying out any operations on xenon headlight units, it is recommended that protective gloves and safety glasses are worn. It is essential that the wiring connectors are disconnected from the rear of the headlight unit, then wait until the bulbs have cooled down before removal. DO NOT switch the headlights on with the bulb removed, as it is harmful to the eyes.

1 Remove the front bumper as described in this Chapter 11.

2 Remove the three headlight mounting bolts (two above and one below), then release the retaining clip and withdraw the light unit from its location **(see illustrations)**.

3 Disconnect the wiring plug from the back of the light, and remove it from the vehicle **(see illustration)**.

4 Refitting is a reversal of removal, bearing in mind the following points.

a) *Ensure that the retaining clip at the top corner of the light unit engages with the wing panel.*

b) *Refit the radiator grille and front bumper (where applicable) as described in Chapter 11.*

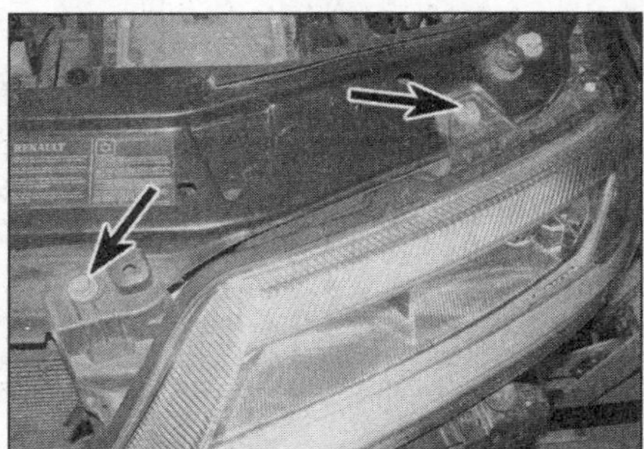
7.2a Undo the upper mounting bolts (arrowed) . . .

7.2b . . . the lower mounting bolt (arrowed) . . .

7.2c . . . and release the retaining clip

7.3 Disconnect the wiring connectors from the light unit

7.7 Undo the mounting screws – arrowed

7.9 Foglight adjuster – viewed from under front bumper

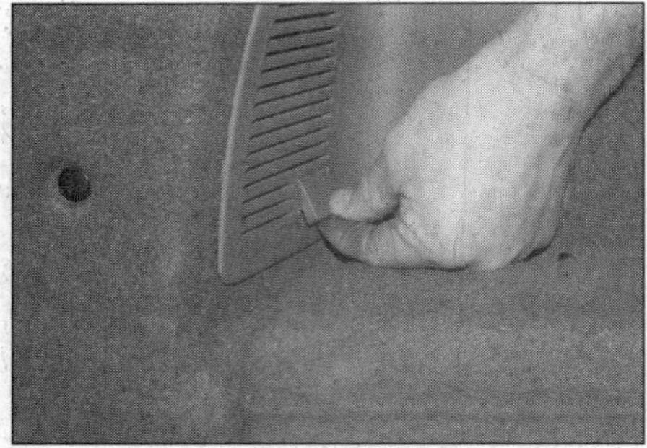

7.13 Unclip the cover from inside the luggage compartment

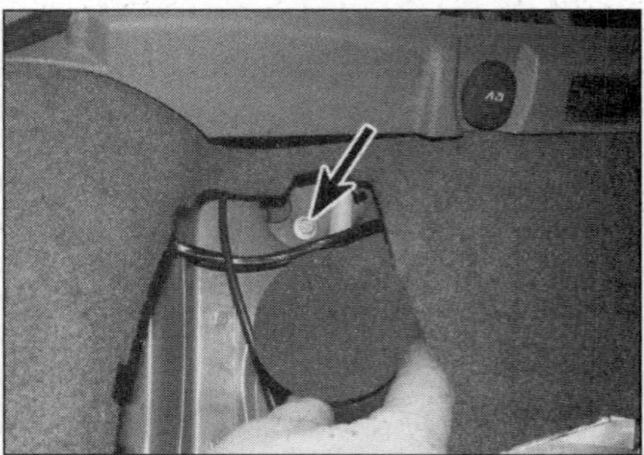

7.14 Remove the insulation to access the upper mounting bolt – arrowed

c) On completion, have the headlight beam alignment checked at the earliest opportunity with reference to Section 8.

Front foglight

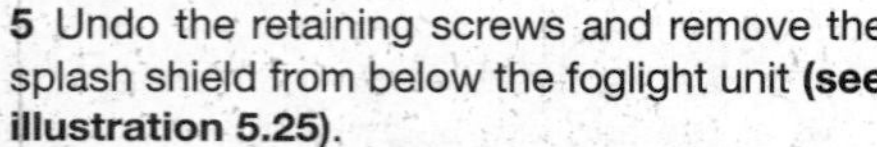

5 Undo the retaining screws and remove the splash shield from below the foglight unit **(see illustration 5.25)**.

6 Reach up behind the foglight and disconnect the wiring connector **(see illustration 5.26)**.

7 Working at the rear of the light unit, undo the two retaining screws and remove the foglight from the rear of the bumper **(see illustration)**.

8 Refitting is a reversal of removal.

9 If necessary, the foglight beam alignment can be adjusted using the screw provided at the bottom of the light unit **(see illustration)**.

Front direction indicator light

10 The direction indicator light is incorporated in the headlight unit and cannot be removed separately. Remove the headlight unit ass described previously in this Section.

Front direction indicator side repeater light

11 Removal and refitting procedure is described as part of the bulb renewal procedure in Section 5, paragraphs 21 to 24.

Rear wing-mounted lights

Hatchback

12 Removal and refitting procedure is described as part of the bulb renewal procedure in Section 5, paragraphs 32 to 36.

Estate

13 Open the tailgate, then release the retaining clip, and remove the cover panel from the rear of the luggage compartment for access to the light assembly **(see illustration)**.

14 Pull out the sound insulation to expose the rear of the light unit and the inner retaining bolt **(see illustration)**.

15 Disconnect the wiring from the bulbholder on the rear of the light unit.

16 Undo the retaining screws, and then withdraw the light unit from the rear of the wing panel **(see illustrations)**.

17 Refitting is a reversal of removal, but ensure that the light unit is correctly seated in the rear wing panel.

Tailgate-mounted lights

18 Removal and refitting procedure is described as part of the bulb renewal procedure in Section 5, paragraphs 42 to 46.

High-level stop-light

Hatchback

19 Open the tailgate, and unclip the cover from the centre of the tailgate trim panel, carefully pull out the sound insulation to expose the back of the high level brake light **(see illustration 5.47)**.

20 Release the retaining clips and from outside the tailgate withdraw the high-level brake light **(see illustrations)**. Disconnect the wiring connector.

21 Refitting is a reversal of removal.

Estate

22 Open the tailgate and undo the screws at each end, securing the plastic inner trim cover and remove it from the tailgate glass **(see illustrations)**.

23 Undo the two retaining screws and from the outside of the tailgate glass withdraw the high-level brake light **(see illustrations)**.

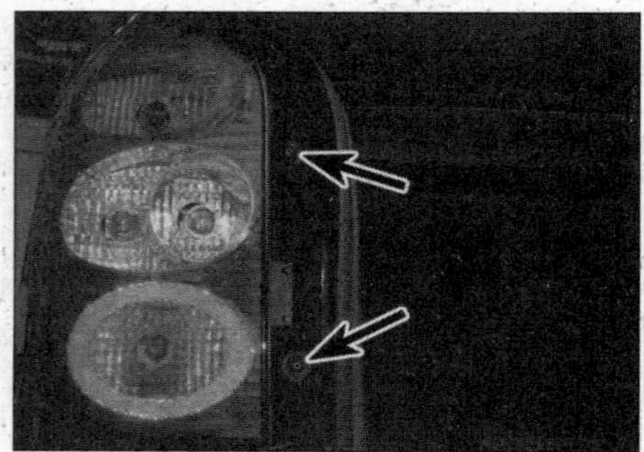

7.16a Undo the mounting screws (arrowed) . . .

7.16b . . . and carefully unclip the light from the wing panel

24 Disconnect the stop-light wiring connector **(see illustration)**.
25 Refitting is a reversal of removal.

Number plate light

26 Removal and refitting procedure is described as part of the bulb renewal procedure in Section 5, paragraphs 52 to 55.

8 Headlight beam alignment - general information

1 Accurate adjustment of the headlight beam is only possible using optical beam-setting equipment, and this work should therefore be carried out by a Renault dealer or suitably-equipped workshop.
2 All vehicles are equipped with a five-position electrical vertical beam adjuster unit – this can be used to adjust the headlight beam, to compensate for the relevant load which the vehicle is carrying. An adjuster switch is provided on the facia, which controls electric adjuster motors located in the rear of the headlight assemblies. The adjuster switch should be positioned as follows, according to the load being carried in the vehicle.

Position 0 *Front seat(s) occupied, luggage compartment empty.*
Position 1 *Front and rear seats occupied, luggage compartment empty.*
Position 2 *Front and rear seats occupied, luggage compartment empty.*
Position 3 *Front and rear seats occupied and luggage compartment loaded.*
Position 4 *Driver's seat occupied and luggage or load reaching the maximum permissible load.*

3 To make a temporary adjustment of the headlights, position the car on a level surface 10 metres from a wall. The tyres must all be at the correct pressure, and the manual adjustment switch inside the car set at 0. Use the adjuster screws at the rear of the headlight to reset the beams accordingly **(see illustration)**.
4 Models with xenon headlights have an automatic levelling system. If a fault occurs in the system, a warning light will show up on the instrument panel, and the headlights will be angled down to avoid dazzling oncoming traffic. If this happens, the driving speed must be adjusted accordingly to allow for decreased visibility.

9 Headlight beam adjustment components - removal and refitting

General

1 Refer to Section 8.

Adjuster switch

2 Removal and refitting procedure is described in Section 4, paragraphs 29 to 31.

7.20a Release the retaining clips (arrowed) . . .

7.20b . . . and withdraw the light unit

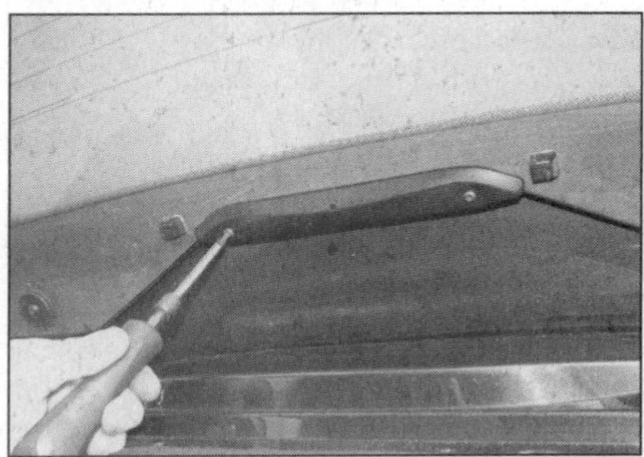
7.22a Remove the two retaining screws . . .

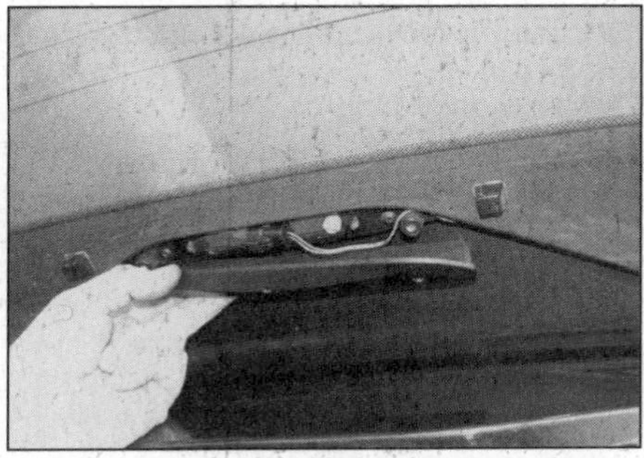
7.22b . . . and remove the trim cover

Adjuster motor

Removal

3 If required, remove the relevant headlight unit as described in Section 7.
4 If not already done, disconnect the wiring connector from the adjuster motor.
5 Twist the adjuster motor through an eighth of a turn to the outside of the car, then slide the unit upwards to release the motor balljoint

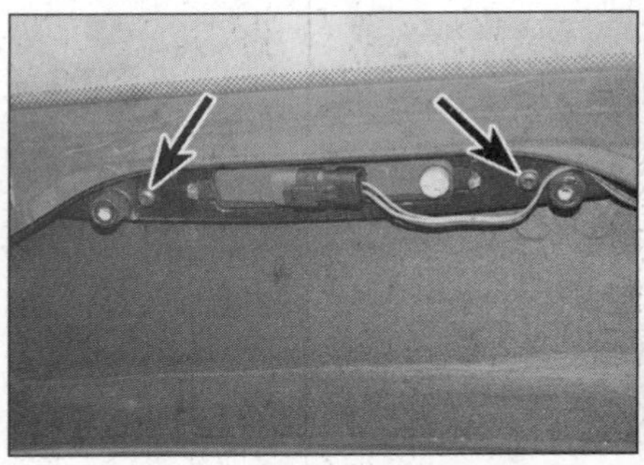
7.23a Remove the two retaining screws (arrowed) . . .

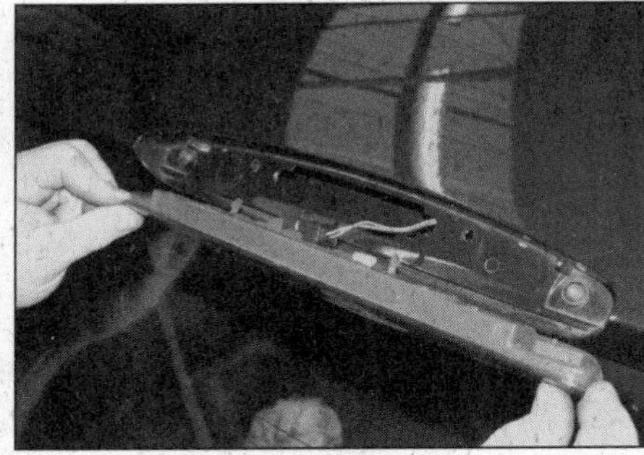
7.23b . . . and remove the high-level brake light

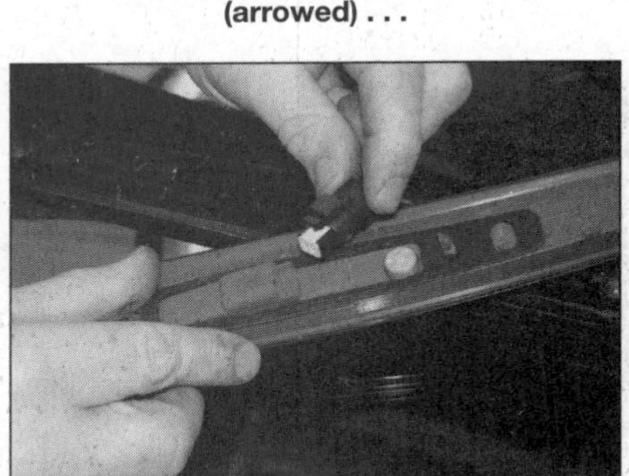
7.24 Disconnect the wiring connector

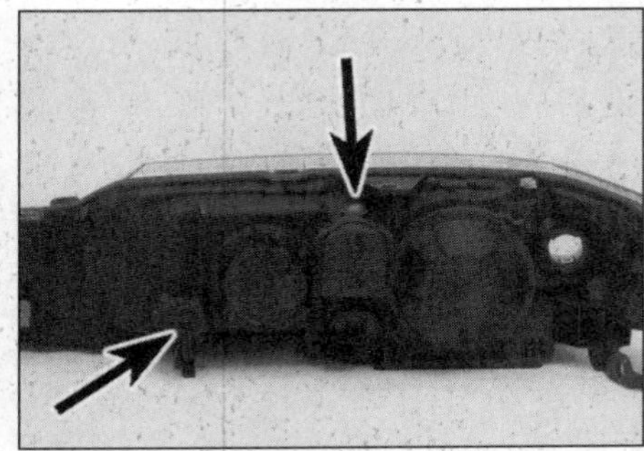
8.3 Adjust upper screw for vertical and lower screw for horizontal

9.5a Twist the motor towards the outside of the car . . .

9.5b . . . then unclip the balljoint from the lever – arrowed

from the slot in the adjuster lever **(see illustrations)**. Take care, as the adjuster lever is easily broken.

6 Withdraw the motor.

Refitting

7 If a new adjuster motor is being fitted, first turn the manual adjusting screw in about six turns before fitting.

8 Slide the motor balljoint into engagement with the slot in the headlight adjuster lever, then engage the motor casing with the headlight, and twist it towards the middle of the car to lock the motor in position.

9 With a new adjuster motor is fitted to the headlight unit; now turn the manual adjusting screw out about six turns.

10 Reconnect the wiring plug back to the adjuster motor

11 Refit the headlight as described in Section 7. ***Note:*** *On completion, have the headlight beam alignment checked at the earliest opportunity with reference to Section 8.*

10 Instrument panel – removal and refitting

Removal

1 Disconnect the battery negative terminal (refer to *Disconnecting the battery* in the Reference Section of this manual).

2 Remove the steering column shrouds as described in Chapter 11, Section 27.

3 Unclip the switch panel from the right-hand bottom corner of the instrument panel **(see illustration).**

4 Unclip the instrument panel surround from the facia, and then withdraw it from the instrument panel **(see illustration)**.

5 Remove the instrument panel lower securing screw **(see illustration).**

6 Twist the instrument panel upwards and unclip it from the facia, and then release the securing clips and disconnect the wiring connectors as it is removed **(see illustrations)**.

Refitting

7 Refitting is a reversal of removal, but ensure that the wiring connector securing clips are securely reconnected.

11 Auxiliary display unit – removal and refitting

Auxiliary display unit

1 Depending on model, the display unit could have the following functions:

a) Radio display.
b) Tyre pressure reading/monitoring.
c) Door closure warning light.
d) Seat belt reminder.
e) Navigation.

Removal

2 Disconnect the battery negative terminal (refer to *Disconnecting the battery* in the Reference Section of this manual).

3 Carefully unclip the upper display from the top of the facia panel; release the securing clips and disconnect the wiring connectors as it is removed **(see illustrations).**

10.3 Unclip the switch trim panel

10.4 Unclip the instrument panel surround

10.5 Undo the securing screw – arrowed

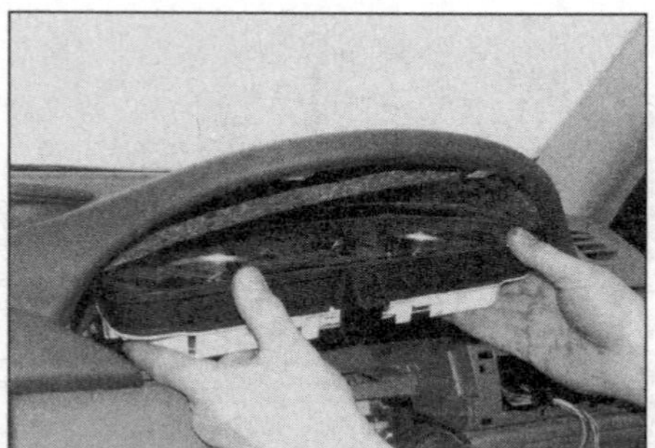
10.6a Unclip the instrument panel . . .

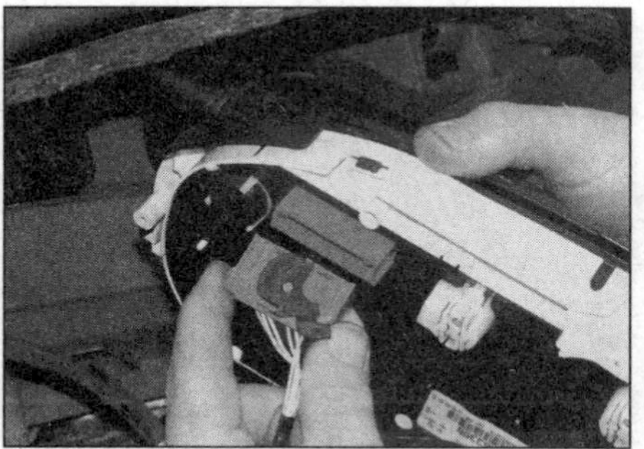
10.6b . . . and disconnect the wiring connectors

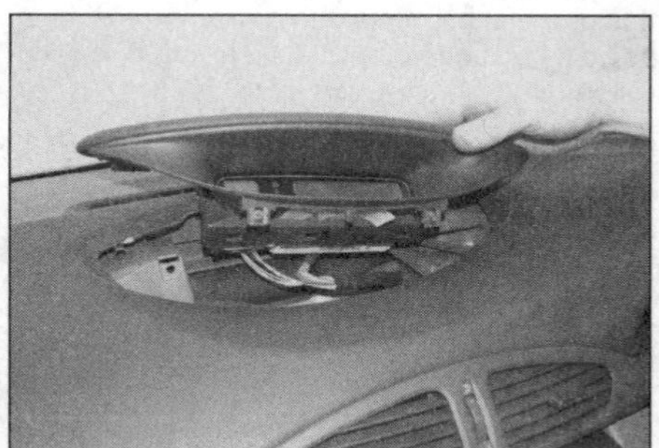
11.3a Unclip the display from the top of the facia . . .

11.3b . . . and disconnect the wiring connectors

4 Each unit can then be unclipped from the display plastic surround.

Refitting

5 Refitting is a reversal of removal.

Exterior temperature sensor

6 The exterior temperature sensor is located in the right-hand exterior mirror; see Chapter 3, Section 11, for the removal and refitting procedure.

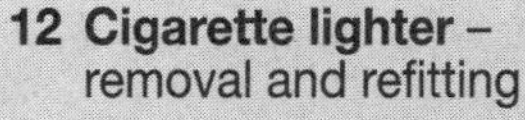

12 Cigarette lighter – removal and refitting

Removal

1 Disconnect the battery negative terminal (refer to *Disconnecting the battery* in the Reference Section of this manual).

2 Unclip the ashtray from its housing.

3 Remove the upper switch trim panel from the centre console as described in Chapter 11, Section 26.

4 Disconnect the wiring connector from the cigarette lighter **(see illustration).**

5 Pull the cigarette lighter element from the metal sleeve.

6 To remove the metal sleeve, push the rear of the sleeve, and simultaneously depress the two securing lugs on the inner face of the sleeve.

7 To remove the plastic housing, push the housing, from the rear, out of the housing.

Refitting

8 Refitting is a reversal of removal.

13 Tyre pressure monitoring system – general information, removal and refitting

General information

1 The purpose of this system is to inform the driver when the tyres are not within the recommended pressures. The tyre pressure monitoring system consists of:

a) Four pressure sensors (one per wheel).
b) A receiver.

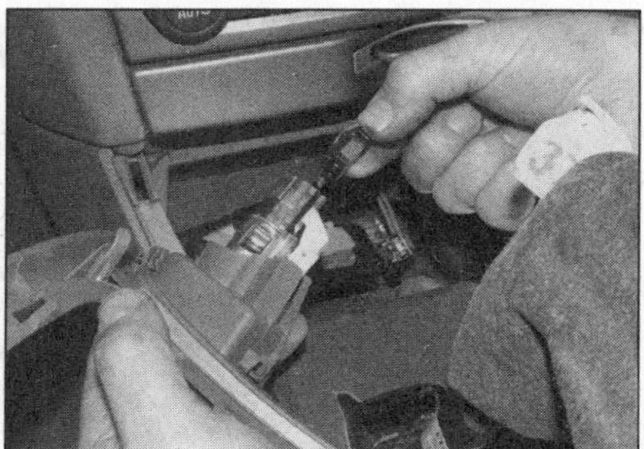

12.4 Disconnecting the wiring connector from the cigarette lighter

13.5a Unclip the receiver . . .

c) Multi-timer unit (UCH).
d) A display unit.

Pressure sensors

2 There are four pressure sensors, which are incorporated in each tyre valve on all the four wheels (not fitted to the spare wheel). Each wheel sensor is identified by a coloured marking around the valve **(see illustration)**, so each wheel can only be fitted back to its original location.

Green	*Front left tyre*
Yellow	*Front right tyre*
Red	*Rear left tyre*
Black	*Rear right tyre*

3 It is recommended that the renewal of these tyre pressure valves be entrusted to a qualified tyre fitter.

Receiver

4 The receiver is located under the vehicle on the left-hand side, near the centre. It collects information from the tyre pressure sensors, and then decodes the information and sends it to the multi-timer unit (UCH).

5 To remove, unclip the sensor from the floor panel, disconnect the wiring connector and remove it from the car **(see illustrations).**

6 Refitting is a reversal of removal.

14.3 Remove the splash shield – arrowed

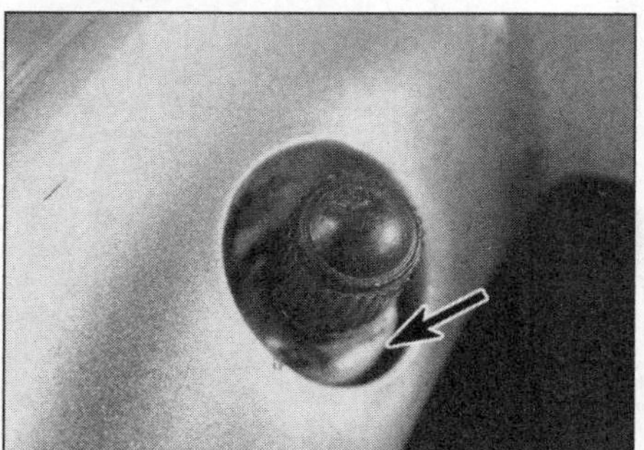

13.2 Coloured ring (arrowed) around the valve

13.5b . . . and disconnect the wiring connector

Multi-timer unit

7 For information on the multi-timer unit, see Section 26.

Display unit

8 For information on the auxiliary display unit, see Section 11.

14 Horn – removal and refitting

Removal

1 There are two horns, which are located behind the left-hand side of the bumper.

2 Disconnect the battery negative terminal (refer to *Disconnecting the battery* in the Reference Section of this manual).

3 Working under the vehicle, remove the splash shield from under the left-hand front of the bumper **(see illustration)**.

4 Disconnect the wiring connector from the lower horn **(see illustration). Note:** *The wiring to the upper horn is a link wire from the lower horn.*

5 Unscrew the securing bolt and remove the

14.4 Disconnect the lower wire connector - arrowed

two horns from the car **(see illustration)**. If required, each individual horn can then be unbolted from the mounting bracket.

Refitting

6 Refitting is a reversal of removal.

15 Wiper arm – removal and refitting

Removal

1 Operate the wiper motor, then switch it off so that the wiper arm returns to the at-rest position. Mark the position of the blade on the glass with adhesive tape, as a guide to refitting.

2 Lift the hinged cover or unclip the plastic

14.5 Horn mounting bracket securing bolt - arrowed

cap, and then slacken and remove the spindle nut. Lift the blade off the glass, and pull the wiper arm off its spindle **(see illustrations)**. Note that on some models, the wiper arms may be very tight on the spindle splines – it should be possible to lever the arm off the spindle, using a flat-bladed screwdriver (take care not to damage the scuttle cover panel). If the arm cannot be levered off, a puller must be used.

Refitting

3 Ensure that the wiper arm and spindle splines are clean and dry, and then refit the arm to the spindle. Where applicable, align the wiper blade with the tape fitted on removal.

4 Refit the spindle nut, tightening it securely, and clip the nut cover back into position.

16 Windscreen wiper motor and linkage – removal and refitting

Removal

1 Disconnect the battery negative terminal (refer to *Disconnecting the battery* in the Reference Section of this manual).

2 Remove the wiper arms as described in Section 15.

3 Fully open the bonnet.

4 Remove the scuttle cover panels as described in Chapter 11, Section 22.

5 Unclip the wiper operating arm balljoint from the linkage arm on the wiper motor **(see illustrations)**.

6 Disconnect the windscreen wiper motor wiring connector, which is positioned behind the coolant expansion bottle **(see illustration)**.

7 Unscrew the three bolts securing the wiper motor mounting bracket to the scuttle, then lift the motor and bracket from the scuttle **(see illustrations)**.

8 If desired, the motor can be separated from the linkage and mounting bracket as follows.

a) Make alignment marks on the linkage drive link and the motor spindle, and then unscrew the spindle nut.

b) Unscrew the three nuts securing the motor to the mounting plate, then withdraw the motor.

9 Where applicable, unscrew the three

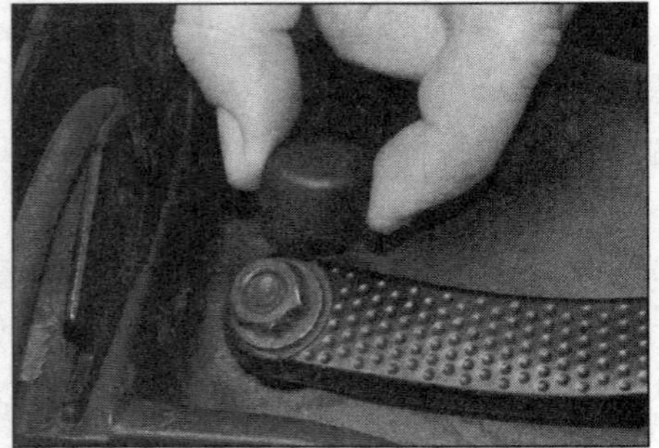

15.2a Unclip the cover . . .

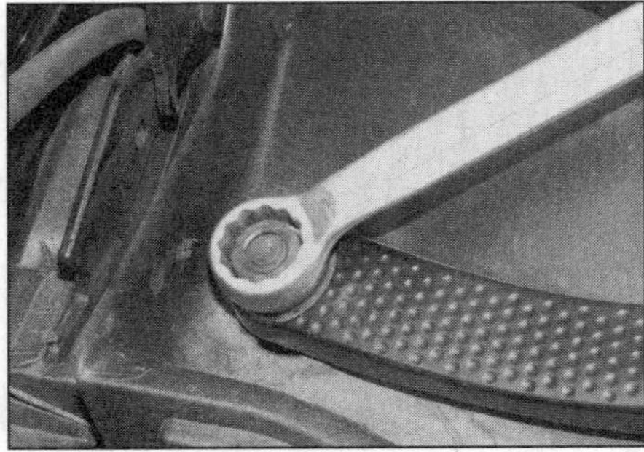

15.2b . . . undo the retaining nut . . .

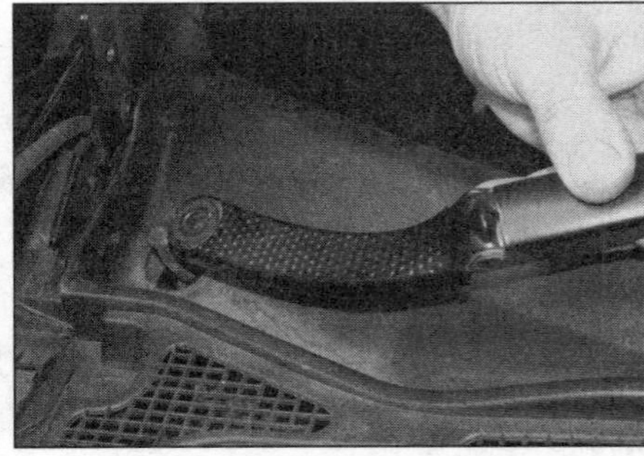

15.2c . . . and remove the wiper arm

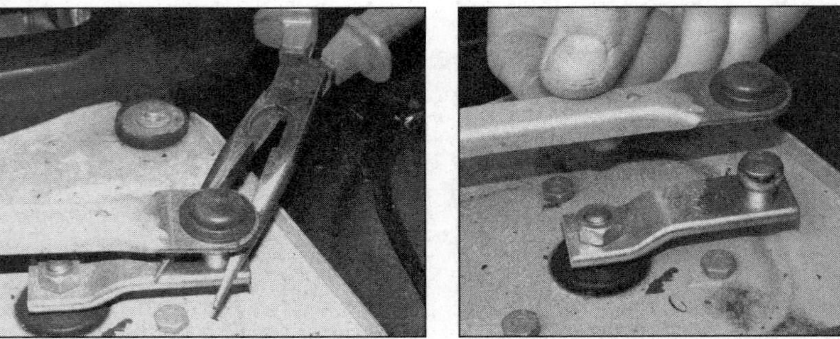

16.5a Using a pair of long-nose pliers . . .

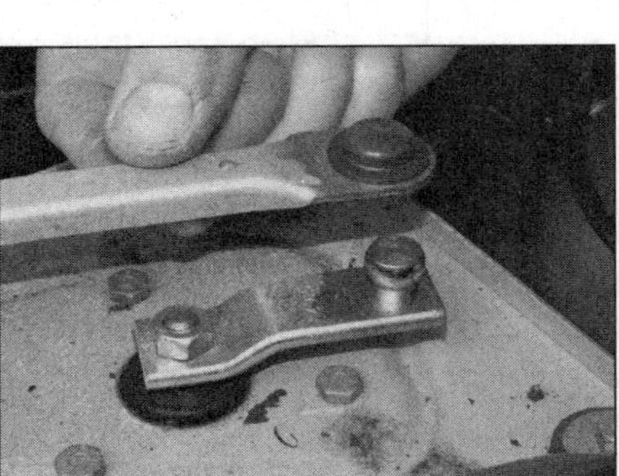

16.5b . . . unclip the balljoint on the wiper linkage

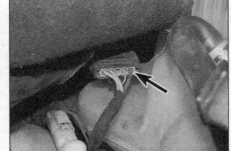

16.6 Disconnect the wiring connector - arrowed

mounting bolts, and lift the wiper linkage assembly from the scuttle **(see illustration)**.

Refitting

10 Refitting is a reversal of removal, noting the following points.

a) Ensure that the motor is in the 'parked' position before refitting.

b) If the motor has been removed from the linkage, ensure that the marks made on the linkage drive link and motor spindle are aligned on refitting.

c) Refit the scuttle panels with reference to Chapter 11, Section 22.

d) Refit the wiper arms with reference to Section 15.

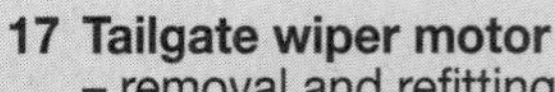

17 Tailgate wiper motor – removal and refitting

Wiper motor

Removal

1 Disconnect the battery negative terminal (refer to *Disconnecting the battery* in the Reference Section of this manual).

2 Remove the wiper arm (see Section 15).

3 Remove the securing screws, and unclip the tailgate rear (inner) trim panel. **Note:** *On Hatchback models, there are two securing screws, which are located in the handle recesses in the panel one at each side.*

4 Disconnect the tailgate wiper motor wiring plug **(see illustration)**.

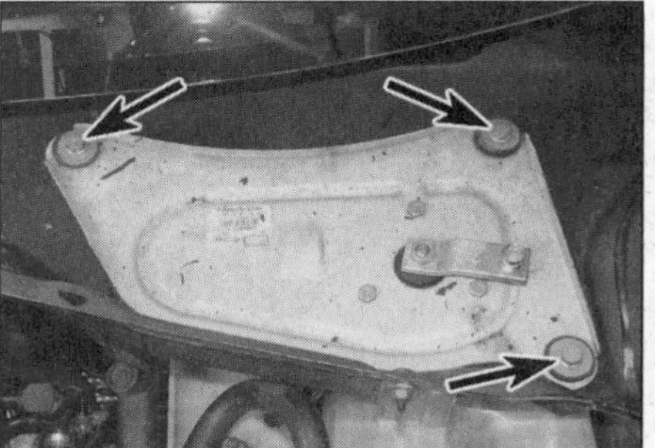

16.7a Undo the mounting bolts (arrowed) . . .

16.7b . . . and withdraw the motor from the scuttle

5 On Hatchback models, working on the outside of the tailgate, unclip the plastic cover from the wiper spindle nut, undo the securing nut and remove the plastic washer.

6 Working back inside the tailgate, unscrew the three bolts securing the motor mounting plate to the tailgate, then remove the motor from the tailgate **(see illustrations)**.

Refitting

7 Refitting is a reversal of the removal procedure.

Wiper linkage – Estate models

Removal

8 Remove the wiper arm (see Section 15).

9 Working on the outside of the tailgate, unclip the plastic cover from the wiper spindle nut, undo the securing nut and remove the plastic washer **(see illustrations)**.

16.9 Undo the mounting bolts (arrowed) to remove the linkage

10 Working on the inside of the tailgate glass, unclip the trim cover, undo the retaining nut and remove the wiper linkage from the tailgate glass **(see illustrations)**.

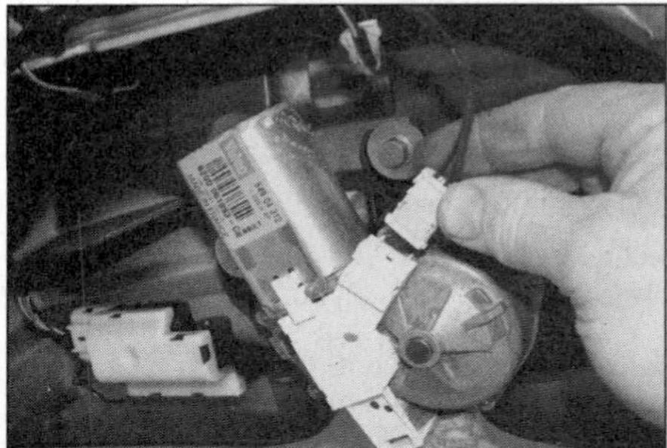

17.4 Disconnect the wiring connector from the wiper motor

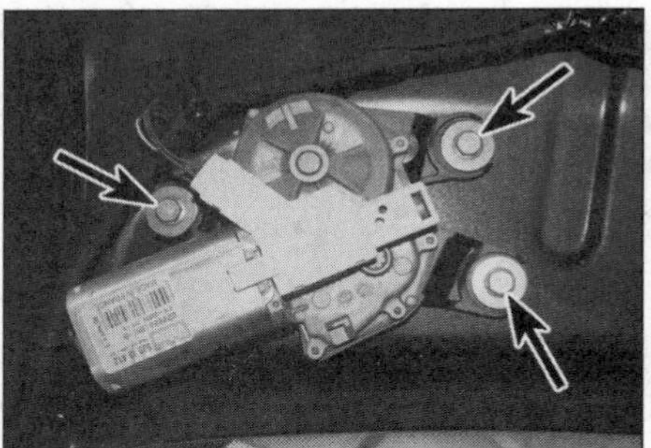

17.6a Mounting bolts (arrowed) – Hatchback

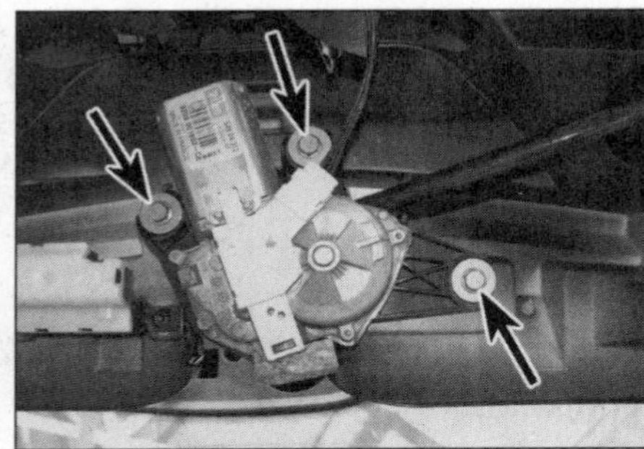

17.6b Mounting bolts (arrowed) – Estate

17.9a Unclip the cover . . .

17.9b . . . undo the spindle nut . . .

17.9c . . . and remove the plastic washer

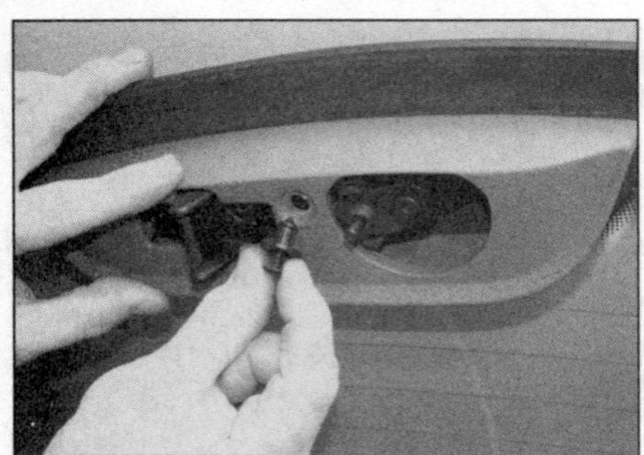
17.10a Unclip the trim cover . . .

17.10b . . . undo the retaining nut (arrowed) . . .

17.10c . . . and remove the wiper linkage

Refitting

11 Refitting is a reversal of the removal procedure.

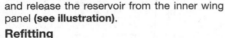

18 Windscreen/tailgate washer system components – removal and refitting

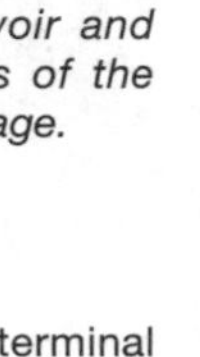

Note: *Prior to removing the reservoir and washer pumps, empty the contents of the reservoir, or be prepared for fluid spillage.*

Washer fluid reservoir

Removal

1 Disconnect the battery negative terminal (refer to *Disconnecting the battery* in the Reference Section of this manual).

2 Remove the front bumper as described in Chapter 11, Section 6.

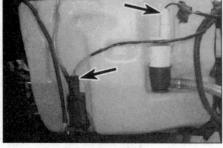

3 Disconnect the wiring plugs from the windscreen washer pump and the headlamp washer pump **(see illustration)**.

4 Unscrew upper securing bolt, then disconnect the fluid hoses from the pumps, and release the reservoir from the inner wing panel **(see illustration)**.

Refitting

5 Refitting is a reversal of removal.

Washer fluid pumps

Removal

6 Proceed as described in paragraphs 1 to 3.

7 Carefully pull the pump from the sealing grommet in the reservoir **(see illustrations)**.

8 Mark the fluid hoses to ensure that they are reconnected in their original locations, and then disconnect the hoses from the pump.

Refitting

9 Refitting is a reversal of removal, but check the condition of the sealing grommet, and renew if necessary.

Windscreen washer jet

Removal

10 Working at the rear of the bonnet, release the securing clips, and push the jet out of the panel.

11 Disconnect fluid hose from the jet.

Refitting

12 Refitting is a reversal of removal.

Tailgate washer jet

Removal

13 On Hatchback models, release the securing clips, and lower the rear of the headlining from the roof. Reach in and unscrew the securing nut, then manipulate the jet out through the top of the roof panel.

14 On Estate models, release the retaining clips and withdraw the jet from the upper spoiler trim panel **(see illustration)**. For further information see the tailgate glass removal and refitting procedure in Chapter 11, Section 15.

15 Disconnect the fluid hose from the jet. Make sure that the hose does not fall into the roof or tailgate whilst the jet is removed.

Refitting

16 Refitting is a reversal of removal.

18.3 Disconnect the wiring connectors (arrowed) from the washer pumps

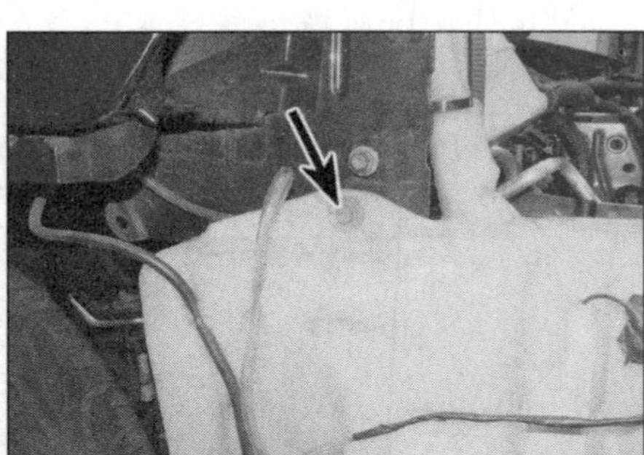
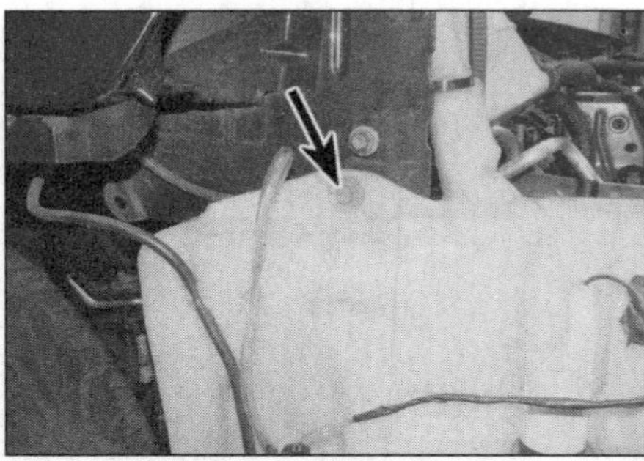
18.4 Undo the reservoir mounting bolt – arrowed

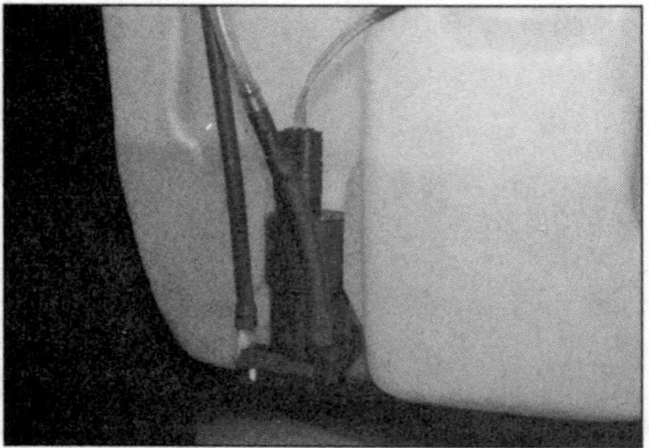
18.7a Windscreen washer fluid pump

18.7b Headlamp washer fluid pump

18.14 Washer jet fitted to the rear spoiler

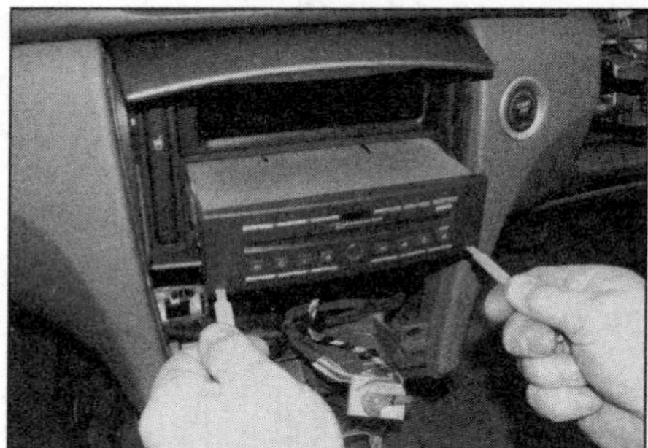

19.5a Using tools to remove the radio/ cassette player . . .

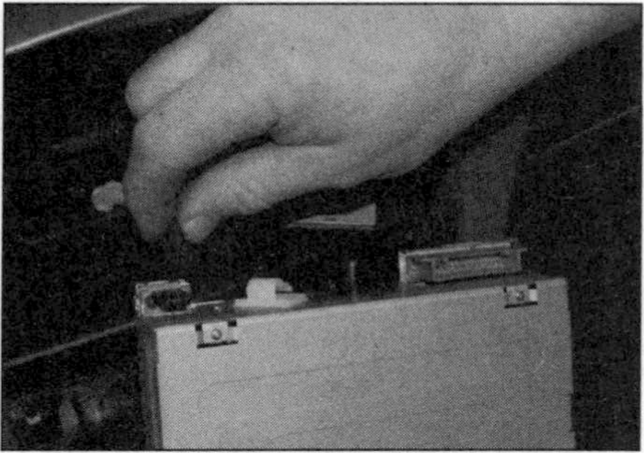

19.5b . . . and disconnect the wiring connectors

19 Radio/cassette/CD player – removal and refitting

Note: *On models with a security-coded radio/ cassette/CD player, once the battery has been disconnected, the unit cannot be re-activated until the appropriate security code has been entered. Do not remove the unit unless the appropriate code is known. The following information applies to radio/cassette players having standard fixings.*

Removal

1 Disconnect the battery negative terminal (refer to *Disconnecting the battery* in the Reference Section of this manual).
2 Open the radio/cassette player cover.
3 In order to release the retaining clips, two removal tools will be required. These tools comprise two flat pieces of metal, which engage with the radio/cassette player securing clips (these tools are often supplied with the vehicle when new if a standard audio unit is fitted). Suitable tools can easily be obtained from car accessory shops or audio specialists.
4 Slide the removal tools into the holes in the front of the radio/cassette player, until they are felt to engage with the securing clips.
5 Pull the unit from the facia using the tools, until the wiring connector(s) and aerial lead can be disconnected from the rear of the unit **(see illustrations)**.

Refitting

6 Reconnect the wiring plug(s) and the aerial lead, then push the unit into its housing until the securing clips engage.
7 On completion, reconnect the battery negative lead and, where applicable, enter the security code.

20 Speakers – removal and refitting

1 Disconnect the battery negative terminal (refer to *Disconnecting the battery* in the Reference Section of this manual).

Facia-mounted speakers

Removal

2 Carefully unclip the speaker trim panel from the facia **(see illustration)**.
3 Unclip the speaker and withdraw it from the facia panel, disconnect the wiring connector as it is removed **(see illustrations)**.

Refitting

4 Refitting is a reversal of removal.

Front door-mounted speakers

Removal

5 Starting at the bottom, carefully unclip the loudspeaker cover panel **(see illustration)**.
6 Unscrew the securing screws, then withdraw the loudspeaker from the housing in the door, and disconnect the wiring **(see illustrations)**.

Refitting

7 Refitting is a reversal of removal.

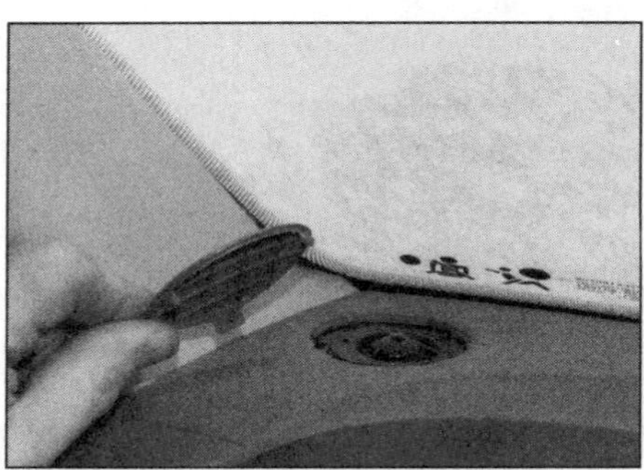

20.2 Unclip the speaker cover

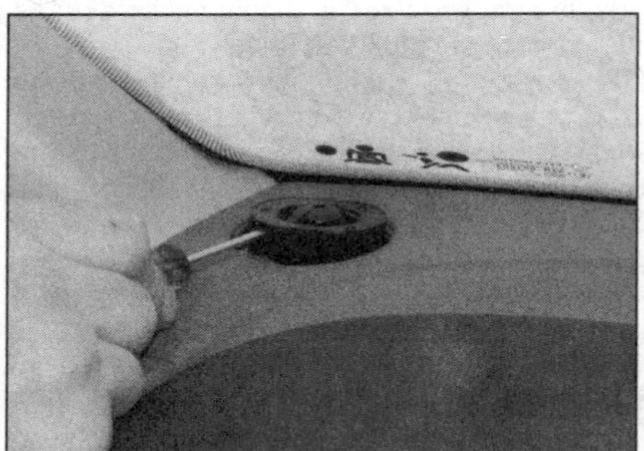

20.3a Remove the speaker . . .

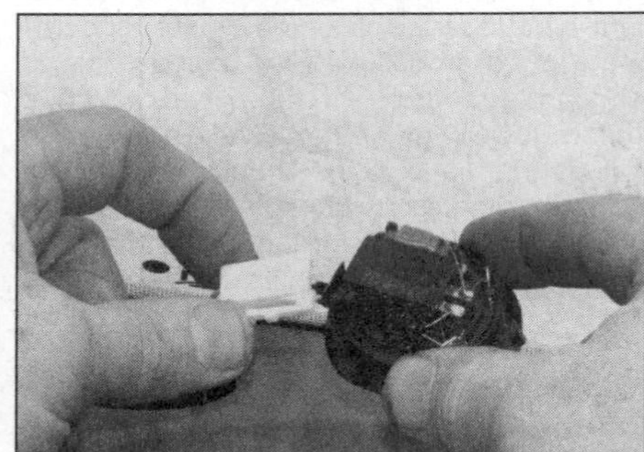

20.3b . . . and disconnect the wiring connector

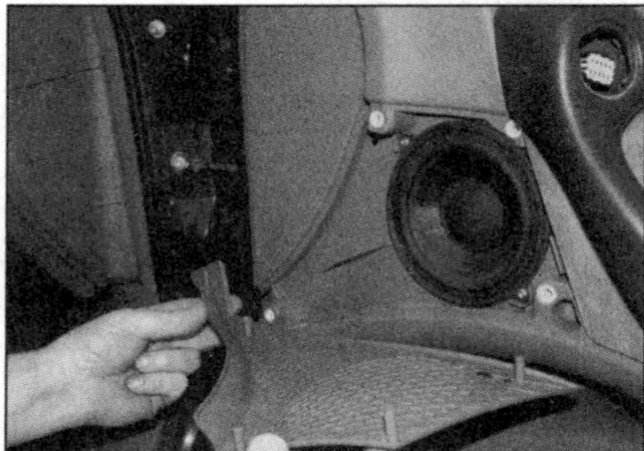

20.5 Unclip the speaker cover

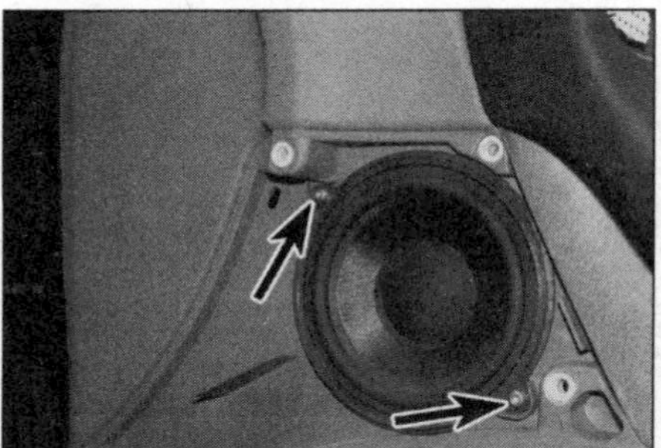

20.6a Undo the retaining screws (arrowed) . . .

20.6b . . . and disconnect the wiring connector

20.8 Unclip the speaker cover

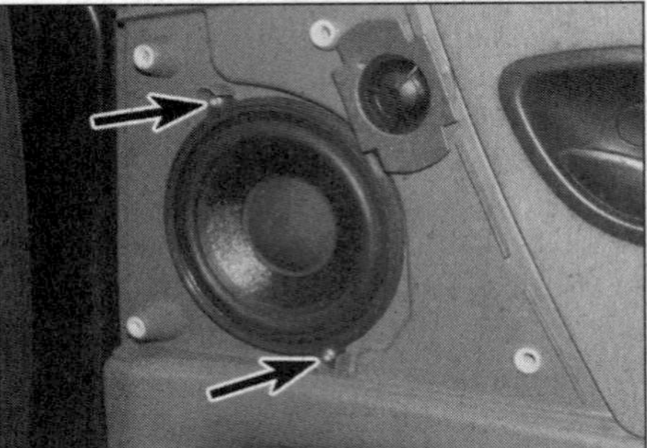

20.9a Undo the retaining screws (arrowed) . . .

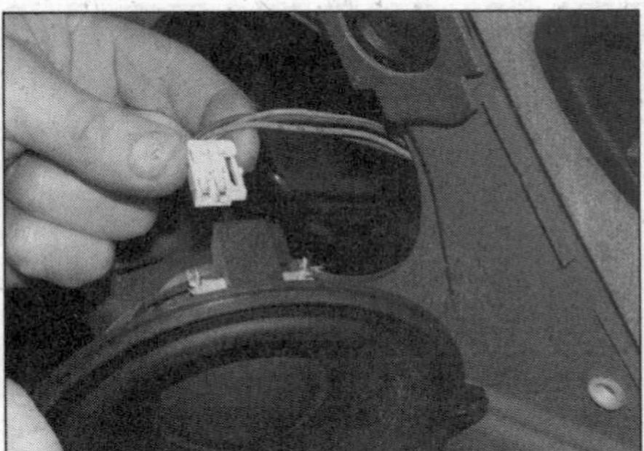

20.9b . . . and disconnect the wiring connector

Rear door-mounted speakers

Removal

8 Starting at the bottom, carefully unclip the loudspeaker cover panel **(see illustration)**.

9 Unscrew the securing screws, then withdraw the loudspeaker from the housing in the door, and disconnect the wiring **(see illustrations)**.

10 With the main speaker removed, the small speaker (tweeter) can be unclipped from the door trim panel, through the main speaker aperture.

Refitting

11 Refitting is a reversal of removal.

21 Radio aerial – general information

The aerial is located at the top of the rear screen (on Hatchback models) and on the rear right-hand quarter glass (on Estate models). There is an amplifier in the system that is fed via the radio by an aerial lead, which is routed down through the vehicle behind the various trim panels. The amplifier is fitted to the rear tailgate on Hatchback models **(see illustration)** and behind the inner rear right-hand quarter panel trim on Estate models.

22 Anti-theft alarm system and engine immobiliser – general information

Certain models are fitted with an anti-theft alarm system, which uses various sensing systems and warning sirens, depending on model. No information was available for the alarm systems at the time of writing. Any faults should be referred to a Renault dealer for diagnosis.

All models are fitted with an engine immobiliser device, which is activated by the coded ignition keycard. When the immobiliser is armed, the indicator light on the instrument panel will flash continuously. When the keycard is inserted, the code from the card is read by the card reader unit and transmits it to the interior multi-timer unit (see Section 26). If the multi-timer unit recognises the code, the engine can be started.

23 Airbag system – general information, precautions and system de-activation

General information

All Renault models are equipped with a comprehensive airbag system. In addition to adaptive front airbags for the driver and front passenger, there are side airbags fitted to the front seats, and side curtain airbags, which are deployed from modules in the headlining. Rear side airbags are available as an option.

The airbag system is triggered in the event of a heavy frontal or side impact above a predetermined force; depending on the point of impact, not all the airbags will necessarily be fired. The airbags inflate within milliseconds to form a safety cushion, which prevents contact with the internal surfaces of the car, greatly reducing the risk of injury. The airbags then deflate almost immediately.

The system is armed only when the ignition is on. However, a reserve power source maintains power to the system in the event of a break in the main electrical supply for a short period – for this reason, it is essential to wait before disconnecting any of the system wiring.

The system is activated by a 'g' sensor (deceleration sensor), incorporated in the electronic control unit, fitted under the rear of the centre console. Note that the airbag control unit also controls the seat belt tensioners. Impact sensors in the B-pillars detect side impacts which, if severe enough, will cause the side and curtain airbags to be fired on the side concerned.

21.1 Aerial amplifier – Hatchback

The airbags are inflated by gas generators, which force the bags out from their locations. Although these are safety items, their deployment is violently rapid, and this may cause injury if they are triggered unintentionally.

Linked to the airbag system are the seat belt tensioners fitted to each seat belt (except the centre belt on the rear seat). All models have two tensioners fitted to the front seats. The seat belt tensioners are fired with the airbags in the event of an accident, to take up the slack in the belts, and hold the occupants in their seats.

Precautions

Warning: The following precautions must be observed to prevent the possibility of personal injury.

a) Do not disconnect the battery with the engine running.

b) Before carrying out any work in the vicinity of the airbag, removal of any of the airbag components, or any welding work on the vehicle, de-activate the system as described in the following sub-Section.

c) Do not attempt to test any of the airbag system circuits using test meters or any other test equipment.

d) If the airbag warning light comes on, or any fault in the system is suspected, consult a Renault dealer without delay. Do not attempt to carry out fault diagnosis, or any dismantling of the components.

Precautions when handling an airbag

a) Transport the airbag by itself, bag upward.

b) Do not put your arms around the airbag.

c) Carry the airbag close to the body, bag outward.

d) Do not drop the airbag or expose it to impacts.

e) Do not attempt to dismantle the airbag unit.

f) Do not connect any form of electrical equipment to any part of the airbag circuit.

Precautions when storing an airbag

a) Store the unit in a cupboard with the airbag upward.

b) Do not expose the airbag to temperatures above 80°C.
c) Do not expose the airbag to flames.
d) Do not attempt to dispose of the airbag – consult a Renault dealer.
e) Never refit an airbag that is known to be faulty or damaged.

De-activation of airbag system

The system must be de-activated as follows, before carrying out any work on the airbag components or surrounding area.

a) Switch off the ignition.
b) Remove the ignition keycard – on models with the 'hands-free' system, the keycard should be kept well away from the car.
c) Switch off all electrical equipment.
d) Disconnect the battery negative terminal.
e) Insulate the battery negative terminal and the end of the battery negative lead to prevent any possibility of contact.
f) Remove the airbag/seat belt tensioner system fuse from the fusebox.
g) ***Wait for at least five minutes*** *before carrying out any further work.*

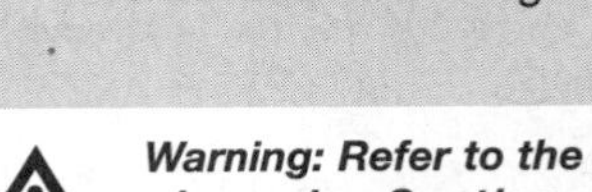

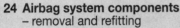

24 Airbag system components – removal and refitting

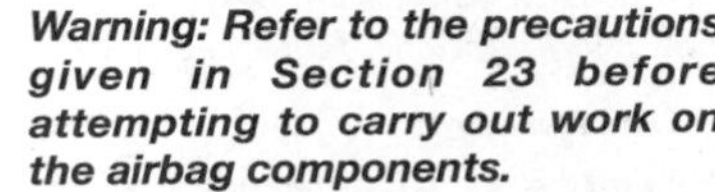

Warning: Refer to the precautions given in Section 23 before attempting to carry out work on the airbag components.

1 Disconnect the battery negative lead and wait for at least five minutes. This will allow the reserve power capacitors in the control unit to discharge and disable the airbag system. De-activate the system as described in Section 23, before removing any of these components.

Driver's airbag unit

Removal

2 Use a small screwdriver in the hole provided at the back of the wheel, prise the end of the spring clip used to retain the airbag – as this is done, pull gently on the steering wheel centre pad to release it **(see illustration)**.

3 The airbag is released first by pulling it carefully upwards. Pull the airbag out from the wheel, to access the two airbag wiring plugs. Release the plugs by prising out the yellow locking clip with a small screwdriver, and disconnect them **(see illustrations)**.

4 Remove the airbag from the car, taking care not to knock or drop it, and keeping the front uppermost. Store it somewhere safe while it is removed.

Refitting

5 Ensure that the wiring connectors are securely reconnected and seat the airbag unit centrally in the steering wheel, making sure the wires do not become trapped. Slide the airbag downwards, and press it squarely into place until the retaining clip at the base engages.

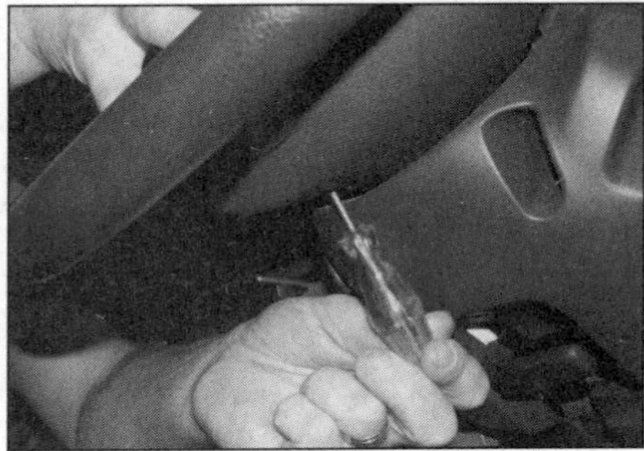

24.2 Release the securing clip

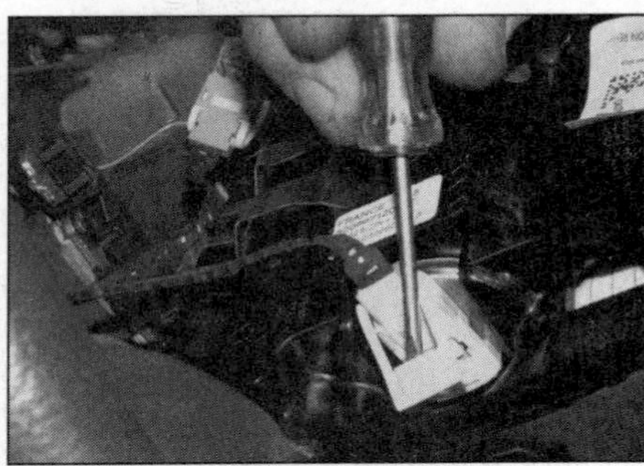

24.3a Release the locking clip . . .

24.3b . . . and disconnect the wiring connector

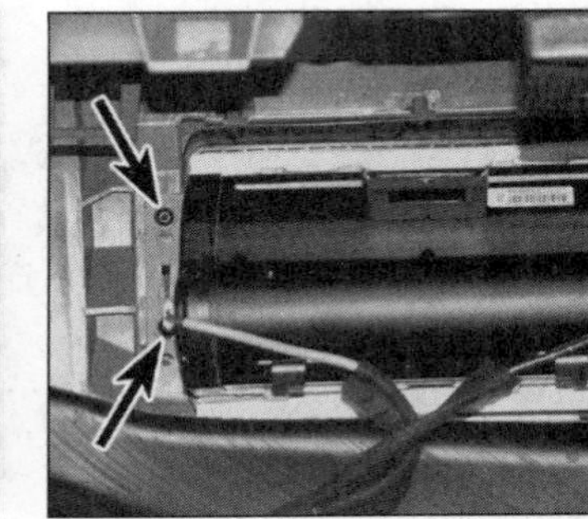

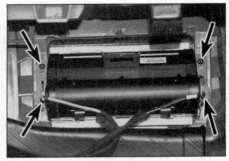

24.8 Passenger's airbag securing screws – arrowed

6 Ensuring no one is sitting in the driver's seat inside the car, reconnect the battery. From the passenger seat, insert the keycard and check the operation of the airbag warning light.

Passenger's airbag unit

Note: *If the passenger's airbag unit has been triggered, the complete facia panel will need to be renewed.*

Removal

7 The passenger's airbag unit is mounted on the underside of the facia panel. Remove the complete facia panel as described in Chapter 11, Section 27.

8 Turn the facia panel over, and remove the four airbag unit mounting screws from behind **(see illustration)**. Withdraw the airbag unit from the inside of the facia panel.

Refitting

9 Refitting is a reversal of removal.

Electronic control unit

Removal

10 The electronic control unit controls the airbag(s) and the seat belt tensioners, and is mounted under the centre console.

11 To remove the control unit, you will first need to remove the centre console as described in Chapter 11.

12 The airbag control unit is located in front of the gear/selector lever, behind the lower floor air vents. To access the unit, a cut must be made in the carpet and sound insulation.

13 Unclip the lower air ducts from the heater housing **(see illustration)**.

14 Fold back the carpeting; this may need to be cut slightly to access the control unit.

15 Unclip the cover fitted over the unit, disconnect the wiring plug after releasing the locking catch, then unscrew the three mounting nuts and remove the unit **(see illustration)**.

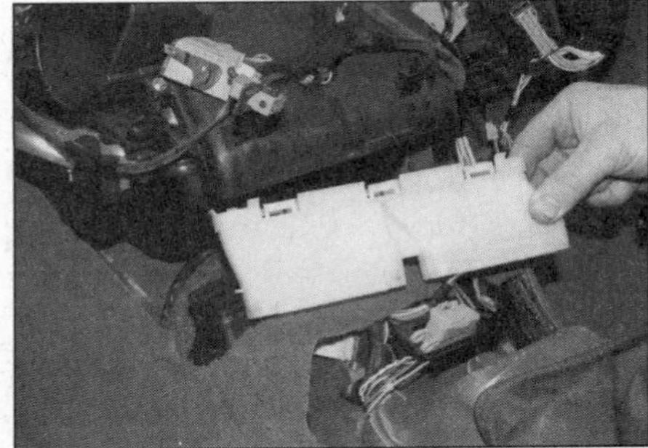

24.13 Unclip the air vents – facia removed for clarity

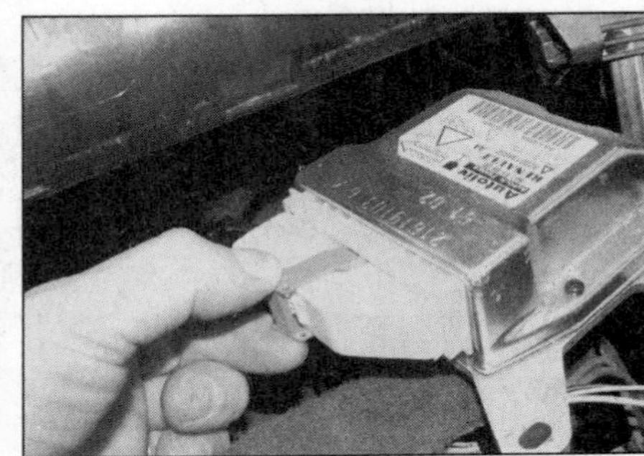

24.15 Release the locking clip to disconnect the wiring connector

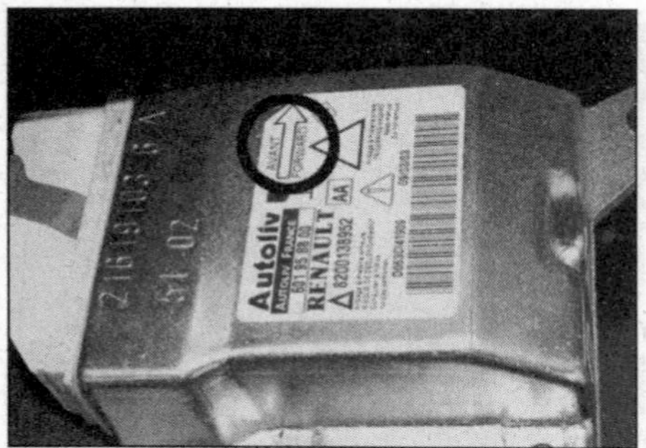

24.16 Arrow on control unit facing forward

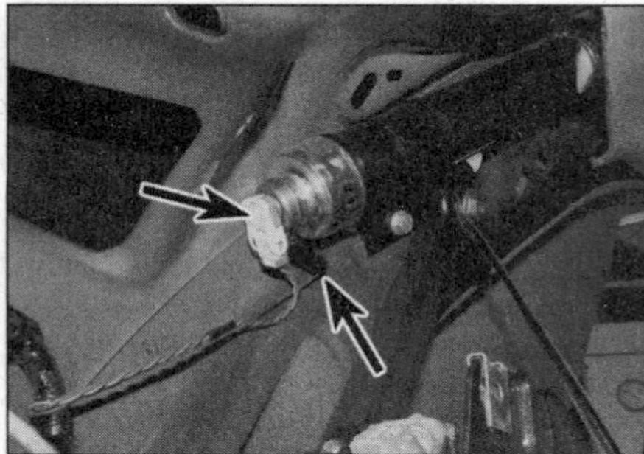

24.23 Disconnect the wiring connectors – arrowed

24.24a Undo the side airbag mounting bolts (arrowed) – Hatchback

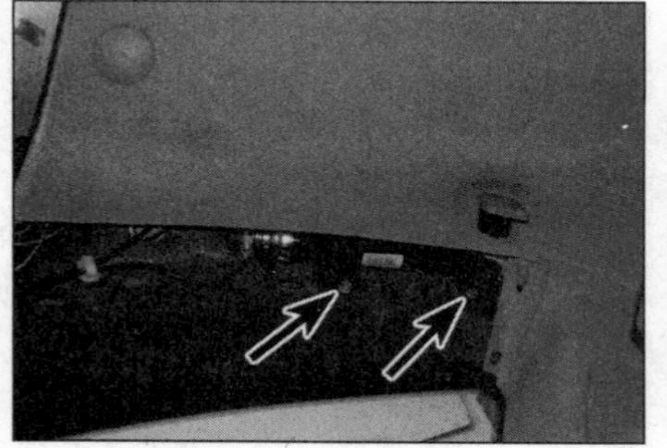

24.24b Undo the side airbag mounting bolts (arrowed) – Estate

Refitting

16 Refit the control unit, tightening the mounting nuts to the specified torque setting. Make sure the control unit is fitted the correct way around with the arrow facing to the front of the vehicle **(see illustration).**

17 Reconnect the wiring connector, and secure with the locking catch. Clip on the unit's cover.

18 Refit the air vents and the centre console as described in Chapter 11.

19 Ensuring no one is sitting inside the car, reconnect the battery. From the passenger seat, insert the keycard and check the operation of the airbag warning light.

Airbag rotary switch

20 Refer to Section 4, paragraphs 10 to 14.

Front side airbags

21 The side airbags are located internally within the front seat backrest, and no attempt should be made to remove them. Any suspected problems with the side airbag system should be referred to a Renault dealer.

25.4 Mounting bolt (arrowed) – with left-hand thread

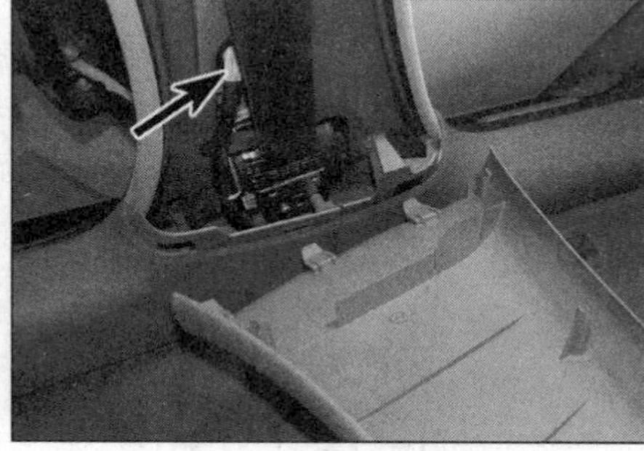

24.28 Location of side impact sensor – arrowed

Rear side airbags

Removal

22 Remove the rear inner trim panels from the C-pillar back, as described in Chapter 11, Section 25.

23 Release the locking clip and disconnect the wiring plug from the airbag, also disconnect the earth connection **(see illustration).**

24 Remove the two airbag unit mounting bolts, and withdraw the unit from the car **(see illustrations).**

Refitting

25 Refitting is a reversal of removal.

Side curtain airbags

26 The modules for the side curtain airbags are located at the sides of the headlining. It is strongly recommended that any work that requires the removal of the headlining and the side curtain airbags be referred to a Renault dealer.

Side impact sensors

Removal

27 Remove the B-pillar lower trim panel as described in Chapter 11, Section 25.

28 Disconnect the wiring plug, then unscrew the mounting bolt and remove the sensor **(see illustration).**

Refitting

29 Refitting is a reversal of removal. Tighten the impact sensor mounting bolt securely.

25 Steering column lock – removal and refitting

1 The steering column lock is located at the lower part of the steering column and is electrically-operated by the interior multi-timer unit when the keycard is inserted or removed. **Note:** *The steering column lock can only be removed when it is in its unlocked state, meaning that the keycard has to be in its slot.*

Removal

2 Remove the steering column shrouds and the lower facia trim panels as described in Chapter 11, Section 27.

3 Disconnect the wiring plug from the front of the steering column lock.

4 Remove the single bolt securing the lock **(see illustration)**, and withdraw it from the column. This bolt has a **left-hand thread** – ie, it unscrews **clockwise**.

Refitting

5 Refitting is a reversal of removal. **Note:** *New steering column lock units are supplied un-coded. Coding is achieved by inserting the keycard in its slot for a few seconds, remove the keycard and the engine immobiliser will be activated after a few seconds. The lock is then coded and the steering column is locked.*

26 Multi-timer unit – general information, removal and refitting

General information

1 The multi-timer unit is located under the right-hand side of the facia panel, and is secured by retaining clips to the fuse/relay box. Note that once removed, the immobiliser, remote control, engine configuration, etc, will all need reprogramming, if this is not done correctly it will prevent the vehicle from starting. Because of the specialised equipment

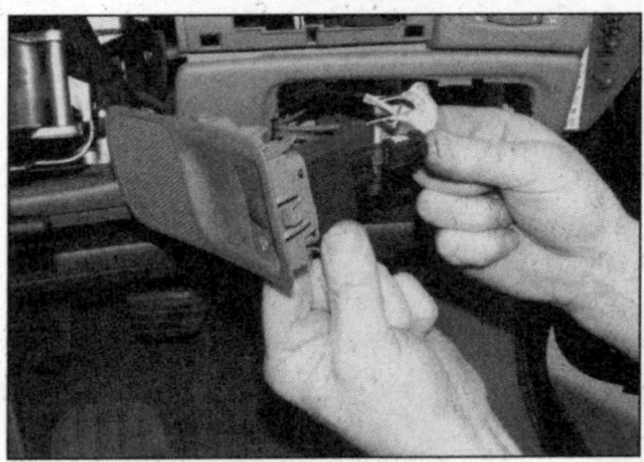
26.4 Unclip the switch panel

26.5 Unclip the right-hand side trim panel

26.6 Undo the securing screw – arrowed

required, this may need to be entrusted to your local Renault dealer.

2 There are different types of multi-timer units available, depending on the equipment level in the vehicle.

Controlling:

- *Indicators and hazard warning lights.*
- *Daytime running lights.*
- *Sidelights.*
- *Bulb failure.*
- *Front and rear wipers.*
- *Headlight washer controls.*
- *Door and window controls.*
- *Door locking when driving (unlocking on impact).*
- *One-touch windows.*
- *Door opening indicator light*
- *Central door locking indicator light.*
- *Timed courtesy lighting.*
- *Radio frequency remote control.*
- *Hands-free remote control.*
- *Engine immobiliser.*
- *Starter positive after ignition supply/relay control.*
- *Passenger compartment buzzer.*
- *Engine overspeed.*
- *External temperature.*
- *Electric seats and rear view mirrors.*
- *Alarm connections.*
- *Variable power steering.*
- *Multiplex network interface.*
- *Interface with fault finding.*
- *Light sensors.*
- *Rain sensors.*

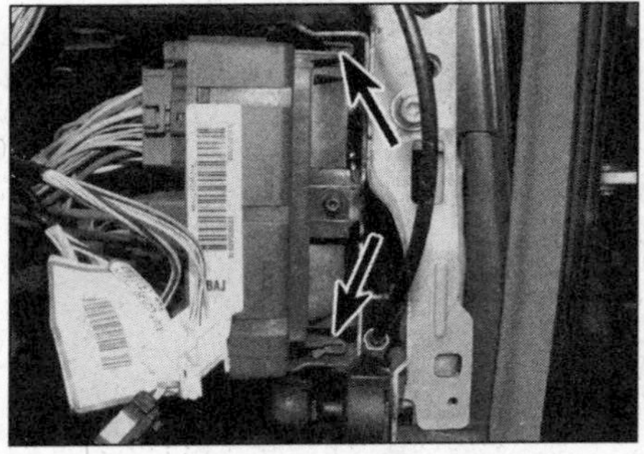
26.8a Release the securing clips (arrowed) . . .

Removal

3 Disconnect the battery negative terminal (refer to *Disconnecting the battery* in the Reference Section of this manual).

4 Unclip the switch panel from the right-hand side of the facia panel and move it to one side **(see illustration)**.

5 Open the driver's side front door and carefully prise off the trim panel from the right-hand side of the facia panel **(see illustration).**

6 Undo the fusebox retaining screw **(see illustration).**

7 To make removal easier it may be necessary to remove the bonnet release lever as described in Chapter 11, Section 9.

8 Release the securing clips at the top and bottom of the multi-timer unit and lower it out from under the facia **(see illustrations)**.

26.8b . . . and remove the fusebox/timer unit – facia removed for clarity

9 Disconnect the wiring block connectors and, if required, unclip the relays from the multi-timer unit. It may be necessary to cut the plastic cable tie to release wiring harness.

10 The multi-timer unit can now be unclipped from the fuse/relay box.

Refitting

11 Refitting is a reversal of removal, bearing in mind the following points.

12 Make sure that the multi-timer unit is secured to the fuse/relay box and is located correctly behind the facia panel.

13 Ensure that the wiring is routed as noted before removal.

RENAULT LAGUNA wiring diagrams

Diagram 1

Key to symbols

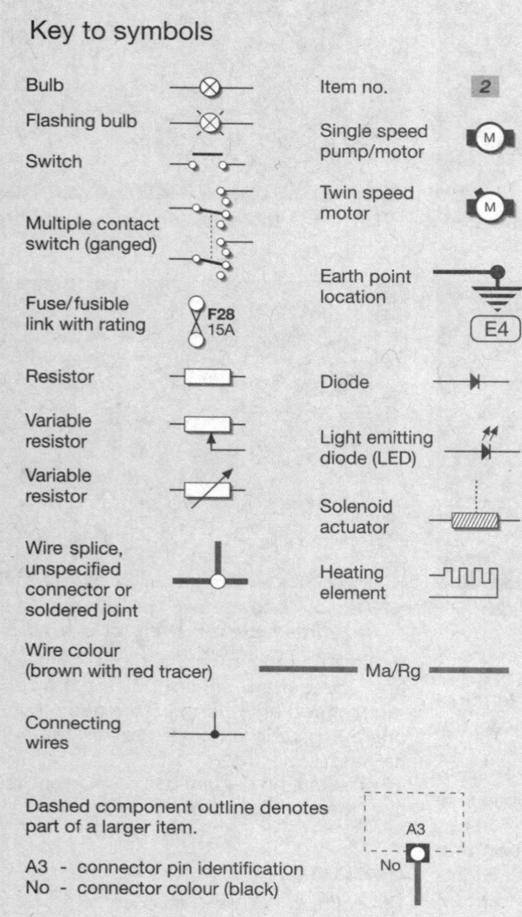

Key to circuits

Diagram 1	Information for wiring diagrams
Diagram 2	Starting, charging, horn, cigar lighter, heated screens & engine cooling fan
Diagram 3	Basic heater, headlight washer, fron & rear wash/wipe
Diagram 4	Side, head, stop, fog & reversing lights
Diagram 5	Direction indicators & hazard warning lights, courtesy lights & luggage compartment light, footwell illumination, glovebox & door lighting
Diagram 6	Front & rear electric windows, electric mirrors
Diagram 7	Central locking

Earth locations

E1	LH inner wing
E2	At LH front footwell
E3	Behind horn
E4	On front of engine
E5	RH side of rear window
E6	At RH front footwell
E7	Below LH rear light
E8	At RH front footwell

Passenger compartment fusebox 1 (4)

Fuse	Rating	Circuit protected
F1	20A	Main beam headlights
F2	10A	Passenger fusebox 1 supply, card reader, push button
F3	10A	Voice synthesiser, discharge bulb computer, instrument cluster, heater outlets, headlight levelling
F4	20A	Reversing lights, heating & ventilation, parking aid, alarm + after ignition feed signal, switch lighting, rain sensor, air conditioning compressor, wiper motor signal, autodimming rear-view mirror
F5	15A	Timed interior lighting
F6	20A	Stop lights, wiper stalk, diagnostic socket, tyre pressure monitor display, child lock indicator light, rear electric lock indicator light, electric window switch lighting, cruise control, hands-free set
F7	15A	LH dipped beam, discharge bulb computer
F8	7.5A	RH sidelights
F9	15A	Hazard warning lights
F10	10A	Communications system, radio, seat relays, seat position memory computer
F11	30A	Voice synthesiser, instrument cluster, front foglights, tailgate electric lock, air conditioning
F12	5A	Airbags & pretensioners
F13	5A	ABS computer, electronic braking distribution
F14	15A	Horn
F15	30A	Driver's electric window, electric door mirror, electric window multiplexing unit
F16	30A	Passenger's electric window, electric window multiplexing unit
F17	10A	Rear foglights
F18	10A	Heated door mirrors
F19	15A	RH dipped beam
F20	7.5A	LH sidelights, lighting dimmer, glovebox light, number plate light, cigarette lighter, switch lighting (except doors and hazard warning lights)
F21	30A	Front/rear windscreen wipers
F22	30A	Central locking
F23	15A	Rear accessories socket, car phone
F24	15A	Cigar lighter, boot accessories socket
F25	10A	Steering lock, heated rear screen relay

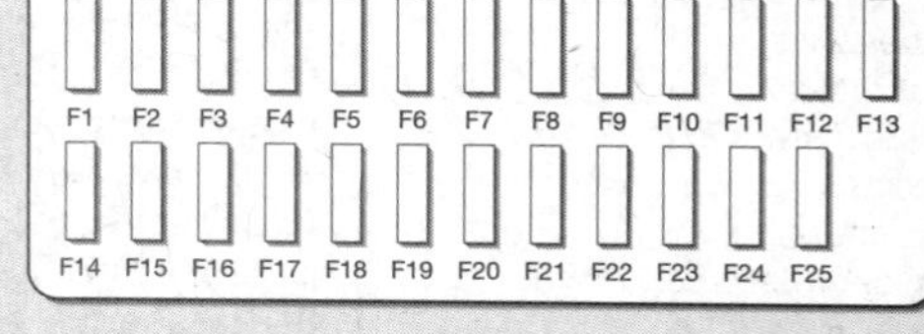

Passenger compartment fusebox 2 (84)

Fuse	Rating	Circuit protected
F26	30A	Caravan socket
F27	30A	Sunroof
F28	-	Not used
F29	30A	Rear electric windows
F30	15A	Steering wheel angle sensor
F31	-	Not used

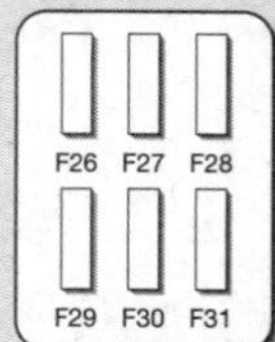

Passenger compartment fusebox 3 (36)

Fuse	Rating	Circuit protected
F32	-	Not used
F33	-	Not used
F34	15A	Driver's electric seat supply
F35	20A	Driver's & passenger's heated seats
F36	20A	Driver's electric seat
F37	20A	Passenger's electric seat

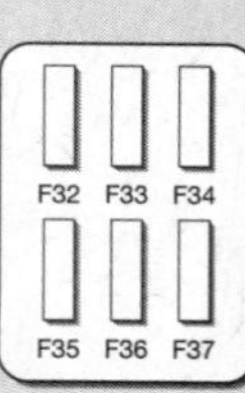

H33352

Diagram 2

Wire colours

Ba	White	**No**	Black
Be	Blue	**Or**	Orange
Bj	Beige	**Rg**	Red
Cy	Crystal	**Sa**	Pink
Gr	Grey	**Ve**	Green
Ja	Yellow	**Vi**	Violet
Ma	Brown		

Key to items

1 Battery
2 Starter
3 Alternator
4 Passenger compartment fusebox 1
5 Cigar lighter
6 Engine fusebox
7 Horn
8 Multifunction switch
9 Steering wheel clock springs
10 Horn switch
11 Engine cooling fan
12 Engine management relay
13 Fan low speed relay
14 Engine management control unit
15 Engine coolant temperature sensor
16 Heated rear window relay
17 Interference supressor (saloon)
18 Heated rear window
19 LH heated front screen relay
20 RH heated front screen relay
21 Heated front screen

H33353

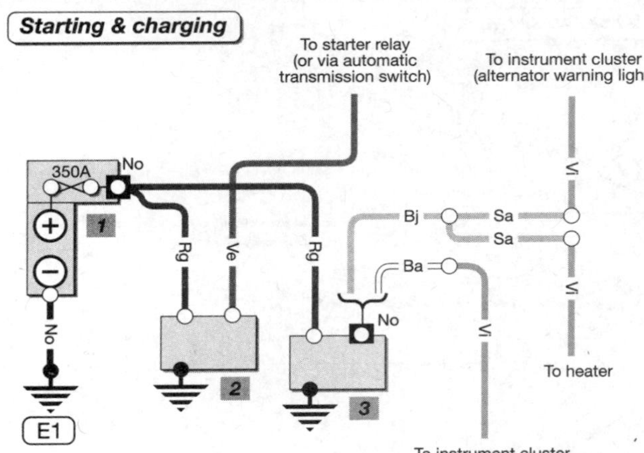

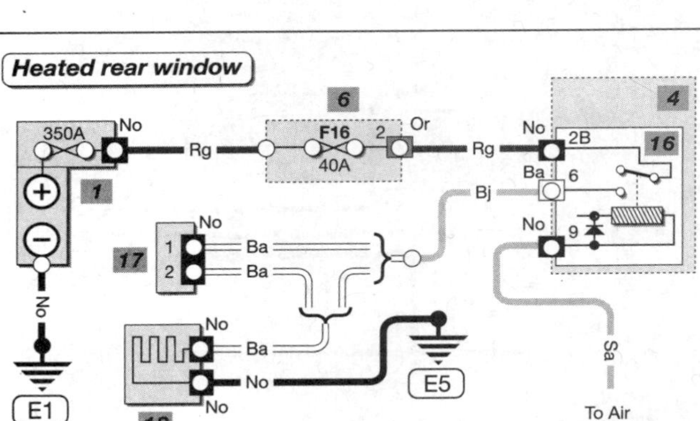

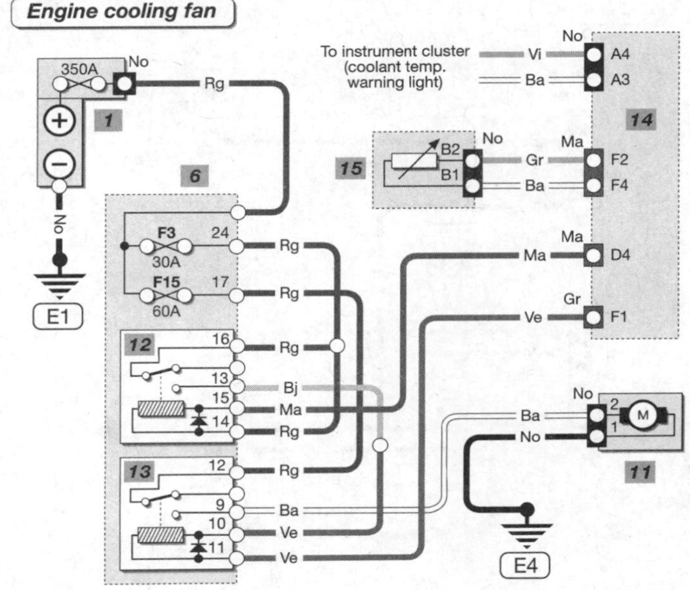

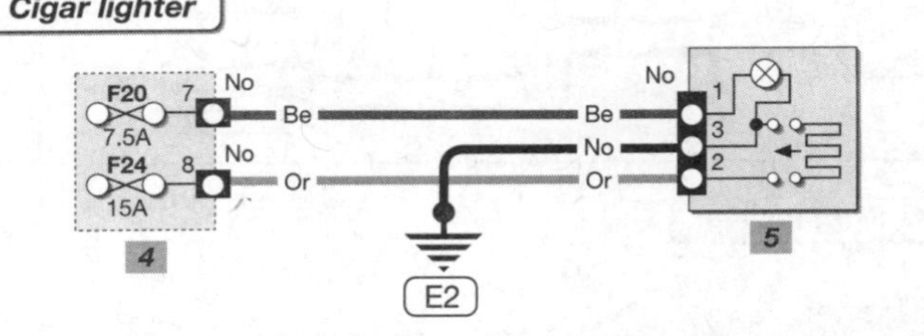

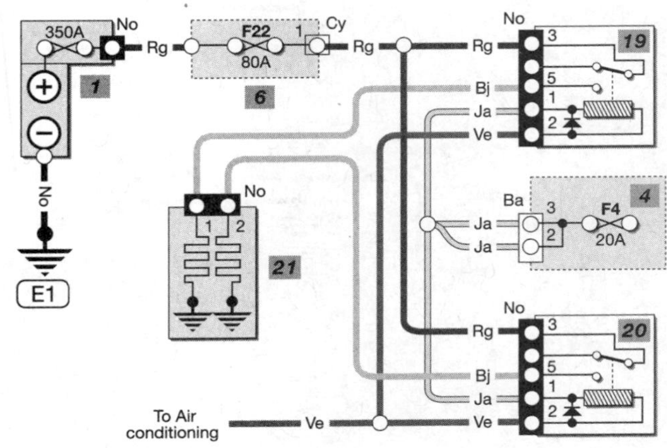

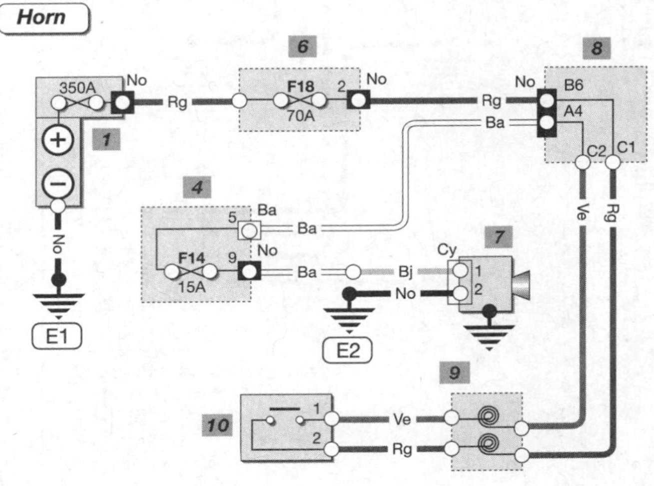

Diagram 3

Wire colours

Ba	White	**No**	Black
Be	Blue	**Or**	Orange
Bj	Beige	**Rg**	Red
Cy	Crystal	**Sa**	Pink
Gr	Grey	**Ve**	Green
Ja	Yellow	**Vi**	Violet
Ma	Brown		

Key to items

1 Battery
4 Passenger compartment fusebox 1
6 Engine fusebox
25 Air conditioning control unit
26 Heater blower resistor pack
27 Heater blower motor
28 Recycling motor
29 Evaporator sensor
30 Front/rear washer pump
31 Front wiper motor
32 Rear wiper motor
33 Wash/wipe switch
34 Rear wiper diode
35 Rain/light sensor
36 Passenger compartment fusebox 3
37 Headlight washer relay
38 Headlight washer pump

H33354

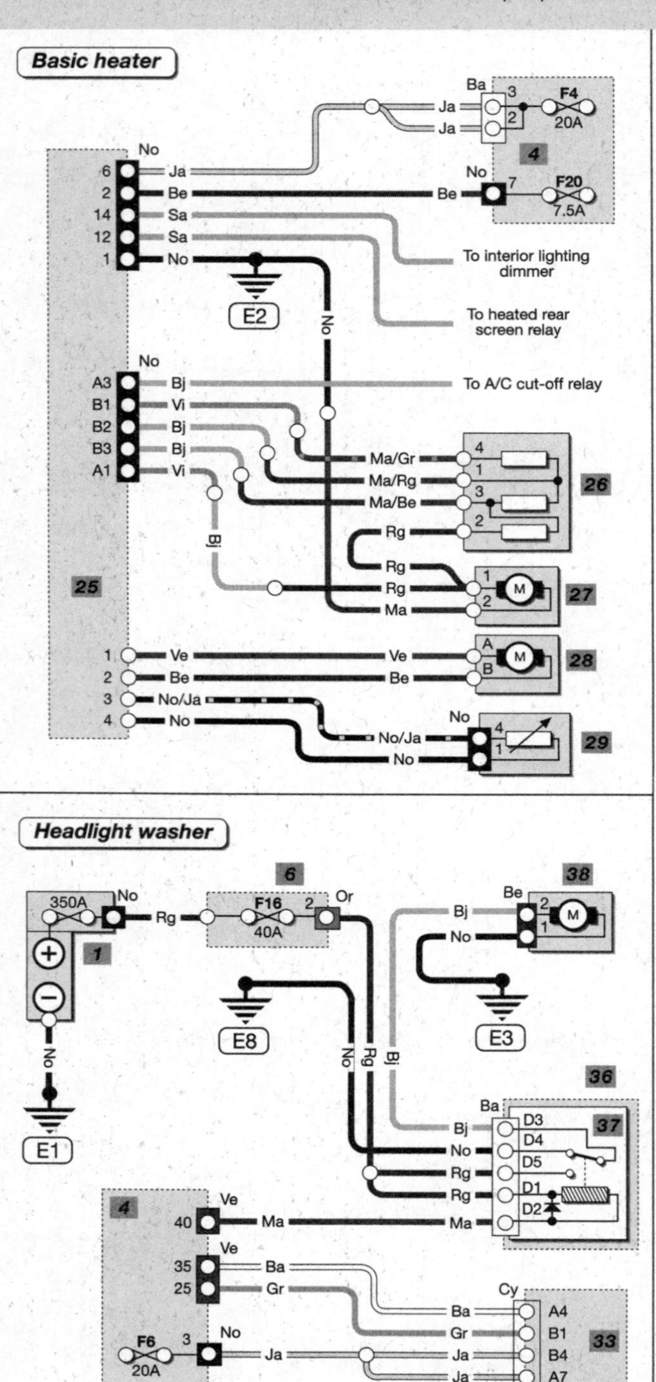

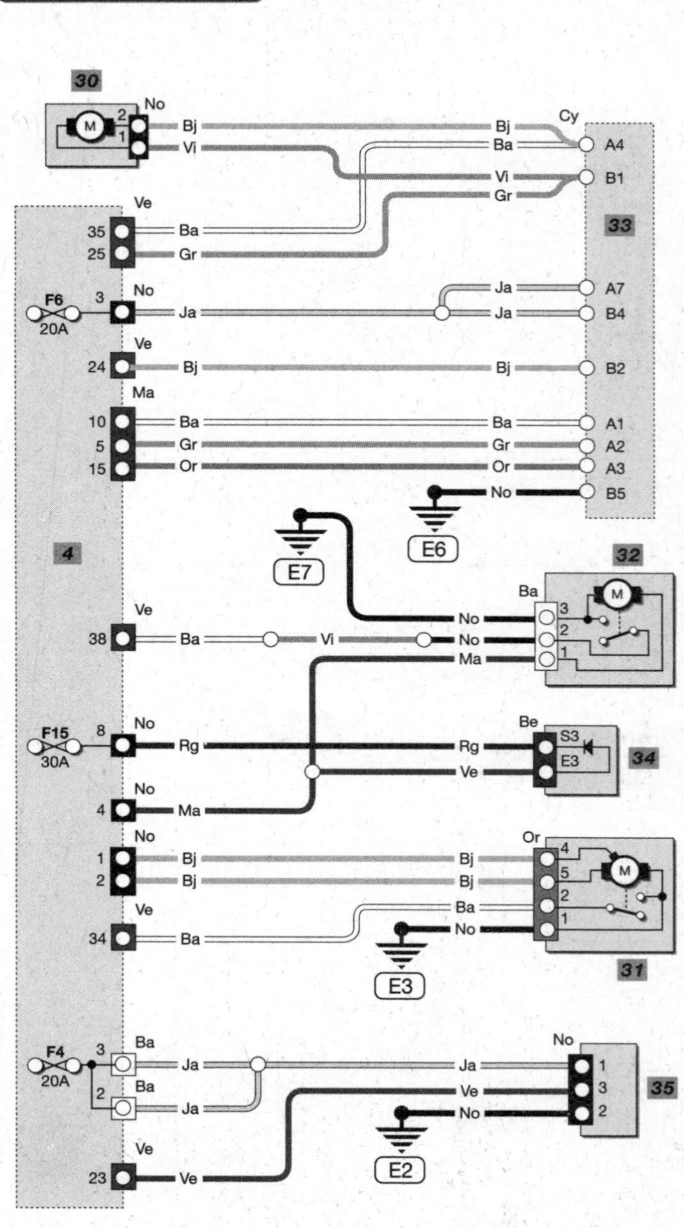

Diagram 4

Wire colours

Ba	White	**No**	Black
Be	Blue	**Or**	Orange
Bj	Beige	**Rg**	Red
Cy	Crystal	**Sa**	Pink
Gr	Grey	**Ve**	Green
Ja	Yellow	**Vi**	Violet
Ma	Brown		

Key to items

1 Battery
4 Passenger compartment fusebox 1
6 Engine fusebox
8 Multifunction switch
36 Passenger compartment fusebox 3
40 LH number plate light
41 RH number plate light
42 LH headlight
 a = sidelight
 b = dip beam
 c = main beam
43 RH headlight
 a = sidelight
 b = dip beam
 c = main beam
44 LH tailgate light unit
 a = tail light
 b = reversing light
45 RH tailgate light unit
 a = tail light
 b = reversing light
46 LH rear light unit
 a = tail light
 b = reversing light
 c = foglight
47 RH rear light unit
 a = tail light
 b = reversing light
 c = foglight
48 High level brake light
49 Reversing light switch
50 Stop light switch
51 Front foglight relay
52 LH front foglight
53 RH front foglight

H33355

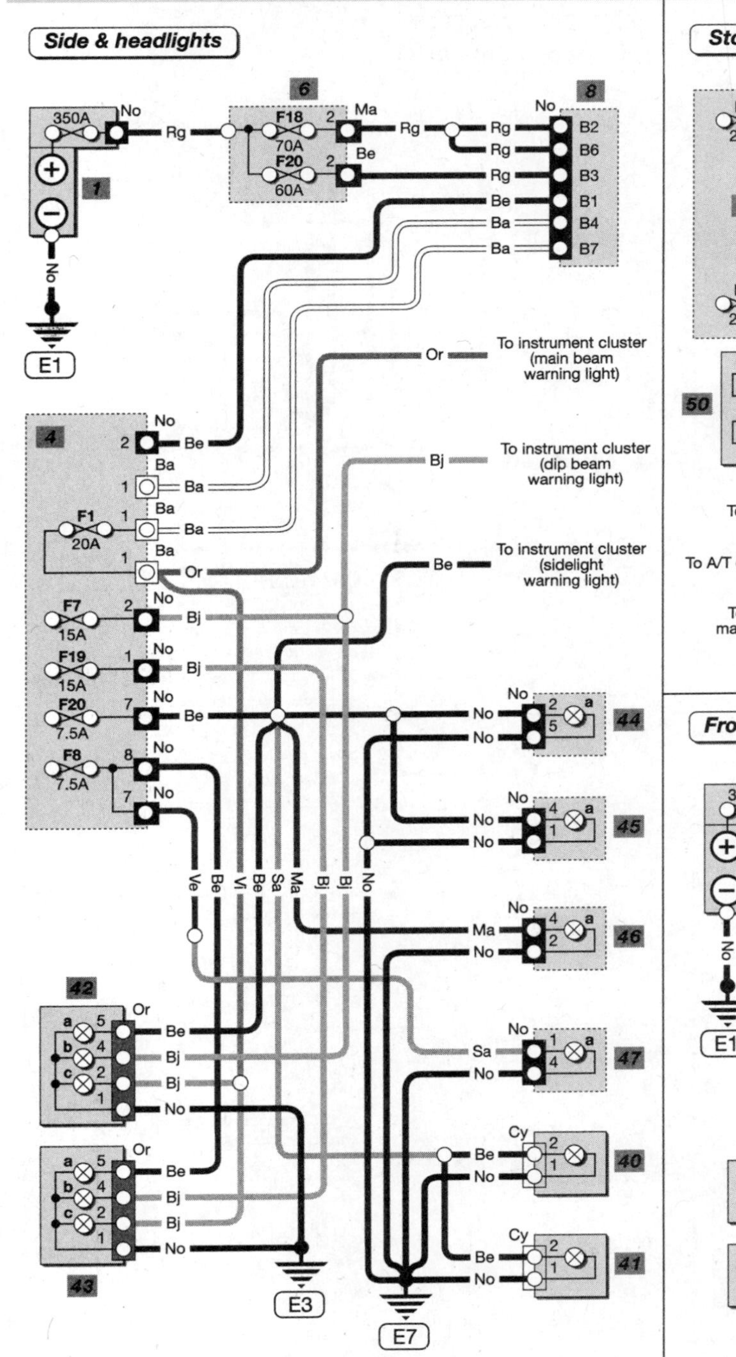

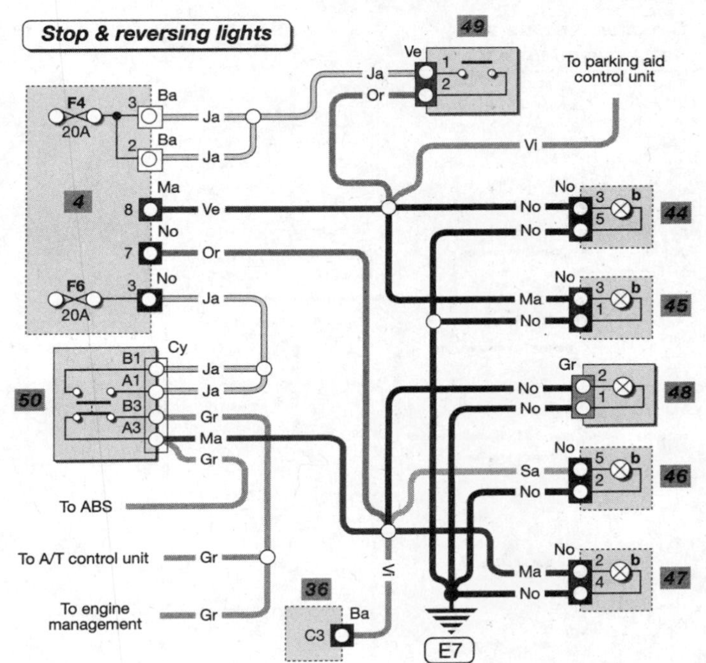

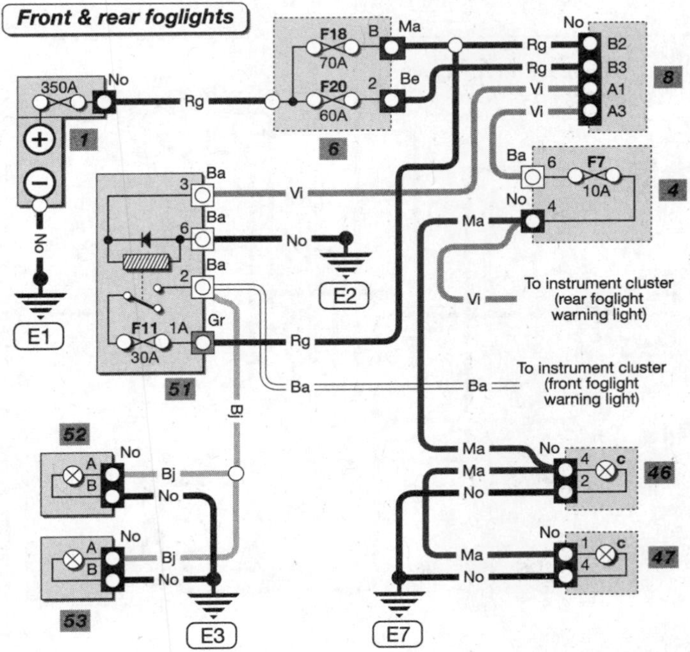

Diagram 5

Wire colours

Ba	White	**No**	Black
Be	Blue	**Or**	Orange
Bj	Beige	**Rg**	Red
Cy	Crystal	**Sa**	Pink
Gr	Grey	**Ve**	Green
Ja	Yellow	**Vi**	Violet
Ma	Brown		

Key to items

4 Passenger compartment fusebox 1
8 Multifunction switch
46 LH rear light unit
  d = direction indicator
47 RH rear light unit
  d = direction indicator
55 Hazard warning light switch
56 LH front direction indicator
57 RH front direction indicator
58 LH indicator side repeater
59 RH indicator side repeater
60 LH rear footwell illumination
61 LH front footwell illumination
62 RH rear footwell illumination
63 RH front footwell illumination
64 Glovebox light
65 Luggage compartment light
66 Driver's door light
67 Passenger's door light
68 LH rear door light
69 RH rear door light
70 LH Vanity mirror light
71 RH vanity mirror light
72 Vanity mirror light switch
73 Front interior light
74 LH rear interior light
75 RH rear interior light
76 Luggage compartment light/switch

H33356

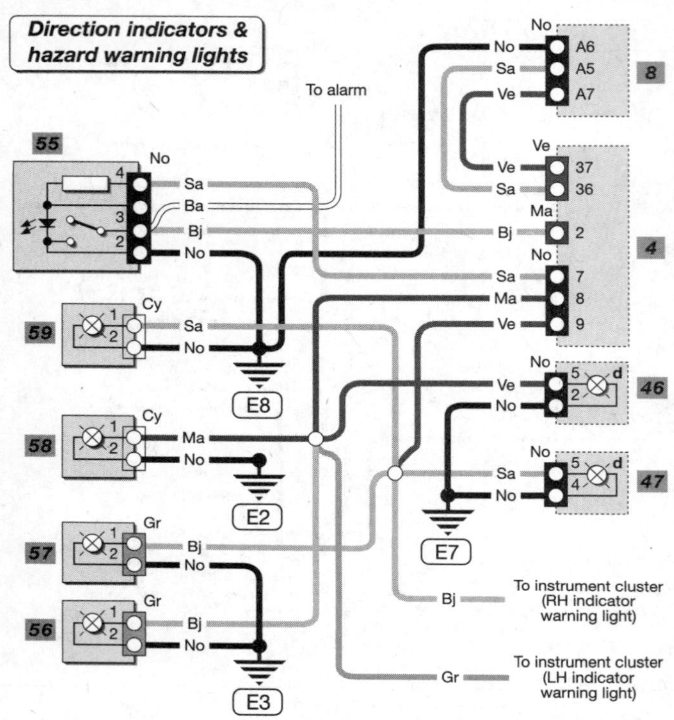

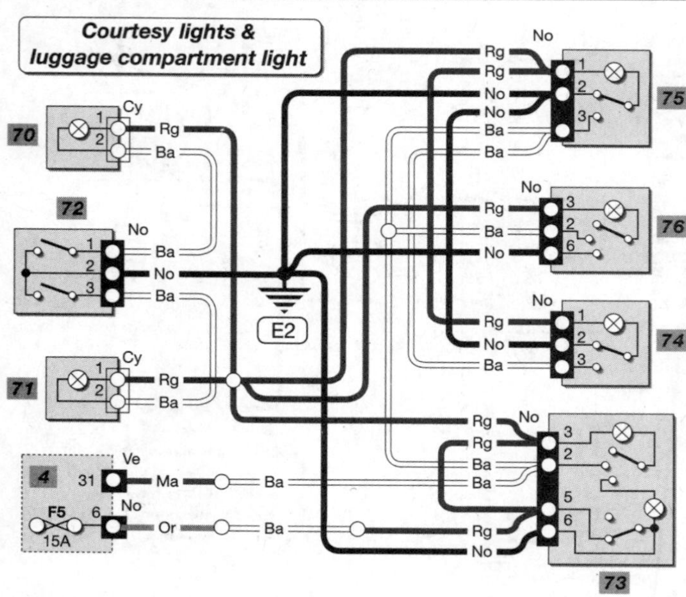

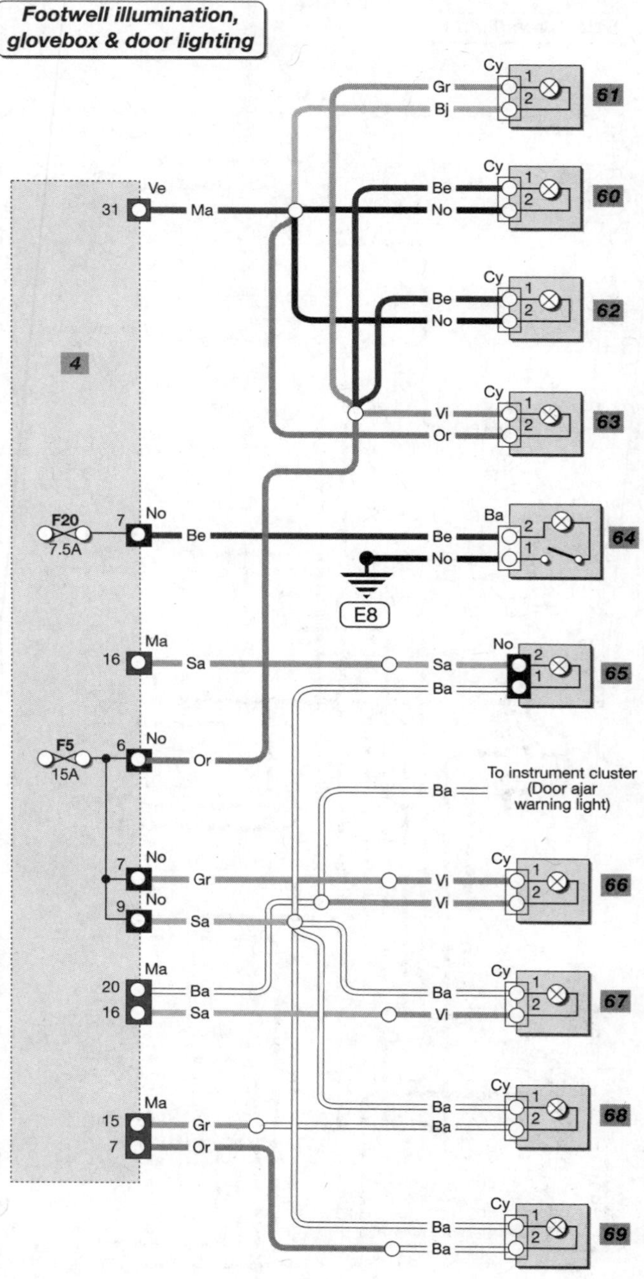

Diagram 6

Wire colours

Ba	White	**No**	Black
Be	Blue	**Or**	Orange
Bj	Beige	**Rg**	Red
Cy	Crystal	**Sa**	Pink
Gr	Grey	**Ve**	Green
Ja	Yellow	**Vi**	Violet
Ma	Brown		

Key to items

4 Passenger compartment fusebox 1
80 Driver's electric window switch
81 Passenger's electric window switch
82 Driver's window motor
83 Passenger's window motor
84 Passenger fusebox 2
85 Rear window safety switch
86 Rear window control switch
87 LH rear window switch
88 LH rear window motor
89 RH rear window switch
90 RH rear window motor
91 LH mirror assembly
92 RH mirror assembly
93 Mirror control switch

H33357

Front electric windows

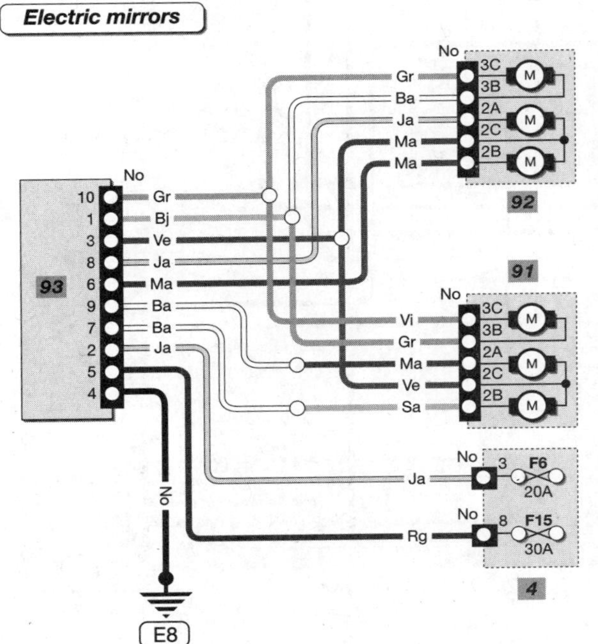

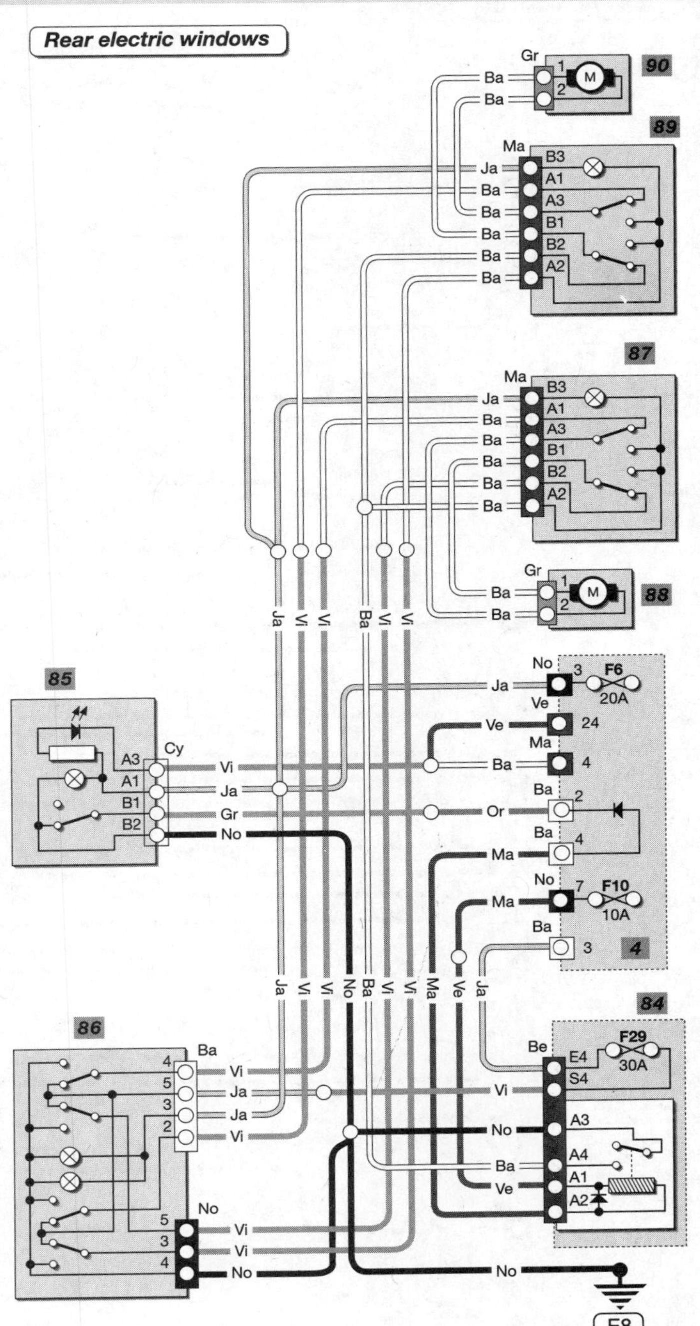

Diagram 7

Wire colours

Ba	White	**No**	Black
Be	Blue	**Or**	Orange
Bj	Beige	**Rg**	Red
Cy	Crystal	**Sa**	Pink
Gr	Grey	**Ve**	Green
Ja	Yellow	**Vi**	Violet
Ma	Brown		

Key to items

4	Passenger compartment fusebox 1
95	Driver's door lock motor
96	Passenger's door lock motor
97	LH rear door lock motor
98	RH rear door lock motor
99	Fuel filler flap lock motor
100	Central locking control switch
101	Diode unit
102	Tailgate release motor
103	Tailgate release switch

H33358

Central locking

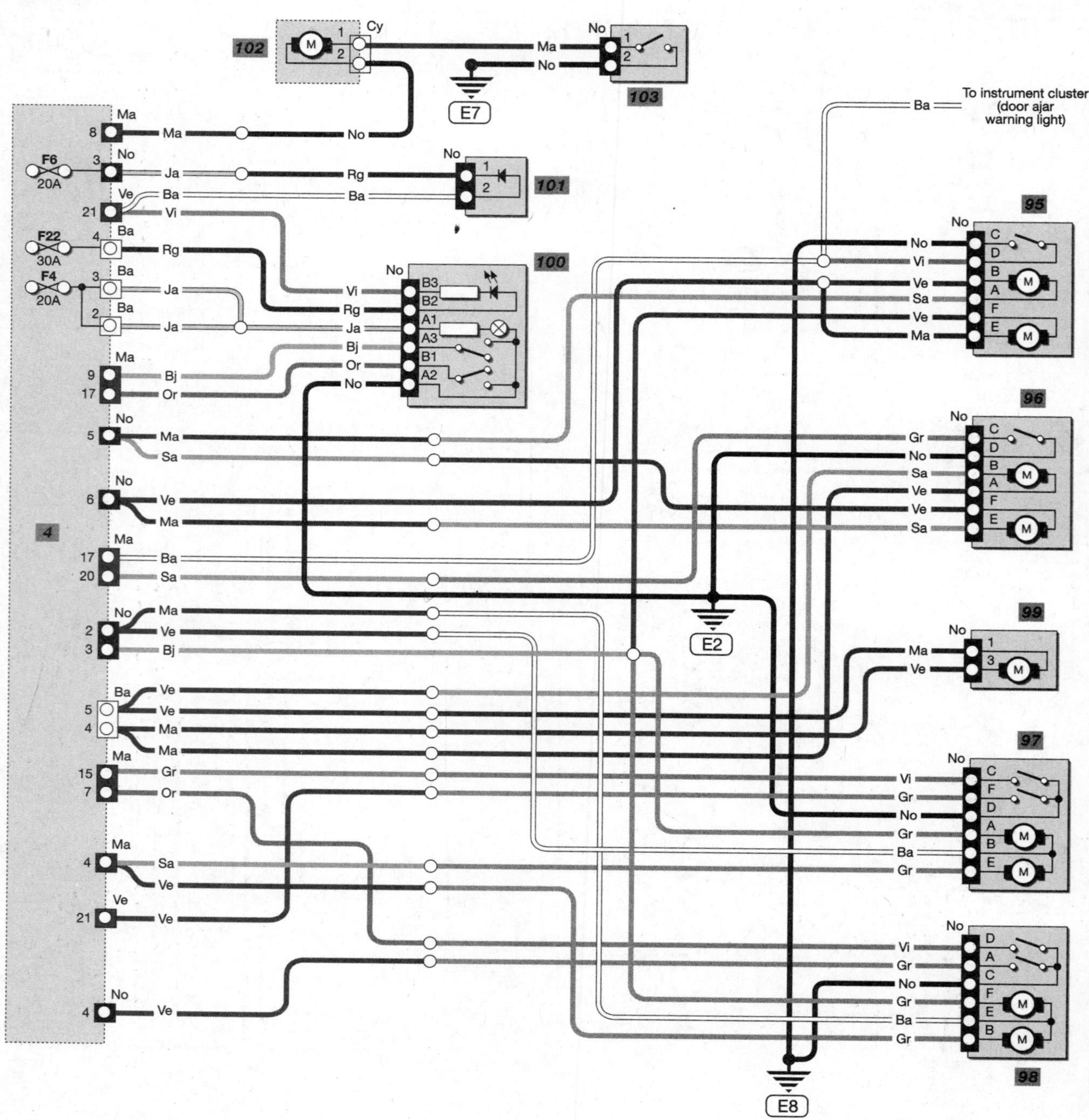

Dimensions and weights

Note: *All figures are approximate, and may vary according to model. Refer to manufacturer's data for exact figures.*

Dimensions

Overall length:	
Hatchback models	4576 mm
Estate models	4695 mm
Overall width (excluding wing mirrors)	2060 mm
Overall height (unladen):	
Hatchback models	1429 mm
Estate models	1443 mm
Wheelbase:	
Hatchback models	2743 mm
Estate models	2745 mm

Weights

Kerb weight*	1305 to 1555 kg
Maximum towing weight**:	
Unbraked trailer	650 kg
Braked trailer	900 to 1500 kg
Maximum roof rack load	80 kg

** Depending on model and specification.*
*** Refer to a Renault dealer for exact recommendations*

Conversion factors

Length (distance)

Inches (in)	x 25.4	= Millimetres (mm)	x 0.0394	= Inches (in)
Feet (ft)	x 0.305	= Metres (m)	x 3.281	= Feet (ft)
Miles	x 1.609	= Kilometres (km)	x 0.621	= Miles

Volume (capacity)

Cubic inches (cu in; in^3)	x 16.387	= Cubic centimetres (cc; cm^3)	x 0.061	= Cubic inches (cu in; in^3)
Imperial pints (Imp pt)	x 0.568	= Litres (l)	x 1.76	= Imperial pints (Imp pt)
Imperial quarts (Imp qt)	x 1.137	= Litres (l)	x 0.88	= Imperial quarts (Imp qt)
Imperial quarts (Imp qt)	x 1.201	= US quarts (US qt)	x 0.833	= Imperial quarts (Imp qt)
US quarts (US qt)	x 0.946	= Litres (l)	x 1.057	= US quarts (US qt)
Imperial gallons (Imp gal)	x 4.546	= Litres (l)	x 0.22	= Imperial gallons (Imp gal)
Imperial gallons (Imp gal)	x 1.201	= US gallons (US gal)	x 0.833	= Imperial gallons (Imp gal)
US gallons (US gal)	x 3.785	= Litres (l)	x 0.264	= US gallons (US gal)

Mass (weight)

Ounces (oz)	x 28.35	= Grams (g)	x 0.035	= Ounces (oz)
Pounds (lb)	x 0.454	= Kilograms (kg)	x 2.205	= Pounds (lb)

Force

Ounces-force (ozf; oz)	x 0.278	= Newtons (N)	x 3.6	= Ounces-force (ozf; oz)
Pounds-force (lbf; lb)	x 4.448	= Newtons (N)	x 0.225	= Pounds-force (lbf; lb)
Newtons (N)	x 0.1	= Kilograms-force (kgf; kg)	x 9.81	= Newtons (N)

Pressure

Pounds-force per square inch (psi; lbf/in^2; lb/in^2)	x 0.070	= Kilograms-force per square centimetre (kgf/cm^2; kg/cm^2)	x 14.223	= Pounds-force per square inch (psi; lbf/in^2; lb/in^2)
Pounds-force per square inch (psi; lbf/in^2; lb/in^2)	x 0.068	= Atmospheres (atm)	x 14.696	= Pounds-force per square inch (psi; lbf/in^2; lb/in^2)
Pounds-force per square inch (psi; lbf/in^2; lb/in^2)	x 0.069	= Bars	x 14.5	= Pounds-force per square inch (psi; lbf/in^2; lb/in^2)
Pounds-force per square inch (psi; lbf/in^2; lb/in^2)	x 6.895	= Kilopascals (kPa)	x 0.145	= Pounds-force per square inch (psi; lbf/in^2; lb/in^2)
Kilopascals (kPa)	x 0.01	= Kilograms-force per square centimetre (kgf/cm^2; kg/cm^2)	x 98.1	= Kilopascals (kPa)
Millibar (mbar)	x 100	= Pascals (Pa)	x 0.01	= Millibar (mbar)
Millibar (mbar)	x 0.0145	= Pounds-force per square inch (psi; lbf/in^2; lb/in^2)	x 68.947	= Millibar (mbar)
Millibar (mbar)	x 0.75	= Millimetres of mercury (mmHg)	x 1.333	= Millibar (mbar)
Millibar (mbar)	x 0.401	= Inches of water (inH_2O)	x 2.491	= Millibar (mbar)
Millimetres of mercury (mmHg)	x 0.535	= Inches of water (inH_2O)	x 1.868	= Millimetres of mercury (mmHg)
Inches of water (inH_2O)	x 0.036	= Pounds-force per square inch (psi; lbf/in^2; lb/in^2)	x 27.68	= Inches of water (inH_2O)

Torque (moment of force)

Pounds-force inches (lbf in; lb in)	x 1.152	= Kilograms-force centimetre (kgf cm; kg cm)	x 0.868	= Pounds-force inches (lbf in; lb in)
Pounds-force inches (lbf in; lb in)	x 0.113	= Newton metres (Nm)	x 8.85	= Pounds-force inches (lbf in; lb in)
Pounds-force inches (lbf in; lb in)	x 0.083	= Pounds-force feet (lbf ft; lb ft)	x 12	= Pounds-force inches (lbf in; lb in)
Pounds-force feet (lbf ft; lb ft)	x 0.138	= Kilograms-force metres (kgf m; kg m)	x 7.233	= Pounds-force feet (lbf ft; lb ft)
Pounds-force feet (lbf ft; lb ft)	x 1.356	= Newton metres (Nm)	x 0.738	= Pounds-force feet (lbf ft; lb ft)
Newton metres (Nm)	x 0.102	= Kilograms-force metres (kgf m; kg m)	x 9.804	= Newton metres (Nm)

Power

Horsepower (hp)	x 745.7	= Watts (W)	x 0.0013	= Horsepower (hp)

Velocity (speed)

Miles per hour (miles/hr; mph)	x 1.609	= Kilometres per hour (km/hr; kph)	x 0.621	= Miles per hour (miles/hr; mph)

Fuel consumption*

Miles per gallon, Imperial (mpg)	x 0.354	= Kilometres per litre (km/l)	x 2.825	= Miles per gallon, Imperial (mpg)
Miles per gallon, US (mpg)	x 0.425	= Kilometres per litre (km/l)	x 2.352	= Miles per gallon, US (mpg)

Temperature

Degrees Fahrenheit = (°C x 1.8) + 32

Degrees Celsius (Degrees Centigrade; °C) = (°F - 32) x 0.56

** It is common practice to convert from miles per gallon (mpg) to litres/100 kilometres (l/100km), where mpg x l/100 km = 282*

Whenever servicing, repair or overhaul work is carried out on the car or its components, observe the following procedures and instructions. This will assist in carrying out the operation efficiently and to a professional standard of workmanship.

Joint mating faces and gaskets

When separating components at their mating faces, never insert screwdrivers or similar implements into the joint between the faces in order to prise them apart. This can cause severe damage which results in oil leaks, coolant leaks, etc upon reassembly. Separation is usually achieved by tapping along the joint with a soft-faced hammer in order to break the seal. However, note that this method may not be suitable where dowels are used for component location.

Where a gasket is used between the mating faces of two components, a new one must be fitted on reassembly; fit it dry unless otherwise stated in the repair procedure. Make sure that the mating faces are clean and dry, with all traces of old gasket removed. When cleaning a joint face, use a tool which is unlikely to score or damage the face, and remove any burrs or nicks with an oilstone or fine file.

Make sure that tapped holes are cleaned with a pipe cleaner, and keep them free of jointing compound, if this is being used, unless specifically instructed otherwise.

Ensure that all orifices, channels or pipes are clear, and blow through them, preferably using compressed air.

Oil seals

Oil seals can be removed by levering them out with a wide flat-bladed screwdriver or similar implement. Alternatively, a number of self-tapping screws may be screwed into the seal, and these used as a purchase for pliers or some similar device in order to pull the seal free.

Whenever an oil seal is removed from its working location, either individually or as part of an assembly, it should be renewed.

The very fine sealing lip of the seal is easily damaged, and will not seal if the surface it contacts is not completely clean and free from scratches, nicks or grooves. If the original sealing surface of the component cannot be restored, and the manufacturer has not made provision for slight relocation of the seal relative to the sealing surface, the component should be renewed.

Protect the lips of the seal from any surface which may damage them in the course of fitting. Use tape or a conical sleeve where possible. Lubricate the seal lips with oil before fitting and, on dual-lipped seals, fill the space between the lips with grease.

Unless otherwise stated, oil seals must be fitted with their sealing lips toward the lubricant to be sealed.

Use a tubular drift or block of wood of the appropriate size to install the seal and, if the seal housing is shouldered, drive the seal down to the shoulder. If the seal housing is unshouldered, the seal should be fitted with its face flush with the housing top face (unless otherwise instructed).

Screw threads and fastenings

Seized nuts, bolts and screws are quite a common occurrence where corrosion has set in, and the use of penetrating oil or releasing fluid will often overcome this problem if the offending item is soaked for a while before attempting to release it. The use of an impact driver may also provide a means of releasing such stubborn fastening devices, when used in conjunction with the appropriate screwdriver bit or socket. If none of these methods works, it may be necessary to resort to the careful application of heat, or the use of a hacksaw or nut splitter device.

Studs are usually removed by locking two nuts together on the threaded part, and then using a spanner on the lower nut to unscrew the stud. Studs or bolts which have broken off below the surface of the component in which they are mounted can sometimes be removed using a stud extractor. Always ensure that a blind tapped hole is completely free from oil, grease, water or other fluid before installing the bolt or stud. Failure to do this could cause the housing to crack due to the hydraulic action of the bolt or stud as it is screwed in.

When tightening a castellated nut to accept a split pin, tighten the nut to the specified torque, where applicable, and then tighten further to the next split pin hole. Never slacken the nut to align the split pin hole, unless stated in the repair procedure.

When checking or retightening a nut or bolt to a specified torque setting, slacken the nut or bolt by a quarter of a turn, and then retighten to the specified setting. However, this should not be attempted where angular tightening has been used.

For some screw fastenings, notably cylinder head bolts or nuts, torque wrench settings are no longer specified for the latter stages of tightening, "angle-tightening" being called up instead. Typically, a fairly low torque wrench setting will be applied to the bolts/nuts in the correct sequence, followed by one or more stages of tightening through specified angles.

Locknuts, locktabs and washers

Any fastening which will rotate against a component or housing during tightening should always have a washer between it and the relevant component or housing.

Spring or split washers should always be renewed when they are used to lock a critical component such as a big-end bearing retaining bolt or nut. Locktabs which are folded over to retain a nut or bolt should always be renewed.

Self-locking nuts can be re-used in non-critical areas, providing resistance can be felt when the locking portion passes over the bolt or stud thread. However, it should be noted that self-locking stiffnuts tend to lose their effectiveness after long periods of use, and should then be renewed as a matter of course.

Split pins must always be replaced with new ones of the correct size for the hole.

When thread-locking compound is found on the threads of a fastener which is to be re-used, it should be cleaned off with a wire brush and solvent, and fresh compound applied on reassembly.

Special tools

Some repair procedures in this manual entail the use of special tools such as a press, two or three-legged pullers, spring compressors, etc. Wherever possible, suitable readily-available alternatives to the manufacturer's special tools are described, and are shown in use. In some instances, where no alternative is possible, it has been necessary to resort to the use of a manufacturer's tool, and this has been done for reasons of safety as well as the efficient completion of the repair operation. Unless you are highly-skilled and have a thorough understanding of the procedures described, never attempt to bypass the use of any special tool when the procedure described specifies its use. Not only is there a very great risk of personal injury, but expensive damage could be caused to the components involved.

Environmental considerations

When disposing of used engine oil, brake fluid, antifreeze, etc, give due consideration to any detrimental environmental effects. Do not, for instance, pour any of the above liquids down drains into the general sewage system, or onto the ground to soak away. Many local council refuse tips provide a facility for waste oil disposal, as do some garages. If none of these facilities are available, consult your local Environmental Health Department, or the National Rivers Authority, for further advice.

With the universal tightening-up of legislation regarding the emission of environmentally-harmful substances from motor vehicles, most vehicles have tamperproof devices fitted to the main adjustment points of the fuel system. These devices are primarily designed to prevent unqualified persons from adjusting the fuel/air mixture, with the chance of a consequent increase in toxic emissions. If such devices are found during servicing or overhaul, they should, wherever possible, be renewed or refitted in accordance with the manufacturer's requirements or current legislation.

OIL CARE
FOLLOW THE CODE
OIL BANK LINE
0800 66 33 66
www.oilbankline.org.uk

Note: It is antisocial and illegal to dump oil down the drain. To find the location of your local oil recycling bank, call this number free.

Buying spare parts

Spare parts are available from many sources, including maker's appointed garages, accessory shops, and motor factors. To be sure of obtaining the correct parts, it will sometimes be necessary to quote the vehicle identification number. If possible, it can also be useful to take the old parts along for positive identification. Items such as starter motors and alternators may be available under a service exchange scheme – any parts returned should be clean.

Our advice regarding spare parts is as follows.

Officially appointed garages

This is the best source of parts which are peculiar to your car, and which are not otherwise generally available (eg, badges, interior trim, certain body panels, etc). It is also the only place at which you should buy parts if the vehicle is still under warranty.

Accessory shops

These are very good places to buy materials and components needed for the maintenance of your car (oil, air and fuel filters, light bulbs, drivebelts, greases, brake pads, tough-up paint, etc). Components of this nature sold by a reputable shop are of the same standard as those used by the car manufacturer.

Besides components, these shops also sell tools and general accessories, usually have convenient opening hours, charge lower prices, and can often be found close to home. Some accessory shops have parts counters where components needed for almost any repair job can be purchased or ordered.

Motor factors

Good factors will stock all the more important components which wear out comparatively quickly, and can sometimes supply individual components needed for the overhaul of a larger assembly (eg, brake seals and hydraulic parts, bearing shells, pistons, valves). They may also handle work such as cylinder block reboring, crankshaft regrinding, etc.

Tyre and exhaust specialists

These outlets may be independent, or members of a local or national chain. They frequently offer competitive prices when compared with a main dealer or local garage, but it will pay to obtain several quotes before making a decision. When researching prices, also ask what 'extras' may be added – for instance fitting a new valve and balancing the wheel are both commonly charged on top of the price of a new tyre.

Other sources

Beware of parts or materials obtained from market stalls, car boot sales or similar outlets. Such items are not invariably sub-standard, but there is little chance of compensation if they do prove unsatisfactory. In the case of safety-critical components such as brake pads, there is the risk not only of financial loss, but also of an accident causing injury or death.

Second-hand components or assemblies obtained from a car breaker can be a good buy in some circumstances, but his sort of purchase is best made by the experienced DIY mechanic.

Vehicle identification

Modifications are a continuing and unpublicised process in vehicle manufacture, quite apart from major model changes. Spare parts manuals and lists are compiled upon a numerical basis, the individual vehicle identification numbers being essential to correct identification of the component concerned.

When ordering spare parts, always give as much information as possible. Quote the car model; year of manufacture, body and engine numbers as appropriate.

The VIN plate is an adhesive label located at the base of the B-pillar on the right-hand side of the vehicle. The *Vehicle Identification Number (VIN)* can be viewed through the bottom of the windscreen at the left-hand side of the vehicle **(see illustrations)**.

The *body number and paint code numbers* are located on the vehicle identification plate.

The *engine number* is stamped on the cylinder block. Even with the engine top cover removed (where applicable), the number can be hard to see **(see illustration)**.

Vehicle identification plate is at the base of the B-pillar

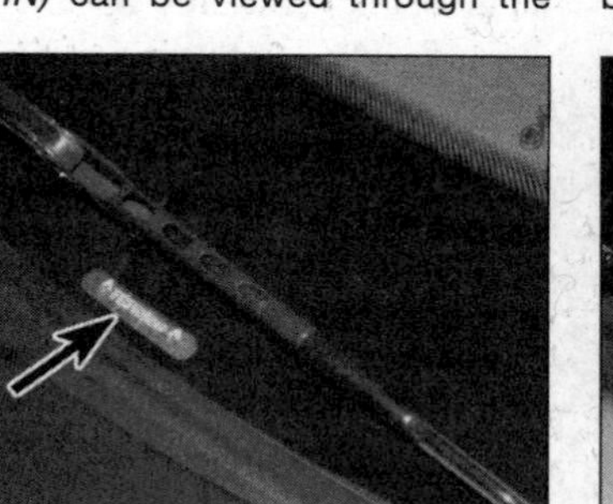

Vehicle identification Number (VIN) can be seen through the windscreen

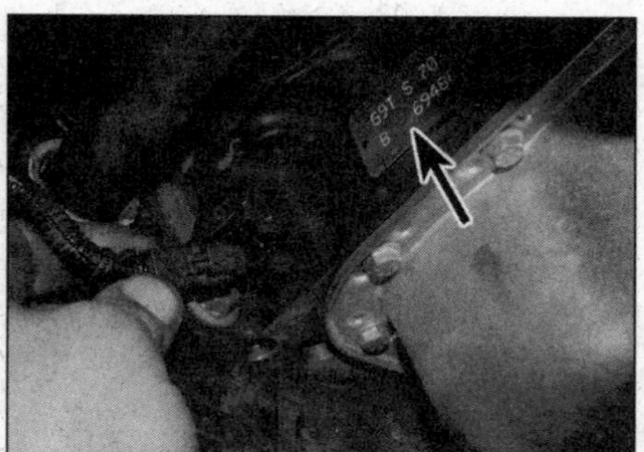

Engine number location (arrowed) – 2.2 litre diesel

Jacking and vehicle support

The jack supplied with the car's tool kit should only be used for changing the roadwheels – see *Wheel changing* at the front of this book. When carrying out any other kind of work, raise the car using a hydraulic (or 'trolley') jack, and always supplement the jack with axle stands positioned under the jacking/support points. If the roadwheels do not have to be removed, consider using wheel ramps – if wished, these can be placed under the wheels once the car has been raised using a hydraulic jack, and then lowered onto the ramps so that it is resting on its wheels.

Only ever jack the car up on a solid, level surface. If there is even a slight slope, take great care that the car cannot move as the wheels are lifted off the ground. Jacking up on an uneven or gravelled surface is not recommended, as the weight of the car will not be evenly distributed, and the jack may slip as the car is raised.

As far as possible, do not leave the car unattended once it has been raised, particularly if children are playing nearby.

Before jacking up the front of the car, ensure that the handbrake is firmly applied. When jacking up the rear of the car, place wooden chocks in front of the front wheels, and engage first gear.

To raise the front of the car, position the jack head underneath the front subframe, on or near one of the mounting bolts, and use a flat piece of wood to spread the load. Always supplement the jack with axle stands under the sill jacking points.

At the rear, provided that work is not being carried out on the rear suspension, if care is taken and a substantial trolley jack is used, the jack can be placed under the rear spring – note, however, that this must only be attempted with the car on solid, level ground. Otherwise, place a wide, flat piece of wood centrally under the rear jacking point to spread the load, and position the jack head and axle stand as close together either side of the jacking point as possible.

Do not jack the car under any other part of the sill, sump, floor pan, or (except as described) directly under any of the steering or suspension components.

Never work under, around, or near a raised vehicle, unless it is adequately supported on stands. Do not rely on a jack alone, as even a hydraulic jack could fail under load.

Warning: Never work under, around, or near a raised vehicle, unless it is adequately supported in at least two places.

Disconnecting the battery

Several systems fitted to the vehicle require battery power to be available at all times, either to ensure their continued operation (such as the clock) or to maintain control unit memories which could be erased if the battery were to be disconnected. Whenever the battery is to be disconnected therefore, first note the following, to ensure that there are no unforeseen consequences of this action:

a) *First, on any vehicle with central locking, it is a wise precaution to remove the keycard, and to keep it with you, so that it does not get locked in, if the central locking should engage accidentally when the battery is reconnected.*

b) *On cars equipped with an engine management system, the system's ECU will lose the information stored in its memory when the battery is disconnected. This includes idling and operating values, and any fault codes detected – in the case of the fault codes, if it is thought likely that the system has developed a fault for which the corresponding code has been logged, the car must be taken to a Renault dealer for the codes to be read, using the special diagnostic equipment necessary for this. Whenever the battery is disconnected, the information relating to idle speed control and other operating values will have to be re-programmed into the unit's memory. The ECU does this by itself, but until then, there may be surging, hesitation, erratic idle and a generally inferior level of performance. To allow the ECU to relearn these values, start the engine and run it as close to idle speed as possible until it reaches its normal operating temperature, then run it for approximately two minutes at 1200 rpm. Next, drive the car as far as necessary – approximately 5 miles of varied driving conditions is usually sufficient – to complete the relearning process.*

c) *If the battery is disconnected while the alarm system is armed or activated, the alarm will remain in the same state when the battery is reconnected. The same applies to the engine immobiliser system.*

d) *If a Renault audio unit is fitted, and the unit and/or the battery is disconnected, the unit will not function again on reconnection until the correct security code is entered. Details of this procedure, which varies according to the unit and model year, are given in the audio operating guide supplied with the car when new. Ensure you have the correct code before you disconnect the battery. For obvious security reasons, the procedure is not given in this manual. If you do not have the code or details of the correct procedure, but can supply proof of ownership and a legitimate reason for wanting this information, the car's selling dealer may be able to help.*

e) *Where electric windows with 'one-touch' operation are fitted, this function may not work correctly until each window has been reset. This is done by fully opening the window with the button pressed, then keeping the button pressed for a few seconds after opening, so the system can 'learn' the fully-open position. Close the window, and again keep the button pressed for a few seconds after closing.*

Devices known as 'memory-savers' (or 'code-savers') can be used to avoid some of the above problems. Precise details vary according to the device used. Typically, it is plugged into the cigarette lighter, and is connected by its own wires to a spare battery; the car's own battery is then disconnected from the electrical system, leaving the 'memory-saver' to pass sufficient current to maintain audio unit security codes and ECU memory values, and also to run permanently-live circuits such as the clock, all the while isolating the battery in the event of a short-circuit occurring while work is carried out.

Warning: Some of these devices allow a considerable amount of current to pass, which can mean that many of the vehicle's systems are still operational when the main battery is disconnected. If a 'memory saver' is used, ensure that the circuit concerned is actually 'dead' before carrying out any work on it!

Introduction

A selection of good tools is a fundamental requirement for anyone contemplating the maintenance and repair of a motor vehicle. For the owner who does not possess any, their purchase will prove a considerable expense, offsetting some of the savings made by doing-it-yourself. However, provided that the tools purchased meet the relevant national safety standards and are of good quality, they will last for many years and prove an extremely worthwhile investment.

To help the average owner to decide which tools are needed to carry out the various tasks detailed in this manual, we have compiled three lists of tools under the following headings: *Maintenance and minor repair, Repair and overhaul*, and *Special*. Newcomers to practical mechanics should start off with the *Maintenance and minor repair* tool kit, and confine themselves to the simpler jobs around the vehicle. Then, as confidence and experience grow, more difficult tasks can be undertaken, with extra tools being purchased as, and when, they are needed. In this way, a *Maintenance and minor repair* tool kit can be built up into a *Repair and overhaul* tool kit over a considerable period of time, without any major cash outlays. The experienced do-it-yourselfer will have a tool kit good enough for most repair and overhaul procedures, and will add tools from the *Special* category when it is felt that the expense is justified by the amount of use to which these tools will be put.

Maintenance and minor repair tool kit

The tools given in this list should be considered as a minimum requirement if routine maintenance, servicing and minor repair operations are to be undertaken. We recommend the purchase of combination spanners (ring one end, open-ended the other); although more expensive than open-ended ones, they do give the advantages of both types of spanner.

- ☐ *Combination spanners:*
  Metric - 8 to 19 mm inclusive
- ☐ *Adjustable spanner - 35 mm jaw (approx.)*
- ☐ *Spark plug spanner (with rubber insert) - petrol models*
- ☐ *Spark plug gap adjustment tool - petrol models*
- ☐ *Set of feeler gauges*
- ☐ *Brake bleed nipple spanner*
- ☐ *Screwdrivers:*
  Flat blade - 100 mm long x 6 mm dia
  Cross blade - 100 mm long x 6 mm dia
  Torx - various sizes (not all vehicles)
- ☐ *Combination pliers*
- ☐ *Hacksaw (junior)*
- ☐ *Tyre pump*
- ☐ *Tyre pressure gauge*
- ☐ *Oil can*
- ☐ *Oil filter removal tool*
- ☐ *Fine emery cloth*
- ☐ *Wire brush (small)*
- ☐ *Funnel (medium size)*
- ☐ *Sump drain plug key (not all vehicles)*

Repair and overhaul tool kit

These tools are virtually essential for anyone undertaking any major repairs to a motor vehicle, and are additional to those given in the *Maintenance and minor repair* list. Included in this list is a comprehensive set of sockets. Although these are expensive, they will be found invaluable as they are so versatile - particularly if various drives are included in the set. We recommend the half-inch square-drive type, as this can be used with most proprietary torque wrenches.

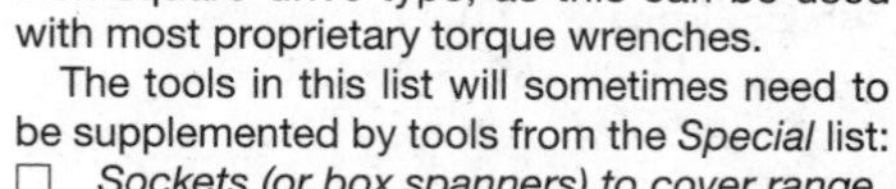

The tools in this list will sometimes need to be supplemented by tools from the *Special* list:

- ☐ *Sockets (or box spanners) to cover range in previous list (including Torx sockets)*
- ☐ *Reversible ratchet drive (for use with sockets)*
- ☐ *Extension piece, 250 mm (for use with sockets)*
- ☐ *Universal joint (for use with sockets)*
- ☐ *Flexible handle or sliding T "breaker bar" (for use with sockets)*
- ☐ *Torque wrench (for use with sockets)*
- ☐ *Self-locking grips*
- ☐ *Ball pein hammer*
- ☐ *Soft-faced mallet (plastic or rubber)*
- ☐ *Screwdrivers:*
  Flat blade - long & sturdy, short (chubby), and narrow (electrician's) types
  Cross blade – long & sturdy, and short (chubby) types
- ☐ *Pliers:*
  Long-nosed
  Side cutters (electrician's)
  Circlip (internal and external)
- ☐ *Cold chisel - 25 mm*
- ☐ *Scriber*
- ☐ *Scraper*
- ☐ *Centre-punch*
- ☐ *Pin punch*
- ☐ *Hacksaw*
- ☐ *Brake hose clamp*
- ☐ *Brake/clutch bleeding kit*
- ☐ *Selection of twist drills*
- ☐ *Steel rule/straight-edge*
- ☐ *Allen keys (inc. splined/Torx type)*
- ☐ *Selection of files*
- ☐ *Wire brush*
- ☐ *Axle stands*
- ☐ *Jack (strong trolley or hydraulic type)*
- ☐ *Light with extension lead*
- ☐ *Universal electrical multi-meter*

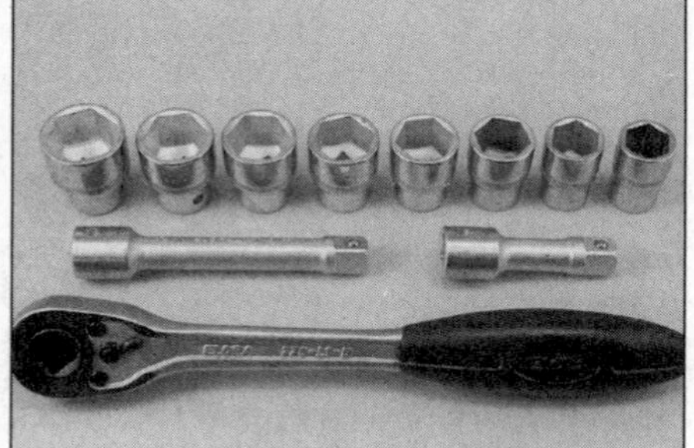

Sockets and reversible ratchet drive

Brake bleeding kit

Torx key, socket and bit

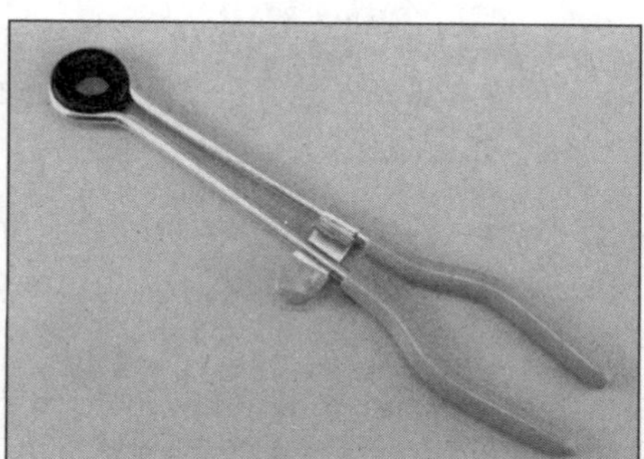

Hose clamp

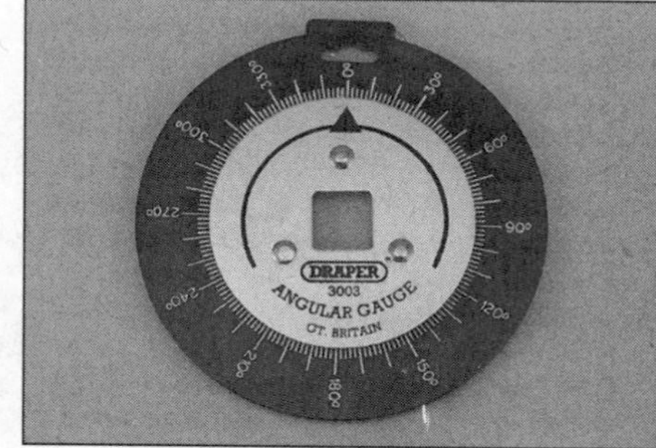

Angular-tightening gauge

Special tools

The tools in this list are those which are not used regularly, are expensive to buy, or which need to be used in accordance with their manufacturers' instructions. Unless relatively difficult mechanical jobs are undertaken frequently, it will not be economic to buy many of these tools. Where this is the case, you could consider clubbing together with friends (or joining a motorists' club) to make a joint purchase, or borrowing the tools against a deposit from a local garage or tool hire specialist. It is worth noting that many of the larger DIY superstores now carry a large range of special tools for hire at modest rates.

The following list contains only those tools and instruments freely available to the public, and not those special tools produced by the vehicle manufacturer specifically for its dealer network. You will find occasional references to these manufacturers' special tools in the text of this manual. Generally, an alternative method of doing the job without the vehicle manufacturers' special tool is given. However, sometimes there is no alternative to using them. Where this is the case and the relevant tool cannot be bought or borrowed, you will have to entrust the work to a dealer.

- ☐ *Angular-tightening gauge*
- ☐ *Valve spring compressor*
- ☐ *Valve grinding tool*
- ☐ *Piston ring compressor*
- ☐ *Piston ring removal/installation tool*
- ☐ *Cylinder bore hone*
- ☐ *Balljoint separator*
- ☐ *Coil spring compressors (where applicable)*
- ☐ *Two/three-legged hub and bearing puller*
- ☐ *Impact screwdriver*
- ☐ *Micrometer and/or vernier calipers*
- ☐ *Dial gauge*
- ☐ *Stroboscopic timing light*
- ☐ *Dwell angle meter/tachometer*
- ☐ *Fault code reader*
- ☐ *Cylinder compression gauge*
- ☐ *Hand-operated vacuum pump and gauge*
- ☐ *Clutch plate alignment set*
- ☐ *Brake shoe steady spring cup removal tool*
- ☐ *Bush and bearing removal/installation set*
- ☐ *Stud extractors*
- ☐ *Tap and die set*
- ☐ *Lifting tackle*
- ☐ *Trolley jack*

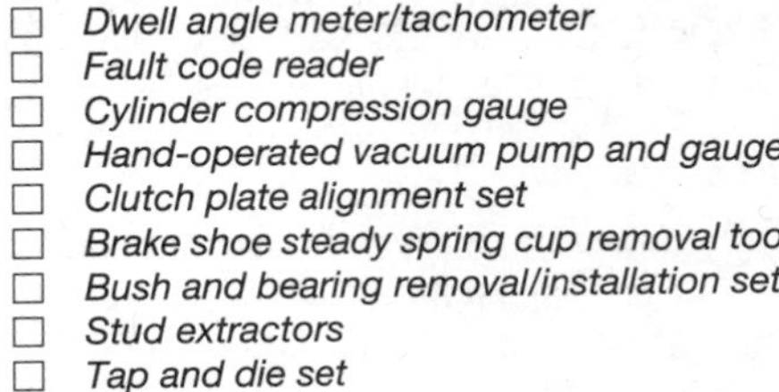

Buying tools

Reputable motor accessory shops and superstores often offer excellent quality tools at discount prices, so it pays to shop around.

Remember, you don't have to buy the most expensive items on the shelf, but it is always advisable to steer clear of the very cheap tools. Beware of 'bargains' offered on market stalls or at car boot sales. There are plenty of good tools around at reasonable prices, but always aim to purchase items which meet the relevant national safety standards. If in doubt, ask the proprietor or manager of the shop for advice before making a purchase.

Care and maintenance of tools

Having purchased a reasonable tool kit, it is necessary to keep the tools in a clean and serviceable condition. After use, always wipe off any dirt, grease and metal particles using a clean, dry cloth, before putting the tools away. Never leave them lying around after they have been used. A simple tool rack on the garage or workshop wall for items such as screwdrivers and pliers is a good idea. Store all normal spanners and sockets in a metal box. Any measuring instruments, gauges, meters, etc, must be carefully stored where they cannot be damaged or become rusty.

Take a little care when tools are used. Hammer heads inevitably become marked, and screwdrivers lose the keen edge on their blades from time to time. A little timely attention with emery cloth or a file will soon restore items like this to a good finish.

Working facilities

Not to be forgotten when discussing tools is the workshop itself. If anything more than routine maintenance is to be carried out, a suitable working area becomes essential.

It is appreciated that many an owner-mechanic is forced by circumstances to remove an engine or similar item without the benefit of a garage or workshop. Having done this, any repairs should always be done under the cover of a roof.

Wherever possible, any dismantling should be done on a clean, flat workbench or table at a suitable working height.

Any workbench needs a vice; one with a jaw opening of 100 mm is suitable for most jobs. As mentioned previously, some clean dry storage space is also required for tools, as well as for any lubricants, cleaning fluids, touch-up paints etc, which become necessary.

Another item which may be required, and which has a much more general usage, is an electric drill with a chuck capacity of at least 8 mm. This, together with a good range of twist drills, is virtually essential for fitting accessories.

Last, but not least, always keep a supply of old newspapers and clean, lint-free rags available, and try to keep any working area as clean as possible.

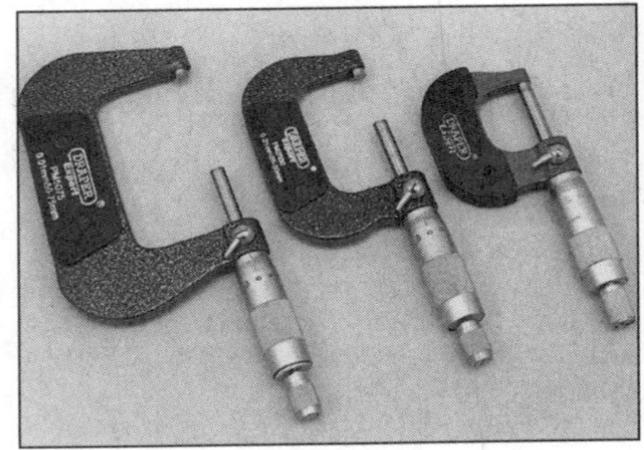

Micrometers

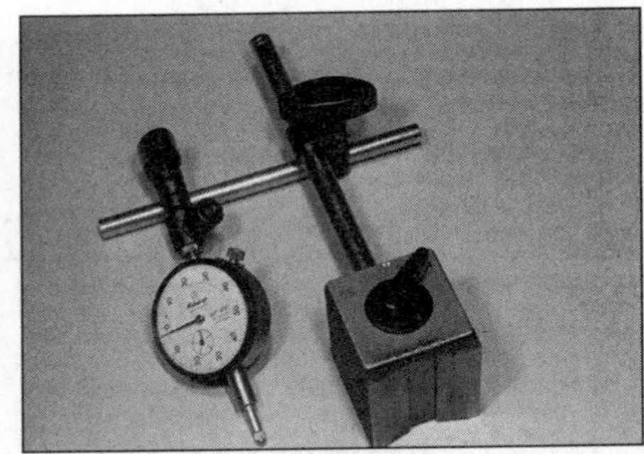

Dial test indicator ("dial gauge")

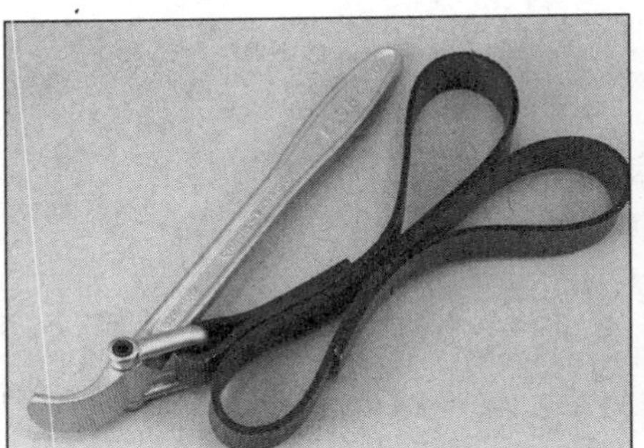

Strap wrench

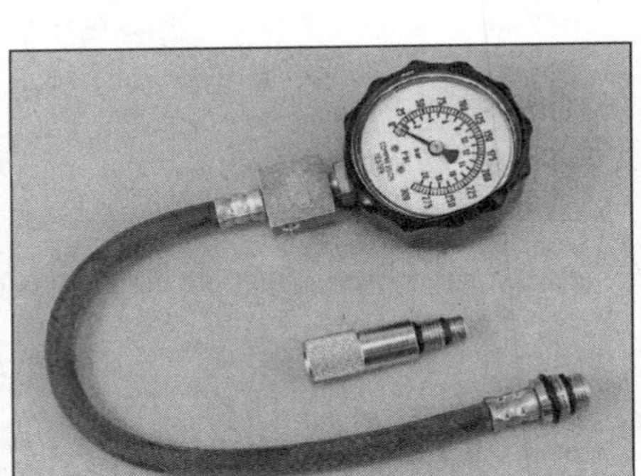

Compression tester

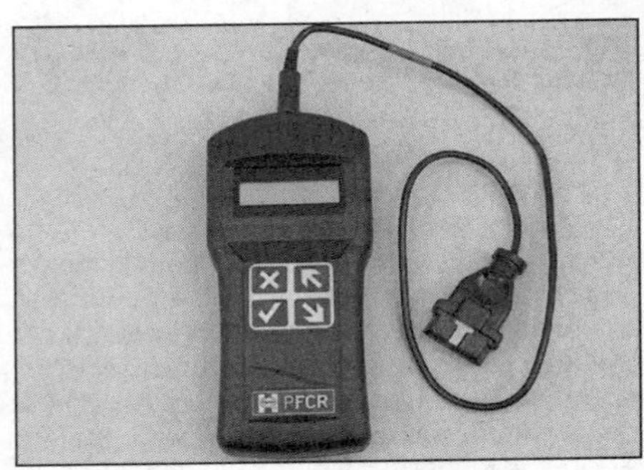

Fault code reader

MOT test checks

This is a guide to getting your vehicle through the MOT test. Obviously it will not be possible to examine the vehicle to the same standard as the professional MOT tester. However, working through the following checks will enable you to identify any problem areas before submitting the vehicle for the test.

It has only been possible to summarise the test requirements here, based on the regulations in force at the time of printing. Test standards are becoming increasingly stringent, although there are some exemptions for older vehicles.

An assistant will be needed to help carry out some of these checks.

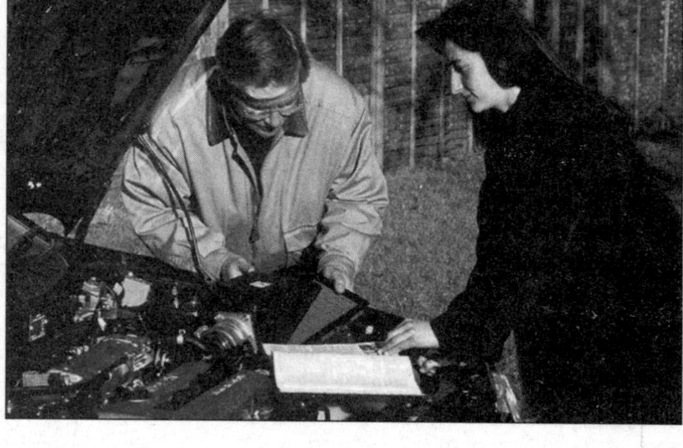

The checks have been sub-divided into four categories, as follows:

1 Checks carried out **FROM THE DRIVER'S SEAT**

2 Checks carried out **WITH THE VEHICLE ON THE GROUND**

3 Checks carried out **WITH THE VEHICLE RAISED AND THE WHEELS FREE TO TURN**

4 Checks carried out on **YOUR VEHICLE'S EXHAUST EMISSION SYSTEM**

1 Checks carried out FROM THE DRIVER'S SEAT

Handbrake

☐ Test the operation of the handbrake. Excessive travel (too many clicks) indicates incorrect brake or cable adjustment.

☐ Check that the handbrake cannot be released by tapping the lever sideways. Check the security of the lever mountings.

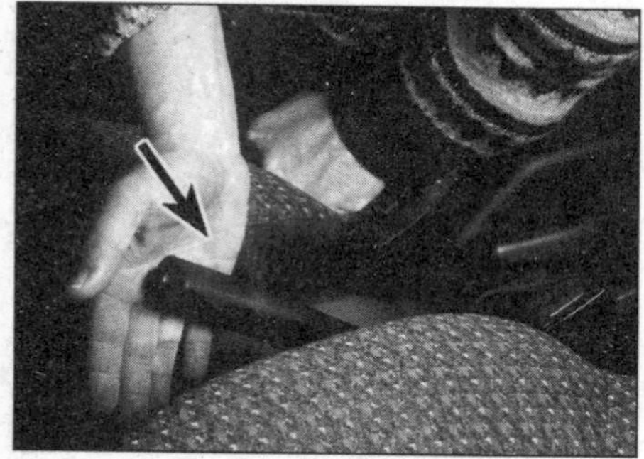

Footbrake

☐ Depress the brake pedal and check that it does not creep down to the floor, indicating a master cylinder fault. Release the pedal, wait a few seconds, then depress it again. If the pedal travels nearly to the floor before firm resistance is felt, brake adjustment or repair is necessary. If the pedal feels spongy, there is air in the hydraulic system which must be removed by bleeding.

☐ Check that the brake pedal is secure and in good condition. Check also for signs of fluid leaks on the pedal, floor or carpets, which would indicate failed seals in the brake master cylinder.

☐ Check the servo unit (when applicable) by operating the brake pedal several times, then keeping the pedal depressed and starting the engine. As the engine starts, the pedal will move down slightly. If not, the vacuum hose or the servo itself may be faulty.

Steering wheel and column

☐ Examine the steering wheel for fractures or looseness of the hub, spokes or rim.

☐ Move the steering wheel from side to side and then up and down. Check that the steering wheel is not loose on the column, indicating wear or a loose retaining nut. Continue moving the steering wheel as before, but also turn it slightly from left to right.

☐ Check that the steering wheel is not loose on the column, and that there is no abnormal

movement of the steering wheel, indicating wear in the column support bearings or couplings.

Windscreen, mirrors and sunvisor

☐ The windscreen must be free of cracks or other significant damage within the driver's field of view. (Small stone chips are acceptable.) Rear view mirrors must be secure, intact, and capable of being adjusted.

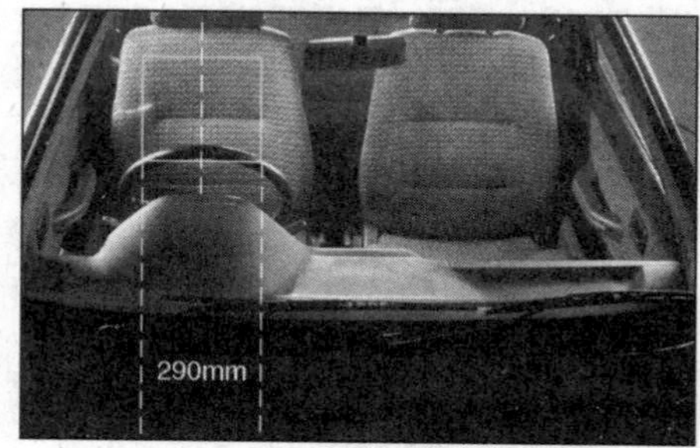

☐ The driver's sunvisor must be capable of being stored in the "up" position.

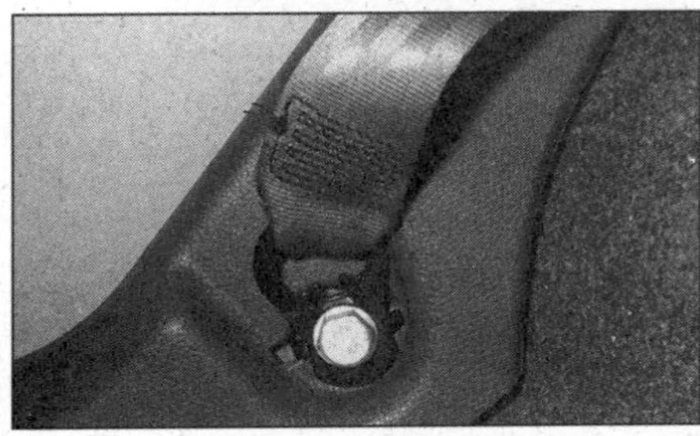

Seat belts and seats

Note: *The following checks are applicable to all seat belts, front and rear.*

☐ Examine the webbing of all the belts (including rear belts if fitted) for cuts, serious fraying or deterioration. Fasten and unfasten each belt to check the buckles. If applicable, check the retracting mechanism. Check the security of all seat belt mountings accessible from inside the vehicle.

☐ Seat belts with pre-tensioners, once activated, have a "flag" or similar showing on the seat belt stalk. This, in itself, is not a reason for test failure.

☐ The front seats themselves must be securely attached and the backrests must lock in the upright position.

Doors

☐ Both front doors must be able to be opened and closed from outside and inside, and must latch securely when closed.

2 Checks carried out WITH THE VEHICLE ON THE GROUND

Vehicle identification

☐ Number plates must be in good condition, secure and legible, with letters and numbers correctly spaced – spacing at (A) should be at least twice that at (B).

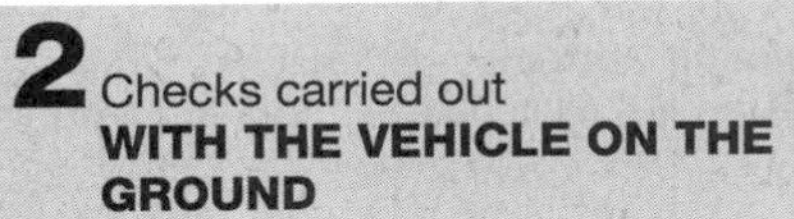

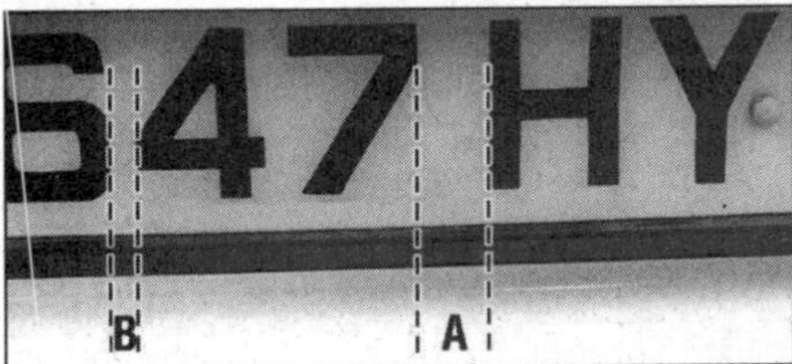

☐ The VIN plate and/or homologation plate must be legible.

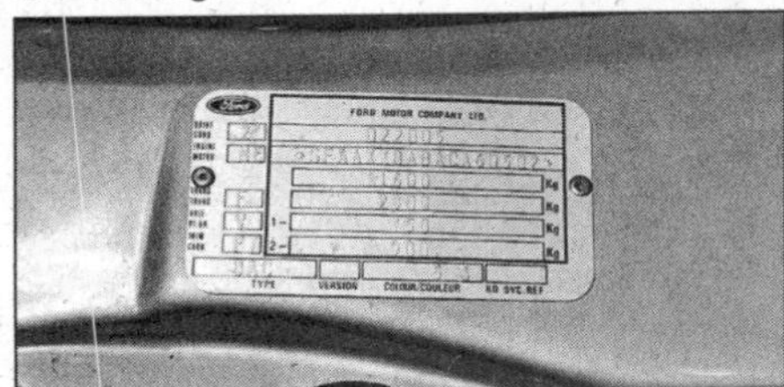

Electrical equipment

☐ Switch on the ignition and check the operation of the horn.

☐ Check the windscreen washers and wipers, examining the wiper blades; renew damaged or perished blades. Also check the operation of the stop-lights.

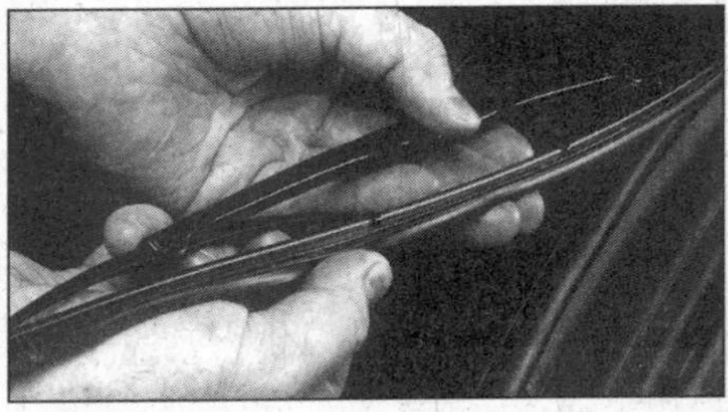

☐ Check the operation of the sidelights and number plate lights. The lenses and reflectors must be secure, clean and undamaged.

☐ Check the operation and alignment of the headlights. The headlight reflectors must not be tarnished and the lenses must be undamaged.

☐ Switch on the ignition and check the operation of the direction indicators (including the instrument panel tell-tale) and the hazard warning lights. Operation of the sidelights and stop-lights must not affect the indicators - if it does, the cause is usually a bad earth at the rear light cluster.

☐ Check the operation of the rear foglight(s), including the warning light on the instrument panel or in the switch.

☐ The ABS warning light must illuminate in accordance with the manufacturers' design. For most vehicles, the ABS warning light should illuminate when the ignition is switched on, and (if the system is operating properly) extinguish after a few seconds. Refer to the owner's handbook.

Footbrake

☐ Examine the master cylinder, brake pipes and servo unit for leaks, loose mountings, corrosion or other damage.

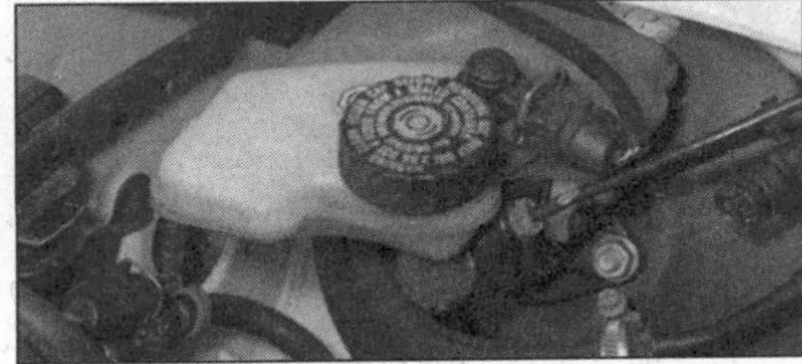

☐ The fluid reservoir must be secure and the fluid level must be between the upper (**A**) and lower (**B**) markings.

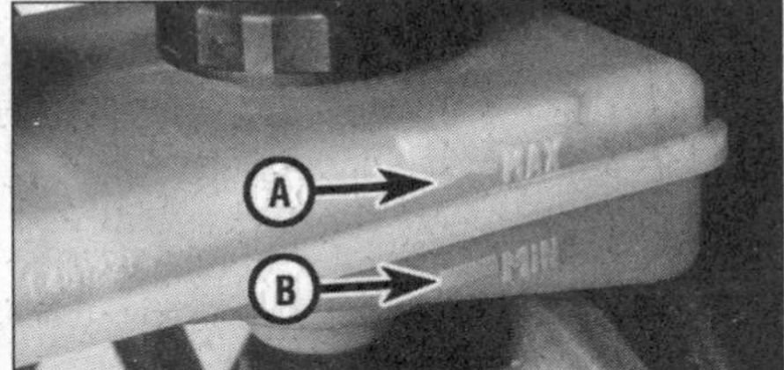

☐ Inspect both front brake flexible hoses for cracks or deterioration of the rubber. Turn the steering from lock to lock, and ensure that the hoses do not contact the wheel, tyre, or any part of the steering or suspension mechanism. With the brake pedal firmly depressed, check the hoses for bulges or leaks under pressure.

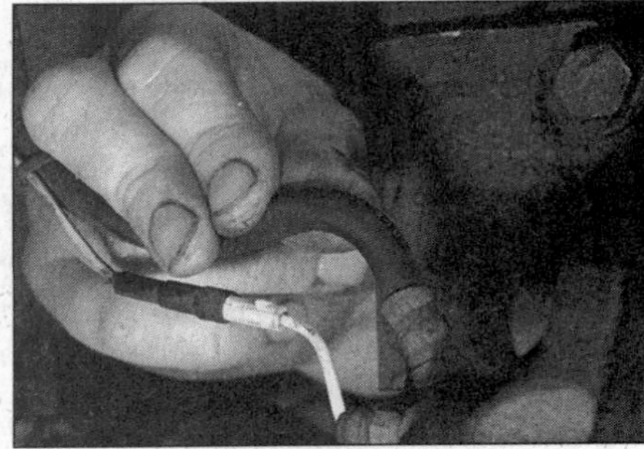

Steering and suspension

☐ Have your assistant turn the steering wheel from side to side slightly, up to the point where the steering gear just begins to transmit this movement to the roadwheels. Check for excessive free play between the steering wheel and the steering gear, indicating wear or insecurity of the steering column joints, the column-to-steering gear coupling, or the steering gear itself.

☐ Have your assistant turn the steering wheel more vigorously in each direction, so that the roadwheels just begin to turn. As this is done, examine all the steering joints, linkages, fittings and attachments. Renew any component that shows signs of wear or damage. On vehicles with power steering, check the security and condition of the steering pump, drivebelt and hoses.

☐ Check that the vehicle is standing level, and at approximately the correct ride height.

Shock absorbers

☐ Depress each corner of the vehicle in turn, then release it. The vehicle should rise and then settle in its normal position. If the vehicle continues to rise and fall, the shock absorber is defective. A shock absorber which has seized will also cause the vehicle to fail.

Exhaust system

☐ Start the engine. With your assistant holding a rag over the tailpipe, check the entire system for leaks. Repair or renew leaking sections.

3 Checks carried out WITH THE VEHICLE RAISED AND THE WHEELS FREE TO TURN

Jack up the front and rear of the vehicle, and securely support it on axle stands. Position the stands clear of the suspension assemblies. Ensure that the wheels are clear of the ground and that the steering can be turned from lock to lock.

Steering mechanism

☐ Have your assistant turn the steering from lock to lock. Check that the steering turns smoothly, and that no part of the steering mechanism, including a wheel or tyre, fouls any brake hose or pipe or any part of the body structure.

☐ Examine the steering rack rubber gaiters for damage or insecurity of the retaining clips. If power steering is fitted, check for signs of damage or leakage of the fluid hoses, pipes or connections. Also check for excessive stiffness or binding of the steering, a missing split pin or locking device, or severe corrosion of the body structure within 30 cm of any steering component attachment point.

Front and rear suspension and wheel bearings

☐ Starting at the front right-hand side, grasp the roadwheel at the 3 o'clock and 9 o'clock positions and rock gently but firmly. Check for free play or insecurity at the wheel bearings, suspension balljoints, or suspension mountings, pivots and attachments.

☐ Now grasp the wheel at the 12 o'clock and 6 o'clock positions and repeat the previous inspection. Spin the wheel, and check for roughness or tightness of the front wheel bearing.

☐ If excess free play is suspected at a component pivot point, this can be confirmed by using a large screwdriver or similar tool and levering between the mounting and the component attachment. This will confirm whether the wear is in the pivot bush, its retaining bolt, or in the mounting itself (the bolt holes can often become elongated).

☐ Carry out all the above checks at the other front wheel, and then at both rear wheels.

Springs and shock absorbers

☐ Examine the suspension struts (when applicable) for serious fluid leakage, corrosion, or damage to the casing. Also check the security of the mounting points.

☐ If coil springs are fitted, check that the spring ends locate in their seats, and that the spring is not corroded, cracked or broken.

☐ If leaf springs are fitted, check that all leaves are intact, that the axle is securely attached to each spring, and that there is no deterioration of the spring eye mountings, bushes, and shackles.

☐ The same general checks apply to vehicles fitted with other suspension types, such as torsion bars, hydraulic displacer units, etc. Ensure that all mountings and attachments are secure, that there are no signs of excessive wear, corrosion or damage, and (on hydraulic types) that there are no fluid leaks or damaged pipes.

☐ Inspect the shock absorbers for signs of serious fluid leakage. Check for wear of the mounting bushes or attachments, or damage to the body of the unit.

Driveshafts (fwd vehicles only)

☐ Rotate each front wheel in turn and inspect the constant velocity joint gaiters for splits or damage. Also check that each driveshaft is straight and undamaged.

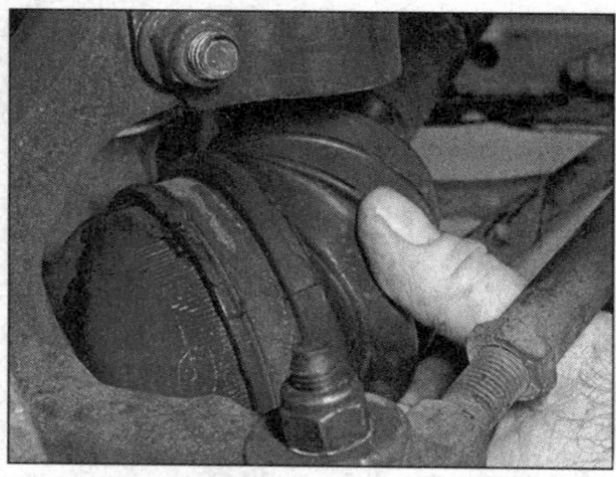

Braking system

☐ If possible without dismantling, check brake pad wear and disc condition. Ensure that the friction lining material has not worn excessively, (A) and that the discs are not fractured, pitted, scored or badly worn (B).

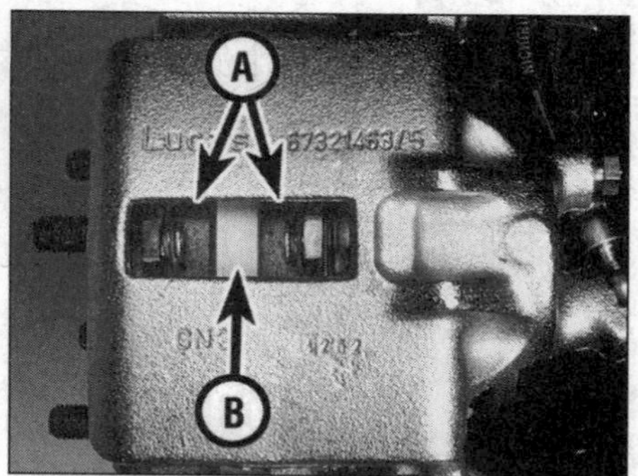

☐ Examine all the rigid brake pipes underneath the vehicle, and the flexible hose(s) at the rear. Look for corrosion, chafing or insecurity of the pipes, and for signs of bulging under pressure, chafing, splits or deterioration of the flexible hoses.

☐ Look for signs of fluid leaks at the brake calipers or on the brake backplates. Repair or renew leaking components.

☐ Slowly spin each wheel, while your assistant depresses and releases the footbrake. Ensure that each brake is operating and does not bind when the pedal is released.

☐ Examine the handbrake mechanism, checking for frayed or broken cables, excessive corrosion, or wear or insecurity of the linkage. Check that the mechanism works on each relevant wheel, and releases fully, without binding.

☐ It is not possible to test brake efficiency without special equipment, but a road test can be carried out later to check that the vehicle pulls up in a straight line.

Fuel and exhaust systems

☐ Inspect the fuel tank (including the filler cap), fuel pipes, hoses and unions. All components must be secure and free from leaks.

☐ Examine the exhaust system over its entire length, checking for any damaged, broken or missing mountings, security of the retaining clamps and rust or corrosion.

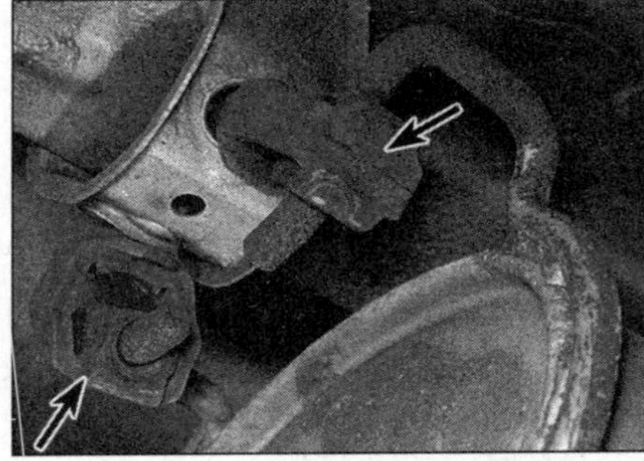

Wheels and tyres

☐ Examine the sidewalls and tread area of each tyre in turn. Check for cuts, tears, lumps, bulges, separation of the tread, and exposure of the ply or cord due to wear or damage. Check that the tyre bead is correctly seated on the wheel rim, that the valve is sound and properly seated, and that the wheel is not distorted or damaged.

☐ Check that the tyres are of the correct size for the vehicle, that they are of the same size and type on each axle, and that the pressures are correct.

☐ Check the tyre tread depth. The legal minimum at the time of writing is 1.6 mm over at least three-quarters of the tread width. Abnormal tread wear may indicate incorrect front wheel alignment.

Body corrosion

☐ Check the condition of the entire vehicle structure for signs of corrosion in load-bearing areas. (These include chassis box sections, side sills, cross-members, pillars, and all suspension, steering, braking system and seat belt mountings and anchorages.) Any corrosion which has seriously reduced the thickness of a load-bearing area is likely to cause the vehicle to fail. In this case professional repairs are likely to be needed.

☐ Damage or corrosion which causes sharp or otherwise dangerous edges to be exposed will also cause the vehicle to fail.

4 Checks carried out on YOUR VEHICLE'S EXHAUST EMISSION SYSTEM

Petrol models

☐ The engine should be warmed up, and running well (ignition system in good order, air filter element clean, etc).

☐ Before testing, run the engine at around 2500 rpm for 20 seconds. Let the engine drop to idle, and watch for smoke from the exhaust. If the idle speed is too high, or if dense blue or black smoke emerges for more than 5 seconds, the vehicle will fail. Typically, blue smoke signifies oil burning (engine wear); black smoke means unburnt fuel (dirty air cleaner element, or other fuel system fault).

☐ An exhaust gas analyser for measuring carbon monoxide (CO) and hydrocarbons (HC) is now needed. If one cannot be hired or borrowed, have a local garage perform the check.

CO emissions (mixture)

☐ The MOT tester has access to the CO limits for all vehicles. The CO level is measured at idle speed, and at 'fast idle' (2500 to 3000 rpm). The following limits are given as a general guide:

At idle speed – Less than 0.5% CO
At 'fast idle' – Less than 0.3% CO
Lambda reading – 0.97 to 1.03

☐ If the CO level is too high, this may point to poor maintenance, a fuel injection system problem, faulty lambda (oxygen) sensor or catalytic converter. Try an injector cleaning treatment, and check the vehicle's ECU for fault codes.

HC emissions

☐ The MOT tester has access to HC limits for all vehicles. The HC level is measured at 'fast idle' (2500 to 3000 rpm). The following limits are given as a general guide:

At 'fast idle' – Less then 200 ppm

☐ Excessive HC emissions are typically caused by oil being burnt (worn engine), or by a blocked crankcase ventilation system ('breather'). If the engine oil is old and thin, an oil change may help. If the engine is running badly, check the vehicle's ECU for fault codes.

Diesel models

☐ The only emission test for diesel engines is measuring exhaust smoke density, using a calibrated smoke meter. The test involves accelerating the engine at least 3 times to its maximum unloaded speed.

Note: *On engines with a timing belt, it is VITAL that the belt is in good condition before the test is carried out.*

☐ With the engine warmed up, it is first purged by running at around 2500 rpm for 20 seconds. A governor check is then carried out, by slowly accelerating the engine to its maximum speed. After this, the smoke meter is connected, and the engine is accelerated quickly to maximum speed three times. If the smoke density is less than the limits given below, the vehicle will pass:

Non-turbo vehicles: 2.5m-1
Turbocharged vehicles: 3.0m-1

☐ If excess smoke is produced, try fitting a new air cleaner element, or using an injector cleaning treatment. If the engine is running badly, where applicable, check the vehicle's ECU for fault codes. Also check the vehicle's EGR system, where applicable. At high mileages, the injectors may require professional attention.

Engine

- ☐ Engine fails to rotate when attempting to start
- ☐ Engine rotates, but will not start
- ☐ Engine difficult to start when cold
- ☐ Engine difficult to start when hot
- ☐ Starter motor noisy or excessively-rough in engagement
- ☐ Engine starts, but stops immediately
- ☐ Engine misfires, or idles unevenly
- ☐ Engine stalls or lacks power
- ☐ Engine backfires
- ☐ Engine noises
- ☐ Oil consumption excessive
- ☐ Oil pressure warning light illuminated with engine running

Cooling system

- ☐ Overheating
- ☐ Overcooling
- ☐ External coolant leakage
- ☐ Internal coolant leakage
- ☐ Corrosion

Fuel and exhaust systems

- ☐ Excessive fuel consumption
- ☐ Fuel leakage and/or fuel odour
- ☐ Black smoke in exhaust
- ☐ Blue or white smoke in exhaust
- ☐ Excessive noise or fumes from exhaust system

Clutch

- ☐ Pedal travels to floor – no pressure or very little resistance
- ☐ Clutch fails to disengage (unable to select gears)
- ☐ Clutch slips (engine speed increases, with no increase in vehicle speed)
- ☐ Judder as clutch is engaged
- ☐ Noise when depressing or releasing clutch pedal

Manual transmission

- ☐ Noisy in neutral with engine running
- ☐ Noisy in one particular gear
- ☐ Difficulty engaging gears
- ☐ Jumps out of gear
- ☐ Vibration
- ☐ Lubricant leaks

Automatic transmission

- ☐ Fluid leakage
- ☐ Transmission fluid brown, or has burned smell
- ☐ General gear selection problems
- ☐ Transmission will not downshift (kickdown) with accelerator fully depressed
- ☐ Engine will not start in any gear, or starts in gears other than Park or Neutral
- ☐ Transmission slips, shifts roughly, is noisy, or has no drive in forward or reverse gears

Driveshafts

- ☐ Clicking or knocking noise on turns (at slow speed on full-lock)
- ☐ Vibration when accelerating or decelerating

Braking system

- ☐ Vehicle pulls to one side under braking
- ☐ Noise (grinding or high-pitched squeal) when brakes applied
- ☐ Excessive brake pedal travel
- ☐ Brake pedal feels spongy when depressed
- ☐ Excessive brake pedal effort required to stop vehicle
- ☐ Judder felt through brake pedal or steering wheel when braking
- ☐ Brakes binding
- ☐ Rear wheels locking under normal braking

Suspension and steering systems

- ☐ Vehicle pulls to one side
- ☐ Wheel wobble and vibration
- ☐ Excessive pitching and/or rolling around corners, or during braking
- ☐ Wandering or general instability
- ☐ Excessively-stiff steering
- ☐ Excessive play in steering
- ☐ Lack of power assistance
- ☐ Tyre wear excessive

Electrical system

- ☐ Battery will not hold a charge for more than a few days
- ☐ Ignition/no-charge warning light remains illuminated with engine running
- ☐ Ignition/no-charge warning light fails to come on
- ☐ Lights inoperative
- ☐ Instrument readings inaccurate or erratic
- ☐ Horn inoperative, or unsatisfactory in operation
- ☐ Windscreen/tailgate wipers inoperative, or unsatisfactory in operation
- ☐ Windscreen/tailgate washers inoperative, or unsatisfactory in operation
- ☐ Electric windows inoperative, or unsatisfactory in operation
- ☐ Central locking system inoperative, or unsatisfactory in operation

Introduction

The vehicle owner who does his or her own maintenance according to the recommended service schedules should not have to use this section of the manual very often. Modern component reliability is such that, provided those items subject to wear or deterioration are inspected or renewed at the specified intervals, sudden failure is comparatively rare. Faults do not usually just happen as a result of sudden failure, but develop over a period of time. Major mechanical failures in particular are usually preceded by characteristic symptoms over hundreds or even thousands of miles. Those components which do occasionally fail without warning are often small and easily carried in the vehicle.

With any fault-finding, the first step is to decide where to begin investigations. Sometimes this is obvious, but on other occasions, a little detective work will be necessary. The owner who makes half a dozen haphazard adjustments or replacements may be successful in curing a fault (or its symptoms), but will be none the wiser if the fault recurs, and ultimately may have spent more time and money than was necessary. A calm and logical approach will be found to be more satisfactory in the long run. Always take into account any warning signs or abnormalities that may have been noticed in the period preceding the fault – power loss, high or low gauge readings, unusual smells, etc – and remember that failure of components such as fuses or spark plugs may only be pointers to some underlying fault.

The pages which follow provide an easy-reference guide to the more common problems which may occur during the operation of the vehicle. These problems and their possible causes are grouped under headings denoting various components or systems, such as Engine, Cooling system, etc. The general Chapter which deals with the problem is also shown in brackets; refer to the relevant part of that Chapter for system-specific information. Whatever the fault, certain basic principles apply. These are as follows:

Verify the fault. This is simply a matter of being sure that you know what the symptoms are before starting work. This is particularly important if you are investigating a fault for someone else, who may not have described it very accurately.

Don't overlook the obvious. For example, if the vehicle won't start, is there petrol in the tank? (Don't take anyone else's word on this particular point, and don't trust the fuel gauge either!) If an electrical fault is indicated, look for loose or broken wires before digging out the test gear.

Cure the disease, not the symptom. Substituting a flat battery with a fully-charged one will get you off the hard shoulder, but if the underlying cause is not attended to, the new battery will go the same way. Similarly, changing oil-fouled spark plugs for a new set will get you moving again, but remember that the reason for the fouling (if it wasn't simply an incorrect grade of plug) will have to be established and corrected.

Don't take anything for granted. Particularly, don't forget that a 'new' component may itself be defective (especially if it's been rattling around in the boot for months), and don't leave components out of a fault diagnosis sequence just because they are new or recently-fitted. When you do finally diagnose a difficult fault, you'll probably realise that all the evidence was there from the start.

Engine

Engine fails to rotate when attempting to start

- ☐ Battery terminal connections loose or corroded (*Weekly Checks*).
- ☐ Battery discharged or faulty (Chapter 5).
- ☐ Broken, loose or disconnected wiring in the starting circuit (Chapter 5).
- ☐ Defective starter solenoid or switch (Chapter 5).
- ☐ Defective starter motor (Chapter 5).
- ☐ Starter pinion or flywheel ring gear teeth loose or broken (Chapters 2 and 5).
- ☐ Engine earth strap broken or disconnected (Chapter 5).
- ☐ Automatic transmission not in Park/Neutral position, or multi-function switch faulty or incorrectly adjusted (Chapter 7).

Engine rotates, but will not start

- ☐ Fuel tank empty.
- ☐ Battery discharged (engine rotates slowly) (Chapter 5).
- ☐ Battery terminal connections loose or corroded (*Weekly Checks*).
- ☐ Ignition components damp or damaged (Chapters 1 and 5).
- ☐ Broken, loose or disconnected wiring in the ignition circuit (Chapters 1 and 5).
- ☐ Worn, faulty or incorrectly-gapped spark plugs (Chapter 1).
- ☐ Fuel injection system fault (Chapter 4).
- ☐ Major mechanical failure (eg camshaft drive) (Chapter 2).

Engine difficult to start when cold

- ☐ Battery discharged (Chapter 5).
- ☐ Battery terminal connections loose or corroded (*Weekly Checks*).
- ☐ Worn, faulty or incorrectly-gapped spark plugs (Chapter 1).
- ☐ Fuel injection system fault (Chapter 4).
- ☐ Other ignition system fault (Chapters 1 and 5).
- ☐ Low cylinder compressions (Chapter 2).

Engine difficult to start when hot

- ☐ Air filter element dirty or clogged (Chapter 1).
- ☐ Fuel injection system fault (Chapter 4).
- ☐ Other ignition system fault (Chapters 1 and 5).
- ☐ Low cylinder compressions (Chapter 2).

Starter motor noisy or excessively-rough in engagement

- ☐ Starter pinion or flywheel ring gear teeth loose or broken (Chapter 2).
- ☐ Starter motor mounting bolts loose or missing (Chapter 5).
- ☐ Starter motor internal components worn or damaged (Chapter 5).

Engine starts, but stops immediately

- ☐ Loose or faulty electrical connections in the ignition circuit (Chapters 1 and 5).
- ☐ Vacuum leak at the throttle body/housing or inlet manifold (Chapter 4).
- ☐ Blocked injector/fuel injection system fault (Chapter 4).
- ☐ Fuel very low in tank.
- ☐ Restriction in fuel feed or return.
- ☐ Air in diesel fuel system (Chapter 4B).
- ☐ Air cleaner dirty or blockage in air intake system (Chapter 1A, 1B, 4A or 4B).
- ☐ Blockage in exhaust system (Chapter 4A or 4B).

Engine misfires, or idles unevenly

- ☐ Air filter element clogged (Chapter 1).
- ☐ Vacuum leak at the throttle body/housing, inlet manifold or associated hoses (Chapter 4).
- ☐ Worn, faulty or incorrectly-gapped spark plugs (Chapter 1).
- ☐ Uneven or low cylinder compressions (Chapter 2).
- ☐ Camshaft lobes worn (Chapter 2).
- ☐ Timing belt incorrectly fitted (Chapter 2).
- ☐ Blocked injector/fuel injection system fault (Chapter 4).
- ☐ Vacuum leak at the throttle body/housing, inlet manifold or associated hoses (Chapter 4).
- ☐ Blocked injector/fuel injection system fault (Chapter 4).
- ☐ Disconnected, leaking, or perished crankcase ventilation hoses (Chapter 4).
- ☐ Overheating (Chapter 3).

Engine stalls or lacks power

- ☐ Vacuum leak at the throttle body/housing, inlet manifold or associated hoses (Chapter 4).
- ☐ Fuel filter choked (Chapter 1).
- ☐ Fuel pump faulty, or delivery pressure low (Chapter 4).
- ☐ Fuel tank vent blocked, or fuel pipes restricted (Chapter 4).
- ☐ Blocked injector/fuel injection system fault (Chapter 4).
- ☐ Blocked catalytic converter (Chapter 4A or 4B).
- ☐ Engine overheating (Chapter 3).
- ☐ Timing belt incorrectly fitted (Chapter 2).
- ☐ Throttle position sensor fault (Chapter 4A or 4B).
- ☐ Engine warning light on (fault code in system) (Chapter 4A or 4B).
- ☐ Uneven or low cylinder compressions (Chapter 2).
- ☐ Worn, faulty or incorrectly-gapped spark plugs (Chapter 1).
- ☐ Brakes binding (Chapters 1 and 9).
- ☐ Clutch slipping – manual transmission models (Chapter 6).

Engine (continued)

Engine backfires

- ☐ Timing belt incorrectly fitted (Chapter 2).
- ☐ Vacuum leak at the throttle body/housing, inlet manifold or associated hoses (Chapter 4).
- ☐ Blocked injector/fuel injection system fault (Chapter 4).
- ☐ Ignition coil faulty – petrol models (Chapter 5B).

Engine noises

Pre-ignition (pinking) or knocking during acceleration or under load

- ☐ Ignition system fault (Chapters 1 and 5).
- ☐ Incorrect grade of spark plug (Chapter 1).
- ☐ Incorrect grade of fuel (Chapter 1).
- ☐ Vacuum leak at the throttle body/housing, inlet manifold or associated hoses (Chapter 4).
- ☐ Excessive carbon build-up in engine (Chapter 2).
- ☐ Blocked injector/fuel injection system fault (Chapter 4).

Whistling or wheezing noises

- ☐ Leaking inlet manifold or throttle body/housing gasket (Chapter 4).
- ☐ Leaking exhaust manifold gasket or pipe-to-manifold joint (Chapter 4).
- ☐ Leaking vacuum hose (Chapter 4).
- ☐ Blowing cylinder head gasket (Chapter 2).

Tapping or rattling noises

- ☐ Worn valve gear or camshaft (Chapter 2).
- ☐ Ancillary component fault (coolant pump, alternator, etc) (Chapters 3, 5, etc).
- ☐ Air in diesel fuel system (Chapter 4B).

Knocking or thumping noises

- ☐ Worn big-end bearings (regular heavy knocking, perhaps less under load) (Chapter 2).
- ☐ Worn main bearings (rumbling and knocking, perhaps worsening under load) (Chapter 2).
- ☐ Piston slap (most noticeable when cold) (Chapter 2).
- ☐ Ancillary component fault (coolant pump, alternator, etc) (Chapters 3, 5, etc).
- ☐ Engine mountings worn or defective (Chapter 2A, 2B or 2C).
- ☐ Front suspension or steering components worn (Chapter 10).

Oil consumption excessive

- ☐ External leakage (standing or running) – eg sump gasket, crankshaft oil seals (Chapter 2A, 2B or 2C).
- ☐ New engine not yet run-in.
- ☐ Engine oil incorrect grade/poor quality, or oil level too high (*Weekly Checks*).
- ☐ Crankcase ventilation system obstructed (Chapter 1 or 4C).
- ☐ Burning oil due to general engine wear – pistons and/or bores, valve stem oil seals, etc (Chapter 2D).

Oil pressure warning light illuminated with engine running

- ☐ Low oil level, or incorrect oil grade (*Weekly Checks*).
- ☐ Faulty oil pressure sensor (Chapter 5).
- ☐ Worn engine bearings and/or oil pump (Chapter 2).
- ☐ High engine operating temperature (Chapter 3).
- ☐ Oil pressure relief valve defective (Chapter 2).
- ☐ Oil pick-up strainer clogged (Chapter 2).

Cooling system

Overheating

- ☐ Insufficient coolant in system (*Weekly Checks*).
- ☐ Thermostat faulty (Chapter 3).
- ☐ Radiator core blocked, or grille restricted (Chapter 3).
- ☐ Radiator electric cooling fan(s) or coolant temperature sensor faulty (Chapter 3).
- ☐ Pressure cap faulty (Chapter 3).
- ☐ Ignition system fault (Chapters 1 and 5).
- ☐ Inaccurate temperature gauge sender unit (Chapter 3).
- ☐ Airlock in cooling system (Chapter 1).
- ☐ Engine management system fault (Chapter 4A or 4B).
- ☐ Blockage in exhaust system (Chapter 4A or 4B).
- ☐ Cylinder head gasket blown (Chapter 2A, 2B or 2C).

Overcooling

- ☐ Thermostat faulty (Chapter 3).
- ☐ Inaccurate temperature gauge sender unit (Chapter 3).

External coolant leakage

- ☐ Deteriorated or damaged hoses or hose clips (Chapter 1).
- ☐ Radiator core or heater matrix leaking (Chapter 3).
- ☐ Pressure cap faulty (Chapter 3).
- ☐ Coolant pump seal leaking (Chapter 3).
- ☐ Boiling due to overheating (Chapter 3).
- ☐ Cylinder block core plug leaking (Chapter 2).

Internal coolant leakage

- ☐ Leaking cylinder head gasket (Chapter 2).
- ☐ Cracked cylinder head or cylinder bore (Chapter 2).

Corrosion

- ☐ Infrequent draining and flushing (Chapter 1).
- ☐ Incorrect coolant mixture or inappropriate coolant type (Chapter 1).

Fuel and exhaust systems

Excessive fuel consumption

- ☐ Air filter element dirty or clogged (Chapter 1).
- ☐ Fuel injection system fault (Chapter 4).
- ☐ Ignition system fault (Chapters 1 and 5).
- ☐ Tyres under-inflated (*Weekly Checks*).
- ☐ Brakes binding (Chapter 1 or 9).
- ☐ Fuel leak, causing apparent high consumption (Chapter 1A, 1B, 4A or 4B).
- ☐ Valve timing incorrect, possibly through a poorly-fitted timing belt (Chapter 2A, 2B or 2C).

Fuel leakage and/or fuel odour

- ☐ Damaged or corroded fuel tank, pipes or connections (Chapter 4).
- ☐ Evaporative emissions system fault – petrol models (Chapter 4C).

Black smoke in exhaust

- ☐ Air cleaner element dirty, or blockage in air intake system (Chapter 1A, 1B, 4A or 4B).
- ☐ Turbo boost pressure inadequate – diesel models (Chapter 4B).
- ☐ Exhaust gas recirculation system fault – diesel models (Chapter 4C).
- ☐ Fuel system fault (Chapter 4A or 4B).

Blue or white smoke in exhaust

- ☐ Engine oil incorrect grade or poor quality, or fuel passing into sump (worn piston rings/bores).
- ☐ Diesel glow plug(s) defective (white smoke at start-up only) (Chapter 5C).
- ☐ Air cleaner element dirty, or blockage in air intake system (Chapter 1A, 1B, 4A or 4B).
- ☐ Injector(s) faulty (Chapter 4A or 4B).
- ☐ Blocked or damaged emissions system hoses or components (Chapter 4C).
- ☐ General engine wear – pistons and/or bores, valve stem oil seals, etc (Chapter 2D).

Excessive noise or fumes from exhaust system

- ☐ Leaking exhaust system or manifold joints (Chapters 1 and 4).
- ☐ Leaking, corroded or damaged silencers or pipe (Chapters 1 and 4).
- ☐ Exhaust gas recirculation system fault – diesel models (Chapter 4C).
- ☐ Oxygen sensors loose or damaged – petrol models (Chapter 4C).
- ☐ Broken mountings causing body or suspension contact (Chapter 1).

Clutch

Pedal travels to floor – no pressure or very little resistance

- ☐ Air in hydraulic system/faulty master or slave cylinder (Chapter 6).
- ☐ Faulty hydraulic release system (Chapter 6).
- ☐ Broken clutch release bearing or fork (Chapter 6).
- ☐ Broken diaphragm spring in clutch pressure plate (Chapter 6).

Clutch fails to disengage (unable to select gears).

- ☐ Air in hydraulic system/faulty master or slave cylinder (Chapter 6).
- ☐ Faulty hydraulic release system (Chapter 6).
- ☐ Clutch plate sticking on gearbox input shaft splines (Chapter 6).
- ☐ Clutch plate sticking to flywheel or pressure plate (Chapter 6).
- ☐ Faulty pressure plate assembly (Chapter 6).
- ☐ Clutch release mechanism worn or incorrectly assembled (Chapter 6).

Clutch slips (engine speed increases, with no increase in vehicle speed).

- ☐ Faulty hydraulic release system (Chapter 6).
- ☐ Clutch plate linings excessively worn (Chapter 6).
- ☐ Clutch plate linings contaminated with oil or grease (Chapter 6).
- ☐ Faulty pressure plate or weak diaphragm spring (Chapter 6).

Judder as clutch is engaged

- ☐ Clutch plate linings contaminated with oil or grease (Chapter 6).
- ☐ Clutch plate linings excessively worn (Chapter 6).
- ☐ Faulty or distorted pressure plate or diaphragm spring (Chapter 6).
- ☐ Worn or loose engine or gearbox mountings (Chapter 2).
- ☐ Clutch plate hub or gearbox input shaft splines worn (Chapter 6).

Noise when depressing or releasing clutch pedal

- ☐ Worn clutch release bearing (Chapter 6).
- ☐ Worn or dry clutch pedal bushes (Chapter 6).
- ☐ Faulty pressure plate assembly (Chapter 6).
- ☐ Pressure plate diaphragm spring broken (Chapter 6).
- ☐ Broken clutch plate cushioning springs (Chapter 6).

Manual transmission

Noisy in neutral with engine running

- ☐ Lack of oil (Chapter 1A or 1B).
- ☐ Input shaft bearings worn (noise apparent with clutch pedal released, but not when depressed) (Chapter 7A).*
- ☐ Clutch release bearing worn (noise apparent with clutch pedal depressed, possibly less when released) (Chapter 6).

Noisy in one particular gear

- ☐ Worn, damaged or chipped gear teeth (Chapter 7A).*

Difficulty engaging gears

- ☐ Clutch fault (Chapter 6).
- ☐ Oil level low (Chapter 1).
- ☐ Worn or damaged gearchange linkage (Chapter 7A).
- ☐ Incorrectly-adjusted gearchange linkage (Chapter 7A).
- ☐ Worn synchroniser units (Chapter 7A).*

Jumps out of gear

- ☐ Worn or damaged gearchange linkage (Chapter 7A).
- ☐ Incorrectly-adjusted gearchange linkage (Chapter 7A).
- ☐ Worn synchroniser units (Chapter 7A).*
- ☐ Worn selector forks (Chapter 7A).*

Vibration

- ☐ Lack of oil (Chapter 1).
- ☐ Worn bearings (Chapter 7A).*

Lubricant leaks

- ☐ Leaking differential output oil seal (Chapter 7A).
- ☐ Leaking housing joint (Chapter 7A).*
- ☐ Leaking input shaft oil seal (Chapter 7A).*

**Although the corrective action necessary to remedy the symptoms described is beyond the scope of the home mechanic, the above information should be helpful in isolating the cause of the condition, so that the owner can communicate clearly with a professional mechanic.*

Automatic transmission

Note: *Due to the complexity of the automatic transmission, it is difficult for the home mechanic to properly diagnose and service this unit. For problems other than the following, the vehicle should be taken to a dealer service department or automatic transmission specialist. Do not be too hasty in removing the transmission if a fault is suspected, as most of the testing is carried out with the unit still fitted.*

Fluid leakage

- ☐ Automatic transmission fluid is usually dark in colour. Fluid leaks should not be confused with engine oil, which can easily be blown onto the transmission by airflow.
- ☐ To determine the source of a leak, first remove all built-up dirt and grime from the transmission housing and surrounding areas using a degreasing agent, or by steam-cleaning. Drive the vehicle at low speed, so airflow will not blow the leak far from its source. Raise and support the vehicle, and determine where the leak is coming from. The following are common areas of leakage:

a) Oil pan – where applicable (Chapter 1).
b) Dipstick tube – where applicable (Chapter 1).
c) Transmission-to-fluid cooler pipes/unions (Chapter 7B).

Transmission fluid brown, or has burned smell

- ☐ Transmission fluid level low, or fluid in need of renewal (Chapter 1).

General gear selection problems

- ☐ Chapter 7B deals with checking and adjusting the selector cable on automatic transmissions. The following are common problems, which may be caused by a poorly adjusted cable:

a) Engine starting in gears other than Park or Neutral.
b) Indicator panel indicating a gear other than the one actually being used.
c) Vehicle moves when in Park or Neutral.
d) Poor gearshift quality or erratic gearchanges

- ☐ Refer to Chapter 7B for the selector cable adjustment procedure.

Transmission will not downshift (kickdown) with accelerator pedal fully depressed

- ☐ Low transmission fluid level (Chapter 1).
- ☐ Incorrect selector cable adjustment (Chapter 7B).
- ☐ Incorrect kickdown cable adjustment (Chapter 7B).
- ☐ Electronic control system fault (Chapter 7B).

Engine will not start in any gear, or starts in gears other than Park or Neutral

- ☐ Incorrect selector cable adjustment (Chapter 7B).
- ☐ Incorrect multi-function switch adjustment (Chapter 7B).

Transmission slips, is noisy, or has no drive in forward or reverse gears

- ☐ There are many probable causes for the above problems, but the home mechanic should be concerned with only one possibility – fluid level. Before taking the vehicle to a dealer or transmission specialist, check the fluid level and condition of the fluid as described in Chapter 1. Correct the fluid level as necessary, or change the fluid and filter if needed. If the problem persists, professional help will be necessary.

Driveshafts

Clicking or knocking noise on turns (at slow speed on full-lock).

- ☐ Lack of constant velocity joint lubricant, possibly due to damaged gaiter (Chapter 8).
- ☐ Worn outer constant velocity joint (Chapter 8).
- ☐ Worn intermediate bearing (Chapter 8).
- ☐ Loose or damaged driveshaft nut (Chapter 1A, 1B or 8).

Vibration when accelerating or decelerating

- ☐ Lack of constant velocity joint lubricant, possibly due to damaged gaiter (Chapter 8).
- ☐ Worn inner constant velocity joint (Chapter 8).
- ☐ Worn intermediate bearing (Chapter 8).
- ☐ Bent or distorted driveshaft (Chapter 8).

Braking system

Note: *Before assuming that a brake problem exists, make sure that the tyres are in good condition and correctly inflated, that the front wheel alignment is correct, and that the vehicle is not loaded with weight in an unequal manner. Apart from checking the condition of all pipe and hose connections, any faults occurring on the anti-lock braking system should be referred to a Nissan dealer for diagnosis.*

Vehicle pulls to one side under braking

- ☐ Worn, defective, damaged or contaminated brake pads/shoes on one side (Chapters 1 and 9).
- ☐ Seized or partially-seized front brake caliper or rear wheel cylinder/caliper piston (Chapters 1 and 9).
- ☐ A mixture of brake pad/shoe lining materials fitted between sides (Chapters 1 and 9).
- ☐ Brake caliper or backplate mounting bolts loose (Chapter 9).
- ☐ Worn or damaged steering or suspension components (Chapters 1 and 10).

Noise (grinding or high-pitched squeal) when brakes applied

- ☐ Brake pad or shoe friction lining material worn down to metal backing (Chapters 1 and 9).
- ☐ Excessive corrosion of brake disc or drum. (May be apparent after the vehicle has been standing for some time (Chapters 1 and 9).
- ☐ Foreign object (stone chipping, etc) trapped between brake disc and shield (Chapters 1 and 9).

Excessive brake pedal travel

- ☐ Faulty master cylinder (Chapter 9).
- ☐ Air in hydraulic system (Chapter 9).
- ☐ Faulty vacuum servo unit (Chapters 1 and 9).

Brake pedal feels spongy when depressed

- ☐ Air in hydraulic system (Chapter 9).
- ☐ Deteriorated flexible rubber brake hoses (Chapters 1 and 9).
- ☐ Master cylinder mounting nuts loose (Chapter 9).
- ☐ Faulty master cylinder (Chapter 9).

Excessive brake pedal effort required to stop vehicle

- ☐ Faulty vacuum servo unit (Chapters 1 and 9).
- ☐ Disconnected, damaged or insecure brake servo vacuum hose (Chapter 9).
- ☐ Primary or secondary hydraulic circuit failure (Chapter 9).
- ☐ Brake vacuum pump leaking or faulty – diesel models (Chapter 9).
- ☐ Seized brake caliper or wheel cylinder piston(s) (Chapter 9).
- ☐ Brake pads or brake shoes incorrectly fitted (Chapter 9).
- ☐ Incorrect grade of brake pads or brake shoes fitted (Chapter 9).
- ☐ Brake pads or brake shoe linings contaminated (Chapter 9).

Judder felt through brake pedal or steering wheel when braking

- ☐ Excessive run-out or distortion of discs/drums (Chapter 9).
- ☐ Brake pad or brake shoe linings worn (Chapters 1 and 9).
- ☐ Brake caliper or brake backplate mounting bolts loose (Chapter 9).
- ☐ Wear in suspension or steering components or mountings (Chapters 1 and 10).

Brakes binding

- ☐ Seized brake caliper or wheel cylinder piston(s) (Chapter 9).
- ☐ Incorrectly-adjusted handbrake mechanism (Chapter 1).
- ☐ Faulty master cylinder (Chapter 9).

Rear wheels locking under normal braking

- ☐ Rear brake pad/shoe linings contaminated (Chapters 1 and 9).
- ☐ Faulty brake pressure regulator (Chapter 9).

Suspension and steering

Note: *Before diagnosing suspension or steering faults, be sure that the trouble is not due to incorrect tyre pressures, mixtures of tyre types, or binding brakes.*

Vehicle pulls to one side

- ☐ Defective tyre (*Weekly Checks*).
- ☐ Excessive wear in suspension or steering components (Chapters 1 and 10).
- ☐ Incorrect front/rear wheel alignment (Chapter 1).
- ☐ Accident damage to steering or suspension components (Chapter 1).

Wheel wobble and vibration

- ☐ Front roadwheels out of balance (vibration felt mainly through the steering wheel) (Chapters 1 and 10).
- ☐ Rear roadwheels out of balance (vibration felt throughout the vehicle) (Chapters 1 and 10).
- ☐ Roadwheels damaged or distorted (Chapters 1 and 10).
- ☐ Faulty or damaged tyre (*Weekly Checks*).
- ☐ Worn steering or suspension joints, bushes or components (Chapters 1 and 10).
- ☐ Wear in driveshaft joint, or loose driveshaft nut (vibration worst when under load) (Chapter 1A, 1B or 8).
- ☐ Wheel bolts loose (Chapters 1 and 10).

Excessive pitching and/or rolling around corners, or during braking

- ☐ Defective shock absorbers (Chapters 1 and 10).
- ☐ Broken or weak spring and/or suspension component (Chapters 1 and 10).
- ☐ Worn or damaged anti-roll bar or mountings (Chapter 10).

Wandering or general instability

- ☐ Incorrect front/rear wheel alignment (Chapter 1).
- ☐ Worn steering or suspension joints, bushes or components (Chapters 1 and 10).
- ☐ Roadwheels out of balance (Chapters 1 and 10).
- ☐ Faulty or damaged tyre (*Weekly Checks*).
- ☐ Wheel bolts loose (Chapters 1 and 10).
- ☐ Defective shock absorbers (Chapters 1 and 10).

Excessively-stiff steering

- ☐ Lack of steering gear lubricant (Chapter 10).
- ☐ Seized track rod end balljoint or suspension balljoint (Chapters 1 and 10).
- ☐ Broken or incorrectly-adjusted auxiliary drivebelt – power steering (Chapter 1).
- ☐ Incorrect front wheel alignment (Chapter 1).
- ☐ Steering rack or column bent or damaged (Chapter 10).

Excessive play in steering

- ☐ Worn steering track rod end balljoints (Chapters 1 and 10).
- ☐ Worn rack-and-pinion steering gear (Chapter 10).
- ☐ Worn steering or suspension joints, bushes or components (Chapters 1 and 10).

Lack of power assistance

- ☐ Broken or incorrectly-adjusted auxiliary drivebelt (Chapter 1).
- ☐ Incorrect power steering fluid level (*Weekly Checks*).
- ☐ Restriction in power steering fluid hoses (Chapter 1).
- ☐ Faulty power steering pump (Chapter 10).
- ☐ Faulty rack-and-pinion steering gear (Chapter 10).

Tyre wear excessive

Tyres worn on inside or outside edges

- ☐ Tyres under-inflated (wear on both edges) (*Weekly Checks*).
- ☐ Incorrect camber or castor angles (wear on one edge only) (Chapter 1).
- ☐ Worn steering or suspension joints, bushes or components (Chapters 1 and 10).
- ☐ Excessively-hard cornering.
- ☐ Accident damage.

Tyre treads exhibit feathered edges

- ☐ Incorrect toe setting (Chapter 1).

Tyres worn in centre of tread

- ☐ Tyres over-inflated (*Weekly Checks*).

Tyres worn on inside and outside edges

- ☐ Tyres under-inflated (*Weekly Checks*).

Tyres worn unevenly

- ☐ Tyres/wheels out of balance (Chapter 1).
- ☐ Excessive wheel or tyre run-out (Chapter 1).
- ☐ Worn shock absorbers (Chapters 1 and 10).
- ☐ Faulty tyre (*Weekly Checks*).

Electrical system

Note: *For problems associated with the starting system, refer to the faults listed under Engine earlier in this Section.*

Battery will not hold a charge for more than a few days

- ☐ Battery defective internally (Chapter 5).
- ☐ Battery electrolyte level low (Chapter 5A).
- ☐ Battery terminal connections loose or corroded (*Weekly Checks*).
- ☐ Auxiliary drivebelt worn or incorrectly adjusted (Chapter 1).
- ☐ Alternator not charging at correct output (Chapter 5).
- ☐ Alternator or voltage regulator faulty (Chapter 5).
- ☐ Short-circuit causing continual battery drain (Chapters 5 and 12).

Ignition/no-charge warning light remains illuminated with engine running

- ☐ Auxiliary drivebelt broken, worn, or incorrectly adjusted (Chapter 1).
- ☐ Alternator brushes worn, sticking, or dirty (Chapter 5).
- ☐ Alternator brush springs weak or broken (Chapter 5).
- ☐ Internal fault in alternator or voltage regulator (Chapter 5).
- ☐ Broken, disconnected, or loose wiring in charging circuit (Chapter 5).

Ignition/no-charge warning light fails to come on

- ☐ Warning light bulb blown (Chapter 12).
- ☐ Broken, disconnected, or loose wiring in warning light circuit (Chapter 12).
- ☐ Alternator faulty (Chapter 5).

Lights inoperative

- ☐ Bulb blown (Chapter 12).
- ☐ Corrosion of bulb or bulbholder contacts (Chapter 12).
- ☐ Blown fuse (Chapter 12).
- ☐ Faulty relay (Chapter 12).
- ☐ Broken, loose, or disconnected wiring (Chapter 12).
- ☐ Faulty switch (Chapter 12).
- ☐ Multi-timer unit fault (Chapter 12).

Instrument readings inaccurate or erratic

Gauges give no reading

- ☐ Faulty gauge sender unit (Chapters 3 and 4).
- ☐ Wiring open-circuit (Chapter 12).
- ☐ Faulty gauge (Chapter 12).

Gauges give continuous maximum reading

- ☐ Faulty gauge sender unit (Chapters 3 and 4).
- ☐ Wiring short-circuit (Chapter 12).
- ☐ Faulty gauge (Chapter 12).

Horn inoperative, or unsatisfactory in operation

Horn operates all the time

- ☐ Horn push either earthed or stuck down (Chapter 12).
- ☐ Horn cable-to-horn push earthed (Chapter 12).

Horn fails to operate

- ☐ Blown fuse (Chapter 12).
- ☐ Cable or cable connections loose, broken or disconnected (Chapter 12).
- ☐ Faulty horn (Chapter 12).

Horn emits intermittent or unsatisfactory sound

- ☐ Cable connections loose (Chapter 12).
- ☐ Horn mountings loose (Chapter 12).
- ☐ Faulty horn (Chapter 12).

Windscreen/tailgate wipers inoperative, or unsatisfactory in operation

Wipers fail to operate, or operate very slowly

- ☐ Wiper blades stuck to screen, or linkage seized or binding (Chapters 1 and 12).
- ☐ Blown fuse (Chapter 12).
- ☐ Cable or cable connections loose, broken or disconnected (Chapter 12).
- ☐ Faulty relay (Chapter 12).
- ☐ Faulty wiper motor (Chapter 12).

Wiper blades sweep over too large or too small an area of the glass

- ☐ Wiper arms incorrectly positioned on spindles (Chapter 1).
- ☐ Excessive wear of wiper linkage (Chapter 12).
- ☐ Wiper motor or linkage mountings loose or insecure (Chapter 12).

Wiper blades fail to clean the glass effectively

- ☐ Wiper blade rubbers worn or perished (*Weekly Checks*).
- ☐ Wiper arm tension springs broken, or arm pivots seized (Chapter 12).
- ☐ Insufficient windscreen washer additive to adequately remove road film (*Weekly Checks*).

Electrical system (continued)

Windscreen/tailgate washers inoperative, or unsatisfactory in operation

One or more washer jets inoperative

- ☐ Blocked washer jet (Chapter 1 or 12).
- ☐ Disconnected, kinked or restricted fluid hose (Chapter 12).
- ☐ Insufficient fluid in washer reservoir (*Weekly Checks*).

Washer pump fails to operate

- ☐ Broken or disconnected wiring or connections (Chapter 12).
- ☐ Blown fuse (Chapter 12).
- ☐ Faulty washer switch (Chapter 12).
- ☐ Faulty washer pump (Chapter 12).

Washer pump runs for some time before fluid is emitted from jets

- ☐ Faulty one-way valve in fluid supply hose (Chapter 12).

Electric windows inoperative, or unsatisfactory in operation

Window glass will only move in one direction

- ☐ Faulty switch (Chapter 12).

Window glass slow to move

- ☐ Incorrectly-adjusted door glass guide channels (Chapter 11).
- ☐ Regulator seized or damaged, or in need of lubrication (Chapter 11).
- ☐ Door internal components or trim fouling regulator (Chapter 11).
- ☐ Faulty motor (Chapter 11).

Window glass fails to move

- ☐ Incorrectly-adjusted door glass guide channels (Chapter 11).
- ☐ Blown fuse (Chapter 12).
- ☐ Faulty relay (Chapter 12).
- ☐ Broken or disconnected wiring or connections (Chapter 12).
- ☐ Faulty motor (Chapter 11).

Central locking system inoperative, or unsatisfactory in operation

Complete system failure

- ☐ Blown fuse (Chapter 12).
- ☐ Faulty relay (Chapter 12).
- ☐ Broken or disconnected wiring or connections (Chapter 12).
- ☐ Faulty control unit (Chapter 11).

Latch locks but will not unlock, or unlocks but will not lock

- ☐ Faulty master switch (Chapter 12).
- ☐ Broken or disconnected latch operating rods or levers (Chapter 11).
- ☐ Faulty relay (Chapter 12).
- ☐ Faulty control unit (Chapter 11).

One solenoid/motor fails to operate

- ☐ Broken or disconnected wiring or connections (Chapter 12).
- ☐ Faulty solenoid/motor (Chapter 11).
- ☐ Broken, binding or disconnected latch operating rods or levers (Chapter 11).
- ☐ Fault in door latch (Chapter 11).

A

ABS (Anti-lock brake system) A system, usually electronically controlled, that senses incipient wheel lockup during braking and relieves hydraulic pressure at wheels that are about to skid.
Air bag An inflatable bag hidden in the steering wheel (driver's side) or the dash or glovebox (passenger side). In a head-on collision, the bags inflate, preventing the driver and front passenger from being thrown forward into the steering wheel or windscreen.
Air cleaner A metal or plastic housing, containing a filter element, which removes dust and dirt from the air being drawn into the engine.
Air filter element The actual filter in an air cleaner system, usually manufactured from pleated paper and requiring renewal at regular intervals.

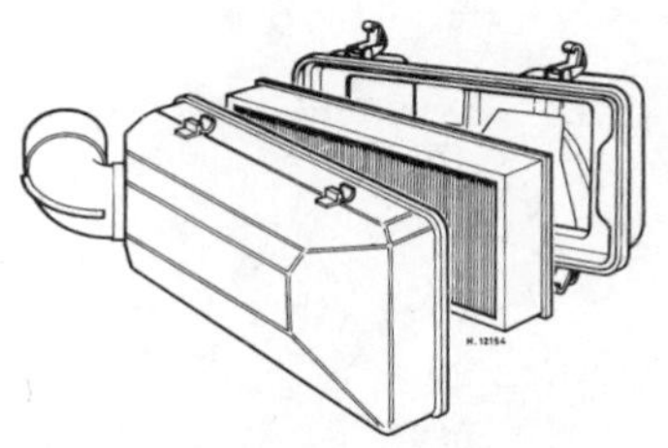

Air filter

Allen key A hexagonal wrench which fits into a recessed hexagonal hole.
Alligator clip A long-nosed spring-loaded metal clip with meshing teeth. Used to make temporary electrical connections.
Alternator A component in the electrical system which converts mechanical energy from a drivebelt into electrical energy to charge the battery and to operate the starting system, ignition system and electrical accessories.

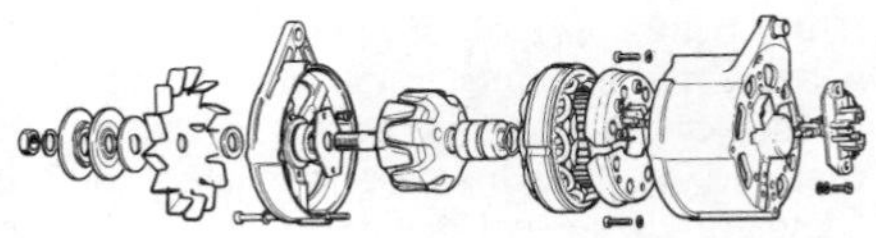

Alternator (exploded view)

Ampere (amp) A unit of measurement for the flow of electric current. One amp is the amount of current produced by one volt acting through a resistance of one ohm.
Anaerobic sealer A substance used to prevent bolts and screws from loosening. Anaerobic means that it does not require oxygen for activation. The Loctite brand is widely used.
Antifreeze A substance (usually ethylene glycol) mixed with water, and added to a vehicle's cooling system, to prevent freezing of the coolant in winter. Antifreeze also contains chemicals to inhibit corrosion and the formation of rust and other deposits that would tend to clog the radiator and coolant passages and reduce cooling efficiency.
Anti-seize compound A coating that reduces the risk of seizing on fasteners that are subjected to high temperatures, such as exhaust manifold bolts and nuts.

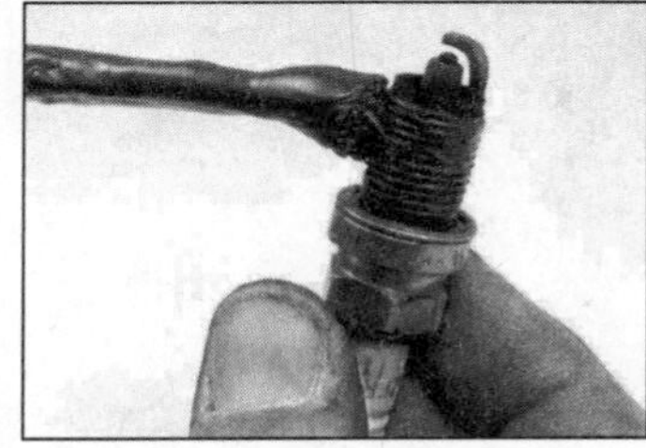

Anti-seize compound

Asbestos A natural fibrous mineral with great heat resistance, commonly used in the composition of brake friction materials. Asbestos is a health hazard and the dust created by brake systems should never be inhaled or ingested.
Axle A shaft on which a wheel revolves, or which revolves with a wheel. Also, a solid beam that connects the two wheels at one end of the vehicle. An axle which also transmits power to the wheels is known as a live axle.

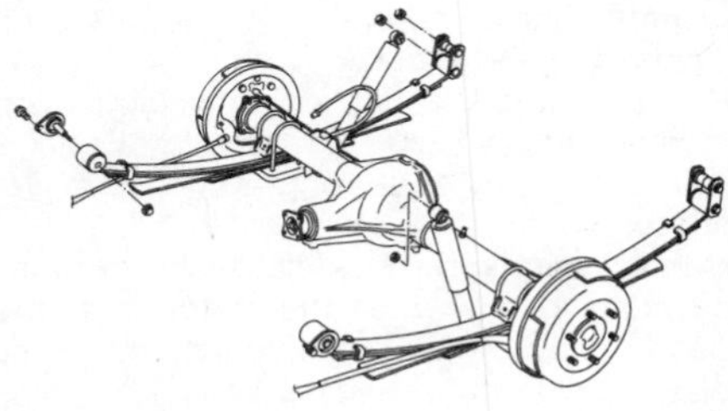

Axle assembly

Axleshaft A single rotating shaft, on either side of the differential, which delivers power from the final drive assembly to the drive wheels. Also called a driveshaft or a halfshaft.

B

Ball bearing An anti-friction bearing consisting of a hardened inner and outer race with hardened steel balls between two races.

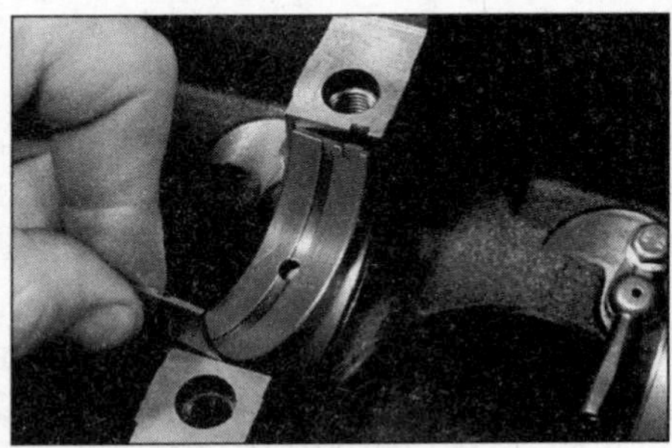

Bearing

Bearing The curved surface on a shaft or in a bore, or the part assembled into either, that permits relative motion between them with minimum wear and friction.
Big-end bearing The bearing in the end of the connecting rod that's attached to the crankshaft.
Bleed nipple A valve on a brake wheel cylinder, caliper or other hydraulic component that is opened to purge the hydraulic system of air. Also called a bleed screw.

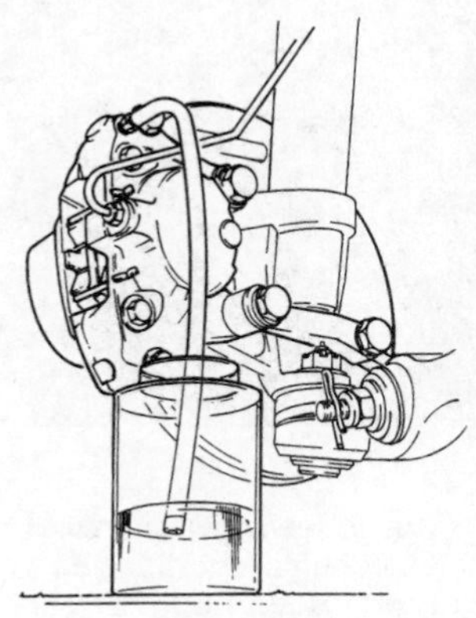

Brake bleeding

Brake bleeding Procedure for removing air from lines of a hydraulic brake system.
Brake disc The component of a disc brake that rotates with the wheels.
Brake drum The component of a drum brake that rotates with the wheels.
Brake linings The friction material which contacts the brake disc or drum to retard the vehicle's speed. The linings are bonded or riveted to the brake pads or shoes.
Brake pads The replaceable friction pads that pinch the brake disc when the brakes are applied. Brake pads consist of a friction material bonded or riveted to a rigid backing plate.
Brake shoe The crescent-shaped carrier to which the brake linings are mounted and which forces the lining against the rotating drum during braking.
Braking systems For more information on braking systems, consult the *Haynes Automotive Brake Manual*.
Breaker bar A long socket wrench handle providing greater leverage.
Bulkhead The insulated partition between the engine and the passenger compartment.

C

Caliper The non-rotating part of a disc-brake assembly that straddles the disc and carries the brake pads. The caliper also contains the hydraulic components that cause the pads to pinch the disc when the brakes are applied. A caliper is also a measuring tool that can be set to measure inside or outside dimensions of an object.

Camshaft A rotating shaft on which a series of cam lobes operate the valve mechanisms. The camshaft may be driven by gears, by sprockets and chain or by sprockets and a belt.

Canister A container in an evaporative emission control system; contains activated charcoal granules to trap vapours from the fuel system.

Canister

Carburettor A device which mixes fuel with air in the proper proportions to provide a desired power output from a spark ignition internal combustion engine.

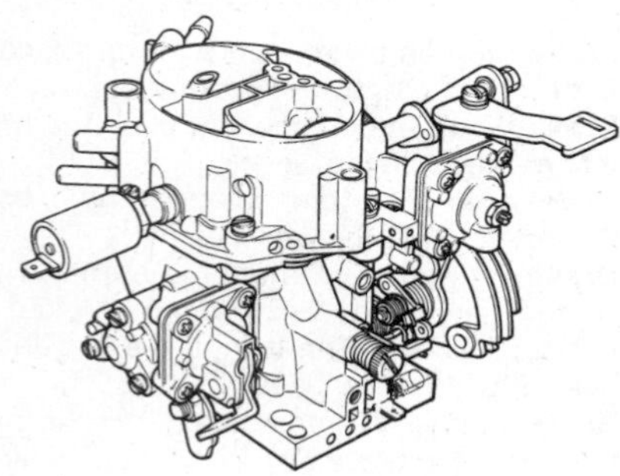

Carburettor

Castellated Resembling the parapets along the top of a castle wall. For example, a castellated balljoint stud nut.

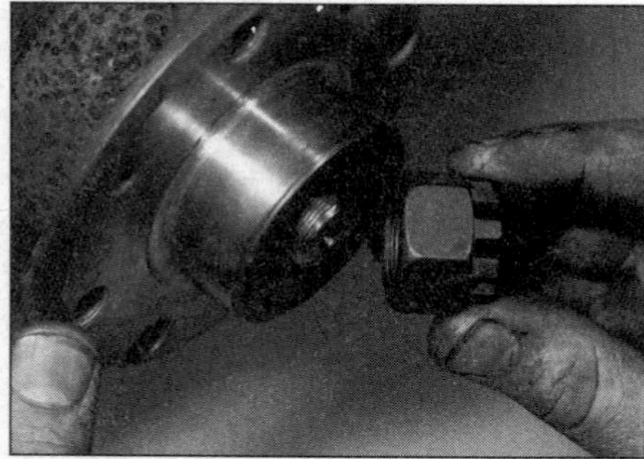

Castellated nut

Castor In wheel alignment, the backward or forward tilt of the steering axis. Castor is positive when the steering axis is inclined rearward at the top.

Catalytic converter A silencer-like device in the exhaust system which converts certain pollutants in the exhaust gases into less harmful substances.

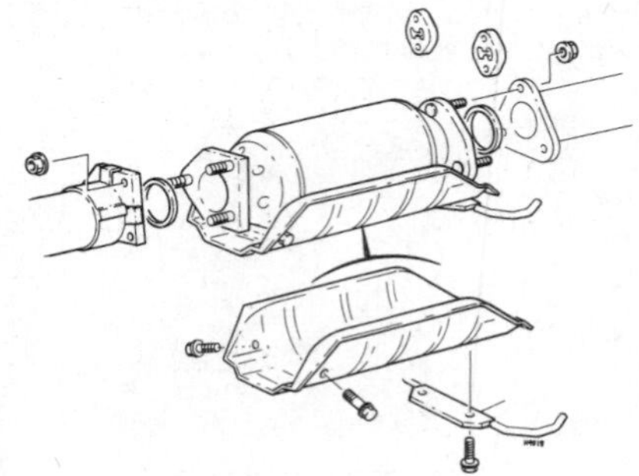

Catalytic converter

Circlip A ring-shaped clip used to prevent endwise movement of cylindrical parts and shafts. An internal circlip is installed in a groove in a housing; an external circlip fits into a groove on the outside of a cylindrical piece such as a shaft.

Clearance The amount of space between two parts. For example, between a piston and a cylinder, between a bearing and a journal, etc.

Coil spring A spiral of elastic steel found in various sizes throughout a vehicle, for example as a springing medium in the suspension and in the valve train.

Compression Reduction in volume, and increase in pressure and temperature, of a gas, caused by squeezing it into a smaller space.

Compression ratio The relationship between cylinder volume when the piston is at top dead centre and cylinder volume when the piston is at bottom dead centre.

Constant velocity (CV) joint A type of universal joint that cancels out vibrations caused by driving power being transmitted through an angle.

Core plug A disc or cup-shaped metal device inserted in a hole in a casting through which core was removed when the casting was formed. Also known as a freeze plug or expansion plug.

Crankcase The lower part of the engine block in which the crankshaft rotates.

Crankshaft The main rotating member, or shaft, running the length of the crankcase, with offset "throws" to which the connecting rods are attached.

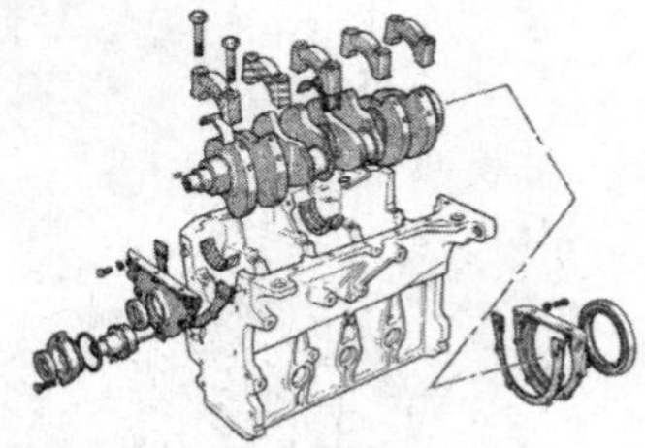

Crankshaft assembly

Crocodile clip See Alligator clip

D

Diagnostic code Code numbers obtained by accessing the diagnostic mode of an engine management computer. This code can be used to determine the area in the system where a malfunction may be located.

Disc brake A brake design incorporating a rotating disc onto which brake pads are squeezed. The resulting friction converts the energy of a moving vehicle into heat.

Double-overhead cam (DOHC) An engine that uses two overhead camshafts, usually one for the intake valves and one for the exhaust valves.

Drivebelt(s) The belt(s) used to drive accessories such as the alternator, water pump, power steering pump, air conditioning compressor, etc. off the crankshaft pulley.

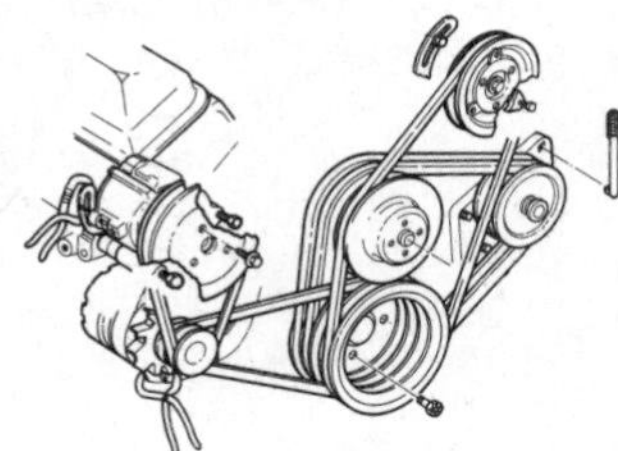

Accessory drivebelts

Driveshaft Any shaft used to transmit motion. Commonly used when referring to the axleshafts on a front wheel drive vehicle.

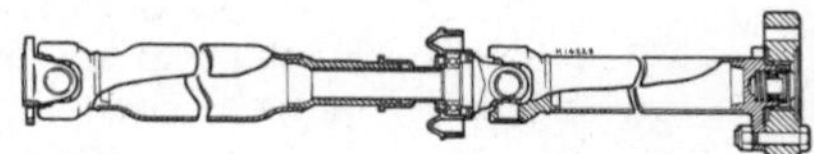

Driveshaft

Drum brake A type of brake using a drum-shaped metal cylinder attached to the inner surface of the wheel. When the brake pedal is pressed, curved brake shoes with friction linings press against the inside of the drum to slow or stop the vehicle.

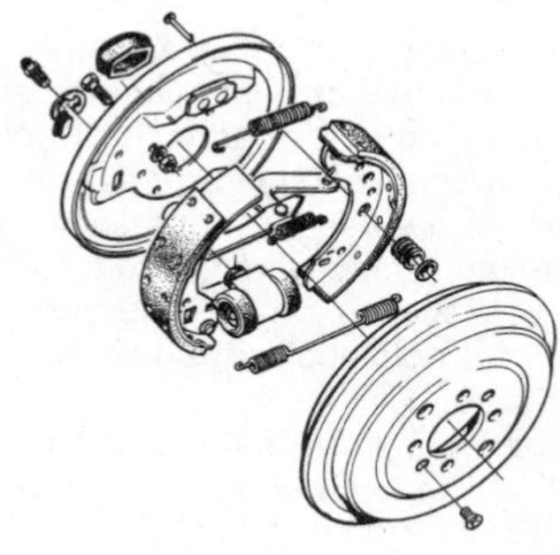

Drum brake assembly

E

EGR valve A valve used to introduce exhaust gases into the intake air stream.

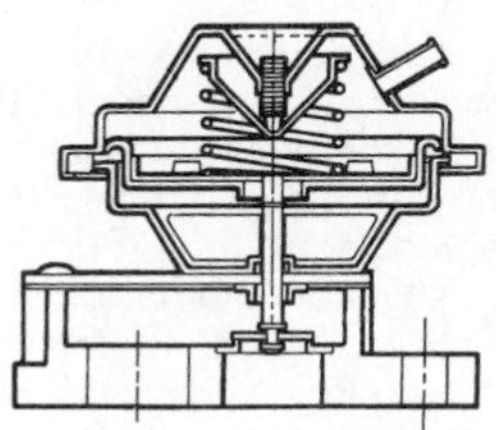

EGR valve

Electronic control unit (ECU) A computer which controls (for instance) ignition and fuel injection systems, or an anti-lock braking system. For more information refer to the *Haynes Automotive Electrical and Electronic Systems Manual.*

Electronic Fuel Injection (EFI) A computer controlled fuel system that distributes fuel through an injector located in each intake port of the engine.

Emergency brake A braking system, independent of the main hydraulic system, that can be used to slow or stop the vehicle if the primary brakes fail, or to hold the vehicle stationary even though the brake pedal isn't depressed. It usually consists of a hand lever that actuates either front or rear brakes mechanically through a series of cables and linkages. Also known as a handbrake or parking brake.

Endfloat The amount of lengthwise movement between two parts. As applied to a crankshaft, the distance that the crankshaft can move forward and back in the cylinder block.

Engine management system (EMS) A computer controlled system which manages the fuel injection and the ignition systems in an integrated fashion.

Exhaust manifold A part with several passages through which exhaust gases leave the engine combustion chambers and enter the exhaust pipe.

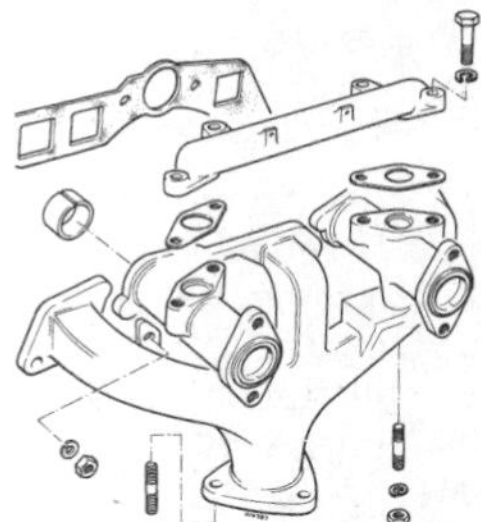

Exhaust manifold

F

Fan clutch A viscous (fluid) drive coupling device which permits variable engine fan speeds in relation to engine speeds.

Feeler blade A thin strip or blade of hardened steel, ground to an exact thickness, used to check or measure clearances between parts.

Feeler blade

Firing order The order in which the engine cylinders fire, or deliver their power strokes, beginning with the number one cylinder.

Flywheel A heavy spinning wheel in which energy is absorbed and stored by means of momentum. On cars, the flywheel is attached to the crankshaft to smooth out firing impulses.

Free play The amount of travel before any action takes place. The "looseness" in a linkage, or an assembly of parts, between the initial application of force and actual movement. For example, the distance the brake pedal moves before the pistons in the master cylinder are actuated.

Fuse An electrical device which protects a circuit against accidental overload. The typical fuse contains a soft piece of metal which is calibrated to melt at a predetermined current flow (expressed as amps) and break the circuit.

Fusible link A circuit protection device consisting of a conductor surrounded by heat-resistant insulation. The conductor is smaller than the wire it protects, so it acts as the weakest link in the circuit. Unlike a blown fuse, a failed fusible link must frequently be cut from the wire for replacement.

G

Gap The distance the spark must travel in jumping from the centre electrode to the side electrode in a spark plug. Also refers to the spacing between the points in a contact breaker assembly in a conventional points-type ignition, or to the distance between the reluctor or rotor and the pickup coil in an electronic ignition.

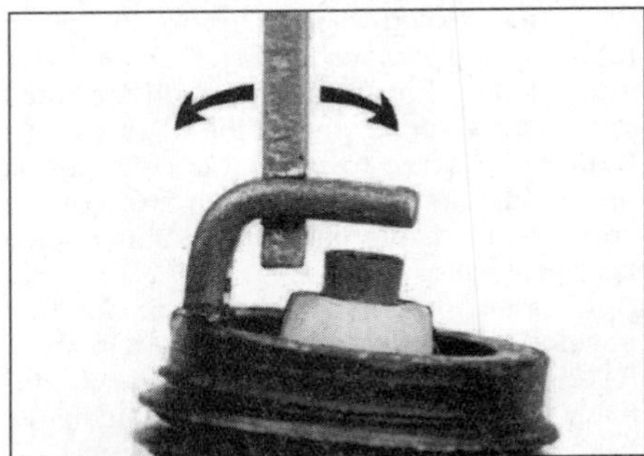

Adjusting spark plug gap

Gasket Any thin, soft material - usually cork, cardboard, asbestos or soft metal - installed between two metal surfaces to ensure a good seal. For instance, the cylinder head gasket seals the joint between the block and the cylinder head.

Gasket

Gauge An instrument panel display used to monitor engine conditions. A gauge with a movable pointer on a dial or a fixed scale is an analogue gauge. A gauge with a numerical readout is called a digital gauge.

H

Halfshaft A rotating shaft that transmits power from the final drive unit to a drive wheel, usually when referring to a live rear axle.

Harmonic balancer A device designed to reduce torsion or twisting vibration in the crankshaft. May be incorporated in the crankshaft pulley. Also known as a vibration damper.

Hone An abrasive tool for correcting small irregularities or differences in diameter in an engine cylinder, brake cylinder, etc.

Hydraulic tappet A tappet that utilises hydraulic pressure from the engine's lubrication system to maintain zero clearance (constant contact with both camshaft and valve stem). Automatically adjusts to variation in valve stem length. Hydraulic tappets also reduce valve noise.

I

Ignition timing The moment at which the spark plug fires, usually expressed in the number of crankshaft degrees before the piston reaches the top of its stroke.

Inlet manifold A tube or housing with passages through which flows the air-fuel mixture (carburettor vehicles and vehicles with throttle body injection) or air only (port fuel-injected vehicles) to the port openings in the cylinder head.

J

Jump start Starting the engine of a vehicle with a discharged or weak battery by attaching jump leads from the weak battery to a charged or helper battery.

L

Load Sensing Proportioning Valve (LSPV) A brake hydraulic system control valve that works like a proportioning valve, but also takes into consideration the amount of weight carried by the rear axle.

Locknut A nut used to lock an adjustment nut, or other threaded component, in place. For example, a locknut is employed to keep the adjusting nut on the rocker arm in position.

Lockwasher A form of washer designed to prevent an attaching nut from working loose.

M

MacPherson strut A type of front suspension system devised by Earle MacPherson at Ford of England. In its original form, a simple lateral link with the anti-roll bar creates the lower control arm. A long strut - an integral coil spring and shock absorber - is mounted between the body and the steering knuckle. Many modern so-called MacPherson strut systems use a conventional lower A-arm and don't rely on the anti-roll bar for location.

Multimeter An electrical test instrument with the capability to measure voltage, current and resistance.

N

NOx Oxides of Nitrogen. A common toxic pollutant emitted by petrol and diesel engines at higher temperatures.

O

Ohm The unit of electrical resistance. One volt applied to a resistance of one ohm will produce a current of one amp.

Ohmmeter An instrument for measuring electrical resistance.

O-ring A type of sealing ring made of a special rubber-like material; in use, the O-ring is compressed into a groove to provide the sealing action.

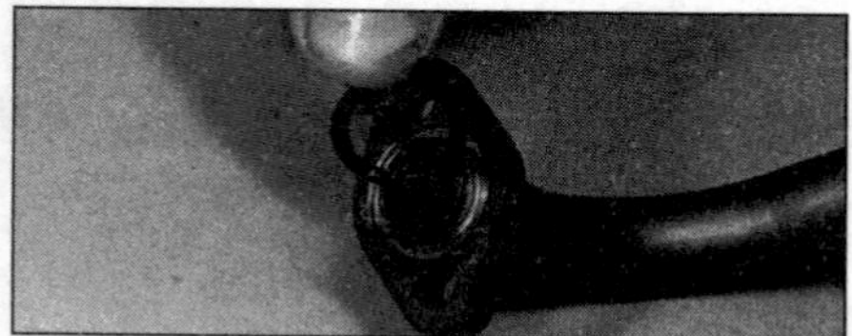

O-ring

Overhead cam (ohc) engine An engine with the camshaft(s) located on top of the cylinder head(s).

Overhead valve (ohv) engine An engine with the valves located in the cylinder head, but with the camshaft located in the engine block.

Oxygen sensor A device installed in the engine exhaust manifold, which senses the oxygen content in the exhaust and converts this information into an electric current. Also called a Lambda sensor.

P

Phillips screw A type of screw head having a cross instead of a slot for a corresponding type of screwdriver.

Plastigage A thin strip of plastic thread, available in different sizes, used for measuring clearances. For example, a strip of Plastigage is laid across a bearing journal. The parts are assembled and dismantled; the width of the crushed strip indicates the clearance between journal and bearing.

Plastigage

Propeller shaft The long hollow tube with universal joints at both ends that carries power from the transmission to the differential on front-engined rear wheel drive vehicles.

Proportioning valve A hydraulic control valve which limits the amount of pressure to the rear brakes during panic stops to prevent wheel lock-up.

R

Rack-and-pinion steering A steering system with a pinion gear on the end of the steering shaft that mates with a rack (think of a geared wheel opened up and laid flat). When the steering wheel is turned, the pinion turns, moving the rack to the left or right. This movement is transmitted through the track rods to the steering arms at the wheels.

Radiator A liquid-to-air heat transfer device designed to reduce the temperature of the coolant in an internal combustion engine cooling system.

Refrigerant Any substance used as a heat transfer agent in an air-conditioning system. R-12 has been the principle refrigerant for many years; recently, however, manufacturers have begun using R-134a, a non-CFC substance that is considered less harmful to the ozone in the upper atmosphere.

Rocker arm A lever arm that rocks on a shaft or pivots on a stud. In an overhead valve engine, the rocker arm converts the upward movement of the pushrod into a downward movement to open a valve.

Rotor In a distributor, the rotating device inside the cap that connects the centre electrode and the outer terminals as it turns, distributing the high voltage from the coil secondary winding to the proper spark plug. Also, that part of an alternator which rotates inside the stator. Also, the rotating assembly of a turbocharger, including the compressor wheel, shaft and turbine wheel.

Runout The amount of wobble (in-and-out movement) of a gear or wheel as it's rotated. The amount a shaft rotates "out-of-true." The out-of-round condition of a rotating part.

S

Sealant A liquid or paste used to prevent leakage at a joint. Sometimes used in conjunction with a gasket.

Sealed beam lamp An older headlight design which integrates the reflector, lens and filaments into a hermetically-sealed one-piece unit. When a filament burns out or the lens cracks, the entire unit is simply replaced.

Serpentine drivebelt A single, long, wide accessory drivebelt that's used on some newer vehicles to drive all the accessories, instead of a series of smaller, shorter belts. Serpentine drivebelts are usually tensioned by an automatic tensioner.

Serpentine drivebelt

Shim Thin spacer, commonly used to adjust the clearance or relative positions between two parts. For example, shims inserted into or under bucket tappets control valve clearances. Clearance is adjusted by changing the thickness of the shim.

Slide hammer A special puller that screws into or hooks onto a component such as a shaft or bearing; a heavy sliding handle on the shaft bottoms against the end of the shaft to knock the component free.

Sprocket A tooth or projection on the periphery of a wheel, shaped to engage with a chain or drivebelt. Commonly used to refer to the sprocket wheel itself.

Starter inhibitor switch On vehicles with an automatic transmission, a switch that prevents starting if the vehicle is not in Neutral or Park.
Strut See MacPherson strut.

T

Tappet A cylindrical component which transmits motion from the cam to the valve stem, either directly or via a pushrod and rocker arm. Also called a cam follower.
Thermostat A heat-controlled valve that regulates the flow of coolant between the cylinder block and the radiator, so maintaining optimum engine operating temperature. A thermostat is also used in some air cleaners in which the temperature is regulated.
Thrust bearing The bearing in the clutch assembly that is moved in to the release levers by clutch pedal action to disengage the clutch. Also referred to as a release bearing.
Timing belt A toothed belt which drives the camshaft. Serious engine damage may result if it breaks in service.
Timing chain A chain which drives the camshaft.
Toe-in The amount the front wheels are closer together at the front than at the rear. On rear wheel drive vehicles, a slight amount of toe-in is usually specified to keep the front wheels running parallel on the road by offsetting other forces that tend to spread the wheels apart.
Toe-out The amount the front wheels are closer together at the rear than at the front. On front wheel drive vehicles, a slight amount of toe-out is usually specified.
Tools For full information on choosing and using tools, refer to the *Haynes Automotive Tools Manual.*
Tracer A stripe of a second colour applied to a wire insulator to distinguish that wire from another one with the same colour insulator.
Tune-up A process of accurate and careful adjustments and parts replacement to obtain the best possible engine performance.
Turbocharger A centrifugal device, driven by exhaust gases, that pressurises the intake air. Normally used to increase the power output from a given engine displacement, but can also be used primarily to reduce exhaust emissions (as on VW's "Umwelt" Diesel engine).

U

Universal joint or U-joint A double-pivoted connection for transmitting power from a driving to a driven shaft through an angle. A U-joint consists of two Y-shaped yokes and a cross-shaped member called the spider.

V

Valve A device through which the flow of liquid, gas, vacuum, or loose material in bulk may be started, stopped, or regulated by a movable part that opens, shuts, or partially obstructs one or more ports or passageways. A valve is also the movable part of such a device.
Valve clearance The clearance between the valve tip (the end of the valve stem) and the rocker arm or tappet. The valve clearance is measured when the valve is closed.
Vernier caliper A precision measuring instrument that measures inside and outside dimensions. Not quite as accurate as a micrometer, but more convenient.
Viscosity The thickness of a liquid or its resistance to flow.
Volt A unit for expressing electrical "pressure" in a circuit. One volt that will produce a current of one ampere through a resistance of one ohm.

W

Welding Various processes used to join metal items by heating the areas to be joined to a molten state and fusing them together. For more information refer to the *Haynes Automotive Welding Manual.*
Wiring diagram A drawing portraying the components and wires in a vehicle's electrical system, using standardised symbols. For more information refer to the *Haynes Automotive Electrical and Electronic Systems Manual.*

Note: *References throughout this index are in the form* **"Chapter number" • "Page number"**. *So, for example, 2C•15 refers to page 15 of Chapter 2C.*

Note: *References throughout this index are in the form* **"Chapter number"** • **"Page number"***. So, for example, 2C•15 refers to page 15 of Chapter 2C.*

Note: *References throughout this index are in the form* **"Chapter number" • "Page number"**. *So, for example, 2C•15 refers to page 15 of Chapter 2C.*

Note: *References throughout this index are in the form* **"Chapter number"** • **"Page number"**. *So, for example, 2C•15 refers to page 15 of Chapter 2C.*

M

N

O

P

R

Note: *References throughout this index are in the form* **"Chapter number" • "Page number"**. *So, for example, 2C•15 refers to page 15 of Chapter 2C.*

S

T

Note: *References throughout this index are in the form* **"Chapter number" • "Page number"**. *So, for example, 2C•15 refers to page 15 of Chapter 2C.*

Haynes Manuals – The Complete **UK Car** List

Title	Book No.
ALFA ROMEO Alfasud/Sprint (74 - 88) up to F *	0292
Alfa Romeo Alfetta (73 - 87) up to E *	0531
AUDI 80, 90 & Coupe Petrol (79 - Nov 88) up to F	0605
Audi 80, 90 & Coupe Petrol (Oct 86 - 90) D to H	1491
Audi 100 & 200 Petrol (Oct 82 - 90) up to H	0907
Audi 100 & A6 Petrol & Diesel (May 91 - May 97) H to P	3504
Audi A3 Petrol & Diesel (96 - May 03) P to 03	4253
Audi A4 Petrol & Diesel (95 - 00) M to X	3575
Audi A4 Petrol & Diesel (01 - 04) X to 54	4609
AUSTIN A35 & A40 (56 - 67) up to F *	0118
Austin/MG/Rover Maestro 1.3 & 1.6 Petrol (83 - 95) up to M	0922
Austin/MG Metro (80 - May 90) up to G	0718
Austin/Rover Montego 1.3 & 1.6 Petrol (84 - 94) A to L	1066
Austin/MG/Rover Montego 2.0 Petrol (84 - 95) A to M	1067
Mini (59 - 69) up to H *	0527
Mini (69 - 01) up to X	0646
Austin/Rover 2.0 litre Diesel Engine (86 - 93) C to L	1857
Austin Healey 100/6 & 3000 (56 - 68) up to G *	0049
BEDFORD CF Petrol (69 - 87) up to E	0163
Bedford/Vauxhall Rascal & Suzuki Supercarry (86 - Oct 94) C to M	3015
BMW 316, 320 & 320i (4-cyl) (75 - Feb 83) up to Y *	0276
BMW 320, 320i, 323i & 325i (6-cyl) (Oct 77 - Sept 87) up to E	0815
BMW 3- & 5-Series Petrol (81 - 91) up to J	1948
BMW 3-Series Petrol (Apr 91 - 99) H to V	3210
BMW 3-Series Petrol (Sept 98 - 03) S to 53	4067
BMW 520i & 525e (Oct 81 - June 88) up to E	1560
BMW 525, 528 & 528i (73 - Sept 81) up to X *	0632
BMW 5-Series 6-cyl Petrol (April 96 - Aug 03) N to 03	4151
BMW 1500, 1502, 1600, 1602, 2000 & 2002 (59 - 77) up to S *	0240
CHRYSLER PT Cruiser Petrol (00 - 03) W to 53	4058
CITROËN 2CV, Ami & Dyane (67 - 90) up to H	0196
Citroën AX Petrol & Diesel (87 - 97) D to P	3014
Citroën Berlingo & Peugeot Partner Petrol & Diesel (96 - 05) P to 55	4281
Citroën BX Petrol (83 - 94) A to L	0908
Citroën C15 Van Petrol & Diesel (89 - Oct 98) F to S	3509
Citroën C3 Petrol & Diesel (02 - 05) 51 to 05	4197
Citroën CX Petrol (75 - 88) up to F	0528
Citroën Saxo Petrol & Diesel (96 - 04) N to 54	3506
Citroën Visa Petrol (79 - 88) up to F	0620
Citroën Xantia Petrol & Diesel (93 - 01) K to Y	3082
Citroën XM Petrol & Diesel (89 - 00) G to X	3451
Citroën Xsara Petrol & Diesel (97 - Sept 00) R to W	3751
Citroën Xsara Picasso Petrol & Diesel (00 - 02) W to 52	3944
Citroën ZX Diesel (91 - 98) J to S	1922
Citroën ZX Petrol (91 - 98) H to S	1881
Citroën 1.7 & 1.9 litre Diesel Engine (84 - 96) A to N	1379
FIAT 126 (73 - 87) up to E *	0305
Fiat 500 (57 - 73) up to M *	0090
Fiat Bravo & Brava Petrol (95 - 00) N to W	3572
Fiat Cinquecento (93 - 98) K to R	3501
Fiat Panda (81 - 95) up to M	0793
Fiat Punto Petrol & Diesel (94 - Oct 99) L to V	3251
Fiat Punto Petrol (Oct 99 - July 03) V to 03	4066
Fiat Regata Petrol (84 - 88) A to F	1167
Fiat Tipo Petrol (88 - 91) E to J	1625
Fiat Uno Petrol (83 - 95) up to M	0923
Fiat X1/9 (74 - 89) up to G *	0273
FORD Anglia (59 - 68) up to G *	0001
Ford Capri II (& III) 1.6 & 2.0 (74 - 87) up to E *	0283
Ford Capri II (& III) 2.8 & 3.0 V6 (74 - 87) up to E	1309
Ford Cortina Mk I & Corsair 1500 ('62 - '66) up to D*	0214
Ford Cortina Mk III 1300 & 1600 (70 - 76) up to P *	0070
Ford Escort Mk I 1100 & 1300 (68 - 74) up to N *	0171
Ford Escort Mk I Mexico, RS 1600 & RS 2000 (70 - 74) up to N *	0139
Ford Escort Mk II Mexico, RS 1800 & RS 2000 (75 - 80) up to W *	0735
Ford Escort (75 - Aug 80) up to V *	0280
Ford Escort Petrol (Sept 80 - Sept 90) up to H	0686
Ford Escort & Orion Petrol (Sept 90 - 00) H to X	1737
Ford Escort & Orion Diesel (Sept 90 - 00) H to X	4081
Ford Fiesta (76 - Aug 83) up to Y	0334
Ford Fiesta Petrol (Aug 83 - Feb 89) A to F	1030
Ford Fiesta Petrol (Feb 89 - Oct 95) F to N	1595
Ford Fiesta Petrol & Diesel (Oct 95 - Mar 02) N to 02	3397
Ford Fiesta Petrol & Diesel (Apr 02 - 05) 02 to 54	4170
Ford Focus Petrol & Diesel (98 - 01) S to Y	3759
Ford Focus Petrol & Diesel (Oct 01 - 05) 51 to 05	4167
Ford Galaxy Petrol & Diesel (95 - Aug 00) M to W	3984
Ford Granada Petrol (Sept 77 - Feb 85) up to B *	0481
Ford Granada & Scorpio Petrol (Mar 85 - 94) B to M	1245
Ford Ka (96 - 02) P to 52	3570
Ford Mondeo Petrol (93 - Sept 00) K to X	1923
Ford Mondeo Petrol & Diesel (Oct 00 - Jul 03) X to 03	3990
Ford Mondeo Petrol & Diesel (July 03 - 07) 03 to 56	4619
Ford Mondeo Diesel (93 - 96) L to N	3465
Ford Orion Petrol (83 - Sept 90) up to H	1009
Ford Sierra 4-cyl Petrol (82 - 93) up to K	0903
Ford Sierra V6 Petrol (82 - 91) up to J	0904
Ford Transit Petrol (Mk 2) (78 - Jan 86) up to C	0719
Ford Transit Petrol (Mk 3) (Feb 86 - 89) C to G	1468
Ford Transit Diesel (Feb 86 - 99) C to T	3019
Ford 1.6 & 1.8 litre Diesel Engine (84 - 96) A to N	1172
Ford 2.1, 2.3 & 2.5 litre Diesel Engine (77 - 90) up to H	1606
FREIGHT ROVER Sherpa Petrol (74 - 87) up to E	0463
HILLMAN Avenger (70 - 82) up to Y	0037
Hillman Imp (63 - 76) up to R *	0022
HONDA Civic (Feb 84 - Oct 87) A to E	1226
Honda Civic (Nov 91 - 96) J to N	3199
Honda Civic Petrol (Mar 95 - 00) M to X	4050
Honda Civic Petrol & Diesel (01 - 05) X to 55	4611
Honda Jazz (01 - Feb 08) 51 - 57	4735
HYUNDAI Pony (85 - 94) C to M	3398
JAGUAR E Type (61 - 72) up to L *	0140
Jaguar MkI & II, 240 & 340 (55 - 69) up to H *	0098
Jaguar XJ6, XJ & Sovereign; Daimler Sovereign (68 - Oct 86) up to D	0242
Jaguar XJ6 & Sovereign (Oct 86 - Sept 94) D to M	3261
Jaguar XJ12, XJS & Sovereign; Daimler Double Six (72 - 88) up to F	0478
JEEP Cherokee Petrol (93 - 96) K to N	1943
LADA 1200, 1300, 1500 & 1600 (74 - 91) up to J	0413
Lada Samara (87 - 91) D to J	1610
LAND ROVER 90, 110 & Defender Diesel (83 - 07) up to 56	3017
Land Rover Discovery Petrol & Diesel (89 - 98) G to S	3016
Land Rover Discovery Diesel (Nov 98 - Jul 04) S to 04	4606
Land Rover Freelander Petrol & Diesel (97 - Sept 03) R to 53	3929
Land Rover Freelander Petrol & Diesel (Oct 03 - Oct 06) 53 to 56	4623
Land Rover Series IIA & III Diesel (58 - 85) up to C	0529
Land Rover Series II, IIA & III 4-cyl Petrol (58 - 85) up to C	0314
MAZDA 323 (Mar 81 - Oct 89) up to G	1608
Mazda 323 (Oct 89 - 98) G to R	3455
Mazda 626 (May 83 - Sept 87) up to E	0929
Mazda B1600, B1800 & B2000 Pick-up Petrol (72 - 88) up to F	0267
Mazda RX-7 (79 - 85) up to C *	0460
MERCEDES-BENZ 190, 190E & 190D Petrol & Diesel (83 - 93) A to L	3450
Mercedes-Benz 200D, 240D, 240TD, 300D & 300TD 123 Series Diesel (Oct 76 - 85)	1114
Mercedes-Benz 250 & 280 (68 - 72) up to L *	0346
Mercedes-Benz 250 & 280 123 Series Petrol (Oct 76 - 84) up to B *	0677
Mercedes-Benz 124 Series Petrol & Diesel (85 - Aug 93) C to K	3253
Mercedes-Benz C-Class Petrol & Diesel (93 - Aug 00) L to W	3511
MGA (55 - 62) *	0475
MGB (62 - 80) up to W	0111
MG Midget & Austin-Healey Sprite (58 - 80) up to W *	0265
MINI Petrol (July 01 - 05) Y to 05	4273
MITSUBISHI Shogun & L200 Pick-Ups Petrol (83 - 94) up to M	1944
MORRIS Ital 1.3 (80 - 84) up to B	0705
Morris Minor 1000 (56 - 71) up to K	0024
NISSAN Almera Petrol (95 - Feb 00) N to V	4053
Nissan Almera & Tino Petrol (Feb 00 - 07) V to 56	4612
Nissan Bluebird (May 84 - Mar 86) A to C	1223
Nissan Bluebird Petrol (Mar 86 - 90) C to H	1473
Nissan Cherry (Sept 82 - 86) up to D	1031
Nissan Micra (83 - Jan 93) up to K	0931
Nissan Micra (93 - 02) K to 52	3254
Nissan Primera Petrol (90 - Aug 99) H to T	1851
Nissan Stanza (82 - 86) up to D	0824
Nissan Sunny Petrol (May 82 - Oct 86) up to D	0895
Nissan Sunny Petrol (Oct 86 - Mar 91) D to H	1378
Nissan Sunny Petrol (Apr 91 - 95) H to N	3219
OPEL Ascona & Manta (B Series) (Sept 75 - 88) up to F *	0316
Opel Ascona Petrol (81 - 88)	3215
Opel Astra Petrol (Oct 91 - Feb 98)	3156
Opel Corsa Petrol (83 - Mar 93)	3160
Opel Corsa Petrol (Mar 93 - 97)	3159
Opel Kadett Petrol (Nov 79 - Oct 84) up to B	0634
Opel Kadett Petrol (Oct 84 - Oct 91)	3196
Opel Omega & Senator Petrol (Nov 86 - 94)	3157
Opel Rekord Petrol (Feb 78 - Oct 86) up to D	0543
Opel Vectra Petrol (Oct 88 - Oct 95)	3158
PEUGEOT 106 Petrol & Diesel (91 - 04) J to 53	1882
Peugeot 205 Petrol (83 - 97) A to P	0932
Peugeot 206 Petrol & Diesel (98 - 01) S to X	3757
Peugeot 206 Petrol & Diesel (02 - 06) 51 to 06	4613
Peugeot 306 Petrol & Diesel (93 - 02) K to 02	3073
Peugeot 307 Petrol & Diesel (01 - 04) Y to 54	4147
Peugeot 309 Petrol (86 - 93) C to K	1266
Peugeot 405 Petrol (88 - 97) E to P	1559
Peugeot 405 Diesel (88 - 97) E to P	3198
Peugeot 406 Petrol & Diesel (96 - Mar 99) N to T	3394
Peugeot 406 Petrol & Diesel (Mar 99 - 02) T to 52	3982
Peugeot 505 Petrol (79 - 89) up to G	0762
Peugeot 1.7/1.8 & 1.9 litre Diesel Engine (82 - 96) up to N	0950
Peugeot 2.0, 2.1, 2.3 & 2.5 litre Diesel Engines (74 - 90) up to H	1607
PORSCHE 911 (65 - 85) up to C	0264

* Classic reprint

Title	Book No.
Porsche 924 & 924 Turbo (76 - 85) up to C	**0397**
PROTON (89 - 97) F to P	**3255**
RANGE ROVER V8 Petrol (70 - Oct 92) up to K	**0606**
RELIANT Robin & Kitten (73 - 83) up to A *	**0436**
RENAULT 4 (61 - 86) up to D *	**0072**
Renault 5 Petrol (Feb 85 - 96) B to N	**1219**
Renault 9 & 11 Petrol (82 - 89) up to F	**0822**
Renault 18 Petrol (79 - 86) up to D	**0598**
Renault 19 Petrol (89 - 96) F to N	**1646**
Renault 19 Diesel (89 - 96) F to N	**1946**
Renault 21 Petrol (86 - 94) C to M	**1397**
Renault 25 Petrol & Diesel (84 - 92) B to K	**1228**
Renault Clio Petrol (91 - May 98) H to R	**1853**
Renault Clio Diesel (91 - June 96) H to N	**3031**
Renault Clio Petrol & Diesel (May 98 - May 01) R to Y	**3906**
Renault Clio Petrol & Diesel (June '01 - '05) Y to 55	**4168**
Renault Espace Petrol & Diesel (85 - 96) C to N	**3197**
Renault Laguna Petrol & Diesel (94 - 00) L to W	**3252**
Renault Laguna Petrol & Diesel (Feb 01 - Feb 05) X to 54	**4283**
Renault Mégane & Scénic Petrol & Diesel (96 - 99) N to T	**3395**
Renault Mégane & Scénic Petrol & Diesel (Apr 99 - 02) T to 52	**3916**
Renault Megane Petrol & Diesel (Oct 02 - 05) 52 to 55	**4284**
Renault Scenic Petrol & Diesel (Sept 03 - 06) 53 to 06	**4297**
ROVER 213 & 216 (84 - 89) A to G	**1116**
Rover 214 & 414 Petrol (89 - 96) G to N	**1689**
Rover 216 & 416 Petrol (89 - 96) G to N	**1830**
Rover 211, 214, 216, 218 & 220 Petrol & Diesel (Dec 95 - 99) N to V	**3399**
Rover 25 & MG ZR Petrol & Diesel (Oct 99 - 04) V to 54	**4145**
Rover 414, 416 & 420 Petrol & Diesel (May 95 - 98) M to R	**3453**
Rover 45 / MG ZS Petrol & Diesel (99 - 05) V to 55	**4384**
Rover 618, 620 & 623 Petrol (93 - 97) K to P	**3257**
Rover 75 / MG ZT Petrol & Diesel (99 - 06) S to 06	**4292**
Rover 820, 825 & 827 Petrol (86 - 95) D to N	**1380**
Rover 3500 (76 - 87) up to E *	**0365**
Rover Metro, 111 & 114 Petrol (May 90 - 98) G to S	**1711**
SAAB 95 & 96 (66 - 76) up to R *	**0198**
Saab 90, 99 & 900 (79 - Oct 93) up to L	**0765**
Saab 900 (Oct 93 - 98) L to R	**3512**
Saab 9000 (4-cyl) (85 - 98) C to S	**1686**
Saab 9-3 Petrol & Diesel (98 - Aug 02) R to 02	**4614**
Saab 9-5 4-cyl Petrol (97 - 04) R to 54	**4156**
SEAT Ibiza & Cordoba Petrol & Diesel (Oct 93 - Oct 99) L to V	**3571**
Seat Ibiza & Malaga Petrol (85 - 92) B to K	**1609**
SKODA Estelle (77 - 89) up to G	**0604**
Skoda Fabia Petrol & Diesel (00 - 06) W to 06	**4376**
Skoda Favorit (89 - 96) F to N	**1801**
Skoda Felicia Petrol & Diesel (95 - 01) M to X	**3505**
Skoda Octavia Petrol & Diesel (98 - Apr 04) R to 04	**4285**
SUBARU 1600 & 1800 (Nov 79 - 90) up to H *	**0995**
SUNBEAM Alpine, Rapier & H120 (67 - 74) up to N *	**0051**
SUZUKI SJ Series, Samurai & Vitara (4-cyl) Petrol (82 - 97) up to P	**1942**
Suzuki Supercarry & Bedford/Vauxhall Rascal (86 - Oct 94) C to M	**3015**
TALBOT Alpine, Solara, Minx & Rapier (75 - 86) up to D	**0337**

Title	Book No.
Talbot Horizon Petrol (78 - 86) up to D	**0473**
Talbot Samba (82 - 86) up to D	**0823**
TOYOTA Avensis Petrol (98 - Jan 03) R to 52	**4264**
Toyota Carina E Petrol (May 92 - 97) J to P	**3256**
Toyota Corolla (80 - 85) up to C	**0683**
Toyota Corolla (Sept 83 - Sept 87) A to E	**1024**
Toyota Corolla (Sept 87 - Aug 92) E to K	**1683**
Toyota Corolla Petrol (Aug 92 - 97) K to P	**3259**
Toyota Corolla Petrol (July 97 - Feb 02) P to 51	**4286**
Toyota Hi-Ace & Hi-Lux Petrol (69 - Oct 83) up to A	**0304**
Toyota Yaris Petrol (99 - 05) T to 05	**4265**
TRIUMPH GT6 & Vitesse (62 - 74) up to N *	**0112**
Triumph Herald (59 - 71) up to K *	**0010**
Triumph Spitfire (62 - 81) up to X	**0113**
Triumph Stag (70 - 78) up to T *	**0441**
Triumph TR2, TR3, TR3A, TR4 & TR4A (52 - 67) up to F *	**0028**
Triumph TR5 & 6 (67 - 75) up to P *	**0031**
Triumph TR7 (75 - 82) up to Y *	**0322**
VAUXHALL Astra Petrol (80 - Oct 84) up to B	**0635**
Vauxhall Astra & Belmont Petrol (Oct 84 - Oct 91) B to J	**1136**
Vauxhall Astra Petrol (Oct 91 - Feb 98) J to R	**1832**
Vauxhall/Opel Astra & Zafira Petrol (Feb 98 - Apr 04) R to 04	**3758**
Vauxhall/Opel Astra & Zafira Diesel (Feb 98 - Apr 04) R to 04	**3797**
Vauxhall/Opel Astra Petrol (04 - 07) 04 - 07	**4732**
Vauxhall/Opel Astra Diesel (04 - 07) 04 - 07	**4733**
Vauxhall/Opel Calibra (90 - 98) G to S	**3502**
Vauxhall Carlton Petrol (Oct 78 - Oct 86) up to D	**0480**
Vauxhall Carlton & Senator Petrol (Nov 86 - 94) D to L	**1469**
Vauxhall Cavalier Petrol (81 - Oct 88) up to F	**0812**
Vauxhall Cavalier Petrol (Oct 88 - 95) F to N	**1570**
Vauxhall Chevette (75 - 84) up to B	**0285**
Vauxhall/Opel Corsa Diesel (Mar 93 - Oct 00) K to X	**4087**
Vauxhall Corsa Petrol (Mar 93 - 97) K to R	**1985**
Vauxhall/Opel Corsa Petrol (Apr 97 - Oct 00) P to X	**3921**
Vauxhall/Opel Corsa Petrol & Diesel (Oct 00 - Sept 03) X to 53	**4079**
Vauxhall/Opel Corsa Petrol & Diesel (Oct 03 - Aug 06) 53 to 06	**4617**
Vauxhall/Opel Frontera Petrol & Diesel (91 - Sept 98) J to S	**3454**
Vauxhall Nova Petrol (83 - 93) up to K	**0909**
Vauxhall/Opel Omega Petrol (94 - 99) L to T	**3510**
Vauxhall/Opel Vectra Petrol & Diesel (95 - Feb 99) N to S	**3396**
Vauxhall/Opel Vectra Petrol & Diesel (Mar 99 - May 02) T to 02	**3930**
Vauxhall/Opel Vectra Petrol & Diesel (June 02 - Sept 05) 02 to 55	**4618**
Vauxhall/Opel 1.5, 1.6 & 1.7 litre Diesel Engine (82 - 96) up to N	**1222**
VW 411 & 412 (68 - 75) up to P *	**0091**
VW Beetle 1200 (54 - 77) up to S	**0036**
VW Beetle 1300 & 1500 (65 - 75) up to P	**0039**
VW 1302 & 1302S (70 - 72) up to L *	**0110**
VW Beetle 1303, 1303S & GT (72 - 75) up to P	**0159**
VW Beetle Petrol & Diesel (Apr 99 - 01) T to 51	**3798**
VW Golf & Jetta Mk 1 Petrol 1.1 & 1.3 (74 - 84) up to A	**0716**
VW Golf, Jetta & Scirocco Mk 1 Petrol 1.5, 1.6 & 1.8 (74 - 84) up to A	**0726**

Title	Book No.
VW Golf & Jetta Mk 1 Diesel (78 - 84) up to A	**0451**
VW Golf & Jetta Mk 2 Petrol (Mar 84 - Feb 92) A to J	**1081**
VW Golf & Vento Petrol & Diesel (Feb 92 - Mar 98) J to R	**3097**
VW Golf & Bora Petrol & Diesel (April 98 - 00) R to X	**3727**
VW Golf & Bora 4-cyl Petrol & Diesel (01 - 03) X to 53	**4169**
VW Golf & Jetta Petrol & Diesel (04 - 07) 53 to 07	**4610**
VW LT Petrol Vans & Light Trucks (76 - 87) up to E	**0637**
VW Passat & Santana Petrol (Sept 81 - May 88) up to E	**0814**
VW Passat 4-cyl Petrol & Diesel (May 88 - 96) E to P	**3498**
VW Passat 4-cyl Petrol & Diesel (Dec 96 - Nov 00) P to X	**3917**
VW Passat Petrol & Diesel (Dec 00 - May 05) X to 05	**4279**
VW Polo & Derby (76 - Jan 82) up to X	**0335**
VW Polo (82 - Oct 90) up to H	**0813**
VW Polo Petrol (Nov 90 - Aug 94) H to L	**3245**
VW Polo Hatchback Petrol & Diesel (94 - 99) M to S	**3500**
VW Polo Hatchback Petrol (00 - Jan 02) V to 51	**4150**
VW Polo Petrol & Diesel (02 - May 05) 51 to 05	**4608**
VW Scirocco (82 - 90) up to H *	**1224**
VW Transporter 1600 (68 - 79) up to V	**0082**
VW Transporter 1700, 1800 & 2000 (72 - 79) up to V *	**0226**
VW Transporter (air-cooled) Petrol (79 - 82) up to Y *	**0638**
VW Transporter (water-cooled) Petrol (82 - 90) up to H	**3452**
VW Type 3 (63 - 73) up to M *	**0084**
VOLVO 120 & 130 Series (& P1800) (61 - 73) up to M *	**0203**
Volvo 142, 144 & 145 (66 - 74) up to N *	**0129**
Volvo 240 Series Petrol (74 - 93) up to K	**0270**
Volvo 262, 264 & 260/265 (75 - 85) up to C *	**0400**
Volvo 340, 343, 345 & 360 (76 - 91) up to J	**0715**
Volvo 440, 460 & 480 Petrol (87 - 97) D to P	**1691**
Volvo 740 & 760 Petrol (82 - 91) up to J	**1258**
Volvo 850 Petrol (92 - 96) J to P	**3260**
Volvo 940 petrol (90 - 98) H to R	**3249**
Volvo S40 & V40 Petrol (96 - Mar 04) N to 04	**3569**
Volvo S40 & V50 Petrol & Diesel (Mar 04 - Jun 07) 04 to 07	**4731**
Volvo S70, V70 & C70 Petrol (96 - 99) P to V	**3573**
Volvo V70 / S80 Petrol & Diesel (98 - 05) S to 55	**4263**
AUTOMOTIVE TECHBOOKS	
Automotive Electrical and Electronic Systems Manual	**3049**
Automotive Gearbox Overhaul Manual	**3473**
Automotive Service Summaries Manual	**3475**
Automotive Timing Belts Manual – Austin/Rover	**3549**
Automotive Timing Belts Manual – Ford	**3474**
Automotive Timing Belts Manual – Peugeot/Citroën	**3568**
Automotive Timing Belts Manual – Vauxhall/Opel	**3577**
DIY MANUAL SERIES	
The Haynes Air Conditioning Manual	**4192**
The Haynes Car Electrical Systems Manual	**4251**
The Haynes Manual on Bodywork	**4198**
The Haynes Manual on Brakes	**4178**
The Haynes Manual on Carburettors	**4177**
The Haynes Manual on Diesel Engines	**4174**
The Haynes Manual on Engine Management	**4199**
The Haynes Manual on Fault Codes	**4175**
The Haynes Manual on Practical Electrical Systems	**4267**
The Haynes Manual on Small Engines	**4250**
The Haynes Manual on Welding	**4176**

* Classic reprint

Preserving Our Motoring Heritage

The Model J Duesenberg Derham Tourster. Only eight of these magnificent cars were ever built – this is the only example to be found outside the United States of America

Almost every car you've ever loved, loathed or desired is gathered under one roof at the Haynes Motor Museum. Over 300 immaculately presented cars and motorbikes represent every aspect of our motoring heritage, from elegant reminders of bygone days, such as the superb Model J Duesenberg to curiosities like the bug-eyed BMW Isetta. There are also many old friends and flames. Perhaps you remember the 1959 Ford Popular that you did your courting in? The magnificent 'Red Collection' is a spectacle of classic sports cars including AC, Alfa Romeo, Austin Healey, Ferrari, Lamborghini, Maserati, MG, Riley, Porsche and Triumph.

A Perfect Day Out

Each and every vehicle at the Haynes Motor Museum has played its part in the history and culture of Motoring. Today, they make a wonderful spectacle and a great day out for all the family. Bring the kids, bring Mum and Dad, but above all bring your camera to capture those golden memories for ever. You will also find an impressive array of motoring memorabilia, a comfortable 70 seat video cinema and one of the most extensive transport book shops in Britain. The Pit Stop Cafe serves everything from a cup of tea to wholesome, home-made meals or, if you prefer, you can enjoy the large picnic area nestled in the beautiful rural surroundings of Somerset.

John Haynes O.B.E., Founder and Chairman of the museum at the wheel of a Haynes Light 12.

Graham Hill's Lola Cosworth Formula 1 car next to a 1934 Riley Sports.

The Museum is situated on the A359 Yeovil to Frome road at Sparkford, just off the A303 in Somerset. It is about 40 miles south of Bristol, and 25 minutes drive from the M5 intersection at Taunton.

Open 9.30am - 5.30pm (10.00am - 4.00pm Winter) 7 days a week, *except Christmas Day, Boxing Day and New Years Day*

Special rates available for schools, coach parties and outings Charitable Trust No. 292048